Issue

Holding

Facts

Procedural Posture

Rationale

Dissenting Opinion

CASES AND PROBLEMS ON
CONTRACTS
Fourth Edition

By

The Late John D. Calamari
Late Agnes and Ignatius M. Wilkinson Professor of Law
Fordham University

Joseph M. Perillo
Distinguished Professor of Law, Emeritus
Fordham University

Helen Hadjiyannakis Bender
Associate Professor of Law
Fordham University

AMERICAN CASEBOOK SERIES®

THOMSON
* ™
WEST

Mat #40146018

TEXT IS PRINTED ON 10% POST CONSUMER RECYCLED PAPER

Preface to the Fourth Edition

The scope of the material that a student should master in a basic contracts course has increased disproportionately to the amount of curricular time available for its mastery. The temptation is to give the student fleeting exposure to masses of issues to the detriment of honing of analytical skills and to the sacrifice of an in-depth mastery of the subject.

The methodology used in this casebook started as an experiment and we deem the experiment a success. The problem method in tandem with case dissection engenders student interest, enlarges their store of knowledge and, most important, requires them to exercise analytic thinking not only in the classroom, but also while doing their assignments.

The principal cases have been edited, but less drastically than in many of the recent casebooks. Numbered footnotes are from the original materials and retain their original numbering. When the editors have added footnotes or other materials, these are indicated by the abbreviation, "Ed."

We lament the passing of our late co-editor, John D. Calamari, but his ideas continue to animate ours.

We welcome comments on the form and content of this coursebook. Send them to JPerillo@law.fordham.edu, or to Hbender@law.fordham.edu.

JOSEPH M. PERILLO
HELEN HADJIYANNAKIS BENDER

*

Copyright Acknowledgements

We are grateful to the following authors, law reviews and publishers for their gracious permission to reprint copyrighted materials: (1) Fordham Law Review for B. Harnett & J. V. Thornton, "The Insurance Condition Subsequent: A Needle in a Semantic Haystack," 17 Fordham Law Review 220 (1948); (2) New York Law School Review for "When in an Actor Unique, Unusual or Extraordinary," 65 U.S.L.Rev. 354 (1931); (3) New York University Law Review for R. Childres, "Conditions in the Law of Contracts," 45 N.Y.U.L.Rev. 33 (1970); (4) Larry Di Matteo for permission to use an excerpt from his book, The Evolution of Contractual Intent 55–56 (1998); (5) Daniel Friedman for an excerpt from "The Efficient Breach Fallacy," 18 J.Leg.Stud. 1 (1989); (6) Alan Schwartz for "The Case for Specific Performance," 89 Yale L.J. 272 (1989); (7) the Journal of Legal Studies for Richard A. Posner, Gratuitous Promises in Economics and Law, 6 J.Leg.Stud. 411 (1977); (8) The Harvard Law School Record for Jorie Roberts, "Hawkins Case: A Hair-Raising Experience," Harvard Law Record, Vol. 66, No. 6, March 17, 1978; (9) the Journal of Legal Studies, The University of Chicago, and A.W. Brian Simpson for A.W.B. Simpson, "Quackery and Contract Law: The Case of the Carbolic Smoke Ball," 14 J.Leg.Stud. 345 (1985). Copyright 1985 by The University of Chicago. All rights reserved.

*

Summary of Contents

vii

*

Table of Contents

*

Table of Cases

The principal cases are in bold type. Cases cited or discussed in the text are roman type. References are to pages. Cases cited in principal cases and within other quoted materials are not included.

*

CASES AND PROBLEMS ON
CONTRACTS

*

Chapter 1

THE AGREEMENT PROCESS

SECTION 1. INTENT TO CONTRACT

(Calamari & Perillo 5th §§ 1.1—1.7, 2.1—2.4, 2.7)

LUCY v. ZEHMER

Supreme Court of Appeals of Virginia, 1954.
196 Va. 493, 84 S.E.2d 516.

BUCHANAN, JUSTICE. This suit was instituted by W.O. Lucy and J.C. Lucy, complainants, against A.H. Zehmer and Ida S. Zehmer, his wife, defendants, to have specific performance of a contract by which it was alleged the Zehmers had sold to W.O. Lucy a tract of land owned by A.H. Zehmer in Dinwiddie county containing 471.6 acres, more or less, known as the Ferguson farm, for $50,000. J.C. Lucy, the other complainant, is a brother of W.O. Lucy, to whom W.O. Lucy transferred a half interest in his alleged purchase.

The instrument sought to be enforced was written by A.H. Zehmer on December 20, 1952, in these words: "We hereby agree to sell to W.O. Lucy the Ferguson Farm complete for $50,000.00, title satisfactory to buyer," and signed by the defendants, A.H. Zehmer and Ida S. Zehmer.

The answer of A.H. Zehmer admitted that at the time mentioned W.O. Lucy offered him $50,000 cash for the farm, but that he, Zehmer, considered that the offer was made in jest; that so thinking, and both he and Lucy having had several drinks, he wrote out "the memorandum" quoted above and induced his wife to sign it; that he did not deliver the memorandum to Lucy, but that Lucy picked it up, read it, put it in his pocket, attempted to offer Zehmer $5 to bind the bargain, which Zehmer refused to accept, and realizing for the first time that Lucy was serious, Zehmer assured him that he had no intention of selling the farm and that the whole matter was a joke. Lucy left the premises insisting that he had purchased the farm.

Depositions were taken and the decree appealed from was entered holding that the complainants had failed to establish their right to specific performance, and dismissing their bill. The assignment of error is to this action of the court.

* * *

1

The defendants insist that the evidence was ample to support their contention that the writing sought to be enforced was prepared as a bluff or dare to force Lucy to admit that he did not have $50,000; that the whole matter was a joke; that the writing was not delivered to Lucy and no binding contract was ever made between the parties.

It is an unusual, if not bizarre defense. When made to the writing admittedly prepared by one of the defendants and signed by both, clear evidence is required to sustain it.

In his testimony Zehmer claimed that he "was high as a Georgia pine," and that the transaction "was just a bunch of two doggoned drunks bluffing to see who could talk the biggest and say the most." That claim is inconsistent with his attempt to testify in great detail as to what was said and what was done. It is contradicted by other evidence as to the condition of both parties, and rendered of no weight by the testimony of his wife that when Lucy left the restaurant she suggested that Zehmer drive him home. The record is convincing that Zehmer was not intoxicated to the extent of being unable to comprehend the nature and consequences of the instrument he executed, and hence that instrument is not to be invalidated on that ground. C.J.S., Contracts, § 133, b., p. 483; Taliaferro v. Emery, 124 Va. 674, 98 S.E. 627. It was in fact conceded by defendants' counsel in oral argument that under the evidence Zehmer was not too drunk to make a valid contract.

The evidence is convincing also that Zehmer wrote two agreements, the first one beginning "I hereby agree to sell." Zehmer first said he could not remember about that, then that "I don't think I wrote but one out." Mrs. Zehmer said that what he wrote was "I hereby agree," but that the "I" was changed to "We" after that night. The agreement that was written and signed is in the record and indicates no such change. Neither are the mistakes in spelling that Zehmer sought to point out readily apparent.

The appearance of the contract, the fact that it was under discussion for forty minutes or more before it was signed; Lucy's objection to the first draft because it was written in the singular, and he wanted Mrs. Zehmer to sign it also; the rewriting to meet that objection and the signing by Mrs. Zehmer; the discussion of what was to be included in the sale, the provision for the examination of the title, the completeness of the instrument that was executed, the taking possession of it by Lucy with no request or suggestion by either of the defendants that he give it back, are facts which furnish persuasive evidence that the execution of the contract was a serious business transaction rather than a casual, jesting matter as defendants now contend.

* * *

If it be assumed, contrary to what we think the evidence shows, that Zehmer was jesting about selling his farm to Lucy and that the transaction was intended by him to be a joke, nevertheless the evidence shows that Lucy did not so understand it but considered it to be a serious business transaction and the contract to be binding on the Zehmers as well as on himself. The very next day he arranged with his brother to put up half the money and take a half interest in the land. The day after that he employed an attorney to examine the title. The next night, Tuesday, he was back at Zehmer's place and there Zehmer told him for the first time, Lucy said, that he wasn't going to sell and he told Zehmer, "You know you sold that place fair and square." After receiving the report from his attorney that the title was good he wrote to Zehmer that he was ready to close the deal.

Not only did Lucy actually believe, but the evidence shows he was warranted in believing, that the contract represented a serious business transaction and a good faith sale and purchase of the farm.

In the field of contracts, as generally elsewhere, "We must look to the outward expression of a person as manifesting his intention rather than to his secret and unexpressed intention. 'The law imputes to a person an intention corresponding to the reasonable meaning of his words and acts.' " First Nat. Exchange Bank of Roanoke v. Roanoke Oil Co., 169 Va. 99, 114, 192 S.E. 764, 770.

At no time prior to the execution of the contract had Zehmer indicated to Lucy by word or act that he was not in earnest about selling the farm. They had argued about it and discussed its terms, as Zehmer admitted, for a long time. Lucy testified that if there was any jesting it was about paying $50,000 that night. The contract and the evidence show that he was not expected to pay the money that night. Zehmer said that after the writing was signed he laid it down on the counter in front of Lucy. Lucy said Zehmer handed it to him. In any event there had been what appeared to be a good faith offer and a good faith acceptance, followed by the execution and apparent delivery of a written contract. Both said that Lucy put the writing in his pocket and then offered Zehmer $5 to seal the bargain. Not until then, even under the defendants' evidence, was anything said or done to indicate that the matter was a joke. Both of the Zehmers testified that when Zehmer asked his wife to sign he whispered that it was a joke so Lucy wouldn't hear and that it was not intended that he should hear.

The mental assent of the parties is not requisite for the formation of a contract. If the words or other acts of one of the parties have but one reasonable meaning, his undisclosed intention is immaterial except when an unreasonable meaning which he attaches to his manifestations is known to the other party. Restatement of the Law of Contracts, Vol. I, § 71, p. 74.

* * *

Whether the writing signed by the defendants and now sought to be enforced by the complainants was the result of a serious offer by Lucy and a serious acceptance by the defendants, or was a serious offer by Lucy and an acceptance in secret jest by the defendants, in either event it constituted a binding contract of sale between the parties.

* * *

The complainants are entitled to have specific performance of the contract sued on. The decree appealed from is therefore reversed and the cause is remanded for the entry of a proper decree requiring the defendants to perform the contract in accordance with the prayer of the bill.

Reversed and remanded.

BALFOUR v. BALFOUR

Court of Appeal, 1919.
2 K.B. 571.

Appeal from a decision of SARGANT, J., sitting as an additional judge of the King's Bench Division.

[The plaintiff and the defendant (her husband), had been married in England in 1900. They were living in Ceylon where the husband was Director of Irrigation. In 1915 they returned to England to spend his leave. In 1916 when his leave was up he had to return to Ceylon. However, plaintiff, who was suffering from rheumatoid arthritis, decided, on doctor's advice, to spend a few more months in England. Before his departure, the husband promised to send her £30 per month for her support. Later, differences developed and they agreed to live apart. She sued and obtained an order for alimony. In the present suit, she sued him for money she claimed to be due under his agreement to send her £30 per month.]

Wife argues: *FACTS*

* * *

SARGANT, J. held that the husband was under an obligation to support his wife, and the parties had contracted that the extent of that obligation should be defined in terms of so much a month. The consent of the wife to that arrangement was a sufficient consideration to constitute a contract which could be sued upon.

He accordingly gave judgment for the plaintiff.

The husband appealed.

[Concurring opinions of DUKE, L.J. and WARRINGTON, L.J. are omitted.]

ATKIN, L.J. The defence to this action on the alleged contract is that the defendant, the husband, entered into no contract with his wife, and for the determination of that it is necessary to remember that there are agreements between parties which do not result in contracts within the meaning of that term in our law. The ordinary example is where two parties agree to take a walk together, or where there is an offer and an acceptance of hospitality. Nobody would suggest in ordinary circumstances that those agreements result in what we know as a contract, and one of the most usual forms of agreement which does not constitute a contract appears to me to be the arrangements which are made between husband and wife. It is quite common, and it is the natural and

LC *Husband's response:*

inevitable result of the relationship of husband and wife, that the two spouses should make arrangements between themselves—agreements such as are in dispute in this action—agreements for allowances, by which the husband agrees that he will pay to his wife a certain sum of money, per week, or per month, or per year, to cover either her own expenses or the necessary expenses of the household and of the children of the marriage, and in which the wife promises either expressly or impliedly to apply the allowance for the purpose for which it is given. To my mind those agreements, or many of them, do not result in contracts at all[;] * * * they are not contracts because the parties did not intend that they should be attended by legal consequences. To my mind it would be of the worst possible example to hold that agreements such as this resulted in legal obligations which could be enforced in the Courts. It would mean this, that when the husband makes his wife a promise to give her an allowance of 30s. or 2l. a week, whatever he can afford to give her, for the maintenance of the household and children, and she promises so to apply it, not only could she sue him for his failure in any week to supply the allowance, but he could sue her for non-performance of the obligation, express or implied, which she had undertaken upon her part. All I can say is that the small Courts of this country would have to be multiplied one hundredfold if these arrangements were held to result in legal obligations. They are not sued upon, not because the parties are reluctant to enforce their legal rights when the agreement is broken, but because the parties, in the inception of the arrangement, never intended that they should be sued upon. Agreements such as these are outside the realm of contracts altogether. * * * In respect of these promises each house is a domain into which the King's writ does not seek to run, and to which his officers do not seek to be admitted.

The only question in this case is whether or not this promise was of such a class or not. For the reasons given by my brethren it appears to me to be plainly established that the promise here was not intended by either party to be attended by legal consequences. I think the onus was upon the plaintiff, and the plaintiff has not established any contract. The parties were living together, the wife intending to return. The suggestion is that the husband bound himself to pay 30l. a month under all circumstances, and she bound herself to be satisfied with that sum under all circumstances, and, although she was in ill-health and alone in this country, that out of that sum she undertook to defray the whole of the medical expenses that might fall upon her, whatever might be the development of her illness, and in whatever expenses it might involve her. To my mind neither party contemplated such a result. * * * For these reasons I think the judgment of the Court below was wrong and that this appeal should be allowed.

Appeal allowed.

SANCHEZ v. LIFE CARE CENTERS
OF AMERICA, INC.

Supreme Court of Wyoming, 1993.
855 P.2d 1256.

BROWN, JUSTICE (Retired).

This case is a wrongful employee termination action brought by appellant Marie Sanchez, against appellee Life Care Centers of America, Inc. (Life Care). The district court granted summary judgment against appellant.* * * *Procedure*

During a portion of 1990, appellant was employed by Life Care. At the time of her employment, she was issued a Handbook of Employment Guidelines. This handbook contained a "handbook disclaimer." * * *

Detailed facts surrounding appellant's termination are disputed, but * * * we do know that appellant called in on July 20, 1990, to inform her employer that she could not come in the following day due to fatigue; that she was told to "forget coming in"; and that she was removed from the work schedule, which effectively terminated her employment.

The district court's order granting summary judgment was filed December 23, 1991. The district court's order granting summary judgment was filed December 23, 1991. The court ruled in favor of Life Care, holding that (1) the handbook disclaimer was conspicuous as a matter of *Holding* law and did not modify the at-will status of appellant's employment; and (2) that no majority of the Wyoming Supreme Court had recognized a cause of action based on promissory estoppel in wrongful termination cases in Wyoming and, therefore, appellant did not state a claim upon which relief could be granted.

Our standard of review in cases involving the granting of summary judgment has been stated many times. W.R.C.P. 56(c) provides in pertinent part:

> The judgment sought shall be rendered forthwith if the pleadings, depositions, answers to interrogatories, and admissions on file, together with the affidavits, if any, show that there is no genuine issue as to any material fact and that the moving party is entitled to a judgment as a matter of law.

* * *

Normally, the construction and interpretation of a contract is for the court as a matter of law. If the meaning of a contract is ambiguous or not apparent, it may be necessary to determine the intention of the parties from evidence other than the contract itself, and interpretation becomes a mixed question of law and fact. *McDonald v. Mobil Coal Producing, Inc.*, 820 P.2d 986, 988 (Wyo.1991) (quoting *Mobil Coal Producing, Inc. v. Parks*, 704 P.2d 702, 706 (Wyo.1985)).

In Wyoming, employment is presumed to be at-will; however, "[a] handbook may change the employer's unfettered right to discharge an employee." *Leithead v. American Colloid Company*, 721 P.2d 1059, 1062 (Wyo.1986); *Alexander v. Phillips Oil Company*, 707 P.2d 1385 (Wyo. 1985); *Mobil Coal Producing, Inc.*, 704 P.2d 702.

The disposition of this case depends on construction of the purported disclaimer along with other provisions in the Handbook in the nature of disclaimers. "The Handbook of Employment Guidelines" given to appellant when she was employed contained a disclaimer on page 2 as follows:

HANDBOOK DISCLAIMER

The guidelines outlined in this handbook are for the mutual benefit of this nursing center and its associates. These guidelines include methods of procedure which, when implemented, can effectively enhance the management of a successful nursing center. The executive director and supervisors must therefore reserve all the customary rights of management, including the right to supervise and control all operations; direct all work; interpret, change or cancel all personnel policies with or without notice; hire, schedule, terminate, layoff, transfer, promote, reward, discipline, or otherwise manage associates and select the manner, method and means of doing so. This handbook is not a contract and contains no promises, guarantees, representations, agreements, or warranties upon which any prospective, current or prior associates of this nursing center can reasonably maintain or create any expectations of such.

Life Care points to provisions in the handbook disclaimer to support its contention:

The executive director and supervisors * * * reserve * * * the right * * * to * * * interpret, change or cancel all personnel policies *with or without notice*; hire, schedule, *terminate*, layoff, transfer, promote, reward, *discipline*, or otherwise manage associates *and select the manner, method and means of doing so.* This handbook is not a contract and *contains no promises, guarantees, representations, agreements, or warranties* * * *. (Emphasis added.)

The "Handbook of Employment Guidelines" contains twenty-five numbered pages and five unnumbered pages, including the "Table of Contents." The contents were in fine print—topic headings were in larger print and bold-faced. Under the caption "Discipline and Termination," thirty-nine examples of unacceptable employee conduct are listed. The paragraph at the top of page 21 cautions:

The list that follows, though not all-inclusive, gives examples of violations of the nursing center principles of conduct which may subject the offender to disciplinary action. Such action includes, but is not limited to, warning notices, suspension and/or discharge.

Under the caption "Disciplinary Procedures" of the handbook, a four-step progressive discipline approach is outlined which the employer will "generally" apply. The first paragraph states that "[t]he nursing center may, depending on the severity of the offense terminate an associate after the first offense." After listing the four disciplinary steps, the handbook further states:

> This will be our usual and preferred process for administering discipline. However, conduct of any type which causes the center to lose confidence in your ability to perform adequately your assigned job may result in immediate discharge.

The handbook contains a tear-out "Acknowledgment Card," in which the employee states that she will familiarize herself with its contents. Appellant signed her acknowledgment card December 4, 1989.

In *McDonald*, 820 P.2d at 986, this court adopted the rules set forth in *Jimenez v. Colorado Interstate Gas Company*, 690 F.Supp. 977, 980 (D.Wyo.1988) * * * which state:

> For this disclaimer to be effective against plaintiff, it must be conspicuous. Whether a disclaimer is conspicuous is a question of law. * * *

Defendant was not obligated to write [standard operating procedures ("SOPs")] and to post them in an employee area. Because it has done so, the court is now faced with a "strong equitable and social policy reasons militating against allowing employers to promulgate for their employees potentially misleading personnel manuals while reserving the right to deviate from them at their own caprice." These policy reasons help explain why an effective disclaimer must be conspicuous. The disclaimer in question is not set off in any way that would attract attention. It falls under the heading "GENERAL INSTRUCTIONS" and the subheading "CONTENTS." Nothing is capitalized that would give notice of a disclaimer. The type size equals that of other provisions on the same page. No border sets the disclaimer apart from any other paragraph on the page. The disclaimer is not conspicuous. Therefore, this court grants summary judgment that the SOPs create implied contract rights.

In *McDonald*, 820 P.2d at 986, we quoted with approval *Woolley v. Hoffmann–La Roche, Inc.*, 99 N.J. 284, 491 A.2d 1257 (1985), mod., 101 N.J. 10, 499 A.2d 515 (1985). In *Woolley*, the court set out an example of what need be done if the employer does not want the manual to be capable of being construed by the court as a binding contract. The court said:

> It would be unfair to allow an employer to distribute a policy manual that makes the workforce believe that certain promises have been made and then to allow the employer to renege on those promises. What is sought here is basic honesty: if the employer, for whatever reason, does not want the manual to be capable of being construed by the court as a binding contract, there are simple ways to attain that goal. All that need be done is the inclusion in a very prominent position of an appropriate statement that there is no promise of any kind by the employer contained in the manual; that regardless of what the manual says or provides, the employer promises nothing and remains free to

change wages and all other working conditions without having to consult anyone and without anyone's agreement; and that the employer continues to have the absolute power to fire anyone with or without good cause. *Woolley*, 491 A.2d at 1271.

* * *

In the case before us, the disclaimer is in the "Introduction" section of the handbook, subtitled "Handbook Disclaimer." The language of the disclaimer speaks in terms of "mutual benefit," management "enhancement" and the right to supervise. It does not say that the employer retains the right to deviate from the terms of the handbook at its own caprice. It does not say that the employer remains free to change wages and all other working conditions without consulting the employee or obtaining his agreement, nor that the employer retains absolute power to fire anyone with or without good cause. Instead, there is an inference in the disclaimer that it is a guide for "mutual benefit," that certain procedures contained therein would be "implemented" to "enhance the management of a successful nursing center," and that the "customary rights" of the employer were set forth in the handbook.

The operative language in the disclaimer is not bold lettered; it is buried in introductory paragraphs. It is not designed to attract attention and is stated in language which does not tell the employee what he needs to know. We are reluctant to specify language and the placement of a disclaimer in order that it be effective. Perhaps this could be accomplished in numerous ways. Additionally, the handbook listed misconduct that could result in discharge, thus implying that cause is required. *Jimenez*, 690 F.Supp. at 980. Detailing stages of progressive discipline results in a further implication that cause is required to discharge. Most likely a lawyer would have told appellant that, under her employment arrangement, she could be discharged without cause. An employee should not have to hire a lawyer to learn that.

In summary, we determine that the disclaimer was not physically conspicuous and its contents were ambiguous in that there was language that inferred that Life Care intended to modify the at-will employment to an employment which could only be terminated for cause. Furthermore, listing numerous types of misconduct that could result in termination coupled with progressive stages of discipline inferred that cause is required to discharge. * * *

Rationale

The meaning and effect of the employment relationship in this case, a mixed question of law and fact, remains unresolved. Therefore, we must reverse summary judgment. The case is remanded to the trial court for determination of whether the employee handbook modified the employment relationship from one terminable at will to one terminable only for cause.

CARDINE, JUSTICE, dissenting, with whom TAYLOR, J., joins.

This is yet another case to come before us in which an employer has tried to satisfy the court's secret concept of an adequate disclaimer in an employee handbook. The employer was, in essence, told: "Sorry, you failed again—but keep trying—you may get it right." Why don't we just tell litigants what is "right?"

Rationale

I dissent because the disclaimer in this employee handbook was clear, explicit and adequate to inform any reasonable employee that the at-will employment relationship was preserved. I dissent also because the court fails once again to inform an employer what is acceptable as an effective disclaimer in an employee handbook. * * *

[The disclaimer] appears on page two of the handbook. It is conspicuous. It cannot be misunderstood. Nevertheless, the court found that the above disclaimer in this case was insufficient. I believe the court, in fairness to litigants, should now say what is sufficient. The most the court has said thus far is that the disclaimer must be conspicuous under the standards adopted in *Jimenez v. Colorado Interstate Gas Co.*, 690 F.Supp. 977, 980 (D.Wyo.1988), and that even if the disclaimer is conspicuous, it still may be negated by a course of conduct which implies that cause is required in order to terminate an employee. *McDonald* . . . , 820 P.2d at 990–91.

Our rulings discourage employers from providing their employees with a manual. This deprives employees of useful information about company policies. The dilemma businesses face was well described in this law review article:

> Employers who have large numbers of employees or who have complicated company policies find themselves in a precarious position. If these employers do not promulgate any sort of policy manual, they may be required to formulate employee policy on an ad hoc basis and face administrative chaos. Conversely, if they do issue a manual and comply with its procedures to such a degree that their employees reasonably expect them to continue to do so in the future, they may be subjected to unintended contractual liability.

> Michael [Rhodes] Wallace, *"Employee Manuals as Implied Contracts: The Guidelines That Bind,"* 27 Tulsa L.J. 263, 263–64 (1991) (hereinafter: *"Employee Manuals as Implied Contracts"*).

My other concern with discouraging employers from issuing manuals is that employees will be deprived of useful safety information that is sometimes contained in the employee manuals. Without a handbook, employees are not apprised of communication processes within the company that are important for maintaining a positive work environment. The time is now for the court to clearly state what would be sufficient, not just continue ruling ad hoc that the particular disclaimer before the court is insufficient.

I would adopt a straight-forward rule that gives clear guidance to employers. * * *

K. D. v. EDUCATIONAL TESTING SERVICE

Supreme Court, New York County, 1976.
87 Misc.2d 657, 386 N.Y.S.2d 747.

ARNOLD GUY FRAIMAN, JUSTICE: This is a motion to dismiss the complaint, pursuant to CPLR Rule 3211(a) pars. 1, 7 and subd. (c) on the grounds that there is a defense founded upon documentary evidence and that the complaint fails to state a cause of action.

Plaintiff is a 37 year old college graduate, having entered college at the age of 32. Seeking to attend law school, he took the Law School Admission Test (LSAT) twice within a four month period in 1973–74. Defendant is a non-profit corporation engaged in the business of preparing and administering various well-known educational tests, including the LSAT, for use by colleges and graduate schools throughout the nation. It has administered the LSAT since 1954. The LSAT is an objective test designed to measure general aptitude for the study of law of candidates seeking admission to law school. It consists of approximately 130 so-called multiple choice questions and it also has a section of about 70 questions of a similar nature designed to test writing ability. Defendant administers the LSAT for the Law School Admissions Council (LSAC), a non-profit membership association of graduate schools of law. The LSAC sets policy for administration of the examinations and the reporting of scores.

Test scores play an important role in determining whether a candidate will be admitted to law school. To insure that they accurately reflect the candidate's own effort, the administration of the tests are carefully monitored, and after they are scored, individual scores are checked by computer against any previous scores by the same candidate. Where an increase of more than 150 points (out of a total of 800) is found, defendant conducts an investigation before the candidate's score is reported to the law schools.

Each candidate who applies to take the LSAT is sent a booklet entitled "Law School Admissions Bulletin" and a registration form. Upon receipt of the completed form, defendant sends the candidate an admission card to take the examination on a specified date at a designated testing center. The registration form requires the applicant to write out in longhand the following statement and to sign it: "I accept the conditions set forth in the Bulletin concerning the administration of the test and the reporting of information to law schools."

Plaintiff took the examination in December 1973 and again in April 1974. Before each examination, he was sent a copy of the Bulletin and completed in his own handwriting the statement above on his registration forms. The Bulletins received by plaintiff each contained the following language under the heading "Scores Cancelled by ETS":

"We are concerned with reporting only valid scores. On rare occasions, misconduct * * * or circumstances beyond the candidate's control * * * may render scores invalid. If doubts are raised about your score because of these or other circumstances, we will expect you to cooperate in our investigation. We reserve the right to cancel any test score if, in our sole opinion, there is adequate reason to question its validity. Before exercising this right, we will offer you an opportunity to take the test again at no additional fee.

"If we cancel a score, we will notify the law schools that received, or were to receive, the scores as well as the schools receiving subsequent reports."

On his December, 1973 examination plaintiff received a score of 399 on the LSAT portion and 26 on the writing ability portion. His April, 1974 LSAT score was 637, or 238 points higher, and his writing ability score was 62. The 238 point discrepancy between the two LSAT scores prompted an investigation by defendant which disclosed striking similarities between plaintiff's answers and the answers of one "KL," the candidate seated adjacent to plaintiff. Plaintiff answered 39 of the 130 multiple choice questions on the LSAT portion of the test incorrectly. Of these, 27 were the same incorrect answers as those selected by KL. The significance of this correlation is made evident from an analysis by defendant of the answer sheets of ten other candidates taking the same LSAT who obtained scores in the same range as plaintiff and KL. Comparing their incorrect answers with plaintiff's, discloses that, on average, there were only 7 incorrect responses identical to plaintiff's. Of the ten other answer sheets analyzed, the most incorrect responses on any one answer sheet which were identical to those of plaintiff was 11. A comparison and analysis of plaintiff's writing ability answer sheet with KL's and the ten other candidates disclosed a similar result.*

On the basis of the foregoing, defendant wrote to plaintiff requesting that he furnish any information which he believed was relevant to his questioned scores. In addition, he was offered an opportunity to take the examination again at a regularly scheduled time at no cost. If he elected to do so, and his retest score came within 50 points of the questioned score, defendant stated that the questioned score would be forwarded to the law schools. On the other hand, if the retest score failed to confirm the questioned score, or if plaintiff refused to take the retest, defendant indicated that it would cancel the questioned score and notify the law schools that plaintiff's score was cancelled "due to serious doubt as to [its] authenticity."

In response to this letter, plaintiff submitted a sworn statement that he did not cheat on the examination. However, he refused to take a retest. He then commenced the instant action for a declaratory judgment and an injunction restraining defendant from cancelling his April, 1974 test score; from notifying the law schools that this action was taken because of the score's doubtful authenticity; and compelling defendant to report the April, 1974 score to the law schools as a valid score.

---

* The scores of KL, who was unknown to plaintiff, were not questioned because he had achieved scores in the same range as those on the April, 1974 examination on two prior occasions on which he took the LSAT.

In support of its motion to dismiss the complaint, defendant alleges that plaintiff is barred by the contract he entered into when he agreed on his registration forms to accept the conditions set forth in the Bulletin concerning the administration of the test and the reporting of results to the law schools. Defendant contends that its actions are in full accord with the following provisions in the Bulletin:

> "We reserve the right to cancel any test score if, in our sole opinion, there is adequate reason to question its validity. * * * If we cancel a score, we will notify the law schools that * * * were to receive the score."

* * *

We turn now to a consideration of that portion of the injunctive relief sought by plaintiff wherein he seeks to restrain defendant from cancelling his April, 1974 test scores and to compel it to forward the scores to the law schools. As noted above, the right to cancel any test score if in its opinion there was adequate reason to question its validity was expressly reserved to itself by defendant in the Bulletin, and plaintiff accepted that as well as all other conditions set forth in the Bulletin when he completed his registration form. Nevertheless, plaintiff contends that he is not bound by his agreement, because, he argues, his contract with defendant is a contract of adhesion, and therefore void. A contract of adhesion is one entered into between parties with unequal bargaining power. They are typically standard contracts which are offered by the party with strong bargaining power to the weaker party on a take it or leave it basis. The instant agreement would appear to fit this description. Almost every accredited law school in the United States requires a candidate for admission to take the LSAT. Thus, when plaintiff decided to attend law school he had no alternative but to accept the standard conditions fixed by defendant for all test takers. Plaintiff could neither contract with a party other than defendant to take a law school aptitude test, since no such entity exists, or indicate to defendant that the terms contained in the Bulletin were not acceptable to him. In the latter case it is clear that if he had done so he would not have been permitted to take the examination.

However, while plaintiff's description of the agreement herein as a contract of adhesion may be justified, his conclusion that it is therefore void, is not. Where the court finds that an agreement is a contract of adhesion, effort will frequently be made to protect the weaker party from the agreement's harsher terms by a variety of pretexts, while still keeping the elementary rules of the law of contracts intact. Kessler, "Contracts of Adhesion—Some Thoughts about Freedom of Contract", 43 Col.L.Rev. 629 (1943) at p. 633. The Court may, for example, find the obnoxious clause "ambiguous", even where no ambiguity exists, and then construe it against its author; or it may find the clause to be against public policy and declare it unenforceable; or finally, the court may hold that although the offending clause prohibits a recovery by plaintiff *ex contractu*, it does not prohibit a recovery in tort.

Thus, the issue in the instant case is whether the clause reserving to defendant itself the right to cancel plaintiff's test score if there is a question about its validity, and requiring him to take a retest in such event, is so unfair and unreasonable that the court, having found it a part of a contract of adhesion, will disregard it by means of one or more of the pretexts above. The issue as thus stated must be answered in the negative. To the extent that defendant can accurately predict the aptitude of a candidate for law school by means of its test results, it performs a highly valuable service not only to the law schools but to the public as well. Moreover, the accuracy of its predictions is defendant's sole stock in trade. The less accurate as a forecaster its tests are, the less value they have to the law schools. Thus, if defendant reasonably believed that the test scores of plaintiff as scored on the April, 1974 test, did not accurately reflect his aptitude for law school, it acted within its right to protect its own image as well as its obligation to the schools who are its clients in cancelling plaintiff's scores and requiring him to take a retest. * * *

In the instant case, the evidence that plaintiff did not achieve his scores on the April, 1974 LSAT unaided was sufficient to justify the action contemplated by defendant. Moreover, its offer of a free retest under normal testing conditions with the understanding that it would forward plaintiff's April, 1974 scores if the retest score came within 50 points of the earlier scores was eminently fair and reasonable under the circumstances. * * *

For all the foregoing reasons, the motion to dismiss so much of the complaint as seeks to enjoin defendant from cancelling plaintiff's April, 1974 test scores, and to compel it to forward those scores to the law schools is granted.

MCC–MARBLE CERAMIC CENTER, INC. v. CERAMICA NUOVA D'AGOSTINO

United States Court of Appeals, Eleventh Circuit, 1998.
144 F.3d 1384.

[Plaintiff claimed not to be bound by certain terms written on the reverse side of a printed contract for a variety of reasons, including the fact that the agreement signed in Italy was in the Italian language. Part of footnote 9 of the opinion is reproduced here.]

MCC makes much of the fact that the written order form is entirely in Italian and that Monzon, who signed the contract on MCC's behalf directly below this provision incorporating the terms on the reverse of the form, neither spoke nor read Italian. This fact is of no assistance to MCC's position. We find it nothing short of astounding that an individual purportedly experienced in commercial matters, would sign a contract in a foreign language and expect not to be bound simply because he could not comprehend its terms. We find nothing in the CISG [Convention on International Sale of Goods] that might counsel this type of reckless behavior and nothing that signals any retreat from the proposition that parties who sign contracts will be bound by them regardless of whether they have read them or understood them. * * *

Problems

Students should read the following problems and propose an answer based upon the foregoing cases and the sections of Calamari & Perillo 5th cited at the beginning of this section.

1.   A owned a $200 set of harness which was stolen from him. While in a state of wrath and in a boastful and blustering manner, A proclaimed in the presence of a group of persons including the plaintiff that he would pay $2,500 to anyone who recovered the harness. Plaintiff recovered the harness and sues A for the reward. Does Plaintiff recover?

2.   D came home one evening and found his house on fire. He was very upset. He called out, "I will give $500,000 to anyone who will rescue my wife from the building, dead or alive." P, who was watching the fire, went into the building and brought out the dead body of D's wife. P sues D. What result?

3.   An influential moral philosopher posed the following question: Tamerlane promised the garrison of Sebastia that, if they would surrender, no blood would be shed. The garrison surrendered. Tamerlane buried them all alive. Did Tamerlane break his promise?

4.   Plaintiff was in the business of manufacturing automobile parts. Plaintiff's customers were the major auto manufacturers. Plaintiff wished to sell to other buyers, particularly to sellers of replacement auto parts (such as Midas Muffler), but it had reason to believe that its automobile manufacturer customers would be displeased and might cease doing business with plaintiff. To achieve secrecy, plaintiff set up a subsidiary to distribute its products. It then entered into a detailed formalized writing with defendant, a trusted employee, which stated that defendant agreed to purchase all shares of the subsidiary for $50,000 and plaintiff agreed to sell the shares at that price. It was orally agreed between plaintiff and defendant that the agreement would not be carried out. For twenty years the parties proceeded without a transfer of the shares or of the money. As far as the business world knew, defendant was the sole owner of the distribution business. Between the parties, however, the defendant acted as a loyal employee of the plaintiff. Then the plaintiff decided to end its arrangement with the defendant and to let it be known to the trade that it was operating the distribution business.

Defendant tenders $50,000 and demands that plaintiff transfer the shares of stock pursuant to the written agreement. Plaintiff starts an action demanding a declaratory judgment to the effect that the written agreement is not binding. Will plaintiff succeed?

5.   A written agreement regulating the commercial relations of the parties (B and S) contained the following clause: "This arrangement is not entered into, nor is the memorandum written as a formal or legal agreement and shall not be subject to legal jurisdiction in the law courts either of the United States or England but it is only a definite expression and record of

the purpose and of the intention of the parties concerned to which they each honorably pledge themselves with the fullest confidence based on past business with each other, that it will be carried through by each of these parties with mutual loyalty and friendly cooperation." Before the parties' relationship had broken off, B had given and S had shipped some orders for goods pursuant to this agreement and S had accepted others which had not been shipped.

  (a) Does B have a cause of action against S for refusal to ship goods pursuant to orders which S had accepted?

  (b) Does S have a cause of action against B for refusing to pay for goods accepted by B?

  6.   H is living in harmony with his wife, W. Before H leaves on a trip, W and H assess W's financial need and agree that H will remit $1000 per month for her support. Is there a contract?

  7.   Would the result be different in Problem 6 if the parties had made their agreement in writing and added this clause, "We intend to make this a legally binding agreement."

  8.   Would the result be different in Problem 6 if the parties had separated in the sense that they had mutually agreed that they were incompatible and would live apart.

  9.   Jim invited Amy to join him to see a play. She agreed, and it was further agreed that he would pick her up at her home at a specified date and time. He drove from San Francisco to San Jose to pick her up at the agreed time. She wasn't home. He sued, claiming $38—the cost of the ticket and the estimated cost of the wasted eighty-mile round trip. (a) Resolve the law suit. (b) Would the result be different if the parties had agreed that there would be a binding obligation?

  10.   Would your answer to Problem 9(a) be any different if Jim had flown cross-country at considerable expense, rented a car to pick her up and she wasn't home at the agreed time?

SECTION 2.   THE OFFER

  (a) Offers Distinguished From Expressions of Opinion, Advertisements, Etc.

———

(Calamari & Perillo 5th §§ 2.5 and 2.6)

COLLINS v. REYNARD

Supreme Court of Illinois, 1992.
154 Ill.2d 48, 607 N.E.2d 1185, 180 Ill.Dec. 672.

JUSTICE HEIPLE delivered the opinion of the court: This is a case of professional malpractice brought by a client against her lawyer. The gist of the complaint is that the lawyer, in drafting certain sales documents for the client, failed to protect the client's security interest in the property being sold, thus causing a financial loss to the client.

The complaint against the lawyer, in separate counts, couched its claims in separate theories of both contract and tort. At the trial level, the lawyer defendant moved to dismiss the tort portion of the complaint for failure to state a cause of action. The motion was denied. The lawyer defendant then took an interlocutory appeal. A unanimous appellate court reversed the trial court and stated, in essence, that the plaintiff's complaint for lawyer malpractice is cognizable in contract but not in tort. 195 Ill.App.3d 1067, 142 Ill.Dec. 719, 553 N.E.2d 69.

On further appeal to this court, we issued a decision affirming the appellate court. Thereafter the plaintiff's petition for rehearing was. *[Procedure]* allowed (134 Ill.2d R. 367), and the case was reargued.

Today we rule that a complaint against a lawyer for professional malpractice may be couched in either contract or tort and that recovery may be sought in the alternative. In so ruling, we adhere to that long line of Illinois cases allowing pleading and recovery in tort for lawyer malpractice. [Citations omitted]. Our ruling is grounded on historical precedent rather than logic. If something has been handled in a certain way for a long period of time and if people are familiar with the practice and accustomed to its use, it is reasonable to continue with that practice until and unless good cause is shown to change the rule. Certainty in the law enables parties to understand their relative rights and duties and facilitates rationality and planning in matters of commerce and social intercourse. Uncertainty, on the other hand, introduces disfunction and chaos.

The appellate court, in attempting to extend the rationale of the *Moorman*, doctrine to the case at hand, ruled contrary to the ruling we announce today. (*Moorman Manufacturing Co. v. National Tank Co.* (1982), 91 Ill.2d 69, 61 Ill.Dec. 746, 435 N.E.2d 443.) While we do not fault its logic, we do not follow its ruling. Rather, we adhere to long established practice and custom. Logic may be a face card but custom is a trump.

Moorman attempted to distinguish between recovery in tort and recovery in contract by looking to the nature of the damage suffered rather than to the relationship between the parties or to the act which caused the damage. In reaching its conclusion, the *Moorman* analysis began at the end of the transaction and reasoned in reverse. It defined a special category of damages as not cognizable in tort. A different analysis might have started at the beginning with a first consideration given to the relationship between the parties under a traditional contract or tort analysis. Though the ultimate decision in that case might yet have been the same, it would have been reached by a different route.

Contract law applies to voluntary obligations freely entered into *[Rule]* between parties. Damages recoverable under a breach of contract theory *[Rational]* are based upon the mutual expectations of the parties. The basic principle for the measurement of contract damages is that the injured party is entitled to recover an amount that will put him in as good a position as he would have been in had the contract been performed as agreed.

Tort law, on the other hand, applies in situations where society recognizes a duty to exist wholly apart from any contractual undertaking. Tort obligations are general obligations that impose liability when a person negligently, carelessly or purposely causes injury to others. These obligations have been recognized by society to protect fellow citizens from unreasonable risks of harm. Whether a duty will be recognized under tort law depends upon the foreseeability of the injury, the likelihood of the injury, the magnitude of the burden of guarding against the injury, and the consequences of placing that burden on the defendant. [Citations omitted.]

Although the common law distinctions between contract and tort have been both modified and confused by different courts in different situations, differences between tort theories and contract theories still have validity. (Feinman, *The Jurisprudence of Classification*, 41 Stan. L.Rev. 661 (1989); Bertschy, *Negligent Performance of Service Contracts and the Economic Loss Doctrine*, 17 J.Mar.L.Rev. 249 (1984); W. Keeton, Prosser & Keeton on Torts § 92, at 655 (5th ed. 1984).) For all of that, a punch in the nose remains, for all practical purposes, a tort and not a breach of contract. In the field of contract, however, some breaches have crossed the line and become cognizable in tort. [Citations omitted].

Finally, it is to be noted that the ruling we announce today is limited to the specific field of lawyer malpractice as an exception to the so-called *Moorman* doctrine and to the distinctions separating contract from tort. Today's decision neither changes the duties a lawyer owes his client, nor does it change the circumstances under which a lawyer may be sued for malpractice, nor does it change the damages recoverable. We merely restate the long standing Illinois practice in this matter.

Disposition

* * *

Appellate court reversed; circuit court affirmed; cause remanded. [A concurring opinion is omitted.]

Holding

HAWKINS v. McGEE

Supreme Court of New Hampshire, 1929.
146 A. 641, 84 N.H. 114.

Defendant's motions for a nonsuit and for a directed verdict on the count in assumpsit were denied, and the defendant excepted. During the argument of plaintiff's counsel to the jury, the defendant claimed certain exceptions, and also excepted to the denial of his requests for instructions and to the charge of the court upon the question of damages, as more fully appears in the opinion. The defendant seasonably moved to set aside the verdict upon the grounds that it was (1) contrary to the evidence; (2) against the weight of the evidence; (3) against the weight of the law and evidence; and (4) because the damages awarded by the jury were excessive. The court denied the motion upon the first three grounds, but found that the damages were excessive, and made an order that the verdict be set aside, unless the plaintiff elected to remit all in excess of $500. The plaintiff having refused to remit, the verdict was set aside "as excessive and against the weight of the evidence," and the plaintiff excepted.

The foregoing exceptions were transferred by Scammon, J. The facts are stated in the opinion.

BRANCH, J. 1. The operation in question consisted in the removal of a considerable quantity of scar tissue from the palm of the plaintiff's right hand and the grafting of skin taken from the plaintiff's chest in place thereof. The scar tissue was the result of a severe burn caused by contact with an electric wire, which the plaintiff received about nine years before the time of the transactions here involved. There was evidence to the effect that before the operation was performed the plaintiff and his father went to the defendant's office, and that the defendant, in answer to the question, "How long will the boy be in the hospital?" replied, "Three or four days, not over four; then the boy can go home and it will be just a few days when he will go back to work with a good hand." Clearly this and other testimony to the same effect would not justify a finding that the doctor contracted to complete the hospital treatment in three or four days or that the plaintiff would be able to go back to work within a few days thereafter. The above statements could only be construed as expressions of opinion or predictions as to the probable duration of the treatment and plaintiff's resulting disability, and the fact that these estimates were exceeded would impose no contractual liability upon the defendant. The only substantial basis for the plaintiff's claim is the testimony that the defendant also said before the operation was decided upon, "I will guarantee to make the hand a hundred per cent perfect hand or a hundred per cent good hand." The plaintiff was present when these words were alleged to have been spoken, and, if they are to be taken at their face value, it seems obvious that proof of their utterance would establish the giving of a warranty in accordance with his contention.

The defendant argues, however, that, even if these words were uttered by him, no reasonable man would understand that they were used with the intention of entering "into any contractual relation whatever," and that they could reasonably be understood only "as his expression in strong language that he believed and expected that as a result of the operation he would give the plaintiff a very good hand." It may be conceded, as the defendant contends, that, before the question of the making of a contract should be submitted to a jury, there is a preliminary question of law for the trial court to pass upon, i.e. "whether the words could possibly have the meaning imputed to them by the party who founds his case upon a certain interpretation," but it cannot be held that the trial court decided this question erroneously in the present case. It is unnecessary to determine at this time whether the argument of the defendant, based upon "common knowledge of the uncertainty which attends all surgical operations," and the improbability that a surgeon would ever contract to make a damaged part of the human body "one hundred per cent perfect," would, in the absence of countervailing considerations, be regarded as conclusive, for there were other factors in the present case which tended to support the contention of the plaintiff. There was evidence that the defendant repeatedly solicited from the plaintiff's father the opportunity to perform this operation, and the theory was advanced by plaintiff's counsel in cross-examination of defendant that he sought an opportunity to "experiment on skin grafting," in which he had had little previous experience. If the jury accepted this part of plaintiff's contention, there would be a reasonable basis for the further conclusion that, if defendant spoke the words attributed to him, he did so with the intention that they should be accepted at their face value, as an inducement for the granting of consent to the operation by the plaintiff and his father, and there was ample evidence that they were so accepted by them. The question of the making of the alleged contract was properly submitted to the jury.

2. The substance of the charge to the jury on the question of damages appears in the following quotation: "If you find the plaintiff entitled to anything, he is entitled to recover for what pain and suffering he has been made to endure and for what injury he has sustained over and above what injury he had before." To this instruction the defendant seasonably excepted. By it, the jury was permitted to consider two elements of damage: (1) Pain and suffering due to the operation; and (2) positive ill effects of the operation upon the plaintiff's hand. Authority for any specific rule of damages in cases of this kind seems to be lacking, but, when tested by general principle and by analogy, it appears that the foregoing instruction was erroneous.

"By 'damages,' as that term is used in the law of contracts, is intended compensation for a breach, measured in the terms of the contract." Davis v. New England Cotton Yarn Co., 77 N. H. 403, 404, 92 A. 732, 733. The purpose of the law is "to put the plaintiff in as good a position as he would have been in had the defendant kept his contract." 3 Williston Cont. § 1338; Hardie–Tynes Mfg. Co. v. Eastern Cotton Oil Co., 150 N. C. 150, 63 S. E. 676, 134 Am. St. Rep. 899. The measure of recovery "is based upon what the defendant should have given the plaintiff, not what the plaintiff has given the defendant or otherwise expended." 3 Williston Cont. § 1341. "The only losses that can be said fairly to come within the terms of a contract are such as the parties must have had in mind when the contract was made, or such as they either knew or ought to have known would probably result from a failure to comply with its terms." Davis v. New England Cotton Yarn Co., 77 N. H. 403, 404, 92 A. 732, 733, Hurd v. Dunsmore, 63 N. H. 171.

The present case is closely analogous to one in which a machine is built for a certain purpose and warranted to do certain work. In such cases, the usual rule of damages for breach of warranty in the sale of chattels is applied, and it is held that the measure of damages is the difference between the value of the machine, if it had corresponded with the warranty and its actual value, together with such incidental losses as the parties knew, or ought to have known, would probably result from a failure to comply with its terms. [Citations omitted.] * * *

The rule thus applied is well settled in this state. "As a general rule, the measure of the vendee's damages is the difference between the value of the goods as they would have been if the warranty as to quality had been true, and the actual value at the time of the sale, including gains prevented and losses sustained, and such other damages as could be reasonably anticipated by the parties as likely to be caused by the vendor's failure to keep his agreement, and could not by reasonable care on the part of the vendee have been avoided." Union Bank v. Blanchard, 65 N. H. 21, 23, 18 A. 90, 91; Hurd v. Dunsmore, supra; Noyes v. Blodgett, 58 N. H. 502; P. L. ch. 166, § 69, subd. 7. We therefore conclude that the true measure of the plaintiff's damage in the present case is the difference between the value to him of a perfect hand or a good hand, such as the jury found the defendant promised him, and the value of his hand in its present condition, including any incidental consequences fairly within the contemplation of the parties when they made their contract. 1 Sutherland, Damages (4th Ed.) § 92. Damages not thus limited, although naturally resulting, are not to be given.

The extent of the plaintiff's suffering does not measure this difference in value. The pain necessarily incident to a serious surgical operation was a part of the contribution which the plaintiff was willing to make to his joint undertaking with the defendant to produce a good hand. * * * It represented a part of the price which he was willing to pay for a good hand, but it furnished no test of the value of a good hand or the difference between the value of the hand which the defendant promised and the one which resulted from the operation.

It was also erroneous and misleading to submit to the jury as a separate element of damage any change for the worse in the condition of the plaintiff's hand resulting from the operation, although this error was probably more prejudicial to the plaintiff than to the defendant. Any such ill effect of the operation would be included under the true rule of damages set forth above, but damages might properly be assessed for the defendant's failure to improve the condition of the hand, even if there were no evidence that its condition was made worse as a result of the operation.

It must be assumed that the trial court, in setting aside the verdict, undertook to apply the same rule of damages which he had previously given to the jury, and, since this rule was erroneous, it is unnecessary for us to consider whether there was any evidence to justify his finding that all damages awarded by the jury above $500 were excessive.

* * *

New trial.

McGEE v. UNITED STATES FIDELITY
& GUARANTY CO.

United States Court of Appeals, First Circuit, 1931.
53 F.2d 953.

Disposition

☆

[After the decision in the principal case, Dr. McKee settled by paying Hawkins $1,400. In this case he sued his malpractice insurance carrier which denied coverage on the ground that the verdict had been for breach of a contract to achieve a promised result and not for the tort of malpractice. The insurance company's defense was sustained. In the opinion we learn more about the condition of Hawkins' hand as described in Hawkins' complaint. "[T]he new tissue grafted upon said hand became matted, unsightly, and so healed and attached to said hand as to practically fill the hand with an unsightly growth, restricting the motion of the plaintiff's hand so that said hand has become useless to the plaintiff wherein, previous to said operation by the said defendant, it was a practical, useful hand . . . ." We also learn that Hawkins spent three months in the hospital.]

Jorie Roberts, *Hawkins Case: A Hair–Raising Experience*, HARVARD LAW RECORD, March 17, 1978 at 1, 7, 13 (based on interviews and correspondence with plaintiff's brother and sister-in-law, Howard and Edith, plaintiff's sister, and a local lawyer).

* * * The case originated in 1922 in Berlin, New Hampshire, a small mill town near the Canadian border, when Dr. Edward McGee, a general practitioner, promised to restore George Hawkins' slightly scarred hand to "perfect condition" through surgery. * * *

George Hawkins was born in January, 1904—the second of Rose Wilkinson and Charles Augustus Hawkins' six children. * * * Charles Hawkins hailed from Canada. In Berlin, Charles Hawkins first worked as a manual laborer, then became night superintendent at a local factory.

One morning in 1915, 11–year–old George burned his right hand while preparing breakfast for his father on the family's wood-burning stove. At the time, George was trying to turn on the kitchen light to illuminate the stove, but an electrical storm the night before had damaged the wiring so that George received a severe shock. One of George's younger brothers, Howard Hawkins, now an insurance agent in Berlin, described George's initial scar as a "small pencil-size scar" which was between his thumb and index finger and did not substantially affect his use of the hand. Nevertheless, Charles Hawkins took his son George to skin specialists in Montreal after the accident; but the doctors advised the Hawkinses against doing anything to restore the hand.

During this period, the family physician, Edward McGee, while treating one of George's younger brothers for pneumonia, also became aware of George's scarred hand. Later, in 1919, after returning from several years of medical service in Europe during World War I, McGee requested George and his parents to let him operate on the hand in order to restore it to "perfect" condition.

According to ... George's younger sister, McGee claimed to have done a number of similar skin grafts on soldiers in Germany during the war, although he later admitted that he had really only observed such operations.

[His sister] recollects that McGee, in persuading George to undergo the surgery, emphasized the social problems which his scarred hand might create. McGee encouraged the Hawkinses to allow him to operate on the hand for three years, until finally George agreed shortly after his 18th birthday. [W]hile [his] parents had strong doubts about the operation, they trusted McGee's judgment and were hesitant to oppose George's decision and the physician's advice. * * *

McGee operated on George's hand ... in March of 1922. The skin graft operation was supposed to be quick, simple, and effective, and to require only a few days of hospitalization. Instead, [his sister] recalls that her brother bled very badly for several days....

* * * George was, in the words of his brother Howard, "in the throes of death" for quite a while after the operation because of his extensive bleeding and the ensuing infection. Moreover, the post-operation scar covered his thumb and two fingers and was densely covered with hair. Howard Hawkins remembers that George's hand was partially closed up and continued to bleed periodically throughout his life. * * *

The jury only awarded the Hawkins [sic] $3,000 for damages, and the final settlement was for $1,400 and lawyers [sic] fees. * * * Charles Hawkins took the $1,400 and his injured son back to Montreal to see if any subsequent operations would alleviate George's deformity, but the doctors there said that the grafted skin was so tough that nothing more could be done. * * *

Although McGee had been the Hawkinses' family physician for a number of years prior to the operation, ... [his sister] recalls that she and her mother went to McGee's office right after their first visit to see George in the hospital and that McGee asserted then that he had nothing at all to say to the Hawkinses concerning the operation. The Hawkinses then engaged another doctor to handle George's post-operative case. * * *

Hawkins' crippled hand affected his employment and outlook throughout his lifetime. After the operation, George Hawkins never returned to high school, even though, in Howard's opinion, "George was very bright, learned quickly, and had a pleasing personality." He was encouraged by his parents to finish school, but would not because, in his siblings' view, he was embarrassed by his hand.

George also gave up tennis and riflery after the operation, although previously he had won several medals as a marksman for the State Home Guard. Because of his hand, George was unable to perform any heavy manual labor or learn to type. He worked for many years in the printing division of the Brown Company, a pulp and paper manufacturer in Berlin, and later in a tire store. * * *

George married late in life and never had any children. * * * According to his family members, George was always very sensitive about his hand and suffered lifelong emotional distress. His parents also grieved until their deaths because of the tragic and unnecessary crippling of their son's hand.

The Hawkins family was unaware of the widespread study of *Hawkins v. McGee* in law schools until, in 1964, Howard and Edith Hawkins' daughter Gail encountered the case early in her contracts course at Boston University Law School. * * *

Howard Hawkins, however, believes that George was somewhat aware of the case's importance before his 1958 death. Howard states: "I think he became aware of the importance of his case though a lawyer friend. . . . I think it gave him a sense of importance, in that this was bringing the facts out in the public eye, but this was only temporary, as he really lived with this incapacity all his life, and he did suffer mentally as well as physically."

GEORGE BERNARD SHAW, THE DOCTOR'S DILEMMA

In George Bernard Shaw's play, "The Doctor's Dilemma" (1906), a financially successful physician, Dr. Schutzmacher, reveals the secret of his financial success to his former classmate, Dr. Ridgeon, in the following dialog:

"Schutzmacher. Oh, in my case the secret was simple enough, though I suppose I should have got into trouble if it had attracted any notice. And I'm afraid you'll think it rather infra dig.

Ridgeon. Oh, I have an open mind. What was the secret?

Schutzmacher. Well, the secret was just two words.

Ridgeon. Not Consultation Free, was it?

Schutzmacher [shocked]. No, no. Really!

Ridgeon [apologetic]. Of course not. I was only joking.

Schutzmacher. My two words were simply Cure Guaranteed.

Ridgeon [admiring]. Cure Guaranteed!

Schutzmacher. Guaranteed. After all, that's what everybody wants from a doctor, isn't it?"

LEONARD v. PEPSICO, INC.

United States District Court, S.D. New York, 1999.
88 F.Supp.2d 116.

Kimba M. Wood, District Judge.

Plaintiff brought this action seeking, among other things, specific performance of an alleged offer of a Harrier Jet, featured in a television advertisement for defendant's "Pepsi Stuff" promotion. Defendant has moved for summary judgment pursuant to Federal Rule of Civil Procedure 56. For the reasons stated below, defendant's motion is granted.

I. Background

This case arises out of a promotional campaign conducted by defendant, the producer and distributor of the soft drinks Pepsi and Diet Pepsi. The promotion, entitled "Pepsi Stuff," encouraged consumers to collect "Pepsi Points" from specially marked packages of Pepsi or Diet Pepsi and redeem these points for merchandise featuring the Pepsi logo. Before introducing the promotion nationally, defendant conducted a test of the promotion in the Pacific Northwest from October 1995 to March 1996. A Pepsi Stuff catalog was distributed to consumers in the test market, including Washington State. Plaintiff is a resident of Seattle, Washington. While living in Seattle, plaintiff saw the Pepsi Stuff commercial that he contends constituted an offer of a Harrier Jet.

A. The Alleged Offer

Because whether the television commercial constituted an offer is the central question in this case, the Court will describe the commercial in detail. The commercial opens upon an idyllic, suburban morning, where the chirping of birds in sun-dappled trees welcomes a paperboy on his morning route. As the newspaper hits the stoop of a conventional two-story house, the tattoo of a military drum introduces the subtitle, "MONDAY 7:58 AM." The stirring strains of a martial air mark the appearance of a well-coiffed teenager preparing to leave for school, dressed in a shirt emblazoned with the Pepsi logo, a red-white-and-blue ball. While the teenager confidently preens, the military drumroll again sounds as the subtitle "T–SHIRT 75 PEPSI POINTS" scrolls across the screen. Bursting from his room, the teenager strides down the hallway wearing a leather jacket. The drumroll sounds again, as the subtitle "LEATHER JACKET 1450 PEPSI POINTS" appears. The teenager opens the door of his house and, unfazed by the glare of the early morning sunshine, puts on a pair of sunglasses. The drumroll then accompanies the subtitle "SHADES 175 PEPSI POINTS." A voiceover then intones, "Introducing the new Pepsi Stuff catalog," as the camera focuses on the cover of the catalog (the "Catalog").**

The scene then shifts to three young boys sitting in front of a high school building. The boy in the middle is intent on his Pepsi Stuff Catalog, while the boys on either side are each drinking Pepsi. The three boys gaze in awe at an object rushing overhead, as the military march builds to a crescendo. The Harrier Jet is not yet visible, but the observer senses the presence of a mighty plane as the extreme winds generated by its flight create a paper maelstrom in a classroom devoted to an otherwise dull physics lesson. Finally, the Harrier Jet swings into view and lands by the side of the school building, next to a bicycle rack. Several students run for cover, and the velocity of the wind strips one hapless faculty member down to his underwear. While the faculty member is being deprived of his dignity, the voiceover announces: "Now the more Pepsi you drink, the more great stuff you're gonna get."

** At this point, the following message appears at the bottom of the screen: "Offer not available in all areas. See details on specially marked packages."

The teenager opens the cockpit of the fighter and can be seen, helmetless, holding a Pepsi. "[L]ooking very pleased with himself," the teenager exclaims, "Sure beats the bus," and chortles. The military drumroll sounds a final time, as the following words appear: "HARRIER FIGHTER 7,000,000 PEPSI POINTS." A few seconds later, the following appears in more stylized script: "Drink Pepsi—Get Stuff." With that message, the music and the commercial end with a triumphant flourish.

Inspired by this commercial, plaintiff set out to obtain a Harrier Jet. Plaintiff explains that he is "typical of the 'Pepsi Generation' . . . he is young, has an adventurous spirit, and the notion of obtaining a Harrier Jet appealed to him enormously." Plaintiff consulted the Pepsi Stuff Catalog. The Catalog features youths dressed in Pepsi Stuff regalia or enjoying Pepsi Stuff accessories, such as "Blue Shades" ("As if you need another reason to look forward to sunny days."), "Pepsi Tees" ("Live in 'em. Laugh in 'em. Get in 'em."), "Bag of Balls" ("Three balls. One bag. No rules."), and "Pepsi Phone Card" ("Call your mom!"). The Catalog specifies the number of Pepsi Points required to obtain promotional merchandise. The Catalog includes an Order Form which lists, on one side, fifty-three items of Pepsi Stuff merchandise redeemable for Pepsi Points (the "Order Form"). Conspicuously absent from the Order Form is any entry or description of a Harrier Jet. The amount of Pepsi Points required to obtain the listed merchandise ranges from 15 (for a "Jacket Tattoo" ("Sew 'em on your jacket, not your arm.")) to 3300 (for a "Fila Mountain Bike" ("Rugged. All-terrain. Exclusively for Pepsi.")). It should be noted that plaintiff objects to the implication that because an item was not shown in the Catalog, it was unavailable.

The rear foldout pages of the Catalog contain directions for redeeming Pepsi Points for merchandise. These directions note that merchandise may be ordered "only" with the original Order Form. The Catalog notes that in the event that a consumer lacks enough Pepsi Points to obtain a desired item, additional Pepsi Points may be purchased for ten cents each; however, at least fifteen original Pepsi Points must accompany each order.

Although plaintiff initially set out to collect 7,000,000 Pepsi Points by consuming Pepsi products, it soon became clear to him that he "would not be able to buy (let alone drink) enough Pepsi to collect the necessary Pepsi Points fast enough." Reevaluating his strategy, plaintiff "focused for the first time on the packaging materials in the Pepsi Stuff promotion," and realized that buying Pepsi Points would be a more promising option. Through acquaintances, plaintiff ultimately raised about $700,000.

B. Plaintiff's Efforts to Redeem the Alleged Offer

On or about March 27, 1996, plaintiff submitted an Order Form, fifteen original Pepsi Points, and a check for $700,008.50. Plaintiff appears to have been represented by counsel at the time he mailed his check; the check is drawn on an account of plaintiff's first set of attorneys. At the bottom of the Order Form, plaintiff wrote in "1

Harrier Jet" in the "Item" column and "7,000,000" in the "Total Points" column. In a letter accompanying his submission, plaintiff stated that the check was to purchase additional Pepsi Points "expressly for obtaining a new Harrier jet as advertised in your Pepsi Stuff commercial."

On or about May 7, 1996, defendant's fulfillment house rejected plaintiff's submission and returned the check, explaining that:

> The item that you have requested is not part of the Pepsi Stuff collection. It is not included in the catalogue or on the order form, and only catalogue merchandise can be redeemed under this program.

> The Harrier jet in the Pepsi commercial is fanciful and is simply included to create a humorous and entertaining ad. We apologize for any misunderstanding or confusion that you may have experienced and are enclosing some free product coupons for your use.

Plaintiff's previous counsel responded on or about May 14, 1996, as follows:

> Your letter of May 7, 1996 is totally unacceptable. We have reviewed the video tape of the Pepsi Stuff commercial ... and it clearly offers the new Harrier jet for 7,000,000 Pepsi Points. Our client followed your rules explicitly ... .

> This is a formal demand that you honor your commitment and make immediate arrangements to transfer the new Harrier jet to our client. If we do not receive transfer instructions within ten (10) business days of the date of this letter you will leave us no choice but to file an appropriate action against Pepsi....

This letter was apparently sent onward to the advertising company responsible for the actual commercial, BBDO New York ("BBDO"). In a letter dated May 30, 1996, BBDO Vice President Raymond E. McGovern, Jr., explained to plaintiff that:

> I find it hard to believe that you are of the opinion that the Pepsi Stuff commercial ("Commercial") really offers a new Harrier Jet. The use of the Jet was clearly a joke that was meant to make the Commercial more humorous and entertaining. In my opinion, no reasonable person would agree with your analysis of the Commercial.

On or about June 17, 1996, plaintiff mailed a similar demand letter to defendant.

* * *

II. DISCUSSION

A. *The Legal Framework*

* * * On a motion for summary judgment, a court "cannot try issues of fact; it can only determine whether there are issues to be tried." * * * To prevail on a motion for summary judgment, the moving party therefore must show that there are no such genuine issues of material fact to be tried, and that he or she is entitled to judgment as a matter of law. * * *

* * *

B. Defendant's Advertisement Was Not An Offer

Advertisements as Offers

The general rule is that an advertisement does not constitute an offer. The *Restatement (Second) of Contracts* explains that:

> Advertisements of goods by display, sign, handbill, newspaper, radio or television are not ordinarily intended or understood as offers to sell. The same is true of catalogues, price lists and circulars, even though the terms of suggested bargains may be stated in some detail. It is of course possible to make an offer by an advertisement directed to the general public (*see* § 29), but there must ordinarily be some language of commitment or some invitation to take action without further communication.

Restatement (Second) of Contracts § 26 cmt. b (1979). Similarly, a leading treatise notes that:

> It is quite possible to make a definite and operative offer to buy or sell goods by advertisement, in a newspaper, by a handbill, a catalog or circular or on a placard in a store window. *It is not customary to do this, however; and the presumption is the other way....* Such advertisements are understood to be mere requests to consider and examine and negotiate; and no one can reasonably regard them as otherwise unless the circumstances are exceptional and the words used are very plain and clear.

1 Arthur Linton Corbin & Joseph M. Perillo, *Corbin on Contracts* § 2.4, at 116–17 (rev. ed.1993) (emphasis added); *see also* 1 E. Allan Farnsworth, *Farnsworth on Contracts* § 3.10, at 239 (2d ed.1998); 1 Samuel Williston & Richard A. Lord, *A Treatise on the Law of Contracts* § 4:7, at 286–87 (4th ed.1990). * * *

An advertisement is not transformed into an enforceable offer merely by a potential offeree's expression of willingness to accept the offer through, among other means, completion of an order form. In *Mesaros v. United States*, 845 F.2d 1576 (Fed.Cir.1988), for example, the plaintiffs sued the United States Mint for failure to deliver a number of Statue of Liberty commemorative coins that they had ordered. When demand for the coins proved unexpectedly robust, a number of individuals who had sent in their orders in a timely fashion were left empty-handed. See id. at 1578–80. The court began by noting the "well-established" rule that advertisements and order forms are "mere notices and solicitations for offers which create no power of acceptance in the recipient." Id. at 1580; * * * Restatement (Second) of Contracts § 26 ("A manifestation of willingness to enter a bargain is not an offer if the person to whom it is addressed knows or has reason to know that the person making it does not intend to conclude a bargain until he has made a further manifestation of assent."). The spurned coin collectors could not maintain a breach of contract action because no contract would be formed until the advertiser accepted the order form and processed payment. * * * Under these principles, plaintiff's letter of March 27, 1996, with the Order Form and the appropriate number of Pepsi Points, constituted the offer. There would be no enforceable contract until defendant accepted the Order Form and cashed the check.

The exception to the rule that advertisements do not create any power of acceptance in potential offerees is where the advertisement is "clear, definite, and explicit, and leaves nothing open for negotiation," in that circumstance, "it constitutes an offer, acceptance of which will complete the contract." *Lefkowitz v. Great Minneapolis Surplus Store,* 251 Minn. 188, 86 N.W.2d 689, 691 (1957). In *Lefkowitz,* defendant had published a newspaper announcement stating: "Saturday 9 AM Sharp, 3 Brand New Fur Coats, Worth to $100.00, First Come First Served $1 Each." Mr. Morris Lefkowitz arrived at the store, dollar in hand, but was informed that under defendant's "house rules," the offer was open to ladies, but not gentlemen. The court ruled that because plaintiff had fulfilled all of the terms of the advertisement and the advertisement was specific and left nothing open for negotiation, a contract had been formed. * * *

The present case is distinguishable from *Lefkowitz.* First, the commercial cannot be regarded in itself as sufficiently definite, because it specifically reserved the details of the offer to a separate writing, the Catalog. The commercial itself made no mention of the steps a potential offeree would be required to take to accept the alleged offer of a Harrier Jet. The advertisement in *Lefkowitz,* in contrast, "identified the person who could accept." Corbin, *supra,* § 2.4, at 119. *See generally United States v. Braunstein,* 75 F.Supp. 137, 139 (S.D.N.Y.1947) ("Greater precision of expression may be required, and less help from the court given, when the parties are merely at the threshold of a contract."); Farnsworth, *supra,* at 239 ("The fact that a proposal is very detailed suggests that it is an offer, while omission of many terms suggests that it is not."). Second, even if the Catalog had included a Harrier Jet among the items that could be obtained by redemption of Pepsi Points, the advertisement of a Harrier Jet by both television commercial and catalog would still not constitute an offer. As the *Mesaros* court explained, the absence of any words of limitation such as "first come, first served," renders the alleged offer sufficiently indefinite that no contract could be formed. *See Mesaros,* 845 F.2d at 1581. "A customer would not usually have reason to believe that the shopkeeper intended exposure to the risk of a multitude of acceptances resulting in a number of contracts exceeding the shopkeeper's inventory." Farnsworth, *supra,* at 242. There was no such danger in *Lefkowitz,* owing to the limitation "first come, first served."

The Court finds, in sum, that the Harrier Jet commercial was merely an advertisement. * * *

* * *

C. An Objective, Reasonable Person Would Not Have Considered the Commercial an Offer

* * *

* * * An obvious joke, of course, would not give rise to a contract. See, e.g., Graves v. Northern N.Y. Pub. Co., 260 A.D. 900, 22 N.Y.S.2d 537 (1940) (dismissing claim to offer of $1000, which appeared in the "joke column" of the newspaper, to any person who could provide a commonly available phone number). On the other hand, if there is no indication that the offer is "evidently in jest," and that an objective, reasonable person would find that the offer was serious, then there may be a valid offer. See ... Lucy v. Zehmer, 196 Va. 493, 84 S.E.2d 516, 518, 520 (1954) (ordering specific performance of a contract to purchase a farm despite defendant's protestation that the transaction was done in jest as " 'just a bunch of two doggoned drunks bluffing' ").

Whether the Commercial Was "Evidently Done In Jest"

* * * The commercial is the embodiment of what defendant appropriately characterizes as "zany humor."

First, the ... implication of the commercial is that Pepsi Stuff merchandise will inject drama and moment into hitherto unexceptional lives. * * * A reasonable viewer would understand such advertisements as mere puffery, not as statements of fact * * * and refrain from interpreting the promises of the commercial as being literally true.

Second, the callow youth featured in the commercial is a highly improbable pilot, one who could barely be trusted with the keys to his parents' car, much less the prize aircraft of the United States Marine Corps. * * *

Third, the notion of traveling to school in a Harrier Jet is an exaggerated adolescent fantasy. * * *

Fourth, * * * [i]n light of the Harrier Jet's well-documented function in attacking and destroying surface and air targets, armed reconnaissance and air interdiction, and offensive and defensive anti-aircraft warfare, depiction of such a jet as a way to get to school in the morning is clearly not serious even if, as plaintiff contends, the jet is capable of being acquired "in a form that eliminates [its] potential for military use."

Fifth, the * * * cost of a Harrier Jet is roughly $23 million dollars, a fact of which plaintiff was aware when he set out to gather the amount he believed necessary to accept the alleged offer. Even if an objective, reasonable person were not aware of this fact, he would conclude that purchasing a fighter plane for $700,000 is a deal too good to be true.

Plaintiff argues that a reasonable, objective person would have understood the commercial to make a serious offer of a Harrier Jet because there was "absolutely no distinction in the manner" in which the items in the commercial were presented. * * * [Plaintiff's argument suggests] merely that the humor of the promotional campaign was tongue in cheek. * * * In light of the obvious absurdity of the commercial, the Court rejects plaintiff's argument that the commercial was not clearly in jest.

* * *

III. Conclusion

In sum, there are three reasons why plaintiff's demand cannot prevail as a matter of law. First, the commercial was merely an advertisement * * *. Second, the tongue-in-cheek attitude of the commercial would not cause a reasonable person to conclude that a soft drink company would be giving away fighter planes as part of a promotion. Third, there is no writing between the parties sufficient to satisfy the Statute of Frauds.

For the reasons stated above, the Court grants defendant's motion for summary judgment. * * *

Defendant won: No cause of action

Problems

11. P, a developer, brings an action against D, an architectural firm, as a result of a defective grading of a trailer park. P alleges D agreed to supervise the grading construction and to check the grades on completion to insure their compliance with the architectural plan. D carelessly supervised the grading construction. As a result, drainage problems were caused. Too much dirt had been removed and P was forced to spend additional sums of money to bring the park to grade. P brings an action in tort (malpractice) and for breach of contract. The tort claim is barred by the statute of limitations, but the contract claim is not. Is P entitled to sue for breach of contract? *Yes*

12. P retained D, an attorney, to represent her in her claim for personal injuries as a result of the negligent driving of X. D agreed to handle the case, but, being very busy, D failed to do anything for several months. When he picked up the file to pursue P's claim, he noticed that the statute of limitations had run out the week before. P sues for breach of contract and for the tort of malpractice. Should either or both claims be dismissed? *No D is responsible*

13. When the plaintiff, Mrs. Stewart, conceived at the age of 37 after two previous stillbirths, she was convinced that she could not have a normal delivery. Consequently, when she and her husband consulted with the defendant, Dr. Bunyan, they demanded that a Caesarian section be performed. The defendant replied that he was not qualified to perform such an operation but that he would see to it that Dr. Kesten was available and a Caesarian would be performed. Because the defendant's medical opinion was that a Caesarian was not indicated he made no effort to contact Dr. Kesten. When the plaintiff, at full term, arrived at the hospital in labor, she again demanded a Caesarian. If a Caesarian were to be done, this was the time to do it, but the defendant, instead of arranging for the Caesarian, told her not

to worry and to go home. The baby was dead by the time the plaintiff was admitted to the hospital the next day. Does the plaintiff have a cause of action for breach of contract?   Yes

14.   A and B owed P $221. P was about to commence legal action when D, who apparently is B's attorney or insurance broker, sent the following letter to P: "I am attempting to adjust an automobile case for B, resulting from his being seriously injured a year ago this month. If I am successful in settling this matter, the balance due will be paid at that time. If I am not successful A will doubtlessly be called upon to pay it. I would suggest that you allow the matter to remain in status quo for a short period to determine whether or not I can effect a settlement." P refrained from suit and B received a large settlement in the automobile case but soon spent the money without paying P. P alleges that D is obligated to make the payment. Is D so obligated? Yes

15.   D, a lawyer handling a tort claim, wrote to the client's landlord, who had a claim for overdue rent, "if there is a favorable settlement or verdict herein, I will protect your monies for you for this rent." A large verdict was entered, but neither D nor D's client has paid the rent in full. Is D liable to the landlord for the unpaid rent? Yes

16.   The Chicago Tribune, a daily newspaper, publishes a booklet called "General Advertising Rates" which lists its charges for advertisements and another booklet called "The Chicago Tribune Advertising Acceptability Guide" which indicates that the Tribune will refuse advertising which is dishonest, indecent or illegal. The plaintiff, a labor union, tendered to the Tribune an advertisement urging readers not to patronize a certain department store because of its policy of featuring imported clothing made by low wage foreign labor. The tendered advertisement was concededly not dishonest, indecent or illegal. The union also tendered sufficient funds to pay for the advertisement in accordance with the "General Advertising Rates." The Tribune refused to print the advertisement. Does plaintiff have a cause of action for breach of contract?   No

17.   D inserted the following ad in a newspaper:

"OPPORTUNITY KNOCKS

We want enthusiastic, ambitious salespeople to represent us locally. Professional training program with $1950 monthly guarantee if qualified. Enthusiasm and ambition quickly rewarded with advancement."

P came to the office, applied for the position, and was hired. P started to work but did not receive the amount of pay specified in the ad. P was told that he had generated insufficient sales to merit the $1950 monthly amount. After two months P resigned. P brought an action for breach of contract. What result? No

18.   D, a medical school, distributed a catalog stating terms under which applications for admission would be evaluated. P received the catalog, applied for admission, paid a fee and was rejected. The catalog provided: "Students are selected on the basis of scholarship, character and motivation without regard to race, creed or sex. The student's potential for the study and practice of medicine will be evaluated on the basis of academic achieve-

ment, Medical College Admission Test results and personal appraisals by a pre-professional advisory committee or individual instructors."

P alleged that D evaluated such applications according to the ability of applicants or their families to make large monetary contributions to the school. Has P stated a cause of action for breach of contract? No

(b) Bids and Auction Sales

(Calamari & Perillo 5th §§ 1.7 and 2.6)

HOFFMAN v. HORTON

Supreme Court of Virginia, 1972.
212 Va. 565, 186 S.E.2d 79.

CARRICO, JUSTICE. The question involved in this case is whether an auctioneer at a foreclosure sale may reopen the bidding when an overbid is made immediately prior to or simultaneously with the falling of the hammer in acceptance of a lower bid. *Issue*

The question arises from an auction sale conducted to foreclose a deed of trust in the sum of $100,000 upon the "Field Tract" in Arlington County, owned by the defendants Howard P. Horton and wife and Ralph R. Kaul and wife. At the sale and after spirited bidding, a bid of $177,000 was made by Hubert N. Hoffman, the plaintiff, and received by the auctioneer. When no other bids appeared to be forthcoming, the auctioneer asked, "Are you all through bidding, gentlemen?" After a pause, he stated, "Going once for $177,000.00, going twice for $177,000.00, sold for $177,000.00." Whereupon, he struck the palm of his left hand with his right fist.

Immediately, one of the trustees, who had been standing nearby, rushed up to the auctioneer and told him that he had missed a bid of $178,000. The auctioneer, who had neither seen nor heard the bid, stated, "If I missed a bid, you people had better speak up. I am going ahead with the sale." The plaintiff then stepped forward and said, "Gentlemen, I have purchased this property for $177,000.00." The auctioneer and the trustee both disagreed with the plaintiff, and the auctioneer announced to the crowd that he had a bid of $178,000. The bidding proceeded, and the property was finally knocked down to the plaintiff for $194,000.

The plaintiff paid the $5,000 deposit required by the terms of the foreclosure but insisted that he had purchased the property for $177,000. Later, he paid the balance of the $194,000 under protest and brought an action against the former owners and the trustees to recover the $17,000 difference between the two bids in dispute. The trial court denied the plaintiff's claim, and we granted a writ of error to review the judgment. *Procedure*

* * *

The trial court found as a matter of fact, and this finding is not questioned by the plaintiff, that the $178,000 bid was made "prior to or simultaneously with" the falling of the auctioneer's fist in acceptance of the plaintiff's bid of $177,000. Based upon its finding of fact, the court held that "the bid for $178,000.00 was made before the bid for $177,000.00 had been accepted" and that the auctioneer had "acted within the discretion permitted" him in reopening the bidding and continuing with the sale.

In holding that the auctioneer was vested with discretion to reopen the bidding, the trial court relied upon Code § 8.2–328(2), a part of the Uniform Commercial Code. The statutory language so relied upon reads as follows:

Rule

"A sale by auction is complete when the auctioneer so announces by the fall of the hammer or in other customary manner. Where a bid is made while the hammer is falling in acceptance of a prior bid the auctioneer may in his discretion reopen the bidding or declare the goods sold under the bid on which the hammer was falling."

We disagree with the trial court that the transaction in this case, involving the sale of land, is controlled by § 8.2–328(2) of the Uniform Commercial Code. Title 8.2 of the Commercial Code applies only to transactions relating to "goods." Code §§ 8.2–105,–107.

However, while the Uniform Commercial Code is not controlling here, we think it appropriate to borrow from it to establish the rule applicable to the transaction at hand. To vest the auctioneer crying a sale of land with the same discretion to reopen bidding that he has in the sale of goods is to achieve uniformity and, of more importance, to recognize a rule which is both necessary and fair.

Holding

We hold, therefore, that the auctioneer in this case was vested with discretion to reopen the bidding for the land which was being sold. And we agree with the trial court that the auctioneer "acted within" his discretion in reopening the bidding and continuing with the sale when it was made apparent to him that a higher bid had been submitted "prior to or simultaneously with" the falling of his fist in acceptance of the plaintiff's lower bid.

Accordingly, the judgment of the trial court will be affirmed.

Affirmed. *Disposition*

Problems

19. Defendant caused circulars to be distributed to dealers throughout the country announcing that an auction would be conducted without reserve of the famous Smith Collection of antiques. Plaintiff flew from California to New York, the announced site of the auction. On arrival plaintiff discovered that the auction had been canceled because of a recession in the antiques market. Does the plaintiff have a cause of action?

20. Defendant Finance Company announced that a 1998 Jaguar which it had repossessed because of a default in payments would be auctioned.

Defendant did not give notice that its agent would be bidding. The auction was not well attended. A, the only legitimate bidder, bid $500. B, defendant's agent, bid $1,000 and the car was ostensibly knocked down to B. A subsequently discovered what had actually occurred. Does A have a cause of action for breach of contract?

21. What is the result in the following bidding sequences assuming always that B is the agent of the auctioneer and that "notice has not been given that liberty for such bidding is reserved" and that a forced sale is not involved?

(a) A 5   B 8   A 12

(b) A 5   B 8   A 12   B 16   A 20

(c) A 5   B 8   C 20   A 21

(d) A 5   B 8   C 20

(e) B 8   A 12

22. P submitted a bid in response to an invitation from the City of Jordan to bid for garbage collection services. P was the lowest bidder and the City agreed to award the contract to P. Subsequently, the City changed its mind and awarded the contract to the next lowest bidder. Does P have a cause of action against the City?

(c) Offers Distinguished From Preliminary Negotiations and Price Quotations

---

(Calamari & Perillo 5th § 2.6)

UNITED STATES v. BRIGGS MANUFACTURING CO.

United States Court of Appeals, Ninth Circuit, 1972.
460 F.2d 1195.

PER CURIAM. The United States brought this action to recover for freight, lighterage and longshoring, and terminal charges, from Briggs for a shipment from Seattle to Point Barrow, Alaska. The trial court found for the United States on several grounds. We need not discuss them all, for it is clear that, from the findings of the court which are not clearly erroneous, Briggs is bound by custom and usage of the business (Hostetter v. Park, 137 U.S. 30, 11 S.Ct. 1, 34 L.Ed. 568) and as the charge made by the government was in accordance therewith, the judgment in that regard must be and is affirmed.

* * *

The defendant Briggs filed a third-party complaint against Toombs, alleging that by its contract with Toombs it was entitled to judgment against Toombs for all sums adjudged against Briggs in favor of the United States. Among other findings the court found that as an inducement for Toombs to purchase the housing involved, Briggs quoted prices on freight, terminal, longshoring and lightering charges. And while these quotations were "estimated", both parties anticipated they would be reasonably accurate and Toombs was entitled to rely on the estimate. These findings are not clearly erroneous. The State of Washington recognizes the doctrine of equitable estoppel. Kessinger v. Anderson, 31 Wash.2d 157, 196 P.2d 289 (1948). There are sufficient factual findings to support the decision of the district court that Briggs must bear the loss under the doctrine of equitable estoppel.

The judgment of the district court on the third-party complaint is affirmed. Disposition

LONERGAN v. SCOLNICK

District Court of Appeal, Fourth District, California, 1954.
129 Cal.App.2d 179, 276 P.2d 8.

BARNARD, PRESIDING JUSTICE.

* * *

The stipulated facts are as follows: During March, 1952, the defendant placed an ad in a Los Angeles paper reading, so far as material here, "Joshua Tree vic. 40 acres, * * * need cash, will sacrifice." In response to an inquiry resulting from this ad the defendant, who lived in New York, wrote a letter to the plaintiff dated March 26, briefly describing the property, giving directions as to how to get there, stating that his rock-bottom price was $2,500 cash, and further stating that "This is a form letter." On April 7, the plaintiff wrote a letter to the defendant saying that he was not sure he had found the property, asking for its legal description, asking whether the land was all level or whether it included certain jutting rock hills, and suggesting a certain bank as escrow agent "should I desire to purchase the land." On April 8, the defendant wrote to the plaintiff saying "From your description you have found the property"; that this bank "is O.K. for escrow agent"; that the land was fairly level; giving the legal description; and then saying, "If you are really interested, you will have to decide fast, as I expect to have a buyer in the next week or so." On April 12, the defendant sold the property to a third party for $2,500. The plaintiff received defendant's letter of April 8 on April 14. On April 15 he wrote to the defendant thanking him for his letter "confirming that I was on the right land", stating that he would immediately proceed to have the escrow opened and would deposit $2,500 therein "in conformity with your offer", and asking the defendant to forward a deed with his instructions to the escrow agent. On April 17, 1952, the plaintiff started an escrow and placed in the hands of the escrow agent $100, agreeing to furnish an additional $2,400 at an unspecified time, with the provision that if the escrow was not closed by May 15, 1952, it should be completed as soon thereafter as possible unless a written demand for a return of the money or instruments was made by either party after that date. It was further stipulated that the plaintiff was ready and willing at all times to deposit the $2,400.

* * *

There can be no contract unless the minds of the parties have met and mutually agreed upon some specific thing. This is usually evidenced by one party making an offer which is accepted by the other party. Section 25 of the Restatement of the Law on Contracts reads:

Rule

> "If from a promise, or manifestation of intention, or from the circumstances existing at the time, the person to whom the promise or manifestation is addressed knows or has reason to know that the person making it does not intend it as an expression of his fixed purpose until he has given a further expression of assent, he has not made an offer."

The language used in Niles v. Hancock, 140 Cal. 157, 73 P. 840, 842, "It is also clear from the correspondence that it was the intention of the defendant that the negotiations between him and the plaintiff were to be purely preliminary," is applicable here. The correspondence here indicates an intention on the part of the defendant to find out whether the plaintiff was interested, rather than an intention to make a definite offer to the plaintiff. The language used by the defendant in his letters of March 26 and April 8 rather clearly discloses that they were not intended as an expression of fixed purpose to make a definite offer, and was sufficient to advise the plaintiff that some further expression of assent on the part of the defendant was necessary.

Issue

The advertisement in the paper was a mere request for an offer. The letter of March 26 contains no definite offer, and clearly states that it is a form letter. It merely gives further particulars, in clarification of the advertisement, and tells the plaintiff how to locate the property if he was interested in looking into the matter. The letter of April 8 added nothing in the way of a definite offer. It merely answered some questions asked by the plaintiff, and stated that if the plaintiff was really interested he would have to act fast. The statement that he expected to have a buyer in the next week or so indicated that the defendant intended to sell to the first-comer, and was reserving the right to do so. From this statement, alone, the plaintiff knew or should have known that he was not being given time in which to accept an offer that was being made, but that some further assent on the part of the defendant was required. Under the language used the plaintiff was not being given a right to act within a reasonable time after receiving the letter; he was plainly told that the defendant intended to sell to another, if possible, and warned that he would have to act fast if he was interested in buying the land.

Holding

Regardless of any opinion previously expressed, the court found that no contract had been entered into between these parties, and we are in accord with the court's conclusion on that controlling issue. The court's construction of the letters involved was a reasonable one, and we think the most reasonable one, even if it be assumed that another construction was possible.

The judgment is affirmed. *Disposition*

FAIRMOUNT GLASS WORKS v. CRUNDEN–MARTIN WOODENWARE CO.

Court of Appeals of Kentucky, 1899.
106 Ky. 659, 51 S.W. 196.

HOBSON, J. On April 20, 1895, appellee wrote appellant the following letter:

> "St. Louis, Mo., April 20, 1895. Gentlemen: Please advise us the lowest price you can make us on our order for ten car loads of Mason green jars, complete, with caps, packed one dozen in a case, either delivered here, or f.o.b. cars your place, as you prefer. State terms and cash discount. Very truly, Grunden–Martin W.W. Co."

To this letter appellant answered as follows:

> "Fairmount, Ind., April 23, 1895. Grunden–Martin Wooden Ware Co., St. Louis, Mo.—Gentlemen: Replying to your favor of April 20, we quote you Mason fruit jars, complete, in one-dozen boxes, delivered in East St. Louis, Ill.: Pints $4.50, quarts $5.00, half gallons $6.50, per gross, for immediate acceptance, and shipment not later than May 15, 1895; sixty days' acceptance, or 2 off, cash in ten days. Yours, truly, Fairmount Glass Works.
>
> "Please note that we make all quotations and contracts subject to the contingencies of agencies or transportation, delays or accidents beyond our control."

For reply thereto, appellee sent the following telegram on April 24, 1895:

> "Fairmount Glass Works, Fairmount, Ind.: Your letter twenty-third received. Enter order ten car loads as per your quotation. Specifications mailed. Grunden–Martin W.W. Co."

In response to this telegram, appellant sent the following:

> "Fairmount, Ind., April 24, 1895. Grunden–Martin W.W. Co., St. Louis, Mo.: Impossible to book your order. Output all sold. See letter. Fairmount Glass Works."

Appellee insists that, by its telegram sent in answer to the letter of April 23d, the contract was closed for the purchase of 10 car loads of Mason fruit jars. Appellant insists that the contract was not closed by this telegram, and that it had the right to decline to fill the order at the time it sent its telegram of April 24. This is the chief question in the case. The court below gave judgment in favor of appellee, and appellant has appealed, earnestly insisting that the judgment is erroneous.

We are referred to a number of authorities holding that a quotation of prices is not an offer to sell, in the sense that a completed contract will arise out of the giving of an order for merchandise in accordance with the proposed terms. There are a number of cases holding that the transaction is not completed until the order so made is accepted. 7 Am.

& Eng.Enc.Law (2d Ed.) p. 138; Smith v. Gowdy, 8 Allen 566; Beaupre v. Telegraph Co., 21 Minn. 155. But each case must turn largely upon the language there used. In this case we think there was more than a quotation of prices, although appellant's letter uses the word "quote" in stating the prices given. The true meaning of the correspondence must be determined by reading it as a whole. Appellee's letter of April 20th, which began the transaction, did not ask for a quotation of prices. It reads: "Please advise us the lowest price you can make us on our order for ten car loads of Mason green jars. * * * State terms and cash discount." From this appellant could not fail to understand that appellee wanted to know at what price it would sell it ten car loads of these jars; so when, in answer, it wrote: "We quote you Mason fruit jars * * * pints $4.50, quarts $5.00, half gallons $6.50, per gross, for immediate acceptance; * * * 2 off, cash in ten days,"—it must be deemed as intending to give appellee the information it had asked for. We can hardly understand what was meant by the words "for immediate acceptance," unless the latter was intended as a proposition to sell at these prices if accepted immediately. In construing every contract, the aim of the court is to arrive at the intention of the parties. In none of the cases to which we have been referred on behalf of appellant was there on the face of the correspondence any such expression of intention to make an offer to sell on the terms indicated. * * * It will be observed that the telegram of acceptance refers to the specifications mailed. These specifications were contained in the following letter: "St. Louis, Mo., April 24, 1895. Fairmount Glass–Works Co., Fairmount, Ind.—Gentlemen: We received your letter of 23rd this morning, and telegraphed you in reply as follows: 'Your letter 23rd received. Enter order ten car loads as per your quotation. Specifications mailed,'—which we now confirm. We have accordingly entered this contract on our books for the ten cars Mason green jars, complete, with caps and rubbers, one dozen in case, delivered to us in East St. Louis at $4.50 per gross for pint, $5.00 for quart, $6.50 for one-half gallon. Terms, 60 days' acceptance, or 2 per cent. for cash in ten days, to be shipped not later than May 15, 1895. The jars and caps to be strictly first-quality goods. You may ship the first car to us here assorted: Five gross pint, fifty-five gross quart, forty gross one-half gallon. Specifications for the remaining 9 cars we will send later. Grunden–Martin W.W. Co." It is insisted for appellant that this was not an acceptance of the offer as made; that the stipulation, "The jars and caps to be strictly first-quality goods," was not in their offer; and that, it not having been accepted as made, appellant is not bound. But it will be observed that appellant declined to furnish the goods before it got this letter, and in the correspondence with appellee it nowhere complained of these words as an addition to the contract. Quite a number of other letters passed, in which the refusal to deliver the goods was placed on other grounds, none of which have been sustained by the evidence. Appellee offers proof tending to show that these words, in the trade in which parties were engaged, conveyed the same meaning as the words used in appellant's letter, and were only a different form of expressing the same idea. Appellant's conduct would seem to confirm this evidence.

Appellant also insists that the contract was indefinite, because the quantity of each size of the jars was not fixed, that 10 car loads is too indefinite a specification of the quantity sold, and that appellee had no right to accept the goods to be delivered on different days. The proof shows that "10 car loads" is an expression used in the trade as equivalent to 1,000 gross, 100 gross being regarded a car load. The offer to sell the different sizes at different prices gave the purchaser the right to name the quantity of each size, and, the offer being to ship not later than May 15th, the buyer had the right to fix the time of delivery at any time before that. * * * Judgment affirmed. Disposition

Problems

23. A states to B that he would like certain work done and asks B for an estimate. B says that he estimates he could do the work for $5,000. A says "I accept." Is there a contract?

24. A states to B that he would like certain plumbing work done and asks B for an estimate. B gives an estimate of $31,000. A says "Go ahead" and B does the work. Upon completion of the work B presents a bill for $42,000, which is in fact the reasonable price. May B collect $42,000?

25. Would the result be different in Problem 24 if A had said "Go ahead and do it at that price" and B did the work?

26. A writes to B: "I am eager to sell my house. I would consider $200,000 for it." B promptly replies: "I will buy your house for $200,000." Is there a contract?

27. On December 9 plaintiff asked defendant if he would consider selling certain property. Defendant stated that if plaintiff made an offer defendant would consider it. Plaintiff named a sum and defendant refused. Plaintiff then stated, "Will you accept $49,000?" Defendant answered, "I will not sell it for less than $56,000." Plaintiff said, "I accept." Was there a contract?

28. Defendant wrote to plaintiff: "In consequence of a rupture in the salt trade we are authorized to offer Michigan fine salt in full carload lots of 80 to 95 bbls. delivered at your city at 85¢ per bbl. At this price it is a bargain as the price in general remains unchanged. Shall be pleased to receive your order." Plaintiff answered: "You may ship me 2,000 barrels Michigan fine salt, as offered in your letter." Was there a contract?

29. Defendant, a farmer who raises millet seed, wrote the following letter to a number of seed dealers including plaintiff: "I have 1800 bu. of millet seed of which I am mailing you a sample. This millet is recleaned and was grown on sod and is good seed. I want $2.25 per hundredweight for this seed f.o.b. Lowell." Plaintiff answered, "I accept your offer." Is there a contract?

30. Defendant knew that plaintiff was planning to bid as general contractor on a State construction project. Defendant sent an unsolicited letter to plaintiff, stating: "In connection with the above job we are pleased to quote a job price of $14,450 covering items 4, 11, 11a, 12, 13, 14, 16, 17, and 23." Plaintiff used defendant's quote in calculating its bid. Plaintiff was

awarded the State contract and accepted defendant's "offer." Defendant argues that the quote was not an offer. Resolve the issue.

SECTION 3. INTENT TO MEMORIALIZE AND INDEFINITENESS

————

(Calamari & Perillo 5th §§ 1.7, 1.8, 2.8 and 2.9)

TEXACO, INC. v. PENNZOIL, CO.
Court of Appeals of Texas, Houston (1st Dist.), 1987.
729 S.W.2d 768.

WARREN, JUSTICE.

This is an appeal from a judgment awarding Pennzoil damages for Texaco's tortious interference with a contract between Pennzoil and the "Getty entities" (Getty Oil Company, the Sarah C. Getty Trust, and the J. Paul Getty Museum).

The jury found, among other things, that:

(1) At the end of a board meeting on January 3, 1984, the Getty entities intended to bind themselves to an agreement providing for the purchase of Getty Oil stock, whereby the Sarah C. Getty Trust would own 4/7th of the stock and Pennzoil the remaining 3/7th; and providing for a division of Getty Oil's assets, according to their respective ownership if the Trust and Pennzoil were unable to agree on a restructuring of Getty Oil by December 31, 1984;

(2) Texaco knowingly interfered with the agreement between Pennzoil and the Getty entities;

(3) As a result of Texaco's interference, Pennzoil suffered damages of $7.53 billion;

(4) Texaco's actions were intentional, willful, and in wanton disregard of Pennzoil's rights; and,

(5) Pennzoil was entitled to punitive damages of $3 billion.

* * *

Though many facts are disputed, the parties' main conflicts are over the inferences to be drawn from, and the legal significance of, these facts. There is evidence that for several months in late 1983, Pennzoil had followed with interest the well-publicized dissension between the board of directors of Getty Oil Company and Gordon Getty, who was a director of Getty Oil and also the owner, as trustee, of approximately 40.2% of the outstanding shares of Getty Oil. On December 28, 1983, Pennzoil announced an unsolicited, public tender offer for 16 million shares of Getty Oil at $100 each.

Soon afterwards, Pennzoil contacted both Gordon Getty and a representative of the J. Paul Getty Museum, which held approximately 11.8% of the shares of Getty Oil, to discuss the tender offer and the possible purchase of Getty Oil. In the first two days of January 1984, a "Memorandum of Agreement" was drafted to reflect the terms that had been reached in conversations between representatives of Pennzoil, Gordon Getty, and the Museum.

* * *

The Memorandum of Agreement stated that it was subject to approval of the board of Getty Oil, and it was to expire by its own terms if not approved at the board meeting that was to begin on January 2. Pennzoil's CEO, Liedtke, and Gordon Getty, for the Trust, signed the Memorandum of Agreement before the Getty Oil board meeting on January 2, and Harold Williams, the president of the Museum, signed it shortly after the board meeting began. Thus, before it was submitted to the Getty Oil board, the Memorandum of Agreement had been executed by parties who together controlled a majority of the outstanding shares of Getty Oil.

The Memorandum of Agreement was then presented to the Getty Oil board, which had previously held discussions on how the company should respond to Pennzoil's public tender offer. * * *

The board voted to reject recommending Pennzoil's tender offer to Getty's shareholders, then later also rejected the Memorandum of Agreement price of $110 per share as too low. Before recessing at 3 a.m., the board decided to make a counter-proposal to Pennzoil of $110 per share plus a $10 debenture. * * * In the morning of January 3, Getty Oil's investment banker, Geoffrey Boisi, began calling other companies, seeking a higher bid than Pennzoil's for the Getty Oil shares.

When the board reconvened at 3 p.m. on January 3, a revised Pennzoil proposal was presented, offering $110 per share plus a $3 "stub" that was to be paid after the sale of a Getty Oil subsidiary ("ERC"), from the excess proceeds over $1 billion. Each shareholder was to receive a pro rata share of these excess proceeds, but in any case, a minimum of $3 per share at the end of five years. * * *

The Museum's lawyer told the board that, based on his discussions with Pennzoil, he believed that if the board went back "firm" with an offer of $110 plus a $5 stub, Pennzoil would accept it. After a recess, the Museum's president (also a director of Getty Oil) moved that the Getty board should accept Pennzoil's proposal provided that the stub be raised to $5, and the board voted 15 to 1 to approve this counter-proposal to Pennzoil. The board then voted themselves and Getty's officers and advisors indemnity for any liability arising from the events of the past few months. Additionally, the board authorized its executive compensation committee to give "golden parachutes" (generous termination benefits) to the top executives whose positions "were likely to be affected" by the change in management. There was evidence that during another brief recess of the board meeting, the counter-offer of $110 plus a $5 stub was presented to and accepted by Pennzoil. After Pennzoil's acceptance was conveyed to the Getty board, the meeting was adjourned, and most board members left town for their respective homes.

That evening, the lawyers and public relations staff of Getty Oil and the Museum drafted a press release describing the transaction between Pennzoil and the Getty entities. The press release, announcing an agreement in principle on the terms of the Memorandum of Agreement but with a price of $110 plus a $5 stub, was issued on Getty Oil letterhead the next morning, January 4, and later that day, Pennzoil issued an identical press release.

On January 4, Boisi continued to contact other companies, looking for a higher price than Pennzoil had offered. After talking briefly with Boisi, Texaco management called several meetings with its in-house financial planning group, which over the course of the day studied and reported to management on the value of Getty Oil, the Pennzoil offer terms, and a feasible price range at which Getty might be acquired. Later in the day, Texaco hired an investment banker, First Boston, to represent it with respect to a possible acquisition of Getty Oil. Meanwhile, also on January 4, Pennzoil's lawyers were working on a draft of a formal "transaction agreement" that described the transaction in more detail than the outline of terms contained in the Memorandum of Agreement and press release.

On January 5, the Wall Street Journal reported on an agreement reached between Pennzoil and the Getty entities, describing essentially the terms contained in the Memorandum of Agreement. The Pennzoil board met to ratify the actions of its officers in negotiating an agreement with the Getty entities, and Pennzoil's attorneys periodically attempted to contact the other parties' advisors and attorneys to continue work on the transaction agreement.

The board of Texaco also met on January 5, authorizing its officers to make an offer for 100% of Getty Oil and to take any necessary action in connection therewith. Texaco first contacted the Museum's lawyer, Lipton, and arranged a meeting to discuss the sale of the Museum's shares of Getty Oil to Texaco. Lipton instructed his associate, on her way to the meeting in progress of the lawyers drafting merger documents for the Pennzoil/Getty transaction, to not attend that meeting, because he needed her at his meeting with Texaco. At the meeting with Texaco, the Museum outlined various issues it wanted resolved in any transaction with Texaco, and then agreed to sell its 11.8% ownership in Getty Oil.

That evening, Texaco met with Gordon Getty to discuss the sale of the Trust's shares. He was informed that the Museum had agreed to sell its shares to Texaco. Gordon Getty's advisors had previously warned him that the Trust shares might be "locked out" in a minority position if Texaco bought, in addition to the Museum's shares, enough of the public shares to achieve over 50% ownership of the company. Gordon Getty accepted Texaco's offer of $125 per share and signed a letter of his intent to sell his stock to Texaco, as soon as a California temporary restraining order against his actions as trustee was lifted.

At noon on January 6, Getty Oil held a telephone board meeting to discuss the Texaco offer. The board voted to withdraw its previous counter-proposal to Pennzoil and unanimously voted to accept Texaco's offer. Texaco immediately issued a press release announcing that Getty Oil and Texaco would merge.

Soon after the Texaco press release appeared, Pennzoil telexed the Getty entities, demanding that they honor their agreement with Pennzoil. * * * The merger agreement between Texaco and Getty Oil was signed on January 6; the stock purchase agreement with the Museum was signed on January 6; and the stock exchange agreement with the Trust was signed on January 8, 1984.

* * *

SPECIAL ISSUE NO. 1

Texaco contends that under controlling principles of New York law, there was insufficient evidence to support the jury's finding that at the end of the Getty Oil board meeting on January 3, the Getty entities intended to bind themselves to an agreement with Pennzoil.

Pennzoil responds that the question of the parties' intent is a fact question, and the jury was free to accept or reject Texaco's after-the-fact testimony of subjective intent. Pennzoil contends that the evidence showed that the parties intended to be bound to the terms in the Memorandum of Agreement plus a price term of $110 plus a $5 stub, even though the parties may have contemplated a later, more formal document to memorialize the agreement already reached. * * *

Under New York law, if parties do not intend to be bound to an agreement until it is reduced to writing and signed by both parties, then there is no contract until that event occurs. * * * If there is no understanding that a signed writing is necessary before the parties will be bound, and the parties have agreed upon all substantial terms, then an informal agreement can be binding, even though the parties contemplate evidencing their agreement in a formal document later. * * * *R.G. Group, Inc. v. Horn & Hardart Co.,* 751 F.2d 69, 74 (2d Cir.1984).

If the parties do intend to contract orally, the mere intention to commit the agreement to writing does not prevent contract formation before execution of that writing, *Winston v. Mediafare Entertainment Corp.,* 777 F.2d 78, 80 (2d Cir.1985), and even a failure to reduce their promises to writing is immaterial to whether they are bound. * * *

However, if either party communicates the intent not to be bound before a final formal document is executed, then no oral expression of agreement to specific terms will constitute a binding contract. *Winston,* 777 F.2d at 80; *R.G. Group,* 751 F.2d at 74.

Thus, under New York law, the parties are given the power to obligate themselves informally or only by a formal signed writing, as they wish. *R.G. Group,* 751 F.2d at 74. The emphasis in deciding when a binding contract exists is on intent rather than on form. *Reprosystem,*

B.V. v. SCM Corp., 727 F.2d 257, 261 (2d Cir.), *cert. denied,* 469 U.S. 828, 105 S.Ct. 110, 83 L.Ed.2d 54 (1984).

It is the parties' expressed intent that controls which rule of contract formation applies. To determine intent, a court must examine the words and deeds of the parties, because these constitute the objective signs of such intent. *Winston,* 777 F.2d at 80; *R.G. Group,* 751 F.2d at 74. Only the outward expressions of intent are considered—secret or subjective intent is immaterial to the question of whether the parties were bound. * * *

Several factors have been articulated to help determine whether the parties intended to be bound only by a formal, signed writing: (1) whether a party expressly reserved the right to be bound only when a written agreement is signed; (2) whether there was any partial performance by one party that the party disclaiming the contract accepted; (3) whether all essential terms of the alleged contract had been agreed upon; and (4) whether the complexity or magnitude of the transaction was such that a formal, executed writing would normally be expected. *Winston,* 777 F.2d at 80; *R.G. Group,* 751 F.2d at 76.

Evaluating the first factor, Texaco contends that the evidence of expressed intent not to be bound establishes conclusively that there was no contract at the time of Texaco's alleged inducement of breach. Texaco argues that this expressed intent is contained in (1) the press releases issued by the Getty entities and Pennzoil, which stated that "the transaction is subject to execution of a definitive merger agreement"; (2) the phrasing of drafts of the transaction agreement, which Texaco alleges "carefully stated that the parties' obligations would become binding only 'after the execution and delivery of this Agreement' "; and (3) the deliberate reference by the press releases to the parties' understanding as an "agreement in principle."

In its brief, Texaco asserts that, as a matter of black letter New York law, the "subject to" language in the press release established that the parties were not then bound and intended to be bound only after signing a definitive agreement, citing *Banking & Trading Corp. v. Reconstruction Finance Corp.,* 147 F.Supp. 193, 204 (S.D.N.Y.1956), *aff'd,* 257 F.2d 765 (2d Cir.1958). The court in that case stated that "if the agreement is expressly subject to the execution of a formal contract, this intent must be respected and no contract found until then." However, the court went on to say that where intent is less sharply expressed, the trier of fact must determine it as best he can. *Id.* at 204–05. Although the intent to formalize an agreement is some evidence of an intent not to be bound before signing such a writing, it is not conclusive. *Id.* at 204. The issue of when the parties intended to be bound is a fact question to be decided from the parties' acts and communications. *Id.; see Chromalloy American Corp. v. Universal Housing Systems of America, Inc.,* 495 F.Supp. 544, 550 (S.D.N.Y.1980), *aff'd,* 697 F.2d 289 (2d Cir.1982).

The press release issued first by Getty, then by Pennzoil, on January 4, 1984, stated:

Getty Oil Company, The J. Paul Getty Museum and Gordon Getty, as Trustee of the Sarah C. Getty Trust, announced today that they have agreed in principle with Pennzoil Company to a merger of Getty Oil and a newly formed entity owned by Pennzoil and the Trustee.

In connection with the transaction, the shareholders of Getty Oil ... *will* receive $110 per share cash plus the right to receive a deferred cash consideration in a formula amount. The deferred consideration *will* be equal to a pro rata share of the ... proceeds, in excess of $1 billion, ... of ERC Corporation, ... and *will* be paid upon the disposition. In any event, under the formula, each shareholder *will* receive at least $5 per share within five years.

Prior to the merger, Pennzoil *will* contribute approximately $2.6 billion in cash and the Trustee and Pennzoil *will* contribute the Getty Oil shares owned by them to the new entity. Upon execution of a definitive merger agreement, the ... tender offer by a Pennzoil subsidiary for shares of Getty Oil stock *will* be withdrawn.

The agreement in principle also provides that Getty Oil *will* grant to Pennzoil an option to purchase eight million treasury shares for $110 per share.

The transaction is *subject to* execution of a definitive merger agreement, approval by the stockholders of Getty Oil and completion of various governmental filing and waiting period requirements.

Following consummation of the merger, the Trust *will* own 4/7ths of the ... stock of Getty Oil and Pennzoil *will* own 3/7ths. The Trust and Pennzoil have also agreed in principle that following consummation of the merger they *will* endeavor in good faith to agree upon a plan for restructuring Getty Oil [within a year] and that if they are unable to reach such an agreement then they *will* cause a division of assets of the company. (Emphasis added.)

Any intent of the parties not to be bound before signing a formal document is not so clearly expressed in the press release to establish, as a matter of law, that there was no contract at that time. The press release does refer to an agreement "in principle" and states that the "transaction" is subject to execution of a definitive merger agreement. But the release as a whole is worded in indicative terms, not in subjunctive or hypothetical ones. The press release describes what shareholders *will* receive, what Pennzoil *will* contribute, that Pennzoil *will* be granted an option, etc.

The description of the transaction as subject to a definitive merger agreement also includes the need for stockholder approval and the completion of various governmental filing and waiting requirements. There was evidence that this was a paragraph of routine details, that the referred to merger agreement was a standard formal document required in such a transaction under Delaware law, and that the parties considered these technical requirements of little consequence.

There is also an arguable difference between a "transaction" being subject to various requirements and the formation of the agreement itself being dependent upon completion of these matters. In *F.W. Berk & Co. v. Derecktor*, 301 N.Y. 110, 92 N.E.2d 914 (1950), cited in Texaco's brief, the defendant's very acceptance of the plaintiff's order was made subject to the occurrence of certain events. The court defined the phrase "subject to" as being the equivalent of "conditional upon or depending on" and held that making the acceptance of an offer subject to a condition was not the kind of assent required to make it a binding promise. However, making the acceptance of an offer conditional, or expressly making an agreement itself conditional, is a much clearer expression of an intent not to be bound than the use of the more ambiguous word "transaction."

Other cases cited by Texaco involved writings that specifically stated that no party would be committed until a written contract was executed. *See, e.g., Reprosystem, B.V.,* 727 F.2d at 260 (draft agreements clearly stated that formal execution was required before the contract would have any binding effect); *Chromalloy American Corp.,* 495 F.Supp. at 547–48 (letter of intent stated that neither party would be committed until a contract was executed). Yet, despite the clear language of reservation in those cases, the parties' intent to be bound was still evaluated as a question of fact to be determined from all the circumstances of the case. *Reprosystem, B.V.,* 727 F.2d at 261–62; *Chromalloy American Corp.,* 495 F.Supp. at 550.

So it is here. Regardless of what interpretation we give to the conditional language in the press release, we conclude that it did not so clearly express the intent of the parties not to be bound to conclusively resolve that issue, as Texaco asserts.

Texaco also contends that explicit language of reservation in drafts of Pennzoil's transaction agreement indicates the parties' expressed intent not to be bound without a signed writing. Texaco asserts that "Pennzoil's lawyers carefully stated that the parties' obligations would become binding only 'after the execution and delivery of this Agreement.'"

That assertion is not accurate. In fact, "after the execution and delivery of this Agreement" was merely used as an introductory phrase before each party's obligations were described, e.g., after the execution and delivery of this Agreement, Pennzoil shall terminate the tender offer; ... Pennzoil and the Company shall terminate all legal proceedings; ... the Company shall purchase all shares held by the Museum; etc. Other clauses in the transaction agreement did not contain that phrase, e.g., the Company *hereby* grants to Pennzoil the option to purchase up to 8 million shares of treasury stock; *on or prior to the effective date,* Pennzoil and the Trustee shall form the merging company; etc.

A reasonable conclusion from reading the entire drafts is that the phrase "after the execution and delivery of this Agreement" was used chiefly to indicate the timing of various acts that were to occur, and not to impose an express precondition to the formation of a contract.

Next, Texaco states that the use of the term "agreement in principle" in the press release was a conscious and deliberate choice of words to convey that there was not yet any binding agreement. Texaco refers to defense testimony that lawyers for Getty Oil and the Museum changed the initial wording of the press release from "agreement" to "agreement in principle" because they understood and intended that phrase to mean that there was no binding contract with Pennzoil.

* * *

Pennzoil and Texaco presented conflicting evidence at trial on the common business usage and understanding of the term "agreement in principle." * * *

* * * There was sufficient evidence at trial on the common business usage of the expression "agreement in principle" and on its meaning in this case for the jury reasonably to decide that its use in the press release did not necessarily establish that the parties did not intend to be bound before signing a formal document.

A second factor that may indicate whether the parties intended to be bound only by a signed, formal writing is whether there was partial performance by one party that the party disclaiming the contract accepted. *Winston,* 777 F.2d at 80; *R.G. Group,* 751 F.2d at 76.

Texaco asserts that there was no partial performance that would indicate an intent to be bound, but conversely, that the conduct of the parties here was inconsistent with the existence of a binding contract.

* * *

Other than the preliminary financial arrangements made by Pennzoil, we find little relevant partial performance in this case that might show that the parties believed that they were bound by a contract. However, the absence of relevant part performance in this short period of time does not compel the conclusion that no contract existed. Texaco has pointed out that there was some conduct inconsistent with the existence of an intent to be bound to a contract. But partial performance, and on the other hand, conduct that is inconsistent with an intent to be bound, are again merely circumstances that the finder of fact could consider in reaching a decision on whether the parties intended to be bound. The evidence on the parties' conduct was presented to the jury, which could either accept or reject the inferences the parties asked it to draw from these facts.

The next factor showing intent to be bound is whether there was agreement on all essential terms of the alleged agreement. Texaco contends that numerous items of "obvious importance" were still being negotiated at the time Pennzoil claims a contract had been formed.

First, Texaco asserts that there was no agreement on which party would buy the Museum's stock [based on later discussions that since Getty Oil's purchase of the Museum's shares might trigger a tax penalty to Getty Oil, Pennzoil might purchase the Museum's shares instead, Ed.]. Pennzoil contends that its contract was formed on January 3, and that intent to be bound must be determined as of that date. The jury specifically found, in response to Special Issue No. 6, that at the end of the January 3 board meeting, the Getty Oil Company, the Museum, the Trust, and Pennzoil each intended to be bound to an agreement that provided that Getty Oil would purchase the Museum's shares forthwith as provided in the Memorandum of Agreement. There is evidence in the record to support this finding.

* * *

There was sufficient evidence for the jury to conclude that the parties had reached agreement on all essential terms of the transaction with only the mechanics and details left to be supplied by the parties' attorneys. Although there may have been many specific items relating to the transaction agreement draft that had yet to be put in final form, there is sufficient evidence to support a conclusion by the jury that the parties did not consider any of Texaco's asserted "open items" significant obstacles precluding an intent to be bound.

The fourth factor that Texaco discusses as showing that the parties did not intend to be bound before executing a formal contract is the magnitude and complexity of the transaction. There is little question that the transaction by which Getty Oil was to be taken private by the Trust and Pennzoil involved an extremely large amount of money. It is unlikely that parties to such a transaction would not have expected a detailed written document, specifically setting out the parties' obligations and the exact mechanics of the transaction, whether it was to be executed before the parties intended to be bound or only to memorialize an agreement already reached.

We agree with Texaco that this factor tends to support its position that the transaction was such that a signed contract would ordinarily be expected before the parties would consider themselves bound. However, we cannot say, as a matter of law, that this factor alone is determinative of the question of the parties' intent.

The trial of this case lasted many weeks, with witnesses for both sides testifying extensively about the events of those first days of January 1984. Eyewitnesses and expert witnesses interpreted and explained various aspects of the negotiations and the alleged agreement, and the jury was repeatedly made aware of the value of Getty Oil's assets and how much money would be involved in the company's sale. There was testimony on how the sale of the company could be structured and on the considerations involved in buying and restructuring, or later liquidating, the company. But there was also testimony that there were companies that in the past had bound themselves to short two-page acquisition agreements involving a lot of money, and Getty's [investment] banker testified that the Texaco transaction included "one page back-of-the-envelope kinds of agreements" that were formalized. The

Memorandum of Agreement containing the essential terms of the Pennzoil/Getty agreement was only four pages long.

Although the magnitude of the transaction here was such that normally a signed writing would be expected, there was sufficient evidence to support an inference by the jury that that expectation was satisfied here initially by the Memorandum of Agreement, signed by a majority of shareholders of Getty Oil and approved by the board with a higher price, and by the transaction agreement in progress that had been intended to memorialize the agreement previously reached.

* * *

Texaco next claims that even if the parties intended to bind themselves before a definitive document was signed, no binding contract could result because the terms that they intended to include in their agreement were too vague and incomplete to be enforceable as a matter of law. Texaco attacks the terms, found by the jury, of the alleged agreement as being so uncertain as to render the alleged contract fatally indefinite.

* * * [T]he case at bar is distinguishable from those cited by Texaco that involved writings stating specifically that certain essential terms were "to be agreed upon" in the future. *See, e.g., Joseph Martin, Jr., Delicatessen, Inc. v. Schumacher,* 52 N.Y.2d 105, 436 N.Y.S.2d 247, 417 N.E.2d 541 (1981); *Willmott v. Giarraputo,* 5 N.Y.2d 250, 184 N.Y.S.2d 97, 157 N.E.2d 282 (1959).

For a contract to be enforceable, the terms of the agreement must be ascertainable to a reasonable degree of certainty. *Candid Productions, Inc. v. International Skating Union,* 530 F.Supp. 1330, 1333 (S.D.N.Y. 1982). The question of whether the agreement is sufficiently definite to be enforceable is a difficult one. The facts of the individual case are decisively important. *Mason v. Rose,* 85 F.Supp. 300, 311 (S.D.N.Y.1948), *aff'd,* 176 F.2d 486 (2d Cir.1949). "The agreement need not be so definite that all the possibilities that might occur to a party in bad faith are explicitly provided for, but it must be sufficiently complete so that parties in good faith can find in the agreement words that will fairly define their respective duties and liabilities." *Id.* On review, the agreement must be sufficiently definite for the court to be able to recognize a breach and to fashion a remedy for that breach. *Candid Productions, Inc.,* 530 F.Supp. at 1333–34.

Texaco does not assert that a specific essential term was completely omitted from the agreement, but rather alleges very briefly why the terms of the agreement found by the jury are fatally incomplete. Texaco cites to the lack of description of the mechanics of various aspects of the transaction, e.g., how and when the determined price would be paid to shareholders, how the agreed stock ownership ratio was to be achieved, how a potential tax penalty on Getty's purchasing the Museum shares would be resolved, and what limitations, if any, existed on the option granted to Pennzoil to buy 8 million shares of Getty Oil stock.

Texaco's attempts to create additional "essential" terms from the mechanics of implementing the agreement's existing provisions are unpersuasive. The terms of the agreement found by the jury are supported by the evidence, and the promises of the parties are clear enough for a court to recognize a breach and to determine the damages resulting from that breach. Point of Error 47 is overruled.

[Texaco raised numerous points of error relating to jury submissions and instructions.] Special Issue no. 1 asked:

Do you find from a preponderance of the evidence that at the end of the Getty Oil board meeting of January 3, 1984, Pennzoil and each of the Getty entities, to wit, the Getty Oil Company, the Sarah C. Getty Trust and the J. Paul Getty Museum, intended to bind themselves to an agreement that included the following terms:

> a.   all Getty Oil shareholders except Pennzoil and the Sarah C. Getty Trust ... were to receive $110 per share, plus [a $5 stub];
>
> b.   Pennzoil was to own 3/7th ... and the Sarah C. Getty Trust was to own ... 4/7ths of the stock of Getty Oil; and
>
> c.   Pennzoil and the Sarah C. Getty Trust were to endeavor in good faith to agree upon a plan for restructuring Getty Oil on or before December 31, 1984, and if they were unable to reach such agreement then they would divide the assets also on a 3/7ths/4/7ths basis.
> * * *

The accompanying instructions ... state:

Instructions

1.   An agreement may be an oral, it may be written or it may be partly written and partly oral. Where an agreement is fully or partially in writing, the law provides that persons may bind themselves to that agreement even though they do not sign it, where their assent is otherwise indicated.

2.   In answering Issue No. 1, you should look to the intent of Pennzoil and the Getty entities as outwardly or objectively demonstrated to each other by their words and deeds. The question is not determined by the parties' secret, inward, or subjective intentions.

3.   Persons may intend to be bound to an agreement even though they plan to sign a more formal and detailed document at a later time. On the other hand, parties may intend not to be bound until such a document is signed.

4.   There is no legal requirement that parties agree on all the matters incidental to their agreement before they can intend to be bound. Thus, even if certain matters were left for future negotiations, those matters may not have been regarded by Pennzoil and the Getty entities as essential to their agreement, if any, on January 3. On the other hand, you may find that the parties did not intend to be bound until each and every term of their transaction was resolved.

5. Every binding agreement carries with it a duty of good faith performance. If Pennzoil and the Getty entities intended to be bound at the end of the Getty Oil board meeting of January 3, they were obliged to negotiate in good faith the terms of the definitive merger agreement and to carry out the transaction.

6. Modification or discussions to modify an agreement do not defeat or nullify a prior intention to be bound. Parties may always, by mutual consent and understanding, add new provisions spelling out additional terms that were not included in their original agreement.

* * *

[Other portions of the court's opinion are omitted. The judgment of the trial court was affirmed on condition that Pennzoil file a remittitur agreeing to the reduction of punitive damages from $3 billion to $1 billion. The judgment for $7.3 billion compensatory damages was unaffected by the remittitur.]

HAINES v. CITY OF NEW YORK

Court of Appeals of New York, 1977.
41 N.Y.2d 769, 396 N.Y.S.2d 155, 364 N.E.2d 820.

GABRIELLI, JUDGE. In the early 1920's, respondent City of New York and intervenors Town of Hunter and Village of Tannersville embarked upon negotiations for the construction of a sewage system to serve the village and a portion of the town. These negotiations were prompted by the city's need and desire to prevent the discharge of untreated sewage by residents of the area into Gooseberry Creek, a stream which fed a reservoir of the city's water supply system in the Schoharie watershed.

In 1923, the Legislature enacted enabling legislation authorizing the city to enter into contracts with municipalities in the watershed area "for the purpose of providing, maintaining [and] operating systems and plants for the collection and disposal of sewage" (L.1923, ch. 630, § 1). The statute further provided that any such contracts would be subject to the approval of the New York City Board of Estimate and Apportionment.

The negotiations culminated in an agreement in 1924 between the city and intervenors. By this agreement, the city assumed the obligation of constructing a sewage system consisting of a sewage disposal plant and sewer mains and laterals, and agreed that "all costs of construction and subsequent operation, maintenance and repair of said sewerage system with the house connections thereof and said disposal works shall be at the expense" of the city. The agreement also required the city to extend the sewer lines when "necessitated by future growth and building constructions of the respective communities". The village and town were obligated to and did obtain the necessary easements for the construction of the system and sewage lines.

The Board of Estimate, on December 9, 1926, approved the agreement and authorized the issuance of $500,000 of "corporate stock" of the City of New York for construction of the system by appropriate resolution. It is interesting to here note that a modification of the original agreement occurred in 1925 wherein the village agreed to reimburse the city for a specified amount representing the expense of changing the location of certain sewer lines. The plant was completed and commenced operation in 1928. The city has continued to maintain the plant through the ensuing years and in 1958 expended $193,000 to rehabilitate and expand the treatment plant and facilities.

Presently, the average flow of the plant has increased from an initial figure of 118,000 gallons per day to over 600,000 gallons daily and the trial court found that the plant "was operating substantially in excess of design capacity". The city asserts, and it is not disputed by any of the parties in this action, that the system cannot bear any significant additional "loadings" because this would result in inadequate treatment of all the sewage and consequently harm the city's water supply. The instant controversy arose when plaintiff, who is the owner of a tract of unimproved land which he seeks to develop into 50 residential lots, applied to the city for permission to connect houses, which he intends to construct on the lots, to existing sewer lines. The city refused permission on the ground that it had no obligation to further expand the plant, which is presently operating at full capacity, to accommodate this new construction.

Plaintiff then commenced this action for declaratory and injunctive relief, in which intervenors town and village joined as plaintiffs, maintaining that the 1924 agreement is perpetual in duration and obligates the city to expend additional capital funds to enlarge the existing plant or build a new one to accommodate the present and future needs of the municipalities. Both the trial court and the Appellate Division, by a divided court, held in favor of plaintiff and intervenors concluding, that, while the contract did not call for perpetual performance, the city was bound to construct additional facilities to meet increased demand until such time as the village or town is legally obligated to maintain a sewage disposal system. Two members of the court dissented in part stating that the agreement should not be construed as requiring the city to construct new or additional facilities.

We conclude that the city is presently obligated to maintain the existing plant but is not required to expand that plant or construct any new facilities to accommodate plaintiff's substantial, or any other increased demands on the sewage system. The initial problem encountered in ascertaining the nature and extent of the city's obligation pursuant to the 1924 agreement, is its duration. We reject, as did the courts below, the plaintiff's contention that the city is perpetually bound under the agreement. The contract did not expressly provide for perpetual performance and both the trial court and the Appellate Division found that the parties did not so intend. Under these circumstances, the law will not imply that a contract calling for continuing performance is perpetual in duration (*Mitler v. Freideberg*, 32 Misc.2d 78, 85, 222 N.Y.S.2d 480, 488; *Warner–Lambert Pharm. Co. v. John J. Reynolds, Inc.*, 178 F.Supp. 655, affd. 2 Cir., 280 F.2d 197; *Holt v. St. Louis Union Trust Co.*, 4 Cir., 52 F.2d 1068, 1069; *Town of Readsboro v. Hoosac Tunnel & Wilmington R.R. Co.*, 2 Cir., 6 F.2d 733 [L. Hand, J.]; *Borough of West Caldwell v. Borough of Caldwell*, 26 N.J. 9, 28–29, 138 A.2d 402, 1 Williston, Contracts [3d ed.], § 38, p. 113).

On the other hand, the city's contention that the contract is terminable at will because it provides for no express duration should also be rejected. In the absence of an express term fixing the duration of a contract, the courts may inquire into the intent of the parties and supply the missing term if a duration may be fairly and reasonably fixed by the surrounding circumstances and the parties' intent (*Warner–Lambert Pharm. Co. v. John J. Reynolds, Inc., supra*, p. 661; *Benham v. World Airways*, 9 Cir., 432 F.2d 359, 361; *Town of Readsboro v. Hoosac Tunnel & Wilmington R.R. Co., supra*, p. 735). It is generally agreed that where a duration may be fairly and reasonably supplied by implication, a contract is not terminable at will (1 Williston, *op.cit.*, p. 112; 10 N.Y.Jur., Contracts, § 412, p. 426; 17 Am.Jur.2d, Contracts, § 487, p. 957; C.J.S. Contracts § 398, p. 480; see, also, Restatement, Contracts 2d [Tent.Draft No. 7], § 230) [now § 204, ed.].

While we have not previously had occasion to apply it, the weight of authority supports the related rule that where the parties have not clearly expressed the duration of a contract, the courts will imply that they intended performance to continue for a reasonable time (*Colony Liq. Distrs. v. Daniel Distillery–Lem Motlow Prop.*, 22 A.D.2d 247, 249–250, 254 N.Y.S.2d 547, 549, 550 [Aulisi, J.]; *Metal Assoc. v. East Side Metal Spinning & Stamping Corp.*, 2 Cir., 165 F.2d 163, 165; *Borough of West Caldwell v. Borough of Caldwell, supra*, 138 A.2d p. 412; Simpson, Contracts, § 48, p. 74; 1 Williston, *op.cit.*, pp. 116–117; 10 N.Y.Jur., Contracts, § 413, p. 427). * * * Thus, we hold that it is reasonable to infer from the circumstances of the 1924 agreement that the parties intended the city to maintain the sewage disposal facility until such time as the city no longer needed or desired the water, the purity of which the plant was designed to insure. * * *

Having determined the duration of the city's obligation, the scope of its duty remains to be defined. By the agreement, the city obligated itself to build a specifically described disposal facility and to extend the lines of that facility to meet future increased demand. At the present time, the extension of those lines would result in the overloading of the system. Plaintiff claims that the city is required to build a new plant or expand the existing facility to overcome the problem. We disagree. The city should not be required to extend the lines to plaintiffs' property if to do so would overload the system and result in its inability to properly treat sewage. In providing for the extension of sewer lines, the contract does not obligate the city to provide sewage disposal services for properties in areas of the municipalities not presently served or even to new properties in areas which are presently served where to do so could reasonably be expected to significantly increase the demand on present plant facilities.

Thus, those paragraphs of the judgment which provide that the city is obligated to construct any additional facilities required to meet increased demand and that plaintiff is entitled to full use of the sewer lines should be stricken.

Accordingly, the order of the Appellate Division should be modified and the case remitted to Supreme Court, Greene County, for the entry of judgment in accordance with the opinion herein and, as so modified, affirmed, with costs to appellants against plaintiffs-respondents only.

WAGENSELLER v. SCOTTSDALE MEMORIAL HOSPITAL

Supreme Court of Arizona, En Banc, 1985.
147 Ariz. 370, 710 P.2d 1025.

FELDMAN, JUSTICE. Catherine Sue Wagenseller petitioned this court to review a decision of the court of appeals affirming in part the trial court's judgment in favor of Scottsdale Memorial Hospital and certain Hospital employees (defendants). The trial court had dismissed all causes of action on defendants' motion for summary judgment. The court of appeals affirmed in part and remanded, ruling that the only cause of action available to plaintiff was the claim against her supervisor, Kay Smith. * * * We granted review to consider the law of this state with regard to the employment-at-will doctrine. The issues we address are:

1. Is an employer's right to terminate an at-will employee limited by any rules which, if breached, give rise to a cause of action for wrongful termination?

2. If "public policy" or some other doctrine does form the basis for such an action, how is it determined?

3. Did the trial court err, in view of *Leikvold v. Valley View Community Hospital,* 141 Ariz. 544, 688 P.2d 170 (1984), when it determined as a matter of law that the terms of Scottsdale Memorial Hospital's personnel policy manual were not part of the employment contract?

4. Do employment contracts contain an implied covenant of "good faith and fair dealing," and, if so, what is the nature of the covenant?

* * *

FACTUAL BACKGROUND

Catherine Wagenseller began her employment at Scottsdale Memorial Hospital as a staff nurse in March 1975, having been personally recruited by the manager of the emergency department, Kay Smith. Wagenseller was an "at-will" employee—one hired without specific contractual term. Smith was her supervisor. In August 1978, Wagenseller was assigned to the position of ambulance charge nurse, and approximately one year later was promoted to the position of paramedic coordinator, a newly approved management position in the emergency department. Three months later, on November 1, 1979, Wagenseller was terminated.

Most of the events surrounding Wagenseller's work at the Hospital and her subsequent termination are not disputed, although the parties differ in their interpretation of the inferences to be drawn from and the significance of these events. For more than four years, Smith and Wagenseller maintained a friendly, professional, working relationship. In May 1979, they joined a group consisting largely of personnel from other hospitals for an eight-day camping and rafting trip down the Colorado River. According to Wagenseller, "an uncomfortable feeling" developed between her and Smith as the trip progressed—a feeling that Wagenseller ascribed to "the behavior that Kay Smith was displaying." Wagenseller states that this included public urination, defecation and bathing, heavy drinking, and "grouping up" with other rafters. Wagenseller did not participate in any of these activities. She also refused to join in the group's staging of a parody of the song "Moon River," which allegedly concluded with members of the group "mooning" the audience. Smith and others allegedly performed the "Moon River" skit twice at the Hospital following the group's return from the river, but Wagenseller declined to participate there as well.

Wagenseller contends that her refusal to engage in these activities caused her relationship with Smith to deteriorate and was the proximate cause of her termination. She claims that following the river trip Smith began harassing her, using abusive language and embarrassing her in the company of other staff. Other emergency department staff reported a similar marked change in Smith's behavior toward Wagenseller after the trip, although Smith denied it.

Up to the time of the river trip, Wagenseller had received consistently favorable job performance evaluations. Two months before the trip, Smith completed an annual evaluation report in which she rated Wagenseller's performance as "exceed[ing] results expected," the second highest of five possible ratings. In August and October 1979, Wagenseller met first with Smith and then with Smith's successor, Jeannie Steindorff, to discuss some problems regarding her duties as paramedic coordinator and her attitude toward the job. On November 1, 1979, following an exit interview at which Wagenseller was asked to resign and refused, she was terminated.

She appealed her dismissal in letters to her supervisor and to the Hospital administrative and personnel department, answering the Hospital's stated reasons for her termination, claiming violations of the disciplinary procedure contained in the Hospital's personnel policy manual, and requesting reinstatement and other remedies. When this appeal was denied, Wagenseller brought suit against the Hospital, its personnel administrators, and her supervisor, Kay Smith.

Wagenseller, an "at-will" employee, contends that she was fired for reasons which contravene public policy and without legitimate cause related to job performance. She claims that her termination was wrongful, and that damages are recoverable under both tort and contract theories. The Hospital argues that an "at-will" employee may be fired for cause, without cause, or for "bad" cause. We hold that in the absence of contractual provision such an employee may be fired for good cause or for no cause, but not for "bad" cause.

THE EMPLOYMENT-AT-WILL DOCTRINE

History

As early as 1562, the English common law presumed that an employment contract containing an annual salary provision or computation was for a one-year term. Murg & Scharman, *Employment at Will: Do the Exceptions Overwhelm the Rule?* 23 B.C.L.Rev. 329, 332 (1982). * * *

* * * The late nineteenth century, however, brought the Industrial Revolution; with it came the decline of the master-servant relationship and the rise of the more impersonal employer-employee relationship. In apparent response to the economic changes sweeping the country, American courts abandoned the English rule and adopted the employment-at-will doctrine. Murg & Scharman, *supra*, at 334. This new doctrine gave the employer freedom to terminate an at-will employee for any reason, good or bad.

The at-will rule has been traced to an 1877 treatise by H.G. Wood, in which he wrote:

> With us the rule is inflexible, that a general or indefinite hiring is *prima facie* a hiring at will, and if the servant seeks to make it out a yearly hiring, the burden is upon him to establish it by proof.... [I]t is an indefinite hiring and is determinable at the will of either party....
>
> *H.G. Wood, Law of Master and Servant* § 134 at 273 (1877). As commentators and courts later would point out, none of the four cases cited by Wood actually supported the rule. * * *

However unsound its foundation, Wood's at-will doctrine was adopted by the New York courts in *Martin v. New York Life Insurance Co.,* 148 N.Y. 117, 42 N.E. 416 (1895), and soon became the generally accepted American rule. In 1932, this court first adopted the rule for Arizona: "The general rule in regard to contracts for personal services, ... where no time limit is provided, is that they are terminable at pleasure by either party, or at most upon reasonable notice." *Dover Copper Mining Co. v. Doenges,* 40 Ariz. 349, 357, 12 P.2d 288, 291–92 (1932). Thus, an employer was free to fire an employee hired for an indefinite term "for good cause, for no cause, or even for cause morally wrong, without being thereby guilty of legal wrong." Blades, *Employment at Will v. Individual Freedom: On Limiting the Abusive Exercise of Employer Power,* 67 Colum.L.Rev. 1404, 1405 (1967)....

Present–Day Status of the At–Will Rule

In recent years there has been apparent dissatisfaction with the absolutist formulation of the common law at-will rule. The Illinois

Supreme Court is representative of courts that have acknowledged a need for a less mechanical application of the rule:

> With the rise of large corporations conducting specialized operations and employing relatively immobile workers who often have no other place to market their skills, recognition that the employer and employee do not stand on equal footing is realistic. In addition, unchecked employer power, like unchecked employee power, has been seen to present a distinct threat to the public policy carefully considered and adopted by society as a whole. As a result, it is now recognized that a proper balance must be maintained among the employer's interest in operating a business efficiently and profitably, the employee's interest in earning a livelihood, and society's interest in seeing its public policies carried out.

Palmateer v. International Harvester Co., 85 Ill.2d 124, 129, 52 Ill.Dec. 13, 15, 421 N.E.2d 876, 878 (1981) (citation omitted). Today, courts in three-fifths of the states have recognized some form of a cause of action for wrongful discharge. Lopatka, *The Emerging Law of Wrongful Discharge—A Quadrennial Assessment of the Labor Law Issue of the 80s,* 40 Bus.Law. 1 (1984).

The trend has been to modify the at-will rule by creating exceptions to its operation. Three general exceptions have developed. The most widely accepted approach is the "public policy" exception, which permits recovery upon a finding that the employer's conduct undermined some important public policy. The second exception, based on contract, requires proof of an implied-in-fact promise of employment for a specific duration, as found in the circumstances surrounding the employment relationship, including assurances of job security in company personnel manuals or memoranda. Under the third approach, courts have found in the employment contract an implied-in-law covenant of "good faith and fair dealing" and have held employers liable in both contract and tort for breach of that covenant. Wagenseller raises all three doctrines.

THE PUBLIC POLICY EXCEPTION

The public policy exception to the at-will doctrine began with a narrow rule permitting employees to sue their employers when a statute expressly prohibited their discharge. *See Kouff v. Bethlehem–Alameda Shipyard,* 90 Cal.App.2d 322, 202 P.2d 1059 (1949) (statute prohibiting discharge for serving as an election officer). This formulation was then expanded to include any discharge in violation of a statutory expression of public policy. *See Petermann v. Teamsters Local 396,* 174 Cal.App.2d 184, 344 P.2d 25 (1959) (discharge for refusal to commit perjury). Courts later allowed a cause of action for violation of public policy, even in the absence of a specific statutory prohibition. *See Nees v. Hocks,* 272 Or. 210, 536 P.2d 512 (1975) (discharge for being absent from work to serve on jury duty). The New Hampshire Supreme Court announced perhaps the most expansive rule when it held an employer liable for discharging an employee who refused to go out with her foreman. The court concluded that termination "motivated by bad faith or malice or based on retaliation is not [in] the best interest of the economic system or the public good and constitutes a breach of the employment contract." *Monge v. Beebe Rubber Co.,* 114 N.H. 130, 133, 316 A.2d 549, 551 (1974).[3] Although no other court has gone this far, a majority of the states have now either recognized a cause of action based on the public policy exception or have indicated their willingness to consider it, given appropriate facts.[4] The key to an employee's claim in all of these cases is the proper definition of a public policy that has been violated by the employer's actions.

* * *

It is difficult to justify this court's further adherence to a rule which permits an employer to fire someone for "cause morally wrong." So far as we can tell, no court faced with a termination that violated a "clear mandate of public policy" has refused to adopt the public policy exception. Certainly, a court would be hard-pressed to find a rationale to hold that an employer could with impunity fire an employee who refused to commit perjury. Why should the law imply an agreement which would give the employer such power? It may be argued, of course, that our economic system functions best if employers are given wide latitude in dealing with employees. We assume that it is in the public interest that employers continue to have that freedom. We also believe, however, that the interests of the economic system will be fully served if employers may fire for good cause or without cause. The interests of society as a whole will be promoted if employers are forbidden to fire for cause which is "morally wrong."

We therefore adopt the public policy exception to the at-will termination rule. We hold that an employer may fire for good cause or for no cause. He may not fire for bad cause—that which violates public policy. To the extent that it is contrary to the foregoing, we overrule *Dover Copper Mining Co. v. Doenges, supra.*

We turn then to the questions of where "public policy" may be found and how it may be recognized and articulated. As the expressions of our founders and those we have elected to our legislature, our state's constitution and statutes embody the public conscience of the people of this state. It is thus in furtherance of their interests to hold that an employer may not with impunity violate the dictates of public policy found in the provisions of our statutory and constitutional law.

---

3. Although *Monge* held that the aggrieved employee had a cause of action for breach of her employment contract based on the employer's "bad faith," the New Hampshire Supreme Court later restricted the reach of *Monge,* construing it to apply "only to a situation where an employee is discharged because he performed an act that public policy would encourage, or re- fused to do that which public policy condemned." *Howard v. Dorr Woolen Co.,* 120 N.H. 295, 297, 414 A.2d 1273, 1274 (1980).

4. Twelve states have recognized a wrongful discharge cause of action for violation of public policy; fifteen additional states have acknowledged a willingness to consider it, if presented with appropriate facts. * * *

We do not believe, however, that expressions of public policy are contained only in the statutory and constitutional law, nor do we believe that all statements made in either a statute or the constitution are expressions of public policy. Turning first to the identification of other sources, we note our agreement with the following:

> Public policy is usually defined by the political branches of government. Something "against public policy" is something that the Legislature has forbidden. But the Legislature is not the only source of such policy. In common-law jurisdictions the courts too have been sources of law, always subject to legislative correction, and with progressively less freedom as legislation occupies a given field. It is the courts, to give one example, that originated the whole doctrine that certain kinds of businesses—common carriers and innkeepers— must serve the public without discrimination or preference. In this sense, then, courts make law, and they have done so for years.

Lucas v. Brown & Root, 736 F.2d 1202, 1205 (8th Cir.1984). * * * Thus, we believe that reliance on prior judicial decisions, as part of the body of applicable common law, is appropriate, although we agree with the Hawaii Supreme Court that "courts should proceed cautiously if called upon to declare public policy absent some prior legislative or judicial expression on the subject." *Parnar v. Americana Hotels,* 65 Hawaii at 380, 652 P.2d at 631. Thus, we will look to the pronouncements of our founders, our legislature, and our courts to discern the public policy of this state.

All such pronouncements, however, will not provide the basis for a claim of wrongful discharge. Only those which have a singularly *public* purpose will have such force. * * * Where the interest involved is merely private or proprietary, the exception does not apply. In *Pierce v. Ortho Pharmaceutical Corp.,* [84 N.J. 58, 417 A.2d 505 (1980)] * * * for instance, the court held that the plaintiff did not have a cause of action for wrongful discharge based on her refusal to do certain research, where she had failed to articulate a clear public policy that had been violated. Citing the personal nature of Dr. Pierce's opposition [to do research on artificial sweeteners], the court stated:

> Chaos would result if a single doctor engaged in research were allowed to determine, according to his or her individual conscience, whether a project should continue. An employee does not have a right to continued employment when he or she refuses to conduct research simply because it would contravene his or her personal morals. An employee at will who refuses to work in answer to a call of conscience should recognize that other employees and their employer might heed a different call.

84 N.J. at 75, 417 A.2d at 514 (citation omitted). Although an employee facing such a quandary may refuse to do the work believed to violate her moral philosophy, she may not also claim a right to continued employment. *Id.* * * *

However, some legal principles, whether statutory or decisional, have a discernible, comprehensive public purpose. A state's criminal code provides clear examples of such statutes. Thus, courts in other jurisdictions have consistently recognized a cause of action for a discharge in violation of a criminal statute. * * *

Although we do not limit our recognition of the public policy exception to cases involving a violation of a criminal statute, we do believe that our duty will seldom be clearer than when such a violation is involved. * * *

In the case before us, Wagenseller refused to participate in activities which arguably would have violated our indecent exposure statute, A.R.S. § 13–1402. She claims that she was fired because of this refusal. The statute provides:

§ 13–1402. Indecent exposure; classifications

A. A person commits indecent exposure if he or she exposes his or her genitals or anus or she exposes the areola or nipple of her breast or breasts and another person is present, and the defendant is reckless about whether such other person, as a reasonable person, would be offended or alarmed by the act.

B. Indecent exposure is a class 1 misdemeanor. Indecent exposure to a person under the age of fifteen years is a class 6 felony.

While this statute may not embody a policy which "strikes at the heart of a citizen's social right, duties and responsibilities" (*Palmateer, supra*) as clearly and forcefully as a statute prohibiting perjury, we believe that it was enacted to preserve and protect the commonly recognized sense of public privacy and decency. The statute does, therefore, recognize bodily privacy as a "citizen's social right." We disagree with the court of appeals' conclusion that a minor violation of the statute would not violate public policy. (Slip op. at 6.) The nature of the act, and not its magnitude, is the issue. The legislature has already concluded that acts fitting the statutory description contravene the public policy of this state. We thus uphold this state's public policy by holding that termination for refusal to commit an act which might violate A.R.S. § 13–1402 may provide the basis of a claim for wrongful discharge. The relevant inquiry here is not whether the alleged "mooning" incidents were either felonies or misdemeanors or constituted purely technical violations of the statute, but whether they contravened the important public policy interests embodied in the law. The law enacted by the legislature establishes a clear policy that public exposure of one's anus or genitals is contrary to public standards of morality. We are compelled to conclude that termination of employment for refusal to participate in public exposure of one's buttocks[5] is a termination contrary to the policy

---

5. We have little expertise in the techniques of mooning. We cannot say as a matter of law, therefore, whether mooning would always violate the statute by revealing the mooner's anus or genitalia. That question could only be determined, we suppose, by an examination of the facts of each case. We deem such an inquiry unseemly and unnecessary in a civil case. Compelled exposure of the bare buttocks, on pain of of this state, even if, for instance, the employer might have grounds to believe that all of the onlookers were voyeurs and would not be offended. In this situation, there might be no crime, but there would be a violation of public policy to compel the employee to do an act ordinarily proscribed by the law.

From a theoretical standpoint, we emphasize that the "public policy exception" which we adopt does not require the court to make a new contract for the parties. In an at-will situation, the parties have made no express agreement regarding the duration of employment or the grounds for discharge. The common law has presumed that in so doing the parties have intended to allow termination at any time, with or without good cause. It might be more properly argued that the law has recognized an implied covenant to that effect. Whether it be presumption or implied contractual covenant, we do not disturb it. We simply do not raise a presumption or imply a covenant that would require an employee to do that which public policy forbids or refrain from doing that which it commands.

Thus, in an at-will hiring we continue to recognize the presumption or to imply the covenant of termination at the pleasure of either party, whether with or without cause. Firing for bad cause—one against public policy articulated by constitutional, statutory, or decisional law—is not a right inherent in the at-will contract, or in any other contract, even if expressly provided. *See 1 A. Corbin, Contracts* § 7; *6A A. Corbin, Contracts* §§ 1373–75 (1962). Such a termination violates rights guaranteed to the employee by law and is tortious. *See Prosser & Keeton on Torts* § 92 at 655 (5th ed. 1984).

The "Personnel Policy Manual" Exception

Although an employment contract for an indefinite term is presumed to be terminable at will, that presumption, like any other presumption, is rebuttable by contrary evidence. * * *

An implied-in-fact contract term * * * is inferred from the statements or conduct of the parties. It is not a promise defined by the law, but one made by the parties, though not expressly. Courts have found such terms in an employer's policy statements regarding such things as job security and employee disciplinary procedures, holding that by the conduct of the parties these statements may become part of the contract, supplementing the verbalized at-will agreement, and thus limiting the employer's absolute right to discharge an at-will employee. * * * Arizona is among the jurisdictions that have recognized the implied-in-fact contract term as an exception to the at-will rule. In *Leikvold v. Valley View Community Hospital,* [141 Ariz. 544, 688 P.2d 170 (1984)] this court held that a personnel manual can become part of an employment contract and remanded the cause for a jury determination as to whether the particu-

---

termination of employment, is a sufficient violation of the *policy* embodied in the statute to support the action, even if there would have been no technical violation of the statute.

lar manual given to Leikvold had become part of her employment contract with Valley View. 141 Ariz. at 548, 688 P.2d at 174.

The relevant facts in the case before us are not dissimilar to those in *Leikvold.* In October 1978, Scottsdale Memorial Hospital established a four-step disciplinary procedure to achieve the Hospital's stated policy of "provid[ing] fair and consistent discipline as required to assist with the improvement of employees' behavior or performance." Subject to 32 listed exceptions, prior to being terminated a Hospital employee must be given a verbal warning, a written performance warning, a letter of formal reprimand, and a notice of dismissal. The manual further qualifies the mandatory procedure by providing that the 32 exceptions "are not inclusive and are only guidelines." In appealing her dismissal, Wagenseller cited violations of this procedure, but the trial court ruled as a matter of law that the manual had not become part of the employment contract between Wagenseller and the Hospital. The court of appeals held that the Hospital's failure to follow the four-step disciplinary procedure did not violate Wagenseller's contract rights because she failed to prove her reliance on the procedure as a part of her employment contract. (Slip op. at 14.) We disagree with both of these rulings.

First, we need look only to *Leikvold* for the rule governing the determination of whether a particular statement by an employer becomes a part of an employment contract:

> Whether any particular personnel manual modifies any particular employment-at-will relationship and becomes part of the particular employment contract is a *question of fact.* Evidence relevant to this factual decision includes the language used in the personnel manual as well as the employer's course of conduct and oral representations regarding it.

141 Ariz. at 548, 688 P.2d at 174 (emphasis added). Thus, we held in *Leikvold* that entry of summary judgment was inappropriate "[b]ecause a material question—whether the policies manual was incorporated into and became part of the terms of the employment contract—remain[ed] in dispute." *Id.* The court may determine as a matter of law the proper construction of contract terms which are "clear and unambiguous." *Id.* Here, the court of appeals ruled, in effect, that the Hospital had adequately disclaimed any liability for failing to follow the procedure it had established. It found this disclaimer in the final item in the Hospital's list of exceptions to its disciplinary procedure: "20. These major and minor infractions are not inclusive and are only guidelines." The court concluded that the effect of this "clear" and "conspicuous" provision was "to create, by its terms, no rights at all." (Slip op. at 14.)

We do not believe this document, read in its entirety, has the clarity that the court of appeals attributed to its individual portions. One reading the document might well infer that the Hospital had established a procedure that would generally apply in disciplinary actions taken against employees. Although such a person would also note the long list of exceptions, he might not conclude from reading the list that an exception would apply in every case so as to swallow the general rule completely. We do not believe that the provision for unarticulated exceptions destroys the entire articulated general policy as a matter of law. Not only does such a result defy common sense, it runs afoul of our reasoning in *Leikvold,* where we addressed this problem directly:

> Employers are certainly free to issue no personnel manual at all or to issue a personnel manual that clearly and conspicuously tells their employees that the manual is not part of the employment contract and that their jobs are terminable at the will of the employer with or without reason. Such actions, either not issuing a personnel manual or issuing one with clear language of limitation, instill no reasonable expectations of job security and do not give employees any reason to rely on representations in the manual. However, if an employer does choose to issue a policy statement, in a manual or otherwise, and, by its language or by the employer's actions, encourages reliance thereon, the employer cannot be free to only selectively abide by it. Having announced a policy, the employer may not treat it as illusory.

141 Ariz. at 548, 688 P.2d at 174.

* * *

The general rule is that the determination whether in a particular case a promise should be implied in fact is a question of fact. 1 *A. Corbin, supra,* § 17 at 38; *see also Leikvold,* 141 Ariz. at 548, 688 P.2d at 174. * * * We believe that reasonable persons could differ in the inferences and conclusions they would draw from the Hospital's published manual regarding disciplinary policy and procedure. Thus, there are questions of fact as to whether this policy and procedure became a part of Wagenseller's employment contract. *See Leikvold,* 141 Ariz. at 548, 688 P.2d at 174. The trial court therefore erred in granting summary judgment on this issue.

The court of appeals' resolution of the reliance issue also was incorrect. A party may enforce a contractual provision without showing reliance. *Leikvold* does not require a plaintiff employee to show reliance in fact. The employee's reliance on an announced policy is only one of several factors that are relevant in determining whether a particular policy was intended by the parties to modify an at-will agreement. The employer's course of conduct and oral representations regarding the policy, as well as the words of the policy itself, also may provide evidence of such a modification. *Leikvold,* 141 Ariz. at 548, 688 P.2d at 174.

THE "GOOD FAITH AND FAIR DEALING" EXCEPTION

We turn next to a consideration of implied-in-law contract terms which may limit an employer's right to discharge an at-will employee. Wagenseller claims that discharge without good cause breaches the implied-in-law covenant of good faith and fair dealing contained in every contract. * * * In the context of this case, she argues that discharge without good cause violates the covenant of good faith and is, therefore, wrongful. The covenant requires that neither party do anything that will injure the right of the other to receive the benefits of their agreement. * * * The duty not to act in bad faith or deal unfairly thus becomes a part of the contract, and, as with any other element of the contract, the remedy for its breach generally is on the contract itself. * * * In certain circumstances, breach of contract, including breach of the covenant of good faith and fair dealing, may provide the basis for a tort claim. * * *

The question whether a duty to terminate only for good cause should be implied into all employment-at-will contracts has received much attention in the case law and other literature. * * * Courts have generally rejected the invitation to imply such a duty in employment contracts, voicing the concern that to do so would place undue restrictions on management and would infringe the employer's "legitimate exercise of management discretion." *Pugh v. See's Candies,* 116 Cal. App.3d at 330, 171 Cal.Rptr. at 928. * * * We think this concern is appropriate.

California has come closer than any other jurisdiction to implying a good cause duty in all employment-at-will contracts. The case most often cited for this rule is *Cleary v. American Airlines,* 111 Cal.App.3d 443, 168 Cal.Rptr. 722 (1980). In *Cleary,* the plaintiff was discharged after eighteen years of employment with the defendant. He alleged that the discharge violated both an express policy of the company regarding employee grievances and the implied covenant of good faith and fair dealing. *Id.* at 448, 168 Cal.Rptr. at 725. The court agreed:

> Termination of employment without legal cause after such a period of time offends the implied-in-law covenant of good faith and fair dealing contained in all contracts, including employment contracts. As a result of this covenant, a duty arose on the part of the employer . . . to do nothing which would deprive plaintiff, the employee, of the benefits of the employment bargain—benefits described in the complaint as having accrued during plaintiff's 18 years of employment.

Id. at 455, 168 Cal.Rptr. at 729. Thus, the court held that the employer could not discharge this employee without good cause, based on both the longevity of the employee's service and the express policy of the employer. *Id.* If the plaintiff could sustain his burden of proving that he had been terminated unjustly, the court held further that his cause of action would sound in tort as well as contract. *Id.* Only one other court has allowed a tort recovery for breach of the implied covenant of good faith in an employment contract, and, in that case as well as in *Cleary,* the court relied in part upon the existence of an employee handbook on which plaintiff had relied. *Gates v. Life of Montana Insurance Co.,* [638 P.2d 1063 (Mont. 1982)]. . . . *Cf. Moore v. Home Insurance Co.,* 601 F.2d 1072 (9th Cir.1979) (applying Arizona law, court held that the good faith duty did not limit employment discharges to those for which good cause could be shown).

* * *

We find neither the logic of the California cases nor their factual circumstances compelling for recognition of so broad a rule in the case before us. Were we to adopt such a rule, we fear that we would tread perilously close to abolishing completely the at-will doctrine and establishing by judicial fiat the benefits which employees can and should get *only* through collective bargaining agreements or tenure provisions. * * *

In reaching this conclusion, however, we do not feel that we should treat employment contracts as a special type of agreement in which the law refuses to imply the covenant of good faith and fair dealing that it implies in all other contracts. As we noted above, the implied-in-law covenant of good faith and fair dealing protects the right of the parties to an agreement to receive the benefits of the agreement that they have entered into. The denial of a party's right to those benefits, whatever they are, will breach the duty of good faith implicit in the contract. Thus, the relevant inquiry always will focus on the contract itself, to determine what the parties did agree to. In the case of an employment-at-will contract, it may be said that the parties have agreed, for example, that the employee will do the work required by the employer and that the employer will provide the necessary working conditions and pay the employee for work done. What cannot be said is that one of the agreed benefits to the at-will employee is a guarantee of continued employment or tenure. The very nature of the at-will agreement precludes any claim for a prospective benefit. Either employer or employee may terminate the contract at any time.

We do, however, recognize an implied covenant of good faith and fair dealing in the employment-at-will contract, although that covenant does not create a duty for the employer to terminate the employee only for good cause. The covenant does not protect the employee from a "no cause" termination because tenure was never a benefit inherent in the at-will agreement. The covenant does protect an employee from a discharge based on an employer's desire to avoid the payment of benefits already earned by the employee, such as the sales commissions in *Fortune* [*v. National Cash Register,* 364 N.E.2d 1251 (Mass. 1977)], but not the tenure required to earn the pension and retirement benefits in *Cleary, supra.* Thus, plaintiff here has a right to receive the benefits that were a part of her employment agreement with defendant Hospital. To the extent, however, that the benefits represent a claim for prospective employment, her claim must fail. The terminable-at-will contract between her and the Hospital made no promise of continued employment. To the contrary, it was, by its nature, subject to termination by either party at any time, subject only to the legal prohibition that she could not be fired for reasons which contravene public policy.

Thus, because we are concerned not to place undue restrictions on the employer's discretion in managing his workforce and because tenure is contrary to the bargain in an at-will contract, we reject the argument that a no cause termination breaches the implied covenant of good faith and fair dealing in an employment-at-will relationship.

* * *

SUMMARY AND CONCLUSIONS

The trial court granted summary judgment against Wagenseller on the count alleging the tort of wrongful discharge in violation of public policy. We adopt the "public policy" exception to the at-will termination rule and hold that the trial court erred in granting judgment against plaintiff on this theory. On remand plaintiff will be entitled to a jury trial if she can make a prima facie showing that her termination was caused by her refusal to perform some act contrary to public policy, or her performance of some act which, as a matter of public policy, she had a right to do. The obverse, however, is that mere dispute over an issue involving a question of public policy is not equivalent to establishing causation as a matter of law and will not automatically entitle plaintiff to judgment. In the face of conflicting evidence or inferences as to the actual reason for termination, the question of causation will be a question of fact.

The trial court granted summary judgment against Wagenseller on the count alleging breach of implied-in-fact provisions of the contract. We hold that this was error. On this record, there is a jury question as to whether the provisions of the employment manual were part of the contract of employment.

We affirm the grant of summary judgment on the count seeking recovery for breach of the implied covenant of good faith and fair dealing. We recognize that covenant as part of this and other contracts, but do not construe it to give either party to the contract rights—such as tenure—different from those for which they contracted.

* * *

For the foregoing reasons, we affirm in part and reverse in part. The decision of the court of appeals is vacated and the case remanded to the trial court for proceedings not inconsistent with this opinion.

[The dissenting and specially concurring opinion of Holohan, C.J., and the supplemental opinion of Feldman, J., are omitted.]

SOUTHWEST ENGINEERING CO. v. MARTIN TRACTOR CO., INC.

Supreme Court of Kansas, 1970.
205 Kan. 684, 473 P.2d 18.

FONTRON, JUSTICE. This is an action to recover damages for breach of contract. Trial was had to the court which entered judgment in favor of the plaintiff. The defendant has appealed.

Southwest Engineering Company, Inc., the plaintiff, is a Missouri corporation engaged in general contracting work, while the defendant,

Martin Tractor Company, Inc., is a Kansas corporation. The two parties will be referred to hereafter either as plaintiff, or Southwest, on the one hand and defendant, or Martin, on the other.

We glean from the record that in April, 1966, the plaintiff was interested in submitting a bid to the United States Corps of Engineers for the construction of certain runway lighting facilities at McConnell Air Force Base at Wichita. However, before submitting a bid, and on April 11, 1966, the plaintiff's construction superintendent, Mr. R.E. Cloepfil, called the manager of Martin's engine department, Mr. Ken Hurt, who at the time was at Colby, asking for a price on a standby generator and accessory equipment. Mr. Hurt replied that he would phone him back from Topeka, which he did the next day, quoting a price of $18,500. This quotation was re-confirmed by Hurt over the phone on April 13.

Southwest submitted its bid on April 14, 1966, using Hurt's figure of $18,500 for the generator equipment, and its bid was accepted. On April 20, Southwest notified Martin that its bid had been accepted. Hurt and Cloepfil thereafter agreed over the phone to meet in Springfield on April 28. On that date Hurt flew to Springfield, where the two men conferred at the airfield restaurant for about an hour. Hurt took to the meeting a copy of the job specifications which the government had supplied Martin prior to the letting.

At the Springfield meeting it developed that Martin had upped its price for the generator and accessory equipment from $18,500 to $21,500. Despite this change of position by Martin, concerning which Cloepfil was understandably amazed, the two men continued their conversation and, according to Cloepfil, they arrived at an agreement for the sale of a D353 generator and accessories for the sum of $21,500. * * *

* * *

On May 2, 1966, Cloepfil addressed a letter to the Martin Tractor Company, directing Martin to proceed with shop drawings and submittal documents for the McConnell lighting job and calling attention to the fact that applicable government regulations were required to be followed. Further reference to this communication will be made when necessary.

Some three weeks thereafter, on May 24, 1966, Hurt wrote Cloepfil the following letter:

"MARTIN TRACTOR COMPANY, INC.

Topeka Chanute Concordia Colby

CATERPILLAR*

"P.O. Box 1698
Topeka, Kansas
May 24, 1966
Mr. R.E. Cloepfil
Southwest Engineering Co., Inc.
P.O. Box 3314, Glenstone Station
Springfield, Missouri 65804

Dear Sir:

Due to restrictions placed on Caterpillar products, accessory suppliers, and other stipulations by the district governing agency, we cannot accept your letter to proceed dated May 2, 1966, and hereby withdraw all verbal quotations.

Regretfully,

/s/ Ken Hurt
Ken Hurt, Manager Engine
Division"

* * *

It is quite true, as the trial court found, that terms of payment were not agreed upon at the Springfield meeting. Hurt testified that as the memorandum was being made out, he said they wanted 10 per cent with the order, 50 per cent on delivery and the balance on acceptance, but he did not recall Cloepfil's response. Cloepfil's version was somewhat different. He stated that after the two had shaken hands in the lobby preparing to leave, Hurt said their terms usually were 20 per cent down and the balance on delivery; while he (Cloepfil) said the way they generally paid was 90 per cent on the tenth of the month following delivery and the balance on final acceptance. It is obvious the parties reached no agreement on this point.

However, a failure on the part of Messrs. Hurt and Cloepfil to agree on terms of payment would not, of itself, defeat an otherwise valid agreement reached by them. K.S.A. 84–2–204(3) [this is the Kansas enactment of UCC § 2–204(3) ed.] reads:

"Even though one or more terms are left open a contract for sale does not fail for indefiniteness if the parties have intended to make a contract and there is a reasonably certain basis for giving an appropriate remedy."

The official U.C.C. Comment is enlightening:

"Subsection (3) states the principle as to 'open terms' underlying later sections of the Article. If the parties intend to enter into a binding agreement, this subsection recognizes that agreement as valid in law despite missing terms, if there is any reasonably certain basis for granting a remedy. The test is not certainty as to what the parties were to do nor as to the exact amount of damages due the plaintiff. Nor is the fact that one or more terms are left to be agreed upon enough of itself to defeat an otherwise adequate agreement. Rather, commercial standards on the point of 'indefiniteness' are intended to be applied, this Act making provision elsewhere for missing terms needed for performance, open price, remedies and the like.

"The more terms the parties leave open, the less likely it is that they have intended to conclude a binding agreement, but their actions may be frequently conclusive on the matter despite the omissions."

The above Code provision and accompanying Comment were quoted in *Pennsylvania Co. v. Wilmington Trust Co.*, 39 Del.Ch. 453, 166 A.2d 726, where the court made this observation:

"There appears to be no pertinent court authority interpreting this rather recent but controlling statute. In an article entitled 'The Law of Sales In the Proposed Uniform Commercial Code,' 63 Harv. Law Rev. 561, 576, Mr. Williston wanted to limit omissions to 'minor' terms. He wanted 'business honor' to be the only compulsion where 'important terms' are left open. Nevertheless, his recommendation was rejected (see note on p. 561). This shows that those drafting the statute intended that the omission of even an important term does not prevent the finding under the statute that the parties intended to make a contract." (pp. 731, 732.)

So far as the present case is concerned, K.S.A. 84–2–310 supplies the omitted term. This statute provides in pertinent part:

"Unless otherwise agreed

"(*a*) payment is due at the time and place at which the buyer is to receive the goods even though the place of shipment is the place of delivery;"

In our view, the language of the two Code provisions is clear and positive. Considered together, we take the two sections to mean that where parties have reached an enforceable agreement for the sale of goods, but omit therefrom the terms of payment, the law will imply, as part of the agreement, that payment is to be made at time of delivery. In this respect the law does not greatly differ from the rule this court laid down years ago.

* * *

We do not mean to infer that terms of payment are not of importance under many circumstances, or that parties may not condition an agreement on their being included. However, the facts before us hardly indicate that Hurt and Cloepfil considered the terms of payment to be significant, or of more than passing interest. Hurt testified that while he stated his terms he did not recall Cloepfil's response, while Cloepfil stated that as the two were on the point of leaving, each stated their usual terms and that was as far as it went. The trial court found that only a brief and casual conversation ensued as to payment, and we think that is a valid summation of what took place.

Moreover, it is worthy of note that Martin first mentioned the omission of the terms of payment, as justifying its breach, in a letter written by counsel on September 15, 1966, more than four months after the memorandum was prepared by Hurt. On prior occasions Martin attributed its cancellation of the Springfield understanding to other causes. In its May 24 letter, Martin ascribed its withdrawal of "all verbal quotations" to "restrictions placed on Caterpillar products, accessory suppliers, and other stipulations by the district governing agency." In explaining the meaning of the letter to Cloepfil, Hurt said that Martin was doing work for the Corps of Engineers in the Kansas City and Tulsa districts and did not want to take on additional work with them at this time.

The entire circumstances may well give rise to a suspicion that Martin's present insistence that future negotiations were contemplated concerning terms of payment, is primarily an afterthought, for use as an escape hatch. Doubtless the trial court so considered the excuse in arriving at its findings.

We are aware of Martin's argument that Southwest's letter of May 2, 1966, referring to the sale is evidence that no firm contract had been concluded. Granted that some of the language employed might be subject to that interpretation, the trial court found, on what we deem to be substantial, competent evidence, that an agreement of sale *was* concluded at Springfield. Under our invariable rule those findings are binding upon this court on appeal even though there may have been evidence to the contrary. (See cases in 1 Hatcher's Kansas Digest [Rev.Ed.] Appeal & Error, §§ 507, 508.)

The defendant points particularly to the following portion of the May 2 letter, as interjecting a new and unacceptable term in the agreement made at Springfield.

" ... We are not prepared to make a partial payment at the time of placing of this order. However, we will be able to include 100% of the engine-generator price in our first payment estimate after it is delivered, and only 10% will have to be withheld pending acceptance. Ordinarily this means that suppliers can expect payment of 90% within about thirty days after delivery."

It must be conceded that the terms of payment proposed in Southwest's letter had not been agreed to by Martin. However, we view the proposal as irrelevant. Although terms of payment had not been mutually agreed upon, K.S.A. 84–2–310 supplied the missing terms, i.e., payment on delivery, which thus became part of the agreement already concluded. In legal effect the proposal was no more than one to change the terms of payment implied by law. Since Martin did not accept the change, the proposal had no effect, either as altering or terminating the agreement reached at Springfield. * * *

* * *

We find no error in this case and the judgment of the trial court is affirmed.

JOSEPH MARTIN, JR., DELICATESSEN, INC. v. SCHUMACHER

Court of Appeals of New York, 1981.
52 N.Y.2d 105, 436 N.Y.S.2d 247, 417 N.E.2d 541.

FUCHSBERG, JUDGE. This case raises an issue fundamental to the law of contracts. It calls upon us to review a decision of the Appellate Division, 70 A.D.2d 1, 419 N.Y.S.2d 558 which held that a realty lease's provision that the rent for a renewal period was "to be agreed upon" may be enforceable.

The pertinent factual and procedural contexts in which the case reaches this court are uncomplicated. In 1973, the appellant, as landlord, leased a retail store to the respondent for a five-year term at a rent graduated upwards from $500 per month for the first year to $650 for the fifth. The renewal clause stated that "[t]he Tenant may renew this lease for an additional period of five years at annual rentals to be agreed upon; Tenant shall give Landlord thirty (30) days written notice, to be mailed certified mail, return receipt requested, of the intention to exercise such right". It is not disputed that the tenant gave timely notice of its desire to renew or that, once the landlord made it clear that he would do so only at a rental starting at $900 a month, the tenant engaged an appraiser who opined that a fair market rental value would be $545.41.

The tenant thereupon commenced an action for specific performance in Supreme Court, Suffolk County, to compel the landlord to extend the lease for the additional term at the appraiser's figure or such other sum as the court would decide was reasonable. For his part, the landlord in due course brought a holdover proceeding in the local District Court to evict the tenant. On the landlord's motion for summary judgment, the Supreme Court, holding that a bald agreement to agree on a future rental was unenforceable for uncertainty as a matter of law, dismissed the tenant's complaint. Concordantly, it denied as moot the tenant's motion to remove the District Court case to the Supreme Court and to consolidate the two suits.

It was on appeal by the tenant from these orders that the Appellate Division, expressly overruling an established line of cases in the process, reinstated the tenant's complaint and granted consolidation. In so doing, it reasoned that "a renewal clause in a lease providing for future agreement on the rent to be paid during the renewal term is enforceable if it is established that the parties' intent was not to terminate in the event of a failure to agree". It went on to provide that, if the tenant met that burden, the trial court could proceed to set a "reasonable rent". One of the Justices, concurring, would have eliminated the first step and required the trial court to proceed directly to the fixation of the rent. Each party now appeals by leave of the Appellate Division pursuant to CPLR 5602 (subd. [b], par. 1). The tenant seeks only a modification adopting the concurrer's position. The question formally certified to us by the Appellate Division is simply whether its order was properly made. Since we conclude that the disposition at the Supreme Court was the correct one, our answer must be in the negative.

We begin our analysis with the basic observation that, unless otherwise mandated by law (e.g., residential emergency rent control statutes), a contract is a private "ordering" in which a party binds himself to do, or not to do, a particular thing (*Fletcher v. Peck,* 6 Cranch [10 U.S.] 87, 136; 3 L.Ed. 162. Hart and Sachs, Legal Process, 147–148 [1958]). This liberty is no right at all if it is not accompanied by freedom not to contract. The corollary is that, before one may secure redress in our courts because another has failed to honor a promise, it must appear that the promisee assented to the obligation in question.

It also follows that, before the power of law can be invoked to enforce a promise, it must be sufficiently certain and specific so that what was promised can be ascertained. Otherwise, a court, in intervening, would be imposing its own conception of what the parties should or might have undertaken, rather than confining itself to the implementation of a bargain to which they have mutually committed themselves. Thus, definiteness as to material matters is of the very essence in contract law. Impenetrable vagueness and uncertainty will not do (1 Corbin, Contracts, § 95, p. 394; 6 Encyclopedia of New York Law, Contracts, § 301; Restatement, Contracts 2d, § 32, Comment *a*).

Dictated by these principles, it is rightfully well settled in the common law of contracts in this State that a mere agreement to agree, in which a material term is left for future negotiations, is unenforceable (*Willmott v. Giarraputo,* 5 N.Y.2d 250, 253, 184 N.Y.S.2d 97, 157 N.E.2d 282; *Sourwine v. Truscott,* 17 Hun. 432, 434). This is especially true of the amount to be paid for the sale or lease of real property (see *Forma v. Moran,* 273 App.Div. 818, 76 N.Y.S.2d 232; *Huber v. Ruby,* 187 Misc. 967, 969, 65 N.Y.S.2d 462, app. dsm'd 271 App.Div. 927, 67 N.Y.S.2d 710, see, generally, 58 A.L.R.3d 500, Validity and Enforceability of Provision for Renewal of Lease at Rental to be Fixed by Subsequent Agreement of the Parties). The rule applies all the more, and not the less, when, as here, the extraordinary remedy of specific performance is sought (11 Williston, Contracts [Jaeger 3d ed.], § 1424; Pomeroy, Equity Jurisprudence, § 1405).

This is not to say that the requirement for definiteness in the case before us now could only have been met by explicit expression of the rent to be paid. The concern is with substance, not form. It certainly would have sufficed, for instance, if a methodology for determining the rent was to be found within the four corners of the lease, for a rent so arrived at would have been the end product of agreement between the parties themselves. Nor would the agreement have failed for indefiniteness because it invited recourse to an objective extrinsic event, condition or standard on which the amount was made to depend. All of these, *inter alia,* would have come within the embrace of the maxim that what can be made certain is certain (9 Coke, 47a). (Cf. *Backer Mgt. Corp. v. Acme Quilting Co.,* 46 N.Y.2d 211, 219, 413 N.Y.S.2d 135, 385 N.E.2d 1062 [escalation of rent keyed to building employees' future wage increases]; *City of Hope v. Fisk Bldg. Assoc.,* 63 A.D.2d 946, 406 N.Y.S.2d 472 [rental increase to be adjusted for upward movement in US Consumer Price Index]; see, generally, 87 A.L.R.3d 986; Lease Provisions Providing for Rent Adjustment Based on Event or Formula Outside Control of Parties.)

But the renewal clause here in fact contains no such ingredients. Its unrevealing, unamplified language speaks to no more than "annual rentals to be agreed upon". Its simple words leave no room for legal construction or resolution of ambiguity. Neither tenant nor landlord is bound to any formula. There is not so much as a hint at a commitment to be bound by the "fair market rental value" which the tenant's expert reported or the "reasonable rent" the Appellate Division would impose, much less any definition of either. Nowhere is there an inkling that either of the parties directly or indirectly assented, upon accepting the clause, to subordinate the figure on which it ultimately would insist, to one fixed judicially, as the Appellate Division decreed be done, or, for that matter, by an arbitrator or other third party.

Finally, in this context, we note that the tenant's reliance on *May Metropolitan Corp. v. May Oil Burner Corp.,* 290 N.Y. 260, 49 N.E.2d 13 is misplaced. There the parties had executed a franchise agreement for the sale of oil burners. The contract provided for annual renewal, at which time each year's sales quota was "to be mutually agreed upon". In holding that the defendant's motion for summary judgment should have been denied, the court indicated that the plaintiff should be given an opportunity to establish that a series of annual renewals had ripened into a course of dealing from which it might be possible to give meaning to an otherwise uncertain term. This decision, in the more fluid sales setting in which it occurred, may be seen as a precursor to the subsequently enacted Uniform Commercial Code's treatment of open terms in contracts for the sale of goods (see Uniform Commercial Code, § 1–205, subd. [1]; § 2–204, subd. [3]; see, also, Restatement, Contracts 2d, § 249). As the tenant candidly concedes, the code, by its very terms, is limited to the sale of goods. The *May* case is therefore not applicable to real estate contracts. Stability is a hallmark of the law controlling such transactions (see *Heyert v. Orange & Rockland Utilities,* 17 N.Y.2d 352, 362, 271 N.Y.S.2d 201, 218 N.E.2d 263).

For all these reasons, the order of the Appellate Division should be reversed, with costs, and the orders of the Supreme Court, Suffolk County, reinstated. The certified question, therefore, should be answered in the negative. As to the plaintiff's appeal, since that party was not aggrieved by the order of the Appellate Division, the appeal should be dismissed (CPLR 5511), without costs.

MEYER, JUDGE (concurring). While I concur in the result because the facts of this case do not fit the rule of *May Metropolitan Corp. v. May Oil Burner Corp.* 290 N.Y. 260, 49 N.E.2d 13, I cannot concur in the majority's rejection of that case as necessarily inapplicable to litigation concerning leases. That the setting of that case was commercial and that its principle is now incorporated in a statute (the Uniform Commercial Code) which by its terms is not applicable to real estate is irrelevant to the question whether the principle can be applied in real estate cases.

As we recognized in *Farrell Lines v. City of New York,* 30 N.Y.2d 76, 82, 330 N.Y.S.2d 358, 281 N.E.2d 162, quoting from *A.Z.A. Realty Corp. v. Harrigan's Café,* 113 Misc. 141, 147, 185 N.Y.S. 212: "An agreement of lease possesses no peculiar sanctity requiring the application of rules of construction different from those applicable to an ordinary contract." To the extent that the majority opinion can be read as holding that no course of dealing between the parties to a lease could make a clause providing for renewal at a rental "to be agreed upon" enforceable I do not concur.

JASEN, JUDGE (dissenting in part). While I recognize that the traditional rule is that a provision for renewal of a lease must be "certain" in order to render it binding and enforceable, in my view the better rule would be that if the tenant can establish its entitlement to renewal under the lease, the mere presence of a provision calling for renewal at "rentals to be agreed upon" should not prevent judicial intervention to fix rent at a reasonable rate in order to avoid a forfeiture. Therefore, I would affirm the order of the Appellate Division for the reasons stated in the opinion of JUSTICE LEON D. LAZER at the Appellate Division.

COOKE, C.J., and GABRIELLI, JONES and WACHTLER, JJ., concur with FUCHSBERG, J. MEYER, J., concurs in a memorandum. JASEN, J., dissents in part and on defendant's appeal votes to affirm in a memorandum.* * *

COPELAND v. BASKIN ROBBINS U.S.A.

Court of Appeal, Second District, 2002.
96 Cal.App.4th 1251, 117 Cal.Rptr.2d 875.

JOHNSON, ACTING P.J. We address an unsettled question in California: may a party sue for breach of a contract to negotiate an agreement or is such a "contract" merely an unenforceable "agreement to agree?" We hold a contract to negotiate an agreement is distinguishable from a so-called "agreement to agree" and can be formed and breached just like any other contract. We further hold, however, even if the plaintiff in this case could establish the defendant's liability for breach of contract he is limited to reliance damages—a form of recovery he has disavowed and defendant has shown he cannot prove. For this reason we affirm the trial court's judgment for defendant.

FACTS AND PROCEEDINGS BELOW

The following facts are undisputed. Baskin Robbins operated an ice cream manufacturing plant in the city of Vernon. When the company announced its intention to close the plant, Copeland expressed an interest in acquiring it. The parties commenced negotiations. Copeland made clear from the outset his agreement to purchase the plant was contingent on Baskin Robbins agreeing to purchase the ice cream he manufactured there. Copeland testified at his deposition the ice cream purchase arrangement, known as "co-packing," was "critical" and "a key to the deal." Without co-packing, Copeland testified, "this deal doesn't work." Baskin Robbins does not deny the co-packing arrangement was an indispensable part of the contract to purchase the plant.

After several months of negotiations an agreement took shape under which Copeland would purchase the plant's manufacturing assets and sublease the plant property. Baskin Robbins would purchase seven million gallons of ice cream from Copeland over a three year period.

In May 1999 Baskin Robbins sent Copeland a letter, which stated in relevant part:

> "This letter details the terms which our Supply Chain executives have approved for subletting and sale of our Vernon manufacturing facility/equipment and a product supply agreement.... (1) Baskin Robbins will sell [Copeland] Vernon's ice cream manufacturing equipment ... for $1,300,000 cash.... (2) Baskin Robbins would agree, subject to a separate co-packing agreement and negotiated pricing, to provide [Copeland] a three year co-packing agreement for 3,000,000 gallons in year 1, 2,000,000 gallons in year 2 and 2,000,000 in year 3.... If the above is acceptable please acknowledge by returning a copy of this letter with a non-refundable check for three thousand dollars.... We should be able to coordinate a closing [within] thirty days thereafter."

Copeland signed a statement at the bottom of the letter agreeing "[t]he above terms are acceptable" and returned the letter to Baskin Robbins along with the $3000 deposit.

After Copeland accepted the terms in the May 1999 letter, the parties continued negotiating over the terms of the co-packing agreement. Among the issues to be settled were the price Baskin Robbins would pay for the ice cream, the flavors Copeland would produce, quality standards and controls, who would bear the loss from spoilage, and trademark protection. Copeland testified he believed in June 1999 he reached an oral agreement with Baskin Robbins on a price for the ice cream of his cost plus 85 cents per tub. He conceded, however, the parties had not agreed on how the cost component was to be determined and so far as he knew there was no written memorandum of this pricing agreement. None of the other issues were settled before Baskin Robbins allegedly breached the contract.

In July 1999, Baskin Robbins wrote to Copeland breaking off negotiations over the co-packing arrangement and returning his $3000 deposit. The letter explained Baskin Robbins' parent company had "recently ... made strategic decisions around the Baskin Robbins business" and "the proposed co-packing arrangement [is] out of alignment with our strategy." Therefore, Baskin Robbins informed Copeland, "we will not be engaging in any further negotiations of a co-packing arrangement." Although Baskin Robbins offered to proceed with the agreement for the sale and lease of the Vernon plant assets it did not insist on doing so, apparently accepting Copeland's view the lack of a co-packing agreement was a "deal-breaker."

In his suit for breach of contract, Copeland alleged he and Baskin Robbins entered into a contract which provided Baskin Robbins would enter into a co-packing agreement with Copeland under the terms set out in the May 1999 letter and additional terms to be negotiated. Baskin Robbins breached this contract by "unreasonably and wrongfully refusing to enter into any co-packing agreement with [Copeland]." As a result of this breach of contract Copeland suffered expectation damages "in the form of lost profits . . . as well as lost employment opportunities and injury to his reputation." In response to a discovery request, Copeland stated his damages consisted of "lost profits from [the] three year co-packing agreement with defendants" as well as lost profits from other sales he could have made had he acquired the plant and the profit he could have earned from selling the plant equipment. Copeland's discovery responses did not provide or allege he could provide evidence of damages he suffered as a result of his relying on Baskin Robbins' promise to negotiate a co-packing agreement.

The trial court granted Baskin Robbins' motion for summary judgment based on the undisputed facts described *ante*. The court concluded the May 1999 letter was susceptible to several interpretations but no matter how it was interpreted it failed as a contract because the essential terms of the co-packing deal were never agreed to and there was no reasonable basis upon which to determine them. Copeland filed a timely appeal from the subsequent judgment. For the reasons discussed below we affirm the judgment albeit on a ground different from those relied upon by the trial court.

DISCUSSION * * *

When Baskin Robbins refused to continue negotiating the terms of the co-packing agreement Copeland faced a dilemma. "Many millions of dollars" in anticipated profits had melted away like so much banana ripple ice cream on a hot summer day. True enough, he could proceed with the contract for the purchase and lease of the Vernon plant's assets and use those assets to produce ice cream for other retailers. But, as he explained in his deposition, without the Baskin Robbins co-packing agreement he could not afford to purchase the assets and pay the ongoing costs of operating the plant while he searched for other business. Alternatively he could attempt to sue Baskin Robbins for breach of the co-packing agreement on the theory the terms of the agreement set out in the May 1999 letter plus additional terms supplied by the court constituted an enforceable contract. Such a suit, however, had a slim prospect of success. While courts have been increasingly liberal in supplying missing terms in order to find an enforceable contract they do so only where the "reasonable intentions of the parties" can be ascertained. It is still the general rule that where any of the essential elements of a promise are reserved for the future agreement of both parties, no legal obligation arises "until such future agreement is made."

Here, the parties agreed in the May 1999 letter as to the amount of ice cream Baskin Robbins would purchase over a three year period but, as Copeland candidly admitted, "a variety of complex terms" remained for agreement before the co-packing contract could be completed. These included price, the flavors to be manufactured, quality control standards, and responsibility for waste.

Copeland chose a third course. Rather than insist the parties had formed a co-packing contract and Baskin Robbins had breached it, he claimed the May 1999 letter constituted a contract to negotiate the remaining terms of the co-packing agreement and Baskin Robbins breached this contract by refusing without excuse to continue negotiations or, alternatively, by failing to negotiate in good faith. This path too has its difficulties. No reported California case has held breach of a contract to negotiate an agreement gives rise to a cause of action for damages. On the other hand numerous California cases have expressed the view the law provides no remedy for breach of an "agreement to agree" in the future. We believe, however, these difficulties could be overcome in an appropriate case.

Initially, we see no reason why in principle the parties could not enter into a valid, enforceable contract to negotiate the terms of a co-packing agreement. * * * Persons are free to contract to do just about anything that is not illegal or immoral[7]. Conducting negotiations to buy and sell ice cream is neither.

Furthermore, as we will demonstrate below, purported contracts which the courts have dismissed as mere "agreements to agree" are distinguishable from contracts to negotiate in at least two respects.

A contract to negotiate the terms of an agreement is not, in form or substance, an "agreement to agree." If, despite their good faith efforts, the parties fail to reach ultimate agreement on the terms in issue the contract to negotiate is deemed performed and the parties are discharged from their obligations. Failure to agree is not, itself, a breach of the contract to negotiate.[8] A party will be liable only if a failure to reach ultimate agreement resulted from a breach of that party's obligation to negotiate or to negotiate in good faith.[9] For these reasons, criticisms of an "agreement to agree" as "absurd" and a "contradiction in terms" do not apply to a contract to negotiate an agreement.

In addition, it is important to note courts which have found purported contracts to be unenforceable "agreements to agree" have focused on the enforceability of the underlying substantive contract, not on whether the agreement to negotiate the terms of that contract is enforceable in its own right. In *Autry v. Republic Productions,* for example, after stating

---

7. Under Civil Code section 1667 persons are not permitted to enter into contracts which are: "1. Contrary to an express provision of law; 2. Contrary to the policy of express law, though not expressly prohibited; or, 3. Otherwise contrary to good morals."

8. *Itek Corporation v. Chicago Aerial Industries, Inc.* (Del.1968) 248 A.2d 625, 629.

9. [*Id.*]; and see Farnsworth, "Precontractual Liability and Preliminary Agreements: Fair Dealing and Failed Negotiations" (1987) 87 Colum. L. Rev. 217, 251. (Hereafter Farnsworth.)

the law "provides [no] remedy for breach of an agreement to agree" the court explained this was so because "[t]he court may not imply what the parties will agree upon."

Most jurisdictions which have considered the question have concluded a cause of action will lie for breach of a contract to negotiate the terms of an agreement.[15]

The *Channel Home Centers* case is illustrative. There the parties executed a letter of intent to enter into the lease of a store in a shopping center. The letter stated, inter alia, Grossman the lessor " 'will withdraw the store from the rental market, and only negotiate the above described leasing transaction to completion.' " After Channel Home Centers expended approximately $25,000 in activities associated with the negotiations, Grossman unilaterally terminated negotiations. The following day Grossman leased the store to one of Channel Home Centers' competitors, Mr. Good Buys. Channel Home Centers sued Grossman for breach of contract based on the letter of intent. After a court trial, the court awarded judgment to Grossman. The Third Circuit Court of Appeals reversed. Distinguishing this case from one alleging merely the breach of an agreement to agree the court pointed out: "[I]t is Channel's position that [the letter of intent] is enforceable as a mutually binding obligation *to negotiate in good faith*. By unilaterally terminating negotiations with Channel and precipitously entering into a lease agreement with Mr. Good Buys, Channel argues, Grossman acted in bad faith and breached his promise to 'withdraw the Store from the rental market and only negotiate the above-described leasing transaction to completion.' " The court concluded under Pennsylvania law an agreement to negotiate in good faith is an enforceable contract.

Baskin Robbins maintains there are sound public policy reasons for not enforcing a contract to negotiate an agreement. In doing so, we would be injecting a covenant of good faith and fair dealing into the negotiation process whether or not the parties specifically agreed to such a term.[18] Citing Professor Farnsworth,[19] Baskin Robbins argues that instead of having a salutary effect on contract negotiations, imposing a regime of good faith and fair dealing would actually discourage parties from entering into negotiations, especially where the chances of success were slight. Alternatively, such an obligation might increase the pressure on the parties to bring the negotiations to a hasty, even if unsatisfactory conclusion, rather than risk being charged with the ill-defined wrong of bad faith negotiation. Most parties, Baskin Robbins suggests, would prefer to risk losing their out-of-pocket costs if the negotiation fails rather than risk losing perhaps millions of dollars in expectation damages if their disappointed negotiating partner can prove bad faith. Finally, Baskin Robbins argues, any precontractual wrong-doing can be

15. *Channel Home Centers, Grace Retail v. Grossman* (3d Cir.1986) 795 F.2d 291, 293–294, 299 (applying Pennsylvania law); see also *Venture Associates v. Zenith Data Systems* (7th Cir.1993) 987 F.2d 429, 433 (applying Illinois law)....

18. In California, a covenant of good faith and fair dealing is implied in every contract. *Foley v. Interactive Data Corp.* (1988) 47 Cal.3d 654, 684, 254 Cal.Rptr. 211, 765 P.2d 373.)

19. See footnote 9, above.

adequately remedied by existing causes of action for unjust enrichment, promissory fraud and promissory estoppel.

We find Baskin Robbins' policy arguments unpersuasive.

Allowing a party to sue for breach of a contract to negotiate an agreement would not inject a covenant of good faith and fair dealing into the negotiation process in violation of the parties' intent. When two parties, under no compulsion to do so, engage in negotiations to form or modify a contract neither party has any obligation to continue negotiating or to negotiate in good faith. Only when the parties are under a contractual compulsion to negotiate does the covenant of good faith and fair dealing attach, as it does in every contract. In the latter situation the implied covenant of good faith and fair dealing has the salutary effect of creating a disincentive for acting in bad faith in contract negotiations.

Professor Farnsworth's criticisms were not directed toward a cause of action for breach of a contract to negotiate the terms of an agreement. On the contrary, Farnsworth supports such a cause of action.[22] Rather, his criticisms were directed at the theory propounded by some European courts and legal scholars that, even absent a contractual agreement to negotiate, a general obligation of fair dealing arises out of the negotiations themselves.[23] * * *

Arguing bad faith is an uncertain concept which could cost the defendant millions of dollars in expectation damages is also without merit. For the reasons we explain below, the appropriate remedy for breach of a contract to negotiate is not damages for the injured party's lost expectations under the prospective contract but damages caused by the injured party's reliance on the agreement to negotiate.[26] Furthermore, we disagree with those who say the courts, unlike the National Labor Relations Board or labor arbitrators, are ill equipped to determine whether people are negotiating with each other in good faith.[27] While few of us will ever negotiate a multi-million dollar contract, each of us participates in some form of negotiation nearly every day. In most cases the question whether the defendant negotiated in good faith will be a question of fact for the jury. In our view ordinary citizens applying their experience and common sense are very well equipped to determine whether the parties negotiated with each other in good faith.

Recovery for unjust enrichment in the context of contract negotiations is usually based on ideas disclosed or services rendered during the negotiations.[28] Where, as here, the negotiations are over the sale of

---

22. Farnsworth, 87 Colum. L.Rev. at pp. 251, 263–269.

23. Farnsworth, 87 Colum. L.Rev. at pp. 239–243.

26. See Farnsworth, 87 Colum. L.Rev. at p. 267.

27. See e.g., *Venture Associates v. Zenith Data Systems* (7th Cir.1996) 96 F.3d 275, 277. (Venture Associates II.)

28. See e.g., *Blaustein v. Burton* (1970) 9 Cal.App.3d 161, 184, 88 Cal.Rptr. 319 [idea for motion picture disclosed to defendants in discussing production contract]; *Hill v. Waxberg* (9th Cir.1956) 237 F.2d 936, 938–939 [services of architect rendered to contractor during negotiation for building contract].

goods, the subject matter of the contract is not an idea nor does the potential seller typically confer a precontractual service on the potential buyer.

A cause of action for promissory fraud is based on "[a] promise made without any intention of performing it."[29] In many cases the defendant may have intended to negotiate in good faith when it contracted to do so but changed its mind later when, for example, a more attractive contracting partner came along.

Thus, we conclude neither unjust enrichment nor promissory fraud provide a party an adequate vehicle for relief when its negotiating partner breaks off negotiations or negotiates in bad faith.

The doctrine of promissory estoppel is generally used to enforce the defendant's clear and unambiguous promise when the plaintiff has reasonably and foreseeably relied on it. We agree a cause of action for promissory estoppel might lie if the defendant made a clear, unambiguous promise to negotiate in good faith and the plaintiff reasonably and foreseeably relied on that promise in incurring expenditures connected with the negotiation.[32] We may also assume for the sake of argument such a cause of action could be based on an implied promise to negotiate in good faith.[33] If these propositions are correct, then promissory estoppel is just a different rubric for determining the enforceability of a contract to negotiate an agreement.

Finally, we believe there are sound public policy reasons for protecting parties to a business negotiation from bad faith practices by their negotiating partners. Gone are the days when our ancestors sat around a fire and bargained for the exchange of stone axes for bear hides. Today the stakes are much higher and negotiations are much more complex. Deals are rarely made in a single negotiating session. Rather, they are the product of a gradual process in which agreements are reached piecemeal on a variety of issues in a series of face-to-face meetings, telephone calls, e-mails and letters involving corporate officers, lawyers, bankers, accountants, architects, engineers and others. As Professor Farnsworth observes, contracts today are not formed by discrete offers, counter-offers and acceptances. Instead they result from a gradual flow of information between the parties followed by a series of compromises and tentative agreements on major points which are finally refined into contract terms.[36] These slow contracts are not only time-consuming but costly. For these reasons, the parties should have some assurance "their investments in time and money and effort will not be wiped out by the other party's footdragging or change of heart or taking advantage of a vulnerable position created by the negotiation."[37] * * *

For obvious reasons, damages for breach of a contract to negotiate an agreement are measured by the injury the plaintiff suffered in relying

---

29. Civ.Code, § 1572 subdivision 4. . . .

32. See *Arcadian Phosphates, Inc. v. Arcadian Corp.* (2d Cir.1989) 884 F.2d 69, 74.

33. See *Drennan v. Star Paving Co.* (1958) 51 Cal.2d 409, 333 P.2d 757. . . .

36. Farnsworth, 87 Colum. L.Rev. at p. 219.

37. *Venture Associates II,* 96 F.3d at p. 278. . . .

on the defendant to negotiate in good faith. This measure encompasses the plaintiff's out-of-pocket costs in conducting the negotiations and may or may not include lost opportunity costs.[40] The plaintiff cannot recover for lost expectations (profits) because there is no way of knowing what the ultimate terms of the agreement would have been or even if there would have been an ultimate agreement.* * *

[The court concluded that Baskin Robbins is entitled to summary judgment because it showed that Copeland could not establish reliance damages. Ed.]

DISPOSITION

The judgment is affirmed.

[WOODS and PERLUSS, JJ. concurred]

OGLEBAY NORTON CO. v. ARMCO, INC.

Supreme Court of Ohio, 1990.
52 Ohio St.3d 232, 556 N.E.2d 515.

On January 9, 1957, Armco Steel Corporation, n.k.a. Armco, Inc., appellant, entered into a long-term contract with Columbia Transportation Company, which later became a division of Oglebay Norton Company, appellee. The principal term of this contract required Oglebay to have adequate shipping capacity available and Armco to utilize such shipping capacity if Armco wished to transport iron ore on the Great Lakes from mines in the Lake Superior district to Armco's plants in the lower Great Lakes region.

In the 1957 contract, Armco and Oglebay established a primary and a secondary price rate mechanism which stated:

"*Armco agrees to pay* * * * for all iron ore transported hereunder *the regular net contract rates for the season* in which the ore is transported, *as recognized by the leading iron ore shippers* in such season for the transportation of iron ore * * *. *If*, in any season of navigation hereunder, *there is no regular net contract rate recognized by the leading iron ore shippers* for such transportation, *the parties shall mutually agree upon a rate* for such transportation, *taking into consideration the contract rate being charged for similar transportation* by the leading independent vessel operators engaged in transportation of iron ore from The Lake Superior District." (Emphasis added.)

During the next twenty-three years, Armco and Oglebay modified the 1957 contract four times. With each modification Armco agreed to extend the time span of the contracts beyond the original date. Both parties acknowledged that the ever-increasing requirements capacity Armco sought from Oglebay would require a substantial capital invest-

---

40. Farnsworth, 87 Colum. L.Rev. at pp. 225–229. Because Copeland cannot establish lost opportunity costs in this case we need not decide whether, in principle, such damages are recoverable for breach of a contract to negotiate. * * *

ment from Oglebay to maintain, upgrade, and purchase iron ore carrier vessels.

The fourth amendment, signed in 1980, required Oglebay to modify and upgrade its fleet to give each Oglebay vessel that Armco utilized a self-unloading capability. It is undisputed that Oglebay began a $95 million capital improvement program at least in part to accommodate Armco's new shipping needs. For its part, Armco agreed to pay an additional twenty-five cents per ton for ore shipped in Oglebay's self-unloading vessels and agreed to extend the running of the contract until December 31, 2010.

During trial, the court recognized Armco's and Oglebay's close and long-standing business relationship, which included a seat for Armco on Oglebay's Board of Directors, Armco's owning Oglebay Norton stock, and a partnership in another venture. In fact, one of Oglebay's vessels was named "The Armco."

This relationship is perhaps best characterized by the language contained in the 1962 amendment, wherein the parties provided:

> " * * * Armco has a vital and unique interest in the continued dedication of * * * [Oglebay's] bulk vessel fleet * * * since such service is a necessary prerequisite to Armco's operation as a major steel producer. * * * Armco's right to require the dedication of * * * [Oglebay's] bulk vessels to Armco's service * * * is the essence of this Agreement[.] * * *." The amendment also granted to Armco the right to seek a court order for specific performance of the terms of the contract.

From 1957 through 1983 the parties established the contract shipping rate that Oglebay charged Armco by referring to a specified rate published in "Skillings Mining Review," in accordance with the 1957 contract's primary price mechanism. The published rate usually represented the price that Innerlake Steamship Company, a leading independent iron ore shipper, charged its customers for a similar service. Oglebay would quote this rate to Armco, which would then pay it to Oglebay.

Unfortunately, in 1983 the iron and steel industry suffered a serious downturn in business. Thus, in late 1983, when Oglebay quoted Armco the shipping rate for the 1984 season, Armco challenged that rate. Due to its weakened economic position, Armco requested that Oglebay reduce the rate Oglebay was going to charge Armco. The parties then negotiated a mutually satisfactory rate for the 1984 season.

In late 1984 the parties were unable to establish a mutually satisfactory shipping rate for the 1985 season. Oglebay billed Armco $7.66 ($.25 self-unloading vessel surcharge included) per gross ton, and Armco reduced the invoice amount to $5 per gross ton. Armco then paid the $5 per ton figure, indicating payment in full language on the check to Oglebay, and explaining its position in an accompanying letter. In late 1985, the parties again attempted to negotiate a rate, this time for the 1986 season. Again they failed to reach a mutually satisfactory rate.

On April 11, 1986, Oglebay filed a declaratory judgment action requesting the court to declare the rate set forth in the contract to be the correct rate, or in the absence of such a rate, to declare a reasonable rate for Oglebay's services. Armco's answer denied that the $7.41 rate sought by Oglebay was the "contract rate," and denied that the trial court had jurisdiction to declare this rate of its own accord, as a "reasonable rate" or otherwise.

During the 1986 season, Oglebay continued to ship iron ore for Armco. Armco paid Oglebay $4.22 per gross ton for ore shipped prior to August 1, 1986 and $3.85 per gross ton for ore shipped after August 1, 1986.

On August 12, 1987, Armco filed a supplemental counterclaim seeking a declaration that the contract was no longer enforceable, because the contract had failed of its purpose due to the complete breakdown of the rate pricing mechanisms.

After a lengthy bench trial, the trial court on November 20, 1987 issued its declaratory judgment, which made four basic findings of fact and law. First, the court held that it was apparent from the evidence presented that Oglebay and Armco intended to be bound by the 1957 contract, even though the rate or price provisions in the contract were not settled.

Second, the court held that where the parties intended to be bound, but where a service contract pricing mechanism based upon the mutual agreement of the parties fails, " * * * then the price shall be the price that is 'reasonable' under all the circumstances at the time the service is rendered."

Third, the trial court held that the parties must continue to comply with the alternative pricing provision contained within paragraph two of the 1957 contract. That alternative pricing provision mandates that the parties consider rates charged for similar services by leading independent iron ore vessel operators.

Fourth, the trial court held that if the parties were unable to agree upon a rate for the upcoming seasons, then the parties must notify the court immediately. Upon such notification, the court, through its equitable jurisdiction, would appoint a mediator and require the parties' chief executive officers " * * * to meet for the purpose of mediating and determining the rate for such season, i.e., that they 'mutually agree upon a rate.' "

The court of appeals affirmed the judgment of the trial court.

* * *

PER CURIAM. This case presents three mixed questions of fact and law. First, did the parties intend to be bound by the terms of this contract despite the failure of its primary and secondary pricing mechanisms? Second, if the parties did intend to be bound, may the trial court establish $6.25 per gross ton as a reasonable rate for Armco to pay Oglebay for shipping Armco ore during the 1986 shipping season? Third, may the trial court continue to exercise its equitable jurisdiction over the parties, and may it order the parties to utilize a mediator if they are unable to mutually agree on a shipping rate for each annual shipping season? We answer each of these questions in the affirmative and for the reasons set forth below affirm the decision of the court of appeals.

I

Appellant Armco argues that the complete breakdown of the primary and secondary contract pricing mechanisms renders the 1957 contract unenforceable, because the parties never manifested an intent to be bound in the event of the breakdown of the primary and secondary pricing mechanisms. Armco asserts that it became impossible after 1985 to utilize the first pricing mechanism in the 1957 contract, i.e., examining the published rate for a leading shipper in the "Skillings Mining Review," because after 1985 a new rate was no longer published. Armco asserts as well that it also became impossible to obtain the information necessary to determine and take into consideration the rates charged by leading independent vessel operators in accordance with the secondary pricing mechanism. This is because that information was no longer publicly available after 1985 and because the trial court granted the motions to quash of non-parties, who were subpoenaed to obtain this specific information. Armco argues that since the parties never consented to be bound by a contract whose specific pricing mechanisms had failed, the trial court should have declared the contract to be void and unenforceable.

The trial court recognized the failure of the 1957 contract pricing mechanisms. Yet the trial court had competent, credible evidence before it to conclude that the parties intended to be bound despite the failure of the pricing mechanisms. The evidence demonstrated the long-standing and close business relationship of the parties, including joint ventures, interlocking directorates and Armco's ownership of Oglebay stock. As the trial court pointed out, the parties themselves contractually recognized Armco's vital and unique interest in the combined dedication of Oglebay's bulk vessel fleet, and the parties recognized that Oglebay could be required to ship up to 7.1 million gross tons of Armco iron ore per year.

Whether the parties intended to be bound, even upon the failure of the pricing mechanisms, is a question of fact properly resolved by the trier of fact. *Normandy Place Assoc. v. Beyer* (1982), 2 Ohio St.3d 102, 106, 2 OBR 653, 656, 443 N.E.2d 161, 164. Since the trial court had ample evidence before it to conclude that the parties did so intend, the court of appeals correctly affirmed the trial court regarding the parties' intent. We thus affirm the court of appeals on this question.

II

Armco also argues that the trial court lacked jurisdiction to impose a shipping rate of $6.25 per gross ton when that rate did not conform to the 1957 contract pricing mechanisms. The trial court held that it had the authority to determine a reasonable rate for Oglebay's services, even though the price mechanism of the contract had failed, since the parties intended to be bound by the contract. The court cited 1 Restatement of the Law 2d, Contracts (1981) 92, Section 33, and its relevant comments to support this proposition. Comment *e* to Section 33 explains in part:

"* * * Where * * * [the parties] * * * intend to conclude a contract for the sale of goods * * * and the price is not settled, the price is a reasonable price at the time of delivery if * * * (c) the price is to be fixed in terms of some agreed market or other standard as set or recorded by a third person or agency and it is not so set or recorded. Uniform Commercial Code § 2–305(1)." *Id.* at 94–95.

As the trial court noted, Section 33 was cited with approval by the Court of Appeals for Cuyahoga County in *Mr. Mark Corp. v. Rush, Inc.* (1983), 11 Ohio App.3d 167, 11 OBR 259, 464 N.E.2d 586, and in *North Coast Cookies, Inc. v. Sweet Temptations, Inc.* (1984), 16 Ohio App.3d 342, 16 OBR 391, 476 N.E.2d 388. Restatement Section 33, Comment *e* follows virtually identical language contained in Section 2–305(1) of the Uniform Commercial Code, which was adopted in Ohio as R.C. 1302.18(A). Moreover the Court of Appeals for Cuyahoga County applied R.C. 1302.18 by analogy to a contract for services involving an open price term in *Winning Sheet Metal Mfg. Co. v. Heat Sealing Equip. Mfg. Co.* (Sept. 30, 1982), Cuyahoga App. No. 44365, unreported, at 3–4, 1982 WL 5944.

The court therefore determined that a reasonable rate for Armco to pay to Oglebay for transporting Armco's iron ore during the 1986 shipping season was $6.00 per gross ton with an additional rate of twenty-five cents per gross ton when self-unloading vessels were used. The court based this determination upon the parties' extensive course of dealing, "* * * the detriment to the parties respectively, and valid comparisons of market price which reflect [the] economic reality of current depressed conditions in the American steel industry."

The court of appeals concluded that the trial court was justified in setting $6.25 per gross ton as a "reasonable rate" for Armco to pay Oglebay for the 1986 season, given the evidence presented to the trial court concerning various rates charged in the industry and given the intent of the parties to be bound by the agreement.

The court of appeals also held that an open price term could be filled by a trial court, which has the authority to review evidence and establish a "reasonable price," when the parties clearly intended to be bound by the contract. To support this holding, the court cited Restatement of the Law 2d, Contracts, *supra*, at 92, Section 33, and its comments, and 179, Section 362, and its comments.

Section 33, Comment *a* provides in part:

"* * * [T]he actions of the parties may show conclusively that they have intended to conclude a binding agreement, even though one or more terms are missing or are left to be agreed upon. In such cases courts endeavor, if possible, to attach a sufficiently definite meaning to the bargain.

"An offer which appears to be indefinite may be given precision by usage of trade or by course of dealing between the parties. Terms may be supplied by factual implication, and in recurring situations the law often supplies a term in the absence of agreement to the contrary. * * * " *Id.* at 92.

As the court of appeals noted, we have held that "agreements to agree," such as the pricing mechanisms in the 1957 contract, are enforceable when the parties have manifested an intention to be bound by their terms and when these intentions are sufficiently definite to be specifically enforced. *Normandy Place Assoc., supra,* 2 Ohio St.3d at 105–106, 2 OBR at 656, 443 N.E.2d at 164. We have also held that "[i]f it is found that the parties intended to be bound, the court should not frustrate this intention, if it is reasonably possible to fill in some gaps that the parties have left, and reach a fair and just result." *Litsinger Sign Co. v. American Sign Co.* (1967), 11 Ohio St.2d 1, 14, 40 O.O.2d 30, 37, 227 N.E.2d 609, 619.

The court of appeals conducted an extensive review of the evidence presented to the trial court and concluded that the $6.25 per gross ton figure was a "reasonable rate" in this situation. The court of appeals noted that Oglebay presented evidence from Jesse J. Friedman, an economic and financial expert, who testified that $7.44 per gross ton was a reasonable rate for such services. Further evidence showed that Armco paid $5.00 per gross ton to Oglebay for the 1985 season, even though the published rate for that season was $7.41 per gross ton.

There was also testimony that Oglebay quoted Armco $5.66 per gross ton as the rate for the 1987 season. The evidence also showed that LTV Steel, prior to its bankruptcy renegotiations with Oglebay, had paid Oglebay the published rate of $7.41 per gross ton. Evidence also indicated that American Steamship Co. had quoted Armco a $5.90 per gross ton rate for the 1986 season.

The court of appeals concluded that the $6.25 per gross ton figure fell acceptably between the rate range extremes proven at trial. The court found this to be a reasonable figure. We find there was competent, credible evidence in the record to support this holding and affirm the court of appeals on this question.

III

Armco also argues that the trial court lacks equitable jurisdiction to order the parties to negotiate or in the failure of negotiations, to mediate, during each annual shipping season through the year 2010. The court of appeals ruled that the trial court did not exceed its jurisdiction in issuing such an order.

3 Restatement of the Law 2d, Contracts (1981) 179, Section 362, entitled "Effect of Uncertainty of Terms," is similar in effect to Section 33 and states:

"Specific performance or an injunction will not be granted unless the terms of the contract are sufficiently certain to provide a basis for an appropriate order."

Comment *b* to Section 362 explains:

" * * * Before concluding that the required certainty is lacking, however, a court will avail itself of all of the usual aids in determining the scope of the agreement. * * * Expressions that at first appear incomplete may not appear so after resort to usage * * * or the addition of a term supplied by law * * *." *Id.* at 179.

Ordering specific performance of this contract was necessary, since, as the court of appeals pointed out, " * * * the undisputed dramatic changes in the market prices of great lakes shipping rates and the length of the contract would make it impossible for a court to award Oglebay accurate damages due to Armco's breach of the contract." We agree with the court of appeals that the appointment of a mediator upon the breakdown of court-ordered contract negotiations neither added to nor detracted from the parties' significant obligations under the contract.

It is well-settled that a trial court may exercise its equitable jurisdiction and order specific performance if the parties intend to be bound by a contract, where determination of long-term damages would be too speculative. See 3 Restatement of the Law 2d, Contracts, *supra*, at 171–172, Section 360(a), Comment *b*; *Columbus Packing Co. v. State, ex rel. Schlesinger* (1919), 100 Ohio St. 285, 294, 126 N.E. 291, 293–294. Indeed, the court of appeals pointed out that under the 1962 amendment, Armco itself had the contractual right to seek a court order compelling Oglebay to specifically perform its contractual duties.

The court of appeals was correct in concluding that ordering the parties to negotiate and mediate during each shipping season for the duration of the contract was proper, given the unique and long-lasting business relationship between the parties, and given their intent to be bound and the difficulty of properly ascertaining damages in this case. The court of appeals was also correct in concluding that ordering the parties to negotiate and mediate with each shipping season would neither add to nor detract from the parties' significant contractual obligations. This is because the order would merely facilitate in the most practical manner the parties' own ability to interact under the contract. Thus we affirm the court of appeals on this question.

The court of appeals had before it competent, credible evidence from which to conclude that the parties intended to be bound by the terms of the contract, to conclude that the $6.25 per gross ton figure was a "reasonable rate" under the circumstances, and to conclude that the trial court's exercise of continuing equitable jurisdiction was proper in this situation. Accordingly, we affirm the decision of the court of appeals.

Judgment affirmed. MOYER, C.J. and SWEENEY, HOLMES, DOUGLAS, WRIGHT, HERBERT R. BROWN and RESNICK, JJ., concur.

ECKLES v. SHARMAN

United States Court of Appeals, Tenth Circuit, 1977.
548 F.2d 905.

BREITENSTEIN, CIRCUIT JUDGE. This is an action by the owner of a professional basketball team for breach of contract by a former coach and for the inducement of that breach by the owner of another professional basketball team. Judgment was entered on a jury verdict for $250,000 against the coach and for $175,000 against the inducing owner. We reverse and remand with directions.

After these appeals were filed, the plaintiff-appellee Mountain States Sports, Inc., became bankrupt and R.T. Eckles, trustee in bankruptcy, was substituted as the appellee in each case. References herein will be to Mountain States rather than to the trustee.

Defendant-appellant Sharman was the coach of the San Francisco Warriors, a professional basketball team of the National Basketball Association, NBA. In 1968 he was persuaded to leave the San Francisco team and to coach the Los Angeles Stars of the newly formed American Basketball Association, ABA. The contract between Sharman and the Los Angeles team was for seven years and called for a starting salary of $55,000 with yearly increases of 5%. Provisions of the contract pertinent to these cases are:

(1)—Sharman was given an "option to purchase 5% ownership of the Club" at a price to be agreed upon between him and the owner.

(2)—Sharman was to participate in a "pension plan" of an undefined nature.

(3)—The parties agreed that: "In the event any one paragraph of this Agreement is invalid, this Agreement will not fail by reason thereof but will be interpreted as if the invalid portion were omitted."

(4)—California law governs the agreement.

In 1970 the Los Angeles Stars were sold for $345,000 to plaintiff Mountain States Sports, Inc., a Colorado corporation, of which Bill Daniels was the president and principal stockholder. An addendum to the sale agreement provided:

"Buyer shall not be obligated to assume the Sharman contract unless he shall have confirmed his willingness to transfer to the city selected by Buyer for operation of the team. Seller states that Sharman has orally expressed his willingness to do so."

The team was moved to Salt Lake City, Utah, and became the Utah Stars. Without anything in writing pertaining to his participation in the move, Sharman went to Salt Lake City with the team. Sharman coached the Utah Stars during the 1970–1971 season and the team won the ABA championship.

During the two years that the team was in Los Angeles with Sharman as coach nothing was done with regard to the option and pension provisions of the contract. Boryla, the general manager of the Utah Stars, told Sharman that the pension provision would be worked out. Later Sharman and Daniels, the president of Mountain States, had numerous communications, both oral and written, concerning Sharman's pension rights. No final agreement was reached. In June, 1971, Sharman resigned as coach of the Utah Stars and, in July, signed a contract to coach the Los Angeles Lakers of the NBA.

Mountain States brought suit in Utah state court charging Sharman with breach of contract. The complaint was amended to assert a claim against defendant-appellant California Sports, Inc., the owner of the Los Angeles Lakers, and two individuals for the tortious inducement of Sharman's breach of contract. * * *

* * *

* * * At the conclusion of the plaintiff's case, Judge Ritter denied a defense motion to dismiss saying that the claim of contract invalidity because of the option and pension clauses presented nothing but a "red herring" and that Sharman and the owners of the Utah Stars had made a "good faith" effort to "clear up those terms." At the conclusion of all of the evidence, Judge Ritter directed a verdict against Sharman on the question of liability.

The case went to the jury on the questions of damages recoverable from Sharman, liability of the other defendants charged with inducement of contract breach and, if there was inducement, the damages resulting therefrom. The jury returned verdicts (1) in favor of the individuals sued for inducement, (2) against Sharman in the amount of $250,000, and (3) against California Sports in the amount of $175,000.

Implicit in the direction of a verdict against Sharman on the question of liability is a ruling that as a matter of law (1) the contract between Sharman and the Los Angeles Stars was valid and enforceable, (2) the contract was validly assigned to Mountain States Sports, and (3) the option and pension provisions of the contract were severable from the remainder thereof.

The option clause was unenforceable because it was nothing more than an agreement to agree. The pension clause did not state (1) the amount of pension, (2) the manner in which it would be funded, and (3) the age at which the pension would begin. The plaintiff does not seriously contest the defense claim that the pension clause is ambiguous.

Plaintiff relies on the severance clause which says that "[i]n the event any one paragraph of this Agreement is invalid," the agreement will not fail but will be interpreted as if the invalid portion was omitted. We have a failure of two paragraphs. Sharman and representatives of the plaintiff negotiated for about 15 months over the two mentioned clauses, principally that pertaining to the pension.

Good faith negotiations over various terms of an agreement do not make a fatally ambiguous contract valid and enforceable. The controlling

California law is that for there to be an enforceable contract the parties must agree on the essential and material terms. See e.g. *Coleman Engineering Co. v. North America Aviation*, 65 Cal.2d 396, 55 Cal.Rptr. 1, 420 P.2d 713, and *Ablett v. Clauson*, 43 Cal.2d 280, 272 P.2d 753. If a contract has been agreed upon and all that remains is good faith negotiations or elaboration of non-essential terms, the contract will be held legally cognizable despite the uncertainties. See *White Point Co. v. Herrington*, 268 Cal.App.2d 458, 73 Cal.Rptr 885, 889. The question is not whether good faith negotiations had taken place but whether the option and pension were so essential to the contract that failure to agree on the pertinent terms made the contract unenforceable.

Moffat Tunnel Improvement Dist. v. Denver & S.L. Ry. Co., 10 Cir., 45 F.2d 715, 731, says that a severability clause "is but an aid to construction, and will not justify a court in declaring a clause as divisible when, considering the entire contract, it obviously is not." The crucial question is whether the clauses to be severed are essential to the contract. Essentiality depends on the intent of the parties. * * *

The intent evidence is not all one way. Sharman testified that without the option and pension provisions he would not have left the well-established NBA for the newly-established ABA. His testimony was corroborated by other witnesses. On the other hand, the record reveals that Sharman never made any serious efforts to clarify or enforce the option clause. Nothing was done about the pension clause during the two years that Sharman and the team were in Los Angeles. During the fifteen months that Sharman was with the Utah Stars many communications, both written and verbal, passed between Sharman and representatives of the team owners. Nothing was accomplished. From the evidence in the record a reasonable man could have drawn an inference one way or the other on the question of intent.

We have repeatedly held that a verdict may not be directed unless the evidence all points one way and is susceptible of no reasonable inferences which sustain the position of the party against whom the motion is made. * * * On the record presented it may not be said, as a matter of law, that the option and pension clauses were unessential and hence severable. Neither can it be said, as a matter of law, that without the resolution of the controversy over those clauses Sharman agreed to the assignment of the contract to the owners of the Utah Stars. The pertinent intent questions required factual determination by the jury under proper instructions. The court erred in directing a verdict against Sharman and in favor of Mountain States on the liability issue.

The liability of California Sports depends on whether the contract between Sharman and the owner of the Los Angeles Stars was valid and whether the contract was enforceable by the owner of the Utah Stars against Sharman. If the contract was not valid, and if the contract was not enforceable by the Utah Stars, California Sports is not liable under the claim of tortious inducement of breach. The error of the court in directing a verdict on the question of Sharman's liability requires the reversal of the judgment against California Sports.

* * *

[Retrial ordered. Ed.]

Problems

31. O owned a resort hotel. O was approached by the defendant railroad company which asked for a right-of-way across O's land adjacent to the hotel. O granted the right-of-way in exchange for the railroad's promise to build "a neat and tasteful railway station" at a specified spot near O's hotel. The railroad was built on the right-of-way but no station was built at or near the specified spot. Does O have a contractual right to have a station built?

32. Is an agreement to remodel in accordance with blueprints for $27,000 void where the blueprints do not specify the materials to be used?

33. If the vendor and vendee agree to sell and purchase a parcel of real property, but do not have a price term in their agreement, is there a contract?

34. A offers to hire B at $52,000 per year payable $1,000 per week and B agrees to take the job. Are the parties bound for a year?

35. Howard is a young lawyer who practices in a jurisdiction that does not recognize a cause of action for the abusive discharge of an at-will employee. Howard was employed by a large law firm and became aware of various violations of the rules of professional conduct by one of his fellow associates. He reported these violations to the proper disciplinary authorities. As a result, he was fired. He asserts that the discharge creates a cause of action because a disciplinary rule states that a lawyer has an obligation to report information "that raises a substantial question as to another lawyer's honesty, trustworthiness or fitness ... " Does he have a cause of action against the law firm?

36. P was an employee of D. In 1982, P wrote a lengthy letter to the editor of a local newspaper that was highly critical of the company and several of its officers. The letter was published and as a result P was fired. Does P have an enforceable claim?

37. A agrees to sell and B agrees to buy 1000 widgets. All of the terms are set out except that the parties "agree to agree" on the price at a later date. Is there a contract? If so, what are the legal consequences if they fail to agree?

38. A agrees to sell and B agrees to buy widgets, "the quantity to be agreed upon from time to time." Is there a contract?

39. "A and B shall make every reasonable effort to agree upon and have prepared as quickly as possible a contract providing for the foregoing purchase by A and sale by B, subject to the approval of A's stockholders, embodying the above terms and such other terms and conditions as the parties shall agree upon. If the parties fail to agree upon and execute such a

contract they shall be under no further obligation to one another." What are the obligations, if any, of the parties under this provision?

40. V gave P a six month option to buy real property which P accepted within the six month period. The option agreement described the property, the price and the amount of the purchase money mortgage. The agreement also provided with respect to the mortgage: "The payment of interest and amortization of principal shall be mutually agreed upon at the time of entering into a more formal contract." (a) Was there a contract? (b) Would the result be different if the subject matter was a tractor?

SECTION 4.   THE ACCEPTANCE

(a) *Preliminary Problems With Respect to Acceptance*

———

(Calamari & Perillo 5th §§ 2.10(a), 2.11—2.17)

———

STATE v. MALM

Supreme Court of Errors of Connecticut, 1956.
143 Conn. 462, 123 A.2d 276.

BALDWIN, ASSOCIATE JUSTICE: The petitioner, hereinafter called the plaintiff, brought a motion to the Superior Court under § 8268 of the General Statutes claiming a reward offered by the governor in the matter of State v. Malm, 142 Conn. 113, 111 A.2d 685. Her motion was denied and she has appealed. The question is whether she fulfilled the terms of the offer for the reward.

On December 10, 1953, the body of Irene Fiederowicz was discovered in the rear yard of a dwelling house in the southwestern part of Hartford. She had been strangled by a scarf tied around her neck, and it was suspected that she had been criminally assaulted. The plaintiff read the account of the murder in "The Hartford Times" late in the afternoon of December 10. [Plaintiff] had been criminally assaulted on November 22, 1953, and her assailant had not been apprehended. She was impressed by the similarity of the circumstances in the Fiederowicz case and her own. The next day, December 11, she communicated with the police and furnished information concerning her assailant which placed Malm under suspicion. He was taken into custody on December 12 and was identified by the plaintiff as the one who had assaulted her. On December 13, after questioning by the police, Malm confessed to the assault on the plaintiff. On December 14, the governor caused to be published an offer of reward in the Fiederowicz case "to the person or persons who shall give information leading to the arrest and conviction" of the guilty person. On December 15, Malm confessed to the murder of Irene Fiederowicz. Prior to the offer of the reward, the plaintiff had furnished to the police all the information within her possession and

Malm had been taken into custody. The trial court concluded that she had failed to comply with the terms of the offer of reward.

Section 8269 of the General Statutes authorizes the governor, when any crime punishable by death or imprisonment in the state prison has been committed, to offer publicly, upon application of the state's attorney in the county wherein the crime was committed, "a reward not exceeding three thousand dollars, to the person who shall give information leading to the arrest and conviction of the guilty person * * *, which reward shall be paid to the informer by the state, by order of the court before which such conviction is had." In *Atwood v. Buckingham*, 78 Conn. 423, 428, 62 A. 616, 618, we said that a statute authorizing the offer of a reward "contain[s] the conditions of a contract." See also In the Matter of Kelly, 39 Conn. 159, 162. Section 8269, by its express terms, empowers the governor to make an offer of a reward. So long as this offer continues in force it can be accepted only by compliance with its terms. This concept of an offer of a reward as an offer to enter into a contractual relationship which can be accepted by the performance of an act or series of acts is the one which has been generally accepted by the courts. * * *

There is a divergence of view on whether the performance must be with knowledge of the offer in mind, or in other words whether the person claiming the reward must act in response to the offer. 1 Corbin, Contracts, pp. 181, 218; 1 Williston, Contracts (Rev.Ed.) p. 85 § 33, p. 88 § 33a. Where the offer has been made by an agency of the government, some courts have subscribed to the proposition that knowledge of the offer and action based upon it are essential to recovery. Glover v. District of Columbia, D.C.Mun.App., 77 A.2d 788, 790; 1 Corbin, op. cit., p. 181 & n. 15; Restatement, 1 Contracts § 53. Others have taken the position that such an offer is in effect a grant and that the ordinary rules of contract do not apply. Smith v. State, 38 Nev. 477, 480, 151 P. 512, L.R.A.1916A, 1276; 1 Corbin, op. cit., p. 182 & n. 16. The application of any general rule as decisive of a particular case is not altogether satisfactory. Of necessity, much depends upon the peculiar terms of the offer and the facts of each individual case. For example, in MacFarlane v. Bloch, 59 Or. 1, 3, 115 P. 1056, the published offer was "Lost— Pocketbook. Return to county judge's office; $100.00 reward." The court held that even though the pocketbook was found before the offer of reward was published, the return of the pocketbook entitled the plaintiff to the reward. Similarly, in cases where the public authorities have offered a reward for information leading to the apprehension and conviction of a criminal, some courts have held that even though the performance was begun before knowledge of the reward and completed afterwards, the person rendering the performance was entitled to recover.* * *

The facts of the instant case do not bring it within the comprehension of the rule generally accepted by the courts. The terms of the statute and the offer of the reward made pursuant to it are prospective. The reward is for the person "who shall give information leading to the arrest and conviction" of the guilty person. The manifest purpose of the statute was to elicit information not already available. See In the Matter of Kelly, 39 Conn. 159, 162. It contemplated performance in reliance upon the offer. It was not its purpose to provide recompense to one who had wholly performed before the offer was made. In this important respect our statute differs from the one under consideration in the case of Smith v. State, 38 Nev. 477, 480, 151 P. 512, L.R.A.1916A, 1276, which subscribes to the so-called "grant" theory. Our statute does not admit of an interpretation such as the court gave the Nevada statute. In the Kelly case, supra, we intimated that rewards which were offered pursuant to a statute were distinguishable from those which were not and therefore presumably rested on contract. It does not appear in the Kelly case, supra, whether the petitioner actually knew of the reward but, as a matter of fact, the services for which the reward was claimed were performed after the offer of reward had been published. The reward had been offered by the selectmen under a statute, Rev. 1866, p. 294, § 274, which contained language similar to that in § 8269.

We said in In the Matter of Kelly, 39 Conn. 159, 162: "The object of this statute [Rev. 1866, p. 294, § 274] manifestly is to encourage private citizens to aid and assist the public authorities in detecting and punishing crime. Not every one who merely gives information is entitled to a reward; that would be enlarging the meaning of the statute; it ought to receive an equitable, not a strict or technical, construction." While § 8269 should receive an equitable construction, courts cannot read into the terms of a statute something which manifestly is not there in order to reach what the court thinks would be a just result. "[A]n offer of reward * * * is not the recognition of an equitable duty of the government to the informer, but a mere act of public policy, the giving or withholding of which, and whose terms, are wholly within the discretion of the government. Whoever claims under such an offer must bring himself within its terms. Failing to do that, his compensation is the consolation which comes to every citizen from the discharge of a public duty, which is the common obligation of all." United States v. Connor, 138 U.S. 61, 66, 11 S.Ct. 229, 231, 34 L.Ed. 860. In the field of legislation, the legislature is supreme. Courts must apply legislative enactments according to their plain terms.

There is no error. In this opinion the other Judges concurred.

"INDUSTRIAL AMERICA", INC. v. FULTON INDUSTRIES, INC.

Supreme Court of Delaware, 1971.
285 A.2d 412.

[Plaintiff, acting through its president, Deutsch, was a broker specializing in mergers. B–H, Inc. wished to consummate a merger and so informed plaintiff and other brokers. Plaintiff tried to negotiate several mergers for B–H but these all fell through. Later, B–H changed its mind about using the services of a broker but never informed plaintiff of that decision. Later, plaintiff noticed Fulton's advertisement in the Wall Street Journal to the effect that Fulton wanted to acquire a machinery product line by purchase or merger and stating: "brokers fully protected." Deutsch brought the parties together. Eventually, B–H merged into Fulton even though plaintiff was frozen out of the final negotiations. The case involved the liability of Fulton on the quoted guaranty. The jury found as a fact that plaintiff was the procuring cause of the merger.]

HERRMANN, JUSTICE.

* * *

The basic question for decision in this appeal, in our view, is whether the plaintiff had the burden of proving a subjective intent on the part of Deutsch to accept the offer of guaranty which had been made in the advertisement by Fulton under the jury's findings.

We are of the opinion that Deutsch's subjective intent was not a relevant issue; that, rather, the relevant issues were (1) whether Fulton's offer of guaranty invited acceptance by performance; (2) whether Deutsch knew of the offer; and (3) whether Deutsch's course of action constituted a performance amounting to an acceptance.

It is basic that overt manifestation of assent—not subjective intent—controls the formation of a contract; that the "only intent of the parties to a contract which is essential is an intent to say the words or do the acts which constitute their manifestation of assent"; that "the intention to accept is unimportant except as manifested." Restatement of Contracts, § 20; 1 Williston on Contracts (3d Ed.) § 21, p. 39, § 66, p. 213; compare Western Natural Gas v. Cities Service Gas Co., Del.Supr., 223 A.2d 379, 383 (1966); Canister Co. v. National Can Corp. (D.Del.), 63 F.Supp. 361, 365 (1945).

Where an offeror requests an act in return for his promise and the act is performed, the act performed becomes the requisite overt manifestation of assent if the act is done intentionally; i.e., if there is a "conscious will" to do it. Restatement of Contracts, § 20; 1 Williston on Contracts (3d Ed.) § 68. But "it is not material what induces the will," Restatement of the Law of Contracts, § 20, Comment (a). Otherwise stated, motive in the manifestation of assent is immaterial. There may be primary and secondary reasons or motives for a performance constituting manifestation of assent to an offer inviting acceptance by performance; and the "chief reason" or the prevailing motive need not necessarily be the offer itself. A unilateral contract may be enforceable when the promisor has received the desired service even though the service was primarily motivated by a reason other than the offer. The "motivating causes of human action are always complex and are frequently not clearly thought out or expressed by the actor himself. This being true, it is desirable that not much weight should be given to the motives of an offeree and that no dogmatic requirement should be embodied in a stated rule of law." 1 Corbin on Contracts, § 58, p. 244, § 59, p. 246. It follows that a unilateral contract may arise even though at the time of performance the offeree did not "rely" subjectively upon, i.e., was not primarily motivated by, the offer. See Simmons v. United States (4 Cir.) 308 F.2d 160 (1962); Eagle v. Smith (Del.) 4 Houst. 293 (1871); Carbill [sic] v. Carbolic Smoke Ball Co. [1893] Q.B. 256; Restatement of Contracts, § 55, Comment b (1932): " * * * contracts may exist where if the offer is in any sense a cause of the acceptor's action it is so slight a factor that a statement that the acceptance is caused by the offer is misleading."

The clear trend and development of the law in this connection is demonstrated by a proposed change in the status of Section 55 of the Restatement of Contracts (1932).[2] The development of this facet of the law of contracts became apparent in Section 55 [now § 53, ed.] of the 1964 Tentative Draft of Restatement of Contracts, Second.[3] A comparison of the 1932 and the 1964 versions of Section 55 indicates that under the currently developing rule of law, an offer that invites an acceptance by performance will be deemed accepted by such performance unless there is a manifestation of intention to the contrary. See 1 Williston on Contracts (3d Ed.) § 67. Thus, in the establishment of a contractual obligation, the favored rule shifts the emphasis away from a manifestation of intent to accept to a manifestation of intent not to accept; thereby establishing, it would appear, a rebuttable presumption of acceptance arising from performance when the offer invites acceptance by performance. See Braucher, Offer and Acceptance in Second Restatement, 74 Yale L.J. 302, 308 (1964). The law thus rightfully imputes to a person an intention corresponding to the reasonable meaning of his words and deeds.

The defendants contend that, because an offer of guaranty is here involved, the issue is whether the plaintiff gave to Fulton the necessary notice of acceptance of the offer, citing 1 Williston on Contracts (3d Ed.) § 69AA, p. 223. The position is untenable in the light of the following portion of the *Williston* statement upon which the defendants rely:

> "Ordinarily there is no occasion to notify the offeror of the acceptance of such an offer, if the doing of the act is sufficient acceptance, and the promisor knows that he is bound when he sees that action has been taken on the faith of his offer. * * *."

2. Section 55 provided:

"ACCEPTANCE OF OFFER FOR UNILATERAL CONTRACT; NECESSITY OF INTENT TO ACCEPT

"If an act or forbearance is requested by the offeror as the consideration for a unilateral contract, the act or forbearance must be given with the intent of accepting the offer."

3. The Draft contains the following:

"ACCEPTANCE BY PERFORMANCE; MANIFESTATION OF INTENTION NOT TO ACCEPT

"(1) An offer may be accepted by the rendering of a performance only if the offer invites such an acceptance. (2) Except as stated in § 72, [now § 69, ed.] the rendering of a performance does not constitute an acceptance if within a reasonable time the offeree exercises reasonable diligence to notify the offeror of nonacceptance. (3) Where an offer of a promise invites acceptance by performance and does not invite a promissory acceptance, the rendering of the invited performance does not constitute an acceptance if before the offeror performs his promise the offeree manifests an intention not to accept."

See also Restatement of Contracts, § 56 (1932); 1 Corbin on Contracts, § 68, fn. 91. The facts of this case meet the test. In this connection, the Trial Judge ruled that Fulton's knowledge of the plaintiff's submission of B–H's name to it was notice to Fulton of an act constituting acceptance of its offer. We concur in that ruling.

Applying the law we find applicable to the facts of this case: we conclude that the Trial Court erred in submitting the issue of subjective reliance to the jury under Interrogatory No. 4. We hold that there was no relevant issue of fact as to the plaintiff's subjective reliance upon Fulton's offer. As a matter of law, it appears unquestionable that Fulton's offer invited acceptance by performance; it is uncontroverted that Deutsch knew of the offer at the time of performance; by the jury's finding of procuring cause, it has been established that the plaintiff did in fact and in law perform. It follows as a matter of law, in the absence of any manifestation of intention to the contrary, that the plaintiff's performance constituted an acceptance of the offer of Fulton which was found by the jury to be an offer of guaranty outstanding and viable at the time of the performance.

The necessary result of the foregoing chain is that the plaintiff is entitled to judgments against Fulton ... as a matter of law upon the basis of the judgment against B–H, unless there is validity in any of the grounds of the defendants' appeals herein.

* * *

Accordingly, upon the bases of the jury's answers to the special interrogatories and of the conclusions we have reached herein, we conclude that as a matter of law the plaintiff is entitled to judgments against Fulton ... as well as against B–H upon the verdict of $125,000. The cause is remanded for further proceedings consistent herewith.

CARLILL v. CARBOLIC SMOKE BALL CO.

Court of Appeal, 1893.
1 Q.B. 256.

Appeal from a decision of HAWKINS, J., [1892] 2 Q.B. 484.

The defendants, who were the proprietors and vendors of a medical preparation called "The Carbolic Smoke Ball," inserted in the *Pall Mall Gazette* of November 13, 1891, and in other newspapers, the following advertisement:

"£100 reward will be paid by the Carbolic Smoke Ball Company to any person who contracts the increasing epidemic influenza, colds or any disease caused by taking cold, after having used the ball three times daily for two weeks according to the printed directions supplied with each ball. £1000 is deposited with the Alliance Bank, Regent Street shewing our sincerity in the matter.

"During the last epidemic of influenza many thousand carbolic smoke balls were sold as preventives against the disease, and in no ascertained case was the disease contracted by those using the carbolic smoke ball.

"One carbolic smoke ball will last a family several months, making it the cheapest remedy in the world at the price, 10s., post free. The ball can be refilled at a cost of 5s. Address, Carbolic Smoke Ball Company, 27, Princes Street, Hanover Square, London."

The plaintiff, a lady, on the faith of this advertisement, bought one of the balls at a chemist's and used it as directed, three times a day, from November 20, 1891, to January 17, 1892, when she was attacked by influenza. Hawkins, J., held that she was entitled to recover the £100. The defendants appealed.

LINDLEY, L.J. * * *

* * * We are dealing with an express promise to pay £100 in certain events. Read the advertisement how you will, and twist it about as you will, here is a distinct promise expressed in language which is perfectly unmistakable: "£100 reward will be paid by the Carbolic Smoke Ball Company to any person who contracts the influenza after having used the ball three times daily for two weeks according to the printed directions supplied with each ball."

We must first consider whether this was intended to be a promise at all, or whether it was a mere puff which meant nothing. Was it a mere puff? My answer to that question is "No," and I base my answer upon this passage: "£1000 is deposited with the Alliance Bank, shewing our sincerity in the matter." Now, for what was that money deposited or that statement made except to negative the suggestion that this was a mere puff and meant nothing at all? The deposit is called in aid by the advertiser as proof of his sincerity in the matter, that is, the sincerity of his promise to pay this £100 in the event which he has specified. I say this for the purpose of giving point to the observation that we are not inferring a promise; there is the promise, as plain as words can make it.

Then it is contended that it is not binding. In the first place, it is said that it is not made with anybody in particular. Now that point is common to the words of this advertisement and to the words of all other advertisements offering rewards. They are offers to anybody who performs the conditions named in the advertisement, and anybody who does perform the conditions accepts the offer. In point of law this advertisement is an offer to pay £100 to anybody who will perform these conditions, and the performance of the conditions, is the acceptance of the offer. That rests upon a string of authorities, the earliest of which is *Williams v. Carwardine*, 4 Barn. & Adol. 621, which has been followed by many other decisions upon advertisements offering rewards.

* * *

It appears to me, therefore, that the defendants must perform their promise, and, if they have been so unwary as to expose themselves to a great many actions, so much the worse for them.

Bowen, L.J. I am of the same opinion. * * *

* * *

Then it was said that there was no notification of the acceptance of the contract. One cannot doubt that, as an ordinary rule of law, an acceptance of an offer made ought to be notified to the person who makes the offer, in order that the two minds may come together. Unless this is done the two minds may be apart, and there is not that consensus which is necessary according to the English law—I say nothing about the laws of other countries—to make a contract. But there is this clear gloss to be made upon that doctrine, that is notification of acceptance is required for the benefit of the person who makes the offer, the person who makes the offer may dispense with notice to himself if he thinks it desirable to do so, and I suppose there can be no doubt that where a person in an offer made by him to another person, expressly or impliedly intimates a particular mode of acceptance as sufficient to make the bargain binding, it is only necessary for the other person to whom such offer is made to follow the indicated method of acceptance; and if the person making the offer, expressly or impliedly intimates in his offer that it will be sufficient to act on the proposal without communicating acceptance of it to himself, performance of the condition is a sufficient acceptance without notification.

* * *

Now, if that is the law, how are we to find out whether the person who makes the offer does intimate that notification of acceptance will not be necessary in order to constitute a binding bargain? In many cases you look to the offer itself. In many cases you extract from the character of the transaction that notification is not required, and in the advertisement cases it seems to me to follow as an inference to be drawn from the transaction itself that a person is not to notify his acceptance of the offer before he performs the condition, but that if he performs the condition notification is dispensed with. It seems to me that from the point of view of common sense no other idea could be entertained. If I advertise to the world that my dog is lost, and that anybody who brings the dog to a particular place will be paid some money, are all the police or other persons whose business it is to find lost dogs to be expected to sit down and write a note saying that they have accepted my proposal? Why, of course, they at once look after the dog, and as soon as they find the dog they have performed the condition. The essence of the transaction is that the dog should be found, and it is not necessary under such circumstances, as it seems to me, that in order to make the contract binding there should be any notification of acceptance. It follows from the nature of the thing that the performance of the condition is sufficient acceptance without the notification of it, and a person who makes an offer in an advertisement of that kind makes an offer which must be read by the light of that common sense reflection. He does, therefore, in his offer impliedly indicate that he does not require notification of the acceptance of the offer.

* * *

Appeal dismissed.

———

A. W. Brian Simpson, *Quackery and Contract Law: The Case of the Carbolic Smoke Ball,* **14 J. Leg. Stud. 345 (1985):** * * * Happily, a considerable volume of material survives that makes it possible to recreate at least something of the historical background and significance of this landmark in the history of contract law and its relationship to the seedy world of the late nineteenth-century vendors of patent medical appliances. * * *

The Patenting of the Smoke Ball

On October 30, 1889, one Frederick Augustus Roe, "of 202 Regent St. in the County of Middlesex, Gentleman," submitted an application to patent what he described as "An Improved Device for Facilitating the Distribution, Inhalation and Application of Medicated and Other Powder." * * * As described in the specification, the improved device "comprises a compressible hollow ball or receptacle of India Rubber or other suitable elastic material, having an orifice or nozzle provided with a porous or perforated disc or diaphragm consisting of muslin, silk, wire or gauze, perforated sheet metal or the like, through which, when the ball or receptacle is compressed, the powder will be forced *in a cloud of infinitesimally small particles resembling smoke.*" * * * By a fortunate chance the directions for use of the ball as marketed survive. . . :

> Hold the ball by the loose end below the silk floss, with the thumb and forefinger in front of the mouth. Snap or flip rapidly on the side of the ball, on the place marked "S" and a fine powder resembling smoke will arise. Inhale this smoke or powder as it arises, as shown in the above illustration. This will cause sneezing, and for a few moments you will feel as if you were taking cold. This feeling will soon pass away and the cure has commenced. If you do not feel the effects at the first inhalation by it making you sneeze, take a second in the same manner. * * *

Patent records also show that Roe was from New York; . . . though in 1885 he was living [in] London. . . . The American origin of the smoke ball is confirmed by an advertising leaflet . . . which describes it as the "New American Remedy" and the "Standard Remedy of America."

The Marketing of the Ball

Whether the ball was in fact marketed in America, perhaps as "the Pulverator," is unknown, but late in 1889 or early in 1890 Roe began to market his Carbolic Smoke Ball in England, moving his premises to 27 Princes Street, Hanover Square, at about this time. The influenza epidemic which had begun ... in December of 1889, must have come as a godsend to his new enterprise, but the utility of the ball was by no means restricted to this single ailment. The earliest of his advertisements that I have located appeared in the *Illustrated London News* on January 11, 1890. He claimed that the ball, to be had from the Carbolic Smoke Ball Company at their new premises for a price of ten shillings, "Will positively cure Influenza, Catarrh, Asthma, Bronchitis, Hay Fever, Neuralgia, Throat Deafness, Hoarseness, Loss of Voice, Whooping Cough, Croup, Coughs, Colds, and all other ailments caused by Taking Cold." Behind this optimism lay a theory, more fully articulated in some of his later advertisements. It was that all these ailments arose from a single cause, taking cold, and were therefore all amenable to the same single remedy, the Carbolic Smoke Ball. * * *

Frederick Roe was only one of many advertisers who made claims to cure or ward off influenza. It was the practice of the patent medicine vendors to adapt their claims, rather than their products, to the current needs of the market, and Roe was merely doing what was normal in the trade. The product remained the same; its function changed. * * *

During 1890 the appliance does not seem to have been heavily advertised.... During 1891, however, the ball was heavily and imaginatively advertised.... * * * An appeal was also made to the snobbery of the readers by providing a list of distinguished people who, it was claimed, used the ball; the use of such testimonials, which could be fraudulent, was standard practice in the quack medicine world. * * *

The Recurrence of Influenza, 1891–92

Influenza again became established in London during 1891, first in June and July and again during the winter of 1891–92. * * * [T]hough no such company had in fact been formally incorporated, Roe ... was trading as the Carbolic Smoke Ball Company....

The advertisement that gave rise to the litigation first appeared ... in the *Pall Mall Gazette* on November 13, 1891, and again on November 24 and December 8; apparently it also appeared in substantially the same form in other newspapers.... * * *

To the lasting benefit of the law of contract, Mrs. Carlill saw this ·advertisement on the evening of November 13, 1891.

The Carlill Family

Her full name was Louisa Elizabeth Carlill. She used the name Elizabeth. [S]he was born ... on October 22, 1845.... * * * She was the third of ten children. On December 17, 1873 ... she married James Briggs Carlill. [A]ccording to family tradition he was an actuary. [A]lthough his family had connections with insurance, I have not been able to confirm his occupation. Whatever he eventually became, he was originally a solicitor. * * * There were three children of the marriage, a son and two daughters.... * * * As for Mrs. Carlill herself, she was described by counsel in the legal proceedings as "a literary lady." This was a slightly mocking expression at the time, but it is clear that she had, as a writer, an income of her own. * * *

Mrs. Carlill saw the advertisement, and on November 20 she purchased a smoke ball from Messrs. Wilcox and Company, who operated a druggist's shop at 239 Oxford Street. She paid for the ball out of her literary earnings. The vendors, as we have seen, were actively promoting the ball at the time. According to her account of the matter, which was given in evidence at the trial and not disputed, she assiduously used the ball three times daily for two weeks, in accordance with the already quoted printed instructions supplied with it: "In the morning before breakfast, at about 2 o'clock, and again when I went to bed." Whether she continued to use the ball thereafter does not appear. On January 17, that is, at the height of the epidemic, she contracted influenza. She remained ill under the care of a Dr. Robertson for some two weeks.

On January 20 her husband, James Briggs Carlill, wrote to the Carbolic Smoke Ball Company informing them of what had occurred; possibly her letter was only one of many received at this time:

Dear Sir,

Seeing your offer of a reward, dated July 20, in the "Pall Mall Gazette" of November 13, my wife purchased one of your smoke balls, and has used it three times a day since the beginning of December. She was, however, attacked by influenza. Dr. Robertson, of West Dulwich, attended, and will no doubt be able to certify in the matter. I think it right to give you notice of this, and shall be prepared to answer any inquiry or furnish any evidence you require. I am, yours obediently,

J. B. Carlill.

This was ignored. He wrote again, threatening to place the matter in the hands of his solicitors, and received in reply a post card saying the matter would receive attention. He wrote a third time, and received in reply a printed circular, undated, endorsed "In answer to your letter of January 20." This remarkable document read:

Re reward of £100—The Carbolic Smoke Ball Company, seeing that claims for the above reward have been made by persons who have either not purchased the smoke ball at all, or else have failed to use it as directed, consider it necessary that they should state the conditions in which alone such reward would be paid. They have such confidence in the efficacy of the carbolic smoke ball, if used according to the printed directions supplied to each person, that they made the aforesaid offer in entire good faith, believing it impossible for the influenza to be taken during the daily inhalation of the smoke ball as prescribed. In order to protect themselves against all fraudulent claims, the Carbolic Smoke Ball Company require that the smoke ball be administered, free of charge, at their office, to those who have already purchased it. Intending claimants must attend three times daily for three weeks, and inhale the smoke ball under the directions of the Smoke Ball Company. These visits will be specially recorded by the secretary in a book. 27 Princes St., Hanover Square, London.

Why this gem was not quoted in the law reports must forever remain a mystery, for it goes a long way toward explaining the hostile judicial attitude to the company. It certainly irritated James Briggs Carlill, who replied, insisting his claim was perfectly honest. To this Roe replied that "the company considered his letter impertinent and gave him the names of his solicitors." And so it was that on February 15 an action was commenced to claim the £100 promised. * * *

[The case] came on for trial ... on June 16, 1892.... * * * Neither side appears to have been parsimonious in securing the very best legal representation. Indeed the plaintiff's expenditure on counsel supports the suggestion that principle, not money, was at issue. * * * The defense was led by no less than Herbert Henry Asquith, Q.C., future prime minister.... * * *

Roe Goes Public

The litigation with Mrs. Carlill took from February 15 to December 7, 1892, to wend its way through the courts. * * * The scale of his advertising suggests that many balls had indeed been sold during the epidemic of 1891–92, and the reward had been offered over a period of just under three months, through the peak of the epidemic. * * *

This was not the only development in 1892. On December 16, shortly after the decision had gone against him in the Court of Appeal, Frederick Roe, together with one Henry Ewin Teasdale Turner, agreed to form a limited company to market the ball.... * * * The Carbolic Smoke Ball Company, Ltd. was duly incorporated on December 19.... * * *

Now it might be supposed that December 1892, just after the loss of the action, was hardly the moment for forming the new company. [H]is personal liability for the payment of the £100 rewards would in no way be affected by the later acquisition of limited liability. * * * But in fact no flood of claims seems to have occurred. On February 25 we find the managing director of the new company boldly publishing in the *Illustrated London News* a new advertisement, cunningly framed in order to turn the whole affair to his advantage. In it he pointed out that a reward of £100 pounds had recently been promised to anyone who contracted influenza, or eleven other diseases "caused by taking cold," after using the ball according to the instructions. The text continues: "Many thousand Carbolic Smoke Balls were sold on these advertisements, but only three persons claimed the reward of £100, thus proving conclusively that this invaluable remedy will prevent and cure the above mentioned diseases. THE CARBOLIC SMOKE BALL COMPANY LTD. now offer £200 REWARD to the person who purchases a Carbolic Smoke Ball and afterwards contracts any of the following diseases...." There followed a list of nineteen ailments: influenza, coughs, cold in the head, cold in the chest, catarrh, asthma, bronchitis, sore throat, hoarseness, throat deafness, loss of voice, laryngitis, snoring, sore eyes, diphtheria, croup, whooping cough, neuralgia, headache.... It will be noted that this offer appears to envisage only a single prize, and the small print went on to restrict the scope of the offer still further in a way which suggests legal advice: "This offer is made to those who have purchased a Carbolic Smoke Ball since Jan. 1, 1893, and is subject to conditions to be obtained on application, a duplicate of which must be signed and deposited with the Company in London by the applicant before commencing the treatment specified in the conditions. This offer will remain open only till March 31, 1893."

What these conditions were, or whether anyone succeeded in claiming the reward, does not appear. But no similar offer appears to have been made in later advertisements, so perhaps the experiment proved costly. The ball continued to be advertised enthusiastically in the early part of 1893. . . . In June 1893, however, there took place a curious reorganization of the business, which involved the formation of a second limited liability company and a transfer of control.

The new company, called the Carbolic Smoke Ball Company (1893), Ltd., was incorporated on June 10, 1893. . . . * * *

* * * The smoke ball continued to be advertised in the later part of 1893, though under the new management the scale and flamboyance of the advertisements declined. * * * The business seems to have fallen on hard times, for on June 19, 1895, a resolution was passed to wind the company up since it could not, because of its liabilities, remain in business. * * * Why the company failed is obscure. A decline in the prevalence of influenza does not explain the matter, and in any event the other ailments for which the ball was sold remained common. It may be that the new management had failed to grasp the fact that vigorous advertising was essential to success in the quack medicine field. * * *

Records . . . show that Roe . . . died of tuberculosis and valvular heart disease on June 3, 1899 . . . ; he was fifty-seven, and his occupation of "Patent Medicine Proprietor" failed to protect him. He left a widow, but no will. * * *

Epilogue.

[A]s for Louisa Elizabeth Carlill . . . she long survived her adventure with the law. After her husband died on October 6, 1930, she lived in a flat in Blackheath, but by 1939 she was established in a hotel on the south coast . . . where she was renowned for her punctuality and her settled practice of drinking one glass of claret with her lunch. She then went to live with her daughter. . . . There she died on March 10, 1942, at the age of ninety-six years, principally, as her death certificate records, of old age.

The other cause noted by her medical man, Dr. Joseph M. Yarman, was influenza.

Problems

41. Grandfather says to granddaughter, if you make Phi Beta Kappa, I will pay you $20,000. Granddaughter promises to attain membership. Is there a contract?

42. On June 10, the defendants executed an instrument for the purpose of having the plaintiff reroof their residence. The document contained all of the material terms and in addition, the following provision: "This agreement shall become binding only upon written acceptance hereof or upon performance of the work." Does this offer look to a unilateral or a bilateral contract or some variation thereof?

43. A says to B, "If you promise to rake my lawn I promise to pay you $25." B starts to rake in A's presence. Is there a contract?

44. On January 2, A promises B to pay $7,500 if B paints the outside of A's summer house at Point Lookout within two weeks from January 2. A further states that this offer is open for three days. B makes no promise but begins the job on January 4 and completes it on January 9. Is there a contract?

45. S has been B's regular supplier of various component parts for machinery manufactured by B. Lately S has been unwilling to sell to B on credit terms. B sends a telex message to S, reading, "Will you ship 15, catalog No. 337K, at $5,000 each? Urgent. Need to have your reply today. We have deposited $75,000 to your account in Geneva." Does the order look to a unilateral or bilateral contract or some variation thereof?

46. Jim Casey was the owner of a sporting goods store in Oshkosh and did business under the trade name "Sportserama." Everyone in town knew that Casey was the owner of Sportserama. Bill Daly sent in an order addressed to Jim Casey for a particular rod and reel. Casey owed money to Daly and Daly assumed that the price of the rod and reel would be offset from Casey's debt. On the day that the order was received, Casey had sold out to Schwartz, a recent transplant from New York. The order was filled without notifying Daly of the change in ownership. Must Daly pay Schwartz?

47. Kreimeyer worked for Hercules, Inc. Hercules had published a personnel manual, promising that if any employee had to be laid off because of a need to cut the work force, such lay-offs would strictly be on a seniority basis. When Hercules decided it needed to cut the work force, it asked its supervisory personnel to rank the employees they supervised. Kreimeyer was ranked 13th out of 14 in his job classification and was laid off despite his greater seniority than some of the employees in his job classification who were retained. At trial, Kreimeyer admitted that he had never seen the personnel manual before his dismissal and was unaware of any company policy on the subject of lay offs. Assuming the jurisdiction has the same attitude toward personnel manuals as Wyoming (see *Sanchez, supra,* p. 6), does Kreimeyer have a cause of action?

48. A found a lost article and, knowing the owner, decided to return it. A went to the owner's house for that purpose but before arriving A learned that a reward had been offered for the return of the article and returned the article without mentioning the reward. Later A claimed it. Is A entitled to the reward?

49. An ingot of platinum was stolen from a warehouse. An insurance company paid the claim to the owners and published an offer of reward for information leading to the recovery of the platinum. Mrs. A learned that her son had been involved in the theft when he gave her a sampling with a

request that she have it analyzed to verify its purity. A few days later, Mrs. A was arrested for shoplifting and retained Mr. X, an attorney, to represent her. She revealed to him that she knew where some platinum was located and asked him to help her market it. He refused. Knowing of the offered reward, Mr. X asked a police inspector what he knew about recently stolen platinum. The inspector proceeded to interrogate Mr. X who then revealed his conversation with Mrs. A. Soon thereafter, Mrs. A was called to police headquarters for questioning. She requested the presence of her lawyer. When Mr. X arrived, he advised her to talk freely as she had committed no crime with respect to the platinum. She gave the police a full statement inculpating her son. The son was arrested and the platinum was recovered. Mr. X and Mrs. A make separate claims against the insurance company for the offered reward. Is either or both of them entitled to the reward?

50.   D, Harry Eaton's brother, in Nova Scotia, wrote P, in Illinois: "If Harry needs money, let him have it, or assist him in getting it, and I will see that it is paid." The following month P helped Harry borrow money by signing Harry's note as guarantor. After signing, P so notified D by letter which D never received. Harry did not pay the debt at maturity. P paid and sued D. What result?

51.   On March 15, P signed an agreement to purchase specific residential property from D Corp. The agreement was not signed by anyone for D Corp. The agreement provided as follows: "This Agreement has been obtained by Seller's salesman or agent who has no authority to bind Seller to this Agreement. This Agreement becomes a contract when accepted by Buyer and signed by Seller at its executive office within thirty (30) calendar days from the date below."

(a) D Corp. never signed the agreement. Is there a contract?

(b) Would the result be different if D Corp. signed within 30 days but did not notify P and later attempted to withdraw?

(c) Suppose the language had been, "This agreement shall not be binding upon Seller unless signed by Seller within 30 days?"

52.   G called E about reroofing G's residence. E's salesman and G signed a document which set out the details of the work and the price. The document contained a provision that, "this agreement shall become binding only upon written acceptance hereof by the home office or upon commencing performance of the work." Does this offer look to unilateral or bilateral contract or some variation thereof?

(b) Acceptance by Silence and Conduct

(Calamari & Perillo 5th §§ 1.8, 2.12, 2.18 and 2.19)

GEM BROADCASTING, INC. v. MINKER

District Court of Appeal of Florida, Fourth District, 2000.
763 So.2d 1149.

GROSS, J.

Gem Broadcasting, Inc. ("Gem") appeals a final judgment awarding appellee Gary Minker $10,550 in damages, along with pre-judgment interest and costs. Finding competent, substantial evidence to support the damage award, we affirm.

After a bench trial, the judge found that a contract implied in fact existed between Minker and Gem for Minker to provide the corporation with consulting services.

In a non-jury trial, it is the obligation of the trial judge to reconcile conflicts, to determine the credibility of witnesses, and to evaluate the reasonableness and weight of the evidence presented. An appellate court must accept "a determination of facts made by the trial judge where the record discloses testimony from which the trial judge could have determined the facts...." *Casey v. Cohan*, 740 So.2d 59, 60 (Fla. 4th DCA 1999) (quoting *Pergament v. Pergament*, 117 So.2d 26, 29 (Fla. 2d DCA 1959)) (citations omitted).

The judge accepted Minker's trial testimony that he worked a total of thirty days. An abundance of evidence at trial supported the trial court's valuation of Minker's services at $385 per day. Contrary to Gem's contention on appeal, the trial court was not precluded from considering Minker's unaccepted proposal for a contract when assessing the reasonable value of Minker's services. *See Fred McGilvray, Inc. v. Delphian Group, Inc.*, 424 So.2d 891, 892 (Fla. 3d DCA 1982).

Gem also argues that Minker may not recover on a "quantum meruit" claim because he failed to establish that he conferred a benefit on the company. Gem's argument confuses a contract implied in fact with a contract implied in law. In *Commerce Partnership 8098 Limited Partnership v. Equity Contracting Co.*, 695 So.2d 383 (Fla. 4th DCA 1997) (en banc), we recognized that the term "quantum meruit" has been applied to contracts implied in fact as well as to those implied in law. We wrote in *Commerce Partnership* that:

> A contract implied in fact is one form of an enforceable contract; it is based on a tacit promise, one that is inferred in whole or in part from the parties' conduct, not solely from their words. Where an agreement is arrived at by words, oral or written, the contract is said to be "express." A contract implied in fact is not put into promissory words with sufficient clarity, so a fact finder must examine and interpret the parties' conduct to give definition to their unspoken agreement. It is to this process of defining an enforceable agreement that Florida courts have referred when they have indicat-

ed that contracts implied in fact "rest upon the assent of the parties."

* * *

Common examples of contracts implied in fact are where a person performs services at another's request, or "where services are rendered by one person for another without his expressed request, but with his knowledge, and under circumstances" fairly raising the presumption that the parties understood and intended that compensation was to be paid. In these circumstances, the law implies the promise to pay a reasonable amount for the services.

Id. at 385–86 (citations omitted).

In contrast to a contract implied in fact, "[a] contract implied in law, or quasi contract, is not based upon the finding, by a process of implication from the facts, of an agreement between the parties." *Id.* at 386.

A contract implied in law is a legal fiction, an obligation created by the law without regard to the parties' expression of assent by their words or conduct. The fiction was adopted to provide a remedy where one party was unjustly enriched, where that party received a benefit under circumstances that made it unjust to retain it without giving compensation.

Id. (citations omitted).

A necessary element of a cause of action for a contract implied in law is that the plaintiff has conferred a benefit on the defendant. *See id.* However, the enforceability of a contract implied in fact is based on an implied promise, "not on whether the defendant has received something of value." *See id.* at 387. In *Commerce Partnership*, we gave an example that is similar to the fact situation in this case:

[A] common form of contract implied in fact is where one party has performed services at the request of another without discussion of compensation. These circumstances justify the inference of a promise to pay a reasonable amount for the service. The enforceability of this obligation turns on the implied promise, not on whether the defendant has received something of value. A contract implied in fact can be enforced even where a defendant has received nothing of value.

Id. For these reasons, it was unnecessary for Minker to prove that he conferred a benefit on Gem in order to recover a judgment. * * *

AFFIRMED. Stevenson, J., and Bailey, Jennifer D., Associate Judge, concur.

CAN BOTH THE OFFER AND ACCEPTANCE BE SILENT?

Nathaniel Hawthorne's Novel, *The Marble Faun*, is set in Rome. In this story, Donatello, a youth, is very much in love with Miriam, an older (20 something?) beauty. Miriam is being stalked by a man she knows and obviously loathes. Neither Donatello nor the reader knows the identity of this man.

Miriam and Donatello, together with other friends, take a late night stroll to the Capitoline Hill. The friends leave but Miriam and Donatello linger behind. The stalker appears. Donatello grabs him, looks at Miriam and then shoves the stalker off the cliff, sending him to his death. Miriam, in horror, whispers "What have you done." Donatello replies, "I did what your eyes bade me do, when I asked them with mine, as I held the wretch over the precipice."

"These last words struck Miriam like a bullet. Could it be so? Had her eyes provoked or assented to this deed?"

Several chapters later Miriam visits Hilda, one of the friends who had been with her just before the killing. Hilda reveals that she had left the group to return to the Capitoline Hill to talk to Miriam and had witnessed the killing.

Hilda says, "It was all like a flash of lightening. A look passed from your eyes to Donatello's—a look—* * * It revealed your heart, Miriam, * * * a look of hatred, triumph, vengeance, and, as it were, joy at some unhoped for relief."

" 'Ah, Donatello was right, then,' murmured Miriam, who shook throughout all her frame. 'My eyes bade him do it.' "

Assuming that the criminal law in effect would find that a person who entered into an agreement to have another killed is equally guilty as the killer, is Miriam guilty?

WILHOITE v. BECK

Appellate Court of Indiana, Division No. 1, 1967.
141 Ind.App. 543, 230 N.E.2d 616.

FAULCONER, JUDGE. Appellant's decedent, Flossie B. Lawrence, arrived at the home of appellee Ruth Beck in 1939 or 1940, apparently uninvited, unannounced and unexpected, and stayed until her death on July 12, 1963. After decedent's death appellee filed a claim against the estate of decedent for room, board and care and companionship allegedly furnished decedent from January 15, 1942 until July 12, 1963, all of the total value of $27,837, for which appellee prayed judgment. The claim was tried by the court, without a jury, and the court found for the claimant—appellee here—and entered judgment in the sum of $11,368. Appellant's motion for new trial was overruled and such action is the only error assigned on this appeal.

The specifications of appellant's motion for new trial argued on this appeal are * * * 2) the decision of the court is not sustained by sufficient evidence; 3) the decision of the court is contrary to law; and 4) * * *

* * *

Appellant groups, for the purpose of argument, specifications 2 and 3 of her motion for new trial, that the evidence is insufficient and the decision of the court is contrary to law.

"Where one accepts valuable services from another the law implies a promise to pay for them and the contract implied by law may support a claim against his estate. To warrant a finding of an implied contract of decedent to pay for services rendered by claimant, the elements of intention to pay and expectation of payment must be found to exist. The intention of decedent to pay for services rendered and claimant's expectation of compensation may be inferred from conduct, where equity and justice require compensation, as well as from direct communications between the parties * * *, or such inference of compensation may arise from the relation and situation of the parties, the nature and character of the services rendered, and any other facts and circumstances shedding light on the question at issue." C.J.S. Executors and Administrators § 784, pp. 853–854; * * *

Appellant argues that the evidence shows that appellee and decedent were second cousins and, therefore, there is a presumption that such services and accommodations were rendered gratuitously.

The evidence clearly establishes that appellee and decedent were distant cousins, second or third. To our knowledge our courts have not ruled upon such a relationship in this type of action.

We are of the opinion, after a review of the text writers and decisions of those jurisdictions having passed upon the issue, that the relationship of second or third cousins in and of itself is insufficient to raise the presumption of gratuity. * * *

However, the presumption that such services were rendered gratuitously may also arise where the parties live together as a family which alone, or in conjunction with blood relationship, may raise the presumption.

"This presumption affecting members of a household applies to all who actually live together as a family, however related, or whether related, or not, by blood or affinity, though the presumption may be strengthened or weakened by the closeness or remoteness of the relation and intimacy of the parties as a circumstance of the case." Crampton v. Logan (1902), 28 Ind.App. 405, 407, 408, 63 N.E. 51, 52; Walting v. Brown (1965), Ind.App., 211 N.E.2d 803, 805, 806, (Transfer denied).

Such presumption is rebuttable by proof of a contract, express or implied. The presumption of gratuity indulged as to persons living as members of the same family may be rebutted by an express contract to pay and a recovery may be had upon the contract, or it may be rebutted by facts and circumstances which exclude the intention on the part of such persons that the thing furnished or services rendered were gratuitous, and raise an inference that compensation was intended and in justice and fairness under the circumstances they ought to have made a contract to pay; under such circumstances the law will imply a contract and require payment. Hill v. Hill (1889), 121 Ind. 255, 260, 23 N.E. 87; Wainwright Trust Co., Admr. v. Kinder (1918), 69 Ind.App. 88, 97, 98, 120 N.E. 419.

* * *

"[T]he term 'family' means a collection of persons who form one household, under one head and one domestic government, and who have reciprocal, natural or moral duties to support and care for each other." 58 Am.Jur., Work and Labor, § 11, p. 520.

Although decedent lived in claimant's home for more than 20 years, we are of the opinion that the evidence in the record is not such that we could say, as a matter of law, that reasonable minds could reach only the conclusion that there existed a family relationship between them. There is evidence that the decedent was an independent person in the extreme, came and went when and as she pleased; and most of the time she took her meals alone, cooked for herself and entertained her own guests alone. Although she did some chores around the house they were evidently voluntary on her part as she was never asked to do anything.

Since there was no contention that there existed an express contract between decedent and appellee, the trial court was concerned with whether an implied contract was proven. We are unable to determine, from its general finding for claimant-appellee, whether the trial court, in arriving at its finding, found there were facts or reasonable inferences therefrom establishing an implied contract sufficient to rebut the presumption of gratuity having first determined either a blood relationship or family relationship or both, existed, or whether it first determined that no such relationship existed and, therefore, claimant had the benefit of the general presumption of intention to pay and expectation of payment.

We will on appeal however adopt that theory, within the pleadings and proof, which will uphold the action of the trial court as all presumptions are indulged in favor of the trial court's findings.

" '[A]n implied contract or promise is inferred from the conduct, situation or mutual relations of the parties, and is enforced by the law on the ground of justice.' " Hays v. McConnell (1873), 42 Ind. 285, 286–287; Wainwright Trust Co., Admr. v. Kinder, supra (1918), 69 Ind.App. 88, 97, 120 N.E. 419; Crampton v. Logan, supra (1902), 28 Ind.App. 405, 408, 63 N.E. 51.

* * *

Although during the time decedent lived at appellee's home there is no evidence of any conversation between them concerning the matter of payment, we are of the opinion that the facts and reasonable inferences therefrom meet the requirement that the finding of an implied contract be supported by substantial evidence of probative value. Nor can we say that reasonable minds could not so conclude.

There was evidence that decedent first occupied a basement room; that she later shared a room on the second floor with claimant's mother, and when the latter was taken to a nursing home decedent occupied said room alone until her death. Although decedent could go anywhere in the house she was not treated, nor did she expect to be treated, as one of the family. Decedent was employed most of the time she lived in the house.

One definite strain runs throughout the record of the evidence in this cause as related by several witnesses, and that is the fact that decedent was an independent woman in the extreme, that she did not want charity and in fact, when her meals were brought to her room it was necessary to tell her someone brought them to her or that they were "left-overs." There was further evidence that claimant instructed her hired girl to keep an eye on decedent, but not to allow decedent to suspect it as she would be resentful. Claimant-appellee testified that she never intended to give the services and accommodations gratuitously. There was evidence that at one time appellee decided to move but cancelled the move because decedent resented the fact that no room would be available for her. One reading this record can hardly conceive that decedent did not intend to pay for these accommodations. She was an intelligent woman, "well read", and employed in a responsible position most of the time. One is impressed by the apparent attitude taken by all parties of giving decedent "a wide berth", so to speak, due to her independence and pride in "taking care of herself."

Appellant further argues that decedent named appellee as beneficiary in her will, thus carrying out a statement of decedent to a third party that claimant "would be taken care of." This does not, however, necessarily preclude recovery by a beneficiary of a legitimate claim for services rendered decedent against decedent's estate. Witt v. Witt, Executrix (1938), 105 Ind.App. 415, 421, 12 N.E.2d 1013; Allen, Exr. v. Etter (1931), 92 Ind.App. 297, 307, 308, 175 N.E. 286. It is only an element to be considered in determining whether there was an express or implied contract to pay and be paid.

An examination of the will discloses that decedent left $500 to each of four persons, unrelated to her, and the residue of her estate to six cousins, including appellee, to share equally. There is no evidence of the value of decedent's estate or of what it consisted.

The trial court, in our opinion, could reasonably conclude from the facts and circumstances of this cause, and from the fact that decedent directed her executrix to pay "all of my [her] just debts", that she did not intend such bequest to appellee to compensate for such accommodations and services provided her by claimant. At least we could not hold otherwise as a matter of law. It is further evident from the record that none of the other beneficiaries offered or performed more than perfunctory and infrequent services for the decedent during this time although at least some of them were aware of her needs and failure to pay claimant.

No general rule can be set forth as to what facts are necessary to prove the existence of an implied contract. We are of the opinion, on reviewing the evidence in the record before us, the circumstances, and the inferences the court could have drawn therefrom, that the finding of the trial court and the judgment entered thereon is just and fair and should be affirmed.

Judgment affirmed.

MILLER v. NBD BANK, N.A.

Court of Appeals of Indiana, 1998.
701 N.E.2d 282.

[Some students wax indignant at the decision in *Wilhoite v. Beck*, wondering why plaintiff and decedent had not discussed compensation. Maybe such discussions had taken place but could not be placed in the record. This excerpt may explain].

* * *

Indiana Code § 34–1–14–6 (repealed, now codified at Indiana Code § 34–45–2–4), commonly known as the "Dead Man's Statute," provided in relevant part:

> In suits or proceedings in which an executor or administrator is a party, involving matters which occurred during a lifetime of the decedent, where a judgment or allowance may be made or rendered for or against the estate represented by such executor or administrator; any person who is a necessary party to the issue or record, whose interest is adverse to such estate, shall not be a competent witness as to such matters against such estate. . . .

One purpose of the statute is to prevent persons from testifying against the estate as to transactions, acts or conversations of the decedent when the decedent's "lips are sealed by death." *In re Sutherland's Estate*, 246 Ind. 234, 240–41, 204 N.E.2d 520, 523 (1965). "It is, in fact, a statute for the prevention of fraud." *Id*. at 241, 204 N.E.2d at 523. Rather than excluding evidence, the statute prevents a particular class of witnesses from testifying regarding claims against an estate. *Fisher v. Estate of Haley*, 695 N.E.2d 1022, 1027 (Ind.Ct.App.1998).

* * *

HOBBS v. MASSASOIT WHIP CO.

Supreme Judicial Court of Massachusetts, 1893.
158 Mass. 194, 33 N.E. 495.

* * *

HOLMES, J. This is an action for the price of eel skins sent by the plaintiff to the defendant, and kept by the defendant some months, until they were destroyed. It must be taken that the plaintiff received no notice that the defendants declined to accept the skins. The case comes before us on exceptions to an instruction to the jury that, whether there was any prior contract or not, if skins are sent to the defendant, and it sees fit, whether it has agreed to take them or not, to lie back, and to say nothing, having reason to suppose that the man who has sent them believes that it is taking them, since it says nothing about it, then, if it fails to notify, the jury would be warranted in finding for the plaintiff.

Standing alone, and unexplained, this proposition might seem to imply that one stranger may impose a duty upon another, and make him a purchaser, in spite of himself, by sending goods to him, unless he will take the trouble, and bear the expense, of notifying the sender that he will not buy. The case was argued for the defendant on that interpretation. But, in view of the evidence, we do not understand that to have been the meaning of the judge, and we do not think that the jury can have understood that to have been his meaning. The plaintiff was not a stranger to the defendant, even if there was no contract between them. He had sent eel skins in the same way four or five times before, and they had been accepted and paid for. On the defendant's testimony, it was fair to assume that if it had admitted the eel skins to be over twenty-two inches in length, and fit for its business, as the plaintiff testified and the jury found that they were, it would have accepted them; that this was understood by the plaintiff; and, indeed, that there was a standing offer to him for such skins. In such a condition of things, the plaintiff was warranted in sending the defendant skins conforming to the requirements, and even if the offer was not such that the contract was made as soon as skins corresponding to its terms were sent, sending them did impose on the defendant a duty to act about them; and silence on its part, coupled with a retention of the skins for an unreasonable time, might be found by the jury to warrant the plaintiff in assuming that they were accepted, and thus to amount to an acceptance. See *Bushel v. Wheeler*, 15 Q.B. 442; Benj. Sales, (6th Amer.Ed.) §§ 162–164; *Taylor v. Dexter Engine Co.*, 146 Mass. 613, 615, 16 N.E.Rep. 462. The proposition stands on the general principle that conduct which imports acceptance or assent is acceptance or assent, in the view of the law, whatever may have been the actual state of mind of the party,—a principle sometimes lost sight of in the cases. *O'Donnell v. Clinton*, 145 Mass. 461, 463, 14 N.E.Rep. 747; *McCarthy v. Boston & Lowell Railroad*, 148 Mass. 550, 552, 20 N.E.Rep. 182.

Exceptions overruled.

39 UNITED STATES CODE

39 U.S.C. § 3009. Mailing of unordered merchandise

(a) Except for (1) free samples clearly and conspicuously marked as such, and (2) merchandise mailed by a charitable organization soliciting contributions, the mailing of unordered merchandise or of communications prohibited by subsection (c) of this section constitutes an unfair method of competition and an unfair trade practice in violation of section 45(a)(1) of title 15.

(b) Any merchandise mailed in violation of subsection (a) of this section, or within the exceptions contained therein, may be treated as a gift by the recipient, who shall have the right to retain, use, discard, or dispose of it in any manner he sees fit without any obligation whatsoever to the sender. All such merchandise shall have attached to it a clear and conspicuous statement informing the recipient that he may treat the merchandise as a gift to him and has the right to retain, use, discard, or dispose of it in any manner he sees fit without any obligation whatsoever to the sender.

(c) No mailer of any merchandise mailed in violation of subsection (a) of this section, or within the exceptions contained therein, shall mail to any recipient of such merchandise a bill for such merchandise or any dunning communications.

(d) For the purposes of this section, "unordered merchandise" means merchandise mailed without the prior expressed request or consent of the recipient.

[Many state statutes adopt the same principle, but go beyond mailing to any sending. E.g., McKinney's New York General Business Law § 396. Ed.]

ProCD, INC. v. ZEIDENBERG

United States Court of Appeals, Seventh Circuit, 1996.
86 F.3d 1447.

EASTERBROOK, CIRCUIT JUDGE.

Must buyers of computer software obey the terms of shrinkwrap licenses? The district court held not, for two reasons: first, they are not contracts because the licenses are inside the box rather than printed on the outside; second, federal law forbids enforcement even if the licenses are contracts. 908 F.Supp. 640 (W.D.Wis.1996). The parties and numerous amici curiae have briefed many other issues, but these are the only two that matter—and we disagree with the district judge's conclusion on each. Shrinkwrap licenses are enforceable unless their terms are objectionable on grounds applicable to contracts in general (for example, if they violate a rule of positive law, or if they are unconscionable). Because no one argues that the terms of the license at issue here are troublesome, we remand with instructions to enter judgment for the plaintiff.

I

ProCD, the plaintiff, has compiled information from more than 3,000 telephone directories into a computer database. We may assume that this database cannot be copyrighted, although it is more complex, contains more information (nine-digit zip codes and census industrial codes), is organized differently, and therefore is more original than the single alphabetical directory at issue in *Feist Publications, Inc. v. Rural Telephone Service Co.*, 499 U.S. 340, 111 S.Ct. 1282, 113 L.Ed.2d 358 (1991). See Paul J. Heald, The Vices of Originality, 1991 Sup.Ct. Rev. 143, 160–68. ProCD sells a version of the database, called SelectPhone (trademark), on CD–ROM discs. (CD–ROM means "compact disc—read only memory." The "shrinkwrap license" gets its name from the fact that retail software packages are covered in plastic or cellophane "shrinkwrap," and some vendors, though not ProCD, have written licenses that become effective as soon as the customer tears the wrapping from the package. Vendors prefer "end user license," but we use the more common term.) A proprietary method of compressing the data serves as effective encryption too. Customers decrypt and use the data with the aid of an application program that ProCD has written. This program, which is copyrighted, searches the database in response to users' criteria (such as "find all people named Tatum in Tennessee, plus all firms with 'Door Systems' in the corporate name"). The resulting lists (or, as ProCD prefers, "listings") can be read and manipulated by other software, such as word processing programs.

The database in SelectPhone (trademark) cost more than $10 million to compile and is expensive to keep current. It is much more valuable to some users than to others. The combination of names, addresses, and SIC codes enables manufacturers to compile lists of potential customers. Manufacturers and retailers pay high prices to specialized information intermediaries for such mailing lists; ProCD offers a potentially cheaper alternative. People with nothing to sell could use the database as a substitute for calling long distance information, or as a way to look up old friends who have moved to unknown towns, or just as an electronic substitute for the local phone book. ProCD decided to engage in price discrimination, selling its database to the general public for personal use at a low price (approximately $150 for the set of five discs) while selling information to the trade for a higher price. It has adopted some intermediate strategies too: access to the SelectPhone (trademark) database is available via the America Online service for the price America Online charges to its clients (approximately $3 per hour), but this service has been tailored to be useful only to the general public.

If ProCD had to recover all of its costs and make a profit by charging a single price—that is, if it could not charge more to commercial users than to the general public—it would have to raise the price substantially over $150. The ensuing reduction in sales would harm consumers who value the information at, say, $200. They get consumer surplus of $50 under the current arrangement but would cease to buy if the price rose substantially. If because of high elasticity of demand in the consumer segment of the market the only way to make a profit turned out to be a price attractive to commercial users alone, then all consumers would lose out—and so would the commercial clients, who would have to pay more for the listings because ProCD could not obtain any contribution toward costs from the consumer market.

To make price discrimination work, however, the seller must be able to control arbitrage. An air carrier sells tickets for less to vacationers than to business travelers, using advance purchase and Saturday-night-stay requirements to distinguish the categories. A producer of movies segments the market by time, releasing first to theaters, then to pay-per-view services, next to the videotape and laserdisc market, and finally to cable and commercial tv. Vendors of computer software have a harder task. Anyone can walk into a retail store and buy a box. Customers do not wear tags saying "commercial user" or "consumer user." Anyway, even a commercial-user-detector at the door would not work, because a consumer could buy the software and resell to a commercial user. That arbitrage would break down the price discrimination and drive up the minimum price at which ProCD would sell to anyone.

Instead of tinkering with the product and letting users sort themselves—for example, furnishing current data at a high price that would be attractive only to commercial customers, and two-year-old data at a low price—ProCD turned to the institution of contract. Every box containing its consumer product declares that the software comes with restrictions stated in an enclosed license. This license, which is encoded on the CD–ROM disks as well as printed in the manual, and which appears on a user's screen every time the software runs, limits use of the application program and listings to non-commercial purposes.

Matthew Zeidenberg bought a consumer package of SelectPhone (trademark) in 1994 from a retail outlet in Madison, Wisconsin, but decided to ignore the license. He formed Silken Mountain Web Services, Inc., to resell the information in the SelectPhone (trademark) database. The corporation makes the database available on the Internet to anyone willing to pay its price—which, needless to say, is less than ProCD charges its commercial customers. Zeidenberg has purchased two additional SelectPhone (trademark) packages, each with an updated version of the database, and made the latest information available over the World Wide Web, for a price, through his corporation. ProCD filed this suit seeking an injunction against further dissemination that exceeds the rights specified in the licenses (identical in each of the three packages Zeidenberg purchased). The district court held the licenses ineffectual because their terms do not appear on the outside of the packages. The court added that the second and third licenses stand no different from the first, even though they are identical, because they *might* have been different, and a purchaser does not agree to—and cannot be bound by— terms that were secret at the time of purchase. 908 F.Supp. at 654.

II

Following the district court, we treat the licenses as ordinary contracts accompanying the sale of products, and therefore as governed by the common law of contracts and the Uniform Commercial Code. Whether there are legal differences between "contracts" and "licenses" (which may matter under the copyright doctrine of first sale) is a subject for another day. See *Microsoft Corp. v. Harmony Computers & Electronics, Inc.*, 846 F.Supp. 208 (E.D.N.Y.1994). Zeidenberg does not argue that Silken Mountain Web Services is free of any restrictions that apply to Zeidenberg himself, because any effort to treat the two parties as distinct would put Silken Mountain behind the eight ball on ProCD's argument that copying the application program onto its hard disk violates the copyright laws. Zeidenberg does argue, and the district court held, that placing the package of software on the shelf is an "offer," which the customer "accepts" by paying the asking price and leaving the store with the goods. *Peeters v. State*, 154 Wis. 111, 142 N.W. 181 (1913). In Wisconsin, as elsewhere, a contract includes only the terms on which the parties have agreed. One cannot agree to hidden terms, the judge concluded. So far, so good—but one of the terms to which Zeidenberg agreed by purchasing the software is that the transaction was subject to a license. Zeidenberg's position therefore must be that the printed terms on the outside of a box are the parties' contract—except for printed terms that refer to or incorporate other terms. But why would Wisconsin fetter the parties' choice in this way? Vendors can put the entire terms of a contract on the outside of a box only by using microscopic type, removing other information that buyers might find more useful (such as what the software does, and on which computers it works), or both. The "Read Me" file included with most software, describing system requirements and potential incompatibilities, may be equivalent to ten pages of type; warranties and license restrictions take still more space. Notice on the outside, terms on the inside, and a right to return the software for a refund if the terms are unacceptable (a right that the license expressly extends), may be a means of doing business valuable to buyers and sellers alike. See E. Allan Farnsworth, 1 *Farnsworth on Contracts* § 4.26 (1990); *Restatement (2d) of Contracts* § 211 comment a (1981) ("Standardization of agreements serves many of the same functions as standardization of goods and services; both are essential to a system of mass production and distribution. Scarce and costly time and skill can be devoted to a class of transactions rather than the details of individual transactions."). Doubtless a state could forbid the use of standard contracts in the software business, but we do not think that Wisconsin has done so.

Transactions in which the exchange of money precedes the communication of detailed terms are common. Consider the purchase of insurance. The buyer goes to an agent, who explains the essentials (amount of coverage, number of years) and remits the premium to the home office, which sends back a policy. On the district judge's understanding, the terms of the policy are irrelevant because the insured paid before receiving them. Yet the device of payment, often with a "binder" (so that the insurance takes effect immediately even though the home office reserves the right to withdraw coverage later), in advance of the policy, serves buyers' interests by accelerating effectiveness and reducing transactions costs. Or consider the purchase of an airline ticket. The traveler calls the carrier or an agent, is quoted a price, reserves a seat, pays, and gets a ticket, in that order. The ticket contains elaborate terms, which the traveler can reject by canceling the reservation. To use the ticket is to accept the terms, even terms that in retrospect are disadvantageous. See *Carnival Cruise Lines, Inc. v. Shute*, 499 U.S. 585, 111 S.Ct. 1522, 113 L.Ed.2d 622 (1991); see also *Vimar Seguros y Reaseguros, S.A. v. M/V Sky Reefer*, 515 U.S.528, 115 S.Ct. 2322, 132 L.Ed.2d 462 (1995) (bills of lading). Just so with a ticket to a concert. The back of the ticket states that the patron promises not to record the concert; to attend is to agree. A theater that detects a violation will confiscate the tape and escort the violator to the exit. One *could* arrange things so that every concertgoer signs this promise before forking over the money, but that cumbersome way of doing things not only would lengthen queues and raise prices but also would scotch the sale of tickets by phone or electronic data service.

Consumer goods work the same way. Someone who wants to buy a radio set visits a store, pays, and walks out with a box. Inside the box is a leaflet containing some terms, the most important of which usually is the warranty, read for the first time in the comfort of home. By Zeidenberg's lights, the warranty in the box is irrelevant; every consumer gets the standard warranty implied by the UCC in the event the contract is silent; yet so far as we are aware no state disregards warranties furnished with consumer products. Drugs come with a list of ingredients on the outside and an elaborate package insert on the inside. The package insert describes drug interactions, contraindications, and other vital information—but, if Zeidenberg is right, the purchaser need not read the package insert, because it is not part of the contract.

Next consider the software industry itself. Only a minority of sales take place over the counter, where there are boxes to peruse. A customer may place an order by phone in response to a line item in a catalog or a review in a magazine. Much software is ordered over the Internet by purchasers who have never seen a box. Increasingly software arrives by wire. There is no box; there is only a stream of electrons, a collection of information that includes data, an application program, instructions, many limitations ("MegaPixel 3.14159 cannot be used with BytePusher 2.718"), and the terms of sale. The user purchases a serial number, which activates the software's features. On Zeidenberg's arguments, these unboxed sales are unfettered by terms—so the seller has made a broad warranty and must pay consequential damages for any shortfalls in performance, two "promises" that if taken seriously would drive prices through the ceiling or return transactions to the horse-and-buggy age.

According to the district court, the UCC does not countenance the sequence of money now, terms later. (Wisconsin's version of the UCC does not differ from the Official Version in any material respect, so we use the regular numbering system. Wis. Stat. § 402.201 corresponds to UCC § 2–201, and other citations are easy to derive.) One of the court's reasons—that by proposing as part of the draft Article 2B a new UCC § 2–2203 that would explicitly validate standard-form user licenses, the American Law Institute and the National Conference of Commissioners on Uniform Laws have conceded the invalidity of shrinkwrap licenses under current law, see 908 F.Supp. at 655–56—depends on a faulty inference. To propose a change in a law's *text* is not necessarily to propose a change in the law's *effect*. New words may be designed to fortify the current rule with a more precise text that curtails uncertainty. To judge by the flux of law review articles discussing shrinkwrap licenses, uncertainty is much in need of reduction—although businesses seem to feel less uncertainty than do scholars, for only three cases (other than ours) touch on the subject, and none directly addresses it. See *Step-Saver Data Systems, Inc. v. Wyse Technology*, 939 F.2d 91 (3d Cir.1991); *Vault Corp. v. Quaid Software Ltd.*, 847 F.2d 255, 268–70 (5th Cir.1988); *Arizona Retail Systems, Inc. v. Software Link, Inc.*, 831 F.Supp. 759 (D.Ariz.1993). As their titles suggest, these are not consumer transactions. *Step-Saver* is a battle-of-the-forms case, in which the parties exchange incompatible forms and a court must decide which prevails. See *Northrop Corp. v. Litronic Industries*, 29 F.3d 1173 (7th Cir.1994) (Illinois law); Douglas G. Baird & Robert Weisberg, *Rules, Standards, and the Battle of the Forms: A Reassessment of § 2–207*, 68 Va. L.Rev. 1217, 1227–31 (1982). Our case has only one form; UCC § 2–207 is irrelevant. *Vault* holds that Louisiana's special shrinkwrap-license statute is preempted by federal law, a question to which we return. And *Arizona Retail Systems* did not reach the question, because the court found that the buyer knew the terms of the license before purchasing the software.

What then does the current version of the UCC have to say? We think that the place to start is § 2–204(1): "A contract for sale of goods may be made in any manner sufficient to show agreement, including conduct by both parties which recognizes the existence of such a contract." A vendor, as master of the offer, may invite acceptance by conduct, and may propose limitations on the kind of conduct that constitutes acceptance. A buyer may accept by performing the acts the vendor proposes to treat as acceptance. And that is what happened. ProCD proposed a contract that a buyer would accept by *using* the software after having an opportunity to read the license at leisure. This Zeidenberg did. He had no choice, because the software splashed the license on the screen and would not let him proceed without indicating acceptance. So although the district judge was right to say that a contract can be, and often is, formed simply by paying the price and walking out of the store, the UCC permits contracts to be formed in other ways. ProCD proposed such a different way, and without protest Zeidenberg agreed. Ours is not a case in which a consumer opens a package to find an insert saying "you owe us an extra $10,000" and the seller files suit to collect. Any buyer finding such a demand can prevent formation of the contract by returning the package, as can any consumer who concludes that the terms of the license make the software worth less than the purchase price. Nothing in the UCC requires a seller to maximize the buyer's net gains.

Section 2–606, which defines "acceptance of goods", reinforces this understanding. A buyer accepts goods under § 2–606(1)(b) when, after an opportunity to inspect, he fails to make an effective rejection under § 2–602(1). ProCD extended an opportunity to reject if a buyer should find the license terms unsatisfactory; Zeidenberg inspected the package, tried out the software, learned of the license, and did not reject the goods. We refer to § 2–606 only to show that the opportunity to return goods can be important; acceptance of an offer differs from acceptance of goods after delivery, see *Gillen v. Atalanta Systems, Inc.*, 997 F.2d 280, 284 n. 1 (7th Cir.1993); but the UCC consistently permits the parties to structure their relations so that the buyer has a chance to make a final decision after a detailed review.

Some portions of the UCC impose additional requirements on the way parties agree on terms. A disclaimer of the implied warranty of merchantability must be "conspicuous." UCC § 2–316(2), incorporating UCC § 1–201(10). Promises to make firm offers, or to negate oral modifications, must be "separately signed." UCC §§ 2–205, 2–209(2). These special provisos reinforce the impression that, so far as the UCC is concerned, other terms may be as inconspicuous as the forum-selection clause on the back of the cruise ship ticket in *Carnival Lines*. Zeidenberg has not located any Wisconsin case—for that matter, any case in any state—holding that under the UCC the ordinary terms found in shrin-kwrap licenses require any special prominence, or otherwise are to be undercut rather than enforced. In the end, the terms of the license are conceptually identical to the contents of the package. Just as no court would dream of saying that SelectPhone (trademark) must contain 3,100 phone books rather than 3,000, or must have data no more than 30 days old, or must sell for $100 rather than $150—although any of these changes would be welcomed by the customer, if all other things were held constant—so, we believe, Wisconsin would not let the buyer pick and choose among terms. Terms of use are no less a part of "the product" than are the size of the database and the speed with which the software compiles listings. Competition among vendors, not judicial revision of a package's contents, is how consumers are protected in a market economy. *Digital Equipment Corp. v. Uniq Digital Technologies, Inc.*, 73 F.3d 756 (7th Cir.1996). ProCD has rivals, which may elect to compete by offering superior software, monthly updates, improved terms of use, lower price, or a better compromise among these elements. As we stressed above, adjusting terms in buyers' favor might help Matthew Zeidenberg today (he already has the software) but would lead to a response, such as a higher price, that might make consumers as a whole worse off.

* * *

REVERSED AND REMANDED.

Problems

53. A made an offer to sell B 1000 Mason Green jars (gallons) at $85 per hundred. B answered with an offer to pay $82.50 per hundred. A did not reply. Is there a contract?

54. A makes an unsolicited offer to B by mail and states: "If I do not hear from you by next Tuesday I shall assume you accept." B does not reply. Is there a contract?

55. P and D, an unmarried couple, had been living together. When the relationship ended, P claimed D was contractually obligated to pay for her services in preparing his meals, doing his laundry, etc. Is she right?

56. At about the same time that P began courting Carolyn, her parents bought a piece of real property on which they intended to build a house for Carolyn. Construction began and P married Carolyn later that year. P helped with the work of constructing the house. After a dispute involving the

house, the marriage broke up. P sued his in-laws for the value of his services. (Title to the house remained at all times in the parents-in-law.) What result?

57. A invited a number of brokers to submit proposals for fire and theft insurance on certain property. Later upon A's request B, one of the brokers, revised his bid several times, presenting a favorable proposal from the Niagara Insurance Co. A's vice-president in charge took the proposal to a close friend who was an insurance broker who contacted Niagara and acted as broker in the transaction on the same terms that B had negotiated. B sues to recover the costs incurred in preparing the bid and its various revisions. What result?

58. On August 23, P ordered for prompt shipment 942 cases of shortening at 70½ cents per pound through Tweedy, D's traveling salesman. This order was sent to D by Tweedy, who had no authority to accept. On September 4, P called to ascertain what happened to his order and he was told that the order had been declined. Tweedy had represented D in the area for eight months, and during that time he had taken several orders from P, which orders in every case had been accepted and shipped, without any communication from D. In an action by P against D, what result?

59. Plaintiff fell and suffered serious permanent injuries allegedly the result of the negligence of the landowner of the place where she had fallen. She wrote to the defendant, an attorney, requesting that he represent her in bringing a claim against the landowner. The defendant's partner replied, sending a copy to the defendant, saying that defendant was in the State capital, serving a term in the legislature. He added that defendant would return about March 15, and would contact her at that time. Defendant returned to his office as scheduled and found a large backlog of paperwork on his desk. On May 11th, plaintiff wrote inquiring about the status of her case. Defendant replied that spurred by her letter he had examined the file and was shocked to learn that the statute of limitations had run out on May 8th. Plaintiff sues for malpractice, arguing that defendant's allowing the statute of limitations to run was negligent. Defendant denies the existence of an attorney-client relation, arguing that therefore he owed plaintiff no duty. Was there an attorney-client relation?

Answer problems 60 through 62 as a common law proposition without reference to the statute quoted on pp. 115–116 *supra*.

60. A sends a one-volume edition of Shakespeare with a letter saying "If you wish to buy this book send me $36.50 within one week after receipt hereof, otherwise notify me and I will forward postage for return." B examines the book and without replying makes a gift of it to his wife. What result?

61. The facts being otherwise as stated in Case 60, B examines the book and without replying carefully lays it on a shelf to await A's messenger. What result?

62. The facts being otherwise as stated in Case 60, B examines the book and uses it or gives it to his wife, writing A at the same time that he has taken the book, but that it is worth only $25 and that he will pay no more. What result?

63. In answering this problem, take into account a statute similar to the statute reproduced on pages 115–116 that covers "sending" of merchandise. S, a manufacturer, by mistake sent a carload of 64 refrigerators to Hayes, a retailer who had frequently dealt with S. The mistake was caused by the error of a clerk who had filed an order from a Mr. Hays in a folder for Hayes. When the shipment arrived, Hayes instructed his personnel to unload the shipment and place the refrigerators in his store. He then displayed them for sale. Must Hayes pay S for the refrigerators?

64. Under a claim of right made in error but in good faith, B digs a well on A's unused land and takes water therefrom which has no market value and no value to A, doing no injury to the value of the land. A notifies B that B will have to pay $500 a day for every day on which B takes water from this source. Does B accept A's offer by taking water?

65. B was the owner of an unimproved piece of realty. B spent the summer in Europe and upon returning found a beautiful house where the empty lot had been. As B was about to enter, A came up to B and informed B that A had caused the structure to be built and that, if B used it, B would be *contractually* obligated to pay. Is A correct?

66. P and D, the City of Shady Grove, entered into an agreement by which P gave D an option to acquire a perpetual right of way for sewer lines across P's property. In exchange, P was to be allowed a specified number of sewer connections. By the terms of the agreement, D was to exercise the option by giving written notice in a specified way. D never gave such notice but it did proceed to install sewer lines across P's property. When P discovered this, P asked for the promised sewer connections and D refused. In an action by P against D, what result?

67. Assume the facts of the *ProCD* case with one factual change. Suppose the exterior of the box did not contain any notice that a licensing agreement was contained within the box. Would the result be the same?

Bank and Credit Card Problems

Bank cards are issued to depositors to provide them with identification for cashing checks at branches of the bank and to allow them electronic access to their bank accounts at automatic teller machines. *Credit* cards are issued to customers of banks and other financial services institutions to allow them to make purchases on credit at cooperating retailers and to borrow directly against their credit card accounts with no red tape.

Consider the following two paragraphs. Under what common law theories did the attorneys for the banks draft the quoted provisions?

(a) A form agreement pursuant to which bank cards were issued to depositors contains a provision with respect to changes in the agreement which provides as follows: "We can change this Agreement at any time. We will mail you a copy of any changes by ordinary mail. You must notify us within ten days of your nonacceptance of the changes. If you do not, you will have agreed to the changes."

(b) A notice to holders of Visa credit cards issued by a bank informed them of an increase both in annual fees and in the interest rate. The notice contained the following provision: "This change will not apply to your account unless you accept it. If you incur any further indebtedness for purchases under your Visa account after March 1, that will constitute your acceptance of the change."

SECTION 5. WHEN MAY AN OFFER LOOKING TO A UNILATERAL CONTRACT NO LONGER BE REVOKED?

———

(Calamari & Perillo 5th § 2.22)

PETTERSON v. PATTBERG

New York Court of Appeals, 1928.
248 N.Y. 86, 161 N.E. 428.

KELLOGG, J. The evidence given upon the trial sanctions the following statement of facts: John Petterson, of whose last will and testament the plaintiff is the executrix, was the owner of a parcel of real estate in Brooklyn, known as 5301 Sixth avenue. The defendant was the owner of a bond executed by Petterson, which was secured by a third mortgage upon the parcel. On April 4, 1924, there remained unpaid upon the principal the sum of $5,450. This amount was payable in installments of $250 on April 25, 1924, and upon a like monthly date every three months thereafter. Thus the bond and mortgage had more than five years to run before the entire sum became due. Under date of the 4th of April, 1924, the defendant wrote Petterson as follows:

"I hereby agree to accept cash for the mortgage which I hold against premises 5301 6th Ave., Brooklyn, N.Y. It is understood and agreed as a consideration I will allow you $780 providing said mortgage is paid on or before May 31, 1924, and the regular quarterly payment due April 25, 1924, is paid when due."

On April 25, 1924, Petterson paid the defendant the installment of principal due on that date. Subsequently, on a day in the latter part of May, 1924, Petterson presented himself at the defendant's home, and knocked at the door. The defendant demanded the name of his caller. Petterson replied: "It is Mr. Petterson. I have come to pay off the mortgage." The defendant answered that he had sold the mortgage. Petterson stated that he would like to talk with the defendant, so the defendant partly opened the door. Thereupon Petterson exhibited the cash and said he was ready to pay off the mortgage according to the agreement. The defendant refused to take the money. Prior to this conversation Petterson had made a contract to sell the land to a third person free and clear of the mortgage to the defendant. Meanwhile, also, the defendant had sold the bond and mortgage to a third party. It, therefore, became necessary for Petterson to pay to such person the full amount of the bond and mortgage. It is claimed that he thereby sustained a loss of $780, the sum which the defendant agreed to allow upon the bond and mortgage if payment in full of principal, less that sum, was made on or before May 31, 1924. The plaintiff has had a recovery for the sum thus claimed, with interest.

Clearly the defendant's letter proposed to Petterson the making of a unilateral contract, the gift of a promise in exchange for the performance of an act. The thing conditionally promised by the defendant was the reduction of the mortgage debt. The act requested to be done, in consideration of the offered promise, was payment in full of the reduced principal of the debt prior to the due date thereof. "If an act is requested, that very act and no other must be given." Williston on Contracts, § 73. "In case of offers for a consideration, the performance of the consideration is always deemed a condition." Langdell's Summary of the Law of Contracts, § 4. It is elementary that any offer to enter into a unilateral contract may be withdrawn before the act requested to be done has been performed. Williston on Contracts, § 60; Langdell's Summary, § 4; Offord v. Davies, 12 C.B.(N.S.) 748. A bidder at a sheriff's sale may revoke his bid at any time before the property is struck down to him. Fisher v. Seltzer, 23 Penn.St. 308. The offer of a reward in consideration of an act to be performed is revocable before the very act requested has been done. Shuey v. United States, 92 U.S. 73; Biggers v. Owen, 79 Ga. 658; Fitch v. Snedaker, 38 N.Y. 248. So, also, an offer to pay a broker commissions, upon a sale of land for the offeror, is revocable at any time before the land is sold, although prior to revocation the broker performs services in an effort to effectuate a sale. Stensgaard v. Smith, 43 Minn. 11; Smith v. Cauthen, 98 Miss. 746.

An interesting question arises when, as here, the offeree approaches the offeror with the intention of proffering performance and, before actual tender is made, the offer is withdrawn. Of such a case Williston says:

> "The offeror may see the approach of the offeree and know that an acceptance is contemplated. If the offeror can say 'I revoke' before the offeree accepts, however brief the interval of time between the two acts, there is no escape from the conclusion that the offer is terminated." Williston on Contracts, § 60–b.

In this instance Petterson, standing at the door of the defendant's house, stated to the defendant that he had come to pay off the mortgage. Before a tender of the necessary moneys had been made the defendant informed Petterson that he had sold the mortgage. That was a definite notice to Petterson that the defendant could not perform his offered promise and that a tender to the defendant, who was no longer the creditor, would be ineffective to satisfy the debt. "An offer to sell property may be withdrawn before acceptance without any formal notice to the person to whom the offer is made. It is sufficient if that person has actual knowledge that the person who made the offer has done some act inconsistent with the continuance of the offer, such as selling the property to a third person." Dickinson v. Dodds, 2 Ch.Div. 463, head-note. To the same effect is Coleman v. Applegarth, 68 Md. 21, 11 A. 284. Thus, it clearly appears that the defendant's offer was withdrawn before its acceptance had been tendered. It is unnecessary to determine, therefore, what the legal situation might have been had tender been made before withdrawal. It is the individual view of the writer that the same result would follow. This would be so, for the act requested to be performed was the completed act of payment, a thing incapable of performance unless assented to by the person to be paid. Williston on Contracts, § 60–b. Clearly an offering party has the right to name the precise act performance of which would convert his offer into a binding promise. Whatever the act may be until it is performed the offer must be revocable. However, the supposed case is not before us for decision. We think that in this particular instance the offer of the defendant was withdrawn before it became a binding promise, and, therefore, that no contract was ever made for the breach of which the plaintiff may claim damages.

The judgment of the Appellate Division and that of the Trial Term should be reversed and the complaint dismissed, with costs in all courts.

LEHMAN, J. (dissenting). The defendant's letter to Petterson constituted a promise on his part to accept payment at a discount of the mortgage he held, provided the mortgage is paid on or before May 31, 1924. Doubtless by the terms of the promise itself, the defendant made payment of the mortgage by the plaintiff, before the stipulated time, a condition precedent to performance by the defendant of his promise to accept payment at a discount. If the condition precedent has not been performed, it is because the defendant made performance impossible by refusing to accept payment, when the plaintiff came with an offer of immediate performance. "It is a principle of fundamental justice that if a promisor is himself the cause of the failure of performance either of an obligation due him or of a condition upon which his own liability depends, he cannot take advantage of the failure." Williston on Contracts, § 677. The question in this case is not whether payment of the mortgage is a condition precedent to the performance of a promise made by the defendant, but, rather, whether at the time the defendant refused the offer of payment, he had assumed any binding obligation, even though subject to condition.

The promise made by the defendant lacked consideration at the time it was made. Nevertheless the promise was not made as a gift or mere gratuity to the plaintiff. It was made for the purpose of obtaining from the defendant something which the plaintiff desired. It constituted an offer which was to become binding whenever the plaintiff should give, in return for the defendant's promise, exactly the consideration which the defendant requested.

Here the defendant requested no counter promise from the plaintiff. The consideration requested by the defendant for his promise to accept payment was, I agree, some act to be performed by the plaintiff. Until the act requested was performed, the defendant might undoubtedly revoke his offer. Our problem is to determine from the words of the letter read in the light of surrounding circumstances what act the defendant requested as consideration for his promise.

The defendant undoubtedly made his offer as an inducement to the plaintiff to "pay" the mortgage before it was due. Therefore, it is said, that "the act requested to be performed was the completed act of payment, a thing incapable of performance unless assented to by the person to be paid." In unmistakable terms the defendant agreed to accept payment, yet we are told that the defendant intended, and the plaintiff should have understood, that the act requested by the defendant, as consideration for his promise to accept payment, included performance by the defendant himself of the very promise for which the act was to be consideration. The defendant's promise was to become binding only when fully performed; and part of the consideration to be furnished by the plaintiff for the defendant's promise was to be the performance of that promise by the defendant. So construed, the defendant's promise or offer, though intended to induce action by the plaintiff, is but a snare and delusion. The plaintiff could not reasonably suppose that the defendant was asking him to procure the performance by the defendant of the very act which the defendant promised to do, yet we are told that even after the plaintiff had done all else which the defendant requested, the defendant's promise was still not binding because the defendant chose not to perform.

I cannot believe that a result so extraordinary could have been intended when the defendant wrote the letter. "The thought behind the phrase proclaims itself misread when the outcome of the reading is injustice or absurdity." See opinion of Cardozo, C. J., in Surace v. Danna, 248 N.Y. 18, 161 N.E. 315. If the defendant intended to induce payment by the plaintiff and yet reserve the right to refuse payment when offered he should have used a phrase better calculated to express his meaning than the words: "I agree to accept." A promise to accept payment, by its very terms, must necessarily become binding, if at all, not later than when a present offer to pay is made.

I recognize that in this case only an offer of payment, and not a formal tender of payment, was made before the defendant withdrew his offer to accept payment. Even the plaintiff's part in the act of payment was then not technically complete. Even so, under a fair construction of the words of the letter I think the plaintiff had done the act which the defendant requested as consideration for his promise. The plaintiff offered to pay with present intention and ability to make that payment. A formal tender is seldom made in business transactions, except to lay the foundation for subsequent assertion in a court of justice of rights which spring from refusal of the tender. If the defendant acted in good faith in making his offer to accept payment, he could not well have intended to draw a distinction in the act requested of the plaintiff in return, between an offer which unless refused would ripen into completed payment, and a formal tender. Certainly the defendant could not have expected or intended that the plaintiff would make a formal tender of payment without first stating that he had come to make payment. We should not read into the language of the defendant's offer a meaning which would prevent enforcement of the defendant's promise after it had been accepted by the plaintiff in the very way which the defendant must have intended it should be accepted, if he acted in good faith.

The judgment should be affirmed.

STATE v. WHEELER

Washington Supreme Court, 1981.
95 Wash.2d 799, 803, 631 P.2d 376, 379.

UTTER, J. * * * The defendant seeks specific performance of the prosecutor's initial offer. He contends that the prosecutor could not legally rescind the offer until he had an opportunity to accept it. The issue, as framed by his argument, is one of first impression in this state.

The weight of authority is that, absent some detrimental reliance by the defendant, the State may withdraw from any plea agreement prior to the actual entry of a guilty plea. *Government v. Scotland*, 614 F.2d 360 (3d Cir. 1980); [other citations omitted.] That result has been reached by strictly applying contract principles and characterizing the plea bargain as a unilateral contract. That is, only the defendant's plea, or some other detrimental reliance upon the arrangement, constitutes an acceptance of the agreement; and consequently the bargain can be revoked if neither has occurred. Those courts have further reasoned that enforcing bargains made before the plea would inhibit the prosecutor's use of plea bargaining; and that the defendant, because she or he can still get a jury trial, has an adequate remedy for the State's revocation.

* * *

MOTEL SERVICES, INC. v. CENTRAL MAINE POWER CO.

Supreme Judicial Court of Maine, 1978.
394 A.2d 786.

POMEROY, JUSTICE.

This is an appeal from a final judgment entered in favor of Central Maine Power Company (CMP), the defendant and third party plaintiff. The third party action against Waterville Housing Authority (WHA) was dismissed. No cross-appeal was taken. The case was heard by a single Justice, sitting without a jury.

On August 5, 1971 Motel Services, Inc. entered into an agreement with WHA whereby Motel Services would build two housing projects for WHA on a *"turnkey"* basis. After the agreement became effective, appellant sought to change the construction specifications to provide for an electrical rather than an oil heating system. Appellant sought this change in order to qualify for a promotional allowance given by CMP to the *owner of a home either new or existing which is initially built for or converted to the use of electricity as the primary method of heating ... , provided that the installation of such electric heating equipment complies with the Company's* "Standard Requirement Electric Service and Meter Installation" And "Standards of Insulation For Use with Electric House Heating."

Appellant took the initiative in persuading WHA and the Federal Department of Housing and Urban Development (HUD) to consent to the modifications. Appellant, with CMP's assistance, demonstrated that electric heating was ultimately more economical; appellant also promised to reduce its contract price by $16,000 if the change was approved. Both WHA and HUD agreed to the modification. Appellant never informed either agency of the existence of the promotional allowance, however, despite the fact that approximately $8,000 of the $16,000 reduction was due to appellant's expectation of receiving the allowance.

After the electrical system had been completely installed, but before all the *"Standards"* required by CMP had been complied with, appellant conveyed both premises to WHA. This conveyance prior to final completion was designed primarily to avoid the imposition upon appellant of the tax to be exacted on April 1. The projects, however, were completed after closing to the full satisfaction of WHA and in compliance with the CMP standards.

After inspection of the premises by a CMP employee, the appropriate forms for receipt of the allowance were prepared. Unaware that appellant expected the allowance, the employee sent the forms and eventually the allowance to WHA, the owner on the date of completion of the projects. Appellant brought this action against CMP, claiming it was entitled to the allowance. CMP sued WHA in a third party action seeking return of the allowance in the event of a judgment in appellant's favor.

The Justice below made findings of fact and conclusions of law. Most significantly, these included a finding that appellant had not fully complied with the requirements of the allowance policy prior to conveyance of the property. Having concluded that CMP's policy was a standing offer to enter into a unilateral contract, the presiding Justice ruled that appellant did not fully perform prior to relinquishing ownership, and no enforceable contract was therefore produced.

I.

Our first conclusion, which we have little difficulty in reaching, is that WHA is not entitled to the allowance. Not having known of it prior to completion of the construction, WHA provided no consideration, and did not bargain for it. The completion of the claim forms does not constitute performance of the acts requested by the offer * * *

II.

The Court below correctly characterized CMP's marketing policy as an offer to enter into a unilateral contract. Despite the general rule that contracts are presumed to be bilateral, Restatement of Contracts, § 31, the presumption is rebutted by the clear import of the offer, which requested not a promise to perform, but complete performance in accordance with its terms. Such is the essential hallmark of a unilateral contract.

We find error, however, in the presiding Justice's interpretation of the law of unilateral contracts. Specifically, the Court erred in ruling as a matter of law that *"[i]f an act is required in return for a promise, that act and only that act and the whole of that act must be performed or there is no contract."* Brackenbury v. Hodgkin, 116 Me. 399, 401, 102 A. 106 (1917).* * * Professor Corbin discusses *Brackenbury* in some detail, as illustrative of the rule that part performance by the promisee renders an offer of a unilateral contract irrevocable. *See Corbin on Contracts*, § 49. [This last sentence was in a footnote. Ed.]

* * *

In the instant case, it is clear that when appellant undertook to install the heating system in accordance with CMP's policy, it was not only entitled as owner of the homes to accept the offer, but in fact did so. Appellant's failure to notify CMP of its acceptance, in the context of an offer of a unilateral contract, does not undermine the validity of the acceptance. *See 1 Williston on Contracts*, § 68 (3rd ed. 1957).

However, while CMP's offer was rendered irrevocable by appellant's acceptance, payment of the allowance remained contingent upon appellant's completion of the required performance.

III.

Appellees set forth two grounds by which they contend that appellant failed completely to perform. First, appellant did not complete the final steps necessary to claim the allowance, namely, the submission of the forms to CMP. Second, appellant was no longer the owner of the buildings at the time it fully complied with CMP's construction standards.

The first contention is unpersuasive. Appellant failed to fill out the requisite forms because CMP sent them to WHA, and instructed WHA on how to complete them to claim the allowance. It is undisputed that, had CMP provided the forms, appellant would have completed this final requirement.

Where the offeree of a unilateral contract is prevented from completing performance by the actions of the offeror, such failure will not be a defense to an action by the offeree on the contract. *Brackenbury v. Hodgkin, supra*, at 402, 102 A. 106; *1 Williston*, § 74A, p. 246.

Appellee's second argument presents a more substantial issue, but is likewise unpersuasive, in the last analysis. The failure of appellant to maintain his *"owner"* status through the period of completion of work does not, we think, preclude recovery.

CMP extended its offer

to the owner of a home ... which is initially built for or converted to the use of electricity as the primary method of heating.... An allowance will be paid at the above stated rate [also] to owners of homes, which use electricity ... who install additional electric heating....

Appellant was the owner of the buildings under construction until April 1, when it persuaded WHA to accept an early conveyance of the property in order to protect themselves from an imminent property tax imposition. Appellees contend that such transfer, occurring prior to full compliance with CMP's standards, precluded appellant from entitlement to the allowance.

We do not agree.

The offeror is the master of his offer, and is entitled to establish such standards of acceptance, notice, and the like as he sees fit. Among such powers is the right to designate the person, persons, or class of persons entitled to accept the offer. * * * In this case, CMP's offer was explicitly limited to acceptance by *"owners"*. Appellant, at the time it undertook to perform the requested acts, was owner of the buildings and entitled to, and did, accept the offer.

CMP contends that a major purpose of its policy of requiring adequate insulation as a prerequisite to payment of the allowance was to insure that the customer would obtain satisfactory results from his heating system. Therefore, it urges, the emphasis in the quoted passage should be upon the word *"use"*; The allowance was intended to go to the *"user"* of the system, who was in most cases also the owner. Thus the crucial determinant respecting entitlement to the allowance was the identity of the user, rather than the owner.

CMP's management aims in developing its policy, however, are less important than its outward manifestations. We believe that a plain reading of the offer leads to the conclusion that the class of offerees consisted of owners of homes who undertook to install electrical heating equipment. No conditions are attached to the offer plainly indicating a requirement that the owner occupy the home and use the system after installation. Indeed CMP admitted that no such requirement had ever been imposed. Any emphasis CMP chose to place on who the *"ultimate user"* was is absent from the terms of the offer. It is to those terms that we must look in determining the class of persons empowered by CMP to accept its offer.

* * *

Here, CMP received what it had bargained for by the terms of its offer. The owner of a home undertook to install an electric heating system; 90% of the work was completed before the property was conveyed, the remaining details shortly thereafter. Had appellant retained title to the property until it received the allowance, and conveyed it immediately thereafter, there is no doubt but that the case would not be before us. We are not convinced that the conveyance should change the result.

* * *

Appeal sustained; remanded with instructions to enter judgment for appellant on its claim.

Problems

68. A, a property owner, says to B, the CEO of a railroad, "if you extend your lines to my property (up to a spot that A designated on a map), I will pay your company" a specified amount. When the railroad company had extended its rails halfway to the designated spot, A sent B a notice of revocation. Should the railroad continue to extend its rails? Does the railroad have an action for breach of contract against A?

69. A promises B to rake her lawn in return for $25 paid in advance. B tenders $25 within a reasonable time. A refuses to accept the tender. What result?

70. Mortgagee agreed to accept a smaller amount than the total mortgage debt in satisfaction, if mortgagor would pay it within 90 days. In reliance on the promise, mortgagor completed a bank loan. Mortgagee revoked. Advise mortgagor.

71. A appointed B as her agent for 90 days to sell certain property and promised to pay B a 5% commission in case B brought about a sale within that time. B spent time and money in an effort to procure a purchaser. The property was sold by another broker within the 90 day period. This fact was communicated to B. In an action by B against A, what result?

SECTION 6.   ACCEPTANCE OF INDIFFERENT OFFERS AND ACCEPTANCE BY PROMISE

(Calamari & Perillo 5th §§ 2.10(b) & (c) and 2.23)

BRACKENBURY v. HODGKIN

Supreme Judicial Court of Maine, 1917.
116 Me. 399, 102 A. 106.

CORNISH, C.J. The defendant Mrs. Sarah D.P. Hodgkin on the 8th day of February, 1915, was the owner of certain real estate—her home farm, situated in the outskirts of Lewiston. She was a widow and was living alone. She was the mother of six adult children, five sons, one of whom, Walter, is the codefendant, and one daughter, who is the coplaintiff. The plaintiffs were then residing in Independence, Mo. Many letters had passed between mother and daughter concerning the daughter and her husband returning to the old home and taking care of the mother, and finally on February 8, 1915, the mother sent a letter to the daughter and her husband which is the foundation of this bill in equity. In this letter she made a definite proposal, the substance of which was that if the Brackenburys would move to Lewiston, and maintain and care for Mrs. Hodgkin on the home place during her life, and pay the moving expenses, they were to have the use and income of the premises, together with the use of the household goods, with certain exceptions, Mrs. Hodgkin to have what rooms she might need. The letter closed, by way of postscript, with the words, "you to have the place when I have passed away."

Relying upon this offer, which was neither withdrawn nor modified, and in acceptance thereof, the plaintiffs moved from Missouri to Maine late in April, 1915, went upon the premises described and entered upon the performance of the contract. Trouble developed after a few weeks, and the relations between the parties grew most disagreeable. The mother brought two suits against her son-in-law on trifling matters, and finally ordered the plaintiffs from the place, but they refused to leave. Then on November 7, 1916, she executed and delivered to her son, Walter C. Hodgkin, a deed of the premises, reserving a life estate in herself. Walter, however, was not a bona fide purchaser for value without notice, but took the deed with full knowledge of the agreement between the parties and for the sole purpose of evicting the plaintiffs. On the very day the deed was executed he served a notice to quit upon Mr. Brackenbury, as preliminary to an action of forcible entry and detainer which was brought on November 13, 1916. This bill in equity was brought by the plaintiffs to secure a reconveyance of the farm from Walter to his mother, to restrain and enjoin Walter from further prosecuting his action of forcible entry and detainer, and to obtain an adjudication that the mother holds the legal title impressed with a trust in favor of the plaintiffs in accordance with their contract.

The sitting justice made an elaborate and carefully considered finding of facts and signed a decree, sustaining the bill with costs against Walter C. Hodgkin, and granting the relief prayed for. The case is before the law court on the defendants' appeal from this decree.

Four main issues are raised.

1. As to the completion and existence of a valid contract.

A legal and binding contract is clearly proven. The offer on the part of the mother was in writing, and its terms cannot successfully be disputed. There was no need that it be accepted in words, nor that a counter promise on the part of the plaintiffs be made. The offer was the basis, not of a bilateral contract, requiring a reciprocal promise, a promise for a promise, but of a unilateral contract requiring an act for a promise. "In the latter case the only acceptance of the offer that is necessary is the performance of the act. In other words, the promise becomes binding when the act is performed." 6 R.C.L. 607. This is elementary law.

The plaintiffs here accepted the offer by moving from Missouri to the mother's farm in Lewiston and entering upon the performance of the specified acts, and they have continued performance since that time so far as they have been permitted by the mother to do so. The existence of a completed and valid contract is clear.

* * *

Appeal dismissed.

CANTU v. CENTRAL EDUCATION AGENCY

Court of Appeals of Texas, Austin 1994.
884 S.W.2d 565.

BEA ANNE SMITH, JUSTICE. Appellant Maria Diosel Cantu sued for judicial review of a final order of the State Commissioner of Education, Lionel Meno. The district court affirmed the Commissioner's decision. We will affirm the trial-court judgment.

BACKGROUND

The facts in this cause are undisputed. Cantu was hired as a special-education teacher by the San Benito Consolidated Independent School District under a one-year contract for the 1990–91 school year. On Saturday, August 18, 1990, shortly before the start of the school year, Cantu hand-delivered to her supervisor a letter of resignation, effective August 17, 1990. In this letter, Cantu requested that her final paycheck be forwarded to an address in McAllen, Texas, some fifty miles from the San Benito office where she tendered the resignation. The San Benito superintendent of schools, the only official authorized to accept resignations on behalf of the school district, received Cantu's resignation on Monday, August 20. The superintendent wrote a letter accepting Cantu's resignation the same day and deposited the letter, properly stamped and addressed, in the mail at approximately 5:15 p.m. that afternoon. At about 8:00 a.m. the next morning, August 21, Cantu hand-delivered to the superintendent's office a letter withdrawing her resignation. This letter contained a San Benito return address. In response, the superintendent hand-delivered that same day a copy of his letter mailed the previous day to inform Cantu that her resignation had been accepted and could not be withdrawn.

The State Commissioner of Education concluded that, because the school district's acceptance of Cantu's resignation was effective when mailed, an agreement to rescind Cantu's employment contract was in force when she attempted to withdraw her offer of resignation and the school district's refusal to honor her contract was not unlawful.

DISCUSSION

The sole legal question presented for our review is the proper scope of the "mailbox rule"[4] under Texas law and whether the rule was correctly applied by the Commissioner and district court. None of the

---

4. The mailbox rule provides that the properly addressed acceptance of an offer is effective when deposited in the mail, unless otherwise agreed or provided by law. Black's Law Dictionary 952 (6th ed. 1990).

parties to this appeal disputes that an agreement to rescind Cantu's employment contract requires the elements of an offer, acceptance, and consideration. See *Texas Gas Util. Co. v. Barrett*, 460 S.W.2d 409, 414 (Tex.1970). Rather, Cantu contends in a single point of error that the trial court erred in ruling that the agreement to rescind her contract of employment became effective when the superintendent deposited his letter accepting Cantu's resignation in the mail. Cantu argues that, under Texas law, an acceptance binds the parties in contract on mailing only if the offeror has sent the offer by mail or has expressly authorized acceptance by mail. There was no express authorization for the school district to accept Cantu's offer by mail. The question presented is whether authorization to accept by mail may be implied only when the offer is delivered by mail or also when the existing circumstances make it reasonable for the offeree to so accept.

The aphorism "the offeror is the master of his offer" reflects the power of the offeror to impose conditions on acceptance of an offer, specify the manner of acceptance, or withdraw the offer before the offeree has effectively exercised the power of acceptance. However, more often than not, an offeror does not expressly authorize a particular mode, medium, or manner of acceptance. Consequently, particularly with parties communicating at a distance, a rule of law is needed to establish the point of contract formation and allocate the risk of loss and inconvenience that inevitably falls to one of the parties between the time that the offeree exercises, and the offeror receives, the acceptance. See 1 Arthur L. Corbin, Contracts § 78 (1963).

As Professor Corbin notes, courts could adopt a rule that no acceptance is effective until received, absent express authorization by the offeror; however, the mailbox rule, which makes acceptance effective on dispatch, closes the deal and enables performance more promptly, and places the risk of inconvenience on the party who originally has power to control the manner of acceptance. *Id.* Moreover, "the mailing of a letter has long been a customary and expected way of accepting [an] offer." *Id.* Therefore, "[e]ven though the offer was not made by mail and there was no [express] authorization, the existing circumstances may be such as to make it reasonable for the offeree to accept by mail and to give the offeror reason to know that the acceptance will be so made." *Id.* In short, acceptance by mail is impliedly authorized if reasonable under the circumstances.

The Restatement approves and adopts this approach: an acceptance by any medium reasonable under the circumstances is effective on dispatch, absent a contrary indication in the offer. Restatement (Second) of Contracts §§ 30(2), 63(a), 65, 66 (1979). In addition, the Restatement specifically recognizes that acceptance by mail is ordinarily reasonable if the parties are negotiating at a distance or *even if a written offer is delivered in person to an offeree in the same city. Id.* § 65 cmt. c (emphasis added). The same standard, *viz.*, whether the manner of acceptance is reasonable under the circumstances, governs offer and acceptance in commercial transactions under the Texas Business and

Commerce Code. See Tex.Bus. & Com.Code Ann. [UCC] § 2.206 (West 1968).

* * * We hold that it is proper to consider whether acceptance by mail is reasonably implied under the circumstances, whether or not the offer was delivered by mail.

Looking at the circumstances presented for our review, we agree with the Commissioner and the trial court that it was reasonable for the superintendent to accept Cantu's offer of resignation by mail. Cantu tendered her resignation shortly before the start of the school year—at a time when both parties could not fail to appreciate the need for immediate action by the district to locate a replacement. In fact, she delivered the letter on a Saturday, when the Superintendent could neither receive nor respond to her offer, further delaying matters by two days. Finally, Cantu's request that her final paycheck be forwarded to an address some fifty miles away indicated that she could no longer be reached in San Benito and that she did not intend to return to the school premises or school-district offices. The Commissioner of Education and district court properly concluded that it was reasonable for the school district to accept Cantu's offer by mail. We overrule appellant's point of error.

Conclusion

We affirm the trial-court judgment that the Commission correctly determined that the school district accepted Cantu's resignation, rescinding her employment contract, before Cantu attempted to withdraw her offer of resignation.

FUJIMOTO v. RIO GRANDE PICKLE CO.

United States Court of Appeals, Fifth Circuit, 1969.
414 F.2d 648.

Goldberg, Circuit Judge:

This appeal involves claims by George Fujimoto and Jose Bravo against the Rio Grande Pickle Company upon written contracts of employment. The questions before us are of contract formation and construction.

Rio Grande Pickle Company, a Colorado corporation engaged in the business of raising and selling cucumbers for the pickling industry, hired Fujimoto in the Spring of 1965 and Bravo in the following Fall. Both of these employees were given important jobs. Fujimoto was employed as the supervisor of the planting and growing operations, while Bravo functioned as the labor recruiter.

In order to encourage them to work with zeal and not to leave the company's employ, Rio Grande offered contracts with profit sharing bonus provisions to both Fujimoto and Bravo. Prior to the offer of the written contracts, the company had responded to the offerees' demands for more compensation by orally agreeing to pay them a salary plus a bonus of ten per cent of the company's annual profits. Bravo told the president of Rio Grande that he wanted the agreement in writing, and the president replied "I will prepare one and send you a contract in writing." The contractual documents sent to Fujimoto and Bravo did not specify how the offers could be accepted or how the acceptances should be communicated to the company. Under these circumstances Fujimoto and Bravo signed their respective contracts but did not return them to the company. Believing that they had accepted the company's offers and that they were working under the proffered bonus contracts, the two employees remained in the employ of Rio Grande until November 30, 1966.

The written contracts called for the employees to devote their best efforts to Rio Grande and promised in return that the company would pay each offeree a bonus amounting to ten per cent of the company's net profits for each fiscal year. Each employee was to agree to return half of his bonus to the company as an investment in company stock.

* * *

In answer to special interrogatories the jury found that Fujimoto and Bravo each had entered into a written contract in October, 1965. * * *

On appeal Rio Grande argues that there is insufficient evidence in the record to support the jury's finding that Fujimoto and Bravo had accepted the offered bonus contracts. * * *

I.

Rio Grande argues that there were no contracts because Fujimoto and Bravo did not accept the written bonus offers by signing and returning the written instruments to the company. Each contract was signed by the respective employee, but neither was returned. Thus the first issue is whether the offers, which by their terms did not specify the means by which they could be accepted, could be accepted by a mode other than the return of the signed instruments.

Professor Corbin has summarized the law on this issue as follows:

"In the first place, there is no question that the offeror can require notice of acceptance in any form that he pleases. He can require that it shall be in any language and transmitted in any manner. He may require notice to be given by a nod of the head, by flags, by wig-wag, by a smoke signal on a high hill. He may require that it be by letter, telegraph or radio, and that there shall be no contract unless and until he is himself made conscious of it.

"Secondly, the offeror can specify a mode of making an acceptance of his offer, without making that method exclusive of all others. If the mode that he specifies is one that may not bring home to him the knowledge that his offer has been accepted, then such knowledge by him is not a requisite. The offeror can specify a mode of acceptance without any knowledge of the law of contract and without thinking in terms of offer and acceptance at all. This will be considered below.

> "Thirdly, if the offeror specifies no mode of acceptance, the law requires no more than that the mode adopted shall be in accord with the usage and custom of men in similar cases. If proof of such usage and custom is wanting or is uncertain, the court must consider probable convenience and results and then help by its decision to establish a custom for the future and a rule of law." Corbin on Contracts § 67, p. 109 [Student Ed.1952].

See also Allied Steel & Conveyors, Inc. v. Ford Motor Company, 6 Cir.1960, 277 F.2d 907, 910–911.

This case falls within the third of Professor Corbin's rules. Neither written offer specified a particular mode of acceptance, and there is no evidence that Rio Grande ever manifested any intent that the offers could be accepted only by the return of the signed instruments. Moreover, there is substantial and convincing evidence to the contrary. The record is replete with evidence that the company conditioned the bonus offers primarily upon the offerees remaining in the company's employment and that the employees understood that they did not have to return the signed contracts in order to have contracts under which they would each get a ten per cent bonus.

Since we have found that the return of the signed documents was not the exclusive means by which the offerees could convey their acceptances, we must now determine whether Fujimoto and Bravo in fact adequately communicated such acceptances to the company. Where, as here, the offer and surrounding circumstances are silent as to permissible modes of acceptance, the law requires only that there be some clear and unmistakable expression of the offeree's intention to accept. In the words of Professor Corbin:

> "Whenever the case is such as to require a notice of acceptance, it is not enough for the offeree to express mental assent, or even to do some overt act that is not known to the offeror and is not one that constitutes a customary method of giving notice. *If the overt act is one that clearly expresses an intention* to accept the specific offer and is in fact known by the offeror, there is an effective acceptance. This is because the offeror has actual knowledge." [Emphasis added.] Corbin on Contracts, *supra*, § 67 at p. 111.

As Professor Corbin indicates, the mode of expressing assent is inconsequential so long as it effectively makes known to the offeror that his offer has been accepted. One usually thinks of acceptance in terms of oral or written incantations, but in many situations acts or symbols may be equally effective communicative media. See Restatement of Contracts § 21. In the words of Chief Judge Brown in Aetna Casualty & Surety Co. v. Berry, 5 Cir.1965, 350 F.2d 49, 54:

> "That the communication from the Berry Companies to Aetna was not in words express goes only to the weight and clarity of the message, but it does not mean that no contract came into existence.

Of necessity, the law has long recognized the efficacy of nonverbal communications. From the formation of contracts by an offeree's silence, nod, hand signal "√" or "x" on an order blank to the doctrine of admission by silence, the law has legally realized that to offer guidance and comment meaningfully on the full range of human conduct, cognizance must be taken of communications other than by words. Symbols for words often suffice. Lawyers and Judges live by them, as the citation to this very case may sometime demonstrate."

See also McCarty v. Langdeau, Tex.Civ.App.1960, 337 S.W.2d 407, 412 (writ ref'd n.r.e.).

In the case at bar there is substantial evidence to support the jury's finding that the company knew that the offerees had agreed to the terms of the proffered bonus contracts. Of particular importance is the fact that Fujimoto and Bravo, who had threatened to quit unless their remuneration was substantially increased, continued to work for the company for fourteen months after receiving the offers. Moreover, during this fourteen-month period they did not again express dissatisfaction with their compensation. There is also evidence that Fujimoto and Bravo discussed the bonus contracts with the company president in such circumstances and in such a manner that their assent and acceptance should have been unmistakable to him. In view of these circumstances, Rio Grande could not have been besieged with any Hamlet-like doubts regarding the existence of a contract. Since Rio Grande knew that Fujimoto and Bravo had accepted its offer, there was a valid and binding contract. See Williston on Contracts § 90 (1957).

* * *

Affirmed in part and reversed and remanded in part.

Problems

72. A writes to B, "If you will paint my fence next week, I will pay you $200." B paints but not in A's presence. Is there a contract?

73. A writes to B, "If you paint my fence next week, I promise to pay you $200." B replies, "I'll do it." Is there a contract?

74. P sent a purchase order to D requesting the prompt shipment of certain items. D sent a written promise to ship the goods that were ordered. Is there a contract?

75. B sent S a purchase order for 200,000 blue medical bottles at $1 each. S responded by shipping 200,000 clear medical bottles the market price of which was 90 cents per bottle. B accepted the bottles, notified S of breach and sued S for breach of contract. What result?

76. B sent a purchase order to S which amounted to an offer to buy goods. S began to execute B's order. B knew that S was beginning performance. (a) Was B entitled to cancel the order? (b) Would B be entitled to cancel the order if B was unaware of the beginning of performance?

77. B sends an offer to Y stating, "You can accept this offer only by signing your name on the line provided below my signature." Y sends a letter of acceptance. Is there a contract?

78. Seller mailed Buyer a letter offering to sell specified goods which Seller was prepared to purchase from a third party. The letter contained the sentence, "Please reply by fax at once so I can make a deposit and close the deal." Buyer called Seller and "accepted" on the phone. Is there a contract?

79. A made an offer to B stating, "This offer shall be accepted by signing in the appropriate place and by returning it to me." B called A and stated that the offer was accepted. Is there a contract?

80. A makes an offer by mail to sell her used car to B. B immediately sends an acceptance by mail, changes his mind, and then sends a rejection by fax. The fax is received before the acceptance is received. a) In a suit by A against B for breach of contract, what result? b) Suppose A had sold her car to C after she had received the message of rejection but before she had received the letter of acceptance. In an action by B against A for breach of contract, what result?

81. A calls B on the telephone. A is in New York and B is in New Jersey. A makes an offer. B speaks words of acceptance into the phone which A does not hear because of the fault of the Telephone Company. Is there a contract?

82. A made an offer to B by mail. A's offer stated, "your acceptance is effective when sent provided that it is received." B's mailed acceptance was lost and was never received by A. What result?

83. The defendant sent an offer to the plaintiff by mail. The last sentence in the offer read: "As soon as the acceptance is received we shall send amongst the farmers and secure the first lots." The plaintiff promptly sent a letter of acceptance which was lost and never received. Was there a contract?

84. What legal error appears in this excerpt from the *New York Times'* obituary of football-great Mel Hein? "For all the glory of his career with the Giants, it happened largely by accident and through a violation of sacred postal regulations. In 1931, Mr. Hein wrote to several N.F.L. teams, including the Giants and the Providence Steamrollers, offering his services. When the Providence team was the first to respond, offering him a $125-a-game contract, Mr. Hein signed it and mailed it back. The next day a Giants contract, offering him $150 a game, arrived, and Mr. Hein sent a wire begging the postmaster in Providence to intercept the other contract and return it. The official obliged and the rest is Giants history."

85. A makes B an offer to be accepted by mail or messenger, and B promptly sends an acceptance by his own employee. When does the contract arise? Would the result be different if the acceptance were given to a private messenger service?

SECTION 7. MISTAKE IN TRANSMISSION

(Calamari & Perillo 5th § 2.24)

Problems

86. S made an offer to sell a certain quantity of oranges to B at $2.60 per box. When transmitted by the telegraph company the offer read $1.60 per box. B accepted this offer when the market price was $2.30 per box. B had reason to know that at the time and place of the offer the oranges were worth at least $2.30 per box. In an action by B against S for refusal to deliver for $1.60 per box, what result?

87. A writes an offer to B which he encloses in an envelope and addresses and stamps. Shortly afterwards A decides not to send the offer but by mistake deposits it in the mail. It is delivered to B who "accepts" the offer. What result?

Would the result be different if A sent the offer while sleepwalking?

SECTION 8. TERMINATION OF A REVOCABLE OFFER AND ACCEPTANCE VARYING FROM OFFER

(Calamari & Perillo 5th §§ 2.20 and 2.21)

SWIFT & CO. v. SMIGEL

Superior Court of New Jersey, Appellate Division, 1971.
115 N.J.Super. 391, 279 A.2d 895, aff'd 60 N.J. 348, 289 A.2d 793.

CONFORD, P.J.A.D. Plaintiff Swift & Company instituted an action in the Superior Court against Erwin Smigel, executor of the estate of Joseph O. Smigel, for $8,509.60, the amount of merchandise it supplied the Pine Haven Nursing Home & Sanitarium, Inc. ("Pine Haven") upon credit. Plaintiff held continuing guaranties by decedent Smigel and third-party defendant Abe Kraig for payment of the indebtedness. The trial court granted defendant Erwin Smigel's motion for summary judgment, and entered judgment dismissing Swift's complaint and Smigel's third-party complaint against Kraig. Swift appeals from that judgment.

The action of the trial court was predicated upon Joseph Smigel's adjudication as an incompetent prior to the delivery of any of the merchandise for which claim is here made, and upon the authority of the supposed rule that mental incompetency of an offeror prior to acceptance by the offeree terminates the offer whether or not the offeree had notice of the incompetency at the time of the acceptance. *Restatement, Contracts*, § 48 at 56 (1932). The justification for any such rule, which has not heretofore been passed upon in any reported New Jersey case, is the main question before us for resolution.

The undisputed facts which emerge from the pleadings, motion papers, briefs and oral argument are these. To induce plaintiff to sell provisions to Pine Haven, the two equal owners of its stock, decedent Smigel and one Abe Kraig, on November 11, 1962 each entered into a written agreement of "continuing guaranty" with plaintiff undertaking to pay at maturity all indebtedness of Pine Haven for goods to be sold and delivered to it by plaintiff. Among other provisions, the agreement signed by Smigel purported to cover all liabilities the buyer might incur until ten days after receipt of notice from the guarantor or his legal representatives of withdrawal of the guaranty. No notice of withdrawal was ever given by Smigel or his representatives. Plaintiff asserts, and for the purpose of this appeal it must be accepted as a fact, that it never had knowledge of Smigel's incompetency during the period of delivery of the merchandise giving rise to the present claims, or previously.

We are without information on the basis of which it could be determined whether plaintiff reasonably should have known or been put on inquiry of facts which would have disclosed Smigel's incompetence. Smigel was adjudicated incompetent January 16, 1966, and letters of guardianship were issued to his son, the present defendant, on February 1, 1966. The unpaid-for merchandise was delivered during the period from January 4, 1967 to October 12, 1967. What the course of deliveries and payments therefor previously may have been is not disclosed by the record.

* * *

Neither of the parties to this appeal disputes that the agreement upon which this action was brought was a continuing guaranty of the kind "which is not limited to a particular transaction * * * but which is intended to cover future transactions". See *Fidelity Union Trust Co. v. Galm*, 109 N.J.L. 111, 116, 160 A. 645 (E. & A.1932). A continuing guaranty is at its inception an offer from the guarantor and is accepted by the creditor each time the latter does a specified act (*e.g.*, extending credit to the debtor). Typically, as here, such a guaranty reserves in the guarantor the power to revoke it unilaterally prior to action by way of acceptance by the creditor. 38 *Am.Jur.2d, Guaranty,* § 63 at 1064.

The specific question which concerns us here—whether an adjudication of mental incompetency of a guarantor operates automatically to revoke a continuing guaranty—has not been decided in any American case disclosed by research of the parties or our own. An English trial court decided that the continuing efficacy of the guaranty ceased only when the creditor became aware of the guarantor's insanity. The issue, however, was not involved in the reported appeal. *Bradford Old Bank v. Sutcliffe*, 2 K.B. 833 (Ct.App.1918).

The treatment of the question in the texts has been subsumed under the assumed analogy of death of the guarantor. Most of the few decided cases on the latter point have held that death terminates the guaranty without regard to knowledge by the creditor, on the purported general principle that the death of an offeror destroys one of the two essential assenting entities to a contract. See 10 *Williston, Contracts* (Jaeger–3d ed. 1967) § 1253 at 809–810; 1 *id.* § 62 at 206–207 (1957); *Restatement, Contracts*, § 48 at 56 (1932); *Restatement, Security*, § 87 at 250–252 (1941). A New Jersey trial court followed the general rule. *Teplitz*

Thrown Silk Co. v. Rich, 13 N.J.Misc. 494, 179 A. 305 (Cir.Ct.1935). Other typical such cases are *Jordan v. Dobbins,* 122 Mass. 168 (Sup.Jud. Ct.1877); *Aitken v. Lang,* 106 Ky. 652, 51 S.W. 154 (Ct.App.1899). The leading case to the contrary is *Gay v. Ward,* 67 Conn. 147, 34 A. 1025 (Sup.Ct.Err.1895), which stressed the diminished business utility of continuing guaranties if terminable without notice on death. Professor Corbin treats that case as representative of the preferred rule. 1 *Corbin, Contracts* (1963) § 54 at 229. See *infra.*

The conceptual underpinning of the notion that an offer should be deemed automatically revoked upon death or insanity of the offeror despite good-faith action by way of acceptance thereof by an unknowing offeree has been criticized by the leading writers on the subject.

Corbin comments:

It is very generally said that the death of the offeror terminates the offeree's power of acceptance even though the offeree has no knowledge of such death. Such general statements arose out of the earlier notion that a contract cannot be made without an actual meeting of minds at a single moment of time, a notion that has long been abandoned. The rule has also been supposed to follow by some logical necessity from the dictum that it takes two persons to make a contract. It is not contrary to that dictum to deny that death terminates power to accept; the offer was made by a living man and is accepted by another living man.

* * *

It has even been held, *and justly,* that the doing of the requested acts after the death of the offeror, but in ignorance thereof, consummates a contract. Thus, where through an agent an offeror orders the shipment of goods to the agent, and the offeree ships the goods in ignorance that the offeror has died, the offeree can collect the price from the offeror's estate. So, also, where one has given his promise to guarantee payment for goods to be sold, money to be lent, or service to be rendered to another, the sale or loan or service in ignorance of the promisor's death has been held to enable the promisee to enforce the promise of guaranty against the guarantor's estate. Some cases have held the contrary, however; and also it has been held that the offeree can not accept after he has knowledge that the offeror is dead. [1 *Corbin, op. cit.,* § 54 at 227–228, 229; emphasis added]

The case for terminating the offer on subsequent insanity of the offeror without knowledge of the offeree is found by Corbin "even more doubtful than the rule as to the offeror's death" as "[i]nsanity is far less easily determinable as a fact than is death, either by the contracting parties themselves or by a court." *Id.* at 231.

* * *

It is noteworthy, in the same vein, that the American Law Institute, although retaining in proposed *Restatement, Contracts 2d* (Tent.Dr. No. 1, 1964) the substance of section 48 of the *Restatement,* terminating an offeree's power of acceptance when the offeror (or offeree) dies or is deprived of legal capacity to enter into the proposed contract, apparently does so reluctantly and critically. Comment (a) to section 48 in *Restatement 2d*, reads:

Death of offeror. The offeror's death terminates the power of the offeree without notice to him. *This rule seems to be a relic of the obsolete view* that a contract requires a "meeting of minds," and it is out of harmony with the modern doctrine that a manifestation of assent is effective without regard to actual mental assent. See § 21. Some inroads have been made on the rule by statutes and decisions with respect to bank deposits and collections, and by legislation with respect to powers of attorney given by servicemen. See Uniform Commercial Code § 4–405; *Restatement of Agency Second* § 120 and Comment a. In the absence of legislation, the rule remains in effect. [Emphasis added]

See the comparable criticism of the rationale of the principle of automatic revocation of offers on death or insanity of the offeror in Oliphant, "Duration and Termination of an Offer," 18 Mich.L.Rev. 201, 209–211 (1919), and in Note, 24 Colum.L.Rev. 294 (1924), in both of which that rule is found to violate the reasonable expectations of an offeree without knowledge of the offeror's death or other disability. In the latter the observation is made:

Contract and tort liabilities pass to personal representatives. Why not liability under an offer? If we adopt a test objective as to the offeror and ask, "What is the scope of the offeree's reasonable expectation?," it would seem that notice of the death should be required to terminate the offer. [at 295]

In view of the foregoing criticisms of the conventional approach, which strike us as persuasive, we are not disposed, in determination of this first-instance litigation on the point, routinely to follow existing standard formulations on the subject. The search should be for the rule which will accord with the reasonable expectations of persons in the business community involved in transactions of this kind. In that regard, moreover, we bear no responsibility in this case for determining the rule in the case of death of the guarantor but only in that of his adjudication of incompetency. There may be material differences in the respective situations, as noted in the excerpt quoted from *Corbin, supra*. Furthermore, our New Jersey cases on the effect of insanity on contract liability, as will be seen *infra*, also call for a special approach to the guaranty question in the insanity context.

In broad terms, the law of contracts has been said to "attempt[s] the realization of reasonable expectations that have been induced by the making of a promise." 1 *Corbin, op. cit.*, § 1 at 2. In the present instance decedent promised plaintiff to make good any bills for provisions incurred by a corporate business enterprise in which he had a one-half stock interest. Had he not done so plaintiff presumably would not have taken on the business risk of selling to the corporation. It would seem to us that if plaintiff neither knew nor had any reason to know of decedent's later adjudication as an incompetent during any portion of the time it was making the deliveries which gave rise to the debts here sued on, plaintiff's reasonable expectations based on decedent's original continuing promise would be unjustifiably defeated by denial of recovery.

If the situation is judged in terms of relative convenience, it would seem easier and more expectable for the guardian of the incompetent to notify at least those people with whom the incompetent had been doing business of the fact of adjudication than for the holder of a guaranty such as here to have to make a specific inquiry as to competency of the guarantor on each occasion of an advance of credit to the principal debtor. *Cf. Gay v. Ward*, supra, 34 A., at 1026.

We have thus far been considering the problem presented on the theory that decedent's accountability should soundly be appraised on the basis of reasonable expectations and reliance of others stemming from his act of execution of the guaranty. On that approach his subsequent incompetency would be irrelevant, for he was competent when he acted. The theoretical basis for the conventional view of automatic termination of the continuing guaranty on insanity, however, is that there is a renewal of the offer on each occasion of acceptance thereof by the offeree, and that renewal cannot be effected by one without legal capacity at the time. See Note, 24 Colum.Law Rev., *op. cit.*, at p. 295. But even if we adhered to that concept of the jural conduct of the guarantor in a continuing guaranty, immunity of defendant in the present situation as a matter of law would not square with existing New Jersey cases as to the liability of persons who, lacking mental capacity, contract with others having no knowledge of that fact and parting with valuable consideration.

In *Manufacturers Trust Co. v. Podvin*, 10 N.J. 199, 207–208, 89 A.2d 672 (1952), the court approved the rule declared in the early case of *Drake v. Crowell*, 40 N.J.L. 58, 59 (Sup.Ct.1878), to the effect that:

> The law in this state is settled, that contracts with lunatics and insane persons are invalid, subject to the qualification that a contract made in good faith with a lunatic, for a full consideration, which has been executed without knowledge of the insanity, or such information as would lead a prudent person to the belief of the incapacity, will be sustained.

The qualification stated was applied by the court in the *Drake* case in favor of an unknowing party dealing with the alleged incompetent. In accord, *South Orange Trust Co. v. Hartley*, 29 N.J.Super. 58, 60, 101 A.2d 616 (Ch.Div.1953). * * *

It is thus clear that whatever view is taken as to the appropriate theoretical basis for determining the decedent's liability in this fact pattern, the decisive consideration should be the presence or absence of knowledge by plaintiff, actual or reasonably to be imputed, of decedent's incompetency at the time of each advance of credit pursuant to the guaranty.

Moreover, if at the trial plaintiff's knowledge is established by defendant, the issue of decedent's incompetency would not necessarily be concluded by proof of the fact of adjudication of incompetency. The decisions in this State leave no doubt that that fact is not conclusive but only *prima facie* evidence of legal incompetency. *Eckman v. Wood*, 108 N.J.L. 105, 108, 154 A. 862 (E. & A.1931); *American National Red Cross v. Lester*, 129 N.J.Eq. 28, 18 A.2d 295 (E. & A.1941); *Coombs v. Witte*, 104 N.J.L. 519, 140 A. 408 (E. & A.1928).

The entire judgment, including the dismissal of the third-party complaint, is reversed and the cause is remanded to the Law Division for further proceedings consonant with this opinion.

Disposition [handwritten annotation in left margin]

Problems

88.   On January 29, D sent a letter dated January 29, which stated, "Will give you eight days to accept or reject." P received the offer on February 2. On February 8, P sent an acceptance which was received by D on February 9th. (a) Was the acceptance timely? (b) Would the result be different if there was a delay in transmission of the offer and without the delay the offer would have arrived on January 30th?

89.   A sends a telegraphic offer to sell oil at a fixed price which at the time is subject to rapid fluctuations in price. The offer is received near the close of business hours, and a telegraphic acceptance is sent the next day, after the offeree has learned of a sharp price rise. Is there a contract?

90.   On May 27, 1837 the City of Boston caused the following reward offer to be published: "The frequent and successful repetition of incendiary attempts renders it necessary that the most vigorous efforts should be made to prevent their recurrence. One thousand dollars will be paid by the City for information leading to the apprehension and conviction of any person engaged in these nefarious practices." The offer was published for one week. No attempt was ever made to withdraw it. From the time of the reward notice until early 1841 there were very few fires in Boston. The fire in question was set in January of 1841 and the conviction occurred in March of 1841. Is the plaintiff entitled to the reward if he supplied information leading to the apprehension and conviction of an arsonist?

91.   The defendant offered a reward of $200 for information leading to the conviction of the person who set a specific fire. Three years and 2 months later the culprit was convicted as a result of information supplied by the plaintiff three months before the trial. Is the plaintiff entitled to the reward?

92.   D was interviewed live for a late-night TV news show in which viewers were encouraged to call in. The name of the show and the telephone number were flashed periodically on the screen. During the interview, D stated that "If anybody calls this show and cites any section of the Internal Revenue Code that says an individual is required to file a tax return, I'll pay them $100,000." A few hours later a taped segment of this interview was rebroadcast on the morning news. P saw the rebroadcast, researched income tax law and the following day called the morning news show (at a different number than had been flashed on the screen during the original broadcast) and cited the appropriate Code sections. D refused to pay. P sues D. What result?

93. A made an offer to B relating to certain hay on June 15. Slightly after the passage of a reasonable time, on June 20, B sent a card of acceptance. A never replied. Was there a contract?

94. O, the owner of Greenacre sent offers to sell the property on specified terms to a number of prospective buyers. Each offer contained the phrase, "subject to prior sale." Within a reasonable time, A accepted the offer. Thereafter, but still within a reasonable time, B sent an acceptance to O. Is O liable to both A and B?

95. B offered to buy from S a specified quantity of a certain pesticide. While the offer was still open the Environmental Protection Agency promulgated a rule banning the sale or use of the pesticide. S immediately dispatched an acceptance of the offer. Is there a contract?

96. Hoover offered to buy certain real property from Clements. Soon thereafter they talked on the telephone. Clements expressed a strong interest in accepting and suggested that they meet to discuss certain details. Hoover then said: "We have not decided, we might not want to go through with it." Clements immediately responded, "I accept your offer." Was there a contract?

97. A, a newspaper, publishes an offer of prizes to the persons who procure the largest number of subscriptions as evidenced by cash or checks received by a specified time. B completes and mails an entry blank giving B's name and address, that is received by A. Thereafter during the contest, A publishes a notice that personal checks will not be counted; B does not see the notice. Is B bound by the notice?

98. Defendant railroad posted a notice that the ticket price for passage from Norwich to New London was 50 cents if purchased in advance and 55 cents if purchased from the conductor on board the train. Plaintiff boarded with no ticket and tendered 50 cents to the conductor, explaining that he went to the ticket office a reasonable time before the train's departure, but the office was closed. When he refused to pay the 55 cent fare, the conductor and another railroad employee seized him and threw him off the train onto the ground while the train was not in motion. As the train was starting up again, plaintiff grabbed onto the rear of the car in an attempt to climb aboard when a railroad employee kicked him in the face, throwing him back on the ground breaking his kneecap. [It would make a nice movie vignette starring Clint Eastwood as the passenger.] Does Plaintiff have a claim for breach of contract?

99. S makes an offer to sell a piece of real property to A and then makes the same offer to B; A accepts; B learns of A's acceptance. May B accept?

100. A offers to work as a full-time typist in B's office during the next year, the offer to remain open for 10 days. B then hears reliable information that A has agreed to work for C during the same year. May B accept A's offer?

101. B offers to hire A as a typist and A hears reliable information that B hired another typist for his office for the same period. May A accept B's offer?

SECTION 9. COUNTER–OFFERS AND THE BATTLE OF THE FORMS

(Calamari & Perillo 5th § 2.21 and 2.12)

DORTON v. COLLINS & AIKMAN CORP.

United States Court of Appeals, Sixth Circuit, 1972.
453 F.2d 1161.

CELEBREZZE, CIRCUIT JUDGE.

* * *

The primary question before us on appeal is whether the District Court, in denying Collins & Aikman's motion for a stay pending arbitration, erred in holding that The Carpet Mart was not bound by the arbitration agreement appearing on the back of Collins & Aikman's acknowledgment forms. * * *

In each of the more than 55 transactions, one of the partners in The Carpet Mart, or, on some occasions, Collins & Aikman's visiting salesman, telephoned Collins & Aikman's order department in Dalton, Georgia, and ordered certain quantities of carpets listed in Collins & Aikman's catalogue. There is some dispute as to what, if any, agreements were reached through the telephone calls and through the visits by Collins & Aikman's salesman. After each oral order was placed, the price, if any, quoted by the buyer was checked against Collins & Aikman's price list, and the credit department was consulted to determine if The Carpet Mart had paid for all previous shipments. After it was found that everything was in order, Collins & Aikman's order department typed the information concerning the particular order on one of its printed acknowledgment forms. Each acknowledgment form bore one of three legends: "Acknowledgment," "Customer Acknowledgment," or "Sales Contract." The following provision was printed on the face of the forms bearing the "Acknowledgment" legend:

> "The acceptance of your order is subject to all of the terms and conditions on the face and reverse side hereof, including arbitration, all of which are accepted by buyer; it supersedes buyer's order form, if any. It shall become a contract either (a) when signed and delivered by buyer to seller and accepted in writing by seller, or (b) at Seller's option, when buyer shall have given to seller specification of assortments, delivery dates, shipping instructions, or instructions to bill and hold as to all or any part of the merchandise herein described, or when buyer has received delivery of the whole or any part thereof, or when buyer has otherwise assented to the terms and conditions hereof."

Similarly, on the face of the forms bearing the "Customer Acknowledgment" or "Sales Contract" legends the following provision appeared:

> "This order is given subject to all of the terms and conditions on the face and reverse side hereof, including the provisions for arbitration

and the exclusion of warranties, all of which are accepted by Buyer, supersede Buyer's order form, if any, and constitute the entire contract between Buyer and Seller. This order shall become a contract as to the entire quantity specified either (a) when signed and delivered by Buyer to Seller and accepted in writing by Seller or (b) when Buyer has received and retained this order for ten days without objection, or (c) when Buyer has accepted delivery of any part of the merchandise specified herein or has furnished to Seller specifications or assortments, delivery dates, shipping instructions, or instructions to bill and hold, or when Buyer has otherwise indicated acceptance of the terms hereof.''

The small print on the reverse side of the forms provided, among other things, that all claims arising out of the contract would be submitted to arbitration in New York City. Each acknowledgment form was signed by an employee of Collins & Aikman's order department and mailed to The Carpet Mart on the day the telephone order was received or, at the latest, on the following day. The carpets were thereafter shipped to The Carpet Mart, with the interval between the mailing of the acknowledgment form and shipment of the carpets varying from a brief interval to a period of several weeks or months. Absent a delay in the mails, however, The Carpet Mart always received the acknowledgment forms prior to receiving the carpets. In all cases The Carpet Mart took delivery of and paid for the carpets without objecting to any terms contained in the acknowledgment form.

Holding

In holding that no binding arbitration agreement was created between the parties through the transactions above, the District Court relied on T.C.A. § 47–2–207 [UCC § 2–207], which provides:

"(1) A definite and seasonable expression of acceptance or a written confirmation which is sent within a reasonable time operates as an acceptance even though it states terms additional to or different from those offered or agreed upon, unless acceptance is expressly made conditional on assent to the additional or different terms.

"(2) The additional terms are to be construed as proposals for addition to the contract. Between merchants such terms become part of the contract unless: (a) the offer expressly limits acceptance to the terms of the offer; (b) they materially alter it; or (c) notification of objection to them has already been given or is given within a reasonable time after notice of them is received.

"(3) Conduct by both parties which recognizes the existence of a contract is sufficient to establish a contract for sale although the writings of the parties do not otherwise establish a contract. In such case the terms of the particular contract consist of those terms on which the writings of the parties agree, together with any supplementary terms incorporated under any other provisions of chapters 1 through 9 of this title.''

The District Court found that Subsection 2–207(3) controlled the instant case, quoting the following passage from 1 W. Hawkland, A Transactional Guide to the Uniform Commercial Code § 1.090303, at 19–20 (1964):

> "If the seller . . . ships the goods and the buyer accepts them, a contract is formed under subsection (3). The terms of this contract are those on which the purchase order and acknowledgment agree, and the additional terms needed for a contract are to be found throughout the U.C.C.
>
> . . . [T]he U.C.C. does not impose an arbitration term on the parties where their contract is silent on the matter. Hence, a conflict between an arbitration and an no-arbitration clause would result in the no-arbitration clause becoming effective."

Under this authority alone the District Court concluded that the arbitration clause on the back of Collins & Aikman's sales acknowledgment had not become a binding term in the 50–odd transactions with The Carpet Mart.

* * *

As Official Comment No. 1 indicates, UCC § 2–207 was intended to apply to two situations:

> "The one is where an agreement has been reached either orally or by informal correspondence between the parties and is followed by one or both of the parties sending formal acknowledgments or memoranda embodying the terms so far as agreed upon and adding terms not discussed. The other situation is one in which a wire or letter expressed and intended as the closing or confirmation of an agreement adds further minor suggestions or proposals such as 'ship by Tuesday,' 'rush,' 'ship draft against bill of lading inspection allowed,' or the like." T.C.A. § 47–2–207 [UCC § 2–207], Official Comment 1.

Although Comment No. 1 is itself somewhat ambiguous, it is clear that Section 2–207, and specifically Subsection 2–207(1), was intended to alter the "ribbon matching" or "mirror" rule of common law, under which the terms of an acceptance or confirmation were required to be identical to the terms of the offer or oral agreement, respectively. 1 W. Hawkland, *supra*, at 16; R. Nordstrom, Handbook of the Law of Sales, Sec. 37, at 99–100 (1970). Under the common law, an acceptance or a confirmation which contained terms additional to or different from those of the offer or oral agreement constituted a rejection of the offer or agreement and thus became a counter-offer. The terms of the counter-offer were said to have been accepted by the original offeror when he proceeded to perform under the contract without objecting to the counter-offer. Thus, a buyer was deemed to have accepted the seller's counter-offer if he took receipt of the goods and paid for them without objection.

Under Section 2–207 the result is different. This section of the Code recognizes that in current commercial transactions, the terms of the offer and those of the acceptance will seldom be identical. Rather, under the current "battle of the forms," each party typically has a printed form drafted by his attorney and containing as many terms as could be envisioned to favor that party in his sales transactions. Whereas under common law the disparity between the fine-print terms in the parties' forms would have prevented the consummation of a contract when these forms are exchanged, Section 2–207 recognizes that in many, but not all, cases the parties do not impart such significance to the terms on the printed forms. *See* 1 W. Hawkland, *supra*; § 1.0903, at 14, § 1.090301, at 16. Subsection 2–207(1) therefore provides that "[a] definite and season-able expression of acceptance or a written confirmation ... operates as an acceptance even though it states terms additional to or different from those offered or agreed upon, unless acceptance is expressly made conditional on assent to the additional or different terms." Thus, under Subsection (1), a contract is recognized notwithstanding the fact that an acceptance or confirmation contains terms additional to or different from those of the offer or prior agreement, provided that the offeree's intent to accept the offer is definitely expressed, *see* Sections 2–204 and 2–206, and provided that the offeree's acceptance is not expressly conditioned on the offeror's assent to the additional or different terms. When a contract is recognized under Subsection (1), the additional terms are treated as "proposals for addition to the contract" under Subsection (2), which contains special provisions under which such additional terms are deemed to have been accepted when the transaction is between merchants. Conversely, when no contract is recognized under Subsection 2–207(1)—either because no definite expression of acceptance exists or, more specifically, because the offeree's acceptance is expressly conditioned on the offeror's assent to the additional or different terms—the entire transaction aborts at this point. If, however, the subsequent conduct of the parties—particularly, performance by both parties under what they apparently believe to be a contract—recognizes the existence of a contract, under Subsection 2–207(3) such conduct by both parties is sufficient to establish a contract, notwithstanding the fact that no contract would have been recognized on the basis of their writings alone. Subsection 2–207(3) further provides how the terms of contracts recognized thereunder shall be determined.

With the above analysis and purposes of Section 2–207 in mind, we turn to their application in the present case. We initially observe that the affidavits and the acknowledgment forms themselves raise the question of whether Collins & Aikman's forms constituted acceptances or confirmations under Section 2–207. The language of some of the acknowledgment forms ("The acceptance of your order is subject to ... ") and the affidavit of Mr. William T. Hester, Collins & Aikman's marketing operations manager, suggest that the forms were the only acceptances issued in response to The Carpet Mart's oral offers. However, in his affidavit Mr. J.A. Castle, a partner in The Carpet Mart, asserted that when he personally called Collins & Aikman to order carpets, someone from the latter's order department would agree to sell the requested carpets, or, alternatively, when Collins & Aikman's visiting salesman took the order, he would agree to the sale, on some occasions after he had used The Carpet Mart's telephone to call Collins & Aikman's order department. Absent the District Court's determination of whether Collins & Aikman's acknowledgment forms were acceptances or, alternatively, confirmations of prior oral agreements, we will consider the application of Section 2–207 to both situations for the guidance of the District Court on remand.

Viewing Collins & Aikman's acknowledgment forms as acceptances under Subsection 2–207(1), we are initially faced with the question of whether the arbitration provision in Collins & Aikman's acknowledgment forms were in fact "additional to or different from" the terms of The Carpet Mart's oral offers. In the typical case under Section 2–207, there exist both a written purchase order and a written acknowledgment, and this determination can be readily made by comparing the two forms. In the present case, where the only written forms were Collins & Aikman's sales acknowledgments, we believe that such a comparison must be made between the oral offers and the written acceptances. Although the District Court apparently assumed that The Carpet Mart's oral orders did not include in their terms the arbitration provision which appeared in Collins & Aikman's acknowledgment forms, we believe that a specific finding on this point will be required on remand.

Assuming, for purposes of analysis, that the arbitration provision was an addition to the terms of The Carpet Mart's oral offers, we must next determine whether or not Collins & Aikman's acceptances were "expressly made conditional on assent to the additional ... terms" therein, within the proviso of Subsection 2–207(1). As set forth in full above, the provision appearing on the face of Collins & Aikman's acknowledgment forms stated that the acceptances (or orders) were "subject to all of the terms and conditions on the face and reverse side hereof, including arbitration, all of which are accepted by buyer." The provision on the "Acknowledgment" forms further stated that Collins & Aikman's terms would become the basis of the contract between the parties

> "either (a) when signed and delivered by buyer to seller and accepted in writing by seller, or (b) at Seller's option, when buyer shall have given to seller specification of assortments, delivery dates, shipping instructions, or instructions to bill and hold as to all or any part of the merchandise herein described, or when buyer has received delivery of the whole or any part thereof, or when buyer has otherwise assented to the terms and conditions hereof."

Similarly, the provision on the "Customer Acknowledgment" and "Sales Contract" forms stated that the terms therein would become the basis of the contract

> "either (a) when signed and delivered by Buyer to Seller and accepted in writing by Seller or (b) when Buyer has received and retained this order for ten days without objection, or (c) when Buyer

has accepted delivery of any part of the merchandise specified herein or has furnished to Seller specifications or assortments, delivery dates, shipping instructions to bill and hold, or when Buyer has otherwise indicated acceptance of the terms hereof."

Although Collins & Aikman's use of the words "subject to" suggests that the acceptances were conditional to some extent, we do not believe the acceptances were "expressly made conditional on [the buyer's] assent to the additional or different terms," as specifically required under the Subsection 2–207(1) proviso. In order to fall within this proviso, it is not enough that an acceptance is expressly conditional on additional or different terms; rather, an acceptance must be *expressly* conditional on the offeror's *assent* to those terms. Viewing the Subsection (1) proviso within the context of the rest of that Subsection and within the policies of Section 2–207 itself, we believe that it was intended to apply only to an acceptance which clearly reveals that the offeree is unwilling to proceed with the transaction unless he is assured of the offeror's assent to the additional or different terms therein. *See* 1 W. Hawkland, *supra*, § 1.090303, at 21. That the acceptance is predicated on the offeror's assent must be "directly and distinctly stated or expressed rather than implied or left to inference." Webster's Third International Dictionary (defining "express").

Although the UCC does not provide a definition of "assent," it is significant that Collins & Aikman's printed acknowledgment forms specified at least seven types of action or inaction on the part of the buyer which—sometimes at Collins & Aikman's option—would be deemed to bind the buyer to the terms therein. These ranged from the buyer's signing and delivering the acknowledgment to the seller—which indeed could have been recognized as the buyer's assent to Collins & Aikman's terms—to the buyer's retention of the acknowledgment for ten days without objection—which could never have been recognized as the buyer's assent to the additional or different terms where acceptance is expressly conditional on that assent.

To recognize Collins & Aikman's acceptances as "expressly conditional on [the buyer's] assent to the additional ... terms" therein, within the proviso of Subsection 2–207(1), would thus require us to ignore the specific language of that provision. Such an interpretation is not justified in view of the fact that Subsection 2–207(1) is clearly designed to give legal recognition to many contracts where the variance between the offer and acceptance would have precluded such recognition at common law.

Because Collins & Aikman's acceptances were not expressly conditional on the buyer's assent to the additional terms within the proviso of Subsection 2–207(1), a contract is recognized under Subsection (1), and the additional terms are treated as "proposals" for addition to the contract under Subsection 2–207(2). Since both Collins & Aikman and The Carpet Mart are clearly "merchants" as that term is defined in Subsection 2–104(1), the arbitration provision will be deemed to have been accepted by The Carpet Mart under Subsection 2–207(2) unless it materially altered the terms of The Carpet Mart's oral offers. T.C.A. § 47–2–207(2)(b) [UCC § 2–207(2)(b)]. We believe that the question of whether the arbitration provision materially altered the oral offer under Subsection 2–207(2)(b) is one which can be resolved only by the District Court on further findings of fact in the present case. If the arbitration provision did in fact materially alter The Carpet Mart's offer, it could not become a part of the contract "unless expressly agreed to" by The Carpet Mart. T.C.A. § 47–2–207 [UCC § 2–207], Official Comment No. 3.

We therefore conclude that if on remand the District Court finds that Collins & Aikman's acknowledgments were in fact acceptances and that the arbitration provision was additional to the terms of The Carpet Mart's oral orders, contracts will be recognized under Subsection 2–207(1). The arbitration clause will then be viewed as a "proposal" under Subsection 2–207(2) which will be deemed to have been accepted by The Carpet Mart unless it materially altered the oral offers.

If the District Court finds that Collins & Aikman's acknowledgment forms were not acceptances but rather were confirmations of prior oral agreements between the parties, an application of Section 2–207 similar to that above will be required. Subsection 2–207(1) will require an initial determination of whether the arbitration provision in the confirmations was "additional to or different from" the terms orally agreed upon. Assuming that the District Court finds that the arbitration provision was not a term of the oral agreements between the parties, the arbitration clause will be treated as a "proposal" for addition to the contract under Subsection 2–207(2), as was the case when Collins & Aikman's acknowledgments were viewed as acceptances above. The provision for arbitration will be deemed to have been accepted by The Carpet Mart unless the District Court finds that it materially altered the prior oral agreements, in which case The Carpet Mart could not become bound thereby absent an express agreement to that effect.

As a result of the above application of Section 2–207 to the limited facts before us in the present case, we find it necessary to remand the case to the District Court for the following findings: (1) whether oral agreements were reached between the parties prior to the sending of Collins & Aikman's acknowledgment forms; if there were no such oral agreements, (2) whether the arbitration provision appearing in Collins & Aikman's "acceptances" was additional to the terms of The Carpet Mart's oral offers; and, if so, (3) whether the arbitration provision materially altered the terms of The Carpet Mart's oral offers. Alternatively, if the District Court does find that oral agreements were reached between the parties before Collins & Aikman's acknowledgment forms were sent in each instance, it will be necessary for the District Court to make the following findings: (1) whether the prior oral agreements embodied the arbitration provision appearing in Collins & Aikman's "confirmations"; and, if not, (2) whether the arbitration provision materially altered the prior oral agreements. Regardless of whether the District Court finds Collins & Aikman's acknowledgment forms to have been acceptances or confirmations, if the arbitration provision was additional to, and a material alteration of, the offers or prior oral agreements, The Carpet Mart will not be bound to that provision absent a finding that it expressly agreed to be bound thereby.

* * *

[Remanded for further findings.]

DIAMOND FRUIT GROWERS, INC. v. KRACK CORP.

United States Court of Appeals, Ninth Circuit, 1986.
794 F.2d 1440.

WIGGINS, CIRCUIT JUDGE:

Procedure

Metal–Matic, Inc. (Metal–Matic) appeals from judgment entered after a jury verdict in favor of Krack Corporation (Krack) on Krack's third-party complaint against Metal–Matic. Metal–Matic also appeals from the district court's denial of its motion for judgment n.o.v. We have jurisdiction under 28 U.S.C. § 1291 (1982) and affirm.

FACTS AND PROCEEDINGS BELOW

Krack is a manufacturer of cooling units that contain steel tubing it purchases from outside suppliers. Metal–Matic is one of Krack's tubing suppliers. At the time this dispute arose, Metal–Matic had been supplying tubing to Krack for about ten years. The parties followed the same course of dealing during the entire ten years. At the beginning of each year, Krack sent a blanket purchase order to Metal–Matic stating how much tubing Krack would need for the year. Then, throughout the year as Krack needed tubing, it sent release purchase orders to Metal–Matic requesting that tubing be shipped. Metal–Matic responded to Krack's release purchase orders by sending Krack an acknowledgment form and then shipping the tubing.[5]

Metal–Matic's acknowledgment form disclaimed all liability for consequential damages and limited Metal–Matic's liability for defects in the tubing to refund of the purchase price or replacement or repair of the tubing. As one would expect, these terms were not contained in Krack's purchase order. The following statement was printed on Metal–Matic's form: "Metal–Matic, Inc.'s acceptance of purchaser's offer or its offer to purchaser is hereby expressly made conditional to purchaser's acceptance of the terms and provisions of the acknowledgment form." This statement and the disclaimer of liability were on the back of the acknowledgment form. However, printed at the bottom of the front of the form in bold-face capitals was the following statement: "SEE REVERSE SIDE FOR TERMS AND CONDITIONS OF SALE."

---

5. The blanket purchase order apparently did no more than establish Krack's willingness to purchase an amount of tubing during the year. The parties' conduct indicates that they intended to establish their contract based on Krack's release purchase orders and Metal–Matic's acknowledgments sent in response to those purchase orders.

On at least one occasion during the ten-year relationship between Metal–Matic and Krack, Allen Zver, Krack's purchasing manager, discussed the limitation of warranty and disclaimer of liability terms contained in Metal–Matic's acknowledgment form with Robert Van Krevelen, Executive Vice President of Metal–Matic. Zver told Van Krevelen that Krack objected to the terms and tried to convince him to change them, but Van Krevelen refused to do so. After the discussions, Krack continued to accept and pay for tubing from Metal–Matic.

In February 1981, Krack sold one of its cooling units to Diamond Fruit Growers, Inc. (Diamond) in Oregon, and in September 1981, Diamond installed the unit in a controlled-atmosphere warehouse. In January 1982, the unit began leaking ammonia from a cooling coil made of steel tubing.

After Diamond discovered that ammonia was leaking into the warehouse, Joseph Smith, the engineer who had been responsible for building Diamond's controlled-atmosphere warehouses, was called in to find the source of the leak. Smith testified that he found a pinhole leak in the cooling coil of the Krack cooling unit. Smith inspected the coil while it was still inside the unit. He last inspected the coil on April 23, 1982. The coil then sat in a hall at Diamond's warehouse until May, 1984, when John Myers inspected the coil for Metal–Matic.

Myers cut the defective tubing out of the unit and took it to his office. At his office, he did more cutting on the tubing. After Myers inspected the tubing, it was also inspected by Bruce Wong for Diamond and Paul Irish for Krack.

Diamond sued Krack to recover the loss in value of fruit that it was forced to remove from the storage room as a result of the leak. Krack in turn brought a third-party complaint against Metal–Matic and Van Huffel Tube Corporation (Van Huffel), another of its tubing suppliers, seeking contribution or indemnity in the event it was held liable to Diamond. At the close of the evidence, both Metal–Matic and Van Huffel moved for a directed verdict on the third party complaint. The court granted Van Huffel's motion based on evidence that the failed tubing was not manufactured by Van Huffel. The court denied Metal–Matic's motion.

The jury returned a verdict in favor of Diamond against Krack. It then found that Krack was entitled to contribution from Metal–Matic for thirty percent of Diamond's damages. Metal–Matic moved for judgment n.o.v. The court denied that motion and entered judgment on the jury verdict.

Metal–Matic raises two grounds for reversal. First, Metal–Matic contends that as part of its contract with Krack, it disclaimed all liability for consequential damages and specifically limited its liability for defects in the tubing to refund of the purchase price or replacement or repair of the tubing. Second, Metal–Matic asserts that the evidence does not support a finding that it manufactured the tubing in which the leak developed or that it caused the leak. We address each of these contentions in turn.

* * *

DISCUSSION

A. *Metal–Matic's Disclaimer of Liability for Consequential Damages*

If the contract between Metal–Matic and Krack contains Metal–Matic's disclaimer of liability, Metal–Matic is not liable to indemnify Krack for part of Diamond's damages. Therefore, the principal issue before us on this appeal is whether Metal–Matic's disclaimer of liability became part of the contract between these parties.

Relying on Uniform Commercial Code (U.C.C.) § 2–207, Or.Rev. Stat. § 72.2070 (1985), Krack argues that Metal–Matic's disclaimer did not become part of the contract. Metal–Matic, on the other hand, argues that section 2–207 is inapplicable to this case because the parties discussed the disclaimer, and Krack assented to it.

Krack is correct in its assertion that section 2–207 applies to this case. One intended application of section 2–207 is to commercial transactions in which the parties exchange printed purchase order and acknowledgment forms. *See* U.C.C. § 2–207 comment 1. The drafters of the U.C.C. recognized that "[b]ecause the [purchase order and acknowledgment] forms are oriented to the thinking of the respective drafting parties, the terms contained in them often do not correspond." *Id.* Section 2–207 is an attempt to provide rules of contract formation in such cases. In this case, Krack and Metal–Matic exchanged purchase order and acknowledgment forms that contained different or additional terms. This, then, is a typical section 2–207 situation. The fact that the parties discussed the terms of their contract after they exchanged their forms does not put this case outside section 2–207. *See* 3 R. Duesenburg & L. King, *Sales and Bulk Transfers under the Uniform Commercial Code* (Bender's U.C.C. Service) § 3.05[2] (1986). Section 2–207 provides rules of contract formation in cases such as this one in which the parties exchange forms but do not agree on all the terms of their contact.

A brief summary of section 2–207 is necessary to an understanding of its application to this case.[5] Section 2–207 changes the common law's

---

5. U.C.C. § 2–207, Or.Rev.Stat. § 72.2070, provides:

Additional terms in acceptance or confirmation.

(1) A definite and seasonable expression of acceptance or a written confirmation which is sent within a reasonable time operates as an acceptance even though it states terms additional to or different from those offered or agreed upon, unless acceptance is expressly made conditional on assent to the additional or different terms.

(2) The additional terms are to be construed as proposals for addition to the contract. Between merchants such terms become part of the contract unless:

(a) The offer expressly limits acceptance to the terms of the offer;

(b) They materially alter it; or

(c) Notification of objection to them has already been given or is given within a reasonable time after notice of them is received.

(3) Conduct by both parties which recognizes the existence of a contract is suf-

mirror–image rule for transactions that fall within article 2 of the U.C.C. At common law, an acceptance that varies the terms of the offer is a counteroffer and operates as a rejection of the original offer. *See Idaho Power Co. v. Westinghouse Electric Corp.*, 596 F.2d 924, 926 (9th Cir. 1979). If the offeror goes ahead with the contract after receiving the counteroffer, his performance is an acceptance of the terms of the counteroffer. *See C. Itoh & Co. v. Jordan International Co.*, 552 F.2d 1228, 1236 (7th Cir.1977); J. White & R. Summers, *Handbook of the Law Under the Uniform Commercial Code*, § 1–2 at 34 (2d ed. 1980).

Generally, section 2–207(1) "converts a common law counteroffer into an acceptance even though it states additional or different terms." *Idaho Power*, 596 F.2d at 926; *see* U.C.C. § 2–207(1). The only requirement under section 2–207(1) is that the responding form contain a definite and seasonable expression of acceptance. The terms of the responding form that correspond to the offer constitute the contract. Under section 2–207(2), the additional terms of the responding form become proposals for additions to the contract. Between merchants the additional terms become part of the contract unless the offer is specifically limited to its terms, the offeror objects to the additional terms, or the additional terms materially alter the terms of the offer. U.C.C. § 2–207(2); *see* J. White & R. Summers, § 1–2 at 32.

However, section 2–207(1) is subject to a proviso. If a definite and seasonable expression of acceptance expressly conditions acceptance on the offeror's assent to additional or different terms contained therein, the parties' differing forms do not result in a contract unless the offeror assents to the additional terms. *See* J. White & R. Summers, § 1–2 at 32–33. If the offeror assents, the parties have a contract and the additional terms are a part of that contract. If, however, the offeror does not assent, but the parties proceed with the transaction as if they have a contract, their performance results in formation of a contract. U.C.C. § 2–207(3). In that case, the terms of the contract are those on which the parties' forms agree plus any terms supplied by the U.C.C. *Id.; see Boise Cascade Corp. v. Etsco, Ltd.*, 39 U.C.C.Rep.Serv. (Callaghan) 410, 414 (D.Or.1984); J. White & R. Summers, § 1–2 at 34.

In this case, Metal–Matic expressly conditioned its acceptance on Krack's assent to the additional terms contained in Metal–Matic's acknowledgment form. That form tracks the language of the section 2–207(1) proviso, stating that "Metal–Matic, Inc.'s acceptance . . . is hereby *expressly made conditional* to purchaser's acceptance of the terms and provisions of the acknowledgment form." (emphasis added). *See C. Itoh & Co.*, 552 F.2d at 1235. Therefore, we must determine whether Krack assented to Metal–Matic's limitation of liability term.

ficient to establish a contract for sale although the writings of the parties do not otherwise establish a contract. In such case the terms of the particular contract consist of those terms on which the writings of the parties agree, together with any supplementary terms incorporated under any other provisions of the Uniform Commercial Code.

Metal–Matic argues that Krack did assent to the limitation of liability term. This argument is based on the discussions between Zver for Krack and Van Krevelen for Metal–Matic. Some time during the ten-year relationship between the companies, these two men discussed Krack's objections to the warranty and liability limitation terms in Metal–Matic's acknowledgment form. Krack attempted to persuade Metal–Matic to change its form, but Metal–Matic refused to do so. After the discussions, the companies continued to do business as in the past. Metal–Matic contends that Krack assented to the limitation of liability term when it continued to accept and pay for tubing after Metal–Matic insisted that the contract contain its terms.

To address Metal–Matic's argument, we must determine what constitutes assent to additional or different terms for purposes of section 2–207(1). The parties have not directed us to any cases that analyze this question and our research has revealed none.[1] We therefore look to the language and structure of section 2–207 and to the purposes behind that section to determine the correct standard.

One of the principles underlying section 2–207 is neutrality. If possible, the section should be interpreted so as to give neither party to a contract an advantage simply because it happened to send the first or in some cases the last form. *See* J. White & R. Summers, § 1–2 at 26–27. Section 2–207 accomplishes this result in part by doing away with the common law's "last shot" rule. *See* 3 R. Duesenberg & L. King, § 3.05[1][a][iii] at 3–73. At common law, the offeree/counterofferor gets all of its terms simply because it fired the last shot in the exchange of forms. Section 2–207(3) does away with this result by giving neither party the terms it attempted to impose unilaterally on the other. *See id.* at 3–71. Instead, all of the terms on which the parties' forms do not agree drop out, and the U.C.C. supplies the missing terms.

Generally, this result is fair because both parties are responsible for the ambiguity in their contract. The parties could have negotiated a contract and agreed on its terms, but for whatever reason, they failed to do so. Therefore, neither party should get its terms. *See* 3 R. Duesenberg & L. King, § 3.05[2] at 3–88. However, as White and Summers point out, resort to section 2–207(3) will often work to the disadvantage of the seller because he will "wish to undertake less responsibility for the quality of his goods than the Code imposes or else wish to limit his damages liability more narrowly than would the Code." J. White & R. Summers, § 1–2 at 34. Nevertheless, White and Summers recommend that section 2–207(3) be applied in such cases. *Id.* We agree. Application of section 2–207(3) is more equitable than giving one party its terms simply because it sent the last form. Further, the terms imposed by the

---

1. The United States District Court for the District of Columbia has decided a case on this issue. However, the case is of little precedential value because the court provided no analysis to support its decision. In *McKenzie v. Alla–Ohio Coals, Inc.,* 29 U.C.C.Rep.Serv. (Callaghan) 852, 855 (D.D.C.1979), the offeror objected to a term in the offeree's form. The offeree reaffirmed that term, and the offeror made no further objection. The court held that the term was part of the contract because the parties continued to behave as if they had a contract after the offeree reaffirmed the term.

code are presumably equitable and consistent with public policy because
they are statutorily imposed. *See* 3 R. Duesenberg & L. King, § 3.05[2]
at 3–88.

With these general principles in mind, we turn now to Metal–Matic's
argument that Krack assented to the disclaimer when it continued to
accept and pay for tubing once Metal–Matic indicated that it was willing
to sell tubing only if its warranty and liability terms were part of the
contract. Metal–Matic's argument is appealing. Sound policy supports
permitting a seller to control the terms on which it will sell its products,
especially in a case in which the seller has indicated both in writing and
orally that those are the only terms on which it is willing to sell the
product. Nevertheless, we reject Metal–Matic's argument because we
find that these considerations are outweighed by the public policy
reflected by Oregon's enactment of the U.C.C.

If we were to accept Metal–Matic's argument, we would reinstate to
some extent the common law's last shot rule. To illustrate, assume that
the parties in this case had sent the same forms but in the reverse order
and that Krack's form contained terms stating that Metal–Matic is liable
for all consequential damages and conditioning acceptance on Metal–
Matic's assent to Krack's terms. Assume also that Metal–Matic objected
to Krack's terms but Krack refused to change them and that the parties
continued with their transaction anyway. If we applied Metal–Matic's
argument in that case, we would find that Krack's term was part of the
contract because Metal–Matic continued to ship tubing to Krack after
Krack reaffirmed that it would purchase tubing only if Metal–Matic were
fully liable for consequential damages. Thus, the result would turn on
which party sent the last form, and would therefore be inconsistent with
section 2–207's purpose of doing away with the last shot rule.

That result is avoided by requiring a specific and unequivocal
expression of assent on the part of the offeror when the offeree conditions its acceptance on assent to additional or different terms. If the
offeror does not give specific and unequivocal assent but the parties act
as if they have a contract, the provisions of section 2–207(3) apply to fill
in the terms of the contract. Application of section 2–207(3) is appropriate in that situation because by going ahead with the transaction
without resolving their dispute, both parties are responsible for introducing ambiguity into the contract. Further, in a case such as this one,
requiring the seller to assume more liability than it intends is not
altogether inappropriate. The seller is most responsible for the ambiguity because it inserts a term in its form that requires assent to additional
terms and then does not enforce that requirement. If the seller truly
does not want to be bound unless the buyer assents to its terms, it can
protect itself by not shipping until it obtains that assent. *See C. Itoh &
Co.*, 552 F.2d at 1238.

We hold that because Krack's conduct did not indicate unequivocally
that Krack intended to assent to Metal–Matic's terms, that conduct did

not amount to the assent contemplated by section 2–207(1). *See* 3 R. Duesenberg & L. King, § 3.05[1][a][iii] at 3–74.

* * *

The jury verdict is supported by the evidence and consistent with the U.C.C. Therefore, the district court did not err in denying Metal–Matic's motion for a directed verdict.

AFFIRMED.

HILL v. GATEWAY 2000, INC.

United States Court of Appeals, Seventh Circuit, 1997.
105 F.3d 1147.

EASTERBROOK, CIRCUIT JUDGE. A customer picks up the phone, orders a computer, and gives a credit card number. Presently a box arrives, containing the computer and a list of terms, said to govern unless the customer returns the computer within 30 days. Are these terms effective as the parties' contract, or is the contract term-free because the order-taker did not read any terms over the phone and elicit the customer's assent?

One of the terms in the box containing a Gateway 2000 system was an arbitration clause. Rich and Enza Hill, the customers, kept the computer more than 30 days before complaining about its components and performance. They filed suit in federal court arguing, among other things, that the product's shortcomings make Gateway a racketeer (mail and wire fraud are said to be the predicate offenses), leading to treble damages under RICO for the Hills and a class of all other purchasers. Gateway asked the district court to enforce the arbitration clause; the judge refused, writing that "[t]he present record is insufficient to support a finding of a valid arbitration agreement between the parties or that the plaintiffs were given adequate notice of the arbitration clause." Gateway took an immediate appeal, as is its right. 9 U.S.C. § 16(a)(1)(A).

The Hills say that the arbitration clause did not stand out: they concede noticing the statement of terms but deny reading it closely enough to discover the agreement to arbitrate, and they ask us to conclude that they therefore may go to court. Yet an agreement to arbitrate must be enforced "save upon such grounds as exist at law or in equity for the revocation of any contract." 9 U.S.C. § 2. *Doctor's Associates, Inc. v. Casarotto*, 517 U.S. 681, 116 S.Ct. 1652, 134 L.Ed.2d 902 (1996), holds that this provision of the Federal Arbitration Act is inconsistent with any requirement that an arbitration clause be prominent. A contract need not be read to be effective; people who accept take the risk that the unread terms may in retrospect prove unwelcome. *Carr v. CIGNA Securities, Inc.*, 95 F.3d 544, 547 (7th Cir.1996); *Chicago Pacific Corp. v. Canada Life Assurance Co.*, 850 F.2d 334 (7th Cir.1988). Terms inside Gateway's box stand or fall together. If they constitute the parties' contract because the Hills had an opportunity to return the computer after reading them, then all must be enforced.

ProCD, Inc. v. Zeidenberg, 86 F.3d 1447 (7th Cir.1996), holds that terms inside a box of software bind consumers who use the software after an opportunity to read the terms and to reject them by returning the product. Likewise, *Carnival Cruise Lines, Inc. v. Shute*, 499 U.S. 585, 111 S.Ct. 1522, 113 L.Ed.2d 622 (1991), enforces a forum-selection clause that was included among three pages of terms attached to a cruise ship ticket. ProCD and Carnival Cruise Lines exemplify the many commercial transactions in which people pay for products with terms to follow; ProCD discusses others. 86 F.3d at 1451–52. The district court concluded in ProCD that the contract is formed when the consumer pays for the software; as a result, the court held, only terms known to the consumer at that moment are part of the contract, and provisos inside the box do not count. Although this is one way a contract could be formed, it is not the only way: "A vendor, as master of the offer, may invite acceptance by conduct, and may propose limitations on the kind of conduct that constitutes acceptance. A buyer may accept by performing the acts the vendor proposes to treat as acceptance." *Id.* at 1452. Gateway shipped computers with the same sort of accept-or-return offer ProCD made to users of its software. ProCD relied on the Uniform Commercial Code rather than any peculiarities of Wisconsin law; both Illinois and South Dakota, the two states whose law might govern relations between Gateway and the Hills, have adopted the UCC; neither side has pointed us to any atypical doctrines in those states that might be pertinent; ProCD therefore applies to this dispute.

Plaintiffs ask us to limit ProCD to software, but where's the sense in that? ProCD is about the law of contract, not the law of software. Payment preceding the revelation of full terms is common for air transportation, insurance, and many other endeavors. Practical considerations support allowing vendors to enclose the full legal terms with their products. Cashiers cannot be expected to read legal documents to customers before ringing up sales. If the staff at the other end of the phone for direct-sales operations such as Gateway's had to read the four-page statement of terms before taking the buyer's credit card number, the droning voice would anesthetize rather than enlighten many potential buyers. Others would hang up in a rage over the waste of their time. And oral recitation would not avoid customers' assertions (whether true or feigned) that the clerk did not read term X to them, or that they did not remember or understand it. Writing provides benefits for both sides of commercial transactions. Customers as a group are better off when vendors skip costly and ineffectual steps such as telephonic recitation, and use instead a simple approve-or-return device. Competent adults are bound by such documents, read or unread. For what little it is worth, we add that the box from Gateway was crammed with software. The computer came with an operating system, without which it was useful only as a boat anchor. See *Digital Equipment Corp. v. Uniq Digital Technologies, Inc.*, 73 F.3d 756, 761 (7th Cir.1996). Gateway also included many application programs. So the Hills' effort to limit ProCD to software would not avail them factually, even if it were sound legally—which it is not.

For their second sally, the Hills contend that ProCD should be limited to executory contracts (to licenses in particular), and therefore does not apply because both parties' performance of this contract was complete when the box arrived at their home. This is legally and factually wrong: legally because the question at hand concerns the formation of the contract rather than its performance, and factually because both contracts were incompletely performed. ProCD did not depend on the fact that the seller characterized the transaction as a license rather than as a contract; we treated it as a contract for the sale of goods and reserved the question whether for other purposes a "license" characterization might be preferable. 86 F.3d at 1450. All debates about characterization to one side, the transaction in ProCD was no more executory than the one here: Zeidenberg paid for the software and walked out of the store with a box under his arm, so if arrival of the box with the product ends the time for revelation of contractual terms, then the time ended in ProCD before Zeidenberg opened the box. But of course ProCD had not completed performance with delivery of the box, and neither had Gateway. One element of the transaction was the warranty, which obliges sellers to fix defects in their products. The Hills have invoked Gateway's warranty and are not satisfied with its response, so they are not well positioned to say that Gateway's obligations were fulfilled when the motor carrier unloaded the box. What is more, both ProCD and Gateway promised to help customers to use their products. Long-term service and information obligations are common in the computer business, on both hardware and software sides. Gateway offers "lifetime service" and has a round-the-clock telephone hotline to fulfil this promise. Some vendors spend more money helping customers use their products than on developing and manufacturing them. The document in Gateway's box includes promises of future performance that some consumers value highly; these promises bind Gateway just as the arbitration clause binds the Hills.

Next the Hills insist that ProCD is irrelevant because Zeidenberg was a "merchant" and they are not. Section 2–207(2) of the UCC, the infamous battle-of-the-forms section, states that "additional terms [following acceptance of an offer] are to be construed as proposals for addition to a contract. Between merchants such terms become part of the contract unless . . .". Plaintiffs tell us that ProCD came out as it did only because Zeidenberg was a "merchant" and the terms inside ProCD's box were not excluded by the "unless" clause. This argument pays scant attention to the opinion in ProCD, which concluded that, when there is only one form, "sec. 2–207 is irrelevant." 86 F.3d at 1452. The question in ProCD was not whether terms were added to a contract after its formation, but how and when the contract was formed—in particular, whether a vendor may propose that a contract of sale be formed, not in the store (or over the phone) with the payment of money or a general "send me the product," but after the customer has had a chance to inspect both the item and the terms. ProCD answers "yes," for merchants and consumers alike. Yet again, for what little it is worth we observe that the Hills misunderstand the setting of ProCD. A "merchant" under the UCC "means a person who deals in goods of the kind or otherwise by his occupation holds himself out as having knowledge or skill peculiar to the practices or goods involved in the transaction", § 2–104(1). Zeidenberg bought the product at a retail store, an uncommon place for merchants to acquire inventory. His corporation put ProCD's database on the Internet for anyone to browse, which led to the litigation but did not make Zeidenberg a software merchant.

At oral argument the Hills propounded still another distinction: the box containing ProCD's software displayed a notice that additional terms were within, while the box containing Gateway's computer did not. The difference is functional, not legal. Consumers browsing the aisles of a store can look at the box, and if they are unwilling to deal with the prospect of additional terms can leave the box alone, avoiding the transactions costs of returning the package after reviewing its contents. Gateway's box, by contrast, is just a shipping carton; it is not on display anywhere. Its function is to protect the product during transit, and the information on its sides is for the use of handlers rather than would-be purchasers.

Perhaps the Hills would have had a better argument if they were first alerted to the bundling of hardware and legal-ware after opening the box and wanted to return the computer in order to avoid disagreeable terms, but were dissuaded by the expense of shipping. What the remedy would be in such a case—could it exceed the shipping charges?—is an interesting question, but one that need not detain us because the Hills knew before they ordered the computer that the carton would include some important terms, and they did not seek to discover these in advance. Gateway's ads state that their products come with limited warranties and lifetime support. How limited was the warranty—30 days, with service contingent on shipping the computer back, or five years, with free onsite service? What sort of support was offered? Shoppers have three principal ways to discover these things. First, they can ask the vendor to send a copy before deciding whether to buy. The Magnuson–Moss Warranty Act requires firms to distribute their warranty terms on request, 15 U.S.C. § 2302(b)(1)(A); the Hills do not contend that Gateway would have refused to enclose the remaining terms too. Concealment would be bad for business, scaring some customers away and leading to excess returns from others. Second, shoppers can consult public sources (computer magazines, the Web sites of vendors) that may contain this information. Third, they may inspect the documents after the product's delivery. Like Zeidenberg, the Hills took the third option. By keeping the computer beyond 30 days, the Hills accepted Gateway's offer, including the arbitration clause.

* * * The decision of the district court is vacated, and this case is remanded with instructions to compel the Hills to submit the dispute to arbitration.

KLOCEK v. GATEWAY, INC.

United States District Court, District of Kansas, 2000.
104 F.Supp.2d 1332.

MEMORANDUM AND ORDER

VRATIL, DISTRICT JUDGE. William S. Klocek brings suit against Gateway, Inc. ... on claims arising from purchases of a Gateway computer.... * * * For reasons stated below, the Court overrules Gateway's motion to dismiss....

A. Gateway's Motion to Dismiss

Plaintiff brings individual and class action claims against Gateway, alleging that it induced him and other consumers to purchase computers and special support packages by making false promises of technical support. Individually, plaintiff also claims breach of contract and breach of warranty, in that Gateway breached certain warranties that its computer would be compatible with standard peripherals and standard internet services.

Gateway asserts that plaintiff must arbitrate his claims under Gateway's Standard Terms and Conditions Agreement ("Standard Terms"). Whenever it sells a computer, Gateway includes a copy of the Standard Terms in the box which contains the computer battery power cables and instruction manuals. At the top of the first page, the Standard Terms include the following notice:

NOTE TO THE CUSTOMER:

This document contains Gateway 2000's Standard Terms and Conditions. By keeping your Gateway 2000 computer system beyond five (5) days after the date of delivery, you accept these Terms and Conditions.

The notice is in emphasized type and is located inside a printed box which sets it apart from other provisions of the document. The Standard Terms are four pages long and contain 16 numbered paragraphs. Paragraph 10 provides the following arbitration clause:

DISPUTE RESOLUTION. Any dispute or controversy arising out of or relating to this Agreement or its interpretation shall be settled exclusively and finally by arbitration. The arbitration shall be conducted in accordance with the Rules of Conciliation and Arbitration of the International Chamber of Commerce. The arbitration shall be conducted in Chicago, Illinois, U.S.A. before a sole arbitrator. Any award rendered in any such arbitration proceeding shall be final and binding on each of the parties, and judgment may be entered thereon in a court of competent jurisdiction.[2]

2. Gateway states that after it sold plaintiff's computer, it mailed all existing customers in the United States a copy of its quarterly magazine, which contained notice of a change in the arbitration policy set forth in the Standard Terms. The new arbi-

Gateway urges the Court to dismiss plaintiff's claims under the Federal Arbitration Act ("FAA"), 9 U.S.C. § 1 et seq. The FAA ensures that written arbitration agreements * * * involving interstate commerce are "valid, irrevocable, and enforceable." 9 U.S.C. § 2.[3]

* * *

Gateway bears an initial summary-judgment-like burden of establishing that it is entitled to arbitration. * * * Thus, Gateway must present evidence sufficient to demonstrate the existence of an enforceable agreement to arbitrate. * * * If Gateway makes such a showing, the burden shifts to plaintiff to submit evidence demonstrating a genuine issue for trial. * * * In this case, Gateway fails to present evidence establishing the most basic facts regarding the transaction. The gaping holes in the evidentiary record preclude the Court from determining what state law controls the formation of the contract in this case and, consequently, prevent the Court from agreeing that Gateway's motion is well taken.

Before granting a stay or dismissing a case pending arbitration, the Court must determine that the parties have a written agreement to arbitrate. * * * The existence of an arbitration agreement "is simply a matter of contract between the parties; [arbitration] is a way to resolve those disputes—but only those disputes—that the parties have agreed to submit to arbitration." * * *

Before evaluating whether the parties agreed to arbitrate, the Court must determine what state law controls the formation of the contract in this case. * * * Kansas courts apply the doctrine of *lex loci contractus*, which requires that the Court interpret the contract according to the law of the state in which the parties performed the last act necessary to form the contract. * * *

The parties do not address the choice of law issue, and the record is unclear where they performed the last act necessary to complete the contract. Gateway * * * provides no details regarding the transaction. * * * [I]t appears that the parties may have performed the last act necessary to form the contract in Kansas (with plaintiff purchasing the computer in Kansas), Missouri (with Gateway shipping the computer to plaintiff in Missouri), or some unidentified other states (with Gateway agreeing to ship plaintiff's catalog order and/or Gateway actually shipping the order).

tration policy afforded customers the option of arbitrating before the International Chamber of Commerce ("ICC"), the American Arbitration Association ("AAA"), or the National Arbitration Forum ("NAF") in Chicago, Illinois, or any other location agreed upon by the parties. Plaintiff denies receiving notice of the amended arbitration policy. Neither party explains why—if the arbitration agreement was an enforceable contract—Gateway was entitled to unilater-

ally amend it by sending a magazine to computer customers.

3. The FAA does not create independent federal-question jurisdiction; rather, "there must be diversity of citizenship or some other independent basis for federal jurisdiction" before the Court may act. *Moses H. Cone Memorial Hosp. v. Mercury Const. Corp.*, 460 U.S. 1, 25 n. 32, 103 S.Ct. 927, 74 L.Ed.2d 765 (1983). In this case, plaintiff asserts diversity jurisdiction.

The Court discerns no material difference between the applicable substantive law in Kansas and Missouri and—as to those two states—it perhaps would not need to resolve the choice of law issue at this time. * * *

The Uniform Commercial Code ("UCC") governs the parties' transaction under both Kansas and Missouri law. * * * [T]he issue is whether the contract of sale includes the Standard Terms as part of the agreement.

State courts in Kansas and Missouri apparently have not decided whether terms received with a product become part of the parties' agreement. Authority from other courts is split. Compare *Step–Saver*, 939 F.2d 91 (printed terms on computer software package not part of agreement); *Arizona Retail Sys., Inc. v. Software Link, Inc.*, 831 F.Supp. 759 (D.Ariz.1993) (license agreement shipped with computer software not part of agreement); and *U.S. Surgical Corp. v. Orris, Inc.*, 5 F.Supp.2d 1201 (D.Kan.1998) (single use restriction on product package not binding agreement); with *Hill v. Gateway 2000, Inc.*, 105 F.3d 1147 (7th Cir.), cert. denied, 522 U.S. 808, 118 S.Ct. 47, 139 L.Ed.2d 13 (1997) (arbitration provision shipped with computer binding on buyer); *ProCD, Inc. v. Zeidenberg*, 86 F.3d 1447 (7th Cir.1996) (shrinkwrap license binding on buyer);[6] and *M.A. Mortenson Co., Inc. v. Timberline Software Corp.*, 140 Wash.2d 568, 998 P.2d 305 (2000) (following Hill and ProCD on license agreement supplied with software).[7] It appears that at least in part, the cases turn on whether the court finds that the parties formed their contract before or after the vendor communicated its terms to the purchaser. Compare *Step–Saver*, 939 F.2d at 98 (parties' conduct in shipping, receiving and paying for product demonstrates existence of contract; box top license constitutes proposal for additional terms under § 2–207 which requires express agreement by purchaser); *Arizona Retail*, 831 F.Supp. at 765 (vendor entered into contract by agreeing to ship goods, or at latest by shipping goods to buyer; license agreement constitutes proposal to modify agreement under § 2–209 which requires express assent by buyer); and *Orris*, 5 F.Supp.2d at 1206 (sales contract concluded when vendor received consumer orders; single-use language on product's label was proposed modification under § 2–209 which requires express assent by purchaser); with *ProCD*, 86 F.3d at 1452

---

6. The term "shrinkwrap license" gets its name from retail software packages that are covered in plastic or cellophane "shrinkwrap" and contain licenses that purport to become effective as soon as the customer tears the wrapping from the package. *See ProCD*, 86 F.3d at 1449.

7. The Mortenson court also found support for its holding in the proposed Uniform Computer Information Transactions Act ("UCITA") (formerly known as proposed UCC Article 2B) (text located at www.law.upenn.edu/library/ulc/ucita/UCITA_99.htm), which the National Conference of Commissioners on Uniform State Laws approved and recommended for enactment by the states in July 1999. See Mortenson, 998 P.2d at 310 n. 6, 313 n. 10. The proposed UCITA, however, would not apply to the Court's analysis in this case. The UCITA applies to computer information transactions, which are defined as agreements "to create, modify, transfer, or license computer information or informational rights in computer information." UCITA, §§ 102(11) and 103. In transactions involving the sale of computers, such as our case, the UCITA applies only to the computer programs and copies, not to the sale of the computer itself. *See* UCITA § 103(c)(2).

(under § 2–204 vendor, as master of offer, may propose limitations on kind of conduct that constitutes acceptance; § 2–207 does not apply in case with only one form); *Hill*, 105 F.3d at 1148–49 (same); and *Mortenson*, 998 P.2d at 311–314 (where vendor and purchaser utilized license agreement in prior course of dealing, shrinkwrap license agreement constituted issue of contract formation under § 2–204, not contract alteration under § 2–207).

Gateway urges the Court to follow the Seventh Circuit decision in *Hill*. That case involved the shipment of a Gateway computer with terms similar to the Standard Terms in this case, except that Gateway gave the customer 30 days—instead of 5 days—to return the computer. In enforcing the arbitration clause, the Seventh Circuit relied on its decision in *ProCD*, where it enforced a software license which was contained inside a product box. See Hill, 105 F.3d at 1148–50. In *ProCD*, the Seventh Circuit noted that the exchange of money frequently precedes the communication of detailed terms in a commercial transaction. See *ProCD*, 86 F.3d at 1451. Citing UCC § 2–204, the court reasoned that by including the license with the software, the vendor proposed a contract that the buyer could accept by using the software after having an opportunity to read the license.[8] *ProCD*, 86 F.3d at 1452. Specifically, the court stated:

> A vendor, as master of the offer, may invite acceptance by conduct, and may propose limitations on the kind of conduct that constitutes acceptance. A buyer may accept by performing the acts the vendor proposes to treat as acceptance.

ProCD, 86 F.3d at 1452. The Hill court followed the *ProCD* analysis, noting that "[p]ractical considerations support allowing vendors to enclose the full legal terms with their products." *Hill*, 105 F.3d at 1149.[9]

---

8. Section 2–204 provides: "A contract for sale of goods may be made in any manner sufficient to show agreement, including conduct by both parties which recognizes the existence of such contract."

9. Legal commentators have criticized the reasoning of the Seventh Circuit in this regard. See, e.g., Jean R. Sternlight, *Gateway Widens Doorway to Imposing Unfair Binding Arbitration on Consumers*, Fla. Bar J., Nov. 1997, at 8, 10–12 (outcome in Gateway is questionable on federal statutory, common law and constitutional grounds and as a matter of contract law and is unwise as a matter of policy because it unreasonably shifts to consumers search cost of ascertaining existence of arbitration clause and return cost to avoid such clause); Thomas J. McCarthy *et al., Survey: Uniform Commercial Code*, 53 Bus. Law. 1461, 1465–66 (Seventh Circuit finding that UCC § 2–207 did not apply is inconsistent with official comment); Batya Goodman, *Honey, I Shrink–Wrapped the Consumer: the Shrink–Wrap Agreement as an Adhesion*

Contract, 21 Cardozo L.Rev. 319, 344–352 (Seventh Circuit failed to consider principles of adhesion contracts); Jeremy Senderowicz, *Consumer Arbitration and Freedom of Contract: A Proposal to Facilitate Consumers' Informed Consent to Arbitration Clauses in Form Contracts*, 32 Colum. J.L. & Soc. Probs. 275, 296–299 (judiciary (in multiple decisions, including Hill) has ignored issue of consumer consent to an arbitration clause). Nonetheless, several courts have followed the Seventh Circuit decisions in Hill and *ProCD*. See, e.g., *M.A. Mortenson Co., Inc. v. Timberline Software Corp.*, 140 Wash.2d 568, 998 P.2d 305 (license agreement supplied with software); *Rinaldi v. Iomega Corp.*, 1999 WL 1442014, Case No. 98C–09–064–RRC (Del.Super. Sept. 3, 1999) (warranty disclaimer included inside computer Zip drive packaging); *Westendorf v. Gateway 2000, Inc.*, 2000 WL 307369, Case No. 16913 (Del. Ch. March 16, 2000) (arbitration provision shipped with computer); *Brower v. Gateway 2000*, Inc., 246 A.D.2d 246, 676 N.Y.S.2d 569 (N.Y.App.Div.

The Court is not persuaded that Kansas or Missouri courts would follow the Seventh Circuit reasoning in Hill and *ProCD*. In each case the Seventh Circuit concluded without support that UCC § 2–207 was irrelevant because the cases involved only one written form. *See ProCD*, 86 F.3d at 1452 (citing no authority); *Hill*, 105 F.3d at 1150 (citing *ProCD*). This conclusion is not supported by the statute or by Kansas or Missouri law. Disputes under § 2–207 often arise in the context of a "battle of forms," *see, e.g., Daitom, Inc. v. Pennwalt Corp.*, 741 F.2d 1569, 1574 (10th Cir.1984), but nothing in its language precludes application in a case which involves only one form.* * * By its terms, § 2–207 applies to an acceptance or written confirmation. It states nothing which requires another form before the provision becomes effective. In fact, the official comment to the section specifically provides that §§ 2–207(1) and (2) apply "where an agreement has been reached orally ... and is followed by one or both of the parties sending formal memoranda embodying the terms so far agreed and adding terms not discussed." Official Comment 1 of UCC § 2–207. Kansas and Missouri courts have followed this analysis. * * * Thus, the Court concludes that Kansas and Missouri courts would apply § 2–207 to the facts in this case. * * *

In addition, the Seventh Circuit provided no explanation for its conclusion that "the vendor is the master of the offer." See *ProCD*, 86 F.3d at 1452 (citing nothing in support of proposition); *Hill*, 105 F.3d at 1149 (citing *ProCD*). In typical consumer transactions, the purchaser is the offeror, and the vendor is the offeree. *See Brown Mach., Div. of John Brown, Inc. v. Hercules, Inc.*, 770 S.W.2d 416, 419 (Mo.App.1989) (as general rule orders are considered offers to purchase); *Rich Prods. Corp. v. Kemutec Inc.*, 66 F.Supp.2d 937, 956 (E.D.Wis.1999) (generally price quotation is invitation to make offer and purchase order is offer). While it is possible for the vendor to be the offeror, *see Brown Machine*, 770 S.W.2d at 419 (price quote can amount to offer if it reasonably appears from quote that assent to quote is all that is needed to ripen offer into contract), Gateway provides no factual evidence which would support such a finding in this case. [The Court therefore assumes for purposes of the motion to dismiss that plaintiff offered to purchase the computer (either in person or through catalog order) and that Gateway accepted plaintiff's offer (either by completing the sales transaction in person or by agreeing to ship and/or shipping the computer to plaintiff).[11] *Accord Arizona Retail*, 831 F.Supp. at 765 (vendor entered into contract by agreeing to ship goods, or at latest, by shipping goods).

Under § 2–207, the Standard Terms constitute either an expression of acceptance or written confirmation. As an expression of acceptance, the Standard Terms would constitute a counter-offer only if Gateway

1998) (same); *Levy v. Gateway* 2000, Inc., 1997 WL 823611, 33 UCC Rep. Serv.2d 1060 (N.Y.Sup. Oct. 31, 1997) (same).

11. UCC § 2–206(b) provides that "an order or other offer to buy goods for prompt or current shipment shall be construed as inviting acceptance either by a prompt promise to ship or by the prompt or current shipment ... " The official comment states that "[e]ither shipment or a prompt promise to ship is made a proper means of acceptance of an offer looking to current shipment." UCC § 2–206, Official Comment 2.

expressly made its acceptance conditional on plaintiff's assent to the additional or different terms. * * * "[T]he conditional nature of the acceptance must be clearly expressed in a manner sufficient to notify the offeror that the offeree is unwilling to proceed with the transaction unless the additional or different terms are included in the contract." *Brown Machine*, 770 S.W.2d at 420.[12] Gateway provides no evidence that at the time of the sales transaction, it informed plaintiff that the transaction was conditioned on plaintiff's acceptance of the Standard Terms. Moreover, the mere fact that Gateway shipped the goods with the terms attached did not communicate to plaintiff any unwillingness to proceed without plaintiff's agreement to the Standard Terms. *See, e.g., Arizona Retail*, 831 F.Supp. at 765 (conditional acceptance analysis rarely appropriate where contract formed by performance but goods arrive with conditions attached); *Leighton Indus., Inc. v. Callier Steel Pipe & Tube, Inc.*, 1991 WL 18413, *6, Case No. 89–C–8235 (N.D.Ill. Feb. 6, 1991) (applying Missouri law) (preprinted forms insufficient to notify offeror of conditional nature of acceptance, particularly where form arrives after delivery of goods).

Because plaintiff is not a merchant, additional or different terms contained in the Standard Terms did not become part of the parties' agreement unless plaintiff expressly agreed to them. * * * Gateway argues that plaintiff demonstrated acceptance of the arbitration provision by keeping the computer more than five days after the date of delivery. Although the Standard Terms purport to work that result, Gateway has not presented evidence that plaintiff expressly agreed to those Standard Terms. Gateway states only that it enclosed the Standard Terms inside the computer box for plaintiff to read afterwards. It provides no evidence that it informed plaintiff of the five-day review-and-return period as a condition of the sales transaction, or that the parties

12. Courts are split on the standard for a conditional acceptance under § 2–207. See *Daitom*, 741 F.2d at 1576 (finding that Pennsylvania would most likely adopt "better" view that offeree must explicitly communicate unwillingness to proceed with transaction unless additional terms in response are accepted by offeror). On one extreme of the spectrum, courts hold that the offeree's response stating a materially different term solely to the disadvantage of the offeror constitutes a conditional acceptance. See *Daitom*, 741 F.2d at 1569 (citing *Roto–Lith, Ltd. v. F.P. Bartlett & Co.*, 297 F.2d 497 (1st Cir.1962)). At the other end of the spectrum, courts hold that the conditional nature of the acceptance should be so clearly expressed in a manner sufficient to notify the offeror that the offeree is unwilling to proceed without the additional or different terms. *See Daitom*, 741 F.2d at 1569 (citing *Dorton v. Collins & Aikman Corp.*, 453 F.2d 1161 (6th Cir.1972)). The middle approach requires that the response predicate acceptance on clarification, addi-

tion or modification. See *Daitom*, 741 F.2d at 1569 (citing *Construction Aggregates Corp. v. Hewitt–Robins, Inc.*, 404 F.2d 505 (7th Cir.1968)). The First Circuit has since overruled its decision in *Roto–Lith, see Ionics, Inc. v. Elmwood Sensors, Inc.*, 110 F.3d 184, and the Court finds that neither Kansas nor Missouri would apply the standard set forth therein. *See Boese–Hilburn Co. v. Dean Machinery Co.*, 616 S.W.2d 520, (Mo. App.1981) (rejecting Roto–Lith standard); *Owens-Corning Fiberglas Corp. v. Sonic Dev. Corp.*, 546 F.Supp. 533, 538 (D.Kan. 1982) (acceptance is not counteroffer under Kansas law unless it is made conditional on assent to additional or different terms (citing Roto–Lith as comparison)); Daitom, 741 F.2d at 1569 (finding that Dorton is "better" view). Because Gateway does not satisfy the standard for conditional acceptance under either of the remaining standards (Dorton or Construction Aggregates), the Court does not decide which of the remaining two standards would apply in Kansas and/or Missouri.

contemplated additional terms to the agreement.[14] *See Step–Saver*, 939 F.2d at 99 (during negotiations leading to purchase, vendor never mentioned box-top license or obtained buyer's express assent thereto).

- The Court finds that the act of keeping the computer past five days was not sufficient to demonstrate that plaintiff expressly agreed to the Standard Terms. *Accord Brown Machine*, 770 S.W.2d at 421 (express assent cannot be presumed by silence or mere failure to object). Thus, because Gateway has not provided evidence sufficient to support a finding under Kansas or Missouri law that plaintiff agreed to the arbitration provision contained in Gateway's Standard Terms, the Court overrules Gateway's motion to dismiss.

The motion also must be overruled because Kansas and Missouri law may not apply. * * * If Gateway contends that the issue of contract formation is governed by some law other than that of Kansas or Missouri, it shall file a supplemental motion which cites the factual and legal basis for its position. The Court will review that submission and decide whether to order a jury trial on the existence of an agreement to arbitrate. * * *

* * *

Problems

102.   A offers to sell B Blackacre for $5,000, the offer to be open for 30 days.

(a) B replies immediately, "I'll pay $4,800." A refuses; B accepts within 30 days. Is there a contract?

(b) B replies immediately, "I'll pay $4,800." A replies, "Cannot reduce price." B accepts within 30 days. Is there a contract?

(c) B says, "Won't you take $4,800?" A refuses. B accepts within 30 days. Is there a contract?

(d) B says "I am keeping your offer under advisement but if you wish to close the deal now I'll give you $4,800." A refuses. B accepts within 30 days. Is there a contract?

(e) B replies immediately, "I accept but I still insist that you are driving a hard bargain." Is there a contract?

103.   A makes a written offer to B to sell him Blackacre. B replies: "I accept your offer if you can convey me a good title." Is there a contract?

104.   After negotiations, the State Department of Transportation ("DOT") offered to renew Express Industries' expired lease for the use of a state-owned pier for a four-year period for $3,500,000. The offeree's president signified acceptance of the offer by signing and returning it. An

---

14. The Court is mindful of the practical considerations which are involved in commercial transactions, but it is not unreasonable for a vendor to clearly communicate to a buyer—at the time of sale—either the complete terms of the sale or the fact that the vendor will propose additional terms as a condition of sale, if that be the case.

environmental group, HRC, had been a party to the negotiations. The offeree's cover letter returning the offer stated that "certain parts of the deal are still under discussion with the HRC and when Mr. McGowan of that group returns from vacation we can resolve an outstanding issue: the exclusion of 70,000 square feet of the truck yard from the lease." Upon receipt of the letter and signed offer, the DOT received an offer of $4,500,000 from another party and proceeded to accept the higher offer. Express Industries sues the State for breach of contract. What result?

105.   A makes an offer for the sale of goods to B and B accepts but adds: "Prompt acknowledgment must be made of receipt of this letter." Is there a contract? If so, what are its terms?

106.   B made an offer to buy goods, S sent a letter to B accepting the offer but made its acceptance expressly conditional on assent to its limited warranty terms and to certain payment terms. B then requested a change in the payment terms and S agreed. S then delivered the goods which B accepted. Do S's limited warranty terms form part of the contract, or do the implied warranty terms of the Code form part of the contract?

107.   X and Y exchanged correspondence and entered into a contract containing terms A, B and C.

    (a) If X sent a written confirmation listing terms A, B, C and D what would be the result?

    (b) If X's memo states that the terms are A, B and D, what result?

    (c) Suppose that both parties send memos. X's memo lists terms A, B, C and D and Y's memo sets forth terms A, B, C and specifically states not D. What result?

108.   B and S entered into a verbal agreement for the sale of certain restaurant equipment at which time they discussed an approximate price. An invoice was delivered with the equipment. B accepted the goods without reading the invoice and did not contest the invoice price, which was several thousand dollars higher than the approximate price discussed, until 90 days later. S sues to recover the invoice price. Does the invoice operate as a confirmation? If so, what is the result?

SECTION 10.   E–COMMERCE

SPECHT v. NETSCAPE COMMUNICATIONS CORP.

United States Court of Appeals, Second Circuit, 2002.
306 F.3d 17.

SOTOMAYOR, CIRCUIT JUDGE. This is an appeal from a judgment of the Southern District of New York denying a motion by defendants-appellants Netscape Communications Corporation and its corporate parent, America Online, Inc. (collectively, "defendants" or "Netscape"), to compel arbitration and to stay court proceedings. In order to resolve the central question of arbitrability presented here, we must address issues of contract formation in cyberspace. * * *

We * * * affirm the district court's denial of defendants' motion to compel arbitration and to stay court proceedings.

BACKGROUND

I. Facts

* * * [P]laintiffs alleged that when they first used Netscape's Communicator—a software program that permits Internet browsing—the program created and stored on each of their computer hard drives a small text file known as a "cookie" that functioned "as a kind of electronic identification tag for future communications" between their computers and Netscape. Plaintiffs further alleged that when they installed SmartDownload—a separate software "plug-in"[2] that served to enhance Communicator's browsing capabilities—SmartDownload created and stored on their computer hard drives another string of characters, known as a "Key," which similarly functioned as an identification tag in future communications with Netscape. According to the complaints in this case, each time a computer user employed Communicator to download a file from the Internet, SmartDownload "assume[d] from Communicator the task of downloading" the file and transmitted to Netscape the address of the file being downloaded together with the cookie created by Communicator and the Key created by SmartDownload. These processes, plaintiffs claim, constituted unlawful "eavesdropping" on users of Netscape's software products as well as on Internet websites from which users employing SmartDownload downloaded files [in violation of two federal statutes, the Electronic Communications Privacy Act, 18 U.S.C. §§ 2510 *et seq*, and the Computer Fraud and Abuse Act, 18 U.S.C. § 1030].

In the time period relevant to this litigation, Netscape offered on its website various software programs, including Communicator and Smart-Download, which visitors to the site were invited to obtain free of charge. It is undisputed that ... plaintiffs ... downloaded Communicator from the Netscape website. [P]laintiffs acknowledge that when they proceeded to initiate installation[3] of Communicator, they were automatically shown a scrollable text of that program's license agreement and were not permitted to complete the installation until they had clicked on a "Yes" button to indicate that they accepted all the license terms.[4] If a user

---

2. Netscape's website defines "plug-ins" as "software programs that extend the capabilities of the Netscape Browser in a specific way—giving you, for example, the ability to play audio samples or view video movies from within your browser." (http://wp.netscape.com/plugins/) Smart-Download purportedly made it easier for users of browser programs like Communicator to download files from the Internet without losing their progress when they paused to engage in some other task, or if their Internet connection was severed. See [*Specht v. Netscape Communications Corp.*, 150 F.Supp.2d 585, 587 (S.D.N.Y.2001)].

3. There is a difference between downloading and installing a software program.

When a user downloads a program from the Internet to his or her computer, the program file is stored on the user's hard drive but typically is not operable until the user installs or executes it, usually by double-clicking on the file and causing the program to run.

4. This kind of online software license agreement has come to be known as "click-wrap" (by analogy to "shrinkwrap," used in the licensing of tangible forms of software sold in packages) because it "presents the user with a message on his or her computer screen, requiring that the user manifest his or her assent to the terms of the license agreement by clicking on an icon. The product cannot be obtained or used unless and attempted to install Communicator without clicking "Yes," the installation would be aborted. All five named user plaintiffs expressly agreed to Communicator's license terms by clicking "Yes." The Communicator license agreement that these plaintiffs saw made no mention of Smart-Download or other plug-in programs, and stated that "[t]hese terms apply to Netscape Communicator and Netscape Navigator"[6] and that "all disputes relating to this Agreement (excepting any dispute relating to intellectual property rights)" are subject to "binding arbitration in Santa Clara County, California."

Although Communicator could be obtained independently of Smart-Download, ... plaintiffs ... downloaded and installed Communicator in connection with downloading SmartDownload. [P]laintiffs allegedly arrived at a Netscape webpage[8] captioned "SmartDownload Communicator" that urged them to "Download With Confidence Using SmartDownload!" At or near the bottom of the screen facing plaintiffs was the prompt "Start Download" and a tinted button labeled "Download." By clicking on the button, plaintiffs initiated the download of SmartDownload. Once that process was complete, SmartDownload, as its first plug-in task, permitted plaintiffs to proceed with downloading and installing Communicator, an operation that was accompanied by the clickwrap display of Communicator's license terms described above.

The signal difference between downloading Communicator and downloading SmartDownload was that no clickwrap presentation accompanied the latter operation. Instead, once plaintiffs ... had clicked on the "Download" button located at or near the bottom of their screen, and the downloading of SmartDownload was complete, ... plaintiffs encountered no further information about the plug-in program or the existence of license terms governing its use.[9] The sole reference to SmartDownload's license terms on the "SmartDownload Communicator" webpage was located in text that would have become visible to

until the icon is clicked." *Specht*, 150 F.Supp.2d at 593–94 (footnote omitted). Just as breaking the shrinkwrap seal and using the enclosed computer program after encountering notice of the existence of governing license terms has been deemed by some courts to constitute assent to those terms in the context of tangible software, *see, e.g., ProCD, Inc. v. Zeidenberg,* 86 F.3d 1447, 1451 (7th Cir.1996), so clicking on a webpage's clickwrap button after receiving notice of the existence of license terms has been held by some courts to manifest an Internet user's assent to terms governing the use of downloadable intangible software, *see, e.g., Hotmail Corp. v. Van$ Money Pie Inc.,* 47 U.S.P.Q.2d 1020, 1025 (N.D.Cal.1998).

6. While Navigator was Netscape's "stand-alone" Internet browser program during the period in question, Communicator was a "software suite" that comprised Navigator and other software products. * * *

8. For purposes of this opinion, the term "webpage" or "page" is used to designate a document that resides, usually with other webpages, on a single Internet website and that contains information that is viewed on a computer monitor by scrolling through the document. To view a webpage in its entirety, a user typically must scroll through multiple screens.

9. Plaintiff Kelly, a relatively sophisticated Internet user, testified that when he clicked to download SmartDownload, he did not think that he was downloading a software program at all, but rather that Smart-Download "was merely a piece of download technology." He later became aware that SmartDownload was residing as software on his hard drive when he attempted to download electronic files from the Internet.

plaintiffs only if they had scrolled down to the next screen. [SmartDownload's license terms included an identical arbitration clause. Ed.]

Had plaintiffs scrolled down instead of acting on defendants' invitation to click on the "Download" button, they would have encountered the following invitation: "Please review and agree to the terms of the *Netscape SmartDownload software license agreement* before downloading and using the software." Plaintiffs ... averred in their affidavits that they never saw this reference to the SmartDownload license agreement when they clicked on the "Download" button. * * *

In sum, plaintiffs ... allege that the process of obtaining Smart-Download contrasted sharply with that of obtaining Communicator. Having selected SmartDownload, they were required neither to express unambiguous assent to that program's license agreement nor even to view the license terms or become aware of their existence before proceeding with the invited download of the free plug-in program. Moreover, once ... plaintiffs had initiated the download, the existence of Smart-Download's license terms was not mentioned while the software was running or at any later point in plaintiffs' experience of the product. * * *

II. *Proceedings Below*

In the district court, defendants moved to compel arbitration and to stay court proceedings pursuant to the Federal Arbitration Act ("FAA"), 9 U.S.C. § 4.... Finding that Netscape's webpage, unlike typical examples of clickwrap, neither adequately alerted users to the existence of SmartDownload's license terms nor required users unambiguously to manifest assent to those terms as a condition of downloading the product, the court held that the ... plaintiffs had not entered into the SmartDownload license agreement. *Specht,* 150 F.Supp.2d at 595–96.

The district court also ruled that the separate license agreement governing use of Communicator, even though the user plaintiffs had assented to its terms, involved an independent transaction that made no mention of SmartDownload and so did not bind plaintiffs to arbitrate their claims relating to SmartDownload. *Id.* at 596. * * *

DISCUSSION

* * * The FAA provides that a "written provision in any ... contract evidencing a transaction involving commerce to settle by arbitration a controversy thereafter arising out of such contract or transaction ... shall be valid, irrevocable, and enforceable, save upon such grounds as exist at law or in equity for the revocation of any contract."[11] 9 U.S.C. § 2. * * *

---

11. The parties do not dispute ... that the agreement is a "written provision" despite being provided to users in a downloadable electronic form. The ... point has been settled by the Electronic Signatures in Global and National Commerce Act ("E-Sign Act"), Pub.L. No. 106–229, 114 Stat. 464 (2000) (codified at 15 U.S.C. §§ 7001 *et seq.*), which provides that "a signature, contract, or other record relating to such transaction may not be denied legal effect, validity, or enforceability solely because it is in

II. Whether This Court Should Remand
for a Trial on Contract Formation

* * * [W]e conclude that the district court properly decided the question of reasonable notice and objective manifestation of assent as a matter of law on the record before it, and we decline defendants' request to remand for a full trial on that question.

III. Whether the User Plaintiffs Had Reasonable Notice
of and Manifested Assent to the SmartDownload
License Agreement

Whether governed by the common law or by Article 2 of the Uniform Commercial Code ("UCC"), a transaction, in order to be a contract, requires a manifestation of agreement between the parties. *See Windsor Mills, Inc. v. Collins & Aikman Corp.*, 25 Cal.App.3d 987, 991, 101 Cal.Rptr. 347, 350 (1972) ("[C]onsent to, or acceptance of, the arbitration provision [is] necessary to create an agreement to arbitrate."); *see also* Cal. Com.Code § 2204(1) ("A contract for sale of goods may be made in any manner sufficient to show agreement, including conduct by both parties which recognizes the existence of such a contract.").[13] Mutual manifestation of assent, whether by written or spoken word or by conduct, is the touchstone of contract. Binder v. Aetna Life Ins. Co., 75 Cal.App.4th 832, 848, 89 Cal.Rptr.2d 540, 551 (1999); *cf.* Restatement (Second) of Contracts § 19(2) (1981) ("The conduct of a party is not effective as a manifestation of his assent unless he intends to engage in the conduct and knows or has reason to know that the other party may infer from his conduct that he assents."). Although an onlooker observing the disputed transactions in this case would have seen each of the user plaintiffs click on the SmartDownload "Download" button ... a consumer's clicking on a download button does not communicate assent to contractual terms if the offer did not make clear to the consumer that clicking on the download button would signify assent to those terms.... California's common law is clear that "an offeree, regardless of apparent manifestation of his consent, is not bound by inconspicuous contractual provisions of which he is unaware, contained in a document whose contractual nature is not obvious." [*Cedars Sinai Med. Ctr. v. Mid–West Life Ins. Co.*, 118 F.Supp.2d 1002, 1008 (C.D. Cal. 2000)].... * * *

Arbitration agreements are no exception to the requirement of manifestation of assent. * * *

A. The Reasonably Prudent Offeree of Downloadable Software

Defendants argue that plaintiffs must be held to a standard of reasonable prudence and that, because notice of the existence of Smart-

---

electronic form." *Id.* § 7001(a)(1); *see also* Cal. Civ.Code § 1633.7(b) ("A contract may not be denied legal effect or enforceability solely because an electronic record was used in its formation.").

13. [See Editors' note at the conclusion of the opinion.]

Download license terms was on the next scrollable screen, plaintiffs were on "inquiry notice" of those terms.[14] We disagree with the proposition that a reasonably prudent offeree in plaintiffs' position would necessarily have known or learned of the existence of the SmartDownload license agreement prior to acting, so that plaintiffs may be held to have assented to that agreement with constructive notice of its terms. * * * It is true that "[a] party cannot avoid the terms of a contract on the ground that he or she failed to read it before signing." *Marin Storage & Trucking,* 89 Cal.App.4th at 1049, 107 Cal.Rptr.2d at 651. But courts are quick to add: "An exception to this general rule exists when the writing does not appear to be a contract and the terms are not called to the attention of the recipient. In such a case, no contract is formed with respect to the undisclosed term." *Id.* . . .

Most of the cases cited by defendants in support of their inquiry-notice argument are drawn from the world of paper contracting. * * *

Receipt of a physical document containing contract terms or notice thereof is frequently deemed, in the world of paper transactions, a sufficient circumstance to place the offeree on inquiry notice of those terms. * * * These principles apply equally to the emergent world of online product delivery, pop-up screens, hyperlinked pages, clickwrap licensing, scrollable documents, and urgent admonitions to "Download Now!". What plaintiffs saw when they were being invited by defendants to download this fast, free plug-in called SmartDownload was a screen containing praise for the product and, at the very bottom of the screen, a "Download" button. Defendants argue that . . . a "fair and prudent person using ordinary care" would have been on inquiry notice of SmartDownload's license terms. * * * Plaintiffs were responding to an offer that did not carry an immediately visible notice of the existence of license terms or require unambiguous manifestation of assent to those terms. Thus, plaintiffs' "apparent manifestation of . . . consent" was to terms "contained in a document whose contractual nature [was] not obvious." *Windsor Mills,* 25 Cal.App.3d at 992, 101 Cal.Rptr. at 351. Moreover, the fact that, given the position of the scroll bar on their computer screens, plaintiffs may have been aware that an unexplored portion of the Netscape webpage remained below the download button does not mean that they reasonably should have concluded that this portion contained a notice of license terms. In their deposition testimony, plaintiffs variously stated that they used the scroll bar "[o]nly if there is something that I feel I need to see that is on—that is off the page," or that the elevated position of the scroll bar suggested the presence of "mere[ ] formalities, standard lower banner links" or "that the page is bigger than what I can see." Plaintiffs testified, and defendants did not refute, that plaintiffs were in fact unaware that defendants intended to attach license terms to the use of SmartDownload. * * *

---

14. "Inquiry notice" is "actual notice of circumstances sufficient to put a prudent man upon inquiry." *Cal. State Auto. Ass'n Inter–Ins. Bureau v. Barrett Garages, Inc.,* 257 Cal.App.2d 71, 64 Cal.Rptr. 699, 703 (Cal.Ct.App.1967) (internal quotation marks omitted).

Internet users may have, as defendants put it, "as much time as they need[ ]" to scroll through multiple screens on a webpage, but there is no reason to assume that viewers will scroll down to subsequent screens simply because screens are there. When products are "free" and users are invited to download them in the absence of reasonably conspicuous notice that they are about to bind themselves to contract terms, the transactional circumstances cannot be fully analogized to those in the paper world of arm's-length bargaining. * * *

B. Shrinkwrap Licensing and Related Practices

Defendants cite certain well-known cases involving shrinkwrap licensing and related commercial practices in support of their contention that plaintiffs became bound by the SmartDownload license terms by virtue of inquiry notice. For example, in *Hill v. Gateway 2000, Inc.*, 105 F.3d 1147 (7th Cir.1997), the Seventh Circuit held that where a purchaser had ordered a computer over the telephone, received the order in a shipped box containing the computer along with printed contract terms, and did not return the computer within the thirty days required by the terms, the purchaser was bound by the contract. *Id.* at 1148–49. In *ProCD, Inc. v. Zeidenberg,* the same court held that where an individual purchased software in a box containing license terms which were displayed on the computer screen every time the user executed the software program, the user had sufficient opportunity to review the terms and to return the software, and so was contractually bound after retaining the product. *ProCD,* 86 F.3d at 1452; *cf. Moore v. Microsoft Corp.,* 293 A.D.2d 587, 587, 741 N.Y.S.2d 91, 92 (2d Dep't 2002) (software user was bound by license agreement where terms were prominently displayed on computer screen before software could be installed and where user was required to indicate assent by clicking "I agree"); *Brower v. Gateway 2000, Inc.*, 246 A.D.2d 246, 251, 676 N.Y.S.2d 569, 572 (1st Dep't 1998) (buyer assented to arbitration clause shipped inside box with computer and software by retaining items beyond date specified by license terms); *M.A. Mortenson Co. v. Timberline Software Corp.,* 93 Wash.App. 819, 970 P.2d 803, 809 (1999) (buyer manifested assent to software license terms by installing and using software), *aff'd,* 140 Wash.2d 568, 998 P.2d 305 (2000); . . . . These cases do not help defendants. To the extent that they hold that the purchaser of a computer or tangible software is contractually bound after failing to object to printed license terms provided with the product, *Hill* and *Brower* do not differ markedly from the cases involving traditional paper contracting discussed in the previous section. Insofar as the purchaser in *ProCD* was confronted with conspicuous, mandatory license terms every time he ran the software on his computer, that case actually undermines defendants' contention that downloading in the absence of conspicuous terms is an act that binds plaintiffs to those terms. In *Mortenson,* the full text of license terms was printed on each sealed diskette envelope inside the software box, printed again on the inside cover of the user manual, and notice of the terms appeared on the computer screen every time the purchaser executed the program.

Mortenson, 970 P.2d at 806. In sum, the foregoing cases are clearly distinguishable from the facts of the present action.

C. Online Transactions

Cases in which courts have found contracts arising from Internet use do not assist defendants, because in those circumstances there was much clearer notice than in the present case that a user's act would manifest assent to contract terms. See, e.g., ... *Caspi v. Microsoft Network, L.L.C.,* 323 N.J.Super. 118, 732 A.2d 528, 530, 532–33 (N.J.Super.Ct.App.Div.1999) (upholding forum selection clause where subscribers to online software were required to review license terms in scrollable window and to click "I Agree" or "I Don't Agree"); *Barnett v. Network Solutions, Inc.,* 38 S.W.3d 200, 203–04 (Tex.App.2001) (upholding forum selection clause in online contract for registering Internet domain names that required users to scroll through terms before accepting or rejecting them).... [17]

After reviewing the California common law and other relevant legal authority, we conclude that under the circumstances here, plaintiffs' downloading of SmartDownload did not constitute acceptance of defendants' license terms. Reasonably conspicuous notice of the existence of contract terms and unambiguous manifestation of assent to those terms by consumers are essential if electronic bargaining is to have integrity

---

17. Although the parties here do not refer to it, California's consumer fraud statute, Cal. Bus. & Prof.Code § 17538, is one of the few state statutes to regulate online transactions in goods or services. The statute provides that in disclosing information regarding return and refund policies and other vital consumer information, online vendors must legibly display the information either:

(i) [on] the first screen displayed when the vendor's electronic site is accessed, (ii) on the screen on which goods or services are first offered, (iii) on the screen on which a buyer may place the order for goods or services, (iv) on the screen on which the buyer may enter payment information, such as a credit card account number, or (v) for nonbrowser-based technologies, in a manner that gives the user a reasonable opportunity to review that information. *Id.* § 17538(d)(2)(A).

The statute's clear purpose is to ensure that consumers engaging in online transactions have relevant information before they can be bound. Although consumer fraud as such is not alleged in the present action, and § 17538 protects only California residents, we note that the statute is consistent with the principle of conspicuous notice of the existence of contract terms that is also found in California's common law of contracts.

In addition, the model code, UCITA, discussed [in note 13] generally recognizes the importance of conspicuous notice and unambiguous manifestation of assent in online sales and licensing of computer information. For example, § 112, which addresses manifestation of assent, provides that a user's opportunity to review online contract terms exists if a "record" (or electronic writing) of the contract terms is "made available in a manner that ought to call it to the attention of a reasonable person and permit review." UCITA, § 112(e)(1) (rev. ed. Aug.23, 2001) (available at *www.ucitaonline.com/ucita.html*). * * *

We hasten to point out that UCITA, which has been enacted into law only in Maryland and Virginia, does not govern the parties' transactions in the present case, but we nevertheless find that UCITA's provisions offer insight into the evolving online "circumstances" that defendants argue placed plaintiffs on inquiry notice of the existence of the SmartDownload license terms. UCITA has been controversial as a result of the perceived breadth of some of its provisions. * * * Nonetheless, UCITA's notice and assent provisions seem to be consistent with well-established principles governing contract formation and enforcement. * * *

and credibility. We hold that a reasonably prudent offeree in plaintiffs' position would not have known or learned, prior to acting on the invitation to download, of the reference to SmartDownload's license terms hidden below the "Download" button on the next screen. We affirm the district court's conclusion that the ... plaintiffs ... are not bound by the arbitration clause contained in those terms.

IV. Whether Plaintiffs' Assent to Communicator's License Agreement Requires Them To Arbitrate Their Claims Regarding SmartDownload

Plaintiffs do not dispute that they assented to the license terms governing Netscape's Communicator. The parties disagree, however, over the scope of that license's arbitration clause. Defendants contend that the scope is broad enough to encompass plaintiffs' claims regarding SmartDownload, even if plaintiffs did not separately assent to Smart-Download's license terms and even though Communicator's license terms did not expressly mention SmartDownload. Thus, defendants argue, plaintiffs must arbitrate.* * *

To begin with, we find that the underlying dispute in this case—whether defendants violated plaintiff's rights under the Electronic Communications Privacy Act and the Computer Fraud and Abuse Act—involves matters that are clearly collateral to the Communicator license agreement. * * *

Having determined this much, we next ... must determine whether plaintiffs by their particular allegations have brought the dispute within the license terms. Defendants argue that plaintiffs' complaints "literally bristled with allegations that Communicator and Smart Download operated in conjunction with one another to eavesdrop on Plaintiffs' Internet communications." We disagree. * * * In the course of their description of the installation and downloading process, plaintiffs keep SmartDownload separate from Communicator and clearly indicate that it is Smart-Download that performed the allegedly unlawful eavesdropping and made use of the otherwise innocuous Communicator cookie as well as its own "Key" and "UserID" to transmit plaintiffs' information to Netscape * * *

After careful review of these allegations, we conclude that ... the claims of the ... plaintiffs are beyond the scope of the arbitration clause contained in the Communicator license agreement. Because those claims are not arbitrable under that agreement or under the SmartDownload license agreement, to which plaintiffs never assented, we affirm the district court's holding that the ... plaintiffs may not be compelled to arbitrate their claims. * * *

CONCLUSION

For the foregoing reasons, we affirm the district court's denial of defendants' motion to compel arbitration and to stay court proceedings.

Editors' note on Software and Information under the UCC:
In footnote 13 of the *Specht* opinion, the court reviewed the question of
whether the UCC governed the transaction. It found it unnecessary to
decide the question. That footnote is reproduced here:

The district court concluded that the SmartDownload transactions
here should be governed by "California law as it relates to the sale of
goods, including the Uniform Commercial Code in effect in California."
Specht, 150 F.Supp.2d at 591. It is not obvious, however, that UCC
Article 2 ("sales of goods") applies to the licensing of software that is
downloadable from the Internet. * * * There is no doubt that a sale of
tangible goods over the Internet is governed by Article 2 of the UCC.
See, e.g., Butler v. Beer Across Am., 83 F.Supp.2d 1261, 1263–64 & n. 6
(N.D.Ala.2000) (applying Article 2 to an Internet sale of bottles of beer).
Some courts have also applied Article 2, occasionally with misgivings, to
sales of off-the-shelf software in tangible, packaged formats. *See, e.g.,
ProCD*, 86 F.3d at 1450. * * *

Downloadable software, however, is scarcely a "tangible" good, and,
in part because software may be obtained, copied, or transferred effort-
lessly at the stroke of a computer key, licensing of such Internet
products has assumed a vast importance in recent years. Recognizing
that "a body of law based on images of the sale of manufactured goods ill
fits licenses and other transactions in computer information," the National Conference of Commissioners on Uniform State Laws has promulgated the Uniform Computer Information Transactions Act ("UCITA"),
a code resembling UCC Article 2 in many respects but drafted to reflect
emergent practices in the sale and licensing of computer information.
UCITA, prefatory note (rev. ed. Aug.23, 2001) (available at www.ucitaon-
line.com/ucita.html). UCITA—originally intended as a new Article 2B to
supplement Articles 2 and 2A of the UCC but later proposed as an
independent code—has been adopted by two states, Maryland and Virginia. *See* Md.Code Ann. Com. Law §§ 22–101 *et seq.;* Va.Code Ann.
§§ 59.1–501.1 *et seq.*

We need not decide today whether UCC Article 2 applies to Internet
transactions in downloadable products. The district court's analysis and
the parties' arguments on appeal show that, for present purposes, there
is no essential difference between UCC Article 2 and the common law of
contracts. We therefore apply the common law, with exceptions as noted.

Editors' note on the proposed revision of the UCC: The
definition of "goods" in revised § 2–103(1)(k) provides that "[t]he term
does not include information. . . ."

The probable explanation for the exclusion of information transactions from the UCC is that NCCUSL, co-sponsor with the ALI of the
UCC, had embraced UCITA (Uniform Computer Information Transactions Act) even though UCITA was rejected by the ALI. Only Virginia
and Maryland have enacted UCITA. More states have enacted Anti–
UCITA legislation, for example, providing that a choice of law clause
that would lead to the application of UCITA is void. See, e.g., Iowa–St.

§ 554D.104. At this writing, August 2003, NCCUSL has announced that it is no longer pressing for UCITA's adoption.

Why is there hostility toward UCITA? Opponents argue that it is too strongly pro-licensor. For example, it permits license agreements to curtail a licensee's rights under Federal copyright law and it bars evidence of terms that are not contained in the written or downloaded license. Consumer protection advocates find many other faults in the formulation of the Act.

SECTION 11. OPTION CONTRACTS

(Calamari & Perillo 5th § 2.25 and 2.26)

PLANTATION KEY DEVELOPERS, INC. v. COLONIAL MORTGAGE CO. OF INDIANA, INC.

United States Court of Appeals, Fifth Circuit, 1979.
589 F.2d 164.

FAY, CIRCUIT JUDGE: This is an action brought by a condominium project builder, Plantation Key Developers, Inc. ("Plantation"), against its permanent lender, Colonial Mortgage Co.[1] ("Colonial"), based on breach of contract and fraud.[2] The trial court directed a verdict against Plantation on its fraud claim. The jury returned a verdict of $60,000 in favor of Plantation on its contract claim. The Court entered judgment thereon for $60,000 plus interest and costs. Colonial raises three points on appeal: 1) the breach of contract issue should not have been submitted to the jury. [Discussion of the two other points is omitted].

The dispute arose from a loan arrangement between Colonial and Plantation. Plantation was formed for the purpose of constructing a condominium project on Plantation Key, Florida. Through a mortgage broker Plantation contacted Colonial, a mortgage lender, for the purpose of obtaining permanent financing[3] for the condominium project.

---

1. There are actually two defendants in this action: Colonial Mortgage Co. and Southern Colonial Mortgage Co., a subsidiary. They are both referred to as "Colonial."

2. Jurisdiction is based on diversity of citizenship. 28 U.S.C. § 1332.

3. In order to facilitate an understanding of this opinion, we provide a brief description of the business relationships involved here. The builder is in the business of building condominiums for resale. In order to finance a construction project, the builder obtains a construction loan. The permanent lender agrees to make mortgage loans to purchasers of the units. This serves the function of encouraging sales. Part of the money which the purchaser pays to the builder goes to the construction lender, who is eventually paid off entirely. If the builder wants to be certain, at the commencement of construction, that mortgage loans will be available to prospective purchasers at the completion of the project, he pays the permanent lender a commitment fee in exchange for the lender's agreement to offer mortgage loans at a certain rate for a specified period of time. In making such a commitment, the permanent lender runs the risk that interest rates may rise and it is committed to offering loans at less than the market rate.

In November 1973 Colonial promised to provide permanent mortgage funds through 1975 to Plantation. The agreement provided for performance in three parts. First, Colonial agreed to provide mortgage money through December 31, 1974 at the rate of 9% plus a loan service fee (points) of 3½% of the loan amount. Second, Plantation had the option to extend the commitment for six months "with adjustments in interest and points made if market conditions so demand." Finally, the agreement provided for another six month extension of the commitment with the same interest and point adjustments. Plantation paid a nonrefundable commitment fee of $60,000. In addition, Plantation agreed to pay $30,000 each time it chose to bind Colonial to a six month extension.

The dispute is based on Colonial's adjustment of the interest rates and service fees for the first extension, January 1, 1975 to July 1, 1975. Colonial proposed to extend the commitment with the rate changed to 9¾% and 9 points. Plantation contended that these rates were inconsistent with Colonial's promise to make rate adjustments only in response to "market conditions." Plantation refused to pay $30,000 for an extension at the rates of 9¾% interest and 9 points. Instead, it brought this action.

I. Breach of Contract

Colonial presents an arsenal of legal theories as the grounds upon which it is excused from performance of the first six month option, regardless of the reasonableness of its adjustment of the rates. It argues: 1) Plantation's payment of the extension fee was a condition precedent to suit; 2) the quotation and extension fee were dependent covenants; 3) the quotation and the extension fee were concurrent conditions; 4) Plantation's failure to tender the extension fee was a breach which excused Colonial from performance; and 5) the option lapsed due to Plantation's failure to exercise it. The essence of Colonial's argument is that Plantation cannot complain that the quoted rates were violative of the contract since it did not tender the $30,000 for the six month extension. Both the authorities and the reasoning relied upon by Colonial are unpersuasive.

Colonial fails to recognize its agreement for what it is, an option contract. An option contract has two elements: 1) the underlying contract which is not binding until accepted; and 2) the agreement to hold open to the optionee the opportunity to accept. *Frissell v. Nichols,* 94 Fla. 403, 114 So. 431, 433 (1927). Both the option and the underlying contract must be supported by consideration. *Donahue v. Davis,* 68 So.2d 163 (Fla.1953); *Koplin v. Bennett,* 155 So.2d 568 (Fla. 1st DCA 1963). In this case, the consideration for the option to bind Colonial to a six month extension was the $60,000 which Plantation had already paid. Plantation was obligated to pay the additional $30,000 only if it chose *to exercise* its option and *to bind* Colonial to the quoted rates for the extended period. Viewed in this manner, it is clear that Colonial's contractual duty to quote a rate for the six month extension period was in no way dependent upon Plantation's payment of the $30,000. It would be absurd to say that

Plantation should pay $30,000 for Colonial's commitment before Colonial has stated the terms, especially when Plantation had already paid Colonial $60,000 to do just that.

Thus, the trial court correctly left to the jury the decision of whether Colonial's quoted rate of 9¾% and 9 points was in compliance with Colonial's obligation to change its rates only if market conditions so demanded. The jury found in a special verdict that the interest rate and closing fees were not in compliance with the commitment letter.

Our inquiry on review is whether there was sufficient evidence to support the jury's decision. "[I]t is the function of the jury as the traditional finder of the facts, and not the Court, to weigh conflicting evidence and inferences, and determine the credibility of witnesses." *Boeing Co. v. Shipman,* 411 F.2d 365, 375 (5th Cir.1969) (footnote omitted). The evidence supports the jury's decision that Colonial's rate quotation did not comply with the contract. Plantation presented several witnesses who testified that the rates charged on projects comparable to Plantation's were in the range of 9¾% interest and 3 points. In addition, money was available through the J.I. Kislak Company, one of the country's largest mortgage brokers, for permanent condominium loans at 9¾% interest and 3 points. Finally, an expert witness testified that points had been fairly constant at about 3½ to 4½% of the amount of the loan. Based upon this testimony, the jury reasonably could have found that Colonial's rate of 9¾% and 9 points was not in compliance with the contractual provision requiring quotations to be in accord with market conditions. * * *

The jury verdict is affirmed. * * *

Problems

109. A makes an offer to B by mail which states that the offer will be open for thirty days. Before B accepts, A calls and revokes the offer. Is the revocation effective? Would the result be different if the offer had read: "This offer is irrevocable for 30 days"; "This is a firm offer for 30 days"; "I must have your answer within 30 days"?

110. A, in a signed writing, sent B an offer that stated: "This offer is not subject to revocation for thirty days." B immediately rejected the offer and A then purported to revoke the offer. Was the offer still open so that it could be accepted?

111. In June 1980 L agreed to lease certain commercial premises to T for a term of 10 years. A clause of the lease gave T a right of first refusal to purchase the property during the term of the lease. This clause provided that if L decided to sell the property and found a bona fide purchaser ready to buy it, L would give T immediate notification of the terms of the proposed sale. T then had the right for 30 days to purchase the property on the same terms as those negotiated with the third party purchaser. On June 24, 1988, T received a letter from L notifying T of the proposed sale to C, enclosing a copy of the contract signed by L and C and giving T 30 days to exercise its

right of first refusal. On July 22, 1988, T sent a notice of exercise to L which was received on August 6. Is T entitled to purchase the property?

First Examination Question

Case owned a tractor located in the woods near Oswego, New York. On February 16, Thompson called Case about buying the tractor. Case said: "I will sell the tractor to you, or to anybody else for that matter, for $450. Upon an agreement you may take possession of the tractor." On March 1st Thompson picked up the tractor and brought it to his place and so informed Case on March 15. On March 1st Peterson, who had learned of the offer from Thompson, sent in a notice of acceptance.

(a) Discuss the rights of the parties.

(b) Would the result be different if Case had not said "Upon an agreement you may take possession of the Tractor?"

(c) What would be the result if instead of picking up the tractor on March 1, Thompson had sent a letter stating: "This letter is sent to confirm that I am purchasing the tractor of which we spoke on the terms indicated. Naturally, I expect that an arbitration clause is part of our deal."

Second Examination Question

Proctor & Gamble (P & G) manufactures Pampers, a brand of disposable diapers. For some years each package of Pampers bore a Teddy Bear symbol and this legend:

> Save these Teddy Bear points and use them to save money on toys, clothes, furniture and lots of other baby things when you shop the Pampers Baby Catalog. For your free copy of the Catalog send your name, complete address and youngest baby's date of birth to: Pampers Baby Catalog, P.O. Box 8634, Clinton Iowa 52736.

In April 1989, P & G sent out its final catalog. On the front cover was a statement that the offer would expire on February 28, 1990.

Plaintiffs are a class of individuals who had faithfully collected Teddy Bear symbols, and had not seen the April 1989 catalog, were unaware of the February 28, 1990 expiration statement, and who have sued P & G.

Discuss the rights of the parties including theories available, probable defenses, and your estimate of the likely result of the lawsuit.

Multiple Choice Question

John and his 9–year old daughter visited Tony, a breeder of golden retrievers, in response to Tony's newspaper ad for sale of puppies. During the visit, John offered to buy a specific 8–week old puppy selected by his daughter for $600, payment to be made when the puppy is picked up at 10 weeks of age. Tony indicated that another customer had expressed an interest in this particular puppy and that he would check with that customer and get back to John. In fact, though he gave Tony no reason to know this, John had no intention of buying the puppy but had made the offer just to please his daughter. Two days later Tony sent John a fax stating that he accepted John's offer.

a) John is not contractually bound to buy the puppy because he did not intend to make an offer.

b) John is not contractually bound to buy the puppy because his offer, made in a face-to face conversation, lapsed before acceptance.

c) John is not contractually bound to buy the puppy because the fax was an unreasonable medium to transmit the acceptance.

d) John is contractually bound to buy the puppy.

Chapter 2

CONSIDERATION

SECTION 1.   WHAT IS CONSIDERATION?

(Calamari & Perillo 5th §§ 4.1—4.8, 4.14—4.15)

ADAM SMITH, THE WEALTH OF NATIONS
1776

In almost every other race of animals each individual, when it is grown up to maturity, is entirely independent, and in its natural state has occasion for the assistance of no other living creature. But man has almost constant occasion for the help of his brethren, and it is in vain for him to expect it from their benevolence only. He will be more likely to prevail if he can interest their self-love in his favour, and show them that it is for their own advantage to do for him what he requires of them. Whoever offers to another a bargain of any kind, proposed to do this. Get me that which I want and you shall have this which you want, is the meaning of each offer; and it is in this manner that we obtain from one another the far greater part of those good offices which we stand in need of. It is not from the benevolence of the butcher, the brewer, or the baker that we expect our dinner, but from their regard to their own interest.

HAMER v. SIDWAY
Court of Appeals of New York, 1891.
124 N.Y. 538, 27 N.E. 256.

Appeal from an order of the general term of the supreme court in the fourth judicial department, made July 1, 1890, which reversed a judgment in favor of the plaintiff entered upon a decision of the court on trial at Special Term and granted a new trial.

This action was brought upon an alleged contract.

The plaintiff presented a claim to the executor of William E. Story, Sr., for $5,000 and interest from the 6th day of February, 1875. She acquired it through several mesne assignments from William E. Story, 2d. The claim being rejected by the executor, this action was brought. It appears that William E. Story, Sr., was the uncle of William E. Story, 2d;

that at the celebration of the golden wedding of Samuel Story and wife, father and mother of William E. Story, Sr., on the 20th day of March, 1869, in the presence of the family and invited guests, he promised his nephew that if he would refrain from drinking, using tobacco, swearing, and playing cards or billiards for money until he became 21 years of age, he would pay him the sum of $5,000. The nephew assented thereto, and fully performed the conditions inducing the promise. When the nephew arrived at the age of 21 years, and on the 31st day of January, 1875, he wrote to his uncle, informing him that he had performed his part of the agreement, and had thereby become entitled to the sum of $5,000. The uncle received the letter, and a few days later, and on the 6th day of February, he wrote and mailed to his nephew the following letter:

"Buffalo, Feb. 6, 1875.

"W.E. Story, Jr.:

"Dear Nephew—Your letter of the 31st ult. came to hand all right, saying that you had lived up to the promise made to me several years ago. I have no doubt but you have, for which you shall have five thousand dollars, as I promised you. I had the money in the bank the day you was twenty-one years old that I intend for you, and you shall have the money certain. * * *

"P.S.—You can consider this money on interest."

The nephew received the letter, and thereafter consented that the money should remain with his uncle in accordance with the terms and conditions of the letter. The uncle died on the 29th day of January, 1887, without having paid over to his nephew any portion of the said $5,000 and interest.

PARKER, J. (after stating the facts as above.) The question which provoked the most discussion by counsel on this appeal, and which lies at the foundation of plaintiff's asserted right of recovery, is whether by virtue of a contract defendant's testator, William E. Story, became indebted to his nephew, William E. Story, 2d, on his twenty-first birthday in the sum of $5,000. The trial court found as a fact that "on the 20th day of March, 1869, * * * William E. Story agreed to and with William E. Story, 2d, that if he would refrain from drinking liquor, using tobacco, swearing, and playing cards or billiards for money until he should become twenty-one years of age, then he, the said William E. Story, would at that time pay him, the said William E. Story, 2d, the sum of $5,000 for such refraining, to which the said William E. Story, 2d, agreed," and that he "in all things fully performed his part of said agreement."

The defendant contends that the contract was without consideration to support it, and therefore invalid. He asserts that the promisee, by refraining from the use of liquor and tobacco, was not harmed, but benefited; that that which he did was best for him to do, independently of his uncle's promise,—and insists that it follows that, unless the promisor was benefited, the contract was without consideration,—a contention which, if well founded, would seem to leave open for controversy in many cases whether that which the promisee did or omitted to do was in fact of such benefit to him as to leave no consideration to support the enforcement of the promisor's agreement. Such a rule could not be tolerated, and is without foundation in the law. The exchequer chamber in 1875 defined "consideration" as follows: "A valuable consideration, in the sense of the law, may consist either in some right, interest, profit, or benefit accruing to the one party, or some forbearance, detriment, loss, or responsibility given, suffered, or undertaken by the other." Courts "will not ask whether the thing which forms the consideration does in fact benefit the promisee or a third party, or is of any substantial value to any one. It is enough that something is promised, done, forborne, or suffered by the party to whom the promise is made as consideration for the promise made to him." (Anson's Prin. of Con. 63.)

"In general a waiver of any legal right at the request of another party is a sufficient consideration for a promise." (Parsons on Contracts, 444.)

"Any damage, or suspension, or forbearance of a right will be sufficient to sustain a promise." (Kent, vol 2, 465, 12th ed.)

Pollock in his work on Contracts, page 166, after citing the definition given by the exchequer chamber, already quoted, says: "The second branch of this judicial description is really the most important one. Consideration means not so much that one party is profiting as that the other abandons some legal right in the present, or limits his legal freedom of action in the future, as an inducement for the promise of the first."

Now, applying this rule to the facts before us, the promisee used tobacco, occasionally drank liquor, and he had a legal right to do so. That right he abandoned for a period of years upon the strength of the promise of the testator that for such forbearance he would give him $5,000. We need not speculate on the effort which may have been required to give up the use of those stimulants. It is sufficient that he restricted his lawful freedom of action within certain prescribed limits upon the faith of his uncle's agreement, and now, having fully performed the conditions imposed, it is of no moment whether such performance actually proved a benefit to the promisor, and the court will not inquire into it; but, were it a proper subject of inquiry, we see nothing in this record that would permit a determination that the uncle was not benefited in a legal sense. Few cases have been found which may be said to be precisely in point, but such as have been, support the position we have taken.

* * *

In *Lakota v. Newton*, (an unreported case in the superior court of Worcester, Mass.,) the complaint averred defendant's promise that "if you (meaning the plaintiff) will leave off drinking for a year I will give you $100," plaintiff's assent thereto, performance of the condition by him, and demanded judgment therefor. Defendant demurred, on the ground, among others, that the plaintiff's declaration did not allege a valid and sufficient consideration for the agreement of the defendant. The demurrer was overruled.

In *Talbott v. Stemmons*, [12 S.W.Rep. 297,] * * * the stepgrandmother of the plaintiff made with him the following agreement: "I do promise and bind myself to give my grandson Albert R. Talbott $500 at my death if he will never take another chew of tobacco or smoke another cigar during my life, from this date up to my death; and if he breaks this pledge he is to refund double the amount to his mother." The executor of Mrs. Stemmons demurred to the complaint on the ground that the agreement was not based on a sufficient consideration. The demurrer was sustained, and an appeal taken therefrom to the court of appeals, where the decision of the court below was reversed. In the opinion of the court it is said that "the right to use and enjoy the use of tobacco was a right that belonged to the plaintiff, and not forbidden by law. The abandonment of its use may have saved him money, or contributed to his health; nevertheless, the surrender of that right caused the promise, and, having the right to contract with reference to the subject-matter, the abandonment of the use was a sufficient consideration to uphold the promise." Abstinence from the use of intoxicating liquors was held to furnish a good consideration for a promissory note in *Lindell v. Rokes*, (60 Mo. 249).

The cases cited by the defendant on this question are not in point. * * *

The order appealed from should be reversed and the judgment of the Special Term affirmed, with costs payable out of the estate.

All concur.

KIRKSEY v. KIRKSEY

Supreme Court of Alabama, 1845.
8 Ala. 131.

The plaintiff was the wife of defendant's brother, but had for some time been a widow, and had several children. In 1840, the plaintiff resided on public land, under a contract of lease, she had held over and was comfortably settled, and would have attempted to secure the land she lived on. The defendant resided in Talladega county, some sixty, or seventy miles off. On the 10th October, 1840, he wrote to her the following letter:

"Dear sister Antillico—Much to my mortification, I heard, that brother Henry was dead, and one of his children. I know that your situation is one of grief, and difficulty. You had a bad chance before, but a great deal worse now. I should like to come and see you, but cannot with convenience at present. * * * I do not know whether you have a preference on the place you live on, or not. If you had, I would advise you to obtain your preference, and sell the land and quit the country, as I understand it is very unhealthy, and I know society is very bad. If you will come down and see me, I will let you have a place to raise your family, and I have more open land than I can tend; and on the account of your situation, and that of your family, I feel like I want you and the children to do well."

Within a month or two after the receipt of this letter, the plaintiff abandoned her possession, without disposing of it, and removed with her family, to the residence of the defendant, who put her in comfortable houses, and gave her land to cultivate for two years, at the end of which time he notified her to remove, and put her in a house, not comfortable, in the woods, which he afterwards required her to leave.

A verdict being found for the plaintiff, for two hundred dollars, the above facts were agreed, and if they will sustain the action, the judgment is to be affirmed, otherwise it is to be reversed.

* * *

ORMOND, J. The inclination of my mind, is, that the loss and inconvenience, which the plaintiff sustained in breaking up, and moving to the defendant's, a distance of sixty miles, is a sufficient consideration to support the promise, to furnish her with a house, and land to cultivate, until she could raise her family. My brothers, however think, that the promise on the part of the defendant, was a mere gratuity, and that an action will not lie for its breach. The judgment of the Court below must therefore be reversed, pursuant to the agreement of the parties.

GOTTLIEB v. TROPICANA HOTEL AND CASINO

United States District Court, E.D. Pennsylvania, 2000.
109 F.Supp.2d 324.

BARTLE, DISTRICT JUDGE. * * *

Tropicana, a New Jersey corporation that operates a gambling casino in Atlantic City, offers people membership in its "Diamond Club." In order to become a Diamond Club member, an individual must visit a promotional booth in the casino, obtain and fill out an application form, and show identification. There is no charge. The application form lists the individual's name, address, telephone number, and e-mail address, and the information provided is entered into the casino's computer database. Each member receives a Diamond Club card bearing a unique identification number. The member then presents or "swipes" the card in a machine each time he or she plays a game at the casino, and the casino obtains information about the member's gambling habits. The casino's marketing department then uses that information to tailor its promotions.

Ms. Gottlieb was, and had been for a number of years, a member of Tropicana's Diamond Club. Upon entering the casino on July 24, 1999, she immediately went to the Fun House Million Dollar Wheel Promotion ("Million Dollar Wheel") and waited in line for approximately five minutes before it was her turn to play. Diamond Club members were entitled to one free spin of the Million Dollar Wheel each day. As its name suggests, the promotion offered participants the chance to win a grand prize of $1 million. Ms. Gottlieb had played the game several times before. In both New Jersey and Pennsylvania, Tropicana had advertised the Million Dollar Wheel in newspapers, magazines, and with direct mailings, although there is no evidence that the Gottliebs saw any of the advertisements.

Not surprisingly, the parties do not agree as to everything that happened once Ms. Gottlieb started play. However, they do agree that she presented her Diamond Club card, a casino operator swiped it through the card reader, she pressed a button to activate the wheel, and the Million Dollar Wheel began spinning. Ms. Gottlieb contends that the wheel landed on the $1 million grand prize, but that when it did so, the casino attendant immediately swiped another card through the machine, reactivated the wheel, and then the wheel landed on a prize of two show tickets. Tropicana avers that the wheel simply landed on the lesser prize. The casino says the wheel never landed on $1 million, and the attendant never intervened and reactivated the wheel.

I.

* * *

Under both Pennsylvania and New Jersey law, adequate consideration is necessary in order to form an enforceable contract. *See Continental Bank of Pennsylvania v. Barclay Riding Academy, Inc.*, 93 N.J. 153, 459 A.2d 1163, 1171 (1983); *Stelmack v. Glen Alden Coal Co.*, 339 Pa. 410, 413–14, 14 A.2d 127 (1940). Consideration is a bargained for exchange, and it may take the form of either a detriment to the promisee or a benefit to the promisor. *See Continental Bank*, 459 A.2d at 1172; *Stelmack*, 339 Pa. at 414, 14 A.2d at 128. In support of its contention that New Jersey law holds that no valid consideration exists when a person participates in a promotion, Tropicana cites only one case, a 1985 unpublished transcript of a ruling of the Superior Court of New Jersey. There, the Resorts International Hotel, Inc., a licensed casino operator in New Jersey, sued the New Jersey Division of Gaming Enforcement seeking a declaratory judgment that three promotions it was conducting, a gin rummy tournament and two stock market games, did not violate New Jersey law. *See Resorts Int'l Hotel, Inc. v. New Jersey Div. of Gaming Enforcement*, No. L39436–85, slip op. (N.J.Super. Ct. Law Div., Atlantic Co. Oct. 25, 1985). The question before the court was whether "something of value" passed from the player to the casino, making the promotions illegal gambling in violation of New Jersey law.[3] The court

---

3. According to the court, New Jersey law defined "something of value" as "any money or property, any token, object or article exchangeable for money or property or any form of credit or promise directly or indirectly contemplating transfer of money or property or of any interest therein or involving extension of a service, entertainment or a privilege of playing at a game or scheme without charge." Id. at 12 (citing N.J. Stat. Ann. § 2C:37–1(d)).

did not determine whether a contract had been formed. It did observe, however, that in the past the presence of only "minute consideration" made a promotion illegal gambling under New Jersey law. *Id.* at 11. Over time, though, the scope of "something of value" had been restricted and "strictly defined." *Id.* at 12. In other words, "something of value" requires more than the minimum consideration that would support the formation of a contract. The court concluded that nothing "of value" had passed from player to casino in the course of the three promotions. *Id.* at 13. It did not decide, as Tropicana contends, that participation in a promotion cannot constitute adequate consideration for a contract.

We find the decision of the New Jersey Supreme Court in *Lucky Calendar Co. v. Cohen*, 19 N.J. 399, 117 A.2d 487 (1955), *op. adhered to on reh'g*, 20 N.J. 451, 120 A.2d 107 (1956), to be on point. There, an advertising company brought a declaratory judgment action against the Camden County prosecutor, seeking a determination that its promotional advertisement campaign for Acme Super Markets did not violate New Jersey's Lottery Act. The centerpiece of the campaign was a calendar that had Acme coupons bordering it, which was distributed by mass mailings. *See Lucky Calendar*, 117 A.2d at 489–90. The calendar contained an explanation of the "Lucky Calendar Prize Contest." Entrants had the opportunity to win prizes in monthly drawings. All they had to do to enter was tear the entry form off of the calendar, enter a name, address, and phone number, and have the form deposited in a box at any Acme store. There was no charge, and they were not required to be present for the drawing. *See Id.* at 490.

The question in *Lucky Calendar* was whether there had been consideration for participation in the drawings. The Supreme Court of New Jersey noted that, assuming consideration was required in order for something to qualify as an illegal lottery under the Lottery Act, it need only be the minimum consideration that is necessary to form a contract. *See Id.* at 495. It explained:

> [T]he consideration in a lottery, as in any form of simple contract, need not be money or the promise of money. Nor need it be of intrinsic value; "a rose, a hawk or a peppercorn" will suffice, provided it is what is asked for by the promisor and is not illegal. . . . Whether a "peppercorn" or the filling in and delivering of a coupon is sufficient consideration for a promise depends only on whether it was the requested detriment to the promisee induced by the promise. That is consideration which is regarded as such by the parties.

Id. (citing *Williston on Contracts* (rev. ed.1936), §§ 100 n. 8 and 115).[4]

The court determined that consideration was present "both in the form of a detriment or inconvenience to the promisee at the request of the promisor and of a benefit to the promisor." *Id.* "Completing the coupon and arranging for the deposit of it in the box" at the store was

---

4. The legislature of New Jersey has repealed the Lottery Act that was in effect at the time of this case.

the detriment to the promisee, and the "increase in volume of business" was the benefit to the promisor and its customer, the owner of the Acme stores. *Id.* at 496. As the court pointed out, "The motives of the plaintiff and its customer [in offering the Lucky Calendar Prize Contest] ... are in nowise altruistic." *Id.*

In *Cobaugh v. Klick–Lewis, Inc.*, 385 Pa.Super. 587, 561 A.2d 1248, (1989), the Superior Court of Pennsylvania decided that there was adequate consideration to form a binding contract where a golfer, who was participating in a tournament, shot a hole-in-one after seeing a contest announcement offering a new car to anyone who could ace the particular hole. See *Cobaugh*, 561 A.2d at 1249–50. The court noted that the promisor benefitted from the publicity of the promotional advertising, and the golfer performed an act that he was under no legal obligation to perform. *See Id.* at 1250.

The laws of New Jersey and Pennsylvania similarly hold that the minimal detriment to a participant in a promotional contest is sufficient consideration for a valid contract. As there is no conflict between the laws of the two states, we need not engage in any conflict of laws analysis. It simply does not matter which law we apply.

Ms. Gottlieb had to go to the casino to participate in the promotion. She had to wait in line to spin the wheel. By presenting her Diamond Club card to the casino attendant and allowing it to be swiped into the casino's machine, she was permitting the casino to gather information about her gambling habits. Additionally, by participating in the game, she was a part of the entertainment that casinos, by their very nature, are designed to offer to all of those present. All of these detriments to Ms. Gottlieb were "the requested detriment[s] to the promisee induced by the promise" of Tropicana to offer her a chance to win $1 million. *Lucky Calendar*, 117 A.2d at 495. Tropicana's motives in offering the promotion were "in nowise altruistic." *Id.* at 496. It offered the promotion in order to generate patronage of and excitement within the casino. In short, Ms. Gottlieb provided adequate consideration to form a contract with Tropicana.

* * *

Tropicana's motion for summary judgment against Ms. Gottlieb on Count I of the complaint will be denied.

BATSAKIS v. DEMOTSIS

Court of Civil Appeals of Texas, El Paso, 1949.
226 S.W.2d 673.

McGill, Justice.

This is an appeal from a judgment of the 57th judicial District Court of Bexar County. * * *

Plaintiff sued defendant to recover $2,000 with interest at the rate of 8% per annum from April 2, 1942, alleged to be due on the following instrument, being a translation from the original, which is written in the Greek language:

"Peiraeus [sic]
April 2, 1942

"Mr. George Batsakis
Konstantinou Diadohou #7
Peiraeus [sic]

"Mr. Batsakis:

"I state by my present (letter) that I received today from you the amount of two thousand dollars ($2,000.00) of United States of America money, which I borrowed from you for the support of my family during these difficult days and because it is impossible for me to transfer dollars of my own from America.

"The above amount I accept with the expressed promise that I will return to you again in American dollars either at the end of the present war or even before in the event that you might be able to find a way to collect them (dollars) from my representative in America to whom I shall write and give him an order relative to this. You understand until the final execution (payment) to the above amount an eight per cent interest will be added and paid together with the principal.

"I thank you and I remain yours with respects.

"The recipient,

(Signed) Eugenia The. Demotsis."

Trial to the court without the intervention of a jury resulted in a judgment in favor of plaintiff for $750.00 principal, and interest at the rate of 8% per annum from April 2, 1942 to the date of judgment, totaling $1163.83, with interest thereon at the rate of 8% per annum until paid. Plaintiff has perfected his appeal.

The court sustained certain special exceptions of plaintiff to defendant's first amended original answer on which the case was tried, and struck therefrom paragraphs II, III and V. Defendant excepted to such action of the court, but has not cross-assigned error here. The answer, stripped of such paragraphs, consisted of a general denial contained in paragraph I thereof, and of paragraph IV, which is as follows:

"IV. That under the circumstances alleged in Paragraph II of this answer, the consideration upon which said written instrument sued upon by plaintiff herein is founded, is wanting and has failed to the extent of $1975.00, and defendant pleads specially under the verification hereinafter made the want and failure of consideration stated, and now tenders, as defendant has heretofore tendered to plaintiff, $25.00 as the value of the loan of money received by defendant from plaintiff, together with interest thereon.

"Further, in connection with this plea of want and failure of consideration defendant alleges that she at no time received from plaintiff himself or from anyone for plaintiff any money or thing of value other than, as hereinbefore alleged, the original loan of 500,000 drachmae. That at the time of the loan by plaintiff to defendant of said 500,000 drachmae the value of 500,000 drachmae in the Kingdom of Greece in dollars of money of the United States of America, was $25.00, and also at said time the value of 500,000 drachmae of Greek money in the United States of America in dollars was $25.00 of money of the United States of America. The plea of want and failure of consideration is verified by defendant as follows."

The allegations in paragraph II which were stricken, referred to in paragraph IV, were that the instrument sued on was signed and delivered in the Kingdom of Greece on or about April 2, 1942, at which time both plaintiff and defendant were residents of and residing in the Kingdom of Greece, and

"*Plaintiff* (emphasis ours) avers that on or about April 2, 1942 she owned money * * * in the United States of America, but was then and there in the Kingdom of Greece in straitened financial circumstances due to the conditions produced by World War II and could not make use of her money and property and credit existing in the United States of America. That in the circumstances the plaintiff agreed to and did lend to defendant the sum of 500,000 drachmae, which at that time, on or about April 2, 1942, had the value of $25.00 in money of the United States of America. That the said plaintiff, knowing defendant's financial distress and desire to return to the United States of America, exacted of her the written instrument plaintiff sues upon, which was a promise by her to pay to him the sum of $2,000.00 of United States of America money."

Plaintiff specially excepted to paragraph IV because the allegations thereof were insufficient to allege either want of consideration or failure of consideration, in that it affirmatively appears therefrom that defendant received what was agreed to be delivered to her, and that plaintiff breached no agreement. The court overruled this exception, and such action is assigned as error. Error is also assigned because of the court's failure to enter judgment for the whole unpaid balance of the principal of the instrument with interest as therein provided.

Defendant testified that she did receive 500,000 drachmas from plaintiff. It is not clear whether she received all the 500,000 drachmas or only a portion of them before she signed the instrument in question. Her testimony clearly shows that the understanding of the parties was that plaintiff would give her the 500,000 drachmas if she would sign the instrument. She testified:

"Q . . . . who suggested the figure of $2,000.00?

A.   That was how he asked me from the beginning. He said he will give me five hundred thousand drachmas provided I signed that I would pay him $2,000.00 American money."

The transaction amounted to a sale by plaintiff of the 500,000 drachmas in consideration of the execution of the instrument sued on, by defendant. It is not contended that the drachmas had no value. Indeed, the judgment indicates that the trial court placed a value of $750.00 on them or on the other consideration which plaintiff gave defendant for the instrument if he believed plaintiff's testimony. Therefore the plea of want of consideration was unavailing. A plea of want of consideration amounts to a contention that the instrument never became a valid obligation in the first place. National Bank of Commerce v. Williams, 125 Tex. 619, 84 S.W.2d 691.

Mere inadequacy of consideration will not void a contract. 10 Tex. Jur., Contracts, Sec. 89, p. 150; Chastain v. Texas Christian Missionary Society, Tex.Civ.App., 78 S.W.2d 728, loc. cit. 731(3), Wr. Ref.

Nor was the plea of failure of consideration availing. Defendant got exactly what she contracted for according to her own testimony. The court should have rendered judgment in favor of plaintiff against defendant for the principal sum of $2,000.00 evidenced by the instrument sued on, with interest as therein provided. We construe the provision relating to interest as providing for interest at the rate of 8% per annum. The judgment is reformed so as to award appellant a recovery against appellee of $2,000.00 with interest thereon at the rate of 8% per annum from April 2, 1942. Such judgment will bear interest at the rate of 8% per annum until paid on $2,000.00 thereof and on the balance interest at the rate of 6% per annum. As so reformed, the judgment is affirmed.

Reformed and affirmed.

WHITE v. McBRIDE

Supreme Court of Tennessee, 1996.
937 S.W.2d 796.

DROWOTA, JUSTICE.

This case presents the question of whether the plaintiff, attorney Frank White, may recover attorney's fees from the estate of Kasper McGrory. This broad question may, in turn, be divided into two specific subissues: (1) whether the contingency fee contract between White and McGrory is "clearly excessive" under Disciplinary Rule 2–106 of the Code of Professional Responsibility, Tenn. Sup.Ct. R. 8, and is, thus, unenforceable; and (2) if the contingency fee contract is unenforceable, whether White may, nevertheless, recover attorney's fees on a *quantum meruit* basis. For the reasons that follow, we hold that the contract is unenforceable and that White is not entitled to recover under the theory of *quantum meruit*. Because the probate court and the Court of Appeals held that White could not recover under the contract, but could recover on a *quantum meruit* basis, we reverse the latter part of the judgment.

FACTS AND PROCEDURAL HISTORY

* * * The plaintiff, Frank White, was a friend and legal representative of Kasper McGrory and his wife Ruby Leigh Anglin McGrory for several years; in the early 1970s, he drafted wills for them in which each left all his or her assets to the surviving spouse. The McGrorys' relationship, however, apparently deteriorated thereafter. In the fall of 1990,

while suffering from an illness that would eventually result in her death, Leigh wrote a holographic will in which she left several specific bequests to family members and friends, but made no mention whatsoever of Kasper. This will was placed in her safe, which contained a great many of her assets, including jewelry, deeds to real property in Texas, and numerous stock certificates.

During Leigh's illness her brother, Roma Anglin, traveled to Memphis from his home in Texas and, with White's assistance, secured a durable power of attorney [from] her. * * * [D]ays before her death, Roma Anglin and Vincent Smith, one of Kasper's nephews, opened Leighs's safe and made a detailed inventory of its contents. After completing the inventory, Roma removed the contents and placed them, pursuant to his power of attorney, in a safe deposit box at a First Tennessee Bank in Memphis. At some point after the inventory was taken, Vincent Smith provided copies of that document to both Kasper McCrory and White.

Leigh died on December 22, 1990; after the funeral, Roma Anglin returned to Texas, taking the holographic will with him. [It later came to light that Roma Anglin had taken the entire contents of the safe deposit back to Texas.] Soon thereafter Kasper expressed a desire to put Leigh's estate in order, and he asked White to assist him. White agreed to help, and he apparently contacted Roma and Leigh's other relatives in Texas to find out if they would be willing to come to Shelby County and have the estate probated there. Evidently, White did not receive a positive response from these Texas relatives, and he advised Kasper to wait and see what would happen. Kasper continued, however, to insist on taking action with regard to the estate. Thus, on February 28, 1991, he and White entered into an agreement in which White was "to force the probate of Leigh McGrory's estate in Shelby County, Tennessee to ascertain assets, 1/3 of which belong to the husband, in order to recover same." For these services White was to be paid a $2,500 retainer plus "one-third of gross recovery above and in excess of retainer."

[Under Tennessee law, a surviving spouse is allowed to elect to take 1/3 of his or her deceased spouse's estate despite the provisions of the decedent's will. Ed.]

On March 8, 1991, White filed, in the Shelby County Probate Court, a petition to open Leigh McGrory's estate and to issue letters of administration. * * *

On March 11, 1991, the probate court entered an order appointing James Allison as administrator of Leigh McGrory's estate. * * *

On March 27, 1991, Verda Hogue, Leigh's sister living in Texas, filed a petition in the probate court asking it to (1) admit the will taken from the safe to probate; (2) appoint Verda Hogue executrix of the estate; and (3) revoke the letters of administration previously issued to James Allison. * * *

[The contents of the Tennessee safe deposit box with the exception of the jewelry, were returned to the probate court.]

* * * [I]n its April 25, 1991, order denying Verda Hogue's petition to be named executrix, the probate court stated that "an injunction shall issue enjoining all heirs and interested parties from disposition of, or removing from this jurisdiction any personal property belonging to the deceased."

After this initial flurry of activity, the administration of Leigh McGrory's estate languished in the probate court; when Kasper McGrory died on July 22, 1992, no assets had yet been distributed.[2] Kasper left a will in which he bequeathed virtually his entire estate to the Catholic Diocese of Memphis; he also named Hubert McBride as executor of the will. McBride, in turn, hired attorney James Bland to represent Kasper's estate.

In the fall of 1993, James Kleiser, the chief financial officer of the Memphis Diocese, expressed concern about the fact that the administration of Leigh McGrory's estate was not still complete, and that Kasper's estate had received nothing therefrom. After conferring with Bland, Kleiser decided that it would be preferable to relieve White of his representation of Kasper's interest in Leigh's estate. Bland, thus, wrote White a letter on October 27, 1992, informing him of the decision. In this letter, Bland offered to pay White a reasonable fee for his prior representation of Kasper's interest in Leigh's estate.

White refused to accept this proposal, citing his February 28, 1991, contingency fee contract with Kasper. Thereafter, Kasper's estate filed a petition to substitute Bland as counsel and for approval of attorney's fees, which White opposed. On January 25, 1993, the probate court entered an order substituting counsel; it also set a hearing for March 2, 1993, for a determination of a reasonable fee due White.

Before the hearing was held, however, White filed a claim against Kasper's estate for $108,291.00; this figure represented approximately one-third of $349,000, the amount of Leigh's estate to which Kasper was entitled by law. McBride filed an exception to this claim, alleging that the claimed fee was "clearly excessive" under DR 2–106 and was, therefore, unenforceable.

After hearing evidence on these issues, including the testimony of two former probate judges and White's sworn statement as to the amount of time he had expended on the case, the probate court filed a memorandum opinion in January 1994. In this opinion, the probate court held that the fee sought to be charged by White violated DR 2–106. It reasoned as follows:

> There is no proof in this record that there was ever any doubt that Mr. McGrory was Ruby Leigh McGrory's surviving spouse and an heir at law, and therefore entitled to, at a minimum, 1/3 of his wife's estate. The record reflects no will contest, no issue raised as to Mr.

---

2. The record reveals that relatively little was done with regard to the estate. The only meaningful pleading is White's petition on behalf of Kasper for an elective share on May 31, 1991, and this petition was never acted upon. Furthermore, several essential matters, such as taxation requirements, were not taken care of by the administrator. * * *

McGrory being the surviving spouse and no other suit or challenge of any kind in this matter undertaken or defended by Mr. White. Therefore, the only genuine contingency involved was how large a disbursement Mr. McGrory would ultimately receive by operation of law.

[White] in support of his fee request points to the fact that he had to resist the efforts of Mrs. McGrory's relatives to take her assets to Texas. Mr. Allison testified that Mr. White was instrumental in helping him get those assets returned to Memphis. Although Mr. White did help get those assets back, there was never any doubt that these assets belonged to Mrs. McGrory's estate and it was in the power of this court to order them to be returned . . . .

[White also] defends his contingent fee contract by claiming that Mr. McGrory was fully advised of the situation when he entered into the subject contract. The fact that an attorney fully informs his client of the contingent fee contract and its implications does not validate it. The court in *Florida Bar v. Moriber*, 314 So.2d 145, 149 (Fla.1975), faced a similar defense and stated "even if we presume that the client were an educated, experienced party dealing at arm's length with Respondent, it is our view that an attorney may still be disciplined for overreaching when fees charged are grossly dispropor- tionate to the services rendered." In the instant case even if Mr. White fully explained the contingent fee contract to Mr. McGrory, it does not validate the agreement in this case. It is quite possible that Mr. McGrory did not fully understand the matter and had no idea what other attorneys in the area would charge for similar services to obtain his legal share of his wife's estate, which he would have received by operation of law. The duty must therefore be placed on the attorney to deal fairly and in good faith with his clients in setting fees.

. . . The court finds and so holds that the fee sought to be charged by [White], under said contract, was grossly disproportionate to the services he rendered. The court further finds that the fee sought by [White] under said agreement was clearly excessive and unreason- able, and the court therefore holds that the subject contingent fee contract was in violation of Disciplinary Rule 2–106(a) and said contract was unenforceable. Therefore, [White] cannot recover un- der it.

Although it rejected White's claim pursuant to the fee contract, the probate court went on to note that Tennessee law permits a recovery under the theory of *quantum meruit* even if a fee contract were unen- forceable. Believing that it was required to award a fee based on *quantum meruit*, the probate court multiplied White's time on the case, approximately 114 hours, by $150 per hour—a rate established by expert testimony as the maximum allowable for probate matters.[3] After making some minor deductions, the probate court set the fee at $12,500.

* * *

I.

The first issue for our consideration is whether the contingency fee contract itself and the subsequent attempt to enforce that contract contravened DR 2–106. That rule provides:

(A) A lawyer shall not enter into an agreement for, charge, or attempt to collect an illegal or clearly excessive fee.

(B) A fee is clearly excessive when, after a review of the facts, a lawyer of ordinary prudence would be left with a definite and firm conviction that the fee is in excess of a reasonable fee. Factors to be considered as guides in determining the reasonableness of a fee include the following:

(1) The time and labor required, the novelty and difficulty of the questions involved, and the skill requisite to perform the legal service properly.

(2) The likelihood, if apparent to the client, that the acceptance of the particular employment will preclude other employment by the lawyer.

(3) The fee customarily charged in the locality for similar legal services.

(4) The amount involved and the results obtained.

(5) The time limitations imposed by the client or by the circumstances.

(6) The nature and length of the professional relationship with the client.

(7) The experience, reputation, and ability of the lawyer or lawyers performing the services.

(8) Whether the fee is fixed or contingent.

(C) A lawyer shall not enter into an arrangement for, charge, or collect a contingent fee for representing a defendant in a criminal case.

Although these factors are to be used as guides, *Connors v. Connors*, 594 S.W.2d 672, 676 (Tenn.1980), ultimately the reasonableness of the fee must depend upon the particular circumstances of the individual case. *Hail v. Nashville Trust Co.*, 31 Tenn.App. 39, 212 S.W.2d 51 (1948).

* * *

---

3. Two former Shelby County probate judges, Joseph Evans and James Watson, testified that $150 per hour was the maximum rate they would award for probate work.

Having rejected White's proffered justification of the fee contract, we have no doubt that the probate court was correct in holding that the fee contract violated DR 2–106. Although this estate matter was not without problems, it was, in the scheme of things, not terribly complicated or novel. Certainly it did not require any special skill or expertise, DR 2–106(B)(1), and White does not hold himself out as a probate specialist, worthy of an extraordinarily high fee. DR 2–106(B)(7). There is no indication that this matter prohibited White from undertaking other employment. DR 2–106(B)(2). Furthermore, the results obtained by White were not particularly good, DR 2–106(B)(4), as Kasper had received nothing from Leigh's estate as of the date of his death. Finally, and most dramatically, we note that if White were to be paid in accordance with the fee contract, he would have earned approximately $950 per hour. This figure is grossly in excess of the $150 hourly rate, which, judging from the expert testimony, we consider to be at the upper end of "the fee customarily charged in the locality for similar legal services." DR 2–106(B)(3).

Because we agree that the fee sought to be charged was clearly excessive under DR 2–106, we therefore affirm the probate court's holding on this issue.

II.

The next issue for our consideration is whether White may recover fees on a *quantum meruit* basis despite the fact that the fee contract is violative of DR 2–106 and, thus, unenforceable. White argues that settled Tennessee law provides that an attorney may recover fees on the theory of *quantum meruit* even if the fee contract itself is determined to be unenforceable. * * *

The estate, for its part, concedes that Tennessee law does sanction a recovery in *quantum meruit* even if the fee contract were deemed to be unenforceable. However, it argues that this rule is flawed and that attorneys who attempt to charge a fee that is clearly excessive under the disciplinary rules of this court should not be permitted to recover on a theory of *quantum meruit* if that fee is disallowed. To allow such a practice, the estate contends, encourages unscrupulous attorneys to try and exact unreasonable fees from their clients, confident that they will receive a reasonable amount of compensation if their unethical efforts are thwarted.

Initially, we note that the parties are correct in their assessment of Tennessee case law on this point. These decisions, however, have been almost entirely devoid of any supporting rationale for the rule. * * *

* * *

* * * We agree that attorneys should not be penalized for innocent snafus, such as an oversight in drafting that might render their fee contracts unenforceable. To do so would be unfair to the lawyer who had otherwise diligently pursued the client's interests, and it would result in a windfall to the client who had benefitted from these services. Thus, a

recovery under a theory of *quantum meruit* is warranted in these situations.

We are of the opinion, however, that an attorney who enters into a fee contract, or attempts to collect a fee, that is clearly excessive under DR 2–106 should not be permitted to take advantage of the *Cummings* rule [allowing recovery despite innocent violations of the rules—ed.]. A violation of DR 2–106 is an ethical transgression of a most flagrant sort as it goes directly to the heart of the fiduciary relationship that exists between attorney and client. To permit an attorney to fall back on the theory of *quantum meruit* when he unsuccessfully fails to collect a clearly excessive fee does absolutely nothing to promote ethical behavior. On the contrary, this interpretation would encourage attorneys to enter exorbitant fee contracts, secure that the safety net of *quantum meruit* is there in case of a subsequent fall.

We do not agree with White's dire prediction that this holding will have a chilling effect on attorneys' willingness to enter contingent fee contracts. Disciplinary Rule 2–106 is not a weapon that a recalcitrant client can employ at will to nullify the fee contract and thereby escape all liability for legal services. Rather, by its very terms the rule condemns only those fees that a lawyer of ordinary prudence would definitely and firmly believe to be excessive and sets forth a list of factors to determine when a fee is reasonable. Because of the high threshold embodied in the rule, we are confident that DR 2–106 will serve to deny recovery only to those who truly deserve it.

Having so concluded, we reverse that portion of the lower courts' judgment awarding fees on a *quantum meruit* basis. Any prior authority in conflict with this opinion is hereby expressly overruled.

ELEANOR THOMAS v. BENJAMIN THOMAS

Queen's Bench, 1842.
114 Eng.Rep. 330, 2 Q.B. 851.

[Assumpsit upon an agreement, a part of which follows:] "And whereas the said testator, shortly before his death, declared, in the presence of several witnesses, that he was desirous his said wife should have and enjoy during her life, or so long as she should continue his widow, all and singular the dwelling-house," & c., "or 100*l.* out of his personal estate," in addition to the respective legacies and bequests given her in and by his said will; "but such declaration and desire was not reduced to writing in the life-time of the said John Thomas and read over to him; but the said Samuel Thomas and Benjamin Thomas are fully convinced and satisfied that such was the desire of the said testator, and are willing and desirous that such intention should be carried into full effect: Now these presents witness, and it is hereby agreed and declared by and between the parties, that, in consideration of such desire and of the premises," the executors would convey the dwelling-house, & c., to the plaintiff and her assigns during her life, or for so long a time as she should continue a widow and unmarried: "provided nevertheless, and it is hereby further agreed and declared, that the said Eleanor Thomas or her assigns shall and will, at all times during which she shall have possession of the said dwelling-house, & c., pay to the said Samuel Thomas and Benjamin Thomas, their executors, & c., the sum of 1*l*. yearly towards the ground-rent payable in respect of the said dwelling-house and other premises thereto adjoining, and shall and will keep the said dwelling-house and premises in good and tenable repair:" with other provisions not affecting the questions in this case.

The plaintiff was left in possession of the dwelling-house and premises for some time; but the defendant, after the death of his co-executor, refused to execute a conveyance tendered to him for execution pursuant to the agreement, and shortly before the trial brought an ejectment, under which he turned the plaintiff out of possession. * * * Ultimately a verdict was found for the plaintiff on all the issues; and, in Easter term last, a rule nisi was obtained pursuant to the leave reserved.

* * *

LORD DENMAN, C.J. There is nothing in this case but a great deal of ingenuity, and a little wilful blindness to the actual terms of the instrument itself. There is nothing whatever to show that the ground-rent was payable to a superior landlord; and the stipulation for the payment of it is not a mere proviso, but an express agreement. (His Lordship here read the proviso.) This is in terms an express agreement, and shows a sufficient legal consideration quite independent of the moral feeling which disposed the executors to enter into such a contract. Mr. Williams' definition of consideration is too large: the word causa in the passage referred to means one which confers what the law considers a benefit on the party. Then the obligation to repair is one which might impose charges heavier than the value of the life estate.

PATTESON, J. It would be given to causa too large a construction if we were to adopt the view urged for the defendant: it would be confounding consideration with motive. Motive is not the same thing with consideration. Consideration means something which is of some value in the eye of the law, moving from the plaintiff: it may be some detriment to the plaintiff, or some benefit to the defendant; but at all events it must be moving from the plaintiff. Now that which is suggested as the consideration here—a pious respect for the wishes of the testator—does not in any way move from the plaintiff: it moves from the testator; therefore, legally speaking, it forms no part of the consideration. Then it is said that, if that be so, there is no consideration at all, it is a mere voluntary gift: but when we look at the agreement we find that this is not a mere proviso that the donee shall take the gift with the burthens; but it is an express agreement to pay what seems to be a fresh apportionment of a ground-rent, and which is made payable not to a superior landlord but to the executors. So that this rent is clearly not something incident to the assignment of the house; for in that case, instead of being payable to the executors, it would have been payable to the landlord. Then as to the repairs: these houses may very possibly be held under a lease containing covenants to repair; but we know nothing about it: for any thing that appears, the liability to repair is first created by this instrument. The proviso certainly struck me at first as Mr. Williams put it, that the rent and repairs were merely attached to the gift by the donors; and, had the instrument been executed by the donors only, there might have been some ground for that construction; but the fact is not so. Then it is suggested that this would be held to be a mere voluntary conveyance as against a subsequent purchaser for value: possibly that might be so: but suppose it would: the plaintiff contracts to take it, and does take it, whatever it is, for better or worse: perhaps a bona fide purchase for a valuable consideration might override it; but that cannot be helped.

COLERIDGE, J. The concessions made in the course of the arguments have in fact disposed of the case. It is conceded that mere motive need not be stated; and we are not obliged to look for the legal consideration in any particular part of the instrument, merely because the consideration is usually stated in some particular part: ut res magis valeat, we may look to any part. In this instrument, in the part where it is usual to state the consideration, nothing certainly is expressed but a wish to fulfil the intentions of the testator; but in another part we find an express agreement to pay an annual sum for a particular purpose, and also a distinct agreement to repair. If these had occurred in the first part of the instrument, it could hardly have been argued that the declaration was not well drawn, and supported by the evidence. As to the suggestion of this being a voluntary conveyance, my impression is that this payment of 1*l.* annually is more than a good consideration: it is a valuable consideration: it is clearly a thing newly created, and not part of the old ground rent.

Rule discharged.

FIEGE v. BOEHM

Court of Appeals of Maryland, 1956.
210 Md. 352, 123 A.2d 316.

DELAPLAINE, JUDGE.

This suit was brought in the Superior Court of Baltimore City by Hilda Louise Boehm against Louis Gail Fiege to recover for breach of a contract to pay the expenses incident to the birth of his bastard child and to provide for its support upon condition that she would refrain from prosecuting him for bastardy.

Plaintiff alleged in her declaration substantially as follows: (1) that early in 1951 defendant had sexual intercourse with her although she was unmarried, and as a result thereof she became pregnant, and defendant acknowledged that he was responsible for her pregnancy; (2) that on September 29, 1951, she gave birth to a female child; that defendant is the father of the child; and that he acknowledged on many occasions that he is its father; (3) that before the child was born, defendant agreed to pay all her medical and miscellaneous expenses and to compensate her for the loss of her salary caused by the child's birth, and also to pay her ten dollars per week for its support until it reached the age of 21, upon condition that she would not institute bastardy proceedings against him as long as he made the payments in accordance with the agreement; (4) that she placed the child for adoption on July 13, 1954, and she claimed the following sums: Union Memorial Hospital, $110; Florence Crittenton Home, $100; Dr. George Merrill, her physician, $50; medicines, $70.35; miscellaneous expenses, $20.45; loss of earnings for 26 weeks, $1,105; support of the child, $1,440; total, $2,895.80; and (5) that defendant paid her only $480, and she demanded that he pay her the further sum of $2,415.80, the balance due under the agreement, but he failed and refused to pay the same.

Defendant demurred to the declaration on the ground that it failed to allege that in September, 1953, plaintiff instituted bastardy proceedings against him in the Criminal Court of Baltimore, but since it had been found from blood tests that he could not have been the father of the child, he was acquitted of bastardy. The Court sustained the demurrer with leave to amend.

Plaintiff then filed an amended declaration, which contained the additional allegation that, after the breach of the agreement by defendant, she filed a charge with the State's Attorney that defendant was the father of her bastard child; and that on October 8, 1953, the Criminal Court found defendant not guilty solely on a physician's testimony that "on the basis of certain blood tests made, the defendant can be excluded as the father of the said child, which testimony is not conclusive upon a jury in a trial court."

Defendant also demurred to the amended declaration, but the Court overruled that demurrer.

Plaintiff, a typist, now over 35 years old, who has been employed by the Government in Washington and Baltimore for over thirteen years, testified in the Court below that she had never been married, but that at about midnight on January 21, 1951, defendant, after taking her to a moving picture theater on York Road and then to a restaurant, had sexual intercourse with her in his automobile. She further testified that he agreed to pay all her medical and hospital expenses, to compensate her for loss of salary caused by the pregnancy and birth, and to pay her ten dollars per week for the support of the child upon condition that she would refrain from instituting bastardy proceedings against him. She further testified that between September 17, 1951, and May, 1953, defendant paid her a total of $480.

Defendant admitted that he had taken plaintiff to restaurants, had danced with her several times, had taken her to Washington, and had brought her home in the country; but he asserted that he had never had sexual intercourse with her. He also claimed that he did not enter into any agreement with her. He admitted, however, that he had paid her a total of $480. His father also testified that he stated "that he did not want his mother to know, and if it were just kept quiet, kept principally away from his mother and the public and the courts, that he would take care of it."

Defendant further testified that in May, 1953, he went to see plaintiff's physician to make inquiry about blood tests to show the paternity of the child; and that those tests were made and they indicated that it was not possible that he could have been the child's father. He then stopped making payments. Plaintiff thereupon filed a charge of bastardy with the State's Attorney.

The testimony which was given in the Criminal Court by Dr. Milton Sachs, hematologist at the University Hospital, was read to the jury in the Superior Court. In recent years the blood-grouping test has been employed in criminology, in the selection of donors for blood transfusions, and as evidence in paternity cases. The Landsteiner blood-grouping test is based on the medical theory that the red corpuscles in human blood contain two affirmative agglutinating substances, and that every individual's blood falls into one of the four classes and remains the same throughout life. According to Mendel's law of inheritance, this blood individuality is an hereditary characteristic which passes from parent to child, and no agglutinating substance can appear in the blood of a child which is not present in the blood of one of its parents. The four Landsteiner blood groups, designated as AB, A, B, and O, into which human blood is divided on the basis of the compatibility of the corpuscles and serum with the corpuscles and serum of other persons, are characterized by different combinations of two agglutinogens in the red blood cells and two agglutinins in the serum. Dr. Sachs reported that Fiege's blood group was Type O, Miss Boehm's was Type B, and the infant's was Type A. He further testified that on the basis of these tests, Fiege could not have been the father of the child, as it is impossible for a mating of Type O and Type B to result in a child of Type A.

Although defendant was acquitted by the Criminal Court, the Superior Court overruled his motion for a directed verdict. In the charge to the jury the Court instructed them that defendant's acquittal in the Criminal Court was not binding upon them. The jury found a verdict in favor of plaintiff for $2,415.80, the full amount of her claim.

Defendant filed a motion for judgment n.o.v. or a new trial. The Court overruled that motion also, and entered judgment on the verdict of the jury. Defendant appealed from that judgment.

Defendant contends that, even if he did enter into the contract as alleged, it was not enforceable, because plaintiff's forbearance to prosecute was not based on a valid claim, and hence the contract was without consideration. He, therefore, asserts that the Court erred in overruling (1) his demurrer to the amended declaration, (2) his motion for a directed verdict, and (3) his motion for judgment n.o.v. or a new trial.

It was originally held at common law that a child born out of wedlock is *filius nullius,* and a putative father is not under any legal liability to contribute to the support of his illegitimate child, and his promise to do so is unenforceable because it is based on purely a moral obligation. * * *

However, where statutes are in force to compel the father of a bastard to contribute to its support, the courts have invariably held that a contract by the putative father with the mother of his bastard child to provide for the support of the child upon the agreement of the mother to refrain from invoking the bastardy statute against the father, or to abandon proceedings already commenced, is supported by sufficient consideration. Jangraw v. Perkins, 77 Vt. 375, 60 A. 385; Beach v. Voegtlen, 68 N.J.L. 472, 53 A. 695; Thayer v. Thayer, 189 N.C. 502, 127 S.E. 553, 39 A.L.R. 428.

In Maryland it is now provided by statute that whenever a person is found guilty of bastardy, the court shall issue an order directing such person (1) to pay for the maintenance and support of the child until it reaches the age of eighteen years, such sum as may be agreed upon, if consent proceedings be had, or in the absence of agreement, such sum as the court may fix, with due regard to the circumstances of the accused person; and (2) to give bond to the State of Maryland in such penalty as the court may fix, with good and sufficient securities, conditioned on making the payments required by the court's order, or any amendments thereof. Failure to give such bond shall be punished by commitment to the jail or the House of Correction until bond is given but not exceeding two years. Code Supp.1955, art. 12, § 8.

Prosecutions for bastardy are treated in Maryland as criminal proceedings, but they are actually civil in purpose. Kennard v. State, 177 Md. 549, 10 A.2d 710; Kisner v. State, Md., 122 A.2d 102. While the prime object of the Maryland Bastardy Act is to protect the public from the burden of maintaining illegitimate children, it is so distinctly in the interest of the mother that she becomes the beneficiary of it. Accordingly a contract by the putative father of an illegitimate child to provide for its support upon condition that bastardy proceedings will not be instituted is a compromise of civil injuries resulting from a criminal act, and not a contract to compound a criminal prosecution, and if it is fair and reasonable, it is in accord with the Bastardy Act and the public policy of the State.

Of course, a contract of a putative father to provide for the support of his illegitimate child must be based, like any other contract, upon sufficient consideration. * * *

In 1867 the Maryland Court of Appeals, in the opinion delivered by Judge Bartol in Hartle v. Stahl, 27 Md. 157, 172, held: (1) that forbearance to assert a claim before institution of suit, if not in fact a legal claim, is not of itself sufficient consideration to support a promise; but (2) that a compromise of a doubtful claim or a relinquishment of a pending suit is good consideration for a promise; and (3) that in order to support a compromise, it is sufficient that the parties entering into it thought at the time that there was a *bona fide* question between them, although it may eventually be found that there was in fact no such question.

We have thus adopted the rule that the surrender of, or forbearance to assert, an invalid claim by one who has not an honest and reasonable belief in its possible validity is not sufficient consideration for a contract. 1 Restatement, Contracts, sec. 76(b). We combine the subjective requisite that the claim be *bona fide* with the objective requisite that it must have a reasonable basis of support. Accordingly a promise not to prosecute a claim which is not founded in good faith does not of itself give a right of action on an agreement to pay for refraining from so acting, because a release from mere annoyance and unfounded litigation does not furnish valuable consideration.

Professor Williston was not entirely certain whether the test of reasonableness is based upon the intelligence of the claimant himself, who may be an ignorant person with no knowledge of law and little sense as to facts; but he seemed inclined to favor the view that "the claim forborne must be neither absurd in fact from the standpoint of a reasonable man in the position of the claimant, nor, obviously unfounded in law to one who has an elementary knowledge of legal principles." 1 Williston on Contracts, Rev.Ed., sec. 135. We agree that while stress is placed upon the honesty and good faith of the claimant, forbearance to prosecute a claim is insufficient consideration if the claim forborne is so lacking in foundation as to make its assertion incompatible with honesty and a reasonable degree of intelligence. Thus, if the mother of a bastard knows that there is no foundation, either in law or fact, for a charge against a certain man that he is the father of the child, but that man promises to pay her in order to prevent bastardy proceedings against him, the forbearance to institute proceedings is not sufficient consideration.

On the other hand, forbearance to sue for a lawful claim or demand is sufficient consideration for a promise to pay for the forbearance if the party forbearing had an honest intention to prosecute litigation which is not frivolous, vexatious, or unlawful, and which he believed to be well founded. Snyder v. Cearfoss, 187 Md. 635, 643, 51 A.2d 264; Pullman Co. v. Ray, 201 Md. 268, 94 A.2d 266. Thus the promise of a woman who is expecting an illegitimate child that she will not institute bastardy proceedings against a certain man is sufficient consideration for his promise to pay for the child's support, even though it may not be certain whether the man is the father or whether the prosecution would be successful, if she makes the charge in good faith. * * *

* * *

Another analogous case is Thompson v. Nelson, 28 Ind. 431. There the plaintiff sought to recover back money which he had paid to compromise a prosecution for bastardy. He claimed that the prosecuting witness was not pregnant and therefore the prosecution was fraudulent. It was held by the Supreme Court of Indiana, however, that the settlement of the prosecution was a good consideration for the payment of the money and it could not be recovered back, inasmuch as it appeared from the evidence that the prosecution was instituted in good faith, and at that time there was reason to believe that the prosecuting witness was pregnant, although it was found out afterwards that she was not pregnant.

* * *

In the case at bar there was no proof of fraud or unfairness. Assuming that the hematologists were accurate in their laboratory tests and findings, nevertheless plaintiff gave testimony which indicated that she made the charge of bastardy against defendant in good faith. For these reasons the Court acted properly in overruling the demurrer to the amended declaration and the motion for a directed verdict.

* * *

Judgment affirmed, with costs.

Problems

1. F had prepared a will by the terms of which he divided his estate equally among his three children. One of them, P, told F that she was pregnant but did not intend to marry. Thereupon, F revoked his will and executed a new one in which he eliminated P as a co-equal beneficiary. He promised P that he would execute another will according to his original plan if she would have an abortion. P had an abortion and notified her father. However, he died without changing his will. P sues the estate. What result?

2. A promises B that A will sell and deliver a set of books to B if B's father, C, pays $150 for the set. C pays, but A fails to deliver the books. May B enforce A's promise?

3. A and B entered into a contract under which A would do specified work and B would pay $10,000 when the work was done. After the work was completed, B said to A, "You have done such a good job that I'll pay you $5,000 extra." B paid A $15,000. May B recover $5,000?

4. H and W were living in a house owned by H's father (F). H made valuable improvements upon the property. Upon H's death F wrote to W and stated: "In view of the fact that my son has made improvements upon the property for which I feel that you should receive adequate compensation, I give you the privilege of purchasing said property for the sum of $230,000 at my death." F signed and mailed the letter which was received by W. F is now deceased and W wishes to purchase the property. Does she have an enforceable right to purchase it for $230,000?

5. D promised P that, if P continued to deliver specified kinds of merchandise to D's brother, D would pay for the items already delivered and for the items to be delivered. P duly performed. Does P have a cause of action against D?

6. Defendant put a notice in a trade magazine stating that it needed a reporter with stated qualifications for a "permanent position." The plaintiff replied and was eventually hired. The plaintiff left a job as a baker in which he was receiving the sum of $50 per week and took the job with the defendant at $40 per week. After 3 years the plaintiff was fired. Does he have a cause of action for breach of contract?

7. P gave a lease to J.S. for life. J.S. transferred the lease to D. P demanded rent from D. D replied that his understanding was that J.S. had fully paid for the lease and no rent was due. D also stated that, if P would

show him a deed proving that rent was due, he would pay it. P showed him such a deed. May P recover on D's promise?

8. D, father, conveyed property to his daughter, P, and stated that it was a Christmas present. As part of the same transaction D agreed to continue to pay off two mortgages that encumbered the property. At the same time one of P's brothers gave P a dollar which in turn she gave to her father. Is there consideration to support D's promise?

9. R Corp. owns a restaurant. S is a supplier of restaurant equipment. D is R Corp.'s principal shareholder. D gave S the following guarantee signed by D: "For and in consideration of $1 paid by S (receipt of which is hereby acknowledged) I hereby guarantee to S any indebtedness of R Corp. to the extent of $10,000." The $1 mentioned was not in fact paid.

At the time D gave S the guarantee, R Corp. was not indebted to S but did become indebted to S in the amount of $5,000 for restaurant equipment delivered on credit. Is the guarantee enforceable? What result if the $5,000 debt had been incurred before the guarantee was given?

SECTION 2.   PRE–EXISTING DUTY RULE

(Calamari & Perillo 5th §§ 4.9—4.11)

SCHWARTZREICH v. BAUMAN–BASCH, INC.

New York Court of Appeals, 1921.
231 N.Y. 196, 131 N.E. 887.

CRANE, J. On the 31st day of August, 1917, the plaintiff entered into the following employment agreement with the defendant:

"BAUMAN-BASCH, INC.,
"Coats & Wraps
"31–33 East 32nd Street
"New York

"Agreement entered into this 31st day of August, 1917, by and between Bauman–Basch, Inc., a domestic corporation, party of the first part, and Louis Schwartzreich, of the Borough of Bronx, City of New York, party of the second part, *Witnesseth*:

"The party of the first part does hereby employ the party of the second part, and the party of the second part agrees to enter the services of the party of the first part as a designer of coats and wraps.

"The employment herein shall commence on the 22nd day of November, 1917, and shall continue for twelve months thereafter. The party of the second part shall receive a salary of Ninety ($90.00) per week, payable weekly.

"The party of the second part shall devote his entire time and attention to the business of the party of the first part, and shall use his best energies and endeavors in the furtherance of its business.

"*In witness whereof,* the party of the first part has caused its seal to be affixed hereto and these presents to be signed, and the party of the second part has hereunto set his hand and seal the day and year first above written.

BAUMAN–BASCH, INC.

"S. Bauman

"LOUIS SCHWARTZREICH

"In the presence of:"

In October the plaintiff was offered more money by another concern. Mr. Bauman, an officer of the Bauman–Basch, Inc., says that in that month he heard that the plaintiff was going to leave and thereupon had with him the following conversation.

"A. I called him in the office, and I asked him, 'Is that true that you want to leave us?' and he said 'Yes,' and I said, 'Mr. Schwartzreich, how can you do that; you are under contract with us?' He said, 'Somebody offered me more money.' * * * I said, 'How much do they offer you?' He said, 'They offered him $115 a week.' * * * I said, 'I cannot get a designer now, and, in view of the fact that I have to send my sample line out on the road, I will give you a hundred dollars a week rather than to let you go.' He said, 'If you will give me $100, I will stay.'"

Thereupon Mr. Bauman dictated to his stenographer a new contract, dated October 17, 1917, in the exact words of the first contract and running for the same period, the salary being $100 a week, which contract was duly executed by the parties and witnessed. Duplicate originals were kept by the plaintiff and defendant.

Simultaneously with the signing of this new contract, the plaintiff's copy of the old contract was either given to or left with Mr. Bauman. He testifies that the plaintiff gave him the paper but that he did not take it from him. The signatures to the old contract plaintiff tore off at the time according to Mr. Bauman.

The plaintiff's version as to the execution of the new contract is as follows:

"A. I told Mr. Bauman that I have an offer from Scheer & Mayer of $110 a week, and I said to him, 'Do you advise me as a friendly matter—will you advise me as a friendly matter what to do; you see I have a contract with you, and I should not accept the offer of $110 a week, and I ask you, as a matter of friendship, do you advise me to take it or not.' At the minute he did not say anything, but the day afterwards he came to me in and he said, 'I will give you $100 a week, and I want you to stay with me.' I said, 'All right, I will accept it; it is very nice of you that you do that, and I appreciate it very much.'"

The plaintiff says that on the 17th of October when the new contract was signed, he gave his copy of the old contract back to Mr. Bauman, who said: "You do not want this contract any more because the new one takes its place."

The plaintiff remained in the defendant's employ until the following December when he was discharged. He brought this action under the contract of October 17th for his damages.

The defense, insisted upon through all the courts, is that there was no consideration for the new contract as the plaintiff was already bound under his agreement of August 31, 1917, to do the same work for the same period at $90 a week.

Defendant argues ★

The trial justice submitted to the jury the question whether there was a cancellation of the old contract and charged as follows:

Trial Court agrees with Plaintiff

"If you find that the $90 contract was prior to or at the time of the execution of the $100 contract cancelled and revoked by the parties by their mutual consent, then it is your duty to find that there was a consideration for the making of the contract in suit, viz., the $100 contract and, in that event, the plaintiff would be entitled to your verdict for such damages as you may find resulted proximately, naturally and necessarily in consequence of the plaintiff's discharge prior to the termination of the contract period of which I shall speak later on."

Defendant's counsel thereupon excepted to that portion of the charge in which the court permitted the jury to find that the prior contract may have been canceled simultaneously with the execution of the other agreement. Again the court said:

"The test question is whether by word or by act, either prior to or at the time of the signing of the $100 contract, these parties mutually agreed that the old contract from that instant should be null and void."

The jury having rendered a verdict for the plaintiff the trial justice set it aside and dismissed the complaint on the ground that there was not sufficient evidence that the first contract was canceled to warrant the jury's findings.

The above quotations from the record show that a question of fact was presented and that the evidence most favorable for the plaintiff would sustain a finding that the first contract was destroyed, canceled or abrogated by the consent of both parties.

The Appellate Term was right in reversing this ruling. Instead of granting a new trial, however, it reinstated the verdict of the jury and the judgment for the plaintiff. The question remains, therefore, whether the charge of the court as above given, was a correct statement of the law or whether on all the evidence in the plaintiff's favor a cause of action was made out.

Can a contract of employment be set aside or terminated by the parties to it and a new one made or substituted in its place? If so, is it competent to end the one and make the other at the same time?

It has been repeatedly held that a promise made to induce a party to do that which he is already bound by contract to perform is without consideration. But the cases in this state, while enforcing this rule, also recognize that a contract may be canceled by mutual consent and a new one made. Thus *Vanderbilt v. Schreyer* (91 N.Y. 392, 402) held that it was no consideration for a guaranty that a party promise to do only that which he was before legally bound to perform. This court stated, however:

"It would doubtless be competent for parties to cancel an existing contract and make a new one to complete the same work at a different rate of compensation, but it seems that it would be essential to its validity that there should be a valid cancellation of the original contract. Such was the case of *Lattimore v. Harsen* (14 Johns. 330)."

In *Cosgray v. New England Piano Co.* (10 App.Div. 351, 353) it was decided that where the plaintiff had bound himself to work for a year at $30 a week, there was no consideration for a promise thereafter made by the defendant that he should notwithstanding receive $1,800 a year. Here it will be noticed there was no termination of the first agreement which gave occasion for BARTLETT, J., to say in the opinion:

"The case might be different if the parties had, by word of mouth, agreed wholly to abrogate and do away with a pre-existing written contract in regard to service and compensation, and had substituted for it another agreement."

Any change in an existing contract, such as a modification of the rate of compensation, or a supplemental agreement, must have a new consideration to support it. In such a case the contract is continued, not ended. Where, however, an existing contract is terminated by consent of both parties and a new one executed in its place and stead, we have a different situation and the mutual promises are again a consideration. Very little difference may appear in a mere change of compensation in an existing and continuing contract and a termination of one contract and the making of a new one for the same time and work, but at an increased compensation. There is, however, a marked difference in principle. Where the new contract gives any new privilege or advantage to the promisor, a consideration has been recognized, though in the main it is the same contract. (*Triangle Waist Co., Inc. v. Todd*, 223 N.Y. 27.)

If this which we are now holding were not the rule, parties having once made a contract would be prevented from changing it no matter how willing and desirous they might be to do so, unless the terms conferred an additional benefit to the promisor.

All concede that an agreement may be rescinded by mutual consent and a new agreement made thereafter on any terms to which the parties may assent. Prof. Williston in his work on Contracts says (Vol. I, § 130a): "A rescission followed shortly afterwards by a new agreement in regard to the same subject-matter would create the legal obligations provided in the subsequent agreement."

The same effect follows in our judgment from a new contract entered into at the same time the old one is destroyed and rescinded by mutual consent. The determining factor is the rescission by consent. Provided this is the expressed and acted upon intention, the time of the rescission, whether a moment before or at the same time as the making of the new contract, is unimportant.

The decisions are numerous and divergent where one of the parties to a contract refuses to perform unless paid an additional amount. Some states hold the new promise to pay the demand binding though there be no rescission. It is said that the new promise is given to secure performance in place of an action for damages for not performing *(Parrot v. Mexican Central Railway Co.*, 207 Mass. 184), or that the new contract is evidence of the rescission of the old one and it is the same as if no previous contract had been made (*Coyner v. Lynde*, 10 Ind. 282; *Connelly v. Devoe*, 37 Conn. 570; *Goebel v. Linn*, 47 Mich. 489), or that unforeseen difficulties and hardships modify the rule (*King v. Duluth, M. & N. Ry. Co.*, 61 Minn. 482), or that the new contract is an attempt to mitigate the damages which may flow from the breach of the first. (*Endriss v. Belle Isle Ice Co.*, 49 Mich. 279.) (See Anson's Law of Contract [Huffcut's Amer.Ed.], p. 114, sec. 138.) * * *

The contrary has been held in such cases as *Carpenter v. Taylor* (164 N.Y. 171); *Price v. Press Publishing Co.* (117 App.Div. 854); *Davis & Company v. Morgan* (117 Ga. 504); *Alaska Packers' Association v. Domenico* (117 Fed.Rep. 99); *Conover v. Stillwell* (34 N.J.L. 54, 57); *Erny v. Sauer* (234 Penn.St. 330). In none of these cases, however, was there a full and complete rescission of the old contract and it is this with which we are dealing in this case. Rescission is not presumed; it is expressed; the old contract is not continued with modifications; it is ended and a new one made.

The efforts of the courts to give a legal reason for holding good a promise to pay an additional compensation for the fulfillment of a pre-existing contract is commented upon in note upon *Abbott v. Doane* (163 Mass. 433) in 34 L.R.A. 33, 39, and the result reached is stated as follows: "The almost universal rule is that without any express rescission of the old contract, the promise is made simply for additional compensation, making the new promise a mere *nudum pactum.*" As before stated, in this case we have an express rescission and a new contract.

There is no reason that we can see why the parties to a contract may not come together and agree to cancel and rescind an existing contract, making a new one in its place. We are also of the opinion that reason and authority support the conclusion that both transactions can take place at the same time.

For the reasons here stated, the charge of the trial court was correct, and the judgments of the Appellate Division and the Appellate Term should be affirmed, with costs.

Judgments affirmed.

ANGEL v. MURRAY

Supreme Court of Rhode Island, 1974.
113 R.I. 482, 322 A.2d 630.

ROBERTS, CHIEF JUSTICE.

This is a civil action brought by Alfred L. Angel and others against John E. Murray, Jr ., Director of Finance of the City of Newport, the city of Newport, and James L. Maher, alleging that Maher had illegally been paid the sum of $20,000 by the Director of Finance and praying that the defendant Maher be ordered to repay the city such sum. The case was heard by a justice of the Superior Court, sitting without a jury, who entered a judgment ordering Maher to repay the sum of $20,000 to the city of Newport. Maher is now before this court prosecuting an appeal.

The record discloses that Maher has provided the city of Newport with a refuse-collection service under a series of five-year contracts beginning in 1946. On March 12, 1964, Maher and the city entered into another such contract for a period of five years commencing on July 1, 1964, and terminating on June 30, 1969. The contract provided, among other things, that Maher would receive $137,000 per year in return for collecting and removing all combustible and noncombustible waste materials generated within the city.

In June of 1967 Maher requested an additional $10,000 per year from the city council because there had been a substantial increase in the cost of collection due to an unexpected and unanticipated increase of 400 new dwelling units. Maher's testimony, which is uncontradicted, indicates the 1964 contract had been predicated on the fact that since 1946 there had been an average increase of 20 to 25 new dwelling units per year. After a public meeting of the city council where Maher explained in detail the reasons for his request and was questioned by members of the city council, the city council agreed to pay him an additional $10,000 for the year ending on June 30, 1968. Maher made a similar request again in June of 1968 for the same reasons, and the city council again agreed to pay an additional $10,000 for the year ending on June 30, 1969.

The trial justice found that each such $10,000 payment was made in violation of law. His decision, as we understand it, is premised on two independent grounds. * * * Second, he found that Maher was not entitled to extra compensation because the original contract already required him to collect all refuse generated within the city and, therefore, included the 400 additional units. The trial justice further found that these 400 additional units were within the contemplation of the parties when they entered into the contract. It appears that he based this portion of the decision upon the rule that Maher had a preexisting duty to collect the refuse generated by the 400 additional units, and thus there was no consideration for the two additional payments.

[The court points out that it is illegal for a municipality to pay out money as a gift; if there is no consideration the payments were illegal gifts. Ed.]

* * *

It is generally held that a modification of a contract is itself a contract, which is unenforceable unless supported by consideration. *See* Simpson, [Contracts] § 93 [(2d ed. 1965)]. In Rose v. Daniels, 8 R.I. 381 (1866), this court held that an agreement by a debtor with a creditor to discharge a debt for a sum of money less than the amount due is unenforceable because it was not supported by consideration.

Rose is a perfect example of the preexisting duty rule. Under this rule an agreement modifying a contract is not supported by consideration if one of the parties to the agreement does or promises to do something that he is legally obligated to do or refrains or promises to refrain from doing something he is not legally privileged to do. *See* Calamari & Perillo, Contracts § 60 (1970); 1A Corbin, Contracts §§ 171–72 (1963); 1 Williston, [Contracts] § 130 [(Jaeger 3d ed. 1957)]; Annot., 12 A.L.R.2d 78 (1950). In *Rose* there was no consideration for the new agreement because the debtor was already legally obligated to repay the full amount of the debt.

Although the preexisting duty rule is followed by most jurisdictions, a small minority of jurisdictions, Massachusetts, for example, find that there is consideration for a promise to perform what one is already legally obligated to do because the new promise is given in place of an action for damages to secure performance. *See* Swartz v. Lieberman, 323 Mass. 109, 80 N.E.2d 5 (1948); Munroe v. Perkins, 26 Mass. (9 Pick.) 298 (1830). *Swartz* is premised on the theory that a promisor's forbearance of the power to breach his original agreement and be sued in an action for damages is consideration for a subsequent agreement by the promisee to pay extra compensation. This rule, however, has been widely criticized as an anomaly. *See* Calamari & Perillo, *supra*, § 61; Annot., 12 A.L.R.2d 78, 85–90 (1950).

The primary purpose of the preexisting duty rule is to prevent what has been referred to as the "hold-up game." *See* 1A Corbin, *supra*, § 171. A classic example of the "hold-up game" is found in Alaska Packers' Ass'n v. Domenico, 117 F. 99 (9th Cir.1902). There 21 seamen entered into a written contract with Domenico to sail from San Francisco to Pyramid Harbor, Alaska. They were to work as sailors and fishermen out of Pyramid Harbor during the fishing season of 1900. The contract specified that each man would be paid $50 plus two cents for each red salmon he caught. Subsequent to their arrival at Pyramid Harbor, the men stopped work and demanded an additional $50. They threatened to return to San Francisco if Domenico did not agree to their demand. Since it was impossible for Domenico to find other men, he agreed to pay the men an additional $50. After they returned to San Francisco, Domenico refused to pay the men an additional $50. The court found that the subsequent agreement to pay the men an additional $50 was not supported by consideration because the men had a preexisting duty to work on the ship under the original contract, and thus the subsequent agreement was unenforceable.

Another example of the "hold-up game" is found in the area of construction contracts. Frequently, a contractor will refuse to complete work under an unprofitable contract unless he is awarded additional compensation. The courts have generally held that a subsequent agreement to award additional compensation is unenforceable if the contractor is only performing work which would have been required of him under the original contract. * * *

These examples clearly illustrate that the courts will not enforce an agreement that has been procured by coercion or duress and will hold the parties to their original contract regardless of whether it is profitable or unprofitable. However, the courts have been reluctant to apply the preexisting duty rule when a party to a contract encounters unanticipated difficulties and the other party, not influenced by coercion or duress, voluntarily agrees to pay additional compensation for work already required to be performed under the contract. For example, the courts have found that the original contract was rescinded, Linz v. Schuck, 106 Md. 220, 67 A. 286 (1907); abandoned, Connelly v. Devoe, 37 Conn. 570 (1871), or waived, Michaud v. McGregor, 61 Minn. 198, 63 N.W. 479 (1895).

Although the preexisting duty rule has served a useful purpose insofar as it deters parties from using coercion and duress to obtain additional compensation, it has been widely criticized as a general rule of law. With regard to the preexisting duty rule, one legal scholar has stated: "There has been a growing doubt as to the soundness of this doctrine as a matter of social policy. * * * In certain classes of cases, this doubt has influenced courts to refuse to apply the rule, or to ignore it, in their actual decisions. Like other legal rules, this rule is in process of growth and change, the process being more active here than in most instances. The result of this is that a court should no longer accept this rule as fully established. It should never use it as the major premise of a decision, at least without giving careful thought to the circumstances of the particular case, to the moral deserts of the parties, and to the social feelings and interests that are involved. It is certain that the rule, stated in general and all-inclusive terms, is no longer so well-settled that a court must apply it though the heavens fall." 1A Corbin, *supra*, § 171; *see also* Calamari & Perillo, *supra*, § 61.

The modern trend appears to recognize the necessity that courts should enforce agreements modifying contracts when unexpected or unanticipated difficulties arise during the course of the performance of a contract, even though there is no consideration for the modification, as long as the parties agree voluntarily.

Under the Uniform Commercial Code, § 2–209(1), which has been adopted by 49 states, "[a]n agreement modifying a contract [for the sale of goods] needs no consideration to be binding." See G.L.1956 (1969 Reenactment) § 6A–2–209(1). Although at first blush this section appears to validate modifications obtained by coercion and duress, the comments to this section indicate that a modification under this section must meet the test of good faith imposed by the Code, and a modification obtained by extortion without a legitimate commercial reason is unenforceable.

The modern trend away from a rigid application of the preexisting duty rule is reflected by § 89D(a) [now 89(a), Ed.] of the American Law Institute's Restatement Second of the Law of Contracts, which provides:

"A promise modifying a duty under a contract not fully performed on either side is binding (a) if the modification is fair and equitable in view of circumstances not anticipated by the parties when the contract was made * * *."

We believe that § 89D(a) is the proper rule of law and find it applicable to the facts of this case. It not only prohibits modifications obtained by coercion, duress, or extortion but also fulfills society's expectation that agreements entered into voluntarily will be enforced by the courts. *See generally* Horwitz, The Historical Foundations of Modern Contract Law, 87 Harv.L.Rev. 917 (1974). Section 89D(a), of course, does not compel a modification of an unprofitable or unfair contract; it only enforces a modification if the parties voluntarily agree and if (1) the promise modifying the original contract was made before the contract was fully performed on either side, (2) the underlying circumstances which prompted the modification were unanticipated by the parties, and (3) the modification is fair and equitable.

The evidence, which is uncontradicted, reveals that in June of 1968 Maher requested the city council to pay him an additional $10,000 for the year beginning on July 1, 1968, and ending on June 30, 1969. This request was made at a public meeting of the city council, where Maher explained in detail his reasons for making the request. Thereafter, the city council voted to authorize the Mayor to sign an amendment to the 1964 contract which provided that Maher would receive an additional $10,000 per year for the duration of the contract. Under such circumstances we have no doubt that the city voluntarily agreed to modify the 1964 contract.

Having determined the voluntariness of this agreement, we turn our attention to the three criteria delineated above. First, the modification was made in June of 1968 at a time when the five-year contract which was made in 1964 had not been fully performed by either party. Second, although the 1964 contract provided that Maher collect all refuse generated within the city, it appears this contract was premised on Maher's past experience that the number of refuse-generating units would increase at a rate of 20 to 25 per year. Furthermore, the evidence is uncontradicted that the 1967–1968 increase of 400 units "went beyond any previous expectation." Clearly, the circumstances which prompted the city council to modify the 1964 contract were unanticipated. Third, although the evidence does not indicate what proportion of the total this increase comprised, the evidence does indicate that it was a "substantial" increase. In light of this, we cannot say that the council's agreement to pay Maher the $10,000 increase was not fair and equitable in the circumstances.

The judgment appealed from is reversed, and the cause is remanded to the Superior Court for entry of judgment for the defendants.

CONVENTION ON CONTRACTS FOR THE INTERNATIONAL SALE OF GOODS

Article 29 (1).

A contract may be modified or terminated by the mere agreement of the parties.

DE CICCO v. SCHWEIZER

New York Court of Appeals, 1917.
221 N.Y. 431, 117 N.E. 807.

[In reading this decision the student should be aware that an engagement to marry was a binding contract in New York State until the legally binding effect of engagements was abolished by what is now McKinney's N.Y. Civil Rights Law § 80–a. Ed.]

* * *

CARDOZO, J. On January 16, 1902, "articles of agreement" were executed by the defendant Joseph Schweizer, his wife Ernestine, and Count Oberto Gulinelli. The agreement is in Italian. We quote from a translation the part essential to the decision of this controversy: "Whereas, Miss Blanche Josephine Schweizer, daughter of said Mr. Joseph Schweizer and of said Mrs. Ernestine Teresa Schweizer, is now affianced to and is to be married to the above said Count Oberto Giacomo Giovanni Francesco Maria Gulinelli, Now, in consideration of all that is herein set forth the said Mr. Joseph Schweizer promises and expressly agrees by the present contract to pay annually to his said daughter Blanche, during his own life and to send her, during her lifetime, the sum of Two Thousand Five Hundred dollars, or the equivalent of said sum in Francs, the first payment of said amount to be made on the 20th day of January, 1902." Later articles provide that "for the same reason heretofore set forth," Mr. Schweizer will not change the provision made in his will for the benefit of his daughter and her issue, if any. The yearly payments in the event of his death are to be continued by his wife.

On January 20, 1902, the marriage occurred. On the same day, the defendant made the first payment to his daughter. He continued the payments annually till 1912. This action is brought to recover the installment of that year. The plaintiff holds an assignment executed by the daughter, in which her husband joined. The question is whether there is any consideration for the promised annuity.

That marriage may be a sufficient consideration is not disputed. The argument for the defendant is, however, that Count Gulinelli was already affianced to Miss Schweizer, and that the marriage was merely the fulfilment of an existing legal duty. For this reason, it is insisted, consideration was lacking. The argument leads us to the discussion of a vexed problem of the law which has been debated by courts and writers with much subtlety of reasoning and little harmony of results. There is general acceptance of the proposition that where A is under a contract with B, a promise made by one to the other to induce performance is void. The trouble comes when the promise to induce performance is made by C, a stranger. Distinctions are then drawn between bilateral and unilateral contracts; between a promise by C in return for a new promise by A, and a promise by C in return for performance by A. Some jurists hold that there is consideration in both classes of cases (Ames, Two Theories of Consideration, 12 Harvard Law Review, 515; 13 *Id.* 29, 35; Langdell, Mutual Promises as a Consideration, 14 *Id.* 496; Leake, Contracts, p. 622). Others hold that there is consideration where the promise is made for a new promise, but not where it is made for performance (Beale, Notes on Consideration, 17 Harvard Law Review, 71; 2 Street, Foundations of Legal Liability, pp. 114, 116; Pollock, Contracts [8th ed.], 199; Pollock, Afterthoughts on Consideration, 17 Law Quarterly Review, 415; 7 Halsbury, Laws of England, Contracts, p. 385; *Abbott v. Doane*, 163 Mass. 433). Others hold that there is no consideration in either class of cases (Williston, Successive Promises of the Same Performance, 8 Harvard Law Review, 27, 34; Consideration in Bilateral Contracts, 27*Id.* 503, 521; Anson on Contracts [11th ed.], p. 92).

* * *

The courts of this state are committed to the view that a promise by A to B to induce him not to *break* his contract with C is void (*Arend v. Smith*, 151 N.Y. 502; *Vanderbilt v. Schreyer*, 91 N.Y. 392; *Seybolt v. N.Y., L.E. & W.R.R. Co.*, 95 N.Y. 562; *Robinson v. Jewett*, 116 N.Y. 40). If that is the true nature of this promise, there was no consideration. We have never held, however, that a like infirmity attaches to a promise by A, not merely to B, but to B and C jointly, to induce them not to *rescind* or *modify* a contract which they are free to abandon. To determine whether that is in substance the promise before us, there is need of closer analysis.

The defendant's contract, if it be one, is not bilateral. It is unilateral (*Miller v. McKenzie*, 95 N.Y. 575). The consideration exacted is not a promise, but an act. The Count did not promise anything. In effect the defendant said to him: If you and my daughter marry, I will pay her an annuity for life. Until marriage occurred, the defendant was not bound. It would not have been enough that the Count remained willing to marry. The plain import of the contract is that his bride also should be willing, and that marriage should follow. The promise was intended to affect the conduct, not of one only, but of both. This becomes the more evident when we recall that though the promise ran to the Count, it was intended for the benefit of the daughter (*Durnherr v. Rau*, 135 N.Y. 219). When it came to her knowledge, she had the right to adopt and enforce it (*Gifford v. Corrigan*, 117 N.Y. 257; *Buchanan v. Tilden*, 158 N.Y. 109; *Lawrence v. Fox*, 20 N.Y. 268). In doing so, she made herself a party to the contract (*Gifford v. Corrigan*, *supra*). If the contract had been bilateral, her position might have been different. Since, however, it was unilateral, the consideration being performance (*Miller v. McKenzie, supra*), action on the faith of it put her in the same position as if she had been in form the promisee. That she learned of the promise before the marriage is a legitimate inference from the relation of the parties and from other attendant circumstances. The writing was signed by her parents; it was delivered to her intended husband; it was made four days before the marriage; it called for a payment on the day of the marriage; and on that day payment was made, and made to her. From all these circumstances, we may infer that at the time of the marriage the promise was known to the bride as well as the husband, and that both acted upon the faith of it.

The situation, therefore, is the same in substance as if the promise had run to husband and wife alike, and had been intended to induce performance by both. They were free by common consent to terminate their engagement or to postpone the marriage. If they forebore from exercising that right and assumed the responsibilities of marriage in reliance on the defendant's promise, he may not now retract it. The distinction between a promise by A to B to induce him not to break his contract with C, and a like promise to induce him not to join with C in a voluntary rescission, is not a new one. It has been suggested in cases where the new promise ran to B solely, and not to B and C jointly (Pollock, Contracts [8th ed.], p. 199; Williston, 8 Harv.L.Rev. 36). The criticism has been made that in such circumstances there ought to be some evidence that C was ready to withdraw (Williston, *supra*, at pp. 36, 37. Whether that is true of contracts to marry is not certain. Many elements foreign to the ordinary business contract enter into such engagements. It does not seem a far-fetched assumption in such cases that one will release where the other has repented. We shall assume, however, that the criticism is valid where the promise is intended as an inducement to only one of the two parties to the contract. It may then be sheer speculation to say that the other party could have been persuaded to rescind. But where the promise is held out as an inducement to both parties alike, there are new and different implications. One does not commonly apply pressure to coerce the will and action of those who are anxious to proceed. The attempt to sway their conduct by new inducements is an implied admission that both may waiver; that one equally with the other must be strengthened and persuaded; and that rescission or at least delay is something to be averted, and something, therefore, within the range of not unreasonable expectation. If pressure, applied to both, and holding both to their course, is not the purpose of the promise, it is at least the natural tendency and the probable result.)

The defendant knew that a man and a woman were assuming the responsibilities of wedlock in the belief that adequate provision had been made for the woman and for future offspring. He offered this inducement to both while they were free to retract or to delay. That they neither retracted nor delayed is certain. It is not to be expected that they should lay bare all the motives and promptings, some avowed and conscious, others perhaps half-conscious and inarticulate, which swayed their conduct.* It is enough that the natural consequence of the defendant's promise was to induce them to put the thought of rescission or delay aside. From that moment, there was no longer a real alternative. There was no longer what philosophers call a "living" option. This in itself permits the inference of detriment (*Smith v. Chadwick*, 9 App.Cas. 187, 196; *Smith v. Land & House Corp.*, 28 Ch.D. 7, 16; *Voorhis v. Olmstead*, 66 N.Y. 113, 118; *Fottler v. Moseley*, 179 Mass. 295). "If it is proved that the defendants with a view to induce the plaintiff to enter into a contract made a statement to the plaintiff of such a nature as would be likely to induce a person to enter into the contract, it is a fair inference of fact that he was induced to do so by the statement" (BLACKBURN, L.J., in *Smith v. Chadwick, supra*). The same inference follows, not so inevitably, but still legitimately, where the statement is made to induce the preservation of a contract. It will not do to divert the minds of others from a given line of conduct, and then to urge that because of the diversion the opportunity has gone by to say how their minds would otherwise have acted. If the tendency of the promise is to induce them to persevere, reliance and detriment may be inferred from the mere fact of performance. The springs of conduct are subtle and varied. One who meddles with them must not insist upon too nice a measure of proof that the spring which he released was effective to the exclusion of all others.

One other line of argument must be considered. The suggestion is made that the defendant's promise was not made *animo contrahendi*. It was not designed, we are told, to sway the conduct of any one; it was merely the offer of a gift which found its *motive* in the engagement of the daughter to the Count. Undoubtedly, the prospective marriage is not to be deemed a consideration for the promise "unless the parties have dealt with it on that footing" (Holmes, Common Law, p. 292; *Fire Ins. Assn. v. Wickham*, 141 U.S. 564, 579). "Nothing is consideration that is not regarded as such by both parties" (*Philpot v. Gruninger*, 14 Wall. 570, 577; *Fire Ins. Assn. v. Wickham, supra*). But here the very formality of the agreement suggests a purpose to affect the legal relations of the signers. One does not commonly pledge one's self to generosity in the language of a covenant. That the parties believed there was a consideration is certain. The document recites the engagement and the coming marriage. It states that these are the "consideration" for the promise. The failure to marry would have made the promise ineffective. In these circumstances we cannot say that the promise was not intended to control the conduct of those whom it was designed to benefit. Certainly we cannot draw that inference as one of law. Both sides moved for the direction of a verdict, and the trial judge became by consent the trier of the facts. If conflicting inferences were possible, he chose those favorable to the plaintiff.

* ["It is an object eagerly sought by low rich to buy for their daughters a High-Caste husband." Ah–Chin–Le, Some Observations on the Civilization of the Western Barbarians 151 (J.Y.S. Transl. 1876). Ed.]

The conclusion to which we are thus led is reinforced by those considerations of public policy which cluster about contracts that touch the marriage relation. The law favors marriage settlements, and seeks to uphold them. It puts them for many purposes in a class by themselves (*Phalen v. U.S. Trust Co.*, 186 N.Y. 178, 181). It has enforced them at times where consideration, if present at all, has been dependent upon doubtful inference (*McNutt v. McNutt*, 116 Ind. 545; *Appleby v. Appleby*, 100 Minn. 408). It strains, if need be, to the uttermost the interpretation of equivocal words and conduct in the effort to hold men to the honorable fulfilment of engagements designed to influence in their deepest relations the lives of others.

The judgment should be affirmed with costs.

CRANE, J. (concurring). I concur for affirmance and agree with what JUDGE CARDOZO has said about the law of consideration, but I prefer other reasons for my conclusions in this case.

Marriage settlements are usually made between husband and wife; but marriage settlements by third parties have been recognized by law. (Schouler's Dom.Rel. [5th ed.] sec. 178; *Phalen v. U.S. Trust Co.*, 186 N.Y. 178.) The policy of the law to uphold and enforce such contracts is applicable to both classes.

* * *

Judgment affirmed.

IN RE MORTON ALLAN SEGALL, ATTORNEY

Supreme Court of Illinois, 1987.
117 Ill.2d 1, 509 N.E.2d 988, 109 Ill.Dec. 149.

* * *

JUSTICE THOMAS J. MORAN delivered the opinion of the court:

The Administrator of the Attorney Registration and Disciplinary Commission filed a three-count complaint charging respondent, Morton Allan Segall, with professional misconduct. Count I of the complaint charged that respondent's attempts to settle a lawsuit brought against him by the Carte Blanche Corporation violated Rules 1–102(a)(4), 1–102(a)(5) and 7–104(a)(1) of the Code of Professional Responsibility (87 Ill.2d Rules 1–102(a)(4), 1–102(a)(5), 7–104(a)(1)). Count II charged the same violations with regard to respondent's attempts to settle a lawsuit brought against him by the Amoco Oil Company. Count III charged that respondent's repeated refusal to allow Amoco to take his deposition violated Rule 1–102(a)(5) (87 Ill.2d R. 1–102(a)(5)). The Hearing Board found no ethical violation with regard to count III, but found against respondent on counts I and II. The Hearing Board recommended that he be censured. The Review Board agreed with the Hearing Board's findings but recommended that a two-year suspension be imposed. Respondent filed exceptions in this court pursuant to Rule 753(e)(5) (103 Ill.2d R. 753(e)(5)).

The issue before this court is what, if any, sanctions should be imposed.

The complaint in the Carte Blanche suit alleged that respondent incurred numerous credit card charges, beginning on May 18, 1979. As of the date of the complaint, November 24, 1981, the unpaid balance on the account was alleged to be $12,837.42. On February 8, 1982, a default judgment was entered in favor of Carte Blanche for $12,837.42, plus costs.

Respondent moved to vacate the default judgment, claiming lack of notice. On October 4, 1982, while this motion was pending, respondent, who was in Florida at the time, directed his secretary to send a check for $95.60 directly to Carte Blanche. He knew at the time that Carte Blanche was represented by counsel, but he nonetheless bypassed that counsel. Typed on the reverse of the check was an attempted limitation, stating that "acceptance, negotiation or endorsement of this draft shall constitute a full and final release in settlement of all claims and causes of action for Acct. No. 944–148–645–4 in the name of Mort A. Segall." Allegedly accompanying the check was a letter which referenced the pending lawsuit, and read as follows:

"Gentlemen:

In order to settle all pending claims and disputes in connection with the above entitled litigation for the above account, and to avoid the expense and effort of further litigation, I am enclosing herewith and tendering my check in the sum of $95.60 in full settlement and payment of any and all claims, causes of action and matters in dispute as referenced above and now pending so that all claims between your company and the undersigned can be resolved amicably and finally.

If you agree with this offer of settlement to resolve all pending disputes and all claims with reference to the above, then your acceptance, negotiation or endorsement of the enclosed check shall constitute a full and final release, settlement and satisfaction of all claims and disputed actions with reference to all pending disputes, claims and accounts as referenced above, and you need not acknowledge this letter as the cancelled check will be sufficient for my records to show that you have agreed to accept the enclosed payment in full satisfaction and settlement and release of all pending matters and claims and accounts disputed as referenced above."

On November 22, 1982, respondent's first motion to vacate the judgment was denied. On December 10, 1982, respondent filed another motion to vacate the judgment. Attached to the motion were copies of the above letter and the negotiated check. In support of the motion respondent claimed that the negotiated check evidenced a settlement of Carte Blanche's claims. The trial court, however, found that there had been no accord and satisfaction, and dismissed the motion.

Respondent appealed, but the appellate court affirmed the trial court's judgment in an unpublished order *(Carte Blanche Corp. v. Segall*

(1983), 115 Ill.App.3d 1158, 78 Ill.Dec. 253, 461 N.E.2d 1087). * * * On May 24, 1984, more than 10 months after the appellate court order was issued, respondent paid the judgment in full.

The facts in the Amoco case were very similar. Amoco's amended complaint alleged that respondent, as of August 26, 1980, owed a balance of $11,238.16 for credit purchases between January 1, 1979, and June 1, 1980. On October 4, 1982, the same date as his letter and check to Carte Blanche, respondent directed his secretary to send Amoco a letter and a check for $48.76. Except for the account number and the lawsuit referenced, the letter and the endorsement restriction on the check were identical to those in the Carte Blanche case. As in the Carte Blanche case, respondent knowingly bypassed Amoco's lawyers, sending the check directly to Amoco.

On November 10, 1982, respondent filed a motion to dismiss Amoco's suit, claiming that the negotiated check evidenced a settlement. Respondent also filed a motion to "quash" his own deposition, for which he had failed to appear despite two court orders specifically requiring him to do so. On December 16, 1982, respondent's motions were denied, and a judgment for $11,238.16, plus costs, was entered against him as a sanction for his repeated refusal to be deposed. This judgment was upheld by the appellate court. (For further details, see *Amoco Oil Co. v. Segall* (1983), 118 Ill.App.3d 1002, 74 Ill.Dec. 447, 455 N.E.2d 876.) Approximately three months later respondent paid the judgment in full.

Disciplinary Rule 7–104 states, in part:

"(a) During the course of his representation of a client a lawyer shall not

(1) communicate or cause another to communicate on the subject of the representation with a party he knows to be represented by a lawyer in that matter unless he has the prior consent of the lawyer representing such other party or is authorized by law to do so." (87 Ill.2d R. 7–104(a)(1).)

Respondent admits that in each of the lawsuits he knowingly contacted a party represented by counsel without obtaining counsel's consent. He argues, however, that these contacts were made on his own behalf as a litigant and thus were not "[d]uring the course of his representation of a client." We disagree. An attorney who is himself a party to the litigation represents himself when he contacts an opposing party. Rule 7–104(a)(1) is designed to protect litigants represented by counsel from direct contacts by opposing counsel. A party, having employed counsel to act as an intermediary between himself and opposing counsel, does not lose the protection of the rule merely because opposing counsel is also a party to the litigation. Consequently, an attorney who is himself a litigant may be disciplined under Rule 7–104(a)(1) when, as in the case at bar, he directly contacts an opposing party without permission from that party's counsel.

The Administrator also alleges that respondent's conduct violated Disciplinary Rules 1–102(a)(4) and (5). Rule 1–102 reads in pertinent part:

"(a) A lawyer shall not

* * *

(4) engage in conduct involving dishonesty, fraud, deceit, or misrepresentation; or

(5) engage in conduct that is prejudicial to the administration of justice." 87 Ill.2d R. 1–102.

The Administrator argues that respondent's conduct was deceptive and was an attempt to defraud Carte Blanche and Amoco, in violation of Rule 1–102(a)(4). The Administrator also argues that, by representing to the court in each case that the suit had been settled, respondent attempted a fraud on the court, in violation of Rule 1–102(a)(5).

In both circuit court cases the court found that the plaintiff's negotiation of respondent's check did not establish an accord and satisfaction because respondent did not sufficiently prove that the letter explaining the conditional settlement was actually sent along with the checks. In the Amoco case, for example, the appellate court pointed out that respondent claimed that his secretary, Barbara Butts, sent the letter at his direction while he was in Florida. However, Butts neither testified nor supplied an affidavit, so there was no evidence as to when and where the letter was sent, or if it was sent at all. (*Amoco Oil Co. v. Segall* (1983), 118 Ill.App.3d 1002, 1012, 74 Ill.Dec. 447, 455 N.E.2d 876.) If the Administrator had been able to prove that respondent knew that the letters had never been sent, then it would have been obvious that respondent had committed fraud. The Administrator, however, specifically alleged that respondent *did* send the letters to Amoco and Carte Blanche. Since this allegation was admitted by respondent we must assume that the letters were in fact sent. The Administrator nonetheless argues that the letters, together with the circumstances under which they were sent, amounted to an attempted fraud.

This court has applied a broad definition of fraud, finding fraud whenever there is conduct "calculated to deceive." (*In re Armentrout* (1983), 99 Ill.2d 242, 251, 75 Ill.Dec. 703, 457 N.E.2d 1262; accord, *People ex rel. Chicago Bar Association v. Gilmore* (1931), 345 Ill. 28, 46, 177 N.E. 710.) We agree with the Hearing Board and the Review Board that respondent's conduct, taken as a whole, was calculated to deceive Carte Blanche and Amoco by obtaining settlements of large claims for *de minimis* amounts. Respondent bypassed each plaintiff's attorney in these cases and sent each plaintiff a letter which was designed to make the plaintiffs' agents believe that the minimal amount tendered was the amount actually due. The letters did not state the actual amount due, and, in the Carte Blanche case, did not even mention that the dispute had been reduced to a judgment. We agree with the Review Board that there is "no rational basis upon which we can believe that Respondent thought that he could actually settle claims of $12,837.42 and $11,238.16 for $95.60 and $48.76, respectively." We therefore agree that his conduct violated Rule 1–102(a)(4).

Also, by filing motions to dismiss the suits due to the purported settlements, respondent attempted to involve the courts in his fraudulent scheme. Involving the courts in such a scheme must be considered "prejudicial to the administration of justice," and thus respondent's conduct also violated Rule 1–102(a)(5).

While respondent's attempted fraud was not successful, an attempted deception is as serious an ethical violation as a successful one. Together with the violation of Rule 7–104(a)(1) we feel that respondent's attempted fraud was serious enough to warrant a substantial suspension. We therefore order that respondent be suspended from the practice of law for a period of two years from the date of this opinion.

Respondent suspended.

[CLARK, C.J., dissented and filed opinion in which SIMON, J., joined.]

KIBLER v. FRANK L. GARRETT & SONS, INC.

Supreme Court of Washington, En Banc, 1968.
73 Wash.2d 523, 439 P.2d 416.

ROSELLINI, JUDGE. This action on a contract was dismissed at the close of the plaintiff's evidence, the trial court finding, although it had not been pleaded, that there had been an accord and satisfaction. The plaintiff has appealed.

The facts are these: The plaintiff was hired by the defendant to harvest his wheat crop. There was no agreement on the price to be paid. According to the plaintiff's evidence, he told the defendant that, if the wheat crop proved to be more than 50 bushels per acre, the price would be 18 cents per bushel and perhaps more, depending on the circumstances. He testified that the crop was in excess of 50 bushels per acre and there were harvesting difficulties which had not been anticipated due to the presence of guy wires, roads, and risers. He sent the defendant a bill based upon a charge of 25 cents per bushel, but later sent a corrected bill for $876.20 based on 20 cents per bushel. The response which he eventually received to this billing was the following letter and a check for $444:

> This check is for $10.00 an acre, and 37 acres is $370.00. This is what you offered to harvest our wheat for. Seeing that the wheat was fairly heavy, we are paying you $2.00 an acre more, which makes a total of $444.00. Your total pay is 50% more than we paid last year for harvesting the same acres, and 20% more than you agreed to do it for. Billing on this acreage for approximately $30.00 an acre is ridiculous.

Upon receipt of these items, the plaintiff called his attorney and asked if he could safely deposit the check. The attorney asked him to read the notations on it. He read the typewritten notation: "Harvesting

Wheat Washington Ranch" and the printed words "Frank L. Garrett & Sons, Inc.", but he did not see a line of fine print on the check which read: "By endorsement this check when paid is accepted in full payment of the following account." The attorney told him he could deposit the check. He did not communicate further with the defendant but proceeded to bring this action.

As we have said, accord and satisfaction was not pleaded as a defense. However, the trial court, observing the fine print on the check and drawing it to the attention of the parties, concluded that, taken in conjunction with the letter, this notation established as a matter of law that there had been an accord and satisfaction.

The rules governing the question of accord and satisfaction are set forth in the leading case of *Graham v. New York Life Ins. Co.*, 182 Wash. 612, 47 P.2d 1029 (1935). They are as follows:

(1) Whether there has been an accord and satisfaction in any given case is generally a mixed question of law and fact.

(2) But where the facts are not in controversy, it is purely a question of law for the court.

(3) To create an accord and satisfaction in law, there must be a meeting of minds of the parties upon the subject and an intention on the part of both to make such an agreement.

(4) An accord and satisfaction is founded on contract, and a consideration therefor is as necessary as for any other contract.

(5) Where the debtor pays what in law he is bound to pay and what he admits that he owes, such payment by the debtor and its acceptance by the creditor, even though tendered as payment in full of a larger indebtedness, do not operate as an accord and satisfaction of the entire indebtedness, because there is no consideration therefor.

(6) Generally speaking, when a debtor sends to his creditor a check in an amount that the debtor is willing to pay, and at the same time informs the creditor that the debtor intends the check to be considered as full payment, then, by accepting and cashing the check, the creditor agrees to the settlement and cannot thereafter seek additional compensation.

(7) But the rule just stated does not apply where there is an agreement that a certain sum shall be paid on account and not in full settlement, and the sending of a check stating that it is in full settlement does not, as a matter of law, under such circumstances, effect an accord and satisfaction.

(8) Nor does that rule apply where the debt or amount is liquidated or certain and due, unless there is a new consideration.

(9) Where the amount of a debt or obligation is unliquidated or in dispute, then the tender by the debtor of a certain sum in full payment of the debt, followed by acceptance and retention of the amount tendered, establishes an accord and satisfaction; but if the amount be liquidated or undisputed, then such tender and acceptance do not establish an accord and satisfaction.

The facts are not in dispute in this case, therefore the question is one of law. Did the letter and the check and the cashing of the latter constitute an accord and satisfaction? The claim was unliquidated; therefore, if the check was intended as full payment and that fact was communicated to the plaintiff, his cashing of the check completed the accord.

The important question to determine is whether there was a meeting of the minds. In order for this to have occurred, the defendant must have made his intention clear to the plaintiff. The trial court was of the opinion that the letter, when read in conjunction with the fine print on the check, manifested that intention.

The letter itself does not state that the check is sent in full payment. Such an intent might be gleaned from the language that he considers it all that is reasonably owing to the plaintiff. Yet the last sentence equivocates. The amount asked by the plaintiff is ridiculous, the defendant says, but he does not say, "I will pay no more than the amount enclosed." We think the letter leaves the question of the amount owed open to further negotiation. The fact that the plaintiff did not attempt further negotiation does not alter the import of the language of the letter.

* * *

Since there were no conditions attached to the acceptance of the check in this case, the letter was not an offer of an accord.

Was the condition sufficiently expressed on the check itself? It is unquestioned that the plaintiff did not see the fine print, and his attorney did not see it. The defendant's attorney did not notice it, apparently, until it was called to his attention at the trial. This was a form check, presumably used in the payment of all of the defendant's accounts, whether the payments made were payments in full or partial payments. There was nothing on the check to indicate that the language was particularly applicable to the plaintiff's claim. The trial court felt that the tone of the letter cast upon the plaintiff the duty to examine the check minutely or cash it at his peril. We do not agree. The burden is upon the party alleging an accord and satisfaction to show that there was indeed a meeting of the minds. See *Brear v. Klinker Sand & Gravel Co.*, 60 Wash.2d 443, 374 P.2d 370 (1962). If the language contained in the fine print on the check was of significance in forming an accord, it must appear that the fact of its significance was brought to the plaintiff's attention. The evidence is to the contrary.

* * *

We hold that the proof in this case did not show an accord and satisfaction, since while the claim was disputed, there was no showing that the defendant manifested to the plaintiff his intention to pay no more than the amount which he remitted. To sustain the trial court would necessitate a holding that payment of an amount less than that claimed by the creditor operates as an accord and satisfaction if the amount paid is all that the debtor admits that he owes. This is contrary to the rule we have quoted from *Ingram v. Sauset,* supra, and would place a creditor at a disadvantage in accepting partial payments from a reluctant debtor, since by doing so he would be jeopardizing his right to receive the balance, even though in law that balance was in fact due him. It is true that the courts look with favor on compromise, but this means genuine compromise, arrived at through mutual agreement, and not compromise fallen into inadvertently.

The plaintiff's witnesses testified that the reasonable value of his services was close to the amount which he claimed was due him. The defendant did not present evidence on this question, since the court dismissed the action at the close of the plaintiff's case. As the record now stands, there is no evidence of overreaching on the part of the plaintiff.

The judgment is reversed and the cause remanded for a new trial.

* * *

HALE, J. (dissenting). The facts of this case, in my judgment, present a classic example of accord and satisfaction, and I would, therefore, affirm the trial court. After all, the question of whether the parties have resolved their differences by an accord and satisfaction is largely a question of fact to be determined by the jury, or, as in this case, by the court as trier of the fact. 1 Am.Jur.2d, *Accord & Satisfaction* § 11.

I agree that the printed notation on the check was insufficient to engender an accord and satisfaction, but the events leading up to the delivery of the check and the circumstance of its cashing provided more than adequate evidence, in my view, to support the trial court's factual finding that Mr. Kibler knowingly cashed the check in full payment and satisfaction of the debt for which it had been tendered. Here are the circumstances as I see them which led inexorably to an accord and satisfaction.

* * *

The instant case began with an unliquidated claim, an agreement to harvest the wheat for an unspecified sum running from $10 per acre to a greater amount, depending vaguely on unspecified contingencies. Then the creditor sent a bill demanding 25 cents per bushel for a total demand of $1,095.25. A few days later he sent his debtor a corrected or new billing at 20 cents per bushel in the total sum of $876.20, thus conclusively establishing the unliquidated and uncertain nature of the obligation. The debt at the outset was unliquidated and for an uncertain amount; it remained so through the first erroneous billing for $1,095.25 and the second billing at $876.20.

It was still unliquidated and uncertain when defendant sent plaintiff a check for $444 on November 3, 1965, and stated specifically that the check was for the agreed price of $10 per acre, with an added $2 per acre because the wheat was very heavy. The assertions in the letter of transmittal that the enclosed check was 50 per cent more than plaintiff agreed to do the work for, and that the billing sent by plaintiff at nearly

$30 an acre was ridiculous, all unmistakably convey the notion that the check was tendered in full payment. Under these circumstances, it should have been clear to a person of ordinary understanding that cashing the check constituted an acceptance of the $444 in full payment and discharge of plaintiff's claim for harvesting defendant's 37 acres.

I would, therefore, affirm.

* * *

Problems

Analyze these problems from a common law perspective. Ignore any statutory changes and the doctrine of duress.

10. A bank in Kentucky was robbed. A bankers' association offered a reward of $5,000 to anyone who apprehended the robber. Within a week, P, who was a police officer in the jurisdiction in which the bank was located, apprehended the robber who was convicted. P sues the association. What result?

11. Angela applied to the Village of Homewood to become a firefighter. Under State law, the Village was required to process her application; the processing included a physical agility test. Prior to administering the test, the Village required Angela to sign a release of liability for all injuries she might suffer as a result of the test. During the test, she fell and was injured. She claims that the injuries were the result of the Village's negligence. The Village raises the release as a defense. Will the defense succeed?

12. Plaintiffs were sailors on defendant's vessel and agreed to work for a certain sum for a particular voyage. Midway through the voyage the plaintiffs demanded an increase in wages and defendant promised to pay $X more. Was the defendant's promise enforceable?

13. Plaintiff and defendant entered into a contract for the sale and delivery (in installments) of 4,000 wooden display stands at a price of 65 cents each. After 2,000 stands had been delivered and paid for, the plaintiff told defendant that due to increased costs he would have to charge 75 cents for each stand and defendant agreed to pay the higher rate. Plaintiff delivered the stands. At what rate is plaintiff entitled to be paid?

14. P was employed by D under a contract for the year. D got into financial difficulties and during the contract year, P agreed with other key personnel that they all would accept a lesser salary for the balance of the year. Is there consideration for P's promise to take less?

15. D bought a tractor-trailer and financed the purchase through C, a bank. D missed a number of payments. C declared D in default on the loan agreement and threatened to exercise its right of repossession. D and C reached an agreement whereby D promised to have the broker, for whom D worked, subtract the money D owed C from D's paycheck and give it directly to C in exchange for C's promise not to exercise its right of repossession. The next day the tractor-trailer was repossessed on C's order. D sued C. Was there a binding agreement?

16. A, a subcontractor, contracts with B, a general contractor, to install heating units in houses being built by B for C. A discontinues work without

justification. C promises to pay A an additional amount if A completes the installation in accordance with A's contract with B. A performs. Is there consideration for C's promise?

17. Plaintiff, as landlord, entered into a lease with defendant as tenant. The lease was for a five-year period at the agreed rental of $500 per month. Two years later, the parties entered into an oral agreement whereby rentals were reduced to $450. The reduced rent was paid and plaintiff now seeks to recover the $50 per month that was not paid.

18. Tenant terminated its lease as it was empowered to do by a clause in the lease providing that Tenant could terminate the lease by paying a termination fee of $380,000. It delivered a check in that amount clearly marked that it was tendered in full satisfaction of all claims Landlord had against Tenant. Landlord protested the language on the check but deposited it into its account. Landlord now sues Tenant, claiming damages for Tenant's breach of an obligation to restore the premises to their pre-rental condition. Tenant pleads the affirmative defense of accord and satisfaction. How can Landlord meet this defense?

19. The plaintiff sold and delivered to defendant at various times bricks for which defendant was billed for the total of $820. On May 12th plaintiff sent bricks which would have been worth $448 if they had conformed to the contract. The defendant rejected them as non-conforming and asked plaintiff what to do with the bricks. On August 3 the defendant wrote the plaintiff as follows:

> "Enclosed find check for $820 which pays our account up to July 1st. We have deducted the $448 for non-conforming bricks.

> Please advise us what disposition we shall make of these bricks for you."

Plaintiff received and cashed the check and now sues for the $448, alleging that the bricks are conforming. (a) If you were representing the defendant what would you set forth in your answer? (b) What issues will arise as to the validity of this defense?

20. Bridget bought a new Honda from a dealer, Honda of Rapid City, Inc. To pay for it, she applied for and received partial financing from First National Bank. The bank issued a check in the amount of $11,000 payable to the dealer. On the back of the check the bank had rubber-stamped this legend: "On accepting this check the dealer will cause to be recorded in the appropriate record offices and on the title to the vehicle a notice of a lien on the vehicle in favor of the First National Bank." Bridget delivered the check to the sales representative at the dealer's premises. The sales representative delivered the check to the bookkeeper who rubber-stamped it "Honda of Rapid City, Inc." and deposited it. No notice of lien was recorded. The car was delivered to Bridget who soon thereafter lost her job and sold the Honda for cash to a *bona fide* purchaser who had no notice of any lien. First National Bank sues Honda of Rapid City, Inc. What result?

SECTION 3.   DURESS AND STATUTORY CHANGES

(Calamari & Perillo 5th §§ 5.12—5.17 and 9.6)

U.C.C. § 1–102. Purposes; Rules of Construction; Variation by Agreement

* * *

(3) The effect of provisions of this Act may be varied by agreement, except as otherwise provided in this Act and except that the obligations of good faith, diligence, reasonableness and care prescribed by this Act may not be disclaimed by agreement but the parties may by agreement determine the standards by which the performance of such obligations is to be measured if such standards are not manifestly unreasonable.

U.C.C. § 1–203. Obligation of Good Faith

Every contract or duty within this Act imposes an obligation of good faith in its performance or enforcement.

U.C.C. § 1–201. General Definitions

Subject to additional definitions contained in the subsequent Articles of this Act which are applicable to specific Articles or Parts thereof, and unless the context otherwise requires, in this Act:

* * *

(19) "Good faith" means honesty in fact in the conduct or transaction concerned.

U.C.C. § 2–103. Definitions and Index of Definitions

(1) In this Article unless the context otherwise requires

* * *

(b) "Good faith" in the case of a merchant means honesty in fact and the observance of reasonable commercial standards of fair dealing in the trade.

ROTH STEEL PRODUCTS v. SHARON STEEL CORP.

United States Court of Appeals, Sixth Circuit, 1983.
705 F.2d 134.

CELEBREZZE, SENIOR CIRCUIT JUDGE.

This diversity action for breach of contract involves issues which require us to explore some relatively uncharted areas of Article Two of the Uniform Commercial Code, Ohio Rev.Code Sec. 1302.01 *et seq*. We vacate the district court's judgment, however, to the extent that it concludes that adequate notice of breach was given in 1974 and remand this question for more comprehensive findings of fact.

I.

The plaintiffs-appellees (cross-appellants), Roth Steel Products Company and Toledo Steel Tube Company, are subsidiaries of Roth Industries, Inc. Roth Steel produces welded straight tubing for a variety of uses; Toledo Steel Tube produces fabricated steel tubing for use in automobile exhaust systems. Mr. Howard Guerin, vice-president for purchasing, Roth Industries, served as the purchasing agent for both corporations until April, 1973, when he was replaced by Mr. Richard Mecaskey.

Sharon Steel Corporation, defendant-appellant (cross-appellee), is a subsidiary of NVF Corporation. In 1973, Sharon was an integrated steel producer which accounted for approximately one percent of the steel produced in this country. It produced hot rolled and cold rolled sheet steel in carbon and alloy grades, as well as pickled and oiled sheet steel. The plaintiffs used sheet steel to produce tubing. Mr. Frank Metzger, Sharon's Northern Ohio Sales Manager, was responsible for all sales to the plaintiffs.

A.   In 1972, the steel industry operated at approximately 70% of its capacity. Steel prices were highly competitive and discounts from published prices were given customers in an effort to increase the productive use of steel making capacity. On November 14, 1972, Metzger, Sharon's representative, met with Guerin and offered to sell the plaintiffs specific quantities of hot rolled, cold rolled and pickled steel at prices substantially lower than Sharon's "book price". Testimony indicated that these prices and quantities were to be effective from January 1 until December 31, 1973.

On November 17, 1972, Metzger forwarded a communication in the form of a letter to Guerin confirming the discussions of November 14. The letter indicated that Sharon would sell the plaintiffs 200 tons of hot rolled pickled steel each month for $148.00 per ton and that it would sell plaintiffs hot rolled black steel on an open schedule basis for $140.00 per ton. The letter also discussed "the probability" that Sharon could sell 500 tons of cold rolled to both Roth Steel and Toledo at varying prices depending on the type of cold rolled steel ordered. Metzger testified that a few days after the letter was sent, the plaintiffs agreed to purchase 1,000 tons of cold rolled steel (500 tons each) at the prices indicated in the letter.

On February 15, 1973, Metzger and Guerin met to discuss the tonnages of hot rolled steel mentioned in the November 17 letter. During the meeting, Metzger and Guerin agreed to increase the monthly tonnage of hot rolled pickled steel that Sharon would sell to the plaintiffs from 200 tons to 300 tons each month. Metzger also agreed, on behalf of Sharon, to sell the plaintiffs 300 tons of hot rolled black steel until May, 1973, when the monthly tonnage would be increased to 400 tons per month for the remainder of 1973. To confirm the agreement, Metzger noted these increased tonnages on Guerin's copy of the November 17 letter.

In early 1973, several factors influenced the market for steel. Federal price controls discouraged foreign producers from importing steel; conversely, domestic producers exported a substantial portion of the steel produced domestically, in an effort to avoid federal price controls.

Thus, the domestic steel supply was sharply reduced. In addition, the industry experienced substantial increases in demand as well as increases in labor, raw material, and energy costs. These increased labor, raw material, and energy costs compelled steel producers to increase prices. The increased demand and the attractive export market caused the entire industry to operate at full capacity in 1973 and 1974. Consequently, nearly every domestic producer experienced substantial delays in delivery.

As a result of the changed market conditions, Sharon decided to withdraw all price concessions, including those it had given the plaintiffs. The plaintiffs were notified of this decision on March 23, 1973 and they immediately protested, asserting that the price increase was a breach of the November, 1972 agreement, as modified in February. As a result of this protest, discussions ensued and Sharon agreed to continue to sell steel to the plaintiffs at the discount prices of November, 1972 until June 30, 1973. For the remainder of 1973, Sharon proposed to sell rolled steel to plaintiffs at modified prices; these prices were higher than the prices set forth in the November 17 letter, but were lower than the published prices which Sharon charged its other customers. Sharon clearly indicated to plaintiffs that Sharon would sell no steel to plaintiffs after June 30, 1973 except at modified prices. Although plaintiffs initially . were reluctant to accept Sharon's compromise, they finally agreed to Sharon's compromise proposal primarily because they were unable to purchase sufficient steel elsewhere to meet their production requirements.

In the second half of 1973, Sharon also experienced difficulties in filling orders in a timely fashion. In most of 1973 and 1974, Sharon's mill was operating at full capacity; because it could not produce any more steel, Sharon implemented a "blanking" policy in an effort to reduce the backlog of orders. Pursuant to the blanking policy, Sharon would refuse to accept purchase orders that requested delivery for a particular "blanked" month and all the steel produced that month was used to fill overdue orders. Because of this policy Sharon refused several purchase orders issued by plaintiffs: it refused to book Roth's orders of 300 tons of hot rolled pickled steel and 400 tons of hot rolled black steel for delivery in October, 1973 and Toledo's order of 425 tons of cold rolled steel for delivery in December, 1973. Both October and December were "blanked" months.

B. Sharon and the plaintiffs conducted business differently in 1974. In 1974, contracts were formed separately on an order-by-order basis. Normally, the plaintiffs issued a purchase order which indicated the type and amount of steel sought, and the requested delivery date; the purchase orders were offers to purchase steel and were not effective until accepted by Sharon. Sharon accepted an offer by issuing an acknowledgment form; in this form, Sharon agreed to ship a quantity of steel by a specific date, usually the date requested by the purchaser. The acknowledgment form indicated that the price for the shipment would be the "[s]eller's prices prevailing at the time of shipment."

In 1974, the steel market became even less predictable than in 1973: overall demand increased, deliveries of steel became more erratic, and acknowledged delivery dates were rarely observed. Sharon's actual delivery dates were three to five months after the promised delivery dates. Throughout 1974, the price of steel steadily rose; as a consequence, Sharon's late deliveries had the effect of increasing the price of the goods.

Although Sharon's shipments to the plaintiffs were consistently delinquent throughout 1974, the plaintiffs continued to accept the late shipments and to place new orders with Sharon. The plaintiffs apparently acquiesced in this pattern of late shipments and higher prices for two reasons: they had no practical alternative source of steel and they believed Sharon's assurances that the late deliveries resulted from the general shortage of raw materials and the need to equitably allocate its limited production among all of its customers.

In May, 1974, the plaintiffs discovered facts that caused them to believe that the delays in shipment were not entirely the result of raw material shortages and Sharon's allocation system. Specifically, the plaintiffs learned on May 9, 1974, that Sharon was selling substantial amounts of rolled steel to its subsidiary Ohio Metal Processing Company. Ohio Metal Processing was operating as a warehouse and selling steel at premium prices. By selling through its warehouse-subsidiary, Sharon was able to obtain higher prices than federal price controls otherwise permitted. In 1974, approximately fifteen percent (20,000 tons per month) of Sharon's monthly steel production was sold to Ohio Metal Processing. Thus, the plaintiffs assert that they first learned that Sharon's late deliveries were not entirely the result of raw material shortages and an allocation system when they learned that steel was being sold to Ohio Metal Processing.

The plaintiffs did not immediately act upon this information. Instead, they allowed the remaining unfilled orders to pend during the summer. In September, 1974, Roth's orders were placed on "hold" due to [a] labor dispute. Most of plaintiffs' orders were cancelled [in] October, 1974. One final delivery was made by Sharon on October 31, 1974; although this order had been inadvertently overlooked by the plaintiffs and thus not cancelled, the plaintiffs rejected this shipment because delivery had been made nearly one year after the agreed delivery date.

C. The plaintiffs commenced this action in April, 1975, alleging breach of contract and seeking to recover their expenses in "covering". In March, 1976, the plaintiffs sought leave to file an amended complaint. The complaint, as amended, asserted 41 counts; plaintiffs sought damages based on the difference between the contract price and the market price for the goods at the time breach was discovered. The amended complaint sought total damages of $896,174.60. Sharon's answer denied the existence of a contract for the calendar year 1973 and raised several defenses: the statute of frauds, modification of the oral contract, commercial impracticability and failure to give notice of breach. It also counterclaimed for damages based upon the steel shipment which was rejected by Toledo Steel in October, 1974.

Following discovery, the district court granted plaintiffs' motion for partial summary judgment, concluding that the statute of frauds did not bar the enforcement of the November, 1972 oral agreement. Following a five day trial, the district court issued a lengthy and exhaustive memorandum of opinion. In the opinion, the district court concluded that an oral contract was formed in November, 1972; that Sharon's attempt, in June, 1973, to modify the contract was ineffective; and that Sharon had breached the contract by charging prices higher than agreed upon in the November, 1972 contract, by refusing to sell steel in October and December, 1973, and by failing to make timely delivery of some orders issued pursuant to the 1972 agreement. With regard to the 1974 transactions, the district court concluded that Sharon had breached several contracts for delivery of steel by failing to make a timely delivery or by failing to make delivery at all. It also concluded that the plaintiffs had given adequate notice of breach with regard to those late shipments which they accepted. It granted the plaintiffs damages of $555,968.46, but denied their motion for prejudgment interest. Finally, it dismissed Sharon's counterclaim, because it concluded that Toledo properly rejected the late shipment.

Sharon has appealed from the district court's order granting the plaintiffs' claim for damages and the order dismissing its counterclaim. The plaintiffs have cross-appealed from the district court's order denying prejudgment interest.

II.

* * *

C.   In March, 1973, Sharon notified its customers that it intended to charge the maximum permissible price for all of its products; accordingly, all price concessions, including those made to the plaintiffs, were to be rescinded effective April 1, 1973. On March 23, 1973, Guerin indicated to Metzger that the plaintiffs considered the proposed price increase to be a breach of the November, 1972 contract. In an effort to resolve the dispute, Guerin met with representatives of Sharon on March 28, 1973 and asked Sharon to postpone any price increases until June or July, 1973. Several days later, Richard Mecaskey, Guerin's replacement, sent a letter to Sharon which indicated that the plaintiffs believed that the November, 1972 agreement was enforceable and that the plaintiffs were willing to negotiate a price modification if Sharon's cost increases warranted such an action. As a result of this letter, another meeting was held between Sharon and the plaintiffs. At this meeting, Walter Gregg, Sharon's vice-president and chairman of the board, agreed to continue charging the November, 1972 prices until June 30, 1973 and offered, for the remainder of 1973, to charge prices that were lower than Sharon's published prices but higher than the 1972 prices. Although the plaintiffs initially rejected the terms offered by Sharon for the second half of 1973, Mecaskey reluctantly agreed to Sharon's terms on June 29, 1973.

Before the district court, Sharon asserted that it properly increased prices because the parties had modified the November, 1973 contract to reflect changed market conditions. The district court, however, made several findings which, it believed, indicated that Sharon did not seek a modification to avoid a loss on the contract. The district court also found that the plaintiffs' inventories of rolled steel were "alarmingly deficient" at the time modification was sought and that Sharon had threatened to cease selling steel to the plaintiffs in the second-half of 1973 unless the plaintiffs agreed to the modification. Because Sharon had used its position as the plaintiffs' chief supplier to extract the price modification, the district court concluded that Sharon had acted in bad faith by seeking to modify the contract. In the alternative, the court concluded that the modification agreement was voidable because it was extracted by means of economic duress; the tight steel market prevented the plaintiffs from obtaining steel elsewhere at an affordable price and, consequently, the plaintiffs were forced to agree to the modification in order to assure a continued supply of steel. *See e.g. Oskey Gasoline & Oil Co. v. Continental Oil Co.,* 534 F.2d 1281 (8th Cir.1976). Sharon challenges these conclusions on appeal.

The ability of a party to modify a contract which is subject to Article Two of the Uniform Commercial Code is broader than common law, primarily because the modification needs no consideration to be binding. O.R.C. Sec. 1302.12 (U.C.C. Sec. 2–209(1)). A party's ability to modify an agreement is limited only by Article Two's general obligation of good faith. * * * In determining whether a particular modification was obtained in good faith, a court must make two distinct inquiries: whether the party's conduct is consistent with "reasonable commercial standards of fair dealing in the trade," *U.S. for Use and Benefit of Crane Co. v. Progressive Enterprises,* 418 F.Supp. 662, 664 n. 1 (E.D.Va.1976), and whether the parties were in fact motivated to seek modification by an honest desire to compensate for commercial exigencies. *See Ralston Purina Co. v. McNabb,* 381 F.Supp. at 183 (subjective purpose [to maximize damages] of extending time of performance under contract indicates bad faith and renders modification invalid); O.R.C. Sec. 1302.01(A)(2) (U.C.C. Sec. 2–103). The first inquiry is relatively straightforward; the party asserting the modification must demonstrate that his decision to seek modification was the result of a factor, such as increased costs, which would cause an ordinary merchant to seek a modification of the contract. *See* Official Comment 2, O.R.C. Sec. 1302.12 (U.C.C. Sec. 2–209) (reasonable commercial standards may require objective reason); J. White & R. Summers, Handbook of Law under the U.C.C. at 41. The second inquiry, regarding the subjective honesty of the parties, is less clearly defined. Essentially, this inquiry requires the party asserting the modification to demonstrate that he was, in fact, motivated by a legitimate commercial reason and that such a reason is not offered merely as a pretext. *Ralston Purina Co. v. McNabb,* 381 F.Supp. at 183–84.

Moreover, the trier of fact must determine whether the means used to obtain the modification are an impermissible attempt to obtain a modification by extortion or overreaching. * * *

Sharon argues that its decision to seek a modification was consistent with reasonable commercial standards of fair dealing because market exigencies made further performance entail a substantial loss. The district court, however, made three findings which caused it to conclude that economic circumstances were not the reason that Sharon sought a modification: it found that Sharon was partially insulated from raw material price increases, that Sharon bargained for a contract with a slim profit margin and thus implicitly assumed the risk that performance might come to involve a loss, and that Sharon's overall profit in 1973 and its profit on the contract in the first quarter of 1973 were inconsistent with Sharon's position that the modification was sought to avoid a loss. Although all of these findings are marginally related to the question whether Sharon's conduct was consistent with reasonable commercial standards of fair dealing, we do not believe that they are sufficient to support a finding that Sharon did not observe reasonable commercial standards by seeking a modification. In our view, these findings do not support a conclusion that a reasonable merchant, in light of the circumstances, would not have sought a modification in order to avoid a loss. For example, the district court's finding that Sharon's steel slab contract[26] insulated it from industry wide cost increases is correct, so far as it goes. Although Sharon was able to purchase steel slabs at pre–1973 prices, the district court's findings also indicate that it was not able to purchase, at those prices, a sufficient tonnage of steel slabs to meet its production requirements. The district court also found that Sharon experienced substantial cost increases for other raw materials, ranging from 4% to nearly 20%. In light of these facts, the finding regarding the fixed-price contract for slab steel, without more, cannot support an inference that Sharon was unaffected by the market shifts that occurred in 1973. Similarly, the district court's finding that Sharon entered a contract in November, 1972 which would yield only a slim profit does not support a conclusion that Sharon was willing to risk a loss on the contract. Absent a finding that the market shifts and the raw material price increases were foreseeable at the time the contract was formed—a finding which was not made—Sharon's willingness to absorb a loss cannot be inferred from the fact that it contracted for a smaller profit than usual. Finally, the findings regarding Sharon's profits are not sufficient, by themselves, to warrant a conclusion that Sharon was not justified in seeking a modification. Clearly, Sharon's initial profit on the

26. Sharon was a party to a contract with United States Steel which allowed it to make monthly purchases of slab steel ranging from a minimum of 25,000 tons per month to a maximum of 45,000 tons per month. It was also a party to a contract with Wierton Steel which allowed it to purchase slab steel in amounts varying between 10,000 to 20,000 tons per month. Both of these contracts were entered prior to 1973, at a very attractive price. When the market strengthened in 1973, however, Sharon was unable to obtain the maximum monthly tonnages permitted under these contracts: U.S. Steel delivered only 30,000 tons per month and Wierton 10,000 tons per month.

contract is an important consideration; the district court's findings indicate, however, that at the time modification was sought substantial future losses were foreseeable. A party who has not actually suffered a loss on the contract may still seek a modification if a future loss on the agreement was reasonably foreseeable. Similarly, the overall profit earned by the party seeking modification is an important factor; this finding, however, does not support a conclusion that the decision to seek a modification was unwarranted. The more relevant inquiry is into the profit obtained through sales of the product line in question. This conclusion is reinforced by the fact that only a few product lines may be affected by market exigencies; the opportunity to seek modification of a contract for the sale of goods of a product line should not be limited solely because some other product line produced a substantial profit.

In the final analysis, the single most important consideration in determining whether the decision to seek a modification is justified in this context is whether, because of changes in the market or other unforeseeable conditions, performance of the contract has come to involve a loss. In this case, the district court found that Sharon suffered substantial losses by performing the contract as *modified.* * * * We are convinced that unforeseen economic exigencies existed which would prompt an ordinary merchant to seek a modification to avoid a loss on the contract; thus, we believe that the district court's findings to the contrary are clearly erroneous. * * *

The second part of the analysis, honesty in fact, is pivotal. The district court found that Sharon "threatened not to sell Roth and Toledo any steel if they refused to pay increased prices after July 1, 1973" and, consequently, that Sharon acted wrongfully. Sharon does not dispute the finding that it threatened to stop selling steel to the plaintiffs. Instead, it asserts that such a finding is merely evidence of bad faith and that it has rebutted any inference of bad faith based on that finding. We agree with this analysis; although coercive conduct is evidence that a modification of a contract is sought in bad faith, that prima facie showing may be effectively rebutted by the party seeking to enforce the modification. *E.g., Business Incentives Co., Inc. v. Sony Corp. of America,* 397 F.Supp. 63, 69 (S.D.N.Y.1975) (in context of economic duress, coercive conduct permissible in light of contractual right to terminate). *See Jamestown Farmers Elevator, Inc. v. General Mills,* 552 F.2d 1285, 1290 (8th Cir.1977) ("good faith insistence upon a legal right [with coercive effect] which one believes he has usually is not duress, even if it turns out that that party is mistaken and, in fact, has no such right"); White & Summers, *supra,* at 41 (good faith exists if a party believes that contract permits party seeking modification to refuse to perform if modification not effected). Although we agree with Sharon's statement of principles, we do not agree that Sharon has rebutted the inference of bad faith that rises from its coercive conduct. Sharon asserts that its decision to unilaterally raise prices was based on language in the November 17, 1972 letter which allowed it to raise prices to the extent of any general industry-wide price increase. Because prices in the steel industry had increased, Sharon concludes that it was justified in raising its prices. Because it was justified in raising the contract price, the plaintiffs were bound by the terms of the contract to pay the increased prices. Consequently, any refusal by the plaintiffs to pay the price increase sought by Sharon must be viewed as a material breach of the November, 1972 contract which would excuse Sharon from any further performance. Thus, Sharon reasons that its refusal to perform absent a price increase was justified under the contract and consistent with good faith.

This argument fails in two respects. First, the contractual language on which Sharon relies only permits, at most, a price increase for cold rolled steel; thus, even if Sharon's position were supported by the evidence, Sharon would not have been justified in refusing to sell the plaintiffs hot rolled steel because of the plaintiffs' refusal to pay higher prices for the product. More importantly, however, the evidence does not indicate that Sharon ever offered this theory as a justification until this matter was tried. Sharon's representatives, in their testimony, did not attempt to justify Sharon's refusal to ship steel at 1972 prices in this fashion. Furthermore, none of the contemporaneous communications contain this justification for Sharon's action. In short, we can find no evidence in the record which indicates that Sharon offered this theory as a justification at the time the modification was sought. Consequently, we believe that the district court's conclusion that Sharon acted in bad faith by using coercive conduct to extract the price modification is not clearly erroneous. Therefore, we hold that Sharon's attempt to modify the November, 1972 contract, in order to compensate for increased costs which made performance come to involve a loss, is ineffective because Sharon did not act in a manner consistent with Article Two's requirement of honesty in fact when it refused to perform its remaining obligations under the contract at 1972 prices.[31]

* * *

We have exhaustively reviewed the record, and have considered nearly every facet of the district court's decision. We believe, for the most part, that the district court has correctly resolved the factual and legal questions which the parties have so bitterly contested for the past eight years. Regrettably, however, we cannot bring this long and costly litigation to an end; we must remand this case for factual findings regarding the timeliness of plaintiffs' notice of breach in 1974.

---

31. The district court also found, as an alternative ground, that the modification was voidable because the plaintiffs agreed to the modification due to economic duress. *See, e.g., Oskey Gasoline & Oil Co. v. Continental Oil,* 534 F.2d 1281 (8th Cir.1976). Because we conclude that the modification was ineffective as a result of Sharon's bad faith, we do not reach the issue whether the contract modification was also voidable because of economic duress. We note, however, that proof that coercive means were used is necessary to establish that a contract is voidable because of economic duress. Id. at 1286. Normally, it cannot be used to void a contract modification which has been sought in good faith; if a contract modification has been found to be in good faith, then presumably no wrongful coercive means have been used to extract the modification.

Accordingly, we affirm in part, vacate in part, and remand for further proceedings not inconsistent with this opinion.

MERRITT, CIRCUIT JUDGE, concurring in part and dissenting in part. [Opinion omitted. Ed.]

AUSTIN INSTRUMENT, INC. v. LORAL CORP.

Court of Appeals of New York, 1971.
29 N.Y.2d 124, 324 N.Y.S.2d 22, 272 N.E.2d 533.

FULD, CHIEF JUDGE. The defendant, Loral Corporation, seeks to recover payment for goods delivered under a contract which it had with the plaintiff Austin Instrument, Inc., on the ground that the evidence establishes, as a matter of law, that it was forced to agree to an increase in price on the items in question under circumstances amounting to economic duress.

In July of 1965, Loral was awarded a $6,000,000 contract by the Navy for the production of radar sets. The contract contained a schedule of deliveries, a liquidated damages clause applying to late deliveries and a cancellation clause in case of default by Loral. The latter thereupon solicited bids for some 40 precision gear components needed to produce the radar sets, and awarded Austin a subcontract to supply 23 such parts. That party commenced delivery in early 1966.

In May, 1966, Loral was awarded a second Navy contract for the production of more radar sets and again went about soliciting bids. Austin bid on all 40 gear components but, on July 15, a representative from Loral informed Austin's president, Mr. Krauss, that his company would be awarded the subcontract only for those items on which it was low bidder. The Austin officer refused to accept an order for less than all 40 of the gear parts and on the next day he told Loral that Austin would cease deliveries of the parts due under the existing subcontract unless Loral consented to substantial increases in the prices provided for by that agreement—both retroactively for parts already delivered and prospectively on those not yet shipped—and placed with Austin the order for all 40 parts needed under Loral's second Navy contract. Shortly thereafter, Austin did, indeed, stop delivery. After contacting 10 manufacturers of precision gears and finding none who could produce the parts in time to meet its commitments to the Navy,[1] Loral acceded to Austin's demands; in a letter dated July 22, Loral wrote to Austin that "We have feverishly surveyed other sources of supply and find that because of the prevailing military exigencies, were they to start from scratch as would have to be the case, they could not even remotely begin to deliver on time to meet the delivery requirements established by the Government. * * * Accordingly, we are left with no choice or alternative but to meet your conditions."

---

1. The best reply Loral received was from a vendor who stated he could commence deliveries sometime in October.

Loral thereupon consented to the price increases insisted upon by Austin under the first subcontract and the latter was awarded a second subcontract making it the supplier of all 40 gear parts for Loral's second contract with the Navy.[2] Although Austin was granted until September to resume deliveries, Loral did, in fact, receive parts in August and was able to produce the radar sets in time to meet its commitments to the Navy on both contracts. After Austin's last delivery under the second subcontract in July, 1967, Loral notified it of its intention to seek recovery of the price increases.

On September 15, 1967, Austin instituted this action against Loral to recover an amount in excess of $17,750 which was still due on the second subcontract. On the same day, Loral commenced an action against Austin claiming damages of some $22,250—the aggregate of the price increases under the first subcontract—on the ground of economic duress. The two actions were consolidated and, following a trial, Austin was awarded the sum it requested and Loral's complaint against Austin was dismissed on the ground that it was not shown that "it could not have obtained the items in question from other sources in time to meet its commitment to the Navy under the first contract." A closely divided Appellate Division affirmed (35 A.D.2d 387, 316 N.Y.S.2d 528, 532). There was no material disagreement concerning the facts; as Justice Steuer stated in the course of his dissent below, "[t]he facts are virtually undisputed, nor is there any serious question of law. The difficulty lies in the application of the law to these facts." (35 A.D.2d 392, 316 N.Y.S.2d 534.)

The applicable law is clear and, indeed, is not disputed by the parties. A contract is voidable on the ground of duress when it is established that the party making the claim was forced to agree to it by means of a wrongful threat precluding the exercise of his free will. (See *Allstate Med. Labs., Inc. v. Blaivas*, 20 N.Y.2d 654, 282 N.Y.S.2d 268, 229 N.E.2d 50; *Kazaras v. Manufacturers Trust Co.*, 4 N.Y.2d 930, 175 N.Y.S.2d 172, 151 N.E.2d 356; *Adams v. Irving Nat. Bank*, 116 N.Y. 606, 611, 23 N.E. 7, 9; see, also, 13 Williston, Contracts [3d ed., 1970], § 1603, p. 658.) The existence of economic duress or business compulsion is demonstrated by proof that "immediate possession of needful goods is threatened" (*Mercury Mach. Importing Corp. v. City of New York*, 3 N.Y.2d 418, 425, 165 N.Y.S.2d 517, 520, 144 N.E.2d 400) or, more particularly, in cases such as the one before us, by proof that one party to a contract has threatened to breach the agreement by withholding goods unless the other party agrees to some further demand. * * * However, a mere threat by one party to breach the contract by not delivering the required items, though wrongful, does not in itself constitute economic duress. It must also appear that the threatened party could not obtain the goods from another source of supply and that the ordinary remedy of an action for breach of contract would not be adequate.

2. Loral makes no claim in this action on the second subcontract.

We find without any support in the record the conclusion reached by the courts below that Loral failed to establish that it was the victim of economic duress. On the contrary, the evidence makes out a classic case, as a matter of law, of such duress.

It is manifest that Austin's threat—to stop deliveries unless the prices were increased—deprived Loral of its free will. As bearing on this, Loral's relationship with the Government is most significant. As mentioned above, its contract called for staggered monthly deliveries of the radar sets, with clauses calling for liquidated damages and possible cancellation on default. Because of its production schedule, Loral was, in July, 1966, concerned with meeting its delivery requirements in September, October and November, and it was for the sets to be delivered in those months that the withheld gears were needed. Loral had to plan ahead, and the substantial liquidated damages for which it would be liable, plus the threat of default, were genuine possibilities. Moreover, Loral did a substantial portion of its business with the Government, and it feared that a failure to deliver as agreed upon would jeopardize its chances for future contracts. These genuine concerns do not merit the label " 'self-imposed, undisclosed and subjective' " which the Appellate Division majority placed upon them. It was perfectly reasonable for Loral, or any other party similarly placed, to consider itself in an emergency, duress situation.

Austin, however, claims that the fact that Loral extended its time to resume deliveries until September negates its alleged dire need for the parts. A Loral official testified on this point that Austin's president told him he could deliver some parts in August and that the extension of deliveries was a formality. In any event, the parts necessary for production of the radar sets to be delivered in September were delivered to Loral on September 1, and the parts needed for the October schedule were delivered in late August and early September. Even so, Loral had to "work * * * around the clock" to meet its commitments. Considering that the best offer Loral received from the other vendors it contacted was commencement of delivery sometime in October, which, as the record shows, would have made it late in its deliveries to the Navy in both September and October, Loral's claim that it had no choice but to accede to Austin's demands is conclusively demonstrated.

We find unconvincing Austin's contention that Loral, in order to meet its burden, should have contacted the Government and asked for an extension of its delivery dates so as to enable it to purchase the parts from another vendor. Aside from the consideration that Loral was anxious to perform well in the Government's eyes, it could not be sure when it would obtain enough parts from a substitute vendor to meet its commitments. The only promise which it received from the companies it contacted was for *commencement* of deliveries, not full supply, and, with vendor delay common in this field, it would have been nearly impossible to know the length of the extension it should request. It must be remembered that Loral was producing a needed item of military hardware. Moreover, there is authority for Loral's position that nonperformance by a subcontractor is not an excuse for default in the main contract. (See, e.g., McBride & Wachtel, Government Contracts, § 35.10, [11].) In light of all this, Loral's claim should not be held insufficiently supported because it did not request an extension from the Government.

Loral, as indicated above, also had the burden of demonstrating that it could not obtain the parts elsewhere within a reasonable time, and there can be no doubt that it met this burden. The 10 manufacturers whom Loral contacted comprised its entire list of "approved vendors" for precision gears, and none was able to commence delivery soon enough. As Loral was producing a highly sophisticated item of military machinery requiring parts made to the strictest engineering standards, it would be unreasonable to hold that Loral should have gone to other vendors, with whom it was either unfamiliar or dissatisfied, to procure the needed parts. As Justice Steuer noted in his dissent, Loral "contacted all the manufacturers whom it believed capable of making these parts" (35 A.D.2d at p. 393, 316 N.Y.S.2d at p. 534), and this was all the law requires.

It is hardly necessary to add that Loral's normal legal remedy of accepting Austin's breach of the contract and then suing for damages would have been inadequate under the circumstances, as Loral would still have had to obtain the gears elsewhere with all the concomitant consequences mentioned above. In other words, Loral actually had no choice, when the prices were raised by Austin, except to take the gears at the "coerced" prices and then sue to get the excess back.

Austin's final argument is that Loral, even if it did enter into the contract under duress, lost any rights it had to a refund of money by waiting until July, 1967, long after the termination date of the contract, to disaffirm it. It is true that one who would recover moneys allegedly paid under duress must act promptly to make his claim known. (See *Oregon Pacific R.R. Co. v. Forrest*, 128 N.Y. 83, 93, 28 N.E. 137, 139; *Port Chester Elec. Constr. Corp. v. Hastings Terraces*, 284 App.Div. 966, 967, 134 N.Y.S.2d 656, 658.) In this case, Loral delayed making its demand for a refund until three days after Austin's last delivery on the second subcontract. Loral's reason—for waiting until that time—is that it feared another stoppage of deliveries which would again put it in an untenable situation. Considering Austin's conduct in the past, this was perfectly reasonable, as the possibility of an application by Austin of further business compulsion still existed until all of the parts were delivered.

In sum, the record before us demonstrates that Loral agreed to the price increases in consequence of the economic duress employed by Austin. Accordingly, the matter should be remanded to the trial court for a computation of its damages.

The order appealed from should be modified, with costs, by reversing so much thereof as affirms the dismissal of defendant Loral Corporation's claim and, except as so modified, affirmed.

BERGAN, JUDGE (dissenting). Whether acts charged as constituting economic duress produce or do not produce the damaging effect attributed to them is normally a routine type of factual issue.

Here the fact question was resolved against Loral both by the Special Term and by the affirmance at the Appellate Division. It should not be open for different resolution here.

In summarizing the Special Term's decision and its own, the Appellate Division decided that "the conclusion that Loral acted deliberately and voluntarily, without being under immediate pressure of incurring severe business reverses, precludes a recovery on the theory of economic duress" (35 A.D.2d 387, 391, 316 N.Y.S.2d 528, 532).

When the testimony of the witnesses who actually took part in the negotiations for the two disputing parties is examined, sharp conflicts of fact emerge. Under Austin's version the request for a renegotiation of the existing contract was based on Austin's contention that Loral had failed to carry out an understanding as to the items to be furnished under that contract and this was the source of dissatisfaction which led both to a revision of the existing agreement and to entering into a new one.

This is not necessarily and as a matter of law to be held economic duress. On this appeal it is needful to look at the facts resolved in favor of Austin most favorably to that party. Austin's version of events was that a threat was not made but rather a request to accommodate the closing of its plant for a customary vacation period in accordance with the general understanding of the parties.

Moreover, critical to the issue of economic duress was the availability of alternative suppliers to the purchaser Loral. The demonstration is replete in the direct testimony of Austin's witnesses and on cross-examination of Loral's principal and purchasing agent that the availability of practical alternatives was a highly controverted issue of fact. On that issue of fact the explicit findings made by the Special Referee were affirmed by the Appellate Division. Nor is the issue of fact made the less so by assertion that the facts are undisputed and that only the application of equally undisputed rules of law is involved.

Austin asserted and Loral admitted on cross-examination that there were many suppliers listed in a trade registry but that Loral chose to rely only on those who had in the past come to them for orders and with whom they were familiar. It was, therefore, at least a fair issue of fact whether under the circumstances such conduct was reasonable and made what might otherwise have been a commercially understandable renegotiation an exercise of duress.

The order should be affirmed.

* * *

Problems

21. Assume you have purchased an appliance directly from the manufacturer and have opened the box to find a limited warranty document that promises some protection but disclaims the implied warranties of the UCC. You also found a postcard asking for some information about your purchase. You filled out the card and mailed it. Your appliance develops problems not covered by the limited warranty but which would be covered by the implied warranties of the UCC. You bring action against the seller for breach of the UCC warranty. What will be the result?

22. Assume you bought a used truck. The bill of sale says "AS IS, WITHOUT WARRANTY." Soon after you had inspected the truck and accepted delivery, defects showed up. The seller, a dealer, agrees to repair the truck at no cost to you. The dealer makes major engine repairs and bills you $19,000. Is the dealer bound by the promise to repair without charging anything?

SECTION 4. CONSIDERATION IN BILATERAL CONTRACTS AND MUTUALITY OF OBLIGATION

(Calamari & Perillo 5th §§ 4.12—4.16)

RIDGE RUNNER FORESTRY v. ANN M. VENEMAN, SECRETARY OF AGRICULTURE

United States Court of Appeals, Federal Circuit, 2002.
287 F.3d 1058.

MAYER, CHIEF JUDGE. Ridge Runner Forestry appeals from the decision of the Department of Agriculture Board of Contract Appeals dismissing its cause of action for lack of jurisdiction pursuant to 41 U.S.C. §§ 601–613. In re Ridge Runner Forestry, AGBCA No. 2000–161–1, 2001 WL 170915 (Feb. 13, 2001). Because no contract had been formed, we affirm the board's decision.

BACKGROUND

Ridge Runner Forestry is a fire protection company located in the Pacific Northwest. In response to a request for quotations ("RFQ") issued by the Forestry Service, Ridge Runner submitted a proposal and ultimately signed a document entitled Pacific Northwest Interagency Engine Tender Agreement ("Tender Agreement"). The Tender Agreement incorporated the RFQ in its entirety, including the following two provisions in bold faced lettering: (1) "Award of an Interagency Equipment Rental Agreement based on response to this Request for Quotations (RFQ) does not preclude the Government from using any agency or cooperator or local EERA resources"; and (2) "Award of an Interagency

Equipment Rental Agreement does not guarantee there will be a need for the equipment offered nor does it guarantee orders will be placed against the awarded agreements." *Request for Quotation*, No. R6–99–117 (March 29, 1999). Additionally, because the government could not foresee its actual equipment needs, the RFQ contained language that allowed the contractor to decline the government's request for equipment for any reason: "Because the equipment needs of the government and availability of contractor's equipment during an emergency cannot be determined in advance, it is mutually agreed that, upon request of the government, the contractor shall furnish the equipment offered herein *to the extent the contractor is willing and able at the time of order.*" *Id.* (emphasis added). The RFQ also included a clause informing bidders that they would not be reimbursed for any costs incurred in submitting a quotation. Ridge Runner signed Tender Agreements in 1996, 1997, 1998, and 1999. In 1999, it presented a claim for $180,000 to the contracting officer alleging that the Forestry Service had violated an "implied duty of good faith and fair dealing" because Ridge Runner had been "systematically excluded for the past several years from providing services to the Government." In response, the contracting officer told Ridge Runner that she lacked the proper authority to decide the claim. Ridge Runner timely appealed the decision to the Department of Agriculture Board of Contract Appeals. The board granted the government's motion to dismiss concluding that because no contract had been entered into, it lacked jurisdiction under the Contract Disputes Act ("CDA"), 41 U.S.C. §§ 601–613.

DISCUSSION

We have jurisdiction over an appeal from a decision of an agency board of contract appeals by virtue of 28 U.S.C. § 1295(a)(10). The board's jurisdiction under the CDA requires, at a minimum, a contract between an agency and another party. 41 U.S.C. § 607(d) (1994, amended in 2000). Therefore, the threshold matter is whether the Tender Agreements constituted contracts between the parties, which is a question of law that we review de novo. See *Oman–Fischbach Int'l v. Pirie*, 276 F.3d 1380, 1383 (Fed.Cir.2002).

"To be valid and enforceable, a contract must have both consideration to ensure mutuality of obligation ... and sufficient definiteness so as to 'provide a basis for determining the existence of a breach and for giving an appropriate remedy.'" *Ace-Federal Reporters, Inc. v. Barram*, 226 F.3d 1329, 1332 (Fed.Cir.2000) (internal citations omitted). "To constitute consideration, a performance or a return promise must be bargained for." Restatement (Second) of Contracts § 71(1) (1979). And the "promise or apparent promise is not consideration if by its terms the promisor or purported promisor reserves a choice of alternative performances...." *Id.* § 77.

Ridge Runner argues that the Tender Agreement was a binding contract that placed specific obligations upon the government; namely, the government was obligated to call upon Ridge Runner, and the other winning vendors, for its fire fighting needs, and in return, the vendors were to remain ready with acceptable equipment and trained staff to answer the government's call. This, Ridge Runner argues, places the alleged contract squarely within our holding in *Ace–Federal*, 226 F.3d 1329.

Ace–Federal involved a requirements contract whereby the government was obligated to use, with limited exceptions, enumerated suppliers. Following a request for proposals, Ace Federal, as well as other vendors, contracted with the government to provide court reporting and transcription services for various federal agencies. Included in each of the contracts was the standard requirements clause found in Federal Acquisition Regulation § 52.216–21(c) which provides "[e]xcept as this contract otherwise provides, the Government shall order from the Contractor all the supplies or services specified in the Schedule that are required to be purchased by the Government activity or activities specified in the Schedule." 48 C.F.R. § 52.216–21(c) (1988). Each contract also included a termination for convenience clause that limited government liability should the General Services Administration ("GSA") choose to cancel any contract. During the relevant term, some of the covered agencies contracted for transcription services from non-contract sources without obtaining the necessary waiver. We held that "each time an agency that did not obtain a GSA waiver arranged for services covered under the contract from a non-contract source, the government did not act within the limited exception and breached the contract." *Ace–Federal*, 226 F.3d at 1332–33.

The contract in *Ace–Federal* is quite distinct from the Tender Agreements at issue in this case. That contract obligated the government to fulfill all of its requirements for transcription services from enumerated vendors or obtain a waiver. The Tender Agreements here are nothing but illusory promises. By the phrase illusory promise is meant words in promissory form that promise nothing; they do not purport to put any limitation on the freedom of the alleged promisor, but leave his future action subject to his own future will, just as it would have been had he said no words at all. *Torncello v. United States*, 231 Ct.Cl. 20, 681 F.2d 756, 769 (1982) (quoting 1 *Corbin on Contracts* § 145 (1963)). The government had the option of attempting to obtain firefighting services from Ridge Runner or any other source, regardless of whether that source had signed a tender agreement. The Agreements contained no clause limiting the government's options for firefighting services; the government merely "promised" to consider using Ridge Runner for firefighting services. Also, the Tender Agreement placed no obligation upon Ridge Runner. If the government came calling, Ridge Runner "promised" to provide the requested equipment only if it was "willing and able." It is axiomatic that a valid contract cannot be based upon the illusory promise of one party, much less illusory promises of both parties. See Restatement (Second) of Contracts § 71(1).

CONCLUSION

Accordingly, the decision of the Department of Agriculture Board of Contract Appeals is affirmed.

WOOD v. LUCY, LADY DUFF–GORDON

New York Court of Appeals, 1917.
222 N.Y. 88, 118 N.E. 214.

CARDOZO, J. The defendant styles herself "a creator of fashions." Her favor helps a sale. Manufacturers of dresses, millinery and like articles are glad to pay for a certificate of her approval. The things which she designs, fabrics, parasols and what not, have a new value in the public mind when issued in her name. She employed the plaintiff to help her to turn this vogue into money. He was to have the exclusive right, subject always to her approval, to place her indorsements on the designs of others. He was also to have the exclusive right to place her own designs on sale, or to license others to market them. In return, she was to have one-half of "all profits and revenues" derived from any contracts he might make. The exclusive right was to last at least one year from April 1, 1915, and thereafter from year to year unless terminated by notice of ninety days. The plaintiff says that he kept the contract on his part, and that the defendant broke it. She placed her indorsement on fabrics, dresses and millinery without his knowledge, and withheld the profits. He sues her for the damages, and the case comes here on demurrer.

The agreement of employment is signed by both parties. It has a wealth of recitals. The defendant insists, however, that it lacks the elements of a contract. She says that the plaintiff does not bind himself to anything. It is true that he does not promise in so many words that he will use reasonable efforts to place the defendant's indorsements and market her designs. We think, however, that such a promise is fairly to be implied. The law has outgrown its primitive stage of formalism when the precise word was the sovereign talisman, and every slip was fatal. It takes a broader view to-day. A promise may be lacking, and yet the whole writing may be "instinct with an obligation," imperfectly expressed (SCOTT, J., in *McCall Co. v. Wright*, 133 App.Div. 62; *Moran v. Standard Oil Co.*, 211 N.Y. 187, 198). If that is so, there is a contract.

The implication of a promise here finds support in many circumstances. The defendant gave an exclusive privilege. She was to have no right for at least a year to place her own indorsements or market her own designs except through the agency of the plaintiff. The acceptance of the exclusive agency was an assumption of its duties (*Phoenix Hermetic Co. v. Filtrine Mfg. Co.*, 164 App.Div. 424; *W.G. Taylor Co. v. Bannerman*, 120 Wis. 189; *Mueller v. Bethesda Mineral Spring Co.*, 88 Mich. 390). We are not to suppose that one party was to be placed at the mercy of the other (*Hearn v. Stevens & Bro.*, 111 App.Div. 101, 106; *Russell v. Allerton*, 108 N.Y. 288). Many other terms of the agreement point the same way. We are told at the outset by way of recital that "the said Otis F. Wood possesses a business organization adapted to the placing of such indorsements as the said Lucy, Lady Duff–Gordon has approved." The implication is that the plaintiff's business organization will be used for the purpose for which it is adapted. But the terms of the defendant's compensation are even more significant. Her sole compensation for the grant of an exclusive agency is to be one-half of all the profits resulting from the plaintiff's efforts. Unless he gave his efforts, she could never get anything. Without an implied promise, the transaction cannot have such business "efficacy as both parties must have intended that at all events it should have" (BOWEN, L.J., in *The Moorcock*, 14 P.D. 64, 68). But the contract does not stop there. The plaintiff goes on to promise that he will account monthly for all moneys received by him, and that he will take out all such patents and copyrights and trademarks as may in his judgment be necessary to protect the rights and articles affected by the agreement. It is true, of course, as the Appellate Division has said, that if he was under no duty to try to market designs or to place certificates of indorsement, his promise to account for profits or take out copyrights would be valueless. But in determining the intention of the parties, the promise *has* a value. It helps to enforce the conclusion that the plaintiff *had* some duties. His promise to pay the defendant one-half of the profits and revenues resulting from the exclusive agency and to render accounts monthly, was a promise to use reasonable efforts to bring profits and revenues into existence. For this conclusion, the authorities are ample. . . .

The judgment of the Appellate Division should be reversed, and the order of the Special Term affirmed, with costs in the Appellate Division and in this court.

* * *

MEZZANOTTE v. FREELAND

Court of Appeals of North Carolina, 1973.
20 N.C.App. 11, 200 S.E.2d 410.

This is an action seeking specific performance of a contract of sale and damages for breach of contract.

On 2 May 1972 plaintiffs and defendants executed a contract under the terms of which plaintiffs agreed to buy and defendants agreed to sell a tract of land in Orange County, together with improvements and facilities, known as the Daniel Boone Complex. The contract set out the sales price and terms of payment which included a good faith deposit by plaintiffs of $5,000.00. * * *

* * *

Among the other provisions of the 2 May 1972 agreement were the following:

"2. This agreement is contingent upon parties of the second part [plaintiffs] being able to secure a second mortgage from North Carolina National Bank on such terms and conditions as are satisfactory to them in order to finance the closing and to secure additional working capital * * *

* * *

BALEY, J. * * *

The second contention of the defendants that the contract on May 2 was not supported by valid consideration is dependent upon the interpretation to be placed upon the promise of plaintiffs to purchase the properties in accordance with the terms of the contract. Defendants assert that since the agreement was contingent upon the plaintiffs' obtaining "satisfactory" financing from North Carolina National Bank the promise to buy was illusory and cannot constitute consideration.

It seems clear that the parties in signing the contract of sale intended to be mutually bound to comply with its terms. They understood that plaintiffs would make an honest good faith effort to acquire financing satisfactory to themselves from NCNB. The contract implies that plaintiffs would in good faith seek proper financing from NCNB and that such financing in keeping with reasonable business standards could not be rejected at the personal whim of plaintiffs but only for a satisfactory cause. Where a contract confers on one party a discretionary power affecting the rights of the other, this discretion must be exercised in a reasonable manner based upon good faith and fair play. The record here indicates that the parties so understood their obligation and that plaintiffs applied for a loan from NCNB and obtained a verbal commitment but were not able to secure the loan and arranged other financing in order to meet their obligations under the contract. A promise conditioned upon an event within the promisor's control is not illusory if the promisor also "impliedly promises to make reasonable effort to bring the event about or to use good faith and honest judgment in determining whether or not it has in fact occurred." 1 Corbin on Contracts, § 149, at 659. The implied promise is enforceable by the promisee, and it constitutes a legal detriment to the promisor; therefore it furnishes sufficient consideration to support a return promise. In *Helicopter Corp. v. Realty Co.*, 263 N.C. 139, 147, 139 S.E.2d 362, 368, our court approved this language concerning consideration:

> "It has been held that 'there is a consideration if the promisee, in return for the promise, does anything legal which he is not bound to do, or refrains from doing anything which he has a right to do, whether there is any actual loss or detriment to him or actual benefit to the promisor or not.'"

Although there are no North Carolina cases specifically in point, courts in other jurisdictions have recognized that a conditional promise may be accompanied by an implied promise of good faith and reasonable effort, and that it need not be illusory.

For example, in *Jay Dreher Corp. v. Delco Appliance Corp.*, 93 F.2d 275 (2d Cir.1937), defendant granted plaintiff a franchise to sell its products in a certain territory. Plaintiff agreed to sell these products and build up defendant's business in the specified territory. Defendant reserved the right to reject any order sent in by plaintiff, and plaintiff contended that this made defendant's promise illusory. In an opinion by Judge Learned Hand, the court held that the contract was supported by consideration, finding an implied promise "that the defendant will use an honest judgment in passing upon orders submitted." Id. at 277.

In *Commercial Credit Co. v. Insular Motor Corp.*, 17 F.2d 896 (1st Cir.1927), defendant, an automobile dealer, agreed to sell plaintiff all the time sales obligations of its customers for two years, and plaintiff agreed to purchase these obligations. The contract provided that plaintiff would purchase only "acceptable" time sales obligations. The court rejected defendant's contention that the contract lacked consideration. It held that the contract did not allow plaintiff to refuse arbitrarily to purchase defendant's obligations. "Acceptable does not mean acceptable by whim; it means acceptable within the usual business meaning of the word as applied to this kind of business dealings." Id. at 899–900.

In *Richard Bruce & Co. v. J. Simpson & Co.*, 40 Misc.2d 501, 243 N.Y.S.2d 503 (Sup.Ct.1963), plaintiff agreed to underwrite a public offering of defendant's stock, and defendant agreed to pay plaintiff a commission. Defendant violated the agreement, and plaintiff sued for breach of contract. Defendant asserted that the contract was void for lack of consideration, pointing to a provision allowing plaintiff to terminate the contract if it "in its absolute discretion, shall determine that market conditions or the prospects of the public offering are such as to make it undesirable or inadvisable." The court held the contract enforceable, stating that plaintiff's discretion was only "a discretion based upon fair dealing and good faith—a reasonable discretion." Id. at 504, 243 N.Y.S.2d at 506.

Several cases have upheld the validity of contracts quite similar to the one involved in the present case. In *Mattei v. Hopper*, 51 Cal.2d 119, 330 P.2d 625 (1958), plaintiff agreed to buy a tract of land from defendant. The contract provided that it was "[s]ubject to Coldwell Banker & Company obtaining leases satisfactory to the purchaser." The court held that plaintiff was bound by an implied promise to use good faith in determining whether Coldwell Banker's leases were "satisfactory." Therefore, his promise was not illusory and the contract was enforceable.

In *Kays v. Brack*, 350 F.Supp. 1243 (D.Idaho 1972), plaintiffs agreed to lease a tract of land and buy some corporate stock from defendants. The contract provided: "The buyer's agreement to purchase is contingent upon the buyer being able to secure financing acceptable to the buyer, and if the buyer is unable, despite his best efforts, to obtain such financing within 10 days after all sellers have signed this agreement, the buyer shall notify the sellers and either party shall have the right to cancel this transaction." The court held that plaintiffs' promise was not illusory, since they were required to use their best efforts to obtain financing. A similar case is *White & Bollard, Inc. v. Goodenow*, 58 Wash.2d 180, 361 P.2d 571 (1961).

Most closely in point is *Sheldon Simms Co. v. Wilder*, 108 Ga.App. 4, 131 S.E.2d 854 (1963). Here plaintiff entered into a contract to purchase real property from defendant. The contract provided: "This contract is contingent upon the purchaser's ability to obtain a loan on said property of $24,000.00 with maximum interest of 6¼ percent per annum, for a maximum period of twenty years." The court held that the contract was valid and supported by consideration. Plaintiff was required to make "a diligent effort" to obtain a loan. Id. at 5, 131 S.E.2d at 855. He could not frustrate the contract by deciding at whim not to get a loan.

All of these cases tend to indicate that the agreement signed on 2 May 1972 by the Mezzanottes and the Freelands was a valid and enforceable contract, supported by consideration. The contract included an implied promise by the Mezzanottes to use reasonable effort to procure a loan and to exercise good faith in deciding whether the terms of the loan were satisfactory.

* * *

Affirmed.

MIAMI COCA–COLA BOTTLING CO.
v. ORANGE CRUSH CO.

Circuit Court of Appeals, Fifth Circuit, 1924.
296 F. 693.

BRYAN, CIRCUIT JUDGE. This is an appeal from an order dismissing appellant's bill, which seeks to enjoin the cancellation by the appellee of a contract and to compel its specific performance. The contract is in the form of a license, whereby the appellee grants to the appellant the exclusive right, within a designated territory, to manufacture a certain drink called "orange crush," and to bottle and distribute it in bottles under appellee's trade-mark. The appellee agreed, among other things, to supply its concentrate to be used in the manufacture of orange crush at stated prices, and to do certain advertising. The appellant agreed to purchase a specified quantity of the concentrate, to maintain a bottling plant, to solicit orders, and generally to undertake to promote the sale of orange crush, and to develop an increase in the volume of sales. The license granted was perpetual, but contained a proviso to the effect that the appellant might at any time cancel the contract.

The bill avers that the appellant bought a quantity of the concentrate, manufactured orange crush, and was engaged in the performance of its obligations, when, about a year after the contract was entered into, the appellee gave written notice that it would no longer be bound.

We agree with the District Judge that the contract was void for lack of mutuality. It may be conceded that the appellee is liable to the appellant for damages for the period during which the contract was performed; but for such damages the appellant has an adequate remedy at law. So far, however, as the contract remains executory, it is not binding, since it can be terminated at the will of one of the parties to it.

The consideration was a promise for a promise. But the appellant did not promise to do anything, and could at any time cancel the contract. According to the great weight of authority such a contract is unenforceable. Marble Co. v. Ripley, 10 Wall. 339, 359, 19 L.Ed. 955; Willard Sutherland & Co. v. United States, 262 U.S. 489, 43 Sup.Ct. 592, 67 L.Ed. 1086; Velie Motor Car Co. v. Kopmeier Motor Car Co., 194 Fed. 324, 114 C.C.A. 284; McCaffrey v. Knight (D.C.) 282 Fed. 334; Fowler Utilities Co. v. Gray, 168 Ind. 1, 79 N.E. 897, 7 L.R.A. (N.S.) 726, 120 Am.St.Rep. 344; 6 R.C.L. 691; 1 Williston, pp. 219, 222. The contract cannot be upheld upon the theory that the appellant had a continuing option, because an option to be valid must be supported by a consideration. 6 R.C.L. 687.

* * *

The decree is affirmed.

TEXAS GAS UTILITIES COMPANY v. S.A. BARRETT

Supreme Court of Texas, 1970.
460 S.W.2d 409.

STEAKLEY, JUSTICE. This is a suit for minimum payments under a contract for natural gas service. It was instituted by petitioner, Texas Gas Utilities Company, sometimes called the gas company, against respondents S.A. Barrett, John Barrett and James Beavers. After trial to a jury, the trial court ruled in response to respondents' motion for judgment that they were entitled to judgment on the jury verdict and as a matter of law. A take nothing judgment was accordingly rendered against petitioner. The court of civil appeals affirmed upon the holding that the contract is unenforceable for lack of mutuality of obligation. 452 S.W.2d 508. Our views are otherwise which, in turn, calls for consideration of points not discussed by the intermediate court.

The contract upon which suit was brought was dated April 21, 1964 and was for a term of five years with an option to renew for an additional five years. The signatories were Associated Oil and Gas Company, petitioner's predecessor-assignor (the assignment being dated January 1, 1965) and respondents. The purpose of the contract was the supplying of natural gas for use by respondents in fueling irrigation water well pumps on farm properties which they held under a five year agricultural lease dated January 17, 1964. The contract required an annual minimum payment during the life of the contract of $7.50 per 1400 h.p. for each engine installed.[1] A five mile pipe line to the proper-

---

1. Article II provided that "Customer shall be billed monthly and will on or before the tenth day from date of billing pay company for gas delivered or made available hereunder between the last two meter readings (called 'Billing Period') at the following rates and amounts.

　1.　55 cents per each 1,000 cubic feet of gas.

2. An annual minimum payable in equal monthly installments, whether used or not, of $7.50 per horsepower for each engine installed, the original engines installed hereunder having 1400 horsepower. In event the original engines

ties was constructed by petitioner's predecessor in March, 1964, at an expense in excess of $100,000 and deliveries of natural gas were commenced on April 6, 1964. Subsequent to the execution of the contract, and prior to its assignment to petitioner on January 1, 1965, respondents were evicted from the leased properties by their lessors. The contract is silent concerning the obligations of the parties in such event. It does not appear to be disputed that natural gas was available at all times; that the gas company furnished gas as ordered by respondents; and that the gas company delivered gas to the successors of respondents, billed them therefor, and will credit respondents with the sums paid by such successors.

The basic obligation assumed by Associated Oil and Gas Company, and by petitioner as assignee of the contract in question, was the delivery of natural gas to respondents as set forth in Article I:

> "Subject to the terms and conditions herein stated Company will from April 21, 1964 to April 21st, 1969 until the expiration or other termination of this agreement (unless prevented by one or more of the causes mentioned in Article VI hereof) deliver to Customer at a meter installed by Company on the service line owned by Customer downstream of Billing Meter, set at various water well locations on a 4100.33 Acre Farm, * * * natural gas for use by Customer for the following purposes only: Fuel for irrigation purposes for approximately twenty (20) water wells."

The obligation to furnish gas was subject, however, to these provisions in Article VI of the contract:

> "Company will make reasonable provision to insure a continuous supply of natural gas but does not guarantee a continuous supply of natural gas, and shall not be liable for damages occasioned by interruptions to service or failure to commence delivery, caused by conditions beyond its reasonable control, by an Act of God or the public enemy, inevitable accident, floods, fire, explosions, strikes, riots, war, delay in receiving shipments of required material, order of court or judge granted in any bonafide adverse legal proceedings or actions, or any order of any commission or tribunal having jurisdiction in the premises or without limitation by the preceding enumeration any other act or thing reasonably beyond its control or interruptions necessary for repairs or changes in Company's distributing system. No payment, however, shall be required from Customer for service which Company herein agrees but fails to furnish.

> "*It is further and distinctly understood and agreed that the Company assumes no obligation whatever regarding the quantity or quality of gas delivered hereunder, or the continuity of service, and shall not be liable therefor,* but Company will endeavor to supply the requirements of Customer for the above class of service to the extent of the

be abandoned or replaced by ones of lesser horsepower, the original engine horsepower rate shall apply; if replaced by one of greater horsepower the new shall apply."

amount of gas available for such service and to the extent permitted under any agreement between Company and any producer of gas available to Company for the supply of natural gas to Company, and subject to such limitations in the sale of gas for this class of service as in Company's opinion may be necessary for the continued maintenance of the supply of gas for domestic use, it being recognized that Company is dependent for gas to be supplied hereunder upon gas produced by [sic] Company by other producers." (Italics are added.)

It was the view of the court of civil appeals that under Article VI, particularly the italicized portion, the gas company was not obligated to furnish gas and for this reason the contract was unenforceable as lacking in mutuality of obligation. This, in respondents' words, is their "first and foremost" position in asserting non-liability for the minimum payments which petitioner seeks to recover.

As has been noted by recognized legal scholars, a commonly repeated statement by the courts is that mutuality of obligation is a requisite in the formation of a contract, and that both parties to a contract must be bound or neither is bound. See 1 Williston on Contracts § 105A, at 420 (1957); 1A Corbin on Contracts § 152, at 2 (1963); 1 Page on Contracts § 565, at 949 (1920). The Williston treatise suggests that however limited, this is but a way of stating that there must be valid consideration. Professor Corbin urges the view that mutuality of obligations should be used solely to express the idea that each party is under a legal duty to the other; each has made a promise and each is an obligor. This is said to be the meaning with which the term is commonly used and that it is more correct to say that it is consideration that is necessary, not mutuality of obligation. But it has also been concluded "that logic is as powerless to disprove the existence of the mutuality rule as it has been shown to be powerless to establish its existence * * * that no logic is able to connect the supposed mutuality rule with any formulation of the doctrine of consideration and no other logical justification for it has ever been suggested." Oliphant, Mutuality of Obligation in Bilateral Contracts at Law, 25 Colum.L.Rev. 705 (1925); 28 Colum.L.Rev. 997 (1928).

Be all of this as it may, this Court in Texas Farm Bureau Cotton Ass'n v. Stovall, 113 Tex. 273, 253 S.W. 1101 (1923) spoke quite succinctly of the rule of mutuality of obligation when it said:

"Reduced to its last analysis, the rule is simply that a contract must be based upon a valid consideration, and that a contract in which there is no consideration moving from one party, or no obligation upon him, lacks mutuality, is unilateral, and unenforceable. * * * It is quite elementary that the promise of one party is a valid consideration for the promise of the other party."

In speaking of mutual reciprocal obligations as consideration, the rule was stated in Clement v. Producers' Refining Co., 277 S.W. 634 (Tex.Comm.App.1925) that "where no other consideration is shown, mutual obligations by the parties to the agreement will furnish a sufficient consideration to constitute a binding contract." See also Johnson v. Breckenridge–Stephens Title Co., 257 S.W. 223, (Tex.Comm.App. 1924) and Roberts v. Anthony, 185 S.W. 423, (Tex.Civ.App.—Amarillo 1916, no writ.) It is presumed that when parties make an agreement they intend it to be effectual, not nugatory. Portland Gasoline Co. v. Superior Marketing Co., Inc., 150 Tex. 533, 243 S.W.2d 823 (1951). A contract will be construed in favor of mutuality, Carpenter Paper Co. v. Calcasieu Paper Co., Inc., 164 F.2d 653 (5th Cir.1947). The modern decisional tendency is against lending the aid of courts to defeat contracts on technical grounds of want of mutuality. Armstrong v. Southern Production Co., Inc., 182 F.2d 238 (5th Cir.1950).

It is clear to us that the agreement here in question is a binding and enforceable contract. The writing embodies an exchange of obligations of value to each contracting party, reciprocally or mutually induced. The gas company was bound to deliver natural gas to the various water well delivery points specified in the contract; to make reasonable provisions to insure a continuous supply of natural gas; to endeavor to supply the requirements of respondents; and to install the necessary metering equipment at its own expense. Respondents were in turn bound to pay for the gas delivered to their wells upon their order and to pay the minimum charges provided in the contract. These mutually imposed obligations are not negated by the language used. See Portland Gasoline Co. v. Superior Marketing Co., Inc., supra. The gas company explicitly bound itself in Article I to deliver natural gas to respondents "unless prevented by one or more of the causes mentioned in Article VI hereof." The exculpatory clause in Article VI did not relieve the gas company of this obligation. It would have been subject to liability for breach of contract if it had failed upon order to furnish gas to respondents for causes other than those specified in Article VI. The extent of the exculpatory clause is that the gas company assumed no obligation—made no guarantee—either that gas would always be available or that gas of a particular quality would always be available. It was bound, however, to supply *available* natural gas to respondents within the restrictions of Article 6057, R.C.S. of Texas, 1925.[2] Cf. Standard Oil Company of Texas v. Lopeno Gas Company, 240 F.2d 504 (5th Cir.1957).

We accordingly hold that the contract upon which petitioner sued is enforceable against respondents. * * *

* * *

The judgments below will therefore be reversed and the cause remanded to the trial court for entry of judgment consistent with this opinion.

It is so ordered.

2. "No such pipe line public utility shall discriminate in favor of or against any person, place or corporation, either in apportioning the supply of natural gas or in its charges therefor; nor shall any such utility directly or indirectly charge, demand, collect or receive from any one a greater or less compensation for any service rendered than from another for a like and contemporaneous service; provided this shall not limit the right of the Commission to prescribe different rates and regulations for the use of natural gas for manufacturing and similar purposes, or to prescribe rates and regulations for service from or to other or different places, as it may determine."

CANUSA CORPORATION v. A & R LOBOSCO, INC.

U.S. District Court, E.D.N.Y., 1997.
986 F.Supp. 723.

Trager, District Judge.

This diversity action for breach of contract raises a surprisingly novel question: what is the effect of an estimate in an output contract when the supplier produces less than the stated estimate? I conclude that New York law would hold that good faith, rather than the stated estimate, would control whether a breach has occurred.

Background

Plaintiff Canusa seeks damages for lost sales as a result of an alleged breach of contract by defendants Lobosco as well as attorneys' fees in connection with an equipment lease to Lobosco. The case was tried without a jury, where the following facts are found.

Plaintiff Canusa is a Maryland corporation that recycles and brokers waste paper. A & R Lobosco ("Lobosco") is a New York corporation that receives, collects, cleans and resells this recyclable paper to paper mills or brokers like Canusa. Michael Lobosco is A & R Lobosco's president.

In late 1992, Lobosco entered into an agreement with the City of New York to accept 850 tons per week (3,400–3,500 tons per month) of material to be recycled. * * * To handle this paper, Lobosco needed a baler, a piece of equipment to process and bale the recyclable paper. At about the same time, Canusa heard from a third party also in the paper recycling business that Lobosco had obtained a City contract and might be looking for a baler. * * * Lobosco had put down a deposit on a baler with another firm, but ultimately decided to enter into an arrangement with Canusa because Canusa would finance the baler, while the other arrangement obligated Lobosco to obtain separate financing. * * *

* * *

The Agreement (captioned an "Output Agreement") recited that the parties were entering into an output contract with a five-year term, but it also contained language stating that Lobosco would initially ship 1100 tons per month of number 8 quality old news print (ONP 8) per month to Canusa in 1993, and 1500 tons per month thereafter (1994–97). Both parties presented evidence that they understood this number to mean the minimum number of tons Lobosco was obligated to provide to Canusa. * * * The Agreement also provided that the price per ton of ONP would be set each month between the parties and defined acceptable ONP. Fleming described ONP 8 as "anything that normally comes in a household newspaper." * * * Materials that have no relationship to paper, such as garbage, masonry, metal, etc., are called prohibitives. Materials that are acceptable in small amounts are called outthrows. Examples of outthrows include Sunday newspaper magazines and coupon circulars. * * * Some paper products, most notably telephone books, are also considered prohibitives. The Agreement specified that no prohibited materials would be accepted, and that total outthrows could not exceed one quarter of one percent (.25%) by weight. * * * [T]he Agreement provided for the application of New York law.

From the beginning, the relationship was a rocky one. Canusa provided documentation demonstrating the actual tons of material shipped to it from 1993 into May 1994, Lobosco's last shipment date. Only in the very first month of the contract, April 1993, did Lobosco come close to the estimate in the Agreement, shipping 942 tons. Michael Lobosco gave several reasons for his firm's inability to meet the schedule set in the Agreement. First, he stated that the materials from the City had a much higher proportion of garbage than what he had previously obtained from similar programs in the suburbs. * * * Second, he noted that he did not always get the amount promised under the City contract. * * * He also testified, without contradiction, that of the material he received from the City, ultimately 28% was convertible into ONP 8. Michael Lobosco derived this figure as follows: he testified that 30% of each load from the City consisted of prohibitives such as garbage, thus leaving 70% of the initial amount. Of this remainder, Lobosco estimated that 40% of it was ONP 8. * * * During this time, Lobosco also received about 150 tons per month of newspaper from other sources. * * *

At the same time Lobosco was not meeting the specification of the Agreement, it was shipping another paper product to Mandala Recycling. * * * Lobosco testified that this product contained "50–60%" newspaper. * * * There was no direct testimony by the buyer or the seller as to the outthrow content of this proprietary package, which was to be sent overseas, but the principal of Mandala, Stephen Batty, testified that he was allowed "a little more latitude" in the material that he shipped to Indonesia. * * *

Beginning in September 1993, after a series of attempts to have Lobosco's output conform to ONP 8, Canusa offered to modify the Agreement. Specifically, Canusa offered to accept 500 tons per month of ONP 7/8 (also known as "export news") instead of the higher quality ONP 8. * * * Michael Lobosco never signed this agreement; however, he testified that he acted pursuant to his understanding of it. * * * Lobosco also testified that he told Knight not to ship this product to a newsprint mill because it would be rejected, but that Knight went ahead and did so. * * * Knight's testimony was similar, except that Knight stated that the material was rejected because it had rotted due to moisture. * * * In the month following this amendment (October, 1993), the amount of paper Lobosco shipped to Canusa almost doubled.

Although Lobosco had shipped 440 tons in January of 1994, that number decreased to 270 in February and zero in March. In January 1994, Canusa offered to accept a "baler fee" payment of $3.00 per ton, relieving Lobosco of any obligation under the Agreement. * * * In March 1994, Canusa again offered to modify the Agreement. Lobosco would pay, in addition to the regular baler payment, $3,000.00 per month. This amount was computed on the basis of a $2 per ton profit on the 1500 tons that Lobosco was to have shipped to Canusa. In return, Canusa would release Lobosco from its obligation under the Output Agreement. * * * Lobosco never accepted this proposal. * * * Canusa filed its complaint on June 27, 1994.

Canusa sought damages for breach of contract, fraudulent inducement, and replevin of the baler. The parties entered into a stipulation of partial settlement on June 30, 1994, which provided that Lobosco would purchase the baler from Canusa, settling the replevin and rent claims, but that Canusa reserved all of its other rights under the Equipment Lease, guarantee, and Agreement. * * * At trial, Canusa's fraudulent inducement claim was dismissed; thus, only the action for breach of contract under the Agreement and fees and costs associated with the replevin action remain to be decided.

DISCUSSION

* * *

Canusa contends that Lobosco breached its contract by failing to meet the minimum set forth in the Agreement. Lobosco contends that there was no breach because it supplied Canusa with all the ONP 8 that it produced. The initial dispute, then, is over the meaning of an estimate in an output contract. Canusa argues that under the Agreement it is entitled to the minimum tonnage specified, while Lobosco argues that output agreements like this one are subject only to the requirement of good faith. Significantly, Canusa did not offer any evidence to prove, nor advance the theory at trial, that this contract was a fixed quantity contract; indeed, it would be difficult to do so given the document itself. In fact, Knight testified at trial that Canusa subsequently changed its contracts to supply contracts to ensure that it would receive a specified amount. * * * Thus, there is no dispute that the Agreement is an output contract; the issue is what weight should be given to the Agreement's estimate.

Output contracts are governed by § 2–306, which provides in part:

> A term which measures the quantity by the output of the seller or the requirements of the buyer means such actual output or requirements as may occur in good faith, except that no quantity unreasonably disproportionate to any stated estimate or in the absence of a stated estimate to any normal or otherwise comparable prior output or requirements may be tendered or demanded.

N.Y.U.C.C. § 2–306(1) (McKinney 1993). Prior to the introduction of the UCC, estimates in output contracts were just that: estimates. *See Orange and Rockland Utils., Inc. v. Amerada Hess Corp.*, 59 A.D.2d 110, 115, 397 N.Y.S.2d 814 (2d Dep't 1977). Comment 3 to § 2–306 provides: "Any minimum or maximum set by the agreement shows a clear limit on the intended elasticity. In similar fashion, the agreed estimate is to be regarded as a center around which the parties intend the variation to occur." N.Y.U.C.C. § 2–306, cmt.3 (McKinney 1993). In contrast, comment 2 states: "The essential test is whether the party is acting in good faith." *Id.*, cmt. 2. Taken together, these comments do not provide much guidance as to the importance of the estimate in a reduced output context, because the weight given an estimate in an output or requirement contract usually only becomes an issue in the context of an increase, either in the seller's output or in the buyer's demand. The former case is illustrated by *Philadelphia Corp. v. Niagara Mohawk Power Corp.*, 207 A.D.2d 176, 621 N.Y.S.2d 237 (3d Dep't 1995). There, the court held that the plaintiffs, who sought to increase their electrical output, could not "increase their electrical output beyond the reasonable expectations of the parties as quantified by the stated estimates." Id. at 179, 621 N.Y.S.2d 237 (citation and footnote omitted). In *Orange and Rockland Utilities*, the court held that in a rising market the doubling of an estimated demand for fuel oil under a fixed price contract was unreasonably disproportionate. *See* 59 A.D.2d at 115, 397 N.Y.S.2d 814.

Because these decisions do not address the concerns that arise in the specific factual context of this case they are inapposite. Three cases do, however, shed light on this issue. The first, a leading case in New York, is *Feld v. Henry S. Levy & Sons, Inc.*, 37 N.Y.2d 466, 373 N.Y.S.2d 102, 335 N.E.2d 320 (N.Y.1975). In *Feld*, plaintiff entered into a contract to purchase all of the output of the defendant seller's bread crumbs. Defendant stopped production of bread crumbs after several months of production, and dismantled the equipment for making them. Defendant argued that its total cessation of production ended its duty under the contract. The reason given for the cessation was that it was no longer economically feasible for the firm to produce the product. The court noted that "good faith cessation of production terminates any further obligations thereunder and excuses further performance by the party discontinuing production," Id. at 470–71, 373 N.Y.S.2d 102, 335 N.E.2d 320 (citations omitted), and that while an imperiling of defendant's business might warrant cessation, the fact of a lesser return than expected on the contract would not. Thus, although there was no estimate in the contract, the court held that the only appropriate test was one of good faith. The court did not discuss the issue of disproportionate variation.

The second relevant case is *Empire Gas Corp. v. American Bakeries Co.*, 840 F.2d 1333 (7th Cir.1988). In *Empire Gas*, the parties entered into a requirements contract to convert several thousand of defendant's vehicles to gas; the defendant never converted a single vehicle under the contract. On appeal, the defendant contended it was error for the trial judge to read § 2–306 verbatim to the jury, because the "unreasonably disproportionate" language, without explanation, might effectively have produced a directed verdict for plaintiff, since taking nothing under the contract could easily be "unreasonably disproportionate." Writing for the court, Judge Posner held that when a buyer takes less, rather than more than the stated estimate in a requirements contract, the unreasonably disproportionate provision of § 2–306 does not apply, and the sole test is good faith. *See Id.* at 1339. Thus, a buyer could reduce his or her requirements to zero under a requirements contract, provided that he or she did so in good faith. *See Id.* at 1338.

The court began its analysis of the disproportionate proviso by noting that case law distinguishes between overdemanding and underdemanding cases, and that at common law the sole test of underdemanding was good faith. *See Id.* at 1337 (citing cases) The court then read the statute to mean that the "unreasonably disproportionate" language as providing a specific articulation of good faith, the general standard, in the context of an overdemanding case. *See Id.* at 1338. Thus, the "unreasonably disproportionate" language of § 2–306(1) has no application in the context of an underdemanding case.

At least one circuit court has adopted the reasoning of *Empire Gas* in a factual setting similar to this case. In *Atlantic Track & Turnout Co. v. Perini Corp.*, 989 F.2d 541 (1st Cir.1993), Perini had contracted to remove material as part of a railroad track rehabilitation project, and then sought to sell this material to Atlantic Track. Perini supplied on[ly] 15% of the material estimated in Atlantic Track's purchase orders because the rehabilitation contract was modified and then terminated, and because some of the material from the project was contaminated and apparently unusable. Atlantic Track argued that under § 2–306, Perini was obligated to provide material in conformity with the estimates in plaintiff's purchase orders, which also stated that Perini was to furnish "all available material." *Id.* at 542–43. Rejecting this argument, the First Circuit held that the unreasonably disproportionate language of § 2–306 does not apply to an output contract where the seller tenders less than the estimate, and that the sole test in this context is good faith. *See Id.* at 544–45. In reaching its conclusion, the court first adopted the reasoning in *Empire Gas* that the "unreasonably disproportionate" language represented a specified articulation of good faith, and that a requirements contract "represents a risk allocation." *Id.* at 544 (citing *Empire Gas*, 840 F.2d at 1340). Interpreting Massachusetts law, the court went on to hold that the risk allocation rationale articulated in *Empire Gas* "supports different treatment of cases such as the present one, in which the seller in an output contract tenders less than the stated estimate, from cases in which the seller tenders more." *Atlantic Track*, 989 F.2d at 545 (citation omitted). Here, "the output contract allocates to the buyer the risk of a change in the seller's business that makes continuation costly, while the seller assumes the risk of a less urgent change in circumstances." *Id.*

Although *Atlantic Track* is not controlling and although neither *Feld* nor *Empire Gas* is directly on point, the reasoning of these three cases is compelling here. First, as the *Feld* court noted, good faith is the general standard by which output contracts are measured. *See Feld*, 37 N.Y.2d at 470, 373 N.Y.S.2d 102, 335 N.E.2d 320. Second, as the *Empire Gas* court found, the "unreasonably disproportionate" language in § 2–306 is a specific construction of good faith in the context of increased output or demand, and has no relationship to a good faith analysis of a decrease.

See Empire Gas, 840 F.2d at 1338. In a requirements contract, the seller takes the risk that the buyer may in good faith reduce its requirements to zero. *See Id.* Given the premise that a seller will want to maximize its output, the good faith standard provides a sufficient test to measure a reducing seller's performance against. *See HML Corp. v. General Foods Corp.*, 365 F.2d 77, 81 (3rd Cir.1966) (applying New York law). So too, in an output contract, the buyer takes the risk that the seller may reduce its production to zero. *See Feld*, 37 N.Y.2d at 470–71, 373 N.Y.S.2d 102, 335 N.E.2d 320. Applying good faith rather than an estimate does not give the seller an un-bargained for advantage; rather, it merely preserves the essential character of contracts that lack a fixed term, albeit through the somewhat elusive concept of good faith. *See Empire Gas*, 840 F.2d at 1339 (calling good faith a "chameleon"); *see also Bloor v. Falstaff Brewing Corp.*, 601 F.2d 609, 612–15 (2d Cir.1979) (Friendly, J.) (discussing a "best efforts" clause under New York law and noting at n. 7 that "the New York law is far from clear.").

Moreover, a mechanical adherence to the estimate in the contract would essentially convert all output contracts with an estimate into fixed contracts. The fallacy of this proposition is illustrated by this case: having bargained for the flexibility of an output contract, Canusa now seeks to treat it as a fixed goods contract. An output agreement is not transformed into a fixed quantity contract by the insertion of an estimate. Thus, where an output contract provides for a certain amount of goods to be produced, the appropriate test for a seller's reduction in output is good faith rather than the estimate in the contract.

After discounting the estimate in the Agreement as the appropriate yardstick, the baseline for the defendant's good faith must be set at Michael Lobosco's own estimate of the ONP 8 he could produce from the City's material, because Canusa failed to establish any other basis. Despite being given the opportunity, Canusa did not offer *any* evidence of other percentages of ONP production from *any* city's recycling program. Measured by its own standard, however, Lobosco's performance does not comport with good faith. When asked why he failed to produce ONP 8 in quantities consistent with his own production estimate, Michael Lobosco's only explanation was that it would have taken more time to sort the material. * * * The fact that it would cost more to clean the material to reach the ONP 8 standard does not demonstrate good faith; nor does it provide an excuse, *see Feld*, 37 N.Y.2d at 471–72, 373 N.Y.S.2d 102, 335 N.E.2d 320, especially where there is no showing that the additional costs would not have made the contract unprofitable. Thus, because Lobosco failed to supply the ONP 8 that its president testified it could produce, it breached the Output Agreement.

Lobosco did not raise the defense of waiver at trial. Even if it had, Canusa's efforts to work with Lobosco is not a waiver of the good faith requirement, because a party need not terminate the contract, but may instead seek to resolve the problem. *See Horn Waterproofing Corp. v. Bushwick Iron & Steel Co., Inc.*, 66 N.Y.2d 321, 326–31, 497 N.Y.S.2d 310, 488 N.E.2d 56 (N.Y.1985) (holding that UCC § 1–207 permitted the reservation of rights by a creditor who endorsed defendant's check). Indeed, as a matter of policy, the law ought to encourage Canusa's attempt to avoid litigation.

* * *

CONCLUSION

* * * Judgment to be entered against A & R Lobosco, Incorporated, in the amount $125,597.59. . . . The Clerk of the Court is directed to enter judgment accordingly and close the case.

CENTRAL ADJUSTMENT BUREAU, INC. v. INGRAM

Supreme Court of Tennessee, 1984.
678 S.W.2d 28.

DROWOTA, JUSTICE.

This appeal * * * involves non-competition clauses in employment contracts. It raises an issue regarding the consideration necessary to support such a covenant when it is entered into after employment has begun. * * *

I

The plaintiff-employer, Central Adjustment Bureau, a Texas corporation whose home office is in Dallas, Texas, is qualified to do business in Tennessee as a collector of past-due debts. It has 25 branch offices throughout the United States, including a branch in Nashville, Tennessee. The defendants are former employees who left Central Adjustment Bureau (hereinafter CAB) in 1979 to form Ingram & Associates, a company which competed directly with CAB. All of the defendants had signed covenants not to compete with CAB. After the defendants left, CAB brought suit in Chancery Court seeking both compensatory and injunctive relief. According to CAB's allegations, the defendants were liable in tort and for breach of the non-competition covenants.

The Chancellor found that the non-competition covenants were unreasonably broad with regard to geographical and time limitations. The Chancellor, however, modified these restrictions enforcing them as modified by injunctive relief. In addition, the Chancellor awarded the plaintiff $80,000.00 in damages for the breach of the covenants and for the torts of unfair competition and breach of the duty of loyalty.

The Court of Appeals reversed the Chancellor on the issue of the covenant not to compete, holding that the covenants were unenforceable for lack of consideration. * * *

II

* * *

Defendant Henry Preston Ingram was hired on March 1, 1970, by CAB as a salesman in North Carolina with a base salary of $600.00

monthly plus commissions. A week after he began working, CAB informed him that he must sign a covenant not to compete. Ingram initially refused to sign, but under threat of termination, he signed two weeks later.

In June, 1972, CAB promoted Ingram to manager of the Nashville district. Ingram was promoted in June, 1977, to manager of the northern region of CAB. CAB is divided into three regions nationwide. The northern region which was headquartered in Nashville included Kentucky and Tennessee as well as most of the states in the midwestern, northeastern and mid-Atlantic areas of the United States. As a regional manager, Ingram was employed in the highest corporate position outside that of an officer.

Ingram resigned from CAB on February 22, 1979. At that time, he was the fifth highest paid employee at CAB. In 1978, he received more than $59,000.00 in compensation.

Defendant Richard B. Goostree was hired as a collector in the Nashville office on March 6, 1972, at a base salary of $500.00 monthly plus commissions. Prior to beginning employment, he was not informed that he would be required to sign a covenant not to compete. It was presented to him and signed on March 7, 1972.

Goostree received a promotion to collections manager in April, 1973. In June, 1977, he was promoted to district manager of the Nashville office.

Defendant James Bjorkholm was hired as a salesman for the Nashville office on May 5, 1977, at a base salary of $750.00 a month plus commissions and an automobile allowance. He signed a non-competition covenant three weeks later. This agreement was lost, however, and another was signed on August 8, 1977. Bjorkholm received one $50.00 raise in his base salary while at CAB, but no promotions.

The covenant was identical in each case, providing as follows:

"I, /s/_____, the undersigned, during the term of my employment with Central Adjustment Bureau, Inc., and/or its wholly-owned subsidiaries, and at any time within two years of termination thereof, shall not compete within the United States, either directly or indirectly, with the corporation (1) by owning, operating, managing, being employed by, having a proprietary interest of any kind in, or extending financial credit to any person, enterprise, firm or corporation which is engaged in any business in which the corporation is engaged or directly or indirectly competes with the corporation in any manner; (2) by divulging any information pertaining to the business, trade secrets, and/or confidential data of the corporation, or make any use whatsoever of the same; or (3) by contacting any client or customer of the corporation who has been a client or customer of the corporation during the term of employment.

"I fully understand that the corporation will rely on this covenant in employing me, and I agree that in the event of any breach of this covenant that the corporation's damages are irreparable and that the corporation shall be entitled to injunctive relief, in addition to such other and further relief as may be proper. It is further agreed that if at any time it shall be determined that this covenant is unreasonable as to time or area, or both, by any court of competent jurisdiction, the corporation shall be entitled to enforce this covenant for such period of time and within such area as may be determined to be reasonable by such court. In the event of breach of this covenant, I agree to pay all costs of enforcement of the said covenant, including, but not limited to, reasonable attorney's fees."

* * *

Ingram resigned from CAB on February 22, 1979; Goostree and Bjorkholm resigned in March, 1979. On March 10, 1979, Ingram, Goostree and Bjorkholm of the Nashville CAB office met with Kathleen Garrison, David Powers and Anthony Schweitzer to finalize the formation of Ingram & Associates. Ingram was to hold sixty per cent of the outstanding stock with Powers, Bjorkholm, Garrison and Goostree each holding ten per cent.

On or about March 22, 1979, Ingram & Associates began actively functioning in the collection agency business. Both prior and subsequent to this date, the new venture solicited CAB customers, making use of personal contacts gained by the defendants while employed by CAB.

The Chancellor found that the defendants

"... utilized valuable knowledge and personal contacts gained and developed while they were CAB employees. They know which potential customers are likely to be profitable, and how to secure, retain and service customers. They have been able to profit from the personal relationships they developed with CAB customers...."

The record amply supports the findings. It is undisputed that defendant Ingram made plans and took actions prior to his resignation to acquire a proprietary interest in a collection agency, which was intended to operate in direct competition with CAB. For instance, prior to leaving CAB, defendant Ingram obtained from various CAB branch officers client information sheets deemed confidential by CAB. These sheets set forth information valuable to any competitor of CAB, including the names of the client contacts, collection, legal, accounting and special requirements of each client as well as the commission charged each client by CAB. Through its access to this and similar information, Ingram & Associates was able to make proposals to major CAB clients which undercut the CAB rate of commission. Other documents indicate that Ingram & Associates in its effort to attract clients made extensive use of the good will and personal contacts developed by the defendants while working for CAB.

III

As a general rule, restrictive covenants in employment contracts will be enforced if they are reasonable under the particular circumstances.

Allright Auto Parks, Inc. v. Berry, 219 Tenn. 280, 409 S.W.2d 361 (1966). The rule of reasonableness applies to consideration as well as to other matters such as territorial and time limitations. *Di Deeland v. Colvin,* 208 Tenn. 551, 554, 347 S.W.2d 483, 484 (1961). Whether there is adequate consideration to support a non-competition covenant signed during an on-going employment relationship depends upon the facts of each case. *Davies & Davies Agency, Inc. v. Davies,* 298 N.W.2d 127 (Minn.1980).

The first question before us is whether future employment of an at-will employee constitutes consideration for a non-competition covenant. In *Ramsey v. Mutual Supply Co.,* 58 Tenn.App. 164, 427 S.W.2d 849 (1968), Ramsey agreed to a non-competition covenant with his employer, Mutual Supply Company, "at the time of such employment." 427 S.W.2d at 850. Ramsey's employment lasted nearly two and a half years before he left to work for a competitor. When Mutual Supply brought suit to enforce the covenant, Ramsey argued that employment was not sufficient consideration. The court rejected that argument, holding

> "that employment, even for an indefinite period of time, subject to termination at the option of the employer is sufficient consideration to support such a contract." Id. 427 S.W.2d at 852.

Ramsey is thus authority for the proposition that employment is sufficient consideration for a covenant which is part of the original employment agreement. The contention is made, however, that the employee must be informed of the covenant during employment negotiations before beginning employment. It is argued that if the covenant is not presented to the employee until the first day at work or shortly thereafter, the covenant is not the subject of free bargaining.

Such an argument, if accepted, threatens to vitiate any agreement between an employee already working and his or her employer. *See McQuown v. Lakeland Window Cleaning Co.,* 136 So.2d 370 (Fla.App. 1962). We hold that a covenant signed prior to, contemporaneously with or shortly after employment begins is part of the original agreement, and that therefore, under *Ramsey,* it is supported by adequate consideration.

For this reason, we find that there is adequate consideration to support defendant Goostree's covenant. According to an exhibit filed by CAB, Goostree began working for CAB on March 6, 1972. He signed the covenant not to compete on March 7, 1972. Under these circumstances, the covenant was clearly part of the original employment agreement.[2]

Even when the covenant is not signed until after employment has begun, courts in the following states have found continued employment to be sufficient consideration: Alabama, Connecticut, Florida, Georgia, Iowa, Kentucky, Massachusetts, Mississippi, Missouri, New Hampshire, New Jersey and Texas. *See* generally Annot. 51 A.L.R.3d 825 (1973). Some of these courts reason that the mutual promises of the parties as

---

2. In so holding, we view the record in the light most favorable to the defendant. The covenant itself is dated March 3, 1972. Goostree's testimony suggests that he began working on that same day.

to continued employment form a binding bilateral contract with the promise of employment constituting sufficient consideration. *See, e.g. Sherman v. Pfefferkorn,* 241 Mass. 468, 135 N.E. 568 (1922); *Reed, Roberts Associates, Inc. v. Bailenson,* 537 S.W.2d 238 (Mo.App.1976). Other courts, however, regard the mere promise of continued employment as not binding on the employee where the employment is one at-will. They nevertheless regard the covenant as binding if there is actual performance of the promise of continued employment.

In *Thomas v. Coastal Industrial Services,* 214 Ga. 832, 108 S.E.2d 328 (1959), the court stated its reasoning as follows:

"Though a promise may be *nudum pactum* when made because the promisee is not bound, it becomes binding when he subsequently furnishes the consideration contemplated by doing what he was expected to do." *Id.* 108 S.E.2d at 329.

The court thus held that although there was no mutuality or consideration to bind the employer when an employee, already employed, signed a non-competition covenant, performance under the contract supplied the mutuality and consideration necessary to make the contract binding. The Kentucky Court of Appeals relied on *Thomas v. Coastal Industrial Services, Inc.,* in holding that a covenant is enforceable "provided the employer continues to employ the employee for an appreciable length of time after he signs the covenant, and the employee severs his relationship with his employer by voluntarily resigning." *CAB v. Ingram, supra,* 622 S.W.2d at 685. *See also,* * * * *Roessler v. Burwell,* 119 Conn. 289, 176 A. 126 (1934) (Employed over 4 years after signing covenant); *Hogan v. Bergen Brunswig Corp.,* 153 N.J.Super. 37, 378 A.2d 1164 (1977) (continuation of employment for 3 years held sufficient consideration) * * *

The defendant contends, however, that Tennessee has rejected this reasoning, adhering instead to the rule that the mere fact of continued employment will not support a non-competition covenant signed subsequent to employment, relying on *Associated Dairies, Inc. v. Ray Moss Farms, Inc.,* et al., 205 Tenn. 268, 326 S.W.2d 458 (1959). In *Ray Moss,* the non-competition covenant signed by the defendant employee was not part of the original agreement, although the opinion does not state how long the employee, Ralph Byrum, had worked for Associated Dairies when he signed the covenant. In consideration for the covenant, Associated Dairies agreed only to retain Byrum in employment at will. The Court held that there was no consideration since Associated Dairies was not bound by the agreement to retain Byrum for even a single day.

We disagree with the defendants' interpretation of *Ray Moss.* The court there decided only the question of whether the *promise* of continued employment standing alone is sufficient consideration for a non-competition covenant signed after employment has begun. It did not address the issue of consideration when employment has in fact continued for an appreciable period of time. Indeed, the opinion does not indicate how long Byrum remained with Associated Dairies after he signed the covenant.

Thus, if there has been actual performance in the form of continued employment, the inquiry must move beyond *Ray Moss.* In *Hoyt v. Hoyt,* 213 Tenn. 117, 372 S.W.2d 300 (1963), this Court stated:

> "The authorities are uniform in holding that where there has been full or substantial performance by one party to a bilateral contract, originally invalid for want of mutuality of obligation, the other party cannot refuse performance after receiving the promised benefits. [Citations omitted] ... Williston and Corbin contend that once performance is made of the counter-promise (Appellee's here) the other promise (Appellant's promise) becomes binding as sufficient consideration has been received for it. By this view a binding unilateral contract is forged out of a former, invalid bilateral contract."

Id. at 128–29, 372 S.W.2d at 305.

We are persuaded that the doctrine stated in *Hoyt* should be applied in cases involving non-competition covenants. Such an approach is in agreement with the decisions of our sister state courts cited above. Moreover, it does not require that we overrule *Ray Moss;* rather, *Ray Moss* remains good law when the only consideration is the promise of continued employment.

Whether performance is sufficient to support a covenant not to compete depends upon the facts and circumstances of each case. The requirement that consideration for a non-competition covenant be reasonable remains. *Di Deeland v. Colvin, supra.* It is possible, for instance, that employment for only a short period of time would be insufficient consideration under the circumstances. *See, e.g., Frierson v. Sheppard Building Supply Co.,* 247 Miss. 157, 154 So.2d 151, 154 (1963) ("If appellant had been discharged shortly after signing the agreement, this Court would probably hold the agreement was not supported by consideration"). Another factor affecting reasonableness is the circumstances under which an employee leaves. Although an at-will employee can be discharged for any reason without breach of the contract, a discharge which is arbitrary, capricious or in bad faith clearly has a bearing on whether a court of equity should enforce a non-competition covenant. *Id.,* 154 So.2d at 155; Gibson's Suits in Chancery § 18 (6th ed. 1982).

We find that because of the length of employment of each defendant, the covenant is binding against them. Defendants Ingram and Goostree remained with CAB for seven years after signing the covenants while defendant Bjorkholm was employed for two years. Each defendant left voluntarily; there is no evidence that CAB acted in bad faith or with unclean hands. It is unnecessary at this time to say how long employment must continue before there is substantial performance under the doctrine of *Hoyt v. Hoyt* discussed above. The length of employment of each defendant in this case is sufficient to constitute substantial performance.

In addition, we note that defendant Ingram received numerous salary increases while employed at CAB. Beginning as a salesman, Ingram advanced until at the time of his resignation, he occupied one of the highest positions in the company. Defendant Goostree also received numerous salary increases as well as two promotions. He had risen to the position of Nashville district manager at the time he resigned from CAB in order to compete with it in the Nashville area.

Some courts which have required additional consideration other than continued employment have held that a beneficial change in an employee's status constitutes sufficient consideration to support a restrictive covenant agreed to after the initial taking of employment. *See M.S. Jacobs and Associates, Inc. v. Duffley,* 452 Pa. 143, 303 A.2d 921 (1973); *Faw, Casson & Co. v. Cranston,* 375 A.2d 463 (Del.Ch.1977). In *Davies & Davies Agency, Inc. v. Davies,* 298 N.W.2d 127 (Minn.1980), the employee signed the covenant after his employment began. In enforcing the covenant, the court found decisive the fact that because he had signed the covenant, he had advanced to a responsible selling position in his ten years with the firm, and had in effect taken over one aspect of the firm's business which had become identified with him.

As in *Davies & Davies,* defendants Ingram and Goostree received additional benefits above and beyond continued employment which they would not have received had they not signed the covenants. The fact of these additional benefits shows the extent to which CAB performed under its contracts with Ingram and Goostree. For this additional reason, we hold that the covenants are supported by sufficient consideration.

* * *

The judgment of the Court of Appeals as to all defendants is reversed and the judgment of the Chancellor is affirmed. Costs are taxed against the defendants.

COOPER, C.J., and HARBISON, J., concur. FONES and BROCK, JJ., dissent in separate opinion.

BROCK, JUSTICE, dissenting.

* * * In *Associated Dairies, Inc. v. Ray Moss Farms, Inc.,* 205 Tenn. 268, 326 S.W.2d 458 (1959), this Court held that continued employment is no consideration for a restrictive covenant imposed after an employment relationship has begun. In *Ray Moss,* a competitor of the employer, who was in the dairy business, allegedly began to hire the employer's sales drivers and to use those drivers to solicit the employer's business. In response, the employer required its drivers, including the defendant, to sign a noncompetition agreement. In refusing to enforce the agreement, this Court found as follows:

> "In the case at bar there was no agreement that the complainant would retain the defendant for as much as one day.... In these circumstances there was no consideration to sustain the contract which purports to restrain the defendant from engaging in the

solicitation of business for another." *Id.,* 205 Tenn. at 275, 326 S.W.2d at 461.

Thus, if the terms of the original employment agreement do not include a covenant not to compete, any subsequent covenant must be supported by some consideration other than mere continued employment under a contract terminable at will. *See, e.g., Di Deeland v. Colvin,* 208 Tenn. 551, 347 S.W.2d 483 (1961) (new obligation to give two weeks' notice before employment terminated held to be adequate consideration).

Ray Moss is supported by the following reasoning in *Pemco Corp. v. Rose,* 163 W.Va. 420, 257 S.E.2d 885, 890 (1979):

> "The argument that the employer's consideration for the non-competition covenant is the forebearance of the legal right of discharge we find unavailing but not without logical support.... Common law principles governing employment contracts should not be employed to supply consideration for a non-competition covenant where such a provision was not freely bargained for by the parties."

In the instant case, CAB did not present the covenants to the defendants until after they had terminated their previous employment and begun work for CAB. Although the covenants were presented to the defendants as soon as or shortly after they began working, at that point the covenants were no longer the subject of free bargaining. As the Court of Appeals observed, "[e]ven if he [the employee] is notified of the restrictive covenant on the first day of his new employment, he has foreclosed his other options at that point and has little choice but to sign."

The *Ray Moss* rule that an employee's anticompetitive covenant executed after the commencement of his employment is unenforceable because without consideration is followed in a number of other states. * * * We are urged to hold in this case that consideration may be found to have consisted of promotions and increases in compensation granted to the defendants-employees over the years of their employment with the appellant. *Davies & Davies Agcy., Inc. v. Davies,* Minn., 298 N.W.2d 127 (1980) is cited as authority for such a holding. I decline this invitation because of the fundamental doctrine that in order for an act to constitute consideration for a promise it must have been "bargained for and given in exchange for that very promise." Section 75, Restatement of Contracts, American Law Institute. There is simply no indication in this record whatever for a conclusion that promotions and increases in compensation, given years after the covenants not to compete were executed, were bargained for and given in exchange for those covenants. The covenants not to compete in the instant case were not bargained for at all but were merely imposed upon the employees after their employment began. I would hold that these covenants fail for lack of consideration. The majority finds consideration where there is none.

* * *

Problems

23. Defendant leased to plaintiff 75 acres of land for 99 years for the sum of 5 cents for each ton of sand and gravel taken therefrom. The plaintiff did not by any express terms agree to take any sand and gravel. Was there a contract?

24. On April 30, B and S signed a contract which provided that B agreed to buy and S to sell special pre-mixed barbecue sauce, at a designated price per gallon, to be used in toasted buns in B's restaurant. S also agreed to give B an exclusive right to use this sauce in the State of Oregon. The agreement was for a period of 10 years. Beginning in May, B began purchasing several gallons of sauce per month. In October, B decided it could make a similar sauce for less money. Thus, B did not place an order for sauce that month and informed S that it did not expect to buy any additional sauce. Does S have a cause of action against B?

25. D, an oil company, agreed to supply P, a public utility, with P's requirements for fuel oil at one of its generators. The contract was for a five-year period at a fixed rate per barrel and contained estimates of the amounts of oil which P would require per year. These estimates were made based upon the assumption that P would primarily burn gas. At the time the agreement was signed, gas was less expensive than oil and, in the agreement, P explicitly reserved the right to burn as much gas as it chose.

Within five months of the signing of the agreement, the market price of oil increased sharply. P revised its requirements for oil, demanding a 63 percent increase over the contract estimate. D refused to meet the increased demand but supplied P with the amount of the contract estimate plus ten percent.

The increase in P's demand was occasioned by a sixfold increase in sales of electricity by P to other utilities. In addition, P proposed to sell to a supplier of gas a large quantity of gas that it could have used to produce electricity. P sued D for failure to deliver its increased demands of oil. What result?

26. Kemp owned and operated a gasoline station. He entered into a contract with plaintiff, a petroleum company, agreeing to purchase all his supplies of gasoline from plaintiff for a period of 7 years. In the second year of performance, Kemp formed a corporation wholly owned by himself and transferred the gasoline station and all its assets to this corporation. He then informed plaintiff that he had no further requirements for gasoline. Kemp's corporation then began purchasing gasoline from one of plaintiff's competitors. Plaintiff sues. What result?

27. A enters into a bilateral contract with B in which A promises to ride B's horse in the Derby in return for B's promise to pay $1,000. A threatens not to ride. C, a stranger, promises A an additional $1,000 if A will promise to ride. A makes the promise and rides. Does the doctrine of forging a good unilateral contract out of a bad bilateral contract apply to this case?

28. A promises to work for B for one year in return for B's promise to pay him a fair share of the profits. A performs. Does the doctrine of forging a good unilateral contract out of a bad bilateral contract apply to this case?

29.   P and D, who were brothers, owned adjacent parcels of land. There was a dock on D's parcel. They entered into an agreement which permitted P to use the dock for 10 years in exchange for P's promise to pay one half of the maintenance expenses each year. By the terms of the agreement, P was permitted to terminate the agreement at will. After five years D refused to allow P to continue to use the dock. P brings an action against D for breach of contract and D sets up a defense of mutuality of obligation. During the five years prior to the commencement of the suit P had paid one half of the maintenance expenses of the dock. Make one or more arguments for P.

30.   S and B entered into an agreement by the terms of which S agreed to sell and B agreed to buy 12 carloads of Ko–Hi flasks at a stipulated price. There was a clause in the agreement which read as follows: "It is agreed that Buyer may have the privilege of increasing quantity by an additional 13 carloads shown herein during the period covered by this agreement." An additional 13 carloads were ordered but not delivered. What are the rights of the parties?

31.   The defendant, acting under its power of eminent domain, took title to the plaintiff's building. The defendant promised plaintiff to pay plaintiff's moving expenses if the plaintiff promised (1) to depart the premises peacefully and expeditiously without requiring the defendant to resort to legal action; (2) to relocate its business elsewhere in the same community and not liquidate. Plaintiff so promised. Was defendant's promise supported by consideration?

32.   Plaintiff was employed by the defendant in Wyoming at a time when the employer's personnel manual made clear promises of job security. (Review the *Sanchez* decision on page 6. It represents Wyoming law on personnel manuals). Subsequently, the employer informed each employee that the personnel manual was withdrawn and that from that moment on all personnel were under a hiring at will. As part of a downsizing operation, plaintiff was later discharged. (a) Does plaintiff have a claim based on the original manual? (b)Would the answer or analysis be different if the manual had expressly stated that it would be subject to change by the employer?

Chapter 3

MORAL OBLIGATION AND CONSIDERATION

(Calamari & Perillo 5th §§ 5.1—5.11 and 5.18)

SHELDON v. BLACKMAN

Supreme Court of Wisconsin, 1925.
188 Wis. 4, 205 N.W. 486.

* * *

This is an appeal from the judgment of the county court of Walworth county in probate, rendered in favor of the respondent for a claim against the estate of Henry J. Wilkinson, deceased. The claim, the allowance of which is the subject of this appeal, is based upon a written promise of the deceased to compensate the respondent in the sum of $30,000 for services rendered, and to pay reasonable value for services rendered him subsequently to the date of the written instrument. The instrument in question reads as follows:

"$30,000.00.

"Whitewater, Wisconsin, May 10, 1919.

"At the date of my death, for value received, I promise to pay to Julia H. Sheldon, of Whitewater, Wisconsin, the sum of thirty thousand ($30,000) dollars, without interest.

"The consideration for this note is the services rendered by the said Julia H. Sheldon for me, at my request, in the care of my home and the care of myself and wife during the thirty years next preceding the date hereof, for which services so rendered to date I am indebted to her in the above amount, no part of which has been paid.

"And it is hereby understood and agreed that for future services rendered by her she shall be paid their reasonable value from my estate, at the time of my decease, the amount to be paid for future services however, not to cause the abatement of any general legacies provided for by my last will and testament now made or that hereafter may be made.

"[$6.00 Rev. Stamps.]

"H.J. Wilkinson. [Seal.]"

The respondent, a niece of the wife of the deceased, came to live with Mr. Wilkinson and his wife in 1889, at the request of Mr. Wilkinson and upon the understanding that she would receive his property upon the death of himself and his wife, if she cared for them until the death of

277

both of them. The respondent performed the services required for 34 years, giving up a dress making establishment which she was operating in Woodstock, Ill., at the time the request for her services was made. In May, 1919, the written instrument set out above and a will were made; the latter, after providing for certain small legacies, leaving the residue of the property of the deceased to the respondent. The will has been lost or destroyed, and upon filing a claim against the estate of the deceased, based upon the written instrument, it was opposed by the next of kin and the administrator, upon the grounds that it was not properly delivered, that there was not sufficient consideration for it, and that it was testamentary in character, but not properly attested to take effect as a will.

Mr. Wilkinson was a banker, and, so far as appears from the record, of good business ability. The nearest other relatives were cousins. Mrs. Wilkinson was quite deaf and dim of vision. Her health for many years was poor, and she required much personal physical care before she died. The claimant always assisted her to dress, and when she went upon the street attended her. Mr. Wilkinson had serious bladder trouble, and was cared for by the claimant, acting as a trained nurse, who catheterized him for about 10 years. In other respects she performed delicate and disagreeable services for him. The claimant lived in and was treated as a member of the family, but performed all kinds of domestic service. During the period she bought a house, for which she paid $1,500, but title was taken in the name of the deceased. When she commenced rendering service, she was 42 years old. Mrs. Wilkinson died at the age of 84 and Mr. Wilkinson died at the age of 94.

When the writing in question and the last will of the deceased were executed, they were prepared by the attorney of Mr. Wilkinson at his home, and although the claimant was in the house, she was not present when the note was signed, and did not know the contents of the will, but saw it in a box thereafter, and had access to the box and its contents. The first time she saw the note, or knew of its existence, was August 5, 1920, about 15 months after its execution, when Mr. Wilkinson had it in his hand. She took the note to Mr. Ferris, attorney for the deceased, for safe-keeping on August 6, 1920, and took a receipt. Mr. Ferris held the note thereafter, and produced it at the trial. On the 28th of June, 1917, both Mr. and Mrs. Wilkinson executed wills, in which each devised all of his or her estate to the other in case of survival, but in the event that the other did not survive certain small legacies were given to various people, and all the rest and residue was bequeathed to the claimant, and she was named executrix without bond.

It is admitted that the respondent has a claim for services upon a quantum meruit basis. The probate court found that the instrument in question was a nonnegotiable promissory note for good and sufficient consideration, and allowed the sum of $30,000 and the reasonable value of the services of the respondent from the date of the instrument until the date of the death of the deceased, at $30 a week, in all $35,925, with interest. From this judgment this appeal is brought.

* * *

Jones, J. (after stating the facts as above). It is the first broad contention of the appellant's counsel that there was no consideration for the writing in question; that, since it appeared that Wilkinson's property included real estate when the original parol agreement was made, it was void under the statute of frauds. It is further argued that the relations between the parties were such that no compensation could be recovered without an express contract; that under the arrangement then made the deceased would owe the claimant nothing at any particular time, as she could recover only on complete performance. As bearing on these propositions, counsel cite the following cases: [Citations omitted.]

It is conceded, however, that under these decisions, although a parol agreement of this nature is void, it may be resorted to, to rebut the presumption that the services rendered were gratuitous, and it is claimed that the cause of action accrues only after the services have been rendered, and unless there is an open mutual account, or partial payments, the claim for services for more than 6 years is barred by the statute of limitations. It is argued that at best the deceased owed the claimant merely the reasonable value of her services for the 6 years next preceding the execution of the written instrument. The complaint was in two counts. One claimed compensation for the reasonable value of the services during the 34 years, and the other was based upon the written instrument. The defendant's counsel offered proof of the reasonable value of the services, which was ruled out on objection, and the question is thus raised whether this ruling was correct.

Mr. and Mrs. Wilkinson, when 60 and 54 years of age, respectively, seemed to realize since they had no children or near relatives, that they might need, as old age approached, faithful and competent care, and they were willing that the bulk of their property should be devoted to that object. They selected the claimant as the person best fitted to comply with their wishes, and Mr. Wilkinson made with her the arrangement that, if she should faithfully serve them during their lives, she should have the residue of their estate. Although this parol agreement was invalid, it showed the intention that she should be paid and well paid. This intention was again manifested by the two wills executed in 1917. The failing health they had anticipated came in due time. Their later years were clouded by such physical ailments as called for the most devoted service, and they were not favored with an "old age serene and bright."

No question is raised that the claimant did not perform in full measure the arduous task she had assumed. In 1919, after the aged couple had enjoyed and had the benefit of this service for 30 years, Mr. Wilkinson, after advice of its legal effect, made the note in question. If the last will had been proven, the claimant would have received more than the sum stipulated in the note, since probably no valid objection could have been made to it; and yet Mr. Wilkinson may have shared the fear and dread of many laymen, lest a will may be contested. With all this background he deliberately executed the note now relied on by the claimant. * * *

In this case the services had been rendered under such conditions and were of so intimate and delicate a character that their value could be estimated with no degree of mathematical certainty. No one knew their value so well as Mr. and Mrs. Wilkinson, and if he had not appreciated their value he would have been guilty of gross ingratitude. Evidently he did realize their worth, and desired to make liberal compensation, which he had the perfect right to do. If he deliberately chose to pay more than the services were really worth, he had the right to do so. To receive the consideration and respect of others, and to be able to be generous in later life, are among the motives which prompt men to practice economy and self-denial. There had been a consideration of inestimable value for the execution of the note, and it was in no sense a gift. The utmost that can be fairly claimed is that the consideration for the note was inadequate. But under such facts as here exist mere inadequacy does not amount to a failure or partial failure of consideration. Of course, that may be a circumstance relevant to the issue, where fraud or duress or undue influence is claimed; but in this case there is no suggestion of such a claim. There might be circumstances under which the inadequacy of consideration might be so grossly disproportionate to the value of the benefit received or the services rendered that a court might feel justified in refusing to enforce the contract.

In this case, where there was no element of fraud or misrepresentation, the value of the services may be measured by the wants of the persons benefited. To hold that this agreement, deliberately made, should be set aside or impaired, would be a denial of the right of parties to make their own contracts. There is abundant authority for the rule that, when the value of services is indefinite or indeterminate, or largely a matter of opinion, the courts will not substitute their judgments for that of the contracting parties. * * *

* * *

It does not follow that, because the note was not to take effect until after the maker's death, it was testamentary. As often happens, the title was vested in the payee on delivery and acceptance, although the enjoyment was postponed. "The mere fact that a writing is to become effective only on the death of the maker is not sufficient to give it a testamentary character." Schouler on Wills, § 350. * * *

In this connection there is some argument by counsel for the appellants that the plan of the execution of the note and the will at the same time was adopted with the purpose of evading in part, at least, the inheritance tax. We are aware that there are some persons who regard the inheritance taxes as a new and added terror to death, and that they sometimes adopt ingenious devices to shield their survivors from its burdens. But the argument in this respect rests in sheer speculation, and there is not a scintilla of evidence to support it.

It is our conclusion that the findings and judgment of the trial court should be sustained.

Judgment affirmed.

ESTATE OF LOVEKAMP

Court of Civil Appeals of Oklahoma, Division No. 1, 2001.
24 P.3d 894.

CARL B. JONES, JUDGE:

¶ 1 Louise Serrato appeals an order denying her claim against the Estate of Donald L. Lovekamp. Appellant's claim was for $60,000.00 and was denied by operation of law. Pursuant to 58 O.S.1991 § 339, she brought the instant action as an ancillary proceeding in the probate case. This Court's review is *de novo*.

¶ 2 Appellant and the decedent were previously married but had been divorced for eighteen years. She alleged that at the time of the divorce she and decedent entered into an oral agreement that he would pay her $60,000.00. The agreement, she alleged, was "to prevent the forced sale and partition of the ranch and cattle jointly held by the parties." In Appellant's deposition and answers to interrogatories, however, she clarified that the agreement was not entered into at the time of the divorce in 1975, but rather in July, 1981.

They did not own any property jointly at that time. The circumstances were that several months after the divorce Appellant and decedent began residing together again. One evening decedent had been feeling ill and, according to Appellant, talked about selling his house and 80 acre ranch. He said he was going to ask $120,000.00 for it. He then gave Appellant a check for $60,000.00 and told her it was for coming back and staying with him after they divorced. He told her that she could cash the check if he sold the property or if something happened to him. The check was dated July 29, 1981. When decedent died in September, 1999, the check, of course, was too old to cash, thus this claim was asserted against the estate.

¶ 3 The Appellant and the Personal Representative of the estate both filed motions for summary judgment. The trial court, in granting the Personal Representative's motion for summary judgment, made numerous findings of fact and conclusions of law. Pertinent findings include that Appellant and decedent were divorced in 1975 after being married for approximately 10 years. The divorce decree awarded all real property to the decedent as his sole and separate property. The divorce decree was not appealed. There was no mention in the decree of any agreement to give Appellant $60,000.00. These facts were undisputed.

¶ 4 The trial court held that there was no valid contract because there was a lack of consideration. The court stated:

"As a matter of law, under these facts, the decedent giving the claimant a check for $60,000.00 to cash if he sold the place or if something happened to him in consideration of claimant having come back and stayed the rest of the years until 1981, fails as a contract between the parties, as claimant coming back and staying with the decedent until 1981 fails as a past consideration."

The court cited Johnson v. Hazaleus, 1959 OK 62, 338 P.2d 345; Kennedy v. Marshall, 1945 OK 213, 160 P.2d 397; and, Intercon Mfg. Inc. v. Centrifugal Casting Machine Co., 1993 OK CIV APP 143, 875 P.2d 1149. Kennedy, supra, at 398–399 states what has long been the law in Oklahoma.

"By the great weight of authority a past consideration, if it imposed no legal obligation at the time it was furnished, will support no promise whatever; or, as the rule has been stated otherwise, an executed consideration is no consideration for any promise other than that which the law would imply. A past consideration, it is said, is some act or forbearance in time past by which a man has benefitted without thereby incurring any legal liability; if afterward, whether from good feeling or from interested motives, he makes a promise to the person by whose act or forbearance he has benefitted, and that promise is made on no other consideration than the past benefit, it is gratuitous and cannot be enforced; it is based on motive and not on consideration."

¶ 5 Appellant insists that she and the decedent had an express oral contract. Oral or otherwise, consideration is still a necessary element of a binding contract. 15 O.S.1991 § 2. And as the cited cases show, consideration was lacking which would make this agreement enforceable.

¶ 6 For the reasons discussed, the order granting summary judgment to the Appellee, Personal Representative of the Estate of Donald L. Lovekamp is affirmed. * * *

BANCO DO BRASIL S.A v. STATE OF ANTIGUA AND BARBUDA

N.Y. Appellate Division, First Department 2000.
268 A.D.2d 75, 707 N.Y.S.2d 151.

LERNER, J. In this action for breach of a loan agreement and associated promissory notes and guarantees, we are called upon to determine whether defendants' 1997 letter regarding their loan agreement, sent to plaintiffs after the Statute of Limitations had run, constituted an acknowledgment or promise within the meaning of General Obligations Law § 17–101 and was sufficient to revive plaintiffs' time-barred claims.

On or about November 12, 1981, plaintiff Banco do Brasil, a Brazilian banking corporation with its principal place of business in Brasilia, Brazil, entered into a loan agreement with defendant, the State of Antigua and Barbuda ("the State"), wherein Banco do Brasil agreed to grant the State a loan in the principal amount of $3,000,000 plus interest. In connection with the loan agreement, the State executed certain promissory notes providing for the repayment of the loan with interest. Under the terms of the loan agreement, defendant, the Ministry of Finance of the State of Antigua and Barbuda ("the Ministry"), agreed to act as guarantor of the loan and the promissory notes on behalf of the State. As guarantor, the Ministry agreed to pay the amount due under the loan agreement and the promissory notes in the event of the State's default.

The State failed to pay the amount due within the time period provided in the promissory notes. The last payment was due on January 21, 1985. By letter dated October 5, 1989, the Ministry wrote to Banco do Brasil, confirming its obligation to pay the amount due under the loan agreement. However, the Ministry advised that due to the damages which the State sustained from Hurricane Hugo, it needed to reschedule its loan payments and requested six months to devise a plan for repayment.

In a second letter signed by its financial secretary and dated February 24, 1997, the Ministry confirmed the then-current balances (principal plus interest) due under the original loan agreement. The letter set forth the original loan amount, accrued interest, past-due interest and the total of $11,400,810.96 due and owing on that date.

Despite repeated demands, defendants failed to pay the amount due and owing under the loan agreement. Plaintiffs commenced the instant action for breach of the loan agreement, breach of promissory notes and breach of the guarantee agreement.

Defendants moved to dismiss plaintiffs' complaint upon the ground that plaintiffs' claims were barred under CPLR 213(2), the applicable six-year Statute of Limitations. Defendants argued that neither their October 5, 1989 letter, nor their February 24, 1997 letter satisfied the requirements of General Obligations Law § 17–101 that these writings indicate an absolute and unqualified intention to repay the debt owed to the plaintiffs.

The IAS court denied defendants' motion to dismiss and concluded that the six-year Statute of Limitations was revived under General Obligations Law § 17–101, because the 1997 letter constituted a plain admission of indebtedness and nothing in the letter was inconsistent with a clear intent to repay the loan.

General Obligations Law § 17–101 states, in pertinent part, as follows:

> An acknowledgment or promise contained in a writing signed by the party to be charged thereby is the only competent evidence of a new or continuing contract whereby to take an action out of the operation of the provisions of limitations of time for commencing actions under the civil practice law and rules ...

"This section restates the rule that a written acknowledgment or promise will toll the Statute of Limitations ... The writing, in order to constitute an acknowledgment, must recognize an existing debt and must contain nothing inconsistent with an intention on the part of the debtor to pay it" (Lew Morris Demolition Co. v. Board of Education of the City of New York, 40 N.Y.2d 516, 520–521, 387 N.Y.S.2d 409, 355 N.E.2d 369; *see also* Flynn v. Flynn, 175 A.D.2d 51, 52, 572 N.Y.S.2d 307, *lv. denied* 78 N.Y.2d 863, 578 N.Y.S.2d 878, 586 N.E.2d 61).

The motion court correctly held that defendants' 1997 letter to plaintiffs constituted an "acknowledgment or promise" within the meaning of General Obligations Law § 17–101 that revived plaintiffs' otherwise time-barred claims. In its entirety, such letter refers to the parties' 1981 loan agreement and then "confirms" four "balances", namely, the original loan amount, accrued interest, past-due interest, and, adding up the first three balances, the "total amount". Even if this recital of a repayment obligation that is current and increasing with time is something less than a new promise to pay a past-due debt, it clearly conveys and is consistent with an intention to pay, which is all that need be shown in order to satisfy section 17–101. [Citations omitted.]

Further, there is no merit to defendants' contention that their motion to dismiss should have been held in abeyance for disclosure on the issue of whether their letter imported an intention to repay. Defendants do not need to discover their own intention.

Accordingly, the order of the Supreme Court, New York County (Charles Ramos, J.), entered February 17, 1999, which denied defendants' motion to dismiss the complaint as time barred, should be affirmed, with costs.

HARRINGTON v. TAYLOR

Supreme Court of North Carolina, 1945.
225 N.C. 690, 36 S.E.2d 227.

PER CURIAM.

The plaintiff in this case sought to recover of the defendant upon a promise made by him under the following peculiar circumstances:

The defendant had assaulted his wife, who took refuge in plaintiff's house. The next day the defendant gained access to the house and began another assault upon his wife. The defendant's wife knocked him down with an axe, and was on the point of cutting his head open or decapitating him while he was laying on the floor, and the plaintiff intervened, caught the axe as it was descending and the blow intended for defendant fell upon her hand, mutilating it badly, but saving defendant's life.

Subsequently, defendant orally promised to pay the plaintiff her damages; but, after paying a small sum, failed to pay anything more. So, substantially, states the complaint.

The defendant demurred to the complaint as not stating a cause of action, and the demurrer was sustained. Plaintiff appealed.

The question presented is whether there was a consideration recognized by our law as sufficient to support the promise. The Court is of the opinion that, however much the defendant should be impelled by common gratitude to alleviate the plaintiff's misfortune, a humanitarian act of this kind, voluntarily performed, is not such consideration as would entitle her to recover at law.

The judgment sustaining the demurrer is

Affirmed.

WEBB v. McGOWIN

Court of Appeals of Alabama, 1935.
27 Ala.App. 82, 168 So. 196, cert. denied 232 Ala. 374, 168 So. 199.

Action by Joe Webb against N. Floyd McGowin and Joseph F. McGowin, as executors of the estate of J. Greeley McGowin, deceased. From a judgment of nonsuit, plaintiff appeals.

* * *

BRICKEN, PRESIDING JUDGE.

This action is in assumpsit. The complaint as originally filed was amended. The demurrers to the complaint as amended were sustained, and because of this adverse ruling by the court the plaintiff took a nonsuit, and the assignment of errors on this appeal are predicated upon said action or ruling of the court.

A fair statement of the case presenting the questions for decision is set out in appellant's brief, which we adopt.

"On the 3d day of August, 1925, appellant while in the employ of the W.T. Smith Lumber Company, a corporation, and acting within the scope of his employment, was engaged in clearing the upper floor of mill No. 2 of the company. While so engaged he was in the act of dropping a pine block from the upper floor of the mill to the ground below; this being the usual and ordinary way of clearing the floor, and it being the duty of the plaintiff in the course of his employment to so drop it. The block weighed about 75 pounds.

"As appellant was in the act of dropping the block to the ground below, he was on the edge of the upper floor of the mill. As he started to turn the block loose so that it would drop to the ground, he saw J. Greeley McGowin, testator of the defendants, on the ground below and directly under where the block would have fallen had appellant turned it loose. Had he turned it loose it would have struck McGowin with such force as to have caused him serious bodily harm or death. Appellant could have remained safely on the upper floor of the mill by turning the block loose and allowing it to drop, but had he done this the block would have fallen on McGowin and caused him serious injuries or death. The only safe and reasonable way to prevent this was for appellant to hold to the block and divert its direction in falling from the place where McGowin was standing and the only safe way to divert it so as to prevent its coming into contact with McGowin was for appellant to fall with it to the ground below. Appellant did this, and by holding to the block and falling with it to the ground below, he diverted the course of its fall in such way that McGowin was not injured. In thus preventing the injuries to McGowin appellant himself received serious bodily injuries, resulting in his right leg being broken, the heel of his right foot torn off and his right arm broken. He was badly crippled for life and rendered unable to do physical or mental labor.

"On September 1, 1925, in consideration of appellant having prevented him from sustaining death or serious bodily harm and in consideration of the injuries appellant had received, McGowin agreed with him to care for and maintain him for the remainder of appellant's life at the rate of $15 every two weeks from the time he sustained his injuries to and during the remainder of appellant's life; it being agreed that McGowin would pay this sum to appellant for his maintenance. Under the agreement McGowin paid or caused to be paid to appellant the sum so agreed on up until McGowin's death on January 1, 1934. After his death the payments were continued to and including January 27, 1934, at which time they were discontinued. Thereupon plaintiff brought suit to recover the unpaid installments accruing up to the time of the bringing of the suit.

"The material averments of the different counts of the original complaint and the amended complaint are predicated upon the foregoing statement of facts."

* * *

1. The averments of the complaint show that appellant saved McGowin from death or grievous bodily harm. This was a material benefit to him of infinitely more value than any financial aid he could have received. Receiving this benefit, McGowin became morally bound to compensate appellant for the services rendered. Recognizing his moral obligation, he expressly agreed to pay appellant as alleged in the complaint and complied with this agreement up to the time of his death; a period of more than 8 years.

Had McGowin been accidentally poisoned and a physician, without his knowledge or request, had administered an antidote, thus saving his life, a subsequent promise by McGowin to pay the physician would have been valid. Likewise, McGowin's agreement as disclosed by the complaint to compensate appellant for saving him from death or grievous bodily injury is valid and enforceable.

Where the promisee cares for, improves, and preserves the property of the promisor, though done without his request, it is sufficient consideration for the promisor's subsequent agreement to pay for the service, because of the material benefit received. Pittsburg Vitrified Paving & Building Brick Co. v. Cerebus Oil Co., 79 Kan. 603, 100 P. 631; Edson v. Poppe, 24 S.D. 466, 124 N.W. 441, 26 L.R.A. (N.S.) 534; Drake v. Bell, 26 Misc. 237, 55 N.Y.S. 945.

In Boothe v. Fitzpatrick, 36 Vt. 681, the court held that a promise by defendant to pay for the past keeping of a bull which had escaped from defendant's premises and been cared for by plaintiff was valid, although there was no previous request, because the subsequent promise obviated that objection; it being equivalent to a previous request. On the same principle, had the promisee saved the promisor's life or his body from grievous harm, [the promisor's] subsequent promise to pay for the services rendered would have been valid. Such service would have been far more material than caring for his bull. Any holding that saving a man from death or grievous bodily harm is not a material benefit sufficient to uphold a subsequent promise to pay for the service, necessarily rests on the assumption that saving life and preservation of the body from harm have only a sentimental value. The converse of this is true. Life and preservation of the body have material, pecuniary values, measurable in dollars and cents. Because of this, physicians practice their profession charging for services rendered in saving life and curing the body of its ills, and surgeons perform operations. The same is true as to the law of negligence, authorizing the assessment of damages in personal injury cases based upon the extent of the injuries, earnings, and life expectancies of those injured.

In the business of life insurance, the value of a man's life is measured in dollars and cents according to his expectancy, the soundness of his body, and his ability to pay premiums. The same is true as to health and accident insurance.

It follows that if, as alleged in the complaint, appellant saved J. Greeley McGowin from death or grievous bodily harm, and McGowin subsequently agreed to pay him for the service rendered, it became a valid and enforceable contract.

2. It is well settled that a moral obligation is a sufficient consideration to support a subsequent promise to pay where the promisor has received a material benefit, although there was no original duty or liability resting on the promisor. * * *

The case at bar is clearly distinguishable from that class of cases where the consideration is a mere moral obligation or conscientious duty unconnected with receipt by promisor of benefits of a material or pecuniary nature. Park Falls State Bank v. Fordyce, [206 Wis. 628, 238 N.W. 516]. Here the promisor received a material benefit constituting a valid consideration for his promise.

3. Some authorities hold that, for a moral obligation to support a subsequent promise to pay, there must have existed a prior legal or equitable obligation, which for some reason had become unenforceable, but for which the promisor was still morally bound. This rule, however, is subject to qualification in those cases where the promisor, having received a material benefit from the promisee, is morally bound to compensate him for the services rendered and in consideration of this obligation promises to pay. In such cases the subsequent promise to pay is an affirmance or ratification of the services rendered carrying with it the presumption that a previous request for the service was made. * * *

Under the decisions above cited, McGowin's express promise to pay appellant for the services rendered was an affirmance or ratification of what appellant had done raising the presumption that the services had been rendered at McGowin's request.

4. The averments of the complaint show that in saving McGowin from death or grievous bodily harm, appellant was crippled for life. This was part of the consideration of the contract declared on. McGowin was benefited. Appellant was injured. Benefit to the promisor or injury to the promisee is a sufficient legal consideration for the promisor's agreement to pay. * * *

5. Under the averments of the complaint the services rendered by appellant were not gratuitous. The agreement of McGowin to pay and the acceptance of payment by appellant conclusively shows the contrary.

* * *

The cases of Shaw v. Boyd, 1 Stew. & P. 83, and Duncan v. Hall, 9 Ala. 128, are not in conflict with the principles here announced. In those cases the lands were owned by the United States at the time the alleged improvements were made, for which subsequent purchasers from the government agreed to pay. These subsequent purchasers were not the owners of the lands at the time the improvements were made. Consequently, they could not have been made for their benefit.

From what has been said, we are of the opinion that the court below erred in the ruling complained of; that is to say, in sustaining the demurrer, and for this error the case is reversed and remanded.

Reversed and remanded.

SAMFORD, JUDGE (concurring). The questions involved in this case are not free from doubt, and perhaps the strict letter of the rule, as stated by judges, though not always in accord, would bar a recovery by plaintiff, but following the principle announced by Chief Justice Marshall in Hoffman v. Porter, Fed.Cas. No. 6,577, 2 Brock. 156, 159, where he says, "I do not think that law ought to be separated from justice, where it is at most doubtful," I concur in the conclusions reached by the court.

RICHARD A. POSNER, GRATUITOUS PROMISES IN ECONOMICS AND LAW

6 J. Legal Studies 411 (1977).

* * *

B. PAST CONSIDERATION

Among the exceptions to the general principle that gratuitous promises will not be enforced are several which are grouped under the rubric of "past consideration." A subsequent promise to pay a debt barred by the statute of limitations, or to pay a debt discharged in bankruptcy, [the bankruptcy cases have since been overturned by Congress, Ed.] or to pay a debt that is uncollectable because the debtor was minor at the time the debt was contracted, is legally enforceable even though there is no fresh consideration for the promise. These are classes of promise in which the utility of the promise to the promisor is often great and the costs of enforcement low. First, as regards utility, it should be noted not only that the stakes are often substantial (these are formal debts after all) but that the *incremental* gain in utility from the enforceable character of the promise may be great. The legal promise conveys information (which a mere stated intention to pay would not) about the promisor's attitude toward the payment of debts barred by a technicality. The information conveyed enhances the promisor's reputation for credit-worthiness and may induce people—not necessarily the promisee himself, which is why the promise itself may not be bilateral—to extend credit to him in the future. And enforcement costs are likely to be low or at least no higher than in conventional bilateral-contract cases because the underlying obligation—the original debt—is fully bilateral. The original debt is not directly enforceable only because of a condition which in the case of the statute of limitations slightly, and in the case of discharge in bankruptcy or voidable by reason of minority not at all, increases the likelihood of error compared to what it would have been in a suit on the original bilateral contract that gave rise to the debt.

The foregoing are cases where, although the promise is not bilateral, the promisor's intent is not donative, that is, not motivated by interdependence between the promisor's and the promisee's utility functions. Another class of "past consideration" cases, however, is best understood on the premise of the law's (implicit) recognition of the existence of interdependent utility functions. These are cases involving promises to compensate rescuers or others who have rendered an unbargained but valuable service to the promisor. The existence of a promise in such a case is strongly attested by the presence of circumstances likely to induce an act of altruism by the promisor toward the promisee. A sees B about to be run down by a speeding car and pushes him out of the way. He saves him but sustains a serious injury in the process. In economic terms, A rescued B because at the moment of danger B's expected utility or wealth was very low; the rescue was like a gift to a starving man. But after the rescue the wealth positions of the parties are dramatically reversed: now A's wealth is low relative to B's since B is whole and A is injured. Hence it is to be expected that B would promise to reward A. The presence of altruistic motivation makes the promise a more plausible one—*i.e.*, one less likely to be a figment of the promisee's imagination—than in the standard unilateral promise case. Stated otherwise, the legal-error costs of enforcing the promise are lower in the rescue case.

The facts of a leading rescue past consideration case, *Webb v. McGowin*, illustrate the benefits that may accrue to the promisor in such cases if the promise is legally enforceable, over and above the benefits of the transfer itself. The rescued person promised to pay his rescuer $15 every two weeks for the rest of the rescuer's life. This was a generous gift to the extent that the promise was enforceable but a much less generous one to the extent it was not. Had the promisor believed that such a promise was unenforceable, he might have decided instead to make a one-time transfer that might have had a much lower present value than that of the annuity which he in fact promised. Both parties would have been made worse off by this alternative. Hence, it is not surprising that the court held the promise to be enforceable.

Lon Fuller in a well-known article suggested a different rationale for the past-consideration doctrine. Proceeding from the premise that the requirement of consideration is designed in part to prevent people from making promises on the spur of the moment—promises they do not really mean to make and therefore should not be forced to honor (the "cautionary" function of consideration)—he argues that where the promise is to do what the promisor is morally obligated to do anyway, we need not worry whether he is acting deliberately or not—he *should* have made the promise and that is all that is important. This paternalistic approach is both difficult to square with the basic premises of contract law and an unnecessary embellishment to a theory of the enforcement of gratuitous promises. Fuller is aware of the relevance of economic considerations in explaining the pattern of enforcement and only fails to see that economic analysis can also explain the past-consideration cases.

* * *

Problems

1. Mrs. V. owed $13,500 to each of her two adult sons. She died without having paid any part of these debts. Mr. V., the stepfather of Mrs. V.'s sons, gave each of these stepsons a promissory note signed by him in the amount of $13,500. He died without having made any payments on these notes. The stepsons filed claims against his estate. Should the executor honor the claims?

2. A told B, a builder, that A needed a stable. B said he would do the job and began construction before agreeing on a price. B did a fine job and upon seeing the stable for the first time A promised B that he would pay him $10,000. The reasonable value of the work was only $7,200. Before B assented to this figure, A withdrew his promise. B brought suit based on A's promise. What result?

3. A is employed by B to repair a vacant house. By mistake A repairs the house next door which belongs to C. C subsequently promises to pay A the value of repairs. Is C's promise binding? What result if the value of the repairs was $385 and C, who promised to pay $515, later refused to pay and A sued?

4. Father's coal company was near bankruptcy, owing $18,000 to creditors. Son contracted with Father to enter the business and assume all of the company's prior debts. Two years later, Father told Son that by assuming the debts he had saved the company and that he could have an option to purchase Father's stock. Father then wrote a memorandum to Son stating: "Upon my death my son has an irrevocable option to buy all of my stock in Black's Coal Company." Father died and Son brought suit to enforce the writing. What result?

5. Defendant defaulted under contracts with the Army for the production of carbine bolts and flash suppressors. The Government contracting officer assessed a certain sum as being owed the Army because of the

default. Under the contract defendant was entitled to appeal to the Armed Services Board of Contract Appeals (ASBCA). Pending appeal to ASBCA a signed, written "deferral agreement" was entered into between defendant and the Army whereby defendant agreed to pay the amount found owing by ASBCA promptly within 45 days of the decision. The defendant failed to pay the amount found by the ASBCA to be owing. Suit was brought by the Government. It would be time barred if the cause of action accrued at the initial default, but not if calculated from the date of the breach of the deferral agreement. Is it time barred?

6. Plaintiff, a construction contractor, completed work on a project for the Board of Education. The agreed price was $18,850. Plaintiff billed the Board for $25,000 alleging extra work had been done at the request of the Board. The Board disputed the additional sum. Moreover, the Board insisted on withholding funds pending the outcome of a wrongful death claim filed against the Board and Plaintiff by the estate of a person who had been killed at the job site. After negotiations, the Board paid Plaintiff $13,000 pursuant to a written agreement which stated that this sum was disbursed as a "partial settlement without prejudice to the rights of either party." The wrongful death action resulted in the exoneration of Plaintiff. Plaintiff sues for $12,000. The defendant Board pleads the statute of limitations. The statutory period has run if computed from the time of the initial claim, but not if calculated from the date of the partial settlement agreement. What result?

Chapter 4

PROMISSORY ESTOPPEL

(Calamari & Perillo 5th §§ 6.1—6.4)

FEINBERG v. PFEIFFER CO.

Court of Appeals of Missouri, 1959.
322 S.W.2d 163.

DOERNER, COMMISSIONER.

This is a suit brought in the Circuit Court of the City of St. Louis by plaintiff, a former employee of the defendant corporation, on an alleged contract whereby defendant agreed to pay plaintiff the sum of $200 per month for life upon her retirement. A jury being waived, the case was tried by the court alone. Judgment below was for plaintiff for $5,100, the amount of the pension claimed to be due as of the date of the trial, together with interest thereon, and defendant duly appealed.

The parties are in substantial agreement on the essential facts. Plaintiff began working for the defendant, a manufacturer of pharmaceuticals, in 1910, when she was but 17 years of age. By 1947 she had attained the position of bookkeeper, office manager, and assistant treasurer of the defendant, and owned 70 shares of its stock out of a total of 6,503 shares issued and outstanding. Twenty shares had been given to her by the defendant or its then president, she had purchased 20, and the remaining 30 she had acquired by a stock split or stock dividend. Over the years she received substantial dividends on the stock she owned, as did all of the other stockholders. Also, in addition to her salary, plaintiff from 1937 to 1949, inclusive, received each year a bonus varying in amount from $300 in the beginning to $2,000 in the later years.

On December 27, 1947, the annual meeting of the defendant's Board of Directors was held at the Company's offices in St. Louis, presided over by Max Lippman, its then president and largest individual stockholder. The other directors present were George L. Marcus, Sidney Harris, Sol Flammer, and Walter Weinstock, who, with Max Lippman, owned 5,007 of the 6,503 shares then issued and outstanding. At that meeting the Board of Directors adopted the following resolution, which, because it is the crux of the case, we quote in full:

"The Chairman thereupon pointed out that the Assistant Treasurer, Mrs. Anna Sacks Feinberg, has given the corporation many years of long and faithful service. Not only has she served the corporation devotedly, but with exceptional ability and skill. The

292

President pointed out that although all of the officers and directors sincerely hoped and desired that Mrs. Feinberg would continue in her present position for as long as she felt able, nevertheless, in view of the length of service which she has contributed provision should be made to afford her retirement privileges and benefits which should become a firm obligation of the corporation to be available to her whenever she should see fit to retire from active duty, however many years in the future such retirement may become effective. It was, accordingly, proposed that Mrs. Feinberg's salary which is presently $350.00 per month, be increased to $400.00 per month, and that Mrs. Feinberg would be given the privilege of retiring from active duty at any time she may elect to see fit so to do upon a retirement pay of $200.00 per month for life, with the distinct understanding that the retirement plan is merely being adopted at the present time in order to afford Mrs. Feinberg security for the future and in the hope that her active services will continue with the corporation for many years to come. After due discussion and consideration, and upon motion duly made and seconded, it was—

"Resolved, that the salary of Anna Sacks Feinberg be increased from $350.00 to $400.00 per month and that she be afforded the privilege of retiring from active duty in the corporation at any time she may elect to see fit so to do upon retirement pay of $200.00 per month, for the remainder of her life."

At the request of Mr. Lippman his sons-in-law, Messrs. Harris and Flammer, called upon the plaintiff at her apartment on the same day to advise her of the passage of the resolution. Plaintiff testified on cross-examination that she had no prior information that such a pension plan was contemplated, that it came as a surprise to her, and that she would have continued in her employment whether or not such a resolution had been adopted. It is clear from the evidence that there was no contract, oral or written, as to plaintiff's length of employment, and that she was free to quit, and the defendant to discharge her, at any time.

Plaintiff did continue to work for the defendant through June 30, 1949, on which date she retired. In accordance with the foregoing resolution, the defendant began paying her the sum of $200 on the first of each month. Mr. Lippman died on November 18, 1949, and was succeeded as president of the company by his widow. Because of an illness, she retired from that office and was succeeded in October, 1953, by her son-in-law, Sidney M. Harris. Mr. Harris testified that while Mrs. Lippman had been president she signed the monthly pension check paid plaintiff, but fussed about doing so, and considered the payments as gifts. After his election, he stated, a new accounting firm employed by the defendant questioned the validity of the payments to plaintiff on several occasions, and in the Spring of 1956, upon its recommendation, he consulted the Company's then attorney, Mr. Ralph Kalish. Harris testified that both Ernst and Ernst, the accounting firm, and Kalish told him there was no need of giving plaintiff the money. He also stated that he had concurred in the view that the payments to plaintiff were mere gratuities rather than amounts due under a contractual obligation, and that following his discussion with the Company's attorney plaintiff was sent a check for $100 on April 1, 1956. Plaintiff declined to accept the reduced amount, and this action followed. Additional facts will be referred to later in this opinion.

* * *

Appellant's next complaint is that there was insufficient evidence to support the court's finding that plaintiff would not have quit defendant's employ had she not known and relied upon the promise of defendant to pay her $200 a month for life, and the finding that, from her voluntary retirement until April 1, 1956, plaintiff relied upon the continued receipt of the pension installments. The trial court so found, and, in our opinion, justifiably so. Plaintiff testified, and was corroborated by Harris, defendant's witness, that knowledge of the passage of the resolution was communicated to her on December 27, 1947, the very day it was adopted. She was told at that time by Harris and Flammer, she stated, that she could take the pension as of that day, if she wished. She testified further that she continued to work for another year and a half, through June 30, 1949; that at that time her health was good and she could have continued to work, but that after working for almost forty years she thought she would take a rest. Her testimony continued:

"Q. Now, what was the reason—I'm sorry. Did you then quit the employment of the company after you—after this year and a half? A. Yes.

"Q. What was the reason that you left? A. Well, I thought almost forty years, it was a long time and I thought I would take a little rest.

"Q. Yes. A. And with the pension and what earnings my husband had, we figured we could get along.

"Q. Did you rely upon this pension? A. We certainly did.

"Q. Being paid? A. Very much so. We relied upon it because I was positive that I was going to get it as long as I lived.

"Q. Would you have left the employment of the company at that time had it not been for this pension? A. No.

"Mr. Allen: Just a minute, I object to that as calling for a conclusion and conjecture on the part of this witness.

"The Court: It will be overruled.

"Q. (Mr. Agatstein continuing): Go ahead, now. The question is whether you would have quit the employment of the company at that time had you not relied upon this pension plan? A. No, I wouldn't.

"Q. You would not have. Did you ever seek employment while this pension was being paid to you—A. (interrupting): No.

"Q. Wait a minute, at any time prior—at any other place? A. No sir.

"Q. Were you able to hold any other employment during that time? A. Yes, I think so.

"Q. Was your health good? A. My health was good."

It is obvious from the foregoing that there was ample evidence to support the findings of fact made by the court below.

We come, then, to the basic issue in the case. While otherwise defined in defendant's third and fourth assignments of error, it is thus succinctly stated in the argument in its brief: " * * * whether plaintiff has proved that she has a right to recover from defendant based upon a legally binding contractual obligation to pay her $200 per month for life."

It is defendant's contention, in essence, that the resolution adopted by its Board of Directors was a mere promise to make a gift, and that no contract resulted either thereby, or when plaintiff retired, because there was no consideration given or paid by the plaintiff. It urges that a promise to make a gift is not binding unless supported by a legal consideration; that the only apparent consideration for the adoption of the foregoing resolution was the "many years of long and faithful service" expressed therein; and that past services are not a valid consideration for a promise. Defendant argues further that there is nothing in the resolution which made its effectiveness conditional upon plaintiff's continued employment, that she was not under contract to work for any length of time but was free to quit whenever she wished, and that she had no contractual right to her position and could have been discharged at any time.

Plaintiff concedes that a promise based upon past services would be without consideration, but contends that there were two other elements which supplied the required element: First, the continuation by plaintiff in the employ of the defendant for the period from December 27, 1947, the date when the resolution was adopted, until the date of her retirement on June 30, 1949. And second, her change of position, i.e., her retirement, and the abandonment by her of her opportunity to continue in gainful employment, made in reliance on defendant's promise to pay her $200 per month for life.

We must agree with the defendant that the evidence does not support the first of these contentions. There is no language in the resolution predicating plaintiff's right to a pension upon her continued employment. She was not required to work for the defendant for any period of time as a condition to gaining such retirement benefits. She was told that she could quit the day upon which the resolution was adopted, as she herself testified, and it is clear from her own testimony that she made no promise or agreement to continue in the employ of the defendant in return for its promise to pay her a pension. Hence there was lacking that mutuality of obligation which is essential to the validity of a contract. * * *

But as to the second of these contentions we must agree with plaintiff. By the terms of the resolution defendant promised to pay plaintiff the sum of $200 a month upon her retirement. * * *

Section 90 of the Restatement of the Law of Contracts states that: "A promise which the promisor should reasonably expect to induce action or forbearance of a definite and substantial character on the part of the promisee and which does induce such action or forbearance is binding if injustice can be avoided only by enforcement of the promise." * * *

Rule

* * *

Was there such an act on the part of plaintiff, in reliance upon the promise contained in the resolution, as will estop the defendant, and therefore create an enforceable contract under the doctrine of promissory estoppel? We think there was. One of the illustrations cited under Section 90 of the Restatement is: "2. A promises B to pay him an annuity during B's life. B thereupon resigns a profitable employment, as A expected that he might. B receives the annuity for some years, in the meantime becoming disqualified from again obtaining good employment. A's promise is binding." This illustration is objected to by defendant as not being applicable to the case at hand. The reason advanced by it is that in the illustration B became "disqualified" from obtaining other employment *before* A discontinued the payments, whereas in this case the plaintiff did not discover that she had cancer and thereby became unemployable until *after* the defendant had discontinued the payments of $200 per month. We think the distinction is immaterial. The only reason for the reference in the illustration to the disqualification of A is in connection with that part of Section 90 regarding the prevention of injustice. The injustice would occur regardless of when the disability occurred. Would defendant contend that the contract would be enforceable if the plaintiff's illness had been discovered on March 31, 1956, the day before it discontinued the payment of the $200 a month, but not if it occurred on April 2nd, the day after? Furthermore, there are more ways to become disqualified for work, or unemployable, than as the result of illness. At the time she retired plaintiff was 57 years of age. At the time the payments were discontinued she was over 63 years of age. It is a matter of common knowledge that it is virtually impossible for a woman of that age to find satisfactory employment, much less a position comparable to that which plaintiff enjoyed at the time of her retirement.

The fact of the matter is that plaintiff's subsequent illness was not the "action or forbearance" which was induced by the promise contained in the resolution. As the trial court correctly decided, such action on plaintiff's part was her retirement from a lucrative position in reliance upon defendant's promise to pay her an annuity or pension. * * *

The Commissioner therefore recommends, for the reasons stated, that the judgment be affirmed.

Per Curiam.

The foregoing opinion by DOERNER, C., is adopted as the opinion of the court. The judgment is, accordingly, affirmed.

SHOEMAKER v. COMMONWEALTH BANK

Superior Court of Pennsylvania, 1997.
700 A.2d 1003.

JOHNSON, JUDGE: We are asked to determine whether a mortgagor who is obligated by a mortgage to maintain insurance on the mortgaged property can establish a cause of action in promissory estoppel based upon an oral promise made by the mortgagee to obtain insurance. We find no merit in those portions of the instant case sounding in fraud and breach of contract. We conclude, nevertheless, that a mortgagee's promise to obtain insurance can be actionable on a theory of promissory estoppel. Accordingly, on this appeal from the order granting summary judgment to the mortgagee, we affirm in part, reverse in part and remand for further proceedings.

Lorraine and Robert S. Shoemaker obtained a $25,000 mortgage on their home from Commonwealth Bank (Commonwealth). The mortgage agreement provided that the Shoemakers were required to "carry insurance" on the property. By January 1994, the Shoemakers had allowed the home-owners' insurance policy covering their home to expire. In 1995, the Shoemakers' home, still uninsured, was destroyed by fire. The parties disagree as to the series of events that occurred after the insurance had lapsed.

The Shoemakers allege that Commonwealth sent a letter to them, dated January 20, 1994, that informed them that their insurance had been cancelled and that if they did not purchase a new insurance policy, Commonwealth might "be forced to purchase [insurance] and add the premium to [their] loan balance." The Shoemakers further allege that Mrs. Shoemaker received a telephone call from a representative of Commonwealth in which the representative informed her that if the Shoemakers did not obtain insurance, Commonwealth would do so and would add the cost of the premium to the balance of the mortgage. The Shoemakers assert that they assumed, based on the letter and phone conversation, that Commonwealth had obtained insurance on their home. They also contend that they received no further contact from Commonwealth regarding the insurance and that they continued to pay premiums as a part of their loan payments. Only after the house burned, the Shoemakers allege, did they learn that the house was uninsured.

Commonwealth, on the other hand, admits that it sent the letter of January 20, but denies the Shoemakers' allegations regarding the contents of the alleged conversation between its representative and Mrs. Shoemaker. Commonwealth further claims that it obtained insurance coverage for the Shoemakers' home and notified them of this fact by a letter dated February 4, 1994. Commonwealth also asserts that it elected to allow this coverage to expire on December 1, 1994, and that, by the letter dated October 25, 1994, it informed the Shoemakers of this fact and reminded them of their obligation under the mortgage to carry insurance on the property. The Shoemakers deny receiving any letter from Commonwealth regarding the insurance other than the letter dated January 20, 1994, that informed them that their policy had expired.

After the house burned down, Mrs. Shoemaker sued Commonwealth, alleging causes of action in fraud, promissory estoppel and breach of contract; the basis for all three causes of action was Commonwealth's alleged failure to obtain insurance coverage for the Shoemaker home. By order of the court, Mr. Shoemaker was joined as an involuntary plaintiff. Commonwealth then filed a motion for summary judgment.

The trial court granted Commonwealth's motion. The court noted that, even if Commonwealth had promised to obtain insurance on the Shoemakers' home, it made no representation regarding the duration of that coverage. The court concluded that because Commonwealth had actually obtained insurance, even though the policy later expired, it had fulfilled its promise to the Shoemakers. Thus, the court reasoned that because Commonwealth had made no misrepresentation and breached no promise, the Shoemakers could not prevail on any of their causes of action. Mrs. Shoemaker now appeals.

* * *

On appeal, Mrs. Shoemaker argues that the trial court erred by entering summary judgment on their fraud and promissory estoppel claims. To prevail on a fraud cause of action, a plaintiff must prove that: (1) the defendant made a misrepresentation that is material to the transaction at hand; (2) the misrepresentation was made with knowledge of the statement's falsity or with reckless disregard as to whether it was true or false; (3) the defendant made the misrepresentation with the intent of inducing reliance; (4) the plaintiff justifiably relied upon the misrepresentation; and (5) the resulting injury was proximately caused by the reliance. *Gibbs v. Ernst*, 538 Pa. 193, 207, 647 A.2d 882, 889 (1994).

Mrs. Shoemaker argues that Commonwealth made a misrepresentation to her when its representative, in a telephone conversation, stated that Commonwealth would purchase insurance coverage and add the cost of the premium to the cost of her and her husband's loan. * * *

It is well-established that the breach of a promise to do something in the future is not actionable in fraud. *Krause v. Great Lakes Holdings, Inc.*, 387 Pa.Super. 56, 67, 563 A.2d 1182, 1187 (1989); *Edelstein v. Carole House Apartments, Inc.*, 220 Pa.Super. 298, 303, 286 A.2d 658, 661 (1971). The Shoemakers base their fraud claim on Commonwealth's alleged promise that it would obtain an insurance policy for their home if they failed to do so. Commonwealth was, therefore, promising to take future action. Thus, Commonwealth's promise cannot form the basis of a cause of action in fraud. *See Krause, supra*, at 67, 563 A.2d at 1187 (an oral representation that a party would assume a debt obligation in exchange for the forbearance from legal action was not actionable in fraud because the representation was a promise to do something in the future); *Edelstein, supra,* at 304, 286 A.2d at 661 (a promise to relieve person of liability if certain condition was met is not actionable in fraud because representation was promise to do something in the future). We therefore hold that the trial court properly granted summary judgment on the fraud claim.

Mrs. Shoemaker next argues that the trial court erred by granting summary judgment on their promissory estoppel claim. The doctrine of promissory estoppel allows a party, under certain circumstances, to enforce a promise even though that promise is not supported by consideration. *See Thatcher's Drug Store of West Goshen, Inc. v. Consolidated Supermarkets, Inc.,* 535 Pa. 469, 476, 636 A.2d 156, 160 (1994); Restatement (Second) of Contracts § 90. To establish a promissory estoppel cause of action, a party must prove that: (1) the promisor made a promise that he should have reasonably expected would induce action or forbearance on the part of the promisee; (2) the promisee actually took action or refrained from taking action in reliance on the promise; and (3) injustice can be avoided only by enforcing the promise. *Holewinski v. Children's Hospital of Pittsburgh,* 437 Pa.Super. 174, 178, 649 A.2d 712, 714 (1994). . . .

In their complaint, the Shoemakers allege that Commonwealth promised that it would purchase "adequate insurance" and add the cost of the premium to the cost of their loan. They further allege that they relied on this promise by not purchasing the insurance on their own and that injustice can be avoided only by enforcing Commonwealth's promise. Commonwealth, on the other hand, argues that the Shoemakers cannot enforce their claim through promissory estoppel because of the Shoemakers' contractual obligation to maintain insurance under the mortgage. Further, Commonwealth argues that even if such a promise was actionable, the facts alleged by the Shoemakers are insufficient to support their claim because they have not alleged that Commonwealth promised to maintain such insurance for a particular duration.

Our research has not discovered any Pennsylvania cases that have addressed the question of whether a mortgagor who is obligated by a mortgage to maintain insurance on their property can establish a cause of action in promissory estoppel based upon an oral promise made by the mortgagee to obtain insurance. We have, however, discovered cases from other jurisdictions that have addressed this question, and the weight of this authority holds that such promises are actionable.

In *Graddon v. Knight,* 138 Cal.App.2d 577, 292 P.2d 632 (1956), a California appellate court considered whether homeowners, who were obligated under a deed of trust to procure and maintain fire insurance on their home, could establish a cause of action based upon an oral promise by a bank to obtain the insurance on the homeowners' behalf. The court first considered whether the bank's promise to obtain fire insurance was inconsistent with the ... deed of trust [and] concluded that the bank's promise was not inconsistent with the homeowners' obligation under the deed of trust because the deed required only that the homeowners procure and maintain insurance; the deed did not bar them from making a separate agreement under which another party would procure the insurance on their behalf. *Id.* at 635–36. The court then held that the evidence presented by the plaintiffs was sufficient to establish a cause of action in promissory estoppel because the plaintiffs relied to their detriment on the bank's promise to obtain insurance. *Id.* at 636–37; *cf. Franklin Investment Co., Inc. v. Huffman*, 393 A.2d 119, 122 (D.C.1978) (a gratuitous promise to procure insurance on an automobile obligated the promisor under an estoppel theory to fulfill the promise and obtain insurance); *East Providence Credit Union v. Geremia*, 103 R.I. 597, 239 A.2d 725, 727–28 (1968) (an owner of chattels could recover based on a theory of promissory estoppel where a loan agreement obligated the owner to maintain insurance on the property; the owner relied on the lender's promise to obtain such insurance, the lender failed to do so and property [was] destroyed) (dicta); *Estes v. Lloyd Hammerstad, Inc.*, 8 Wash.App. 22, 503 P.2d 1149, 1152 (1972) (a gratuitous promise to obtain insurance was enforceable under an estoppel theory). In accord with these cases, illustration 13 to comment e of section 90 of the Restatement (Second) of Contracts provides:

> A, a bank, lends money to B on the security of a mortgage on B's new home. The mortgage requires B to insure the property. At the closing of the transaction A promises to arrange for the required insurance, and in reliance on the promise B fails to insure. Six months later the property, still uninsured, is destroyed by fire. The promise is binding.

Restatement (Second) of Contracts § 90, cmt. e, illus. 13. *See also Murphy v. Burke*, 454 Pa. 391, 398, 311 A.2d 904, 908 (1973) (adopting section 90 as Pennsylvania law). We find this authority persuasive and thus we reject Commonwealth's claim that the Shoemakers cannot maintain a cause of action because of their obligation under the mortgage to maintain insurance on the property.

We must next determine whether the Shoemakers' allegations and the evidence that they have presented are sufficient to create genuine issues of material fact with regard to each element of a promissory estoppel cause of action and thus survive Commonwealth's motion for summary judgment. The first element of a promissory estoppel cause of action is that the promisor made a promise that he should reasonably have expected to induce action or forbearance on the part of the promisee. Holewinski, supra, at 178, 649 A.2d at 714. The Shoemakers have alleged that the bank promised to obtain insurance on their behalf and that it would add this cost to their mortgage payment. Mrs. Shoemaker testified in her deposition and swore in an affidavit that a representative from Commonwealth stated that the bank would acquire insurance if she did not and that she instructed the representative to take that action. Because the Shoemakers claim that Commonwealth's promise to obtain insurance was, essentially, conditioned upon the Shoemakers course of conduct, i.e., that Commonwealth would obtain insurance if they did not, we conclude that this evidence, if believed, would be sufficient to allow a jury to find that Commonwealth made a promise upon which it reasonably should have expected the Shoemakers to rely. *See Holewinski, supra.*

The second element of a promissory estoppel cause of action is that the promisee actually relied upon the promise. *Id.* at 178, 649 A.2d at 714. The Shoemakers allege that they actually relied upon Commonwealth's promise and, thus, failed to obtain insurance. In support of this allegation, Mrs. Shoemaker testified in her deposition and swore in her affidavit that she instructed Commonwealth's representative to acquire insurance on her behalf. We conclude that this evidence, if believed, would be sufficient to allow a jury to find that the Shoemakers relied upon Commonwealth's promise to obtain insurance. See *Holewinski, supra.*

The final element of a promissory estoppel cause of action is that injustice can be avoided only by enforcement of the promise. *Id.* at 178, 649 A.2d at 714. One of the factors that a court may consider in determining whether a promisee has satisfied this element is " 'the reasonableness of the promisee's reliance.' " *Thatcher's Drug Store, supra,* at 477, 636 A.2d at 160, quoting Restatement (Second) of Contracts § 90, cmt. b. Mrs. Shoemaker testified that she and her husband received no communication from Commonwealth regarding their insurance after her conversation with a Commonwealth representative in early 1994. Commonwealth, on the other hand, asserts that it sent the Shoemakers letters informing them that their house would be uninsured after December 1, 1994. We conclude that this evidence is sufficient to create a genuine issue of material fact regarding the reasonableness of the Shoemakers' reliance. Accordingly, we hold that the trial court erred by granting summary judgment on the Shoemakers' promissory estoppel claim.

* * *

We therefore reverse that portion of the trial court's order that granted summary judgment on the Shoemakers' promissory estoppel claim and remand for trial on that claim. We affirm the grant of summary judgment on the Shoemakers' fraud and breach of contract claims.

Order AFFIRMED in part, REVERSED in part. Case REMANDED for further proceedings consistent with this Opinion. Jurisdiction RELINQUISHED.

SALSBURY v. NORTHWESTERN BELL TELEPHONE CO.

Supreme Court of Iowa, 1974.
221 N.W.2d 609.

HARRIS, JUSTICE.

* * *

John Salsbury (plaintiff) participated in the efforts to establish Charles City College (the college). He was the first and only chairman of the college's board of trustees. * * * As part of the funding drive Peter Bruno, a professional fund raiser, solicited a subscription from Northwestern Bell Telephone Company (defendant). Defendant's office manager in Charles City was Daryl V. Winder who was also active in the campaign to raise money for the college. Bruno negotiated a number of times with Winder for the subscription from defendant.

* * * Winder lacked authority to bind defendant for a pledge but conveyed the request to superiors in defendant corporation. Winder apparently did not have a pledge form available when he received defendant's consent for the subscription. Accordingly he wrote a letter to Bruno as follows:

> "This is to advise you that the contribution from Northwestern Bell Telephone Co. to the Charles City College has been approved by Mr. E.A. McDaniel, District Manager, Mason City.

> "The $15,000 contribution will be made over a three year period, in three equal payments. Our first $5000 payment will be made in 1968.

> "We are very pleased to add our name to the list of contributors to this fine community undertaking.

> "If I can be of further assistance, please feel free to contact me."

* * *

Cases throughout the country clearly reflect a conflict between the desired goal of enforcing charitable subscriptions and the realities of contract law. The result has been strained reasoning which has been the subject of considerable criticism. This criticism is directed toward efforts by the courts to secure a substitute for consideration in charitable subscriptions. These efforts were thought necessary to bind the subscriber on a contract theory. Yet, in the nature of charitable subscriptions, it is presupposed the promise is made as a gift and not in return for consideration. 1 Williston on Contracts, Third Ed., § 116, page 473.

Consideration sufficient for a binding contract has been found under various criticized theories. Id. at 476–479. We have found consideration in the promises of other subscribers. Brokaw v. McElroy, 162 Iowa 288, 143 N.W. 1087; Trustees v. Noyes, 165 Iowa 601, 146 N.W. 848; In re Estate of Leigh, 186 Iowa 931, 173 N.W. 143; Young Men's Christian Assn. v. Caward, 213 Iowa 408, 239 N.W. 41. This theory is also criticized:

> " * * * The difficulty with this view is its lack of conformity to the facts. It is doubtless possible for two or more persons to make mutual promises that each will give a specified amount to a charity or other object, but in the case of ordinary charitable subscriptions, the promise of each subscriber is made directly to the charity or its trustees, and it is frequently made without any reference to the

subscription of others. If induced at all by previous or expected subscriptions, this inducement only affects the motive of the subscriber; it cannot be said that the previous subscriptions were given in exchange for the later one. Indeed the earlier subscriptions would be open to the objection of being past consideration so far as a later subscription was concerned. * * *." 1 Williston on Contracts, supra, pages 476–477.

In reaction to this widespread criticism a number of courts have turned to promissory estoppel as an alternative for the consideration requirement. 1 Williston on Contracts, Third Ed., § 140, pages 607–619; C.J.S. Subscriptions, § 5b(2), 736 at 737–738; 73 Am.Jur.2d, Subscriptions, § 13, pages 704–705.

If promissory estoppel were to be the standard or criterion for enforcement this defendant probably could not be bound on the pledge. Estoppel can never arise unless there has been reliance. * * * Plaintiff relied on defendant's letter but not the form of it. Plaintiff conceded he had not even seen the letter until shortly before trial. * * *

We acknowledge as valid the criticism of cases which enforce charitable subscriptions only on a fictional finding of consideration. But we are reluctant to adopt promissory estoppel as the sole alternative basis for such enforcement.

" * * * [W]ide variation in reasoning indicates the difficulty of enforcing a charitable subscription on grounds of consideration. Yet, the courts have generally striven to find grounds for enforcement, indicating the depth of feeling in this country that private philanthropy serves a highly important function in our society.

"Of late, courts have tended to abandon the attempt to utilize traditional contract doctrines to sustain subscriptions and have placed their decision on grounds of promissory estoppel. Surprisingly, however, if promissory estoppel, in its traditional form, is widely adopted as the grounds upon which such subscriptions are to be tested, fewer subscriptions are likely to be enforced than previously. Under previous holdings, despite the conceptual inadequacy of the reasoning, promises were frequently enforced without regard to detrimental reliance on the promise. It was enough that the promisor had subscribed. If enforcement of charitable subscriptions is a desirable goal, it would seem sounder to view the preponderance of the cases as supporting the proposition that a charitable subscription is enforceable without consideration and without detrimental reliance. This seems to be the position taken in Restatement Second. Recognition of such a rule would also put an end to the flood of needless litigation created by the caution of executors and administrators who, for self-protection against surcharging, will not pay out on a subscription without a court decree." Calamari & Perillo, Law of Contracts, § 103, pages 177–178.

The tentative draft of Restatement of Contracts, Second, includes a new subparagraph 2. Section 90 now reads as follows:

"(1) A promise which the promisor should reasonably expect to induce action or forbearance on the part of the promisee or a third person and which does induce such action or forbearance is binding if injustice can be avoided only by enforcement of the promise. The remedy granted for breach may be limited as justice requires.

"(2) A charitable subscription or a marriage settlement is binding under Subsection (1) without proof that the promise induced action or forbearance."

We believe public policy supports this view. It is more logical to bind charitable subscriptions without requiring a showing of consideration or detrimental reliance.

Charitable subscriptions often serve the public interest by making possible projects which otherwise could never come about. It is true some fund raising campaigns are not conducted on a plan which calls for subscriptions to be binding. In such cases we do not hesitate to hold them not binding. However where a subscription is unequivocal the pledgor should be made to keep his word.

Affirmed.

DRENNAN v. STAR PAVING CO.

Supreme Court of California, In Bank, 1958.
51 Cal.2d 409, 333 P.2d 757.

TRAYNOR, JUSTICE.

Defendant appeals from a judgment for plaintiff in an action to recover damages caused by defendant's refusal to perform certain paving work according to a bid it submitted to plaintiff.

On July 28, 1955, plaintiff, a licensed general contractor, was preparing a bid on the "Monte Vista School Job" in the Lancaster school district. Bids had to be submitted before 8:00 p.m. Plaintiff testified that it was customary in that area for general contractors to receive the bids of subcontractors by telephone on the day set for bidding and to rely on them in computing their own bids. Thus on that day plaintiff's secretary, Mrs. Johnson, received by telephone between fifty and seventy-five subcontractors' bids for various parts of the school job. As each bid came in, she wrote it on a special form, which she brought into plaintiff's office. He then posted it on a master cost sheet setting forth the names and bids of all subcontractors. His own bid had to include the names of subcontractors who were to perform one-half of one per cent or more of the construction work, and he had also to provide a bidder's bond of ten per cent of his total bid of $317,385 as a guarantee that he would enter the contract if awarded the work.

Late in the afternoon, Mrs. Johnson had a telephone conversation with Kenneth R. Hoon, an estimator for defendant. He gave his name and telephone number and stated that he was bidding for defendant for the paving work at the Monte Vista School according to plans and specifications and that his bid was $7,131.60. At Mrs. Johnson's request he repeated his bid. Plaintiff listened to the bid over an extension telephone in his office and posted it on the master sheet after receiving the bid form from Mrs. Johnson. Defendant's was the lowest bid for the paving. Plaintiff computed his own bid accordingly and submitted it with the name of defendant as the subcontractor for the paving. When the bids were opened on July 28th, plaintiff's proved to be the lowest, and he was awarded the contract.

On his way to Los Angeles the next morning plaintiff stopped at defendant's office. The first person he met was defendant's construction engineer, Mr. Oppenheimer. Plaintiff testified: "I introduced myself and he immediately told me that they had made a mistake in their bid to me the night before, they couldn't do it for the price they had bid, and I told him I would expect him to carry through with their original bid because I had used it in compiling my bid and the job was being awarded them. And I would have to go and do the job according to my bid and I would expect them to do the same."

Defendant refused to do the paving work for less than $15,000. Plaintiff testified that he "got figures from other people" and after trying for several months to get as low a bid as possible engaged L & H Paving Company, a firm in Lancaster, to do the work for $10,948.60.

The trial court found on substantial evidence that defendant made a definite offer to do the paving on the Monte Vista job according to the plans and specifications for $7,131.60, and that plaintiff relied on defendant's bid in computing his own bid for the school job and naming defendant therein as the subcontractor for the paving work. Accordingly, it entered judgment for plaintiff in the amount of $3,817.00 (the difference between defendant's bid and the cost of the paving to plaintiff) plus costs.

Defendant contends that there was no enforceable contract between the parties on the ground that it made a revocable offer and revoked it before plaintiff communicated his acceptance to defendant.

There is no evidence that defendant offered to make its bid irrevocable in exchange for plaintiff's use of its figures in computing his bid. Nor is there evidence that would warrant interpreting plaintiff's use of defendant's bid as the acceptance thereof, binding plaintiff, on condition he received the main contract, to award the subcontract to defendant. In sum, there was neither an option supported by consideration nor a bilateral contract binding on both parties.

Plaintiff contends, however, that he relied to his detriment on defendant's offer and that defendant must therefore answer in damages for its refusal to perform. Thus the question is squarely presented: Did plaintiff's reliance make defendant's offer irrevocable?

Section 90 of the Restatement of Contracts states: "A promise which the promisor should reasonably expect to induce action or forbearance of a definite and substantial character on the part of the promisee and which does induce such action or forbearance is binding if injustice can be avoided only by enforcement of the promise." This rule applies in this state. * * *

Defendant's offer constituted a promise to perform on such conditions as were stated expressly or by implication therein or annexed thereto by operation of law. (See 1 Williston, Contracts [3rd. ed.], § 24A, p. 56, § 61, p. 196.) Defendant had reason to expect that if its bid proved the lowest it would be used by plaintiff. It induced "action ... of a definite and substantial character on the part of the promisee."

Had defendant's bid expressly stated or clearly implied that it was revocable at any time before acceptance we would treat it accordingly. It was silent on revocation, however, and we must therefore determine whether there are conditions to the right of revocation imposed by law or reasonably inferable in fact. In the analogous problem of an offer for a unilateral contract, the theory is now obsolete that the offer is revocable at any time before complete performance. Thus section 45 of the Restatement of Contracts provides: "If an offer for a unilateral contract is made, and part of the consideration requested in the offer is given or tendered by the offeree in response thereto, the offeror is bound by a contract, the duty of immediate performance of which is conditional on the full consideration being given or tendered within the time stated in the offer, or, if no time is stated therein, within a reasonable time." In explanation, comment *b* states that the "main offer includes as a subsidiary promise, necessarily implied, that if part of the requested performance is given, the offeror will not revoke his offer, and that if tender is made it will be accepted. Part performance or tender may thus furnish consideration for the subsidiary promise. Moreover, merely acting in justifiable reliance on an offer may in some cases serve as sufficient reason for making a promise binding (see § 90)."

Whether implied in fact or law, the subsidiary promise serves to preclude the injustice that would result if the offer could be revoked after the offeree had acted in detrimental reliance thereon. Reasonable reliance resulting in a foreseeable prejudicial change in position affords a compelling basis also for implying a subsidiary promise not to revoke an offer for a bilateral contract.

The absence of consideration is not fatal to the enforcement of such a promise. It is true that in the case of unilateral contracts the Restatement finds consideration for the implied subsidiary promise in the part performance of the bargained-for exchange, but its reference to section 90 makes clear that consideration for such a promise is not always necessary. The very purpose of section 90 is to make a promise binding even though there was no consideration "in the sense of something that is bargained for and given in exchange." (See 1 Corbin, Contracts, § 634 et seq.) Reasonable reliance serves to hold the offeror in lieu of the consideration ordinarily required to make the offer binding. In a case involving similar facts the Supreme Court of South Dakota stated that "we believe that reason and justice demand that the doctrine [of section 90] be applied to the present facts. We cannot believe that by accepting this doctrine as controlling in the state of facts before us we will abolish the requirement of a consideration in contract cases, in any different sense than an ordinary estoppel abolishes some legal requirement in its application. We are of the opinion, therefore, that the defendants in executing the agreement [which was not supported by consideration] made a promise which they should have reasonably expected would induce the plaintiff to submit a bid based thereon to the Government, that such promise did induce this action, and that injustice can be avoided only by enforcement of the promise." Northwestern Engineering Co. v. Ellerman, 69 S.D. 397, 408, 10 N.W.2d 879, 884; see also, Robert Gordon, Inc. v. Ingersoll–Rand Co., 7 Cir., 117 F.2d 654, 661; cf. James Baird Co. v. Gimbel Bros., 2 Cir., 64 F.2d 344.

When plaintiff used defendant's offer in computing his own bid, he bound himself to perform in reliance on defendant's terms. Though defendant did not bargain for this use of its bid neither did defendant make it idly, indifferent to whether it would be used or not. On the contrary it is reasonable to suppose that defendant submitted its bid to obtain the subcontract. It was bound to realize the substantial possibility that its bid would be the lowest, and that it would be included by plaintiff in his bid. It was to its own interest that the contractor be awarded the general contract; the lower the subcontract bid, the lower the general contractor's bid was likely to be and the greater its chance of acceptance and hence the greater defendant's chance of getting the paving subcontract. Defendant had reason not only to expect plaintiff to rely on its bid but to want him to. Clearly defendant had a stake in plaintiff's reliance on its bid. Given this interest and the fact that plaintiff is bound by his own bid, it is only fair that plaintiff should have at least an opportunity to accept defendant's bid after the general contract has been awarded to him.

It bears noting that a general contractor is not free to delay acceptance after he has been awarded the general contract in the hope of getting a better price. Nor can he reopen bargaining with the subcontractor and at the same time claim a continuing right to accept the original offer. See, R.J. Daum Const. Co. v. Child, Utah, 247 P.2d 817, 823. In the present case plaintiff promptly informed defendant that plaintiff was being awarded the job and that the subcontract was being awarded to defendant.

Defendant contends, however, that its bid was the result of mistake and that it was therefore entitled to revoke it. It relies on the rescission cases of M.F. Kemper Const. Co. v. City of Los Angeles, 37 Cal.2d 696, 235 P.2d 7, and Brunzell Const. Co. v. G.J. Weisbrod, Inc., 134 Cal. App.2d 278, 285 P.2d 989. See also, Lemoge Electric v. San Mateo County, 46 Cal.2d 659, 662, 297 P.2d 638. In those cases, however, the bidder's mistake was known or should have been known to the offeree, and the offeree could be placed in status quo. Of course, if plaintiff had reason to believe that defendant's bid was in error, he could not justifiably rely on it, and section 90 would afford no basis for enforcing it. Robert Gordon, Inc. v. Ingersoll–Rand, Inc., 7 Cir., 117 F.2d 654, 660. Plaintiff, however, had no reason to know that defendant had made a mistake in submitting its bid, since there was usually a variance of 160 per cent between the highest and lowest bids for paving in the desert around Lancaster. He committed himself to performing the main contract in reliance on defendant's figures. Under these circumstances defendant's mistake, far from relieving it of its obligation, constitutes an additional reason for enforcing it, for it misled plaintiff as to the cost of doing the paving. Even had it been clearly understood that defendant's offer was revocable until accepted, it would not necessarily follow that defendant had no duty to exercise reasonable care in preparing its bid. It presented its bid with knowledge of the substantial possibility that it would be used by plaintiff; it could foresee the harm that would ensue from an erroneous underestimate of the cost. Moreover, it was motivated by its own business interest. Whether or not these considerations alone would justify recovery for negligence had the case been tried on that theory (see Biakanja v. Irving, 49 Cal.2d 647, 650, 320 P.2d 16), they are persuasive that defendant's mistake should not defeat recovery under the rule of section 90 of the Restatement of Contracts. As between the subcontractor who made the bid and the general contractor who reasonably relied on it, the loss resulting from the mistake should fall on the party who caused it.

Leo F. Piazza Paving Co. v. Bebek & Brkich, 141 Cal.App.2d 226, 296 P.2d 368, 371, and Bard v. Kent, 19 Cal.2d 449, 122 P.2d 8, 139 A.L.R. 1032, are not to the contrary. In the Piazza case the court sustained a finding that defendants intended, not to make a firm bid, but only to give the plaintiff "some kind of an idea to use" in making its bid; there was evidence that the defendants had told plaintiff they were unsure of the significance of the specifications. There was thus no offer, promise, or representation on which the defendants should reasonably have expected the plaintiff to rely. The Bard case held that an option not supported by consideration was revoked by the death of the optionor. The issue of recovery under the rule of section 90 was not pleaded at the trial, and it does not appear that the offeree's reliance was "of a definite and substantial character" so that injustice could be avoided "only by the enforcement of the promise."

There is no merit in defendant's contention that plaintiff failed to state a cause of action, on the ground that the complaint failed to allege that plaintiff attempted to mitigate the damages or that they could not have been mitigated. Plaintiff alleged that after defendant's default, "plaintiff had to procure the services of the L & H Co. to perform said asphaltic paving for the sum of $10,948.60." Plaintiff's uncontradicted evidence showed that he spent several months trying to get bids from other subcontractors and that he took the lowest bid. Clearly he acted reasonably to mitigate damages. In any event any uncertainty in plaintiff's allegation as to damages could have been raised by special demurrer. Code Civ.Proc. § 430, subd. 9. It was not so raised and was therefore waived. Code Civ.Proc. § 434.

The judgment is affirmed.

GROUSE v. GROUP HEALTH PLAN, INC.

Supreme Court of Minnesota, 1981.
306 N.W.2d 114.

OTIS, JUSTICE.

Plaintiff John Grouse appeals from a judgment in favor of Group Health Plan, Inc., in this action for damages resulting from repudiation of an employment offer. The narrow issue raised is whether the trial court erred by concluding that Grouse's complaint fails to state a claim upon which relief can be granted. In our view, the doctrine of promissory estoppel entitles Grouse to recover and we, therefore, reverse and remand for a new trial on the issue of damages.

The facts relevant to this appeal are essentially undisputed. Grouse, a 1974 graduate of the University of Minnesota School of Pharmacy, was employed in 1975 as a retail pharmacist at Richter Drug in Minneapolis. He worked approximately 41 hours per week earning $7 per hour. Grouse desired employment in a hospital or clinical setting, however, because of the work environment and the increased compensation and benefits. In the summer of 1975 he was advised by the Health Sciences Placement office at the University that Group Health was seeking a pharmacist.

Grouse called Group Health and was told to come in and fill out an application. He did so in September and was, at that time, interviewed by Cyrus Elliott, Group Health's Chief Pharmacist. Approximately 2 weeks later Elliott contacted Grouse and asked him to come in for an interview with Donald Shoberg, Group Health's General Manager. Shoberg explained company policies and procedures as well as salary and benefits. Following this meeting Grouse again spoke with Elliott who told him to be patient, that it was necessary to interview recent graduates before making an offer.

On December 4, 1975, Elliott telephoned Grouse at Richter Drug and offered him a position as a pharmacist at Group Health's St. Louis Park Clinic. Grouse accepted but informed Elliott that 2 week's notice to Richter Drug would be necessary. That afternoon Grouse received an offer from a Veteran's Administration Hospital in Virginia which he declined because of Group Health's offer. Elliott called back to confirm that Grouse had resigned.

Sometime in the next few days Elliott mentioned to Shoberg that he had hired, or was thinking of hiring, Grouse. Shoberg told him that company hiring requirements included a favorable written reference, a background check, and approval of the general manager. Elliott contacted two faculty members at the School of Pharmacy who declined to give references. He also contacted an internship employer and several pharmacies where Grouse had done relief work. Their responses were that they had not had enough exposure to Grouse's work to form a judgment as to his capabilities. Elliott did not contact Richter because Grouse's application requested that he not be contacted. Because Elliott was unable to supply a favorable reference for Grouse, Shoberg hired another person to fill the position.

On December 15, 1975 Grouse called Group Health and reported that he was free to begin work. Elliott informed Grouse that someone else had been hired. Grouse complained to the director of Group Health who apologized but took no other action. Grouse experienced difficulty regaining full time employment and suffered wage loss as a result. He commenced this suit to recover damages; the trial judge found that he had not stated an actionable claim.

In our view the principle of contract law applicable here is promissory estoppel. Its effect is to imply a contract in law where none exists in fact. *Del Hayes & Sons, Inc. v. Mitchell,* 304 Minn. 275, 230 N.W.2d 588 (1975). On these facts no contract exists because due to the bilateral power of termination neither party is committed to performance and the promises are, therefore, illusory. The elements of promissory estoppel are stated in *Restatement of Contracts* § 90 (1932):

> A promise which the promisor should reasonably expect to induce action or forbearance * * * on the part of the promisee and which does induce such action or forbearance is binding if injustice can be avoided only by enforcement of the promise.

Group Health knew that to accept its offer Grouse would have to resign his employment at Richter Drug. Grouse promptly gave notice to Richter Drug and informed Group Health that he had done so when specifically asked by Elliott. Under these circumstances it would be unjust not to hold Group Health to its promise.

The parties focus their arguments on whether an employment contract which is terminable at will can give rise to an action for damages if anticipatorily repudiated. * * * Group Health contends that recognition of a cause of action on these facts would result in the anomalous rule that an employee who is told not to report to work the day before he is scheduled to begin has a remedy while an employee who is discharged after the first day does not. We cannot agree since under appropriate circumstances we believe section 90 would apply even after employment has begun.

When a promise is enforced pursuant to section 90 "[t]he remedy granted for breach may be limited as justice requires." Relief may be limited to damages measured by the promisee's reliance.

The conclusion we reach does not imply that an employer will be liable whenever he discharges an employee whose term of employment is at will. What we do hold is that under the facts of this case the appellant had a right to assume he would be given a good faith opportunity to perform his duties to the satisfaction of respondent once he was on the job. He was not only denied that opportunity but resigned the position he already held in reliance on the firm offer which respondent tendered him. Since, as respondent points out, the prospective employment might have been terminated at any time, the measure of damages is not so much what he would have earned from respondent as what he lost in quitting the job he held and in declining at least one other offer of employment elsewhere.

Reversed and remanded for a new trial on the issue of damages.

WERNER v. XEROX CORP.

United States Court of Appeals, Seventh Circuit, 1984.
732 F.2d 580.

BAUER, CIRCUIT JUDGE.

Plaintiffs John A. Werner and W & D Services, Inc., appeal the decision of the district court awarding them $19,600 in damages on their promissory estoppel claim against defendant Xerox Corporation. Xerox cross-appeals. We affirm.

I. FACTS

This promissory estoppel action arises from the business relationship between W & D and Xerox. John A. Werner is a consulting engineer with considerable experience in the design and manufacture of special metal working machinery. During the twelve years preceding the trial in this case, Werner had been doing business principally through W & D Services, a corporation which he formed to build special metal working machinery and of which he is the sole owner.

Xerox Corporation, which manufactures photocopying machines, sought to improve the process used in manufacturing metal rollers for its machines. Acting generally through Frank Wolf, a Manufacturing Technology Specialist at Xerox, Xerox conducted a world-wide search for a manufacturer that would produce the machines capable of making these improved rollers. When Wolf completed the search in October 1978, he had discovered only four manufacturers, one of which was W & D, who were capable of producing the machines and rollers.

From April 1978 to November 1979, W & D made prototype rollers and performed developmental work for Xerox on an old lathe which W & D previously had assembled. Although the lathe could not produce rollers to Xerox's specifications, Xerox was sufficiently encouraged by the results to request a price quotation from W & D for designing and building a similar machine. In November 1978, Xerox issued a purchase order to W & D for a new machine. In March and November, 1979, Xerox ordered two additional machines, even though the first had not yet been qualified as meeting Xerox's specifications. During 1980, W & D delivered all three machines to Xerox for installation.

Xerox planned to use these three machines to produce the improved rollers at its plant in Rochester, New York. With regard to these three machines, many of the dealings between Xerox and W & D were expressly covered by a series of agreements embodied in quotations and invoices. The district court found that Xerox fully performed its obligations under these agreements. Neither party contests this finding on appeal.

The basis of this appeal is what, if any, additional obligations Xerox may owe to W & D. Xerox contends that these agreements encompass its entire relationship with W & D, that it has fulfilled all its obligations to W & D, and that W & D has sustained no damage. W & D contends that Xerox is liable for damages which W & D sustained through reliance on Wolf's representations to W & D.

The district court agreed in part with W & D. The district court found that Xerox, through Wolf, offered to make W & D the principal off-load producer of Xerox rollers. At the time Xerox was looking for a company to manufacture the machine that would produce its new rollers, Xerox also was searching for an off-load producer for its improved rollers. Establishing an off-load producer would allow Xerox to meet demands for relatively small quantities of rollers without changing its in-house machines to accommodate the specifications of smaller runs.

The court based its conclusion regarding Wolf's offer to establish Werner as the principal off-load supplier on representations that Wolf made to Werner, two of which were specifically cited by the district court in its order. First, in early 1978, Werner and Wolf visited the Church Metals Spinning Company, which was owned by Don and Gene Verhein. Werner there showed Wolf a machine that Werner had designed for Church Metals, which Werner exhibited as a prototype of the machine he could build for Xerox for its in-house production of the rollers. During this meeting Wolf proposed both that Werner build a machine to manufacture rollers for Xerox and that "if they were 'smart' they would build a machine for themselves and run off parts for Xerox." The district court concluded that Wolf "painted a rosy picture of Werner's future as a off-load supplier of parts for Xerox."

Second, in November 1978, Werner and the Verheins formed the Q.E.D. Corporation, which leased a facility for manufacturing the machines for Xerox. At the same time, Q.E.D. leased additional space for producing off-load rollers. Manufacturing the machines required a facility with heavy equipment, whereas producing rollers required space for raw materials, a machine to produce the parts, inspection equipment, and shipping facilities. According to the district court, Wolf visited Q.E.D., "saw the space that was leased and thought it adequate for a production facility and reassured Werner that producing parts would be a 'nice little business' to get into, and one that would 'really pay.'"

In July 1979, Dr. Charles Downey, the manager of Wolf's department at Xerox, visited the Q.E.D. Corporation. Werner testified at trial that Downey told him and the Verheins that they "would never make parts for Xerox at this facility." Werner further testified that he and the Verheins were astounded by Downey's statement. After Downey's visit, Werner contacted Wolf, who told him to disregard Downey's statements and that Downey "didn't know what he was talking about." On other occasions Wolf continued to reassure Werner that he would be an off-load supplier. Nevertheless, the Verheins sued Werner for a refund of their investment in Q.E.D., basing their suit on misrepresentations and deceit by Werner. Werner, however, used W & D to continue preparing the new facility to be an off-load supplier. In October 1980, after W & D delivered the third machine to Xerox, Xerox prepared to run off-load parts in its own plant and terminated its relationship with Werner.

Werner and W & D sued Xerox to recover damages based on theories of breach of contract, promissory estoppel, and deceit. The court rejected the plaintiffs' claims of breach of contract and deceit, but entered judgment in favor of the plaintiffs for $19,600 based on promissory estoppel. The court found that Werner reasonably had relied on Xerox's representations through July 1979, but that he "had no basis for relying on Wolf after the Downey statements were made." The court thus refused to award Werner damages for expenses he incurred after July 1979.

II. Promissory Estoppel

In the landmark case of *Hoffman v. Red Owl Stores, Inc.*, 26 Wis.2d 683, 133 N.W.2d 267 (1965), the Wisconsin Supreme Court established three conditions for application of promissory estoppel:

(1) Was the promise one which the promisor should reasonably expect to induce action or forbearance of a definite and substantial character on the part of the promisee?

(2) Did the promise induce such action or forbearance?

(3) Can injustice be avoided only by enforcement of the promise?

Id. at 698, 133 N.W.2d at 275.

The first two conditions are questions of fact and we will not set aside the court's findings unless clearly erroneous. F.R.C.P. 52(a). 26 Wis.2d at 698, 133 N.W.2d at 275. The third condition requires the court to make a policy decision that necessarily requires the exercise of discretion, *id.*, which decision we will not reverse absent a showing that the court abused its discretion. We affirm the district court's conclusions on each element of the *Red Owl* test.

First, the district court determined that Xerox, through Wolf, promised Werner that he would be an off-load parts supplier for Xerox. Wolf's promises were more than mere representations regarding what Xerox might do in the future. The district court found that Wolf consistently and actively encouraged Werner to set up an off-load supply facility and that Wolf approved of Werner's progress toward that goal. Xerox should have reasonably expected Wolf's actions to induce W & D's action.[1] The district court found, however, that Werner could not reasonably have relied on Xerox's promises after Downey's visit in July 1979, when

---

1. If Xerox's promise had been merely a promise of some future conduct, this action would fail because such a promise of future conduct on the part of Xerox is not the kind of promise which Xerox "should reasonably expect to induce action or forbearance of a definite and substantial character" on the part of Werner. Such a promise would be unenforceable under theories of promissory estoppel because it would be subject to too many contingencies. *See Gruen Industries, Inc. v. Biller*, 608 F.2d 274, 280–81 (7th Cir.1979).

Downey told Werner and the Verheins that they would never make off-load parts for Xerox. The district court had to weigh much evidence and determine the credibility of the witnesses to find a promise from Xerox to W & D. Both Werner and Wolf testified at length at the trial regarding the extent and nature of the business relationship between W & D and Xerox. The district court specifically found that Werner was "a more credible witness," and that his testimony was "more deserving of belief than that of Mr. Wolf on the aspects of the case where their testimony differs." We will not reweigh those determinations here. Werner's testimony was a crucial part of the district court's finding that Xerox made promises to W & D. These findings are not clearly erroneous.

Second, the district court found that until July 1979, Wolf's promises did induce Werner's action. Werner contends that Xerox's promises induced action on his part through October 1980. The court found, however, that after July 1979 Werner's reliance upon Wolf's statements was not justified. Xerox agrees that any reliance upon Wolf's "reassurances" after July 1979 were not justified in the light of Downey's unequivocal statement to Werner and the Verheins.

Werner claims that the court based this finding upon an improper legal standard. Werner contends that under *Red Owl* the promisee's reliance need only be in the exercise of ordinary care. 26 Wis.2d at 697, 133 N.W.2d at 274. Werner thus suggests that when the district court required that Werner's reliance have been "justifiable," it raised the legal standard beyond ordinary care, even though the "justifiable reliance" language is taken from our decision in *Janke Construction Company v. Vulcan Materials,* 527 F.2d 772, 779 (7th Cir.1976). Xerox counters this argument by contending that whether the promisee's reliance needs to be "in the exercise of ordinary care" or "justifiable" makes no difference under the theory of promissory estoppel. We agree that both terms are merely different ways of expressing the same concept: the promisee's reliance must be reasonable to recover damages. Werner's conduct, as the district court found, was reasonable until July 1979, when Downey's statements were made. At that point, any reliance by Werner on Wolf's representations clearly was unreasonable. No prudent businessman would have considered proceeding as if nothing had happened, as Werner apparently did in this case. The district court's holding on the second prong of *Red Owl* therefore was not clearly erroneous.

Third, the district court held that injustice could be avoided only by enforcement of Wolf's promise. This determination necessarily requires the exercise of the trial court's discretion, 26 Wis.2d at 698, 133 N.W.2d at 275, and we will reverse the court only upon a showing that it has abused that discretion. Here, it was not "very speculative that the plaintiff has actually suffered from his reliance," *Silberman v. Roethe,* 64 Wis.2d 131, 144, 218 N.W.2d 723, 729 (1974), but instead Werner incurred substantial detriment in reliance on Xerox's promises. The trial court found that, to his detriment, Werner "deviated from his usual manner of doing business, . . . leased a large facility[, went] into business with the Verheims (sic) and hired an employee, Robert Parr, to work for the newly created corporation." On the record before us, the court's finding was not an abuse of discretion.

III. DAMAGES

Xerox, on cross-appeal, contends that the $19,600 damage award is unsupported by the facts and the applicable law. Damages in promissory estoppel actions are limited to reliance damages, *Janke Construction*, 527 F.2d at 780, and the trial judge has wide latitude in the affixing of damages. *Harry Alter Co. v. Chrysler Corp.*, 285 F.2d 903, 907 (7th Cir.1961). We will overturn an award of damages only if it is clearly erroneous.

The district court reviewed the large damage claim submitted by plaintiffs, examined the supporting documents, and concluded that a fair and reasonable damage figure, incurred in reliance upon Xerox's promises, was $19,600. Those damages consisted of $3,500 for a portion of Parr's salary, $2,000 for some of the shop supplies and equipment, $5,100 for part of the rent and telephone expenses, and $9,000 for a portion of the costs involved in the Verhein's lawsuit against Werner. Nothing in the record supports a conclusion that this award is clearly erroneous.

* * *

For the above stated reasons, the judgment of the district court is affirmed.

Affirmed.

DELI v. UNIVERSITY OF MINNESOTA

Court of Appeals of Minnesota, 1998.
578 N.W.2d 779.

SHORT, JUDGE.

Katalin Deli seeks to hold the University of Minnesota liable for emotional distress damages arising from its athletic director's breach of an oral promise not to view a videotape that contained both the University's gymnastics team performance at a 1992 Florida competition and Deli's sexual encounter with her husband in a Florida hotel room. On appeal from an award in Deli's favor, the University argues its legal obligation and the doctrine of immunity preclude Deli's promissory estoppel claim. In the alternative, the University argues Deli cannot recover emotional distress damages on a contract-based claim and the trial court erred by submitting Deli's equitable claim to the jury.

FACTS

Deli was head coach of the University of Minnesota women's gymnastics team from 1973 to 1992. Her husband worked as an assistant coach from 1976 to 1992. In January 1992, Deli and her husband videotaped the team's performance at a Florida competition using University equipment. During their Florida stay, Deli's husband also used the University's equipment to videotape the couple having sexual relations in their hotel room. On the airplane home, one student asked Deli's husband if she could borrow the videotape to review the team's performance. Deli's husband gave the student the videotape, which contained both the Florida competition and the Delis' hotel room encounter. Before Deli could recover the videotape, several students and another assistant coach had watched the tape. A parent of one of those students complained to the women's athletic director about the sexually explicit videotape.

The athletic director conducted an investigation. The Delis initially said the sex scenes were accidentally recorded while the camera's batteries were being charged. However, the athletic director discovered students were given a 1991 videotape from a competition at UCLA that also contained an earlier sexual encounter between the Delis. On March 3, 1992, the athletic director asked Deli for the Florida videotape, and orally promised that she would not view it. On March 12, the athletic director sent Deli and her husband confidential memoranda advising that failure to surrender the unaltered tapes of both the Florida and UCLA competitions by noon the following day would result in disciplinary action. On March 13, Deli surrendered only the Florida tape because her husband had erased the UCLA videotape. At the direction of the University's legal counsel, the director reviewed and took notes on the videotape's contents.

On April 12, 1993, the University discharged Deli for reasons unrelated to the Florida videotape. *Deli v. University of Minn.*, 511 N.W.2d 46, 53–54 (Minn.App.1994), *review denied* (Minn. Mar. 23, 1994). [Insubordination, lying to athletic director, violation of rules. Ed.] Following an unsuccessful challenge to her termination, Deli filed this action against the University alleging violation of Minn.Stat. §§ 13.01–.99 (1996) (Data Practices Act), breach of contract, unjust enrichment, and promissory estoppel. The trial court granted summary judgment in the University's favor. We affirmed that judgment in part, but reversed and remanded on the data practices and promissory estoppel claims. *Deli v. Hasselmo*, 542 N.W.2d 649, 658 (Minn.App.1996), *review denied* (Minn. Apr. 26, 1996). Before trial, the court again granted summary judgment on the data practices claim. The jury returned a special verdict in favor of Deli on her promissory estoppel claim. Concluding that injustice could only be avoided through enforcement of the director's promise, the trial court awarded Deli $675,000 in damages for emotional distress suffered to the time of trial.

ISSUE

Absent the existence of an independent tort claim, are emotional distress damages recoverable in Deli's promissory estoppel action?

ANALYSIS

* * *

Promissory estoppel implies a contract in law where no contract exists in fact. *Del Hayes & Sons, Inc. v. Mitchell*, 304 Minn. 275, 283, 230 N.W.2d 588, 593 (1975). Under the doctrine of promissory estoppel, a promise may be enforced when (1) it is clear and definite, (2) the promisor intended to induce the promisee to rely on the promise, (3) the promisee detrimentally relied on the promise, and (4) enforcement of the promise is required to prevent an injustice. *See Cohen v. Cowles Media Co.*, 479 N.W.2d 387, 391 (Minn.1992) (providing elements of promissory estoppel). Thus, a promissory estoppel claim sounds in contract. *See Cohen*, 479 N.W.2d at 390 (concluding promissory estoppel variation of contract theory); *Grouse v. Group Health Plan, Inc.*, 306 N.W.2d 114, 116 (Minn.1981) (concluding promissory estoppel is principle of contract law); *see generally* Comment, *Once More Into the Breach: Promissory Estoppel and Traditional Damage Doctrine*, 37 U. Chi. L.Rev. 559, 562–63 (1970) (noting it is clear from systematics of Restatement and its legislative history that promises enforceable under § 90 entitled to whatever remedy prescribed for breach of contract); *see, e.g., Pine Valley Meats, Inc. v. Canal Capital Corp.*, 566 N.W.2d 357, 363–64 (Minn.App. 1997) (applying contractual damages limitation to promissory estoppel claim), *review denied* (Minn. Sept. 18, 1997).

In the absence of specific statutory provisions, extra-contractual damages, such as emotional distress, are not recoverable for breach of contract except in exceptional cases where the breach is accompanied by an independent tort. * * * [S]ee William Lloyd Prosser, *The Borderland of Tort and Contract, in Selected Topics On the Law of Torts* 380, 426 (1953) (noting in contract actions, there is no recovery for mental suffering). The accompanying independent tort must be willful and support the extra-contractual damages in its own right. *Lickteig [v. Alderson, Ondov, Leonard & Sween, P.A.*, 556 N.W.2d 557, 561 (Minn. 1996)]. A malicious motive in breaking a contract will not convert a contract action into a tort action. *Id.*; *see Wild [v. Rarig*, 302 Minn. 419, 442, 234 N.W.2d at 790 (1975)] (concluding bad faith breach of contract does not become tort).

Extra-contractual damages, such as emotional distress, are limited to those instances in which the breach is accompanied by an independent tort to insure that contract law is not swallowed by tort law. *See, e.g., State Farm Mut. Auto. Ins. Co. v. Ford Motor Co.*, 572 N.W.2d 321, 324 (Minn.App.1997) (holding economic loss doctrine preserves boundary between tort and contract law); *cf.* Grant Gilmore, *The Death of Contract* 87–103 (1974) (arguing approaching point where there will be no viable distinction between liability in contract or tort). The preservation of a boundary between contract and tort law is necessary to protect the specific interests and expectations each embodies. *See Restatement (Second) Contracts* § 1 (1979) (defining contract as promise or set of promises for breach of which law gives remedy, or performance of which law in some way recognizes as duty); W. Page Keeton, et al., *Prosser and Keeton on The Law of Torts* §§ 1–2, at 6–7 (5th ed.1984) (noting common thread of tort law is unreasonable interference with interests of others and its primary purpose is to compensate injured party for damages suffered at expense of wrongdoer); *see also Foley v. Interactive Data Corp.*, 47 Cal.3d 654, 254 Cal.Rptr. 211, 227, 765 P.2d 373, 389 (1988) (holding distinction between tort and contract well grounded in common law, and divergent objectives underlie remedies created in two areas); *see, e.g.*, William Powers, Jr., *Border Wars*, 72 Tex. L.Rev. 1209, 1209–10 n. 3 (1994) (explaining advantages for plaintiffs who attempt to import tort principles into commercial litigation); Prosser, *supra*, at 425–26 (explaining tort remedy often more advantageous to injured party because it will permit greater recovery).

Deli argues promissory estoppel is not "a contract by another name" and the "special circumstances" of her promissory estoppel claim warrant an award of emotional distress damages. *See Cohen*, 479 N.W.2d at 392 (concluding plaintiff in promissory estoppel action entitled to recover damages that arise directly and naturally in course of breach or are consequences of special circumstances known to or reasonably contemplated by parties when contract made); *see also Walser v. Toyota Motor Sales, U.S.A., Inc.*, 43 F.3d 396, 401–02 (8th Cir.1994) (concluding Minnesota courts treat damages decision under Restatement (Second) § 90 as being within discretion of district court). While the inherently personal nature of the images on the videotape make this case unusual, the gravamen of Deli's promissory estoppel claim sounds in contract. *See Cohen*, 479 N.W.2d at 390 (awarding same damages on promissory estoppel claim as available to plaintiff in breach of contract action); *see generally* Susan M. Gilles, *Promises Betrayed: Breach of Confidence as a Remedy for Invasions of Privacy*, 43 Buff. L.Rev. 1, 38 n. 160 (1995) (citing *Cohen* to support proposition that damages under promissory estoppel claim are same damages available in contract action); *cf. McNeill & Assocs., Inc. v. ITT Life Ins. Corp.*, 446 N.W.2d 181, 187 (Minn.App.1989) (refusing to permit recovery for emotional distress where damages caused by tort are same damages caused by breach of contract), *review denied* (Minn. Dec. 1, 1989).

Because promissory estoppel is a contract-based claim, to recover emotional distress damages, Deli was required to plead and prove the existence of an independent tort. Despite protracted litigation in this case, Deli has never alleged the existence of an independent tort. Furthermore, on the facts of this case, the only "tort" sufficient to compensate Deli for "mental distress from having been exposed to public view" is essentially an invasion of privacy tort. *See Time, Inc. v. Hill*, 385 U.S. 374, 384–85 n. 9, 87 S.Ct. 534, 540–41 n. 9, 17 L.Ed.2d 456 (1967) (concluding in right to privacy case, primary damage is mental distress from having been exposed to public view); *Morgan by Chambon v. Celender*, 780 F.Supp. 307, 309–10 (W.D.Pa.1992) (examining elements of judicially created invasion of privacy tort); *Sabrina W. v. Willman*, 4 Neb.App. 149, 540 N.W.2d 364, 368–70 (1995) (examining Nebraska's statutory cause of action for invasion of privacy tort). Because Minnesota does not recognize a statutory or judicially created cause of action for invasion of privacy, to allow Deli to recover for emotional distress would permit her to accomplish in contract that which she is barred from accomplishing in tort. *See Richie v. Paramount Pictures Corp.*, 544 N.W.2d 21, 28 (Minn.1996) (concluding Minnesota has never recognized cause of action for invasion of privacy); *see also Stubbs v. North Mem'l Med. Ctr.*, 448 N.W.2d 78, 81 (Minn.App.1989) (concluding not function of court to establish new cause of action for invasion of privacy), *review denied* (Minn. Jan. 12, 1990). We decline to subvert the law of contract to fashion an exception to fit the unusual facts of this case. *See generally* Daniel A. Farber & John H. Matheson, *Beyond Promissory Estoppel: Contract Law and the "Invisible Handshake,"* 52 U. Chi. L.Rev. 903, 905 (1985) (concluding expansion of promissory estoppel not proof that contract in process of being swallowed by tort, but rather that promissory estoppel being transformed into new theory of distinctly contractual relationships); *cf.* Mark Gergen, *A Cautionary Tale About Contractual Good Faith in Texas*, 72 Tex. L.Rev. 1235, 1236 (1994) (concluding extension of tort of bad faith breach into contract cases to award emotional damages for breach is doctrinally unsound and bad policy).

* * * Because we conclude Deli failed to prove compensable contract damages, we need not address the University's alternative grounds for reversal.

Decision

The trial court erred in awarding emotional distress damages on Deli's contract-based claim because Deli failed to allege or prove the existence of an independent tort.

Reversed.

Problems

1. The Coors Brewing Company decided to market its product in Missouri where it had previously refrained from marketing. It publicly solicited applicants for distributorship, dividing the state into districts. Plaintiff was one of thirty-five applicants for District No. 10. He was the only such applicant selected for an in-house interview. Coors determined that none of the applicants were satisfactory and took over distribution in District No. 10 through a subsidiary. About a year later Coors awarded the distributorship to a company that was not one of the original thirty-five applicants. Plaintiff seeks to prove that he relied on obtaining the distributorship at a heavy cost to himself. Has Plaintiff stated a case?

2. Father (F) promised to give his daughter (D) $17,000 so she could buy a two-family house. She would live in one apartment and he in the other. In reliance on the promise, D paid $2,000 of her own money for an option on a suitable house. F died and his executor refuses to pay the $17,000 promised. What result?

3. Plaintiff (P) is the father of H. P had placed his son (H) and his daughter-in-law (W) in possession of a lot of land and told them that it was

theirs as long as they lived. Thereupon H and W kept possession of the land, cleared the property and made some other improvements upon it. P brought an action in ejectment. The answer set up a claim for specific performance. What result?

4.   Would the result in Kirksey v. Kirksey on p. 191 be different if the doctrine of promissory estoppel had been applied by the court?

5.   A had a mechanic's lien upon B's property. B, who was not personally obligated to A, promised to pay the amount due to A. A did not foreclose his lien during the statutory period. Does A have a cause of action based upon B's promise?

6.   At the request of B, a bank, D gave the bank a note in the sum of $350,000. At the same time B gave D a written statement to the effect that D would not be held liable on the note. The note, however, was treated on B's books as an asset of the bank and was shown to bank examiners. The bank became bankrupt. Can the bank's liquidators enforce the note against D?

7.   Employer delivered to employee a certificate which stated that, if the employee died while still an employee, his beneficiary would receive a lump sum payment of $10,000. The certificate further provided that it was purely voluntary and gratuitous and could be withdrawn or discontinued by employer at any time. Employee worked for employer for 20 years and died while he was still an employee. Must employer pay the death benefit?

8.   A was employed by B and had been so employed for a three-year period. C, whose employees were on strike, offered to give A "permanent employment," after A had stated he would take the job only on a permanent basis and not merely as a strikebreaker. A quit his job and moved near C's place of business. C, as part of its settlement agreement with the strikers, subsequently terminated A's employment. Is C liable to A?

9.   F & B were partners and bound by a lease to C. F desired to withdraw from the business and B agreed. F wanted to go into a new business, but did not want to do so unless he could obtain a release from his obligation under the lease. He told C his plans and C said that he "was perfectly satisfied if B assumed the balance of the lease, as far as I am concerned, just forget about it." B assumed the balance of the lease. After this statement was made, F withdrew from the partnership and entered into a new business. In time, C brought an action against F for rent. What result?

10.   G, a general contractor, requested a bid from S, a subcontractor, to be used by G in connection with a particular project. S replied, "I can't give no bid, because I don't trust those specifications. But it should be about $1.25 per yard. It is O.K. if you want to use this quote and O.K. if you don't want to use it." G used it and was awarded the contract in connection with the project and now claims that S is bound to perform at $1.25 per yard. What result?

11.   During a hospital stay John Togstad suffered a stroke that paralyzed one side of his body and deprived him of the ability to speak. Based on information supplied by the duty nurse, Mrs. Togstad concluded that perhaps her husband was a victim of medical malpractice. She consulted Miller,

an attorney. Miller interviewed her for about an hour and advised her that he did not think that the Togstads had a viable case for malpractice. Miller had no experience in medical practice cases, did no research, and failed to advise Mrs. Togstad that the statute of limitations on a medical malpractice case was about to expire. Miller charged no fee for the consultation. After the statutory period had passed, an experienced medical malpractice lawyer advised Mrs. Togstad that she and her husband had a very good case but it was too late to pursue. In a malpractice action against Miller, the jury found damages of $700,000. Miller appeals, claiming that there never was a contractual relationship between himself and either of the Togstads, and, therefore, no attorney-client relation. Decide the appeal.

Examination Problems

In solving these problems consider relevant material in the Offer and Acceptance, Consideration, and Promissory Estoppel chapters.

I.

The Deadbeat (hereafter "Group") is a rock music group. Hot Sound, Inc., is a nationally known recording company (hereafter "Company"). The parties signed a written agreement under which Group agreed to record exclusively for Company for a five-year period and to record a specified minimum number of records. Company agreed to pay specified royalties on the sale of records and on the sale of sheet music for any songs composed by Group. The instrument also contained the following provision:

> "Company is not obligated to make or sell records manufactured from any master recordings made hereunder or to have Group record any minimum number of record sides. The decision to publish sheet music or other printed editions of any musical composition shall be entirely within the discretion of Company."

Pursuant to the terms of the agreement, at the time of signing Company's president handed Group a check for $1,000 with the notation "non-refundable advance against royalties."

During the 21 months that followed, Group made 4 single recordings and two albums, one of which eventually received a gold record for one million dollars in sales. But during those 21 months, Group was in need of money to pay for recording sessions, traveling expenses, back income taxes and to settle a litigation against them. Company, without obligation to do so, gave Group a total of $80,000 advances against royalties to cover these expenses.

At the end of 24 months, Group signed a contract with a rival recording company.

What issues will arise in Company's action against Group?

II.

On July 1, 1993, Ben E. Factor sent a letter to O. Byer, that read as follows:

Dear Mr. Byer:

I hereby offer to sell you Greenacre for $600,000, closing on or prior to December 31, 1993. The price includes a few of my fine thoroughbred horses that are pasturing there. We can work out which ones at the time of closing. Indicate your acceptance by signing and returning a copy of this letter.

Sincerely, /s/ Ben E. Factor

On November 10, 1993, Factor, after being told about the great charitable work the Plutonian Church was doing and having been advised by his tax lawyer that he should make some charitable donations prior to the end of the year, wrote to Reverend F. Tuck, the head of the Church, the following:

Dear Reverend Tuck:

In consideration of the tremendous work the Plutonian Church has done with the poor and to enable the Church to continue to do its great work with the poor, I promise to convey Greenacre to the Church on or prior to December 31, 1993.

Sincerely, Ben E. Factor.

On November 13, 1993, an article about Factor's donation appeared in the *National Enquiry*, offered for sale in supermarkets, and Byer read it. While he had not intended to accept the July 1, 1993 offer anyway, (the property was not worth the asking price), Byer was infuriated that Factor had not conferred with him prior to the donation. His only thought was that of showing Factor that he couldn't kick Byer around and get away with it. Accordingly, he quickly faxed the following:

I HEREBY ACCEPT YOUR OFFER OF JULY 1 AND EXPECT STRICT ADHERENCE TO THE TERMS OF OUR DEAL. PUT YOUR LAWYERS IN TOUCH WITH ME TO PUT TOGETHER A WRITTEN CONTRACT.

/s/ O. Byer

Byer's intent in sending the fax was simply to scare Factor into paying money to extricate himself from a so-called agreement that Byer believed Factor couldn't perform. He planned to settle his claim against Factor for a modest sum, in the neighborhood of $1,000.

Factor had, in fact, forgotten about the July 1 offer made to Byer and, when he received Byer's fax, felt morally bound to go through with the sale to Byer. Accordingly, on November 14, he telephoned Reverend Tuck at the monastery to tell Tuck about the problem, and suggested a cash gift of $400,000 instead of a gift of Greenacre. Tuck was disappointed, but was not about to express disappointment to Factor. Instead, he agreed to the change, feigned gratitude, and thanked Factor for his kindness. The next day, (November 15), Factor wrote Tuck as follows:

Dear Reverend Tuck:

In accordance with my letter of November 10 and our discussion yesterday, I hereby promise to pay the Plutonian Church $400,000 on or prior to December 31, 1993.

Sincerely, /s/ Ben E. Factor

On receiving the November 15 letter, Tuck immediately purchased on credit a new stereo system for the monastery ($3,000) and a new Mercedes Benz ($50,000) so that the clergy of the Church could finally travel in style.

After Factor had written to Tuck on November 15, he called his lawyer on November 17, and told her to contact Byer and get moving on the sale of the property. She immediately called Byer and said:

"I'm glad to hear that my client has a deal with you. Let's get the draft of a formal agreement together so we can iron out the bumps before the end of the year."

Byer was startled by the call and told Factor's lawyer that the November 13 "acceptance" was a joke which anyone would have known because news of the donation of the property was "public." He concluded by saying that under no circumstances was he going through with the sale.

Factor's lawyer reported the conversation to her client. Factor was furious because he was going to make the $400,000 gift out of the proceeds of the sale of the property. He immediately telephoned Reverend Tuck to advise him that he could not make the gift by the end of the year because some other pressures had come up. Pleading for reconsideration, Tuck referred to purchases already made by the Church. Responding to Factor's questions, Tuck explained the nature of the purchases. Factor expressed his displeasure with the Church and, before hanging up, Factor said, "You'll have to sue to get a cent out of me."

What are the rights of the parties? Discuss all the contracts issues raised by this statement of facts although some may be resolved by subsequent events.

III.

A MODEL ANSWER TO THIS QUESTION IS IN APPENDIX C, ENTITLED "THE PLUMBER AND HIS SUPPLIERS"

B, a plumbing contractor, received a spring catalog from A, a plumbing supplier. S distributed a new catalog quarterly. B wrote to S as follows:

"I see from your catalog that prices have gone up again. You know that we have always bought a lot from you. Right now I am preparing a number of bids, and I would like a favor. Will you promise me that I can buy what I want for the rest of this year at the prices in this spring catalog?"

S wrote in reply:

"You are a most valued customer. We will give you the price protection you seek for the rest of the year. Naturally, however, we insist that you agree to buy all your plumbing supplies from us during this period."

B wrote in reply:

"Thanks for your cooperation. I agree with what you insist on. Of course we have to be flexible though. Sometimes contract specifications call for brand names you don't handle and sometimes when we're in a rush we've got to buy from a local guy. Other special situations sometimes pop up. Like a plumber named Jones is going to jail and I'm trying to buy his stuff at a good price."

This letter was not delivered for three months as the airplane carrying it crashed into Lake Ontario. It has only recently been dredged up.

Soon after this letter was mailed, B bought Jones' inventory of supplies for $20,000 which was paid on the spot. On the same day B was approached by C, another plumbing supplier, who told B that because of a cash shortage, he would supply B at a discount of 30% off his list prices. B, delighted at this, bid for three major plumbing subcontracts using C's list prices less 30% in calculating his costs. He was awarded all three contracts. When he placed his first order with C, C informed him that because of a change in his cash position all supplies would be sold at list price. He then placed the same order with S who informed him that the price he must pay is 10% above the spring catalog price.

Meanwhile, from his jail cell, Jones wrote to B stating:

"I think I was robbed. $20,000 was much too low a price. You took advantage of me. I had to sell in a hurry and I wasn't thinking straight. The materials were worth $60,000, but if you send me another $10,000, I won't pester you none."

B wrote back that he would pay the $10,000.

Discuss all the contract problems raised by this set of facts.

Chapter 5

PAROL EVIDENCE AND INTERPRETATION

SECTION 1. THE PAROL EVIDENCE RULE

(Calamari & Perillo 5th §§ 3.1—3.8)

MITCHILL v. LATH

Court of Appeals of New York, 1928.
247 N.Y. 377, 160 N.E. 646.

ANDREWS, J. In the fall of 1923 the Laths owned a farm. This they wished to sell. Across the road, on land belonging to Lieutenant Governor Lunn, they had an ice house which they might remove. Mrs. Mitchill looked over the land with a view to its purchase. She found the ice house objectionable. Thereupon "the defendants orally promised and agreed, for and in consideration of the purchase of their farm by the plaintiff, to remove the said ice house in the spring of 1924." Relying upon this promise, she made a written contract to buy the property for $8,400, for cash and a mortgage and containing various provisions usual in such papers. Later receiving a deed, she entered into possession and has spent considerable sums in improving the property for use as a summer residence. The defendants have not fulfilled their promise as to the ice house and do not intend to do so. We are not dealing, however, with their moral delinquencies. The question before us is whether their oral agreement may be enforced in a court of equity.

This requires a discussion of the parol evidence rule—a rule of law which defines the limits of the contract to be construed. (*Glackin v. Bennett*, 226 Mass. 316.) It is more than a rule of evidence and oral testimony even if admitted will not control the written contract (*O'Malley v. Grady*, 222 Mass. 202), unless admitted without objection. (*Brady v. Nally*, 151 N.Y. 258.) It applies, however, to attempts to modify such a contract by parol. It does not affect a parol collateral contract distinct from and independent of the written agreement. It is, at times, troublesome to draw the line. Williston, in his work on Contracts (sec. 637) points out the difficulty. "Two entirely distinct contracts," he says, "each for a separate consideration may be made at the same time and will be distinct legally. Where, however, one agreement is entered into wholly or partly in consideration of the simultaneous agreement to enter into another, the transactions are necessarily bound together. * * * Then if one of the agreements is oral and the other is written, the

325

problem arises whether the bond is sufficiently close to prevent proof of the oral agreement." That is the situation here. It is claimed that the defendants are called upon to do more than is required by their written contract in connection with the sale as to which it deals.

The principle may be clear, but it can be given effect by no mechanical rule. As so often happens, it is a matter of degree, for as Professor Williston also says where a contract contains several promises on each side it is not difficult to put any one of them in the form of a collateral agreement. If this were enough written contracts might always be modified by parol. Not form, but substance is the test.

In applying this test the policy of our courts is to be considered. We have believed that the purpose behind the rule was a wise one not easily to be abandoned. Notwithstanding injustice here and there, on the whole it works for good. Old precedents and principles are not to be lightly cast aside unless it is certain that they are an obstruction under present conditions. New York has been less open to arguments that would modify this particular rule, than some jurisdictions elsewhere. Thus in *Eighmie v. Taylor* (98 N.Y. 288) it was held that a parol warranty might not be shown although no warranties were contained in the writing.

Under our decisions before such an oral agreement as the present is received to vary the written contract at least three conditions must exist, (1) the agreement must in form be a collateral one; (2) it must not contradict express or implied provisions of the written contract; (3) it must be one that parties would not ordinarily be expected to embody in the writing; or put in another way, an inspection of the written contract, read in the light of surrounding circumstances must not indicate that the writing appears "to contain the engagements of the parties, and to define the object and measure the extent of such engagement." Or again, it must not be so clearly connected with the principal transaction as to be part and parcel of it.

The respondent does not satisfy the third of these requirements. It may be, not the second. We have a written contract for the purchase and sale of land. The buyer is to pay $8,400 in the way described. She is also to pay her portion of any rents, interest on mortgages, insurance premiums and water meter charges. She may have a survey made of the premises. On their part the sellers are to give a full covenant deed of the premises as described, or as they may be described by the surveyor if the survey is had, executed and acknowledged at their own expense; they sell the personal property on the farm and represent they own it; they agree that all amounts paid them on the contract and the expense of examining the title shall be a lien on the property; they assume the risk of loss or damage by fire until the deed is delivered; and they agree to pay the broker his commissions. Are they to do more? Or is such a claim inconsistent with these precise provisions? It could not be shown that the plaintiff was to pay $500 additional. Is it also implied that the defendants are not to do anything unexpressed in the writing?

That we need not decide. At least, however, an inspection of this contract shows a full and complete agreement, setting forth in detail the obligations of each party. On reading it one would conclude that the reciprocal obligations of the parties were fully detailed. Nor would his opinion alter if he knew the surrounding circumstances. The presence of the ice house, even the knowledge that Mrs. Mitchill thought it objectionable would not lead to the belief that a separate agreement existed with regard to it. Were such an agreement made it would seem most natural that the inquirer should find it in the contract. Collateral in form it is found to be, but it is closely related to the subject dealt with in the written agreement—so closely that we hold it may not be proved.

Where the line between the competent and the incompetent is narrow the citation of authorities is of slight use. Each represents the judgment of the court on the precise facts before it. How closely bound to the contract is the supposed collateral agreement is the decisive factor in each case. * * *

* * * A line of cases in Massachusetts, of which *Durkin v. Cobleigh* (156 Mass. 108) is an example, have to do with collateral contracts made before a deed is given. But the fixed form of a deed makes it inappropriate to insert collateral agreements, however closely connected with the sale. This may be cause for an exception. Here we deal with the contract on the basis of which the deed to Mrs. Mitchill was given subsequently, and we confine ourselves to the question whether its terms may be modified.

* * *

Our conclusion is that the judgment of the Appellate Division and that of the Special Term should be reversed and the complaint dismissed, with costs in all courts.

LEHMAN, J. (dissenting). I accept the general rule as formulated by Judge Andrews. I differ with him only as to its application to the facts shown in the record. The plaintiff contracted to purchase land from the defendants for an agreed price. [The] formal written agreement * * * is on its face a complete contract for the conveyance of the land. It describes the property to be conveyed. It sets forth the purchase price to be paid. All the conditions and terms of the conveyance to be made are clearly stated. I concede at the outset that parol evidence to show additional conditions and terms of the conveyance would be inadmissible. * * *

The parol agreement which the court below found the parties had made was collateral to, yet connected with, the agreement of purchase and sale. It has been found that the defendants induced the plaintiff to agree to purchase the land by a promise to remove an ice house from land not covered by the agreement of purchase and sale. No independent consideration passed to the defendants for the parol promise. To that extent the written contract and the alleged oral contract are bound together. The same bond usually exists wherever attempt is made to prove a parol agreement which is collateral to a written agreement. Hence "the problem arises whether the bond is sufficiently close to prevent proof of the oral agreement." See Judge Andrews' citation from Williston on Contracts, section 637.

Judge Andrews has formulated a standard to measure the closeness of the bond. Three conditions, at least, must exist before an oral agreement may be proven to increase the obligation imposed by the written agreement. I think we agree that the first condition that the agreement "must in form be a collateral one" is met by the evidence. I concede that this condition is met in most cases where the courts have nevertheless excluded evidence of the collateral oral agreement. The difficulty here, as in most cases, arises in connection with the two other conditions.

The second condition is that the "parol agreement must not contradict express or implied provisions of the written contract." Judge Andrews voices doubt whether this condition is satisfied. The written contract has been carried out. The purchase price has been paid; conveyance has been made, title has passed in accordance with the terms of the written contract. The mutual obligations expressed in the written contract are left unchanged by the alleged oral contract. When performance was required of the written contract, the obligations of the parties were measured solely by its terms. By the oral agreement the plaintiff seeks to hold the defendants to other obligations to be performed by them thereafter upon land which was not conveyed to the plaintiff. The assertion of such further obligation is not inconsistent with the written contract unless the written contract contains a provision, express or implied, that the defendants are not to do anything not expressed in the writing. Concededly there is no such express provision in the contract, and such a provision may be implied, if at all, only if the asserted additional obligation is "so clearly connected with the principal transaction as to be part and parcel of it," and is not "one that the parties would not ordinarily be expected to embody in the writing." The hypothesis so formulated for a conclusion that the asserted additional obligation is inconsistent with an implied term of the contract is that the alleged oral agreement does not comply with the third condition as formulated by Judge Andrews. In this case, therefore, the problem reduces itself to the one question whether or not the oral agreement meets the third condition.

I have conceded that upon inspection the contract is complete. "It appears to contain the engagements of the parties, and to define the object and measure the extent of such engagement;" it constitutes the contract between them and is presumed to contain the whole of that contract. (*Eighmie v. Taylor*, 98 N.Y. 288.) That engagement was on the one side to convey land; on the other to pay the price. The plaintiff asserts further agreement based on the same consideration to be performed by the defendants after the conveyance was complete, and directly affecting only other land. It is true, as Judge Andrews points out, that "the presence of the ice house, even the knowledge that Mrs. Mitchill thought it objectionable, would not lead to the belief that a separate agreement existed with regard to it;" but the question we must decide is whether or not, *assuming* an agreement was made for the removal of an unsightly ice house from one parcel of land as an inducement for the purchase of another parcel, the parties would ordinarily or naturally be expected to embody the agreement for the removal of the ice house from one parcel in the written agreement to convey the other parcel. Exclusion of proof of the oral agreement on the ground that it varies the contract embodied in the writing may be based only upon a finding or presumption that the written contract was intended to cover the oral negotiations for the removal of the ice house which lead up to the contract of purchase and sale. To determine what the writing was intended to cover "the document alone will not suffice. What it was intended to cover cannot be known till we know what there was to cover. The question being whether certain subjects of negotiation were intended to be covered, we must compare the writing and the negotiations before we can determine whether they were in fact covered." (Wigmore on Evidence [2d ed.], section 2430.)

The subject-matter of the written contract was the conveyance of land. The contract was so complete on its face that the conclusion is inevitable that the parties intended to embody in the writing all the negotiations covering at least the conveyance. The promise by the defendants to remove the ice house from other land was not connected with their obligation to convey, except that one agreement would not have been made unless the other was also made. The plaintiff's assertion of a parol agreement by the defendants to remove the ice house was completely established by the great weight of evidence. It must prevail unless that agreement was part of the agreement to convey and the entire agreement was embodied in the writing.

The fact that in this case the parol agreement is established by the overwhelming weight of evidence is, of course, not a factor which may be considered in determining the competency or legal effect of the evidence. Hardship in the particular case would not justify the court in disregarding or emasculating the general rule. It merely accentuates the outlines of our problem. The assumption that the parol agreement was made is no longer obscured by any doubts. The problem then is clearly whether the parties are presumed to have intended to render that parol agreement legally ineffective and non-existent by failure to embody it in the writing. Though we are driven to say that nothing in the written contract which fixed the terms and conditions of the stipulated conveyance suggests the existence of any further parol agreement, an inspection of the contract, though it is complete on its face in regard to the subject of the conveyance, does not, I think, show that it was intended to embody negotiations or agreements, if any, in regard to a matter so loosely bound to the conveyance as the removal of an ice house from land not conveyed.

The rule of integration undoubtedly frequently prevents the assertion of fraudulent claims. Parties who take the precaution of embodying their oral agreements in a writing should be protected against the assertion that other terms of the same agreement were not integrated in the writing. The limits of the integration are determined by the writing, read in the light of the surrounding circumstances. A written contract, however complete, yet covers only a limited field. I do not think that in the written contract for the conveyance of land here under consideration we can find an intention to cover a field so broad as to include prior agreements, if any such were made, to do other acts on other property after the stipulated conveyance was made.

In each case where such a problem is presented, varying factors enter into its solution. Citation of authority in this or other jurisdictions is useless, at least without minute analysis of the facts. The analysis I have made of the decisions in this State leads me to the view that the decision of the courts below is in accordance with our own authorities and should be affirmed.

Cardozo, Ch. J., Pound, Kellogg and O'Brien, JJ., concur with Andrews, J.; Lehman, J., dissents in opinion in which Crane, J., concurs.

Judgment accordingly.

LEE v. JOSEPH E. SEAGRAM & SONS, INC.

United States Court of Appeals, Second Circuit, 1977.
552 F.2d 447.

Gurfein, Circuit Judge:

This is an appeal by defendant Joseph E. Seagram & Sons, Inc. ("Seagram") from a judgment entered by the District Court, Hon. Charles H. Tenney, upon the verdict of a jury in the amount of $407,850 in favor of the plaintiffs on a claim asserting common law breach of an oral contract. The court also denied Seagram's motion under Rule 50(b), Fed.R.Civ.P., for judgment notwithstanding the verdict. *Harold S. Lee, et al. v. Joseph E. Seagram and Sons*, 413 F.Supp. 693 (S.D.N.Y.1976). It had earlier denied Seagram's motion for summary judgment. The plaintiffs are Harold S. Lee (now deceased) and his two sons, Lester and Eric ("the Lees"). Jurisdiction is based on diversity of citizenship. We affirm.

The jury could have found the following. The Lees owned a 50% interest in Capitol City Liquor Company, Inc. ("Capitol City"), a wholesale liquor distributorship located in Washington, D.C. The other 50% was owned by Harold's brother, Henry D. Lee, and his nephew, Arthur Lee. Seagram is a distiller of alcoholic beverages. Capitol City carried numerous Seagram brands and a large portion of its sales were generated by Seagram lines.

The Lees and the other owners of Capitol City wanted to sell their respective interests in the business and, in May 1970, Harold Lee, the father, discussed the possible sale of Capitol City with Jack Yogman ("Yogman"), then Executive Vice President of Seagram (and now President), whom he had known for many years. Lee offered to sell Capitol City to Seagram but conditioned the offer on Seagram's agreement to relocate Harold and his sons, the 50% owners of Capitol City, in a new distributorship of their own in a different city.

About a month later, another officer of Seagram, John Barth, an assistant to Yogman, visited the Lees and their co-owners in Washington and began negotiations for the purchase of the assets of Capitol City by Seagram on behalf of a new distributor, one Carter, who would take it over after the purchase. The purchase of the assets of Capitol City was consummated on September 30, 1970 pursuant to a written agreement. The promise to relocate the father and sons thereafter was not reduced to writing.

Harold Lee had served the Seagram organization for thirty-six years in positions of responsibility before he acquired the half interest in the Capitol City distributorship. From 1958 to 1962, he was chief executive officer of Calvert Distillers Company, a wholly-owned subsidiary. During this long period he enjoyed the friendship and confidence of the principals of Seagram.

In 1958, Harold Lee had purchased from Seagram its holdings of Capitol City stock in order to introduce his sons into the liquor distribution business, and also to satisfy Seagram's desire to have a strong and friendly distributor for Seagram products in Washington, D.C. Harold Lee and Yogman had known each other for 13 years.

The plaintiffs claimed a breach of the oral agreement to relocate Harold Lee's sons, alleging that Seagram had had opportunities to procure another distributorship for the Lees but had refused to do so. The Lees brought this action on January 18, 1972, fifteen months after the sale of the Capitol City distributorship to Seagram. They contended that they had performed their obligation by agreeing to the sale by Capitol City of its assets to Seagram, but that Seagram had failed to perform its obligation under the separate oral contract between the Lees and Seagram. The agreement which the trial court permitted the jury to find was "an oral agreement with defendant which provided that if they agreed to sell their interest in Capitol City, defendant in return, within a reasonable time, would provide the plaintiffs a Seagram distributorship whose price would require roughly an amount equal to the capital obtained by the plaintiffs for the sale of their interest in Capitol City, and which distributorship would be in a location acceptable to plaintiffs." No specific exception was taken to this portion of the charge. By its verdict for the plaintiffs, we must assume—as Seagram notes in its brief—that this is the agreement which the jury found was made before the sale of Capitol City was agreed upon.

* * *

I

Judge Tenney, in a careful analysis of the application of the parol evidence rule, decided that the rule did not bar proof of the oral agreement. We agree.

The District Court, in its denial of the defendant's motion for summary judgment, treated the issue as whether the written agreement for the sale of assets was an "integrated" agreement not only of all the mutual agreements concerning the sale of Capitol City assets, but also of *all* the mutual agreements of the parties. Finding the language of the sales agreement "somewhat ambiguous," the court decided that the determination of whether the parol evidence rule applies must await the taking of evidence on the issue of whether the sales agreement was intended to be a complete and accurate integration of all of the mutual promises of the parties.

Seagram did not avail itself of this invitation. It failed to call as witnesses any of the three persons who negotiated the sales agreement on behalf of Seagram regarding the intention of the parties to integrate all mutual promises or regarding the failure of the written agreement to contain an integration clause.

Appellant contends that, as a matter of law, the oral agreement was "part and parcel" of the subject-matter of the sales contract and that failure to include it in the written contract barred proof of its existence. *Mitchill v. Lath*, 247 N.Y. 377, 380, 160 N.E. 646 (1928). The position of appellant, fairly stated, is that the oral agreement was either an inducing cause for the sale or was a part of the consideration for the sale, and in either case, should have been contained in the written contract. In either case, it argues that the parol evidence rule bars its admission.

Appellees maintain, on the other hand, that the oral agreement was a collateral agreement and that, since it is not contradictory of any of the terms of the sales agreement, proof of it is not barred by the parol evidence rule. Because the case comes to us after a jury verdict we must assume that there actually was an oral contract, such as the court instructed the jury it could find. The question is whether the strong policy for avoiding fraudulent claims through application of the parol evidence rule nevertheless mandates reversal on the ground that the jury should not have been permitted to hear the evidence. *See Fogelson v. Rackfay Constr. Co.*, 300 N.Y. 334 at 337–38, 90 N.E.2d 881 (1950).

The District Court stated the cardinal issue to be whether the parties "intended" the written agreement for the sale of assets to be the complete and accurate integration of all the mutual promises of the parties. If the written contract was not a complete integration, the court held, then the parol evidence rule has no application. We assume that the District Court determined intention by objective standards. *See* 3 Corbin on Contracts §§ 573–574. The parol evidence rule is a rule of substantive law. * * *

The law of New York is not rigid or categorical, but is in harmony with this approach. As Judge Fuld said in *Fogelson:*

> "Decision in each case must, of course, turn upon the type of transaction involved, the scope of the written contract and the content of the oral agreement asserted."

300 N.Y. at 338, 90 N.E.2d at 883. And the Court of Appeals wrote in *Ball v. Grady*, 267 N.Y. 470, 472, 196 N.E. 402, 403 (1935):

> "In the end, the court must find the limits of the integration as best it may by reading the writing in the light of surrounding circumstances."

Accord, Fogelson, supra, 300 N.Y. at 338, 90 N.E.2d 881. Thus, certain oral collateral agreements, even though made contemporaneously, are not within the prohibition of the parol evidence rule "because [if] they are separate, independent, and complete contracts, although relating to the same subject ... [t]hey are allowed to be proved by parol, because they were made by parol, and no part thereof committed to writing." *Thomas v. Scutt*, 127 N.Y. 133, 140–41, 27 N.E. 961, 963 (1891).

Although there is New York authority which in general terms supports defendant's thesis that an oral contract inducing a written one or varying the consideration may be barred, *see, e.g., Fogelson v. Rackfay Constr. Co., supra*, 300 N.Y. at 340, 90 N.E.2d 881, the overarching question is whether, in the context of the particular setting, the oral agreement was one which the parties would ordinarily be expected to embody in the writing. *Ball v. Grady, supra*, 267 N.Y. at 470, 196 N.E. 402; *accord, Fogelson v. Rackfay Constr. Co., supra*, 300 N.Y. at 338, 90 N.E.2d 881. *See* Restatement on Contracts § 240. For example, integration is most easily inferred in the case of real estate contracts for the sale of land, *e.g., Mitchill v. Lath, supra*, 247 N.Y. 377, 160 N.E. 646, or leases, *Fogelson, supra*; *Plum Tree, Inc. v. N.K. Winston Corp.*, 351 F.Supp. 80, 83 (S.D.N.Y.1972). In more complex situations, in which customary business practice may be more varied, an oral agreement can be treated as separate and independent of the written agreement even though the written contract contains a strong integration clause. *See Gem Corrugated Box Corp. v. National Kraft Container Corp.*, 427 F.2d 499, 503 (2d Cir.1970).

Thus, as we see it, the issue is whether the oral promise to the plaintiffs, as individuals, would be an expectable term of the contract for the sale of assets by a corporation in which plaintiffs have only a 50% interest, considering as well the history of their relationship to Seagram.

Here, there are several reasons why it would *not* be expected that the oral agreement to give Harold Lee's sons another distributorship would be integrated into the sales contract. In the usual case, there is an identity of parties in both the claimed integrated instrument and in the oral agreement asserted. Here, although it would have been physically possible to insert a provision dealing with only the shareholders of a 50% interest, the transaction itself was a *corporate* sale of assets. Collateral agreements which survive the closing of a corporate deal, such as employment agreements for particular shareholders of the seller or consulting agreements, are often set forth in separate agreements. *See Gem Corrugated Box Corp. v. National Kraft Container Corp., supra*, 427 F.2d at 503 ("it is ... plain that the parties ordinarily would not embody the stock purchase agreement in a writing concerned only with box materials purchase terms"). It was expectable that such an agreement as one to obtain a new distributorship for certain persons, some of whom were not even parties to the contract, would not necessarily be integrated into an instrument for the sale of *corporate* assets. As with an oral condition precedent to the legal effectiveness of an otherwise integrated written contract, which is not barred by the parol evidence rule if it is not directly contradictory of its terms, *Hicks v. Bush*, 10 N.Y.2d 488, 225 N.Y.S.2d 34, 180 N.E.2d 425 (1962); *cf.* 3 Corbin on Contracts § 589, "it is certainly not improbable that parties contracting in these circumstances would make the asserted oral agreement...." 10 N.Y.2d at 493, 225 N.Y.S.2d at 39, 180 N.E.2d at 428.

Similarly, it is significant that there was a close relationship of confidence and friendship over many years between two old men, Harold Lee and Yogman, whose authority to bind Seagram has not been questioned. It would not be surprising that a handshake for the benefit of Harold's sons would have been thought sufficient. In point, as well, is the circumstance that the negotiations concerning the provisions of the sales agreement were not conducted by Yogman but by three other Seagram representatives, headed by John Barth. The two transactions may not have been integrated in their minds when the contract was drafted.[1]

Finally, the written agreement does not contain the customary integration clause, even though a good part of it (relating to warranties and negative covenants) is boilerplate. The omission may, of course, have been caused by mutual trust and confidence, but in any event, there is not such strong presumption of exclusion because of the existence of a detailed integration clause, as was relied upon by the Court of Appeals in *Fogelson, supra*, 300 N.Y. at 340, 90 N.E.2d 881.

Nor do we see any contradiction of the terms of the sales agreement. *Mitchill v. Lath, supra*, 247 N.Y. at 381, 160 N.E. 646; 3 Corbin on Contracts § 573, at 357. The written agreement dealt with the sale of corporate assets, the oral agreement with the relocation of the Lees. Thus, the oral agreement does not vary or contradict the money consideration recited in the contract as flowing to the selling corporation. That is the only consideration recited, and it is still the only consideration to the corporation.

We affirm Judge Tenney's reception in evidence of the oral agreement and his denial of the motion under Rule 50(b) with respect to the parol evidence rule.

* * *

Affirmed.

GEORGE v. DAVOLI

City Court, City of Geneva, N.Y. 1977.
91 Misc.2d 296, 397 N.Y.S.2d 895.

DAVID H. BRIND, JUDGE. At the trial of this matter the Defendant was called by the Plaintiff as his only witness. The Plaintiff's attendance

---

1. Barth in a confidential memorandum dated June 12, 1970 to Yogman and Edgar Bronfman stated that "he [Harold Lee] would very much like to have another distributorship in another area for his two sons." Apparently Barth, who was not present at Harold Lee's meeting with Yogman, assumed that this was a desire on the part of Lee rather than a promise made by Yogman for Seagram.

was waived by his attorney and he did not testify. The gravamen of this action revolves about a sale of certain jewelry on approval. A memorandum of sale was submitted to the Court which was signed by both the Plaintiff and the Defendant. The Memorandum stated that the Plaintiff was purchasing certain Indian jewelry for the sum of $500.00, but if the jewelry were not acceptable, the seller would accept its return and refund $440.00 of the purchase price to the buyer. The memorandum in question is silent as to the time within which such jewelry had to be returned by the buyer to the seller.

The court allowed the Defendant, over the objection of Plaintiff's counsel, to testify to a contemporaneous oral agreement between the buyer and seller to the effect that the jewelry had to be returned by the following Monday evening, or the sale would be deemed completed. The Plaintiff did not contact the Defendant until the following Wednesday of the same week, two days after the orally agreed upon deadline. The Plaintiff at that time tendered the return of the jewelry stating that they were not acceptable and demanded the return of $440.00 of his purchase price. The Defendant refused to accept the jewelry or to return the money, stating the sale had been completed in accordance with the agreement.

The law of this case is governed by the Uniform Commercial Code of the State of New York. * * *

There is no question that under the Uniform Commercial Code *that unless* [otherwise] *agreed upon*, the goods must be returned "seasonably" (UCC 2–326 and 2–327). Returning the merchandise within one week as is the situation in the present case would ordinarily be seasonable or within a reasonable time. However, where there is an agreement setting forth a specific time limit, the Court is bound to enforce such limit.

Section 2–202 of UCC compels a court to allow oral testimony supplementing the written agreement where not inconsistent and where the writing is not intended as a complete and exclusive statement of the terms of the agreement. The court finds the absence of an agreed upon time limit, that type of omission which comes within the area provided for in this statute. There is nothing inconsistent with the Defendant's testimony inasmuch as the written memorandum makes no reference to the time of return of the merchandise. Likewise it cannot be said that the written memorandum is a complete and exclusive statement of the terms of the agreement since the time of return is an important part of the arrangement between the parties. Is it therefore such an additional term that the parties would certainly have included it in the written document if it had been agreed upon and consequently one not to be admitted on trial? The Appellate Division in *Hunt Foods & Ind.* v. *Doliner*, 26 A.D.2d 41, 270 N.Y.S.2d 937; interpreting UCC 2–202 held that under like circumstances the oral testimony must be admitted. The Court held:

> "So the first question presented is whether that term is 'consistent' with the instrument. In a sense any oral provision which would prevent the ripening of the obligations of a writing is inconsistent with the writing. But that obviously is not the sense in which the word is used (*Hicks* v. *Bush*, 10 N.Y.2d 488, 491, 225 N.Y.S.2d 34, 180 N.E.2d 425). To be inconsistent the term must contradict or negate a term of the writing. *A term or condition which has a lesser effect is provable.*

> "The Official Comment prepared by the drafters of the code contains this statement: 'If the additional terms are such that, if agreed upon, they would certainly have been included in the document in the view of the court, then evidence of their alleged making must be kept from the trier of fact.' [UCC § 2–202, (comment 3).]

> "Special Term interpreted this language as not only calling for an adjudication by the court in all instances where proof of an 'additional oral term' is offered, but making that determination exclusively the function of the court. We believe the proffered evidence to be *inadmissible only* where the writing contradicts the existence of the claimed additional term (*Meadow Brook Nat. Bank* v. *Bzura,* 20 A.D.2d 287, 290, 246 N.Y.S.2d 787, 790). The conversations in this case, some of which are not disputed, and the expectation of all the parties for further negotiations, suggest that the alleged oral condition precedent cannot be precluded as a matter of law or as factually impossible. It is not sufficient that the existence of the condition is implausible. *It must be impossible* (cf. *Millerton Agway Co-op.* v. *Briarcliff Farms,* 17 N.Y.2d 57, 63–64, 268 N.Y.S.2d 18, 215 N.E.2d 341)." (emphasis supplied.) (See also 17 A.L.R.3rd 1032, which interprets UCC § 2–202(b) similarly.)

Therefore, the Court finds that parol evidence as to the agreement setting forth the time within which the merchandise was to be returned if not acceptable, is admissable [sic] to supplement the written memorandum and further finds that *Mitchill* v. *Lath*, 247 N.Y. 377, 160 N.E. 646 decided by the Court of Appeals in 1928, cited by the Plaintiff, does not apply herein as its application to the instant case has been changed by legislative enactment (UCC § 2–202(b)) which took effect in 1964.

Since the parol evidence as to such agreement stands unrebutted, the Court must find that the Plaintiff failed to comply with the parties' agreement to the return of the goods by Monday evening, the consequence of which is that title therein passed to the Plaintiff, and the Defendant is under no legal obligation to accept the return thereof.

The complaint of the Plaintiff is hereby dismissed without costs.

VAL–FORD REALTY CORP. v.
J.Z.'S TOY WORLD, INC.

N.Y. Supreme Court, Appellate Division, 1996.
231 A.D.2d 434, 647 N.Y.S.2d 488.

MEMORANDUM DECISION: Order, Supreme Court, New York County (Herman Cahn, J.), entered on or about October 26, 1995, which, insofar as appealed from, denied plaintiff's motion for summary judgment, unanimously affirmed, without costs.

Plaintiff seeks to recover rent due under a written lease executed by the corporate defendant and guaranteed by the individual defendant. Defendants admit executing these documents, but assert that their purpose was to defraud plaintiff's construction lender into advancing additional funds and were never intended by the parties to be enforceable, and that the parties are not strangers in that, among other things, the individual defendant is one of the plaintiff corporation's three directors. We agree with the motion court that this parol evidence offered by defendants raises issues of credibility inappropriate for summary judgment treatment. While parol evidence is generally inadmissible to contradict, vary, add to, or subtract from the terms of an integrated agreement such as the instant lease and guarantee, it is admissible to show that a " 'writing, although purporting to be a contract, is, in fact, no contract at all' " (*Greenleaf v. Lachman*, 216 A.D.2d 65, 66, 628 N.Y.S.2d 268, *lv denied* 88 N.Y.2d 802, 645 N.Y.S.2d 445, 668 N.E.2d 416, quoting Richardson on Evidence § 606 [Prince, 10th ed.]; *see also*, *Paolangeli v. Cowles*, 208 A.D.2d 1174, 617 N.Y.S.2d 936). We have considered plaintiff's other arguments and find them to be without merit. * * *

Problems

1. A and B made an oral agreement and signed a writing that incorporated its terms. However, they were not fully satisfied with the writing and they agreed to have it redrafted. Does this writing constitute an integration?

2. P opened a T-shirt store in D's mall pursuant to a written commercial lease with D as landlord. Subsequently, D leased space in the same mall to X for another T-shirt store. P sued D for breach of P's lease. At trial P offered evidence that it had been orally agreed at the time the lease was signed that P would have the only store of its kind in the mall. The written lease had no such provision. Is P's proffered evidence admissible?

3. P applied for and received a construction loan from D in order to build a house on land owned by P. The house was built by G, a general contractor selected on the advice of D. The construction contract contained an estimated, rather than a fixed, price. P sues D for negligence with the allegation that additional costs were caused by G's incompetence. P offers evidence at trial that D orally agreed to help select the contractor, guarantee the contractor's competence and supervise construction to assure that the house would be built for the estimated price. The loan agreement contained

a merger clause and also a provision that selection of a contractor was the exclusive responsibility of the borrower. Should P's evidence be excluded?

4. Owner and Contractor entered into a written construction contract which did not state a completion date. In Owner's lawsuit against Contractor, Owner offered evidence that there was a contemporaneous conversation in which a completion date was agreed upon. Is this evidence admissible?

5. B entered into a written contract by which S agreed to sell B its requirements of raw material for a stated consideration. There was a merger clause in this agreement. B sues S for breach of a contemporaneous oral agreement that S would sell 50 shares of its stock to B for an agreed price. Is evidence of this agreement admissible?

6. Defendant agreed to create customized software for plaintiff trucking company. A written contract described what the software should be designed to accomplish in terms of tracking the location of individual trucks, planning service intervals, etc. The writing contained the following provision: "There are no promises, verbal understandings or agreements of any kind pertaining to this contract other than specified herein." The instrument was dated Sept. 6. At the trial, plaintiff offered evidence that either on Sept. 5, or 7, S's general manager agreed that B might try out the software for a month and if it did not prove satisfactory, B might delete the software from its computer and have its money back. Is plaintiff's evidence admissible?

7. P had been working for D for about a year as an employee at an agreed fixed salary. Subsequently the parties signed a document which stated that P was an independent contractor. According to this writing, P was to be paid according to the work done and was to carry the necessary Workers' Compensation Insurance. P sues on the initial contract for unpaid salary and offers to testify that the second agreement was not intended to be binding: It's purpose was to enable D to avoid the Compensation Law. Is the evidence admissible?

8. H & W, a young married couple, purchased a home. W's parents made a $70,000 payment toward the purchase price. H & W signed a promissory note in this amount payable to W's parents in which they jointly and severally agreed to be liable for payment on demand. After 12 years, W brought divorce proceedings against H. W's parents demanded payment of the note from H. When he refused to pay, they sued. In defense, he offered testimony to the effect that W's parents had represented that the $70,000 was a gift, specifically, an advance on W's inheritance. Is this testimony admissible?

9. B made an offer to buy S's stock for $5.50 per share. The negotiations at this point were recessed. Since B was afraid that S would use B's offer to obtain a higher price from a third party, B requested and received from S a written option (supported by consideration) to purchase the stock at $5.50 per share. After the negotiations collapsed, B attempted to exercise the option. At the trial S offered evidence that it was orally agreed simultaneously with the granting of the option that the option was not to be exercised unless S sought outside bids for the stock. Is the evidence admissible?

10. P alleges that it was induced to enter into a written contract to purchase a lease of a building because of oral representations, falsely made by D, as to the operating expenses and profits of the building. The contract contains the following language: "The Seller has not made and does not make any representations as to physical condition, rents, leases, expenses, operation or any other matter or thing affecting or related to the aforesaid premises except as herein specifically set forth, and the Purchaser hereby expressly acknowledges that it has inspected the premises and agrees to take the premises as is." There is, in addition, a merger clause and a statement that neither party is relying upon any representation not embodied in the contract. Is P's action for fraud based on D's oral representations precluded by the parol evidence rule?

SECTION 2. INTERPRETATION

(Calamari & Perillo·5th §§ 3.9—3.17)

T.S. ELIOT, BURNT NORTON (FOUR QUARTETS)

Words strain,

Crack and sometimes break, under the burden,

Under the tension, slip, slide, perish,

Decay with imprecision, will not stay in place,

Will not stay still.

LEWIS CARROLL, THROUGH THE LOOKING GLASS

"When I use a word," Humpty Dumpty said . . ., "it means just what I choose it to mean—neither more nor less."

"The question is," said Alice, "whether you can make words mean so many different things."

PACIFIC GAS AND ELEC. CO. v. G. W. THOMAS DRAYAGE & RIGGING CO.

Supreme Court of California, In Bank, 1968.
69 Cal.2d 33, 69 Cal.Rptr. 561, 442 P.2d 641.

Traynor, Chief Justice. Defendant appeals from a judgment for plaintiff in an action for damages for injury to property under an indemnity clause of a contract.

In 1960 defendant entered into a contract with plaintiff to furnish the labor and equipment necessary to remove and replace the upper metal cover of plaintiff's steam turbine. Defendant agreed to perform the work "at [its] own risk and expense" and to "indemnify" plaintiff "against all loss, damage, expense and liability resulting from . . . injury to property, arising out of or in any way connected with the performance of this contract." Defendant also agreed to procure not less than $50,000 insurance to cover liability for injury to property. * * *

During the work the cover fell and injured the exposed rotor of the turbine. Plaintiff brought this action to recover $25,144.51, the amount it subsequently spent on repairs. During the trial it dismissed a count based on negligence and thereafter secured judgment on the theory that the indemnity provision covered injury to all property regardless of ownership.

Defendant offered to prove by admissions of plaintiff's agents, by defendant's conduct under similar contracts entered into with plaintiff, and by other proof that in the indemnity clause the parties meant to cover injury to property of third parties only and not to plaintiff's property. Although the trial court observed that the language used was "the classic language for a third party indemnity provision" and that "one could very easily conclude that . . . its whole intendment is to indemnify third parties," it nevertheless held that the "plain language" of the agreement also required defendant to indemnify plaintiff for injuries to plaintiff's property. Having determined that the contract had a plain meaning, the court refused to admit any extrinsic evidence that would contradict its interpretation.

When a court interprets a contract on this basis, it determines the meaning of the instrument in accordance with the ". . . extrinsic evidence of the judge's own linguistic education and experience." (3 Corbin on Contracts (1960 ed.) [1964 Supp. § 579, p. 225, fn. 56].) The exclusion of testimony that might contradict the linguistic background of the judge reflects a judicial belief in the possibility of perfect verbal expression. (9 Wigmore on Evidence (3d ed. 1940) § 2461, p. 187.) This belief is a remnant of a primitive faith in the inherent potency[2] and inherent meaning of words.[3]

The test of admissibility of extrinsic evidence to explain the meaning of a written instrument is not whether it appears to the court to be plain and unambiguous on its face, but whether the offered evidence is relevant to prove a meaning to which the language of the instrument is reasonably susceptible. * * *

A rule that would limit the determination of the meaning of a written instrument to its four-corners merely because it seems to the court to be clear and unambiguous, would either deny the relevance of the intention of the parties or presuppose a degree of verbal precision and stability our language has not attained.

Some courts have expressed the opinion that contractual obligations are created by the mere use of certain words, whether or not there was

---

2. E.g., "The elaborate system of taboo and verbal prohibitions in primitive groups; the ancient Egyptian myth of Khern, the apotheosis of the word, and of Thoth, the Scribe of Truth, the Giver of Words and Script, the Master of Incantations; the avoidance of the name of God in Brahmanism, Judaism and Islam; totemistic and protective names in mediaeval Turkish and Finno–Ugrian languages; the misplaced verbal scruples of the 'Précieuses'; the Swedish peasant custom of curing sick cattle smitten by witchcraft, by making them swallow a page torn out of the psalter and put in dough. . . ." from Ullman, The Principles of Semantics (1963 ed.) 43. (See also Ogden and Richards, The Meaning of Meaning (rev. ed. 1956) pp. 24–47.)

3. " 'Rerum enim vocabula immutabilia sunt, homines mutabilia,' " (Words are unchangeable, men changeable) from Dig. XXXIII, 10, 7, § 2, *de sup. leg.* as quoted in 9 Wigmore on Evidence, *op. cit. supra*, § 2461, p. 187.

any intention to incur such obligations.[4] Under this view, contractual obligations flow, not from the intention of the parties but from the fact that they used certain magic words. Evidence of the parties' intention therefore becomes irrelevant.

In this state, however, the intention of the parties as expressed in the contract is the source of contractual rights and duties.[5] A court must ascertain and give effect to this intention by determining what the parties meant by the words they used. Accordingly, the exclusion of relevant, extrinsic evidence to explain the meaning of a written instrument could be justified only if it were feasible to determine the meaning the parties gave to the words from the instrument alone.

If words had absolute and constant referents, it might be possible to discover contractual intention in the words themselves and in the manner in which they were arranged. Words, however, do not have absolute and constant referents. "A word is a symbol of thought but has no arbitrary and fixed meaning like a symbol of algebra or chemistry, ..." (*Pearson v. State Social Welfare Board* (1960) 54 Cal.2d 184, 195, 5 Cal.Rptr. 553, 559, 353 P.2d 33, 39.) The meaning of particular words or groups of words varies with the ". . . verbal context and surrounding circumstances and purposes in view of the linguistic education and experience of their users and their hearers or readers (not excluding judges). * * * A word has no meaning apart from these factors; much less does it have an objective meaning, one true meaning." (Corbin, *The Interpretation of Words and the Parol Evidence Rule* (1965) 50 Cornell L.Q. 161, 187.) Accordingly, the meaning of a writing ". . . can only be found by interpretation in the light of all the circumstances that reveal the sense in which the writer used the words. The exclusion of parol evidence regarding such circumstances merely because the words do not appear ambiguous to the reader can easily lead to the attribution to a written instrument of a meaning that was never intended. [Citations omitted.]" (*Universal Sales Corp. v. California Press Mfg. Co.*, * * * 20 Cal.2d 751, 776, 128 P.2d 665, 679 (concurring opinion) * * * 3 Corbin on Contracts (1960 ed.) § 579, pp. 412–431; Ogden and Richards, The Meaning of Meaning, *op. cit.* 15; Ullmann, The Principles of Semantics, *supra*, 61; McBaine, *The Rule Against Disturbing Plain Meaning of Writings* (1943) 31 Cal.L.Rev. 145.)

Although extrinsic evidence is not admissible to add to, detract from, or vary the terms of a written contract, these terms must first be determined before it can be decided whether or not extrinsic evidence is being offered for a prohibited purpose. The fact that the terms of an

---

4. "A contract has, strictly speaking, nothing to do with the personal, or individual, intent of the parties. A contract is an obligation attached by the mere force of law to certain acts of the parties, usually words, which ordinarily accompany and represent a known intent." (*Hotchkiss v. National City Bank of New York* (S.D.N.Y.1911) 200 F. 287, 293. See also *C.H. Pope & Co. v.* *Bibb Mfg. Co.* (2d Cir.1923) 290 F. 586, 587; see 4 Williston on Contracts (3d ed. 1961) § 612, pp. 577–578, § 613, p. 583.)

5. "A contract must be so interpreted as to give effect to the mutual intention of the parties as it existed at the time of contracting, so far as the same is ascertainable and lawful." (Civ.Code, § 1636; see also Code Civ.Proc. § 1859 * * *.)

instrument appear clear to a judge does not preclude the possibility that the parties chose the language of the instrument to express different terms. That possibility is not limited to contracts whose terms have acquired a particular meaning by trade usage,[6] but exists whenever the parties' understanding of the words used may have differed from the judge's understanding.

Accordingly, rational interpretation requires at least a preliminary consideration of all credible evidence offered to prove the intention of the parties.[7] * * * Such evidence includes testimony as to the "circumstances surrounding the making of the agreement ... including the object, nature and subject matter of the writing ..." so that the court can "place itself in the same situation in which the parties found themselves at the time of contracting." *(Universal Sales Corp. v. Cal. Press Mfg. Co., supra,* 20 Cal.2d 751, 761, 128 P.2d 665, 671. * * *) If the court decides, after considering this evidence, that the language of a contract, in the light of all the circumstances, is "fairly susceptible of either one of the two interpretations contended for...." *(Balfour v. Fresno C. & I. Co.* (1895) 109 Cal. 221, 225, 41 P. 876, 877 * * *), extrinsic evidence relevant to prove either of such meanings is admissible.[8]

In the present case the court erroneously refused to consider extrinsic evidence offered to show that the indemnity clause in the contract was not intended to cover injuries to plaintiff's property. Although that evidence was not necessary to show that the indemnity clause was reasonably susceptible of the meaning contended for by defendant, it was nevertheless relevant and admissible on that issue. Moreover, since that clause was reasonably susceptible of that meaning, the offered evidence was also admissible to prove that the clause had that meaning and did

---

6. Extrinsic evidence of trade usage or custom has been admitted to show that the term "United Kingdom" in a motion picture distribution contract included Ireland *(Ermolieff v. R.K.O. Radio Pictures, Inc.* (1942) 19 Cal.2d 543, 549–552, 122 P.2d 3); that the word "ton" in a lease meant a long ton or 2,240 pounds and not the statutory ton of 2,000 pounds *(Higgins v. Cal. Petroleum, etc., Co.* (1898) 120 Cal. 629, 630–632, 52 P. 1080); that the word "stubble" in a lease included not only stumps left in the ground but everything "left on the ground after the harvest time" *(Callahan v. Stanley* (1881) 57 Cal. 476, 477–479); that the term "north" in a contract dividing mining claims indicated a boundary line running along the "magnetic and not the true meridian" *(Jenny Lind Co. v. Bower & Co.* (1858) 11 Cal. 194, 197–199) and that a form contract for purchase and sale was actually an agency contract *(Body–Steffner Co. v. Flotill Products* (1944) 63 Cal.App.2d 555, 558–562, 147 P.2d 84). * * *

7. When objection is made to any particular item of evidence offered to prove the intention of the parties, the trial court may not yet be in a position to determine whether in the light of all of the offered evidence, the item objected to will turn out to be admissible as tending to prove a meaning of which the language of the instrument is reasonably susceptible or inadmissible as tending to prove a meaning of which the language is not reasonably susceptible. In such case the court may admit the evidence conditionally by either reserving its ruling on the objection or by admitting the evidence subject to a motion to strike. * * *

8. Extrinsic evidence has often been admitted in such cases on the stated ground that the contract was ambiguous * * *. This statement of the rule is harmless if it is kept in mind that the ambiguity may be exposed by extrinsic evidence that reveals more than one possible meaning.

not cover injuries to plaintiff's property.[9] Accordingly, the judgment must be reversed.

* * *

TRIDENT CENTER v. CONNECTICUT GENERAL LIFE INSURANCE CO.

United States Court of Appeals, Ninth Circuit, 1988.
847 F.2d 564.

KOZINSKI, CIRCUIT JUDGE:

The parties to this transaction are, by any standard, highly sophisticated business people: Plaintiff is a partnership consisting of an insurance company and two of Los Angeles' largest and most prestigious law firms; defendant is another insurance company. Dealing at arm's length and from positions of roughly equal bargaining strength, they negotiated a commercial loan amounting to more than $56 million. The contract documents are lengthy and detailed; they squarely address the precise issue that is the subject of this dispute; to all who read English, they appear to resolve the issue fully and conclusively.

Plaintiff nevertheless argues here, as it did below, that it is entitled to introduce extrinsic evidence that the contract means something other than what it says. This case therefore presents the question whether parties in California can ever draft a contract that is proof to parol evidence. Somewhat surprisingly, the answer is no.

FACTS

The facts are rather simple. Sometime in 1983 Security First Life Insurance Company and the law firms of Mitchell, Silberberg & Knupp and Manatt, Phelps, Rothenberg & Tunney formed a limited partnership

---

9. The court's exclusion of extrinsic evidence in this case would be error even under a rule that excluded such evidence when the instrument appeared to the court to be clear and unambiguous on its face. The controversy centers on the meaning of the word "indemnify" and the phrase "all loss, damage, expense and liability." The trial court's recognition of the language as typical of a third party indemnity clause and the double sense in which the word "indemnify" is used in statutes and defined in dictionaries demonstrate the existence of an ambiguity. * * *

Plaintiff's assertion that the use of the word "all" to modify "loss, damage, expense and liability" dictates an all inclusive interpretation is not persuasive. If the word "indemnify" encompasses only third-party claims, the word "all" simply refers to all such claims. The use of the words "loss," "damage," and "expense" in addition to the word "liability" is likewise inconclusive.

These words do not imply an agreement to reimburse for injury to an indemnitee's property since they are commonly inserted in third-party indemnity clauses, to enable an indemnitee who settles a claim to recover from his indemnitor without proving his liability. * * *

The provision that defendant perform the work "at his own risk and expense" and the provisions relating to insurance are equally inconclusive. By agreeing to work at its own risk defendant may have released plaintiff from liability for any injuries to defendant's property arising out of the contract's performance, but this provision did not necessarily make defendant an insurer against injuries to plaintiff's property. Defendant's agreement to procure liability insurance to cover damages to plaintiff's property does not indicate whether the insurance was to cover all injuries or only injuries caused by defendant's negligence.

for the purpose of constructing an office building complex on Olympic Boulevard in West Los Angeles. The partnership, Trident Center, the plaintiff herein, sought and obtained financing for the project from defendant, Connecticut General Life Insurance Company. The loan documents provide for a loan of $56,500,000 at 12¼ percent interest for a term of 15 years, secured by a deed of trust on the project. The promissory note provides that "[m]aker shall not have the right to prepay the principal amount hereof in whole or in part" for the first 12 years. * * * In years 13–15, the loan may be prepaid, subject to a sliding prepayment fee. The note also provides that in case of a default during years 1–12, Connecticut General has the option of accelerating the note and adding a 10 percent prepayment fee.

Everything was copacetic for a few years until interest rates began to drop. The 12¼ percent rate that had seemed reasonable in 1983 compared unfavorably with 1987 market rates and Trident started looking for ways of refinancing the loan to take advantage of the lower rates. Connecticut General was unwilling to oblige, insisting that the loan could not be prepaid for the first 12 years of its life, that is, until January 1996.

Trident then brought suit in state court seeking a declaration that it was entitled to prepay the loan now, subject only to a 10 percent prepayment fee. Connecticut General promptly removed to federal court and brought a motion to dismiss, claiming that the loan documents clearly and unambiguously precluded prepayment during the first 12 years. The district court agreed and dismissed Trident's complaint. The court also *"sua sponte,* sanction[ed] the plaintiff for the filing of a frivolous lawsuit." Order of Dismissal, No. CV 87–2712 JMI (Kx), at 3 (C.D.Cal. June 8, 1987). Trident appeals both aspects of the district court's ruling.

Discussion

I

Trident makes two arguments as to why the district court's ruling is wrong. First, it contends that the language of the contract is ambiguous and proffers a construction that it believes supports its position. Second, Trident argues that, under California law, even seemingly unambiguous contracts are subject to modification by parol or extrinsic evidence. Trident faults the district court for denying it the opportunity to present evidence that the contract language did not accurately reflect the parties' intentions.

A. *The Contract*

As noted earlier, the promissory note provides that Trident "shall not have the right to prepay the principal amount hereof in whole or in part before January 1996." * * * It is difficult to imagine language that more clearly or unambiguously expresses the idea that Trident may not unilaterally prepay the loan during its first 12 years. Trident, however, argues that there is an ambiguity because another clause of the note provides that "[i]n the event of a prepayment resulting from a default hereunder or the Deed of Trust prior to January 10, 1996 the prepayment fee will be ten percent (10%)." * * * Trident interprets this clause as giving it the option of prepaying the loan if only it is willing to incur the prepayment fee.

We reject Trident's argument out of hand. In the first place, its proffered interpretation would result in a contradiction between two clauses of the contract; the default clause would swallow up the clause prohibiting Trident from prepaying during the first 12 years of the contract. The normal rule of construction, of course, is that courts must interpret contracts, if possible, so as to avoid internal conflict. *See* ... 4 S. Williston, *A Treatise on the Law of Contracts* § 618, at 714–15 (3d ed. 1961); *id.* § 624, at 825.

In any event, the clause on which Trident relies is not on its face reasonably susceptible to Trident's proffered interpretation. Whether to accelerate repayment of the loan in the event of default is entirely Connecticut General's decision. The contract makes this clear at several points. ... ("in each such event [of default], the entire principal indebtedness, or so much thereof as may remain unpaid at the time, shall, *at the option of Holder,* become due and payable immediately" (emphasis added)); * * * ("[i]n the event Holder exercises its *option to accelerate* the maturity hereof ..." (emphasis added)); ... ("in each such event [of default], Beneficiary *may* declare all sums secured hereby immediately due and payable ..." (emphasis added)). Even if Connecticut General decides to declare a default and accelerate, it "may rescind any notice of breach or default." * * * Finally, Connecticut General has the option of doing nothing at all: "Beneficiary reserves the right at its sole option to waive noncompliance by Trustor with any of the conditions or covenants to be performed by Trustor hereunder." * * *

Once again, it is difficult to imagine language that could more clearly assign to Connecticut General the exclusive right to decide whether to declare a default, whether and when to accelerate, and whether, having chosen to take advantage of any of its remedies, to rescind the process before its completion.

Trident nevertheless argues that it is entitled to precipitate a default and insist on acceleration by tendering the balance due on the note plus the 10 percent prepayment fee. The contract language, cited above, leaves no room for this construction. It is true, of course, that Trident is free to stop making payments, which may then cause Connecticut General to declare a default and accelerate. But that is not to say that Connecticut General would be required to so respond.[2] The contract quite clearly gives Connecticut General other options: It may choose to waive the default, or to take advantage of some other remedy such as the

---

2. See 1 H. Miller & M. Starr, *Current Law of California Real Estate* § 3:62, at 428 ("[w]hen there is a default, acceleration does not occur automatically. It is merely a contractual *option* given to beneficiary for his benefit, and acceleration only occurs when the beneficiary *affirmatively* elects to declare the balance of the principal and interest due" (emphasis original)); *id.* § 3:69, at 449. ...

right to collect "all the income, rents, royalties, revenue, issues, profits, and proceeds of the Property." * * * By interpreting the contract as Trident suggests, we would ignore those provisions giving Connecticut General, not Trident, the exclusive right to decide how, when and whether the contract will be terminated upon default during the first 12 years.

In effect, Trident is attempting to obtain judicial sterilization of its intended default. But defaults are messy things; they are supposed to be. Once the maker of a note secured by a deed of trust defaults, its credit rating may deteriorate; attempts at favorable refinancing may be thwarted by the need to meet the trustee's sale schedule; its cash flow may be impaired if the beneficiary takes advantage of the assignment of rents remedy; default provisions in its loan agreements with other lenders may be triggered. Fear of these repercussions is strong medicine that keeps debtors from shirking their obligations when interest rates go down and they become disenchanted with their loans.[4] That Trident is willing to suffer the cost and delay of a lawsuit, rather than simply defaulting, shows far better than anything we might say that these provisions are having their intended effect. We decline Trident's invitation to truncate the lender's remedies and deprive Connecticut General of its bargained-for protection.

B. Extrinsic Evidence

Trident argues in the alternative that, even if the language of the contract appears to be unambiguous, the deal the parties actually struck is in fact quite different. It wishes to offer extrinsic evidence that the parties had agreed Trident could prepay at any time within the first 12 years by tendering the full amount plus a 10 percent prepayment fee. As discussed above, this is an interpretation to which the contract, as written, is not reasonably susceptible. Under traditional contract principles, extrinsic evidence is inadmissible to interpret, vary or add to the terms of an unambiguous integrated written instrument. *See* 4 S. Williston, *supra* p. 5, § 631, at 948–49 . . . .

Trident points out, however, that California does not follow the traditional rule. Two decades ago the California Supreme Court in *Pacific Gas & Electric Co. v. G.W. Thomas Drayage & Rigging Co.,* 69 Cal.2d 33, 442 P.2d 641, 69 Cal.Rptr. 561 (1968), turned its back on the notion that a contract can ever have a plain meaning discernible by a court without resort to extrinsic evidence. The court reasoned that contractual obligations flow not from the words of the contract, but from the intention of the parties. "Accordingly," the court stated, "the exclusion of relevant, extrinsic, evidence to explain the meaning of a written instrument could be justified only if it were feasible to determine the meaning the parties gave to the words from the instrument alone."

---

4. This provides a symmetry with the situation where interest rates go up and it is the lender who is stuck with a loan it would prefer to turn over at market rates. In an economy where interest rates fluctu- ate, it is all but certain that one side or the other will be dissatisfied with a long-term loan at some time. Mutuality calls for en- forcing the contract as written no matter whose ox is being gored.

69 Cal.2d at 38, 442 P.2d 641, 69 Cal.Rptr. 561. This, the California Supreme Court concluded, is impossible: "If words had absolute and constant referents, it might be possible to discover contractual intention in the words themselves and in the manner in which they were arranged. Words, however, do not have absolute and constant referents." *Id.* In the same vein, the court noted that "[t]he exclusion of testimony that might contradict the linguistic background of the judge reflects a judicial belief in the possibility of perfect verbal expression. This belief is a remnant of a primitive faith in the inherent potency and inherent meaning of words." *Id.* at 37, 442 P.2d 641, 69 Cal.Rptr. 561 (citation and footnotes omitted).[5]

Under *Pacific Gas,* it matters not how clearly a contract is written, nor how completely it is integrated, nor how carefully it is negotiated, nor how squarely it addresses the issue before the court: the contract cannot be rendered impervious to attack by parol evidence. If one side is willing to claim that the parties intended one thing but the agreement provides for another, the court must consider extrinsic evidence of possible ambiguity. If that evidence raises the specter of ambiguity where there was none before, the contract language is displaced and the intention of the parties must be divined from self-serving testimony offered by partisan witnesses whose recollection is hazy from passage of time and colored by their conflicting interests. *See Delta Dynamics, Inc. v. Arioto,* 69 Cal.2d 525, 532, 446 P.2d 785, 72 Cal.Rptr. 785 (1968) (Mosk, J., dissenting). We question whether this approach is more likely to divulge the original intention of the parties than reliance on the seemingly clear words they agreed upon at the time. *See generally Morta v. Korea Ins. Corp.,* 840 F.2d 1452, 1460 (9th Cir.1988).

Pacific Gas casts a long shadow of uncertainty over all transactions negotiated and executed under the law of California. As this case illustrates, even when the transaction is very sizeable, even if it involves only sophisticated parties, even if it was negotiated with the aid of counsel, even if it results in contract language that is devoid of ambiguity, costly and protracted litigation cannot be avoided if one party has a strong enough motive for challenging the contract. While this rule creates much business for lawyers and an occasional windfall to some clients, it leads only to frustration and delay for most litigants and clogs already overburdened courts.

It also chips away at the foundation of our legal system. By giving credence to the idea that words are inadequate to express concepts, *Pacific Gas* undermines the basic principle that language provides a meaningful constraint on public and private conduct. If we are unwilling to say that parties, dealing face to face, can come up with language that binds them, how can we send anyone to jail for violating statutes

---

5. In an unusual footnote, the court compared the belief in the immutable meaning of words with " '[t]he elaborate system of taboo and verbal prohibitions in primitive groups ... [such as] the Swedish peasant custom of curing sick cattle smitten by witchcraft, by making them swallow a page torn out of a psalter and put in dough....' " *Id.* n. 2 (quoting Ullman, *The Principles of Semantics* 43 (1963)).

consisting of mere words lacking "absolute and constant referents"? How can courts ever enforce decrees, not written in language understandable to all, but encoded in a dialect reflecting only the "linguistic background of the judge"? Can lower courts ever be faulted for failing to carry out the mandate of higher courts when "perfect verbal expression" is impossible? Are all attempts to develop the law in a reasoned and principled fashion doomed to failure as "remnant[s] of a primitive faith in the inherent potency and inherent meaning of words"?

Be that as it may. While we have our doubts about the wisdom of *Pacific Gas,* we have no difficulty understanding its meaning, even without extrinsic evidence to guide us. As we read the rule in California, we must reverse and remand to the district court in order to give plaintiff an opportunity to present extrinsic evidence as to the intention of the parties in drafting the contract. It may not be a wise rule we are applying, but it is a rule that binds us. *Erie R.R. Co. v. Tompkins,* 304 U.S. 64, 78, 58 S.Ct. 817, 822, 82 L.Ed. 1188 (1938).

II

In imposing sanctions on plaintiff, the district court stated:

> Pursuant to Fed.R.Civ.P. 11, the Court, *sua sponte,* sanctions the plaintiff for the filing of a frivolous lawsuit. The Court concludes that the language in the note and deed of trust is plain and clear. No reasonable person, much less firms of able attorneys, could possibly misunderstand this crystal-clear language. Therefore, this action was brought in bad faith.

Order of Dismissal at 3. Having reversed the district court on its substantive ruling, we must, of course, also reverse it as to the award of sanctions. While we share the district judge's impatience with this litigation, we would suggest that his irritation may have been misdirected. It is difficult to blame plaintiff and its lawyers for bringing this lawsuit. With this much money at stake, they would have been foolish not to pursue all remedies available to them under the applicable law. At fault, it seems to us, are not the parties and their lawyers but the legal system that encourages this kind of lawsuit. By holding that language has no objective meaning, and that contracts mean only what courts ultimately say they do, *Pacific Gas* invites precisely this type of lawsuit. With the benefit of 20 years of hindsight, the California Supreme Court may wish to revisit the issue. If it does so, we commend to it the facts of this case as a paradigmatic example of why the traditional rule, based on centuries of experience, reflects the far wiser approach.

Conclusion

The judgment of the district court is REVERSED. * * *

BEANSTALK GROUP, INC. v. AM GENERAL CORP.

United States Court of Appeals, Seventh Circuit, 2002.
283 F.3d 856.

[In 1997, at the time of the contract between the plaintiff and defendant, AM General manufactured the Humvee, a military vehicle that is the successor to the Jeep, and it also sold in a civilian version called the "Hummer." In their "representation agreement," AM General appointed Beanstalk as its exclusive agent to find licensees to use AM General's Hummer trademark. Beanstalk would be compensated by a commission of 35% on all gross receipts from such license agreements. The representation agreement was to continue to the end of 2000. In 1999, in a complex transaction described below, AM General entered into a joint-venture agreement with GM in which GM acquired the Hummer trademark. Beanstalk sued AM General for a 35% commission on so much of the consideration running from GM to AM General as is attributable to the value of the Hummer trademark. The District Court dismissed Beanstalk's complaint. Ed.]

POSNER, CIRCUIT JUDGE. The agreement was drafted by Beanstalk, but this fact has little interpretive significance since AM General is a commercially sophisticated party represented by counsel. Most courts now agree with this exception to the principle that contracts are to be construed against the party that drafted it. [Citations omitted.] There are holdouts, illustrated by *Eastern Bus Lines, Inc. v. Board of Education*, 7 Conn.App. 581, 509 A.2d 1071, 1073–74 (1986), where the court, quoting an earlier opinion, said that "the party who actually does the writing of an instrument will presumably be guided by his own interests and goals in the transaction. He may choose shadings of expression, words more specific or more imprecise, according to the dictates of these interests." No doubt; but the other party, if commercially sophisticated and represented by counsel, will insist on clarification. Indiana has yet to take a stand on the exception, though the only case from Indiana that we can find which bears on it, *Nationwide Mutual Ins. Co. v. Neville*, 434 N.E.2d 585, 599 (Ind.App.1982), leans in favor of rejecting it. No matter; AM does not need the rule in order to prevail. We add that the rule is in practice a makeweight rather than a tie breaker.

Beanstalk set about obtaining agreements for the licensing of the Hummer trademark. In 1999, however, two years into the representation agreement with Beanstalk, AM General entered into a joint-venture agreement with General Motors under which GM would design and engineer a new version of the Hummer, would make an interest-free loan of $235 million to AM General for the construction of a factory to manufacture the new version, would promise to buy a minimum number of the new vehicles, would obtain an option to buy up to 40 percent of AM General's common stock—and would acquire the Hummer trademark. GM informed Beanstalk that it had not assumed any of AM General's obligations under the representation agreement and that it would not compensate Beanstalk for any license agreements made or renewed after the effective date of the joint-venture agreement.

Beanstalk argues that the agreement between AM General and GM, although of course not labeled a license agreement, was one because it transferred the Hummer trademark to GM and thus was an "agreement or arrangement, whether in the form of a license or otherwise, granting merchandising or other rights in the Property"; for the transfer gave GM the right, indeed the exclusive right, to merchandise the Hummer trademark, that is, the "Property." The contract thus is clear, Beanstalk argues—the joint venture was an "agreement" that "grant[ed]" GM "merchandising ... rights" in the Hummer trademark and it did not have to be "in the form of a license" because the representation agreement says "in the form of a license or otherwise"—and under accepted principles of contract law we should look no further. Beanstalk wants 35 percent of so much of the consideration running from GM to AM General as represents the value of the Hummer trademark. We do not know what the consideration was, or what that value is, because no evidence has been taken—in fact, the joint-venture agreement is not even in the record, though the sketch we have just given of its terms is not contested.

Beanstalk is correct that written contracts are usually enforced in accordance with the ordinary meaning of the language used in them and without recourse to evidence, beyond the contract itself, as to what the parties meant. This presumption simplifies the litigation of contract disputes and, more important, protects contracting parties against being blindsided by evidence intended to contradict the deal that they thought they had graven in stone by using clear language. It is a strong presumption, motivated by an understandable distrust in the accuracy of litigation to reconstruct contracting parties' intentions, but it is rebuttable—here by two principles of contract interpretation that are closely related in the setting of this suit. The first is that a contract will not be interpreted literally if doing so would produce absurd results, in the sense of results that the parties, presumed to be rational persons pursuing rational ends, are very unlikely to have agreed to seek. [Citations omitted.]

This is an interpretive principle, not a species of paternalism. "The letters between plaintiff and defendant were from one merchant to another. They are to be read as businessmen would read them, and only as a last resort are to be thrown out altogether as meaningless futilities.... If literalness is sheer absurdity, we are to seek some other meaning whereby reason will be instilled and absurdity avoided." *Outlet Embroidery Co. v. Derwent Mills*, 254 N.Y. 179, 172 N.E. 462, 463 (1930) (Cardozo, C.J.). "There is a long tradition in contract law of reading contracts sensibly; contracts—certainly business contracts of the kind involved here—are not parlor games but the means of getting the world's work done.... True, parties can contract for preposterous terms. If contract language is crystal clear or there is independent extrinsic evidence that something silly was actually intended, a party may be held to its bargain, absent some specialized defense." *Rhode Island Charities Trust v. Engelhard Corp.*, 267 F.3d 3, 7 (1st Cir.2001); [further citations omitted]. The second principle is that a contract must be interpreted as a whole. [Citations omitted.] Sentences are not isolated units of meaning, but take meaning from other sentences in the same document.

The second principle thus is linguistic; the first reflects the fact that interpretation is a cultural as well as a linguistic undertaking. To interpret a contract or other document, it is not enough to have a command of the grammar, syntax, and vocabulary of the language in which the document is written. One must know something about the practical as well as the purely verbal context of the language to be interpreted. In the case of a commercial contract, one must have a general acquaintance with commercial practices. This doesn't mean that judges should have an M.B.A. or have practiced corporate or commercial law, but merely that they be alert citizens of a market-oriented society so that they can recognize absurdity in a business context. A blinkered literalism, a closing of one's eyes to the obvious, can produce nonsensical results, as this case illustrates. Beanstalk is in the business of merchandising trademarks. If, while the representation agreement was in effect, a toy company wanted to make a toy Hummer, Beanstalk was authorized to grant the toy company a license in exchange for a fee that it would split 35/65 with AM General. The joint-venture agreement was not that kind of arrangement. It was not an arrangement for the promotion of AM General's trademark. By the agreement creating the joint venture, AM General essentially transferred the Hummer business to General Motors, retaining a role limited to manufacturing, in a factory built with GM's money, a vehicle designed by, engineered by, and to be marketed by (that is the significance of the transfer of the trademark) GM. Quite apart from the option that GM also received to buy a large, doubtless controlling interest in AM General, it's as if AM General had sold its entire business, including its manufacturing assets and all its trademarks, to GM.

Beanstalk is not a business broker. It had nothing to do with the joint venture and indeed didn't even know about it until after it took place. The parties could hardly have intended that Beanstalk should get a commission if AM General decided, as in effect it did, to get out of the Hummer business. A business would not contract to pay an agent for work that the agent did not do but that the business did itself. Beanstalk and AM General must have known when they signed the representation agreement that if AM General ever sold its Hummer business, the trademark would go with it, as the purchaser would need it in order to identify the product, while AM General would no longer have any need or use for it. Indeed, AM General would have nothing to attach the trademark to—and a trademark is an identifier, not a freestanding piece of intellectual property; hence the rule that a trademark cannot be sold in gross, that is, without the assets that create the product that it identifies. [Citations omitted.] The parties would hardly have intended Beanstalk to obtain a commission on the sale of the business merely because the sale would *inevitably* include the trademark. And they would not have wanted to burden the sale with the added cost of allocating the purchase price between the trademark and the other assets involved in the sale, as Beanstalk claims they must do in order to compute the commission to which it is entitled on the joint venture. (Such allocations may be required for tax purposes. See *Thrifticheck Service Corp. v. Commissioner*, 287 F.2d 1, 2, 3–4 (2d Cir.1961) (Friendly, J.). We are not told whether that was the case with the AM General–GM joint venture.)

The unreasonableness of Beanstalk's position can be seen most clearly by imagining that the joint venture had taken place the day after the representation agreement between Beanstalk and AM General went into effect. Then on Beanstalk's interpretation it would be entitled to 35 percent of the entire value of the Hummer trademark even though it had made absolutely no contribution to that value. That makes no sense; it is apparent that the definition of "License Agreement" in the representation agreement covers any agreement that has the function or character of a trademark licensing agreement even if the word "license" or a cognate term does not appear; the sale of a business is an agreement of an entirely different character.

* * *

Affirmed. [The dissenting opinion of Judge Rovner is omitted.]

UNTIEDT v. GRAND LABORATORIES, INC.

Court of Appeals of Minnesota, 1996.
552 N.W.2d 571.

[Untiedt retained Schmidt to represent him in a case concerning a defective cattle vaccine and consumer fraud. After a 10–hour discussion, Schmidt dictated a retainer agreement entitling his firm to a 40% contingent fee. The agreement was signed by Untiedt and Schmidt's secretary on behalf of Schmidt. The jury returned a verdict for $1,038,725 in Untiedt's favor and the court further assessed $366,584.24 in costs and attorneys' fees. Among the disputes between lawyer and client was whether the 40% contingency fee also included 40% of the attorneys' fees awarded Untiedt under the Minnesota consumer fraud statute. The paragraph that required interpretation read:

3. In the event of a cash settlement or jury verdict, I agree to pay said attorneys from any money and or [sic] property paid, received, or collected by action, compromise, or otherwise, 40 percent of any recovery for attorney fees for handling my case to settlement or suit including appeal.

The court noted that the term "recovery" was ambiguous. In ruling for the client the court said the following in a footnote. Ed.]

It is appropriate for us to place the burden of identifying and clarifying ambiguities on the attorney, whose experience places him or her in a better position to discharge the task at the least cost. Moreover, it is consistent with the attorney's fiduciary status, which requires him or her to exercise great caution in the adverse process of selecting the terms that will govern a contingent fee arrangement. *See Cardenas* [*v. Ramsey County*], 322 N.W.2d 191, at 193–94 [(Minn. 1982)] (interpreting the language of a contingent fee agreement in light of the drafting attorney's fiduciary status).

LARRY A. DI MATTEO, CONTRACT THEORY: THE EVOLUTION OF CONTRACTUAL INTENT 55–56 (Michigan State Univ. Press 1998).

Kreis v. Venture Out in America, Inc., [375 F.Supp. 482, 484 (E.D. Tenn.1973)], illustrates the quagmire that courts have immersed themselves in dealing with contractual interpretation. This quagmire is a result of not coming to terms with the dialectic [*i.e.,* the reconciliation of subjective and objective elements in the law of contracts]. "The courts cannot only look to the language of the contract but must ascertain the intention of the parties and make a construction that is fair and reasonable." Conceptually, this statement represents a court that is unsure as to the appropriate approach to contract interpretation. The rudiments of both the objective and subjective approaches are present. The objectivity of the *language of the instrument* is placed on the same plane as the more subjective finding of the *intention of the parties*. The language of the instrument does not prevent the court from straying outside its four corners to find the actual intent of the parties. Both poles of the dialectic are ate work in this court's interpretive exercise. A restrictive reading of contractual intent is disregarded. The use of surrounding circumstances to find the *real* intent of the parties is used to *make a construction that is fair and reasonable.* The reasonable person is seen here as a vehicle to impose a construction that is fair but not necessarily a reflection of the parties' actual intent. (Emphasis in original, footnote omitted).

RAFFLES v. WICHELHAUS

Court of Exchequer, 1864.
2 H. & C. 906, 159 Eng.Rep. 375.

Declaration. For that it was agreed between the plaintiff and the defendants, to wit, at Liverpool, that the plaintiff should sell to the defendants, and the defendants buy of the plaintiff, certain goods, to wit, 125 bales of Surat cotton, guaranteed middling fair merchant's Dhollorah, to arrive ex Peerless from Bombay; and that the cotton should be taken from the quay, and that the defendants would pay the plaintiff for the same at a certain rate, to wit, at the rate of 17¼ *d.* per pound, within a certain time then agreed upon after the arrival of the said goods in England. Averments: that the said goods did arrive by the said ship from Bombay in England, to wit, at Liverpool, and the plaintiff was then and there ready and willing and offered to deliver the said goods to the defendants, etc. Breach: that the defendants refused to accept the said goods or pay the plaintiff for them.

Plea. That the said ship mentioned in the said agreement was meant and intended by the defendants to be the ship called the Peerless, which sailed from Bombay, to wit, in October; and that the plaintiff was not ready and willing, and did not offer, to deliver to the defendants any bales of cotton which arrived by the last-mentioned ship, but instead thereof was only ready and willing, and offered to deliver to the defendants 125 bales of Surat cotton which arrived by another and different ship, which was also called the Peerless, and which sailed from Bombay, to wit, in December.

DEMURRER, and joinder therein.

MILWARD in support of the demurrer. The contract was for the sale of a number of bales of cotton of a particular description, which the plaintiff was ready to deliver. It is immaterial by what ship the cotton was to arrive, so that it was a ship called the Peerless. The words "to arrive ex Peerless," only meant that if the vessel is lost on the voyage, the contract is to be at an end. [Pollock, C.B. It would be a question for the jury whether both parties meant the same ship called the Peerless.] That would be so if the contract was for the sale of a ship called the Peerless; but it is for the sale of cotton on board a ship of that name. [Pollock, C.B. The defendant only bought that cotton which was to arrive by a particular ship. It may as well be said, that if there is a contract for the purchase of certain goods in warehouse A that is satisfied by the delivery of goods of the same description in warehouse B.] In that case there would be goods in both warehouses; here it does not appear that the plaintiff had any goods on board the other Peerless. [Martin, B. It is imposing on the defendant a contract different from that which he entered into. Pollock, C.B. It is like a contract for the purchase of wine coming from a particular estate in France or Spain, where there are two estates of that name.] The defendant has no right to contradict by parol evidence a written contract good upon the face of it. He does not impute misrepresentation or fraud, but only says that he fancied the ship was a different one. Intention is of no avail, unless stated at the time of the contract. [Pollock, C.B. One vessel sailed in October and the other in December.] The time of sailing is no part of the contract.

MELLISH (Cohen with him) in support of the plea. There is nothing on the face of the contract to show that any particular ship called the Peerless was meant; but the moment it appears that two ships called the Peerless were about to sail from Bombay there is a latent ambiguity, and parol evidence may be given for the purpose of showing that the defendant meant one Peerless and the plaintiff another. That being so, there was no consensus ad idem, and therefore no binding contract. He was then stopped by the court.

PER CURIAM. There must be judgment for the defendants.

———

Note on *Raffles*: Was the identity of the ship important? Why? If the case had gone to the jury what would have been the result? Was there a genuine misunderstanding? Can we attribute fault for the misunderstanding? The case has been thoroughly researched by the noted historian, A.W. Brian Simpson, in *Contracts for Cotton to Arrive: The Case of the Two Ships* Peerless, 11 Cardozo L.Rev. 287 (1989). Some of the background relevant to these questions is summarized below:

Raffles was a Liverpool cotton broker. Wichelhaus and Busch were not cotton brokers but "general commission merchants," also from Liverpool. The market price for cotton was very volatile due to the Civil War in America and particularly the North's naval blockade of the South which kept American cotton from the marketplace. American cotton was superior to Indian cotton and the market price for Indian cotton rose and fell depending on news from America regarding the likely duration of the War. (It was erroneously thought that lifting of the blockade would result in flooding the market with large amounts of stored American cotton.) Speculation in cotton was rampant. The contract involved in the *Raffles* case was an example of this speculation. Buyers were not buying for use but in the hopes of a profitable resale (or possibly assignment of their rights to purchase).

Why was the identity of the vessel important? Sellers couldn't promise a delivery date since it was uncertain when, or even if, the sailing vessel would arrive, or when it would be able to unload its cargo. Generally, sellers identified the cotton by the name of the vessel on which it was carried and contracts were made for sale of the cotton while the ship was en route to the destination or even on its arrival. Reliable reports of the movements of ships were available at the time. Thus, the identity of the ship was critical as it enabled the buyers to estimate the approximate date of delivery of the cotton. In a volatile market this date would determine the success or failure of the speculation.

There were no fewer than eleven ships *Peerless* sailing at the time, two registered at Liverpool—the two involved in the litigation. Vessels of the same name were usually differentiated by the name of their captain. Thus, had the parties been aware of two vessels named *Peerless* loading cotton in Bombay, they would have been expected to have identified the vessel not just by name but also by captain, *e.g.*, "*Peerless* (Major)" for the October *Peerless*, whose master was Roger Major, or "*Peerless* (Flavin)" for the December *Peerless*, whose master was Thomas Flavin.

Buyers' claim that they intended the October *Peerless* finds some support in the fact that the October *Peerless* had made a trip to India the year before, whereas the December *Peerless* was newly registered in Liverpool and its previous voyages under Captain Flavin had been to Australia and North America, not to India.

The date of contracting could also shed some light on the plausibility of the parties' conflicting claims. News of the departure of the October *Peerless* from Bombay for Liverpool was published in England on November 21, 1862; but news of the departure of the December *Peerless* did not reach England until January 21, 1863. Buyers' claim that they intended the October *Peerless* is more plausible if the contract was entered into before January 21, 1863. On the other hand, if the contract was entered into after January 21, 1863, Raffles' claim that he intended the December ship becomes more plausible, or at least there could have been reason to know that two ships by the same name were en route from Bombay to Liverpool.

The date of the contract is not known, but the fluctuation in the market price of cotton helps determine the date of contracting. (It is likely that the contract date was no earlier that November 21, 1862, the date that it was known in England that the October *Peerless* had sailed from Bombay.) After a sharp decline in the market, prices were rising due to news from America that indicated prolongation of the Civil War. The contract would probably have been made when the relevant market price for cotton was at or slightly below the contract price (17 1/4d per pound) with the expectation that the market price would rise by the time of delivery. During the week of January 10, 1863 there was a great deal of speculation in cotton, the relevant market price was between 17 and 17 3/8d, and there is evidence that sales of the October shipment from Bombay were being made as well as sales for December shipment. Thus, it appears that the contract was entered into during the week of January 10, 1863, before the departure of the December *Peerless* was known in England. (It is also interesting to note that published reports in England of the *arrival* of the two ships *Peerless* in Bombay were dated September 22 and November 5, 1862, respectively.)

Subsequently prices started to fall. The October *Peerless* arrived in Liverpool on February 18 and was unloading at a time when the relevant market price was between 15 and 15 1/4d. Raffles' counsel stated that his client had no cotton on board that vessel. If he had, he would have surely tendered it to the buyers. The buyers did not complain.

The December *Peerless* arrived in Liverpool on April 19 and was unloading when the relevant market price was at approximately 16 3/4d. Had the buyers accepted delivery they would have suffered a loss, but less of a loss than they would have suffered had the seller tendered delivery from the October *Peerless* in February. "The misunderstanding had in a sense worked in their favor.... " *Id.* at 323.

Had the dispute been submitted to arbitration, which would have been the customary way to proceed, what would have been the result?

> [The] arbitrators might well have decided that the sensible and decent way to handle the problem, the equitable solution, would be to require them to take delivery from Raffles,[168] or even, though this would be less favorable to them, to do something which courts are always reluctant to do—split the difference. Furthermore, if Wichelhaus and Busch deliberately kept quiet when no cotton was tendered by Raffles from *Peerless* (Major), hoping that when the second ship arrived, the price would have moved in their favor, it would hardly seem fair to allow them both to have their cake and eat it by now

---

168. In terms of a money award, compensate Raffles by paying the difference between the contract price and market price.

refusing to accept the cotton when they discovered that their hopes had been in vain." *Id.* at 323–24.

NANAKULI PAVING AND ROCK CO. v. SHELL OIL CO.

United States Court of Appeals, Ninth Circuit, 1981.
664 F.2d 772.

HOFFMAN, DISTRICT JUDGE:

Appellant Nanakuli Paving and Rock Company (Nanakuli) initially filed this breach of contract action against appellee Shell Oil Company (Shell) in Hawaiian State Court in February, 1976. Nanakuli, the second largest asphaltic paving contractor in Hawaii, had bought all its asphalt requirements from 1963 to 1974 from Shell under two long-term supply contracts; its suit charged Shell with breach of the later 1969 contract. The jury returned a verdict of $220,800 for Nanakuli on its first claim, which is that Shell breached the 1969 contract in January, 1974, by failing to price protect Nanakuli on 7200 tons of asphalt at the time Shell raised the price for asphalt from $44 to $76. Nanakuli's theory is that price-protection, as a usage of the asphaltic paving trade in Hawaii, was incorporated into the 1969 agreement between the parties, as demonstrated by the routine use of price protection by suppliers to that trade, and reinforced by the way in which Shell actually performed the 1969 contract up until 1974. Price protection, appellant claims, required that Shell hold the price on the tonnage Nanakuli had already committed because Nanakuli had incorporated that price into bids put out to or contracts awarded by general contractors and government agencies. The District Judge set aside the verdict and granted Shell's motion for judgment n. o. v., which decision we vacate. We reinstate the jury verdict.... * * *

Nanakuli ... argues, all material suppliers to the asphaltic paving trade in Hawaii followed the trade usage of price protection and thus it should be assumed, under the U.C.C., that the parties intended to incorporate price protection into their 1969 agreement. This is so, Nanakuli continues, even though the written contract provided for price to be "Shell's Posted Price at time of delivery," F.O.B. Honolulu. Its proof of a usage that was incorporated into the contract is reinforced by evidence of the commercial context, which under the U.C.C. should form the background for viewing a particular contract. The full agreement must be examined in light of the close, almost symbiotic relations between Shell and Nanakuli on the island of Oahu, whereby the expansion of Shell on the island was intimately connected to the business growth of Nanakuli. The U.C.C. looks to the actual performance of a contract as the best indication of what the parties intended those terms to mean. Nanakuli points out that Shell had price protected it on the two occasions of price increases under the 1969 contract other than the 1974 increase. In 1970 and 1971 Shell extended the old price for four and three months, respectively, after an announced increase. This was done, in the words of Shell's agent in Hawaii, in order to permit Nanakuli's to "chew up" tonnage already committed at Shell's old price.

* * *

Shell presents three arguments for upholding the judgment n.o.v. or, on cross appeal, urging that the District Judge erred in admitting certain evidence. First, it says, the District Court should not have denied Shell's motion *in limine* to define trade, for purposes of trade usage evidence, as the sale and purchase of asphalt in Hawaii, rather than expanding the definition of trade to include other suppliers of materials to the asphaltic paving trade. Asphalt, its argument runs, was the subject matter of the disputed contract and the only product Shell supplied to the asphaltic paving trade. Shell protests that the judge, by expanding the definition of trade to include the other major suppliers to the asphaltic paving trade, allowed the admission of highly prejudicial evidence of routine price protection by all suppliers of aggregate. Asphaltic concrete paving is formed by mixing paving asphalt with crushed rock, or aggregate, in a "hot-mix" plant and then pouring the mixture onto the surface to be paved. Shell's second complaint is that the two prior occasions on which it price protected Nanakuli, although representing the only other instances of price increases under the 1969 contract, constituted mere waivers of the contract's price term, not a course of performance of the contract. A course of performance of the contract, in contrast to a waiver, demonstrates how the parties understand the terms of their agreement. Shell cites two U.C.C. Comments in support of that argument: (1) that, when the meaning of acts is ambiguous, the preference is for the waiver interpretation, and (2) that one act alone does not constitute a relevant course of performance. Shell's final argument is that, even assuming its prior price protection constituted a course of performance and that the broad trade definition was correct and evidence of trade usages by aggregate suppliers was admissible, price protection could not be construed as reasonably consistent with the express price term in the contract, in which case the Code provides that the express term controls.

We hold that the judge did not abuse his discretion in defining the applicable trade, for purposes of trade usages, as the asphaltic paving trade in Hawaii, rather than the purchase and sale of asphalt alone, given the unusual, not to say unique, circumstances: the smallness of the marketplace on Oahu; the existence of only two suppliers on the island; the long and intimate connection between the two companies on Oahu, including the background of how the development of Shell's asphalt sales on Oahu was inextricably linked to Nanakuli's own expansion on the island; the knowledge of the aggregate business on the part of Shell's Hawaiian representative, Bohner; his awareness of the economics of Nanakuli's bid estimates, which included only two major materials, asphalt and aggregate; his familiarity with realities of the Hawaiian marketplace in which all government agencies refused to include escalation clauses in contract awards and thus pavers would face tremendous losses on price increases if all their material suppliers did not routinely offer them price protection; and Shell's determination to build Nanakuli up to compete for those lucrative government contracts with the largest paver on the island, Hawaiian Bitumuls (H.B.), which was supplied by the only other asphalt company on the islands, Chevron, and which was routinely price protected on materials. We base our holding on the reading of the Code Comments as defining trade more broadly than transaction and as binding parties not only to usages of their particular trade but also to usages of trade in general in a given locality. This latter seems an equitable application of usage evidence where the usage is almost universally practiced in a small market such as was Oahu in the 1960's before Shell signed its 1969 contract with Nanakuli. Additionally, we hold that, under the facts of this case, a jury could reasonably have found that Shell's acts on two occasions to price protect Nanakuli were not ambiguous and therefore indicated Shell's understanding of the terms of the agreement with Nanakuli rather than being a waiver by Shell of those terms.[8]

Lastly we hold that, although the express price terms of Shell's posted price of delivery may seem, at first glance, inconsistent with a trade usage of price protection at time of increases in price, a closer reading shows that the jury could have reasonably construed price protection as consistent with the express term. We reach this holding for several reasons. First, we are persuaded by a careful reading of the U.C.C., one of whose underlying purposes is to promote flexibility in the expansion of commercial practices and which rather drastically overhauls this particular area of the law. The Code would have us look beyond the printed pages of the contract to usages and the entire commercial context of the agreement in order to reach the "true understanding" of the parties. Second, decisions of other courts in similar situations have managed to reconcile such trade usages with seemingly contradictory express terms where the prior course of dealings between the parties, trade usages, and the actual performance of the contract by the parties showed a clear intent by the parties to incorporate those usages into the agreement or to give to the express term the particular meaning provided by those usages, even at times varying the apparent meaning of the express terms. Third, the delineation by thoughtful commentators of the degree of consistency demanded between express terms and usage is that a usage should be allowed to modify the apparent agreement, as seen in the written terms, as long as it does not totally negate it. We believe the usage here falls within the limits set forth by commentators and generally followed in the better reasoned decisions. The manner in which price protection was actually practiced in Hawaii was that it only came into play at times of price increases and only for work committed prior to

8. In addition, Shell's Bohner volunteered on direct for Shell that Shell price protected Nanakuli again after 1974 on the only two occasions of later price increases in 1977 and 1978. Although not constituting a course of performance, since the occasions took place under different contracts, these two additional instances of price protection could have reinforced the jury's impression that Shell's earlier actions were a carrying out of the price term.

those increases on non-escalating contracts. Thus, it formed an exception to, rather than a total negation of, the express price term of "Shell's Posted Price at time of delivery." Our decision is reinforced by the overwhelming nature of the evidence that price protection was routinely practiced by all suppliers in the small Oahu market of the asphaltic paving trade and therefore was known to Shell; that it was a realistic necessity to operate in that market and thus vital to Nanakuli's ability to get large government contracts and to Shell's continued business growth on Oahu; and that it therefore constituted an intended part of the agreement, as that term is broadly defined by the Code, between Shell and Nanakuli.

* * *

Perhaps one of the most fundamental departures of the Code from prior contract law is found in the parol evidence rule and the definition of an agreement between two parties. Under the U.C.C., an agreement goes beyond the written words on a piece of paper. " 'Agreement' means the bargain of the parties in fact as found in their language or by implication from other circumstances including course of dealing or usage of trade or course of performance as provided in this chapter (sections 490:1–205 and 490:2–208)." *Id.* § 490:1–201(3). Express terms, then, do not constitute the entire agreement, which must be sought also in evidence of usages, dealings, and performance of the contract itself. The purpose of evidence of usages, which are defined in the previous section, is to help to understand the entire agreement. * * *

A commercial agreement, then, is broader than the written paper and its meaning is to be determined not just by the language used by them in the written contract but "by their action, read and interpreted in the light of commercial practices and other surrounding circumstances. The measure and background for interpretation are set by the commercial context, which may explain and supplement even the language of a formal or final writing." *Id.*, Comment 1. Performance, usages, and prior dealings are important enough to be admitted always, even for a final and complete agreement; only if they cannot be reasonably reconciled with the express terms of the contract are they not binding on the parties. "The express terms of an agreement and an applicable course of dealing or usage of trade shall be construed wherever reasonable as consistent with each other; but when such construction is unreasonable express terms control both course of dealing and usage of trade and course of dealing controls usage of trade." *Id.* § 490:1–205(4).

Of these three, then, the most important evidence of the agreement of the parties is their actual performance of the contract. *Id.* The operative definition of course of performance is as follows: "Where the contract for sale involves repeated occasions for performance by either party with knowledge of the nature of the performance and opportunity for objection to it by the other, any course of performance accepted or acquiesced in without objection shall be relevant to determine the meaning of the agreement." *Id.* § 490:2–208(1). "Course of dealing ... is restricted, literally, to a sequence of conduct between the parties previous to the agreement. However, the provisions of the Act on course of performance make it clear that a sequence of conduct after or under the agreement may have equivalent meaning (Section 2–208)." *Id.* 490:1–205, Comment 2. The importance of evidence of course of performance is explained: "The parties themselves know best what they have meant by their words of agreement and their action under that agreement is the best indication of what that meaning was. This section thus rounds out the set of factors which determines the meaning of the 'agreement' ..." *Id.* § 490:2–208, Comment 1. "Under this section a course of performance is always relevant to determine the meaning of the agreement." *Id.*, Comment 2.

Our study of the Code provisions and Comments, then, form the first basis of our holding that a trade usage to price protect pavers at times of price increases for work committed on nonescalating contracts could reasonably be construed as consistent with an express term of seller's posted price at delivery. Since the agreement of the parties is broader than the express terms and includes usages, which may even add terms to the agreement, and since the commercial background provided by those usages is vital to an understanding of the agreement, we follow the Code's mandate to proceed on the assumption that the parties have included those usages unless they cannot reasonably be construed as consistent with the express terms.

* * *

* * * Here the evidence was overwhelming that all suppliers to the asphaltic paving trade price protected customers under the same types of circumstances. Chevron's contract with H.B. was a similar long-term supply contract between a buyer and seller with very close relations, on a form supplied by the seller, covering sales of asphalt, and setting the price at seller's posted price, with no mention of price protection. * * * Here, the express price term was "Shell's Posted Price at time of delivery." A total negation of that term would be that the buyer was to set the price. It is a less than complete negation of the term that an unstated exception exists at times of price increases, at which times the old price is to be charged, for a certain period or for a specified tonnage, on work already committed at the lower price on nonescalating contracts. Such a usage forms a broad and important exception to the express term, but does not swallow it entirely. Therefore, we hold that, under these particular facts, a reasonable jury could have found that price protection was incorporated into the 1969 agreement between Nanakuli and Shell and that price protection was reasonably consistent with the express term of seller's posted price at delivery.

* * *

Because the jury could have found for Nanakuli on its price protection claim under either theory, we reverse the judgment of the District

Court and reinstate the jury verdict for Nanakuli in the amount of $220,800, plus interest according to law.

* * *

Problems

11. The parties entered into an agreement for the sale and purchase of coal in which the quantity term was expressed in "metric tons" rather than "dry metric tons." One of the parties sought to introduce evidence that there was a course of dealing which showed that there was a common basis between the parties for interpreting "metric tons" to be the equivalent of "dry metric tons." Is the evidence admissible?

12. M–V Corp., a manufacturer, sues B, an authorized dealer, for the price of electronic equipment supplied and delivered. B counterclaims based on S's refusal to accept conforming goods returned for credit. The agreement stated that B had no right to return conforming goods and obtain a credit. B now asserts that the parties continually ignored the agreement and that over a period of time 210 units were returned for credit. May this evidence be introduced as a relevant course of performance? May it be introduced as the basis of a modification?

13. Defendant asked Young, one of his employees, to shop for a surge protector. Young's initial search found surge protectors in the range of $50 to $200. For various reasons, he found that none of them fully met his employer's needs until he found the plaintiff's product. Young asked plaintiff's salesperson the price of the protector. The salesperson replied "fifty-six twenty" which Young took to mean $56.20. The salesperson meant $5,620. The protector was delivered and installed. Defendant immediately realized that it had to cost much more than $56.20 and asked the plaintiff to take it back. Plaintiff refused and sued for the price. What result?

14. Plaintiff subscribed to DIRECTV. The subscription agreement contained this clause: "DIRECTV reserves the right to change these terms and conditions.... If any changes are made DIRECTV will send you a written notice describing the change and its effective date. If a change is not acceptable to you, you may cancel your service. If you do not cancel your service, your continued receipt of any service is considered to be your acceptance of that change." Soon thereafter, in an envelope containing the monthly bill, DIRECTV included a new agreement that differed from the old by a clause that stated that any claim "arising out of, or relating to this agreement ... shall be resolved in according to binding arbitration." Plaintiff did not cancel the service and continued to receive DIRECTV's signal. Plaintiff has brought a court case based on an alleged breach of the agreement. DIRECTV argues that the case should be dismissed and that Plaintiff is bound by the arbitration clause. Think of a successful argument on behalf of Plaintiff based on interpretation.

Examination Problem

A MODEL ANSWER TO THIS QUESTION IS IN APPENDIX C, ENTI-
TLED "FLOOD AND THE WELL"

Lessor leased to Lessee a lot for use as a gasoline station for a term of 10
years at a monthly rental of $1,000. All material terms were included in a
written signed lease. The lease recited that in consideration of $1 B had the
privilege of buying the lot at any time during the term of the lease for the
price of $50,000. The lease also provided that: "Lessor agrees to furnish
Lessee with water for the station insofar as Lessor is able to do so with
Lessor's present water supply. In case Lessor's well fails to supply sufficient
water, Lessor is not responsible and Lessee is required to make his own
arrangements for securing water."

Some months into the lease, the parties had a dispute as to whether the
water supply was adequate. The parties entered into a written, signed
agreement under which an additional well would be drilled on the premises
and each would pay one-half of the cost.

The parties hired Flood, a well-driller, to drill a well to a depth of 200
feet. The agreed price was $3,000. Flood encountered difficulties because
there was more rock than anticipated. When Flood threatened to quit,
Lessor and Lessee agreed to pay Flood an additional $1,000. Flood finished
the work but neither Lessor nor Lessee made any payment. Eventually,
Flood stated in a signed writing that he would take $3,000 in full payment
and Lessor and Lessee sent a check in that amount which Flood cashed.

Subsequently, Lessee decided to exercise the option to purchase and
tendered the $50,000 called for in the lease. Lessor refused to accept the
tender claiming that when the agreement with respect to the new well was
made, the parties had agreed that Lessee was to bear the entire cost of the
well if Lessee exercised the option to purchase.

Discuss all of the contract problems involved in this set of facts.

Chapter 6

CAPACITY OF PARTIES

(Calamari & Perillo 5th §§ 8.1—8.17)

PETTIT v. LISTON

Supreme Court of Oregon, 1920.
97 Or. 464, 191 P. 660.

Plaintiff, a minor, brings this action by his guardian to recover $125 paid by him upon the purchase price of a certain motorcycle purchased from the defendants.

The case involves the question of whether or not a minor who has purchased an article of this kind, and taken and used the same, after paying part or all of the purchase price, can return the article and recover the money paid without making good to the vendors the wear and tear and depreciation of the same while in his hands.

The defendants in the case were engaged in the selling of motorcycles and attachments. The plaintiff purchased from them a motorcycle at the agreed price of $325. He paid $125 down, and was to pay $25 per month upon the purchase price until the payments were completed. He took and used the motorcycle for a little over a month and finally returned the same to the defendants and demanded the return of his money. The defendants answer and allege that plaintiff used the machine, and in so doing damaged it to the amount of $156.65.

There was a demurrer to the answer, which was overruled by the court, and the plaintiff refusing to reply or plead further and standing upon his demurrer, a judgment and order were entered dismissing the cause, from which the plaintiff appeals.

* * *

BENNETT, J. (after stating the facts as above). The amount involved in this proceeding is not large, but the question of law presented is a very important one, and one which has been much disputed in the courts, and about which there is a great and irreconcilable conflict in the authorities, and we have therefore given the matter careful attention.

The courts, in an attempt to protect the minor upon the one hand, and to prevent wrong or injustice to persons who have dealt fairly and reasonably with such minor upon the other, have indulged in many fine distinctions and recognized various slight shades of difference.

In dealing with the right of the minor to rescind his contract and the conditions under which he may do so, the decisions of the courts in the

364

different states have not only conflicted upon the main questions involved, but many of the decisions of the same court in the same state seem to be inconsistent with each other; and oftentimes one court has made its decision turn upon a distinction or difference not recognized by the courts of other states as a distinguishing feature.

The result has been that there are not only two general lines of decisions directly upon the question involved, but there are many others, which diverge more or less from the main line, and make particular cases turn upon real or fancied differences and distinctions, depending upon whether the contract was executory or partly or wholly executed, whether it was for necessaries, whether it was beneficial to the minor, whether it was fair and reasonable, whether the minor still had the property purchased in his possession, whether he had received any beneficial use of the same, etc.

Many courts have held broadly that a minor may so purchase property and keep it for an indefinite time, if he chooses, until it is worn out and destroyed, and then recover the payments made on the purchase price, without allowing the seller anything whatever for the use and depreciation of the property.

Inconsistent Rules

Many other authorities hold that where the transaction is fair and reasonable, and the minor was not overcharged or taken advantage of in any way, and he takes and keeps the property and uses or destroys it, he cannot recover the payments made on the purchase price, without allowing the seller for the wear and tear and depreciation of the article while in his hands.

The plaintiff contends for the former rule, and supports his contention with citations from the courts of last resort of Maine, Connecticut, Indiana, Massachusetts, Vermont, Nebraska, Virginia, Iowa, Mississippi, and West Virginia, most of which (although not all) support his contention. On the contrary, the courts of New York, Maryland, Montana, Illinois, Kentucky, New Hampshire, and Minnesota, with some others, support the latter rule, which seems to be also the English rule.

Some of the cyclopedias and some of the different series of selected cases state the rule contended for by plaintiff, as supported by the strong weight of authority; but we find the decisions rather equally balanced, both in number and respectability.

In Rice v. Butler, 160 N.Y. 578, 55 N.E. 275, 47 L.R.A. 303, 73 Am.St.Rep. 703, in an opinion by Mr. Justice Haight, concurred in by the entire court, it is said:

> "There are numerous authorities bearing upon the question, but they are not in entire harmony. We have examined them with some care, but have found none in this court which appears to settle the question now presented. We, consequently, are left free to adopt such a rule as in our judgment will best promote justice and equity. The contract in this case in its entirety must be held to be executory; for, under its terms, payments were to mature in the future and the title was only to pass to the minor upon making all of the

payments stipulated; but in so far as the payments made were concerned the contract was in a sense executed, for nothing further remained to be done with reference to those payments. Kent, in his Commentaries (volume 2, p. 240), says: 'If an infant pays money on his contract and enjoys the benefit of it and then avoids it when he comes of age he cannot recover back the consideration paid. On the other hand, if he avoids an executed contract when he comes of age on the ground of infancy, he must restore the consideration which he had received. The privilege of infancy is to be used as a shield and not as a sword. He cannot have the benefit of the contract on one side without returning the equivalent on the other.' ''

* * *

Our attention has not been called to any Oregon case bearing upon the question, and as far as our investigation has disclosed, there is none.

In this condition of the authorities, we feel that we are in a position to pass upon the question as one of first impression, and announce the rule which seems to us to be the better one, upon considerations of principle and public policy.

We think, where the minor has not been overreached in any way, and there has been no undue influence, and the contract is a fair and reasonable one, and the minor has actually paid money on the purchase price, and taken and used the article, that he ought not to be permitted to recover the amount actually paid, without allowing the vendor of the goods the reasonable compensation for the use and depreciation of the article, while in his hands.

Of course, if there has been any fraud or imposition on the part of the seller, or if the contract is unfair, or any unfair advantage has been taken of the minor in inducing him to make the purchase, then a different rule would apply. And whether there had been such an over-reaching on the part of the seller would always, in case of a jury trial, be a question for the jury.

We think this rule will fully and fairly protect the minor against injustice or imposition, and at the same time it will be fair to the business man who has dealt with such minor in good faith. This rule is best adapted to modern conditions, and especially to the conditions in our Far Western states.

Here, minors are permitted to and do in fact transact a great deal of business for themselves, long before they have reached the age of legal majority. Most young men have their own time long before reaching that age. They work and earn money and collect it and spend it oftentimes without any oversight or restriction.

No business man questions their right to buy, if they have the money to pay for their purchases. They not only buy for themselves, but they often are intrusted with the making of purchases for their parents and guardians. It would be intolerably burdensome for every one concerned if merchants and other business men could not deal with them safely, in a fair and reasonable way, in cash transactions of this kind.

Again, it will not exert any good moral influence upon boys and young men, and will not tend to encourage honesty and integrity, or lend them to a good and useful business future, if they are taught that they can make purchases with their own money, for their own benefit, and after paying for them in this way, and using them until they are worn out and destroyed, go back and compel the business man to return to them what they have paid upon the purchase price. Such a doctrine, as it seems to us, can only lead to the corruption of young men's principles and encourage them in habits of trickery and dishonesty.

In view of all these considerations, we think that the rule we have indicated, and which is substantially the rule adopted in New York, is the better rule, and we adopt the same in this state.

We must not be understood as deciding at this time what would be the rule where the vendor is seeking to enforce an executory contract against the minor, which is a different question not necessarily involved in this case.

It follows that the judgment of the court below should be affirmed.

ORTELERE v. TEACHERS' RETIREMENT BOARD

Court of Appeals of New York, 1969.
25 N.Y.2d 196, 303 N.Y.S.2d 362, 250 N.E.2d 460.

BREITEL, JUDGE. This appeal involves the revocability of an election of benefits under a public employees' retirement system and suggests the need for a renewed examination of the kinds of mental incompetency which may render voidable the exercise of contractual rights. The particular issue arises on the evidently unwise and foolhardy selection of benefits by a 60–year–old teacher, on leave for mental illness and suffering from cerebral arteriosclerosis, after service as a public school-teacher and participation in a public retirement system for over 40 years. The teacher died a little less than two months after making her election of maximum benefits, payable to her during her life, thus causing the entire reserve to fall in. She left surviving her husband of 38 years of marriage and two grown children.

There is no doubt that any retirement system depends for its soundness on an actuarial experience based on the purely prospective selections of benefits and mortality rates among the covered group, and that retrospective or adverse selection after the fact would be destructive of a sound system. It is also true that members of retirement systems are free to make choices which to others may seem unwise or foolhardy. The issue here is narrower than any suggested by these basic principles. It is whether an otherwise irrevocable election may be avoided for incapacity because of known mental illness which resulted in the election when, except in the barest actuarial sense, the system would sustain no unfavorable consequences.

The husband and executor of Grace W. Ortelere, the deceased New York City schoolteacher, sues to set aside her application for retirement without option, in the event of her death. It is alleged that Mrs. Ortelere, on February 11, 1965, two months before her death from natural causes, was not mentally competent to execute a retirement application. By this application, effective the next day, she elected the maximum retirement allowance (Administrative Code of City of New York, § B20–46.0). She thus revoked her earlier election of benefits under which she named her husband a beneficiary of the unexhausted reserve upon her death. Selection of the maximum allowance extinguished all interests upon her death.

Following a nonjury trial in Supreme Court, it was held that Grace Ortelere had been mentally incompetent at the time of her February 11 application, thus rendering it "null and void and of no legal effect". The Appellate Division, by a divided court, reversed the judgment of the Supreme Court and held that, as a matter of law, there was insufficient proof of mental incompetency as to this transaction (31 A.D.2d 139, 295 N.Y.S.2d 506).

Mrs. Ortelere's mental illness, indeed, psychosis, is undisputed. It is not seriously disputable, however, that she had complete cognitive judgment or awareness when she made her selection. A modern understanding of mental illness, however, suggests that incapacity to contract or exercise contractual rights may exist, because of volitional and affective impediments or disruptions in the personality, despite the intellectual or cognitive ability to understand. It will be recognized as the civil law parallel to the question of criminal responsibility which has been the recent concern of so many and has resulted in statutory and decisional changes in the criminal law (e.g., A.L.I. Model Penal Code, § 4.01; Penal Law, § 30.05; *Durham v. United States*, 214 F.2d 862).

Mrs. Ortelere, an elementary schoolteacher since 1924, suffered a "nervous breakdown" in March, 1964 and went on a leave of absence expiring February 5, 1965. She was then 60 years old and had been happily married for 38 years. On July 1, 1964 she came under the care of Dr. D'Angelo, a psychiatrist, who diagnosed her breakdown as involutional psychosis, melancholia type. Dr. D'Angelo prescribed, and for about six weeks decedent underwent, tranquilizer and shock therapy. Although moderately successful, the therapy was not continued since it was suspected that she also suffered from cerebral arteriosclerosis, an ailment later confirmed. However, the psychiatrist continued to see her at monthly intervals until March, 1965. On March 28, 1965 she was hospitalized after collapsing at home from an aneurysm. She died 10 days later; the cause of death was "Cerebral thrombosis due to H[ypertensive] H[eart] D[isease]."

As a teacher she had been a member of the Teachers' Retirement System of the City of New York (Administrative Code, § B20–3.0). This entitled her to certain annuity and pension rights, preretirement death benefits, and empowered her to exercise various options concerning the payment of her retirement allowance.

Some years before, on June 28, 1958, she had executed a "Selection of Benefits under Option One" naming her husband as beneficiary of the unexhausted reserve. Under this option upon retirement her allowance would be less by way of periodic retirement allowances, but if she died before receipt of her full reserve the balance of the reserve would be payable to her husband. On June 16, 1960, two years later, she had designated her husband as beneficiary of her service death benefits in the event of her death prior to retirement.

Then on February 11, 1965, when her leave of absence had just expired and she was still under treatment, she executed a retirement application, the one here involved, selecting the maximum retirement allowance payable during her lifetime with nothing payable on or after death. She also, at this time, borrowed from the system the maximum cash withdrawal permitted, namely, $8,760. Three days earlier she had written the board, stating that she intended to retire on February 12 or 15 or as soon as she received "the information I need in order to decide whether to take an option or maximum allowance." She then listed eight specific questions, reflecting great understanding of the retirement system, concerning the various alternatives available. An extremely detailed reply was sent, by letter of February 15, 1965, although by that date it was technically impossible for her to change her selection. However, the board's chief clerk, before whom Mrs. Ortelere executed the application, testified that the questions were "answered verbally by me on February 11th." Her retirement reserve totalled $62,165 (after deducting the $8,760 withdrawal), and the difference between electing the maximum retirement allowance (no option) and the allowance under "option one" was $901 per year or $75 per month. That is, had the teacher selected "option one" she would have received an annual allowance of $4,494 or $375 per month, while if no option had been selected she would have received an annual allowance of $5,395 or $450 per month. Had she not withdrawn the cash the annual figures would be $5,247 and $6,148 respectively.

Following her taking a leave of absence for her condition, Mrs. Ortelere had become very depressed and was unable to care for herself. As a result her husband gave up his electrician's job, in which he earned $222 per week, to stay home and take care of her on a full-time basis. She left their home only when he accompanied her. Although he took her to the Retirement Board on February 11, 1965, he did not know why she went, and did not question her for fear "she'd start crying hysterically that I was scolding her. That's the way she was. And I wouldn't upset her."

The Orteleres were in quite modest circumstances. They owned their own home, valued at $20,000, and had $8,000 in a savings account. They also owned some farm land worth about $5,000. Under these circumstances, as revealed in this record, retirement for both of the Orteleres or the survivor of them had to be provided, as a practical matter, largely out of Mrs. Ortelere's retirement benefits.

According to Dr. D'Angelo, the psychiatrist who treated her, Mrs. Ortelere never improved enough to "warrant my sending her back [to teaching]." A physician for the Board of Education examined her on February 2, 1965 to determine her fitness to return to teaching. Although not a psychiatrist but rather a specialist in internal medicine, this physician "judged that she had apparently recovered from the depression" and that she appeared rational. However, before allowing her to return to teaching, a report was requested from Dr. D'Angelo concerning her condition. It is notable that the Medical Division of the Board of Education on February 24, 1965 requested that Mrs. Ortelere report to the board's "panel psychiatrist" on March 11, 1965.

Dr. D'Angelo stated "[a]t no time since she was under my care was she ever mentally competent"; that "[m]entally she couldn't make a decision of any kind, actually, of any kind, small or large." He also described how involutional melancholia affects the judgment process: "They can't think rationally, no matter what the situation is. They will even tell you, 'I used to be able to think of anything and make any decision. Now,' they say, 'even getting up, I don't know whether I should get up or whether I should stay in bed.' Or, 'I don't even know how to make a slice of toast any more.' Everything is impossible to decide, and everything is too great an effort to even think of doing. They just don't have the effort, actually, because their nervous breakdown drains them of all their physical energies."

While the psychiatrist used terms referring to "rationality," it is quite evident that Mrs. Ortelere's psychopathology did not lend itself to a classification under the legal test of irrationality. It is undoubtedly, for this reason, that the Appellate Division was unable to accept his testimony and the trial court's finding of irrationality in the light of the prevailing rules as they have been formulated.

Rule) The well-established rule is that contracts of a mentally incompetent person who has not been adjudicated insane are voidable. Even where the contract has been partly or fully performed it will still be avoided upon restoration of the *status quo*. * * *

Traditionally, in this State and elsewhere, contractual mental capacity has been measured by what is largely a cognitive test (*Aldrich v. Bailey*, 132 N.Y. 85, 30 N.E. 264; 2 Williston, Contracts [3d ed.], § 256; see 17 C.J.S. Contracts § 133(1), subd. e, pp. 860–862). Under this standard the "inquiry" is whether the mind was "so affected as to render him wholly and absolutely incompetent to comprehend and understand the nature of the transaction" (*Aldrich v. Bailey*, *supra*, at p. 89, 30 N.E. at p. 265). A requirement that the party also be able to make a rational judgment concerning the particular transaction qualified the cognitive test (*Paine v. Aldrich*, 133 N.Y. 544, 546, 30 N.E. 725, 726, Note, "Civil Insanity": The New York Treatment of the Issue of Mental Incompetency in Non–Criminal Cases, 44 Cornell L.Q. 76). Conversely, it is also well recognized that contractual ability would be affected by insane delusions intimately related to the particular transaction (*Moritz v. Moritz*, 153 App.Div. 147, 138 N.Y.S. 124, affd 211 N.Y. 580, 105 N.E. 1090, see Green, Judicial Tests of Mental Incompetency, 6 Mo.L.Rev. 141, 151).

These traditional standards governing competency to contract were formulated when psychiatric knowledge was quite primitive. They fail to account for one who by reason of mental illness is unable to control his conduct even though his cognitive ability seems unimpaired. When these standards were evolving it was thought that all the mental faculties were simultaneously affected by mental illness. (Green, Mental Incompetency, 38 Mich.L.Rev. 1189, 1197–1202.) This is no longer the prevailing view (Note, Mental Illness and the Law of Contracts, 57 Mich.L.Rev. 1020, 1033–1036).

Of course, the greatest movement in revamping legal notions of mental responsibility has occurred in the criminal law. The nineteenth century cognitive test embraced in the *M'Naghten* rules has long been criticized and changed by statute and decision in many jurisdictions (see *M'Naghten's Case,* 10 Clark & Fin. 200; 8 Eng.Rep. 718 [House of Lords, 1843]; Weihofen, Mental Disorder as a Criminal Defense [1954], pp. 65– 68; British Royal Comm. on Capital Punishment [1953], ch. 4; A.L.I. Model Penal Code, § 4.01, *supra;* cf. Penal Law, § 30.05).

While the policy considerations for the criminal law and the civil law are different, both share in common the premise that policy consider- ations must be based on a sound understanding of the human mind and, therefore, its illnesses. Hence, because the cognitive rules are, for the most part, too restrictive and rest on a false factual basis they must be re-examined. Once it is understood that, accepting plaintiff's proof, Mrs. Ortelere was psychotic and because of that psychosis could have been incapable of making a voluntary selection of her retirement system benefits, there is an issue that a modern jurisprudence should not exclude, merely because her mind could pass a "cognition" test based on nineteenth century psychology.

There has also been some movement on the civil law side to achieve a modern posture. For the most part, the movement has been glacial and has been disguised under traditional formulations. Various devices have been used to avoid unacceptable results under the old rules by finding unfairness or overreaching in order to avoid transactions (see, e.g., Green, Proof of Mental Incompetency and the Unexpressed Major Prem- ise, 53 Yale L.J. 271, 298–305).

In this State there has been at least one candid approach. In *Faber v. Sweet Style Mfg. Corp.,* 40 Misc.2d 212, at p. 216, 242 N.Y.S.2d 763, at p. 768, Mr. Justice Meyer wrote: "[i]ncompetence to contract also exists when a contract is entered into under the compulsion of a mental disease or disorder but for which the contract would not have been made" (noted in 39 N.Y.U.L.Rev. 356). This is the first known time a court has recognized that the traditional standards of incompetency for contractu- al capacity are inadequate in light of contemporary psychiatric learning and applied modern standards. Prior to this, courts applied the cognitive standard giving great weight to objective evidence of rationality. * * *

It is quite significant that Restatement, 2d, Contracts, states the modern rule on competency to contract. This is in evident recognition, and the Reporter's Notes support this inference, that, regardless of how the cases formulated their reasoning, the old cognitive test no longer explains the results. Thus, the new Restatement section reads: "(1) A person incurs only voidable contractual duties by entering into a transaction if by reason of mental illness or defect . . . (b) he is unable to act in a reasonable manner in relation to the transaction and the other party has reason to know of his condition." (Restatement, 2d, Contracts [T.D. No. 1, April 13, 1964], § 18C.) [Now § 15, Ed.] (See, also, Allen, Ferster, Weihofen, Mental Impairment and Legal Incompetency, p. 253 [Recommendation b] and pp. 260–282; and Note, 57 Mich.L.Rev. 1020, *supra,* where it is recommended "that a complete test for contractual incapacity should provide protection to those persons whose contracts are merely uncontrolled reactions to their mental illness, as well as for those who could not understand the nature and consequences of their actions" [at p. 1036]).

The avoidance of duties under an agreement entered into by those who have done so by reason of mental illness, but who have understanding, depends on balancing competing policy considerations. There must be stability in contractual relations and protection of the expectations of parties who bargain in good faith. On the other hand, it is also desirable to protect persons who may understand the nature of the transaction but who, due to mental illness, cannot control their conduct. Hence, there should be relief only if the other party knew or was put on notice as to the contractor's mental illness. Thus, the Restatement provision for avoidance contemplates that "the other party has reason to know" of the mental illness (*id.*).

When, however, the other party is without knowledge of the contractor's mental illness and the agreement is made on fair terms, the proposed Restatement rule is: "The power of avoidance under subsection (1) terminates to the extent that the contract has been so performed in whole or in part or the circumstances have so changed that avoidance would be inequitable. In such a case a court may grant relief on such equitable terms as the situation requires." (Restatement, 2d, Contracts, *supra,* § 18C, subd. [2] [Now § 15, Ed.].)

The system was, or should have been, fully aware of Mrs. Ortelere's condition. They, or the Board of Education, knew of her leave of absence for medical reasons and the resort to staff psychiatrists by the Board of Education. Hence, the other of the conditions for avoidance is satisfied.

Lastly, there are no significant changes of position by the system other than those that flow from the barest actuarial consequences of benefit selection.

Nor should one ignore that in the relationship between retirement system and member, and especially in a public system, there is not involved a commercial, let alone an ordinary commercial, transaction. Instead the nature of the system and its announced goal is the protection of its members and those in whom its members have an interest. It is not a sound scheme which would permit 40 years of contribution and participation in the system to be nullified by a one-instant act committed by one known to be mentally ill. This is especially true if there would be no substantial harm to the system if the act were avoided. On the record none may gainsay that her selection of a "no option" retirement while under psychiatric care, ill with cerebral arteriosclerosis, aged 60, and with a family in which she had always manifested concern, was so unwise and foolhardy that a factfinder might conclude that it was explainable only as a product of psychosis.

On this analysis it is not difficult to see that plaintiff's evidence was sufficient to sustain a finding that, when she acted as she did on February 11, 1965, she did so solely as a result of serious mental illness, namely, psychosis. Of course, nothing less serious than medically classified psychosis should suffice or else few contracts would be invulnerable to some kind of psychological attack. Mrs. Ortelere's psychiatrist testified quite flatly that as an involutional melancholiac in depression she was incapable of making a voluntary "rational" decision. Of course, as noted earlier, the trial court's finding and perhaps some of the testimony attempted to fit into the rubrics of the traditional rules. For that reason rather than reinstatement of the judgment at Trial Term there should be a new trial under the proper standards frankly considered and applied.

Accordingly, the order of the Appellate Division should be reversed, without costs, and the action remanded to Special Term for a new trial.

JASEN, JUDGE (dissenting). * * *

The evidence conclusively establishes that the decedent, at the time she made her application to retire, understood not only that she was retiring, but also that she had selected the maximum payment during her lifetime.

Indeed, the letter written by the deceased to the Teachers' Retirement System prior to her retirement demonstrates her full mental capacity to understand and to decide whether to take an option or the maximum allowance. The full text of the letter reads as follows:

February 8, 1965

Gentlemen:

    I would like to retire on Feb. 12 or Feb. 15. In other words, just as soon as possible after I receive the information I need in order to decide whether to take an option or maximum allowance. Following are the questions I would like to have answered:

    1.   What is my 'average' five-year salary?

    2.   What is my maximum allowance?

    3.   I am 60 years old. If I select option four-a with a beneficiary (female) 27 years younger, what is my allowance?

    4.   If I select four-a on the pension part only, and take the maximum annuity, what is my allowance?

    5.   If I take a loan of 89% of my year's salary before retirement, what would my maximum allowance be?

6. If I take a loan of $5,000 before retiring, and select option four-a on both the pension and annuity, what would my allowance be?

7. What is my total service credit? I have been on a leave without pay since Oct. 26, 1964.

8. What is the 'factor' used for calculating option four-a with the above beneficiary?

Thank you for your promptness in making the necessary calculations. I will come to your office on Thursday afternoon of this week.

It seems clear that this detailed, explicit and extremely pertinent list of queries reveals a mind fully in command of the salient features of the Teachers' Retirement System. Certainly, it cannot be said that the decedent could possess sufficient capacity to compose a letter indicating such a comprehensive understanding of the retirement system, and yet lack the capacity to understand the answers.

As I read the record, the evidence establishes that the decedent's election to receive maximum payments was predicated on the need for a higher income to support two retired persons—her husband and herself. Since the only source of income available to decedent and her husband was decedent's retirement pay, the additional payment of $75 per month which she would receive by electing the maximal payment was a necessity. Indeed, the additional payments represented an increase of 20% over the benefits payable under option 1. Under these circumstances, an election of maximal income during decedent's lifetime was not only a rational, but a necessary decision.

Further indication of decedent's knowledge of the financial needs of her family is evidenced by the fact that she took a loan for the maximum amount ($8,760) permitted by the retirement system at the time she made application for retirement.

* * *

Decedent's election of the maximum retirement benefits, therefore, was not so contrary to her best interests so as to create an inference of her mental incompetence.

* * *

Nor can I agree with the majority's view that the traditional rules governing competency to contract "are, for the most part, too restrictive and rest on a false factual basis."

The issue confronting the courts concerning mental capacity to contract is under what circumstances and conditions should a party be relieved of contractual obligations freely entered. This is peculiarly a legal decision, although, of course, available medical knowledge forms a datum which influences the legal choice. * * *

* * *

As in every situation where the law must draw a line between liability and nonliability, between responsibility and nonresponsibility, there will be borderline cases, and injustices may occur by deciding erroneously that an individual belongs on one side of the line or the other. To minimize the chances of such injustices occurring, the line should be drawn as clearly as possible.

* * *

Accordingly, I would affirm the order appealed from.

* * *

Order reversed, without costs, and a new trial granted.

Problems

1. P, a fifteen-year-old employee of a Toyota dealership, injured his back in the course of his employment. An adjuster for the dealer's insurer negotiated a settlement of P's worker's compensation claim with P and with P's mother. The final agreed settlement was for $6,136.40. P signed the settlement agreement; P's mother did not. She, however, was aware of its terms and had advised P to accept the offered settlement. P has now declared that he disaffirms the agreement and has filed a petition to reopen his claim. Should it be granted?

2. P, a minor, sold a painting for $100. On reaching the age of majority P received a book on French art. While perusing the book P noticed that the painting was worth $1,500. P immediately brought a suit to recover the painting. (a) What result? (b) Would the result change if two months had passed? Two years?

3. An infant borrowed one hundred dollars from Lender, asserting that the money was needed to purchase food and clothing. Receiving the money, the infant immediately lost it playing five card stud. Lender now sues for the fifty dollars. What result?

4. A 17-year-old high school senior in N.Y. has been accepted by Berkeley. Ace Airlines offers a discount flight for persons under 18 for $150, one-half of the adult fare. To attend the school the student, who cannot afford $150, misrepresents his age in order to obtain a full-fare ticket from the airline on it's "fly now, pay later" plan. (This plan is only available to adults.) Upon arrival in San Francisco the student's grandmother gives the student $200, as she had previously promised to reimburse him for the cost of the flight. The student then disaffirmed the contract and the airline brought suit. What result?

5. In *Ortelere*, suppose that the retirement system had no knowledge of Mrs. Ortelere's disability. (a) Would the result be different? (b) Assuming that arguably it would be different, what reasons can be advanced for distinguishing the cases?

6. In Swift & Co. v. Smigel, p. 142 supra, the court adopted the minority view that supervening adjudication of incompetence does not auto-

matically terminate an offer. Consequently, a series of unilateral contracts had been formed. Are they, then, voidable?

7.   On March 1, Icarus went to a Rolls Royce dealer and bought a Silver Cloud with cash. The deal went smoothly and was fair. Icarus immediately attempted flight and the car was destroyed. Icarus' executor brought suit to recover the purchase price. During the trial it was established that Icarus had been incompetent since February 1, although no adjudication of incompetence had been made. (a) What result? (b) What result if Icarus had been adjudicated incompetent and a guardian of his property appointed on February 1? (c) Would the result be different, assuming no prior adjudication of incompetence, if, when paying, Icarus had made paper planes of the money and, with each plane that landed successfully in the dealer's cash register, jumped up and down shouting, "Not even the sun will stop me now"?

8.   On February 1, A purchased a car on credit. Though normal by all appearances, A was suffering from a mental affliction which deprived A of knowledge of the transaction. By March 1, A had fully recovered, but had no recollection of how the car had been acquired, and continued driving the car for nine months. Could A now successfully disaffirm the contract?

9.   Jill had long sought Pete's Stradivarius to no avail. One night she plied Pete with a pint of Vodka and convinced Pete to part with the instrument for a fair price. When once again sober, could Pete disaffirm the contract?

10.   For the fifth time in as many years Mr. Smith had his lawyer, Ms. Jones, attempt to gain his release from guardianship. She again failed and the guardian refused to pay for the legal services. Would the lawyer be successful if she brought suit for the reasonable value of her services?

Chapter 7

AVOIDANCE FOR MISCONDUCT OR MISTAKE

SECTION 1. DURESS

(Calamari & Perillo 5th §§ 9.1—9.8)

GALLON v. LLOYD–THOMAS CO.

United States Court of Appeals, Eighth Circuit, 1959.
264 F.2d 821.

Matthes, Circuit Judge.

For the second time we are asked to review the action of the trial court in rendering judgment for defendant notwithstanding the verdict favorable to appellant (plaintiff) on Counts I and IX of plaintiff's amended complaint. * * *

* * *

As reference to our former opinion will reveal, in Count I plaintiff alleged that on October 13, 1954, as the result of defendant's duress, threats and coercion, he was compelled to sign an agreement with respect to his employment. In this count plaintiff prayed for rescission and cancellation of the contract, and for $25,000 actual damages. The jury awarded him $100 as damages. Count IX sought punitive damages and thereon plaintiff received a verdict for $20,000.

The court's judgment n.o.v. on Counts I and IX, was predicated on the conclusion that if the contract of October 13, 1954, was entered into by plaintiff under duress, it was nevertheless ratified in all respects by him as a matter of law.

* * *

Plaintiff was employed by defendant in November, 1949. In March, 1950, he was appointed district manager in St. Louis, Missouri. For his services in selling appraisal service to business concerns, plaintiff received 15 per cent commission of the initial appraisal charge as well as the annual service charge. In 1952, for reasons not here material, plaintiff was transferred by defendant to New York with a drawing account of $225, with the oral understanding that defendant would not

377

charge any overdrafts which plaintiff might incur in New York against his commissions earned in St. Louis. Plaintiff's operations in New York proved unsuccessful. His draw or advancement of $225 a week exceeded his earnings of 15 per cent of the defendant's fee on all contracts closed by plaintiff, and in September, 1954, defendant reduced plaintiff's drawing account to $175 a week. Pursuant to a telephone call from Ernest E. Goran, president of defendant company, plaintiff met Mr. Goran at the Sheraton Park Plaza Hotel in New York on or about October 12, 1954. Plaintiff testified that in the telephone conversation Goran said, " * * * that I had stuck my neck out too far and that a few days or weeks earlier he had received a call from an officer of the Department of Justice in Chicago; that they were investigating my character; that the investigator asked Goran if he knew that I was a bigamist; that he, Goran, didn't want to be implicated so he turned the investigator over to Mr. Gatenbey (vice-president of defendant) to deal with." Getting down to the events in the hotel, it appears that plaintiff's wife was with him, but Goran would not permit her to accompany plaintiff and Goran to the latter's room in the hotel. Plaintiff stated that he was very upset; that he and Goran found Gatenbey in the room and the latter began reading from a paper " * * * and telling me that I was a bad man, a bigamist, promiscuous or maybe worse and went on for nearly an hour and a half or two *until I was completely broken down.*" Continuing, plaintiff testified that Gatenbey "said that if he had had his way he would have fired me long ago; that I would have to get out of the country in twelve hours or else take the consequences." From other testimony we learn that plaintiff came to the United States from England in November, 1949; that he first married Ethel Charle, apparently in England; he then married one Margaret Duffin in Gretna Green, Scotland; he again [was] married in East St. Louis, Illinois, to a woman whom he had met in Toronto, Canada. This marriage was annulled in New York in September, 1953, and on August 10, 1954, plaintiff married his fourth and present wife. At the time of the Sheraton Plaza Hotel incident on October 12, 1954, plaintiff had not been naturalized, and it is apparent that the statements made by Gatenbey in the hotel room caused plaintiff great anxiety and fear that he would be deported from the United States. Following the encounter with Gatenbey, above related, and after Gatenbey had gone into the washroom, Goran informed plaintiff that he had told Gatenbey "not to be so hard on me"; that Gatenbey's friend (a prominent citizen of New York, then an official of that state) would be contacted in an effort to delay the investigation. According to plaintiff's testimony, when he left the hotel room he was so sick that Mr. Goran had to walk him around in the hall before he was in a condition to be taken downstairs.

Mrs. Gallon testified that when she and her husband met Goran in the hotel lobby he stated to plaintiff: "John, you've gone too far this time. We're going to have a terrible time to keep the investigators from bothering you and I am afraid you will be deported, but we will see (what) Mr. Gatenbey and I can figure out about it." Mrs. Gallon stated she waited in the hotel lobby from two until four o'clock p.m. while her husband was with Goran and Gatenbey. That when Mr. Gallon appeared "he was very, very sick. I do not know what he went through, but he really went through something with those people, believe me. My husband was very, very upset. He had been crying you could see." While in the cocktail lounge later in the day, Goran again stated that he and Gatenbey would try to figure out what could be done to prevent the investigation, and plaintiff would be advised. Out of the foregoing came the contract which materially changed plaintiff's remuneration. From further testimony, it seems that following the events above set forth, and within a day or two thereafter, Goran and Gatenbey presented the contract to plaintiff who expressed some reluctance on signing it. Thereupon, Gatenbey lost his temper and stated he was in favor of firing plaintiff right then. In this setting, and with plaintiff still laboring under the fear of deportation, he signed the October 13, 1954, contract. The inference is clear from his testimony that he was then assured by Goran and Gatenbey that the investigation relating to deportation of plaintiff would be stopped and everything would be all right.

The salient features and terms of the October 13, 1954, contract were: Plaintiff acknowledged his services had not been performed satisfactorily; defendant was to retain plaintiff in its employ as long as his services were satisfactory, and his compensation was to be in an amount agreed upon between the parties; plaintiff acknowledged that he was overdrawn in his account with defendant in an amount in excess of $15,000, and authorized defendant to apply any and all credits and moneys due plaintiff from defendant toward payment of the overdraft (this terminated plaintiff's right to continue drawing commission on St. Louis business); plaintiff authorized defendant to pay out of moneys due him the sum of $200 to Mrs. Georgina Bird Gallon, one of his former wives, being the amount of a note held by her.

It is clear to us that the genuine trial issue revolved around and was focused upon the circumstances under which plaintiff entered into the October 13, 1954, contract. Was it the result of duress? That was the question. Plaintiff's testimony was sufficient to warrant a jury in finding that the contract came into existence as the direct result of the threats of Goran and Gatenbey, and that such threats caused plaintiff to be bereft of the quality of mind essential to the making of a contract.[2] * * *

Did plaintiff ratify the contract as a matter of law? Appellee insists that in view of plaintiff's actions and conduct, and his attitude toward the contract following its execution, the question must be answered in the affirmative. We agree. In resolving this crucial issue, we are mindful of the well-established principle of law that a contract entered into as the result of duress is not void, but merely voidable, and is capable of being

---

2. "Under the modern doctrine there is no legal standard of resistance with which the victim must comply at the peril of being remediless for duress imposed, and no general rule respecting the sufficiency of facts to produce duress; the question in each case is whether or not the victim was so acted on by threats of the person claiming the benefit of the contract, as to be bereft of the quality of mind essential to the making of a contract, and whether or not the contract was thereby so obtained." 17 C.J.S. Contracts § 175. * * *

ratified after the duress is removed. Ratification results if the party who executed the contract under duress accepts the benefits flowing from it or remains silent or acquiesces in the contract for any considerable length of time after opportunity is afforded to annul or void it. * * * An essential element in the doctrine of ratification is intention: indeed, it has authoritatively been said that it is " * * * at the foundation of the doctrine of waiver or ratification." 17A Am.Jur., Duress and Undue Influence § 26 at page 594.

Measured by the foregoing standard, the conclusion is inevitable that plaintiff ratified the contract in question. It appears without dispute that at the time the contract was signed, plaintiff was represented by an attorney, and in November or December, 1954, plaintiff informed his attorney of the conference in the hotel room preceding the execution of the contract, and also asked his attorney whether he could in fact be deported. From the time plaintiff signed the contract until he left defendant's employ in July, 1955, he never on a single occasion voiced any objection to the circumstances leading up to the contract nor did he at any time, after the alleged duress was removed, protest to Goran, Gatenbey or any other official of defendant that he had been pressured into signing the contract. To the contrary, he recognized the contract in all of its terms and provisions. He made weekly reports to defendant, in which he requested payment of his draw allowance of $175, which had been agreed upon. The commissions on the St. Louis, Missouri, business, which accrued after the contract was executed, were retained by defendant; the $200 due plaintiff's former wife was sent to her by defendant in accordance with one of the contract provisions, and in plaintiff's own words: "I never asked them (Goran and Gatenbey) to set the contract aside at anytime until after I resigned from the company. I never made such a claim to Goran, and I never made such a claim to Gatenbey until after I left the company." * * *

In June or the early part of July, 1955, defendant reduced plaintiff's drawing account from $175 to $125 a week. This brought two letters from plaintiff, both written July 21, 1955. In one plaintiff proposed that his headquarters be transferred to Syracuse with a territory in out-state New York, and that he be permitted to draw $175 a week against his earnings. The other letter constituted his resignation to take effect within thirty days in the event his proposal was rejected. In neither letter did plaintiff question the validity of the contract. When defendant remained firm in its prior decision to reduce the weekly draw to $125, the parties parted company—and it was not until September, 1955, that plaintiff decided to take legal action to rescind or cancel the contract on the ground of duress in its procurement.

Without further discussion of undisputed testimony, bearing on ratification, we are of the opinion and so hold that when all of the facts and circumstances, viewed collectively, are fairly considered, only one conclusion can be reached and that is that plaintiff ratified the contract as a matter of law. Having done so, it necessarily follows that under no theory is plaintiff entitled to actual damages (awarded in Count I) or punitive damages (awarded in Count IX), and that the Court properly entered judgment for defendant on both of said counts.

Affirmed.

AUSTIN INSTRUMENT, INC. v. LORAL CORP.

Court of Appeals of New York, 1971.
29 N.Y.2d 124, 324 N.Y.S.2d 22, 272 N.E.2d 533.

See p. ___ supra.

Problems

1. Loral entered into a number of negotiated fixed-price contracts with the Navy for the manufacture of electronic equipment. The contract prices were based on the Navy's calculation of production costs. The Navy, however, did not adequately calculate rental value of Loral's factory. Despite Loral's protestations on this point, Loral entered into the contracts. Loral is now in court, seeking additional compensation by alleging duress. It argues that since it dealt almost exclusively with the government, it would have committed financial suicide by refusing to enter into the contracts at the Navy's price. What result?

2. P, alleging duress, sues to set aside a more than generous property settlement agreement which he made with his wife three years prior to commencing the action. He alleges that his wife caused private detectives to photograph him in the home of another woman and that she threatened to use the photographs as the basis for an action for alienation of affections against this other woman. Moreover, she threatened to release the photographs in such a way as to cause him, the other woman and the woman's family the greatest embarrassment. Has he stated a cause of action?

3. Several conspirators, including Jill Bird, sent a note to executives of Gulf Oil stating that 10 explosive charges had been placed in Gulf's Cedar Bayou, Texas, plant which were actuated to explode in 120 hours. The conspirators promised that in exchange for $15,000,000 the location of the charges would be revealed along with instructions for their deactivation. In the event Gulf did not comply another Gulf plant in a metropolitan area would be sabotaged as well. The price for the safety of the second plant would be $30,000,000.

The FBI located and disarmed five devices in the Texas plant and arrested the conspirators in Colorado. Among them was John McBride, Bird's husband. McBride offered to divulge all information about the remaining bombs in exchange for a promise that his wife would not be prosecuted. Murphy, the assistant U.S. Attorney in charge of the case in Colorado, agreed, after obtaining the concurrence of Longoria, his counterpart in Texas. Murphy thought that the agreement was similar to a binding plea bargain while Longoria expressed the opinion to Murphy that the agreement was being made under duress and could be set aside after the emergency was over. The coercion consisted of the believed continued threat to persons and property in Texas, an honest belief shared by McBride, Murphy and Longoria.

McBride performed his side of the bargain. As agreed, Murphy sought and obtained a dismissal of charges against Bird in the U.S. District Court in Colorado. Subsequently she was indicted on the same charges in a U.S. District Court in Texas. Assuming contract principles are applicable, should this indictment be dismissed?

4.   Plaintiff's father had made a will in which he treated each of his three children, including Plaintiff, equally. Subsequently, Plaintiff informed her father that she was pregnant and had no intention to marry. He told her that unless she had the pregnancy terminated he would disinherit her. She refused and within a few days he changed his will. Shortly thereafter, he agreed that if she would terminate the pregnancy he would execute a will that was the same as the will he had just revoked. She complied, but he died before carrying out his end of the bargain. In her action against the estate and her siblings, they raise the defense that she had been coerced into making the agreement with the decedent and therefore it is voidable for duress. How viable is the defense?

5.   P operated a large department store. Its fur department was operated by T, a concessionaire. Customers of the store, however, assumed they were dealing with P. Some 400 furs were left with T for cleaning and storage. T, in turn, delivered these to D for cleaning and storage. D was aware that T was an independent contractor. T went bankrupt and P cancelled the concession. In November, P requested D to return the furs, offering to pay for the cleaning and storage. D refused unless P paid $700 due for cleaning and storing the furs plus $3,300 which T owed D on past due accounts. The temperature dropped to 15° F and P's customers were clamoring for the return of the furs. After several days of vehement protests, P paid D $4,000. Two weeks later, it brought this action for restitution of $3,300. What result?

SECTION 2.   UNDUE INFLUENCE

(Calamari & Perillo 5th §§ 9.9—9.12)

FRANCOIS v. FRANCOIS
United States Court of Appeals, Third Circuit, 1979.
599 F.2d 1286, cert. denied 444 U.S. 1021, 100 S.Ct. 679, 62 L.Ed.2d 653 (1980).

Rosenn, Circuit Judge.

We are asked in this appeal to assess whether the district court properly relieved a husband from the disastrous financial consequences of a "Property Settlement and Separation Agreement" (agreement) entered into with his wife. The plaintiff, Victor H. Francois, instituted an action in the district court against his wife, A. Jane Francois, seeking rescission of the agreement and various real and personal property transfers made pursuant to that agreement. The district court declared the agreement and the conveyances to be null and void on the grounds, *inter alia,* that Jane Francois had exerted undue influence over her husband. The district court restored title to one parcel of real property and various securities to Victor Francois in his name alone. From the final order of the district court, Jane Francois appeals alleging that the district court improperly invalidated the agreement and reconveyed properties to her husband. We affirm.

I.

The controversy before us arises out of the troubled and relatively brief marriage of the parties. Victor H. Francois (Victor) and A. Jane Francois (Jane) were married on May 13, 1971 after a brief courtship of several months. At the time of the wedding, Victor was fifty years old, a bachelor residing with his elderly mother. Jane was thirty years old, twice divorced and the mother of two minor children, one approximately sixteen years old, and the other thirteen. Victor was relatively secure financially, possessing an acre lot, Lilliendal and Marienhoj, St. Thomas, V.I. (Lilliendal), with a two story, five bedroom building containing two apartments, a one-fourth interest in his family's hardware business, thirty shares of a family close corporation (Francois Realty), four shares of stock in a multi-family close corporation (21 Queen's Quarter), a portfolio of publicly held stock valued at between $18,000 and $19,000, and two bank accounts. Victor also received income from his job as manager of the family hardware business. Jane was gainfully employed at the time of the marriage but ceased working shortly thereafter. She apparently brought no money or property to the marriage.

The couple began to experience difficulties not long after the marriage. A series of events over the next four years centering on financial disputes led to the deterioration and eventual collapse of the marital relation. Within months of the wedding, Jane began to express anxiety over her financial security in the event that Victor died. To allay his wife's fears, Victor opened a joint savings account into which he deposited $5,000 for her use.

Jane also expressed a continuing desire for a marital homestead. In response, in March of 1972, Victor purchased a fairly large house with a swimming pool (Misgunst) for a sum of $107,000. Victor supplied a $37,000 downpayment from his assets and undertook the responsibility for the monthly mortgage payments in excess of $860 per month. Title was taken by the entireties. The same year, Victor filed a petition seeking adoption of Jane's two children. The court granted the petition after Victor acknowledged under oath that he voluntarily assumed responsibility for the children.

In the fall of 1973, the couple's finances became further consolidated. Victor conveyed all of his interest in his Lilliendal property to Jane and assigned to her a half interest in both his thirty shares of Francois Realty stock and four shares of 21 Queen's Quarter stock. He also gave Jane a power of attorney over his portfolio of publicly held stock. Jane also insisted on having a boat. Victor sold $18,000 of his stock in order to purchase a boat for Jane in her name at the cost of $17,000. Jane sold this boat approximately a year later for $16,000 and personally invested the proceeds for herself. The couple also executed reciprocal wills leaving the entirety of the marital estate to the surviving spouse or, if no spouse survived, to the children.

In September of 1974 a domestic quarrel precipitated the demise of the marriage. The dispute centered on an incident in which Victor allegedly embarrassed Jane by his behavior in front of one of Jane's friends. As a result of the incident, Jane determined to divorce Victor and on October 8, 1974, contacted an attorney, Harold Monoson, to draw up divorce papers. Victor was unaware of his wife's decision to terminate the marriage. Two days later, Jane, without any explanation, invited Victor to accompany her to Monoson's office where Victor, to his complete surprise, was presented for his signature a "Property Settlement and Separation Agreement." Monoson advised Victor that he would need an attorney, but Victor's choice was vetoed by his wife's insistence that this attorney was unacceptable. Monoson then asked a lawyer with an office in the same building, Gregory Ball, to come into the office. Ball read the agreement, which interestingly already had his name on it as Victor's counsel. Ball strenuously advised Victor not to sign the agreement because it would commit him to "financial suicide." When Victor persisted in his determination to sign, Ball informed him that he could not represent him in the matter, and left the office.

Victor, relying on representations made to him by Monoson and Jane, was persuaded that only by signing the agreement could he preserve his marriage. Victor signed the agreement and several related documents apparently in hope of saving his marriage. He conveyed to Jane his one-half interest in the marital home, Misgunst, and assigned to her his stock portfolio and his remaining stock interest in both close corporations. In addition, the agreement required Victor to pay $300 per month in alimony to his wife.

After signing the agreement, however, the parties resumed cohabitation for approximately one year. But early in 1975, Jane informed Victor that she had sold the entire portfolio of publicly held stock for around $20,000. In October of 1975, Jane informed Victor that she had sold the Misgunst and Lilliendal properties in exchange for properties owned in California by AD'M Enterprises, a limited partnership. In mid-October Jane also summarily informed Victor that she was leaving him permanently and promptly left the Virgin Islands. AD'M took title to the properties by a single deed dated October 15, 1975 but before it could record the deed, Victor instituted these proceedings. Apparently when AD'M learned of this litigation, it never recorded the deed but instead sued Jane for rescission of the conveyance.

Victor's suit against Jane and AD'M sought rescission of the agreement and reconveyance of all properties transferred to Jane. AD'M was duly served but never appeared and a default judgment was entered against them from which no appeal has been taken. The case was tried to the court without a jury.

Chief Judge Christian, the trial judge, declared the Property Settlement and Separation Agreement to be null and void as the result of: 1) the cohabitation of the parties subsequent to the signing of the agreement; 2) the undue influence exerted by Jane over Victor in connection with the signing of the agreement; 3) fraud and misrepresentation on the part of Jane; and 4) the unconscionable terms of the agreement. Judge Christian also declared the deed of October 10, 1974 transferring sole title in the Misgunst property to Jane to be null and void and awarded title to the property solely in Victor's name. The court held the attempted transfer of Misgunst and Lilliendal properties by Jane to AD'M to be null and void. The court likewise voided the assignment made to Jane, pursuant to the agreement of Victor's stock in the two close corporations, Francois Realty and 21 Queen's Quarters, and restored sole title to the stock to Victor. The court decreed that title to the Lilliendal property remain in Jane's name because "the circumstances of that transfer were not explicated before the court in the testimony." The court, however, placed a lien against the Lilliendal property to secure Victor's reimbursement for the value of the stock and monies converted by Jane in early 1975. Finally, the district court awarded costs and attorneys fees to Victor.

II.

Jane's first contention on appeal is that the district court erred in setting aside the Property Settlement and Separation Agreement. She challenges each of the four theories underpinning the district court's order of nullification. Because we agree that the district court properly voided the agreement on the grounds of undue influence exerted by Jane over her husband, we need not examine Jane's contentions relating to the three other theories supporting the district court's judgment.

* * *

The key inquiry in the case before us is whether Jane and Victor Francois, as husband and wife, also enjoyed a confidential relationship. The marital relation does not automatically give rise to a confidential relation, but it "arises when one party places confidence in the other with a resulting superiority and influence on the other side." *Yohe* [*v. Yohe,* 353 A.2d 417, 421 (1976)]. Thus, each marriage must be examined on its own facts to determine if a confidential relation exists.

The district court unequivocally found that a confidential relationship existed between Jane and Victor Francois and that Jane was clearly the dominant partner. The district court found the evidence to be "replete with instances" in which Jane was able to secure her wishes simply by badgering Victor into submission. The record reveals that Victor, very early in the marriage, began to turn over the management of his finances to Jane who subsequently used her position to gain control incrementally over most of Victor's assets. The evidence supports the district court's findings that the relationship between the parties was one in which Victor reposed total trust and confidence in Jane who used her superior position in the marriage to Victor's financial detriment.

* * * The trial court, after determining the existence of a confidential relation quite properly allocated the burden of proof to Jane [to demonstrate the fairness of the agreement].

We must now consider whether Jane met her burden of proof to rebut the charge of undue influence. If she failed, a constructive trust may be imposed on the couple's properties in order to prevent Jane's unjust enrichment.

Undue influence is not a concept susceptible of unitary definition. The essence of the idea is the subversion of another person's free will in order to obtain assent to an agreement.

> If a party in whom another reposes confidence misuses that confidence to gain his own advantage while the other has been made to feel that the party in question will not act against his welfare, the transaction is the result of undue influence. The influence must be such that the victim acts in a way contrary to his own best interest and thus in a fashion in which he would not have operated but for the undue influence.

Williston on Contracts, § 1625 at 776–77 (3d ed. 1970) (footnotes omitted).

The degree of persuasion that is necessary to constitute undue influence varies from case to case. The proper inquiry is not just whether persuasion induced the transaction but whether the result was produced by the domination of the will of the victim by the person exerting undue influence. Restatement of Contracts § 497, Comment c. Hence, the particular transaction must be scrutinized to determine if the agreement was truly the product of a free and independent mind. In this respect, the fairness of the agreement must be shown by clear and convincing evidence. *Id.* § 1627B at 823, *Buchanan* [*v. Brentwood Fed'l Sav. & L. Ass'n,* 320 A.2d 117, 127 (1974)].

* * *

The district court found that Jane alone caused the agreement to be made and that she alone benefited from it. The district court described the circumstances under which Victor was urged to obtain legal advice as a charade. There is no evidence that the independent advice received by Victor was from an attorney of his choosing. In fact, the meeting with Attorney Ball was arranged spontaneously and without an opportunity for a full and private consultation. Ball's name was already on the agreement as Victor's counsel. (For importance of independent counseling, *see* Williston, *supra* § 1625 at 778.) Victor was apparently surprised by his wife's decision to terminate the marriage and there is evidence that Monoson and/or Jane misled him into believing that by signing the agreement, the marriage could be salvaged. The district court also found that Jane, at the time the agreement was signed, had no real intent to save the marriage.

The terms of the agreement were hardly fair. Attorney Ball's assessment that the agreement was financial suicide for Victor was accurate. On this record, we conclude that the district court was correct in its finding that Jane had failed to rebut the presumption of undue influence.

We thus have a classic situation in which a constructive trust should be imposed over all the assets acquired by Jane. The district court properly used its equitable power to declare the agreement to be null and void. Equity should fully protect one spouse from exploitation through the exercise of undue influence by the other in whom confidence and trust has been innocently reposed.

* * *

Appellant raises other contentions on appeal, all of which are without merit. Accordingly the judgment of the district court will be affirmed. Costs taxed against appellant.

METHODIST MISSION HOME OF TEXAS
v. N_____ A_____ B_____

Court of Civil Appeals of Texas, 1970.
451 S.W.2d 539.

CADENA, JUSTICE.

Defendant, Methodist Mission Home of Texas, a licensed adoption agency, appeals from a judgment declaring that certain instruments executed by plaintiff, surrendering parental custody and control of her infant illegitimate child to, and permitting placement of the child for adoption by, defendant are void. The judgment is based on a jury finding that the execution of the instruments by plaintiff was the result of undue influence exerted on her by defendant's agents and employees.

Defendant seeks a reversal of the judgment and a remand of the case on the ground that there is insufficient evidence to support the jury finding of undue influence.

The parties agree that, since plaintiff consented to the placement of her child for adoption by an agency licensed by the State of Texas, the consent is revocable only on proof of "fraud, mistake, misrepresentation, overreaching and the like." Catholic Charities of Diocese of Galveston, Inc. v. Harper, 161 Tex. 21, 337 S.W.2d 111, 114–115 (1960). The case was tried below on the theory, not questioned here by either party, that a consent executed as the result of the exertion of undue influence on the consenting natural parent is subject to revocation under the Harper Rule.

The Methodist Mission Home in San Antonio is operated by the United Methodist Church as a maternity home to provide "proper care for the girl or woman who finds herself faced with an out-of-wedlock pregnancy." The United Methodist Church is the principal source of financial support for the Home. Additional sources of revenue include fees paid by girls who are admitted to the Home, contributions made by other religious organizations, and donations made by individuals, including gifts made by persons who adopt the children surrendered to the Home.

In addition to board, lodging and medical care, girls admitted to the Home receive the benefit of counselling by trained social workers who are members of the Home's counselling staff. This counselling concerns the girls' personal problems and vocational plans as well as "plans for the unborn child." Once each week, the residents participate in group counselling sessions, conducted by Rev. Don Lilljedahl, Director of Counselling, assisted by Mrs. Sharon Burrows. In addition, each resident meets privately with her individual counsellor about once a week. Plaintiff's individual counsellor was Mrs. Jo Ann Burns. Plaintiff's claim of undue influence concerns the conduct and statements of Rev. Lilljedahl, Mrs. Burrows and, particularly, Mrs. Burns.

When the question before us concerns the "sufficiency" of the evidence to support a jury finding, we must consider and weigh all of the evidence in the case, not merely that which supports the verdict. We may set aside the verdict and remand the cause for a new trial if we conclude that, in view of all the evidence, the verdict is manifestly unjust, even though the record contains some evidence of probative force in support of the jury finding.

An examination of the entire statement of facts reveals that there is sufficient evidence to support the following conclusions:

1. It is the policy of the Home to encourage unwed mothers to release their children to the Home for placement for adoption.

2. The Home's counselling staff attempted to persuade the residents to release their children for adoption.

3. During the time, prior to the birth of plaintiff's son, that the Home's staff believed plaintiff intended to give up her child no effort was made by the counsellors to induce plaintiff to reconsider her decision.

4. After plaintiff, subsequent to the birth of her son, announced her decision to keep the child, Mrs. Burns initiated a series of interviews with plaintiff, extending over a period of about five days, as the result of which plaintiff consented to the placement of the baby for adoption.

5. Although Mrs. Burns testified that she initiated the interviews for the purpose of discussing with plaintiff the "pros and cons" of the problem, the counsellor's contributions to the discussions consisted solely of a recital of the reasons why plaintiff should give up her baby.

6. Mrs. Burns implanted in plaintiff's mind the belief that plaintiff's parents, who had announced they would support plaintiff in her decision to keep the child, were attempting to take advantage of plaintiff. As a result, plaintiff successfully insisted that her step-father and sister, who had started the journey to Texas for the purpose of driving plaintiff and the child to California, "turn around and go back" to California.

During the period between Tuesday, November 26, and Tuesday, December 3, when plaintiff signed the instruments consenting to the adoption, plaintiff was very weak and Mrs. Burns, according to plaintiff, repeatedly and "emphatically stressed" that if plaintiff "was any sort of person" she would give up the child. Plaintiff described this period as a "nightmare" during which she was able to sleep only about three hours a day. She testified that, as a result of her discussions with Mrs. Burns, she felt "trapped," and that on Monday, December 2, after Mrs. Burns had repeated everything that the counsellor had said before, she consented to the adoption of her child in order to avoid "harassment."

What constitutes "undue influence" depends on the particular facts and circumstances of each case, viewed in the light of applicable principles of law. It is said that a finding of undue influence is justified only where the actor's free agency and will have been destroyed and subverted to the extent that his act, instead of expressing his own will, expresses the will of the person exerting the influence. Rothermel v. Duncan, 369 S.W.2d 917 (Tex.Sup.1963); Winn v. Daniel, 386 S.W.2d 293 (Tex.Civ. App.—Fort Worth 1965, writ ref'd n.r.e.). Such statements of principles of law, since they involve inquiry into the metaphysical concept of will, furnish no concrete guidelines which are helpful in the decisional process. Since each case is more or less *sui generis,* any attempt to formulate a precise definition will be futile.

It is true that exerted influence cannot be branded as "undue" merely because it is persuasive and effective, and that the law does not condemn all persuasion, entreaty, cajolery, importunity, intercession, argument and solicitation. Robinson v. Stuart, 73 Tex. 267, 11 S.W. 275 (1889); Winn v. Daniel, supra. It may be conceded that calling to the attention of an unwed mother the considerations which tend to show that her best interest, and that of her child would best be served by placement of the child for adoption cannot be branded as undue influence, even though she is thereby induced to give up her child. See In re Surrender of Minor Children, 344 Mass. 230, 181 N.E.2d 836, 838 (1962).

But in this case we have testimony which amply supports the conclusion that plaintiff was subjected to excessive persuasion. All of the witnesses agreed that plaintiff was shy and reluctant to discuss her personal problems. Plaintiff's testimony concerning her emotional distress during the critical period following the birth of her child is rendered credible by the fact that an unwed mother who has just given birth is usually emotionally distraught and peculiarly vulnerable to efforts, well-meaning or unscrupulous, to persuade her to give up her child. Immediately following plaintiff's announcement that, contrary to the expectations of Mrs. Burns, she intended to keep her son, she was subjected to an intensive campaign, extending over a five-day period, designed to convince her to give up her baby, rather than to insure that her decision, whatever it might be, would be based on a consideration of all relevant factors. Plaintiff was told, falsely, that she had no right to keep her child. She was accused of being selfish and told that if she "was any kind of person" she would consent to the adoption of her baby. Her parents, the only persons who were willing to accept plaintiff's decision to keep her child, were accused by Mrs. Burns, with no factual support, of acting out of improper motives and with the intention of "putting something over" on plaintiff. What Mrs. Burns described as a discussion of the "pros and cons" consisted entirely of an endless recital only of the "cons"—a repetitive monologue of the reasons why plaintiff should not keep her child. The polemic by Mrs. Burns was in keeping with the policy of the Home to encourage the residents to surrender their children to the Home's placement agency. Further, this concentrated assault on plaintiff's will came from a person to whom plaintiff was encouraged to look for guidance, a member of an organization to which plaintiff was undoubtedly indebted and on which, according to all the testimony, she was dependent for help in finding her employment and a place to live.

Viewing the totality of the situation, we cannot say that, under the evidence, the jury acted unreasonably in concluding that the influence exerted on plaintiff was such as to constrain her to execute a consent which she would not otherwise have executed. Nor can we say that, considering all of the evidence, the finding is such as to "shock the conscience," or that it is "clearly unjust," or that it "clearly indicates bias" so that a court would "have to go blind" in order to accept it. Garwood, The Question of Insufficient Evidence on Appeal, 30 Tex. L.Rev. 803, 811 (1952).

The judgment of the trial court is affirmed.

Problems

6.   Decedent, an enfeebled woman over the age of 80, made a gift of almost all her assets to D, a physician. In addition to being her physician, D was her business adviser, agent and friend. Decedent in her lifetime had spoken of D with much affection and, on one occasion, stated that she regarded him as a son. She left, as surviving relatives, two sisters and their children. There was a conflict of evidence as to whether she had stated her intention to leave her estate to her relatives. Has a prima facie case for undue influence been presented?

7.   P, a woman factory worker, was seriously injured by the negligence of D. An adjuster for D's insurer made numerous visits to P while she was hospitalized. On the last visit, P was still in a cast from multiple fractures received in the accident. For two hours the adjuster repeatedly importuned her to sign a release in return for one-half of the estimated medical expenses. P testified that she became highly nervous and hysterical and signed the release in order to get the adjuster out of the room. The jury returned a verdict on P's negligence claim for damages substantially greater than the amount stated in the release and the trial court entered judgment for P for the amount of the verdict. On appeal, what result?

SECTION 3. MISREPRESENTATION AND NON–DIS-CLOSURE

(Calamari & Perillo 5th §§ 9.13—9.24)

COUSINEAU v. WALKER

Supreme Court of Alaska, 1980.
613 P.2d 608.

BOOCHEVER, JUSTICE.

The question in this case is whether the appellants are entitled to rescission of a land sale contract because of false statements made by the sellers. The superior court concluded that the buyers did not rely on any misrepresentations made by the sellers, that the misrepresentations were not material to the transaction, and that reliance by the buyers was not justified. Restitution of money paid under the contract was denied. We reverse and remand the case to the superior court to determine the amount of damages owed the appellants.

In 1975, Devon Walker and his wife purchased 9.1 acres of land in Eagle River, Alaska, known as Lot 1, Cross Estates. They paid $140,000.00 for it. A little over a year later, in October, 1976, they signed a multiple listing agreement with Pat Davis, an Anchorage realtor. The listing stated that the property had 580 feet of highway frontage on the Old Glenn Highway and that "ENGINEER REPORT SAYS OVER 1 MILLION IN GRAVEL ON PROP." The asking price was $245,000.00.

When the multiple listing expired, Walker signed a new agreement to retain Davis as an exclusive agent. In the broker's contract, the property was again described as having 580 feet of highway frontage, but the gravel content was listed as "minimum 80,000 cubic yds of gravel." The agreement also stated that 2.6 acres on the front of the parcel had been proposed for B–3 zoning (a commercial use), and the asking price was raised to $470,000.00.

An appraisal was prepared to determine the property's value as of December 31, 1976. Walker specifically instructed the appraiser not to include the value of gravel in the appraisal. A rough draft of the appraisal and the appraiser's notes were introduced at trial. Under the heading, "Assumptions and Limiting Conditions," the report stated the appraisal "does not take into account any gravel...." But later in the report the ground was described as "all good gravel base ... covered with birch and spruce trees." The report did not mention the highway frontage of the lot.

Wayne Cousineau, a contractor who was also in the gravel extraction business, became aware of the property when he saw the multiple listing. He consulted Camille Davis, another Anchorage realtor, to see if the property was available. In January, Cousineau and Camille Davis visited the property and discussed gravel extraction with Walker, although according to Walker's testimony commercial extraction was not considered. About this time Cousineau offered Walker $360,000.00 for the property. Cousineau tendered a proposed sales agreement which stated that all gravel rights would be granted to the purchaser at closing.

Sometime after his first offer, Cousineau attempted to determine the lot's road frontage. The property was covered with snow, and he found only one boundary marker. At trial the appraiser testified he could not find any markers. Cousineau testified that he went to the borough office to determine if any regulations prevented gravel extraction.

Despite Walker's reference to an "Engineer Report" allegedly showing "over 1 million in gravel," Walker admitted at trial that he had never seen a copy of the report. According to Walker's agent, Pat Davis, Camille Davis was told that if either she or Cousineau wanted the report they would have to pay for it themselves. It was undisputed that Cousineau never obtained the report.

In February, 1977, the parties agreed on a purchase price of $385,000.00 and signed an earnest money agreement. The sale was contingent upon approval of the zoning change of the front portion of the lot to commercial use. The amount of highway frontage was not included in the agreement. Paragraph 4(e) of the agreement conditionally granted gravel rights to Cousineau.[1] According to the agreement, Cousineau would be entitled to remove only so much gravel as was necessary to establish a construction grade on the commercial portion of the property. To remove additional gravel, Cousineau would be required to pay releases on those portions of ground where gravel was removed. This language was used to prevent Walker's security interest in the property from being impaired before he was fully paid.

Soon after the earnest money agreement was signed, the front portion of the property was rezoned and a month later the parties closed the sale.

There is no reference to the amount of highway frontage in the final purchase agreement. An addendum to a third deed of trust incorporates essentially the same language as the earnest money agreement with regard to the release of gravel rights.

After closing, Cousineau and his partners began developing the commercial portion of the property. They bought a gravel scale for $12,000.00 and used two of Cousineau's trucks and a loader. The partners contracted with South Construction to remove the gravel. According to Cousineau's testimony, he first learned of discrepancies in the real estate listing which described the lot when a neighbor threatened to sue Cousineau because he was removing gravel from the neighbor's adjacent lot. A recent survey shows that there is 415 feet of highway frontage on the property—not 580 feet, as advertised.

At the same time Cousineau discovered the shortage in highway frontage, South Construction ran out of gravel. They had removed 6,000 cubic yards. To determine if there was any more gravel on the property, a South Construction employee bulldozed a trench about fifty feet long

---

1. Paragraph IX of the judge's factual findings states that there was no mention of the amount of gravel or road frontage in the purchase agreement. This statement is correct insofar as the agreement did not mention specific amounts of gravel or frontage, but the agreement plainly does provide for the transfer of gravel rights.

and twenty feet deep. There was no gravel. A soils report prepared in 1978 confirmed that there were no gravel deposits on the property.

After December, 1977, Cousineau and his partners stopped making monthly payments. At that time they had paid a total of $99,000.00 for the property, including a down payment and monthly installments. In March, 1978, they informed Walker of their intention to rescind the contract. A deed of trust foreclosure sale was held in the fall of 1978, and Walker reacquired the property. At a bench trial in December, Cousineau and his partners were denied rescission and restitution.

Among his written findings of fact, the trial judge found:

> At some point in time, between October 24, 1976, and January 11, 1977, there existed a multiple listing advertisement which included information relating to gravel as well as road frontage, said information subsequently determined to be incorrect.

He further found:

> The plaintiffs did not rely on any misinformation or misrepresentations of defendants. The claimed misinformation about gravel on the property and the road frontage was not a material element of the parties' negotiations, and these pieces of information did not appear in the February 16, 1977 purchase agreement document prepared by attorney Harland Davis, attorney for the plaintiffs and signed by the parties.

In part, based on these findings, the court adopted the following conclusions of law:

> The plaintiffs are not entitled to rescission of the contract of sale or restitution as they were not entitled to rely on the alleged misrepresentation.

> · · · · ·

> The information which allegedly formed the basis of the misrepresentation was not material in the instant transaction, the agreement reached by the parties was valid and does not suffer any taint or defect of misrepresentation.

I.   Rescission of the Contract

Numerous cases hold and the Restatement provides that an innocent misrepresentation may be the basis for rescinding a contract. There is no question, as the trial judge's findings of fact state, that the statements made by Walker and his real estate agent in the multiple listing were false.[4] Three questions must be resolved, however, to determine whether Cousineau is entitled to rescission and restitution of the amount paid for the property on the basis of the misrepresentations. First, it must be determined whether Cousineau in fact relied on the statements. Second, it must be determined whether the statements were material to the transaction—that is, objectively, whether a reasonable

---

4. The statements made regarding highway frontage and gravel content in the two listing agreements cannot be characterized as "puffing." They were positive statements "susceptible of exact knowledge" at the time they were made. *Young & Cooper, Inc. v. Vestring,* 214 Kan. 311, 521 P.2d 281, 290 (1974). * * *

person would have considered the statements important in deciding whether to purchase the property. Finally, assuming that Cousineau relied on the statements and that they were material, it must be determined whether his reliance was justified.

A. Reliance on the False Statements

As quoted above, in his findings of fact, the trial judge stated, "The plaintiffs did not rely on any misinformation or misrepresentations of defendants." * * * In our opinion, the trial judge's finding that Cousineau and his partners did not rely on the statements made by Walker is clearly erroneous.

Regardless of the credibility of some witnesses, the uncontroverted facts are that Wayne Cousineau was in the gravel extraction business. He first became aware of the property through a multiple listing that said "1 MILLION IN GRAVEL." The subsequent listing stated that there were 80,000 cubic yards of gravel. Even if Walker might have taken the position that the sale was based on the appraisal, rather than the listings, the appraisal does not disclaim the earlier statements regarding the amount of highway frontage and the existence of gravel. In fact, the appraisal might well reaffirm a buyer's belief that gravel existed, since it stated there was a good gravel base. All the documents prepared regarding the sale from the first offer through the final deed of trust make provisions for the transfer of gravel rights. Cousineau's first act upon acquiring the property was to contract with South Construction for gravel removal, and to purchase gravel scales for $12,000.00. We conclude that the court erred in finding that Cousineau did not rely on Walker's statement that there was gravel on the property.

We are also convinced that the trial court's finding that Cousineau did not rely on Walker's statement regarding the amount of highway frontage was clearly erroneous. The Cousineaus were experienced and knowledgeable in real estate matters. In determining whether to purchase the property, they would certainly have considered the amount of highway frontage to be of importance. Despite Walker's insistence that Cousineau knew the location of the boundary markers, neither Cousineau nor the appraiser ever found them. It is improbable that Cousineau would have started removing gravel from a neighbor's property had he known the correct location of his boundary line.

B. Materiality of the Statements

Materiality is a mixed question of law and fact. A material fact is one "to which a reasonable man might be expected to attach importance in making his choice of action." W. Prosser, Law of Torts § 108, at 719 (4th ed. 1971). It is a fact which could reasonably be expected to influence someone's judgment or conduct concerning a transaction. * * * Under § 306 of the tentative draft of the Restatement (Second) of Contracts, a misrepresentation may be grounds for voiding a contract if it is either fraudulent or material. [Now § 164, Ed.] The reason behind the rule requiring proof of materiality is to encourage stability in contractual relations. The rule prevents parties who later become disappointed at the outcome of their bargain from capitalizing on any insignificant discrepancy to void the contract.

We conclude as a matter of law that the statements regarding highway frontage and gravel content were material. A reasonable person would be likely to consider the existence of gravel deposits an important consideration in developing a piece of property. Even if not valuable for commercial extraction, a gravel base would save the cost of obtaining suitable fill from other sources. Walker's real estate agent testified that the statements regarding gravel were placed in the listings because gravel would be among the property's "best points" and a "selling point." It seems obvious that the sellers themselves thought a buyer would consider gravel content important.

The buyers received less than three-fourths of the highway frontage described in the listings. Certainly the amount of highway frontage on a commercial tract would be considered important. * * *

C. Justifiable Reliance

The trial judge concluded as a matter of law that the plaintiffs "were not entitled to rely on the alleged misrepresentation."

The bulk of the appellee's brief is devoted to the argument that Cousineau's unquestioning reliance on Walker and his real estate agent was imprudent and unreasonable. Cousineau failed to obtain and review the engineer's report. He failed to obtain a survey or examine the plat available at the recorder's office. He failed to make calculations that would have revealed the true frontage of the lot. Although the property was covered with snow, the plaintiffs, according to Walker, had ample time to inspect it. The plaintiffs were experienced businessmen who frequently bought and sold real estate. Discrepancies existed in the various property descriptions which should have alerted Cousineau and his partners to potential problems. In short, the appellees urge that the doctrine of caveat emptor precludes recovery.

In fashioning an appropriate rule for land sale contracts, we note initially that, in the area of commercial and consumer goods, the doctrine of caveat emptor has been nearly abolished by the Uniform Commercial Code and imposition of strict products liability. In real property transactions, the doctrine is also rapidly receding. Alaska has passed the Uniform Land Sales Practices Act, AS 34.55.004–.046, which imposes numerous restrictions on vendors of subdivided property. Criminal penalties may be imposed for violations. The Uniform Residential Landlord and Tenant Act, AS 34.03.010–.380, has greatly altered the common law of landlord and tenant in favor of tenants. Many states now imply warranties of merchantability in new home sales. Wyoming has recently extended this warranty beyond the initial purchaser to subsequent buyers. *Moxley v. Laramie Builders, Inc.,* 600 P.2d 733, 735–36 (Wyo.1979).

There is a split of authority regarding a buyer's duty to investigate a vendor's fraudulent statements, but the prevailing trend is toward placing a minimal duty on a buyer. Recently, a Florida appellate court reversed long-standing precedent which held that a buyer must use due diligence to protect his interest, regardless of fraud, if the means for acquiring knowledge concerning the transaction were open and available. In the context of a building sale the court concluded:

> A person guilty of fraudulent misrepresentation should not be permitted to hide behind the doctrine of *caveat emptor*.

> *Upledger v. Vilanor, Inc.,* 369 So.2d 427, 430 (Fla.App.), *cert. denied,* 378 So.2d 350 (Fla.1979).

The Supreme Court of Maine has also recently reversed a line of its prior cases, concluding that a defense based upon lack of due care should not be allowed in land sales contracts where a reckless or knowing misrepresentation has been made. *Letellier v. Small,* 400 A.2d 371, 375 (Me.1979). This is also the prevailing view in California, Idaho, Kansas, Massachusetts, and Oregon. On the other hand, some jurisdictions have reaffirmed the doctrine of caveat emptor, but as noted in Williston on Contracts,

> [t]he growing trend and tendency of the courts will continue to move toward the doctrine that negligence in trusting in a misrepresentation will not excuse positive willful fraud or deprive the defrauded person of his remedy.

W. Jaeger, Williston on Contracts § 1515B at 487 (3d ed. 1970).

There is also authority for not applying the doctrine of caveat emptor even though the misrepresentation is innocent. The Restatements, case law, and a ready analogy to express warranties in the sale of goods support this view.

The recent draft of the Restatement of Contracts allows rescission for an innocent material misrepresentation unless a buyer's fault was so negligent as to amount to "a failure to act in good faith and in accordance with reasonable standards of fair dealing." Restatement (Second) of Contracts § 314, Comment b (Tent. Draft. no. 11, 1976). [Now § 172, Ed.]

In *Van Meter v. Bent Construction Co.,* 46 Cal.2d 588, 297 P.2d 644 (1956), the city of San Diego failed to properly mark the area of a reservoir that needed to be cleared of brush. A lower court concluded that the city's failure to mark the area properly was an innocent mistake, and that a bidder's actions in failing to discover the true area to be cleared was negligent. Recovery was denied because the city's misrepresentation was not willful. The California Supreme Court reversed, first noting that a party's negligence does not bar rescission for mutual mistake, and then concluding:

> There is even more reason for not barring a plaintiff from equitable relief where his negligence is due in part to his reliance in good faith upon the false representations of a defendant, although the statements were not made with intent to deceive. A defendant who misrepresents the facts and induces the plaintiff to rely on his

statements should not be heard in an equitable action to assert that the reliance was negligent unless plaintiff's conduct, in the light of his intelligence and information, is preposterous or irrational.

Id. 297 P.2d at 648 (citations omitted). The Massachusetts Supreme Judicial Court has expressed a similar view in *Yorke v. Taylor,* 332 Mass. 368, 124 N.E.2d 912, 916 (1955).

We do not contend that real property transactions are the same as those involving sales of goods. Nevertheless, an analogy to the applicability of the doctrine of caveat emptor under the Uniform Commercial Code is helpful. Under the Code, factual statements regarding the sale of goods constitute an express warranty. AS 45.05.094. The official comment to section 2–316 of the Code (codified as AS 45.05.100), dealing with disclaimers of warranties, states:

> Application of the doctrine of "caveat emptor" in all cases where the buyer examines the goods regardless of statements made by the seller is, however, rejected by this Article. Thus, if the offer of examination is accompanied by words as to their merchantability or specific attributes and the buyer indicates clearly that he is relying on those words rather than on his examination, they give rise to an "express" warranty.

Numerous cases have concluded that a buyer is entitled to rely on an express warranty, regardless of an inadequate examination of the goods.

Furthermore, the protections of the Code extend to highly sophisticated buyers in arms length transactions as well as to household consumers. Other than tradition, no reason exists for treating land sales differently from the sale of commercial goods insofar as application of the doctrine of caveat emptor is involved. We conclude that a purchaser of land may rely on material representations made by the seller and is not obligated to ascertain whether such representations are truthful.

A buyer of land, relying on an innocent misrepresentation, is barred from recovery only if the buyer's acts in failing to discover defects were wholly irrational, preposterous, or in bad faith.

Although Cousineau's actions may well have exhibited poor judgment for an experienced businessman, they were not so unreasonable or preposterous in view of Walker's description of the property that recovery should be denied. Consequently, we reverse the judgment of the superior court.

II. RESTITUTION

Walker received a total of $99,000.00 from Cousineau and his partners, but the appellants are not entitled to restitution of this amount. Cousineau apparently caused extensive damage to one building on the property, and he removed 6,000 cubic yards of gravel. Walker should be allowed some recoupment for these items, plus an amount for the fair rental value of the property less reasonable costs of rental.

It is necessary to remand this case to the trial court to determine the correct amount of damages.

REVERSED and REMANDED.

VOKES v. ARTHUR MURRAY, INC.

District Court of Appeal of Florida, 1968.
212 So.2d 906.

PIERCE, JUDGE.

This is an appeal by Audrey E. Vokes, plaintiff below, from a final order dismissing with prejudice, for failure to state a cause of action, her fourth amended complaint, hereinafter referred to as plaintiff's complaint.

Defendant Arthur Murray, Inc., a corporation, authorizes the operation throughout the nation of dancing schools under the name of "Arthur Murray School of Dancing" through local franchised operators, one of whom was defendant J.P. Davenport whose dancing establishment was in Clearwater.

Plaintiff Mrs. Audrey E. Vokes, a widow of 51 years and without family, had a yen to be "an accomplished dancer" with the hopes of finding "new interest in life". So, on February 10, 1961, a dubious fate, with the assist of a motivated acquaintance, procured her to attend a "dance party" at Davenport's "School of Dancing" where she whiled away the pleasant hours, sometimes in a private room, absorbing his accomplished sales technique, during which her grace and poise were elaborated upon and her rosy future as "an excellent dancer" was painted for her in vivid and glowing colors. As an incident to this interlude, he sold her eight ½–hour dance lessons to be utilized within one calendar month therefrom, for the sum of $14.50 cash in hand paid, obviously a baited "come-on".

Thus she embarked upon an almost endless pursuit of the terpsichorean art during which, over a period of less than sixteen months, she was sold fourteen "dance courses" totalling in the aggregate 2302 hours of dancing lessons for a total cash outlay of $31,090.45, all at Davenport's dance emporium. All of these fourteen courses were evidenced by execution of a written "Enrollment Agreement—Arthur Murray's School of Dancing" with the addendum in heavy black print, "No one will be informed that you are taking dancing lessons. Your relations with us are held in strict confidence", setting forth the number of "dancing lessons" and the "lessons in rhythm sessions" currently sold to her from time to time, and always of course accompanied by payment of cash of the realm.

These dance lesson contracts and the monetary consideration therefor of over $31,000 were procured from her by means and methods of Davenport and his associates which went beyond the unsavory, yet legally permissible, perimeter of "sales puffing" and intruded well into the forbidden area of undue influence, the suggestion of falsehood, the suppression of truth, and the free exercise of rational judgment, if what plaintiff alleged in her complaint was true. From the time of her first contact with the dancing school in February, 1961, she was influenced unwittingly by a constant and continuous barrage of flattery, false praise, excessive compliments, and panegyric encomiums, to such extent that it would be not only inequitable, but unconscionable, for a Court exercising inherent chancery power to allow such contracts to stand.

She was incessantly subjected to overreaching blandishment and cajolery. She was assured she had "grace and poise"; that she was "rapidly improving and developing in her dancing skill"; that the additional lessons would "make her a beautiful dancer, capable of dancing with the most accomplished dancers"; that she was "rapidly progressing in the development of her dancing skill and gracefulness", etc., etc. She was given "dance aptitude tests" for the ostensible purpose of "determining" the number of remaining hours [of instruction] needed by her from time to time.

At one point she was sold 545 additional hours of dancing lessons to be entitled to award of the "Bronze Medal" signifying that she had reached "the Bronze Standard", a supposed designation of dance achievement by students of Arthur Murray, Inc.

Later she was sold an additional 926 hours in order to gain the "Silver Medal", indicating she had reached "the Silver Standard", at a cost of $12,501.35.

At one point, while she still had to her credit about 900 unused hours of instructions, she was induced to purchase an additional 24 hours of lessons to participate in a trip to Miami at her own expense, where she would be "given the opportunity to dance with members of the Miami Studio".

She was induced at another point to purchase an additional 126 hours of lessons in order to be not only eligible for the Miami trip but also to become "a life member of the Arthur Murray Studio", carrying with it certain dubious emoluments, at a further cost of $1,752.30.

At another point, while she still had over 1,000 unused hours of instruction she was induced to buy 151 additional hours at a cost of $2,049.00 to be eligible for a "Student Trip to Trinidad", at her own expense as she later learned.

Also, when she still had 1100 unused hours to her credit, she was prevailed upon to purchase an additional 347 hours at a cost of $4,235.74, to qualify her to receive a "Gold Medal" for achievement, indicating she had advanced to "the Gold Standard".

On another occasion, while she still had over 1200 unused hours, she was induced to buy an additional 175 hours of instruction at a cost of $2,472.75 to be eligible "to take a trip to Mexico".

Finally, sandwiched in between other lesser sales promotions, she was influenced to buy an additional 481 hours of instruction at a cost of $6,523.81 in order to "be classified as a Gold Bar Member, the ultimate achievement of the dancing studio".

All the foregoing sales promotions, illustrative of the entire fourteen separate contracts, were procured by defendant Davenport and Arthur

Murray, Inc., by false representations to her that she was improving in her dancing ability, that she had excellent potential, that she was responding to instructions in dancing grace, and that they were developing her into a beautiful dancer, whereas in truth and in fact she did not develop in her dancing ability, she had no "dance aptitude", and in fact had difficulty in "hearing the musical beat". The complaint alleged that such representations to her "were in fact false and known by the defendant to be false and contrary to the plaintiff's true ability, the truth of plaintiff's ability being fully known to the defendants, but withheld from the plaintiff for the sole and specific intent to deceive and defraud the plaintiff and to induce her in the purchasing of additional hours of dance lessons". It was averred that the lessons were sold to her "in total disregard to the true physical, rhythm, and mental ability of the plaintiff". In other words, while she first exulted that she was entering the "spring of her life", she finally was awakened to the fact there was "spring" neither in her life nor in her feet.

The complaint prayed that the Court decree the dance contracts to be null and void and to be cancelled, that an accounting be had, and judgment entered against the defendants "for that portion of the $31,090.45 not charged against specific hours of instruction given to the plaintiff". The Court held the complaint not to state a cause of action and dismissed it with prejudice. We disagree and reverse.

The material allegations of the complaint must of course be accepted as true for the purpose of testing its legal sufficiency. Defendants contend that contracts can only be rescinded for fraud or misrepresentation when the alleged misrepresentation is as to a material fact, rather than an opinion, prediction or expectation, and that the statements and representations set forth at length in the complaint were in the category of "trade puffing" . . .

It is true that "generally a misrepresentation, to be actionable, must be one of fact rather than of opinion". Tonkovich v. South Florida Citrus Industries, Inc., Fla.App.1966, 185 So.2d 710; Kutner v. Kalish, Fla.App. 1965, 173 So.2d 763. But this rule has significant qualifications, applicable here. It does not apply where there is a fiduciary relationship between the parties, or where there has been some artifice or trick employed by the representor, or where the parties do not in general deal at "arm's length" as we understand the phrase, or where the representee does not have equal opportunity to become apprised of the truth or falsity of the fact represented. 14 Fla.Jur. Fraud and Deceit, § 28; Kitchen v. Long, 1914, 67 Fla. 72, 64 So. 429. As stated by Judge Allen of this Court in Ramel v. Chasebrook Construction Company, Fla.App. 1961, 135 So.2d 876:

> " * * * A statement of a party having * * * superior knowledge may be regarded as a statement of fact although it would be considered as opinion if the parties were dealing on equal terms."

It could be reasonably supposed here that defendants had "superior knowledge" as to whether plaintiff had "dance potential" and as to whether she was noticeably improving in the art of terpsichore. And it would be a reasonable inference from the undenied averments of the complaint that the flowery eulogiums heaped upon her by defendants as a prelude to her contracting for 1944 additional hours of instruction in order to attain the rank of the Bronze Standard, thence to the bracket of the Silver Standard, thence to the class of the Gold Bar Standard, and finally to the crowning plateau of a Life Member of the Studio, proceeded as much or more from the urge to "ring the cash register" as from any honest or realistic appraisal of her dancing prowess or a factual representation of her progress.

Even in contractual situations where a party to a transaction owes no duty to disclose facts within his knowledge or to answer inquiries respecting such facts, the law is if he undertakes to do so he must disclose the *whole truth*. Ramel v. Chasebrook Construction Company, supra; Beagle v. Bagwell, Fla.App.1964, 169 So.2d 43. From the face of the complaint, it should have been reasonably apparent to defendants that her vast outlay of cash for the many hundreds of additional hours of instruction was not justified by her slow and awkward progress, which she would have been made well aware of if they had spoken the "whole truth".

In Hirschman v. Hodges, etc., 1910, 59 Fla. 517, 51 So. 550, it was said that—

"* * * what is plainly injurious to good faith ought to be considered as a fraud sufficient to impeach a contract", and that an improvident agreement may be avoided—

"* * * because of surprise, or mistake, *want of freedom, undue influence, the suggestion of falsehood, or the suppression of truth*". (Emphasis supplied.)

We repeat that where parties are dealing on a contractual basis at arm's length with no inequities or inherently unfair practices employed, the Courts will in general "leave the parties where they find themselves". But in the case sub judice, from the allegations of the unanswered complaint, we cannot say that enough of the accompanying ingredients, as mentioned in the foregoing authorities, were not present which otherwise would have barred the equitable arm of the Court to her. In our view, from the showing made in her complaint, plaintiff is entitled to her day in Court.

It accordingly follows that the order dismissing plaintiff's last amended complaint with prejudice should be and is reversed.

Reversed.

WITHDRAWAL WHEN A LAWYER'S SERVICES WILL OTHERWISE BE USED TO PERPETRATE A FRAUD

ABA Comm. on Ethics and Professional Responsibility
Formal Op. 92–366 (August 8, 1992).

A lawyer who knows or with reason believes that her services or work product are being used or are intended to be used by a client to perpetrate a fraud must withdraw from further representation of the client, and may disaffirm documents prepared in the course of the representation that are being, or will be, used in furtherance of the fraud, even though such a "noisy" withdrawal may have the collateral effect of inferentially revealing client confidences.

When a lawyer's services have been used in the past by a client to perpetrate a fraud, but the fraud has ceased, the lawyer may but is not required to withdraw from further representation of the client; in these circumstances, a "noisy" withdrawal is not permitted.

The Committee has been asked its views on what the ABA Model Rules of Professional Conduct (1983, amended 1992) require, and what the Rules permit, a lawyer to do when she learns that her client has used her work product to perpetrate a fraud, is continuing so to use it, or plans so to use it in the future. The answers to these questions require a somewhat difficult reconciliation of the text and commentary of three Rules: Rule 1.6, imposing a broad requirement of confidentiality; 1.2(d), prohibiting a lawyer from assisting client crime or fraud; and Rule 1.16(a)(1), requiring withdrawal from a representation where continued representation would result in a violation of the Rules.

As more fully explained below, the Committee's conclusions are these:

First, the lawyer must withdraw from any representation of the client that, directly or indirectly, would have the effect of assisting the client's continuing or intended future fraud.

Second, the lawyer may withdraw from all representation of the client, and must withdraw from all representation if the fact of such representation is likely to be known to and relied upon by third persons to whom the continuing fraud is directed, and the representation is therefore likely to assist in the fraud.

Third, the lawyer may disavow any of her work product to prevent its use in the client's continuing or intended future fraud, even though this may have the collateral effect of disclosing inferentially client confidences obtained during the representation. In some circumstances, such a disavowal of work product (commonly referred to as a "noisy" withdrawal) may be necessary in order to effectuate the lawyer's withdrawal from representation of the client.

Fourth and finally, if the fraud is completed, and the lawyer does not know or reasonably believe that the client intends to continue the fraud or commit a future fraud by use of the lawyer's services or work product, the lawyer may withdraw from representation of the client but may not disavow any work product.

* * *

Problems

8.   Plaintiff Gladys McVeigh's former husband, Thomas McConnell owed her $18,000 for past due alimony and child support. McVeigh knew that McConnell had been unemployed and had been on welfare. She did not know he had recently collected a $20,000 inheritance. McConnell's lawyer, McGuerren, met with McVeigh and her lawyer to convince her to abandon any attempt to collect the money owed her by litigation. Although McGuerren knew of the inheritance, he told them that McConnell was broke but could borrow $1,250 from a friend if McVeigh would release her claim for the balance for this amount. She agreed, signed a release, and was paid $1,250. When McVeigh learned of the inheritance, she sued her former husband to have the release set aside and, in a separate action, sued McGuerren in tort for deceit. What will be the result in these actions?

9.   V sold a lot to P, representing falsely that only one-family houses would be built on the remaining lots of the subdivision. P, in an action to rescind, proved the representation, its falsity, V's knowledge of its falsity, and that P would not have purchased the lot but for the representation. The trial judge found for P and ordered V to make restitution on condition that P reconvey the land. On appeal V seeks reversal on the ground that P failed to prove that P suffered any damages as a result of the misrepresentation. What result?

10.   D, an electric power company, formulated a plan to acquire land for a large hydro-electric project. P owned 138 acres of timberland in the area. A, who was D's undisclosed agent, contacted P and offered to purchase P's tract. When P asked him why he wanted the land, A falsely replied that he had come into a large sum of money which he wanted to invest in timber. D agreed to sell the tract for $4100 and the contract was performed. P sues in equity to rescind the deed, alleging that had he known A's and D's true motive, he could have demanded and received $27,000 for the tract. What result?

11.   D operated a small but highly successful chicken processing plant. A key reason for this success was that D had developed machines for stripping meat from chicken necks and emulsifying the meat for use in baby food. These machines were adaptations of existing vegetable pulpers bought from FMC on which FMC held patents. D's application for a patent on the adaptations was pending. P had negotiations with D to purchase D's business. After investigating D's application and discovering that it was an adaptation of FMC's patent, P's patent attorney asked D what was new and novel about D's adaptation. D replied that the key innovation was the precise setting of the gap between the vanes and the blades. P offered to purchase on the condition that the patent application be granted. D refused to accept the condition. P then agreed to purchase after P's patent attorney gave an opinion that the adaptation was patentable. P made the purchase of

the business along with rights in the patent application. The application was denied. P sued to rescind. The trial judge found that D's statement as to the importance of the gap was innocent but incorrect and granted rescission and restitution. On appeal, what are the issues and how should they be resolved?

12. The United States was acquiring land for a reservoir project and had the power to acquire the land by eminent domain, but preferred negotiated settlements. K, an agent of the government, negotiated with S for S's farm. S reluctantly agreed to a price of $230,000, but only if the government would pay within 60 days. K promised that payment would be made in 60 days, but refused to put the promise in the written documents signed by S. K knew from experience that the government rarely paid so swiftly and that he had no control over the time of payment. Payment was not tendered within 60 days. The land has been taken by the United States by condemnation and the trial judge set the land's value at $270,000. The government appeals, arguing that S is bound by the agreed price of $230,000. What result?

13. B, a real estate broker in Orlando, Florida, offered to purchase a 10–acre orange grove from S, a real estate broker in St. Petersburg. After negotiations, the property was sold to B in 1966 for $47,500, a price about 50% above the going rate for orange groves. In 1970, as a result of the construction of Walt Disney World, real property values boomed in the Orlando area. The value of this orange grove was greatly enhanced by its close proximity to a cloverleaf exchange connecting two highways which had been built because of the increased traffic brought about by Walt Disney World. S sues to rescind the sale, alleging that B knew of the proposed location of the cloverleaf and of the impact that Walt Disney World would have on land values. He contends that B, as a broker, owed a duty to disclose these facts before purchasing. Is this contention sound?

14. P contracted to purchase from D a tract of land which was used as a vacation resort. The land was irrigated from Grouse Creek. P inquired about water rights and D replied that the tract had water rights to Grouse Creek. D did not inform P that a neighboring landowner had questioned the water rights and on several occasions had by words and actions asserted rights to the water inconsistent with those of D. Upon discovery of this adverse claim, P seeks to rescind. What result?

15. A and B reach an agreement and agree to reduce it to writing. A prepares a writing, which B reads, that accurately reflects their understanding. Prior to signing the writing, A substitutes a writing that is similar in appearance, but which contains terms that are radically different. B signs this second writing. What is the legal effect of the signed writing?

16. At the request of her husband, W signed a document whereby she personally guaranteed to the plaintiff bank the obligations of a corporation controlled by her husband. Her husband told her that her signature was required by the bank but that she would not be under any liability to the bank. Although literate, she did not read the document. When the corporation defaulted on its obligation to the bank, the latter brought suit against W. Can she rescind?

SECTION 4.   MISTAKE

(Calamari & Perillo 5th §§ 9.25—9.30)

WOOD v. BOYNTON

Supreme Court of Wisconsin, 1885.
64 Wis. 265, 25 N.W. 42.

TAYLOR, J. This action was brought in the circuit court for Milwaukee county to recover the possession of an uncut diamond of the alleged value of $1,000. The case was tried in the circuit court, and after hearing all the evidence in the case, the learned circuit judge directed the jury to find a verdict for the defendants. The plaintiff excepted to such instruction, and, after a verdict was rendered for the defendants, moved for a new trial upon the minutes of the judge. The motion was denied, and the plaintiff duly excepted, and after judgment was entered in favor of the defendants, appealed to this court. The defendants are partners in the jewelry business. On the trial it appeared that on and before the twenty-eighth of December, 1883, the plaintiff was the owner of and in the possession of a small stone of the nature and value of which she was ignorant; that on that day she sold it to one of the defendants for the sum of one dollar. Afterwards it was ascertained that the stone was a rough diamond, and of the value of about $700. After hearing this fact the plaintiff tendered the defendants the one dollar, and ten cents as interest, and demanded a return of the stone to her. The defendants refused to deliver it, and therefore she commenced this action.

The plaintiff testified to the circumstances attending the sale of the stone to *Mr. Samuel B. Boynton*, as follows: "The first time *Boynton* saw that stone he was talking about buying the topaz, or whatever it is, in September or October. I went into the store to get a little pin mended, and I had it in a small box,—the pin,—a small ear-ring; . . . this stone, and a broken sleeve-button were in the box. *Mr. Boynton* turned to give me a check for my pin. I thought I would ask him what the stone was, and I took it out of the box and asked him to please tell me what that was. He took it in his hand and seemed some time looking at it. I told him I had been told it was a topaz, and he said it might be. He says, 'I would buy this; would you sell it?' I told him I did not know but what I would. What would it be worth? And he said he did not know; he would give me a dollar and keep it as a specimen, and I told him I would not sell it; and it was certainly pretty to look at. He asked me where I found it, and I told him in Eagle. He asked about how far out, and I said right in the village, and I went out. Afterwards, and about the twenty-eighth of December, I needed money pretty badly, and thought every dollar would help, and I took it back to *Mr. Boynton* and told him I had brought back the topaz, and he says, 'Well, yes; what did I offer you for it?' and I says, 'One dollar;' and he stepped to the change drawer and gave me the dollar, and I went out."

In another part of her testimony she says: "Before I sold the stone I had no knowledge whatever that it was a diamond. I told him that I had been advised that it was probably a topaz, and he said probably it was. The stone was about the size of a canary bird's egg, nearly the shape of an egg,—worn pointed at one end; it was nearly straw color,—a little darker." She also testified that before this action was commenced she tendered the defendants $1.10, and demanded the return of the stone, which they refused. This is substantially all the evidence of what took place at and before the sale to the defendants, as testified to by the plaintiff herself. She produced no other witness on that point.

The evidence on the part of the defendant is not very different from the version given by the plaintiff, and certainly is not more favorable to the plaintiff. *Mr. Samuel B. Boynton*, the defendant to whom the stone was sold, testified that at the time he bought this stone, he had never seen an uncut diamond; had seen cut diamonds, but they are quite different from the uncut ones; "he had no idea this was a diamond, and it never entered his brain at the time." Considerable evidence was given as to what took place after the sale and purchase, but that evidence has very little if any bearing, upon the main point in the case.

This evidence clearly shows that the plaintiff sold the stone in question to the defendants, and delivered it to them in December, 1883, for a consideration of one dollar. By such sale the title to the stone passed by the sale and delivery to the defendants. How has that title been divested and again vested in the plaintiff? The contention of the learned counsel for the appellant is that the title became vested in the plaintiff by the tender to the *Boyntons* of the purchase money with interest, and a demand of a return of the stone to her. Unless such tender and demand revested the title in the appellant, she cannot maintain her action.

The only question in the case is whether there was anything in the sale which entitled the vendor (the appellant) to rescind the sale and so revest the title in her. The only reasons we know of for rescinding a sale and revesting the title in the vendor so that he may maintain an action at law for the recovery of the possession against his vendee are (1) that the vendee was guilty of some fraud in procuring a sale to be made to him; (2) that there was a mistake made by the vendor in delivering an article which was not the article sold,—a mistake in fact as to the identity of the thing sold with the thing delivered upon the sale. This last is not in reality a rescission of the sale made, as the thing delivered was not the thing sold, and no title ever passed to the vendee by such delivery.

In this case, upon the plaintiff's own evidence, there can be no just ground for alleging that she was induced to make the sale she did by any fraud or unfair dealings on the part of *Mr. Boynton*. Both were entirely ignorant at the time of the character of the stone and of its intrinsic value. *Mr. Boynton* was not an expert in uncut diamonds, and had made no examination of the stone, except to take it in his hand and look at it before he made the offer of one dollar, which was refused at the time, and afterwards accepted without any comment or further examination made by *Mr. Boynton*. The appellant had the stone in her possession for a long time, and it appears from her own statement that she had made some inquiry as to its nature and qualities. If she chose to sell it without further investigation as to its intrinsic value to a person who was guilty of no fraud or unfairness which induced her to sell it for a small sum, she cannot repudiate the sale because it is afterwards ascertained that she made a bad bargain. * * *

There is no pretense of any mistake as to the identity of the thing sold. It was produced by the plaintiff and exhibited to the vendee before the sale was made, and the thing sold was delivered to the vendee when the purchase price was paid. * * * Suppose the appellant had produced the stone, and said she had been told it was a diamond, and she believed it was, but had no knowledge herself as to its character or value, and *Mr. Boynton* had given her $500 for it, could he have rescinded the sale if it had turned out to be a topaz or any other stone of very small value? Could *Mr. Boynton* have rescinded the sale on the ground of mistake? Clearly not, nor could he rescind it on the ground that there had been a breach of warranty, because there was no warranty, nor could he rescind it on the ground of fraud, unless he could show that she falsely declared that she had been told it was a diamond, or, if she had been so told, still she knew it was not a diamond. See *Street v. Blay*, [2 Barn & Adol. 456].

It is urged, with a good deal of earnestness, on the part of the counsel for the appellant that, because it has turned out that the stone was immensely more valuable than the parties at the time of the sale supposed it was, such fact alone is a ground for the rescission of the sale, and that fact was evidence of fraud on the part of the vendee. Whether inadequacy of price is to be received as evidence of fraud, even in a suit in equity to avoid a sale, depends upon the facts known to the parties at the time the sale is made.

When this sale was made the value of the thing sold was open to the investigation of both parties, neither knowing its intrinsic value, and, so far as the evidence in this case shows, both supposed that the price paid was adequate. How can fraud be predicated upon such a sale, even though after-investigation showed that the intrinsic value of the thing sold was hundreds of times greater than the price paid? It certainly shows no such fraud as would authorize the vendor to rescind the contract and bring an action at law to recover the possession of the thing sold. Whether that fact would have any influence in an action in equity to avoid the sale we need not consider. * * *

We can find nothing in the evidence from which it could be justly inferred that *Mr. Boynton*, at the time he offered the plaintiff one dollar for the stone, had any knowledge of the real value of the stone, or that he entertained even a belief that the stone was a diamond. It cannot, therefore, be said that there was a suppression of knowledge on the part of the defendant as to the value of the stone which a court of equity might seize upon to avoid the sale. The following cases show that, in the absence of fraud or warranty, the value of the property sold, as compared with the price paid, is no ground for a rescission of a sale. * * *

However unfortunate the plaintiff may have been in selling this valuable stone for a mere nominal sum, she has failed entirely to make out a case either of fraud or mistake in the sale such as will entitle her to a rescission of such sale so as to recover the property sold in an action at law.

By the Court.— The judgment of the circuit court is affirmed.

LENAWEE COUNTY BOARD OF HEALTH v. MESSERLY

Supreme Court of Michigan, 1982.
417 Mich. 17, 331 N.W.2d 203.

RYAN, JUSTICE. In March of 1977, Carl and Nancy Pickles, appellees, purchased from appellants, William and Martha Messerly, a 600–square–foot tract of land upon which is located a three-unit apartment building. Shortly after the transaction was closed, the Lenawee County Board of Health condemned the property and obtained a permanent injunction which prohibits human habitation on the premises until the defective sewage system is brought into conformance with the Lenawee County sanitation code.

We are required to determine whether appellees should prevail in their attempt to avoid this land contract on the basis of mutual mistake and failure of consideration. We conclude that the parties did entertain a mutual misapprehension of fact, but that the circumstances of this case do not warrant rescission.

I

The facts of the case are not seriously in dispute. In 1971, the Messerlys acquired approximately one acre plus 600 square feet of land. A three-unit apartment building was situated upon the 600–square–foot portion. The trial court found that, prior to this transfer, the Messerlys' predecessor in title, Mr. Bloom, had installed a septic tank on the property without a permit and in violation of the applicable health code. The Messerlys used the building as an income investment property until 1973 when they sold it, upon land contract, to James Barnes who likewise used it primarily as an income-producing investment.[1]

Mr. and Mrs. Barnes, with the permission of the Messerlys, sold approximately one acre of the property in 1976, and the remaining 600 square feet and building were offered for sale soon thereafter when Mr. and Mrs. Barnes defaulted on their land contract. Mr. and Mrs. Pickles evidenced an interest in the property, but were dissatisfied with the terms of the Barnes–Messerly land contract. Consequently, to accommo-

1. James Barnes was married shortly after he purchased the property. Mr. and Mrs. Barnes lived in one of the apartments on the property for three months and, after they moved, Mrs. Barnes continued to aid in the management of the property.

date the Pickleses' preference to enter into a land contract directly with the Messerlys, Mr. and Mrs. Barnes executed a quit-claim deed which conveyed their interest in the property back to the Messerlys. After inspecting the property, Mr. and Mrs. Pickles executed a new land contract with the Messerlys on March 21, 1977. It provided for a purchase price of $25,500. A clause was added to the end of the land contract form which provides:

"17. Purchaser has examined this property and agrees to accept same in its present condition. There are no other or additional written or oral understandings."

Five or six days later, when the Pickleses went to introduce themselves to the tenants, they discovered raw sewage seeping out of the ground. Tests conducted by a sanitation expert indicated the inadequacy of the sewage system. The Lenawee County Board of Health subsequently condemned the property and initiated this lawsuit in the Lenawee Circuit Court against the Messerlys as land contract vendors, and the Pickleses, as vendees, to obtain a permanent injunction proscribing human habitation of the premises until the property was brought into conformance with the Lenawee County sanitation code. The injunction was granted, and the Lenawee County Board of Health was permitted to withdraw from the lawsuit by stipulation of the parties.

When no payments were made on the land contract, the Messerlys filed a cross-complaint against the Pickleses seeking foreclosure, sale of the property, and a deficiency judgment. Mr. and Mrs. Pickles then counterclaimed for rescission against the Messerlys, and filed a third-party complaint against the Barneses, which incorporated, by reference, the allegations of the counterclaim against the Messerlys. In count one, Mr. and Mrs. Pickles alleged failure of consideration. Count two charged Mr. and Mrs. Barnes with willful concealment and misrepresentation as a result of their failure to disclose the condition of the sanitation system. Additionally, Mr. and Mrs. Pickles sought to hold the Messerlys liable in equity for the Barneses' alleged misrepresentation. The Pickleses prayed that the land contract be rescinded.

After a bench trial, the court concluded that the Pickleses had no cause of action against either the Messerlys or the Barneses as there was no fraud or misrepresentation. This ruling was predicated on the trial judge's conclusion that none of the parties knew of Mr. Bloom's earlier transgression or of the resultant problem with the septic system until it was discovered by the Pickleses, and that the sanitation problem was not caused by any of the parties. The trial court held that the property was purchased "as is", after inspection and, accordingly, its "negative * * * value cannot be blamed upon an innocent seller". Foreclosure was ordered against the Pickleses, together with a judgment against them in the amount of $25,943.09.

Mr. and Mrs. Pickles appealed from the adverse judgment. The Court of Appeals unanimously affirmed the trial court's ruling with respect to Mr. and Mrs. Barnes but, in a two-to-one decision, reversed the finding of no cause of action on the Pickleses' claims against the Messerlys. *Lenawee County Board of Health v. Messerly,* 98 Mich.App. 478, 295 N.W.2d 903 (1980). It concluded that the mutual mistake between the Messerlys and the Pickleses went to a basic, as opposed to a collateral, element of the contract, and that the parties intended to transfer income-producing rental property but, in actuality, the vendees paid $25,500 for an asset without value.

We granted the Messerlys' application for leave to appeal. 411 Mich. 900 (1981).

II

We must decide initially whether there was a mistaken belief entertained by one or both parties to the contract in dispute and, if so, the resultant legal significance.

A contractual mistake "is a belief that is not in accord with the facts". 1 Restatement Contracts, 2d § 151, p. 383. The erroneous belief of one or both of the parties must relate to a fact in existence at the time the contract is executed. *Richardson Lumber Co. v. Hoey,* 219 Mich. 643, 189 N.W. 923 (1922); *Sherwood v. Walker,* 66 Mich. 568, 580, 33 N.W. 919 (1887) (Sherwood, J., dissenting). That is to say, the belief which is found to be in error may not be, in substance, a prediction as to a future occurrence or non-occurrence. * * *

The Court of Appeals concluded, after a *de novo* review of the record, that the parties were mistaken as to the income-producing capacity of the property in question. 98 Mich.App. 487–488, 295 N.W.2d 903. We agree. The vendors and the vendees each believed that the property transferred could be utilized as income-generating rental property. All of the parties subsequently learned that, in fact, the property was unsuitable for any residential use.

* * *

Having determined that when these parties entered into the land contract they were laboring under a mutual mistake of fact, we now direct our attention to a determination of the legal significance of that finding.

A contract may be rescinded because of a mutual misapprehension of the parties, but this remedy is granted only in the sound discretion of the court. *Harris v. Axline,* 323 Mich. 585, 36 N.W.2d 154 (1949). Appellants argue that the parties' mistake relates only to the quality or value of the real estate transferred, and that such mistakes are collateral to the agreement and do not justify rescission, citing *A & M Land Development Co. v. Miller,* 354 Mich. 681, 94 N.W.2d 197 (1959).

In that case, the plaintiff was the purchaser of 91 lots of real property. It sought partial rescission of the land contract when it was frustrated in its attempts to develop 42 of the lots because it could not obtain permits from the county health department to install septic tanks on these lots. This Court refused to allow rescission because the mistake, whether mutual or unilateral, related only to the value of the property.

* * *

Appellees contend, on the other hand, that in this case the parties were mistaken as to the very nature of the character of the consideration and claim that the pervasive and essential quality of this mistake renders rescission appropriate. They cite in support of that view *Sherwood v. Walker,* 66 Mich. 568, 33 N.W. 919 (1887), the famous "barren cow" case. In that case, the parties agreed to the sale and purchase of a cow which was thought to be barren, but which was, in reality, with calf. When the seller discovered the fertile condition of his cow, he refused to deliver her. In permitting rescission, the Court stated:

> "It seems to me, however, in the case made by this record, that the mistake or misapprehension of the parties went to the whole substance of the agreement. If the cow was a breeder, she was worth at least $750; if barren, she was worth not over $80. The parties would not have made the contract of sale except upon the understanding and belief that she was incapable of breeding, and of no use as a cow. It is true she is now the identical animal that they thought her to be when the contract was made; there is no mistake as to the identity of the creature. Yet the mistake was not of the mere quality of the animal, but went to the very nature of the thing. A barren cow is substantially a different creature than a breeding one. There is as much difference between them for all purposes of use as there is between an ox and a cow that is capable of breeding and giving milk. If the mutual mistake had simply related to the fact whether she was with calf or not for one season, then it might have been a good sale; but the mistake affected the character of the animal for all time, and for her present and ultimate use. She was not in fact the animal, or the kind of animal, the defendants intended to sell or the plaintiff to buy. She was not a barren cow, and, if this fact had been known, there would have been no contract. The mistake affected the substance of the whole consideration, and it must be considered that there was no contract to sell or sale of the cow as she actually was. The thing sold and bought had in fact no existence. She was sold as a beef creature would be sold; she is in fact a breeding cow, and a valuable one.

> "The court should have instructed the jury that if they found that the cow was sold, or contracted to be sold, upon the understanding of both parties that she was barren, and useless for the purpose of breeding, and that in fact she was not barren, but capable of breeding, then the defendants had a right to rescind, and to refuse to deliver, and the verdict should be in their favor." 66 Mich. 577–578, 33 N.W. 919.

As the parties suggest, the foregoing precedent arguably distinguishes mistakes affecting the essence of the consideration from those which go to its quality or value, affording relief on a per se basis for the former but not the latter. * * *

However, the distinctions which may be drawn from *Sherwood* and *A & M Land Development Co.* do not provide a satisfactory analysis of the nature of a mistake sufficient to invalidate a contract. Often, a mistake relates to an underlying factual assumption which, when discovered, directly affects value, but simultaneously and materially affects the essence of the contractual consideration. It is disingenuous to label such a mistake collateral. * * *

Appellant and appellee both mistakenly believed that the property which was the subject of their land contract would generate income as rental property. The fact that it could not be used for human habitation deprived the property of its income-earning potential and rendered it less valuable. However, this mistake, while directly and dramatically affecting the property's value, cannot accurately be characterized as collateral because it also affects the very essence of the consideration. "The thing sold and bought [income-generating rental property] had in fact no existence". *Sherwood v. Walker*, 66 Mich. 578, 33 N.W. 919.

We find that the inexact and confusing distinction between contractual mistakes running to value and those touching the substance of the consideration serves only as an impediment to a clear and helpful analysis for the equitable resolution of cases in which mistake is alleged and proven. Accordingly, the holdings of *A & M Land Development Co.* and *Sherwood* with respect to the material or collateral nature of a mistake are limited to the facts of those cases.

Instead, we think the better-reasoned approach is a case-by-case analysis whereby rescission is indicated when the mistaken belief relates to a basic assumption of the parties upon which the contract is made, and which materially affects the agreed performances of the parties. * * *[11] Rescission is not available, however, to relieve a party who has assumed the risk of loss in connection with the mistake. * * *[12]

All of the parties to this contract erroneously assumed that the property transferred by the vendors to the vendees was suitable for human habitation and could be utilized to generate rental income. The fundamental nature of these assumptions is indicated by the fact that

---

11. * * * ["Restatement of Contracts (Second)] Section 152 delineates the legal significance of a mistake. § 152. When Mistake of Both Parties Makes a Contract Voidable '(1) Where a mistake of both parties at the time a contract was made as to a basic assumption on which the contract was made has a material effect on the agreed exchange of performances, the contract is voidable by the adversely affected party unless he bears the risk of the mistake under the rule stated in § 154.' '(2) In determining whether the mistake has a material effect on the agreed exchange of performances, account is taken of any relief by way of reformation, restitution, or otherwise.' "

12. [Restatement of Contracts (Second)] "§ 154. When a Party Bears the Risk of a Mistake

"A party bears the risk of a mistake when (a) the risk is allocated to him by agreement of the parties, or (b) he is aware, at the time the contract is made, that he has only limited knowledge with respect to the facts to which the mistake relates but treats his limited knowledge as sufficient, or (c) the risk is allocated to him by the court on the ground that it is reasonable in the circumstances to do so."

their invalidity changed the character of the property transferred, thereby frustrating, indeed precluding, Mr. and Mrs. Pickles' intended use of the real estate. Although the Pickleses are disadvantaged by enforcement of the contract, performance is advantageous to the Messerlys, as the property at issue is less valuable absent its income-earning potential. Nothing short of rescission can remedy the mistake. Thus, the parties' mistake as to a basic assumption materially affects the agreed performances of the parties.

Despite the significance of the mistake made by the parties, we reverse the Court of Appeals because we conclude that equity does not justify the remedy sought by Mr. and Mrs. Pickles.

Rescission is an equitable remedy which is granted only in the sound discretion of the court. *Harris v. Axline,* 323 Mich. 585, 36 N.W.2d 154 (1949); *Hathaway v. Hudson,* 256 Mich. 694, 239 N.W. 859 (1932). A court need not grant rescission in every case in which the mutual mistake relates to a basic assumption and materially affects the agreed performance of the parties.

In cases of mistake by two equally innocent parties, we are required, in the exercise of our equitable powers, to determine which blameless party should assume the loss resulting from the misapprehension they shared.[13] Normally that can only be done by drawing upon our "own notions of what is reasonable and just under all the surrounding circumstances".[14]

Equity suggests that, in this case, the risk should be allocated to the purchasers. We are guided to that conclusion, in part, by the standards announced in § 154 of the Restatement of Contracts 2d, for determining when a party bears the risk of mistake. See fn 12. Section 154(a) suggests that the court should look first to whether the parties have agreed to the allocation of the risk between themselves. While there is no express assumption in the contract by either party of the risk of the property becoming uninhabitable, there was indeed some agreed allocation of the risk to the vendees by the incorporation of an "as is" clause into the contract which, we repeat, provided:

> "Purchaser has examined this property and agrees to accept same in its present condition. There are no other or additional written or oral understandings."

That is a persuasive indication that the parties considered that, as between them, such risk as related to the "present condition" of the property should lie with the purchaser. If the "as is" clause is to have

13. This risk-of-loss analysis is absent in both *A & M Land Development Co.* and *Sherwood,* and this omission helps to explain, in part, the disparate treatment in the two cases. Had such an inquiry been undertaken in *Sherwood,* we believe that the result might have been different. Moreover, a determination as to which party assumed the risk in *A & M Land Development Co.* would have alleviated the need to characterize the mistake as collateral so as to justify the result denying rescission. Despite the absence of any inquiry as to the assumption of risk in those two leading cases, we find that there exists sufficient precedent to warrant such an analysis in future cases of mistake.

14. *Hathaway v. Hudson,* 256 Mich. 702, 239 N.W. 859, quoting 9 C.J., p. 1161.

any meaning at all, it must be interpreted to refer to those defects which were unknown at the time that the contract was executed. Thus, the parties themselves assigned the risk of loss to Mr. and Mrs. Pickles.

We conclude that Mr. and Mrs. Pickles are not entitled to the equitable remedy of rescission and, accordingly, reverse the decision of the Court of Appeals.

WHITE v. BERENDA MESA WATER DIST.

Court of Appeal, Fifth District, 1970.
7 Cal.App.3d 894, 87 Cal.Rptr. 338.

COAKLEY, ASSOCIATE JUSTICE.

The plaintiffs shall be referred to herein as "White" and "Aetna"; the defendant as "The District."

This is an action for declaratory relief in which White and Aetna seek rescission of a construction contract and the return of a bid bond posted by Aetna on behalf of White, the low bidder. The District filed a cross-complaint for damages. Following a trial to the court, judgment was entered in favor of The District on the complaint and on the cross-complaint, and against White and Aetna. The District's damages were fixed at $42,789. * * *

The controversy arose in this way: The District invited bids on a construction project which was divided into four separate entities for bidding purposes. White was low bidder on one segment of the project, i.e., a regulating reservoir. With his bid, White filed a surety bond by Aetna in the sum of $42,789. [A number of jurisdictions require that a bidder on a public contract post a bond that will be forfeited if the bidder withdraws its bid. Ed.]

Eight other bids were received for the work on which White was the low bidder. When the bids were opened, they ran from White's low bid of $427,890 to a high bid of $721,851. The bid next lowest to White's was by Einer Brothers, et al., for $494,320, or $66,430 above White's bid. The estimate of Boyle Engineering, the consulting engineers for The District, was $512,250, or $84,360 above White's bid. Concerned that he had made an error in his bid, White reviewed it in detail and concluded that he had made a mistake in computing item 13, i.e., the cost of excavating 230,000 cubic yards of material. On discovery of his mistake, and prior to acceptance or rejection of any of the bids by The District, White notified The District, in writing, that because of an error in computation, "We hereby withdraw our bid . . . and request the return of the deposit submitted therewith." * * *

Counsel for the board advised the board that if White's error was due to a mistake of fact the bid could not be accepted, but if it was due to a mistake of judgment the bid was binding upon White. The board then voted to accept the bid which White had asked permission to withdraw. Shortly thereafter, White advised the board, in writing, that he rescinded his bid. The District, thereupon, awarded the contract to Einer Brothers, the next lowest bidder. This action by White followed.

* * *

Before preparing his bid, White studied the plans and specifications, visited the site, and made a visual examination of the terrain. While White visited the site, his son, Kelly, called at the office of Boyle Engineering for the purpose of examining a soil report relating to the material to be excavated. There, he examined plates 3 and 4, which were part of the soil report and available for examination by all bidders. Prior to looking at the soil report, he had also examined sheet 10, which was part of the plans and specifications. Plates 3 and 4 show the location of various test holes drilled by the soil engineers. One such hole is marked B–51. Plate 3 also shows a broken line terminating about 100 feet east of point B–51. The broken line represents a proposed penstock alignment, which was not part of the work included in the regulating reservoir phase of the total project. Plate 4 shows "decomposed shale and sandstone" as comprising all but a small portion of the terrain lying west of B–51. Kelly White testified that, on the basis of his examination of plates 3 and 4, he concluded and reported to his father that only a small quantity of hard rock was involved in the work of excavating. His estimate of hard rock was seven percent. White then called Boyle Engineering, and Mr. Thomas of that firm told him that very little hard rock would be encountered. Thereupon, White submitted his bid and surety bond. It is a fact that decomposed shale and sandstone comprised 90 percent or more of the terrain west of point B–51, with hard rock comprising the balance of the terrain. Thus, Kelly White's estimate of only seven percent hard rock was reasonably close for the area west of point B–51.

However, sheet 10 and the plans and specifications, as distinguished from plates 3 and 4 of the soil report, clearly show the penstock alignment terminating at a point 400 feet or more east of point B–51, and not 100 feet as indicated in plate 3. A hill, composed almost exclusively of hard rock, lay between point B–51 and the western terminus of the penstock alignment. Excavation of this hill and the hard rock material was part of item 13 of the bid and, therefore, the responsibility of the excavating contractor.

With reference to the entire area to be excavated as called for by item 13, i.e., 230,000 cubic yards of material, the evidence established that, instead of 10,000 cubic yards of hard rock to be removed, there was 110,000 cubic yards; instead of hard rock constituting only seven percent of the total excavation, as Kelly White had estimated, it constituted approximately 50 percent thereof, with the remaining 50 percent being made up of decomposed shale and sandstone. It was established that hard rock is substantially more costly to excavate than decomposed shale and sandstone.

White had a copy of the specifications which he examined before preparing his bid. Section 108 thereof provided that The District did not warrant the accuracy of the soil report. White was an experienced contractor. As such, he knew that soil reports are prepared in advance of the detailed specifications for a project, and that the specifications, not the soil report, control. There was, therefore, an element of negligence in the preparation of White's bid, more particularly, in White's failure to correlate plates 3 and 4 of the soil report, which White knew from experience were not warranted as accurate, with sheet 10 and the other specifications.

The findings recite only that White made a mistake in estimating the amount of hard rock material to be excavated; that the mistake was material to the contract; and that the mistake was one of judgment.

* * *

Where, as here, the facts are not in dispute, the issue is one of law, and this court is free to draw its own conclusions of law from such undisputed facts. * * * Doing so, we conclude that White's mistake was a mixed mistake of fact and of judgment. White's estimate or calculation of the amount of hard rock to be excavated was judgmental, and in that sense his mistake was one of judgment. On the other hand, his estimate or calculation was predicated on a misunderstanding of the true facts, occasioned in part, at least, by reliance on the soil report (plates 3 and 4) and Mr. Thomas' statement. It is in this posture that we now examine the law on the subject.

THE LAW

We commence our discussion of the law by pointing out that counsel has not cited any case, from California or elsewhere, and our independent research has failed to find such a case, where the mistake, whether of fact or of judgment, so called, was occasioned by circumstances similar to those present in this case.

M.F. Kemper Const. Co. v. City of L.A., 37 Cal.2d 696, 235 P.2d 7, is a leading case on the subject of rescission of bids on a public project. It enumerates the elements essential to rescission for a mistake of fact. They are summarized in headnote 4 of the official report in these words:

> "Recission may be had for mistake of fact if the mistake is material to the contract and is not the result of neglect of a legal duty, if enforcement of the contract as made would be unconscionable, if the other party can be placed in statu quo, if the party seeking relief gives prompt notice of his election to rescind, and if he restores or offers to restore to the other party everything of value which he has received under the contract. (Civ.Code, §§ 1577, 1689, 1691, 3406, 3407.)"

The District's brief acknowledges that all of the elements required for rescission as set forth in *Kemper* are present in our case, except that the mistake was one of judgment, not fact, and the mistake resulted from the neglect of a legal duty. We have held, *supra*, that White's mistake was not solely one of judgment, but was a mixed mistake of fact and of judgment. We shall return to that subject after we first examine the meaning of the term "neglect of a legal duty." (*Kemper, supra.*)

That term appears in Civil Code, section 1577, which reads in part as follows:

> "Mistake of fact is a mistake, not caused by the neglect of a legal duty on the part of the person making the mistake, and consisting in: . . ."

In construing Civil Code, section 1577, the court said in *Kemper, supra*, 37 Cal.2d 696, 702, 235 P.2d 7, 10, that:

> "It has been recognized numerous times that not all carelessness constitutes a 'neglect of legal duty' within the meaning of the section."

* * *

The soil report on which White relied in part, while not warranted as accurate, was a report used by The District's engineers in preparing the specifications; it was available for study by all prospective bidders; Kelly White examined it, and, in a mistaken reliance on plates 3 and 4 of the report, informed his father that hard rock constituted seven percent of the excavation. *After* receiving this information from his son, White spoke with Mr. Thomas of Boyle Engineering and was told by him that very little hard rock would be encountered. The undisputed fact is that almost 50 percent of the material to be excavated was hard rock. We hold, therefore, that White's negligence was ordinary and not gross; that his error "is one which will sometimes occur in the conduct of reasonable and cautious businessmen," and did not constitute neglect of a legal duty. (M.F. Kemper Const. Co. v. City of L.A., *supra*, 37 Cal.2d 696, 702, 235 P.2d 7, 11; . . . .)

We next consider the meaning of mistake of fact "versus" mistake of judgment. Where the mistake in preparing a bid is due to clerical error, e.g., in mathematical computation or in the transposition of figures from work sheets to final bid forms, and where all the other elements calling for rescission are present, the cases uniformly hold the mistake to be one of fact and release the bidder from any obligation under his bid.

Statements appear in some of the cases to the effect that courts of equity will grant relief where the mistake is one of fact, but not where the mistake is one of judgment. Such a statement appears in *Kemper, supra* * * * [p. 703, 235 P.2d at 11]. * * *

We first observe that in *Kemper* the Supreme Court said, "*Generally,* relief is refused for error in judgment." (Emphasis added.) It was careful not to lay down a hard and fast rule to the effect that relief may never be granted for a mistake in judgment.

* * *

In *Kemper, supra*, the contractor brought an action against the city to cancel a bid it had submitted on public construction work and to obtain discharge of its bid bond. The city cross-complained for forfeiture of the bond and damages. The trial court canceled the bid, discharged the bond, and allowed the city nothing on its cross-complaint. In affirming, the Supreme Court said:

> "The sole issue is whether the company is entitled to relief on the ground of unilateral mistake." (37 Cal.2d p. 699, 235 P.2d p. 9.)

The unilateral mistake found by the court in *Kemper* was the typical mistake of fact, i.e., an error in the transposition of figures arrived at by the contractor's estimators, to a final accumulation sheet from which the total amount of the bid was taken. An item of over $300,000 was inadvertently omitted in transposition from the work sheet to the accumulation sheet, and, accordingly, omitted from the final bid. From that point on that case and our case are identical. Thus, there, as here, (1) the contractor was the low bidder; (2) it discovered its mistake shortly after the bids were opened; (3) it immediately explained its mistake to the city's board of public works, and withdrew its bid; (4) a few days later, the bidder again appeared before the board and submitted evidence of its mistake; (5) notwithstanding, the board thereafter passed a resolution accepting the bid; (6) the company refused to enter into a contract at its bid figure; (7) without readvertising, the board awarded the contract to the next lowest bidder; (8) the city then demanded forfeiture of the bond; (9) the company's suit followed to cancel its bid and to discharge the bond.

* * *

The sole distinction between the *Kemper* case and our case is in the nature of the mistake made by the bidder. There the error was in transposing figures and the inadvertent omission of a substantial amount from an accumulation sheet and bid, the classic "mistake of fact". In our case, White's error was his negligence in failing to properly correlate plates 3 and 4 with the plans and specifications, and as a consequence he underestimated or miscalculated the amount of hard rock to be removed.

* * *

* * * In our opinion, the judgment below draws too fine a line between so called mistakes of fact and mistakes of judgment, producing a result which finds no support in equity.

To deny White and Aetna the relief they seek would be grossly unjust and would set a harsh and unnecessary precedent. In our opinion, the fact that White said he made a mistake of judgment and that the court "took him at his word," should not change the result. It is the facts surrounding the mistake, not the label, i.e., "mistake of fact" or "mistake of judgment," which should control.

In holding that White is entitled to withdraw his bid and to a return of the bond, we are not unmindful that the system of public bidding, developed by experience and usual in public contracts, should not be broken down by lightly permitting bidders to withdraw because of a change of mind. Such a course would be unfair to other straightforward bidders, as well as disruptive of public business. But we are confident that our public agencies and our courts are capable of preventing, and will prevent, abuses where, unlike our case, the facts do not justify relieving the low bidder from his bid. (See State of Connecticut v. F.H. McGraw & Co., *supra*, 41 F.Supp. 369, 374.)

The judgment is reversed, and the court below is directed to enter judgment permitting White to withdraw his bid and to return to White and Aetna the bid bond posted by them.

Problems

17.   P bought a 16-day-old bull calf of good breeding stock for $5,000 from D. P and D were both knowledgeable cattle breeders. After a year and a half, medical tests showed that as a result of a congenital condition the bull was sterile. Medically, however, this condition cannot be diagnosed until the bull is one year old. A 16-day-old bull calf not suitable for breeding was worth $30 at the time of sale. P sues for restitution. What result?

18.   S contracted to sell to B a parcel of hilly land on the waterfront. S was aware that B planned to build a residence on the parcel. After contracting, geological reports as well as the practical experience of the local building inspector revealed that a house constructed on the site would have a significant chance of being carried into the water by a landslide. In fact, after contracting, several neighboring houses were totally destroyed by landslides. B notified S that he rescinded the contract and sues for restitution. What result?

19.   P, a tennis and swim club, contracted to purchase a 50-acre estate from D, revealing its intention to relocate its facilities to the estate. Neither party knew that, after P had checked the zoning ordinances and 4 days prior to signing the contract, a new zoning ordinance had been enacted limiting the premises to residential uses. P sues for restitution. What result?

20.   A State official notified S and B, two landowners of adjacent acreage, that the boundary lines described in their deeds were ambiguous and appeared to overlap. The parties met and agreed that S would convey a parcel of land to B for $1,400. A State employee had prepared the description. When asked how much acreage was included in the description, he had said that 15 acres was a "ball park figure." Three years later, a survey commissioned by B showed that 68 acres had been conveyed. B then conveyed the parcel to his wife, without consideration. What remedies, if any, are available to S?

21.   D, a municipality, conducted an auction on March 25th to sell surplus real property which it owned. A brochure described the various properties. On page 73 of the brochure, parcel #212 was carelessly described as "unimproved." In fact, it contained a two-family house. The parcel was knocked down to P, the high bidder, for $6,500. Title was to close on or before May 27th. On April 29th, D learned of its mistake and notified P that it was avoiding the contract. What result?

22.   McLure Electrical bid $145,000 on a Navy contract, the lowest bid submitted. The Navy had estimated the contract at $282,969. The Navy

contracting officer wrote to McLure stating that "you are the apparent low bidder. Please review your worksheets for possible errors or omissions." The letter contained an enclosure showing the amounts of the competing bids and the Navy's estimate. McLure replied, confirming the accuracy of its bid. Later, McLure discovered a clerical error that resulted in the omission of an item it valued at $16,530. McLure sues to reform the contract or to avoid it. What result?

23. McDonald's Corporation, as tenant, leased for 30 years a parcel of land in South Carolina for a fast food establishment. The monthly rental was $375. Because of a delay in the first month's payment, a check for $750 was sent for two months' rent. Negligently, in the belief that $750 was the monthly rent, McDonald's clerk in Chicago prepared checks for $750 each month thereafter for three years. Each month an officer of McDonald's signed the check prepared by the clerk. The checks were sent to the Landlord in South Carolina who cashed them on receipt. McDonald's sues for recovery of the overpayments. What result?

SECTION 5.   REFORMATION

(Calamari & Perillo 5th §§ 9.31—9.36)

BOLLINGER v. CENTRAL PENNSYLVANIA QUARRY STRIPPING AND CONSTR. CO.

Supreme Court of Pennsylvania, 1967.
425 Pa. 430, 229 A.2d 741.

MUSMANNO, JUSTICE.

Mahlon Bollinger and his wife, Vinetta C. Bollinger, filed an action in equity against the Central Pennsylvania Quarry Stripping Construction Company asking that a contract entered into between them be reformed so as to include therein a paragraph alleged to have been omitted by mutual mistake and that the agreement, as reformed, be enforced.

The agreement, as executed, provided that the defendant was to be permitted to deposit on the property of the plaintiffs, construction waste as it engaged in work on the Pennsylvania Turnpike in the immediate vicinity of the plaintiff's property. The Bollingers claimed that there had been a mutual understanding between them and the defendant that, prior to depositing such waste on the plaintiffs' property, the defendant would remove the topsoil of the plaintiffs' property, pile on it the waste material and then restore the topsoil in a way to cover the deposited waste. The Bollingers averred that they had signed the written agreement without reading it because they assumed that the condition just stated had been incorporated into the writing.

When the defendant first began working in the vicinity of the plaintiffs' property, it did first remove the topsoil, deposited the waste on the bare land, and then replaced the topsoil. After a certain period of time, the defendant ceased doing this and the plaintiffs remonstrated. The defendant answered there was nothing in the written contract which required it to make a sandwich of its refuse between the bare earth and the topsoil. It was at this point that the plaintiffs discovered that that feature of the oral understanding had been omitted from the written contract. The plaintiff husband renewed his protest and the defendant's superintendent replied he could not remove the topsoil because his equipment for that operation had been taken away. When he was reminded of the original understanding, the superintendent said, in effect, he couldn't help that.

The plaintiffs then filed their action for reformation of the contract, the Court granted the requested relief, and the defendant firm appealed. We said in *Bugen v. New York Life Insurance Co.*, 408 Pa. 472, 184 A.2d 499:

> "A court of equity has the power to reform the written evidence of a contract and make it correspond to the understanding of the parties.... However, the mistake must be mutual to the parties to the contract."

The fact, however, that one of the parties denies that a mistake was made does not prevent a finding of mutual mistake. *Kutsenkow v. Kutsenkow*, 414 Pa. 610, 612, 202 A.2d 68.

Once a person enters into a written agreement he builds around himself a stone wall, from which he cannot escape by merely asserting he had not understood what he was signing. However, equity would completely fail in its objectives if it refused to break a hole through the wall when it finds, after proper evidence, that there was a mistake between the parties, that it was real and not feigned, actual and not hypothetical.

The Chancellor, after taking testimony, properly concluded:

> "We are satisfied that plaintiffs have sustained the heavy burden placed upon them. Their understanding of the agreement is corroborated by the undisputed evidence. The defendant did remove and set aside the top soil on part of the area before depositing its waste and did replace the top soil over such waste after such depositing. It follows it would not have done so had it not so agreed. Further corroboration is found in the testimony that it acted similarly in the case of plaintiffs' neighbor Beltzner."

* * *

Decree affirmed, costs on the appellant.

Problems

24. S sold to B a large tract of land. It was orally agreed that S could remove mill machinery and the rails of a light railroad that ran through the tract. The deed, however, provided that "all improvements" were conveyed along with the land. S removed the machinery and the rails and B sues for

damages. S counterclaims for reformation, alleging that the parties were unaware that the legal effect of the term "all improvements" was to transfer the machinery and the rails. Does the counterclaim state a claim for relief?

25. Joan was suing her husband Tim for divorce. They agreed that they would split their property evenly. They and their attorneys had protracted negotiations about the value of certain of their holdings. Tim thought that a parcel of realty was worth $450,000 while Joan valued it at $550,000. Joan made an offer of settlement based on the $550,000 value. The offer contained an arithmetical error in Tim's favor of $100,000. Tim, noting the error, accepted the offer, explaining to his accountant that the arithmetical error canceled out his disagreement about the value she had placed upon the realty. Anxious to have the last word, after Joan had obtained her divorce decree, Tim sent her a copy of the calculations with this message: "PLEASE NOTE $100,000 MISTAKE IN YOUR FIGURES." Joan responded with an action for reformation. What result?

26. Hand, an attorney employed by D Corp., lost his job when D restructured its operations. D offered to pay Hand $38,000 in severance pay if he would sign a general release. He refused, contending that he was entitled to this sum under his existing contract. Nonetheless D caused a release document to be drafted and typed and tendered it to Hand renewing its previous offer of $38,000. Hand caused the document to be retyped in identical form and in identical language with the exception of the insertion of a clause stating "except as to claims of age discrimination and breach of contract." He brought this new document to a meeting with an officer of D where both parties signed the document. Thereafter Hand brought this action for age discrimination and breach of contract. D raised the affirmative defense of release, requesting reformation of the release to conform to its original offer. Should the release be reformed?

SECTION 6. UNCONSCIONABILITY AND DUTY TO READ

(Calamari & Perillo 5th §§ 9.37—9.45)

WILLIAMS v. WALKER–THOMAS FURNITURE CO.

United States Court of Appeals, District of Columbia Circuit, 1965.
350 F.2d 445, 18 A.L.R.3d 1297.

J. Skelly Wright, Circuit Judge: Appellee, Walker–Thomas Furniture Company, operates a retail furniture store in the District of Columbia. During the period from 1957 to 1962 each appellant in these cases purchased a number of household items from Walker–Thomas, for which payment was to be made in installments. The terms of each purchase were contained in a printed form contract which set forth the value of the purchased item and purported to lease the item to appellant for a stipulated monthly rent payment. The contract then provided, in substance, that title would remain in Walker–Thomas until the total of all the monthly payments made equaled the stated value of the item, at which time appellants could take title. In the event of a default in the payment of any monthly installment, Walker–Thomas could repossess the item.

The contract further provided that "the amount of each periodical installment payment to be made by (purchaser) to the Company under this present lease shall be inclusive of and not in addition to the amount of each installment payment to be made by (purchaser) under such prior leases, bills or accounts; *and all payments now and hereafter made by (purchaser) shall be credited pro rata on all outstanding leases, bills and accounts* due the Company by (purchaser) at the time each such payment is made." The effect of this rather obscure provision was to keep a balance due on every item purchased until the balance due on all items, whenever purchased, was liquidated. As a result, the debt incurred at the time of purchase of each item was secured by the right to repossess all the items previously purchased by the same purchaser, and each new item purchased automatically became subject to a security interest arising out of the previous dealings.

On May 12, 1962, appellant Thorne purchased an item described as a Daveno, three tables, and two lamps, having total stated value of $391.10. Shortly thereafter, he defaulted on his monthly payments and appellee sought to replevy all the items purchased since the first transaction in 1958. Similarly, on April 17, 1962, appellant Williams bought a stereo set of stated value of $514.95.[1] She too defaulted shortly thereafter, and appellee sought to replevy all the items purchased since December, 1957. The Court of General Sessions granted judgment for appellee. The District of Columbia Court of Appeals affirmed, and we granted appellants' motion for leave to appeal to this court.

Appellants' principal contention, rejected by both the trial and the appellate courts below, is that these contracts, or at least some of them, are unconscionable and, hence, not enforceable. In its opinion in Williams v. Walker–Thomas Furniture Company, 198 A.2d 914, 916 (1964), the District of Columbia Court of Appeals explained its rejection of this contention as follows:

> "Appellant's second argument presents a more serious question. The record reveals that prior to the last purchase appellant had reduced the balance in her account to $164. The last purchase, a stereo set, raised the balance due to $678. Significantly, at the time of this and the preceding purchases, appellee was aware of appellant's financial position. The reverse side of the stereo contract listed the name of appellant's social worker and her $218 monthly stipend from the government. Nevertheless, with full knowledge that appellant had to feed, clothe and support both herself and seven children on this amount, appellee sold her a $514 stereo set.

1. At the time of this purchase her account showed a balance of $164 still owing from her prior purchases. The total of all the purchases made over the years in question came to $1,800. The total payments amounted to $1,400.

"We cannot condemn too strongly appellee's conduct. It raises serious questions of sharp practice and irresponsible business dealings. A review of the legislation in the District of Columbia affecting retail sales and the pertinent decisions of the highest court in this jurisdiction disclose, however, no ground upon which this court can declare the contracts in question contrary to public policy. We note that were the Maryland Retail Installment Sales Act, Art. 83 §§ 128–153, or its equivalent, in force in the District of Columbia, we could grant appellant appropriate relief. We think Congress should consider corrective legislation to protect the public from such exploitive contracts as were utilized in the case at bar."

We do not agree that the court lacked the power to refuse enforcement to contracts found to be unconscionable. In other jurisdictions, it has been held as a matter of common law that unconscionable contracts are not enforceable.[2] While no decision of this court so holding has been found, the notion that an unconscionable bargain should not be given full enforcement is by no means novel. In Scott v. United States, 79 U.S. (12 Wall.) 443, 445, 20 L.Ed. 438 (1870), the Supreme Court stated:

" * * * If a contract be unreasonable and unconscionable, but not void for fraud, a court of law will give to the party who sues for its breach damages, not according to its letter, but only such as he is equitably entitled to. * * * "[3]

Since we have never adopted or rejected such a rule,[4] the question here presented is actually one of first impression.

Congress has recently enacted the Uniform Commercial Code, which specifically provides that the court may refuse to enforce a contract which it finds to be unconscionable at the time it was made. 28 D.C.CODE § 2–302 (Supp. IV 1965). The enactment of this section, which occurred subsequent to the contracts here in suit, does not mean that the common law of the District of Columbia was otherwise at the time of enactment, nor does it preclude the court from adopting a similar rule in the exercise of its powers to develop the common law for the District of Columbia. In fact, in view of the absence of prior authority on the point, we consider the congressional adoption of § 2–302 persuasive authority for following the rationale of the cases from which the section

---

2. Campbell Soup Co. v. Wentz, 3 Cir., 172 F.2d 80 (1948); Indianapolis Morris Plan Corporation v. Sparks, 132 Ind.App. 145, 172 N.E.2d 899 (1961); Henningsen v. Bloomfield Motors, Inc., 32 N.J. 358, 161 A.2d 69, 84–96, 75 A.L.R.2d 1 (1960). Cf. 1 CORBIN, CONTRACTS § 128 (1963).

3. See Luing v. Peterson, 143 Minn. 6, 172 N.W. 692 (1919); Greer v. Tweed, N.Y.C.P., 13 Abb.Pr., N.S., 427 (1872); Schnell v. Nell, 17 Ind. 29 (1861); and see generally the discussion of the English authorities in Hume v. United States, 132 U.S. 406, 10 S.Ct. 134, 33 L.Ed. 393 (1889).

4. While some of the statements in the court's opinion in District of Columbia v. Harlan & Hollingsworth Co., 30 App.D.C. 270 (1908), may appear to reject the rule, in reaching its decision upholding the liquidated damages clause in that case the court considered the circumstances existing at the time the contract was made, see 30 App.D.C. at 279, and applied the usual rule on liquidated damages. See 5 CORBIN, CONTRACTS §§ 1054–1075 (1964); Note, 72 YALE L.J. 723, 746–755 (1963). Compare Jaeger v. O'Donoghue, 57 App.D.C. 191, 18 F.2d 1013 (1927).

is explicitly derived.[5] Accordingly, we hold that where the element of unconscionability is present at the time a contract is made, the contract should not be enforced.

Unconscionability has generally been recognized to include an absence of meaningful choice on the part of one of the parties together with contract terms which are unreasonably favorable to the other party.[6] Whether a meaningful choice is present in a particular case can only be determined by consideration of all the circumstances surrounding the transaction. In many cases the meaningfulness of the choice is negated by a gross inequality of bargaining power.[7] The manner in which the contract was entered is also relevant to this consideration. Did each party to the contract, considering his obvious education or lack of it, have a reasonable opportunity to understand the terms of the contract, or were the important terms hidden in a maze of fine print and minimized by deceptive sales practices? Ordinarily, one who signs an agreement without full knowledge of its terms might be held to assume the risk that he has entered a one-sided bargain.[8] But when a party of little bargaining power, and hence little real choice, signs a commercially unreasonable contract with little or no knowledge of its terms, it is hardly likely that his consent, or even an objective manifestation of his consent, was ever given to all the terms. In such a case the usual rule that the terms of the agreement are not to be questioned[9] should be

5. See Comment, § 2–302, Uniform Commercial Code (1962). Compare Note, 45 VA.L.REV. 583, 590 (1959), where it is predicted that the rule of § 2–302 will be followed by analogy in cases which involve contracts not specifically covered by the section. Cf. 1 STATE OF NEW YORK LAW REVISION COMMISSION, REPORT AND RECORD OF HEARINGS ON THE UNIFORM COMMERCIAL CODE 108–110 (1954) (remarks of Professor Llewellyn).

6. See Henningsen v. Bloomfield Motors, Inc., supra Note 2; Campbell Soup Co. v. Wentz, supra Note 2.

7. See Henningsen v. Bloomfield Motors, Inc., supra Note 2, 161 A.2d at 86, and authorities there cited. Inquiry into the relative bargaining power of the two parties is not an inquiry wholly divorced from the general question of unconscionability, since a one-sided bargain is itself evidence of the inequality of the bargaining parties. This fact was vaguely recognized in the common law doctrine of intrinsic fraud, that is, fraud which can be presumed from the grossly unfair nature of the terms of the contract. See the oft-quoted statement of Lord Hardwicke in Earl of Chesterfield v. Janssen, 28 Eng. Rep. 82, 100 (1751):

"* * * (Fraud) may be apparent from the intrinsic nature and subject of the bargain itself; such as no man in his

senses and not under delusion would make * * *."

And cf. Hume v. United States, supra Note 3, 132 U.S. at 413, 10 S.Ct. at 137, where the Court characterized the English cases as "cases in which one party took advantage of the other's ignorance of arithmetic to impose upon him, and the fraud was apparent from the face of the contracts." See also Greer v. Tweed, supra Note 3.

8. See RESTATEMENT, CONTRACTS § 70 (1932); Note, 63 HARV.L.REV. 494 (1950). See also Daley v. People's Building, Loan & Savings Ass'n, 178 Mass. 13, 59 N.E. 452, 453 (1901), in which Mr. Justice Holmes, while sitting on the Supreme Judicial Court of Massachusetts, made this observation:

"* * * Courts are less and less disposed to interfere with parties making such contracts as they choose, so long as they interfere with no one's welfare but their own. * * * It will be understood that we are speaking of parties standing in an equal position where neither has any oppressive advantage or power * * *."

9. This rule has never been without exception. In cases involving merely the transfer of unequal amounts of the same commodity, the courts have held the bargain unenforceable for the reason that "in such a case, it is clear, that the law cannot abandoned and the court should consider whether the terms of the contract are so unfair that enforcement should be withheld.[10]

In determining reasonableness or fairness, the primary concern must be with the terms of the contract considered in light of the circumstances existing when the contract was made. The test is not simple, nor can it be mechanically applied. The terms are to be considered "in the light of the general commercial background and the commercial needs of the particular trade or case."[11] Corbin suggests the test as being whether the terms are "so extreme as to appear unconscionable according to the mores and business practices of the time and place." 1 CORBIN, op. cit. supra Note 2. We think this formulation correctly states the test to be applied in those cases where no meaningful choice was exercised upon entering the contract.

Because the trial court and the appellate court did not feel that enforcement could be refused, no findings were made on the possible unconscionability of the contracts in these cases. Since the record is not sufficient for our deciding the issue as a matter of law, the cases must be remanded to the trial court for further proceedings.

So ordered.

DANAHER, CIRCUIT JUDGE (dissenting): The District of Columbia Court of Appeals obviously was as unhappy about the situation here presented as any of us can possibly be. Its opinion in the Williams case, quoted in the majority text, concludes: "We think Congress should consider corrective legislation to protect the public from such exploitive contracts as were utilized in the case at bar."

My view is thus summed up by an able court which made no finding that there had actually been sharp practice. Rather the appellant seems to have known precisely where she stood.

There are many aspects of public policy here involved. What is a luxury to some may seem an outright necessity to others. Is public oversight to be required of the expenditures of relief funds? A washing machine, e.g., in the hands of a relief client might become a fruitful source of income. Many relief clients may well need credit, and certain business establishments will take long chances on the sale of items, expecting their pricing policies will afford a degree of protection commensurate with the risk. Perhaps a remedy when necessary will be found within the provisions of the "Loan Shark" law, D.C.CODE §§ 26–601 et seq. (1961).

I mention such matters only to emphasize the desirability of a cautious approach to any such problem, particularly since the law for so long has allowed parties such great latitude in making their own contracts. I dare say there must annually be thousands upon thousands of

indulge in the presumption of equivalence between the consideration and the promise." 1 WILLISTON, CONTRACTS § 115 (3d ed. 1957).

10. See the general discussion of "Boiler–Plate Agreements" in LLEWELLYN, THE COMMON LAW TRADITION 362–371 (1960).

11. Comment, Uniform Commercial Code § 2–307.

installment credit transactions in this jurisdiction, and one can only speculate as to the effect the decision in these cases will have. I join the District of Columbia Court of Appeals in its disposition of the issues.

KNAPP v. AMERICAN GENERAL FINANCE INC.

United States District Court, S.D. West Virginia, 2000.
111 F.Supp.2d 758.

HADEN, CHIEF JUDGE. Pending is Defendants' motion for summary judgment on all issues. The Court GRANTS the motion on Count IV, breach of fiduciary relationship, but DENIES it on all other claims and counts.

I. FACTUAL BACKGROUND

The facts are presented and viewed in a light most favorable to non-movants. The married Plaintiffs sought to borrow a thousand dollars ($1000) to purchase new tires and have money for the Christmas season. They are the parents of five children, ranging in age from 7 to 20. James Knapp telephoned American General Home Equity, Inc. (AGHE) where someone took loan application information and responded the loan was approved.

On November 26, 1997 the Knapps visited the AGHE office in Charleston, where they signed numerous loan documents. The amount financed included:

1) life insurance (James Knapp) Merit Life,	premium:	$119.10
2) life insurance (Pamela Knapp) Merit Life,	premium:	$102.30
3) life insurance (joint)	premium:	$ 25.47
4) property insurance ($1700 coverage)	premium:	$ 64.13
5) non-filing insurance	premium:	$ 4.00
Total insurance		$315.00

The total amount financed was $1353.83, at an annual percentage rate of 30.99%. Loan proceeds of $1,038.83 were actually paid out to the Knapps.

The loan disclosure statement contained a very small print notice:

INSURANCE: Credit life insurance, credit disability insurance, and/or credit involuntary unemployment insurance are not required to obtain credit and will not be provided unless you sign and agree to pay the additional cost. You understand that we and our insurance affiliate anticipate profits from the sale of credit insurance, and you consent thereto if you select such insurance.

The Knapps signed just below under a typed-in statement: "We want joint decreasing credit life insurance." Down within the midst of more small print was a notice in centered caps:

PERSONAL PROPERTY INSURANCE DISCLOSURE

Beneath that was another diminutive statement:

You are not required to purchase property insurance on your household goods to secure this loan. If you choose to have such insurance, you may obtain the insurance from anyone you want. You should consider any homeowner's or other insurance which you may already have when deciding to purchase insurance with this loan.

Once again the Knapps signed under a very small type statement: "You want property insurance."

The Knapps also executed a separate "Non-compulsory Insurance Voluntarily Purchased by the Applicant Schedule" for single-interest property insurance, marking an "X" next to the statement "I do not have any valid insurance to offer the creditor." In fact, the Knapps had prior homeowner's insurance coverage in effect. Finally, the Knapps signed an "Insurance Disclosure Summary" which proclaimed in bold type:

I WANT TO PURCHASE THE INSURANCE NOTED BELOW AND HAVE THE INSURANCE PREMIUM FINANCED AS PART OF MY LOAN. I FULLY UNDERSTAND THAT I DO NOT HAVE TO PURCHASE ANY OF THE FOLLOWING INSURANCE TO GET MY LOAN.

The credit life, credit personal property, and two Merit L.I.F.E. Plus insurance policies, the latter for each Plaintiff, are listed on this document.

Pamela Knapp cannot read or write. As evidenced in her deposition, she has trouble spelling her own name aloud, but she does know how to sign her name. Mr. Knapp attended school through the eighth grade, but cannot see without glasses, and he had none when he signed these documents. Mr. Knapp testified, while he and his wife completed the loan documents, he informed the person with whom he was dealing that he couldn't see the documents. "And she said, 'Well, I'll tell you,' and then she talked to me and I signed it." Mrs. Knapp also told "the girl across the table" she could not read. That person said she would go over the papers and explain things. Both Knapps testify they were told they had to have insurance to get the loan.

The Note and Security Agreement has an "X" typed in a box indicating: "To secure this loan, you give to Payee a security interest under the Uniform Commercial Code in the following personal property." However, no property is listed on this form in the box below. The Federal Disclosure Statement, however, lists: "2 pc fishing tackle, weedeater, fisher CD, pioneer stereo, 2 RCA 19 in tv's." The Knapps testify they never owned, nor suggested they owned, any of this property except a Pioneer stereo. They testify they were informed by AGHE's agent that she needed to "put some stuff on there to make it look good so the loan will go through." Plaintiffs were not given a copy of this document, so they never saw the putative property listing. A Personal Property Appraisal signed by the Knapps also lists the same items of property. Jennifer Mullins, an agent of AGHE, whose name is signed on the form as witnessing it, testified that she did not witness the signing of the document, but signed as a witness some time later and that she back-dated her signature to the date of the Knapps' loan closing.

After making payments of ninety-five dollars ($95.00) a month for five months, the Knapps fell behind in their loan payments. In November 1998, American General Finance (AGF) hired Troy Mynes of Surveillance Technologies to collect or repossess the Knapps' collateral. Mynes went to the Knapps' residence numerous times to collect loan payments or the collateral. Prior to his last visit, Jennifer Mullins told him to "Knock on the door 'til you get them mad enough to come to the door or until they call the Police Department.... That way, that will at least get them outside and then you can get to the property."

Plaintiffs brought this civil action alleging fraud, unconscionable agreement, unfair or deceptive acts or procedures in the sale of insurance, breach of fiduciary relationship, and breach of duty of good faith and fair dealing. Defendants move for summary judgment on all counts.

II. DISCUSSION

[In parts A and B of the discussion, the court discusses procedural matters which we omit. Ed.]

C. *Knapps' Reliance on Misrepresentation*

To prove fraud under West Virginia law Plaintiffs must demonstrate:

> (1) that the act claimed to be fraudulent was the act of the defendant or induced by him;

> (2) that it was material and false; that plaintiff relied on it and was justified under the circumstances in relying on it; and (3) that he was damaged because he relied on it.

Cordial v. Ernst & Young, 199 W.Va. 119, 130, 483 S.E.2d 248, 259 (1996) (citations omitted). Defendants argue the Knapps cannot show justifiable reliance on any alleged misrepresentation by AGHE that they had to purchase insurance to get the loan because 1) they signed numerous documents indicating they knew they did not have to purchase insurance, 2) they did not seek the help of a third party to read the documents to them, and 3) they did not inform AGHE of their inability to read the documents.

It is a widely accepted principle of contracts that, "absent fraud or other wrongful conduct, one who signs or accepts a written instrument will normally be bound in accordance with its written terms and cannot disaffirm the contract simply by contending that he failed to read the contract or understand its contents". *Hager v. American Gen. Fin., Inc.*, 37 F.Supp.2d 778, 788 (S.D.W.Va.1999).... The principle applies where a person who signs a contract cannot read it; in such cases, the individual has a responsibility to have the contract read to him. *See Hager*, 37 F.Supp.2d at 788. . . . Avoidance of the contract may be proper, however, if it can be shown that the other party deceived the person who could not read the contract as to its contents. *Id.* (citing *Gaskin [v. Stumm Handel GmbH]*, 390 F.Supp. [361] at 366).

Mr. Knapp testified he notified the loan closing agent he could not read the documents and she said, "Well, I'll tell you," and then she talked to the Knapps and they signed the documents. (Pls.' Resp., Ex. 1 at 72.) Mrs. Knapp testified she told the "girl sitting across the table" she could not read, and that person responded she did not care, they could go over the papers, and explain things. (Pls.' Resp., Ex. 4 at 16–17.) Both Knapps testified they were told they had to purchase the insurance to get the loan. Whether the Knapps' reliance on AGHE's alleged misrepresentation of the insurance requirements of the contract terms was justifiable poses a jury question. Accordingly, summary judgment is **DENIED** on this issue.

D. *Unconscionability*

"The principle of unconscionability is one of the prevention of oppression and unfair surprise and not the disturbance of reasonable allocation of risks or reasonable advantage because of superior bargaining power or position." *Orlando v. Finance One of West Virginia, Inc.*, 179 W.Va. 447, 369 S.E.2d 882, 885 (1988). A determination of unconscionability must focus on the relative positions of the parties, the adequacy of the bargaining position, and the existence of meaningful alternatives available to the plaintiffs. *Hager*, 37 F.Supp.2d at 786 . . . "Gross inadequacy in bargaining power may exist where consumers are totally ignorant of the implications of what they are signing or where the parties involved in the transaction include a national corporate lender on one side and unsophisticated, uneducated consumers on the other." *Id.* (citations omitted).

Defendants argue Plaintiffs have come forward with no evidence of oppression, unfair surprise or one-sidedness. They assert Plaintiffs were experienced borrowers, who acknowledged obtaining loans and credit from other companies in the past. Indeed, both Knapps conceded they believed such insurance was a mandatory part of obtaining loans because they had signed such agreements on other occasions. This testimony may be susceptible of conflicting inferences, but it does not demonstrate indisputably these consumers, one illiterate and the other with an eighth-grade education, were sophisticated consumers, able to hold their own in bargaining with loan company representatives.

Defendants next argue the parties executed standard loan documents with full disclosures as required by law. Because Plaintiffs point to no particular provision in their loan agreement that was unfair, Defendants maintain the contract cannot be unconscionable, citing *Troy Mining Corp. v. Itmann Coal Co.*, 176 W.Va. 599, 346 S.E.2d 749 (1986):

> A finding that the transaction was flawed, however, still depends on the existence of unfair terms in the contract. A litigant who complains that he was forced to enter into a fair agreement will find no relief on grounds of unconscionability.

Id.

Unconscionability does not, however, manifest only in the contracting, nor only in the contract. As the Restatement of Contracts (Second) instructs:

A bargain is not unconscionable merely because the parties to it are unequal in bargaining position, nor even because the inequality results in an allocation of risks to the weaker party. But *gross inequality of bargaining power, together with terms unreasonably favorable to the stronger party*, may confirm indications that the transaction involved elements of deception or compulsion, or may show that the weaker party had no meaningful choice, no real alternative, or did not in fact assent or appear to assent to the unfair terms. *Factors which may contribute to a finding of unconscionability in the bargaining process include . . . knowledge of the stronger party that the weaker party is unable reasonably to protect his interests by reason of physical or mental infirmities, ignorance, illiteracy or inability to understand the language of the agreement, or similar factors.*

Restatement (Second) of Contracts § 208 cmt. d (1981) (emphasis added by the court). A contract containing facially innocuous insurance purchases may be unconscionable, and unfair, if entered into due to fraudulent misrepresentation that the insurance was necessary, when it was not.

Accordingly, summary judgment on the issue of unconscionability is **DENIED**.

[Part D of the discussion "Statute of Limitations for Unfair Trade Practices Act" is omitted.]

E.   *Breach of Fiduciary Duty*

Plaintiffs claim Defendants breached a fiduciary duty toward them by forcing insurance on them in addition to extending the loan for which Plaintiffs originally contacted them. The fiduciary duty is " '[a] duty to act for someone else's benefit, while subordinating one's personal interests to that of the other person.' " *Elmore v. State Farm Mut. Automobile Ins. Co.*, 202 W.Va. 430, 435, 504 S.E.2d 893, 898 (1998) (quoting Black's Law Dictionary 625 (6th ed.1990)). A fiduciary relationship exists "whenever a trust, continuous or temporary, is specially reposed in the skill or integrity of another." *McKinley v. Lynch*, 58 W.Va. 44, 57, 51 S.E. 4, 9 (1905). "As a general rule, a fiduciary relationship is established only when it is shown that the confidence reposed by one person was actually accepted by the other, and merely reposing confidence in another may not, of itself, create the relationship." *Id.* (quoting C.J.S. Fiduciary at 385 (1961)).

As Defendants contend, the law does not generally recognize a fiduciary relation between creditor and debtor, the fundamental relation between Defendants and the Knapps. * * * Plaintiffs counter, however, the Defendants exceeded the creditor-debtor relationship when they undertook to sell Knapps unnecessary property and life insurance, thus creating a quasi-fiduciary duty. The case Plaintiffs cite for this proposition, however, finds its quasi-fiduciary relationship in the special circumstances and entire pattern of the dealings between an individual borrower and a savings and loan association. *See* Hutson v. Wenatchee Fed. Sav. and Loan Ass'n, 22 Wash.App. 91, 588 P.2d 1192 (1978). No unusual, special, or unique circumstances are alleged in the Knapps' relation to Defendants beyond their contentions that the Knapps were unsophisticated, uneducated borrowers, unable to determine for themselves the terms of their loan agreements.

* * *

Accordingly, Defendants' motion for summary judgment on Count IV of Plaintiffs' complaint, alleging breach of fiduciary relationship, is GRANTED.

F. Breach of Duty of Good Faith and Fair Dealing

Finally, Plaintiffs allege the contract between the parties contained an implied provision requiring Defendants to exercise good faith and fair dealing in the performance of its contractual obligations, a duty breached when Defendants sought to repossess property based on an invalid security agreement and a bogus personal property appraisal, by employing an agent whom they directed to harass Plaintiffs.

West Virginia recognizes the rule that "in every contract there exists an implied covenant of good faith and fair dealing." *Harless v. First Nat. Bank in Fairmont*, 162 W.Va. 116, 122, 246 S.E.2d 270, 274 (1978). Good faith and fair dealing are pervasive requirements in the law; parties to contracts or commercial transactions are bound by this standard. *See Fortune v. Nat'l Cash Register Co.*, 373 Mass. 96, 364 N.E.2d 1251, 1256 (1977) (collecting cases finding requirement of good faith in a variety of contracts). Under the Uniform Commercial Code, "Every contract or duty within this chapter imposes an obligation of good faith in its performance or enforcement." W. Va.Code § 46–1–203. The secured transactions that generated this litigation are covered in Article 9 of Chapter 46 of the Code.

1. Valid security agreement

Defendants argue a valid security agreement existed, embodied in three documents: the note and security agreement, the federal disclosure statement, and the personal property appraisal. These separate documents, they argue, should be construed together and considered to constitute one agreement where the parties and the subject matter are the same and there is clearly a relationship among the documents.... The note and security agreement contains an "X" in the box preceding the language: "To secure this loan you give to Payee a security interest ... in the following personal property," however, no personal property is listed thereunder. While the federal disclosure statement provided by Defendants does list "2 pc fishing tackle, weedeater, fisher CD, pioneer stereo, 2 RCA 19 in tv's," Plaintiffs state the disclosure statement provided to them did not disclose any security. Michael Pauley, who describes himself as branch manager of "American General," (Pls.'

Resp., Ex 5 at 3), testified personal property might not be listed on the federal disclosure statement given to the borrower "when we didn't have the personal property list before the loan was run." The personal property appraisal form was signed by Jennifer Mullins, who testified she signed the document, supposedly as a witness to the closing, more than a year later and that she backdated it to November 1997. She conceded it was blank when she signed it. (*Id.*, Ex. 2 at 5–7.) Plaintiffs also testified except for the Pioneer stereo they owned none of this property, but the American General agent said she needed to "put some stuff on there to make it look good so the loan will go through." As noted, Plaintiffs were never given a copy of the personal property listing. Manager Pauley asserted the company did not require him to give a copy of this form to customers and the form was not part of the loan documents the customer receives. (*Id.*, Ex. 5 at 14–15.)

There is a genuine issue of material fact whether Defendants had a valid security interest in the property they undertook to repossess and, thus, a further question whether Defendants breached the duty of good faith and fair dealing. Summary judgment on this issue is inappropriate as well.

2. Troy Mynes as employee

[The court concludes that there is an issue of fact as to whether the person sent to repossess the alleged collateral was an employee or an independent contractor. Ed.]

III. CONCLUSION

Defendants' motion for summary judgment is **GRANTED** in part as to Count IV. As to all other Counts, it is **DENIED**. The Clerk is directed to send a copy of this Memorandum Opinion and Order to counsel of record and to post it for publication on the Court's website at http://www.wvsd.uscourts.gov.

BROWER v. GATEWAY 2000, INC.

Supreme Court, Appellate Division, First Department, 1998.
246 A.D.2d 246, 676 N.Y.S.2d 569.

MILONAS, JUSTICE Presiding: * * *

Appellants are among the many consumers who purchased computers and software products from defendant Gateway 2000 through a direct-sales system, by mail or telephone order. As of July 3, 1995, it was Gateway's practice to include with the materials shipped to the purchaser along with the merchandise a copy of its "Standard Terms and Conditions Agreement" and any relevant warranties for the products in the shipment. The Agreement begins with a "NOTE TO CUSTOMER," which provides, in slightly larger print than the remainder of the document, in a box that spans the width of the page: "This document contains Gateway 2000's Standard Terms and Conditions. By keeping your Gateway 2000 computer system beyond thirty (30) days after the date of delivery, you accept these Terms and Conditions." The document consists of 16 paragraphs, and, as is relevant to this appeal, paragraph 10 of the agreement, entitled "DISPUTE RESOLUTION," reads as follows:

> Any dispute or controversy arising out of or relating to this Agreement or its interpretation shall be settled exclusively and finally by arbitration. The arbitration shall be conducted in accordance with the Rules of Conciliation and Arbitration of the International Chamber of Commerce. The arbitration shall be conducted in Chicago, Illinois, U.S.A. before a sole arbitrator. Any award rendered in any such arbitration proceeding shall be final and binding on each of the parties, and judgment may be entered thereon in a court of competent jurisdiction.

Plaintiffs commenced this action on behalf of themselves and others similarly situated for compensatory and punitive damages, alleging deceptive sales practices in seven causes of action, including breach of warranty, breach of contract, fraud and unfair trade practices. In particular, the allegations focused on Gateway's representations and advertising that promised "service when you need it," including around-the-clock free technical support, free software technical support and certain on-site services. According to plaintiffs, not only were they unable to avail themselves of this offer because it was virtually impossible to get through to a technician, but also Gateway continued to advertise this claim notwithstanding numerous complaints and reports about the problem.

Insofar as is relevant to appellants, who purchased their computers after July 3, 1995, Gateway moved to dismiss the complaint based on the arbitration clause in the Agreement. Appellants argued that the arbitration clause is invalid under UCC 2–207, unconscionable under UCC 2–302 and an unenforceable contract of adhesion. Specifically, they claimed that the provision was obscure; that a customer could not reasonably be expected to appreciate or investigate its meaning and effect; that the International Chamber of Commerce ("ICC") was not a forum commonly used for consumer matters; and that because ICC headquarters were in France, it was particularly difficult to locate the organization and its rules. To illustrate just how inaccessible the forum was, appellants advised the court that the ICC was not registered with the Secretary of State, that efforts to locate and contact the ICC had been unsuccessful and that apparently the only way to attempt to contact the ICC was through the United States Council for International Business, with which the ICC maintained some sort of relationship.

In support of their arguments, appellants submitted a copy of the ICC's Rules of Conciliation and Arbitration and contended that the cost of ICC arbitration was prohibitive, particularly given the amount of the typical consumer claim involved. For example, a claim of less than $50,000 required advance fees of $4,000 (more than the cost of most Gateway products), of which the $2000 registration fee was nonrefundable even if the consumer prevailed at the arbitration. Consumers would also incur travel expenses disproportionate to the damages sought, which appellants' counsel estimated would not exceed $1,000 per customer in this action, as well as bear the cost of Gateway's legal fees if the consumer did not prevail at the arbitration; in this respect, the ICC rules follow the "loser pays" rule used in England. Also, although Chicago was designated as the site of the actual arbitration, all correspondence must be sent to ICC headquarters in France.

The IAS court dismissed the complaint as to appellants based on the arbitration clause in the Agreements delivered with their computers. We agree with the court's decision and reasoning in all respects but for the issue of the unconscionability of the designation of the ICC as the arbitration body.

First, the court properly rejected appellants' argument that the arbitration clause was invalid under UCC 2–207. Appellants claim that when they placed their order they did not bargain for, much less accept, arbitration of any dispute, and therefore the arbitration clause in the agreement that accompanied the merchandise shipment was a "material alteration" of a preexisting oral agreement. Under UCC 2–207(2), such a material alteration constitutes "proposals for addition to the contract" that become part of the contract only upon appellants' express acceptance. However, as the court correctly concluded, the clause was not a "material alteration" of an oral agreement, but, rather, simply one provision of the sole contract that existed between the parties. That contract, the court explained, was formed and acceptance was manifested not when the order was placed but only with the retention of the merchandise beyond the 30 days specified in the Agreement enclosed in the shipment of merchandise. Accordingly, the contract was outside the scope of UCC 2–207.

In reaching its conclusion, the IAS court took note of the litigation in Federal courts on this very issue, and, indeed, on this very arbitration clause. In *Hill v. Gateway 2000, Inc.*, 105 F.3d 1147, *cert. denied* 522 U.S. 808, 118 S.Ct. 47, 139 L.Ed.2d 13, plaintiffs in a class action contested the identical Gateway contract in dispute before us, including the enforceability of the arbitration clause. As that court framed the issue, the "[t]erms inside Gateway's box stand or fall together. If they constitute the parties' contract because the Hills had an opportunity to return the computer after reading them, then all must be enforced" (*id.* at 1148). The court then concluded that the contract was not formed with the placement of a telephone order or with the delivery of the goods. Instead, an enforceable contract was formed only with the consumer's decision to retain the merchandise beyond the 30–day period specified in the agreement. Thus, the agreement as a whole, including the arbitration clause, was enforceable.

This conclusion was in keeping with the same court's decision in *ProCD, Inc. v. Zeidenberg* (86 F.3d 1447), where it found that detailed terms enclosed within the packaging of particular computer software purchased in a retail outlet constituted the contract between the vendor and the consumer who retained the product. In that case, the Seventh

Circuit held that UCC 2–207 did not apply and indeed was "irrelevant" to such transactions, noting that the section is generally invoked where multiple agreements have been exchanged between the parties in a classic "battle of the forms," whereas *ProCD* (as well as *Hill* and this case) involves but a single form (*id.* at 1452).

The *Hill* decision, in its examination of the formation of the contract, takes note of the realities of conducting business in today's world. Transactions involving "cash now, terms later" have become commonplace, enabling the consumer to make purchases of sophisticated merchandise such as computers over the phone or by mail—and even by computer. Indeed, the concept of "[p]ayment preceding the revelation of full terms" is particularly common in certain industries, such as air transportation and insurance (*id.* at 1149; *ProCD v. Zeidenberg, supra,* at 1451).

While *Hill* and *ProCD*, as the IAS court recognized, are not controlling (although they are decisions of the United States Court of Appeals for the circuit encompassing the forum state designated for arbitration), we agree with their rationale that, in such transactions, there is no agreement or contract upon the placement of the order or even upon the receipt of the goods. By the terms of the Agreement at issue, it is only after the consumer has affirmatively retained the merchandise for more than 30 days—within which the consumer has presumably examined and even used the product(s) and read the agreement—that the contract has been effectuated. In this respect, the case is distinguishable from *S & T Sportswear v. Drake Fabrics*, 190 A.D.2d 598, 593 N.Y.S.2d 799, cited by appellants, where this Court found that an arbitration clause found on the reverse side of defendant's draft sales contract did constitute a "material alteration" where the parties did in fact have a pre-existing oral agreement.

While appellants argue that *Hill* is contrary to the law of New York in that it departs from the holding of cases such as *Matter of Marlene v. Carnac Textiles*, 45 N.Y.2d 327, 408 N.Y.S.2d 410, 380 N.E.2d 239[1] and its progeny, we disagree with their interpretation of both cases: *Hill* not only involves one form only, as distinguished from the "battle of the forms" scenario of the cases appellants cite, but these cases are simply inapplicable because, as explained, no contract was formed here or in *Hill* until the merchandise was retained beyond the 30–day period. The disputed arbitration clause is simply one provision of the sole contract "proposed" between the parties.

Second, with respect to appellants' claim that the arbitration clause is unenforceable as a contract of adhesion, in that it involved no choice or negotiation on the part of the consumer but was a "take it or leave it" proposition (*see, e.g., Matter of State v. Ford Motor Company*, 74 N.Y.2d 495, 503, 549 N.Y.S.2d 368, 548 N.E.2d 906), we find that this argument, too, was properly rejected by the IAS court. Although the parties clearly

---

1. Holding that, as a matter of law, an arbitration clause contained in an acceptance is a material alteration of the offered terms that contain no reference to arbitration. Ed.

do not possess equal bargaining power, this factor alone does not invalidate the contract as one of adhesion. As the IAS court observed, with the ability to make the purchase elsewhere and the express option to return the goods, the consumer is not in a "take it or leave it" position at all; if any term of the agreement is unacceptable to the consumer, he or she can easily buy a competitor's product instead— either from a retailer or directly from the manufacturer—and reject Gateway's agreement by returning the merchandise (*see, e.g., Carnival Cruise Lines v. Shute*, 499 U.S. 585, 593–594, 111 S.Ct. 1522, 1527–1528, 113 L.Ed.2d 622; *Fidelity and Deposit Company of Maryland v. Altman*, 209 A.D.2d 195, 618 N.Y.S.2d 286, *lv. denied* 91 N.Y.2d 805). The consumer has 30 days to make that decision. Within that time, the consumer can inspect the goods and examine and seek clarification of the terms of the agreement; until those 30 days have elapsed, the consumer has the unqualified right to return the merchandise, because the goods or terms are unsatisfactory or for no reason at all.

While returning the goods to avoid the formation of the contract entails affirmative action on the part of the consumer, and even some expense, this may be seen as a trade-off for the convenience and savings for which the consumer presumably opted when he or she chose to make a purchase of such consequence by phone or mail as an alternative to on-site retail shopping. That a consumer does not read the agreement or thereafter claims he or she failed to understand or appreciate some term therein does not invalidate the contract any more than such claim would undo a contract formed under other circumstances (*see, e.g., Morris v. Snappy Car Rental, Inc.*, 84 N.Y.2d 21, 30, 614 N.Y.S.2d 362, 637 N.E.2d 253). We further note that appellants' claim of adhesion is identical to that made and rejected in *Filias v. Gateway 2000, Inc.*, an unreported case brought to our attention by both parties that interprets the same Gateway agreement (No. 97C 2523 [N.D.Ill., January 15, 1998], *transferred by* 1997 U.S. Dist. LEXIS 7115 [E.D.Mich., Apr.8, 1997, Zatkoff, J.]).

Finally, we turn to appellants' argument that the IAS court should have declared the contract unenforceable, pursuant to UCC 2–302, on the ground that the arbitration clause is unconscionable due to the unduly burdensome procedure and cost for the individual consumer. The IAS court found that while a class-action lawsuit, such as the one herein, may be a less costly alternative to the arbitration (which is generally less costly than litigation), that does not alter the binding effect of the valid arbitration clause contained in the agreement. [Citations omitted].

As a general matter, under New York law, unconscionability requires a showing that a contract is "both procedurally and substantively unconscionable when made" (*Gillman v. Chase Manhattan Bank*, 73 N.Y.2d 1, 10, 537 N.Y.S.2d 787, 534 N.E.2d 824). That is, there must be "some showing of 'an absence of meaningful choice on the part of one of the parties together with contract terms which are unreasonably favorable to the other party' [citation omitted]" (*Matter of State of New York v. Avco Financial Service*, 50 N.Y.2d 383, 389, 429 N.Y.S.2d 181, 406

N.E.2d 1075). The *Avco* court took pains to note, however, that the purpose of this doctrine is not to redress the inequality between the parties but simply to ensure that the more powerful party cannot "surprise" the other party with some overly oppressive term (*id.*).

As to the procedural element, a court will look to the contract formation process to determine if in fact one party lacked any meaningful choice in entering into the contract, taking into consideration such factors as the setting of the transaction, the experience and education of the party claiming unconscionability, whether the contract contained "fine print," whether the seller used "high-pressured tactics" and any disparity in the parties' bargaining power (*Gillman v. Chase Manhattan Bank, supra*, at 10–11, 537 N.Y.S.2d 787, 534 N.E.2d 824). None of these factors supports appellants' claim here. Any purchaser has 30 days within which to thoroughly examine the contents of their shipment, including the terms of the Agreement, and seek clarification of any term therein (*e.g., Matter of Ball*, [236 A.D.2d 158,] 161, 665 N.Y.S.2d 444). The Agreement itself, which is entitled in large print "STANDARD TERMS AND CONDITIONS AGREEMENT," consists of only three pages and 16 paragraphs, all of which appear in the same size print. Moreover, despite appellants' claims to the contrary, the arbitration clause is in no way "hidden" or "tucked away" within a complex document of inordinate length, nor is the option of returning the merchandise, to avoid the contract, somehow a "precarious" one. We also reject appellants' insinuation that, by using the word "standard," Gateway deliberately meant to convey to the consumer that the terms were standard within the industry, when the document clearly purports to be no more than *Gateway*'s "standard terms and conditions."

With respect to the substantive element, which entails an examination of the substance of the agreement in order to determine whether the terms unreasonably favor one party (*Gillman v. Chase Manhattan Bank, supra*, 73 N.Y.2d, at 12, 537 N.Y.S.2d 787, 534 N.E.2d 824), we do not find that the possible inconvenience of the chosen site (Chicago) alone rises to the level of unconscionability. We do find, however, that the excessive cost factor that is necessarily entailed in arbitrating before the ICC is unreasonable and surely serves to deter the individual consumer from invoking the process (*see, Matter of Teleserve Systems*, 230 A.D.2d 585, 594, 659 N.Y.S.2d 659, *lv. denied* App.Div., 1st Dept., Sept. 30, 1997, 1997 N.Y.App.Div. LEXIS 10626). Barred from resorting to the courts by the arbitration clause in the first instance, the designation of a financially prohibitive forum effectively bars consumers from this forum as well; consumers are thus left with no forum at all in which to resolve a dispute. In this regard, we note that this particular claim is not mentioned in the *Hill* decision, which upheld the clause as part of an enforceable contract.

While it is true that, under New York law, unconscionability is generally predicated on the presence of both the procedural and substantive elements, the substantive element alone may be sufficient to render the terms of the provision at issue unenforceable (*see, Gillman v. Chase*

Manhattan Bank, supra, at 12, 537 N.Y.S.2d 787, 534 N.E.2d 824; *Matter of State of New York v. Avco Financial Service, supra,* at 389, 429 N.Y.S.2d 181, 406 N.E.2d 1075; *State of New York v. Wolowitz*, 96 A.D.2d 47, 68, 468 N.Y.S.2d 131). Excessive fees, such as those incurred under the ICC procedure, have been grounds for finding an arbitration provision unenforceable or commercially unreasonable (*see, e.g., Matter of Teleserve Systems, supra*, at 593–594, 659 N.Y.S.2d 659).

In the *Filias* case previously mentioned, the Federal District Court stated that it was "inclined to agree" with the argument that selection of the ICC rendered the clause unconscionable, but concluded that the issue was moot because Gateway had agreed to arbitrate before the American Arbitration Association ("AAA") and sought court appointment of the AAA pursuant to Federal Arbitration Act 9 U.S.C. § 5. The court accordingly granted Gateway's motion to compel arbitration and appointed the AAA in lieu of the ICC. Plaintiffs in that action (who are represented by counsel for appellants before us) contend that costs associated with the AAA process are also excessive, given the amount of the individual consumer's damages, and their motion for reconsideration of the court's decision has not yet been decided. While the AAA rules and costs are not part of the record before us, the parties agree that there is a minimum, nonrefundable filing fee of $500, and appellants claim each consumer could spend in excess of $1,000 to arbitrate in this forum.

Gateway's agreement to the substitution of the AAA is not limited to the *Filias* plaintiffs. Gateway's brief includes the text of a new arbitration agreement that it claims has been extended to all customers, past, present and future (apparently through publication in a quarterly magazine sent to anyone who has ever purchased a Gateway product). The new arbitration agreement provides for the consumer's choice of the AAA or the ICC as the arbitral body and the designation of any location for the arbitration by agreement of the parties, which "shall not be unreasonably withheld." It also provides telephone numbers at which the AAA and the ICC may be reached for information regarding the "organizations and their procedures."

As noted, however, appellants complain that the AAA fees are also excessive and thus in no way have they accepted defendant's offer (*see*, UCC 2–209); because they make the same claim as to the AAA as they did with respect to the ICC, the issue of unconscionability is not rendered moot, as defendant suggests. We cannot determine on this record whether the AAA process and costs would be so "egregiously oppressive" that they, too, would be unconscionable (*Avildsen v. Prystay*, 171 A.D.2d 13, 14, 574 N.Y.S.2d 535, *appeal dismissed*, 79 N.Y.2d 841, 580 N.Y.S.2d 193, 588 N.E.2d 91). Thus, we modify the order on appeal to the extent of finding that portion of the arbitration provision requiring arbitration before the ICC to be unconscionable and remand to Supreme Court so that the parties have the opportunity to seek appropriate substitution of an arbitrator pursuant to the Federal Arbitration Act (9 U.S.C. § 1 et seq.), which provides for such court designation of an arbitrator upon application of either party, where, for whatever reason, one is not otherwise designated (9 U.S.C. § 5).

Appellants make the final argument that the arbitration clause does not apply to the cause of action for false advertising (with respect to the promised round-the-clock service) under various sections of the General Business Law on the ground that there is no mention of arbitration in the technical service contract itself. Although they raise this claim for the first time on this appeal, we find the promise of technical support to be within the scope of arbitration as it is clearly a "dispute or controversy arising out or relating to [the] Agreement or its interpretation." Put another way, the service contract does not apply to some separate product that could be retained while the computer products—and the accompanying agreement—could be returned.

Accordingly, the order of Supreme Court, New York County (Beatrice Shainswit, J.), entered October 21, 1997, which, to the extent appealed from, granted defendants' motion to dismiss the complaint as to appellants on the ground that there was a valid agreement to arbitrate between the parties, should be modified, on the law and the facts, to the extent of vacating that portion of the arbitration agreement as requires arbitration before the International Chamber of Commerce, with leave to the parties to seek appointment of an arbitrator pursuant to 9 U.S.C. § 5 and remanding the matter for that purpose, and otherwise affirmed, without costs.

Order, Supreme Court, New York County (Beatrice Shainswit, J.), entered October 21, 1997, modified, on the law and the facts, to the extent of vacating that portion of the arbitration agreement as requires arbitration before the International Chamber of Commerce, with leave to the parties to seek appointment of an arbitrator pursuant to 9 U.S.C. § 5 and remanding the matter for that purpose, and otherwise affirmed, without costs.

WHITE v. McBRIDE

Supreme Court of Tennessee, at Nashville. 1996.
937 S.W.2d 796.

See p. 198 supra.

K.D. v. EDUCATIONAL TESTING SERVICE

Supreme Court, N.Y. County, 1976.
87 Misc.2d 657, 386 N.Y.S.2d 747.

See p. 11 supra.

Chapter 8

CONDITIONS, PERFORMANCE AND BREACH

SECTION 1. THE NATURE AND EFFECT OF EXPRESS CONDITIONS, THE TIME CLASSIFI-CATION OF CONDITIONS

(Calamari & Perillo 5th §§ 11.1—11.8)

AUDETTE v. L'UNION ST. JOSEPH

Supreme Judicial Court of Massachusetts, 1901.
178 Mass. 113, 59 N.E. 668.

Action by Malvina Audette, administratrix of the estate of Louis Audette, deceased, against L'Union St. Joseph. From a judgment in favor of defendant, plaintiff appeals. Affirmed.

A by-law of the defendant association provided that no sick member should receive any benefits before producing a sworn certificate of a physician. The physician who attended plaintiff's intestate in his last sickness refused to give a sworn certificate because of conscientious scruples against making an oath. [The phrase "conscientious scruples," etc., is a standard phrase to indicate a religious belief that an oath is offensive to the Deity. Generally, procedural statutes and the U.S. Constitution allow an "affirmation" to substitute for an oath. Ed.]

LORING, J. This case comes within the rule that where one engages for the act of a stranger he must procure the act to be done, and the refusal of the stranger, without the interference of the other party, is no excuse. That rule has been applied in this commonwealth to the obligation of a person, insured under a fire insurance policy, to furnish to the fire insurance company a certificate, under the hand and seal of a magistrate, notary public, or commissioner of deeds, stating that he has examined the circumstances attending the loss, knows the character and circumstances of the assured, and believes that the assured has, without fraud, sustained loss on the property insured to the amount certified. Johnson v. Insurance Co., 112 Mass. 49. In that case it was held that the plaintiff was not excused from producing such certificate by showing that he applied to two magistrates for such a certificate in vain, and used his best efforts to procure it, accompanied by proof of the facts which were to be certified to. * * * This action, therefore, was prematurely brought; but the plaintiff, on producing a sworn certificate, unless there is some objection to it not now disclosed, can bring a new writ, and recover the sick benefits now sued for. Judgment for the defendant affirmed.

INMAN v. CLYDE HALL DRILLING CO.

Supreme Court of Alaska, 1962.
369 P.2d 498.

DIMOND, JUSTICE. This case involves a claim for damages arising out of an employment contract. The main issue is whether a provision in the contract, making written notice of a claim a condition precedent to recovery, is contrary to public policy.

Inman worked for the Clyde Hall Drilling Company as a derrickman under a written contract of employment signed by both parties on November 16, 1959. His employment terminated on March 24, 1960. On April 5, 1960, he commenced this action against the Company claiming that the latter fired him without justification, that this amounted to a breach of contract, and that he was entitled to certain damages for the breach. In its answer the Company denied that it had breached the contract, and asserted that Inman had been paid in full the wages that were owing him and was entitled to no damages. Later the Company moved for summary judgment on the ground that Inman's failure to give written notice of his claim, as required by the contract, was a bar to his action based on the contract.[1] The motion was granted, and judgment was entered in favor of the Company. This appeal followed.

A fulfillment of the thirty-day notice requirement is expressly made a "condition precedent to any recovery." Inman argues that this provision is void as against public policy. In considering this first question we start with the basic tenet that competent parties are free to make contracts and that they should be bound by their agreements. In the absence of a constitutional provision or statute which makes certain contracts illegal or unenforceable, we believe it is the function of the judiciary to allow men to manage their own affairs in their own way. As a matter of judicial policy the court should maintain and enforce contracts, rather than enable parties to escape from the obligations they have chosen to incur.

---

1. The portion of the contract with which we are concerned reads: "You agree that you will, within thirty (30) days after any claim (other than a claim for compensation insurance) that arises out of or in connection with the employment provided for herein, give written notice to the Company for such claim, setting forth in detail the facts relating thereto and the basis for such claim; and that you will not institute any suit or action against the Company in any court or tribunal in any jurisdiction based on any such claim prior to six (6) months after the filing of the written notice of claim hereinabove provided for, or later than one (1) year after such filing. Any action or suit on any such claim shall not include any item or matter not specifically mentioned in the proof of claim above provided. It is agreed that in any such action or suit, proof by you of your compliance with the provisions of this paragraph shall be a condition precedent to any recovery."

We recognize that "freedom of contract" is a qualified and not an absolute right, and cannot be applied on a strict, doctrinal basis. An established principle is that a court will not permit itself to be used as an instrument of inequity and injustice. As Justice Frankfurter stated in his dissenting opinion in United States v. Bethlehem Steel Corp., "The fundamental principle of law that the courts will not enforce a bargain where one party has unconscionably taken advantage of the necessities and distress of the other has found expression in an almost infinite variety of cases." In determining whether certain contractual provisions should be enforced, the court must look realistically at the relative bargaining positions of the parties in the framework of contemporary business practices and commercial life. If we find those positions are such that one party has unscrupulously taken advantage of the economic necessities of the other, then in the interest of justice—as a matter of public policy—we would refuse to enforce the transaction. But the grounds for judicial interference must be clear. Whether the court should refuse to recognize and uphold that which the parties have agreed upon is a question of fact upon which evidence is required.

The facts in this case do not persuade us that the contractual provision in question is unfair or unreasonable. Its purpose is not disclosed. The requirement that written notice be given within thirty days after a claim arises may have been designed to preclude stale claims; and the further requirement that no action be commenced within six months thereafter may have been intended to afford the Company timely opportunity to rectify the basis for a just claim. But whatever the objective was, we cannot find in the contract anything to suggest it was designed from an unfair motive to bilk employees out of wages or other compensation justly due them.

There was nothing to suggest that Inman did not have the knowledge, capacity or opportunity to read the agreement and understand it; that the terms of the contract were imposed upon him without any real freedom of choice on his part; that there was any substantial inequality in bargaining positions between Inman and the Company. Not only did he attach a copy of the contract to his complaint, which negatives any thought that he really wasn't aware of its provisions, but he also admitted in a deposition that at the time he signed the contract he had read it, had discussed it with a Company representative, and was familiar with its terms. And he showed specific knowledge of the thirty-day notice requirement when, in response to a question as to whether written notice had been given prior to filing suit, he testified:

"A. Well, now, I filed—I started my claim within 30 days, didn't I, from the time I hit here. I thought that would be a notice that I started suing them when I first came to town.

"Q. You thought that the filing of the suit would be the notice?

"A. That is right."

Under these circumstances we do not find that such a limitation on Inman's right of action is offensive to justice. We would not be justified in refusing to enforce the contract and thus permit one of the parties to escape his obligations. It is conceivable, of course, that a thirty-day notice of claim requirement could be used to the disadvantage of a workman by an unscrupulous employer. If this danger is great, the legislature may act to make such a provision unenforceable.[11] But we may not speculate on what in the future may be a matter of public policy in this state. It is our function to act only where an existent public policy is clearly revealed from the facts and we find that it has been violated. That is not the case here.

Inman's claim arose on March 24, 1960. His complaint was served on the Company on April 14. He argues that since the complaint set forth in detail the basis of his claim and was served within thirty days, he had substantially complied with the contractual requirement.

Service of the complaint probably gave the Company actual knowledge of the claim. But that does not serve as an excuse for not giving the kind of written notice called for by the contract. Inman agreed that no suit would be instituted "prior to six (6) months *after the filing of the written notice of claim.*" (emphasis ours) If this means what it says (and we have no reason to believe it does not), it is clear that the commencement of an action and service of the complaint was not an effective substitute for the kind of notice called for by the agreement. To hold otherwise would be to simply ignore an explicit provision of the contract and say that it had no meaning. We are not justified in doing that.

The contract provides that compliance with its requirement as to giving written notice of a claim prior to bringing suit "shall be a condition precedent to any recovery." Inman argues that this is not a true condition precedent—merely being labelled as such by the Company—and that non-compliance with the requirement was an affirmative defense which the Company was required to set forth in its answer under Civ.R. 8(c). He contends that because the answer was silent on this point, the defense was waived under Civ.R. 12(h).

The failure to give advance notice of a claim where notice is required would ordinarily be a defense to be set forth in the answer. But here the parties agreed that such notice should be a condition precedent to any recovery. This meant that the Company was not required to plead lack of notice as an affirmative defense, but instead, that Inman was required to plead performance of the condition or that performance had been waived or excused. The Company may not be charged under Civ.R. 12(h) with having waived a defense which it was not obliged to present in its answer.

Inman's last point is that the trial court erred in entering a final judgment. He argues that the failure to give written notice was merely a matter in abatement of his action until the condition could be performed,

---

11. In Oklahoma the constitution (art. XXIII, § 9) provides: "Any provision of any contract or agreement, express or implied, stipulating for notice or demand other than such as may be provided by law, as a condition precedent to establish any claim, demand, or liability, shall be null and void." See Brakebill v. Chicago, R.I. & P. Ry., 37 Okl. 140, 131 P. 540 (1913).

and that the most the court ought to have done was to dismiss the action without prejudice.

This argument is unsound. At the time judgment was entered Inman could no longer perform the condition precedent to recovery by giving written notice of his claim within thirty days after the claim arose, because this time limitation had expired. In these circumstances his right to seek redress from the court was barred and not merely abated. Final judgment in the Company's favor was proper.

The judgment is affirmed.

FEDERAL RULES OF CIVIL PROCEDURE

Rule 9. Pleading Special Matters

(c) Conditions Precedent. In pleading the performance or occurrence of conditions precedent, it is sufficient to aver generally that all conditions precedent have been performed or have occurred. A denial of performance or occurrence shall be made specifically and with particularity.

B. HARNETT & J.V. THORNTON, THE INSURANCE CONDITION SUBSEQUENT: A NEEDLE IN A SEMANTIC HAYSTACK

17 Fordham L.Rev. 220 (1948).

II.   Customary Theoretical Analyses of Conditions Precedent and Subsequent In General Contract Law

A. *In the Field of Substantive Law*

The customary definition of the condition precedent is a condition which "must exist or occur before a duty of immediate performance of a promise arises. * * * "[4] A condition subsequent, on the other hand, is said to be a condition, the happening of which "will extinguish a duty to make compensation for breach of contract after the breach has occurred."[5]

---

4. Restatement, Contacts § 250(a) (1933). In the same section the Restatement illustrates a condition precedent in this manner: "A writes to B in a distant city, that if B will advance money to C, A will guarantee repayment by C. B advances the money as requested. B's sending within a reasonable time, notice to A that the advance has been made is a condition precedent within the definition of the section. Failure to give such a notice is a condition

subsequent to the existence of a contract; but giving the notice within a reasonable time is a condition precedent to A's duty to make payment and of any right of action against him. * * * "

5. Restatement, Contracts § 250(b) (1933). In the same section the Restatement illustrates a condition subsequent in this manner: "A owes B a matured debt of $100. B delivers to A his promise under seal that the debt shall be discharged by B's death, if

Following through the implications of these conventional definitions it is discovered that they are broad enough to cover many sets of operative facts which are not normally regarded as conditions precedent or subsequent. Manifestly the making of an offer, the rendering of an acceptance, and the transferring of a consideration are all facts which "must exist or occur before a duty of immediate performance of a promise arises." The same is true of other facts such as legality of the subject matter, capacity of the parties, and definiteness of the objectives of the contract. However, while the definition in terms would cover all these operative facts, its ordinary meaning has been modified and narrowed so as to exclude those facts which go to the primary undertaking of the contract itself. In ordinary connotation the condition precedent refers to operative facts which must occur after the formation of the promissory undertaking in order to create the duty of performing the undertaking.[6]

In utilizing the terms "precedent" and "subsequent," however, courts and writers have not always followed this customary formulation, with resultant difficulty. It is hardly possible to manipulate concepts for socially desirable and consistent purposes unless some basic agreement as to the meaning of the concepts is first attained. Yet, as Professor Williston points out,[7] the term "condition precedent" has been used, contrary to its ordinary meaning, to refer to a set of operative facts, such as the manifestation of an acceptance, which must occur before the agreement of the parties becomes a binding contract.[8] The prevalent

prior thereto B has taken no steps for its collection. The debt remains due and enforceable; but B's death is a condition subsequent that will discharge it if no steps have been taken for its collection. B's death is a condition subsequent, since in view of the sealed release it will extinguish an existing debt."

6. The Restatement proceeds to explain its original definition of condition precedent in a comment which narrows the broad scope of the definition so as to bring it in line with ordinary theoretical formulations. " 'Condition' in ordinary legal use is a word of broad signification. In its widest sense as a legal term of art it is, 1, any operative fact that will create some new legal relation or extinguish an existing relation, or, 2, words or other manifestations that indicate that a fact shall have such an operation. In the law governing land and chattels the word is often used for an operative fact which affects their ownership, or for a provision stating that a fact shall have that operation, as for example, the condition in a mortgage or in a conditional sale of a chattel. Even when the use of the word is confined to facts or provisions which have or may have

operation with reference to contractual relations, its logical significance is very broad. Offer, acceptance, consideration, legality and the like are facts that must exist before contractual duties arise, but unless specific qualifying words are used, it is not customary to call these requirements of the law conditions, and they are not so designated in the Restatement * * * the use of the word is confined either to facts the existence of which modifies a promise or promises, though not necessarily promises which are contractually binding, or to the manifestations verbal or otherwise that provide for this effect * * * where conditions are spoken of without restrictive words, it is assumed that a contract has been formed and the questions involved relate to the duties of the promissor." Restatement, Contracts § 250, comments a and b (1933).

7. 3 Williston, Contracts § 666A (1936).

8. See McIsaac v. Hale, 104 Conn. 374, 132 Atl. 916 (1926), defining a condition in terms of operative facts which must occur prior to a contract springing into existence. To like effect is Muwaw v. Western & Southern Life Ins. Co., 97 Ohio St. 1, 119 N.E. 132 (1917).

view clearly is, however, that the condition precedent is a prerequisite to a duty of immediate performance under an already existing contract.[9]

Difficulties stemming from the imprecision of legal semantics become even more pronounced when effort is made to explain the so-called condition subsequent.[10] Traditionally the condition subsequent is said to exist in the instance where the parties insert a provision that "the fulfillment of a condition or the occurrence of an event shall discharge them both from further liabilities under the contract."[11] The equivocal nature of this phraseology is evident, and such a definition, just as in the case of conditions precedent, is meaningless unless a reference point is selected to which the "subsequent" character of the condition is to be referred.

The selection of the point of reference is of paramount importance because the selection of the reference point determines the precedent or subsequent nature of the "condition"—i.e., the set of operative facts—which is being analyzed. "In one sense, all conditions are subsequent; in another all are precedent."[12] Every condition is subsequent to the operative facts and legal relations which have preceded it, and, converse-

---

9. "A *condition precedent* is an operative fact that must exist prior to the existence of some legal relation in which we are interested. The particular relation most commonly in mind when this term is used is either the instant and unconditional duty of performance by a promisor or the secondary duty to pay damages for a breach of such duty of performance." Corbin, Conditions in the Law of Contract, 28 Yale L.J. 739, 747 (1919). Prof. Costigan in The Performance of Contracts 10 (1911) is substantially in accord with this view: "A condition precedent, as applied to a condition which goes to performance under a contract in distinction from a condition which goes to the existence of a contract, is a fact or event which must take place or be waived before the party whose performance it is to precede owes such performance, i.e., before he must perform or be in default under the contract and liable to an action therefor."

10. The semantic problem in conditions precedent and subsequent is not limited to the field of contracts. While in property conceptions the terms do have different connotations than in contract law, still the analogous problem of differentiation exists. One writer reviewing in detail the future interests section of the Restatement of Property has commented: "Just what is this all-important distinction between a condition which is 'precedent' and one which is a mere 'basis for defeasance?' Just what difference does it make to whom and how and why? How does the [American Law] Institute recognize so easily and so surely that any given limitation 'creates' the one or the other? 'The statement that a designated occurrence, such as survival, is a

"condition precedent" of an interest means,' answers comment k, § 249, 'that the designated occurrence must happen before the interest vests, that is, before the interest acquires those characteristics connoted by the term "vested" * * *.' Still, all of these rules about 'characteristics' tell us only what a court is supposed to do once it has determined whether an 'interest' is subject to a condition precedent or a condition of defeasance; they offer no criteria by which 'conditions precedent' and 'conditions as a basis of defeasance' can be identified. By what criteria does the Institute operate and by what criteria is it proposing that courts operate? Are the same criteria relevant for each of these many practical problems which from the perspective of policy norms are so totally different? The present volume offers us no explicit help; its blackletter merely pronounces arbitrarily and summarily * * * that certain 'conditions' are either this or that, fish or fowl." McDougal, Future Interests Restated: Tradition Versus Clarification and Reform, 55 Harv.L.Rev. 1077, 1090 (1942). For a detailed analysis of insurance problems in terms of relevant policy norms, rather than on the level of legal syntax, see Harnett and Thornton, Insurable Interest in Property: A Socio–Economic Reevaluation of a Legal Concept, 48 Col.L.Rev. 1162 (1948).

11. Anson, Contracts § 358 (2d Am. ed., Huffcut, 1907). * * *

12. Holmes, The Common Law 316 (1881). One of the earliest and still one of the best brief analyses of the condition precedent and condition subsequent is that of Justice Holmes.

ly, every condition is precedent to the operative facts and legal relations which come after it.[13] This is readily demonstrable by consideration of one of the traditional conditions precedent, the procurement of an architect's certificate of satisfactory performance as a prerequisite to full payment in the building contract situation. Analytically viewed, it is apparent that this condition, while ordinarily denominated precedent, has within it the elements of either a condition precedent or a condition subsequent depending upon the reference point selected. The procuring of the certificate is subsequent to certain operative facts and legal relations: it is subsequent to those facts which resulted in the legal relation called the "offer," subsequent also to those facts which represented the "acceptance," and subsequent to those facts which amounted in legal effect to "consideration." Yet, at the same time, the procuring of the certificate is precedent to the promisor's duty to make full payment; precedent to the payment itself if made, and precedent to any right to commence a law suit if payment be not made.

Thus it is that the terms "precedent" and "subsequent" are utterly devoid of meaning unless related to a known point of reference.[14] A further complication is that the points of reference which may be selected are virtually limitless in number. At the nadir is the possible selection for a reference point of the first initiation of any form of contract negotiation; any condition appertaining to the contract must needs be subsequent to that point. At the zenith is the use as a reference point of the ultimate performance under the contract, whether primary performance in the sense of actual completion of the contract or secondary performance in the sense of substituted completion of the contract through payment of damages; any condition is necessarily precedent to that point. Between these opposite poles of initial negotiation and ultimate performance are many other points which could be used as reference guides, such as the formation of the contract or the accrual of a duty of performance thereunder. Accordingly as these points are selected, the identical operative facts will shift from the category "precedent" to the classification "subsequent." Attempting legal analysis without recognizing the decisive effect of this reference point factor is like trying to locate a city without the aid of geographic meridians and parallels. For, just as New York is south of New Haven, south of Cambridge, and south of Montreal, but north of Princeton, north of

---

13. Professor Corbin defines the types of conditions in these terms: "A *condition precedent* is an operative fact that must exist prior to the existence of some legal relation in which we are interested. * * * A *condition subsequent* is an operative fact that causes the termination of some previous legal relation in which we are interested." Corbin, Conditions in the Law of Contract, 28 Yale L.J. 739, 747 (1919).

In the same discussion Corbin points out that the legal relation commonly used as the reference point when the term condition precedent is used is the duty of performance by the promisor or the duty to respond in damages for failure to perform. * * *

14. "The terms precedent and subsequent express a relation in *time* between two facts, one of which is the legal relation itself; and before using either one of them it is necessary to determine just what two facts are being considered." Corbin, Conditions in the Law of Contract, 28 Yale L.J. 739, 747 (1919).

Charlottesville, and north of Atlanta, so is any one set of operative facts precedent to some other facts but subsequent to still others.

In recognition of the critical importance of the reference point concept, the leading contract authorities have generally concurred in the selection of the duty of immediate performance as the reference point. Hence any condition prior to the springing up of the duty of immediate performance is conventionally a condition precedent, whereas any condition which thereafter divests the duty of immediate performance is a condition subsequent.[15] A minority current of authority would, however, not select the duty of immediate performance as the point of reference, but rather would choose the existence of the plaintiff's cause of action.[16]

When the conventional reference point, the duty of immediate performance, is selected, the condition subsequent becomes indeed a rare creature. * * * Contrast * * * genuine condition[s] subsequent with a situation often regarded as a condition subsequent but which is in fact a condition precedent. That is the case where a master and servant contract contemplates a hiring for a certain period with the master being given the right to discharge the servant upon becoming in good faith dissatisfied with his services. While often categorized as a condition subsequent, on the theory that the discharge in good faith avoids a duty which would otherwise exist to respond in damages for the breach of the obligation, the true analysis is simply that the master's satisfaction with the servant's services is a condition precedent to the master's liability. There is no question of divesting a liability; for no liability accrued until the performance of the condition precedent, that is, satisfying the master. Furthermore, the noncompliance with any condition precedent would entitle a party not to perform, and from this it follows that since the master had no duty to perform, he is not liable for failing to perform.

* * *

15. 3 Williston, Contracts § 667 (1936). To the same general effect, see Costigan, Performance of Contracts 12 (1911). "A condition subsequent * * * is any fact or event which will relieve the promisor from a default under the contract—i.e., will relieve him from a cause of action which has accrued against him because performance on his part became due and has not been given,—or which will affect in any way the cause of action which arises from such default." Costigan suggests a "rule of thumb" for discovering the true nature of a condition subsequent in form. The method is to try to phrase the condition in precedent form; if its form can be changed, then, to the extent that it can be changed, it is not genuinely a condition subsequent.

Some writers deny that there ever can be a condition subsequent. See Ashley, Conditions in Contract, 14 Yale L.J. 424 (1905). It is believed that the divergent views on the question are due merely to choice of reference points from which the conditions are examined.

16. Seemingly this is Ashley's view since he avers there is no such thing as a condition subsequent, and that extreme position could only be supported on the assumption that the reference point was the plaintiff's cause of action. See Ashley, supra note 15. Holmes apparently uses a similar point of reference. See Holmes, The Common Law 317 (1881), discussing the condition that a policy of insurance shall be void if not sued upon within one year after default in payment.

Problems

1. (a) Husband and wife were lost at sea when the Lusitania was sunk. The husband had a policy on his life which provided: "Five Thousand Dollars * * * to his wife, if living; if not, then to the insured's executors, administrators or assigns." Should the money be paid to the administrator of the wife or husband?

(b) Used industrial machinery was sold with a warranty that it contained no defects. The warranty was to expire unless a certificate issued by XYZ consulting engineers certified to such defects was presented at the seller's office by noon, March 14. Buyer testifies that XYZ's certification of defects was presented at the seller's office at 11:55 a.m., March 14. Seller testifies that it was delivered at 12:05 p.m., March 14. If the jury does not know whom to believe, what should its verdict be on the issue?

2. Plaintiff was a doctor and a partner in a clinic, the defendant herein. By the terms of the partnership agreement, a doctor could withdraw by giving 90 days' notice of his intention to withdraw. The agreement also provided in part: "In the event that the executive committee requests him to revoke his notice of withdrawal prior to the effective date thereof, and he refuses to comply with such request, he promises that he shall not engage in the practice of medicine within a 25 mile radius of the City of Olympia." In an action for a declaratory judgment, the trial court found as a fact that the plaintiff avoided his colleagues after he submitted the required notice and that he would not have retracted the notice if he had been requested to do so. What result?

3. This is an action on a life and disability policy. The policy expressly provided that, if any premium is not paid on the date when due, the policy shall cease and determine with the exception that the Insurance Company will pay all premiums becoming due after receipt of proof of total and permanent disability and the continuance thereof. The insured died on April 10, 1929. The last premium paid was due on May 27, 1927. The next premium was due on Sept. 27, 1927 and neither it nor any subsequent premium was paid. The plaintiff offered evidence tending to show that decedent was permanently and totally disabled from August 1, 1927 to the date of his death. What result?

4. S agrees to sell to B an exercise machine, promising that if B is dissatisfied with the machine after a 30–day trial, B may return it for a full refund. Describe what kind of condition occurs if B is dissatisfied and tenders the return of the machine.

5. (a) A casualty insurance policy provides that no action on the policy can be brought prior to giving proof of loss within 60 days' of the loss and no action can be brought after twelve months from the loss. What kind of conditions are present?

(b) A typical bail bond contains the following language. Is the defendant's appearance before the Court when ordered to do so a condition precedent or a condition subsequent?

I/we understand that if the defendant obeys all the conditions of his/her release and appears before the Court when ordered to do so, then this appearance bond will be void and any deposit returned.

6. D issued a fire insurance policy to P that provided that no liability shall exist under this policy if the building is vacant or unoccupied at the time of loss. The building was destroyed by fire and there was conflicting evidence as to whether the building was vacant. Who has the burden of proof on this issue?

SECTION 2. DOES THE CONTRACT CREATE AN EXPRESS CONDITION, A PROMISE, OR BOTH?

(Calamari & Perillo 5th §§ 11.9—11.15)

GENERAL CREDIT CORP. v. IMPERIAL CASUALTY AND INDEMNITY CO.

Supreme Court of Nebraska, 1959.
167 Neb. 833, 95 N.W.2d 145.

SIMMONS, CHIEF JUSTICE. Plaintiff, as a lienholder, brought this action to recover the amount allegedly due it for damages sustained to two automobiles. The action is on a policy of insurance issued by the defendant to the Service Trucking Company. There was a loss payable clause attached to the policy as follows: "Loss or damage, if any, under the policy shall be payable as interest may appear to General Credit Corp., Hastings, Nebraska and this insurance as to the interest of the Bailment Lessor, Conditional Vendor or Mortgagee or Assignee of Bailment Lessor, Conditional Vendor or Mortgagee (herein called the Lienholder) shall not be invalidated by any act or neglect of the Lessee, Mortgagor or Owner of the within described automobile nor by any change in the title or ownership of the property; provided, however, that the conversion, embezzlement or secretion by the Lessee, Mortgagor or Purchaser in possession of the property insured under a bailment lease, conditional sale, mortgage or other encumbrance is not covered under such policy, unless specifically insured against and premium paid therefor; and provided, also, that in case the Lessee, Mortgagor or Owner shall neglect to pay any premium due under such policy the Lienholder shall, on demand, pay the same."

To the policy was also attached two separate endorsements covering two automobiles and providing that loss should be paid to the insured and the plaintiff as their interests may appear. The premium for the insurance on each automobile was separately stated as $86. The total premium on the policy was stated as $6,701.43. Plaintiff alleged collision damage to the two automobiles totaling $2,016.44, alleging that its insurable interest exceeded the amount of the damages sustained.

Defendant answered admitting the issuing of the policy and the insurance involved, and that the limit of liability for each loss is the reasonable cost of repairs less $50 or the actual value of the automobile less $50, whichever is lower.

Defendant further alleged that there is due it the sum of $1,786.86 unpaid premium; that pursuant to the clause above quoted it had made demand on the plaintiff for that amount and plaintiff had refused to pay it; and that there was due the defendant from the plaintiff the sum of $1,786.86 to which it is entitled to judgment or to have that sum deducted from any amount the plaintiff may be entitled to recover from the defendant. So stated it appears that defendant seeks to recover the unpaid premium on the principal policy, i.e., it is a claim for the payment of a premium.

The cause was tried on a stipulation of facts. It was stipulated that the reasonable cost of repairs to the two automobiles less deductible amount was $1,839.20, that being less than the actual cash value at the time of the losses; and that plaintiff's insurable interest was in excess of that amount.

It was also stipulated that the policy and endorsements were in full force and effect at the time of loss.

We construe the stipulation to mean that plaintiff, as against the defendant, was entitled to recover $1,839.20.

The facts as to defendant's claim against the plaintiff were also stipulated. There was an unpaid premium due on the policy of $1,786.86 which includes $45.92 on the vehicles in which plaintiff had an insurable interest and $1,740.94 on certain vehicles in which plaintiff had no insurable interest. It was further stipulated that "after the said losses had occurred and the policy had been canceled" the defendant had demanded the sum of $1,786.86 from the plaintiff.

A jury was waived. The trial court awarded plaintiff judgment for $1,839.20 with interest and costs. It denied recovery to the defendant.

Defendant appeals.

As stated by defendant the appeal here presents primarily the question of whether the language in the loss payable clause "provided, also, that in case the Lessee, Mortgagor or Owner shall neglect to pay any premium due under such policy the Lienholder shall, on demand, pay the same" is a condition or a covenant.

We conclude that it is a condition and affirm the judgment of the trial court.

In C.J.S. Insurance § 356(d), p. 1335, the status of the decisions on the matter is stated as follows: "There is a conflict of authority on the question whether or not a mortgagee is liable for premiums on a policy containing a clause, usually referred to as a standard mortgage clause, declaring that the policy shall not be invalidated as to the mortgagee's interest by any act or neglect of the mortgagor, 'provided' in case the mortgagor shall neglect to pay any premium the mortgagee shall, on demand, pay it. Some authorities have held that such clause embodies a contract or covenant on the part of the mortgagee to pay the premium on failure of the mortgagor to pay it. Other authorities have held that such clause, or a similar one, imports a condition merely, and not a covenant, and that the mortgagee is not liable for the premium, if he does not continue the policy, * * *.''

* * *

In Restatement, Contracts, § 260, p. 373, it is stated: "If in an agreement words that state that an act is to be performed purport to be the words of the person who is to do the act, the words are interpreted, unless a contrary intention has been manifested, as a promise by that person to perform the act. If the words purport to be those of a party who is not to do the act they are interpreted, unless a contrary intention has been manifested, as limiting the promise of that party by making performance of the act a condition." In the comment it is said: "b. If a contract is clearly unilateral as is the case with many if not most policies of insurance, the answer to the question to whom must the language be attributed admits of no doubt. In such a contract only one party speaks, and that is the convenantor or promisor. Any clause, therefore, in a policy of insurance, requiring any act to be done by the insured, will make that act a condition of the covenant or promise of insurance."

A discussion citing the above statement in Restatement is made by Williston in his work on contracts. 3 Williston on Contracts (Rev.Ed.), § 672, p. 1930. He states: "The matter has been well expressed by Professor Langdell: 'Moreover, the words of such a clause will have, in fact, a different meaning, according to the party who uses them. If they are used in a contract by the party who is to do the act, they plainly import that he binds himself to do it; while, if they are used by the party for whose benefit the act is to be done, they fairly mean that he will require it to be done, i.e., that his own obligation shall be conditional upon its being done. How then shall it be ascertained to whom the language of such a clause is to be imputed? If the contract be clearly unilateral (e.g., a policy of insurance), of course the answer to this question admits of no doubt. In such a contract only one party speaks, and that is the covenantor or promisor. Any clause, therefore, in a policy of insurance, requiring any act to be done by the insured, will be a condition of the covenant or promise of insurance, though its language may more naturally import a covenant or promise by the insured.' "

It is stated in 14 Appleman, Insurance Law and Practice, § 7842, p. 39, that: "One of the most puzzling results reached by the courts arises in connection with the type of mortgage clause which has been variously termed the 'standard', 'New York', or 'union' clause. It will be recalled from the previous discussion that this clause gives great rights to the mortgagee and protects him under circumstances where the mortgagor would receive no indemnification. However, in return for that special protection, the mortgagee is to pay upon demand, if the mortgagor defaults, such premiums as may be due. This would seem to be clear in itself, to be fair, based upon a proper consideration, and to be an agreement of the mortgagee arising through his request of the loss payable clause, acceptance of the policy, or silent acquiescence. However, the vast majority of courts have reached the somewhat surprising conclusion that such agreement to pay is not a covenant on the part of the mortgagee to pay premiums which can be enforced by the insurer, but is merely a condition to his right to recover the insurance proceeds. Mortgagees are not to be blamed for striving to achieve this result, as it places them in the enviable position of being able to harvest a crop without first sowing seed."

* * *

It is stated in Restatement, Contracts, § 236, p. 328, that: "Where words or other manifestations of intention bear more than one reasonable meaning an interpretation is preferred which operates more strongly against the party from whom they proceed, unless their use by him is prescribed by law."

This language is in accord with our decisions. See 4 Nebraska Digest, Contracts, ☞155.

Commenting on the rule [the] Restatement says: "This rule finds frequent application in regard to policies of insurance, which are ordinarily prepared solely by the insurance company, and therefore, the words of the policies are construed most strongly against it." Restatement, Contracts, § 236, p. 330.

We conclude then that the clause here involved is a condition and that the condition requires the plaintiff to pay the premium on the insurance involved from and after the date of the demand if plaintiff desires to keep the insurance in force. Such a conclusion is in accord with the authorities above cited that construe this language to be a condition.

It being stipulated here that the insurance was in full force and effect when the losses involved occurred and that the demand of the defendant to pay the premium was not made until after the losses had occurred and the policy had been canceled, it must necessarily follow that plaintiff is entitled to judgment for the loss proven and is not required to pay the premium demanded.

* * *

Defendant would have us attach to the condition the obligations that result from a covenant and would escape the obligations that result from a condition. That it cannot do. The judgment of the trial court is affirmed.

NEW YORK BRONZE POWDER CO. v. BENJAMIN ACQUISITION CORP.

Court of Appeals of Maryland, 1998.
351 Md. 8, 716 A.2d 230.

MARVIN H. SMITH, JUDGE (retired), Specially Assigned. This case presents the problem of whether a provision in a contract is a condition or a promise or both. The Court of Special Appeals in an unreported opinion reversed a trial court judgment and construed as a condition precedent a provision in a non-negotiable note/contract requiring surrender of the note in order to receive payment.

The facts relevant to this decision may be briefly stated.

New York Bronze Powder Company, Inc. (New York Bronze) entered into an agreement dated March 15, 1990, with Benjamin Acquisition Corporation (Benjamin) under which Benjamin agreed to purchase from New York Bronze the assets of a business then known as Benjamin F. Rich Company (Rich) for $4.5 million, together with the assumption of certain of Rich's liabilities. Closing was to take place on April 30, 1990. Shortly prior to the closing, Benjamin expressed its concerns to New York Bronze over the valuation of certain assets. The matter was resolved by an April 30, 1990 modification of the purchase agreement (Amendment No. 1). Under Amendment No. 1 $350,000 of the $4.5 million purchase price was deferred, and Benjamin executed a non-negotiable note to New York Bronze for $350,000. Under Section 3 of Amendment No. 1 Benjamin undertook, at its expense, to have prepared a balance sheet of Rich accompanied by the opinion of a specifically named accounting firm, and Benjamin promised to use its best efforts to cause that audited balance sheet to be delivered to New York Bronze no later than June 14, 1990. To the extent that the audited balance sheet reflected a net worth of Rich that was less than $4.5 million, Benjamin was entitled under Section 3 of the note to a dollar for dollar credit against the $350,000 deferred purchase price.

* * *

As matters unfolded following the April 30, 1990 closing under the modified asset purchase agreement, the accounting firm specified in Amendment No. 1 never opined on the audited balance sheet, and apparently never completed its audit.

Benjamin never made or tendered any cash payment on the note. In October 1993 New York Bronze sued Benjamin in the Circuit Court for Montgomery County alleging non-payment of the note and breach of the modified asset purchase agreement. After a bench trial the court entered judgment for $350,000 in favor of New York Bronze.

Benjamin appealed to the Court of Special Appeals, raising three issues, but that court found it necessary to address only one. That issue is whether the portion of Section 4.2 of the note, italicized below, should be construed as a condition precedent to payment. That section provides:

4.2 *Payments.* Payments of any portion of the principal of this Note shall be made by check drawn on a United States commercial bank and shall be mailed by registered mail, return receipt requested, on or prior to the date on which such payment is due, to the Noteholder at the address set forth in the Purchase Agreement. If the date on which any payment hereunder is due is not a Business Day, then such payment shall be due on the next succeeding Business Day. *The Noteholder shall be required to surrender this*

Note for cancellation upon the maturity or prepayment in full of this Note in order to receive payment.

(Emphasis added). Section 4.4 of the note provides that it "SHALL BE GOVERNED BY AND CONSTRUED IN ACCORDANCE WITH THE LAWS OF THE STATE OF NEW YORK."

The Court of Special Appeals held that, under New York law, the italicized language created a condition, the non-occurrence of which extinguished Benjamin's obligation to pay the $350,000 or any part thereof. New York Bronze then petitioned this Court for the writ of certiorari, which was granted.

The factual foundation for Benjamin's position that the "condition" was not fulfilled lies in the testimony of New York Bronze's chief financial officer. When New York Bronze attempted to introduce *not* the note but a *copy* of the note, the following colloquy took place:

Q. [Counsel for New York Bronze]: Can you identify Exhibit No. 3?

A. This would be the Benjamin Acquisition subordinated promissory note [due] July 30, 1991 for $350,000.

(The document referred to was marked for identification as Plaintiff's Exhibit 3.)

. . . .

Q. Was anything paid on that note?

A. No, nothing has been received.

Q. Is that a true and accurate copy of the original?

A. It appears to be, yes.

[Counsel for New York Bronze]: Your Honor, I would move Exhibit No. 3 into evidence[.]

The Court: Any objection?

[Counsel for Benjamin]: Yes, Your Honor. *I have a bit of a problem with this exhibit to the extent Plaintiff is suing on a note and exhibiting the copy as opposed to the original.* It causes me a great deal of concern.

The Court: Okay. Can you establish foundation as to the location of the original?

. . . .

Q. [Counsel for New York Bronze]: Do you have the original note?

A. No, I don't.

Q. Have you sold the original note?

A. No, I have not.

Q. Has it been encumbered by anyone? Have you encumbered the original note?

A. I just want to say where the original note is.

Q. Where is it?

A. Because I am not sure about the word encumbered. Perpetual Savings Bank was the lender at the time. They had an interest in all the assets. They kept the original documents.

Q. Is that a true and accurate copy of the original note?

A. Yes.

[Counsel for New York Bronze]: I would move No. 3 into evidence.

The Court: Any further objection?

[Counsel for Benjamin]: Yes, Your Honor. That still raises a question. *Now they are suing us on a note they are not even holding.*

The Court: Well, I will receive this over objection. I think a foundation has been laid.

(Emphasis added.)

* * *

The Court of Special Appeals held that New York Bronze was not entitled to the principal amount of the note, or any part thereof, because it had not surrendered the original note to Benjamin. In reaching that result, the Court of Special Appeals reasoned:

> New York and Maryland law are congruent on the point that words in a contract (or note) are to be given their ordinary meaning. [Citations omitted.] The New York courts have defined a condition precedent as "an act or event, other than a lapse of time, which, unless the condition is excused, must occur before a duty to perform a promise in the agreement arises." Oppenheimer & Co. v. Oppenheim, Appel, Dixon & Co., [86 N.Y.2d 685, 636 N.Y.S.2d 734] 660 N.E.2d 415, 418 (N.Y.1995) * * *.[2]

> The language in § 4.2 of the note clearly fits that definition. The noteholder is required to surrender the note for cancellation "in order to receive payment." Unquestionably, that requirement does qualify the duty to pay. See Gilpin v. Savage, 94 N.E. 656 (N.Y.1911) (requirement of presentment of negotiable instrument construed as condition precedent); Laurel Race Course v. Regal Constr., 274 Md.

---

2. This squares with Maryland law. This Court has defined a condition precedent as " 'a fact, other than mere lapse of time, which, unless excused, must exist or occur before a duty of immediate performance of a promise arises.' " Chirichella v. Erwin, 270 Md. 178, 182, 310 A.2d 555, 557 (1973) (quoting 17 Am.Jur.2d, Contracts, § 320). While "no particular form of words is necessary in order to create an express condition, such words and phrases as 'if' and 'provided that,' are commonly used to indicate that performance has expressly been made conditional, as have the words 'when,' 'after,' 'as soon as,' or 'subject to.' " Id. (citations omitted). The determination of whether a provision in a contract constitutes a condition precedent is a question of "construction dependent on the intent of the parties to be gathered from the words they have employed and, in case of ambiguity, after resort to the other permissible aids to interpretation." Id.

142 [333 A.2d 319] (1975) (where payment under contract due only upon issuance of certificate by architect, production of certificate is condition precedent to liability).

The dominant element in this case is that the note is non-negotiable.[4] The form of the note was an exhibit to Amendment No. 1 to the asset purchase agreement, and the note's provisions concerning set off implement the provisions of Amendment No. 1 concerning the audit. The asset purchase agreement, as amended, is one integrated contract that includes the note. Under these circumstances the controlling issue is whether the last sentence of Section 4.2 of the note is to be construed as a promise on the part of New York Bronze to surrender the note for cancellation, for an unsubstantial breach of which Benjamin would not be excused from performance, or whether the last sentence is a condition precedent to enforcement of Benjamin's promise to pay.

The most recent decision of the Court of Appeals of New York dealing with conditions in contracts is Oppenheimer & Co., Inc. v. Oppenheim, Appel, Dixon & Co., 86 N.Y.2d 685, 636 N.Y.S.2d 734, 660 N.E.2d 415 (1995). In that case there was an agreement concerning a proposed sublease. Oppenheimer, 636 N.Y.S.2d at 735, 660 N.E.2d at 416. The sublessee had furnished the sublessor plans for construction of a telephone communications linkage system on the premises, and the sublessor obligated itself to obtain the underlying landlord's written consent to that work and to deliver that written consent by a specified date. Id. at 735–36, 636 N.Y.S.2d 734, 660 N.E.2d at 416–17. On the specified date the sublessor telephoned the sublessee, advising that the underlying landlord had consented. Id. at 736, 636 N.Y.S.2d 734, 660 N.E.2d at 417. The sublessee refused to sign the proposed sublease. Id. The issue before the Court of Appeals of New York was whether the requirement for the sublessor to obtain written consent was a covenant, in which event non-performance would be subject to the doctrine of substantial performance, or whether that doctrine had no application because the provision was a condition. Id. at 735, 636 N.Y.S.2d 734, 660 N.E.2d at 416.

The agreement in Oppenheimer stated that if the sublessee "had not received the prime landlord's written consent by the agreed date, both the agreement and the sublease were to be deemed 'null and void and of no further force and effect,' and neither party was to have 'any rights against nor obligations to the other.' " Id. at 736, 636 N.Y.S.2d 734, 660 N.E.2d at 417. Another provision of the agreement stated that

---

4. Benjamin does not contend that the note was a negotiable instrument. It did not contain "an unconditional promise or order to pay a sum certain in money," N.Y.U.C.C. § 3–104(1)(b) (McKinney 1991), and it was not "payable to order or to bearer." Id. § 3–104(1)(d). In addition, the note was introduced by a legend stating that it "may not be transferred except in compliance with, or pursuant to an exemption from, applicable securities laws." Section 4.1 of the note repeats the same warning and adds the provision that "[a]ny transferee of this Note shall take this Note subject to the terms hereof, including, without limitation, the provisions relating to subordination and set off."

"the parties 'agree not to execute and exchange the Sublease unless and until ... the conditions set forth in [the paragraph requiring, inter alia, written consent] are timely satisfied.'" Id. The court held that this language created a condition. Id. at 737, 636 N.Y.S.2d 734, 660 N.E.2d at 418.

The court in Oppenheimer gave guidance for interpreting whether a provision is a condition:

> In determining whether a particular agreement makes an event a condition courts will interpret doubtful language as embodying a promise or constructive condition rather than an express condition. This interpretive preference is especially strong when a finding of express condition would increase the risk of forfeiture by the obligee (see, Restatement [Second] of Contracts § 227[1]).

* * *

In addition to illustrating language that undoubtedly creates a condition, Oppenheimer evidences that the Court of Appeals of New York will look to Restatement (Second) of Contracts § 227 (1981) (Restatement) for the preferred interpretation of language argued to create a condition, as well as to Restatement § 229, dealing with excusing the non-occurrence of a condition. [Citations omitted.] Here, the applicable section of the Restatement is § 227(2). In the language of that subsection, the duty to be performed is Benjamin's duty to pay the note, so that Benjamin is the "obligor;" New York Bronze is the "obligee;" and the asserted condition is the surrender of the note. Benjamin's position necessarily is that, as of the time of contract formation, surrender of the note was an event within the control of New York Bronze.

Where the above recited factors are present, the preferred interpretation is set forth in Restatement § 227(2), which reads:

> Unless the contract is of a type under which only one party generally undertakes duties, when it is doubtful whether
>
> (a) a duty is imposed on an obligee that an event occur, or
>
> (b) the event is made a condition of the obligor's duty, or
>
> (c) the event is made a condition of the obligor's duty and a duty is imposed on the obligee that the event occur,
>
> the first interpretation is preferred if the event is within the obligee's control.

Comment d states the rationale for the preferred interpretation as follows:

> The rule in Subsection (2) states a preference for an interpretation that merely imposes a duty on the obligee to do the act and does not make the doing of the act a condition of the obligor's duty. The preferred interpretation avoids the harsh results that might otherwise result from the non-occurrence of a condition and still gives adequate protection to the obligor under the rules ... relating to performances to be exchanged under an exchange of promises.

Under those rules ... the obligee's failure to perform his duty has, if it is material, the effect of the non-occurrence of a condition of the obligor's duty. Unless the agreement makes it clear that the event is required as a condition, it is fairer to apply these more flexible rules. The obligor will, in any case, have a remedy for breach.

Turning to the interpretation of the last sentence of Section 4.2 of the note we conclude, for the reasons hereinafter set forth, that it is "doubtful" that the parties intended to create a condition. Benjamin's interpretation rests entirely on the language "in order to receive payment." Neither in the context of the contract as a whole, nor within the terms themselves, is the creation of a condition so clear that it overcomes the preference for interpretation of the language as a covenant.

The introductory paragraph of the non-negotiable note contains the promise to pay $350,000 and expresses that that promise is "[s]ubject to Sections 2 and 3 below." The former deals with subordination and the latter is the agreement concerning set offs. Had the parties intended the promise to be subject to a condition found in Section 4.2, careful drafting would have included Section 4.2 in the introduction of the note.

Section 4.2 of the note specifies how and when payments "shall be made ... and shall be mailed." This is the language of covenants. No one could seriously maintain that, if Benjamin, in some immaterial fashion, did not comply with the provisions describing the payment checks and their mailing, then a payment received by New York Bronze could be kept by it without crediting the payment against the obligation. The principal clause of the last sentence in Section 4.2 ("The Noteholder shall be required to surrender this Note for cancellation....") similarly is the language of covenant. Thus, under Benjamin's position, the language, "in order to receive payment," must produce a substantially different legal result than do the other provisions of Section 4.2.

Under the New York cases, it would seem that more explicit language than that used is required in order to achieve that result. For example, the interpretation would be much more clear if the critical clause of the last sentence of Section 4.2 read: "and upon failure to surrender this Note [Benjamin's] obligation to pay any outstanding balance will terminate," or "be extinguished." Instead, the note uses the language, "in order to receive payment." The primary meaning of the verb "to receive" is "to take possession or delivery of," as of a gift or of a letter. Webster's Third New International Dictionary 1984 (1976). In the context of the last sentence of Section 4.2, "receive" carries a passive connotation as to the role of New York Bronze while the active role would be that of Benjamin in tendering payment in full of any outstanding balance. Interpreting Section 4.2 as promises to exchange performances is a far cry from interpreting it to provide that the failure to surrender the note causes New York Bronze to lose all rights to take an active role and enforce collection on the note through legal proceedings.

The obvious purpose of the last sentence of Section 4.2 is to protect Benjamin from the risk that the note will fall into the hands of a third party who will in some way force Benjamin to pay twice. If the critical language is interpreted as part of a covenant by New York Bronze, then Benjamin theoretically had a number of options to remedy the breach. Benjamin could take the position that the breach was substantial, thus excusing Benjamin from performance, but that result is not the situation here, as we explain below. Benjamin could demand and possibly obtain from New York Bronze proof satisfactory to Benjamin that Benjamin would not be required to pay twice. Benjamin could claim as damages for the breach the cost of a bond protecting it against double payment. Although the note is non-interest bearing, Benjamin could have utilized the breach by New York Bronze to oppose a claim for the discretionary allowance of interest on any unpaid and overdue balance on the note for the period from maturity until judgment. Further, if after having paid New York Bronze in full a third party claimed against Benjamin on the note, Benjamin could obtain damages from New York Bronze measured by the cost of defending the claim of the third party and demonstrating that payment had been made in full.

Whatever the effect of the critical language might be in an agreement involving a negotiable note, Benjamin's risk of being required to pay twice is *de minimis* in the instant matter because the note is non-negotiable. If we assume that Benjamin paid the full $350,000 without a surrender of the note, an assignee of New York Bronze could not be a holder in due course. That assignee would take the note subject to the defense of payment by Benjamin to New York Bronze.

Under these circumstances it is unlikely that the parties intended to create a condition entitling Benjamin to keep up to $200,000 of assets without paying the agreed consideration. Thus, we apply the preferred construction and hold that the last sentence of Section 4.2 of the note creates a covenant or contractual duty on the part of New York Bronze to surrender the note.

* * *

JUDGMENT REVERSED. * * *

THOS. J. DYER CO. v. BISHOP INTERNATIONAL ENGINEERING CO.

United States Court of Appeals, Sixth Circuit, 1962.
303 F.2d 655.

SHACKELFORD MILLER, JR., CHIEF JUDGE. Appellee, The Thos. J. Dyer Company, a subcontractor on the project hereinafter referred to, brought this action against the appellant, Bishop International Engineering Company, hereinafter referred to as Engineering Company, the general contractor, to recover the sum of $134,684.53 for materials and labor furnished by it in the construction of the project. The appellant, General Insurance Company of America, was also made a defendant as surety on the "Owner's Protective Bond," executed by the Engineering Company as principal.

The following facts were stipulated by the parties. Appellee is an Ohio corporation engaged in the plumbing contracting business. The

Engineering Company is a partnership engaged in the general contracting business. On or about August 19, 1958, the Engineering Company entered into a written contract with The Kentucky Jockey Club, Inc., hereinafter referred to as the Jockey Club, by the terms of which it agreed to provide labor and materials required in connection with the construction of a portion of a Horse Racing Plant, known as Latonia Race Track, upon premises belonging to the Jockey Club, situated in Boone County, Kentucky. That portion of the construction project covered by the contract was described as "Phase One."

On or about April 27, 1959, the appellee entered into a written subcontract with the Engineering Company, by the provisions of which it agreed to provide materials for and to install certain plumbing and utilities required in connection with the completion of the construction work to be performed by the Engineering Company, pursuant to its contract with the Jockey Club, for which it was to receive the sum of $115,000.00. Paragraph 3 of this subcontract reads as follows:

"3. The total price to be paid to Subcontractor shall be _____ Dollars ($115,000.00) lawful money of the United States, no part of which shall be due until five (5) days after Owner shall have paid Contractor therefor, provided however, that not more than _____ per cent (90%) thereof shall be due until thirty-five (35) days after the entire work to be performed and completed under said contract shall have been completed to the satisfaction of Owners, and provided further that Contractor may retain sufficient moneys to fully pay and discharge any and all liens, stop-notices, attachments, garnishments and executions. Nothing herein is to be construed as preventing Contractor from paying to the Subcontractor all or any part of said price at any time hereafter as an advance or otherwise."

The Engineering Company has provided all of the labor and material and has done all things necessary for the completion of the work required of it under the contract of August 19, 1958, and has received payment of the sum of $2,236,908.95, specified by the contract as the consideration to be paid to it for the work to be performed by it thereunder.

From time to time following the execution of the contract of August 19, 1958, the Engineering Company was called upon by the Jockey Club to provide labor, services and materials for the completion of various items of construction relating to the above mentioned Horse Racing Plant which had not been included within Phase One of the construction program of the Jockey Club. The Engineering Company has received compensation for certain portions of such additional labor, services and materials provided by it at the request of the Jockey Club but has not yet received payment for all of it.

* * *

Appellee has provided all the labor and materials and has done all things necessary for the completion of the work required of it under the subcontract, change orders, proposals and acceptances. Appellee completed its work as required on or before August 1, 1959, and the completed project was accepted by the owners on or about August 28, 1959.

The Engineering Company has not been paid by the Jockey Club for any work performed or material supplied by the appellee, other than that required pursuant to the terms of the original contract, dated August 19, 1958, between the Engineering Company and the Jockey Club.

The Engineering Company has paid to appellee for work performed and materials provided under the subcontract, changes orders, proposals and acceptances the sum of $119,133.06. After the payment of $119,133.06 there remained a balance due from the Engineering Company to the appellee of $108,519.11.

Under date of August 19, 1958, the appellant General Insurance Company of America executed a bond to the Jockey Club in the face amount of $2,086,908.75, upon which the Engineering Company was the principal.

On December 4, 1959, the Jockey Club filed in the United States District Court for the Western District of Kentucky, Louisville Division, a proceeding for its reorganization under Chapter X of the Federal Bankruptcy Act. That proceeding is still pending.

The Engineering Company in its defense to the action contends that by the provisions of paragraph 3 of its subcontract with the appellee no payment was due thereunder to the appellee until five days after the Jockey Club, owner of the construction project to which the contract related, had made payment to the Engineering Company; that the Jockey Club has paid to it on account of the work performed and the materials furnished by the appellee certain payments, all of which have been paid by the Engineering Company to the appellee; and that because it has not received any further payment from the Jockey Club, now being reorganized in bankruptcy, it has no obligation to make further payment to the appellee.

Following the filing of the stipulation of facts, the District Judge made findings of fact and conclusions of law, sustained appellee's motion for summary judgment, and entered judgment for the appellee in the principal amount of $108,519.11, together with $9,224.12 as interest due to the date of the judgment.

* * *

The parties devote considerable time to the question of whether paragraph 3 in appellee's subcontract is an enforceable provision of the contract, appellant contending that it is enforceable and appellee contending that it is not. We think this argument misconceives the real issue in the case. It appears to be settled law that contract provisions making certain obligations conditional or contingent upon the happening of a certain event are valid and enforceable. * * * But the question remains whether the contract provision relied upon creates such a conditional or contingent obligation. This presents a question of construction or interpretation of the contract provision, not a question of its validity. Lewis v. Tipton, 10 Ohio St. 88.

In construing the contract sued on in this case, the first question is whether paragraph 3 of the subcontract of April 27, 1959, is applicable not only to the original subcontract but also to the several supplemental contracts between the parties for work additional to that covered by the original subcontract.

Appellee argues in support of the judgment that paragraph 3 in the subcontract of April 27, 1959, was applicable only to the labor and material covered by that instrument, and the subsequent agreements for additional work by it, which work was not contemplated in the original general contract, or in the initial subcontract, constitute separate contracts which do not contain the provisions of paragraph 3. It contends that the defense relied upon under paragraph 3 of the initial subcontract is not applicable to the work performed under the supplemental contracts. This contention appears to be in accord with the general rule. Canister Co. v. Wood & Selick, 73 F.2d 312, 314, C.A.3rd; 17 C.J.S. Contracts §§ 331–336. The subsequent letter proposals and acceptances do not expressly state that they are subject to the provisions of the initial subcontract and each one contains the elements necessary to constitute a separate, independent contract. However, the fundamental question is one of intention to be determined from the language of the parties, the subject matter of the agreement and in the light of all the surrounding circumstances. * * *

We think it is clear that the two change orders of May 25, 1959, and June 9, 1959, are to be considered as part of the original subcontract, to which they specifically refer.

* * *

Accordingly, we come to the crucial issue in the case, namely, whether, as contended by the appellant, paragraph 3 of the subcontract is to be construed as a conditional promise to pay, enforceable only when and if the condition precedent has taken place which in the present case has not occurred, or, as contended by the appellee, it is to be construed as an unconditional promise to pay with the time of payment being postponed until the happening of a certain event, or for a reasonable period of time if it develops that such event does not take place.

Numerous decisions from various courts are cited by the parties in support of their respective contentions. We think that these cases state the basic rule and are examples of its application under the facts of the particular case being considered. For example, in Kentucky, where the contract herein involved was to be performed, the Court of Appeals of Kentucky held in Fox v. Buckingham, supra, 228 Ky. 176, 180–181, 14 S.W.2d 421, that the promise to pay was a conditional one, enforceable only when the condition precedent has taken place. In Mock v. Trustees of First Baptist Church of Newport, 252 Ky. 243, 67 S.W.2d 9, 94 A.L.R. 716, the same Court had before it the case of an architect who had been employed to prepare plans and specifications for a Sunday school building, the construction of which was indefinitely suspended because of unexpected construction costs and the church's financial limitations. In a suit by the architect for the unpaid balance of his fee the Trustees of the church contended that he had agreed to wait for the unpaid balance until such time as the church in its judgment and discretion was financially able and deemed it advisable to erect and complete the building. The Court held that such a promise to pay was not conditional upon the completion of the building, but should be construed to mean that payment was to be made within a reasonable time. * * * The Court of Appeals of Kentucky in making its ruling * * * quoted with approval from section 2100 of Page on Contracts as follows:

> "The time of performance is sometimes made to depend upon the doing of some specified act other than that which the parties to the contract agree to do or it is made to depend upon the happening of some event which the parties to the contract do not covenant to cause to happen. The tendency of the courts is to hold that unless the contract shows clearly that such an action is an express condition, the provision with reference to such act is inserted in order to fix the time of performance, but not to make the doing of such act or the happening of such event a condition precedent. If this is the intention of the parties, the fact that such act is not performed or that such event does not happen, does not discharge the contract, and the act which the parties agree to do upon the performance of such act or upon the happening of such event, is to be performed in at least a reasonable time. This principle has been applied to a promise to pay when the maker has finished a church then building; or to pay when a certain dispute is settled; or 'as soon as the crop can be sold or the money raised from any other source.' "

As pointed out in that statement of the basic rule, it is the intention of the parties which is the controlling factor in each particular case.

It is, of course, basic in the construction business, for the general contractor on a construction project of any magnitude to expect to be paid in full by the owner for the labor and material he puts into the project. He would not remain long in business unless such was his intention and such intention was accomplished. That is a fundamental concept of doing business with another. The solvency of the owner is a credit risk necessarily incurred by the general contractor, but various legal and contractual provisions, such as mechanics' liens and installment payments, are used to reduce this to a minimum. These evidence the intention of the parties that the contractor be paid even though the owner may ultimately become insolvent. This expectation and intention of being paid is even more pronounced in the case of a subcontractor whose contract is with the general contractor, not with the owner. In addition to his mechanic's lien, he is primarily interested in the solvency of the general contractor with whom he has contracted. He looks to him for payment. Normally and legally, the insolvency of the owner will not defeat the claim of the subcontractor against the general contractor. Accordingly, in order to transfer this normal credit risk incurred by the general contractor from the general contractor to the subcontractor, the contract between the general contractor and subcontractor should contain an express condition clearly showing that to be the intention of the parties. Section 2100, Page on Contracts, supra.

In the case before us we see no reason why the usual credit risk of the owner's insolvency assumed by the general contractor should be transferred from the general contractor to the subcontractor. It seems clear to us under the facts of this case that it was the intention of the parties that the subcontractor would be paid by the general contractor for the labor and materials put into the project. We believe that to be the normal construction of the relationship between the parties. If such was not the intention of the parties it could have been so expressed in unequivocal terms dealing with the possible insolvency of the owner. North American Graphite Corp. v. Allan, 87 U.S.App.D.C. 154, 184 F.2d 387, 390. Paragraph 3 of the subcontract does not refer to the possible insolvency of the owner. On the other hand, it deals with the amount, time and method of payment, which are essential provisions in every construction contract, without regard to possible insolvency. In our opinion, paragraph 3 of the subcontract is a reasonable provision designed to postpone payment for a reasonable period of time after the work was completed, during which the general contractor would be afforded the opportunity of procuring from the owner the funds necessary to pay the subcontractor. Stewart v. Herron, 77 Ohio St. 130, 149, 82 N.E. 956. To construe it as requiring the subcontractor to wait to be paid for an indefinite period of time until the general contractor has been paid by the owner, which may never occur, is to give to it an unreasonable construction which the parties did not intend at the time the subcontract was entered into. * * *

The judgment is affirmed.

J.J. SHANE, INC. v. AETNA CAS. & SURETY CO.

District Court of Appeal of Florida, Third District, 1998.
723 So.2d 302.

GREEN, JUDGE. On this appeal, the plaintiff/subcontractor appeals from an adverse final judgment and order taxing attorney's fees and costs entered pursuant to a jury verdict in favor of the general contractor. We reverse and remand with instructions that this case be dismissed without prejudice as being prematurely filed.

Appellant, J.J. Shane, Inc. ("Shane") was a subcontractor to the general contractor, appellee Recchi America, Inc. ("Recchi") during the construction of the Omni extension of the "People Mover" in downtown Miami. The construction project is owned by Metropolitan Dade County. Shane instituted this breach of contract action when Recchi failed to make complete payment for Shane's work on this project. The center of this dispute involves the interpretation of the following payment provision of the written subcontract between the parties.

ARTICLE XIII METHOD OF PAYMENT

a) Subcontractor is relying upon the financial responsibility of Owner in performing the Work. It is understood by Subcontractor that payment for the work is to be made from funds received from Owner by Contractor in respect to the Work.

Recchi maintains that under this provision, its obligation to pay Shane is clearly conditioned upon its receipt of payment from the county/owner. Since it is undisputed herein that Recchi has not been paid for the project by the county/owner and indeed is itself currently embroiled in litigation for such payment, Recchi maintains that its contractual obligation to pay Shane has not yet arisen. Shane, on the other hand, asserts that this payment provision is ambiguous and, as such, must be construed to require Recchi's payment within a reasonable period of time.

In most subcontract agreements, payment by the owner to the contractor ordinarily is not intended to be a condition precedent to the contractor's duty to pay the subcontractor "because small subcontractors, who must have payment for their work in order to remain in business, will not ordinarily assume the risk of the owner's failure to pay the general contractor." Peacock Constr. Co., Inc. v. Modern Air Conditioning, Inc., 353 So.2d 840, 842 (Fla.1977). However, the Peacock court recognized that subcontract agreements such as the one before us, may contain valid payment provisions which shift the risk of payment failure by the owner from the general contractor to the subcontractor. Id.; see also DEC Elec., Inc. v. Raphael Constr. Corp., 558 So.2d 427, 429 (Fla.1990); Pace Constr. Corp. v. OBS Co., Inc., 531 So.2d 737, 738 (Fla. 2d DCA 1988). "But in order to make such a shift the contract must unambiguously express that intention." Peacock, 353 So.2d at 842–43.

Here, we find the subject payment provision to plainly and unambiguously make payment by the county/owner a condition precedent to payment by the general contractor to the subcontractor herein, rather than simply fixing a reasonable time for payment as contended by the subcontractor. Thus, where the owner's non-payment to the general contractor is undisputed, this cause for payment by the subcontractor was prematurely filed. See Robert F. Wilson, Inc. v. Post–Tensioned Structures, Inc., 522 So.2d 79, 80 (Fla. 3d DCA 1988). Accordingly, we reverse the final judgment and the order awarding fees and costs with directions that this case be dismissed without prejudice.

HICKS v. BUSH

Court of Appeals of New York, 1962.
10 N.Y.2d 488, 225 N.Y.S.2d 34, 180 N.E.2d 425.

FULD, JUDGE. In this action for specific performance of a written agreement, we granted the plaintiff leave to appeal to consider whether the parol evidence rule was violated by the receipt of testimony tending to establish that the parties had orally agreed that the legal effectiveness of the written agreement should be subject to a stated condition precedent.

On July 10, 1956, the plaintiff Frederick Hicks, together with defendant Michael Congero and one Jack McGee, executed a written agreement with the individual defendants, members of defendant Clinton G. Bush Company, whereby the parties were to merge their various corporate interests into a single "holding" company in order to achieve more efficient operation and greater financial strength. The document recited, among other things, that the plaintiff would subscribe for some 425,000 shares of stock in the new holding corporation, known as Bush–Hicks Enterprises, Inc., and that the defendants comprising the Bush Company would subscribe for more than a million shares. The other parties to the agreement were to subscribe for a total of less than 50,000 shares. The principal consideration for the subscription was the transfer to the holding company of stock in the operating corporations which the several parties owned.

The written agreement provided expressly that the subscriptions for the stock in Bush–Hicks Enterprises were to be made "within five days after the date of this Agreement" and that, "If within twenty-five days after the date hereof Bush–Hicks shall have failed to accept any of said subscriptions delivered to it * * * then and in any such event the obligations of all of the parties hereto shall be terminated and cancelled." The subscriptions were promptly made and accepted and, although the plaintiff turned over the stock of his corporations, the defendants did not transfer the stock of their companies to Bush–Hicks Enterprises. In consequence, the plaintiff never received the Bush–Hicks stock as provided in the agreement and the merger never eventuated.

Alleging a breach of contract, the plaintiff brought this suit for specific performance and for an accounting. In their answer, the defendants urged, as an affirmative defense, that the written agreement was executed "upon a parol condition" that it "was not to operate" as a contract and that the contemplated merger was not "to become effective" until so-called "equity expansion funds", amounting to $672,500, were first procured. And, to support that allegation, the defendants upon the trial offered evidence of such an oral understanding. The court admitted the evidence, over the plaintiff's objection that it varied and contradicted the terms of the writing, and, finding that the oral condition asserted had actually been agreed on by the parties, rendered judgment in favor of the defendants.

A reading of the record unquestionably supports the decision of the courts below, that the parties, having concluded that $672,500 was essential to successful operation of the proposed merger, agreed that the entire merger deal was to be subject to the condition precedent that that sum be raised. Thus, one witness, the president of the defendant Bush Company, declared that everyone "understood" that the writing was not to become operative as a binding contract until the specified equity expansion funds were obtained. Indeed, his expressive and colorful testimony leaves no doubt as to the nature of the agreement arrived at: "I used the Chinese slang phrase of 'No tickie, no shirtie.' Let's get signed so we would be ready. I said, 'You all know what that means, that if we do not get the funds, this document [the written agreement] does not become operative * * *.' * * * There is only one understanding, verbal understanding that we have had. That speaks of 'Get the money or no deal.' "

The expansion capital of $672,500, which the parties hoped would be procured by December 31, 1956, was never raised.

The applicable law is clear, the relevant principles settled. Parol testimony is admissible to prove a condition precedent to the legal effectiveness of a written agreement (see Saltzman v. Barson, 239 N.Y. 332, 337, 146 N.E. 618, 619; Grannis v. Stevens, 216 N.Y. 583, 587, 111 N.E. 263, 265; Reynolds v. Robinson, 110 N.Y. 654, 18 N.E. 127; see, also, 4 Williston, Contracts [3d ed., 1961], § 634, p. 1021; 3 Corbin Contracts [1960 ed.], § 589, p. 530 et seq.), if the condition does not contradict the express terms of such written agreement. (See Fadex Foreign Trading Corp. v. Crown Steel Corp., 297 N.Y. 903, 79 N.E.2d 739, affg. 272 App.Div. 273, 274–276, 70 N.Y.S.2d 892, 893–894; see, also, Restatement, Contracts, § 241.) A certain disparity is inevitable, of course, whenever a written promise is, by oral agreement of the parties, made conditional upon an event not expressed in the writing. Quite obviously, though, the parol evidence rule does not bar proof of every orally established condition precedent, but only of those which in a real sense contradict the terms of the written agreement. (See, e.g., Illustration to Restatement, Contracts, § 241.) Upon the present appeal, our problem is to determine whether there is such a contradiction.

The Fadex case (297 N.Y. 903, 79 N.E.2d 739, supra) is illustrative. The plaintiff, seeking damages for nondelivery of certain goods, relied upon written agreements which specifically provided that the goods were "Ready now" and that the time of delivery was to be "Prompt" and "Within 4 to 6 weeks, if possible earlier". Despite these express recitals, plus the further explicit notation that no oral arrangement or modification was to be binding upon the parties, the defendant sought to show a contemporaneous oral agreement that the sales were conditioned upon its ability to obtain the goods within a month. In connection with a motion for partial summary judgment, this court decided that an oral condition precedent to the formation of a contract could be established when not contradictory of the written agreement itself, but concluded that the condition attempted to be proved by the defendant Crown Steel Corporation would, if ruled operative, actually annul the express terms of the writing.

The present case differs materially from Fadex. There is here no direct or explicit contradiction between the oral condition and the writing; in fact, the parol agreement deals with a matter on which the written agreement, as in some of the cases cited (10 N.Y.2d 491, 225 N.Y.S.2d 36, 180 N.E.2d 427, supra), is silent. The plaintiff, however, contends that, since the written agreement provides in terms that the obligations of the parties were to be terminated if the merged corporation failed to accept any of their stock subscriptions within 25 days, the additional oral condition—that the writing "was [not] to become operative" and that the merger was "not to become effective" until the expansion funds had been raised—is irreconcilable with the written agreement.

As already indicated, and analysis confirms it, the two conditions may stand side by side. The oral requirement that the writing was not to take effect as a contract until the equity expansion funds were obtained is simply a further condition—a condition added to that requiring the acceptance of stock subscriptions within 25 days—and not one which is contradictory. If both provisions had been contained in the written agreement, it is clear that the defendants would not have been under immediate legal duty to transfer the stock in their companies to Bush–Hicks Enterprises until both conditions had been fulfilled and satisfied. And it is equally clear that evidence of an oral condition is not to be excluded as contradictory or "inconsistent" merely because the written agreement contains other conditions precedent. (See, e.g., Hartford Fire Ins. Co. v. Wilson, 187 U.S. 467, 474, 23 S.Ct. 189, 47 L.Ed. 261; Ware v. Allen, 128 U.S. 590, 595–596, 9 S.Ct. 174, 32 L.Ed. 563; Liebling v. Florida Realty Inv. Corp., 5 Cir., 24 F.2d 688, 689; Golden v. Meier, 129 Wis. 14, 18, 107 N.W. 27; see, also, 3 Corbin, Contracts [1960 ed.], pp. 541–542.) As the Supreme Court wrote in the Hartford Fire Ins. Co. case (187 U.S. 467, 474, 23 S.Ct. 189, 192, supra), "If an instrument containing an absolute promise to pay may be conditionally delivered, it is difficult to perceive any good reason why an instrument containing a promise to pay upon a contingency may not likewise be conditionally delivered."

In short, the parties in the case before us intended that their respective rights and duties with respect to the contemplated transfers of stock in the operating companies to the holding company be subject to two conditions, each independent of the other—the acceptance of the stock subscription within a specified period and the procuring of expansion funds of $672,500. As the courts below found, the parties did not contemplate performance of the written agreement until such funds were first received. In other words, it was their desire and understanding that the merger was to be one of proposal only and that, even though the formal preliminary steps were to be taken, the writing was not to become operative as a contract or the merger effective until $672,500 was raised. It is certainly not improbable that parties contracting in these circumstances would make the asserted oral agreement; the condition precedent at hand is the sort of condition which parties would not be inclined to incorporate into a written agreement intended for public consumption. The challenged evidence was, therefore, admissible and, since there was ample proof attesting to the making of the oral agreement, the trial court was fully warranted in holding that no operative or binding contract ever came into existence.

The judgment appealed from should be affirmed, with costs.

EDMUND J. FLYNN CO. v. SCHLOSSER

District of Columbia Court of Appeals, 1970.
265 A.2d 599.

QUINN, ASSOCIATE JUDGE, Retired. This appeal arises out of an agreement to purchase a cooperative apartment. Appellee was the prospective purchaser and appellant the agent of the seller. Appellee attempted to revoke her "offer" before the time for performance. At trial, by stipulation of both parties, the issues were reduced to one legal question: What effect was to be given a condition contained in the written sales agreement? As stated by the trial court, the question was: "Is it a condition precedent to the existence of a binding contract to purchase the apartment or a condition precedent to the obligation immediately to perform the contract?" The relevant portion of the agreement is as follows:

> It is understood that Purchaser must be approved by the board of directors of the Cooperative, and the time hereinabove specified for full settlement shall be extended for the time necessary to receive the decision of said board of directors, provided said decision shall not have been received by said time appointed for settlement.

> This entire agreement is conditioned upon Purchaser's being approved for occupancy by the board of directors of the Cooperative, as hereinbefore set forth, and the accompanying application for such approval, executed by both Seller and Purchaser, is hereby made a part hereof as fully as though written herein. It is agreed by the parties hereto that the Agent shall promptly submit said application to the said board of directors. In the event approval of the Purchaser shall be denied by the said board of directors, then and in such event, the entire aforesaid deposit shall be returned to Purchaser promptly, and without any deduction therefrom whatsoever, and this agreement shall thereafter be of no further force or effect.

The sole question on this appeal is likewise the legal effect of this condition. The trial court found that the language in the writing was a condition precedent to the existence of a binding contract, and that the appellee was thus free to revoke her offer. We cannot agree.

The term "condition precedent" has led to much confusion in the law. Most of this confusion arises out of the so-called "dual usage" of the term; i.e., condition to the existence of a contract or condition to the duty to perform. In the case at bar, we are directly faced with the single issue of which use of the term is applicable.

When is a condition precedent a prerequisite to the existence of a contract? There is authority for the proposition that this use of the term is a common, often applied, and well established legal principle. An analysis of the case law, however, shows two specific areas where this use of the term has had a consistent application: (1) Where because of a "conditional acceptance" to an offer no mutual assent occurs and thus no contract arises, and (2) where the effect of a contract is conditional on its validation by some "superior" or "higher" authority, reflecting a limited power in an agent to bind a principal. The latter area consists almost entirely of cases in which a government or one of its agencies is one party to the contract.

Much of the confusion in this area of the law can be attributed to the somewhat unfortunate use of the term "condition precedent" when addressing the issue of the formation of a contract. The issue really is not whether a "condition" must occur before a contract comes into existence but whether the parties have mutually assented or agreed to make a binding contract. If there is such mutual assent, agreed on conditions clearly affect only the duty to perform. If no mutual agreement is ever reached, there is no contract: The "condition precedent" to the formation or existence of a contract is thus the mutual assent or agreement of the parties.

The initial issue in this case is: Did the parties mutually agree to the purchase and sale of this cooperative apartment? By their own written agreement, which is the entire evidence before us as to this question, the only possible answer is in the affirmative.[7] Thus, both parties are bound by the agreement and neither has the power to unilaterally revoke.

As stated previously, the other area where the existence of a contract has been held to be conditioned involves approval by an authority higher than one of the contracting parties. Most of these cases involve that area of the law dealing with government contracts. District of Columbia v. Singleton, D.C.Mun.App., 81 A.2d 335 (1951), aff'd, 91 U.S.App.D.C. 91, 198 F.2d 945 (1952), is such a case in this jurisdiction. There it was held that "the statute here involved should * * * be construed to make a contract over the specified limit, which lacks the Commissioners' approval, unenforceable against the District but binding on the other party." 81 A.2d at 337. We hold that the special rules embodied in government contracts law which cover approval by an authorized agent of the sovereign are not applicable in this case between private litigants.

The trial court, however, relied on the case of Detroit Football Co. v. Robinson, 186 F.Supp. 933 (E.D.La.1960), where a government contract was not involved. There the court held that the endorsement of the commissioner of the National Football League was a condition precedent to the formation of a contract between the parties. The agreement had been reduced to writing and the condition read: "This agreement shall become valid and binding upon each party hereto only when, as and if it shall be approved by the Commissioner." 186 F.Supp. at 935. Appellant urges that, as the language in the contract before us is virtually the same, the above law should be applied to this case. We do not agree for the following reasons.

---

7. We are not here faced with the problem of the admissibility of parol evidence to show that no contract was ever entered into. * * * Nor are we faced with the problem of the admissibility of parol evidence to show a failure of a condition precedent to the duty to perform under the contract, no such evidence having been introduced in this case. * * *

First, the circumstances and background of the *Robinson* case, the pre-merger "war" for talent between the National Football League and the American Football League, were quite foreign to the usual background in most contract cases. Second, and certainly not unrelated, the legal principles which eventually evolved from the pre-merger cases were not based on contract law but on principles of equity.[9] Both reasons are most persuasive for not following the "contract rule" set out in the *Robinson* case.

Thus, we hold that the parties to the contract mutually agreed on the purchase and sale of this cooperative apartment. The condition, approval by the board of directors of the cooperative, was also a result of the mutual agreement. Neither party was obligated to perform until the happening of the condition, but neither party could rightfully revoke or withdraw in the meantime. Both parties were bound by the agreement.[10] As this was the only issue presented both on appeal and at trial, the case is

Reversed with instructions to enter judgment for appellant.

Problems

7. A construction contract provided that the owner, a public housing authority, could issue change orders. If the change order resulted in extra work, the contractor was to provide timely notice of claim and documentation to the authority to "enable the Authority to verify whether allegedly extra work is in fact beyond the scope of the contract. . . ." More specifically, the contractor was to provide the authority with daily written statements of claim, documenting the number of workers and the amount of material employed in providing extra work. In the event the authority disputed the claim of extra work, certain procedures were outlined to be followed. The contract further provided that: "Failure to comply strictly with these requirements shall constitute a waiver of any claim for extra compensation or damages on account of the performance of such Work. . . ." The contractor claims that, although it did no comply with the daily reporting requirement, it had done about $1,000,000 of extra work, and that it had by correspondence notified the authority that it considered that certain items of work were extra. The public authority refuses to pay any part of the claimed extra

9. The *Robinson* case was affirmed in Detroit Football Co. v. Robinson, 283 F.2d 657 (5th Cir.1960), on the grounds that no abuse of discretion was shown in the trial court's denial of a preliminary injunction. In New York Football Giants, Inc. v. Los Angeles Chargers Football Club, Inc., 291 F.2d 471 (5th Cir.1961), the same court held that an action for specific performance or injunction should be dismissed on the basis of the clean hands doctrine. Contra, Houston Oilers, Inc. v. Neely, 361 F.2d 36 (10th Cir.1966), cert. denied, 385 U.S. 840, 87 S.Ct. 92, 17 L.Ed.2d 74 (1966) (the contract analysis in this case supports the holding in the case at bar). See also Los Angeles Rams Football Club v. Cannon, 185 F.Supp. 717 (S.D.Cal.1960); 3 Corbin on Contracts § 589, n. 63 (Supp.1964).

10. Appellee's argument that the effect of this holding is to enforce a contract which binds the appellee-purchaser, but not the seller is without merit. The seller cannot withdraw or, for example, sell the apartment to another with impunity. Wetzel v. DeGroot, D.C.Mun.App., 86 A.2d 737 (1952), is not to the contrary. A valid second sale could be made, but it would be conditional on a failure of the condition precedent to the duty to perform in the first sale.

work. In an action by the contractor, the public authority moved to dismiss the complaint. Should the motion be granted?

8. Plaintiff alleges that defendant agreed to sell him a lot and to construct a residence and to landscape the lot and that "it was understood" that the lake on which the lot fronted would be "cleaned out by a named third party and that, when the lake had been lowered by said third party, the defendant would install a sand beach." The plaintiff promised to pay $50,000 when the house was completed. Plaintiff did pay. Later he sues, alleging that defendant failed to clean out the lake and cause it to be lowered and to install the sand beach. Is a cause of action stated?

9. The plaintiff and defendant entered into a contract for the sale and purchase of 30 tons of casein. The contract contained the clause: "Advice of shipment to be made by cable immediately goods are despatched." The goods were shipped on time by plaintiff but no notice of shipment was given to defendant. Tender of the shipment was refused by defendant. The clause in question had been included in the contract upon the demand of the defendant. Does the plaintiff have a cause of action against defendant for breach of contract?

10. S entered into a contract with B to build a yarn-spinning mill for B. The contract provided the standards that had to be met before performance would be deemed completed. The work was not accepted because the machinery supplied by S lacked the capacity to produce the quantity and quality of yarn described in the contract. The contract was ambiguous on the issue of whether S promised to meet these standards. B asserts a claim for damages for breach of contract. S contends that B is entitled only to withhold the unpaid portion of the contract price. Who is right?

11. Vendee entered into a written agreement with Vendor for the purchase and sale of a specific house on specified terms and conditions. The agreement stated: "This contract is contingent upon buyer being able to obtain mortgage loan in the amount of $50,000." (Further terms and conditions of the prospective loan were detailed.) Vendor seeks a declaratory judgment that the alleged contract is void as the purchaser's promise is illusory. The purchaser, he argues, can effectively defeat the "contract" by failing to seek out mortgage financing. What result?

12. In a sale of a steamboat, there is the following clause: "And it is understood and agreed that this sale is upon this express condition that said steamboat or vessel is not within 10 years from the first day of 1867 to be run upon any routes of travel of the State of California or the Columbia River or its tributaries." Plaintiff seller brings an action for damages for breach of contract alleging that defendant violated the aforesaid terms of the contract. What result?

13. The plaintiff agreed to sell its paper mill to the defendant for an agreed price which was to be paid in four annual installments. Payment was to be in paper. The plaintiff also agreed to instruct defendant in the art of manufacturing paper. At the trial the plaintiff-seller proved the agreement and the delivery of possession of the mill, and nonpayment, and then rested. Defendant did not offer any evidence. What result? Would the result be different if payment was to be in money instead of in paper?

14. Plaintiff and defendant agreed to merge their corporate interests into a new entity. Plaintiff deposited shares of stock in accordance with the written agreement. Plaintiff seeks restitution of these shares, claiming there was an express oral condition that the shares would be returned if adequate financing for the new entity was not obtained and that adequate financing had not be received. Is evidence of this alleged oral condition admissible?

SECTION 3. CONSTRUCTIVE CONDITIONS

———

(Calamari & Perillo 5th §§ 11.16—11.19 and 11.21)

STEWART v. NEWBURY

Court of Appeals of New York, 1917.
220 N.Y. 379, 115 N.E. 984.

Action by Alexander Stewart against Herbert A. Newbury and others, doing business under the firm name and style of the Newbury Manufacturing Company. From a judgment of the Appellate Division (163 App.Div. 868, 147 N.Y.Supp. 1144) affirming a judgment for plaintiff, defendants appeal. Reversed, and new trial ordered.

CRANE, J. The defendants are partners in the pipe fitting business under the name of Newbury Manufacturing Company. The plaintiff is a contractor and builder residing at Tuxedo, N.Y.

The parties had the following correspondence about the erection for the defendants of a concrete mill building at Monroe, N.Y.:

"Alexander Stewart,

"Contractor and Builder,

"Tuxedo, N.Y., July 18, 1911

"Newbury Mfg. Company, Monroe, N.Y.:

"Gentlemen: With reference to the proposed work on the new foundry building I had hoped to be able to get up and see you this afternoon, but find that impossible and am, in consequence, sending you these prices, which I trust you will find satisfactory.

"I will agree to do all excavation work required at sixty-five ($.65) cents per cubic yard.

"I will put in the concrete work, furnishing labor and forms only, at two and 05–100 ($2.05) dollars per cubic yard.

"I will furnish labor to put in reenforcing at four ($4.00) dollars per ton.

"I will furnish labor only to set all window and door frames, window sash and doors, including the setting of hardware for one hundred twelve ($112) dollars. As alternative I would be willing to do any or all of the above work for cost plus 10 per cent., furnishing you with first class mechanics and giving the work considerable of my personal time.

"Hoping to hear favorably from you in this regard, I am,

"Respectfully yours,

"[Signed] Alexander Stewart"

"The Newbury Mfg. Co.,

"Steam Fittings, Grey Iron Castings,
"Skylight Opening Apparatus,"

"Monroe, N.Y.

"Telephone Connection. Monroe, N.Y., July 22, 1911.

"Alexander Stewart, Tuxedo Park, N.Y.:

"Dear Sir: Confirming the telephone conversation of this morning we accept your bid of July the 18th to do the concrete work on our new building. We trust that you will be able to get at this the early part of next week.

"Yours truly,

"The Newbury Mfg. Co.,

"H.A. Newbury"

Nothing was said in writing about the time or manner of payment. The plaintiff, however, claims that after sending his letter, and before receiving that of the defendant, he had a telephone communication with Mr. Newbury and said: "I will expect my payments in the usual manner," and Newbury said, "All right, we have got the money to pay for the building." This conversation over the telephone was denied by the defendants. The custom, the plaintiff testified, was to pay 85 per cent. every 30 days or at the end of each month, 15 per cent. being retained till the work was completed.

In July the plaintiff commenced work and continued until September 29th, at which time he had progressed with the construction as far as the first floor. He then sent a bill for the work done up to that date for $896.35. The defendants refused to pay the bill and work was discontinued. The plaintiff claims that the defendants refused to permit him to perform the rest of his contract, they insisting that the work already done was not in accordance with the specifications. The defendants claimed upon the trial that the plaintiff voluntarily abandoned the work after their refusal to pay his bill.

On October 5, 1911, the defendants wrote the plaintiff a letter containing the following:

"Notwithstanding you promised to let us know on Monday whether you would complete the job or throw up the contract, you have not up to this time advised us of your intention. * * * Under the circumstances, we are compelled to accept your action as being an abandonment of your contract and of every effort upon your part to complete your work on our building. As you know, the bill which you sent us and which we declined to pay is not correct, either in items or amount, nor is there anything due you under our contract as we understand it until you have completed your work on our building."

To this letter the plaintiff replied the following day. In it he makes no reference to the telephone communication agreeing, as he testified, to make "the usual payments," but does say this:

"There is nothing in our agreement which says that I shall wait until the job is completed before any payment is due, nor can this be reasonably implied. * * * As to having given you positive date as to when I should let you know what I proposed doing, I did not do so; on the contrary, I told you that I would not tell you positively what I would do until I had visited the job, and I promised that I would do this at my earliest convenience and up to the present time I have been unable to get up there."

The defendant Herbert Newbury testified that the plaintiff "ran away and left the whole thing." And the defendant F.A. Newbury testified that he was told by Mr. Stewart's man that Stewart was going to abandon the job; that he thereupon telephoned Mr. Stewart, who replied that he would let him know about it the next day, but did not.

In this action, which is brought to recover the amount of the bill presented, as the agreed price and $95.68 damages for breach of contract, the plaintiff had a verdict for the amount stated in the bill, but not for the other damages claimed, and the judgment entered thereon has been affirmed by the Appellate Division.

The appeal to us is upon exceptions to the judge's charge. The court charged the jury as follows:

"Plaintiff says that he was excused from completely performing the contract by the defendants' unreasonable failure to pay him for the work he had done during the months of August and September. * * * Was it understood that the payments were to be made monthly? If it was not so understood, the defendants' only obligation was to make payments at reasonable periods, in view of the character of the work, the amount of work being done, and the value of it. In other words, if there was no agreement between the parties respecting the payments, the defendants' obligation was to make payments at reasonable times. * * * But whether there was such an agreement or not, you may consider whether it was reasonable or unreasonable for him to exact a payment at that time and in that amount."

The court further said, in reply to a request to charge:

"I will say in that connection, if there was no agreement respecting the time of payment, and if there was no custom that was understood by both parties, and with respect to which they made the contract, then the plaintiff was entitled to payments at reasonable times."

The defendants' counsel thereupon made the following request, which was refused:

"I ask your honor to instruct the jury that, if the circumstances existed as your honor stated in your last instruction, then the plaintiff was not entitled to any payment until the contract was completed."

The jury was plainly told that if there were no agreement as to payments, yet the plaintiff would be entitled to part payment at reasonable times as the work progressed, and if such payments were refused he could abandon the work and recover the amount due for the work performed.

This is not the law. Counsel for the plaintiff omits to call our attention to any authority sustaining such a proposition and our search reveals none. In fact, the law is very well settled to the contrary. This was an entire contract. Ming v. Corbin, 142 N.Y. 334, 340, 341, 37 N.E. 105. Where a contract is made to perform work and no agreement is made as to payment, the work must be substantially performed before payment can be demanded. * * *

The judgment should be reversed, and a new trial ordered, costs to abide the event.

OLIVER WENDELL HOLMES, JR., THE COMMON LAW (1881)

p. 337

Suppose A promises B to do a day's work for two dollars, and B promises A to pay two dollars for a day's work. There the two promises cannot be performed at the same time. The work will take all day, the payment half a minute. How are you to decide which is to be done first, that is to say, which promise is dependent upon performance of the other side? It is only by reference to the habits of the community and to convenience. It is not enough to say that on the principle of equivalency a man is not presumed to intend to pay for a thing until he has it. The work is payment for the money, as much as the money for the work, and one must be paid for in advance. The question is, why, if one man is not presumed to intend to pay money until he has money's worth, the other is presumed to intend to give money's worth before he has money. An answer cannot be obtained from any general theory. The fact that employers, as a class, can be trusted for wages more safely than the employed for their labor, that the employers have had the power and have been the law-makers, or other considerations, it matters not what, have determined that the work is to be done first. But the grounds of decision are purely practical, and can never be elicited from grammar or from logic.

MONROE STREET PROPERTIES, INC. v. CARPENTER

United States Court of Appeals, Ninth Circuit, 1969.
407 F.2d 379.

HUFSTEDLER, CIRCUIT JUDGE. Appellant, Monroe Street Properties, Inc. ("Monroe"), appeals from a judgment in favor of the defendant Carpenter entered after Carpenter's motion for a summary judgment was granted. Carpenter is a party in his capacity as a trustee for Western Equities, Inc. ("Western"). Federal jurisdiction is based upon diversity of citizenship.

Monroe's action is for claimed breach of a written contract between Monroe and Western in which Western agreed to buy from Monroe ten insured first mortgages and notes having a face value of $1,250,000 in exchange for $1,000,000 worth of Western's common stock. The District Court granted summary judgment on the ground that the uncontroverted facts showed that Monroe neither performed nor tendered performance on its side and, therefore, Western was not in breach of contract. Monroe contends that there was a genuine issue of material fact within the meaning of Rule 56 of the Federal Rules of Civil Procedure: Could Monroe have performed its agreement by delivering clear insured title to the first mortgages during the life of the contract? We reject Monroe's contention and affirm the judgment.

The following facts are undisputed. On March 27, 1962, Western submitted its written offer to Monroe to buy the ten first mortgages and notes. Monroe promptly accepted the offer. Western's offer was expressly subject to "verification by Union Title Company that the ten first mortgages * * * are valid first mortgages." The offer further provided that Monroe would secure a policy of title insurance at its expense, would take the Western stock "as investment stock without plans for redistribution," and would execute voting proxies for the stock in favor of the Executive Committee of Western for three years. Western agreed to have the stock listed on the American Stock Exchange and to seek with due diligence registration of the stock with the Securities and Exchange Commission.

Pursuant to the contract the parties opened an escrow with Union Title Company on March 30, 1962. The escrow agreement provided that the terms and conditions of the agreement were to be complied with "on or before the date upon which [Western] stock has been listed on the American Stock Exchange, and delivered to Union Title Company." The Western stock was listed on the American Stock Exchange sometime before June 29, 1962, although the precise date of the listing is not clearly stated in the affidavits filed in connection with the motion for summary judgment. Monroe never deposited into escrow ten valid first mortgages or the policy of title, and Western never deposited its stock. Monroe did deposit the mortgage instruments in the escrow, but a preliminary title report received by Western on May 7, 1962, revealed that the properties subject to the ten mortgages were also subject to heavy prior encumbrances. After Monroe deposited those instruments in escrow, Monroe sent a demand to Western to deposit the stock. Western did not comply with the demand. Nothing further was done by either of the parties to perform the agreement and Monroe brought this action in October 1966.

According to the facts presented by Monroe in its own affidavits, which are uncontradicted in this respect by Western's affidavits, the only means by which Monroe could have delivered clear title to the first mortgages and could have obtained the policy of title insurance was to hypothecate Western stock to raise the money to pay off the prior encumbrances. Monroe had no ability or means to perform its part of the agreement unless Western deposited its stock in escrow before Monroe performed.

The District Court correctly decided that Monroe never made an adequate tender of its own performance. Monroe's duty to deposit the insured first mortgages and Western's duty to deposit its stock were concurrent conditions. (Wilhorn Builders, Inc. v. Cortaro Management Co. (1957), 82 Ariz. 48, 308 P.2d 251; Groobman v. Kirk (1958), 159 Cal.App.2d 117, 323 P.2d 867.) Neither party could place the other in breach for failure to perform without a tender of its own performance. "Tender" as used in this connection means " 'a readiness and willingness to perform in case of the *concurrent* performance by the other party, with present ability to do so, and notice to the other party of such readiness.' " (Emphasis added. 6 Williston, Contracts (3d ed. 1962) § 833, p. 105.) Monroe's offer to perform its concurrent condition upon condition that Western perform first was not an adequate tender and could not be relied upon by Monroe to place Western in breach of contract.[1]

The judgment is affirmed.

JACOB & YOUNGS, INC. v. KENT

Court of Appeals of New York, 1921.
230 N.Y. 239, 129 N.E. 889.

CARDOZO, J. The plaintiff built a country residence for the defendant at a cost of upwards of $77,000, and now sues to recover a balance of $3,483.46, remaining unpaid. The work of construction ceased in June, 1914, and the defendant then began to occupy the dwelling. There was no complaint of defective performance until March, 1915. One of the specifications for the plumbing work provides that—

"All wrought-iron pipe must be well galvanized, lap welded pipe of the grade known as 'standard pipe' of Reading manufacture."

The defendant learned in March, 1915, that some of the pipe, instead of being made in Reading, was the product of other factories. The plaintiff was accordingly directed by the architect to do the work anew. The plumbing was then encased within the walls except in a few places where it had to be exposed. Obedience to the order meant more than the substitution of other pipe. It meant the demolition at great expense of substantial parts of the completed structure. The plaintiff left the work untouched, and asked for a certificate that the final payment was due. Refusal of the certificate was followed by this suit.

The evidence sustains a finding that the omission of the prescribed brand of pipe was neither fraudulent nor willful. It was the result of the oversight and inattention of the plaintiff's subcontractor. Reading pipe is

---

1. The cases cited by Monroe do not assist it. The cases support the principle that a vendor's failure to have title to property, which is the subject of the sale, before the vendor's performance is due, is not a breach of contract by the vendor. [Citations omitted]. Monroe's problem is not to avoid a charge based on breach attributed to it, but to establish a breach by Western.

distinguished from Cohoes pipe and other brands only by the name of the manufacturer stamped upon it at intervals of between six and seven feet. Even the defendant's architect, though he inspected the pipe upon arrival, failed to notice the discrepancy. The plaintiff tried to show that the brands installed, though made by other manufacturers, were the same in quality, in appearance, in market value, and in cost as the brand stated in the contract—that they were, indeed, the same thing, though manufactured in another place. The evidence was excluded, and a verdict directed for the defendant. The Appellate Division reversed, and granted a new trial.

We think the evidence, if admitted, would have supplied some basis for the inference that the defect was insignificant in its relation to the project. The courts never say that one who makes a contract fills the measure of his duty by less than full performance. They do say, however, that an omission, both trivial and innocent, will sometimes be atoned for by allowance of the resulting damage, and will not always be the breach of a condition to be followed by a forfeiture. Spence v. Ham, 163 N.Y. 220, 57 N.E. 412, 51 L.R.A. 238; Woodward v. Fuller, 80 N.Y. 312; Glacius v. Black, 67 N.Y. 563, 566; Bowen v. Kimbell, 203 Mass. 364, 370, 89 N.E. 542, 133 Am.St.Rep. 302. The distinction is akin to that between dependent and independent promises, or between promises and conditions. Anson on Contracts (Corbin's Ed.) § 367; 2 Williston on Contracts, § 842. Some promises are so plainly independent that they can never by fair construction be conditions of one another. Rosenthal Paper Co. v. Nat. Folding Box & Paper Co., 226 N.Y. 313, 123 N.E. 766; Bogardus v. N.Y. Life Ins. Co., 101 N.Y. 328, 4 N.E. 522. Others are so plainly dependent that they must always be conditions. Others, though dependent and thus conditions when there is departure in point of substance, will be viewed as independent and collateral when the departure is insignificant. 2 Williston on Contracts, §§ 841, 842; Eastern Forge Co. v. Corbin, 182 Mass. 590, 592, 66 N.E. 419; Robinson v. Mollett, L.R., 7 Eng. & Ir.App. 802, 814; Miller v. Benjamin, 142 N.Y. 613, 37 N.E. 631. Considerations partly of justice and partly of presumable intention are to tell us whether this or that promise shall be placed in one class or in another. The simple and the uniform will call for different remedies from the multifarious and the intricate. The margin of departure within the range of normal expectation upon a sale of common chattels will vary from the margin to be expected upon a contract for the construction of a mansion or a "skyscraper." There will be harshness sometimes and oppression in the implication of a condition when the thing upon which labor has been expended is incapable of surrender because united to the land, and equity and reason in the implication of a like condition when the subject-matter, if defective, is in shape to be returned. From the conclusion that promises may not be treated as dependent to the extent of their uttermost minutiae without a sacrifice of justice, the progress is a short one to the conclusion that they may not be so treated without a perversion of intention. Intention not otherwise revealed may be presumed to hold in contemplation the reasonable and probable. If something else is in view, it must not be left to implication. There will be no assumption of a purpose to visit venial faults with oppressive retribution.

Those who think more of symmetry and logic in the development of legal rules than of practical adaptation to the attainment of a just result will be troubled by a classification where the lines of division are so wavering and blurred. Something, doubtless, may be said on the score of consistency and certainty in favor of a stricter standard. The courts have balanced such considerations against those of equity and fairness, and found the latter to be the weightier. The decisions in this state commit us to the liberal view, which is making its way, nowadays, in jurisdictions slow to welcome it. Dakin & Co. v. Lee, 1916, 1 K.B. 566, 579. Where the line is to be drawn between the important and the trivial cannot be settled by a formula. "In the nature of the case precise boundaries are impossible." 2 Williston on Contracts, § 841. The same omission may take on one aspect or another according to its setting. Substitution of equivalents may not have the same significance in fields of art on the one side and in those of mere utility on the other. Nowhere will change be tolerated, however, if it is so dominant or pervasive as in any real or substantial measure to frustrate the purpose of the contract. Crouch v. Gutmann, 134 N.Y. 45, 51, 31 N.E. 271, 30 Am.St.Rep. 608. There is no general license to install whatever, in the builder's judgment, may be regarded as "just as good." Easthampton L. & C. Co., Ltd. v. Worthington, 186 N.Y. 407, 412, 79 N.E. 323. The question is one of degree, to be answered, if there is doubt, by the triers of the facts (Crouch v. Gutmann; Woodward v. Fuller, supra), and, if the inferences are certain, by the judges of the law (Easthampton L. & C. Co., Ltd. v. Worthington, supra). We must weigh the purpose to be served, the desire to be gratified, the excuse for deviation from the letter, the cruelty of enforced adherence. Then only can we tell whether literal fulfillment is to be implied by law as a condition. This is not to say that the parties are not free by apt and certain words to effectuate a purpose that performance of every term shall be a condition of recovery. That question is not here. This is merely to say that the law will be slow to impute the purpose, in the silence of the parties, where the significance of the default is grievously out of proportion to the oppression of the forfeiture. The willful transgressor must accept the penalty of his transgression. Schultze v. Goodstein, 180 N.Y. 248, 251, 73 N.E. 21; Desmond–Dunne Co. v. Friedman–Doscher Co., 162 N.Y. 486, 490, 56 N.E. 995. For him there is no occasion to mitigate the rigor of implied conditions. The transgressor whose default is unintentional and trivial may hope for mercy if he will offer atonement for his wrong. Spence v. Ham, supra.

In the circumstances of this case, we think the measure of the allowance is not the cost of replacement, which would be great, but the difference in value, which would be either nominal or nothing. Some of the exposed sections might perhaps have been replaced at moderate expense. The defendant did not limit his demand to them, but treated the plumbing as a unit to be corrected from cellar to roof. In point of fact, the plaintiff never reached the stage at which evidence of the extent of the allowance became necessary. The trial court had excluded evidence that the defect was unsubstantial, and in view of that ruling there was no occasion for the plaintiff to go farther with an offer of proof. We think, however, that the offer, if it had been made, would not of necessity have been defective because directed to difference in value. It is true that in most cases the cost of replacement is the measure. Spence v. Ham, supra. The owner is entitled to the money which will permit him to complete, unless the cost of completion is grossly and unfairly out of proportion to the good to be attained. When that is true, the measure is the difference in value. Specifications call, let us say, for a foundation built of granite quarried in Vermont. On the completion of the building, the owner learns that through the blunder of a subcontractor part of the foundation has been built of granite of the same quality quarried in New Hampshire. The measure of allowance is not the cost of reconstruction. "There may be omissions of that which could not afterwards be supplied exactly as called for by the contract without taking down the building to its foundations, and at the same time the omission may not affect the value of the building for use or otherwise, except so slightly as to be hardly appreciable." Handy v. Bliss, 204 Mass. 513, 519, 90 N.E. 864, 134 Am.St.Rep. 673. Cf. Foeller v. Heintz, 137 Wis. 169, 178, 118 N.W. 543, 24 L.R.A.,N.S., 327; Oberlies v. Bullinger, 132 N.Y. 598, 601, 30 N.E. 999; 2 Williston on Contracts, § 805, p. 1541. The rule that gives a remedy in cases of substantial performance with compensation for defects of trivial or inappreciable importance has been developed by the courts as an instrument of justice. The measure of the allowance must be shaped to the same end.

The order should be affirmed, and judgment absolute directed in favor of the plaintiff upon the stipulation, with costs in all courts.

McLAUGHLIN, J. I dissent. The plaintiff did not perform its contract. Its failure to do so was either intentional or due to gross neglect which, under the uncontradicted facts, amounted to the same thing, nor did it make any proof of the cost of compliance, where compliance was possible.

* * *

I am of the opinion the trial court was right in directing a verdict for the defendant. The plaintiff agreed that all the pipe used should be of the Reading Manufacturing Company. Only about two-fifths of it, so far as appears, was of that kind. If more were used, then the burden of proving that fact was upon the plaintiff, which it could easily have done, since it knew where the pipe was obtained. The question of substantial performance of a contract of the character of the one under consideration depends in no small degree upon the good faith of the contractor. If the plaintiff had intended to, and had, complied with the terms of the contract except as to minor omissions, due to inadvertence, then he might be allowed to recover the contract price, less the amount necessary to fully compensate the defendant for damages caused by such omissions.

Woodward v. Fuller, 80 N.Y. 312; Nolan v. Whitney, 88 N.Y. 648. But that is not this case. It installed between 2,000 and 2,500 feet of pipe, of which only 1,000 feet at most complied with the contract. No explanation was given why pipe called for by the contract was not used, nor that any effort made to show what it would cost to remove the pipe of other manufacturers and install that of the Reading Manufacturing Company. The defendant had a right to contract for what he wanted. He had a right before making payment to get what the contract called for. It is no answer to this suggestion to say that the pipe put in was just as good as that made by the Reading Manufacturing Company, or that the difference in value between such pipe and the pipe made by the Reading Manufacturing Company would be either "nominal or nothing." Defendant contracted for pipe made by the Reading Manufacturing Company. What his reason was for requiring this kind of pipe is of no importance. He wanted that and was entitled to it. It may have been a mere whim on his part, but even so, he had a right to this kind of pipe, regardless of whether some other kind, according to the opinion of the contractor or experts, would have been "just as good, better, or done just as well." He agreed to pay only upon condition that the pipe installed were made by that company and he ought not to be compelled to pay unless that condition be performed. The rule, therefore, of substantial performance, with damages for unsubstantial omissions, has no application.

* * *

HISCOCK, CH. J., HOGAN and CRANE, JJ., concur with CARDOZO, J.; POUND and ANDREWS, JJ. concur with MCLAUGHLIN, J.

Order affirmed, etc.

JACOB & YOUNGS, INC. v. KENT

Court of Appeals of New York, 1921.
230 N.Y. 656, 130 N.E. 933.

On motion for reargument. Motion denied.

PER CURIAM. The court did not overlook the specification which provides that defective work shall be replaced. The promise to replace, like the promise to install, is to be viewed, not as a condition, but as independent and collateral, when the defect is trivial and innocent. The law does not nullify the covenant, but restricts the remedy to damages.

Suppose that, under protest, Jacob & Youngs had done as the architect ordered. Would plaintiff have a right to compensation for the extra work done? [Ed.]

VRT, INC. v. DUTTON–LAINSON

Supreme Court of Nebraska, 1995.
247 Neb. 845, 530 N.W.2d 619.

CAPORALE, JUSTICE. The plaintiff-appellee seller, VRT, Inc., formerly known as Sanitas, Inc., sought a judgment declaring its right to past and future royalties under a provision within a purchase and sale contract. VRT alleged that the defendant-appellant buyer, Dutton–Lainson Company, breached its contract with VRT by failing to pay VRT royalties contemplated under the royalty provision. The district court ruled that Dutton–Lainson was obligated to pay both past-due and future royalties as provided in the contract. * * * For the reasons hereinafter set forth, we now reverse the judgment of the district court and remand the cause for dismissal.

Sanitas was formed to manufacture, market, and distribute James Vanderheiden's invention, which improved devices used in hospitals and nursing homes to lift and move patients, hereinafter referred to as the patient care equipment.

After retaining an attorney to file a patent application on the patient care equipment, Sanitas sought out a manufacturer. Having been told by Sanitas that a patent application on the patient care equipment had been filed and having been assured by its own patent attorney that there was good reason to expect that a patent would issue, Dutton–Lainson and Sanitas executed a contract whereunder Sanitas sold and Dutton–Lainson purchased those Sanitas assets which related to the patient care equipment. * * *

* * *

The contract further requires Sanitas to deliver to Dutton–Lainson at the closing "[s]pecific assignments to the assets described . . . above as shall be reasonably required by Dutton–Lainson."

At the closing, Sanitas delivered to Dutton–Lainson a document labeled "BILL OF SALE AND ASSIGNMENT," assigning to Dutton–Lainson all of its "current inventions, blueprints, drawings, plans, specifications, procedures and confidential information; all vendor and sales information including customer lists and other marketing information; and the name Sanitas, Inc. and any other related or similar trade name relating to the production and marketing of Sanitas, Inc.'s Patient Care Equipment." Sanitas also delivered documents purporting to assign to Dutton–Lainson the patent application and Sanitas' interest in the invention disclosed therein. Sanitas thereafter changed its name to VRT, Inc. Although the contract refers to patents and applications for patents, there was but one application and it referred to the patent being sought. There was no other patent. Dutton–Lainson produced the patient care equipment and sold it with some modifications to the invention; part of the invention was not being used at all because the design was unstable.

It turns out that Sanitas' attorney had not filed the patent application when he represented that he had and did not file it until after the parties executed the contract. It was stipulated that because of the late filing, a patent could not issue. As a result, VRT filed an action for professional negligence against its attorney, claiming that the attorney had been negligent in failing to file the patent application, in concealing his failure, and in providing false information. VRT further claimed that as a result of those actions, it was forced to incur substantial legal fees to enforce the royalty contract against Dutton–Lainson and sought recovery from its attorney for the loss of royalties beyond the 10th year. In addition, VRT claimed its future royalty payments would be reduced because Dutton–Lainson would not have the exclusive right to manufacture and market the patient care equipment. VRT and its attorney ultimately settled the action.

To successfully bring an action on a contract, a plaintiff must first establish that the plaintiff substantially performed the plaintiff's obligations under the contract. See, ADC–I, Ltd. v. Pan American Fuels, 247 Neb. 71, 525 N.W.2d 190 (1994); First Data Resources, Inc. v. Omaha Steaks Int., Inc., 209 Neb. 327, 307 N.W.2d 790 (1981). To establish substantial performance under a contract, any deviations from the contract must be relatively minor and unimportant. Lange Indus. v. Hallam Grain Co., 244 Neb. 465, 507 N.W.2d 465 (1993). If there is substantial performance, a contract action may be maintained but without prejudice to any showing of damage on the part of the defendant for failure to receive full and complete performance. Church of the Holy Spirit v. Bevco, Inc., 215 Neb. 299, 338 N.W.2d 601 (1983).

* * *

The relationship between attorney and client is one of agency. Spier v. Thomas, 131 Neb. 579, 269 N.W. 61 (1936). [Citations omitted]. Therefore, the general agency rules of law apply to the relation of attorney-client.

Consequently, the omissions and commissions of an attorney are to be regarded as the acts of the client whom the attorney represents, and the attorney's neglect is equivalent to the neglect of the client. [Citations omitted]. Moreover, a principal holding out an agent as having authority to represent the principal and thereby asserting or impliedly admitting that the agent is worthy of trust and confidence is bound by all the agent's acts within the apparent scope of the employment. Hence, the principal may be held responsible for the fraudulent acts of the agent.
* * *

The contract reveals that the very essence of the transaction was to enable Dutton–Lainson to manufacture, market, and distribute the improvements which were the subject of the patent application. While Dutton–Lainson took the risk that, for reasons beyond the control of the parties, a patent might not issue, Dutton–Lainson did not bargain for the certainty that a patent would not issue because, contrary to the representation made to it, no application had been filed.

Thus, VRT's failure to deliver and assign a filed application was not a relatively minor and unimportant deviation from VRT's obligation. As a consequence, VRT's misrepresentation with regard to the application means there was no honest endeavor in good faith on its part to perform its part of the contract. It therefore necessarily follows that there was no substantial performance on its part and that it is precluded from maintaining this action against Dutton–Lainson. * * *

REVERSED AND REMANDED.

WALKER & CO. v. HARRISON

Supreme Court of Michigan, 1957.
347 Mich. 630, 81 N.W.2d 352.

SMITH, JUSTICE. This is a suit on a written contract. The defendants are in the dry-cleaning business. Walker & Company, plaintiff, sells, rents, and services advertising signs and billboards. These parties entered into an agreement pertaining to a sign. The agreement is in writing and is termed a "rental agreement." It specifies in part that:

"The lessor agrees to construct and install, at its own cost, one 18′ 9″ high x 8′ 8″ wide pylon type d.f. neon sign with electric clock and flashing lamps * * *. The lessor agrees to and does hereby lease or rent unto the said lessee the said SIGN for the term, use and rental and under the conditions, hereinafter set out, and the lessee agrees to pay said rental * * *.

"(a) The term of this lease shall be 36 months * * *.

"(b) The rental to be paid by lessee shall be $148.50 per month for each and every calendar month during the term of this lease; * * *.

"(d) Maintenance. Lessor at its expense agrees to maintain and service the sign together with such equipment as supplied and installed by the lessor to operate in conjunction with said sign under the terms of this lease; this service is to include cleaning and repainting of sign in original color scheme as often as deemed necessary by lessor to keep sign in first class advertising condition and make all necessary repairs to sign and equipment installed by lessor. * * *."

At the "expiration of this agreement," it was also provided, "title to this sign reverts to lessee." This clause is in addition to the printed form of agreement and was apparently added as a result of defendants' concern over title, they having expressed a desire "to buy for cash" and the salesman, at one time, having "quoted a cash price."

The sign was completed and installed in the latter part of July, 1953. The first billing of the monthly payment of $148.50 was made August 1, 1953, with payment thereof by defendants on September 3, 1953. This first payment was also the last. Shortly after the sign was installed, someone hit it with a tomato. Rust, also, was visible on the chrome, complained defendants, and in its corners were "little spider cobwebs." In addition, there were "some children's sayings written down in here." Defendant Herbert Harrison called Walker for the maintenance he believed himself entitled to under subparagraph (d) above. It was not forthcoming. He called again and again. "I was getting, you might say, sorer and sorer. * * * Occasionally, when I started calling up, I would walk around where the tomato was and get mad again. Then I would call up on the phone again." Finally, on October 8, 1953, plaintiff not having responded to his repeated calls, he telegraphed Walker that:

> "You Have Continually Voided Our Rental Contract By Not Maintaining Signs As Agreed As We No Longer Have A Contract With You Do Not Expect Any Further Remuneration."

Walker's reply was in the form of a letter. After first pointing out that "your telegram does not make any specific allegations as to what the failure of maintenance comprises," and stating that "We certainly would appreciate your furnishing us with such information," the letter makes reference to a prior collateral controversy between the parties, "wondering if this refusal on our part prompted your attempt to void our rental contract," and concludes as follows:

> "We would like to call your attention to paragraph G in our rental contract, which covers procedures in the event of a Breach of Agreement. In the event that you carry out your threat to make no future monthly payments in accordance with the agreement, it is our intention to enforce the conditions outlined under paragraph G[1] through the proper legal channels. We call to your attention that your monthly rental payments are due in advance at our office not later than the 10th day of each current month. You are now approximately 30 days in arrears on your September payment. Unless we receive both the September and October payments by October 25th, this entire matter will be placed in the hands of our

---

1. "(g) Breach of Agreement. Lessee shall be deemed to have breached this agreement by default in payment of any installment of the rental herein provided for; abandonment of the sign or vacating premises where the sign is located; termination or transfer of lessee's interest in the premises by insolvency, appointment of a receiver for lessee's business; filing of a voluntary or involuntary petition in bankruptcy with respect to lessee or the violation of any of the other terms or conditions hereof. In the event of such default, the lessor may, upon notice to the lessee, which notice shall conclusively be deemed sufficient if mailed or delivered to the premises where the sign was or is located, take possession of the sign and declare the balance of the rental herein provided for to be forthwith due and payable, and lessee hereby agrees to pay such balance upon any such contingencies. Lessor may terminate this lease and without notice, remove and repossess said sign and recover from the lessee such amounts as may be unpaid for the remaining unexpired term of this agreement. Time is of the essence of this lease with respect to the payment of rentals herein provided for. Should lessee after lessor has declared the balance of rentals due and payable, pay the full amount of rental herein provided, he shall then be entitled to the use of the sign, under all the terms and provisions hereof, for the balance of the term of this lease. No waiver by either party hereto of the nonperformance of any term, condition or obligation hereof shall be a waiver of any subsequent breach of, or failure to perform the same, or any other term, condition or obligation hereof. It is understood and agreed that the sign is especially constructed for the lessee and for use at the premises now occupied by the lessee for the term herein provided; that it is of no value unless so used and that it is a material consideration to the lessor in entering into this agreement that the lessee shall continue to use the sign for the period of time provided herein and for the payment of the full rental for such term."

attorney for collection in accordance with paragraph G which stipulates that the entire amount is forthwith due and payable."

No additional payments were made and Walker sued in assumpsit for the entire balance due under the contract, $5,197.50, invoking paragraph (g) of the agreement. Defendants filed answer and claim of recoupment, asserting that plaintiff's failure to perform certain maintenance services constituted a prior material breach of the agreement, thus justifying their repudiation of the contract and grounding their claim for damages. The case was tried to the court without a jury and resulted in a judgment for the plaintiff. The case is before us on a general appeal.

Defendants urge upon us again and again, in various forms, the proposition that Walker's failure to service the sign, in response to repeated requests, constituted a material breach of the contract and justified repudiation by them. Their legal proposition is undoubtedly correct. Repudiation is one of the weapons available to an injured party in event the other contractor has committed a material breach. But the injured party's determination that there has been a material breach, justifying his own repudiation, is fraught with peril, for should such determination, as viewed by a later court in the calm of its contemplation, be unwarranted, the repudiator himself will have been guilty of material breach and himself have become the aggressor, not an innocent victim.

What is our criterion for determining whether or not a breach of contract is so fatal to the undertaking of the parties that it is to be classed as "material"? There is no single touchstone. Many factors are involved. They are well stated in section 275 of Restatement of the Law of Contracts in the following terms:

"In determining the materiality of a failure fully to perform a promise the following circumstances are influential:

"(a) The extent to which the injured party will obtain the substantial benefit which he could have reasonably anticipated;

"(b) The extent to which the injured party may be adequately compensated in damages for lack of complete performance;

"(c) The extent to which the party failing to perform has already partly performed or made preparations for performance;

"(d) The greater or less hardship on the party failing to perform in terminating the contract;

"(e) The wilful, negligent or innocent behavior of the party failing to perform;

"(f) The greater or less uncertainty that the party failing to perform will perform the remainder of the contract."

We will not set forth in detail the testimony offered concerning the need for servicing. Granting that Walker's delay (about a week after defendant Herbert Harrison sent his telegram of repudiation Walker sent out a crew and took care of things) in rendering the service requested was irritating, we are constrained to agree with the trial court that it was not of such materiality as to justify repudiation of the contract, and we are particularly mindful of the lack of preponderant evidence contrary to his determination. Jones v. Eastern Michigan Motorbuses, 287 Mich. 619, 283 N.W. 710. The trial court, on this phase of the case, held as follows:

> "Now Mr. Harrison phoned in, so he testified, a number of times. He isn't sure of the dates but he sets the first call at about the 7th of August and he complained then of the tomato and of some rust and some cobwebs. The tomato, according to the testimony, was up on the clock; that would be outside of his reach, without a stepladder or something. The cobwebs are within easy reach of Mr. Harrison and so would the rust be. I think that Mr. Bueche's argument that these were not materially a breach would clearly be true as to the cobwebs and I really can't believe in the face of all the testimony that there was a great deal of rust seven days after the installation of this sign. And that really brings it down to the tomato. And of course, when a tomato has been splashed all over your clock, you don't like it. But he says he kept calling their attention to it, although the rain probably washed some of the tomato off. But the stain remained, and they didn't come. I really can't find that that was such a material breach of the contract as to justify rescission. I really don't think so."

Nor, we conclude, do we. There was no valid ground for defendants' repudiation and their failure thereafter to comply with the terms of the contract was itself a material breach, entitling Walker, upon this record, to judgment.

* * *

Affirmed. Costs to appellee.

K & G CONSTR. CO. v. HARRIS

Court of Appeals of Maryland, 1960.
223 Md. 305, 164 A.2d 451.

PRESCOTT, JUDGE. Feeling aggrieved by the action of the trial judge of the Circuit Court for Prince George's County, sitting without a jury, in finding a judgment against it in favor of a subcontractor, the appellant, the general contractor on a construction project, appealed.

The principal question presented is: Does a contractor, damaged by a subcontractor's failure to perform a portion of his work in a workman-like manner, have a right, under the circumstances of this case, to withhold, in partial satisfaction of said damages, an installment payment, which, under the terms of the contract, was due the subcontractor, unless the negligent performance of his work excused its payment?

The appeal is presented on a case stated in accordance with Maryland Rule 826g.

The statement, in relevant part, is as follows:

" * * * K & G Construction Company, Inc. (hereinafter called Contractor), plaintiff and counter-defendant in the Circuit Court and appellant herein, was owner and general contractor of a housing subdivision project being constructed (herein called Project). Harris and Brooks (hereinafter called Subcontractor), defendants and counter-plaintiffs in the Circuit Court and appellees herein, entered into a contract with Contractor to do excavating and earth-moving work on the Project. Pertinent parts of the contract are set forth below:

* * *

" Section 4. (b) Progress payments will be made each month during the performance of the work. Subcontractor will submit to Contractor, by the 25th of each month, a requisition for work performed during the preceding month. Contractor will pay these requisitions, less a retainer equal to ten per cent (10%), by the 10th of the months in which such requisitions are received.

" (c) No payments will be made under this contract until the insurance requirements of Sec. 9 hereof have been complied with.

* * *

" Section 8. * * * All work shall be performed in a workmanlike manner, and in accordance with the best practices.

" Section 9. Subcontractor agrees to carry, during the progress of the work, * * * liability insurance against * * * property damage, in such amounts and with such companies as may be satisfactory to Contractor and shall provide Contractor with certificates showing the same to be in force.

"While in the course of his employment by the Subcontractor on the Project, a bulldozer operator drove his machine too close to Contractor's house while grading the yard, causing the immediate collapse of a wall and other damage to the house. The resulting damage to Contractor's house was $3,400.00. Subcontractor had complied with the insurance provision (Sec. 9) of the aforesaid contract. Subcontractor reported said damages to their liability insurance carrier. The Subcontractor and its insurance carrier refused to repair damage or compensate Contractor for damage to the house, claiming that there was no liability on the part of the Subcontractor.

* * *

"Subcontractor performed work under the contract during July, 1958, for which it submitted a requisition by the 25th of July, as required by the contract, for work done prior to the 25th of July payable under the terms of the contract by Contractor on or before August 10, 1958. Contractor was current as to payments due under all preceding monthly requisitions from Subcontractor. The aforesaid bulldozer accident damaging Contractor's house occurred on August 9, 1958. Contractor refused to pay Subcontractor's requisition due on August 10, 1958, because the bulldozer damage to Contractor's house had not been repaired or paid for. Subcontractor continued to work on the project until the 12th of September, 1958, at which time they discontinued working on the project because of Contractor's refusal to pay the said work requisition and notified Contractor by registered letters of their position and willingness to return to the job, but only upon payment. At that time, September 12, 1958, the value of the work completed by Subcontractor on the project for which they had not been paid was $1,484.50.

* * *

" * * * Contractor filed suit against the Subcontractor in two counts: (1), for the aforesaid bulldozer damage to Contractor's house, alleging negligence of the Subcontractor's bulldozer operator, and (2) for the [stipulated] $450.00 costs above the contract price in having another excavating subcontractor complete the uncompleted work in the contract. Subcontractor filed a counter-claim for recovery of work of the [stipulated] value of $1,484.50 for which they had not received payment and for loss of anticipated profits on uncompleted portion of work in the [stipulated] amount of $1,340.00. By agreement of the parties, the first count of Contractor's claim, i.e., for aforesaid bulldozer damage to Contractor's house, was submitted to jury who found in favor of Contractor in the amount of $3,400.00. Following the finding by the jury, the second count of the Contractor's claim and the counter-claims of the Subcontractor, by agreement of the parties, were submitted to the Court for determination, without jury. All of the facts recited herein above were stipulated to by the parties to the Court. Circuit Court Judge Fletcher found for counter-plaintiff Subcontractor in the amount of $2,824.50 from which Contractor has entered this appeal."

The $3,400 judgment has been paid.

It is immediately apparent that our decision turns upon the respective rights and liabilities of the parties under that portion of their contract whereby the subcontractor agreed to do the excavating and earth-moving work in "a workmanlike manner, and in accordance with the best practices," with time being of the essence of the contract, and the contractor agreed to make progress payments therefor on the 10th day of the months following the performance of the work by the subcontractor. The subcontractor contends, of course, that when the contractor failed to make the payment due on August 10, 1958, he breached his contract and thereby released him (the subcontractor) from any further obligation to perform. The contractor, on the other hand, argues that the failure of the subcontractor to perform his work in a workmanlike manner constituted a material breach of the contract, which justified his refusal to make the August 10 payment; and, as there was no breach on his part, the subcontractor had no right to cease performance on September 12, and his refusal to continue work on the project constituted another breach, which rendered him liable to the contractor for damages. The vital question, more tersely stated, remains: Did the contractor have a right, under the circumstances, to refuse to make the progress payment due on August 10, 1958?

The answer involves interesting and important principles of contract law. Promises and counter-promises made by the respective parties to a contract have certain relations to one another, which determine many of the rights and liabilities of the parties. Broadly speaking, they are (1) independent of each other, or (2) mutually dependent, one upon the other. They are independent of each other if the parties intend that *performance* by each of them is in no way conditioned upon *performance* by the other. 5 Page, The Law of Contracts, ¶ 2971. In other words, the parties exchange promises for promises, not the *performance* of promises for the *performance* of promises. 3 Williston, Contracts (Rev.Ed.), ¶ 813, n. 6. A failure to perform an independent promise does not excuse non-performance on the part of the adversary party, but each is required to perform his promise, and, if one does not perform, he is liable to the adversary party for such non-performance. (Of course, if litigation ensues questions of set-off or recoupment frequently arise.) Promises are mutually dependent if the parties intend *performance* by one to be conditioned upon *performance* by the other, and, if they be mutually dependent, they may be (a) precedent, i.e., a promise that is to be performed before a corresponding promise on the part of the adversary party is to be performed, (b) subsequent, i.e., a corresponding promise that is not to be performed until the other party to the contract has performed a precedent covenant, or (c) concurrent, i.e., promises that are to be performed at the same time by each of the parties, who are respectively bound to perform each. Page, op.cit., ¶ ¶ 2941, 2951, 2961.

* * *

In the early days, it was settled law, that covenants and mutual promises in a contract were *prima facie* independent and that they were to be so construed in the absence of language in the contract clearly showing that they were intended to be dependent. Williston, op.cit., ¶ 816; Page, op.cit., ¶ ¶ 2944, 2945. In the case of Kingston v. Preston, 2 Doug. 689, decided in 1774, Lord Mansfield, contrary to three centuries of opposing precedents, changed the rule, and decided that performance of one covenant might be dependent on prior performance of another, although the contract contained no express condition to that effect. Page op.cit. ¶ 2946; Williston op.cit. ¶ 817. The modern rule, which seems to be of almost universal application, is that there is a presumption that mutual promises in a contract are dependent and are to be so regarded, whenever possible. Page, op.cit., ¶ 2946; Restatement, Contracts, ¶ 266. Cf. Williston, op.cit., ¶ 812.

* * *

Considering the presumption that promises and counter-promises are dependent and the statement of the case, we have no hesitation in holding that the promise and counter-promise under consideration here were mutually dependent, that is to say, the parties intended performance by one to be conditioned on performance by the other; and the subcontractor's promise was, by the explicit wording of the contract, precedent to the promise of payment, monthly, by the contractor. In Shapiro Engineering Corp. v. Francis O. Day Co., 215 Md. 373, 380, 137 A.2d 695, we stated that it is the general rule that where a total price for work is fixed by a contract, the work is not rendered divisible by progress payments. It would, indeed present an unusual situation if we were to hold that a building contractor, who has obtained someone to do work for him and has agreed to pay each month for the work performed in the previous month, has to continue the monthly payments, irrespective of the degree of skill and care displayed in the performance of work, and his only recourse is by way of suit for ill-performance. If this were the law, it is conceivable, in fact, probable, that many contractors would become insolvent before they were able to complete their contracts. As was stated by the Court in Measures Brothers Ltd. v. Measures, 2 Ch. 248: "Covenants are to be construed as dependent or independent according to the intention of the parties and the good sense of the case."

We hold that when the subcontractor's employee negligently damaged the contractor's wall, this constituted a breach of the subcontractor's promise to perform his work in a "workmanlike manner, and in accordance with the best practices." And there can be little doubt that the breach was material: the damage to the wall amounted to more than double the payment due on August 10. Speed v. Bailey, 153 Md. 655, 661, 662, 139 A. 534. 3A Corbin, Contracts, § 708, says: "The failure of a contractor's [in our case, the subcontractor's] performance to constitute 'substantial' performance may justify the owner [in our case, the contractor] in refusing to make a progress payment * * *. * * * If the refusal to pay an installment is justified on the owner's [contractor's] part, the contractor [subcontractor] is not justified in abandoning work by reason of that refusal. His abandonment of the work will itself be a wrongful repudiation that goes to the essence, even if the defects in performance did not." See also Restatement, Contracts, § 274 * * * and compare Williston, op.cit., §§ 805, 841 and 842. Professor Corbin, in § 954, states further: "The unexcused failure of a contractor to render a promised performance when it is due is always a breach of contract * * *. Such failure may be of such great importance as to constitute what has been called herein a 'total' breach. * * *. For a failure of performance constituting such a 'total' breach, an action for remedies that are appropriate thereto is at once maintainable. Yet the injured party is not required to bring such action. He has the option of treating the non-performance as a 'partial' breach only * * *." In permitting the subcontractor to proceed with work on the project after August 9, the contractor, obviously, treated the breach by the subcontractor as a partial one. As the promises were mutually dependent and the subcontractor had made a material breach in his performance, this justified the contractor in refusing to make the August 10 payment; hence, as the contractor was not in default, the subcontractor again breached the contract when he, on September 12, discontinued work on the project, which rendered him liable (by the express terms of the contract) to the contractor for his increased cost in having the excavating done—a stipulated amount of $450. Cf. Keystone Engineering Corp. v. Sutter, 196 Md. 620, 628, 78 A.2d 191.

* * * [The appellees] also contend that the contractor had no right to refuse the August 10 payment, because the subcontractor had furnished the insurance against property damage, as called for in the contract. There is little, or no, merit in this suggestion. The subcontractor and his insurance company denied liability. The furnishing of the insurance by him did not constitute a license to perform his work in a careless, negligent, or unworkmanlike manner; and its acceptance by the contractor did not preclude his assertion of a claim for unworkmanlike performance directly against the subcontractor.

Judgment against the appellant reversed; and judgment entered in favor of the appellant against the appellees for $450, the appellees to pay the costs.

Problems

15. P, buyer, and S, seller, entered into a contract for the purchase and sale of four planes. The first plane was to be delivered at S's place of business on June 1 and the others on July 10, subject to no delays by the manufacturer. No delay in fact occurred and S had the planes ready on the dates fixed in the contract. No further action was taken by either party until an action was begun by P against S on October 8. What result?

16. Cope contracted with Grun to have a new roof installed on Cope's house. It was agreed that the roofing shingles were to be "russet glow," a shade of brown. The roof was installed and many of the shingles were discolored, showing streaks of yellow. Grun replaced some of the shingles, but the new shingles did not match the others. The overall appearance of the roof is that it has been patched with nonblending colors. The roof is functional and is guaranteed to be functional for fifteen years. Must Cope pay for the roof?

17. Plaintiff, a professional singer, agreed to sing for the defendant in the Royal Italian Opera in London from March 30 to July 13. The contract provided: "Mr. Bettini shall sing in concerts as well as in operas, but he shall not sing anywhere within a 50 mile radius of London for the year. Mr. Bettini agrees to be in London without fail at least 6 days before the commencement of his engagement for the purpose of rehearsals." Plaintiff performed except that he arrived in London on March 28 because of temporary illness. When plaintiff arrived in London, defendant refused his services. What are the rights of the parties?

18. On Sept. 26 defendant made a contract with plaintiff for the erection of 19 houses on property owned by defendant. This contract

provided that all buildings should be finished by April 1 of the following year and that the contract price should be paid "by the owner to the contractor in installments as follows: 70 per cent of the above amount to be paid on estimated amount of work done as buildings progress." In timely fashion, plaintiff presented an estimate of work already done and requested payment of 70% according to the contract. Defendant failed to pay without any justification. Plaintiff suspended work immediately and three months later declared the contract at an end. Was plaintiff justified in his conduct?

19.   Plaintiff, a contractor, agreed to do certain construction work for defendant for the sum of $800,000. It was stipulated that estimates of the work completed should be furnished on the first of each month and that 85% of the sum found due should be paid on the 20th of the month. In August plaintiff submitted a statement showing $50,000 to be due. Defendant said that $40,000 was due and submitted his check. Plaintiff abandoned the contract six days later. Defendant made an offer to pay at once any amount which could be shown to be due. Plaintiff refused to submit its calculation for inspection and verification; instead, it brought this action. What result?

20.   Plaintiff agreed to sell and defendant agreed to buy certain realty on or before May 1. On May 1, plaintiff was not ready and able to perform. Plaintiff was ready on May 2 and so informed defendant but defendant said that it was "too late." What are the rights of the parties?

21.   The parties entered into a real estate contract that set a closing date of December 15. On the following January 8, P sent a letter to V stating that there had been a delay in obtaining mortgage financing and requested that closing be set on or about February 1. V sent a letter to P notifying P that the new closing date would be January 17. V also advised P that the failure to close on that date would result in default. P did not object to the contents of the letter. On January 17 P appeared at the place set for closing, stated that V's unilateral scheduling of the closing date was ridiculous and demanded a new closing date of January 31. V refused. When V did not appear on January 31, P commenced an action for specific performance. What result?

SECTION 4. CONSTRUCTIVE CONDITIONS UNDER THE UCC

(Calamari & Perillo 5th § 11.20)

BARTUS v. RICCARDI

City Court, City of Utica, 1967.
55 Misc.2d 3, 284 N.Y.S.2d 222.

HAROLD H. HYMES, JUDGE. The plaintiff is a franchised representative of Acousticon, a manufacturer of hearing aids. On January 15, 1966, the defendant signed a contract to purchase a Model A–660 Acousticon hearing aid from the plaintiff. The defendant specified Model A–660 because he had been tested at a hearing aid clinic and had been informed that the best hearing aid for his condition was this Acousticon model. An ear mold was fitted to the defendant and the plaintiff ordered Model A–660 from Acousticon.

On February 2, 1966, in response to a call from the plaintiff the defendant went to the plaintiff's office for his hearing aid. At that time he was informed that Model A–660 had been modified and improved, and that it was now called Model A–665. This newer model had been delivered by Acousticon for the defendant's use. The defendant denies that he understood this was a different model number. The hearing aid was fitted to the defendant. The defendant complained about the noise, but was assured by the plaintiff that he would get used to it.

The defendant tried out the new hearing aid for the next few days for a total use of 15 hours. He went back to the hearing clinic, where he was informed that the hearing aid was not the model that he had been advised to buy. On February 8, 1966, he returned to the plaintiff's office complaining that the hearing aid gave him a headache, and that it was not the model he had ordered. He returned the hearing aid to the plaintiff, for which he received a receipt. At that time the plaintiff offered to get Model A–660 for the defendant. The defendant neither consented to nor refused the offer. No mention was made by either party about canceling the contract, and the receipt given by the plaintiff contained no notation or indication that the plaintiff considered the contract canceled or rescinded.

The plaintiff immediately informed Acousticon of the defendant's complaint. By letter dated February 14, 1966, Acousticon writing directly to the defendant, informed him that Model A–665 was an improved version of Model A–660, and that they would either replace the model that had been delivered to him or would obtain Model A–660 for him. He was asked to advise the plaintiff immediately of his decision so that they could effect a prompt exchange. After receiving this letter the defendant decided that he did not want any hearing aid from the plaintiff, and he refused to accept the tender of a replacement, whether it be Model A–665 or A–660.

The plaintiff is suing for the balance due on the contract. Although he had made a down payment of $80.00, the defendant made no claim for repayment of his down payment until the case was ready to go to trial. The plaintiff objected to the counterclaim as being untimely. There is nothing in the pleadings to show that such a claim had been previously made by the defendant and, therefore, the court will not consider any counterclaim in this matter.

The question before the court is whether or not the plaintiff, having delivered a model which admittedly is not in exact conformity with the contract, can nevertheless recover in view of his subsequent tender of the model that did meet the terms of the contract.

The defendant contends that since there was an improper delivery of goods, the buyer has the right to reject the same under Sections 2–601 and 2–602(2)(c) of the Uniform Commercial Code. He further contends that even if the defendant had accepted delivery he may, under Section

2–608(1)(b) of the U.C.C., revoke his acceptance of the goods because "his acceptance was reasonably induced * * * by the seller's assurances." He also relies on Section 2–711, claiming that he may recover not only the down payment but also consequential damages.

The defendant, however, has neglected to take into account Section 2–508 of the Uniform Commercial Code which has added a new dimension to the concept of strict performance. This section permits a seller to cure a non-conforming delivery under certain circumstances. Sub-paragraph (1) of this section enacts into statutory law what had been New York case law. This permits a seller to cure a non-conforming delivery *before the expiration of the contract time* by notifying the buyer of his intention to so cure and by making a delivery within the contract period. This has long been the accepted rule in New York. (Lowinson v. Newman, 201 App.Div. 266, 194 N.Y.S. 253; Portfolio v. Rubin, 196 App.Div. 316, 187 N.Y.S. 302).

However, the U.C.C. in sub-paragraph (2) of Section 2–508 goes further and extends *beyond the contract time* the right of the seller to cure a defective performance. Under this provision, even where the contract period has expired and the buyer has rejected a non-conforming tender or has revoked an acceptance, the seller may "substitute a conforming tender" if he had "reasonable grounds to believe" that the nonconforming tender would be accepted, and "if he seasonably notifies the buyer" of his intention "to substitute a conforming tender." (51 N.Y.Jur.Sales, p. 41).

This in effect extends the contract period beyond the date set forth in the contract itself unless the buyer requires strict performance by including such a clause in the contract.

"The section (2–508(2) U.C.C.) rejects the time-honored and perhaps time-worn notion that the proper way to assure effective results in commercial transactions is to require strict performance. Under the Code a buyer who insists upon such strict performance must rely on a special term in his agreement or the fact that the seller knows as a commercial matter that strict performance is required." (48 Cornell Law Quarterly 13; 29 Albany Law Review 260).

This section seeks to avoid injustice to the seller by reason of a surprise rejection by the buyer. (Official Comment, McKinney's Cons. Laws of N.Y., Book 62½, Uniform Commercial Code, Section 2–508).

An additional burden, therefore, is placed upon the buyer by this section. "As a result a buyer may learn that even though he rejected or revoked his acceptance within the terms of Sections 2–601 and 2–711, he still may have to allow the seller additional time to meet the terms of the contract by substituting delivery of conforming goods." [Bender's U.C.C. Service–Sales and Bulk Transfers—Vol. 3, Section 14–02(1)(a)(ii)].

Has the plaintiff in this case complied with the conditions of Section 2–508?

The model delivered to the defendant was a newer and improved version of the model than was actually ordered. Of course, the defendant

is entitled to receive the model that he ordered even though it may be an older type. But under the circumstances the plaintiff had reasonable grounds to believe that the newer model would be accepted by the defendant.

The plaintiff acted within a reasonable time to notify the defendant of his tender of a conforming model. (Section 1–204 U.C.C.). The defendant had not purchased another hearing aid elsewhere. His position had not been altered by reason of the original non-conforming tender.

The plaintiff made a proper subsequent conforming tender pursuant to Section 2–508(2) of the Uniform Commercial Code.

Judgment is granted to plaintiff.

A.B. PARKER v. BELL FORD, INC.

Supreme Court of Alabama, 1983.
425 So.2d 1101.

EMBRY, JUSTICE. This appeal is from a judgment entered on a directed verdict in behalf of the defendants Bell Ford, Inc. and Ford Motor Company, Inc. We affirm.

Plaintiff A.B. Parker purchased a 1979 Ford F–100 pickup truck from defendant Bell Ford, Inc. of Atmore, Alabama, on 6 August 1979. The purchase price was $6,155.40. The truck was manufactured by defendant Ford Motor Company, Inc., which provided the new truck warranty on the vehicle. Parker made several complaints to Bell Ford of excessive tire wear requiring replacement of the tires on the vehicle after approximately 4,000 miles of use. Bell Ford gave Parker a purchase order to have the vehicle aligned at Combs & Dailey, an alignment shop in Mobile, where repairs were allegedly made on the vehicle. Parker was not informed as to what had been done to the vehicle at the alignment shop. Whatever work was performed, however, did not cure Parker's complaint of excessive tire wear and his second set of tires had to be replaced shortly thereafter.

Parker never returned the vehicle to Bell Ford for repairs and never registered any further complaint with Bell Ford until Parker initiated suit against Bell Ford and the manufacturer, the Ford Motor Company. At an inspection of the vehicle after this suit was filed, it was determined by the service manager of Peach Ford, Inc. of Brewton, Alabama, that the vehicle had a defective wheel housing, causing the tires to wear excessively.

On 1 July 1980 Parker filed his complaint containing four counts: one against Bell Ford for misrepresentation; one against Bell Ford for breach of contract; one against Bell Ford and Ford Motor Company for breach of warranty; and one against Bell Ford and Ford Motor Company for breach of implied warranty of merchantability. The trial court granted Ford Motor Company's motion to dismiss count four involving implied warranty of merchantability whereupon Parker amended his complaint accordingly. Parker originally demanded damages of $20,000; a later amendment increased that demand for damages to $30,000. After

trial before a jury, upon motion, the trial court directed a verdict in favor of Bell Ford and Ford Motor Company and entered judgment accordingly.

Parker urges as error the trial court's direction of a verdict denying his claims. Parker contends there was a scintilla of evidence in support of the allegations of his complaint; therefore, the trial court should have allowed the case to go to the jury.

We disagree.

Section 7–2–607(3)(a), Code 1975, describes the buyer's obligation upon learning of a defect in a product he has accepted:

> "(3) Where a tender has been accepted:
>
> "(a) The buyer must within a reasonable time after he discovers or should have discovered any breach notify the seller of breach or be barred from any remedy. . . ."

The transaction between Parker and Bell Ford and Ford Motor Company was one that required compliance with § 7–2–607.

This court, on several occasions, has characterized notice, such as required by § 7–2–607, as a condition precedent to recovery. See *Smith v. Pizitz of Bessemer, Inc.,* 271 Ala. 101, 122 So.2d 591 (1960).

* * *

Official notice has been determined to be the degree of notice which at least comports with the notice an ordinary tortfeasor would have of his breach of duty. * * * The evidence adduced at trial reveals that Parker was not satisfied with the repairs made on behalf of Bell Ford by the alignment shop. Parker admits that at no time did he contact Ford Motor Company about this problem, nor did he return the vehicle to Bell Ford after he took the vehicle from the alignment shop.

> ". . . Notice of breach serves two distinct purposes. First, express notice opens the way for settlement through negotiation between the parties. . . . Second, proper notice minimizes the possibility of prejudice to the seller by giving him 'ample opportunity to cure the defect, inspect the goods, investigate the claim or do whatever may be necessary to properly defend himself or minimize his damages while the facts are fresh in the minds of the parties.'"

Standard Alliance Industries, Inc. v. Black Clawson Company, 587 F.2d 813, 826 (6th Cir.1978), *cert. denied,* 441 U.S. 923, 99 S.Ct. 2032, 60 L.Ed.2d 396 (1979), quoting in part from Note, *Notice of Breach and the Uniform Commercial Code,* 25 U.Fla.L.Rev. 520, 522 (1973). Bell Ford had no notice that the work performed by Combs & Dailey did not eliminate Parker's tire wear problem. In fact, Bell Ford never heard from Parker again until six months later when it received the summons initiating this lawsuit. This court held in *Pizitz of Bessemer, supra,* that one reason for the notice requirement is to apprise the vendor that a claim will be made against him and give him an opportunity to prepare a defense or notify his supplier. We expand that rationale to also include

the requirement of notice in order to enable the seller to make adjustments or replacements, or to suggest opportunities for cure, to the end of minimizing the buyer's loss and reducing the seller's own liability to the buyer. See White and Summers, *Uniform Commercial Code,* § 11–9 (1972).

* * *

The judgment in this case is due to be, and is hereby, affirmed.

EMANUEL LAW OUTLINES, INC. v. MULTI–STATE LEGAL STUDIES, INC.

Southern District of New York, 1995.
899 F.Supp. 1081.

BERNARD NEWMAN, SENIOR JUDGE, by designation: Emanuel Law Outlines, Inc. (hereinafter "ELO"), a publisher of study aids for law students, brings this diversity action against Multi–State Legal Studies, Inc., (hereinafter "Multi–State"), a company that conducts state bar review preparation courses. ELO seeks $60,000 in damages for breach of contract; Multi–State counterclaims for $20,000 in damages, alleging breach of contract by ELO. This matter arises under the court's diversity jurisdiction in conformity with 28 U.S.C. § 1332(a), and the case was tried to the court in a one day bench trial. Pursuant to F.R.C.P. Rule 52(a), the following constitutes the court's findings of fact and conclusions of law.

THE RECORD

ELO offered the following two witnesses: Lazar Emanuel (hereinafter Lazar), General Counsel and Vice President of ELO and Steven Emanuel (hereinafter Steven), President of ELO. Multi–State offered one witness, Robert Feinberg, Multi–State's President. The parties submitted 16 documentary exhibits.

CONTENTIONS OF THE PARTIES

ELO contends that Multi–State's failure to pay the base fees for the second and third years of a three year installment contract breaches the agreement. According to the relevant terms of the contract, ELO was to provide Multi–State with a criminal procedure outline supplement (hereinafter "supplement") no later than May 1, 1993. Although the supplement was not delivered until June 3, 1993, ELO maintains that it performed its obligation under the contract. ELO argues that: (1) Multi–State orally agreed to change the May 1, 1993 contractual deadline to early June 1993; (2) any alleged breach was cured under the terms of the contract; (3) any alleged breach by ELO caused by failing to meet the May 1, 1993 deadline was not material; (4) the nonconforming delivery did not substantially impair the value of the entire contract; and (5) Multi–State reinstated the contract by accepting the supplement without seasonably notifying ELO of the breach.

Multi–State maintains that the failure of ELO to provide the supplements by May 1, 1993 constituted a breach of the agreement and excused Multi–State's obligations under the contract. Specifically, Multi–State disputes the existence of any modification or waiver of the May 1, 1993 deadline. It is further asserted by Multi–State that it sent ELO two letters, dated April 27, 1993 and May 7, 1993 respectively, informing ELO that the failure to meet the May 1st deadline would be considered a material breach of the contract. When ELO did not provide the supplement by May 1, 1993, Multi–State claims that ELO breached the agreement and excused any further performance by Multi–State. Multi–State also insists that the failure to timely provide the supplement by the agreed-upon date caused damage to Multi–State's business in the amount of $20,000.

Findings of Fact

Since 1978, ELO (a New York corporation) has been a leading publisher and distributor of study aids for law students. Steven is the main editor and writer of the Emanuel Law Outline series. The corporation is a continuation of the business started by Steven during his first year at Harvard Law School. The company enjoys an outstanding reputation among law students across the country. In addition to writing and editing, Steven negotiates transactions for the corporation. Lazar, Steven's father, is ELO's general counsel and administrative officer. An experienced attorney and businessman, Lazar runs the office, finalizes contracts, oversees all printing and production of materials, and supervises the collections of accounts.

Multi–State Legal Studies, Inc. (a California corporation) conducts bar review courses for law school graduates. The company, which employs approximately 15 people, offers courses in 42 states and is run by its president and founder Robert Feinberg, who is admitted to the bar of several states, including New York and California. As president of the company, Feinberg develops course materials, directs promotion and marketing of the company, and is one of Multi–State's principle lecturers around the country.

In August 1992, Feinberg contacted ELO to propose an agreement whereby ELO would provide materials which could be distributed to students enrolled in Multi–State's course. As a result, the parties entered into a three-year contract beginning September 1, 1992 and ending August 31, 1995. Under the contract, ELO was required to supply at least 950 copies of each of two volumes of capsule summaries in nine subjects tested on the California bar exam in each of the three years. Multi–State agreed to pay ELO a fee of $30,000 per year and in addition pay printing and delivery costs.... For all subjects except Constitutional Law and Criminal Procedure, ELO was required to take verbatim text of the Capsule Summaries it had published in the Emanuel Law Outline for the particular subject and cosmetically change them as required by Multi–State. For Constitutional Law, ELO was to prepare, edit, and revise a text outline from the review portion of the Constitutional Law

Audio Tapes sold commercially by ELO. The Criminal Procedure Supplement was to be created from scratch by ELO, but be similar in format and detail to the other outlines provided to Multi–State.

Under the first year of the contract, ELO agreed to produce two volumes containing materials for eight of the subjects as well as a Criminal Procedure Supplement. The two volumes were to be delivered to ELO's warehouse no later than October 10, 1992, whereas the supplement, because it required more time for preparation, was to be delivered to the warehouse no later than May 1, 1993. There is no dispute that respecting the two volumes, ELO adequately performed under the contract.

In February 1993, Steven underwent quadruple bypass surgery. As a result of a six week convalescent period, he fell behind in his work on the supplement. Multi–State was informed of the upcoming surgery sometime in January 1993. ELO contends that in accordance with an early April telephone conversation between Steven and Feinberg, Multi–State orally agreed to move back the deadline for the production of the supplement. Specifically, Steven testified that he told Feinberg he had fallen behind in his work due to the operation and while he could still meet the May 1, 1993 deadline, he hoped that the deadline could be "relaxed". Steven also stated that Feinberg told him a delay would be acceptable if the supplement was ready by "early June", and that it "doesn't sound like a big deal". The evidence presented by Multi–State directly conflicts with ELO's claim. Feinberg, in his testimony, flatly denies that he ever agreed to any change in the May 1, 1993 deadline. He emphatically stated that "[i]n 17 years of business, I can never remember one oral waiver that I would have agreed to".

Resolving this factual dispute, the court finds that there was insufficient evidence to establish any change in the May 1st deadline. First, ELO failed to produce written confirmation of any waiver. Considering the experience of both Steven and Lazar, it is likely that if such a change in terms of the contract were made, a confirmatory letter would have been sent by ELO to Multi–State. Moreover, it was demonstrated that ELO relied on the letter of the contract as evidenced by its written demand for payment very soon after the December deadline for the second installment. Accordingly, ELO did not treat changes in the terms of the agreement casually. In sum, no writing from Multi–State was ever produced to corroborate ELO's claim that there was any change in the May 1, 1993 deadline. Therefore, considering the experience of Steven and Lazar, the lack of any writing either sent to Multi–State or even kept in ELO's files, the practice of ELO to closely adhere to the contract terms, and the failure to produce any writing from Multi–State, the court finds the weight of the evidence in favor of Multi–State and concludes that there was no oral modification regarding the May 1, 1993 deadline.

However, another factual dispute arises regarding Multi–State's claim that two letters were sent to ELO regarding the May 1 deadline. The first letter, dated April 27, 1993, purportedly notified ELO that failure to meet the May 1 deadline would be considered a material breach of the agreement. The second letter, dated May 7, 1993, purportedly canceled Multi–State's obligations under the contract based on ELO's failure to meet the May 1 deadline. ELO, on the other hand, insists that it did not receive either letter.

The court concludes that ELO did not receive either letter. As a member of the bar of several states including New York, a lecturer on the law, an experienced businessman, and negotiator of the contract, Feinberg must have been aware that the contract specifically called for *receipt* of notice by the breaching party.[2] Additionally, Feinberg admitted knowledge that ELO would hold him to the specifics of the contract. ELO was, in Feinberg's words, "sticklers" regarding the agreement. Further, Feinberg testified that these letters, supposedly notifying ELO of a material breach, were sent by ordinary mail, rather than a method which provides proof of receipt. This is significant because receipt of written notice of a claimed breach by the breaching party was a critical factor under the contract. Finally, if these letters were received, common sense dictates that there would be some response from ELO regarding the letters. Not only was Multi–State unable to produce evidence of any written response from ELO, but Feinberg never clearly demonstrated that there was any oral response. Based on the evidence presented, even if the court were to assume the letters were sent, the evidence is insufficient to find that either letter was received by ELO.

When the May 1 deadline passed, Multi–State contacted ELO by phone stating that the materials were needed, to which ELO replied that the supplement was being rushed and that it would be forthcoming. Regarding the materials, a third factual dispute arises. The parties agree that the ELO materials were to be utilized by Multi–State bar review course to help marketability, improve the quality of the materials, and give the Multi–State students additional materials for study purposes. Feinberg further argues that he needed the supplement to help prepare his criminal procedure "early-bird"[3] lecture. ELO responds that the materials were not meant to be used either for lecture preparation or as reference points in any of the lectures.

The court credits the position of ELO and determines that the primary purpose of the outlines was to act as a supplement to Multi–State's materials and not as a research or reference tool for lecturers. Multi–State had its own outlines, and for seventeen years has been conducting reviews specifically for the multi-state portion of the bar examination of which Criminal Procedure is a part. It is difficult to imagine that a lecturer of Feinberg's experience would need to rely on an outline prepared by another company. Indeed, the fact that the lecture

2. The contract states: "9.(a) Initial Term: Neither party may terminate this Agreement during the Initial Term, except on account of a material breach by the other, which breach shall have gone uncured for 30 days after the breaching party has *received* written notice of breach...." (emphasis added).

3. The "Early Bird Lecture Series" is a short review of each of the multi-state subjects held in mid-May. The regular course schedule began in early June.

was scheduled only 17 days after the contractual due date for the materials to arrive at ELO's warehouse, renders it unlikely that any lecturer would have been able to substantially rely on those materials for preparation. . . .

The supplement did arrive at ELO's warehouse on June 3, 1993. After having the materials shipped by UPS, Multi–State received the materials on June 10, 1993 and distributed them to the students. Multi–State maintains that the late delivery caused substantial damage to its reputation. Stressing that the "key in our business is word of mouth," Multi–State argues that student satisfaction with the course is critical. Although Feinberg testified that there were numerous complaints about the late shipment, no documentary evidence was produced regarding any negative feedback received by Multi–State.[4]

On August 19, 1993 under the terms of the contract, ELO wrote Multi–State requesting instructions for printing and delivery of the materials for the second year of the contract. On August 23, 1993 Multi–State sent a fax to ELO stating that ELO's failure to deliver the supplement by the May 1 deadline constituted a material breach of the contract and consequently Multi–State was excused from all future obligations under the contract. This fax constituted the last correspondence between the parties.

DISCUSSION

By the terms of the contract, this case is governed by New York law. Since this action involves a contract for the sale of goods, New York's version of the Uniform Commercial Code is the applicable legal authority. Because the court concludes that there is insufficient evidence of any modification of the May 1, 1993 deadline for the supplement, the failure to print the supplement by that date constitutes a breach of contract. While the failure to meet the deadline constituted a breach, the court credits ELO's contentions that the breach was subsequently cured as provided by the agreement and in any case, the delay was not a material breach. Accordingly, Multi–State was still bound by the contract.

A. Multi–State did not give ELO adequate notice of the breach as required by the agreement. The contract unequivocally requires that the agreement may not be terminated unless the breaching party receives written notice of the breach and such breach is not cured more than 30 days after the receipt of such notice. New York law states, "[a] person *receives* a notice or notification when (a) it comes to his attention; or (b) it is duly delivered to [his] place of business. . ." N.Y.U.C.C. § 1–201(26) (emphasis in the original). In this case, there was inadequate evidence to prove that ELO received either the April 27th or May 7th letter. Accordingly, ELO did not have notice of the breach.

4. After the 1993 Bar examination, Multi–State decided not to continue its full service California course. Feinberg stated the reason for this decision was "because we entered into a license agreement with Barpassers, another California course, and . . . under the terms of the license agreement, basically we were assigning our rights to certain materials to them and they were assigning their rights to Multi–State question to us. So we made a business decision."

Multi–State's claim that N.Y.U.C.C. § 2–607 does not require notice of a contract breach be received, is inapplicable to this case. While Multi–State accurately states the provision of § 2–607, it ignores the fact that in this case there was a specific provision requiring receipt of written notice of a breach. It is recognized within the Code itself that parties may vary the terms of the statute and determine the standards by which performance of obligation is to be measured under the code, as long as the variations do not disclaim the obligations of good faith, diligence, reasonableness, care and the standards are not manifestly unreasonable. N.Y.U.C.C. § 1–102; see also, *Prompt Elec. Supply Co. v. Allen–Bradley Co.*, 492 F.Supp. 344, 347–48 (E.D.N.Y.1980); *Dulman v. Martin Fein & Co.*, 66 A.D.2d 809, 810, 411 N.Y.S.2d 358, 359 (2d Dept.1978) (the code is to be interpreted "to allow businessmen to make the terms of their own contracts and to allow them to arrange their own affairs among themselves within the bounds of reason and fair play"). It cannot be said that the written receipt of notice requirement is unreasonable. . . .

Since no notice of a breach was received by ELO prior to its performance on June 3, this Court finds that ELO cured any breach within the guidelines of the agreement. Hence, Multi–State presents no valid basis to justify non-performance of the contract.

B. Even if the Court were to agree that there was an uncured breach of contract by ELO, Multi–State's right to be relieved of its obligations requires a demonstration of substantial impairment of the whole contract. Inasmuch as this contract requires the delivery of goods in separate lots to be separately accepted, it is an installment contract as defined by N.Y.U.C.C. § 2–612(1). Under § 2–612(3), Multi–State's right to cancel the entire agreement required a showing of substantial impairment of the whole contract. Whether a breach constitutes "substantial impairment" is a question of fact. *Stinnes Interoil v. Apex Oil Co.*, 604 F.Supp. 978, 981 (1985). * * * Here, there is no evidence to support Multi–States argument that failure to have the supplements ready by May 1, 1993 substantially impaired the entire contract.

Multi–State's only contention with regard to damages is that the company received oral complaints from students enrolled in the course. This claim is tenuous at best, considering that Multi–State offered no proof of any written complaints, nor did it provide any written records of the complaints, and it failed to show that it had to refund any tuition money to students. Moreover, Multi–State's students did in fact receive eight of the nine promised outline [sic] on time and subsequently received the supplement more than a month prior to the bar exam. Finally, Multi–State's own actions demonstrate the minor nature of any breach. When ELO shipped the goods in June, Multi–State made no effort to expedite delivery. Because it was responsible for the cost of shipping, it could have utilized any delivery method it desired, including overnight mail. Instead, Multi–State opted for UPS delivery, which is far from the fastest method. Inasmuch as Multi–State's actions do not indicate significant urgency, it would be very difficult for the court to so find.

Nor can it be said that the June delivery of the supplements had any effect on future enrollment in Multi–State's course. After the 1993 course, Multi–State no longer offered the full service California bar review course. It is undisputed that Multi–State's decision was unrelated to the instant action. Since Multi–State no longer offered the full service course, ELO's breach could not have had any damaging effect whatsoever for subsequent years.

The very purpose of the substantial impairment requirement of N.Y.U.C.C. § 2–612(3) is to preclude a party from canceling the contract for trivial defects. Multi–State has failed to demonstrate any substantial or lingering harm incurred from ELO's failure to have the supplement ready by May 1, 1993. Accordingly, Multi–State had no legal justification for not performing on the contract.

Conclusion

With regard to ELO's claim, the court determines that while ELO's delay in delivering the supplement breached the agreement it was cured under the terms of the contract. Moreover, the delay in delivery did not substantially impair the value of the instant contract with Multi–State. Accordingly, Multi–State was not entitled to cancel its performance thereof. Therefore, ELO shall recover the sum of $60,000 plus prejudgment interest at the New York statutory rate accruing from August 23, 1993, which represents the date when Multi–State repudiated the contract. Further, Multi–State's counterclaim is hereby dismissed. Each party shall bear its own expenses.

The Clerk of the Court is directed to enter judgment accordingly.

IT IS SO ORDERED.

Problems

22.   Pursuant to a contract, the seller tendered delivery of 10,000 widgets. The buyer, motivated by a desire to reject them so as to take advantage of a reduction of the market price, after careful inspection, found a number of defective widgets and rejected the entire shipment. In a suit by the seller against the buyer, what argument can the seller make?

23.   B entered into a contract to buy capacitors from S. S delivered them in the middle of October. B made partial payments in October and November and promised to make up the deficiencies. B also tested the goods and used them after testing. On November 30th, B sent a notice of rejection. S sues for the purchase price. B contends that the goods were defective. What are the issues to be resolved?

24.   B contracted to buy from S a system of equipment designed to process and refine fructose. The system was to produce, as an end product, 55% fructose, which is used as a sweetener in many foods. S warranted that the system could produce a certain minimum quantity of 55% fructose per day. Nine months later the system was put into operation. Although the system did produce 55% fructose it was never able to meet the production guarantee. For the following 10 months S unsuccessfully attempted to bring

the system into compliance with its production guarantee, after which it left B with a list of suggestions for further remedial efforts. Six months later, after B's further unsuccessful attempts to remedy the system, B notified S that it was revoking its acceptance and demanded a refund of the purchase price.

    (a) Was B justified in revoking its acceptance? Was the notice of revocation timely? Did B have to offer to return the equipment?

    (b) B continued to use the equipment during the pendency of the trial. What is the effect of B's post-revocation use of the system?

25. S agreed to sell B a chemical known as "Prussian blue" in stated installments. Payment was to be made on each delivery. B refused to accept the first shipment, claiming it did not meet contract specifications, and also cancelled the contract. S sues for breach of contract. What is the issue to be resolved?

SECTION 5. LESS THAN SUBSTANTIAL PERFORMANCE: QUASI–CONTRACTUAL RECOVERY

(Calamari & Perillo 5th 11.22)

MARTIN v. SCHOENBERGER

Supreme Court of Pennsylvania, 1845.
8 W. &c. S. 367.

* * *

    To permit a man to recover for part performance of an entire contract, or to permit him to recover on his agreement where he has failed to perform, would tend to demoralize the whole country. If the law were so, a man would just perform as much of his contract as would suit his convenience or cupidity; all faith and fair dealing would be at an end, and all confidence between man and man would be destroyed. * * *

N.Y. LAW REVISION COMMISSION, RESTITUTION FOR BENEFITS CONFERRED BY PARTY IN DEFAULT UNDER CONTRACT*

I. General Statement of the Problem

    The legal problem to be discussed in this study is: To what extent is a party to a contract who has partly performed its requirements and who

---

* This is an excerpt from a study by Professor Edwin W. Patterson for the New York Law Revision Commission. 1952 Report of the Law Revision Commission 93, 93–95.

has repudiated or materially defaulted in the performance of the remaining requirements, entitled to recover judgment against the other party for the benefit conferred by the part performance? By "requirements" is meant usually the performance which the defaulting party is under a duty to render, and also (exceptionally) the performance to be rendered by that party as an express condition of the other party's duties under the contract. A previous study, which covered American reported case law down to the summer of 1941, showed that in New York and in most American jurisdictions the defaulting party is not entitled to recover anything for his part performance, with certain exceptions.

A. Principles for and Against the Present Law

The principles invoked to justify this general rule are chiefly these: 1. To deny recovery to the defaulting party is an effective deterrent to contract-breaking, and to allow such recovery would encourage contract-breaking. 2. To require the defendant (nondefaulting party) to pay for the part performance would be to impose a new contract upon him, since it is uncertain whether, and to what extent, he would have been willing to pay for the part performance had he known when the contract was made that the default was going to occur. 3. How can the innocent party prove all of the harm and inconvenience that he suffered by reason of the default, and why should he be obliged to assume this burden? These reasons have seldom been discussed by the courts, since in most of the cases denying recovery the rule that the defaulting plaintiff cannot recover has been stated as if it were axiomatic, or has been supported by a mere citation of precedents. It has often been uncertain whether or not the plaintiff based his claim on quasi-contractual grounds and whether or not the court considered such grounds in reaching its decision. It is possible that some reported cases may be due to such oversights. On the other hand, in some types of situations, such as the defaulting plaintiff who seeks to recover the value of personal services rendered in part performance, the stream of New York cases has been too consistent to be accidental.[1]

The principle that supports recovery by the defaulting plaintiff is that one who has been unjustly enriched at another's expense is under a duty to make restitution to the other.[2] This general principle is implemented by several mitigating doctrines: The rule that the building contractor whose deviations are not wilful can recover for substantial performance; the doctrine of severability by which the contract is split into units and recovery is allowed one party on the units that he has performed even though he has substantially defaulted on the remainder; and the conception of quasi-contract, which is not always clearly distin-

---

1. See cases cited in Leg.Doc. (1942) No. 65(F), p. 40, n. 96.

2. Restatement, Restitution (1937) § 1.

guished from express or implied-in-fact contract. These three mitigating doctrines were discussed more fully in the 1942 study.[3]

B. Exceptional Situations in Which Recovery Is Allowed

Yet these doctrines have not been applied to all types of situations, and the exceptions referred to above, in which the defaulting plaintiff has been allowed recovery for his part performance, may be grouped under the following main headings:

1. The building contractor is, as was indicated above, allowed in New York and in most other jurisdictions to recover judgment for the contract price minus the cost of making good his deficiencies in performance, if his default was inadvertent. However, if the default was wilful or was so great that the performance was not substantial (the cases indicate that anything below 90% is not substantial) and probably if the defect is structural, one that cannot be remedied without partial demolition of the building, the contractor cannot obtain a judgment for the balance due under the contract.[4] Although the New York precedents deny the building contractor any recovery in quasi-contract, the allowance of recovery for substantial performance (in an action on the contract) coupled with the fact that in most instances the contractor receives from the owner progress payments that cover eighty per cent or more of his labor and material costs, indicates that there are few if any cases of severe hardship to the defaulting plaintiff in this type of situation.

2. Personal service contracts for a definite term, such as one year, which provide that the salary shall be payable in specified amounts at specified intervals of time have been held in other jurisdictions to be severable, so that the employee who has worked eight months of the twelve stipulated, and then quits without justification, is entitled to recover any unpaid balance on his salary for eight months, though he is liable to pay the employer damages for his breach of contract. However, some New York cases have ignored severability on facts where it might have been applied.

3. The New York Labor Law provision (§ 196) requiring payment by the employer of the wages of laborers and mechanics for every six days of work probably serves to protect weekly wage-earners from forfeitures (even though only against loss of a few days' pay), yet it is indefinite in scope and does not apply to supervisory employees nor to those in the higher brackets who are under contract for a fixed term.

4. The seller of goods is protected by the Sales Act as adopted in New York, which allows him a recovery for part performance without any restrictions as to whether the default was wilful or otherwise. Before the adoption of the Uniform Sales Act in New York in 1911 the courts

---

3. Leg.Doc. (1942) No. 65(F), pp. 26–30. For a view favoring restitution to a defaulting party, see Thurston, Recent Developments in Restitution, 1940–1947, 45 Mich. L.Rev. 935, 950–953 (1947). For other recent periodical literature, see 34 Marq. L.Rev. 218 (1950–1951); 31 Marq.L.Rev. 295 (1947); 1949 Wis.L.Rev. 796; 97 U. of Pa.L.Rev. 884 (1949); 23 Tulane L. Rev. 559 (1949); Donaldson, An Analysis of Retail Installment Sales Legislation, 19 Rocky Mt. L.Rev. 135, 163 (1947).

4. Leg.Doc. (1942) No. 65(F), pp. 46–50.

had denied the defaulting seller recovery. In this instance the New York law was changed by statute.

5. Without the aid of statute the New York courts have allowed the lessee to recover his lease security deposit from the lessor even though the lessee has wilfully and unjustifiably abandoned the premises and defaulted in payment of rent; the deposit is, however, treated as a security transaction rather than a partial performance of the lessee's obligations. This distinction between a part performance and a security deposit was criticized in the earlier study.

LANCELLOTTI v. THOMAS

Superior Court of Pennsylvania, 1985.
341 Pa.Super. 1, 491 A.2d 117.

SPAETH, PRESIDENT JUDGE. This appeal raises the question of whether a defaulting purchaser of a business who has also entered into a related lease for the property can recover any part of his payments made prior to default. The common law rule precluded a breaching buyer from recovering these payments. Today, we reject this rule, which created a forfeiture of the breaching buyer's payments and unjustly enriched the nonbreaching seller, and adopt § 374 of the Restatement (Second) Contracts (1979), which permits limited restitution. This case is remanded for further proceedings so that the trial court may apply the Restatement rule.

–1–

On July 25, 1973, the parties entered into an agreement in which appellant agreed to purchase appellees' luncheonette business and to rent from appellees the premises on which the business was located. Appellant agreed to buy the name of the business, the goodwill, and equipment; the inventory and real estate were not included in the agreement for the sale of the business. Appellees agreed to sell the business for the following consideration: $25,000 payable on signing of the agreement; appellant's promise that only he would own and operate the business; and appellant's promise to build an addition to the existing building, which would measure 16 feet by 16 feet, cost at least $15,000, and be 75 percent complete by May 1, 1973.[1]

It was also agreed that appellees would lease appellant the property on which the business was operated for a period of five years, with appellant having the option of an additional five-year term. The rent was $8,000 per year for a term from September 1, 1973, to August 31, 1978. A separate lease providing for this rental was executed by the parties on the same date that the agreement was executed. This lease specified that the agreement to build the existing building was a condition of the lease. In exchange for appellant's promise to build the addition, there was to be

---

1. The parties agree that this date was   tended was May 1, 1974.
incorrect, and that the date the parties in-

no rental charge for the property until August 31, 1973. Further, if the addition was not constructed as agreed, the lease would terminate automatically. An addendum, executed by the parties on August 14, 1973, modified this agreement, providing that "if the addition to the building as described in the Agreement is not constructed in accordance with the Agreement, the Buyer shall owe the Sellers $6,665 as rental for the property ..." for the period from July 25, 1973, to the end of that summer season. The addendum also provided that all the equipment would revert to appellees upon the appellant's default in regard to the addition.

Appellant paid appellees the $25,000 as agreed, and began to operate the business. However, at the end of the 1973 season, problems arose regarding the construction of the addition. Appellant claims that the building permit necessary to construct the addition was denied. Appellees claim that they obtained the building permit and presented it to appellant, who refused to begin construction. Additionally appellees claim that appellant agreed to reimburse them if they built the addition. At a cost of approximately $11,000, appellees did build a 20 feet by 40 feet addition. In the spring of 1974 appellees discovered that appellant was no longer interested in operating the business. There is no evidence in the record that appellant paid any rent from September 1, 1973, as the first rental payment was not due until May 15, 1974. Appellees resumed possession of the business and, upon opening the business for the 1974 summer season, found some of their equipment missing.

Appellant's complaint in assumpsit demanded that appellees return the $25,000 plus interest. * * *

–2–

At one time the common law rule prohibiting a defaulting party on a contract from recovering was the majority rule. J. Calamari and J. Perillo, The Law of Contracts § 11–26, at 427 (2d ed.1977). However, a line of cases, apparently beginning with *Britton v. Turner,* 6 N.H. 481 (1834), departed from the common law rule. The merit of the common law rule was its recognition that the party who breaches should not be allowed "to have advantage from his own wrong." Corbin, The Right of a Defaulting Vendee to the Restitution of Instalments Paid, 40 Yale L.J. 1013, 1014 (1931). As Professor Perillo states, allowing recovery "invites contract-breaking and rewards morally unworthy conduct." Restitution in the Second *Restatement of Contracts,* 81 Colum.L.Rev. 37, 50 (1981). Its weakness, however, was its failure to recognize that the nonbreaching party should not obtain a windfall from the breach. The party who breaches after almost completely performing should not be more severely penalized than the party who breaches by not acting at all or after only beginning to act. Under the common law rule the injured party retains more benefit the more completely the breaching party has performed prior to the default. Thus it has been said that "to allow the injured party to retain the benefit of the part performance ..., without making restitution of any part of such value, is the enforcement of a penalty or forfeiture against the contract-breaker." Corbin, *supra,* at 1013.

Critics of the common law rule have been arguing for its demise for over fifty years. *See* Corbin, *supra. See also* Calamari and Perillo, *supra,* at § 11–26; 5A Corbin on Contracts §§ 1122–1135 (1964); 12 S. Williston, A Treatise on the Law of Contracts §§ 1473–78 (3d ed. 1970). In response to this criticism an alternative rule has been adopted in the Restatement of Contracts. * * *

In 1979, this rule was liberalized. Restatement (Second) of Contracts § 374 (1979) provides:

§ 374.   Restitution in Favor of Party in Breach

(1) Subject to the rule stated in Subsection (2), if a party justifiably refuses to perform on the ground that his remaining duties of performance have been discharged by the other party's breach, the party in breach is entitled to restitution for any benefit that he has conferred by way of part performance or reliance in excess of the loss that he has caused by his own breach.

(2) To the extent that, under the manifested assent of the parties, a party's performance is to be retained in the case of breach, that party is not entitled to restitution if the value of the performance as liquidated damages is reasonable in the light of the anticipated or actual loss caused by the breach and the difficulties of proof of loss.

Thus the first Restatement's exclusion of the willful defaulting purchaser from recovery was deleted, apparently in part due to the influence of the Uniform Commercial Code's permitting recovery by a buyer who willfully defaults.[2] *d.,* Reporter's Note at 218. Professor Perillo suggests that the injured party has adequate protection without the common law rule.[3] Choosing "the just path," he therefore rejects the common law rule, explaining this choice by saying that times have changed. "What appears to be just to one generation may be viewed differently by

---

2. In Pennsylvania, 13 Pa.C.S. § 2718, provides:

§ 2718. Liquidation or limitation of damages; deposits

(a) Liquidated damages in agreement.—Damages for breach by either party may be liquidated in the agreement but only at an amount which is reasonable in the light of the anticipated or actual harm caused by the breach, the difficulties of proof of loss, and the inconvenience or nonfeasibility of otherwise obtaining an adequate remedy. A term fixing unreasonably large liquidated damages is void as a penalty.

(b) Right of buyer to restitution.—Where the seller justifiably withholds delivery of goods because of the breach of the buyer, the buyer is entitled to restitution of any amount by which the sum of his payments exceeds:

(1) the amount to which the seller is entitled by virtue of terms liquidating the damages of the seller in accordance with subsection (a); or

(2) in the absence of such terms, 20% of the value of the total performance for which the buyer is obligated under the contract or $500 whichever is smaller.

* * *

3. He identifies four types of protection:

First, the defaulting party's right to recovery is subject to the aggrieved party's right to offset his damages. Second, the measure of benefit is limited to the actual enrichment and cannot exceed a ratable portion of the contract price. Third, restitution is denied to the extent that the criteria for a valid liquidated damages clause are present. Fourth, restitution is denied if the aggrieved party seeks and is entitled to specific performance. Perillo, *supra,* at 50 (footnotes omitted).

another." Perillo, *supra,* at 50. *See also* 12 S. Williston, *supra,* § 1473, at 222 ("The mores of the time and place will often determine which policy will be followed.").

Many jurisdictions have rejected the common law rule and permit recovery by the defaulting party. * * *

This development has been called the modern trend. *See Quillen v. Kelley,* 216 Md. 396, 140 A.2d 517 (1958). *See also* 12 S. Williston, *supra,* § 1473, at 222 (cases permitting recovery are now the weight of the authority); 5A Corbin on Contracts, *supra,* § 1122, at 3 (common law rule is broad statement not supported by the actual decisions). *But see* 1 G. Palmer, *The Law of Restitution* 568 (1978) (no valid generalization may be made regarding when a defaulting vendee can recover). It may be that the growing number of jurisdictions permitting recovery have been influenced by the widespread adoption of the Uniform Commercial Code § 2–718. *See, e.g., Maxey v. Glindmeyer,* 379 So.2d 297 (Miss.1980) (allowing recovery of excess of seller's actual damages in land sale contract by following the logic of the state statute equivalent to § 2–718 of the Uniform Commercial Code). Indeed, the common law rule is no longer intact even with respect to land sales contracts. *See, e.g., Honey v. Henry's Franchise Leasing Corp.,* 64 Cal.2d 801, 415 P.2d 833, 52 Cal.Rptr. 18 (1966); *McLendon v. Safe Realty Corp.,* 401 N.E.2d 80 (Ind.App.1980); *Newcomb v. Ray, supra; De Leon v. Aldrete, supra; and see* 1 G. Palmer, *supra,* at 596 n. 15 (citing cases).

In Pennsylvania, the common law rule has been applied to contracts for the sale of real property. *Kaufman Hotel & Restaurant Co. v. Thomas,* 411 Pa. 87, 190 A.2d 434 (1963); *Luria v. Robbins,* 223 Pa.Super. 456, 302 A.2d 361 (1973). In such cases, however, the seller has several remedies against a breaching buyer, including, in appropriate cases, an action for specific performance or for the purchase price. *See Trachtenburg v. Sibarco Stations, Inc.,* 477 Pa. 517, 384 A.2d 1209 (1978). *See also* 5A Corbin on Contracts, *supra,* § 1145. As long as the seller remains ready, able, and willing to perform a contract for the sale of real property, the breaching buyer has no right to restitution of payments made prior to default. *See* 5A Corbin on Contracts, *supra,* at § 1130.

The common law rule has also been applied in Pennsylvania to contracts for the sale of goods. *Atlantic City Tire and Rubber Corp. v. Southwark Foundry & Machine Co.,* 289 Pa. 569, 137 A. 807 (1927). However, Pennsylvania has since adopted the Uniform Commercial Code, which, as to contracts for the sale of goods, has modified the common law rule by 13 Pa.C.S. § 2718(b), which permits a breaching party to recover restitution. *See* note 2, *supra.*

The viability of the common law rule permitting forfeiture has also been undermined in other areas of Pennsylvania law. In *Estate of Cahen,* 483 Pa. 157, 168 n. 10, 394 A.2d 958, 964 n. 10 (1978), the Supreme Court held that assuming that a breaching fiduciary could recover in unjust enrichment, the basis would be Restatement of Contracts § 357

(1932), which allows recovery by a breaching party to the extent that the benefits exceed the losses sustained by the other party.

–3–

In regard to the present case, § 374 of the Restatement (Second) of Contracts represents a more enlightened approach than the common law rule. "Rules of contract law are not rules of punishment; the contract breaker is not an outlaw." Perillo, *supra*, at 50. The party who committed a breach should be entitled to recover "any benefit ... in excess of the loss that he has caused by his own breach." Restatement (Second) of Contracts § 374(1).

This conclusion leads to the further conclusion that we should remand this case to the trial court. The trial court rested its decision on the common law rule. * * * Thus it never considered whether appellant is entitled to restitution, Restatement (Second) of Contracts § 374(1), nor, if appellant is not entitled to restitution, whether retention of the $25,000 was "reasonable in the light of the anticipated or actual loss caused by the breach and the difficulties of proof of loss," *id.,* § 374(2).

Remanded for further proceedings consistent with this opinion. Jurisdiction relinquished.

* * *

TAMILIA, JUDGE, dissenting: I strongly dissent. In the first instance, the majority does not and cannot cite *any* Pennsylvania authority adopting the rule cited in § 374 of the Second Restatement of Contracts. Although the ostensible basis for remand is the trial court's reliance on outmoded law, the majority relies on law so new as to be virtually unknown in this jurisdiction. The law in Pennsylvania has been and continues to be that where a binding contract exists, and there is no allegation that the contract itself is void or voidable, a breaching party is not entitled to recovery. *Luria v. Robbins,* 223 Pa.Super. 456, 302 A.2d 361 (1973). While our Supreme Court may yet abrogate the forfeiture principle in this Commonwealth, it has not yet seen fit to do so, and we may not usurp its prerogatives, particularly when the result would be unjust.

Problems

26. Buyer agreed to purchase a specified quantity of vegetable oil for $1,000,000, making a down payment of $217,000. Buyer defaulted. In this action Buyer seeks to recover its down payment. Seller counter-claims, alleging it has been damaged because of the drop in value of oil. What, if anything, may Buyer recover?

27. Plaintiff, a consulting engineer, took a part-time job with the defendant in its research and development department. In return for plaintiff's promise to work a minimum of fifteen hours a week for a year, plaintiff was promised $20,000 payable at the end of the year. After six months, plaintiff quit to take jobs elsewhere on more favorable terms. Plaintiff seeks to recover the reasonable value of his services. What result?

SECTION 6. RECOVERY BY A PARTY IN DEFAULT: DIVISIBILITY, INDEPENDENT PROMISES, AND SEPARATE CONTRACTS

(Calamari & Perillo 5th 11.23–11.26)

SCAVENGER, INC. v. GT INTERACTIVE SOFTWARE, INC.

New York Supreme Court, Appellate Division, 2000.
273 A.D.2d 60, 708 N.Y.S.2d 405.

[Scavenger, a computer game developer brought action against computer-game distributor. The Supreme Court, New York County, Barry Cozier, J., granted developer's motion for partial summary judgment on cause of action for payments and entered judgment for $2,411,114 against distributor. Distributor appealed.]

MEMORANDUM DECISION. * * * * Defendant's contract with plaintiff, containing separate production and payment schedules for each of the four CD–ROM games plaintiff was to deliver to defendant, was a divisible contract (see, Christian v. Christian, 42 N.Y.2d 63, 73, 396 N.Y.S.2d 817, 365 N.E.2d 849). Accordingly, plaintiff's right to recover payments guaranteed under the contract for the two CD–ROM games delivered to defendant was not impaired by plaintiff's failure to deliver the two remaining games and, in its award of partial summary judgment, the motion court correctly determined, as a matter of law, that defendant's claim that plaintiff breached the parties' agreement by failing to deliver the CD–ROM games on time, had been waived by defendant's requests for significant modifications in the games and by defendant's acceptance and marketing of the games without objection (see, Fifty States Mgt. v. Niagara Permanent Sav. & Loan, 58 A.D.2d 177, 181, 396 N.Y.S.2d 925).

Problems

28. V owned a parcel of property improved with a building that consisted of residential space as well as a retail store operated by V. P desired to acquire the property primarily so that P's brother could operate the store. V and P subscribed the following writing:

"Received of P $5,000 deposit on property 1900 Penn. Ave., purchase price $140,000, settlement to be made on or before June 25.

"Store fixtures, $7,000. Store inventory to be paid at market prices.

"In case title is not clear, deposit to be returned."

Prior to June 25, V materially breached the contract by selling the inventory to B who paid value and had no notice of the above quoted agreement. V seeks specific performance of the first paragraph of the agreement. P seeks restitution of the down payment. What result?

29. Plaintiff employee entered into a bilateral contract of employment to commence on April 1 for a one-year term, to be paid "$150 per year, payable monthly, if he wishes." At breakfast on July 8, plaintiff, who had not previously requested his pay, demanded that he be paid what was due him by noon of that day. Defendant, not having ready cash because the job site was distant from defendant's business headquarters, refused the demand and plaintiff quit at noon. What, if anything, may plaintiff recover?

30. Lerner entered into an "industrial preparedness contract" with the United States for the production of microwave magic tees. The contract had four "steps," for each of which a separate price was apportioned. Steps I and II required going through pilot production. Step III required the purchase of additional equipment. Substantial performance of these steps was completed by October 1, 1953 when Lerner became insolvent and transferred his assets to an assignee for the benefit of creditors in lieu of bankruptcy. Step IV required volume production, but only on order from the government in the event of national emergency. The assignee sues the government for the balance due for Steps I–III. What result? Bear in mind that the assignment disables Lerner from further performance and operates as a material breach.

31. Defendant, the owner of a motel, contracted for seven signs to be painted and installed by the plaintiff along the roadside. The signs were designed to lead motorists to the motel. Each sign had an apportioned price. Signs number 1, 2, 3, 6, and 7 were duly installed. Sign number 4 was never installed and sign number 5 was installed at a location other than that provided in the contract. Defendant refused to pay anything. The trial judge, sitting without a jury, found the contract to be severable. Defendant appeals. What result?

32. Plaintiff controlled and was the editor of, a small, but successful, specialized publishing corporation. On the same date, he entered into two written agreements with the defendant, a major publisher. Under the first, all the assets of his corporation were sold to the defendant. Under the second, he was to be employed by defendant for a five-year period. The plaintiff was wrongfully discharged under the second contract and has been awarded damages. In the same proceeding, he also seeks to cancel the first contract. What result?

SECTION 7. WRONGFUL PREVENTION AND NON-COOPERATION

———

(Calamari & Perillo 5th §§ 11.27, 11.28, 11.38 and 11.39)

———

*"[C]ontract is, par excellence, the juridical expression of cooperation * * *. To co-operate, in short, is to participate in a common task."*

* * *

"[Contract law] forces us to assume obligations that we have not contracted for, in the exact sense of the word, since we have not deliberated upon
them * * *. We co-operate because we wish to, but our voluntary cooperation creates duties for us that we did not desire."

E.   Durkheim, The Division of Labor in Society 123–24, 214 (Free Press.
ed. 1964)

CANTRELL–WAIND & ASSOCIATES, INC. v. GUILLAUME MOTORSPORTS, INC.

Court of Appeals of Arkansas, 1998.
62 Ark.App. 66, 968 S.W.2d 72.

BIRD, JUDGE. Cantrell–Waind & Associates, Inc., has appealed from a
summary judgment entered for appellee Guillaume Motorsports, Inc., in
its action to recover a real estate brokerage commission. Because we
agree with appellant that the circuit judge erred in his interpretation of
the applicable law and because genuine issues of material fact remain to
be tried, we reverse and remand.

On August 1, 1994, appellee, represented by its president and sole
stock-holder Todd Williams, agreed to lease real property in Bentonville
to Kenneth Bower and Kay Bower. The lease gave the Bowers an option
to purchase and provided for the payment of a commission to appellant,
the real estate broker in this transaction, as follows:

> In the event of the exercise of this option within the first twenty-
> four (24) month period, ten per cent (10%) of the monthly rental
> payments shall apply to the purchase price. Thereafter, this credit
> shall reduce two per cent (2%) per year until the expiration of the
> original lease term hereof, to the effect that the credit will be eight
> per cent (8%) during the third year, six per cent (6%) during the
> fourth year, and four per cent (4%) during the fifth year. The sales
> price shall be $295,000.00. GUILLAUME MOTORSPORTS, INC.,
> agrees [to] pay CANTREL–WAIND & ASSOCIATES, INC., a real
> estate commission of $15,200.00 upon closing of sale of the property
> under this Option to Purchase, provided the closing occurs within
> two (2) years from the date of execution of the Lease with Option to
> Purchase.

The Bowers' attorney, Charles Edward Young, III, notified Williams
in writing on April 23, 1996, that the Bowers chose to exercise the option
to purchase, and that they anticipated closing at the earliest possible
date. Young also sent a copy of this letter to Samuel Reeves, appellee's
attorney. Soon after this, Williams approached Mr. Bower and offered to
credit him with one-half of the appellant's $15,200 commission if he

would agree to delay closing until after August 1, 1996. Mr. Bower declined this offer.

Ruth Ann Whitehead, a loan officer at the Bank of Bentonville, notified Mr. Bower on July 19, 1996, that the loan had been approved and that she awaited notification of a closing date. In his deposition, Young said that he attempted to set a July closing date on behalf of the Bowers but had been told by Ms. Whitehead, Reeves, and a representative of the title company that Williams had told them he would be out of the country in late July and unavailable for closing until after August 1.

Young also said that he had asked Reeves if Williams would utilize a power of attorney for closing before August 1 but Williams refused. Williams did not leave the country and was in Bentonville July 22 through 25. Closing occurred on August 14, 1996, and the commission was not paid.

Appellant filed a complaint against Guillaume Motorsports, Inc., on August 12, 1996, for breach of contract. Appellee moved for summary judgment on the ground that it was under no obligation to close the transaction before August 1. In support of its motion, appellee filed the affidavits of Ms. Whitehead and Mr. Carroll, who stated that, to their knowledge, a closing date was not scheduled before August 14, 1996.

Appellee Williams also filed his affidavit stating that a closing date was not established before August 14, 1996, and that the Bowers had not demanded an earlier closing date. Further, he admitted: "While I did in fact approach Kenneth Bower with a proposal to reduce the purchase price if he would agree to establish a closing date after August 1, 1996, my offer was not accepted and no such agreement was made." He said although it would not have bothered him to put the closing off until after August 1, he did not think it was a "conscious decision" not to be available until after August 1.

In a hearing on the motion for summary judgment, counsel for appellee argued that neither the corporation nor Williams was under any obligation to close prior to August 1. He contended there was no bad faith to be inferred by the deliberate avoidance of a real estate commission that is keyed to a "drop-dead" date. He said the real estate broker agreed to the terms of the contract and was bound by it. Counsel pointed out the two separate terms used in the contract when referring to the option to purchase and the closing. The contract stated that to get the maximum discount in the purchase price the Bowers had to exercise the option before August 1, 1996. However, the clause referring to the commission stated that the transaction had to close by August 1. Counsel stated, "I believe my client had every right to do anything within his power, short of breaching his contract with this buyer, to see that this closing didn't occur earlier than that date so he would not owe the commission."

In response to appellee's motion for summary judgment, appellant argued that appellee (by Williams) had a duty to act in good faith and that, in taking steps to prevent the transaction from closing before August 1, 1996, appellee had not acted in good faith. Appellant contended that all contingencies and requirements for the loan had been satisfied by July 19, 1996, and that Mr. and Ms. Bower had attempted to establish a closing date before August 1, but had been deliberately prevented from doing so by Williams's misrepresentations that he would be out of the country and unavailable to close until after August 1.

* * *

In his order granting summary judgment, the judge stated that appellee had no obligation to appellant to arrange for a closing date that would have entitled appellant to a commission and said that the real estate commission was "clearly avoidable" by appellee. * * *

The term of the contract providing that a commission would be due appellant only if closing occurred before August 1, 1996, is a condition precedent. See Stacy v. Williams, 38 Ark.App.192, 834 S.W.2d 156 (1992). When a contract term leaves a decision to the discretion of one party, that decision is virtually unreviewable; however, courts will become involved when the party making the decision is charged with bad faith. Vigoro Indus., Inc. v. Crisp, 82 F.3d 785 (8th Cir.1996).

In Willbanks v. Bibler, 216 Ark. 68, 224 S.W.2d 33 (1949), the Arkansas Supreme Court held that "he who prevents the doing of a thing shall not avail himself of the nonperformance he has occasioned." Id. at 72, 224 S.W.2d at 35. See also Samuel Williston, The Law of Contracts § 677 (3d ed.1961). * * *

A party has an implied obligation not to do anything that would prevent, hinder, or delay performance. [Citations omitted].

Comment b to section 225 of the Restatement (Second) of Contracts (1981) provides that the non-occurrence of a condition of a duty is said to be "excused" when the condition need no longer occur in order for performance of the duty to become due: "It may be excused by prevention or hindrance of its occurrence through a breach of the duty of good faith and fair dealing." The Restatement (Second) of Contracts § 205 (1981) states: "Every contract imposes upon each party a duty of good faith and fair dealing in its performance and its enforcement." This legal principle also applies to contracts providing for the payment of commissions to real estate agents. McKay and Co. v. Garland, 17 Ark.App. 1, 701 S.W.2d 392 (1986). Accordingly, we hold that the circuit court erred in failing to recognize that a duty of good faith and fair dealing was included in this contract and, therefore, appellee was obligated to not deliberately avoid closing the transaction before August 1, 1996.

Our above holding requires a determination of whether there is a genuine issue of material fact as to whether appellee's actions prevented or hindered the occurrence of the condition precedent. The burden of sustaining a motion for summary judgment is on the moving party. [The court discusses the procedural requirements for summary judgment and determines that summary judgment should be denied]. Accordingly, we reverse the circuit judge's entry of summary judgment for appellee and remand this case for trial.

Reversed and remanded. ROBBINS, C.J., and ROAF, J., agree.

SWARTZ v. WAR MEMORIAL COMMISSION OF ROCHESTER

N.Y. Supreme Court, Appellate Division, Fourth Department, 1966.
25 A.D.2d 90, 267 N.Y.S.2d 253.

PER CURIAM. Plaintiff's complaint, dismissed by Special Term for lack of merit, alleges, inter alia, that by contract with defendant Commission he has the exclusive concession for the sale of food and refreshments in the Rochester War Memorial Building [a sports arena—ed.]; that on November 15, 1965 defendant Commission removed its prohibition against the sale of beer and ale therein and decided that sale thereof be permitted; that plaintiff chose not to sell said beverages; that on November 30, 1965 defendant Commission notified him that unless he made application for a license to sell beer and ale within 30 days he would be removed and would not be permitted to continue as concessionaire in said building. He further alleges that defendants threaten to violate his rights under the contract and he seeks a judgment declaring the rights and legal relations of the parties and decreeing that defendants are precluded by the contract from doing any act which may interfere with his right to continue as sole concessionaire.

* * *

The introductory clause of the agreement recites: "It is the mutual desire of the parties hereto to enter into a contract whereby * * * the Concessionaire shall furnish such services as are hereinafter provided * * * ". The contract provides for sale of food, beverages, novelties, souvenirs, tobacco, cigars, candy, and other items. The contract further provides in paragraph 6 as follows:

> "The privileges and sales rights granted herein shall not include the right to sell any alcoholic beverages during any period or periods in which such sale or sales are prohibited. However, in the event that such prohibition is removed at any time during the term of this agreement, the exclusive sales rights granted herein shall extend to the sale of such alcoholic beverages and the amount to be paid by the Concessionaire to the Commission on such sales as rental shall be identical to that provided for sales of food and beverages."

The agreement recognizes the need of a license to sell beer and ale and provides that the Commission will cooperate with the Concessionaire in obtaining one. Although paragraph 6 contains no express provision requiring the Concessionaire to apply for a license, the thirteenth paragraph provides:

> "Prior to entering into any and all operations contemplated hereunder, the Concessionaire shall obtain and keep in force all necessary local, state and/or federal permits or licenses * * * ".

Considering all the provisions of the contract and the inferences naturally derivable therefrom as to the intent and object of the parties in making it and the result which they intended to accomplish by its performance, we conclude that it was plaintiff's duty to attempt to qualify himself to sell beer and ale by applying for a license to do so.

Here the agreement expressed the mutual intent of the parties that plaintiff should perform the services provided for in the contract, one of which was to sell alcoholic beverages whenever the prohibition against such sale had been removed. The intent and object of the parties and the result which they intended to accomplish by its performance are apparent. Both parties would derive income from its performance. The public would be convenienced by being able to purchase the food, beverages, and merchandise specified in the contract. Acceptance by plaintiff of the exclusive sales right given him by the contract was an assumption of its duties. Unless he sold the items specified in the contract neither party would derive income from it. His promise to pay defendant Commission a percentage of the gross receipts resulting from the exclusive agency was a promise to use reasonable efforts to bring profits and revenues into existence (Wood v. Lucy, Lady Duff–Gordon, 222 N.Y. 88, 91, 92, 118 N.E. 214, 215). It was indispensable to defendant Commission that plaintiff having the exclusive right to sell should use all diligence to the end that sales be made of the specified items including beer and ale. (Booth v. Cleveland Rolling Mill Co., 74 N.Y. 15, 25.) The reasonable efforts and diligence required of plaintiff to bring profits and revenues into existence imposed upon him the duty to apply for a license to sell beer and ale. His failure to do so amounted to a default on his part of an obligation of the contract. The default continued unremedied for thirty days after his receipt of written notice of it, and the contract was terminated in accordance with its terms.

The judgment and order should be modified in accordance with this opinion, and as so modified affirmed.

Judgment and order unanimously modified on the law and facts in accordance with the opinion and as modified affirmed, without costs of this appeal to either party.

STOP & SHOP, INC. v. GANEM

Supreme Judicial Court of Massachusetts, 1964.
347 Mass. 697, 200 N.E.2d 248.

WHITTEMORE, JUSTICE. The defendants in this bill for declaratory relief are lessors under a percentage lease. They have appealed from the final decree in the Superior Court that ruled that the lease does not expressly or impliedly require the plaintiff, as lessee, to use the demised premises for any particular purpose or to keep the premises open and there engage in the supermarket business. Except for brief testimony which is reported, the facts were stipulated.

The lease, dated August 24, 1953, demised a lot and building at 154 Merrimack Street, Haverhill, for thirteen years and six months from September 1, 1953, for "the minimum rental" of $22,000 a year and the further rent of 1¼% "of all gross sales" above $1,269,230.60 "made by the Lessee on the leased premises during each twelve month period." But the percentage rent was to be paid only if sales at the demised premises and at premises in Lawrence exceeded $3,000,000 a year. * * *

The lease required that the lessee should pay the amount of the increases in the annual real estate taxes and should receive the amount of the decreases therein, measured on the 1946 figure.

The lease does not state the purposes for which the premises are to be used. Nothing therein in terms requires that the premises be used for any purpose or bars the opening by the lessee of places of business competitive to the lessee's business in the demised premises. The lease does, however, require the lessee to us (sic) suitable cash registers to record all sales, to keep accurate books, to furnish statements of gross sales on demand, and at the end of each yearly period to furnish such a statement certified by a certified public accountant. The testimony showed that when the lease was made the plaintiff was engaged in the supermarket business and that the lessors knew it. The premises prior to August 24, 1953, had been used for the conduct of a market.

The plaintiff had occupied the premises as a supermarket through 1962. It had paid percentage rent in 1956 ($2,288.15) and in 1957 ($377.21) but in no other year, and had paid excess taxes in each year. The plaintiff intended to cease operating a supermarket in the premises shortly after January 1, 1963, but to continue to pay the minimum rent and any excess real estate taxes and otherwise to conform to the lease. The defendant lessors had threatened suit to compel the continued operation of a supermarket or, alternatively, for damages.

The defendant lessors filed a counterclaim which alleged that the plaintiff beginning in 1956 had opened two competing stores in Haverhill, one within one-half mile and the other within about one mile of the demised premises. The prayers of the counterclaim were (1) that the lease be reformed to provide that the plaintiff continuously operate the premises as a supermarket, (2) that the plaintiff be ordered to pay to the defendants as part of the rent of the demised premises 1¼% of gross sales from all the plaintiff's stores in Haverhill in excess of $1,269,230.60, and (3) for general relief. An interlocutory decree sustained the plaintiff's demurrer to the counterclaim "with leave to amend denied." The lessors took no appeal from that decree.

Other facts are referred to later in the opinion.

The issue presented by the bill for declaratory relief is whether there is in the lease an implied covenant to continue operations.[2] The counterclaim presents the issue whether the lessee may open competing stores and then discontinue operations. We consider first the issue under the bill.

---

2. The cessation of operations was threatened several years before the end of the lease. Hence, we need not consider whether an implied covenant to continue operations would be enforceable shortly be- fore the end of the term. See Selber Bros. Inc. v. Newstadt's Shoe Stores, 203 La. 316, 324, 14 So.2d 10. Compare Orkin's Fashion Stores, Inc. v. S.H. Kress & Co., 68 N.Y.S.2d 766, 767 (N.Y.Supr.Ct.).

The controlling principles are well established. An omission to specify an agreement in a written lease is evidence that there was no such understanding. Snider v. Deban, 249 Mass. 59, 65, 144 N.E. 69. Covenants will not be extended by implication unless the implication is clear and undoubted. Smiley v. McLauthlin, 138 Mass. 363, 364–365; Mutual Paper Co. v. Hoague–Sprague Corp., 297 Mass. 294, 301, 8 N.E.2d 802. Justice, common sense and the probable intention of the parties are guides to construction of a written instrument. Clark v. State St. Trust Co., 270 Mass. 140, 153, 169 N.E. 897. "Since the governing principle * * * is the justifiable assumption by one party of a certain intention on the part of the other, the undertaking of each promisor in a contract must include any promises which a reasonable person in the position of the promisee would be justified in understanding were included." Williston, Contracts (Rev. ed.) § 1293, p. 3682. Russo v. Enterprise Realty Co., Inc., Mass., 199 N.E.2d 689, and cases cited.

The plaintiff contends that notwithstanding the interest of the lessors in having the premises operated so as to give it the benefit of possible percentage rent, the absence of an express requirement to operate together with a more than nominal minimum rent exclude the implication of a covenant to continue operations.

This may state too broad a rule. For even if there is a more than nominal minimum rent, other circumstances such as that the fixed rent is significantly below the fair rental value of the property might justify the conclusion that the parties intended that the lessors have the benefit of the percentage rent throughout the term.

The record does not show the fair rental value of the demised premises. An apparently substantial minimum rent in an apparently complete written lease, in the absence of a showing of disparity between the fixed rent and the fair rental value, gives ground for the inference that fixed rent and the lessee's self-interest in producing sales were the only assurance of rent that the lessor required. Other circumstances may give rise to the same inference. In cases where the minimum rent was not substantial continued operation has been held contemplated.

In Smiley v. McLauthlin, 138 Mass. 363, this court held that where rent under a lease of a brick yard was to be computed on the basis of bricks made with no provision for minimum rent, there was no implied covenant that the lessee would operate the yard. The opinion stressed the extrinsic circumstances attending the making of the lease. "The premises leased were not a brick yard in operation, equipped for work, but barren, unoccupied land. The parties did not know the amount of clay on the land, nor whether brick could be made on the land at a profit * * *. The lease, applied to the subject matter, furnishes indications that the parties regarded the enterprise as experimental, and that any stipulation binding the lessee to work the yard was purposely omitted." Id. 138 Mass. at 365. The questions may be asked whether the parties did not intend a contract, and if so whether an implied covenant at least to try to operate the brick yard was the only consideration given by the lessee. Compare Wood v. Lucy, Lady Duff–Gordon, 222 N.Y. 88, 118 N.E.

214. As to output and requirement contracts see Neofotistos v. Harvard Brewing Co., 341 Mass. 684, 686–687, 171 N.E.2d 865.

The minimum rent in this lease appears to be substantial. The figure of $22,000 is obviously not nominal in a lease that fixes as a base real estate tax figure the 1946 tax of $3,744.90. The total of real estate taxes for 1954 was $5,127.71. This roughly indicates the valuation for tax purposes of the demised premises at about the time the lease was made.

The burden of showing a disparity between fixed rent and fair rental value such as to furnish ground for implying a covenant to operate would be on the lessors.

Had the lessors brought an action for damages for breach of an implied covenant to continue operations they would, of course, have had the burden of showing the covenant. That the lessee initiated the proceeding for declaratory relief does not shift that burden to the lessee.
* * *

* * *

There is in this record no basis for implying a covenant to continue to operate beyond that time when in the business judgment of the lessee operations at the demised location should cease. The lessors have not shown that "a reasonable person in the position of the * * * [lessors] would be justified in understanding" (Williston, Contracts [Rev. ed.] § 1293) that such a covenant was intended and hence implied.

The percentage rent provision of course gave the lessors an interest in the lessee's operations of the demised premises as a retail store. We assume, without deciding, that such interest could be protected against certain acts of the lessee, as for example, discontinuance of operations for spite or to inflict harm. Such issues are outside this record for there is no intimation that the plaintiff has acted or proposes to act in respect of the leased premises otherwise than as its sound business judgment dictates in fairly promoting its retail business in Haverhill.

* * *

The allegations underlying the prayer that the sales of other stores be included in the computation of percentage rent are, that the "plaintiff has not in good faith operated the demised premises so as to obtain the greatest volume of sales at this location, but has opened wrongfully [two] other stores at nearby locations, selling the same merchandise at lower prices." The effect of the two newly opened stores was, it is alleged, to diminish sales.

We assume that the prayer, although cast in terms of a specific form of relief for the alleged wrong, may be taken as asking damages for the wrongful invasion of the lessors' rights. But the counterclaim does not state a basis for the recovery of damages of any kind.

The allegation "not in good faith" adds nothing to the facts stated. In context, it says no more than that the plaintiff has acted in violation of implied obligations of the lease. The lessors do not contend otherwise.

The lessee, being free to disregard the effect on the lessors of its business decisions in respect of stopping operations, was free also to open stores elsewhere. We assume, without deciding, that had the lessee opened a competing store in the same location as the demised premises, that is adjacent, or nearly so, there might have been a basis for requiring it to regard the lessors' interest under the percentage rent provisions in its conduct of the two stores. In such a case the lessee's acts would affirm the business advantage of remaining at the very place at which it had committed itself as tenant of the lessors. * * *

* * *

The interlocutory decree sustaining the demurrer and the final decree (construed as including a dismissal of the counterclaim) are affirmed.

MARKET STREET ASSOCIATES LIMITED PARTNERSHIP v. FREY

United States Court of Appeals, Seventh Circuit, 1991.
941 F.2d 588.

POSNER, CIRCUIT JUDGE. Market Street Associates Limited Partnership and its general partner appeal from a judgment for the defendants, General Electric Pension Trust and its trustees, entered upon cross-motions for summary judgment in a diversity suit that pivots on the doctrine of "good faith" performance of a contract. Cf. Robert Summers, " 'Good Faith' in General Contract Law and the Sales Provisions of the Uniform Commercial Code," 54 Va.L.Rev. 195, 232–43 (1968). Wisconsin law applies—common law rather than Uniform Commercial Code, because the contract is for land rather than for goods, UCC § 2–102; Wis.Stat. § 402.102 * * *

* * *

We come at last to the contract dispute out of which the case arises. In 1968, J.C. Penney Company, the retail chain, entered into a sale and leaseback arrangement with General Electric Pension Trust in order to finance Penney's growth. Under the arrangement Penney sold properties to the pension trust which the trust then leased back to Penney for a term of 25 years. Paragraph 34 of the lease entitles the lessee to "request Lessor [the pension trust] to finance the costs and expenses of construction of additional Improvements upon the Premises," provided the amount of the costs and expenses is at least $250,000. Upon receiving the request, the pension trust "agrees to give reasonable consideration to providing the financing of such additional Improvements and Lessor and Lessee shall negotiate in good faith concerning the construction of such Improvements and the financing by Lessor of such costs and expenses." Paragraph 34 goes on to provide that, should the negotiations fail, the lessee shall be entitled to repurchase the property at a price roughly equal to the price at which Penney sold it to the pension trust in the first place, plus 6 percent a year for each year since the original purchase. So if the average annual appreciation in the property exceeded 6 percent, a breakdown in negotiations over the financing of improvements would entitle Penney to buy back the property for less than its market value (assuming it had sold the property to the pension trust in the first place at its then market value).

One of these leases was for a shopping center in Milwaukee. In 1987 Penney assigned this lease to Market Street Associates, which the following year received an inquiry from a drugstore chain that wanted to open a store in the shopping center, provided (as is customary) that Market Street Associates built the store for it. Whether Market Street Associates was pessimistic about obtaining financing from the pension trust, still the lessor of the shopping center, or for other reasons, it initially sought financing for the project from other sources. But they were unwilling to lend the necessary funds without a mortgage on the shopping center, which Market Street Associates could not give because it was not the owner but only the lessee. It decided therefore to try to buy the property back from the pension trust. Market Street Associates' general partner, Orenstein, tried to call David Erb of the pension trust, who was responsible for the property in question. Erb did not return his calls, so Orenstein wrote him, expressing an interest in buying the property and asking him to "review your file on this matter and call me so that we can discuss it further." At first, Erb did not reply. Eventually Orenstein did reach Erb, who promised to review the file and get back to him. A few days later an associate of Erb called Orenstein and indicated an interest in selling the property for $3 million, which Orenstein considered much too high.

That was in June of 1988. On July 28, Market Street Associates wrote a letter to the pension trust formally requesting funding for $2 million in improvements to the shopping center. The letter made no reference to paragraph 34 of the lease; indeed, it did not mention the lease. The letter asked Erb to call Orenstein to discuss the matter. Erb, in what was becoming a habit of unresponsiveness, did not call. On August 16, Orenstein sent a second letter—certified mail, return receipt requested—again requesting financing and this time referring to the lease, though not expressly to paragraph 34. The heart of the letter is the following two sentences: "The purpose of this letter is to ask again that you advise us immediately if you are willing to provide the financing pursuant to the lease. If you are willing, we propose to enter into negotiation to amend the ground lease appropriately." The very next day, Market Street Associates received from Erb a letter, dated August 10, turning down the original request for financing on the ground that it did not "meet our current investment criteria": the pension trust was not interested in making loans for less than $7 million. On August 22, Orenstein replied to Erb by letter, noting that his letter of August 10 and Erb's letter of August 16 had evidently crossed in the mails, expressing disappointment at the turn-down, and stating that Market Street Associates would seek financing elsewhere. That was the last contact between the parties until September 27, when Orenstein sent

Erb a letter stating that Market Street Associates was exercising the option granted it by paragraph 34 to purchase the property upon the terms specified in that paragraph in the event that negotiations over financing broke down.

The pension trust refused to sell, and this suit to compel specific performance followed. Apparently the price computed by the formula in paragraph 34 is only $1 million. The market value must be higher, or Market Street Associates wouldn't be trying to coerce conveyance at the paragraph 34 price; whether it is as high as $3 million, however, the record does not reveal.

The district judge granted summary judgment for the pension trust on two grounds that he believed to be separate although closely related. The first was that, by failing in its correspondence with the pension trust to mention paragraph 34 of the lease, Market Street Associates had prevented the negotiations over financing that are a condition precedent to the lessee's exercise of the purchase option from taking place. Second, this same failure violated the duty of good faith, which the common law of Wisconsin, as of other states, reads into every contract. [Citations omitted]. In support of both grounds the judge emphasized a statement by Orenstein in his deposition that it had occurred to him that Erb mightn't know about paragraph 34, though this was unlikely (Orenstein testified) because Erb or someone else at the pension trust would probably check the file and discover the paragraph and realize that if the trust refused to negotiate over the request for financing, Market Street Associates, as Penney's assignee, would be entitled to walk off with the property for (perhaps) a song. The judge inferred that Market Street Associates didn't want financing from the pension trust—that it just wanted an opportunity to buy the property at a bargain price and hoped that the pension trust wouldn't realize the implications of turning down the request for financing. Market Street Associates should, the judge opined, have advised the pension trust that it was requesting financing pursuant to paragraph 34, so that the trust would understand the penalty for refusing to negotiate.

* * *

The pension trust's argument, which the district judge bought, is that either as a matter of simple contract interpretation or under the compulsion of the doctrine of good faith, a provision requiring Market Street Associates to remind the pension trust of paragraph 34 should be read into the lease.

It seems to us that these are one ground rather than two. A court has to have a reason to interpolate a clause into a contract. The only reason that has been suggested here is that it is necessary to prevent Market Street Associates from reaping a reward for what the pension trust believes to have been Market Street's bad faith. So we must consider the meaning of the contract duty of "good faith." The Wisconsin cases are cryptic as to its meaning though emphatic about its existence, so we must cast our net wider. We do so mindful of Learned

Hand's warning, that "such words as 'fraud,' 'good faith,' 'whim,' 'caprice,' 'arbitrary action,' and 'legal fraud' ... obscure the issue." Thompson–Starrett Co. v. La Belle Iron Works, 17 F.2d 536, 541 (2d Cir.1927). Indeed they do. Summers, supra, at 207–20; 2 Farnsworth on Contracts § 7.17a, at pp. 328–32. The particular confusion to which the vaguely moralistic overtones of "good faith" give rise is the belief that every contract establishes a fiduciary relationship. A fiduciary is required to treat his principal as if the principal were he, and therefore he may not take advantage of the principal's incapacity, ignorance, inexperience, or even naivete. [Citations omitted]. If Market Street Associates were the fiduciary of General Electric Pension Trust, then (we may assume) it could not take advantage of Mr. Erb's apparent ignorance of paragraph 34, however exasperating Erb's failure to return Orenstein's phone calls was and however negligent Erb or his associates were in failing to read the lease before turning down Orenstein's request for financing.

But it is unlikely that Wisconsin wishes, in the name of good faith, to make every contract signatory his brother's keeper, especially when the brother is the immense and sophisticated General Electric Pension Trust, whose lofty indifference to small (= < $7 million) transactions is the signifier of its grandeur. In fact the law contemplates that people frequently will take advantage of the ignorance of those with whom they contract, without thereby incurring liability. Restatement, supra, § 161, comment d. The duty of honesty, of good faith even expansively conceived, is not a duty of candor. You can make a binding contract to purchase something you know your seller undervalues. [Citations omitted]. That of course is a question about formation, not performance, and the particular duty of good faith under examination here relates to the latter rather than to the former. But even after you have signed a contract, you are not obliged to become an altruist toward the other party and relax the terms if he gets into trouble in performing his side of the bargain. Kham & Nate's Shoes No. 2, Inc. v. First Bank, 908 F.2d 1351, 1357 (7th Cir.1990). Otherwise mere difficulty of performance would excuse a contracting party—which it does not. Northern Indiana Public Service Co. v. Carbon County Coal Co., 799 F.2d 265, 276–78 (7th Cir.1986); Jennie–O Foods, Inc. v. United States, 217 Ct.Cl. 314, 580 F.2d 400, 409 (1978) (per curiam); 2 Farnsworth on Contracts, supra, § 7.17a, at p. 330.

But it is one thing to say that you can exploit your superior knowledge of the market—for if you cannot, you will not be able to recoup the investment you made in obtaining that knowledge—or that you are not required to spend money bailing out a contract partner who has gotten into trouble. It is another thing to say that you can take deliberate advantage of an oversight by your contract partner concerning his rights under the contract. Such taking advantage is not the exploitation of superior knowledge or the avoidance of unbargained-for expense; it is sharp dealing. Like theft, it has no social product, and also like theft it induces costly defensive expenditures, in the form of overelaborate disclaimers or investigations into the trustworthiness of a prospective contract partner, just as the prospect of theft induces expenditures on locks. See generally Steven J. Burton, "Breach of Contract and the Common Law Duty to Perform in Good Faith," 94 Harv.L.Rev. 369, 393 (1980).

The form of sharp dealing that we are discussing might or might not be actionable as fraud or deceit. That is a question of tort law and there the rule is that if the information is readily available to both parties the failure of one to disclose it to the other, even if done in the knowledge that the other party is acting on mistaken premises, is not actionable. [Citations omitted]. All of these cases, however, with the debatable exception of Guyer v. Cities Service Oil Co., 440 F.Supp. 630 (E.D.Wis. 1977), involve failure to disclose something in the negotiations leading up to the signing of the contract, rather than failure to disclose after the contract has been signed. (Guyer involved failure to disclose during the negotiations leading up to a renewal of the contract.) The distinction is important, as we explained in Maksym v. Loesch, 937 F.2d 1237, 1242 (7th Cir.1991). Before the contract is signed, the parties confront each other with a natural wariness. Neither expects the other to be particularly forthcoming, and therefore there is no deception when one is not. Afterwards the situation is different. The parties are now in a cooperative relationship the costs of which will be considerably reduced by a measure of trust. So each lowers his guard a bit, and now silence is more apt to be deceptive. Cf. AMPAT/Midwest, Inc. v. Illinois Tool Works Inc., 896 F.2d 1035, 1040–41 (7th Cir.1990).

Moreover, this is a contract case rather than a tort case, and conduct that might not rise to the level of fraud may nonetheless violate the duty of good faith in dealing with one's contractual partners and thereby give rise to a remedy under contract law. Burton, supra, at 372 n. 17. This duty is, as it were, halfway between a fiduciary duty (the duty of utmost good faith) and the duty merely to refrain from active fraud. Despite its moralistic overtones it is no more the injection of moral principles into contract law than the fiduciary concept itself is. Tymshare, Inc. v. Covell, 727 F.2d 1145, 1152 (D.C.Cir.1984); Summers, supra, at 204–07, 265–66. It would be quixotic as well as presumptuous for judges to undertake through contract law to raise the ethical standards of the nation's business people. The concept of the duty of good faith like the concept of fiduciary duty is a stab at approximating the terms the parties would have negotiated had they foreseen the circumstances that have given rise to their dispute. The parties want to minimize the costs of performance. To the extent that a doctrine of good faith designed to do this by reducing defensive expenditures is a reasonable measure to this end, interpolating it into the contract advances the parties' joint goal.

It is true that an essential function of contracts is to allocate risk, and would be defeated if courts treated the materializing of a bargained-over, allocated risk as a misfortune the burden of which is required to be shared between the parties (as it might be within a family, for example) rather than borne entirely by the party to whom the risk had been allocated by mutual agreement. But contracts do not just allocate risk.

They also (or some of them) set in motion a cooperative enterprise, which may to some extent place one party at the other's mercy. "The parties to a contract are embarked on a cooperative venture, and a minimum of cooperativeness in the event unforeseen problems arise at the performance stage is required even if not an explicit duty of the contract." AMPAT/Midwest, Inc. v. Illinois Tool Works, Inc., supra, 896 F.2d at 1041. The office of the doctrine of good faith is to forbid the kinds of opportunistic behavior that a mutually dependent, cooperative relationship might enable in the absence of rule. " 'Good faith' is a compact reference to an implied undertaking not to take opportunistic advantage in a way that could not have been contemplated at the time of drafting, and which therefore was not resolved explicitly by the parties." Kham & Nate's Shoes No. 2, Inc. v. First Bank, supra, 908 F.2d at 1357. The contractual duty of good faith is thus not some newfangled bit of welfare-state paternalism or (* * * Duncan Kennedy, "Form and Substance in Private Law Adjudication," 89 Harv.L.Rev. 1685, 1721 (1976)) the sediment of an altruistic strain in contract law, and we are therefore not surprised to find the essentials of the modern doctrine well established in nineteenth-century cases, a few examples being Bush v. Marshall, 47 U.S. (6 How.) 284, 291 (1848); Chicago, Rock Island & Pac. R.R. v. Howard, 74 U.S. (7 Wall.) 392, 413, (1868); Marsh v. Masterson, 101 N.Y. 401, 410–11, 5 N.E. 59, 63 (1886), and Uhrig v. Williamsburg City Fire Ins. Co., 101 N.Y. 362, 4 N.E. 745 (1886).

The emphasis we are placing on postcontractual versus precontractual conduct helps explain the pattern that is observed when the duty of contractual good faith is considered in all its variety, encompassing not only good faith in the performance of a contract but also good faith in its formation, Summers, supra, at 220–32, and in its enforcement. Harbor Ins. Co. v. Continental Bank Corp., 922 F.2d 357, 363 (7th Cir.1990). The formation or negotiation stage is precontractual, and here the duty is minimized. It is greater not only at the performance but also at the enforcement stage, which is also postcontractual. "A party who hokes up a phony defense to the performance of his contractual duties and then when that defense fails (at some expense to the other party) tries on another defense for size can properly be said to be acting in bad faith." Id.; see also Larson v. Johnson, 1 Ill.App.2d 36, 46, 116 N.E.2d 187, 191–92 (1953). At the formation of the contract the parties are dealing in present realities; performance still lies in the future. As performance unfolds, circumstances change, often unforeseeably; the explicit terms of the contract become progressively less apt to the governance of the parties' relationship; and the role of implied conditions—and with it the scope and bite of the good-faith doctrine—grows.

We could of course do without the term "good faith," and maybe even without the doctrine. We could, as just suggested, speak instead of implied conditions necessitated by the unpredictability of the future at the time the contract was made. Farnsworth, "Good Faith Performance and Commercial Reasonableness under the Uniform Commercial Code," 30 U.Chi.L.Rev. 666, 670 (1963). * * *

But whether we say that a contract shall be deemed to contain such implied conditions as are necessary to make sense of the contract, or that a contract obligates the parties to cooperate in its performance in "good faith" to the extent necessary to carry out the purposes of the contract, comes to much the same thing. They are different ways of formulating the overriding purpose of contract law, which is to give the parties what they would have stipulated for expressly if at the time of making the contract they had had complete knowledge of the future and the costs of negotiating and adding provisions to the contract had been zero.

The two formulations would have different meanings only if "good faith" were thought limited to "honesty in fact," an interpretation perhaps permitted but certainly not compelled by the Uniform Commercial Code, see Summers, supra, at 207–20—and anyway this is not a case governed by the UCC. We need not pursue this issue. The dispositive question in the present case is simply whether Market Street Associates tried to trick the pension trust and succeeded in doing so. If it did, this would be the type of opportunistic behavior in an ongoing contractual relationship that would violate the duty of good faith performance however the duty is formulated. There is much common sense in Judge Reynolds' conclusion that Market Street Associates did just that. The situation as he saw it was as follows. Market Street Associates didn't want financing from the pension trust (initially it had looked elsewhere, remember), and when it learned it couldn't get the financing without owning the property, it decided to try to buy the property. But the pension trust set a stiff price, so Orenstein decided to trick the pension trust into selling at the bargain price fixed in paragraph 34 by requesting financing and hoping that the pension trust would turn the request down without noticing the paragraph. His preliminary dealings with the pension trust made this hope a realistic one by revealing a sluggish and hidebound bureaucracy unlikely to have retained in its brontosaurus's memory, or to be able at short notice to retrieve, the details of a small lease made twenty years earlier. So by requesting financing without mentioning the lease Market Street Associates might well precipitate a refusal before the pension trust woke up to paragraph 34. It is true that Orenstein's second letter requested financing "pursuant to the lease." But when the next day he received a reply to his first letter indicating that the pension trust was indeed oblivious to paragraph 34, his response was to send a lulling letter designed to convince the pension trust that the matter was closed and could be forgotten. The stage was set for his thunderbolt: the notification the next month that Market Street Associates was taking up the option in paragraph 34. Only then did the pension trust look up the lease and discover that it had been had.

The only problem with this recital is that it construes the facts as favorably to the pension trust as the record will permit, and that of course is not the right standard for summary judgment. * * *

The district judge jumped the gun in choosing between these alternative characterizations. The essential issue bearing on Market Street Associates' good faith was Orenstein's state of mind, a type of inquiry that ordinarily cannot be concluded on summary judgment, and could not be here. If Orenstein believed that Erb knew or would surely find out about paragraph 34, it was not dishonest or opportunistic to fail to flag that paragraph, or even to fail to mention the lease, in his correspondence and (rare) conversations with Erb, especially given the uninterest in dealing with Market Street Associates that Erb fairly radiated. To decide what Orenstein believed, a trial is necessary. * * *

Problems

33.   L owned a building and T desired to rent space for his restaurant. They entered into a lease that described the leasehold as the entire fourth floor of the building. The lease was contingent upon T obtaining financing, title insurance, and a liquor license. T was able to obtain financing and title insurance but could not obtain a liquor license because to obtain the license T was required to develop a floor plan. T developed such a plan and gave it to L who insisted on a different version of the floor plan. L's version showed T sharing space on the fourth floor with another business. This plan did not satisfy the rules of the State Liquor Authority. T canceled and sued L. What result?

34.   The U.S. Government invited contractors to submit bids for the construction of a breakwater. The project required 88,000 tons, more or less, of riprap stone. The invitation requested bidders to submit a statement of the source from which the contractor proposed to obtain the stone along with a sample. D, a bidder, stated that it proposed to supply the stone from a particular quarry in New York State. At that time the quarry in question was under lease to the government. D was awarded the contract. During the project the government neglected to obtain an extension of its lease and the lease expired. D ceased work. In an action by the U.S. against D, what result?

35.   Plaintiff, broker, and defendant, owner, entered into an agreement whereby plaintiff would receive a brokerage commission for his services if he procured a purchaser of defendant's realty at given terms. The commission would be paid "on closing of title." Plaintiff did procure a purchaser who entered into a contract for the purchase of the realty. The purchaser's title search revealed certain curable clouds on title, which, upon demand, defendant refused to cure. Purchaser in an earlier action recovered his downpayment. Plaintiff in this action seeks to recover his brokerage commission. What result?

36.   Plaintiff contracted with the state to erect a building according to state specifications and to lease it to the state. Time was made of the essence in the contract. Plaintiff completed the building two months late. The state cancelled the contract and leased space elsewhere. Plaintiff sues, alleging and proving that the delay was caused by failure of the state to indicate locations for electrical fixtures, outlets and other details as required by the contract. What result?

37.   Plaintiff is the author of several highly successful books on electricity published by defendant under an agreement whereby defendant had an exclusive right to publish the books in return for a 15% royalty for the

plaintiff. Defendant undertook to use "best efforts" to promote plaintiff's works. After plaintiff had refused to lower his royalty rate, defendant hired M to write competing books for a 3% royalty. When the books written by M were published, defendant ceased its advertisements for plaintiff's books and encouraged its sales personnel to devote their efforts to the new series of books. Plaintiff sues for damages and to enjoin defendant from marketing the competing books. What result?

SECTION 8. WAIVER, ESTOPPEL, AND ELECTION

(Calamari & Perillo 5th §§ 11.29—11.34)

SHIPSVIEW CORP. v. BEECHE SYSTEMS CORP.

United States District Court, N.D. New York, 1996.
1996 WL 590910 (N.D.N.Y.), aff'd, 125 F.3d 844 (2d Cir.1997).

MEMORANDUM–DECISION & ORDER. Hurd, United States Magistrate Judge.

I. Introduction

Plaintiff Shipsview Corporation ("Shipsview") brought this 28 U.S.C. § 1332 diversity of citizenship action against defendant Beeche Systems, Inc. ("Beeche") alleging breach of contract. * * *

II. Trial

A two day bench trial was conducted on July 2, and 3, 1996, in Utica, New York. * * *

III. Findings of Fact

A. *The Agreement*

Shipsview is a bridge cleaning and painting contractor with its principal place of business in Plymouth, Massachusetts. In late 1993, Shipsview was the low bidder on a Connecticut bridge painting project. In January 1994, Shipsview contracted with the State of Connecticut to paint six bridges in the Towns of Meriden, Plainville, New Britain, and Hartford. * * *

Shortly after receiving the Connecticut contract, Shipsview began preliminary talks with Beeche regarding a bridge containment system for the Interstate–84 ("I–84") site in Hartford, Connecticut. In response to growing environmental concerns, bridge containment systems have emerged in the bridge painting business in the last five or six years. Before actual painting can begin, the bridge must be stripped of its existing layers of lead-based paint, a process requiring an elaborate system of containment in order to enclose the lead hazard and protect the workers and surrounding community.

The Beeche containment system is composed of three parts: the platform, the attachment apparatus, and the tarp enclosures. Once a containment system is designed and delivered to the site, a considerable amount of time, perhaps as long as two weeks, is spent assembling the platform. Next, the completed platform is erected under the bridge. To this point, approval of DOT [Connecticut Department of Transportation] is not required. DOT approval of the containment system is required, however, prior to hanging of the tarp enclosures and commencement of paint-stripping operations. * * * Approximately 75% of the containment system is composed of interchangeable standard parts which may be reused in future jobs, and the remaining 25% is custom manufactured to suit the individual project.

On March 26, 1994, the parties agreed that Beeche would design and deliver a bridge containment system for the I–84 site at a total cost of $210,435.00. Under the agreement, shipment was to be in eight to ten weeks from receipt of the order and initial deposit. Normally, Beeche required a deposit of fifty percent (50%) to be paid with an order to cover expenditures associated with purchasing parts and fabricating custom components, as well as securing a client's commitment. At Shipsview's request, however, the deposit terms were modified to extend payment over four installments: 15% with the order; 10% on April 4, 1994; 10% on April 11, 1994; and 15% on April 18, 1994.

The initial 15% deposit ($31,565.25) was received on March 29, 1994, thus triggering the eight to ten week delivery window. The next payment, scheduled for April 4, was not made until April 11, at which time Shipsview paid the 10% owing from April 4, and the 10% due on April 11 ($42,087.00). Thereafter, Shipsview became increasingly delinquent in deposit payment.

At the time of agreement, Beeche had only general details of the I–84 site based solely upon a visual inspection of the bridge. Upon Beeche's examination of the structural "as-built" drawings of the bridge, it was determined that a new platform design would better facilitate access to the I–84 site. On April 19, 1994, the parties agreed to an Option–III type platform, a modification of the original contract. Beeche immediately began engineering work on the modified system.

Adoption of the Option–III platform resulted in an increase in the purchase price to $269,514.00 to which both parties agreed. This corresponded with a proportionate increase in the required deposit. By letter of April 19, Beeche informed Shipsview of the modified deposit payment schedule. The original terms providing for four installments based on the original purchase price remained the same; the only change was an additional payment on April 25, 1994, which would account for the balance of the 50% deposit on the amended agreement. All other terms of the original contract remained in force.

B. *Problems in Performance.*

April 18, and 25, the dates of the 15% and remaining balance deposits, respectively, passed without payment being made. Due to the missed payments, an accumulated balance of $61,110.25 remained on the 50% deposit. On May 4, 1994, Beeche forwarded the engineering structural report for the Option–III platform to Shipsview, which in turn submitted it to DOT for approval.

On May 10, 1994, Beeche warned Shipsview that absent payment of the overdue deposit, fabrication of this project would cease and the delivery schedule would be delayed accordingly. Shipsview then tendered $10,000.00 toward payment, well short of the outstanding balance of $61,110.25. On May 13, 1994, Beeche informed Shipsview by letter fax, that the failure to pay the balance left no choice but to pull the project out of production. Later that same day in a second letter sent via fax, Beeche softened its tone, stating that failure to pay the remaining $51,110.25 by May 16, 1994, would result in the system being pulled out of production. Receipt of the funds was necessary in order to continue fabricating parts according to the delivery schedule.

May 16 passed without Shipsview paying the deposit balance. On May 17, 1994, Gregory Beeche spoke with Deligiannidis [president of Shipsview] regarding the final deposit payment. The parties agreed that Shipsview would send a check for $51,110.25 via Federal Express, to cover the entire balance due on the deposit.

On May 18, 1994, the parties exchanged correspondence outlining each other's interpretation of the previous day's discussions. Beeche's letter confirmed that the containment system would be delivered within three to three-and-one-half weeks after receipt of the deposit balance. With receipt of the final deposit payment on May 19, pursuant to Beeche's letter, the target date for delivery became June 13, 1994.

Deligiannidis' letter which contained the final deposit check ($51,110.25), unequivocally stated that payment was being made with the understanding that delivery of the platform was to be made by June 7, 1994. This date is significant because it marked the end of ten weeks from the date of the original contract. According to the letter, failure to deliver by June 7, would result in cancellation of the order and a demand for the return of all deposit funds. Similar language appeared on the back of the check which was deposited in the normal course of business. Both Gregory and Kirk Beeche saw the language regarding the June 7, delivery date on either the letter or check, but neither took the notice seriously.

There was no further oral communication between the parties after May 17, 1994. Gregory Beeche attempted to contact Deligiannidis by telephone three or four times in the ensuing weeks, but his calls went unanswered. On June 3, 1994, Beeche faxed Shipsview inquiring how Deligiannidis wished to proceed absent DOT approval. Beeche did not want to complete fabrication of the nonstandard components without DOT approval unless Deligiannidis provided a formal written order. At this point, Deligiannidis could have ensured both fabrication and shipment of the system, even absent DOT approval, simply by so instructing Beeche. Shipsview did not respond to Beeche's inquiry.

Delivery of the containment system did not occur on June 7, 1994. While DOT approval had not been obtained as of June 7, this was not enough to forestall delivery since assembly and attachment of the platform could have proceeded absent DOT approval. The system, quite simply, was not ready to ship on June 7, because it was only roughly 90% complete. Neither side, however, was preparing for a June 7 delivery. A common carrier was never contacted, much less provided with directions, times, or telephone numbers for delivery. On June 7, 1994, there was no crew, crane, or forklift at the I–84 site to unload the anticipated trailers. Permission was not obtained for storage on one of the nearby lots, and security arrangements had not been made with respect to the portable aluminum cords which are valued as high as $300 a piece.

Deligiannidis testified that he was at the I–84 site on June 7, and that he remained there six to eight hours awaiting delivery of the system. Admitting that he had access to a telephone that day, Deligiannidis nonetheless stated that he made no effort to contact Beeche concerning the delay because he was "in a daze and ... too upset." The next day, June 8, 1994, Shipsview canceled the order and demanded a full refund of the deposit money.

On June 8 or 9, Deligiannidis contacted KTA Environmental ("KTA") regarding the possibility of providing an alternate containment system. On June 14, KTA's proposal for $18,700.00 was accepted by Shipsview, as was the subsequent upward modification of $2,500.00. The I–84 bridge painting job went forward with KTA providing the containment system.

On June 28, 1994, Shipsview commenced the current action alleging that Beeche breached the contract when it failed to deliver by June 7, 1994. At the time of trial, Shipsview claimed the return of the $134,762.50 deposit, and the $21,200.00 cost of designing a new containment system, for a total of $155,962.50 plus interest.

Beeche was "shocked" with Shipsview's cancellation of the contract on June 8. It contended that time was not of the essence, and it was to be allowed a reasonable time in which to deliver the system. Initially, Beeche sought adequate assurances of performance from Shipsview, but realized that it was not forthcoming in light of Shipsview's filing of this action. Beeche then found itself in a precarious financial situation and was forced to sell the system on the open market. On August 4, 1994, Beeche sold the system to EDT Company, another bridge painting company and subsidiary of Abhe & Svoboda, for $135,000.00, the price Beeche would have received if Shipsview had carried through on the contract.

Beeche contends that it did not breach the contract, but that the contract was, in fact, breached by Shipsview when it failed to perform. At trial, defendant claimed damages for lost profits in the amount of $34,141.92 because of plaintiff's alleged breach.

IV. Conclusions of Law

A. Statement of the Law.

The parties have agreed that this action is governed by New York law and the New York U.C.C. Where a contract for the sale of goods fails to provide a time for shipment or delivery, the law requires delivery within a reasonable time. N.Y. U.C.C. § 2–309(1)(McKinney 1993); see also Rosenfeld v. Basquiat, 78 F.3d 84, 93 (2d Cir. 1996)(written contract for sale of goods need not contain delivery date, even though a delivery date was agreed upon). What constitutes a reasonable time is dependent upon "the nature, purpose and circumstances" of performance. N.Y. U.C.C. § 1–204(2).

* * *

Time is never of the essence in an agreement which explicitly or impliedly provides for performance within a reasonable time. John F. Trainor Co. v. G. Amsinck & Co., 236 N.Y. 392, 395 (1923). Nor is time of the essence in an agreement where the parties have waived time as an essential element of the contract. Taylor v. Goelet, 208 N.Y. 253, 259 (1913). Either party, though, may make or restore time as of the essence whenever it desires, simply by giving notice to that effect. Id.; Mawhinney v. Millbrook Woolen Mills, Inc., 234 N.Y. 244, 249 (1922); N.Y. U.C.C. § 2–309(3). The notice must be clear, distinct and unequivocal; fix a reasonable time within which to act; and inform the other party that failure to perform by that date will be considered a default. [Citations omitted]. It does not matter that the date is unilaterally set or that a party does not specifically state that time is of the essence "as long as the notice specifies a time … and warns that failure to [perform] on that date will result in default." Zev [v. Merman], 134 A.D.2d 555, 557 (2d Dep't 1987), aff'd, 73 N.Y.2d 781 (1988).

* * * In the event of delay in a contract where time is of the essence, the nondefaulting party may cancel the contract or extend the time for performance and sue for damages resulting from the delay. Mawhinney, 234 N.Y. at 249.

B. The Original Contract: Time is of the Essence.

The original contract between Shipsview and Beeche executed on March 26, 1994, provided that shipment of the containment system occur within eight to ten weeks of Beeche's receipt of the order and deposit. Since the agreement provided for a definite time of delivery, i.e., eight to ten weeks, time was of the essence in the original contract. * * * It is of no significance that the original agreement did not provide a specific date such as June 7, 1994. A three week window for delivery is as fixed in the mind of the courts as a single day and will be treated with equal stringency. See Mawhinney, 234 N.Y. at 244 (time was of the essence in a contract which provided for delivery [of goods] during the months of May, June and July; therefore, seller defaulted when delivery did not occur by July 31); see also Schenectady Steel Co. v. Bruno

Trimpoli General Constr. Co., 43 A.D.2d 234, 237 (3d Dep't)(where [construction] contract provided that time was of the essence and work was to be completed in 1968, appellant defaulted when the work was not finished on December 31, 1968), aff'd, 34 N.Y.2d 939 (1974). Thus, Beeche contracted to deliver the containment system in the eighth, ninth or tenth week. If delivery did not occur by the end of ten weeks, Beeche would be in default. When the order and deposit were received on March 29, 1994, Beeche had until June 7, 1994, in which to make timely delivery.

The subsequent modification in platform design and corresponding increase in purchase price had no effect on the delivery schedule of the system. Hence, time remained of the essence.

C. The Delay in Deposit Payment: Time is No Longer of the Essence.

Following the modification, Shipsview fell behind in deposit payments notwithstanding the fact that it understood the terms in both the original and modified contracts called for a 50% deposit. In early May 1994, Beeche made clear that delay in receipt of the deposit would stall production of the system and have a similar effect on delivery.

After a series of frustrating communications and apparent misunderstandings, Beeche sent Shipsview two letters via fax on May 13, 1994, and warned that the $51,110.25 deposit must be received by May 16, 1994, in order to continue fabrication of the project. Unless the funds were received by that date, Beeche would have no choice but to pull the project out of production. These notices made time of the essence with respect to the final deposit payment, and were clear, distinct and unequivocal. Moreover, in light of the parties' ongoing discussions and the fact that the full deposit was scheduled to be paid in April, the notices fixed a reasonable time in which to perform. Ballen, 251 N.Y. at 229; Zev, 134 A.D.2d at 557. Finally, the notices informed Shipsview of the consequences of nonperformance—delay in fabrication of the system.

Beeche's notices to Shipsview made the time of deposit an essential element of this contract. When May 16 passed without payment of the balance on deposit, Shipsview defaulted on the contract. At this point, Beeche had the option of canceling the contract or waiving the stipulation as to time and continuing negotiations with Shipsview. Beeche chose the latter course and reached a subsequent agreement with Shipsview regarding payment of the $51,110.25 balance. In continuing negotiations, time was waived as an essential element of this contract. Time was no longer of the essence to either side. Shipsview now had a reasonable time in which to pay, and Beeche had a reasonable time in which to deliver. See Mawhinney, 234 N.Y. at 248.

D. Shipsview's Unsuccessful Attempt to Reimpose Time as of the Essence.

Shipsview soon sought to reimpose time as an essential element of this contract. On May 19, 1994, Beeche received notice from Shipsview, both in the letter and on the back of the accompanying check, that payment was being made with the understanding that delivery of the system would occur no later than June 7, 1994, the deadline provided in the original contract. Shipsview warned Beeche that failure to deliver by June 7, would result in cancellation of the contract and a demand for the return of all funds paid.

At first glance, this notice appears to reinstate time as of the essence in this contract. Not only is it clear, distinct and unequivocal, but it properly informs Beeche that failure to perform by June 7, would be considered a default. The facts and circumstances of this case, however, suggest that a June 7, delivery date no longer constituted a reasonable time in which to perform. See Zev, 73 N.Y.2d at 783 (must determine reasonableness on a case by case basis); N.Y. U.C.C. § 1–204. Devoid of reasonable time, a determining element of sufficient notice, time could not be restored as of the essence in this contract.

Shipsview last made a timely deposit payment on April 11, 1994. The next payment, scheduled one week later, was not made for an entire month, until May 10, 1994, and even then amounted to only partial payment. Significantly, Shipsview was warned that fabrication and ultimate delivery of the system might be delayed if payment was not made. Following the month-long delay in deposit payment, Beeche lacked the interim funds required to fabricate the system according to the original contract schedule.

When the deadline imposed by reasonable notice, May 16, 1994, passed without payment of the deposit balance, Beeche, true to its word, could have taken the system out of production. * * * This would, of course, have made delivery of the system according to the terms of the original contract untenable. Again, Shipsview was notified of the potential consequences. Nothing, not even receipt of the delinquent payment on May 19, could place production of the system back on the original eight to ten week delivery track.

In light of the foregoing, this court finds that June 7, did not constitute a reasonable time for Beeche to perform. The more than thirty day delay in deposit payment in a contract that provided for performance within ten weeks made the attempted reimposition of the same delivery date as set forth in the original contract (June 7, 1994), quite simply, unreasonable. See Zev, 73 N.Y.2d at 783 ("Included within a courts determination of reasonable [time] are the . . . previous conduct of the parties . . . as well as the specific number of days provided for performance."); N.Y. U.C.C. § 1–204. Because it was unreasonable with respect to time, Shipsview's notice to Beeche to perform by June 7, 1994, "was not such a warning . . . as the law requires." Taylor, 208 N.Y. at 260. Thus, time was not made of the essence. Beeche still had a reasonable time in which to deliver.

E.   The Actions of the Parties.

An analysis of the parties' actions up to and beyond June 7, 1994, further supports the conclusion that time, ultimately, was not of the essence. Beeche's letter to Shipsview on May 18, 1994, confirmed delivery within three-and-one-half weeks after receipt of the balance due on deposit. This would have imposed a June 13, 1994, delivery date, a more probable one in light of the delay in deposit receipt. Shipsview, however, made no attempt to contact Beeche regarding the obvious difference in understanding as to delivery terms.

Beeche, in contrast, tried three or four times to contact Shipsview, albeit unsuccessfully, in the period leading up to June 7. Shipsview failed to return Beeche's telephone calls. On June 3, 1994, Beeche again resorted to fax and inquired of Shipsview how it wished to proceed. Again, Shipsview failed to respond; this, at a time when it could have ensured both fabrication and delivery of the system regardless of DOT approval, simply by issuing a written order. Surely, if Shipsview was adamant about a June 7, 1994, delivery date, then the company would have done more than simply exchange the contradictory letters of May 18. Deligiannidis would have done what any ordinary and reasonable businessman would have done—contacted Beeche and clarified delivery date and details.

Besides the failure to communicate with Beeche prior to June 7, Shipsview also failed to make arrangements for delivery. A common carrier was not contacted. No directions, times, or telephone numbers were exchanged between the parties in relation to a containment system delivery at the I–84 bridge site. In the event of delivery, no work crew was available to unload the trailers. Nor was there equipment available to assist in unloading, for example, a crane or forklift. Moreover, no security arrangements were made to oversee this $269,000.00 system which, incidentally, would lie in an empty parking lot until assembled. Without a single one of these preparations being made, Shipsview's claim that it expected delivery on June 7, 1994, is inconceivable.

Equally incredible was Deligiannidis' testimony that he remained at the I–84 site for six to eight hours on June 7, 1994, awaiting delivery. There was no corroborating testimony adduced at trial which placed Deligiannidis at the site on June 7. In any event, it was purposeless for him to be at the site when there was absolutely no indication, absent delivery preparations, that delivery would occur that day. Finally, the court fails to see why, if having a cellular phone on his person, Deligiannidis would not simply call Beeche regarding the delay as opposed to wasting an entire day at the site. The explanation of this experienced businessman, that he was in a daze and too upset, is beyond belief.

Thus, the court finds that the parties' actions leading up to June 7, do not indicate that time was of the essence in this contract. In this period, communications lapsed and delivery arrangements were ignored. On June 7, 1994, neither party was prepared to send or receive the containment system, and the mutual inaction of the parties precludes a finding of time being of the essence.

The more plausible theory in this case is that the parties became increasingly frustrated in their dealings, and that Shipsview imposed a June 7, delivery date, suspecting that it could not be met, in an effort to avoid the contract. Shipsview's immediate contacting and contracting with KTA Environmental for an alternate containment system, and the filing of this action three weeks later, only supports this theory.

V. Conclusion

The defect in Shipsview's case is that it did not take the preliminary steps necessary to exercise the right of cancellation. See Taylor, 208 N.Y. at 261. The missing step, of course, was notice of a reasonable time in which to perform. Because June 7, 1994, did not provide a reasonable time, and because the parties' actions were not synonymous with a finding of time being of the essence, delivery need only have been performed within a reasonable time. Shipsview's cancellation of the contract on June 8, 1994, prior to giving adequate notice was premature, and has the effect of defeating its present claim.

[The court holds that Beeche has failed to prove any damages to sustain its counterclaim.]

Accordingly, it is ORDERED that: 1. The complaint and the counter-claim are both DISMISSED; and 2. Costs are DENIED to both parties.
* * *

Problems

38.   On December 15, S promised to sell B a machine for $1,000 with delivery to be made on or before March 1. On January 1, B told S he would be willing to take delivery on April 1.

(a) S delivered the machine on April 1. B rejected it on grounds of lateness. S sues for breach of contract. What result?

(b) On January 3, B changed his mind and insisted on delivery by March 1. Upon S's failure to deliver on March 1, B cancels the contract. S sues B. What result?

39.   On September 1, X promised to construct a house for Y on Y's land "to be completed by June 30." The parties agreed that time was of the essence. Nonetheless, on December 1, Y told X that he would not insist on the June 30 deadline. X delayed an order for materials needed in the construction of the house. On February 1, Y recanted, telling X he would insist on the June 30 deadline. If X completes the house sometime in August, should he succeed in an action to collect the contract price from Y?

40.   Seller contracted to sell a parcel of realty to buyer. At the request of the buyer, the contract provided that "this contract is contingent upon the purchaser obtaining a rezoning for a mobile home court. This contract is to be void if the rezoning is not obtained within 120 days." After 60 days, buyer notified seller that he would buy the property irrespective of a zoning change. The zoning change was not obtained. The seller refused to convey. In an action by the buyer against the seller, what result?

41.   Plaintiff contracted with defendant for the purchase of unimproved realty, payable in monthly installments. For the first three years plaintiff was punctual in making payment. In the next four years payments were made tardily and at sporadic intervals. The defendant made no protest. Towards the end of the fourth year, the defendant rejected a tardy payment

and declared the contract at an end pursuant to provisions in the contract making time of each payment of the essence (with a 31–day grace period). The contract also provided: "no waiver of a breach or any term or condition shall be a waiver of any other or subsequent breach of the same or any other term or condition." Plaintiff sues to enforce the contract. What result?

42. Defendant insured plaintiff under a liability policy. Plaintiff was involved in an accident and failed to give the notice required by the policy. Plaintiff's late notice was received by the defendant, which proceeded for two months to try to settle the claim. It then called upon the plaintiff for further information and for the papers which had been served in the case. Shortly before the trial of the action, the defendant returned the papers and said that it would not defend the action. What result?

43. D, a contractor, built a structure for P on P's property. After it was completed P formally accepted the building pursuant to its architect's recommendation. Shortly afterwards the roof began to leak. D tried to remedy the situation but failed. There was evidence that the roof could not be repaired. P sues for damages. What result?

44. Flight Airlines entered into a contract with Aluminum Aircraft to purchase 99 jet planes for a price of a half billion dollars. Delivery of the planes, pursuant to a schedule in the contract, was invariably late. Although Flight occasionally grumbled, it took no action until the last plane was delivered when it brought this action for breach of contract claiming damages of $25,000,000 caused by the delays. Aluminum denies liability because Flight accepted deliveries without indicating it intended to hold Aluminum for breach. What result?

SECTION 9.   RELIEF FROM FORFEITURE

———

(Calamari & Perillo 5th §§ 11.35 and 11.36)

SHARP v. HOLTHUSEN

Supreme Court of Montana, 1980.
189 Mont. 469, 616 P.2d 374.

HARRISON, JUSTICE. This is an appeal from a judgment of the District Court, Fourth Judicial District, Missoula County, dismissing plaintiff's claim for forfeiture under a contract for deed.

On October 11, 1976, Ray D. and Freda Sharp, plaintiffs and sellers, and Earnest D. and Donna M. Holthusen, defendants and buyers, entered into a written contract for deed for the sale and purchase of real property located in Lake County. Terms included monthly installment payments to plaintiffs, assumption by defendants of plaintiffs' Veterans Administration loan, and discharge in full of the balance due and the VA loan by October 11, 1977.

Defendants gained possession of the property on October 11, 1976. Defendants have paid $7,000 cash down and monthly payments totaling

$1,081. Defendants also made payments on the assumed Veterans Administration loan. The contract for deed required defendants to make a balloon payment to plaintiffs and refinance the Veterans Administration loan. The parties contemplated that the defendants would refinance the obligations by October 11, 1977, and that plaintiffs would cooperate in this refinancing, if required.

A well supplying the property with water was found to be functioning properly at the time of sale. Both parties believed that the well was functioning properly; however, this was incorrect. It was later discovered that the water well was contaminated. The trial court found neither party in fault for the contamination.

In April 1977 defendants actively sought financing for the obligation due under the contract. The defendants attempted to refinance the balloon payment due on October 11, 1977, rather than make a cash payment from their own resources. Because of numerous reasons, defendants were not able to obtain the necessary financing within the time limit.

On October 21, 1977, a notice of default was sent to defendants as required in the contract. The default was not cured within forty-five days as specified in the contract, and a demand for the return of the escrow documents from the First National Bank was made. Subsequently, the parties entered into settlement negotiations for purposes of compromising such claims as each might have against the other.

Finally in January 1978, financing for the payoff of the entire contract, the balloon payment, as well as the remaining principal and interest due the plaintiffs was obtained through Lomas and Nettleton of Missoula, Montana. Lomas and Nettleton made the closing date of the loan January 16, 1978, but because they required a test of the water purity on the property, the loan could not be closed as a result of the water test showing that the water well was contaminated.

The Montana State Department of Health and Environmental Sciences recommended to defendants to clean, recap and filter the well water. Later, the Department recommended that the well be relocated. Defendants drilled a new well and installed a new pump at a cost of $1,741.

In March 1978 when the well was completed, defendants were given financing from Lomas and Nettleton. Defendants tendered payment to the escrow agent. The escrow agent refused to accept the loan on directions from plaintiffs. Plaintiffs required defendants to pay all attorney fees and release plaintiffs from all claims they may have for misrepresentation of the water supply. Defendants tendered full payment for the attorney fees, but refused to release the plaintiffs from any action of misrepresentation.

Negotiations continued. However, the parties were not able to enter into a settlement agreement. Plaintiffs filed suit against defendants for forfeiture of the contract and for repossession of the real property in May, 1978. Defendants have been ready, willing and able to pay off the entire amount of the contract since April, 1978. Plaintiffs have refused tender of payment.

"Whenever by the terms of an obligation a party thereto incurs a forfeiture or a loss in the nature of a forfeiture by reason of his failure to comply with its provisions, he may be relieved therefrom upon making full compensation to the other party, except in case of a grossly negligent, willful or fraudulent breach of duty." Section 28–1–104, MCA.

This Court has allowed a party to a contract who is in default, and who is subject to a penalty of forfeiture to redeem his right to the property. *Yellowstone County v. Wight* (1944), 115 Mont. 411, 145 P.2d 516; *Parrott v. Heller* (1976), 171 Mont. 212, 557 P.2d 819. Parties are relieved from forfeiture "in any case where he sets forth facts which appeal to the conscience of a court of equity." *Parrott v. Heller,* 557 P.2d 819, 820. This Court has said that section 28–1–104, MCA, was enacted;

"... for the benefit of obligors whose failure to punctually perform would result in loss to them in the matters [with] respect to which they have contracted. The intention of the Legislature in enacting the statute was that it should be operative and that it should be given full force and effect when the circumstances in any case gave it application. The intention of the law under this statute is that a forfeiture should not be needlessly enforced. The courts have established that as the policy of the law in the absence of statute. The rule as it has found expression in both court decisions generally is that both in law and in equity forfeitures are abhorred ..." *Yellowstone County v. Wight,* 115 Mont. 411, 417, 145 P.2d 516, 518.

The parties' contract, which requires forfeiture in the case of default, does not divest a court of equity of its power to relieve a party from the consequences of his default and need not grant forfeiture.

Defendants' actions here were not intentional, willful or fraudulent acts. The record disclosed that defendants made a good faith effort to pay the necessary money at the time it was due, but because of temporary circumstances outside of their control, the condition of the water well, they were unable to secure the necessary financing within the time desired.

Plaintiffs argue that the time period between default and actual tender of payment was not reasonable to allow a court of equity to relieve the defendants from forfeiture under section 28–1–104, MCA. We disagree.

Subsequent to the forty-five day period given the buyers to cure this default, the parties entered into settlement negotiations for the purpose of compromising such claims as each might have against the other. Defendants attended a closing at Lomas and Nettleton in January of 1978. This closing could not be completed because of the condition of the water well. Plaintiffs never objected to defendants' improvements on the land, the drilling and installing of a new water well. When tender was made, plaintiffs were willing to accept tender on the condition defendants released the plaintiffs from possible suit for misrepresentation on the condition of the water well.

The trial court's judgment gives the plaintiffs what they are equitably entitled to, the amount due under the contract, compensation for their personal expenses and attorney fees, as a result of the delay from the time of performance to the time of tender of payment in March, 1978. There comes a time when failure to perform is not reasonable, and the application of the anti-forfeiture statute not applicable, but this is not the case. From the facts presented here, we find the court was correct in its equitable judgment.

It appears from the record that defendants presented to the District Court sufficient evidence to appeal to the "conscience of a court of equity" which resulted in a specific finding that application of the default clause (forfeiture) would be "harsh and inequitable." Defendants made an initial downpayment and monthly payments to plaintiffs. They paid on the Veterans Administration loan. They spent over $1,700 in improvements on the property in order to drill a well to provide clean water to the house and to satisfy requirements of loan application without liability to the plaintiffs. In addition to the above-mentioned losses, the defendants would lose nearly $10,000 in equity in the land if forfeiture occurred.

The facts in this case present a clear case for application of section 28–1–104, MCA. Defendants made tender of all of the amount due, as well as the personal fees, expenses and attorney fees of the plaintiff to date. Plaintiffs suffered no loss. The right to relief under the statute commences when the contracting party is in default and subject to forfeiture. *Kovachich v. Metals Bank and Trust Co.* (1961), 139 Mont. 449, 365 P.2d 639.

We accept plaintiffs argument that defendants were in default of the contract for deed and of their obligations under the contract, but they still retained a right under the antiforfeiture statute to make a tender, to redeem their interest in the property, and to appeal to the equity of the trial court. Defendants were not relieved from their actions of default, only plaintiffs' claim for forfeiture.

Plaintiffs accepted payment of the contract amount but required that defendants also provide a release of all claims arising out of the contract. From the record, the court found that the plaintiffs did not object to the tender, only to the release that was demanded as a condition for the acceptance of tender.

We find that tender of payment was made. Defendants were delinquent in their payment, and they were in default, but under the circumstances as are presented in this case, the antiforfeiture statute allows the defendants to make full payment of interest and attorney fees for the default, and allows the contract to be enforced.

* * *

Affirmed in part and reversed in part according to this opinion.

BURGER KING CORP. v. FAMILY DINING, INC.

United States District Court, E.D. Pennsylvania, 1977.
426 F.Supp. 485.

HANNUM, DISTRICT JUDGE. Presently before the Court is defendant's motion for an involuntary dismissal in accordance with Rule 41(b), Federal Rules of Civil Procedure, advanced at the close of plaintiff's case. The trial is before the Court sitting without a jury.

In bringing the suit plaintiff seeks a determination under the Declaratory Judgment Act, Title 28, United States Code § 2201, that a contract between the parties, by its own terms, is no longer of any force and effect. * * *

FACTS ESTABLISHED IN PLAINTIFF'S CASE

Plaintiff Burger King Corporation (hereinafter "Burger King") is a Florida corporation engaged in franchising the well-known Burger King Restaurants. In 1954, James W. McLamore, founder of Burger King Restaurants, Inc. (the corporate predecessor of Burger King) built the first Burger King Restaurant in Miami, Florida. In 1961 the franchise system was still relatively modest size having only about 60 or 70 restaurants in operation outside of Florida. By 1963, however, Burger King began to experience significant growth and was building and operating, principally through franchisees, 24 restaurants per year. It was also at this time that Burger King's relationship with defendant Family Dining, Inc., (hereinafter "Family Dining") was created.

Family Dining is a Pennsylvania corporation which at the present time operates ten Burger King Restaurants (hereinafter "Restaurant") in Bucks and Montgomery Counties in Pennsylvania. Family Dining was founded and is currently operated by Carl Ferris who had been a close personal friend of McLamore's for a number of years prior to 1963. In fact they had attended Cornell University together in the late 1940's. It would seem that this friendship eventually led to the business relationship between Burger King and Family Dining which was conceived in the "Burger King Territorial Agreement" (hereinafter "Territorial Agreement") entered on May 10, 1963.

In accordance with the Territorial Agreement Burger King agreed that Family Dining would be its sole licensee, and thus have an "exclusive territory," in Bucks and Montgomery Counties provided Family Dining operated each Restaurant pursuant to Burger King license agreements[1] and maintained a specified rate of development. Articles I and II of the Territorial Agreement * * * are pertinent to this dispute. They provide as follows:

I.

For a period of one year, beginning on the date hereof, Company will not operate or license others for the operation of any BURGER

---

1. Each Restaurant is opened pursuant to a separate Burger King license agree-ment.

KING restaurant within the following described territory hereinafter referred to as "exclusive territory," to-wit:

The counties of Bucks and Montgomery, all in the State of Pennsylvania as long as licensee operates each BURGER KING restaurant pursuant to BURGER KING restaurant licenses with Company and faithfully performs each of the covenants contained.

This agreement shall remain in effect and Licensee shall retain the exclusive territory for a period of ninety (90) years from the date hereof, provided that at the end of one, two, three, four, five, six, seven, eight, nine and ten years from the date hereof, and continuously thereafter during the next eighty years, Licensee has the following requisite number of BURGER KING restaurants in operation or under active construction, pursuant to Licenses with Company:

One (1) restaurant at the end of one year;

Two (2) restaurants at the end of two years;

Three (3) restaurants at the end of three years;

Four (4) restaurants at the end of four years;

Five (5) restaurants at the end of five years;

Six (6) restaurants at the end of six years;

Seven (7) restaurants at the end of seven years;

Eight (8) restaurants at the end of eight years;

Nine (9) restaurants at the end of nine years;

Ten (10) restaurants at the end of ten years;

and continually maintains not less than ten (10) restaurants during the next eighty (80) years.

* * *

II.

If at the end of either one, two, three, four, five, six, seven, eight, nine or ten years from the date hereof, or anytime thereafter during the next eighty (80) years, there are less than the respective requisite number of BURGER KING operations or under active construction in the "exclusive territory" pursuant to licenses by Company, this agreement shall terminate and be of no further force and effect. Thereafter, Company may operate or license others for the operation of BURGER KING Restaurants anywhere within the exclusive territory, so long as such restaurants are not within the "Protected Area", as set forth in any BURGER KING Restaurant License to which the Licensee herein is a party.

The prospect of exclusivity for ninety years was clearly intended to be an inducement to Family Dining to develop the territory as prescribed and it appears that it had exactly this effect as Family Dining was to become one of Burger King's most successful franchisees. While Burger King considered Carl Ferris to be somewhat of a problem at various times and one who was overly meticulous with detail, it was nevertheless through his efforts which included obtaining the necessary financing and assuming significant risks, largely without assistance from Burger King, that enabled both parties to benefit from the arrangement.

On August 16, 1963, [nine months early] Family Dining opened the First Restaurant. * * * The second Restaurant was opened on July 2, 1965, [two months late] * * * and the third Restaurant was opened October 19, 1966 [four months late] * * *.

However, by April, 1968, Family Dining had not opened or begun active construction on a fourth Restaurant which, in accordance with the development rate, should have been accomplished by May 10, 1967, and it was apparent that a fifth Restaurant would not be opened by May 10, 1968, the date scheduled. On May 1, 1968, the parties entered into a Modification of the Territorial Agreement (hereinafter "Modification") whereby Burger King agreed to waive Family Dining's failure to comply with the development rate. * * * There is nothing contained in the record which indicates that Burger King received anything of value in exchange for entering this agreement. However, McLamore testified that if the fourth and fifth Restaurants would be built nearly in compliance with the development rate for the fifth year he would overlook the year or so default in the fourth Restaurant. * * * This attitude seems to be consistent with his overall view toward the development rate with respect to which, he testified, was "designed to insure the company of an orderly process of growth which would also enable the company to produce a profit on the sale of its franchises and through the collection of royalties that the restaurants would themselves produce." * * *

The fourth Restaurant was opened on July 1, 1968, [fourteen months late] * * * and the fifth Restaurant was opened on October 17, 1968, [five months late] * * *.

On April 18, 1969, Ferris forwarded a letter to McLamore * * * [expressing] Ferris' concern regarding compliance with the development rate [for the sixth Restaurant]. By letter dated April 26, 1969, from Howard Walker of Burger King, Ferris was granted a month extension in the development rate. * * *

On October 1, 1969, the sixth Restaurant was opened * * *. The seventh Restaurant was opened on February 2, 1970, ahead of schedule * * *.

At this point in time Burger King was no longer a modest sized franchise system. It had became a wholly owned subsidiary of the Pillsbury Company and had, in fact, evolved into a complex corporate entity. McLamore was elevated to Chairman of the Board of Burger King and, while he remained the chief executive officer for a time, Arthur A. Rosewall was installed as Burger King's President. Ferris was no longer able to expect the close, one to one relationship with McLamore that had previously obtained in his dealings with the company. It seems clear that as a result Family Dining began to experience difficulties in its day to day operations with Burger King.

One of the problem areas which arose concerned site selection. * * * [I]n August, 1970, a * * * location selected by Ferris was rejected by [Burger King]. The reasons offered in support of the decision to reject are not entirely clear and it seems that for the most part it was an exercise of discretion. The only plausible reason, given Ferris' expertise, was that the site was 2.7 miles from another Burger King franchise * * * outside Family Dining's exclusive territory. Yet Burger King chose not to exercise its discretion in similar circumstances when it permitted another franchisee to build a Restaurant in Devon, Pennsylvania, approximately 3 miles away from an existing Family Dining Restaurant.

* * * This was during a time, as Burger King management was well aware, where it was one thing to select a location and quite another to actually develop it. That is, local governing bodies were taking a much stricter view toward allowing this type of development. It was also during this time * * * Burger King realized that the Bucks–Montgomery territory was capable of sustaining substantially more Restaurants than originally thought.

Amidst these circumstances, the eighth Restaurant was opened ahead of schedule on October 7, 1970, * * * and in December, 1971, Burger King approved Family Dining's proposed sites for two additional Restaurants in Ambler, Pennsylvania and Levittown, Pennsylvania.

In early 1972, Arthur Rosewell became the chief executive officer of Burger King. At this time it also became apparent that the ninth Restaurant would not be opened or under construction by May 10, 1972. On April 27, 1972, in a telephone conversation with McLamore, Ferris once again expressed his concern to Burger King regarding compliance with the development rate. * * * [McLamore] indicated to him that, due to the fact that he was in the process of developing four sites at this time, the company would consider he had met, substantially, the requirements of exclusivity. * * * McLamore testified that at that time he had in mind a further delay of 3 to 6 months. * * *

In April, 1973, Burger King approved Family Dining's proposed site for a Restaurant in Warminster, Pennsylvania. However, as of May 10, 1973, neither the ninth or the tenth Restaurant had been opened or under active construction.

A letter dated May 23, 1973, from Helen D. Donaldson, Franchise Documents Administrator for Burger King, was sent to Ferris. * * * The letter provides as follows:

Dear Mr. Ferris:

During a periodic review of all territorial agreements we note that as of this date your development schedule requiring ten restaurants to be open or under construction by May 10, 1973, has not been met. Our records reflect eight stores open in Bucks and/or Montgomery County, and one site approved but not manned.

Under the terms of your territorial agreement failure to have the required number of stores in operation or under active construction constitutes a default of your agreement.

If there are extenuating circumstances about which this office is not aware, we would appreciate your earliest advice.

It is doubtful that the Donaldson letter was intended to communicate to Ferris that the Territorial Agreement was terminated. The testimony of both Rosewall * * * and Leslie W. Paszat * * *, an executive of Burger King, who worked closely with Rosewall on the Family Dining matter indicates that even Burger King had not settled its position at this time. * * *

It seems that throughout this period Burger King treated the matter as something of a "hot potato" subjecting Ferris to contact with several different Burger King officials. * * * Ultimately Paszat was given responsibility for Family Dining and it appears that he provided Ferris with the first clear indication that Burger King considered the Territorial Agreement terminated in his letter of November 6, 1973 * * *. Burger King's corporate structure had become so complex that the question of who, when or where the decision was made could not be answered. The abrupt manner in which Burger King's position was communicated to Family Dining, under the circumstances, was not straightforward.

From November, 1973, until some point early in 1975, the parties attempted to negotiate their differences with no success. The reason for the lack of success is understandable given that Burger King from the outset considered exclusivity a non-negotiable item. * * *

Several months before the instant litigation was begun Family Dining informed Burger King that it intended to open a ninth Restaurant on or about May 15, 1975, on Street Road, Warminster, Pennsylvania. * * *

In May, 1975, Burger King filed a complaint, which was the inception of this lawsuit, seeking to enjoin the use of Burger King trademarks by Family Dining at the Warminster Restaurant. * * * On May 13, 1975, the parties reached an agreement on terms under which the Burger King trademarks could be used at the Warminster Restaurant [and at a tenth Restaurant]. Pursuant to the agreement Burger King filed an amended complaint seeking the instant declaratory relief. * * *

DISCUSSION

Family Dining raises several arguments in support of its motion pursuant to Rule 41(b).[2] One of its principal arguments is that the termination provision should be found inoperative because otherwise it would result in a forfeiture to Family Dining. For reasons which have become evident during the presentation of Burger King's case the Court

---

2. It is apparent that if this case were to proceed to the presentation of Family Dining's evidence, Family Dining would attempt to establish that the 1968 Modification modified the development rate and/or that there was an effective waiver of said rate. The Court reaches no conclusion on these grounds.

finds Family Dining's position compelling both on legal and equitable grounds and is thus persuaded that the Territorial Agreement should not be declared terminated. * * *

In bringing this suit Burger King maintains that the Territorial Agreement is a divisible contract wherein Family Dining promised to open or have under active construction one new Restaurant in each of the first ten years of the contract in exchange for which Burger King promised to grant one additional year of exclusivity for each new Restaurant. This, to be followed by an additional eighty years of exclusivity provided the first ten Restaurants were built on time. In support Burger King relies on the opening language of Article I of the Territorial Agreement which provides that "[f]or a period of one year, beginning on the date hereof, Company will not operate or license ..." It is thus argued that since Family Dining clearly failed to perform its promises the Court must, in accordance with the express language of Article II, declare the contract terminated. Burger King further argues that because Family Dining did not earn exclusivity beyond the ninth year, upon termination, it could not be found that Family Dining would forfeit anything in which it had an interest.

Contrary to the analysis offered by Burger King, the Court considers the development rate a condition subsequent, not a promise, which operates to divest Family Dining of exclusivity. Where words in a contract raise no duty in and of themselves but rather modify or limit the promisees' right to enforce the promise such words are considered to be a condition. Whether words constitute a condition or a promise is a matter of the intention of the parties to be ascertained from a reasonable construction of the language used, considered in light of the surrounding circumstances. *Feinberg v. Automobile Banking Corporation,* 353 F.Supp. 508, 512 (E.D.Pa.1973); Williston, Contracts, §§ 665, 666. It seems clear that the true purpose of the Territorial Agreement was to create a longterm promise of exclusivity to act as an inducement to Family Dining to develop Bucks and Montgomery Counties within a certain time frame. A careful reading of the agreement indicates that it raises no duties, as such, in Family Dining. Both Article I and Article II contain language which refers to ninety years of exclusivity subject to limitation. For instance, Article I provides in part that "[t]his Agreement shall remain in effect and licensee shall retain the exclusive territory for a period of ninety (90) years from the date hereof, provided that at the end of one, two ..." Failure to comply with the development rate operates to defeat liability on Burger King's promise of exclusivity. Liability, or at least Family Dining's right to enforce the promise, arose upon entering the contract. The fact that Burger King seeks affirmative relief premised on the development rate and the fact that it calls for a specified performance by Family Dining tend to obscure its true nature. Nevertheless, in the Court's view it is a condition subsequent. 8 P.L.E. Contracts § 264 (1971).

Furthermore, the fact that performance is to occur in installments does not necessarily mean that the contract is divisible. Once again, this is a question of the intention of the parties ascertained, if possible, from a reasonable interpretation of the language used. *Continental Supermarket Food Service, Inc. v. Soboski,* 210 Pa.Super. 304, 232 A.2d 216, 217 (1967). In view of the fact that there was a single promise of exclusivity to have a ninety year duration, assuming the condition subsequent did not occur by a failure to comply with the development rate, the Court believes, consistent with the views previously expressed herein, that the contract was intended to be entire rather than severable.

The question arises whether Burger King has precluded itself from asserting Family Dining's untimeliness on the basis that Burger King did not demand literal adherence to the development rate throughout most of the first ten years of the contract. Nothing is commoner in contracts than for a promisor to protect himself by making his promise conditional. Ordinarily a party would be entitled to have such an agreement strictly enforced, however, before doing so the Court must consider not only the written contract but also the acts and conduct of the parties in carrying out the agreement. As Judge Kraft, in effect, provided in *Dempsey v. Stauffer,* 182 F.Supp. 806, 810 (E.D.Pa.1960), after one party by conduct indicates that literal performance will not be required, he cannot without notice and a reasonable time begin demanding literal performance.

In the early going Burger King did not demand that Family Dining perform in exact compliance with the development schedule. It failed to introduce any evidence indicating that a change in attitude had been communicated to Family Dining. At the time of the Donaldson letter Family Dining's non-compliance with the development rate was no worse than it was with respect to the fourth and fifth Restaurants. The letter itself was sent by a documents administrator rather than a Burger King official and it seems to imply that the Territorial Agreement would not be terminated. Assuming that at some point between May and November, or even at the time of the Donaldson letter, Ferris realized literal performance would be required, the circumstances of this type of development are such that Burger King was unreasonable in declaring a termination such a short time after, if not concurrent with, notice that literal performance would be required.

Considerable time was consumed in negotiations between November, 1973, until shortly before suit although it appears that these efforts were an exercise in futility given Burger King's view on exclusivity. Moreover, it could be expected that Burger King would have sued to enjoin any further progress by Family Dining, during this lengthy period, just as it did when Family Dining attempted to get the ninth Restaurant under way. The upshot being that the hiatus in development from November, 1973, until active construction began on the ninth and tenth Restaurants is not fully chargeable to Family Dining.

Based on the foregoing the Court concludes that Burger King is not entitled to have the condition protecting its promise strictly enforced.

Moreover and more important, even though a suit for declaratory relief can be characterized as neither legal nor equitable, *United States*

Fidelity & Guaranty Co. v. Koch, 102 F.2d 288, 290 (3d Cir.1939), giving strict effect to the termination provision involves divesting Family Dining of exclusivity, which, in the Court's view, would amount to a forfeiture. As a result the Court will not ignore considerations of fairness and believes that equitable principles, as well, ought to govern the outcome of this suit. *Barraclough v. Atlantic Refining,* 230 Pa.Super. 276, 326 A.2d 477 (1974).

The Restatement, Contracts, § 302 provides:

"A condition may be excused without other reason if its requirement

"(a) will involve extreme forfeiture or penalty, and

"(b) its existence or occurrence forms no essential part of the exchange for the promisor's performance."

Taking the latter consideration first, it seems clear that throughout the early duration of the contract Burger King was more concerned with a general development of the territory than it was with exact compliance with the terms of the development rate. Burger King offered no evidence that it ever considered literal performance to be critical. In fact, the evidence indicates quite the contrary. Even though McLamore testified that he never contemplated a delay of the duration which occurred with the ninth and tenth Restaurants, he felt a total delay of approximately 19 months with respect to the fourth and fifth Restaurants was nearly in compliance. On the basis of his prior conduct and his testimony considered in its entirety his comments on this point command little weight.

Clearly Burger King's attitude with respect to the development rate changed. Interestingly enough it was sometime after Burger King realized Bucks and Montgomery Counties could support substantially more than ten Restaurants as had been originally thought. It was also at a time after Rosewall replaced McLamore as chief executive officer.

Burger King maintains that Ferris' conduct indicates that he knew strict compliance with the development rate was required. This is based on the several occasions where Ferris expressed concern over noncompliance. However, during the presentation of Burger King's evidence it was established that Ferris was an individual who was overly meticulous with details which caused him to be, in many respects, ignored by Burger King officials. Given this aspect of his personality and Burger King's attitude toward him very little significance can be attached to Ferris' expressions of concern. In short, the evidence fails to establish that either Burger King or Family Dining considered the development rate critical. If it eventually did become critical it was not until very late in the first ten years and in such a way that, in conscience, it cannot be used to the detriment of Family Dining.

As previously indicated, the Court believes that if the right of exclusivity were to be extinguished by termination it would constitute a forfeiture. In arguing that by termination Family Dining will lose nothing that it earned, Burger King overlooks the risks assumed and the efforts expended by Family Dining, largely without assistance from Burger King, in making the venture successful in the exclusive territory.

While it is true that Family Dining realized a return on its investment, certainly part of this return was the prospect of continued exclusivity. Moreover, this is not a situation where Burger King did not receive any benefit from the relationship.

In making the promise of exclusivity Burger King intended to induce Family Dining to develop its Restaurants in the exclusive territory. There is no evidence that the failure to fulfill the time feature of this inducement was the result of any intentional or negligent conduct on the part of Family Dining. And at the present time there are ten Restaurants in operation which was all the inducement was intended to elicit. Assuming all ten were built on time Burger King would have been able to expect some definable level of revenue, a percentage of which it lost due to the delay. Burger King did not, however, attempt to establish the amount of this loss at trial.

In any event if Family Dining were forced to forfeit the right of exclusivity it would lose something of incalculable value based on its investment of time and money developing the area, the significant risks assumed and the fact that there remains some 76 years of exclusivity under the Territorial Agreement. Such a loss would be without any commensurate breach on its part since the injury caused to Burger King by the delay is relatively modest and within definable limits. Thus, a termination of the Territorial Agreement would result in an extreme forfeiture to Family Dining.

In accordance with the foregoing the Court finds that under the law and based upon the facts adduced in Burger King's case, it is not entitled to a declaration that the Territorial Agreement is terminated. Therefore, Family Dining's Rule 41(b) motion for an involuntary dismissal is granted.

R & R OF CONNECTICUT, INC. v. STIEGLER

Appellate Court of Connecticut, 1985.
4 Conn.App. 240, 493 A.2d 293.

HULL, JUDGE. This case involves the narrow issue of whether a tenant's late notice of intention to renew a lease of commercial property should be excused on equitable principles. The plaintiff tenant sought an injunction to prohibit the defendant landlord from terminating the lease. The defendant, in her counterclaim, sought a declaratory judgment that the lease would expire on December 31, 1984, because of the plaintiff's failure to exercise its option to extend the lease. The defendant appeals from the judgment of the trial court, A. Aronson, J., that the option to extend the lease has been properly exercised. We find error.

The plaintiff is a tenant of premises located at 172 Washington Street, Hartford, where it operates a supermarket. On June 13, 1979, the defendant leased the premises to Pedro Ortiz. On January 27, 1981, Ortiz assigned the lease to the plaintiff. The term of the lease was for five years and six months, from June 15, 1979, to December 31, 1984. Paragraph six of the lease gave the tenant an option to renew the lease for an additional five-year period which could only be exercised by sending written notice to the landlord at least twelve months prior to December 31, 1984, the termination date of the lease. Paragraph 28 of the lease contained a right of first refusal giving the tenant the right to purchase the property first if the landlord received an offer to buy it.

On January 26, 1984, the defendant notified the plaintiff, in writing, that the lease would terminate on its expiration date of December 31, 1984, because of the plaintiff's failure to exercise the renewal option. On February 6, 1984, counsel for the plaintiff wrote to the defendant's agent advising him that Attorney Arnold E. Bayer, who died on December 14, 1983, had been the attorney for the plaintiff, and stating: "I believe it was probably his intention to send a letter of the clients' intention to renew under the terms of said lease." The letter said the plaintiff wanted to exercise the option and asked the defendant for a reconsideration of the notice of termination. On March 23, 1983, the defendant had entered into an agreement to sell the premises for $425,000 to McDonald's Corporation for a McDonald's restaurant. The defendant's appraiser testified at trial that the fair market value of the property was only $225,000. The defendant was required to deliver the premises to the purchaser "free and clear of all tenancies and parties in possession." The purchase agreement contained no performance date but was dependent on the purchaser being able to close title when it purchased adjoining premises from another party and secured necessary zoning approval and other governmental permits. The plaintiff, upon notice of this agreement on February 24, 1984, did not exercise its right of first refusal on the property.

The court found the McDonald's offer to be a bona fide offer but that in reality it was an option to purchase under certain conditions of benefit to the optionee. It concluded that the loss to the landlord was speculative. It further found that the plaintiff had invested $40,000 and borrowed $390,000 from the small business administration to equip the supermarket. The removal of the fixtures and freezers and loss of business would cost the plaintiff $50,000. Further, there is no suitable location in the area for the plaintiff to relocate its neighborhood type store.

The court succinctly stated the issue to be whether a tenant can exercise late an option to renew a lease, by claiming that his attorney would have properly exercised the option for the tenant, but for the attorney's untimely death, and that equitable considerations will prevent a forfeiture of the lease. The court concluded that Bayer's death, the large monetary loss to be suffered by the plaintiff, the speculative loss which the landlord might incur, and the customer loss from the neighborhood community justified equitable relief for the plaintiff.

The law in Connecticut on this issue is well settled. In F.B. Fountain Co. v. Stein, 97 Conn. 619, 118 A. 47 (1922), the plaintiff tenant was four days late in meeting a thirty day notice requirement for renewal of its lease, with the defendant landlord. The lease was for five years with a privilege of four five year renewals. The tenant had occupied the premises for twenty years prior to the time when it failed to give timely notice of intent to renew the lease. Both the tenant and its sublessees had erected buildings and made improvements on the site. The Supreme Court found error in the trial court's denial of equitable relief because of the court's exclusion of evidence of the value of good will of the plaintiff's business in this location. In so doing, the court stated the rule as follows: "We think the better rule to be that in cases of wilful or gross negligence in failing to fulfil a condition precedent of a lease, equity will never relieve. But in case of mere neglect in fulfilling a condition precedent of a lease, which does not fall within accident or mistake, equity will relieve when the delay has been slight, the loss to the lessor small, and when not to grant relief would result in such hardship to the tenant as to make it unconscionable to enforce literally the condition precedent of the lease." Id., 626–27, 118 A. 47.

The case of Xanthakey v. Hayes, 107 Conn. 459, 140 A. 808 (1928), strongly reaffirmed the F.B. Fountain Co. doctrine, in upholding the granting of an injunction ordering the landlord to execute a renewal of the lease despite untimely notice. The lease was for ten years with a five year extension on sixty days notice before the termination of the lease. Proper notice would have been on December 31, 1926. The tenants gave notice on January 3, 1927. The first day of neglect of notice was a holiday, the second a Sunday, and on the following day, Monday, notice was given. The trial court found that without the renewal of the lease the tenants would lose about $4000 in improvements together with a substantial loss of good will to their business, that the lack of notice was due to mere forgetfulness, and that the landlord suffered no damages from the three day delay. The court then found that case "peculiarly one for the interposition of equity to prevent the consummation of unconscionable hardship to the plaintiffs." Id., 476, 140 A. 808.

In Galvin v. Simons, 128 Conn. 616, 25 A.2d 64 (1942), the Supreme Court ruled for the tenants who were awarded an injunction ordering the landlord to renew a lease. The lease ran from October 10, 1938, to April 30, 1941, with a right of renewal for one year based on ninety days notice before its expiration. The landlord told the tenants that she would record the lease but she did not do so. The tenants lost their copy of the lease and were under the impression that the right to renew could be exercised within sixty days of the expiration of the lease. The tenants had spent $500 on improvements and it would cost $100 to move. In finding that the trial court did not abuse its discretion in finding the notice sufficient, the Supreme Court noted (1) that there was no hint of loss to the lessor from the tenants' use of the property for another year; (2) that no space was available in Cheshire for the tenants' purposes; and (3) that thirteen days delay was a small percentage of the notice required.

The defendant argues that the rule of F.B. Fountain Co. v. Stein, supra, has been limited to three types of cases: (1) F.B. Fountain Co. v. Stein, supra, where the forfeiture of the buildings and improvements would unjustly enrich the landlord; (2) Xanthakey v. Hayes, supra, where the delay was very slight; and (3) Galvin v. Simons, supra, where the landlord misrepresented that she would record the lease. The plaintiff claims that the facts of this case bring it within the rules enunciated in these cases.

The plaintiff claims: (1) that the delay was slight, pointing out that in F.B. Fountain Co. the tenant was thirty-seven days late on a thirty day notice and in Galvin the notice was thirteen days late on a ninety day renewal period; (2) that the plaintiff's delay was not wilful since the trial court found that the tenant may have been neglectful or forgetful but this was excused because of Bayer's death; and (3) that the plaintiff would suffer severe hardship if the lease were not renewed.

An analysis of the F.B. Fountain Co. criteria which must be met before equity will grant relief in cases such as this one reveals error in the court's judgment.

(1) Whether the failure to give notice was mere neglect or gross or wilful negligence: "As a general rule a party will not be given relief against a mistake induced by his own culpable negligence.... But the rule is not inflexible and in many cases relief may be granted although the mistake was not unmixed with some element of negligence, particularly where the other party has been in no way prejudiced." F.B. Fountain Co. v. Stein, supra, 626, quoting 21 Corpus Juris, Equity § 64, p. 88; [other citations omitted]. The court, in finding Bayer's death to be justification for equitable intervention, found only that the tenant "may have been forgetful or neglectful" in giving notice.

The court's finding fails to state whether the plaintiff's failure to give notice amounted to wilful or gross negligence which would not allow equitable relief or was merely neglect which would permit such relief under F.B. Fountain Co. The plaintiff's attorney's statement that he believed it was probably Bayer's intention to send a renewal letter is completely devoid of any probative value. Sanctioning the acceptance of such "evidence" would open the courtroom door to myriad statements of interested lawyers favorable to their clients and lacking any factual basis.

(2) Whether or not the delay has been slight: The court made no specific finding in this regard but its reliance on F.B. Fountain Co. in granting relief makes such a finding implicit in the court's judgment. By comparison with F.B. Fountain Co. (four days late on a thirty day notice), Xanthakey (three days late on a sixty day notice), and Galvin (thirteen days late on a sixty day notice, applying a percentage factor) we conclude that the delay was slight.

(3) Whether the loss to the lessor is small: The propriety of considering the possible loss to the landlord of a more advantageous use of its property was not challenged in the trial court or in this court. Since such evidence is immaterial to the question involved in this case we do not consider the issue of error in the court's rejection of the evidence concerning the McDonald's agreement as "speculative." It was error for the court to consider the evidence in any event. The application of the F.B. Fountain Co. rule requires that the landlord be prejudiced by a

change in position during the period between the time when notice was due and the time when it was given. In other words, the delay itself must have caused the loss. [Citations omitted]. "[W]here an option is contained in a lease or other contract involving an estate in land, some courts of equity, especially in recent years, have tended to treat the offer as not automatically lapsing on expiration of the option period, as for instance, in case of renewal of a long term lease, where to do so would involve substantial forfeiture and the lessor has not materially changed his position in reliance on the optionee's failure to exercise his option within the stated time. [F.B.] Fountain [Co.] v. Stein, [supra]; Xanthakey v. Hayes, [supra]; Ammar v. Cohen, 96 W.Va. 550, 123 S.E. 582 [1924]." 1 Williston, Contracts (3d Ed. Jaeger) § 76, pp. 248–49 n. 4.

We do not reach the ultimate question of possible unconscionability if the plaintiff is not granted a renewal of the lease since a new trial is necessary to make a finding on the missing element of the F.B. Fountain Co. criteria, that is, the degree of the plaintiff's negligence in failing to give notice. If the court finds this necessary predicate to relief in the plaintiff's favor it will then be in a position to determine the ultimate equitable question involved.

There is error, the judgment is set aside and the case is remanded for further proceedings in accordance with this opinion.

In this opinion the other Judges concurred.

C & J FERTILIZER, INC. v. ALLIED MUTUAL INS. CO.

Supreme Court of Iowa, 1975.
227 N.W.2d 169.

REYNOLDSON, JUSTICE. This action to recover for burglary loss under two separate insurance policies was tried to the court, resulting in a finding plaintiff had failed to establish a burglary within the policy definitions. Plaintiff appeals from judgment entered for defendant. We reverse and remand.

Trial court made certain findings of fact in support of its conclusion reached. Plaintiff operated a fertilizer plant in Olds, Iowa. At time of loss, plaintiff was insured under policies issued by defendant and titled "BROAD FORM STOREKEEPERS POLICY" and "MERCANTILE BURGLARY AND ROBBERY POLICY." Each policy defined "burglary" as meaning,

> " * * * the felonious abstraction of insured property (1) from within the premises by a person making felonious entry therein by actual force and violence, of which force and violence there are visible marks made by tools, explosives, electricity or chemicals upon, or physical damage to, the exterior of the premises at the place of such entry * * *."

On Saturday, April 18, 1970, all exterior doors to the building were locked when plaintiff's employees left the premises at the end of the business day. The following day, Sunday, April 19, 1970, one of plaintiff's employees was at the plant and found all doors locked and secure. On Monday, April 20, 1970, when the employees reported for work, the exterior doors were locked, but the front office door was unlocked.

There were truck tire tread marks visible in the mud in the driveway leading to and from the plexiglas door entrance to the warehouse. It was demonstrated this door could be forced open without leaving visible marks or physical damage.

There were no visible marks on the exterior of the building made by tools, explosives, electricity or chemicals, and there was no physical damage to the exterior of the building to evidence felonious entry into the building by force and violence.

Chemicals had been stored in an interior room of the warehouse. The door to this room, which had been locked, was physically damaged and carried visible marks made by tools. Chemicals had been taken at a net loss to plaintiff in the sum of $9,582. Office and shop equipment valued at $400.30 was also taken from the building.

Trial court held the policy definition of "burglary" was unambiguous, there was nothing in the record "upon which to base a finding that the door to plaintiff's place of business was entered feloniously, by actual force and violence," and, applying the policy language, found for defendant.

Certain other facts in the record were apparently deemed irrelevant by trial court because of its view the applicable law required it to enforce the policy provision. Because we conclude different rules of law apply, we also consider those facts.

The "BROAD FORM STOREKEEPERS POLICY" was issued April 14, 1969; the "MERCANTILE BURGLARY AND ROBBERY POLICY" on April 14, 1970. Those policies are in evidence. Prior policies apparently were first purchased in 1968. The agent, who had power to bind insurance coverage for defendant, was told plaintiff would be handling farm chemicals. After inspecting the building then used by plaintiff for storage he made certain suggestions regarding security. There ensued a conversation in which he pointed out there had to be visible evidence of burglary. There was no testimony by anyone that plaintiff was then or thereafter informed the policy to be delivered would define burglary to require "visible marks made by tools, explosives, electricity or chemicals upon, or physical damage to, the exterior of the premises at the place of * * * entry."

The import of this conversation with defendant's agent when the coverage was sold is best confirmed by the agent's complete and vocally-expressed surprise when defendant denied coverage. From what the agent saw (tire tracks and marks on the interior of the building) and his contacts with the investigating officers " * * * the thought didn't enter my mind that it wasn't covered * * *." From the trial testimony it was obvious the only understanding was that there should be some hard evidence of a third-party burglary vis-a-vis an "inside job." The latter was in this instance effectively ruled out when the thief was required to break an interior door lock to gain access to the chemicals.

The agent testified the insurance was purchased and "the policy was sent out afterwards." The president of plaintiff corporation, a 37–year–old farmer with a high school education, looked at that portion of the policy setting out coverages, including coverage for burglary loss, the amounts of insurance, and the "location and description." He could not recall reading the fine print defining "burglary" on page three of the policy.

Trial court's "findings" must be examined in light of our applicable rules. Ordinarily in a law action tried to the court its findings of fact having adequate evidentiary support shall not be set aside unless induced by an erroneous view of the law. It follows, the rule does not preclude inquiry into the question whether, conceding the truth of a finding of fact, the trial court applied erroneous rules of law which materially affected the decision. Beneficial Finance Company of Waterloo v. Lamos, 179 N.W.2d 573, 578 (Iowa 1970) and citations.

Extrinsic evidence that throws light on the situation of the parties, the antecedent negotiations, the attendant circumstances and the objects they were thereby striving to attain is necessarily to be regarded as relevant to ascertain the actual significance and proper legal meaning of the agreement. Hamilton v. Wosepka, 261 Iowa 299, 306, 154 N.W.2d 164, 168 (1967); 3 Corbin on Contracts, 1971 pocket part § 543AA, pp. 91–95.

The question of *interpretation,* i.e., the meaning to be given contractual words, is one to be determined by the court unless the interpretation depends on extrinsic evidence or on a choice among reasonable inferences to be drawn from extrinsic evidence. See Restatement (Second) of Contracts § 238, p. 543 (Student Ed., Tent. Drafts Nos. 1–7, 1973). *Construction* of a contract means determination of its legal operation—its effect upon the action of the courts. Porter v. Iowa Power and Light Company, 217 N.W.2d 221, 228 (Iowa 1974); Boyer v. Iowa High School Athletic Association, 260 Iowa 1061, 1069, 152 N.W.2d 293, 298 (1967); 3 Corbin on Contracts § 534, pp. 7–9; 4 Williston on Contracts § 602, p. 320. "[C]onstruction [of a contract] is always a matter of law for the court." 3 Corbin on Contracts § 554, p. 227. "[C]ourts in construing and applying a standardized contract seek to effectuate the reasonable expectations of the average member of the public who accepts it." Restatement (Second) of Contracts, supra, § 237, comment e, p. 540.

* * *

Insofar as trial court was construing the policy—that being a matter of law for the court—we are not bound by its conclusions. See Farmers Insurance Group v. Merryweather, 214 N.W.2d 184, 187 (Iowa 1974); E. Patterson, The Interpretation and Construction of Contracts, 64 Colum.L.Rev. 833, 836–37 (1964). Neither are we bound by trial court's rule this case is controlled by the fineprint "definition" of burglary, if that rule was erroneously applied below. Beneficial Finance Company of Waterloo v. Lamos, supra.

Trial court did find "[T]here does not appear to have been a discussion of the policy provisions between the parties at the time the policy was secured * * *." That finding is well supported: there is no evidence plaintiff knew of the definition of burglary contained in the policy until after the event. But both parties agree there was conversation concerning the type of insurance and the property to be insured. While plaintiff's president's testimony is ambivalent as to whether it occurred before or after the predecessor policies were issued, the defendant's agent was clear the conversation occurred before any policies were delivered.

There is nothing about trial court's factual findings which precludes this court from construing said contract to arrive at a proper determination of its legal operation as between these parties, or from considering whether the decision appealed from resulted from the application of an erroneous rule of law. And if the definition of "burglary" in defendant's policy is not enforceable here, then trial court's finding there was no evidence of forcible entry through an outside door is not controlling in the disposition of this case.

Plaintiff's theories of recovery based on "reasonable expectations," implied warranty and unconscionability must be viewed in light of accelerating change in the field of contracts.

I. REVOLUTION IN FORMATION OF CONTRACTUAL RELATIONSHIPS

Many of our principles for resolving conflicts relating to written contracts were formulated at an early time when parties of equal strength negotiated in the historical sequence of offer, acceptance, and reduction to writing. The concept that both parties assented to the resulting document had solid footing in fact.

Only recently has the sweeping change in the inception of the document received widespread recognition:

"Standard form contracts probably account for more than ninety-nine percent of all contracts now made. Most persons have difficulty remembering the last time they contracted other than by standard form; except for casual oral agreements, they probably never have. But if they are active, they contract by standard form several times a day. Parking lot and theater tickets, package receipts, department store charge slips, and gas station credit card purchase slips are all standard form contracts.

" * * *

" * * * The contracting still imagined by courts and law teachers as typical, in which both parties participate in choosing the language of their entire agreement, is no longer of much more than historical importance."

— W. Slawson, Standard Form Contracts and Democratic Control of Lawmaking Power, 84 Harv.L.Rev. 529 (1971).

With respect to those interested in buying insurance, it has been observed that:

> "His chances of successfully negotiating with the company for any substantial change in the proposed contract are just about zero. The insurance company tenders the insurance upon a 'take it or leave it' basis.
>
> " * * *
>
> " ' * * * Few persons solicited to take policies understand the subject of insurance or the rules of law governing the negotiations, and they have no voice in dictating the terms of what is called the contract. They are clear upon two or three points which the agent promises to protect, and for everything else they must sign ready-made applications and accept ready-made policies carefully concocted to conserve the interests of the company. * * * The subject, therefore, is *sui generis,* and the rules of a legal system devised to govern the formation of ordinary contracts between man and man cannot be mechanically applied to it.' "

— 7 Williston on Contracts § 900, pp. 29–30 (3d Ed.1963).

* * *

It is generally recognized the insured will not read the detailed, cross-referenced, standardized, mass-produced insurance form, nor understand it if he does. 7 Williston on Contracts § 906B, p. 300 ("But where the document thus delivered to him is a contract of insurance the majority rule is that the insured is not bound to know its contents"); 3 Corbin on Contracts § 559, pp. 265–66 ("One who applies for an insurance policy * * * may not even read the policy, the number of its terms and the fineness of its print being such as to discourage him"); Note, Unconscionable Contracts: The Uniform Commercial Code, 45 Iowa L.Rev. 843, 844 (1960) ("It is probably a safe assertion that most involved standardized form contracts are never read by the party who 'adheres' to them. In such situations, the proponent of the form is free to dictate terms most advantageous to himself").

The concept that persons must obey public laws enacted by their own representatives does not offend a fundamental sense of justice: an inherent element of assent pervades the process.

But the inevitable result of enforcing all provisions of the adhesion contract, frequently, as here, delivered subsequent to the transaction and containing provisions never assented to, would be an abdication of judicial responsibility in face of basic unfairness and a recognition that persons' rights shall be controlled by private lawmakers without the consent, express or implied, of those affected. A question is also raised whether a court may constitutionally allow that power to exist in private hands except where appropriate safeguards are present, including a right to meaningful judicial review. See W. Slawson, supra at 553.

* * *

The mass-produced boiler-plate "contracts," necessitated and spawned by the explosive growth of complex business transactions in a burgeoning population left courts frequently frustrated in attempting to arrive at just results by applying many of the traditional contract-construing stratagems. As long as fifteen years ago Professor Llewellyn, reflecting on this situation in his book "The Common Law Tradition—*Deciding Appeals,*" pp. 362–71 wrote,

> "What the story shows thus far is first, scholars persistently off-base while judges grope over well-nigh a century in irregular but dogged fashion for escape from a recurring discomfort of imbalance that rests on what is in fact substantial *non* agreement despite perfect semblance of agreement. (pp. 367–368).

* * *

> "The answer, I suggest, is this: Instead of thinking about 'assent' to boiler-plate clauses, we can recognize that so far as concerns the specific, there is no assent at all. What has in fact been assented to, specifically, are the few dickered terms, and the broad type of transaction, and but one thing more. That one thing more is a blanket assent (not a specific assent) to any not unreasonable or indecent terms the seller may have on his form, which do not alter or eviscerate the reasonable meaning of the dickered terms. The fine print which has not been read has no business to cut under the reasonable meaning of those dickered terms which constitute the dominant and only real expression of agreement, but much of it commonly belongs in." (p. 370)

* * *

Plaintiff's claim it should be granted relief under the legal doctrines of reasonable expectations, implied warranty and unconscionability should be viewed against the above backdrop.

II.   Reasonable Expectations

This court adopted the doctrine of reasonable expectations in Rodman v. State Farm Mutual Ins. Co., 208 N.W.2d 903, 905–908 (Iowa 1973). The *Rodman* court approved the following articulation of that concept:

> " 'The objectively reasonable expectations of applicants and intended beneficiaries regarding the terms of insurance contracts will be honored even though painstaking study of the policy provisions would have negated those expectations.' "

— 208 N.W.2d at 906.

See Gray v. Zurich Insurance Company, 65 Cal.2d 263, 54 Cal.Rptr. 104, 107–108, 419 P.2d 168, 171–172 (1966); Allen v. Metropolitan Life Ins. Co., 44 N.J. 294, 305, 208 A.2d 638, 644 (1965); Restatement (Second) of Contracts, supra, § 237, comments e and f, pp. 540–41; 1 Corbin on Contracts § 1, p. 2 ("That portion of the field of law that is classified and described as the law of contracts attempts the realization of reasonable expectations that have been induced by the making of a promise"); 7 Williston on Contracts § 900, pp. 33–34 ("Some courts, recognizing that very few insureds even try to read and understand the policy or application, have declared that the insured is justified in assuming that the policy which is delivered to him has been faithfully prepared by the company to provide the protection against the risk which he had asked for. * * * Obviously this judicial attitude is a far cry from the old motto 'caveat emptor.' ").

At comment f to § 237 of Restatement (Second) of Contracts, supra pp. 540–41, we find the following analysis of the reasonable expectations doctrine:

"Although customers typically adhere to standardized agreements and are bound by them without even appearing to know the standard terms in detail, they are not bound to unknown terms which are beyond the range of reasonable expectation. A debtor who delivers a check to his creditor with the amount blank does not authorize the insertion of an infinite figure. Similarly, a party who adheres to the other party's standard terms does not assent to a term if the other party has reason to believe that the adhering party would not have accepted the agreement if he had known that the agreement contained the particular term. Such a belief or assumption may be shown by the prior negotiations or inferred from the circumstances. Reason to believe may be inferred from the fact that the term is bizarre or oppressive, from the fact that it eviscerates the non-standard terms explicitly agreed to, or from the fact that it eliminates the dominant purpose of the transaction. The inference is reinforced if the adhering party never had an opportunity to read the term, or if it is illegible or otherwise hidden from view. This rule is closely related to the policy against unconscionable terms and the rule of interpretation against the draftsman."

Nor can it be asserted the above doctrine does not apply here because plaintiff knew the policy contained the provision now complained of and cannot be heard to say it reasonably expected what it knew was not there. A search of the record discloses no such knowledge.

The evidence does show, as above noted, a "dicker" for burglary insurance coverage on chemicals and equipment. The negotiation was for what was actually expressed in the policies' "Insuring Agreements": the insurer's promise "To pay for loss by burglary or by robbery of a watchman, while the premises are not open for business, of merchandise, furniture, fixtures and equipment within the premises * * *."

In addition, the conversation included statements from which the plaintiff should have understood defendant's obligation to pay would not arise where the burglary was an "inside job." Thus the following exclusion should have been reasonably anticipated:

"Exclusions

"This policy does not apply:

" * * *

"(b) to loss due to any fraudulent, dishonest or criminal act by any Insured, a partner therein, or an officer, employee, director, trustee or authorized representative thereof * * *."

But there was nothing relating to the negotiations with defendant's agent which would have led plaintiff to reasonably anticipate defendant would bury within the definition of "burglary" another exclusion denying coverage when, no matter how extensive the proof of a third-party buglary, no marks were left on the exterior of the premises. This escape clause, here triggered by the burglar's talent (an investigating law officer, apparently acquainted with the current modus operandi, gained access to the steel building without leaving any marks by leaning on the overhead plexiglas door while simultaneously turning the locked handle), was never read to or by plaintiff's personnel, nor was the substance explained by defendant's agent.

Moreover, the burglary "definition" which crept into this policy comports neither with the concept a layman might have of that crime, nor with a legal interpretation. * * *

The most plaintiff might have reasonably anticipated was a policy requirement of visual evidence (abundant here) indicating the burglary was an "outside" not an "inside" job. The exclusion in issue, masking as a definition, makes insurer's obligation to pay turn on the skill of the burglar, not on the event the parties bargained for: a bonafide third party burglary resulting in loss of plaintiff's chemicals and equipment.

* * *

III. IMPLIED WARRANTY

Plaintiff should also prevail because defendant breached an implied warranty that the policy later delivered would be reasonably fit for its intended purpose: to set out in writing the obligations of the parties (1) without altering or impairing the fair meaning of the protection bargained for when read alone, and (2) in terms that are neither in the particular nor in the net manifestly unreasonable and unfair. See K. Llewellyn, The Common Law Tradition—*Deciding Appeals,* p. 371.

More than 75 years ago this court, without statutory support, recognized in contracts for sale of tangible property there was a warranty implied by law that the goods sold "were reasonably fit for the purpose for which they were intended." Alpha Check–Rower Co. v. Bradley, 105 Iowa 537, 547, 75 N.W. 369, 372 (1898). This seminal concept of basic fairness grew by progressive court decisions and statutory enactments into that network of protection which today guards the chattel purchaser from exploitation. See, e.g., Hughes v. National Equipment Corporation, 216 Iowa 1000, 250 N.W. 154 (1933) (statement in written sales contract that it contained the entire agreement did not exclude implied warranty); State Farm Mut Auto. Ins. Co. v. Anderson–Weber, Inc., 252 Iowa 1289, 110 N.W.2d 449 (1961) (privity of contract defense to breach of warranty repudiated; terms and limitations of fine-print express warranty do not relieve manufacturer or seller from implied warranty obligations); Turner v. Kunde, 256 Iowa 835, 128 N.W.2d 196 (1964) (voiding disclaimer of implied warranty in sales memorandum delivered to buyer *after* the bargain was made); Dailey v. Holiday Distributing Corporation, 260 Iowa 859, 151 N.W.2d 477 (1967) (fine-print conditions on back of purchase order not brought to buyer's attention no defense to claim of implied warranty); § 554.1102(3), The Code (" * * * the obligations of good faith, diligence, reasonableness and care prescribed by this chapter may not be disclaimed * * * "); § 554.1201(10) (" * * * Language in the body of a form is 'conspicuous' if it is in larger or other contrasting type or color * * * "); § 554.1203 ("Every contract or duty * * * imposes an obligation of good faith in its performance or enforcement"); § 554.2302 (effect of unconscionable contract clauses may be avoided by the court); § 554.2313 (express warranties); §§ 554.2314, 554.2315 (implied warranties); § 554.2316 (writing to exclude implied warranties of merchantability and fitness must be "conspicuous").

> "The final and perhaps most significant characteristic of insurance contracts differentiating them from ordinary, negotiated commercial contract, is the increasing tendency of the public to look upon the insurance policy not as a contract but as a special form of chattel. The typical applicant buys 'protection' much as he buys groceries."

— 7 Williston on Contracts § 900, p. 34.

We would be derelict in our duty to administer justice if we were not to judicially know that modern insurance companies have turned to mass advertising to sell "protection." A person who has been incessantly assured a given company's policies will afford him complete protection is unlikely to be wary enough to search his policy to find a provision nullifying his burglary protection if the burglar breaks open an inside, but not an outside, door.

There is little justification in depriving purchasers of merchandized "protection" of those remedies long available to purchasers of goods:

> "Although implied warranties of fitness for intended purpose have traditionally been attached only to sales of tangible products, there is no reason why they should not be attached to 'sales of promises' as well. Whether a product is tangible or intangible, its creator ordinarily has reason to know of the purposes for which the buyer intends to use it, and buyers ordinarily rely on the creator's skill or judgment in furnishing it. The reasonable consumer for example depends on an insurance agent and insurance company to sell him a

policy that 'works' for its intended purpose in much the same way that he depends on a television salesman and television manufacturer. In neither case is he likely to be competent to judge the fitness of the product himself; in both, he must rely on common knowledge and the creator's advertising and promotion."

— W. Slawson, supra at 546–47.

See also K. Llewellyn, "The Common Law Tradition—Deciding Appeals," pp. 370–71.

Effective imposition of an implied warranty would encourage insurers to make known to insurance buyers those provisions which would limit the implied warranty inherent in the situation. These exclusions would then become part of the initial bargaining. Such provisions, mandated by the Uniform Commercial Code to be "conspicuous" in the sale of goods (§ 554.2316, The Code), should be conspicuously presented by the insurer in the sale of protection. This would be no more difficult than the manner in which they advertise their product's desirable features. See Henningsen v. Bloomfield Motors, Inc., 32 N.J. 358, 400, 161 A.2d 69, 93 (1960). From a public policy viewpoint, such a requirement (in order to enforce what is essentially an exclusion) might promote meaningful competition among insurers in eliminating technical policy provisions which drain away bargained-for protection. The ultimate benefit would be a chance for knowledgeable selection by insurance purchasers among various coverages.

* * *

Ten years ago this court banished the ancient doctrine of caveat emptor as the polestar for business. Syester v. Banta, 257 Iowa 613, 616, 133 N.W.2d 666, 668 (1965). In Mease v. Fox, 200 N.W.2d 791 (Iowa 1972) we joined a scant handful of courts pioneering the concept that implied warranty relief was not the captive of chattel sales law, but was available to resolve long-standing inequities in the law of dwelling leases. It is now time to provide buyers of protection the same safeguards provided for buyers of personalty and lessees of dwellings.

The policy provided by defendant in this instance breached the implied warranty of fitness for its intended purpose. It altered and impaired the fair meaning of the bargain these parties made for plaintiff's insurance protection. This law theory further requires reversal of trial court's decision.

IV. Unconscionability

Plaintiff is also entitled to a reversal because the liability-avoiding provision in the definition of the burglary is, in the circumstances of this case, unconscionable.

We have already noted the policies were not even before the negotiating persons when the protection was purchased. The fair inference to be drawn from the testimony is that the understanding contemplated only visual evidence of bona-fide burglary to eliminate the risk of an "inside job."

The policies in question contain a classic example of that proverbial fine print (six point type as compared with the twenty-four point type appearing on the face of the policies: "BROAD FORM STOREKEEPERS POLICY" and "MERCANTILE BURGLARY AND ROBBERY POLICY") which "becomes visible only after the event." Such print is additionally suspect when, instead of appearing logically in the "exclusions" of the policies, it poses as a part of an esoteric definition of burglary. A similar contract containing a vast volume of printed conditions neither mentioned nor discussed between the parties once elicited the following comment from this court,

> "It is enough at this time to say that, if it be a contract it is like the Apostle's conception of the human frame, 'fearfully and wonderfully made,' and one upon the construction and effect of which a competent and experienced lawyer may spend days of careful study, without exhausting its possibilities."

> — New Prague Flouring Mill Co. v. Spears, 194 Iowa 417, 438–39, 189 N.W. 815, 824 (1922).

The situation before us plainly justifies application of the unconscionability doctrine:

> "Standardized contracts such as insurance policies, drafted by powerful commercial units and put before individuals on the 'accept this or get nothing' basis, are carefully scrutinized by the courts for the purpose of avoiding enforcement of 'unconscionable' clauses."

> — 6A Corbin on Contracts § 1376, p. 21.

The rule of selective elimination of unconscionable provisions is articulated in the tentative draft of the Restatement (Second) of Contracts, supra § 234, p. 528:

> "§ 234. Unconscionable Contract or Term

> "If a contract or term thereof is unconscionable at the time the contract is made a court may refuse to enforce the contract, or may enforce the remainder of the contract without the unconscionable term, or may so limit the application of any unconscionable term as to avoid any unconscionable result."

The following statement appears in comment "a. *Scope:*

> "Particularly in the case of standardized agreements, the rule of this Section permits the court to pass directly on the unconscionability of the contract or clause rather than to avoid unconscionable results by interpretation."

Comment "d. *Weakness in the bargaining process*" incorporates the following observation,

> "[G]ross inequality of bargaining power, together with terms unreasonably favorable to the stronger party, may confirm indications

that the transaction involved elements of deception or compulsion, or may show that the weaker party had no meaningful choice, no real alternative, or did not in fact assent or appear to assent to the unfair terms."

The resources of a court to avoid unconscionable provisions are not exhausted after a determination of inapplicability of the *contra proferentum* rule: "Even in such a case, the court may refuse to enforce an unconscionable provision and may give such remedy as justice requires * * *. A contractor may defeat his own ends by the use of complex printed forms devised with intent to get the most and to give the least." 3 Corbin on Contracts § 559, pp. 270–71. See Campbell Soup Co. v. Wentz, 172 F.2d 80 (3 Cir.1948); Henningsen v. Bloomfield Motors, Inc., supra; § 554.2302, The Code.

The following reference to the *Henningsen* court and to the unconscionability relief in the commercial code (§ 554.2302, The Code) appears in Grismore, supra, § 294, pp. 508–509:

"After an extensive discussion of some of the cases, the court took the forthright position that the attempted disclaimer in the instant case was 'so inimical to the public good as to compel an adjudication of its invalidity.' This court said what it meant instead of interpreting or constructing its way to the just result. This frontier decision may help to guide other courts to add to the development of a doctrine of unconscionability which will gain the necessary certainty by the traditional process of case-by-case adjudication.

"Adding to the probability that unconscionability will be the stated basis for refusing to enforce oppressive contracts or provisions in the future is the Uniform Commercial Code provision which permits courts to police contracts on this basis. * * * [T]he section is an express recognition of the basic principle. Though the Code is technically applicable only to contracts for the sale of goods, its influence cannot help but be felt in other types of transactions so that most of our courts can say what they mean in refusing to enforce harsh contracts or provisions. Those who would obstruct the development of the unconscionability concept on grounds of uncertainty, indefiniteness and judicial lawmaking, must be characterized as misunderstanding the dynamic nature of the common law and statutory interpretation."

The Iowa court quoted extensively from *Henningsen* and adopted its sound reasoning in State Farm Mut. Auto. Ins. Co. v. Anderson–Weber, Inc., supra.

A policy of relying solely on traditional techniques of construction in an effort to avoid the effect of unconscionable provisions ultimately compounds the problem:

"First, since they [such techniques] all rest on the admission that the clauses in question are permissible in purpose and content, they invite the draftsman to recur to the attack. Give him time, and he will make the grade. Second, since they do not face the issue, they fail to accumulate either experience or authority in the needed direction: that of making out for any given type of transaction what the *minimum decencies* are which a court will insist upon as essential to an enforceable bargain of a given type, or as being inherent in a bargain of that type. Third, since they purport to construe, and do not really construe, nor are intended to * * * they seriously embarrass later efforts * * * to get at the true meaning of those wholly legitimate contracts and clauses which call for their meaning to be got at instead of avoided."

— Llewellyn, Book Review, 52 Harv.L.Rev. 700, 703 (1939).

See Note, supra, 45 Iowa L.Rev. at 845–46 (1960). In the same vein, see 3 Corbin on Contracts § 561, p. 279:

"[A] better brand of justice may be delivered by a court that is clearly conscious of its own processes, than by one that states hard-bitten traditional rules and doctrines and then attains an instinctively felt justice by an avoidance of them that is only half-conscious, accompanied by an extended exegesis worthy of a medieval theologian."

It should be observed that even less justice is attained where, as here, trial court simply stopped with the hard-bitten rules.

Commentators suggest a court considering a claim of unconscionability should examine the factors of assent, unfair surprise, notice, disparity of bargaining power and substantive unfairness. W. Slawson, supra at 564, and citations, n. 79. We have already touched on those considerations in the factual discussions, above. In addition, it would seem appropriate, in every trial when the unconscionability of a contractual provision is a viable issue, to permit either party the right granted by § 554.2302(2), The Code:

"When it is claimed or appears to the court that the contract or any clause thereof may be unconscionable the parties shall be afforded a reasonable opportunity to present evidence as to its commercial setting, purpose and effect to aid the court in making the determination."

In the case *sub judice,* plaintiff's evidence demonstrated the definitional provision was unconscionable. Defendant never offered any evidence, let alone evidence which might support a conclusion the provision in issue, considered in its commercial setting, was either a reasonable limitation on the protection it offered or should have been reasonably anticipated by plaintiff.

Trial court's decision must be reversed because the above provision is unconscionable in view of all the circumstances, including the initial negotiations of these parties.

We reverse and remand for judgment in conformance herewith.

Reversed and remanded.

HARRIS and McCORMICK, JJ., concur.

MASON and RAWLINGS, JJ., concur in Divisions I, II and IV and the result.

LEGRAND, J., MOORE, C.J., and REES and UHLENHOPP, JJ., dissent.

LEGRAND, JUSTICE (dissenting). I dissent from the result reached by the majority because it ignores virtually every rule by which we have heretofore adjudicated such cases and affords plaintiff ex post facto insurance coverage which it not only did not buy but which it *knew* it did not buy.

* * *

While it may be very well to talk in grand terms about "mass advertising" by insurance companies and "incessant" assurances as to coverage which mislead the "unwary," particularly about "fine-print" provisions, such discussion should somehow be related to the case under review. Our primary duty, after all, is to resolve *this* dispute for *these* litigants under *this* record.

There is total silence in this case concerning any of the practices the majority finds offensive; nor is there any claim plaintiff was beguiled by such conduct into believing it had more protection than it actually did.

The record is even stronger against the majority's fine-print argument, the stereotype accusation which serves as a coup de grâce in all insurance cases. Except for larger type on the face sheet and black (but not larger) print to designate divisions and sub-headings, the entire policies are of one size and style of print. To compare the *face* sheet with the body of the policy is like comparing a book's jacket cover with the narrative content; and the use of black type or other means of emphasis to separate one part of an instrument from another is an approved editorial expedient which serves to *assist,* not *hinder,* readability. In fact many of our opinions, including that of the majority in the instant case, resort to that device.

Tested by any objective standard, the size and style of type used cannot be fairly described as "fine print." The majority's description, right or wrong, of the plight of consumers generally should not be the basis for resolving the case now before us.

Like all other appeals, this one should be decided on what the record discloses—a fact which the majority concedes but promptly disregards.

Crucial to a correct determination of this appeal is the disputed provision of each policy defining burglary as "the felonious abstraction of insured property * * * by a person making felonious entry * * * by actual force and violence, of which force and violence there are visible marks made by tools, explosives, electricity or chemicals upon, or physical damage to, the exterior of the premises at the place of such entry * * *." The starting point of any consideration of that definition is a determination whether it is ambiguous. Yet the majority does not even mention ambiguity.

The purpose of such a provision, of course, is to omit from coverage "inside jobs" or those resulting from fraud or complicity by the assured.

The overwhelming weight of authority upholds such provisions as legitimate in purpose and unambiguous in application.

Once this indisputable fact is recognized, plaintiff's arguments virtually collapse. We may not—at least we *should* not—by any accepted standard of construction meddle with contracts which clearly and plainly state their meaning simply because we dislike that meaning, even in the case of insurance policies.

Nor can the doctrine of reasonable expectations be applied here. We adopted that rule in Rodman v. State Farm Mutual Automobile Insurance Company, 208 N.W.2d 903, 906, 907 (Iowa 1973). We refused, however to apply it in that case, where we said:

> "The real question here is whether the principle of reasonable expectations should be extended to cases where an ordinary layman would not misunderstand his coverage from a reading of the policy and where there are no circumstances attributable to the insurer which foster coverage expectations. Plaintiff does not contend he misunderstood the policy. He did not read it. He now asserts in retrospect that if he had read it he would not have understood it. He does not say he was misled by conduct or representations of the insurer. He simply asked trial court to rewrite the policy to cover his loss because if he had purchased his automobile insurance from another company the loss would have been covered, he did not know it was not covered, and if he had known it was not covered he would have purchased a different policy. Trial court declined to do so. We believe trial court correctly refused in these circumstances to extend the principle of reasonable expectations to impose liability."

Yet here the majority would extend the doctrine far beyond the point of refusal in *Rodman*. Here we have affirmative and unequivocal testimony from an officer and director of the plaintiff corporation that he knew the disputed provision was in the policies because "it was just like the insurance policy I have on my farm."

I cannot agree plaintiff may now assert it reasonably expected from these policies something it knew was not there.

These same observations should dispose of plaintiff's claim of implied warranty, a theory incidentally for which there is no case authority at all. The majority apparently seeks to bring insurance contracts within the ambit of the Uniform Commercial Code governing sales of *goods*. I believe the definitional section of the Code itself precludes that notion. See § 554.2105, The Code. This *should* put an end to the majority's argument that buying insurance protection is the same as buying groceries. The complete absence of support from other jurisdictions would also suggest it is indefensible. At least it has done so to some courts. See Drabbels v. Skelly Oil Company, 155 Neb. 17, 50 N.W.2d 229, 231 (Neb.1951).

The remaining ground upon which the majority invalidates the policies—unconscionability—has also been disavowed by the great majority of courts which have decided the question, usually in connection with public policy considerations.

For these several reasons—the principal one being that the findings of the trial court have substantial evidentiary support—I would affirm the judgment.

Problems

45. C, a carrier, agreed to carry goods for A. The agreement provided that C would not be liable for damage to A's cargo unless "written notice of claim for loss" is given within 15 days after delivery of goods. C was aware that A's cargo was damaged during the voyage. Within 10 days of delivery, A gave written notice of damage and oral notice of claim, and C inspected the goods. A did not give written notice of claim until 26 days after delivery of the goods. Is A barred from recovery against C?

46. A contracts to make repairs on B's house for which B agrees to pay $10,000 on the express condition that repairs are completed by October 1. The repairs are completed on October 2. Is A entitled to recover the price provided by the agreement?

47. Tenant purchased a restaurant from a prior tenant and with the landlord's consent assumed the existing lease that had six years to run with an option to renew for 24 additional years by giving notice at least six months prior to expiration of the lease. The restaurant was highly successful and the tenant invested heavily in physical improvements. About 2 months prior to the expiration of the lease, Tenant received a note from the landlord inquiring about Tenant's plans to vacate. Tenant consulted his attorney who drafted and sent a notice of exercise of the option to the landlord.

48. Plaintiff deposited $30,000 with an escrow agent pursuant to an agreement with the owner of a department store building. The $30,000 was to be applied to a $555,000 purchase price, the balance to be paid on or before October 31. Plaintiff made no commitment to purchase. The agreement provided that if the balance were not paid by October 31, it would be forfeited to the seller and neither party would have any further rights against the other. Plaintiff failed to tender the balance by October 31 and defendant declared the money forfeited. Soon thereafter, plaintiff tendered the balance and now sues for specific performance or damages. What result? Would your analysis be different if plaintiff had made a commitment to purchase?

SECTION 10.   CONDITIONS OF SATISFACTION

(Calamari & Perillo 5th § 11.37)

WESTERN HILLS, OREGON, LTD. v. PFAU

Supreme Court of Oregon, 1973.
265 Or. 137, 508 P.2d 201.

McALLISTER, JUSTICE. This is a suit to compel specific performance of an agreement to purchase real property. The plaintiff, the owner of the property, is a limited partnership. Defendants are members of a joint venture, formed for the purpose of purchasing the property from plaintiff and developing it. The trial court found that plaintiff was entitled to specific performance of the agreement, and entered its decree accordingly. Defendants appeal, contending that they were excused from performing by a failure of a condition contained in the agreement, and that the agreement is too indefinite to permit specific enforcement.

Plaintiff Western Hills owned a tract of approximately 286 acres in Yamhill County which it had listed for sale with a Salem real estate firm. Defendant Pfau, who is also a real estate broker, heard about this listing early in 1970. He contacted the other defendants, and they jointly submitted a proposal to purchase the property. Their original proposal was not accepted, but negotiations with Western Hills took place which culminated, on or about March 6, 1970, in the execution of the written agreement which is the subject of this suit. The agreement consists of a filled-in form entitled "Exchange Agreement" together with several attached documents. Generally, it provides that in exchange for the Yamhill County property, defendants agreed to pay Western Hills $15,000 in cash, to convey to Western Hills four parcels of real property "subject to appraisal and acceptance" by Western Hills, and to pay a balance of $173,600 on terms specified in the agreement. In addition to other terms not material to this appeal, the agreement provides:

> "Closing of transaction is subject to ability of purchasers to negotiate with City of McMinnville as to a planned development satisfactory to both first and second parties within 90 days from date. A reasonable extension not to exceed 6 months to be granted if necessary."

Defendants made preliminary proposals for a planned development to the McMinnville Planning Commission, but, although the Commission's reaction to these proposals was favorable, defendants abandoned their attempts to secure approval of a development plan. In September, 1970, defendant Pfau, who represented the other defendants in the transaction, met with some of the partners in Western Hills and notified them that defendants did not wish to go through with the purchase. Western Hills refused to release defendants from the agreement. This suit followed.

Defendants contend that their obligation to purchase the property never became absolute because the condition quoted above was never fulfilled. It appears from the evidence that defendants did not proceed with their application for Planning Commission approval of a planned development because they believed the development would be too expensive, primarily because city sewers would not be available to serve the property for several years. Immediate development would have required the developers to provide a private system of sewage treatment and disposal.

It also appears that at the time they executed the agreement, defendants knew that city sewers would not be available for some time. Defendants' initial offer of purchase included a proposal that the closing of the transaction be subject to satisfactory sewer development. This term was deleted from the final agreement because, according to plaintiff's witnesses, the parties knew that sewers would not be available. Pfau testified that he agreed to the deletion of that term because he was led to believe that the provision for approval of a planned development accomplished the same thing.

The question is whether defendants were excused from performing their agreement to purchase the property because they never secured the city's approval of a "satisfactory" planned development, when the evidence shows that they abandoned their application for an approved planned development because the expense of providing an alternative sewer system made the development financially unattractive. In Anaheim Co. v. Holcombe, 246 Or. 541, 426 P.2d 743 (1967) we considered an earnest money agreement which contained a provision making the purchaser's offer "contingent on obtaining a loan of $25,000." We held that when an agreement contains such a term, it imposes upon the vendee an implied condition that he make a reasonable effort to procure the loan. 246 Or. at 547, 426 P.2d 743. See, also, Aldrich v. Forbes, 237 Or. 559, 570, 385 P.2d 618, 391 P.2d 748 (1964). In the present case defendants had a similar duty, arising by implication, to make a reasonable effort to secure the city's approval of a planned development. As related above, defendants abandoned their attempt to secure the approval of the city Planning Commission in spite of that body's favorable reaction to their initial proposals. There was never any indication that defendants' plan was likely to be rejected.

The condition required, however, not only approval of a planned development, but of a development which was "satisfactory" to the parties. When a contract makes a party's duty to perform conditional on his personal satisfaction the courts will give the condition its intended effect. See, generally, 3A Corbin on Contracts, 78–109, §§ 644–648; 5 Williston on Contracts (3d ed. 1961) 189–218, §§ 675A, 675B; Restatement of Contracts § 265. Discussing such contracts, this court said in Johnson v. School District No. 12, 210 Or. 585, 590–591, 312 P.2d 591, 593 (1957):

" * * * Such contracts are generally grouped into two categories:

"(1) Those which involve taste, fancy or personal judgment, the classical example being a commission to paint a portrait. In such cases the promisor is the sole judge of the quality of the work, and his right to reject, if in good faith, is absolute and may not be reviewed by court or jury.

"(2) Those which involve utility, fitness or value, which can be measured against a more or less objective standard. In these cases, although there is some conflict, we think the better view is that performance need only be 'reasonably satisfactory,' and if the promisor refuses the proffered performance, the correctness of his decision and the adequacy of his grounds are subject to review."

The condition with which we are concerned in this case properly belongs in the first of these categories as it requires the exercise of the parties' personal judgment. There is no objective test by which a court or jury could determine whether a particular development plan ought to be "satisfactory" to reasonable men in defendants' position. The condition is similar to that in Mattei v. Hopper, 51 Cal.2d 119, 330 P.2d 625 (1958) in which the purchaser's duty under a land sale contract was "subject to Coldwell Banker & Company obtaining leases satisfactory to the purchaser." In a suit by the purchaser to compel specific performance, the seller contended that because of this provision there was no mutuality of obligation. The court held that there was a valid contract. Discussing the two types of "satisfaction" clauses, the court said:

" * * * However, it would seem that the factors involved in determining whether a lease is satisfactory to the lessor are too numerous and varied to permit the application of a reasonable man standard as envisioned by this line of cases. * * *

"This multiplicity of factors which must be considered in evaluating a lease shows that this case more appropriately falls within the second line of authorities dealing with 'satisfaction' clauses, being those involving fancy, taste, or judgment. Where the question is one of judgment, the promisor's determination that he is not satisfied, when made in good faith, has been held to be a defense to an action on the contract." 330 P.2d at 627.

The condition in the present case is similar to that in *Mattei* in another respect as well. In that case as in this one the question of satisfaction was not concerned with the quality of the other party's performance. The court in *Mattei* held that the general rule was nevertheless applicable:

" * * * Even though the 'satisfaction' clauses discussed in the above-cited cases dealt with performances to be received as parts of the agreed exchanges, the fact that the leases here which determined plaintiff's satisfaction were not part of the performance to be rendered is not material. The standard of evaluating plaintiff's satisfaction—good faith—applies with equal vigor to this type of condition * * *." Id.

As in *Mattei* we are concerned in this case with a "satisfaction" clause of the type requiring the exercise of personal judgment as to a matter which was not part of the other party's agreed performance. The test, as indicated, is the promisor's real, not feigned, dissatisfaction. See Johnson v. School District, supra, 210 Or. at 591, 312 P.2d 591.

It is clear from the authorities, however, that this dissatisfaction must be not only bona fide and in good faith, but also must relate to the specific subject matter of the condition. General dissatisfaction with the bargain will not suffice.

> " * * * Where a promise is conditional, expressly or impliedly, on his own satisfaction, he must give fair consideration to the matter. A refusal to examine the * * * performance, or a rejection of it, not in reality based on its unsatisfactory nature but on fictitious grounds or none at all, will amount to prevention of performance of the condition and excuse it." 5 Williston, op. cit. 203–204.

As Corbin points out, although the promisor is under no duty if, in good faith, he is dissatisfied with a performance to be rendered to his personal satisfaction, nevertheless

> " * * * [n]ot infrequently it is possible to prove that the defendant is satisfied in fact, that the work has been done exactly as he specified, and that his dissatisfaction is either with his own specifications or merely with having to pay money that he prefers to use otherwise. * * * " 3A Corbin, op. cit. 92.

It is inherent in the requirement that dissatisfaction be bona fide and in good faith that the promisor cannot be allowed to base a claim of dissatisfaction on circumstances which were known or anticipated by the parties at the time of contracting. In the present case the evidence is clear that the defendants entered the agreement with full knowledge that city sewer service would not be immediately available and that their development of the property would have to include a sewage disposal system of some kind. The *Brydon* case is in point and its reasoning is persuasive. Although defendants were entitled under the contract to be the judges of their own satisfaction with any development plan that might be approved by the city, they should not be permitted to rely on the "satisfaction" clause in order to reject the contract because of an expense known and contemplated at the time of contracting. We hold, therefore, that defendants were not justified in abandoning their attempts to secure city approval of a development plan simply because of the expense of providing a sewer system which they knew when they entered the contract would have to be provided as a part of the development. Not having performed their duty to use reasonable diligence to obtain city approval of a development plan, defendants may not rely on the nonoccurrence of the condition. Anaheim Co. v. Holcombe, supra.

* * *

The decree of the trial court is affirmed.

VAN IDERSTINE CO., INC. v. BARNET LEATHER CO., INC.

Court of Appeals of New York, 1926.
242 N.Y. 425, 152 N.E. 250.

LEHMAN, J. On or about August 12th, 1920, the plaintiff and the defendant entered into a contract for the sale of 15,000 vealskins, delivery thereof to be made "beginning week of August 16th." The contract was made upon condition that the skins were "to be received by Jules Star & Co.'s representative subject to their approval." On September 10th, 1920, the parties entered into another contract for the sale of 6,000 vealskins, delivery to be made in September, "to be received by Jules Star & Co. subject to their approval." On or about August 16th a representative of Jules Star & Co. examined 15,000 vealskins tendered by the plaintiff in performance of its contract of sale of August 12th, and rejected 3,500 of such skins. It is not disputed that such rejection was justified. In October the plaintiff notified the defendant that it was ready to deliver 3,500 skins in substitution for those previously rejected. The defendant refused to accept or even examine the same on the ground that the time for delivery had expired. About the same time, Jules Star & Co. rejected the entire quantity of 6,000 skins which the plaintiff tendered in attempted performance of its contract of September 10th, 1920, and defendant refused to accept them.

The plaintiff has brought this action to recover damages suffered because of the defendant's refusal to accept the skins which plaintiff offered to deliver. * * * [P]laintiff alleged that any condition for approval by a representative of Jules Star & Co. of the skins to be delivered under the contract of September 10th was waived and excused because the approval was unreasonably withheld * * *. The issues raised by the denial to these allegations were submitted to the jury and decided in favor of the plaintiff.

* * *

We have pointed out that under both contracts sued upon, the seller agreed to make delivery subject to the approval of Jules Star & Co. The parties chose to stipulate that such approval must be given. It constitutes a condition which unless waived or excused must be fulfilled before the buyer can be compelled to accept skins that are tendered. Concededly approval of Jules Star & Co. has not been given. The condition was as matter of law waived by the buyer in regard to the 3,500 skins referred to in the first cause of action, when the buyer refused to accept any skins even if approved by Jules Star & Co. Of course, the condition was waived also in regard to the contract which forms the basis of the second cause of action if refusal of approval by Jules Star & Co. was the result of bad faith on the part of Jules Star & Co. in which the defendant had some share. If by its own interference and wrong the defendant prevented the plaintiff from obtaining the stipulated approval, then the plaintiff may recover without it. We have pointed out that in the second cause of action the plaintiff has pleaded that the condition was waived and excused not only because of wrongful act on the part of the defendant but because approval was "unreasonably withheld," and the serious question raised upon this appeal is whether the plaintiff may recover under its contract upon proof that it offered to deliver skins which in quality complied with the contract requirements, and that the representative of Jules Star & Co. unreasonably withheld its approval of these skins.

The trial judge charged that if "approval was unreasonably withheld, whether Barnet had anything to do with it or not, the plaintiff could recover. Star must have acted honestly. If he showed an honest judgment the defendant is entitled to a verdict." Though the parties have stipulated that the approval of Jules Star & Co. must be obtained for any skins delivered under the contract, under the rule laid down in the charge, the plaintiff may become liable for damages if he insists upon this stipulation being carried out. It places upon the buyer the risk of determining whether Jules Star & Co. have acted reasonably; it makes the buyer determine whether approval should reasonably have been given, though not he but Jules Star & Co. were to approve of the quality of the skins. In effect it makes the buyer a guarantor of both the honesty and the good judgment of Jules Star & Co.

It is said that authority for the rule laid down in the charge may be found in many cases in this and other jurisdictions where the courts have considered the effect of unreasonable or dishonest refusal of architect or engineer to approve of work done or materials furnished, under building contracts when such approval was made a condition precedent to payment. (*Bowery National Bank v. Mayor, etc.*, 63 N.Y. 336; *Mac-Knight Flintic Stone Co. v. Mayor, etc.*, 160 N.Y. 72.) In those cases it must be remembered that by the nature of the contracts, if failure to obtain approval deprived the contractor of right to recover the agreed compensation the result would be that the benefit of work actually performed and materials actually furnished could be appropriated by the owner without payment, though in other respects the contractor had fully complied with his contract. It would cause forfeiture of agreed price for agreed service without any fault on the contractor's part. In the same manner as the courts have evolved the rule that under contracts of that nature there may be recovery for substantial performance, they have evolved a rule which permits recovery without stipulated certificate of approval where the certificate has been wrongfully or unreasonably refused. (*Nolan v. Whitney*, 88 N.Y. 648.) So, too, in some cases where the contract shows that the person whose approval is required under the contract is merely an agent of a buyer selected by the buyer to pass upon the goods in the buyer's place, wrong on the part of the agent is imputed to the principal. (*Lynn v. Baltimore, etc., R.R. Co.*, 60 Md. 404.) Here the contract is of different nature. The parties agree that a designated broker acting as expert and not simply as the buyer's agent must pass upon the goods and delivery must be made subject to the expert's approval. Refusal to approve by the expert does not enable the buyer to obtain property from the seller without payment. According to the terms of the contract it merely permits him to refuse to accept the goods because he stipulated not merely for goods of a certain quality but for goods of that quality approved by a particular expert. To compel him to accept and pay for the goods without such approval is to impose liability upon him which he had not agreed to assume, and gives compensation to the seller for goods not delivered in full compliance with contract. The theoretical soundness of the rule applied to building contracts has not escaped criticism. It rests upon the basis that enforcement of the contract according to its strict terms would cause forfeiture of compensation for work done or materials furnished. The rule should not be extended by analogy where the reason for the rule fails. (See Williston on Contracts, sections 794–797.) Unless the certificate has been withheld dishonestly and in bad faith, and the defendant is a party to that bad faith through control of the expert or collusion with him, there may be no recovery under the second cause of action.

There are cases where parties stipulate for the approval or certificate of a third person not as part of the contractual obligation of either party to the contract but rather as machinery for avoiding dispute between the parties as to whether these obligations have been properly performed. Question may then arise as to whether the stipulated approval or certificate constitutes in full sense a condition precedent to recovery, or whether there may be recovery based on substantial performance, upon proof that in other respects the contract has been fully complied with. Such question we do not now decide. Doubtless there are cases where such hardship would be imposed upon a party who performs work or manufactures goods at the special instance of another if payment were withheld merely because approval is wrongfully refused, that argument may well be made that such result was not intended by the parties. Here we have no such circumstances. The plaintiff's obligation is only to deliver certain goods, and by express stipulation there may be no delivery without approval of a third party. It has done nothing for which it might legally or equitably expect compensation until delivery is made. If approval is withheld the plaintiff cannot perform; it loses the profit which it might have otherwise made by delivery of goods at a contract price higher than the then prevailing market price. It assumed this risk. It still retains the goods and may sell them at market price. The defendant should not be required to pay the contract price unless the plaintiff performs according to contract "subject to the approval" of the third party.

* * *

The judgments should be reversed and a new trial granted, with costs to abide the event.

CARDOZO, POUND and ANDREWS, JJ., concur; HISCOCK, CH. J., McLAUGHLIN and CRANE, JJ., dissent.

Judgments reversed, etc.

LARGENT CONTRACTING, INC. v. GREAT AMERICAN HOMES, INC.

Court of Appeals of Tennessee, Western Section at Jackson, 1990.
1990 WL 176723.

FARMER, JUDGE: The plaintiff, Largent Contracting, Inc., appeals from the trial court's grant of summary judgment in favor of the defendant, Great American Homes, Inc. The parties entered into a contract on September 1, 1982 whereby Largent was to clear land and build a lake upon defendant's land known as Carrollwood Lake Subdivision. The contract itemized the work to be done. The following day, the parties executed an amendment to the contract providing a more detailed itemization but the total price of $133,479.50 remained unchanged.

The complaint alleges that the plaintiff performed additional work as authorized by the defendant or its agent, and seeks the additional amount of $11,612.36. Plaintiff contends that whether it performed additional work for additional compensation is a factual question which precludes summary judgment. It is the defendant's position that the additional amount sought by plaintiff was not approved by the engineer as is required by the contract. Article 5, Progress Payments, provides that the contractor shall make periodic applications for payment to the architect[3] and further provides in part pertinent:

> [A]nd upon Substantial Completion of the entire Work, a sum sufficient to increase the total payments to one hundred percent (100%) of the Contract Sum, less such amounts as the Architect shall determine for all incomplete Work and unsettled claims as provided in the Contract Documents.

> Progress Payments shall be made on a precentage [sic] of completion as work progresses.

Article 6, Final Payment, provides:

> Final payment, constituting the entire unpaid balance of the Contract Sum, shall be paid by the Owner to the Contractor when the Work has been completed, the Contract fully performed, and a final Certificate for Payment has been issued by the Architect.

The amendment to the contract provides in part as follows:

> The following unit prices shall be used to determine progress payments for work performed on the above referenced project.

> The final payment shall be determined by the quantity of units installed for each item and subject to verification and approval by the Owner's engineer.

Gregory–Grace and Associates, Inc. is the designated engineer. The engineer concedes that additional work was performed by Largent and approved by a representative of Gregory–Grace. Applications for pay-

---

3. The contract provides that "Archi-   tect" shall mean "Engineer."

ment which were submitted to the engineer, approved for payment and paid by Great American totaled $143,707.50, or approximately $10,000.00 more than the amount specified in the contract. This amount was paid by three separate requests for payment. The deposition of Amos E. (John) Largent, president of Largent Contracting, Inc., discloses that the work to be performed by Largent was substantially complete on the date the final application for payment was submitted in September, 1984. A statement dated December 5, 1984 was submitted to Gregory–Grace showing an additional amount due of $11,612.36. The December 5 statement seeking the additional amount was directed to Paul Bray of Gregory–Grace.

We have examined the authorities relied upon by the defendant. Railroad v. Central Lumber, etc., Co., 95 Tenn. 538, 32 S.W. 635 (1895) involved a dispute between the railroad and the contractor. The contract provided,

> "All allowances and differences hereunder, on account of such work, must be agreed and settled upon before the same is begun, otherwise the chief engineer of the East Tennessee, Virginia & Georgia Railway Company shall have the sole and absolute right and authority, and the same is hereby given, to fix and determine the amount of such allowance or differences, if any." Railroad v. Central Lumber, 95 Tenn. at 541.

The Supreme Court, in affirming the decision of the chancellor that the estimate of the engineer was conclusive, stated:

> The rule is well settled that where parties to a construction contract of any kind agree to submit the differences, or questions of any character arising in connection with the work, to the decision of an architect or of an engineer, the decision of the arbiter thus selected is final, and all parties are bound by it unless it be shown that the estimate or conclusion is fraudulent or so excessive or so palpably unjust as to imply bad faith or gross neglect. Railroad v. Central Lumber, 95 Tenn. at 543.

Railroad v. Central Lumber, etc., Co., was followed in Cocke County Bd. v. Newport Utilities Bd., 690 S.W.2d 231 wherein the Supreme Court, speaking through Justice Brock, said:

> Under Tennessee law, a clause in a construction contract making the Engineer's decision concerning the acceptability and fitness of work performed under that contract "final and conclusive" is binding on the parties to the contract unless there is fraud or the decision is so unjust as to imply bad faith or gross neglect. Id., at 236–37.

The rights, powers and duties under a provision in a construction contract for approval by the engineer are determined and limited by the terms of the contract. 17A C.J.S. Contracts § 496(3). Where the construction contract makes the engineer's decision or certificate final, it is ordinarily conclusive as to the rights of the parties in the absence of fraud, bad faith, or mistake; but where the contract does not so provide it does not as a rule have that effect. 17A C.J.S. Contracts § 498(8)(a).

The language in the present case is not nearly as strong as that in either Railroad or Cocke County. The engineer is to approve final payment, but the contract does not provide that its decision as to disputes is to be final and conclusive or that the engineer is to be the final arbiter. A contract may provide for inspection or approval by a third party without making that party's judgment conclusive. Midsouth Land Co. v. A.E. Hughes, Jr., Inc., 434 So.2d 239, 244 (Ala.1983).

* * *

The deposition and affidavit of Largent's president, John Largent, states that Largent performed additional work, which was authorized by the engineer and the owner, for which it has not been paid. He further states that the engineer refused to meet and discuss why they refused to authorize the owner to pay. Our review of this record discloses a genuine issue of material fact sufficient to preclude summary judgment.

The judgment of the trial court is reversed and this cause is remanded for trial on the merits. The costs of this appeal are taxed to the appellee, for which execution may issue if necessary.

INDOE v. DWYER

Superior Court of New Jersey, Law Division, 1980.
176 N.J.Super. 594, 424 A.2d 456, 15 A.L.R.4th 752.

GAYNOR, J. S. C. These cross-motions for summary judgment involve primarily the scope and effect of an attorney approval clause in a contract for the purchase of real estate. A secondary question relates to the binding effect upon a husband of such a contract executed solely by the wife where the only evidence of the husband's interest was a provision in the contract providing that the deed was to be taken in both names. The primary issue presented is one of first impression and, in our opinion, must be resolved by an interpretation which permits an unlimited application of the attorney approval provision in the contract.

The facts of the case are not in dispute. In August 1976 plaintiffs listed their home in Bernardsville for sale at a price of $235,000. The property was not sold and it was listed again in 1977 at the same price. In August 1977 defendant Christine Dwyer was shown the house by a realtor in the absence of plaintiffs. She returned the following weekend with her husband, defendant John Dwyer, for a further inspection. No offer was made because defendants determined they were not interested in purchasing the property.

The following February Mrs. Dwyer inquired of the realtor as to whether plaintiffs' home was still available for purchase. Being informed that it was, but that an offer was then being considered, Mrs. Dwyer contacted her husband, who was on a business trip, and obtained his approval to submit a bid for the property. Accordingly, an offer of $225,000 was submitted orally by Mrs. Dwyer to the realtor. Later that day a realtor's printed form of contract for the sale and purchase of real estate was prepared by the realtor and presented to Mrs. Dwyer for signature. Believing the document to be merely a "bid" and that if acceptable to plaintiffs a purchase contract would thereafter be prepared, with the assistance of counsel and which would include terms acceptable to her husband and their attorney, Mrs. Dwyer signed the agreement. That evening the contract was presented to plaintiffs and executed by them.

When a copy of the fully executed document was returned later the same evening to Mrs. Dwyer, she was informed that, contrary to her expectations, plaintiffs did not intend to include the wall-to-wall carpeting in the sale. She thereupon called her attorney who instructed her to deliver a copy of the agreement to him the following morning. Two or three days later Mr. Dwyer returned from his trip and conferred with their attorney concerning the contract. Following this conference defendants' attorney notified plaintiffs and the relator that, as attorney for defendants and in accordance with the provisions of the agreement, he was withholding his approval of the contract, and accordingly defendants would not proceed with the transaction. It was indicated that such disapproval was not based upon the price or financing terms. Pretrial discovery disclosed that such notification was given because the carpeting was not included in the sale and there was no specification in the agreement as to what personal property was indicated; the concern of defendants as to the close proximity of the swimming pool to the kitchen doors; the lack of provisions for potability and septic system tests; the shortness of the time period for satisfaction of the mortgage contingency; the inadequacy of the agreement in that Mr. Dwyer was not a signatory thereto, and other intangible considerations.

As indicated, the form utilized by the realtor was the "Standard Form of Real Estate Contract Adopted by the New Jersey Association of Realtor Boards for Use by New Jersey Realtors." The property was described by reference to the municipal tax map, and the purchase price, deposit and mortgage amount were handwritten insertions. The type of deed to be delivered was specified as "C. vs. Grantor," and the rate of interest on the mortgage to be obtained by the purchaser was stated as "prevailing rate." The agreement contained typed contingency clauses for the obtaining of a $75,000 conventional mortgage within 20 days and a termite inspection within 7 days. No provision was made for the inclusion in the sale of any personal property, except for gas and electric fixtures, etc., if any, as provided by the printed language of the form. The agreement also contained the following typewritten provision, which is being relied upon by defendants in opposing plaintiffs' motion for summary judgment for breach of the contract and in support of their motion for a dismissal of the complaint:

> This contract, except as to price and financing terms (if any), is contingent upon approval by the respective attorneys for purchasers and sellers within three (3) business days of the date hereof. The parties agree that such approval shall be deemed to have been given, and this contingency satisfied or waived, unless an objection or amendment or addition or other express statement witholding (sic)

approval is made in writing within said three day period and delivered to the realtor or exchanged between the respective attorneys if they are known to each other.

Inasmuch as there does not exist any dispute concerning the material facts relating to the issues presented, it is appropriate that the motions of the parties be determined in a summary proceeding. R. 4:46–2; Judson v. Peoples Bank & Trust Co. of Westfield, 17 N.J. 67, 110 A.2d 24 (1954).

It is plaintiffs' contention that defendants breached the contract by their failure to consummate the purchase in accordance with the agreement and that their attorney's notification of disapproval was not sufficient to excuse them from such performance. They assert that the "attorney approval clause" in the contract does not permit disapproval for unspecified reasons nor for any of the reasons as disclosed by defendants' answers to interrogatories. Plaintiffs argue that it would be unreasonable to conclude otherwise because of the specific language precluding an objection based upon price or financing terms. Additionally, they contend that a reasonable interpretation of the clause would not support a claim that the parties intended carte blanche disapproval rights after entering into what purports on its face to be a legally binding contract. Rather, a more logical conclusion is that the intention of the parties was to provide for a disapproval based upon legal deficiencies of the contract, which would be matters within the special expertise of an attorney.

On the other hand, defendants argue that there was no breach of contract as the inclusion of the subject clause in the agreement rendered its efficacy contingent upon the approval of either party's attorney and, so long as there is no showing of bad faith, the contract is not enforceable in the event of a disapproval by the stipulated counselor. Also, defendants suggest that the reasonable expectation of a purchaser and seller of residential property is that such a provision, in a contract presented to them for execution by a real estate broker or salesperson, grants the right to obtain the unfettered approval or disapproval of their attorney.

While a clause providing for approval of the contract, within a specified time, by the attorney for either party, has not been judicially construed or applied, there appears to be varying interpretations ascribed to such a provision by professionals and others who are involved in real estate transactions. Thus, some may interpret it as meaning that the right of approval is restricted to negotiating the inclusion or exclusion of certain standard clauses, or the modification of included provisions, while others consider that the right is unlimited, thereby permitting the attorney to disapprove the contract for any reason. Under the latter interpretation there is no requirement that the disapproval be reasonable or even that the other contracting party be informed of the reasons for such disapproval. The effect of an unlimited right of disapproval is to place the parties in the same position they would have been if they had been able to consult with an attorney before signing the contract. See Horn, Residential Real Estate Law and Practice in New Jersey, § 1.1.

Although the effect of a general attorney approval clause in a contract for the purchase of real estate has not been judicially passed upon, a somewhat analogous issue has been presented in cases involving contractual provisions requiring that title to the subject property be satisfactory to the purchaser's attorney. Varying conclusions have been reached as to the manner in which the attorney may exercise such contractual right of approval or disapproval. One line of cases holds that any dissatisfaction with the title is to be tested by objective standards, the test being whether the title meets the standard of marketability, or whether the objections are reasonable. Beardslee v. Underhill, 37 N.J.L. 309 (Sup.Ct.1875); Dean v. Williams, 56 Wash. 614, 106 P.130 (Sup.Ct. 1910); Ogg v. Herman, 71 Mont. 10, 227 P. 476 (Sup.Ct.1924); Williams v. Belling, 76 Cal.App. 610, 245 P. 455 (D.Ct.App.1926). A different view is represented by the group of cases which consider that such provisions constitute the attorney as the sole judge of his dissatisfaction, subject only to the limitation that the decision be arrived at in good faith and not be arbitrary or capricious. [Citations omitted].

The objective approach, i.e. where the dissatisfaction is tested by the standard of marketability, proceeds on the basis that a clause making the title subject to an attorney's approval is nothing more than an expression of that which is implied in every real estate purchase contract, namely, that the title shall be good and marketable. Accordingly, the purchaser is required to be satisfied with a title which is in fact marketable. Any claim of dissatisfaction must therefore be judged by what the law holds to be a merchantable title, and title cannot be rejected by a simple expression of dissatisfaction based on insufficient legal reason.

Those cases which apply what might be termed the subjective criterion consider that, by providing for an attorney's approval of title, the contracting parties have bargained for something more than a good or marketable title, namely, the attorney's acceptance of the title as satisfactory. It being competent for parties to so stipulate, the attorney's disapproval is conclusive if made in good faith, although in the opinion of others, including the court, the title may be good as a matter of law. Such an interpretation follows the apparent intention of the parties that the attorney be the sole and final arbiter as to the acceptability of the title. To conclude otherwise would deny to the purchaser his right under the contract to the benefit of his attorney's judgment as to the sufficiency of the title. The rationale of this view was expressed in Sanger v. Slayden, supra, in the following terms:

Such a contract is permissible and legal, and, when deliberately executed, should be enforced. It is an express authority to Sanger to disaffirm when he is dissatisfied with the title. To only allow him to disaffirm when his dissatisfaction rests upon some valid and reasonable objection to the title is to practically deny him the exercise of this privilege expressly conferred by the contract, and denies him the right to the exercise of his judgment in the matter, and makes his right depend solely upon what others may think as to the merits of the title he has acquired. It substitutes their judgment for his. Others may be perfectly satisfied with the title, and think that a man of ordinary caution and prudence should be likewise, and that no reasonable ground for dissatisfaction exists. But, on the other hand, Sanger may, with equal good faith, be dissatisfied with the title for reasons that are satisfactory to him, and may think that a man of caution and prudence had grounds for his dissatisfaction. The true rule of construction of contracts of this character, and the one supported, we think, by reason and the weight of authority, is that the vendee may disaffirm the contract if he is dissatisfied, and his reasons or grounds of dissatisfaction may not be determined or inquired into by any one else.

While these rules are not controlling of the present case, it seems that where the contract permits disapproval thereof by either party's attorney as to its sufficiency or acceptability in general, and not only as to the state of the title, there is even more justification for considering that the right granted by such a provision should not be diluted or denied by requiring that the attorney's judgment be measured by some standard, other than good faith, or another's opinion. The purpose of such an attorney approval clause is to provide the purchaser or seller with the opportunity of obtaining legal advice with respect to the transaction, and its value lies in the fact that the contract may be canceled upon receiving such advice. Parties to a real estate transaction are entitled to the benefit of the judgment of a trusted counselor, and an approval contingency is designed to accord this right to those who, for some reason, enter into a purchase and sale agreement before reviewing the matter with their attorney.

Applying these observations to the present case compels the conclusion that the disapproval of the contract by defendants' attorney effectively terminated the contract. The clause in question expressly made the agreement contingent upon the attorney's approval, except as to price and financing terms, and thereby bound the parties to abide the opinion of either party's attorney with respect to the efficacy of the contract, limited only by the requirement that the attorney act in good faith. The disapproval voiced by the defendants' attorney was an exercise of his judgment, and his reasons therefor were not subject to review or contradiction. The contract cannot be rewritten to qualify the clear and express language of the agreement by limiting the applicability of the attorney approval contingency to those circumstances where the reason for disapproval meets some standard or the concurrence of the plaintiffs, or their attorney. Defendants are entitled to the fruits of their bargain. There is no basis for a claim of bad faith or capriciousness on the part of defendants, or their attorney, in the use of this contingency provision, which would render the notice of disapproval ineffective.

We would also note that a contract for the purchase and sale of a residence determines the rights and responsibilities of the parties as to the entire transaction and is of such importance in this respect as to require preparation or, in the least, preliminary review by an attorney. A text writer has described the significance of the contract in the following manner:

> The contract of sale is the key to the real estate transaction. It is the critical document which fixes the fundamental rights and obligations of the parties from the time it is signed through the closing of title and, in many cases, even beyond. (Horn, Residential Real Estate Law and Practice in New Jersey, § 1.1).

The complexity of the law of contracts and of real property demand that one qualified by education and experience determine the legal sufficiency of a real estate sale agreement and advise the prospective seller or purchaser as to the rights and obligations arising thereunder. Objective counseling by one's own attorney as to the practicability or desirability of undertaking the sale or purchase is also often necessary to avoid precipitous actions which may prove to be legally, financially or socially disadvantageous.

The conclusion reached herein is in accord with the public policy as expressed by the Legislature by including the right of rescission in recent statutes pertaining to retail installment sales, financing of home repairs and the disposition of land in subdivisions. See N.J.S.A. 17:16C–61.5; N.J.S.A. 17:16C–99; N.J.S.A. 45:15–16.12(d).

Our determination that the contract was terminated by operation of the attorney approval contingency provision renders it unnecessary to consider the secondary question concerning the liability of defendant John Dwyer.

Accordingly, plaintiffs' motion for summary judgment for damages is denied and defendants' motion for summary judgment dismissing the complaint is granted.

Problems

49. Plaintiff and defendant entered into an agreement which permitted plaintiff to render valet and laundry services at the defendant's hotel for a period of three years. Plaintiff was to pay $325.00 per month for the concession. The agreement also provided: "It is distinctly understood and agreed that the services to be rendered by the second party (plaintiff) shall meet with the approval of the first party (defendant) who shall be the sole judge of the sufficiency and propriety of the services." Before the three-year period was over, defendant discharged plaintiff. Plaintiff sues for breach and defendant counterclaims for breach of contract. Analyze the possible results.

50. A construction contract required payments to be made only upon submission of the certificate of the architect. The architect refused to issue a certificate because "the owner has instructed me to put on mouldings in accordance with his desires, although I have never seen that kind of moulding which he desires, at the same time he states that nothing else will be accepted by him so there is no alternative and I cannot issue the certificate until this has been done." What result?

51. In a construction contract, plaintiff promised to do the work in a workmanlike manner and "to the satisfaction of the architect to be testified to by his certificate." Plaintiff obtained such a certificate. Defendant offered proof that the work had not been performed in a workmanlike manner and plaintiff objected. Is this evidence admissible?

SECTION 11. A "REALIST" LOOKS AT CONDITIONS

(Calamari & Perillo 5th §§ 11.27—11.37)

R. CHILDRES, CONDITIONS IN THE LAW OF CONTRACTS

45 N.Y.U.L.Rev. 33, 33–35 (1970).
© 1970 New York University Law Review.

I

INTRODUCTION

A. *Gamesmanship and the Traditional Rule*

Cardozo once said "[we] are getting away from * * * the conception of a lawsuit * * * as a * * * game."[1] Half a century later, the law of contract conditions still claims to enforce agreed conditions even though they are immaterial to the legitimate interests of the parties. To the extent the claim is true, the law of conditions is pure gamesmanship: people may succeed in contract controversy with arguments which, under the circumstances, are technical only.

According to the traditional rule, parties to a contract are free to condition their obligations as they desire and to invoke judicial aid in enforcing such conditions despite any resulting injustice. Inman v. Clyde Hall Drilling Co.[2] is a modern example of the application of traditional contract condition law. In that case an employment contract required the employee to give notice within thirty days of any claim to be asserted against the employer. It also specified that suit must be brought between six and twelve months after giving notice. Claiming he was fired without justification, the employee brought suit only twelve days after his discharge. The Supreme Court of Alaska, affirming a lower court's decision, held that since suit was brought prematurely, its commencement did not constitute notice. Further, since the thirty day period for notice had passed, the employee had lost any claim he might otherwise have had. A purer instance of gamesmanship cannot be found. The decision ignores the contract interests of the parties and avoids entirely the question of contract performance in good faith and according to reasonable stan-

---

1. B. Cardozo, The Nature of the Judicial Process 101–02 (1921). Reprinted in Selected Writings of Benjamin Nathan Cardozo 149 (M. Hall ed. 1947).

2. 369 P.2d 498 (Alas.1962). See also 4 A.L.R.3d 430 (1965).

dards. In taking this approach the decision is a lonely outpost. Virtually all contemporary American contract decisions refuse to give effect to immaterial conditions, to what this paper will call conditions, or contentions, technical only. And they refuse to allow effect beyond materiality to conditions which are only slightly material (hereinafter, little material conditions).

The following statement reflects modern decisions much more accurately: "Law puts its imprimatur on the accepted moral standards and condemns conduct which fails to match 'the reflection of moral uprightness, of fundamental honesty, fair play and right dealing in the general and business life of members of society.' "[3] When the traditional contract condition rules were fashioned, the courts subordinated the policy of supporting and promoting good faith conduct according to reasonable standards to a literal formalism that claimed to enforce contracts only as written or stated. This was said to be in the interest of freedom of contract. Yesterday's subordinate policy has become almost completely dominant, but the shift too seldom receives explicit acknowledgement.

B.   Subterfuge in Conditions Cases

It is submitted that the traditional rule is a myth,[4] not entirely abandoned verbally, but supplanted sub silentio by the policy of supporting and promoting good faith conduct according to reasonable standards. The way courts too often defend their decisions obscures this fact.

As will become apparent in part III of this article, the law of contracts has been forced by pressure for just decisions to develop numerous doctrines to nullify what is said to be the law of conditions. Waiver, estoppel, substantial performance and abhorrence of forfeitures are among the doctrines which have allowed the law of conditions to survive by making it inoperative. Since most cases end well, it would be a simple matter to conclude that all is well with the law of contract conditions. But the failure to articulate the real ground of decision misleads the profession and thereby promotes uncertainty and litigation.

Some might still argue that the traditional law of conditions is a stabilizing influence in the law of contracts. A look at the present function of the doctrine will show why this is not so. Its sole function today is to allow a disputant to make a fact or event operative beyond the scope of its demonstrated materiality in the circumstances. As in *Inman,*[5] courts still occasionally claim to allow an irrelevancy to be decisive in litigation. This tempts people to try to escape contract duties by asserting irrelevancies. They rarely succeed, but the attempts make

---

3. Blachly v. United States, 380 F.2d 665, 671 (5th Cir.1967), quoting Gregory v. United States, 253 F.2d 104, 109 (5th Cir. 1958), affirming a conviction for violating the mail fraud statute, 18 U.S.C.A. § 1341 (1952).

4. There is no assertion that the rule is a fiction in part because that concept is subject to too many meanings. See Fuller, Legal Fictions, 25 Ill.L.Rev. 363, 513, 865 (1930–1931), now republished with some editing and a new introduction in L. Fuller, Legal Fictions (1967).

5. See text accompanying notes 2–3 supra.

the traditional law of conditions quite the opposite of a stabilizing influence.

Perhaps there should be an explanation of the limited function of the traditional law of conditions. When a disputant relies on a contract default as affecting his duties, contract law has traditionally asked whether there was a default on a condition. The purpose of this question is to determine whether the effect of the default is to be restricted to its materiality in the circumstances. If restricted to materiality, it was a default on a promise; but if and only if the default is to be decisive regardless of its materiality, it must be characterized as a default on a condition.

Because of its function, the law of conditions claims to bar analysis based upon good faith contract performance. In fact, it only drives such analysis underground where it is conducted under the mysterious shrouds of waiver, estoppel and the other various repealers of the law of conditions. The operation of these repealers is not mysterious and obscure by accident. Obscurity is necessary to the survival of rules about the law of conditions. It continues to be said to exist, but it is allowed to be decisive only in cases whose decisions would go unchanged if there were no law of conditions.

On a higher level of generality, all of this has been said before:

"[C]ertainty in the law is largely an illusion at best, and altogether too high a price may be paid in the effort to attain it." Indeed, we may argue that a more satisfactory degree of "certainty" is attained with flexible notions of fairness eliminating the need to circumvent the inflexible application of mechanical rules.[6]

SECTION 12. PROSPECTIVE FAILURE OF CONDITION AND BREACH BY REPUDIATION

(Calamari & Perillo 5th §§ 12.1—12.10)

HOCHSTER v. DE LA TOUR

In the Queen's Bench, 1853.
2 Ellis & Bl. 678, 118 Eng.Rep. 922.

[The plaintiff brought this action on May 22, 1852, for breach of a bilateral contract whereby the defendant had promised to employ the plaintiff to accompany him as a courier on the continent of Europe for three months beginning on June 1, 1852, and to pay , 10 per month for the service. The plaintiff remained ready and willing to begin service on

---

6. Kessler and Fine, Culpa in Contrahendo, Bargaining in Good Faith and Freedom of Contract: A Comparative Study, 77 Harv.L.Rev. 401, 449 (1964), quoting 3 A. Corbin, Contracts § 609, at 689 (1960).

June 1 as agreed; but the defendant wrongfully discharged him and repudiated the contract on May 11. On receiving notice of his discharge the plaintiff obtained similar employment with Lord Ashburton, but this employment would not begin until July.]

The defendant's counsel objected that there could be no breach of the contract before the 1st of June. The learned judge was of a contrary opinion, but reserved leave to enter a nonsuit on this objection. The other questions were left to the jury, who found for plaintiff.

Hugh Hill, in the same term, obtained a rule nisi to enter a nonsuit or arrest the judgment. In last Trinity Term.

Hannen showed cause. * * * If one party to an executory contract gave the other notice that he refused to go on with the bargain, in order that the other side might act upon that refusal in such a manner as to incapacitate himself from fulfilling it, and he did so act, the refusal could never be retracted; and, accordingly, in Cort. v. Ambergate &c. R. Co. (17 Q.B. 127) this court after considering the cases, decided that in such a case the plaintiff might recover, though he was no longer in a position to fulfil his contract. That was a contract under seal to manufacture and supply iron chairs. The purchasers discharged the vendors from manufacturing the goods; and it was held that an action might be maintained by the vendors. It is true, however, that in that case the writ was issued after the time when the chairs ought to have been received. In the present case, if the writ had been issued on the 2nd of June, Cort v. Ambergate &c. R. Co. would be expressly in point. The question, therefore, comes to be: Does it make any difference that the writ was issued before the 1st of June? If the dicta of Parke, B., in Phillpotts v. Evans, 5 M. & W. 475, are to be taken as universally applicable it does make a difference; but they cannot be so taken. In a contract to marry at a future day, a marriage of the man before that day is a breach. Short v. Stone, 8 Q.B. 358. The reason of this is, that the marriage is a final refusal to go on with the contract. It is not on the ground that the defendant has rendered it impossible to fulfil the contract; for, as was urged in vain in Short v. Stone, the first wife might be dead before the day came. So also, on a contract to assign a term of years on a day future, a previous assignment to a stranger is a breach. Lovelock v. Franklyn, 8 Q.B. 371. [Lord Campbell, C.J. It probably will not be disputed that an act on the part of the defendant incapacitating himself from going on with the contract would be a breach. But how does the defendant's refusal in May incapacitate him from travelling in June? It was possible that he might do so.] It was; but the plaintiff, who, so long as the engagement subsisted, was bound to keep himself disengaged and make preparations so as to be ready and willing to travel with the defendant on the 1st of June, was informed by the defendant that he would not go on with the contract, in order that the plaintiff might act upon that information; and the plaintiff then was entitled to engage himself to another, as he did. In Planche v. Colburn (8 Bing. 14) the plaintiff had contracted with defendants to write a work for "The Juvenile Library"; and he was held to be entitled to recover on their discontinuing the publication; yet the time for the completion of the contract, that is for the work being published in "The Juvenile Library," had not arrived, for that would not be till a reasonable time after the author had completed the work. Now in that case the author never did complete the work. [Lord Campbell, C.J. It certainly would have been cruelly hard if the author had been obliged, as a condition precedent to redress, to compose a work which he knew could never be published. Crompton, J. When a party announces his intention not to fulfill the contract, the other side may take him at his word and rescind the contract. That word "rescind" implies that both parties have agreed that the contract shall be at an end as if it had never been. But I am inclined to think that the party may also say: "Since you have announced that you will not go on with the contract, I will consent that it shall be at an end from this time; but I will hold you liable for the damage I have sustained; and I will proceed to make that damage as little as possible by making the best use I can of my liberty." This is the principle of those cases in which there has been a discussion as to the measure of damages to which a servant is entitled on a wrongful dismissal. They were all considered in Elderton v. Emmens (6 C.B. 160). Lord Campbell, C.J. The counsel in support of the rule have to answer a very able argument.]

Hugh Hill and Deighton, contra. In Cort v. Ambergate &c. R. Co., the writ was taken out after the time for completing the contract. That case is consistent with the defendant's position, which is, that an act incapacitating the defendant, in law, from completing the contract is a breach, because it is implied that the parties to a contract shall keep themselves legally capable of performing it; but that an announcement of an intention to break the contract when the time comes is no more than an offer to rescind. It is evidence, till retracted, of a dispensation with the necessity of readiness and willingness on the other side; and, if not retracted, it is, when the time for performance comes, evidence of a continued refusal; but till then it may be retracted. Such is the doctrine in Phillpotts v. Evans (5 M. & W. 475) and Ripley v. McClure (4 Exch. 345). [Crompton, J. May not the plaintiff, on notice that the defendant will not employ him, look out for other employment, so as to diminish the loss?] If he adopts the defendant's notice, which is in legal effect an offer to rescind, he must adopt it altogether. [Lord Campbell, C.J. So that you say the plaintiff, to preserve any remedy at all, was bound to remain idle. Erle, J. Do you go one step further? Suppose the defendant, after the plaintiff's engagement with Lord Ashburton, had retracted his refusal and required the plaintiff to travel with him on the 1st of June, and the plaintiff had refused to do so, and gone with Lord Ashburton instead? Do you say that the now defendant could in that case have sued the now plaintiff for a breach of contract?] It would be, in such a case, a question of fact for a jury, whether there had not been an exoneration. In Phillpotts v. Evans, it was held that the measure of damages was the market price at the time when the contract ought to be completed. If a refusal before that time is a breach, how could these damages be ascertained? [Coleridge, J. No doubt it was possible, in this case, that, before the 1st of June, the plaintiff might die, in which case the plaintiff would have gained nothing had the contract gone on. Lord Campbell, C.J. All contingencies should be taken into account by the jury in assessing the damages. Crompton, J. That objection would equally apply to the action by a servant for dismissing him before the end of his term, and so disabling him from earning his wages; yet that action may be brought immediately on the dismissal; note to Cutter v. Powell (6 T.R. 320)]. It is quite possible that the plaintiff himself might have intended not to go on; no one can tell what intention is. [Lord Campbell, C.J. The intention of the defendant might be proved by showing that he entered in his diary a memorandum to that effect; and certainly, no action would lie for entering such a memorandum. But the question is as to the effect of a communication to the other side, made that he might know that intention and act upon it.]

Cur.adv.vult.

LORD CAMPBELL, C.J., now delivered the judgment of the Court.

On this motion in arrest of judgment, the question arises, Whether, if there be an agreement between A and B, whereby B engages to employ A on and from a future day for a given period of time, to travel with him into a foreign country as a courier, and to start with him in that capacity on that day, A being to receive a monthly salary during the continuance of such service, B may, before the day, refuse to perform the agreement and break and renounce it, so as to entitle A before the day to commence an action against B to recover damages for breach of the agreement; A having been ready and willing to perform it, till it was broken and renounced by B. The defendant's counsel very powerfully contended that, if the plaintiff was not contented to dissolve the contract and to abandon all remedy upon it, he was bound to remain ready and willing to perform it till the day when the actual employment as courier in the service of the defendant was to begin; and that there could be no breach of the agreement before that day to give a right of action. But it cannot be laid down as a universal rule that, where by agreement an act is to be done on a future day, no action can be brought for a breach of the agreement till the day for doing the act has arrived. If a man promises to marry a woman on a future day, and before that day marries another woman, he is instantly liable to an action for breach of promise of marriage. Short v. Stone (8 Q.B. 358). If a man contracts to execute a lease on and from a future day for a certain term, and before that day executes a lease to another for the same term, he may be immediately sued for breaking the contract. Ford v. Tiley (6 B. & C. 325). So, if a man contracts to sell and deliver specific goods on a future day, and before the day he sells and delivers them to another, he is immediately liable to an action at the suit of the person with whom he first contracted to sell and deliver them. Bowdell v. Parsons (10 East, 359). One reason alleged in support of such an action is, that the defendant has, before the day, rendered it impossible for him to perform the contract at the day, but this does not necessarily follow; for prior to the day fixed for doing the act, the first wife may have died, a surrender of the lease executed might be obtained, and the defendant might have repurchased the goods so as to be in a situation to sell and deliver them to the plaintiff. Another reason may be that, where there is a contract to do an act on a future day, there is a relation constituted between the parties in the meantime by the contract, and that they impliedly promise that in the meantime neither will do anything to the prejudice of the other inconsistent with that relation. As an example, a man and woman engaged to marry are affianced to one another during the period between the time of the engagement and the celebration of the marriage.

In this very case of traveller and courier, from the day of the hiring till the day when the employment was to begin, they were engaged to each other; and it seems to be a breach of an implied contract if either of them renounces the engagement. This reasoning seems in accordance with the unanimous decision of the Exchequer Chamber in Elderton v. Emmens (6 C.B. 160), which we have followed in subsequent cases in this court. The declaration in the present case, in alleging a breach, states a great deal more than a passing intention on the part of the defendant which he may repent of, and could only be proved by evidence that he had utterly renounced the contract, or done some act which rendered it impossible for him to perform it.

If the plaintiff has no remedy for breach of the contract unless he treats the contract as in force, and acts upon it down to the 1st of June, 1852, it follows that, till then, he must enter into no employment which will interfere with his promise "to start with the defendant on such travels on the day and year," and that he must then be properly equipped in all respects as a courier for a three months' tour on the continent of Europe. But it is surely much more rational, and more for the benefit of both parties, that, after the renunciation of the agreement by the defendant, the plaintiff should be at liberty to consider himself absolved from any future performance of it, retaining his right to sue for any damage he has suffered from the breach of it. Thus, instead of remaining idle and laying out money in preparations which must be useless, he is at liberty to seek service under another employer, which would go in mitigation to the damages to which he would otherwise be entitled for a breach of the contract. It seems strange that the defendant, after renouncing the contract, and absolutely declaring that he will never act under it, should be permitted to object that faith is given to his assertion, and that an opportunity is not left to him of changing his mind. If the plaintiff is barred of any remedy by entering into an engagement inconsistent with starting as a courier with the defendant on the 1st of June, he is prejudiced by putting faith in the defendant's assertion, and it would be more consonant with principle, if the defendant were precluded from saying that he had not broken the contract when he declared that he entirely renounced it.

Suppose that the defendant, at the time of his renunciation, had embarked on a voyage for Australia, so as to render it physically impossible for him to employ the plaintiff as a courier on the continent of Europe in the months of June, July, and August, 1852, according to decided cases, the action might have been brought before the 1st of June; but the renunciation may have been founded on other facts, to be given in evidence, which would equally have rendered the defendant's performance of the contract impossible. The man who wrongfully renounces a contract into which he has deliberately entered cannot justly complain if he is immediately sued for a compensation in damages by the man whom he has injured; and it seems reasonable to allow an option to the injured party, either to sue immediately, or to wait till the time when the act was to be done, still holding it as prospectively binding for the exercise of this option, which may be advantageous to the innocent party, and cannot be prejudicial to the wrongdoer. An argument against the action before the 1st of June is urged from the difficulty of calculating the damages, but this argument is equally strong against an action before the 1st of September, when the three months would expire. In either case, the jury in assessing the damages would be justified in looking to all that had happened, or was likely to happen, to increase or mitigate the loss of the plaintiff down to the day of trial. We do not find any decision contrary to the view we are taking of this case. * * *

Upon the whole, we think that the declaration in this case is sufficient. It gives us great satisfaction to reflect that, the question being on the record, our opinion may be reviewed in a court of error. In the meantime we must give judgment for the plaintiff.

Judgment for plaintiff.

DANIELS v. NEWTON

Supreme Judicial Court of Massachusetts, 1874.
114 Mass. 530.

WELLS, J. This action is for breach of an agreement in writing, under seal, for the purchase of certain land from the plaintiff by the defendants. The time for performance is indicated by two clauses; one that "said premises are to be conveyed within thirty days from this date;" the other that "in case the said parties of the second part should fail to sell their estate at the expiration of the thirty days, then we agree to extend this agreement for thirty days." The inference from the latter clause is that the defendants were to have the whole thirty days for performance on their part, and, in the contingency mentioned, thirty days more. Such was the effect given to the terms of the written instrument, by the ruling at the trial, and we think correctly.

The plaintiff relied upon a supposed breach of the agreement by the defendants within the thirty days; to wit, May 29, the writing being dated May 15, and thereupon had brought his action May 30. The ruling of the court upon this point was that if * * * "the defendants * * * refused absolutely to perform * * *, that would be a breach of the agreement on their part for which the plaintiff can maintain this action."

* * *

The proposition involved in this ruling, to wit, that there may be a breach of contract, giving a present right of action, before the performance is due by its terms, seems to have been adopted by recent English decisions. *Frost v. Knight,* L.R. 7 Ex. 111 (1872). *Hochster v. De la Tour,* 2 E. & B. 678 (1853).

It is said to be applicable, not only in cases where performance has been rendered impossible by the voluntary conduct of the party, as, in agreements for marriage or conveyance of land, by marriage or conveyance to another, and by way of exception to the general rule formerly maintained, but to the full extent of a general rule; so that an absolute and unqualified declaration of a purpose not to fulfil or be held by the contract, made by one party to the other, may be treated as of itself a present breach of the contract by repudiation, as well before as after the time stipulated for its fulfilment by such party. * * *

The doctrine has never been adopted in this Commonwealth. * * *

A renunciation of the agreement, by declarations or inconsistent conduct, before the time of performance, may give cause for treating it as rescinded, and excuse the other party from making ready for performance on his part, or relieve him from the necessity of offering performance in order to enforce his rights. It may destroy all capacity of the party, so disavowing its obligations, to assert rights under it afterwards, if the other party has acted upon such disavowal. But we are unable to see how it can, of itself, constitute a present violation of any legal rights of the other party, or confer upon him a present right of action. An executory contract ordinarily confers no title or interest in the subject matter of the agreement. Until the time arrives when, by the terms of the agreement, he is or might be entitled to its performance, he can suffer no injury or deprivation which can form a ground of damages. There is neither violation of right, nor loss upon which to found an action. The true rule seems to us to be that in order to charge one in damages for breach of an executory personal contract, the other party must show a refusal or neglect to perform, at a time when and under conditions such that he is or might be entitled to require performance. *Frazier v. Cushman,* 12 Mass. 277. *Pomroy v. Gold,* 2 Met. 500. *Hapgood v. Shaw,* 105 Mass. 276. *Carpenter v. Holcomb,* 105 Mass. 280. Such undoubtedly was the interpretation of the common law in all the earlier decisions. *Phillpotts v. Evans,* 5 M. & W. 475. *Ripley v. M'Clure,* 4 Exch. 345. *Lovelock v. Franklyn,* 8 Q.B. 371.

* * *

We have examined with care the opinions of Lord Chief Justice Cockburn in *Frost v. Knight,* and of Lord Campbell in *Hochster v. De la Tour,* and we are not convinced that the conclusions at which they arrive are founded in sound principles of jurisprudence, or sustained by the authorities cited in their support.

* * *

Hochster v. De la Tour appears to us to be the only case which sustains this position as an adjudication * * *. * * * It was an action upon a contract of hiring to go as courier for the plaintiff from June 1, 1852, at monthly wages. There was notice of renunciation of the employment; and the action brought May 22, 1852, was sustained. * * *

* * *

But the question, in what mode and at what time * * * [the action] may be sought, must depend upon the provisions of his contract, and the nature of the rights to which it entitles him, and which are affected by the conduct of the other party. Throughout the whole discussion both in *Hochster v. De la Tour,* and *Frost v. Knight,* the question as to what conduct of the defendant will relieve the plaintiff from the necessity of showing readiness and an offer to perform at the day, in order to make out a breach by the other, appears to us to be confounded with that of the plaintiff's cause of action; or rather, the question, in what consists the plaintiff's cause of action, is lost sight of; the court dealing only with the conduct of the defendant in repudiating the obligations of his contract.

Much argument is expended in both cases upon the ground of convenience and mutual advantage to the parties from the rule sought to be established. But before that argument can properly have weight, the point to be reached must first be shown to be consistent with logical deductions from the strictly legal aspects of the case. The legal remedy must be founded on some present legal right, and must conform to the nature of that right. Until the plaintiff has either suffered loss or wrong in respect of that which has already vested in him in right, or has been deprived of or prevented from acquiring that which he is entitled to have or demand, he has no ground on which to seek a remedy by way of reparation. The conduct of the defendant is no wrong to the plaintiff until it actually invades some right of his. Actual injury and not anticipated injury is the ground of legal recovery. The plaintiff's rights are invaded by repudiation of the contract only when it produces the effect of non-performance, or prevents him from entering upon or completing performance on his part, at a time when and in the manner in which he is entitled to perform it or to have it performed.

* * *

[The contract's provisions] allow ... [the defendants] thirty days at least within which to fulfil their agreement. The plaintiff could require nothing of them until the expiration of that time; and no conduct on their part or declaration, whether of promise or denial, could give him any cause of action in respect of that agreement of sale. This action therefore cannot be maintained.

DRAKE v. WICKWIRE

Supreme Court of Alaska, 1990.
795 P.2d 195

MATTHEWS, CHIEF JUSTICE. This is a malpractice action against an attorney for allegedly inducing his client to break an earnest money sales agreement. The underlying facts are set forth in Drake v. Hosley, 713 P.2d 1203 (Alaska 1986). We excerpt them at this point:

On March 5, 1984, Paul Drake signed an exclusive listing agreement with The Charles Hosley Company, Realtors (hereafter "Hosley"). The agreement authorized Hosley to act as Drake's agent until March 30, 1984, to sell some land Drake owned in North Pole, Alaska. The agreement provided for payment of a ten percent commission if, during the period of the listing agreement, 1) Hosley located a buyer "willing and able to purchase at the terms set by the seller," or 2) the seller entered into a "binding sale" during the term set by the seller.

Hosley found a group of three buyers, Robert Goldsmith, Dwayne Hofschulte and David Nystrom (hereafter "buyers"), who were interested in the property. On March 23, 1984, Drake signed a purchase and sale agreement, entitled "earnest money receipt," in which he agreed to sell the land to the buyers at a specified price and terms. The buyers also signed the agreement. It provided that closing would occur "within 10 days of clear title" and "ASAP, 1984." [Time was stated to be "of the essence."] A typed addendum stated that Drake agreed to pay Hosley a commission of ten percent of the price paid for the property. Both Drake and Hosley signed the addendum. On April 3, 1984, Hosley received a preliminary commitment for title insurance. The title report listed a judgment in favor of Drake's ex-wife as the sole encumbrance on the title. The next day Hosley called Drake's attorney, Tom Wickwire, to ask about the judgment. Wickwire stated that the judgment would be paid with the cash received at closing.

Two or three days later, attorney Wickwire called Hosley and stated that his client (Drake) wanted the sale closed by April 11. Wickwire explained that he had negotiated a discounted settlement with Drake's ex-wife that required payment by April 11. Wickwire claims that Hosley agreed to close by April 11. Hosley disagrees, and claims he merely stated that he would try to close as quickly as possible.

When Hosley became concerned that the buyers would not be able to close on April 11, he telephoned the attorney for Drake's ex-wife and learned that the April 11 deadline for payment of the judgment had been extended to the end of the month. On April 11, Wickwire called Hosley to set up the closing. Hosley told Wickwire that the buyers could not close that day because they did not have the money and would not have it before May 1. Wickwire indicated that he would advise Drake to call off the sale because the buyers had refused to perform. Wickwire mailed a letter to Hosley, dated April 11, stating that Drake's offer to sell was withdrawn. Hosley received the letter on approximately April 18. On

April 12, Drake sold his property through another broker to different buyers. On April 12, Hosley went to Wickwire's office to close the sale and submitted checks from the buyers totalling $33,000 for the down payment. Wickwire refused the checks, stating that another buyer already had purchased the property.

Id. at 1204–05 (footnote omitted).

In Drake, Hosley sued Drake for his real estate commission. The trial court granted summary judgment to Hosley. On appeal we affirmed, holding that Hosley was Drake's agent, not the agent of the buyers and thus would have had no authority to change the deadline for closing from April 12 or 13 to April 11 as Drake contended.

* * *

However, we are of the view that Wickwire was negligent as a matter of law. In Drake's brief, authored by Wickwire, in the case of Drake v. Hosley, the critical conversation between Hosley and Wickwire relating to the alleged anticipatory repudiation is set forth as follows:

[O]n the morning of April 11 [Wickwire] called Hosley to select a specific time and place for closing. But Hosley's response was that his buyers could not close on that day as they did not have the money but would need until May 1 to get it. Wickwire asked Hosley if the problem was just getting the time to get the money out of the bank or did they not have the downpayment. Hosley replied that the buyers in fact had the money but were "resisting the pressure to close.".

The law of anticipatory repudiation is set forth in sections 253, 250 and 251 of the Restatement (Second) of Contracts (1981) (hereafter Restatement). Section 253(1) of the Restatement provides:

Where an obligor repudiates a duty before he has committed a breach by non-performance and before he has received all of the agreed exchange for it, his repudiation alone gives rise to a claim for damages for total breach.

The concept of repudiation is explained in § 250 as follows: "A repudiation is (a) a statement by the obligor to the obligee indicating that the obligor will commit a breach that would of itself give the obligee a claim for damages...."

The commentary to this section explains that a statement, in order to qualify as a repudiation, must be reasonably clear:

In order to constitute a repudiation, a party's language must be sufficiently positive to be reasonably interpreted to mean that the party will not or cannot perform. Mere expression of doubt as to his willingness or ability to perform is not enough to constitute a repudiation, although such an expression may given an obligee reasonable grounds to believe that the obligor will commit a serious breach and may ultimately result in a repudiation under the rule stated in § 251. However, language that under a fair reading "amounts to a statement of intention not to perform except on conditions which go beyond the contract" constitutes a repudiation.

Restatement § 250, comment b (citation omitted).

In our view, Wickwire did not act reasonably in treating Hosley's statement as a repudiation. As recited by Wickwire, it was ambiguous on its face. Hosley first indicated that the buyers would need until May 1 to get the money. Later, though, Hosley indicated that the buyers had the money but were "resisting the pressure to close." The latter statement itself is ambiguous in that it is unclear whether the buyers were resisting the pressure to close on April 11 as Drake desired, or on April 12 or 13 as the contract required.

If the former meaning was intended, there would have been no anticipatory repudiation because the buyers had no contractual obligation to close on the 11th. If the latter meaning was intended, Wickwire would have had at most reasonable grounds to believe that the buyers would breach the contract. Neither meaning justifies treating the statement as a repudiation. Instead, Wickwire could have sought assurances of performance under the rule stated in § 251 of the Restatement. That rule states:

> (1) Where reasonable grounds arise to believe that the obligor will commit a breach by nonperformance that would of itself give the obligee a claim for damages for total breach ... the obligee may demand adequate assurance of due performance and may, if reasonable, suspend any performance for which he has not already received the agreed exchange until he receives such assurance.
>
> (2) The obligee may treat as a repudiation the obligor's failure to provide within a reasonable time such assurance of due performance as is adequate in the circumstances of the particular case.

Wickwire's negligence in this case was in advising precipitate conduct in the face of an ambiguous statement which was insufficient to indicate that the buyers would breach the contract.

The judgment is REVERSED and this case is REMANDED for further proceedings consistent with this decision.

RABINOWITZ, JUSTICE, dissenting. I dissent from the court's holding that Wickwire was, as a matter of law, guilty of malpractice.

COHEN v. KRANZ

Court of Appeals of New York, 1963.
12 N.Y.2d 242, 238 N.Y.S.2d 928, 189 N.E.2d 473.

BURKE, JUDGE. On September 22, 1959 plaintiff contracted to purchase defendants' one-family house in Nassau County for $40,000. Four thousand dollars was paid on the signing of the contract and the balance due upon delivery of the deed was in the form of $24,500 cash and the assumption of an $11,500 first mortgage. Closing was set for November 15. Plaintiff obtained an adjournment of the closing date to December 15 without any indication that title would be rejected. On November 30, plaintiff's attorney sent defendants' attorney a letter stating: "An investigation has disclosed that the present structure of the premises is not legal and thus title is unmarketable. Unless a check to the order of Lester Cohen, as attorney in fact, for Sarah Cohen is received in five days, we shall be obligated to commence proceedings against your client."

Plaintiff's attorney appeared at the office of defendants' attorney on the adjourned law date and demanded return of the $4,000 deposit, which was refused by the latter. Neither party was then able to perform and neither made any tender. Plaintiff thereafter commenced this action for return of the deposit plus the costs of searching title; defendants counterclaimed for damages for breach of contract.

Trial Term, Nassau County, gave judgment for plaintiff. The court found that the premises were subject to protective covenants filed in the Nassau County Clerk's office and that the insurability clause of the contract was not complied with because a swimming pool on the premises, installed under a permit, lacked a certificate of occupancy from the Oyster Bay Architectural Control Committee. Further, a split rail fence projected beyond the front line of the dwelling. The court also found that plaintiff had notified defendants of the claimed defects prior to the December 15 closing date and that defendants had taken no steps to remedy the defects, nor had it been established that the violations were minor. The court held, therefore, that the defective title excused plaintiff from tender of payment and awarded plaintiff judgment in the amount of her deposit.

The Appellate Division, Second Department, unanimously reversed Trial Term on the law and facts and directed judgment on the counterclaim for $1,500. It is from this judgment that plaintiff appeals.

In reversing Trial Term's findings of fact, the Appellate Division expressly found that plaintiff's letter of November 30 rejecting title and demanding return of the deposit failed to specify the claimed illegality, and that specific objections to title were not raised until January 25, 1960. The letter speaks for itself and the Appellate Division is obviously correct. Plaintiff's arguments directed at the Appellate Division's finding of January 25th as the date when specific objections were first communicated to defendants are unavailing inasmuch as the earliest further communication of objections supported by the evidence took place upon the commencement of this action by plaintiff on December 31st, still more than two weeks after the law date. It was also found, contrary to the trial court, that the objections to title were curable upon proper and timely notice and demand. We think the weight of the evidence supports the Appellate Division here too. The swimming pool was constructed with a permit and lacked only a certificate of occupancy (which was in fact obtained before defendants sold the house to a third person). The fence projection likewise could clearly be found to be a readily curable objection. These were the only two objections that possibly violated the

"Declaration of Protective Covenants" recorded in the Nassau County Clerk's office and to which the title insurer excepted.

The Appellate Division also found that defendants had not waived a tender by plaintiff and that plaintiff's rejection of title in advance was a default precluding her from recovery of the deposit. Since it is undisputed that defendants made no tender, the Appellate Division's award of damages for breach of contract necessarily implies that no such tender was required. We agree.

While a vendee can recover his money paid on the contract from a vendor who defaults on law day without a showing of tender or even of willingness and ability to perform where the vendor's title is incurably defective (Greene v. Barrett, Nephews & Co., 238 N.Y. 207, 144 N.E. 503), a tender and demand are required to put the vendor in default where his title could be cleared without difficulty in a reasonable time. Further, the vendor in such a case is entitled to a reasonable time beyond law day to make his title good (Ballen v. Potter, 251 N.Y. 224, 167 N.E. 424). It is, therefore, clear that plaintiff's advance rejection of title and demand for immediate return of the deposit was unjustified and an anticipatory breach of contract. This position, adhered to throughout, prevented defendants' title defects from ever amounting to a default. Consequently, plaintiff is barred from recovering the deposit from a vendor whose title defects were curable and whose performance was never demanded on law day. Ansorge v. Belfer, 248 N.Y. 145, 150, 161 N.E. 450, 452, is not to the contrary. It merely holds that a vendee may recover his deposit from a clearly defaulting vendor despite his own unjustified refusal to agree to an adjournment of the law date. It does not deny the doctrine that a vendor whose title defects are curable is not automatically in default but, rather, must be put in default by the vendee's tender of performance and demand for a good title deed. The vendor was there put in default by the vendee's tender. The vendor simply never retrieved his default by curing the defects and tendering a good title (as he could have—Harris v. Shorall, 230 N.Y. 343, 130 N.E. 572). True, defendants here never offered to clear their title and perform; but they were never put in default in the first place by a demand for good title. So Ansorge merely holds with respect to curable title defects what Greene v. Barrett, Nephews & Co., supra, held with respect to incurable defects—namely, that where the vendor is in default the deposit can be recovered even though the vendee himself is in default or breach, e.g., no showing of performance of conditions precedent or excuse for nonperformance (the Greene case); or an unjustified refusal to adjourn the closing date (the Ansorge case). The difference is that a vendor with incurable[1] title defects is automatically in default, whereas a vendor with curable title defects must be placed in default by a tender and demand, which was not done here.

1. We use "incurable" to mean not within the vendor's power to remedy within a reasonable time. (See Greene v. Barrett, Nephews & Co., supra, 238 N.Y. pp. 211–212, 144 N.E. pp. 504–505.)

Defendants obtained an affirmative recovery on their counterclaim for breach of contract based on the loss they sustained when they sold the house to a third person for what the courts below found to be its fair market value. This recovery stands on a different footing from their right to retain the deposit. As Judge Andrews pointed out, in speaking of a vendee, in Greene v. Barrett, Nephews & Co., supra, while the vendee's right to recover the deposit from a defaulting vendor can rest solely upon the latter's default an action for *damages* for breach of contract requires a showing that the plaintiff himself (the vendee in the Greene case) has performed all conditions precedent and concurrent, unless excused. In the case of a purchase of real estate, this would be a showing of tender and demand or, if that be unnecessary, an idle gesture, because of the incurable nature of the title defect, then at least a showing at the trial that the plaintiff vendee was in a position to perform had the vendor been willing and able to perform his part. (Greene v. Barrett, Nephews & Co., supra; Stern v. McKee, 70 App.Div. 142, 75 N.Y.S. 157; Norris v. McMechen, 134 Misc. 866, 236 N.Y.S. 486; Restatement, Contracts, § 306.) Likewise, a vendor such as the defendants here must show a basic ability to perform even if actual tender and demand is unnecessary. However, while it cannot be denied that defendants did not have a title conformable to the contract at law date, an applicable corollary of the above rule excuses even inability to perform conditions precedent or concurrent where such inability is caused by advance notice from the other party that he will not perform his part. (Clarke v. Crandall, 27 Barb. 73; Kotcher v. Edelblute, 250 N.Y. 178, 164 N.E. 897; Restatement, Contracts, §§ 270, 284, 306). Not only did plaintiff's unjustified attempt to cancel the contract and recover her deposit before the adjourned law date render unnecessary and wasteful any attempt by defendants to cure the minor defects before that date, but the failure to specify the objections rendered it impossible. The finding of the Appellate Division, supported by the weight of the evidence, that the defects were curable, means that defendants were basically able to perform and whatever technical inability existed in this regard on the law date was caused by plaintiff and is excused fully as much as the lack of formal tender.

The judgment should be affirmed, without costs.

Problems

52. C entered into a contract with O to build a residence for O. Shortly after C began work, O failed to pay a progress payment when due and refused to make any further payments to C. Does C have the usual election available after a material breach by the other party?

53. Plaintiff agreed to build a house for defendant. Plaintiff began work on April 29 and continued until Sept. 11 when plaintiff told defendant that he could not continue unless defendant advanced him money to meet his payroll. In response, defendant ordered plaintiff off the job. (a) Was defendant justified in ordering plaintiff off the job? (b) Assuming that defendant was so justified, would defendant also have a counterclaim?

54. On Jan. 11, D contracted with P to purchase four lots of land from P. Closing was to take place in seven months. D was to commence, on or before Feb. 10, the erection of a house on each of the lots and the houses were to be completed in 7 months. P promised to advance $4,000 on each house to D and D promised to return the $4,000 and to pay an additional $11,000 for each lot when the houses were completed. On the same day the contract was entered into, P conveyed the premises to a third party and D refused to commence erection of the buildings. Before the closing date, the third party reconveyed the property to P who then brought this action for breach of contract. What result?

55. Defendant agreed to convey to plaintiff certain property. In turn, plaintiff agreed to convey to defendant certain lots. At the time of the agreement, plaintiff did not have title to the lots in question but his wife had a contract with the owner that would have permitted plaintiff to perform on time. When defendant learned that plaintiff did not have title, he called off the deal. What result?

56. Plaintiff contracted on April 2 to buy from defendant for immediate delivery 100 coin-operated weighing scales, payment by $1,500 cash as a down payment and the balance by three and six month notes. Plaintiff's check for $1,500 was dishonored for insufficient funds and defendant's subsequent credit investigation of plaintiff revealed unsatisfied judgments against him. Consequently, on April 21, defendant wrote saying that it did not feel justified in delivering the machines on credit, but hoped that plaintiff would consent to a purchase for cash. This plaintiff refused. When defendant refused to deliver on credit, plaintiff sued for breach of contract and proved he was a wealthy man with large cash reserves. Defendant counterclaims. What result?

57. URC, seller, entered into a Gas Purchase Agreement with Panhandle, buyer. The duration of the contract was 15 years. URC was required to tender a specific quantity of gas per year to Panhandle at its pipeline connection (Contract Quantity). The agreement contained a "take-or-pay" clause: a provision requiring Panhandle to take gas, or pay for gas tendered for delivery but not taken (deficiency payments). However, Panhandle could recoup deficiency payments by taking makeup gas (amounts over and above the Contract Quantity) during the succeeding five-year period. Panhandle ran up a large deficiency during the first two years and refused to make deficiency payments. As a result of studies it conducted on the relevant URC wells after execution of the agreement, Panhandle concluded that it would be impossible for URC to supply both the Contract Quantity for the remainder of the term and makeup gas in sufficient quantities to permit full recoupment of the deficiency payments. Panhandle made a written demand for assurances that URC would either provide makeup gas or refund deficiency payments, and URC refused to give such assurances. Was Panhandle justified in refusing to make deficiency payments?

58. The defendant Insurance Company wrote to the plaintiff that it declared his disability policy void, when in fact there was no basis for this assertion. At this point, plaintiff demanded that the defendant honor the policy and offered to supply any necessary proof and further stated that he

had "elected to mature the full indemnity." The defendant did not reply and 30 days later the plaintiff sued for a total breach. What result?

59. Defendant agreed to pay plaintiff a total of $37,500 for certain interests in corporate stock and realty. The agreement required the payment of $5,000 on Jan. 1, 1956, which defendant paid. Defendant, pursuant to the agreement, then gave a series of promissory notes for the balance payable in installments of $5,000. At the same time, plaintiff transferred his interests in the stock and realty to the defendant. Defendant failed to pay the next installment when it was due and notified plaintiff that the balance would not be paid. For how much may plaintiff recover judgment?

60. Defendant purchased and accepted delivery of certain machinery. The contract of sale required it to pay $10,000 within 30 days and the balance in five annual installments and to execute instruments giving the seller a security interest in the machinery. Before the 30 days elapsed and before fulfilling any of its obligations, defendant resold the machinery. Plaintiff immediately brought suit. What result?

Short Essay Examination Question

Plaintiff, the developer of a tract of land, entered into a contract with the defendant whereby the latter would do specified grading and excavation work for $146,000, and, in addition, paving, storm drain and curb installation at specified unit prices, totaling $30,000. When the grading and excavation work was about 98% completed, the parties had a disagreement about whether certain requested excavation work constituted an "extra" or was within the scope of the contract. As a result, defendant ceased performance. Defendant had received $100,000 in progress payments. The paving and installation work had not yet commenced. Plaintiff retained another contractor to perform the balance of the contract at a greater cost. Plaintiff sues. Defendant counterclaims. The court concludes that defendant breached the contract by ceasing to work and refusing to do the requested work which the court determines was within the scope of the contract. Raise and resolve the legal issues presented by these facts.

Shorter Essay Question

In the 1970's a new professional football league, The World Football League, now defunct, was formed. Greenwood, a professional football player with the Pittsburgh Steelers, was offered a position by the Birmingham Americans, a newly formed team in that league. The offer was made in early 1974. The offer was to a three year contract, for services to commence at the beginning of the 1975 season when Greenwood would have fully performed his obligations to the Steelers and would be a free agent. He accepted the offer and a detailed written contract was subscribed by both parties. By terms of the contract, the Americans were to pay Greenwood $375,000. On the signing of the contract he was to receive and did receive $75,000. The balance was to be "1975 --- $90,000; 1976 --- $100,000; 1977 --- $110,000."

Despite a good 1974 playing season, the Birmingham Americans came to be in a precarious financial position. The players were not paid for the last five games of the season and the team was in arrears in paying withholding taxes to the IRS. After the last game, the team's uniforms were seized by the sporting goods dealer who had not received payment for them and the telephone company disconnected service because of nonpayment. Greenwood's lawyer attempted to contact the corporate managers of the Birmingham team, without success. The World Football League canceled the Birmingham franchise. Thereupon. Greenwood signed a contract with the Pittsburgh Steelers for the three year period covered by his contract with the Birmingham team. The Birmingham Americans went out of the football business. They have brought the instant action against Greenwood, seeking restitution of the $75,000 and damages. Discuss the issues that will be argued before the court and their probable resolution.

Chapter 9

IMPOSSIBILITY OR IMPRACTICABILITY, AND FRUSTRATION

(Calamari & Perillo 5th §§ 13.1—13.24)

SECTION 1. HARDSHIP

PARADINE v. JANE

King's Bench, 1647.
Aleyn, 26, 82 Eng.Rep. 897.

In debt the plaintiff declares upon a lease for years rendering rent at the four usual feasts; and for rent behind for three years, ending at the Feast of the Annunciation, 21 Car. brings his action; the defendant pleads, that a certain German prince, by name Prince Rupert, an alien born, enemy to the King and kingdom, had invaded the realm with an hostile army of men; and with the same force did enter upon the defendant's possession, and him expelled, and held out of possession from the 19 of July 18 Car. till the Feast of the Annunciation, 21 Car. whereby he could not take the profits; whereupon the plaintiff demurred, and the plea was resolved insufficient.

* * *

3.   It was resolved, that the matter of the plea was insufficient; for though the whole army had been alien enemies, yet he ought to pay his rent. And this difference was taken, that where the law creates a duty or charge, and the party is disabled to perform it without any default in him, and hath no remedy over, there the law will excuse him. As in the case of waste, if a house be destroyed by tempest, or by enemies, the lessee is excused. Dyer, 33. a. Inst. 53. d. 283. a. 12 H. 4. 6. So of an escape. Co. 4. 84. b. 33 H. 6. 1. So in 9 E. 3. 16. a supersedeas was awarded to the justices, that they should not proceed in a cessavit upon a cesser during the war, but when the party by his own contract creates a duty or charge upon himself, he is bound to make it good, if he may, notwithstanding any accident by inevitable necessity, because he might have provided against it by his contract. And therefore if the lessee covenant to repair a house, though it be burnt by lightning, or thrown down by enemies, yet he ought to repair it. Dyer 33. a. 40 E. 3. 6. h. Now the rent is a duty created by the parties upon the reservation, and had

609

there been a covenant to pay it, there had been no question but the lessee must have made it good, notwithstanding the interruption by enemies, for the law would not protect him beyond his own agreement, no more than in the case of reparations; this reservation then being a covenant in law, and whereupon an action of covenant hath been maintained (as Roll said) it is all one as if there had been an actual covenant. Another reason was added, that as the lessee is to have the advantage of casual profits, so he must run the hazard of casual losses, and not lay the whole burthen of them upon his lessor; and Dyer 56. 6. was cited for this purpose, that though the land be surrounded, or gained by the sea, or made barren by wildfire, yet the lessor shall have his whole rent: and judgment was given for the plaintiff. [Another report of the case gives as an additional reason that the defendant has an action over against the trespassers. Ed.]

SECTION 2. IMPOSSIBILITY

TAYLOR v. CALDWELL

King's Bench, 1863.
3 B. & S. 826, 122 Eng.Rep. 309.

BLACKBURN, J. In this case the plaintiffs and defendants had, on the 27th May, 1861, entered into a contract by which the defendants agreed to let the plaintiffs have the use of The Surrey Gardens and Music Hall on four days then to come, viz., the 17th June, 15th July, 5th August and 19th August, for the purpose of giving a series of four grand concerts, and day and night fêtes at the Gardens and Hall on those days respectively; and the plaintiffs agreed to take the Gardens and Hall on those days, and pay 100*l.* for each day.

The parties inaccurately call this a "letting," and the money to be paid a "rent;" but the whole agreement is such as to shew that the defendants were to retain the possession of the Hall and Gardens so that there was to be no demise of them, and that the contract was merely to give the plaintiffs the use of them on those days. Nothing however, in our opinion, depends on this. The agreement then proceeds to set out various stipulations between the parties as to what each was to supply for these concerts and entertainments, and as to the manner in which they should be carried on. The effect of the whole is to shew that the existence of the Music Hall in the Surrey Gardens in a state fit for a concert was essential for the fulfilment of the contract,—such entertainments as the parties contemplated in their agreement could not be given without it.

After the making of the agreement, and before the first day on which a concert was to be given, the Hall was destroyed by fire. This destruction, we must take it on the evidence, was without the fault of either party, and was so complete that in consequence the concerts could not be given as intended. And the question we have to decide is whether, under these circumstances, the loss which the plaintiffs have sustained is to fall upon the defendants. The parties when framing their agreement evidently had not present to their minds the possibility of such a disaster, and have made no express stipulation with reference to it, so that the answer to the question must depend upon the general rules of law applicable to such a contract.

There seems no doubt that where there is a positive contract to do a thing, not in itself unlawful, the contractor must perform it or pay damages for not doing it, although in consequence of unforeseen accidents, the performance of his contract has become unexpectedly burthensome or even impossible. * * *

* * * But this rule is only applicable when the contract is positive and absolute, and not subject to any condition either express or implied: and there are authorities which, as we think, establish the principle that where, from the nature of the contract, it appears that the parties must from the beginning have known that it could not be fulfilled unless when the time for the fulfilment of the contract arrived some particular specified thing continued to exist, so that, when entering into the contract, they must have contemplated such continuing existence as the foundation of what was to be done; there, in the absence of any express or implied warranty that the thing shall exist, the contract is not to be construed as a positive contract, but as subject to an implied condition that the parties shall be excused in case, before breach, performance becomes impossible from the perishing of the thing without default of the contractor.

There seems little doubt that this implication tends to further the great object of making the legal construction such as to fulfil the intention of those who entered into the contract. For in the course of affairs men in making such contracts in general would, if it were brought to their minds, say that there should be such a condition.

Accordingly, in the Civil law, such an exception is implied in every obligation of the class which they call obligatio de certo corpore. The rule is laid down in the Digest, lib. XLV., tit. 1, de verborum obligationibus, l. 33. "Si Stichus certo die dari promissus, ante diem moriatur: non tenetur promissor." The principle is more fully developed in l. 23. "Si ex legati causa, aut ex stipulatû hominem certum mihi debeas: non aliter post mortem ejus tenearis mihi, quam si per te steterit, quominus vivo eo eum mihi dares: quod ita fit, si aut interpellatus non dedisti, aut occidisti eum." The examples are of contracts respecting a slave, which was the common illustration of a certain subject used by the Roman lawyers, just as we are apt to take a horse; and no doubt the propriety, one might almost say necessity, of the implied condition is more obvious when the contract relates to a living animal, whether man or brute, than when it relates to some inanimate thing (such as in the present case a theatre) the existence of which is not so obviously precarious as that of the live animal, but the principle is adopted in the Civil law as applicable to every obligation of which the subject is a certain thing. The general subject is treated of by Pothier, who in his Traité des Obligations, partie 3, chap. 6, art. 3, § 668 states the result to be that the debtor corporis certi is freed from his obligation when the thing has perished, neither by his act, nor his neglect, and before he is in default, unless by some stipulation he has taken on himself the risk of the particular misfortune which has occurred.

Although the Civil law is not of itself authority in an English Court, if affords great assistance in investigating the principles on which the law is grounded. And it seems to us that the common law authorities establish that in such a contract the same condition of the continued existence of the thing is implied by English law.

There is a class of contracts in which a person binds himself to do something which requires to be performed by him in person; and such promises, e.g., promises to marry, or promises to serve for a certain time, are never in practice qualified by an express exception of the death of the party; and therefore in such cases the contract is in terms broken if the promisor dies before fulfilment. Yet it was very early determined that, if the performance is personal, the executors are not liable; Hyde v. The Dean of Windsor (Cro.Eliz. 552, 553). See 2 Wms.Exors. 1560, 5th ed., where a very apt illustration is given. "Thus," says the learned author, "if an author undertakes to compose a work, and dies before completing it, his executors are discharged from this contract: for the undertaking is merely personal in its nature, and, by the intervention of the contractor's death, has become impossible to be performed." For this he cites a dictum of Lord Lyndhurst in Marshall v. Broadhurst (1 Tyr. 348, 349), and a case mentioned by Patteson J. in Wentworth v. Cook (10 A. & E. 42, 45–46). In Hall v. Wright (E.B. & E. 746, 749), Crompton J., in his judgment, puts another case. "Where a contract depends upon personal skill, and the act of God renders it impossible, as, for instance, in the case of a painter employed to paint a picture who is struck blind, it may be that the performance might be excused."

It seems that in those cases the only ground on which the parties or their executors, can be excused from the consequences of the breach of the contract is, that from the nature of the contract there is an implied condition of the continued existence of the life of the contractor, and, perhaps in the case of the painter of his eyesight. In the instances just given, the person, the continued existence of whose life is necessary to the fulfilment of the contract, is himself the contractor, but that does not seem in itself to be necessary to the application of the principle; as is illustrated by the following example. In the ordinary form of an apprentice deed the apprentice binds himself in unqualified terms to "serve until the full end and term of seven years to be fully complete and ended," during which term it is covenanted that the apprentice his master "faithfully shall serve," and the father of the apprentice in equally unqualified terms binds himself for the performance by the apprentice of all and every covenant on his part. (See the form, 2 Chitty on Pleading, 370, 7th ed. by Greening.) It is undeniable that if the apprentice dies within the seven years, the covenant of the father that he shall perform his covenant to serve for seven years is not fulfilled, yet surely it cannot be that an action would lie against the father? Yet the only reason why it would not is that he is excused because of the apprentice's death.

These are instances where the implied condition is of the life of a human being, but there are others in which the same implication is made as to the continued existence of a thing. For example, where a contract of sale is made amounting to a bargain and sale, transferring presently the property in specific chattels, which are to be delivered by the vendor at a future day; there, if the chattels, without the fault of the vendor, perish in the interval, the purchaser must pay the price and the vendor is excused from performing his contract to deliver, which has thus become impossible.

* * *

It may, we think, be safely asserted to be now English law, that in all contracts of loan of chattels or bailments if the performance of the promise of the borrower or bailee to return the things lent or bailed, becomes impossible because it has perished, this impossibility (if not arising from the fault of the borrower or bailee from some risk which he has taken upon himself) excuses the borrower or bailee from the performance of his promise to redeliver the chattel.

* * *

In none of these cases is the promise in words other than positive, nor is there any express stipulation that the destruction of the person or thing shall excuse the performance; but that excuse is by law implied, because from the nature of the contract it is apparent that the parties contracted on the basis of the continued existence of the particular person or chattel. In the present case, looking at the whole contract, we find that the parties contracted on the basis of the continued existence of the Music Hall at the time when the concerts were to be given; that being essential to their performance.

We think, therefore, that the Music Hall having ceased to exist, without fault of either party, both parties are excused, the plaintiffs from taking the gardens and paying the money, the defendants from performing their promise to give the use of the Hall and Gardens and other things. Consequently the rule must be absolute to enter the verdict for the defendants.

Rule absolute.

CAZARES v. SAENZ

Court of Appeal, Fourth District, Division 1, California, 1989.
208 Cal.App.3d 279, 256 Cal.Rptr. 209.

WIENER, ACTING PRESIDING JUSTICE. On one level, the issue in this case is simply one of attorney's fees. Are plaintiffs Roy Cazares and Thomas Tosdal, former partners in the law firm of Cazares & Tosdal, entitled to one-half of a contingent fee promised them by defendant Phil Saenz when he associated the firm on a particular personal injury case, notwithstanding that Cazares became a municipal court judge before the case was settled? More fundamentally, however, the issue before us requires that we review not only the nature of contingent attorney fee arrangements but also basic contract law regarding frustration of purpose, incapacitation of parties to a contract, and the proper measure of quantum meruit recovery in such circumstances. We decide that where one member of a two-person law firm becomes incapable of performing on a contract of association with another lawyer, the obligations of the parties to the contract are discharged if it was contemplated that the incapacitated attorney would perform substantial services under the agreement. We therefore hold that Cazares and Tosdal are not entitled to 50 percent of the contingent fee as provided in the association agreement. They may, however, recover the reasonable value of the legal services rendered before Cazares's incapacitation, prorated on the basis of the original contract price.

FACTUAL AND PROCEDURAL BACKGROUND

Defendant Phil Saenz was an attorney of limited experience in November 1978 when he was contacted by the Mexican consulate in San Diego regarding a serious accident involving a Mexican national, Raul Gutierrez. Gutierrez had been burned after touching a power line owned by San Diego Gas & Electric Company (SDG & E). He retained Saenz to represent him in a lawsuit against SDG & E and other defendants. The written retainer agreement authorized Saenz to "retain co-counsel if he deems it necessary" and provided that "[a]ttorney fees shall be 33 1/3% of the net recovery; i.e., after all costs and medical expenses."

Saenz shared office space with the law firm of Cazares & Tosdal, which was composed of partners Roy Cazares and Thomas Tosdal, the plaintiffs in this action. In September 1979, Saenz agreed with Cazares to associate Cazares & Tosdal on the Gutierrez case. According to Saenz, he wanted to work with Cazares because Cazares spoke Spanish and could communicate directly with Gutierrez and because he (Saenz) respected Cazares's work in the Mexican–American community. In contrast, Saenz did not feel comfortable with Tosdal: "Basically, he was an Anglo, a surfer. In my opinion, he was just too liberal for me...." Saenz testified he had no reason to doubt Tosdal's competence as a lawyer. In fact, Saenz did not object to Tosdal's working on the case as long as he (Saenz) had nothing to do with him.

Cazares, on behalf of his firm, and Saenz agreed Saenz would continue to maintain client contact with Gutierrez and would handle a pending immigration matter to prevent Gutierrez from being deported. Saenz also wanted to actively assist in the preparation and trial of the case as a learning experience. Cazares & Tosdal was to handle most of the legal work on the case. Saenz and Cazares orally agreed they would evenly divide the contingent fee on the Gutierrez case.[5] Both Cazares

---

5. Rule of Professional Conduct, rule 2–108, in effect at the time of the association agreement, provided that any agreement between lawyers to divide a fee must be and Saenz testified they expected and assumed Cazares would prosecute the case to its conclusion.

Gutierrez's complaint filed in November 1979 listed both Saenz and Cazares & Tosdal as counsel of record. During the next two and one-half years, Cazares performed most of the legal work in the case. Saenz maintained client contact, performed miscellaneous tasks and attended depositions including some defense depositions which Cazares did not attend. For all intents and purposes Tosdal performed no work on the case. Neither Cazares nor Saenz kept time records.

In June 1981, the Cazares & Tosdal partnership dissolved. [Dissolution is only the first step in the termination of a partnership. Ed.] The two partners decided to retain some cases, including the Gutierrez matter, as partnership assets. No formal substitution of counsel was filed in the case. Cazares and Saenz moved to a new office and continued to work on the case together for the next year.

In May 1982 Cazares was appointed a municipal court judge. Cazares urged Saenz to seek Tosdal's help in prosecuting the Gutierrez case. Saenz refused. In January 1983 Tosdal wrote Saenz stating that he remained "ready, willing and available to assist you in any aspect of the preparation of the case in which you may desire my aid."

Saenz never responded to Tosdal's offer. Instead, he associated an experienced personal injury attorney, Isam Khoury, to assist him on the Gutierrez case. Saenz also hired a young attorney, Dan Mazella, to do some research work.

In April 1983, Saenz settled the Gutierrez case for $1.1 million, entitling him to a fee slightly in excess of $366,000. Out of that fee, Saenz paid Khoury $40,000 and Mazella $7,000 for their work on the case. About two weeks later, Saenz visited Cazares and offered to pay him $40,000 for his work on the case. Cazares declined, claiming Saenz owed the now defunct Cazares & Tosdal partnership more than $183,000. This litigation ensued.

The case was tried to a referee by stipulation. (See Code Civ.Proc., § 638.) The referee concluded in pertinent part as follows:

> "The partnership of Tosdal and Cazares entered into an agreement with Saenz, which was in effect a joint venture agreement. The partnership performed fully up until the time Cazares took the bench. At that time, Saenz rejected any help from the remaining partner, therefore preventing the performance by the partnership in further prosecution of the case. The case of Jewel v. Boxer, 156 Cal.App.3d 171 would appear to govern. The joint venture entered into by [the] partnership [with] Saenz entitled the partnership to receive 50% of the fees received by Defendant Saenz."

The referee went on to conclude that Saenz was entitled to deduct the $47,000 paid to Khoury and Mazella before calculating the 50

consented to in writing by the client after full disclosure. Because this rule exists for the benefit of the client, who is not a party to this proceeding, we offer no further comment on the parties' failure to comply with this requirement.

percent due Cazares and Tosdal. Accordingly, judgment was entered in favor of Cazares and Tosdal in the amount of $159,833.00 plus interest.

DISCUSSION

I

The initial question is whether Saenz breached the association agreement with Cazares & Tosdal when, after Cazares's appointment to the municipal court, he refused to work with Tosdal on the Gutierrez case. Here, the referee in effect held that Saenz was obligated to accept Tosdal as a substitute for Cazares even though the record firmly establishes both parties to the association agreement contemplated that most if not all of the work on the Gutierrez case would be performed by Cazares. We conclude that Saenz acted within his rights in refusing to work with Tosdal after Cazares became a judge.

Where a contract contemplates the personal services of a party, performance is excused when that party dies or becomes otherwise incapable of performing. (Rest.2d Contracts, §§ 261, 262; 1 Witkin, Summary of Cal.Law (9th ed. 1987) Contracts, § 782, p. 705.) Here, the parties contemplated Cazares would personally perform the firm's obligations under the contract with Saenz, which he in fact did for two and one-half years after the execution of the contract. Cazares became legally incapable of performing the contract after his appointment to the bench. (See State Bar of California v. Superior Court (1929) 207 Cal. 323, 337, 278 P. 432.) Of course, the contract was not between Saenz and Cazares but between Saenz and the firm of Cazares & Tosdal; thus, performance by the firm was not technically impossible. Nonetheless, the Restatement Second of Contracts, section 262 addresses this issue because its language is not limited to the death or incapacity of a party to the contract: "If the existence of a particular person is necessary for the performance of a duty, his death or such incapacity as makes performance impracticable is an event the non-occurrence of which was a basic assumption on which the contract was made." (Emphasis added.) Here, both Saenz and Cazares testified that Cazares's prosecution of the case to completion was a "basic assumption on which the contract was made."

* * *

It may be helpful to consider a hypothetical situation in which the roles here were reversed, i.e., if Saenz sought to compel Tosdal to perform after Cazares was appointed to the bench. One of the illustrations to Restatement Second of Contracts, section 262 addresses this precise situation, stating the rule that the death or incapacity of one partner discharges the firm's obligations under the contract.[8] At least

---

8. Illustration number 8 reads as follows: "A and B, a firm of architects, contract with C to design a building for C. It is understood by the parties that both A and B shall render services under the contract. A dies and B fails to complete performance. Both A's and B's duties to design the building are discharged, and neither A's estate nor B is liable to C for breach of contract."

where the contract contemplates the unique personal services of a firm member, the rationale of the illustration necessarily leads to the conclusion that the obligations of the party retaining the firm are also discharged in such a situation.

II

Our decision requires that we remand the case to the trial court for a determination of the reasonable value of the services rendered by Cazares & Tosdal on the Gutierrez case. (See Rest.2d Contracts, § 377; Fracasse v. Brent, supra, 6 Cal.3d at p. 791, 100 Cal.Rptr. 385, 494 P.2d 9.) Because the hourly fee is the prevailing price structure in the legal profession, it is sometimes assumed that the quantum meruit standard applied to legal services includes nothing more than a reasonable hourly rate multiplied by the amount of time spent on the case. (See, e.g., Paolillo v. American Export Isbrandtsen Lines, Inc. (S.D.N.Y.1969) 305 F.Supp. 250, 253–254.) As even Saenz's counsel candidly recognizes, however, this is an overly narrow view of the quantum meruit standard applied in the context of a contingent fee agreement which, through no fault of either party, could not be performed.

A.

As a matter of professional responsibility, California lawyers are entitled to charge clients no more than a reasonable fee for legal services. (Rules Prof.Conduct, rule 2 107.) What is reasonable in a given case depends on a host of circumstances. (Ibid.) Moreover, there may be a significant difference between what is reasonable in the context of a negotiated fee and the otherwise calculated reasonable value of legal services rendered. (Aronson, Attorney–Client Fee Arrangements: Regulation and Review (Federal Judicial Center 1980) 18–19.) A party to a contract may agree to pay a higher-than-market price for services, but where the bargaining process is a fair one, courts traditionally defer to the parties' agreement as the best measure of the value of the contract performance. (Ibid.)

The hourly fee is the standard price structure in the legal profession. (See Schwartz & Mitchell, An Economic Analysis of the Contingent Fee in Personal–Injury Litigation (1970) 22 Stan.L.Rev. 1125.) Where a lawyer normally charges for work on the basis of an hourly fee, it is a fairly simple matter to calculate the reasonable value of services rendered even in the absence of a negotiated fee. The lawyer's customary hourly rate can be evaluated by comparison to the rate charged by others in the legal community with similar experience. The number of hours expended by the lawyer can also be evaluated in light of how long it would have taken other attorneys to perform the same tasks. Properly evaluated and adjusted, the product of the hourly rate and the number of hours expended should yield the reasonable value of the work completed.

Where a lawyer has contracted to provide services in exchange for a contingent percentage fee, calculation of the reasonable value of services rendered in partial performance of the contract becomes a more complicated task. It has been repeatedly recognized that a contingent fee " 'may properly provide for a larger compensation than would otherwise be reasonable.' " * * * This is because a contingent fee involves economic considerations separate and apart from the attorney's work on the case.

In addition to compensation for the legal services rendered, there is the raison d'etre for the contingent fee: the contingency. The lawyer on a contingent fee contract receives nothing unless the plaintiff obtains a recovery. Thus, in theory, a contingent fee in a case with a 50 percent chance of success should be twice the amount of a non-contingent fee for the same case. Usually, the fee is contingent not only on the ultimate success of the case but also on the amount recovered; that is, the fee is measured as a percentage of the total recovery. Thus, the lawyer runs the risk that even if successful, the amount recovered will yield a percentage fee which does not provide adequate compensation. (See Schwartz & Mitchell, op. cit. supra, 22 Stan.L.Rev. at p. 1125.)

Finally, even putting aside the contingent nature of the fee, the lawyer under such an arrangement agrees to delay receiving his fee until the conclusion of the case, which is often years in the future. The lawyer in effect finances the case for the client during the pendency of the lawsuit. (Id. at pp. 1125–1126.) If a lawyer was forced to borrow against the legal services already performed on a case which took five years to complete, the cost of such a financing arrangement could be significant.

Where the calculation of an attorney's reasonable fee requires evidence and analysis of all these factors, it can be a formidable undertaking. (Cf. Third Circuit Task Force, Court Awarded Attorney Fees (1985) 108 F.R.D. 237, 246, 249.) Fortunately, when an attorney partially performs on a contingency fee contract, we already have the parties' agreement as to what was a reasonable fee for the entire case. If the trial court can determine what portion of the contract was performed, calculating the reasonable value of that partial performance becomes a relatively simple procedure.

To determine the extent of partial performance, the trial judge must calculate a fraction where the numerator is the value of the legal services rendered by the particular attorney or firm at issue and the denominator is the aggregate value of all the legal services rendered by any attorney in the case. This may be as simple as adding up the total number of hours spent by all attorneys on the matter, but it is by no means limited to "straight time." The trial court may adjust the fraction upward or downward to account for difficulty of the work or other relevant factors.

The fraction thus calculated represents the attorney's or firm's proportionate work on the case and, if multiplied by the total fee due under the contract, should yield a reasonable approximation of the proportional fee due the attorney or firm. In effect, then, the reasonable value of the services rendered is measured by the attorney's or firm's pro rata share of the contract price.

B

* * *

Because "reasonable value" is such an amorphous concept, it makes no sense to ignore the best evidence of that value as expressed in the parties' agreement. Especially in this type of case, where the contract is between associated attorneys, an unforeseen event which renders complete performance by one party impossible should not result in a windfall to the other attorney. In essence, having contracted with the lawyer or firm to pay a particular fee, the associating attorney is estopped to deny that the pro rata contract price accurately measures the reasonable value of the services rendered.

III

We are familiar with and especially sensitive to the rules which govern the relationships among attorneys and between attorneys and clients. This sensitivity is the product not only of our experience as judges, continually exposed to the interaction among lawyers and between lawyers and clients, but also our pre-judicial experience in the practice of law. We suspect that disputes over legal fees may sully whatever remains of the image of law as a noble "profession." The public may perceive the lawyer as simply another variety of business executive, concerned primarily with the bottom line. Realistically, however, neither archetype—business or profession—alone accurately describes the modern practice of law.

In crafting these rules, we must pragmatically recognize that the ability of lawyers to perform their important professional function in society is in the long run dependent on assurances they will be fairly compensated for their work. We believe the standards set forth in this case with respect to the discharge of an associated firm and the compensation of that firm for work performed prior to discharge appropriately consider and balance the interests of clients in effective representation and the financial interests of the various lawyers involved. * * *

The judgment is reversed. The case is remanded to the superior court for further proceedings consistent with this opinion.

AMERICAN TRADING AND PRODUCTION CORP. v. SHELL INT'L MARINE LTD.

United States Court of Appeals, Second Circuit, 1972.
453 F.2d 939.

MULLIGAN, CIRCUIT JUDGE. This is an appeal by American Trading and Production Corporation (hereinafter "owner") from a judgment entered on July 29th, 1971, in the United States District Court for the Southern District of New York, dismissing its claim against Shell International Marine Ltd. (hereinafter "charterer") for additional compensation in the sum of $131,978.44 for the transportation of cargo from Texas to India via the Cape of Good Hope as a result of the closing of the Suez Canal in

June, 1967. The charterer had asserted a counterclaim which was withdrawn and is not in issue. The action was tried on stipulated facts and without a jury before Hon. Harold R. Tyler, Jr. who dismissed the claim on the merits in an opinion dated July 22, 1971.

We affirm.

The owner is a Maryland corporation doing business in New York and the charterer is a United Kingdom corporation. On March 23, 1967 the parties entered into a contract of voyage charter in New York City which provided that the charterer would hire the owner's tank vessel, WASHINGTON TRADER, for a voyage with a full cargo of lube oil from Beaumont/Smiths Bluff, Texas to Bombay, India. The charter party provided that the freight rate would be in accordance with the then prevailing American Tanker Rate Schedule (AT RS), $14.25 per long ton of cargo, plus seventy-five percent (75%), and in addition there was a charge of $.85 per long ton for passage through the Suez Canal. On May 15, 1967 the WASHINGTON TRADER departed from Beaumont with a cargo of 16,183.32 long tons of lube oil. The charter paid the freight at the invoiced sum of $417,327.36 on May 26, 1967. On May 29th, 1967 the owner advised the WASHINGTON TRADER by radio to take additional bunkers at Ceuta due to possible diversion because of the Suez Canal crisis. The vessel arrived at Ceuta, Spanish Morocco on May 30, bunkered and sailed on May 31st, 1967. On June 5th the owner cabled the ship's master advising him of various reports of trouble in the Canal and suggested delay in entering it pending clarification. On that very day, the Suez Canal was closed due to the state of war which had developed in the Middle East. The owner then communicated with the charterer on June 5th through the broker who had negotiated the charter party, requesting approval for the diversion of the WASHING-TON TRADER which then had proceeded to a point about 84 miles northwest of Port Said, the entrance to the Canal. On June 6th the charterer responded that under the circumstances it was "for owner to decide whether to continue to wait or make the alternative passage via the Cape since Charter Party Obliges them to deliver cargo without qualification." In response the owner replied on the same day that in view of the closing of the Suez, the WASHINGTON TRADER would proceed to Bombay via the Cape of Good Hope and "[w]e [are] reserving all rights for extra compensation." The vessel proceeded westward, back through the Straits of Gibraltar and around the Cape and eventually arrived in Bombay on July 15th (some 30 days later than initially expected), traveling a total of 18,055 miles instead of the 9,709 miles which it would have sailed had the Canal been open. The owner billed $131,978.44 as extra compensation which the charterer has refused to pay.

On appeal and below the owner argues that transit of the Suez Canal was the agreed specific means of performance of the voyage charter and that the supervening destruction of this means rendered the contract legally impossible to perform and therefore discharged the owner's unperformed obligation (Restatement of Contracts § 460

(1932)). Consequently, when the WASHINGTON TRADER eventually delivered the oil after journeying around the Cape of Good Hope, a benefit was conferred upon the charterer for which it should respond in quantum meruit. The validity of this proposition depends upon a finding that the parties contemplated or agreed that the Suez passage was to be the exclusive method of performance, and indeed it was so argued on appeal. We cannot construe the agreement in such a fashion. The parties contracted for the shipment of the cargo from Texas to India at an agreed rate and the charter party makes absolutely no reference to any fixed route. It is urged that the Suez passage was a condition of performance because the ATRS rate was based on a Suez Canal passage, the invoice contained a specific Suez Canal toll charge and the vessel actually did proceed to a point 84 miles northwest of Port Said. In our view all that this establishes is that both parties contemplated that the Canal would be the probable route. It was the cheapest and shortest, and therefore it was in the interest of both that it be utilized. However, this is not at all equivalent to an agreement that it be the exclusive method of performance. The charter party does not so provide and it seems to have been well understood in the shipping industry that the Cape route is an acceptable alternative in voyages of this character.

The District of Columbia Circuit decided a closely analogous case, Transatlantic Financing Corp. v. United States, 124 U.S.App.D.C. 183, 363 F.2d 312 (1966). There the plaintiff had entered into a voyage charter with defendant in which it agreed to transport a full cargo of wheat on the CHRISTOS from a United States port to Iran. The parties clearly contemplated a Suez passage, but on November 2, 1956 the vessel reduced speed when war blocked the Suez Canal. The vessel changed its course in the Atlantic and eventually delivered its cargo in Iran after proceeding by way of the Cape of Good Hope. In an exhaustive opinion Judge Skelly Wright reviewed the English cases which had considered the same problem and concluded that "the Cape route is generally regarded as an alternative means of performance. So the implied expectation that the route would be via Suez is hardly adequate proof of an allocation to the promisee of the risk of closure. In some cases, even an express expectation may not amount to a condition of performance." Transatlantic Financing Corp. v. United States, supra, 363 F.2d at 317 (footnote omitted).

Appellant argues that *Transatlantic* is distinguishable since there was an agreed upon flat rate in that case unlike the instant case where the rate was based on Suez passage. This does not distinguish the case in our view. It is stipulated by the parties here that the only ATRS rate published at the time of the agreement from Beaumont to Bombay was the one utilized as a basis for the negotiated rate ultimately agreed upon. This rate was escalated by 75% to reflect whatever existing market conditions the parties contemplated. These conditions are not stipulated. Had a Cape route rate been requested, which was not the case, it is agreed that the point from which the parties would have bargained would be $17.35 per long ton of cargo as against $14.25 per long ton.

Actually, in *Transatlantic* it was argued that certain provisions in the P. & I. Bunker Deviation Clause referring to the direct and/or customary route required, by implication, a voyage through the Suez Canal. The court responded "[a]ctually they prove only what we are willing to accept—that the parties expected the usual and customary route would be used. The provisions in no way condition performance upon non-occurrence of this contingency." Transatlantic Financing Corp. v. United States, supra, 363 F.2d at 317 n. 8. We hold that all that the ATRS rate establishes is that the parties obviously expected a Suez passage but there is no indication at all in the instrument or *dehors* that it was a condition of performance.

This leaves us with the question as to whether the owner was excused from performance on the theory of commercial impracticability (Restatement of Contracts § 454 (1932)). Even though the owner is not excused because of strict impossibility, it is urged that American law recognizes that performance is rendered impossible if it can only be accomplished with extreme and unreasonable difficulty, expense, injury or loss.[1] There is no extreme or unreasonable difficulty apparent here. The alternate route taken was well recognized, and there is no claim that the vessel or the crew or the nature of the cargo made the route actually taken unreasonably difficult, dangerous or onerous. The owner's case here essentially rests upon the element of the additional expense involved—$131,978.44. This represents an increase of less than one third over the agreed upon $417,327.36. We find that this increase in expense is not sufficient to constitute commercial impracticability under either American or English authority.

Mere increase in cost alone is not a sufficient excuse for non-performance (Restatement of Contracts § 467 (1932)). It must be an "extreme and unreasonable"[2] expense (Restatement of Contracts § 454 (1932)).[3] While in the *Transatlantic* case supra, the increased cost amounted to an increase of about 14% over the contract price, the court did cite with approval[4] the two leading English cases Ocean Tramp Tankers Corp. v. V/O Sovfracht (The Eugenia), [1964] 2 Q.B. 226, 233 (C.A.1963) (which expressly overruled Societe Franco Tunisienne D'Armement v. Sidermar S.P.A. (The Messalia), [1961] 2 Q.B. 278 (1960), where the court had found frustration because the Cape route

1. This is the formula utilized in the Restatement of Contracts § 454 (1932).

2. The Restatement gives some examples of what is "extreme and unreasonable"—Restatement of Contracts § 460, Illus. 2 (tenfold increase in costs) and Illus. 3 (costs multiplied fifty times) (1932); compare § 467, Illus. 3. See generally G. Grismore, Principles of the Law of Contracts § 179 (rev. ed. J.E. Murray 1965).

3. Both parties take solace in the Uniform Commercial Code which in comment 4 to Section 2-615 states that the rise in cost must "alter the essential nature of the performance * * *." This is clearly not the case here. The owner relies on a further sentence in the comment which refers to a severe shortage of raw materials or of supplies due to "war, embargo, local crop failure, unforeseen shutdown of major sources of supply or the like, which either causes a marked increase in cost * * *." Since this is not a case involving the sale of goods but transportation of a cargo where there was an alternative which was a commercially reasonable substitute (see Uniform Commercial Code § 2-614(1)) the owner's reliance is misplaced.

4. Transatlantic Financing Corp. v. United States, supra, 363 F.2d at 319 n. 14.

was highly circuitous and involved an increase in cost of approximately 50%), and Tsakiroglou & Co. Lt. v. Noblee Thorl G.m.b.H., [1960] 2 Q.B. 318, 348 aff'd, [1962] A.C., 93 (1961) where the House of Lords found no frustration though the freight costs were exactly doubled due to the Canal closure.[5]

Appellant further seeks to distinguish *Transatlantic* because in that case the change in course was in the mid-Atlantic and added some 300 miles to the voyage while in this case the WASHINGTON TRADER had traversed most of the Mediterranean and thus had added some 9000 miles to the contemplated voyage. It should be noted that although both the time and the length of the altered passage here exceeded those in the *Transatlantic*, the additional compensation sought here is just under one third of the contract price. Aside from this however, it is a fact that the master of the WASHINGTON TRADER was alerted by radio on May 29th, 1967 of a "possible diversion because of Suez Canal crisis," but nevertheless two days later he had left Ceuta (opposite Gibraltar) and proceeded across the Mediterranean. While we may not speculate about the foreseeability of a Suez crisis at the time the contract was entered, there does not seem to be any question but that the master here had been actually put on notice before traversing the Mediterranean that diversion was possible. Had the WASHINGTON TRADER then changed course, the time and cost of the Mediterranean trip could reasonably have been avoided, thereby reducing the amount now claimed. (Restatement of Contracts § 336, Comment *d* to subsection (1) (1932)).

In a case closely in point, Palmco Shipping Inc. v. Continental Ore Corp. (*The "Captain George K"*), [1970] 2 Lloyd's L.Rep. 21 (Q.B.1969), *The Eugenia,* supra, was followed, and no frustration was found where the vessel had sailed to a point three miles northwest of Port Said only to find the Canal blocked. The vessel then sailed back through the Mediterranean and around the Cape of Good Hope to its point of destination, Kandla. The distances involved, 9700 miles via the initially contemplated Canal route and 18,400 miles actually covered by way of the Cape of Good Hope, coincide almost exactly with those in this case. Moreover, in *The "Captain George K"* there was no indication that the master had at anytime after entering the Mediterranean been advised of the possibility of the Canal's closure.

* * *

Matters involving impossibility or impracticability of performance of contract are concededly vexing and difficult. One is even urged on the

---

5. While these are English cases and refer to the doctrine of "frustration" rather than "impossibility" as Judge Skelly Wright pointed out in *Transatlantic,* supra, 363 F.2d at 320 n. 16 the two are considered substantially identical, 6 A. Corbin, Contracts § 1322, at 327 n. 9 (rev. ed. 1962). While *Tsakiroglou* and *The Eugenia* are criticized in Schegal, Of Nuts, and Ships and Sealing Wax, Suez, and Frustrating Things—The Doctrine of Impossibility of Performance, 23 Rutgers L.Rev. 419, 448 (1969), apparently on the theory that the charterer is a better loss bearer, the overruled *Sidermar* case was previously condemned in Berman, Excuse for Nonperformance in the Light of Contract Practices in International Trade, 63 Colum.L.Rev. 1413, 1424–27 (1963).

allocation of such risks to pray for the "wisdom of Solomon." 6 A. Corbin, Contracts § 1333, at 372 (1962). On the basis of all of the facts, the pertinent authority and a further belief in the efficacy of prayer, we affirm.

NORTHERN CORP. v. CHUGACH ELECTRIC ASSOC.

Supreme Court of Alaska, 1974.
518 P.2d 76.

BOOCHEVER, JUSTICE. We are here presented with issues concerning the alleged impossibility of performing a public contract. Northern Corporation (hereafter referred to as Northern), appellant and cross-appellee, entered into a contract with Chugach Electric Association (hereafter Chugach), appellee and cross-appellant, on August 3, 1966 for the repair and protection of the upstream face of the Cooper Lake Dam. The contract was awarded to Northern on the basis of its low bid in the sum of $63,655.

The work to be performed was described as follows:

> It is required that the upstream face of Cooper Lake Dam be regraded and riprap and filter layer stone quarried, hauled and placed on the upstream face and all other appurtenant work accomplished as required, all in accordance with these plans and specification [sic]. There are about 1750 cubic yards of filter material and 3950 cubic yards of riprap to be placed. The Contractor shall furnish all labor, equipment, materials, etc. required for this project.

The contract called for completion of the work within 60 days of notice to proceed, which was given on August 29, 1966.

The major expense in performing the contract was to be the procurement and placing of riprap. The bidders on the contract were advised with respect to quarry areas from which rock could be obtained:

> A quarry area, with suitable rock outcropping on the stream bank, has been located approximately 2500 feet downstream from the dam. A haul road will have to be constructed, either down the stream bed or along the left bank. The quarry area is shown on the vicinity map.

* * *

> The Contractor may, at his option, select a quarry different from the site shown on the drawings. In this event, the Contractor shall pay the costs of all tests required to verify the suitability of the rock for this project.

Northern first discovered boulders in the stream bed which would be more economical than the designated quarry and received permission to use this source. According to Northern, approximately 20 percent of the contract requirements were fulfilled before Northern exhausted the supply located in the stream bed. Then in the first week of September, Northern moved to the designated quarry site and commenced shooting rock. On September 19, 1966, Northern wrote to Chugach informing them that the rock in the designated quarry was unusable, but was directed in a letter the following day from Chugach's engineering firm to proceed with further blasting and exploration of the designated areas. By September 27, however, Chugach conceded that suitable rock was not available at the designated site and reformed the agreement accordingly.

Alternate quarry sites were found at the opposite end of the lake from the dam. As a result of negotiations, Chugach wrote to Northern on September 27, 1966 authorizing completion of the contract by use of these alternate quarry sites. The authorization provided for amendments to reflect the circumstance that suitable rock was not available in the stream bed for mining, nor in the quarry which had been designated in the original contract documents. Paragraph 3 of the letter of authorization specified:

> Rock will be quarried in suitable sizes and quantities to complete the project and will be stockpiled in or near the quarry, or quarries, mentioned above for transport across Cooper Lake to the dam site when such lake is frozen to a sufficient depth to permit heavy vehicle traffic thereon.

The contract price was increased by $42,000. Subsequently, the contract was formally amended in accordance with the September 27, 1966 authorization. Work commenced in the new quarry in October 1966; and within about 30 days, all of the required rock was drilled and shot.

Although there is some question as to who first suggested it or how it came about, it was the agreement of the parties that the rock from the new quarry site would be transported in winter across the ice of Cooper Lake. In December 1966, Northern cleared a road on the ice to permit deeper freezing of the ice. By the time the ice was thought to be sufficiently thick to begin hauling, however, a water overflow on the ice one to two feet in depth prohibited crossings by the trucks. Northern complained to Chugach of unsafe conditions on the lake ice, but Chugach insisted on performance. In March 1967, one of Northern's Euclid loaders went through the ice and sank, and a small crawler tractor subsequently broke through but was recovered. Neither incident involved loss of life. Despite these occurrences, Chugach and its engineering firm continued to insist on performance, threatening default. On March 27, 1967, Chugach again threatened to consider Northern in default unless they immediately commenced hauling operations. Northern attempted to commence operations but continued to meet with difficulties, finally ceasing operations on March 31, 1967, apparently with the approval of Chugach.

On January 8, 1968, Chugach advised Northern that it would consider Northern in default unless all rock was hauled by April 1, 1968. On January 20, Northern informed Chugach that they were returning to Cooper Lake, and wrote on January 30 that they anticipated favorable conditions to start hauling rock on January 31. The ice conditions were apparently different from those encountered in 1967—there was very little snow cover and no overflow problem. The ice varied from 23½ inches to 30 inches thick, and for several days the temperature had been 30 degrees below zero and clear.

On February 1, 1968, Northern started hauling with half-loaded trucks; but within the first few hours, two trucks with their drivers broke through the ice, resulting in the death of the drivers and loss of the trucks. Northern at this point ceased operations; and on February 16, 1968, informed Chugach that it would make no more attempts to haul rock across the lake. On March 28, 1968, Northern advised Chugach that it considered the contract terminated for impossibility of performance.

Northern commenced legal action against Chugach in September, 1968, seeking recovery for costs incurred in attempted completion of the contract less revenues received. The case was tried in superior court without a jury in December 1971. Northern contended that in the original contract there were express and implied warranties that the designated quarry contained sufficient quantities of suitable rock for the job, and that breach of the warranties entitled Northern to damages. In the alternative, Northern argued that the modified contract was impossible of performance, justifying an award to Northern of reasonable costs incurred in attempted performance. Chugach counterclaimed, contending that it overpaid Northern for work performed under the contract, and that it was entitled to liquidated damages for the period between the date of completion specified in the amended contract and the date of its termination by Northern. The superior court discharged the parties from the contract on the ground of impossibility of performance, but denied both parties' claims for damages and attorney's fees. From that decision, Northern appeals and Chugach cross-appeals.

The issues on this appeal may be summarized as follows:

1. Is Northern entitled to damages for breach of alleged express and implied warranties contained in the original contract pertaining to available quantities of rock?

2. In the alternative, was the contract as modified impossible of performance?

3. If the modified contract was impossible of performance, is Northern entitled to reasonable costs incurred in endeavoring to perform it?

4. Is Chugach entitled to liquidated damages for delays in performance of the contract and to costs and attorney's fees.[1]

Our analysis of the events preceding the lawsuit leads us to the conclusion that the dispositive issues pertain to the question of impossibility of performance. It appears clear to us that the original agreement

---

1. Chugach's contention that it overpaid   on appeal.
Northern has apparently been abandoned

between Chugach and Northern was superseded as a result of Chugach's letter to Northern, dated September 27, 1966, and the subsequent formal amendment of the contract in accordance therewith. The amendment recognized that the quarries originally specified did not provide a sufficient quantity of riprap. The original contract price of $63,655 was increased by $42,000 to cover the additional costs incurred and to be incurred by Northern in exploration of the quarry originally designated, in securing rock at the redesignated quarries, in hauling the rock to the dam site, in stockpiling it, and in cleaning up the redesignated quarry areas. The amendment was executed by both parties to the contract. Since the amendment provided for the additional costs incurred by Northern as a result of the absence of a suitable rock supply at the quarry originally designated, we need not concern ourselves with whether express or implied warranties were breached with reference to the quantity of rock available at the originally designated quarry. There is no contention here that the amended contract did not designate quarries containing suitable quantities of rock.

IMPOSSIBILITY

The focal question is whether the amended contract was impossible of performance. The September 27, 1966 directive specified that the rock was to be transported "across Cooper Lake to the dam site when such lake is frozen to a sufficient depth to permit heavy vehicle traffic thereon," and the formal amendment specified that the hauling to the dam site would be done during the winter of 1966–67. It is therefore clear that the parties contemplated that the rock would be transported across the frozen lake by truck. Northern's repeated efforts to perform the contract by this method during the winter of 1966–67 and subsequently in February 1968, culminating in the tragic loss of life, abundantly support the trial court's finding that the contract was impossible of performance by this method.

Chugach contends, however, that Northern was nevertheless bound to perform, and that it could have used means other than hauling by truck across the ice to transport the rock. The answer to Chugach's contention is that, as the trial court found, the parties contemplated that the rock would be hauled by truck once the ice froze to a sufficient depth to support the weight of the vehicles. The specification of this particular method of performance presupposed the existence of ice frozen to the requisite depth. Since this expectation of the parties was never fulfilled, and since the provisions relating to the means of performance was clearly material,[3] Northern's duty to perform was discharged by reason of impossibility.

There is an additional reason for our holding that Northern's duty to perform was discharged because of impossibility. It is true that in order for a defendant to prevail under the original common law doctrine of impossibility, he had to show that no one else could have performed

---

3. The initial contract price was $63,655. Performing by the alternative method (barging) would have cost an additional $59,520.

the contract. However, this harsh rule has gradually been eroded, and the Restatement of Contracts has departed from the early common law rule by recognizing the principle of "commercial impracticability". Under this doctrine, a party is discharged from his contract obligations, even if it is technically possible to perform them, if the costs of performance would be so disproportionate to that reasonably contemplated by the parties as to make the contract totally impractical in the commercial sense.[7] * * * Sec. 465 of the Restatement also provides that a serious risk to life or health will excuse nonperformance.

Alaska has adopted the Restatement doctrine whereby commercial impracticability may under certain circumstances justify regarding a contract as impossible to perform. In Merl F. Thomas Sons, Inc. v. State, this court was confronted with an appeal from a grant of summary judgment against a contractor or who alleged in defense of nonperformance that the contemplated means of performing a clearing contract was to move equipment across the ice on the Susitna River from Talkeetna to the job site. Due to thin ice, this means of performance was impossible. Despite the state's contention that the equipment could be transported across the ice at Hurricane, some 70 miles to the north, we reversed the grant of summary judgment, holding that the contractor's allegation that all parties contemplated that equipment would be moved across the ice at Talkeetna raised a question of fact material to the defense of impossibility of performance. We quoted with approval Professor Williston's analysis of the concept of impossibility:

> The true distinction is not between difficulty and impossibility. As has been seen, a man may contract to do what is impossible, as well as what is difficult. The important question is whether an unanticipated circumstance, the risk of which should not fairly be thrown upon the promisor, has made performance of the promise vitally different from what was reasonably to be expected (footnote omitted).

In the case before us the detailed opinion of the trial court clearly indicates that the appropriate standard was followed. There is ample evidence to support its findings that "[t]he ice haul method of transporting riprap ultimately selected was within the contemplation of the parties and was part of the basis of the agreement which ultimately resulted in amendment No. 1 in October 1966," and that that method was not commercially feasible within the financial parameters of the contract. We affirm the court's conclusion that the contract was impossible of performance.

EASTERN AIR LINES, INC. v. McDONNELL DOUGLAS CORP.

United States Court of Appeals, Fifth Circuit, 1976.
532 F.2d 957.

[A jury returned a verdict of about $24,500,000, in favor of Eastern Airlines against the defendant for breaches of a series of contracts for

---

7. For example, one California case applied this result where it was about ten times as expensive to perform as was con- templated by the parties. Mineral Park Land Co. v. Howard, 172 Cal. 289, 156 P. 458 (1916).

the delivery of approximately 100 jet planes. The breaches consisted of late deliveries. The contracts were negotiated in early 1965 at which time the Vietnam War "was having no significant effect on the American economy," and President Johnson was predicting a reduction in the military budget for the coming fiscal year. Between January 1965 and December 31, 1966, American troops deployed in Vietnam rose from 23,000 to 455,000. There was a concomitant escalation of production of military aircraft. Under the Defense Production Act, directives could be issued by government officials to manufacturers to give priority to military production. The evidence showed, however, that such directives were rarely issued. Instead "jawboning" was preferred. This usually consisted of telephone calls to business executives requesting priority on an informal basis. Implicit in such requests was a threat that a formal directive would be issued if the requests were not honored.

The defendant attributes its delays to government "jawboning" which caused it to subordinate civilian to military production. Similar "jawboning" caused the suppliers of component parts, such as landing gears, to make late deliveries. The trial judge ruled that evidence of government "jawboning" techniques was inadmissible because immaterial.]

AINSWORTH, CIRCUIT JUDGE.

* * *

B. THE "EXCUSABLE DELAY" CLAUSE

McDonnell Douglas contends that the trial judge's instructions to the jury undercut the defense available to it under the excusable delay clause found in all of the contracts at issue in this appeal. In relevant part, the provision reads as follows:

> Seller shall not be responsible nor deemed to be in default on account of delays in performance * * * due to causes beyond Seller's control and not occasioned by its fault or negligence, including but not being limited to * * * any act of government, governmental priorities, allocation regulations or orders affecting materials, equipment, facilities or completed aircraft, * * * failure of vendors (due to causes similar to those within the scope of this clause) to perform their contracts * * *, provided such clause is beyond Seller's control.

1. *Ejusdem Generis and the Applicability of U.C.C. § 2–615*

McDonnell's first contention in this regard is that the District Court unduly narrowed the scope of this clause by instructing the jury that an excusable delay must be the result of "one or more of the listed events in the excusable delay clause of the contracts, or * * * a similar cause beyond the defendant's control. * * * " This instruction, in McDonnell's view, effectively construes the specifically listed excusable causes of delay as restricting the application of the more general phrase which exempts Douglas from liability for delays beyond its control and not due to its negligence. McDonnell feels, therefore, that its affirmative defense was unjustifiably limited to delays caused by events similar to those specifically listed when, in fact, the contracts excused all delays which were not its fault.

The trial judge's construction of the clause, moreover, affords McDonnell Douglas a narrower range of excuses than is available under the modern view of impossibility as it is codified in U.C.C. § 2–615. Simply stated, section 2–615 excuses delay or nondelivery when the agreed upon performance has been rendered "commercially impracticable" by an unforeseen supervening event not within the contemplation of the parties at the time the contract was entered into. Uniform Commercial Code § 2–615 [Cal.Comm.Code § 2615] Comments 1 & 8; see Restatement, Contracts §§ 454, 457 (1932); 6 A. Corbin, Contracts §§ 1321, 1339 (1962).

Under section 2–615, the impossibility defense is available to the seller only if he has not "assumed a greater obligation" than that imposed upon him by this provision. During the trial, the court below ruled that section 2–615 was not applicable for this reason. Although the trial judge failed to explain his holding, it must have been based upon his restrictive construction of the excusable delay clause. Presumably, then, the protections of section 2–615 were deemed to have been waived because the contracts were interpreted as limiting McDonnell's impossibility defense to delays caused by events similar to those specifically provided for in the excusable delay clause.

In support of this approach, Eastern argues that the District Court correctly applied *ejusdem generis,* a canon of judicial construction limiting the application of general terms which follow specific ones to matters similar in kind or classification to those specified. * * *

* * * This maxim, however, "is only an instrumentality for ascertaining the correct meaning of words when there is uncertainty." Gooch v. United States, 297 U.S. 124, 128, 56 S.Ct. 395, 397, 80 L.Ed. 522, 526 (1936); accord, City of Los Angeles v. Superior Court, 1934, 2 Cal.2d 138, 39 P.2d 401. Obviously, the application of the doctrine in this case would make superfluous the unambiguous words "including but not being limited to" which precede the specifically listed excuses for delay. It is clear, then, that by excusing delays not within McDonnell's control nor due to its negligence, "including but not being limited to" governmental acts, priorities, or orders, the parties intended to excuse all delays coming within the general description regardless of their similarity to the listed excuses. Consequently, there is no basis for the trial judge's conclusion that McDonnell waived the protections of section 2–615 and that its contract excuses are narrower than those available under the doctrine of commercial impracticability.

2. The Foreseeability Issue

McDonnell also challenges the trial judge's jury instruction which limited excusable delivery delays to those resulting from events which were not "reasonably foreseeable" at the time a contract was executed. By writing a foreseeability requirement into the excusable delay clause, the District Court appeared to construe the contracts as constituting nothing more than an application of the Code's commercial impracticability rule to those particular events specified in the contracts.[93]

Although there has been some doubt expressed as to whether the Code permits parties to bargain for exemptions broader than those available under section 2–615, this concern is ill-founded. See Hawkland, The Energy Crisis and Section 2–615 of the Uniform Commercial Code, 79 Com.L.J. 75 (1974). Comment 8 to this provision plainly indicates that parties may "enlarge upon or supplant" section 2–615. See United States v. Wegematic Corp., 2 Cir., 1966, 360 F.2d 674, 677 (Friendly, J.).

There appear to be however, certain strictures imposed upon judicial interpretation of such agreements. Comment 8 provides:

> Generally, express agreements as to exemptions designed to enlarge upon or supplant the provisions of this section are to be read in light of mercantile sense and reason, for this section itself sets up the commercial standard for normal and reasonable interpretation and provides a minimum beyond which agreement may not go.

While this provision could have been drafted in less vague terms, we presume that Comment 8 establishes "mercantile sense and reason" as a general standard governing our construction of agreements enlarging upon the protections of section 2–615. As we understand Comment 8, where there is doubt concerning the parties' intention, exemption clauses should not be construed as broadening the excuses available under the Code's impracticability rule. Applying this standard to the excusable delay clause, we cannot, in the absence of evidence to the contrary, hold that McDonnell is exempt from liability for any delay, regardless of its foreseeability, that is due to causes beyond its control. Exculpatory provisions which are phrased merely in general terms have long been construed as excusing only unforeseen events which make performance impracticable * * * Courts have often held, therefore, that if a promisor desires to broaden the protections available under the excuse doctrine he should provide for the excusing contingencies with particularity and not in general language. * * *

We realize, of course, that this rule of construction developed in the pre-U.C.C. era when the scope of the impossibility and frustration doctrines was unclear and varied from jurisdiction to jurisdiction. Be-

---

93. The trial court's instructions on this issue were as follows:

In seeking to excuse its delayed performance on the theory that the delays were due to causes beyond its control and not occasioned by its fault or negligence, the defendant has the burden of proving that any excusing event or occurrence upon which it relies was not reasonably foreseeable at the time the contract was entered into.

cause of the uncertainty surrounding the law of excuse, parties had good reason to resort to general contract provisions relieving the promisor of liability for breaches caused by events "beyond his control." Although the Uniform Commercial Code has ostensibly eliminated the need for such clauses, lawyers, either through an abundance of caution or by force of habit, continue to write them into contract. See generally Squillante & Congalton, Force Majeure, 80 Com.L.J. 4, 8–9 (1975). Thus, even though our interpretation would render the general terms of the excusable delay clause merely duplicative of section 2–615, we will adhere to the established rule of construction because it continues to reflect prevailing commercial practices.

We reiterate, however, that we are applying only a canon of contract interpretation which generally reflects commercial standards of reasonableness. We disagree with the suggestion of one commentator that section 2–615 imposes a fixed standard governing the interpretation of exemption clauses. The Code establishes no absolute requirement that any agreement purporting to enlarge upon section 2–615 must do so in plain and specific language. Even in the absence of detailed wording, trade usage and the circumstances surrounding a particular agreement may indicate that the parties intended to accord the seller an exemption broader than is available under the U.C.C.[96]

While we hold that the provision of the excusable delay clause exempting McDonnell from liability for delays beyond its control should be interpreted as incorporating the Code's commercial impracticability doctrine, we disagree with the trial judge's jury instruction on foreseeability insofar as it implies that the events specifically listed in the excusable delay clause in each contract must have been unforeseeable at the time the agreement was executed. The rationale for the doctrine of impracticability is that the circumstance causing the breach has made performance so vitally different from what was anticipated that the contract cannot reasonably be thought to govern. 6 S. Williston, Contracts § 1963 at 5511 (rev. ed. 1938). However, because the purpose of a contract is to place the reasonable risk of performance on the promisor, he is presumed, in the absence of evidence to the contrary, to have agreed to bear any loss occasioned by an event which was foreseeable at the time of contracting. Underlying this presumption is the view that a promisor can protect himself against foreseeable events by means of an express provision in the agreement.

Intention of parties could no longer be performed.

---

96. As Comment 8 indicates, however, there is a point beyond which any such agreement may not go. Professor Hawkland suggests that the "minimum" established by section 2–615 includes the duty of the seller to allocate deliveries among his customers and to notify the buyer of any delivery delay or nondelivery. Hawkland, supra, at 79. One student commentator, though, appears to construe Comment 8 as limiting the degree to which a seller's protections under section 2–615 can be narrowed. Note, UCC § 2–615: Sharp Inflationary Increases in Cost as Excuse from Performance of Contract, 50 Notre Dame Law. 297, 300–301 (1974). In any event, exemption provisions are limited by those sections of the Code prohibiting agreements which are "manifestly unreasonable" [§ 1–102(3)], in bad faith [§ 1–203], or unconscionable [§ 2–302]. See Transatlantic Financing Corp. v. United States, 1966, 124 U.S.App. D.C. 183, 363 F.2d 312, 315 n. 3.

Therefore, when the promisor has anticipated a particular event by specifically providing for it in a contract, he should be relieved of liability for the occurrence of such event regardless of whether it was foreseeable. See Edward Maurer Co. v. Tubeless Tire Co., 6 Cir., 1922, 285 F. 713, 714–15. As Justice Traynor noted for the California Supreme Court under different but nonetheless analogous circumstances,

> the question whether a risk was foreseeable is quite distinct from the question whether it was contemplated by the parties. * * * When a risk has been contemplated and voluntarily assumed * * * foreseeability is not an issue and the parties will be held to the bargain they made.

In this case, it is clear that Eastern specifically "contemplated and voluntarily assumed" the risk that deliveries would be delayed by governmental acts, priorities, regulations or orders. Moreover, unlike the only case cited to us by Eastern which construes a similar provision, United States v. Brooks–Callaway Co., 318 U.S. 120, 63 S.Ct. 474, 87 L.Ed. 653 (1943), there is no indication from the wording of the excusable delay clause that McDonnell's defenses are to be limited to breaches caused by unforeseeable events. Therefore, we must conclude that the trial judge erred in instructing the jury that the events specifically listed in the excusable delay clause must have been unforeseeable at the time the contracts were entered into for McDonnell to claim exemption from liability.

3. Informal Demands for Priority as an "Act of Government"

Turning next to the question of whether the Government's informal priorities policy came within the ambit of the excusable delay clause, we have seen in Part IV–A of this opinion that McDonnell and its suppliers, in granting priority to the military, were cooperating with the established, publicly announced procurement policy of the Federal Government. Eastern contends, however, that this informal program did not come within the scope of the contract clause specifically excusing "any act of government, governmental priorities, allocations, or orders affecting materials." Asserting that the Defense Production Act authorizes the Government to obtain precedence for certain orders only by means of formal, published regulations, Eastern concludes that any other method is illegal, if not unconstitutional, and therefore cannot be deemed an act of Government. We disagree for the following reasons.

The Defense Production Act, in "a sweeping delegation of power," grants the President broad authority to require that defense-related contracts be given precedence over less essential orders. D.P.A. § 101(a), 50 App.U.S.C. § 2071(a). Congress created no detailed scheme by which this power was to be exercised, providing only that "[t]he President may make such rules, regulations, and orders as he deems necessary or appropriate." D.P.A. § 704, 50 App.U.S.C. § 2154. There is, moreover, nothing in either the legislative history of the D.P.A. or in the wording of the Act itself which gives any indication that the Government may not seek compliance with its priorities policies by informal means. It is reasonable to conclude, therefore, that Congress intended to accord the Executive Branch great flexibility in molding its priorities policies to the frequently unanticipated exigencies of national defense.

This conclusion is reinforced by the fact that the Defense Production Act of 1950 was enacted in the face of established legal authority which had consistently construed previous procurement statutes as authorizing informal and indirect methods of securing compliance with the Government's military priorities policy. It was recognized that, for reasons of practical necessity, urgently needed government orders had to be obtained "by non-mandatory directions based ultimately on the powers of compulsion rather than by the actual exercise of the statutory compulsive powers." Dodd, Impossibility of Performance of Contracts Due to War–Time Regulations, 32 Harv.L.Rev. 789, 798 (1919). The military's need for speed and flexibility in directing the flow of necessary materials precluded a ponderous bureaucratic procurement process. Thus, even though the World War I National Defense Act, 39 Stat. 213 (June 3, 1916), specifically provided that either the President or a department head placed priorities orders, several decisions held that literal compliance with this requirement was not necessary.

* * *

During World War II, a similarly liberal view was taken of the Government's procurement authority. * * *

There can be little question, then, that the Defense Production Act granted the Government authority to seek compliance with its priorities programs by informal means of persuasion whether written or oral. For this reason, many of the decisions relied on by Eastern are inapposite here. E.g. Northern Pacific Ry. v. American Trading Co., 195 U.S. 439, 25 S.Ct. 84, 49 L.Ed. 269 (1904).

We note, moreover, that this case precisely fits an established pattern of decisions rejecting the contention that breaches of contract are excused only by formal or technical acts of Government. Whether predicated on a contractual provision or simply on the common law defense of impossibility these decisions indicate in the clearest terms that fundamentally coercive acts of Government, whatever their form, constitute an excuse for breach. Thus, a promisor is not liable merely because the government order causing a breach is technically deficient. Texas Co. v. Hogarth Shipping Corp., 256 U.S. 619, 41 S.Ct. 612, 65 L.Ed. 1123 (1921). Neither is he required to resist a government requisition in order to be excused from performance. *The Claveresk,* 2 Cir., 1920, 264 F. 276. As the *Claveresk* court observed, "it would be 'a strange law' which required * * * [a promisor] to resist, 'til the hand of power was laid upon him, an order which it was his duty to obey'." 264 F. at 280–81. The Supreme Court, moreover, has excused breaches caused by a promisor's anticipation of government action. *The Kronprinzessin Cecilie,* 244 U.S. 12, 37 S.Ct. 490, 61 L.Ed. 960 (1917). Writing for the Court, Mr. Justice Holmes found the impossibility doctrine applicable to a ship which returned to port in expectation of World War I but before its actual declaration:

> [I]t hardly could change * * * [the ship owner's] liability that he prophetically and rightly had anticipated the * * * [war] by twenty-four hours. We are wholly unable to accept the argument that although a shipowner may give up his voyage to avoid capture after war is declared, he never is at liberty to anticipate war.

244 U.S. at 24, 37 S.Ct. at 492, 61 L.Ed. at 966. Thus, the "apprehension of restraint, something much less than actual government compulsion, may suffice to dissolve the obligation of a contract." *The Claveresk,* supra, 264 F. at 282.

Consequently, we will not permit the form of the military priorities policy to disguise what was in substance a governmental act beyond the control of McDonnell Douglas. The excusable delay clause cannot be made to turn on a distinction which for so long has been held to be entirely artificial and unrealistic. As Mr. Justice Holmes stated in a very similar context, "[b]usiness contracts must be construed with business sense, as they naturally would be understood by intelligent men of affairs." *The Kronprinzessin Cecilie,* supra, 244 U.S. at 24, 37 S.Ct. at 492, 61 L.Ed. at 966.

This approach, moreover, is consistent with that required under the Uniform Commercial Code. In Comment 10 to section 615, the draftsmen of Article 2 stated:

> Following its basic policy of using commercial practicability as a test for excuse, this section * * * disregards any technical distinctions between "law," "regulation," "order" and the like. Nor does it make the present action of the seller depend upon the eventual judicial determination of the legality of the particular governmental action. The seller's good faith belief in the validity of the regulation is the test under this Article and the best evidence of his good faith is the general commercial acceptance of the regulation.

Given McDonnell's unquestioned good faith in complying with the Government's demands for priority and the uncontroverted evidence of the entire aviation industry's acceptance of the policy, we must hold as a matter of law that McDonnell is not liable for any delivery delay proximately resulting from the informal procurement program.

* * *

Problems

1. S, a farmer, entered into a written agreement to sell to B 35,000 bushels of white corn. Due to a drought which struck S's farm, S was unable to produce sufficient corn to fulfill its contract. B sued S for damages for partial non-delivery. At the trial, S offered evidence that there was a contemporaneous oral agreement that the corn was to come from S's farm. Is this evidence admissible?

2.   D contracted to build a building for P on a certain piece of land according to plans prepared by D, annexed to, and made part of, the written contract. Twice in succession the building collapsed after it had been raised to the third floor due to presence of quicksand in the subsoil. D then refused to rebuild and P sued for damages. What result?

3.   Plaintiff contracted to repair a wooden bridge over the Connecticut River and had completed a goodly portion of the repairs when a fire totally destroyed the bridge as well as a large amount of lumber plaintiff had stored near the bridge for use in repairing the bridge. Plaintiff sues. For what, if anything, may plaintiff recover?

4.   Kelley, a mining engineer, was hired by Thompson to supervise the prospecting of coal on a large tract of land. It was agreed that he would be paid $125 per month. In addition, if the prospecting were successful and certain other conditions were met, Thompson agreed to form and manage a corporation to operate a coal mine at the site and to give Kelley a one-eighth interest in the corporation. Kelley located a rich vein of coal and the other conditions occurred. Thompson died before forming a corporation and his representative refused to carry out the promise to form a corporation and to give Kelley a one-eighth interest in it. Kelley sues. What result?

5.   In consideration of a right of way given by plaintiff to defendant, a railroad, the defendant agreed to give to the plaintiff annual passes during plaintiff's life. After about 10 years the Federal Government enacted a law that made it illegal for the defendant to issue any further annual passes. What are the rights of the parties?

6.   G & W, a large corporate conglomerate, sought to take over control of A & P by entering into contracts with plaintiff and others to purchase their holdings of A & P common stock. A & P obtained a preliminary injunction enjoining G & W from taking delivery of or paying for A & P common stock under such contracts on the grounds of alleged violations of the antitrust and securities laws. It is apparent that several years will elapse before it can be determined whether the allegations are sustained and whether the preliminary injunction will be dissolved or made permanent. G & W, in obedience to the court order, refused to perform its contract with plaintiff. Plaintiff sues for breach of contract. What result?

7.   Plaintiff contracted with the defendant for the sale and purchase of certain silk. By the terms of the agreement shipment was to be made by freight before March 4. Shipment was not made until March 12 because of an embargo placed by the Railroad Administration on shipments of silk by freight. What result?

8.   Defendant contracted to purchase specified quantities of corn from the plaintiff, a farmer. The corn was to be delivered at specified intervals from December to July. Various attempts to make deliveries were rebuffed on the truthful grounds that defendant's grain elevators were full and railroad boxcars were unavailable to ship grain out of the elevators. Plaintiff sold the grain elsewhere and sues for damages. What result?

9.   In May, 1950, D agreed to construct a group of small houses within 90 days under a fixed price contract. D began to perform at once but soon materials became unavailable because of the outbreak of the Korean War on

June 25, 1950. In consequence, the houses were not built within the agreed completion date. By February 1951, at which time the materials were again available but at inflated prices, it became evident that D could not overcome the difficulties besetting the project. The following month, P declared the contract in default and brought in another contractor who promptly completed the work but at a cost substantially in excess of the price that D had agreed to. What result in P's action against D?

10. D contracted to deliver to P fixed quantities of pulpwood over a fixed period of time from a particular tract at $5.50 per cord. Before any deliveries were called for under the contract all of the pulpwood on the tract was fortuitously destroyed by fire except the trees on top of a high mountain which could be cut and delivered only at an expense of $20 per cord. D refused to deliver this pulpwood. P sues for damages for failure to deliver pursuant to the terms of the contract. What result? Would the result be different if some of the pulpwood could and should have been delivered prior to the fire?

11. Gasco contracted to deliver to plaintiff all plaintiff's requirements of propane for a five year term up to a total maximum amount. Gasco has numerous other customers, but is not bound by contract to any of the other customers. During the energy crisis of 1973, there was a shortfall of propane available to Gasco. The circumstances were such that the shortfall was due to "a contingency the non-occurrence of which was a basic assumption on which the contract was made." Gasco has notified plaintiff that it would limit deliveries to a stated percentage of plaintiff's actual requirements. Plaintiff sues, contending truthfully that Gasco has adequate supplies to supply plaintiff's requirements. Plaintiff argues that the shortfall should be visited solely upon Gasco's non-contract customers. What result?

12. When a buyer is rightfully told by the seller that because of impracticability he will be shipped only 75% of the quantity of goods he has contracted to buy, must the buyer accept?

13. Plaintiff contracted to excavate certain rock estimated at 110 cubic yards. He was to be paid pursuant to a formula based on the actual amount of rock excavated as determined by the certificate of a registered surveyor. The plaintiff excavated and the surveyor made measurements of the excavation from time to time but because of the destruction of his records by fire the surveyor is unable to certify the quantities, but is able to estimate them. The defendant refuses to pay because of the absence of a certificate. What result?

SECTION 3. FRUSTRATION

KRELL v. HENRY

Court of Appeal, 1903.
[1903] 2 K.B. 740.

Appeal from a decision of DARLING J. The plaintiff, Paul Krell, sued the defendant, C.S. Henry, for 50£, being the balance of a sum of 75£, for which the defendant had agreed to hire a flat at 56A, Pall Mall on the days of June 26 and 27, for the purpose of viewing the processions to be held in connection with the coronation of His Majesty. The defendant denied his liability, and counterclaimed for the return of the sum of 25£, which had been paid as a deposit, on the ground that, the processions not having taken place owing to the serious illness of the King, there had been a total failure of consideration for the contract entered into by him.

The facts, which were not disputed, were as follows. The plaintiff on leaving the country in March, 1902, left instructions with his solicitor to let his suite of chambers at 56A, Pall Mall on such terms and for such period (not exceeding six months) as he thought proper. On June 17, 1902, the defendant noticed an announcement in the windows of the plaintiff's flat to the effect that windows to view the coronation processions were to be let. The defendant interviewed the housekeeper on the subject, when it was pointed out to him what a good view of the processions could be obtained from the premises, and he eventually agreed with the housekeeper to take the suite for the two days in question for a sum of 75£.

On June 20 the defendant wrote the following letter to the plaintiff's solicitor:—

"I am in receipt of yours of the 18th instant, inclosing form of agreement for the suite of chambers on the third floor at 56A, Pall Mall, which I have agreed to take for the two days, the 26th and 27th instant, for the sum of 75£. For reasons given you I cannot enter into the agreement, but as arranged over the telephone I inclose herewith cheque for 25£ as deposit, and will thank you to confirm to me that I shall have the entire use of these rooms during the days (not the nights) of the 26th and 27th instant. You may rely that every care will be taken of the premises and their contents. On the 24th inst. I will pay the balance, viz., 50£, to complete the 75£ agreed upon."

On the same day the defendant received the following reply from the plaintiff's solicitor:—

"I am in receipt of your letter of to-day's date inclosing cheque for 25£ deposit on your agreeing to take Mr. Krell's chambers on the third floor at 56A, Pall Mall for the two days, the 26th and 27th June, and I confirm the agreement that you are to have the entire use of these rooms during the days (but not the nights), the balance, 50£, to be paid to me on Tuesday next the 24th instant."

The processions not having taken place on the days originally appointed, namely, June 26 and 27, the defendant declined to pay the balance of 50£ alleged to be due from him under the contract in writing of June 20 constituted by the above two letters. Hence the present action.

DARLING J., on August 11, 1902, held, upon the authority of *Taylor* v. *Caldwell* and *The Moorcock*, that there was an implied condition in the contract that the procession should take place, and gave judgment for the defendant on the claim and counter-claim.

The plaintiff appealed.

* * *

VAUGHAN WILLIAMS L.J. read the following written judgment:—The real question in this case is the extent of the application in English law of the principle of the Roman law which has been adopted and acted on in many English decisions, and notably in the case of *Taylor* v. *Caldwell*. That case at least makes it clear that "where, from the nature of the contract, it appears that the parties must from the beginning have known that it could not be fulfilled unless, when the time for the fulfilment of the contract arrived, some particular specified thing continued to exist, so that when entering into the contract they must have contemplated such continued existence as the foundation of what was to be done; there, in the absence of any express or implied warranty that the thing shall exist, the contract is not to be considered a positive contract, but as subject to an implied condition that the parties shall be excused in case, before breach, performance becomes impossible from the perishing of the thing without default of the contractor." Thus far it is clear that the principle of the Roman law has been introduced into the English law. The doubt in the present case arises as to how far this principle extends. * * * I do not think that the principle of the civil law as introduced into the English law is limited to cases in which the event causing the impossibility of performance is the destruction or nonexistence of some thing which is the subject-matter of the contract or of some condition or state of things expressly specified as a condition of it. I think that you first have to ascertain, not necessarily from the terms of the contract, but, if required, from necessary inferences, drawn from surrounding circumstances recognised by both contracting parties, what is the substance of the contract, and then to ask the question whether that substantial contract needs for its foundation the assumption of the existence of a particular state of things. If it does, this will limit the operation of the general words, and in such case, if the contract becomes impossible of performance by reason of the nonexistence of the state of things assumed by both contracting parties as the foundation of the contract, there will be no breach of the contract thus limited.

Now what are the facts of the present case? The contract is contained in two letters of June 20 which passed between the defendant and the plaintiff's agent, Mr. Cecil Bisgood. These letters do not mention the coronation, but speak merely of the taking of Mr. Krell's chambers, or, rather, of the use of them, in the daytime of June 26 and 27, for the sum of 75£, 25£ then paid, balance 50£ to be paid on the 24th. But the affidavits, which by agreement between the parties are to be taken as stating the facts of the case, shew that the plaintiff exhibited on his premises, third floor, 56A, Pall Mall, an announcement to the effect that windows to view the Royal coronation procession were to be let, and that the defendant was induced by that announcement to apply to the housekeeper on the premises, who said that the owner was willing to let the suite of rooms for the purpose of seeing the Royal procession for both days, but not nights, of June 26 and 27. In my judgment the use of the rooms was let and taken for the purpose of seeing the Royal procession. It was not a demise of the rooms, or even an agreement to let and take the rooms. It is a licence to use rooms for a particular purpose and none other. And in my judgment the taking place of those processions on the days proclaimed along the proclaimed route, which passed 56A, Pall Mall, was regarded by both contracting parties as the foundation of the contract; and I think that it cannot reasonably be supposed to have been in the contemplation of the contracting parties, when the contract was made, that the coronation would not be held on the proclaimed days, or the processions not take place on those days along the proclaimed route; and I think that the words imposing on the defendant the obligation to accept and pay for the use of the rooms for the named days, although general and unconditional, were not used with reference to the possibility of the particular contingency which afterwards occurred.

It was suggested in the course of the argument that if the occurrence, on the proclaimed days, of the coronation and the procession in this case were the foundation of the contract, and if the general words are thereby limited or qualified, so that in the event of the non-occurrence of the coronation and procession along the proclaimed route they would discharge both parties from further performance of the contract, it would follow that if a cabman was engaged to take some one to Epsom on Derby Day at a suitable enhanced price for such a journey, say 10£, both parties to the contract would be discharged in the contingency of the race at Epsom for some reason becoming impossible; but I do not think this follows, for I do not think that in the cab case the happening of the race would be the foundation of the contract. No doubt the purpose of the engager would be to go to see the Derby, and the price would be proportionately high; but the cab had no special qualifications for the purpose which led to the selection of the cab for this particular occasion. Any other cab would have done as well. Moreover, I think that, under the cab contract, the hirer, even if the race went off, could have said, "Drive me to Epsom; I will pay you the agreed sum; you have nothing to do with the purpose for which I hired the cab," and that if the cabman refused he would have been guilty of a breach of contract, there being nothing to qualify his promise to drive the hirer to Epsom on a particular day. Whereas in the case of the coronation, there is not merely the purpose of the hirer to see the coronation procession, but it is the coronation procession and the relative position of the rooms which is the basis of the contract as much for the lessor as the hirer; and I think that if the King, before the coronation day and after the contract, had died, the hirer could not have insisted on having the rooms on the days named. It could not in the cab case be reasonably said that seeing the Derby race was the foundation of the contract, as it was of the licence in this case. Whereas in the present case, where the rooms were offered and taken, by reason of their peculiar suitability from the position of the rooms for a view of the coronation procession, surely the view of the coronation procession was the foundation of the contract, which is a very different thing from the purpose of the man who engaged the cab—namely, to see the race—being held to be the foundation of the contract. Each case must be judged by its own circumstances. In each case one must ask oneself, first, what, having regard to all the circumstances, was the foundation of the contract? Secondly, was the performance of the contract prevented? Thirdly, was the event which prevented the performance of the contract of such a character that it cannot reasonably be said to have been in the contemplation of the parties at the date of the contract? If all these questions are answered in the affirmative (as I think they should be in this case). I think both parties are discharged from further performance of the contract. I think that the coronation procession was the foundation of this contract, and that the non-happening of it prevented the performance of the contract; and, secondly, I think that the non-happening of the procession, to use the words of Sir James Hannen in *Baily* v. *De Crespigny*, was an event "of such a character that it cannot reasonably be supposed to have been in the contemplation of the contracting parties when the contract was made, and that they are not to be held bound by general words which, though large enough to include, were not used with reference to the possibility of the particular contingency which afterwards happened." The test seems to be whether the event which causes the impossibility was or might have been anticipated and guarded against. It seems difficult to say, in a case where both parties anticipate the happening of an event, which anticipation is the foundation of the contract, that either party must be taken to have anticipated, and ought to have guarded against, the event which prevented the performance of the contract. * * *

I myself am clearly of opinion that in this case, where we have to ask ourselves whether the object of the contract was frustrated by the non-happening of the coronation and its procession on the days proclaimed, parol evidence is admissible to shew that the subject of the contract was rooms to view the coronation procession, and was so to the knowledge of both parties. When once this is established, I see no difficulty whatever in the case. It is not essential to the application of the principle of *Taylor* v. *Caldwell* that the direct subject of the contract should perish or fail to be in existence at the date of performance of the contract. It is sufficient if a state of things or condition expressed in the contract and essential to its performance perishes or fails to be in existence at that time. In the present case the condition which fails and prevents the achievement of that which was, in the contemplation of both parties, the foundation of the contract, is not expressly mentioned either as a condition of the contract or the purpose of it; but I think for the reasons which I have given that the principle of *Taylor* v. *Caldwell* ought to be applied. This disposes of the plaintiff's claim for 50£ unpaid balance of the price agreed to be paid for the use of the rooms. The defendant at one time set up a cross-claim for the return of the 25£ he paid at the date of the contract. As that claim is now withdrawn it is unnecessary to say anything about it. * * *

AH–CHIN–LE, SOME OBSERVATIONS UPON THE CIVILIZATION OF THE WESTERN BARBARIANS, 1876

Of these Civic Spectacles, a *Coronation* is supreme. This only takes place when a new Sovereign is crowned. No one is admitted to the actual

Ceremony but the highest of the High–Castes. The common people, who bear nearly all the taxes to pay for the enormous cost, must be content to get such glimpses of the passing pageant, as is possible to them, at the risk of limb and of life. The whole thing is so guarded by armed bands on horseback and on foot, with fire-arms ready, and swords drawn, that it is only by rushing close to the horsemen, and pressing upon the foot-braves, that any glimpse can be got by the common multitude; and for these mere glances—under the bellies of horses, or between their legs, or through some iron railings, or the like—the devoted barbarians will risk their lives.

WESTERN PROPERTIES v. SOUTHERN UTAH AVIATION, INC.

Court of Appeals of Utah, 1989.
776 P.2d 656.

DEAN E. CONDER, JUDGE: The trial court granted partial summary judgment in this case, awarding plaintiff Western Properties rent accrued to June 27, 1986, from which the defendants appeal. Western Properties appeals from the final judgment dismissing its claims for additional rent and for breach of a lease covenant regarding construction of a building. We affirm both the partial summary judgment and the final judgment.

Western Properties leased from Cedar City certain vacant land at the Cedar City Airport. Western Properties in turn subleased part of the land to the defendants for a 15–year term beginning March 6, 1985, with a covenant that the defendants "shall construct on the premises a maintenance building," which, upon termination of the sublease, was to have become property of Western Properties. In July of 1985, Cedar City approved the sublease in an addendum to it.

The defendants thereafter applied to Cedar City for site plan approval for the maintenance building, but as of the time of trial had not obtained such approval from Cedar City. Cedar City had also not approved a master plan for the airport as a whole. The defendants defaulted in payment of rent and abandoned the subleased land on June 27, 1986, without ever constructing a maintenance building on the land.

Western Properties sued for unpaid rent and the value of the maintenance building that it was to have received following the 15–year term of the sublease. The trial court granted partial summary judgment and awarded rent accrued to the date of abandonment, but reserved issues of further damages. Later, following trial, the trial court dismissed Western Properties' claims for further rent and for the residual income value of the maintenance building, and from that dismissal Western Properties appeals. The defendants have cross-appealed from the earlier summary judgment, arguing that a factual question concerning the intention of an individual defendant to be bound by the sublease precluded summary judgment. [The court concluded that the individual defendant was bound by the sublease through his signature "regardless of whether he read or understood the full import of what he signed." Ed.]

* * *

Impossibility and Frustration

The trial court based its post-trial judgment on grounds of impossibility. Under the contractual defense of impossibility, an obligation is deemed discharged if an unforeseen event occurs after formation of the contract and without fault of the obligated party, which event makes performance of the obligation impossible or highly impracticable. The rationale for this rule is founded on principles of assent and basic equity. Parties are ordinarily thought to have made certain assumptions in visualizing their agreement, and those assumptions comprise part of the basis and extent of their assent. The impossibility defense serves to prevent enforcement where those assumptions, and hence, the parties assent, prove to be faulty.

Rule

In this case, the parties appear to have tacitly assumed that the City would cooperate in the development of the leased land. The lease makes no provision for the prospect that the City would not approve the development. In the absence of any contractual allocation of the risk of the City's non-cooperation, the failure of the City to approve development of the land is an eventuality sufficiently unforeseen[5] for application of the impossibility defense.

The other facts required for application of the impossibility defense appear to have been sufficiently established at trial. The district court found that the defendants "could not build the maintenance building without city approval and the city did not ever give its approval." There appears to be no factual basis for implicating the defendants in the failure of the City to approve, and the defendants seem to have made every effort that could reasonably be required in order to induce the City to give its approval. In the absence of facts which could indicate fault or a lack of diligence on the part of the defendants, we rely on the trial court's findings in concluding that performance of the defendants' obligations was indeed impossible through no fault of their own. We therefore treat the obligation to construct the maintenance building as discharged from the time when performance of their obligations became impossible.

Construction of the promised building was impossible, but occupancy of the land pursuant to the lease was not necessarily precluded by the inability to construct the building. The land was, however, wholly

---

5. We recognize that the City's failure to approve seems, from our present perspective, to be rather easy to foresee. However, the critical fact is not whether the event could have been foreseen, but rather, whether the parties actually did foresee it and provide accordingly in their contract. A dictum in one Utah case on impossibility employs the word "unforeseeable" in describing the event causing impossibility, Holmgren v. Utah–Idaho Sugar Co., 582 P.2d at 861 (Utah 1978); however, the better and more widely accepted rule looks not to whether the parties could or should have foreseen the event, but rather whether, as a fact of assent, they did foresee it. Restatement (Second) of Contracts § 261 & comment b (1981).

undeveloped and uncultivated. Without a way of productively using the land, the purpose of the leasehold was effectively frustrated. Frustration of purpose differs from the defense of impossibility only in that performance of the promise, rather than being impossible or impracticable, is instead pointless. There was no point in leasing this land once its development became impossible. The covenant to pay rent is therefore also discharged, effective as of June 27, 1986.

The judgment is affirmed.

407 EAST 61ST GARAGE, INC. v. SAVOY FIFTH AVENUE CORP.

Court of Appeals of New York, 1968.
23 N.Y.2d 275, 296 N.Y.S.2d 338, 244 N.E.2d 37.

BREITEL, JUDGE. Plaintiff 407 East 61st Garage, Inc., appeals from an order of the Appellate Division unanimously affirming, without opinion, an order of the Supreme Court, New York County. The Supreme Court, in an opinion, denied plaintiff's motion for an order striking defendant's answer, granting summary judgment, and directing an assessment of damages, and instead granted the cross motion of defendant Savoy Fifth Avenue Corporation for summary judgment.

Plaintiff garage seeks damages for defendant Savoy's alleged breach, by termination, of a contract between the parties, resulting from Savoy's discontinuance of its operation of the Savoy Hilton Hotel. Under a written agreement the garage had undertaken to furnish garage services for a period of five years to guests of the Savoy Hilton and to pay Savoy 10% of its gross transient storage charges to the hotel guests. Savoy agreed to use all reasonable efforts to provide the garage with exclusive opportunity for storage of the motor vehicles of the hotel guests.

The issue is whether the closing of the hotel prior to the expiration of the contract period, due to the asserted financial inability of Savoy to remain in the hotel business, subjects it to continued liability under the contract. The Supreme Court, characterizing the agreement as a requirements contract, held that, absent an express contract provision requiring Savoy to remain in the hotel business, and absent allegations of bad faith, Savoy is not liable for anticipatory breach of contract.

It is concluded that, by ceasing operation of its hotel, Savoy is not excused, as a matter of law, from obligations under its agreement with the garage, and that there is, at least, an issue of fact as to implied conditions in the agreement.

Pursuant to the written agreement, dated October 1, 1963, plaintiff garage undertook to furnish adequate garage services and facilities to any guests of the Savoy Hilton Hotel who requested them. The garage was fully responsible for the billing and collection of charges for its services. Any damage to an automobile between its delivery to a representative of the garage and its return was the responsibility of the garage. The garage also agreed to have adequate supplies on hand, to obtain all necessary insurance and permits, to conform to applicable regulations of the Savoy, and to have its employees act in such a manner as to "promote the best interests" of Savoy. Savoy on its part agreed "to use all reasonable efforts to enable [the garage] to have, throughout the term of this agreement, the exclusive right and privilege of storing the motor vehicles of [the hotel's] guests, tenants and patrons". Savoy was not responsible, however, for any charges incurred by its guests for services rendered by the garage. The garage was allowed to maintain, at its own expense, a direct telephone line between the hotel and the garage. In exchange, the garage agreed to pay to Savoy 10% of the transient storage charges incurred by hotel guests. The term of the agreement was from October 1, 1963 to September 30, 1968.

In late June, 1965, due to substantial financial losses, Savoy ceased operating the hotel. The hotel building was demolished and an office building erected on its site. The garage asserts that a one-half interest in the property was sold to General Motors Corporation, and that the office building is owned jointly by General Motors and Savoy. Savoy apparently claims that it sold 50% of its capital stock to General Motors.

The agreement does not explicitly obligate Savoy to remain in the hotel business during the contract term or, put another way, to fulfill its obligations for the term even if it should wish to cease operation of a hotel. On the other hand, the only provision concerning termination allows Savoy to terminate the contract should the garage default in the performance of any condition, including the provision of adequate service, and then fail to cure the default within 30 days after receiving written notice. It was provided further that all duties of each of the parties were to be performed "during the term" of the contract.

The Supreme Court, in granting defendant Savoy's cross motion for summary judgment, relied on Du Boff v. Matam Corp., 272 App.Div. 502, 71 N.Y.S.2d 134, which held that a party to a "requirements" contract may cease doing business in good faith without incurring liability for breach of contract. However, the agreement between the garage and Savoy is not a "requirements" contract, but is akin to the grant of a license or franchise by Savoy to the garage. Thus, services were to be rendered by the garage not to Savoy but to third parties, that is, the guests of the hotel. Savoy did not undertake to compensate the garage, but was instead to be compensated by the garage for the exclusive opportunities granted. The garage benefited by gaining a preferred position in obtaining the hotel guests as customers for its services. The hotel benefited by receiving a guarantee that its guests would be able to obtain adequate garage services when and if they desired them, thus making their stay at the hotel more convenient and desirable.

Categorization of the agreement, whether as a "requirements" contract, a "license" or a "franchise", in order to determine the obligations of the parties, is only partially helpful. Under the "requirements" contract analysis used by the Supreme Court, it would seem that, absent an allegation of bad faith, there was no cause of action stated for breach of contract (see, e.g., Du Boff v. Matam Corp., supra; but see, contra, Wells v. Alexandre, 130 N.Y. 642, 645–646, 29 N.E. 142,

143, 15 L.R.A. 218). Analogically, in the context of agreements for the use of space, if the contract is considered a license or concession, the general rule is that revocation of a license granted for a stipulated term may be a breach of contract and may result in the imposition of liability for damages. Thus, if the garage had been granted a license to operate its enterprise on Savoy's premises, liability might persist after sale of the building.

Additionally, if the contract is construed as one granting an exclusive agency for the rendition of services, then again, Savoy, by ceasing operation of the business to which the services were incident, may be liable for breach of contract. * * *

In ultimate analysis, however, an attempt to categorize or "pigeonhole" the contract is a circuitous way of answering what is basically a simple question of contract interpretation or construction. The real issue in this case is not what kind of contractual relationship is involved, but whether this agreement imports an implication that Savoy was obligated to remain in the hotel business, or, better, had undertaken indefeasible obligations for the full term.

Under familiar rules a promise that a party will continue to remain in business may be implied in fact as part of an agreement for the rendition of services to a business. * * *

Such a promise to remain in business will be implied particularly where the promisee has undertaken certain burdens or obligations in expectation of and reliance upon the promisor's continued activity (Wigand v. Bachmann–Bechtel Brewing Co., 222 N.Y. 272, 118 N.E. 618). Here, the garage may have undertaken certain additional continuing responsibilities, such as the obtaining of adequate insurance and perhaps even the signing of employment contracts and agreements for the purchase of supplies for the lifetime of the contract.

Savoy, based on inferences, contends that the garage was aware, prior to the signing of the agreement, that the hotel was in financial difficulty, and should be charged with acceptance of the likelihood that the hotel would close. Savoy, of course, was at least equally or better aware of this situation. The obvious solution would have been an express provision that the agreement would terminate upon specified notice to the garage or would terminate if the hotel should close. Yet, the only right of termination by Savoy expressed in the agreement was based upon default in performance by the garage. Certainly the inference by Savoy that the garage knew of the hotel's financial difficulties does not give rise, as a matter of law, to the conclusion that the contract implies a conditional termination, should the hotel cease operation. It could be just as easily concluded that such a provision was intentionally omitted and that otherwise the garage would not have entered into the agreement.

There is another inchoate issue raised by Savoy's argument. It emphasizes, as it well might, the incongruity of an enterprise, as large as a metropolitan hotel, being obligated to "continue in the hotel business" merely because of various relatively minor incidental service contracts, such as that involved here. The mere incongruity would not lessen

Savoy's liability, but it does suggest that there may be a custom or usage in this industry to regard incidental service contracts for a period terminable on the hotel's going out of business. If there be such custom and usage, there is nothing in the record to show it. Upon a trial, of course, the hotel would be able to show such a custom and usage, or any other circumstances which would, subject to the parol evidence rule, establish the correct interpretation or understanding of the agreement as to its term. Certainly, the mere statement of a term in this kind of incidental service agreement is not so free from ambiguity to preclude extrinsic evidence.

At the very least, therefore, an issue of fact is presented whether the agreement did import an implied promise by Savoy to fulfill its obligations for an entire five-year period.

Assuming such an implication, Savoy might, nevertheless, assert the hotel's financial situation as a legal excuse for its failure to continue operation of the hotel. It does point out that it was economically impossible (or rather extremely burdensome) for it to remain in the hotel business. Thus, it may be argued that the basic purpose of the contract, to insure that guests of the hotel would receive adequate garage services, was rendered impossible of performance, or, perhaps, was frustrated, when the hotel was no longer in a financial position to cater to guests. Phrased in these terms, the issue is sometimes regarded as a matter of excuse from performance, apart from the contract, rather than being treated as an implied condition for performance derived from the contractual arrangements between the parties.

Generally, however, the excuse of impossibility of performance is limited to the destruction of the means of performance by an act of God, *vis major,* or by law. Thus, where impossibility or difficulty of performance is occasioned only by financial difficulty or economic hardship, even to the extent of insolvency or bankruptcy, performance of a contract is not excused. Notably, in this case, Savoy does not even assert that bankruptcy or insolvency was a likely consequence of continuing operation of the hotel. Further, in view of its admittedly contemporaneous financial difficulties, Savoy could and should have insisted that the agreement provide for the anticipated contingency of economic hardship (cf. Restatement, Contracts, § 457). In sum, performance by Savoy was at all times possible, although unprofitable, since the hotel could simply have remained in business, and the legal excuse of impossibility of performance would not be available to it.

Cases involving frustration of the purpose of the contract are inapposite. Here, the purpose of providing garage services to hotel guests was frustrated only when Savoy itself made a business decision to close the hotel, and did not result from unanticipated circumstances. * * *

In short, the applicable rules do not permit a party to abrogate a contract, unilaterally, merely upon a showing that it would be financially disadvantageous to perform it; were the rules otherwise, they would place in jeopardy all commercial contracts. If, in fact, the agreement expresses or implies a promise that the hotel would remain liable for the contract term, that promise should be honored, regardless of financial hardship.

Concededly, it would not have made sense for Savoy to stay in the hotel business solely to avoid liability for breach of its contract with the garage. Such lack of business reason does not nullify the liability for damages, whatever effect it may have on a right to specific performance. However, if the patronage at the hotel had declined, proof of that situation, although perhaps not justifying termination of the garage's contract right, may have a significant bearing on the measure of damages sustained by the garage through loss of future profits. * * *

Accordingly, the order should be modified, with costs, by denying defendant's cross motion for summary judgment and, as so modified, affirmed.

Problems

14. At time of contracting, no one could operate a limousine service in the City of New York without entering into a franchising agreement. The City granted defendant a ten-year franchise by a contract that provided for the payment of annual fees. The contract also contained a holdover provision to the effect that if the defendant continued to operate a limousine service after the expiration of the contract, it would continue to pay fees in accordance with the contract schedule. During the term of the contract, the state legislature repealed the law that had given the City a veto power over limousine services, and the operator of a limousine service no longer needed a franchise. Defendant duly paid franchise fees for the ten-year term of the contract, but, despite the holdover provision, it refused to pay additional fees after the ten-year term. The City sought an injunction barring the defendant's operation and also sought compensation for the holdover period. What result?

15. Lessees desired to open a federal savings and loan association which required a charter from the Federal Home Loan Bank Board. This federal agency required that the premises used be under lease and approved prior to the issuing of a charter. This requirement was known to both parties. The parties executed a five-year lease which provided that the leased premises were to be used exclusively as office space for a federal savings and loan association. Prior to the execution of the lease the proposed site was inspected by a representative of the federal agency who unofficially assured Lessees that the site would be approved. After the execution of the lease the federal agency refused to issue the charter. Lessee paid rent on the unoccupied premises for three months and refused to make further payments. Lessor sues Lessee for breach of contract. What result?

16. Mr. & Mrs. Hester, now deceased, pledged $25,000 to Cotter College, "in consideration of our interest in Christian education." The pledge was to be used to endow a scholarship for two students to be selected by the President of Cotter College and the Head of the Sacred Literature Department. Before the pledge was paid, the College ran into financial difficulties. To stay afloat, it ended all educational programs except for its

Department of Agriculture. The executor of the Mr. Hester's estate resists payment. Does the estate have a good defense?

17. Plaintiff signed an arbitration agreement with his employer. It provided: "The Arbitrator shall be selected as follows. The AAA shall give each party a list of 11 arbitrators drawn from its panel of labor-management dispute arbitrators. Each party may strike all names on the list it deems unacceptable. If only one common name remains on the list of all parties, that individual shall be designated as the Arbitrator. If more than one common name remains on the lists of all parties, the parties shall strike names alternatively until only one remains. The party who did not initiate the claim shall strike first. If no common name remains on the list of all parties, the AAA shall furnish an additional list or lists until the Arbitrator is selected."

When both parties found the list (of ten, not 11) arbitrators all unacceptable, the AAA followed its own procedures and appointed an arbitrator without submission of an additional list. Because of the discrepancy between the parties agreement and the action of the AAA, the employee brought suit against the employer in federal court. The district court held the arbitration agreement to be void and ordered a stay of the arbitration. On appeal, construct an argument for a reversal, taking into consideration that the court has jurisdiction over the parties and the AAA.

18. Lessor leased certain vending machines to defendant for a five-year term for use in defendant's bowling alley. Approximately one year later the lessee repudiated the contract. Approximately two years later the bowling alley was totally destroyed by fire and was not rebuilt. Lessor seeks damages from the date of the repudiation to the date of the contract's expiration. Defendant contends damages should be calculated from the date of the repudiation to the date of the fire. Which contention is sound?

SECTION 4. IMPRACTICABILITY

POLLARD v. SHAAFFER

Supreme Court of Pennsylvania, 1787.
1 U.S. (1 Dall.) 210, 1 L.Ed. 104, 1 Am.Dec. 239.

Covenant. The Plaintiff, and one Martha Green (now deceased) made a lease by indenture, dated the 1st of March 1773, of a Sugar House &c. to John William Hoffman and his assigns for five years at £ 70 per ann. payable quarterly. The Lessee covenanted for himself, his executors, administrators, and assigns, to keep the demised premises in good repair, and to deliver them up to the Plaintiff, at the end of the term, in such good repair &c. John William Hoffman assigned the lease to the Defendant, who entered into the premises. The breach alledged in this action was, that the Defendant had not paid £ 35. rent in arrear for the last half year, nor delivered up the premises at the end of the term, to wit, the 1st of March 1778, in good order and repair; but that the roof, window-shutters, floors &c. of the Sugar house were in decay, destroyed &c.

The Defendant pleaded performance of covenants, payment, and that an alien enemy, to wit, the British army, commanded by general, Sir William Howe, on the 1st of September 1777, had invaded the city of Philadelphia, had take possession of the premises, and held the same until the end of the term, and afterwards; and that during the period they held possession, they had committed the waste and destruction &c.

To the last plea, the Plaintiff demurred generally; the Defendant joined in demurrer, and issue &c. * * *

M'Kean, Chief Justice. Two questions were made in this cause: 1st, Whether the Defendant as assignee of the lease, is bound by the covenant to repair, as well as the lessee? And 2ndly, Whether the special matter pleaded, is sufficient in law to bar the Plaintiff? [It was held that the assignee was bound by the covenant to repair. Ed.]

The second question is of great difficulty, and of very great importance in its consequence. We cannot find, that it has come directly before any court in England, or in Europe. We wish, that it had come before abler judges than we pretend to be. However, we must give *our* judgment; but we do it with more diffidence than has occurred in any case since we have had the honor to sit here.

As there is no positive law, no adjudged case, nor established rule, or order, to direct the court in this point, we must be guided by the principles of the law; by conscience, that infallible monitor within every judge's breast, and the original and eternal rules of justice. For, equity is part of the law of Pennsylvania. [Citations omitted.]

It is agreed, that if a house be destroyed by lightning, floods, tempests, or enemies, without any concurrence of the lessee, or possibility of his preventing the same, this is no waste in the lessee: For, it is not done by the lessee's negligence, or any wilful act of his; and he cannot be charged with using it improperly, and it would thus have perished, even in the reversioner's possession. * * *

It is also agreed, that where the *law* creates a duty or charge, and the party is disabled to perform it without any default in him, and hath no remedy over, there he shall be excused. * * *

But, it is contended for the Plaintiff, that the Defendant is obliged to pay the rent, and yield up the tenements in good order and repair, because of the *express* covenant. [Citations omitted.]

On the part of the Defendant, it is insisted, that the express covenant in this case does not bind against acts of God or Enemies, but only against all other events; because such acts were not in the contemplation of either party at the time of the lease executed. A risque known and insured ought to be complied with, agreeably to the bargain, but not otherwise. Every contract ought to be construed according to the intention of the parties; and, in the present case, the Defendant had only covenanted to keep the premises in repair &c. against ordinary accidents, and not against a case, which he could by no possibility prevent.

That if the law were otherwise, yet in England relief would be had in a court of chancery; and that as no such action had ever been brought, in a case circumstanced as this is, an argument is furnished, that no such action will lie. [Citations omitted.]

* * *

If a lessor covenants that the lessee shall quietly enjoy against all men, yet in case he is ousted by an Enemy * * * no action of covenant can be maintained against the lessor, notwithstanding the express general covenant. For the enemy he could not oppose * * *. Vaughan 119. & c. This the counsel for the Plaintiff agree to be the law. Why then should the law make the lessee answerable on such a general express covenant to surrender the demised premises in good repair, when they were destroyed by an hostile army? Ought not the two covenants to receive the like favorable and reasonable construction? 'Remedies are to be reciprocal.' 'When the construction of any thing is left to the law, the law, which abhorreth injury and wrong, will never so construe it, as it shall work a wrong.' [Citation omitted.]

To conclude: Our opinion is that the Defendant ought to pay the rent. [This holding was in large part based on the precedent of Paradine v. Jane, supra. Ed.]

But, I am of opinion, that the Defendant is excused from his covenant to deliver up the premises in good repair on the 1st of March 1778; 1st, Because a covenant to do this, against an act of God or an enemy, ought to be special and express, and so clear that no other meaning could be put upon it. 2ndly, Because the Defendant had no consideration, no premium for this risque, and it was not in the contemplation of either party. And, lastly, because equality is equity, and the loss should be divided; he who had the term will loose the temporary profits of the premises, and he, who hath the reversion, will bear the loss done to the permanent buildings. Neither party has been guilty of any default; the injury has been done by a common enemy, whom both together could not possibly resist or prevent, and the premises would have been thus damnified in the possession of the Plaintiff himself. Suppose, when the lease was executed, that the lessee had been asked, Is it your meaning, that, in case the buildings shall be destroyed by an act of God, or public enemies, you are to rebuild or repair them? His answer would have been unquestionably, 'No; I never entertained such an idea.' Should the like question have been put to the lessor, his answer would certainly have been, 'No, I do not expect any thing so unreasonable.'

If there is no case in point in favor of this determination, there is none against it; and since no action of this kind has hitherto been brought, a presumption arises, that the sense of mankind is against it.

TURNER ENTERTAINMENT CO.
v. DEGETO FILM GmbH

United States Court of Appeals, Eleventh Circuit, 1994.
25 F.3d 1512.

ANDERSON, CIRCUIT JUDGE: This is an appeal of (1) the district court's grant of a preliminary injunction to plaintiff-appellee Turner Entertainment Co. ("Turner"), preventing defendants-appellants from broadcasting certain licensed works over the ASTRA satellites, and (2) the district court's denial of appellants' motion to dismiss or stay the American litigation in light of parallel proceedings under way in Germany. In the intervening period between the grant of the preliminary injunction and argument on this appeal, a judgment on the merits was rendered in the action in Germany. The German court found that the appellants should be able to broadcast via ASTRA for an increased fee to be determined at a later date. In light of this foreign judgment, we must decide whether to defer to the German court's judgment and dismiss or stay this action, or to ignore the German decision and continue essentially parallel proceedings. We hold that the preliminary injunction should be vacated, and that a stay of the American litigation is warranted.

I. FACTS AND PROCEEDINGS BELOW

This case involves a dispute over the interpretation of a License Agreement (the "Agreement") between the parties. The Agreement licensed certain entertainment properties to the appellants for television broadcast to the German population. Rapid changes in geopolitics and television technology since the inception of the Agreement led to the instant dispute over the limits of the contract.

A. The Parties

Defendant Degeto Film GmbH ("Degeto") is the exclusive agent for the other defendants. The remaining defendants are German public broadcasters; each serves one of the German political states (the "Lander"). Together the broadcasters, along with three other companies not a party to the American litigation, form a cooperative * * * collectively referred to in this opinion as ARD. ARD is supported by mandatory royalty fees and is obligated by German law to provide programming to the entire German population.

Although Degeto signed the Agreement with MGM/UA in 1984, Turner acquired the rights, through a series of transactions in the 1980's, to a substantial majority of the MGM/UA licensed properties covered by the Agreement. Thus, Turner purchased the rights and obligations under the Agreement as it pertains to those properties, and now stands in the shoes originally filled by MGM/UA.

B. The Agreement

ARD paid at least $60 million for an exclusive license to telecast the licensed works, under German copyright, to the German-speaking public, only in the German language. The licensed works include many old MGM movies, television series and cartoons. The Agreement expressly allows ARD to telecast the licensed works for reception within the licensed territory "by all means and methods now or hereafter known including but not limited to ... DBS [direct broadcasting satellite] and/or communication satellite for purposes of so-called home television reception," so long as the works are broadcast in German. The licensed territory comprises virtually all of German-speaking Europe—the German Democratic Republic, the Federal Republic of Germany, German-speaking Switzerland, Austria, South Tyrol (a region in Italy), Liechtenstein and Luxembourg.

The Agreement states that the telecasts can originate in any place in the universe, but only for reception within the territory. Because the reception area, or "footprint," of satellite broadcasts does not easily conform to the political and cultural boundaries that comprise the licensed territory, the parties included an exception to the strict definition in the contract of the licensed territory. Thus, the contract states that "[t]he telecast can originate any place in the universe for reception only in the Territory as defined ... below (inclusive of legitimate overspill as set forth in Paragraph 2(f) below)." The meaning of the term "overspill" generally, its applicability to ARD and/or ASTRA broadcasts, and the result that should obtain based on such determinations, has been a hotly contested issue in the litigation. Despite the importance of the term to the contract, no clear explanation of the meaning and scope of overspill exists in the contract. Paragraph 2(f) contains only a contextual definition of overspill and states in relevant part:

> Licensees acknowledge that broadcasts by satellite or otherwise in any language originating outside of the Territory might be received by television sets inside the Territory and that such reception shall not be deemed a breach hereof by MGM/UA. Further, notwithstanding the foregoing, if the overspill into the Territory is a result of compliance by MGM/UA's licensees with international conventions or treaties, including but not limited to the 1977 Geneva Convention, binding upon that licensee's territory, the licensee shall not be deemed to be in breach of its agreement with MGM/UA. In the event of illegitimate overspill into the Territory, Degeto shall notify MGM/UA and MGM/UA shall notify the entity whose signal is encroaching into the Territory to cease and desist from such encroaching activity.... MGM/UA shall provide in its own future standard license agreements that MGM/UA's licensees are prohibited from directing their signal into the Territory and from allowing their signal unintentionally to encroach into the Territory (except as to legitimate overspill as set forth above)....

Nothing more exists in the Agreement to define overspill.

* * *

C. Technological and Geopolitical Changes Since the Agreement's Inception

ARD began broadcasting licensed works from Germany, in German, via the ASTRA 1B satellite in April of 1991. ARD maintains that it chose the ASTRA 1B satellite as a means of telecasting programming because (1) a substantial part of the former East German households, absorbed into the Federal Republic of Germany since the Agreement was drafted, can only receive television programming via satellite, apparently because of its poor communications infrastructure; and (2) there were no other satellites that Defendants could effectively use to reach the German-speaking television audience, which ARD is obligated to do by German law, because satellite dishes designed to receive the ASTRA signal are more common in Germany.

The ASTRA 1B is an FSS satellite, which means that it operates in the "fixed satellite service." Although the footprint of a DBS satellite could be as large as that of the ASTRA 1B, there are significant differences between the two satellites such that television reception of ASTRA 1B covers a much larger area. Relatively new technological developments have increased the sensitivity of common home satellite dish antennae and receivers, enabling FSS satellite signals to be received by anyone with a satellite dish in the satellite's service area. In contrast, DBS satellites require expensive decoding equipment that prohibit the common viewer from receiving its signals. Thus, the FSS satellite has revolutionized European television by allowing broadcasters to easily send their signal directly to viewers who own relatively inexpensive satellite reception dishes. Apparently, the home satellite dish is a more popular mode of television reception in Europe, compared to cable television, than in the U.S. The ASTRA 1B has a footprint over five times the size of the licensed territory; the footprint encompasses most of Europe. ASTRA 1B, therefore, is a prime vehicle for reaching a large European television audience. The Agreement's drafters failed to anticipate that such an easy method of reaching a pan-European audience would become a standard mode of broadcasting during the life of the Agreement.

D. The Dispute—Proceedings in Germany and Atlanta

In March 1993, Turner learned that ARD intended to broadcast its major program, "Das Erste," a program which apparently incorporates the use of licensed works, over ASTRA 1B in August 1993. Turner stated its opinion that transmitting licensed works via ASTRA violates the Agreement. After a flurry of communication between the parties, in which Turner attempted to prevent broadcasts via ASTRA and ARD refused Turner's requests, actions were filed by the parties within a week of each other in Germany and the United States. The German and American lawsuits proceeded concurrently.

1. The German proceedings.

The appellants filed a declaratory judgment action against Turner in Germany, on April 29, 1993, seeking judicial support for their interpretation that the Agreement permitted the use of ASTRA 1B. The German action was filed in a German court of first consideration, the Landgericht Frankfurt am Main.

One of the key issues in the litigation concerned the term "overspill," namely, whether (1) overspill applied to the reception of ARD broadcasts outside the licensed territory, (2) whether overspill applied to FSS satellites so that the ASTRA footprint created overspill, and (3) if overspill did apply to the use of ASTRA, whether the overspill of ASTRA's signal was legitimate. The appellants maintained that the oversized footprint of ASTRA 1B comports with the Agreement because overspill as defined in the Agreement applies reciprocally to licensee and licensor, and that the overspill of ASTRA 1B is legitimate because (1) the broadcasts are in German and the licensed territory encompasses all viable markets for German television, rendering the overspill of German-language programming harmless, and (2) ARD receives no profit from the broadcasts.

The appellants made an alternative argument in the German court that the term overspill as used in the Agreement contemplated neither the new technology of FSS satellites nor the necessity of using them in order to obey the legal mandate that ARD reach the entire German population, and therefore that a gap exists in the contract. Appellants invited the German court to fill the gap in the contract, using the German doctrine of supplemental interpretation, by allowing ARD to broadcast Turner-licensed works via ASTRA, or alternatively to allow the broadcasts on ASTRA subject to the payment of an increased fee.

Turner argued that the Agreement's proviso allowing overspill did not apply reciprocally to licensee and licensor. Therefore, according to Turner's interpretation of the Agreement, Turner and its licensees outside Germany can overspill into the licensed territory, but ARD is strictly limited to broadcasting within the territory, and cannot overspill outside the licensed territory. Turner also made an alternative argument to the German court that a gap in the contract existed concerning the present state of affairs in European television; however, contrary to the appellants' proposal, Turner invited the German court to fill the gap by disallowing the use of ASTRA 1B.

The German court heard argument on the merits of the declaratory judgment action in Germany, and rendered a judgment on the merits on November 25, 1993. The German court held that because of its extensive range, ARD had no absolute right under the Agreement to broadcast via ASTRA. However, the court found that the parties had not contemplated the current circumstances involving the new technology and the fact that ARD was compelled as a practical matter to broadcast outside the licensed territory in order to fulfill its legal obligation to bring its telecasts to the German public. Given this gap in the operation of the contract, the German court determined that it was bound to apply the doctrine of good faith dealing to the situation. Id. at 25. The court attempted a supplemental interpretation of the contract to determine a result that parties bargaining in good faith would have negotiated.

The German court determined that Turner should permit ARD to use the satellite in order to properly fulfill its legal obligations. However, the court determined that ARD would have to pay an increased fee for the privilege, to be determined by that court at a later date. The German court relied on several factors in making this decision. The court noted that Turner had not envisioned concretely any additional licensing of German-language programming outside the licensed territory. Also, the court noted that the licensed territory covers such a large proportion of the German-speaking public that, in its opinion, no significant economic interest of Turner was obliterated by ASTRA. More importantly, the court emphasized (1) the wide distribution of ASTRA reception equipment in the license territory, making ASTRA the best method for reaching a wide audience, and (2) the statutory mandate for ARD to reach the German public; and determined that the just result was the payment of increased fees in exchange for the privilege of broadcasting via ASTRA. Both parties have appealed the German decision, and Turner obtained a delay in the fee hearings pending the German appeal.

2. The Atlanta Proceedings.

Turner filed the instant breach of contract action approximately one week after the German action was filed, on May 6, 1993, in Fulton County Superior Court. Appellants removed, based on diversity, to the United States District Court for the Northern District of Georgia. Turner sought a preliminary and permanent injunction and damages caused by Defendants' alleged breach. The appellants countered with a motion to dismiss or stay the American proceedings in deference to the parallel proceedings in Germany.

At the time of the June 29, 1993, hearing on the motion for preliminary injunction and the motion to dismiss or stay, no discovery had taken place in the American litigation; the parties filed affidavits supporting their arguments. The district court denied from the bench the motion to dismiss or stay the proceedings. On September 10, 1993, the district court, finding that Turner had a substantial likelihood of success on the merits of its case, granted Turner's motion for a preliminary injunction restraining ARD from telecasting Turner-owned licensed works from the ASTRA satellites. On September 29, 1993, however, the district court granted a stay of the preliminary injunction until October 28, 1993, conditioned on the posting of bond in the amount of $2 million by the appellants. Appellants filed an emergency motion to expedite this appeal and an emergency motion to stay the injunction pending appeal. On October 19, 1993, this court stayed the injunction pending appeal. Appellants challenge the preliminary injunction and the denial of their motion to dismiss or stay the domestic litigation. The stay of the preliminary injunction remains in effect by order of this court.

II. DISCUSSION

A. *Whether to Dismiss or Stay the Domestic Litigation: International Abstention*

ARD appeals the district court's denial of its Motion to Dismiss or Stay the American Litigation in deference to the parallel German proceedings. In the period since the district court denied the appellants' Motion to Dismiss or Stay the American Litigation, the German court has rendered a decision on the merits of the dispute, although it has not determined the fee to be paid by ARD to Turner. The existence of the German judgment adds new considerations to the decision whether to continue the American litigation. The issue is whether a federal court, which properly has jurisdiction over an action, should exercise its jurisdiction where parallel proceedings are ongoing in a foreign nation and a judgment has been reached on the merits in the litigation abroad.

Federal courts have a "virtually unflagging obligation" to exercise the jurisdiction conferred upon them. Colorado River Water Conser. Dist. v. United States, 424 U.S. 800, 817, 96 S.Ct. 1236, 1246, 47 L.Ed.2d 483 (1976). Nevertheless, in some private international disputes the prudent and just action for a federal court is to abstain from the exercise of jurisdiction. Therefore, federal courts have begun to fashion principles that guide courts' actions in cases of concurrent jurisdiction in a federal court and the court of a foreign nation. * * * [C]ourts have sought to fashion principles that will promote three readily identifiable goals in the area of concurrent international jurisdiction: (1) a proper level of respect for the acts of our fellow sovereign nations—a rather vague concept referred to in American jurisprudence as international comity; (2) fairness to litigants; and (3) efficient use of scarce judicial resources.

* * *

Turner does not argue that the decision was rendered by fraud, or that the German court is not a competent court which follows civilized procedures. Germany's legal system clearly follows procedures that ensure that litigants will receive treatment that satisfies American notions of due process. Turner's sole argument is that the German court's decision is contrary to federal or Georgia public policy because it abrogates Turner's freedom of contract.

Turner has proffered a strained interpretation of the German court opinion in an attempt to portray the decision as something akin to a "forced judicial sale" of Turner's property. Turner argues that the Agreement clearly limited ARD's right to telecast to the licensed territory, defined in Paragraph 4 of the Agreement, and that the German court decision would force an unwilling Turner to enter into additional contractual provisions widening the defined territory at a royalty fee to be fixed by the court, all of which Turner argues is directly inconsistent with Paragraph 4 of the Agreement which defines the licensed territory. For the reasons that follow, we reject Turner's characterization of the

German opinion, and we reject Turner's argument that the German decision violates American or Georgian public policy.

Turner's argument is along the following lines. Although conceding that Georgia law and the general common law of contracts provide for "gap filling" similar to the "supplemental interpretation" employed by the German court, Turner insists that such "gap filling" is impermissible when the result is a provision inconsistent with the provisions of the contract as written.[13] * * *

We conclude, however, that the result of the German court decision is not inconsistent with the Agreement. The Agreement expressly gives ARD a right to telecast "by all means and methods now or hereafter known including but not limited to ... DBS and/or communication satellite for purposes of so-called home television reception." Significantly, the grant also expressly provides that the "telecast can originate any place in the universe for reception only in the Territory as defined in paragraph 4 below (inclusive of legitimate overspill as set forth in ¶ 2(f) below)." Thus, to deny ARD the right to utilize the ASTRA satellite would conflict with the provisions of the Agreement. On the other hand, the German court reasonably concluded that the parties did not contemplate an overspill of the magnitude which results from recent technology, including the ASTRA satellites. Thus, the German court employed its "supplemental interpretation" and filled the gap in the contract in accordance with its determination of good faith dealings by the parties as to unforeseen eventualities. Because we conclude that the utilization of this "gap filling" methodology under these circumstances is consistent with the contract law of both Georgia and the general common law, we reject Turner's argument that the German court decision is in violation

---

13. Indeed, before the German court, Turner invited the court to use supplemental interpretation to fill any gaps that existed in the contract. It is clear that the doctrine of good faith and the use of supplemental interpretation to reach a result consistent with the result that would be reached by parties bargaining in good faith is a common feature of American contract law. See, e.g., Market Street Associates Ltd. Partnership v. Frey, 941 F.2d 588, 595 (7th Cir.1991) ("The concept of the duty of good faith ... is a stab at approximating the terms that parties would have negotiated had they foreseen the circumstances that have given rise to their dispute.") This is exactly what the German court did in employing supplemental interpretation as a device to implement the German doctrine of good faith.

Of course, Turner was not the original party to the Agreement; the Agreement was one of the obligations Turner assumed when it purchased portions of the MGM library. Given the fact that Turner, unlike MGM/UA, is itself a broadcasting company

with the capability to broadcast licensed works via ASTRA, Turner may very well wish that the Agreement had never been consummated. However, Turner assumed the obligation to honor the contract in good faith upon purchasing the works covered by the Agreement.

On the obligations that accompany contracts, the Market Street court stated that "[t]he parties to a contract are embarked on a cooperative venture, and a minimum of cooperativeness in the event unforeseen problems arise at the performance stage is required even if not an explicit duty of the contract." 941 F.2d at 595. A court's purpose is to uphold the "overriding purpose of contract law, which is to give the parties what they would have stipulated for expressly if at the time of making the contract they had complete knowledge of the future and the costs of negotiation and adding provisions to the contract had been zero." Id. at 596. We see nothing within the German doctrine of good faith or the supplemental interpretation device that strays from this purpose.

of Georgia public policy or in violation of fundamental notions of decency and fairness.

* * *

III.   Conclusion

For the foregoing reasons, we vacate the judgment of the district court and remand the case to the district court with instructions to vacate its preliminary injunction and stay the litigation.

Chapter 10

ENFORCEMENT REMEDIES

SECTION 1. DAMAGES

(a) General Principles

(Calamari & Perillo 5th §§ 14.1—14.2, 14.4—14.17)

HAWKINS v. McGEE

Supreme Court of New Hampshire, 1929.
146 A. 641, 84 N.H. 114.

See p. 18 supra

PROTECTORS INSURANCE SERVICE, INC. v. UNITED STATES FIDELITY & GUARANTY COMPANY

United States Court of Appeals, Tenth Circuit, 1998.
132 F.3d 612.

WESLEY E. BROWN, DISTRICT JUDGE.

The defendants (hereinafter "USF & G") appeal a jury verdict in plaintiff's favor totaling $844,650.00. The jury found that USF & G breached a contract with plaintiff and that, as a result, plaintiff lost future profits in the amount of $809,650.00 and received $35,000.00 less than fair market value upon the sale of its business. On appeal, USF & G concedes liability for breaching the contract, but argues that the lost profits award should be vacated because it represents an impermissible double recovery. * * * The parties agree that the law of Colorado governs this contract dispute. * * *

SUMMARY OF FACTS

The plaintiff, a Colorado corporation, was an insurance agency formed in 1979. The sole owner of plaintiff's corporate stock was Earl Colglazier. Plaintiff was an agent of USF & G and had a written contract authorizing it to solicit and submit applications for USF & G insurance. If the applications were accepted, plaintiff would be paid a commission

660

by USF & G. Although plaintiff was an independent agency, it had contracts with only two insurance carriers; thus, over 80% of the insurance it sold from 1979 to 1992 was USF & G business. Insofar as termination of the agency agreement between plaintiff and USF & G was concerned, the contract stated that the parties "agree to make a good faith effort to provide for rehabilitation and thereby avoid termination of this Agreement."

In March of 1992, USF & G notified Colglazier that because of profitability concerns it was establishing a formal rehabilitation program for plaintiff. The program set a goal of achieving certain "earned loss ratios" (which measure the agent's profitability to the insurance company) in plaintiff's commercial and personal lines of insurance in 1992. In October of 1992, USF & G notified Colglazier that it was going to terminate its personal lines contract with plaintiff in 180 days if the goals of the rehabilitation program were not met by the end of 1992. The letter stated that after May 1, 1993, USF & G would not accept any new personal lines business and would nonrenew the current business. In response, Colglazier wrote USF & G and asserted that his personal and commercial accounts were intertwined and that terminating the personal lines, although only 20% of his sales, would effectively put him out of business. Faced with this situation, Colglazier decided to sell all of plaintiff's assets, including the rights, title and interest on its insurance policies, to Centennial Agency, Inc., on January 1, 1993. The purchase agreement called for plaintiff to receive cash payments of slightly over $148,000.00.

Plaintiff later brought this suit alleging that USF & G breached the contract by not making a good faith effort at rehabilitation to avoid termination of the agreement. For our purposes it suffices to say that the jury could reasonably find from the evidence that USF & G breached the agreement by improperly measuring plaintiff's loss ratios, by unfairly changing the goals and criteria of the rehabilitation program, and/or by certain other arbitrary actions.

With respect to damages, plaintiff presented the testimony of John Putnam, an expert in valuation of insurance agencies. Putnam testified that plaintiff's business was sold at a "distressed" price because of the circumstances under which it was sold, including time pressure to make a sale and USF & G's stated intention of terminating the agency's personal lines insurance. Putnam testified that the agency would have been worth approximately $175,000 had it not been sold under distress. Putnam arrived at this value by using three different methods: a multiple of revenues, a price/earnings ratio, and a capitalization of earnings. In addition to this evidence, Earl Colglazier testified that he would have continued to operate the agency for at least ten more years had USF & G not given him the termination notice. Plaintiff also presented rather confusing evidence with respect to its net profits in the years before the sale. According to Colglazier's testimony, Protectors Insurance Service was operated in conjunction with a company called Protectors Management Service, which conducted "all of the office insurance activities, salary, payroll, paying everybody on behalf of Protectors Insurance Service." The returns of Protectors Insurance Service showed reported net income in the years before the sale ranging from a low of about $36,000 to a high of about $84,000, with an average of about $59,000. Plaintiff argues that the returns of the two companies show that plaintiff made under $2,0000.00 [sic] in 1991 and lost over $17,000.00 in 1992.

The district court instructed the jury with respect to damages as follows:

> To the extent that actual damages have been proved by the evidence you shall award as actual damages:

> 1. The amount of net income and earnings the Plaintiff ... would have earned if the Defendants had not breached the contract; and

> 2. The amount which is the difference between the price the Plaintiff ... received for the sale of the agency's business and the reasonable sale value of the agency's business if the Defendants had not breached the contract....

USF & G objected to this instruction, arguing that it permitted plaintiff to obtain a double recovery because the reasonable sale value of the agency was based on the agency's ability to earn future profits and, thus, plaintiff would be compensated twice if it received lost profits on top of the sale price. The district court rejected this, finding that the two items were distinct because the sale value in 1992 was a "snapshot in time" that did not include lost future profits. As indicated previously, the jury returned a special verdict finding $809,650 in lost profits and a $35,000 difference between the actual sale price of the agency and its reasonable sale value.

Discussion

USF & G first argues that the district court's damage instruction was erroneous because it permitted the plaintiff to obtain a double recovery. We agree. In a breach of contract action, the objective is to place the injured party in the same position it would have been in but for the breach. *McDonald's Corp. v. Brentwood Center*, 942 P.2d 1308, 1310 (Colo.App.1997). A double or duplicative recovery for a single injury, however, is invalid. *Westric Battery Co. v. Standard Elec. Co.*, 482 F.2d 1307, 1317 (10th Cir.1973). Plaintiff contends there was no double recovery here because "[t]he record is devoid of any factual basis for believing that the damages for the decreased sales price are based upon or included future lost profits." This assertion is contradicted both by the record and by common sense. The testimony of plaintiff's expert, John Putnam, shows that his determination of the reasonable sale value of the agency was based largely—if not entirely—upon the agency's ability to generate future profits. His testimony makes clear that the value of an agency to a buyer is determined from its potential to generate a future income stream. Putnam conceded that all of the methods he used to determine value took into account the agency's ability to generate future profits. When asked what the reasonable sale price of the agency's business would have been but for the distress factors brought about by the defendant, Putnam replied:

> Well, at the time that it was sold, you know, based upon income, because to a large degree this is what we all—and I am talking about commission revenue, what kind of income is coming into the agency, what kind of expenses they had. In my opinion the agency was worth approximately $175,000 at the time that it was sold had it not been sold under duress or distress.

* * *

Numerous jurisdictions hold to the view that "when the loss of business is alleged to be caused by the wrongful acts of another, damages are measured by one of two alternative methods: (1) the going concern value; or (2) lost future profits." *Malley–Duff & Assoc. v. Crown Life Ins. Co.*, 734 F.2d 133, 148 (3rd Cir.1984). *See also Johnson v. Oroweat Foods Co.*, 785 F.2d 503, 508 (4th Cir.1986) (the courts allow a plaintiff to recover either the present value of lost future earnings or the present market value of the lost business, but not both). The "going concern value" is the price a willing buyer would pay and a willing seller would accept in a free marketplace for the business in question. *Malley–Duff*, 734 F.2d at 148. It measures damages by awarding the difference between the going concern value and the price actually received by the plaintiff upon sale of the business. Cf id. This is clearly the measure of damages that was presented by plaintiff's expert in the instant case and it properly supports the consequent award of $35,000 by the jury. The award of lost profit damages in addition to this amount, however, was an improper double recovery.

Plaintiff contends that *Atlas Building Products Co. v. Diamond Block & Gravel Co.*, 269 F.2d 950 (10th Cir.1959) supports the view that an injured plaintiff can recover lost profits as well as a "diminution in value" of the business. *Atlas* is distinguishable because the plaintiff in that case continued to operate the business despite the injury. Such a plaintiff might not be made whole by receiving lost profits because the business may be left with assets (e.g., intangible assets such as goodwill) that have less value than before the injury. Such a loss would be realized by the owner upon a subsequent sale of the business. But where the business is sold as a going concern and the owner is awarded the fair market value of the business without the injury, the owner has been made whole because that value takes into account the prospect of future profits as well as the unreduced value of all the business' assets. * * *

* * * In sum, we conclude that the judgment must be vacated in part because it awards plaintiff an impermissible double recovery.

Not surprisingly, the parties disagree as to what effect a double recovery has upon disposition of the appeal. Plaintiff argues that only the $35,000 award for diminished sale value should be vacated and that the lost profits award should stand, while USF & G argues just the opposite. Although, as indicated above, the "going concern" and "lost profit" measures are generally considered alternative remedies, in this case we conclude that the award of lost profits must be vacated. [H]ere we have "clear proof in the record of the value of plaintiff's business as a going concern, and that value must necessarily take into consideration its future profit-earning potential." *Albrecht* * * * [v. The Herald Co., 452 F.2d 124, 129 (8th Cir. 1971)]. In fact, plaintiff's expert in this case testified solely to the going concern value and did not make an estimate of lost future profits. Lost future profits may be used as a method of calculating damage where no other reliable method of valuing the business is available, see id., but that was not the case here. Plaintiff has been made whole by receiving the fair market value of the business; he "is not entitled to sell the [business], receive full compensation therefor, and still receive the profits the [business] might have made over his reasonable work-life expectancy." *Id.* * * * Moreover, we note that the lost profits award in this case would still be duplicative even if the $35,000 were vacated because the former fails to take into account the additional sum received by plaintiff (over $148,000) for the sale of the business. Thus, the award of lost profits cannot stand.

Under the circumstances, we conclude that the proper course is to vacate the portion of the judgment awarding $809,650 in lost profit damages. The alternative award of $35,000 for diminution in market value is appropriate and is AFFIRMED. The case is REMANDED to the district court for entry of judgment in accordance with this opinion.

G. HERBERT, JACULA PRUDENTUM (1651).

For want of a nail the shoe was lost;
For want of a shoe the horse was lost;
And for want of a horse the rider was lost;
For the want of a rider the battle was lost;
For the want of the battle the kingdom was lost;
And all for the want of a horseshoe-nail.

HADLEY v. BAXENDALE

Court of Exchequer, 1854.
9 Ex. 341, 156 Eng.Rep. 145.

At the trial before Crompton, J., at the last Gloucester Assizes, it appeared that the plaintiffs carried on an extensive business as millers at Gloucester; and that, on the 11th of May, their mill was stopped by a breakage of the crank shaft by which the mill was worked. The steam-engine was manufactured by Messrs. Joyce & Co., the engineers, at Greenwich, and it became necessary to send the shaft as a pattern for a new one to Greenwich. The fracture was discovered on the 12th, and on the 13th the plaintiffs sent one of their servants to the office of the defendants, who are the well-known carriers trading under the name of

Pickford & Co., for the purpose of having the shaft carried to Greenwich. The plaintiffs' servant told the clerk that the mill was stopped, and that the shaft must be sent immediately; and in answer to the inquiry when the shaft would be taken, the answer was, that if it was sent up by twelve o'clock any day, it would be delivered at Greenwich on the following day. On the following day the shaft was taken by the defendants, before noon, for the purpose of being conveyed to Greenwich, and the sum of 2£. 4s. was paid for its carriage for the whole distance; at the same time the defendants' clerk was told that a special entry, if required, should be made to hasten its delivery. The delivery of the shaft at Greenwich was delayed by some neglect; and the consequence was, that the plaintiffs did not receive the new shaft for several days after they would otherwise have done, and the working of their mill was thereby delayed, and they thereby lost the profits they would otherwise have received.

On the part of the defendants, it was objected that these damages were too remote, and that the defendants were not liable with respect to them. The learned Judge left the case generally to the jury, who found a verdict with £25. damages beyond the amount paid into Court.

Whateley, in last Michaelmas Term, obtained a rule nisi for a new trial, on the ground of misdirection.

* * *

ALDERSON, B. We think that there ought to be a new trial in this case; but, in so doing, we deem it to be expedient and necessary to state explicitly the rule which the Judge, at the next trial, ought, in our opinion, to direct the jury to be governed by when they estimate the damages.

It is, indeed, of the last importance that we should do this; for, if the jury are left without any definite rule to guide them, it will, in such cases as these, manifestly lead to the greatest injustice. The Courts have done this on several occasions; and, in Blake v. Midland Railway Company (18 Q.B. 93), the Court granted a new trial on this very ground, that the rule had not been definitely laid down to the jury by the learned Judge at Nisi Prius.

"There are certain established rules," this Court says, in Alder v. Keighley (15 M. & W. 117), "according to which the jury ought to find." And the Court, in that case, adds: "and here there is a clear rule, that the amount which would have been received if the contract had been kept, is the measure of damages if the contract is broken."

Now we think the proper rule in such a case as the present is this: Where two parties have made a contract which one of them has broken, the damages which the other party ought to receive in respect of such breach of contract should be such as may fairly and reasonably be considered either arising naturally, i.e., according to the usual course of things, from such breach of contract itself, or such as may reasonably be supposed to have been in the contemplation of both parties, at the time they made the contract, as the probable result of the breach of it. Now, if the special circumstances under which the contract was actually made were communicated by the plaintiffs to the defendants, and thus known to both parties, the damages resulting from the breach of such a contract, which they would reasonably contemplate, would be the amount of injury which would ordinarily follow from a breach of contract under these special circumstances so known and communicated. But, on the other hand, if these special circumstances were wholly unknown to the party breaking the contract, he, at the most, could only be supposed to have had in his contemplation the amount of injury which would arise generally, and in the great multitude of cases not affected by any special circumstances, from such a breach of contract. For, had the special circumstances been known, the parties might have specially provided for the breach of contract by special terms as to the damages in that case; and of this advantage it would be very unjust to deprive them. Now the above principles are those by which we think the jury ought to be guided in estimating the damages arising out of any breach of contract. It is said, that other cases such as breaches of contract in the non-payment of money, or in the not making a good title to land, are to be treated as exceptions from this, and as governed by a conventional rule. But as, in such cases, both parties must be supposed to be cognisant of that well-known rule, these cases may, we think, be more properly classed under the rule above enunciated as to cases under known special circumstances, because there both parties may reasonably be presumed to contemplate the estimation of the amount of damages according to the conventional rule.

Now, in the present case, if we are to apply the principles above laid down, we find that the only circumstances here communicated by the plaintiffs to the defendants at the time the contract was made, were, that the article to be carried was the broken shaft of a mill, and that the plaintiffs were the millers of that mill. But how do these circumstances shew reasonably that the profits of the mill must be stopped by an unreasonable delay in the delivery of the broken shaft by the carrier to the third person? Suppose the plaintiffs had another shaft in their possession put up or putting up at the time, and that they only wished to send back the broken shaft to the engineer who made it; it is clear that this would be quite consistent with the above circumstances, and yet the unreasonable delay in the delivery would have no effect upon the intermediate profits of the mill. Or, again, suppose that, at the time of the delivery to the carrier, the machinery of the mill had been in other respects defective, then, also, the same results would follow. Here it is true that the shaft was actually sent back to serve as a model for a new one, and that the want of a new one was the only cause of the stoppage of the mill, and that the loss of profits really arose from not sending down the new shaft in proper time, and that this arose from the delay in delivering the broken one to serve as a model. But it is obvious that, in the great multitude of cases of millers sending off broken shafts to third persons by a carrier under ordinary circumstances, such consequences would not, in all probability, have occurred; and these special circumstances were here never communicated by the plaintiffs to the defendants. It follows, therefore, that the loss of profits here cannot reasonably be considered such a consequence of the breach of contract as could have been fairly and reasonably contemplated by both the parties when they made this contract. For such loss would neither have flowed naturally from the breach of this contract in the great multitude of such cases occurring under ordinary circumstances, nor were the special circumstances, which, perhaps, would have made it a reasonable and natural consequence of such breach of contract, communicated to or known by the defendants. The Judge ought, therefore, to have told the jury, that, upon the facts then before them, they ought not to take the loss of profits into consideration at all in estimating the damages. There must therefore be a new trial in this case.

Rule absolute.

Note on Hadley. The best text on damages states that the Hadley decision "diminishes the risk of business enterprise, and the result harmonized well with the free trade economic philosophy of the Victorian era...." McCormick on Damages p. 567 (1935). Compare, Walter E. Houghton, The Victorian Frame of Mind, 1830–1870 p.61 (1957): "The major worry [of the business class] was 'failure.' In a period when hectic booms alternated with financial panics and there was no such thing as limited liability, the business magnate and the public investor were haunted by specters of bankruptcy and the debtor's jail. So great was the physical and mental strain that many men, it was said, were forced 'to break off (or to break down) in mid-career, shattered, paralyzed, reduced to premature action or senility.' " (Footnotes omitted).

MADER v. STEPHENSON

Supreme Court of Wyoming, 1976.
552 P.2d 1114.

PER CURIAM. Plaintiffs-appellants were awarded a judgment against defendant-appellee in the sum of $1000 with interest from October 11, 1973, the date of the contract, in the sum of $143.86, for a total of $1143.86.

We shall take appellants' words to describe the scope of their appeal: "From this judgment the Plaintiffs have appealed the second finding which denied damages." * * * In their brief they assert and argue the right to recover certain general items of damage, being $500 as the amount of the fee paid to their attorney for prosecuting this action, and also a claim for $212, being for air transportation to return from Kentucky for the trial, and a $500 estimate of the costs for the time spent in travel, for telephone calls, and various expenses in what they style the "pursuit of justice," * * *.

Absent statutory authority, or contractual agreement, attorney fees are not recoverable by a party nor are travel expenses in connection with the suit recoverable. There is no statutory provision for recovery of travel expenses or time for preparation of a lawsuit. Any recovery for costs is purely statutory.

* * *

We are required by Rule 72(k), W.R.C.P., to determine whether there was reasonable cause for the appeal and if we cannot so certify to tax as part of the costs a reasonable fee of not less than $25 nor more than $300 to the counsel of the appellee, and further to adjudge to the appellee damages in such sum as may be reasonable, not exceeding $500. We have found nothing in this record justifying the conclusion that there was reasonable cause for the appeal and therefore direct the clerk to tax as costs herein the sum of $150 as counsel fees for the appellee, and $50 as penalty and damages to the appellee.

Affirmed.

S. J. GROVES & SONS CO. v. WARNER CO.

United States Court of Appeals, Third Circuit.
576 F.2d 524 (1978).

WEIS, CIRCUIT JUDGE. A contract for the concrete work on a bridge being constructed over the Schuylkill River in Southwest Philadelphia resulted in heavy losses for appellant S.J. Groves & Sons Company. Alleging that much of its loss was caused by the performance of its subcontractor who supplied ready-mixed concrete, Groves filed suit against Warner in the district court. At trial, however, efforts to recoup a substantial portion of the loss from the subcontractor met with only partial success. Concluding that disallowance of many of Groves' claims was based upon factual determinations supported by the record, we affirm the judgment of the district court except insofar as it too narrowly interpreted the duty to mitigate damages. As part of a highway improvement program, the Pennsylvania Department of Transportation undertook the erection of the Girard Point Bridge in Southwest Philadelphia and selected American Bridge Company as the prime contractor. Plaintiff-appellant Groves was awarded a subcontract for the placement of the bridge's concrete decks and parapets and contracted with the defendant Warner for the delivery of ready-mixed concrete for use at the Girard Point site. Groves filed this lawsuit claiming extensive losses because of Warner's failure to deliver adequate supplies at scheduled times. The case was tried to the court and after preparing detailed findings of fact and conclusions of law, the trial judge entered judgment in favor of the plaintiff in the amount of $35,401.28. Dissatisfied with the denial of a large part of its claimed damages, Groves appealed.

The contract at issue provided that Warner would supply approximately 35,000 cubic yards of ready-mixed concrete at a rate of 40 cubic yards per hour and at times specified by Groves. Having its plant close to the job site, Warner was equipped to prepare and deliver large quantities of concrete. The agreement was executed in March, 1970, and the first concrete was delivered to the job site in July of that year. Groves' progress was hindered by three lengthy strikes in the spring and summer of 1970, 1971, and 1972 which postponed completion of its contract from July of 1972 to October of 1972. The work was also delayed by rejections of concrete that failed to meet state specifications, although the number of rejections was within expectations on such a project. Although concrete pours were completed at a later date than anticipated, the number of weeks during which the pours were made remained substantially the same as was originally planned. Groves expected to pour concrete for the decks of the bridge in the mornings and then to use some of the crew to construct parapets in the afternoons. This general plan was frustrated by Warner's frequent failures to make deliveries in compliance with Groves' instructions. As a result, deck pours originally scheduled for the mornings often extended into the afternoons and evenings and created overtime labor expense.

Concerned with its lagging progress, Groves considered securing other sources of concrete as early as 1971 but found no real alternatives. It was too expensive to build its own batching plant at the site and the only other source of ready-mixed concrete in the area was the Trap Rock Company, located near the Warner plant. Trap Rock, however, was not certified to do state work in 1971 and its price was higher than Warner's. Moreover, the production facilities at Trap Rock were limited, as was the number of trucks it had available. Meanwhile, Warner continued to assure Groves that deliveries would improve.

Despite its promises, Warner's performance continued to be erratic and on June 21, 1972, the Pennsylvania Department of Transportation ordered all construction at Girard Point halted until the quality of Warner's service could be discussed at a conference. A meeting took place the next day with state officials and representatives from Warner, Groves, and other contractors in attendance. Based on Warner's renewed assurances of improved performance, state officials allowed work to resume on June 26, 1972. From that date until July 20, 1972, Warner's delivery service improved significantly, although it still did not consistently meet Groves' instructions. In the months following and until completion in October of 1972, Warner's performance continued to be uneven and unpredictable.

On June 14, 1972, when Groves again approached Trap Rock, that firm maintained that it could service the job at the desired delivery rate but did not reduce its price. On July 11, 1972, Trap Rock was certified by the state and the next day agreed to accept the same price as Warner. Groves, nevertheless, decided to continue with Warner as its sole supplier.

The district judge found that Warner had acted in bad faith by deliberately overcommitting its ability to manufacture and deliver enough concrete, providing an inadequate number of trucks to service Groves' project, and following a policy of providing delivery at only 75 percent of the ordered rate. * * * In the court's view, on June 15, 1972 Groves had no reasonable expectation that Warner's performance would improve to "totally satisfactory levels" and by July 11, 1972, "there were no practical impediments to employing Trap Rock as a supplemental supplier." The court therefore concluded that "as of July 12, 1972, Groves had an obligation to utilize Trap Rock as a supplemental supplier . . . in order to mitigate any possible 'delay damages' resulting from Warner's service." Accordingly, the court did not award Groves all the delay damages it sought, allowing only $12,534 for overtime which had been paid on days when Warner's deliveries were late before, but not after, July 12, 1972. * * *

Since the first pour on July 9, 1970 resulted in an unacceptable deck panel due to Warner's defective concrete and inadequate workmanship by Groves, the court allocated the cost of removing and replacing the panel. The total expenditure was $42,357.11 and Groves was awarded $10,589.43.

Although Groves sustained heavy losses in its work on the bridge, the district court recognized that not all were properly attributable to Warner. The lengthy strikes occurring each year at the very beginning of the pouring season, adverse weather, and an overly optimistic expectation of the efficiency which could be obtained on a project of this nature were also substantial factors leading to Groves' misfortune. * * * We find it necessary to refer to only two matters both of a legal, rather than purely factual nature.

The plaintiff contends it is entitled to all, not part, of the loss it sustained as a result of the defective slab poured on July 9, 1970. The trial judge found that there was an inadequate amount of retarder in the concrete which caused premature solidification, although the state did not reject the concrete for that reason. In addition, some of the concrete which Warner supplied was too dry and there was failure to observe instructions as to delivery times. The first truck was late in reaching the job site and the following two arrived too soon. Groves' crews, on the other hand, having a case of "first day jitters," functioned inefficiently, and weather conditions were extremely unfavorable. The court determined that Warner's poor performance was "a substantial cause" of the defective slab to the extent of one-fourth of the damages sought by Groves.

Groves contends that Warner did not meet its contractual obligations on July 9 and should be liable for the entire loss. But the court's analysis of the incident demonstrates that the conduct of both parties contributed in some degree to the loss. The burden is on the plaintiff to establish proximate cause between breach and damage and if the loss caused by a breach cannot be isolated from that attributable to other factors, no damages may be awarded. Lichter v. Mellon–Stuart Co., 305 F.2d 216 (3d Cir. 1962). Here, the trial judge might well have decided that there was an inadequate basis for proration between damages precipitated by Warner's conduct and that of Groves, in which event there would have been no recovery. The judge, however, believed that there was enough evidence to determine that 25 percent was a proper allocation.

* * * Any error in the allocation could only be based on a lack of proof establishing the extent of harm caused exclusively by Warner. From that standpoint, Groves is the beneficiary of the district court's ruling and has no ground for complaint. The action of the trial judge in dividing the loss between the parties was a fair solution to a difficult problem and is not reversible in the circumstances here.

The other matter of law which warrants attention is that of mitigation of damages. The district court determined that since the contract was essentially one for the sale of a product with an additional requirement of proper and timely delivery, the Uniform Commercial Code should govern. See Bevard v. Howat Concrete Co., 140 U.S.App.D.C. 96, 433 F.2d 1202 (1970). We agree that in this diversity case the Pennsylvania courts would treat the contract as one for the sale of goods and so we look to the Code.

The court described the transaction between Groves and Warner as an installment contract as that term is defined in Pa.Stat.Ann. tit. 12A, § 2–612(1) (Purdon 1970), that is, an agreement to deliver goods in "separate lots to be separately accepted." Where there is non-conformity with respect to one or more installments which substantially impairs the value of the whole contract, there is a breach of the whole. § 2–612(3). In the district court's view, such a breach occurred as of July 12, 1972 and should have been apparent to Groves. At that time Warner had been recertified by the Pennsylvania Department of Transportation and Trap Rock had also received state approval. The district court reasoned that in order to recover consequential damages for defective performance after that date, Groves had to prove that it had complied with the obligation to "cover" or otherwise mitigate damages incurred after Warner's breach in July, 1972.

Section 2–715 provides that the consequential damages a buyer may recover are those which "could not reasonably be prevented by cover or otherwise." Thus, generally, when a seller refuses to deliver goods, the buyer must attempt to secure similar articles elsewhere as a prerequisite to receiving consequential damages. "Cover" is defined in § 2–712(1):

> "After a breach ... the buyer may 'cover' by making in good faith and without unreasonable delay any reasonable purchase of or contract to purchase goods in substitution for those due from the seller."

Since Trap Rock was available in July, 1972 as a source of readymixed concrete, the district court held that Groves was under "a duty to attempt to prevent the consequential damages .... by obtaining the supplemental supplier" and that Groves' failure to do so barred it, as a matter of law, from receiving such compensation. In this ruling the trial court erred.

The requirement of cover or mitigation of damages is not an absolute, unyielding one, but is subject to the circumstances. Comment 2 to § 2–712 says:

"(t)he test of proper cover is whether at the time and place the buyer acted in good faith and in a reasonable manner, and it is immaterial that hindsight may later prove that the method of cover used was not the cheapest or most effective." Essentially the cover rules are an expression of the general duty to mitigate damages and usually the same principles apply.[5]

* * * The burden of proving that losses could have been avoided by reasonable effort and expense must be borne by the party who has broken the contract. * * * 5 A. Corbin, Contracts § 1039 (1964).

Here, the court found that as of July 12, 1972, Groves had no reasonable expectation that Warner's performance would improve to totally satisfactory levels, that there were no practical impediments to employing Trap Rock as a supplemental supplier, and therefore Groves had a duty to contract with Trap Rock to mitigate delay damages. We do not think that the premises justify the conclusion.

In July, 1972, Groves found itself confronted with a breach by Warner and the consequent necessity to choose among a number of alternative courses of action. In the circumstances, Groves could have:

1. Declared the contract breached, stopped work, and held Warner liable for all damages. This was not a realistic alternative.

2. Set up its own cement batching plant at the job site. Time and expense made this impractical.

3. Accepted Warner's assurances that it would perform satisfactorily in the future, see § 2–609(1).[6] The court, however, found that it would have been unreasonable to have any faith in continued assurances from Warner.

4. Substituted Trap Rock for Warner for the remainder of the contract. The court made no finding on the reasonableness of this choice but it appears questionable whether Trap Rock had the resources to meet all of Groves' requirements.

5. Engaged Trap Rock as a supplemental supplier; or

6. Continued dealing with Warner in the belief that though its performance would not be satisfactory, consequential damages might be less than if the other alternatives were adopted. Of the six alternatives, Groves was seemingly faced with three practical ones all subject to drawbacks. Groves had to: allow Warner to continue in the hope of averting even greater losses; substitute Trap Rock for all of Warner's

---

5. It has been said that there is not a "duty" on the part of a plaintiff to mitigate damages but rather the principle is that he is entitled to only those damages which he could not avoid by reasonable effort. The "duty" to mitigate cannot be enforced and it is only when recovery is sought that the defense may be invoked. See Restatement of Contracts § 336, comment d; 5 A. Corbin, Contracts § 1039 (1964). D. Dobbs, Handbook on the Law of Remedies, § 3.7 at 188 (1973). The test for plaintiff's efforts is

reasonableness, McCormick on Damages § 35 (1935).

6. Section 2–609(1) reads in part: "When reasonable grounds for insecurity arise with respect to the performance of either party the other may in writing demand adequate assurance of due performance and until he receives such assurance may if commercially reasonable suspend any performance for which he has not already received the agreed return."

work a choice made doubtful by Trap Rock's ability to handle the project; or, lastly, use Trap Rock as a supplemental supplier.

The last choice, the option chosen by the district court, was subject to several difficulties which the court did not discuss. Even if Trap Rock supplied part of the contract with perfect scheduling, there would be no guarantee that Warner would do so. The element of erratic deliveries by Warner would not necessarily be cured, nor would the problems with the quality of concrete it delivered to the site. The presence of two independent suppliers acting separately might indeed pose problems more severe than those which existed before. Moreover, the record reveals that Trap Rock received some of its raw material from Warner and Groves suspected that Warner might not have been too cooperative if part of the Girard Bridge contract were taken away by Trap Rock.

Confronted with these alternatives, Groves chose to stay with Warner, a decision with which the district court did not agree. The court's preference may very well have been the best; that, however, is not the test. As Judge Hastie wrote in In re Kellett Aircraft Corp., 186 F.2d 197, 198–99 (3d Cir. 1950): "Where a choice has been required between two reasonable courses, the person whose wrong forced the choice can not complain that one rather than the other was chosen. (McCormick on Damages, § 35 (1935).) The rule of mitigation of damages may not be invoked by a contract breaker as a basis for hypercritical examination of the conduct of the injured party, or merely for the purpose of showing that the injured person might have taken steps which seemed wiser or would have been more advantageous to the defaulter.... One is not obligated to exalt the interest of the defaulter to his own probable detriment."

There are situations in which continuing with the performance of an unsatisfactory contractor will avoid losses which might be experienced by engaging others to complete the project. 5 Corbin, supra, § 1039 at 249. See also Hillman, Keeping the Deal Together After Material Breach Common Law Mitigation Rules, The UCC, and the Restatement (Second) of Contracts, 47 U.Colo.L.Rev. 553 (1976). In such a setting, mitigation is best served by continuing existing arrangements. As the troubled Prince of Denmark once observed we "... rather bear those ills we have, Than fly to others that we know not of...."[8]

* * *

Thus, * * * we hold that the district court erred in imposing on Groves as a matter of law a duty to engage Trap Rock. Accordingly, we vacate that portion of the court's judgment which allowed damages for delay only until July 12, 1972. We remand for assessment of damages from that point to completion of the contract on the same basis as that used for the pre-July 12 delay damages. In all other respects, the judgment of the district court will be affirmed.

8. W. Shakespeare, Hamlet, Act III, scene I, lines 81–82.

GRUBER v. S–M NEWS CO.

United States District Court, S.D. New York, 1954.
126 F.Supp. 442.

MURPHY, DISTRICT JUDGE. Plaintiffs, invoking jurisdiction of this court on the basis of diverse citizenship, seek damages for breach of contract. Plaintiffs allege in the first count of their complaint (the other two have been withdrawn), that a contract between them and defendant was made about September 10, 1945 at their principal place of business in New York. Under this agreement, plaintiffs allege that they promised to manufacture in conformity with samples approved by defendant, 90,000 sets of twelve Christmas greeting cards for the impending Christmas season; to pack every set in a box of design approved by defendant and be ready for shipment to a list of wholesalers to be furnished by defendant not later than the second week in October; to give defendant exclusive sale and distribution rights to these sets. According to plaintiffs' complaint, in consideration of their promises, defendant bound itself to exercise reasonable diligence to sell all of the sets and use its resources for scientific sales promotion, national advertising, newsstand outlets and sales organization. Defendant further agreed, plaintiffs claim, to pay eighty-four cents for each set f.o.b. its wholesalers' respective places of business where, according to defendant's regular checkup, the cards had been sold at retail. Credit was to be allowed for all sets returned to plaintiffs unsold. It is further alleged that plaintiffs manufactured and packed the sets in accordance with the agreement, notified the defendant to this effect on October 2, 1945, and that defendant then refused its promised performance. Damages for $101,800 are demanded.

* * *

(c) It is clear that distribution of samples in September to four out of over 700 wholesalers and jobbers who in turn supply over 90,000 outlets, is not an exercise of "reasonable diligence" to sell, in the face of a binding agreement requiring production by plaintiffs of 90,000 sets by the second week in October. Accordingly, the defense of performance by defendant is far from complete, and defendant must assume liability for breach of this contract.

* * *

For breach of a contract of exclusive distribution and return, plaintiffs should be entitled to damages measured by the difference between what they actually obtained for their cards and what they would have obtained had defendant exercised its promised reasonable diligence. On this, plaintiffs have the burden of proof to the extent of a reasonably certain and definite factual basis of computation. Under the evidence, such basis in this case is too speculative for an award in a sum certain. The past experience of the defendant in distribution of a high proportion of jig-saw puzzles, maps and cleaning fluids is hardly a basis for prophecy with respect to Christmas cards. And a single retailer's opinion that he would have disposed of 50 boxes of the cards is a precarious foundation for generalization with respect to 90,000 such boxes. Accordingly, plaintiffs have not sustained their burden of proof with respect to their expectation under the breached agreement.

However, alternative to damages for loss of their expectation, plaintiffs have demanded at the close of trial at least their out-of-pocket expenses. The basis for these damages is not plaintiffs' expectation of profits but rather their expenditures made in "essential reliance" upon defendant's promise. Defendant, for its part, insists that there can be no recovery upon this theory of essential reliance because there would have been a loss to plaintiffs had defendant fully performed its promise of distribution.

The few cases in point in New York are apparently not entirely in accord with respect to the relationship between anticipated loss in event of full performance by the defendant, on one hand, and a plaintiff's recovery of his out-of-pocket expenses in reliance on defendant's unperformed promise, on the other. There are situations where there is no such relationship, and a plaintiff may recover his expenditures in reliance upon defendant's promise without regard to profit if that promise had been fully performed by defendant, as in actions for restitution and ones based upon fraud. The Restatement has suggested that if full performance by defendant would have resulted in loss to a plaintiff, then this loss must be deducted from plaintiff's expenditures. * * * "[O]n those occasions in which the performance would not have covered the promisee's outlay, such a result [i.e., recovery of expenses by the promisee] imposes the risk of the promisee's contract upon the promisor. We cannot agree that the promisor's default in performance should under this guise make him an insurer of the promisee's venture; * * *."[8]

We accept as the rule that plaintiff's recovery for their out-of-pocket expenses must be diminished by any loss that would result from defendant's full performance. We are not persuaded that defendant has established the probability of such loss. True, plaintiffs were able to obtain merely six cents per box on a sale of 40,000 boxes in 1949, rather than the promised eighty-four cents for sale in 1945 under their agreement with defendant. But the Christmas cards had a novelty appeal, designed as they were to exploit a dozen different nations at the time of the newly-formed United Nations in 1945. The glamour of the caricatures may well have been clouded by the worsening world situation that gathered in the succeeding years.

The burden of proving loss in event of performance properly rests on the defendant who by its wrong has made the question relevant to the rights of the plaintiffs. We do not find that defendant has sustained this burden.

Only the amount of plaintiffs' expenditures reasonably made in performance of the contract or in necessary preparation therefor, may be

---

8. L. Albert & Son v. Armstrong Rubber Co., 2 Cir., 178 F.2d 182, 189. See also Fuller, Reliance Interest in Contract Damages, 46 Yale L.J. 52, 75–80 (1936).

recovered. This does not include, as plaintiffs have requested, the cost of making the plates from which the cards were printed since these had already been fabricated prior to making the contract with defendant. The amount of plaintiffs' expenditures for labor and material reasonably made in essential reliance on defendant's promise was $19,934.44. From this sum must be deducted the *net* amount realized by plaintiffs from sale of 40,000 sets at six cents a set which was $2,080. Accordingly plaintiffs are entitled to $17,854.44 in damages.

Judgment accordingly.

ANGLIA TELEVISION v. REED

House of Lords.
[1971] 3 All E.R. 690.

This was an appeal by the defendant, Robert Reed, from the judgment of Master Elton * * * . The master adjudged that the defendant should pay to the plaintiffs as damages the sum of £2,750.

LORD DENNING [Master of the Rolls]. Anglia Television Ltd were minded in 1968 to make a film of a play for television entitled 'The Man of the Wood.' It portrayed an American married to an English woman. The American has an adventure in an English wood. The film was to last for 90 minutes. Anglia Television made many arrangements in advance. They arranged for a place where the play was to be filmed. They employed a director, a designer and a stage manager, and so forth. They involved themselves in much expense. All this was done before they got the leading man. They required a strong actor capable of holding the play together. He was to be on the scene the whole time. Anglia Television eventually found the man. He was Mr. Robert Reed, an American who has a very high reputation as an actor. He was very suitable for this part. By telephone conversation on 30th August 1968 it was agreed by Mr. Reed through his agent that he would come to England and be available between 9th September and 11th October 1968 to rehearse and play in this film. He was to get a performance fee of £1,050, living expenses of £100 a week, his first class fares to and from the United States, and so forth. It was all subject to the permit of the Ministry of Labour for him to come here. That was duly given on 2nd September 1968. So the contract was concluded. But unfortunately there was some muddle with the bookings. It appears that Mr. Reed's agent had already booked him in America for some other play. So on 3rd September 1968 the agent said that Mr. Reed would not come to England to perform in this play. He repudiated his contract. Anglia Television tried hard to find a substitute but could not do so. So on 11th September they accepted his repudiation. They abandoned the proposed film. They gave notice to the people whom they had engaged and so forth.

Anglia Television then sued Mr. Reed for damages. He did not dispute his liability, but a question arose as to the damages. Anglia Television do not claim their profit. They cannot say what their profit would have been on this contract if Mr. Reed had come here and performed it. So, instead of claim for loss or profits, they claim for the wasted expenditure. They had incurred the director's fees, the designer's fees, the stage manager's and assistant manager's fees, and so on. It comes in all to £2,750. Anglia Television say that all that money was wasted because Mr. Reed did not perform his contract.

Mr. Reed's advisers take a point of law. They submit that Anglia Television cannot recover for expenditure incurred *before* the contract was concluded with Mr. Reed. They can only recover the expenditure *after* the contract was concluded. They say that the expenditure *after* the contract was only £854.65, and that is all that Anglia Television can recover. The master rejected that contention; he held that Anglia Television could recover the whole £2,750; and now Mr. Reed appeals to this court. Counsel for Mr. Reed has referred us to the recent unreported case of *Perestrello & Compania Limitada v. United Paint Co.Ltd* (No 2), in which Thesiger J quoted the words of Lord Tindal CJ in 1835 in *Hodges v. Earl of Litchfield.*

> "The expenses preliminary to the contract ought not to be allowed. The party enters into them for his own benefit at a time when it is uncertain whether there will be any contract or not."

Thesiger J applied those words, saying: "In my judgment pre-contract expenditure, though thrown away, is not recoverable . . ."

I cannot accept the proposition as stated. * * * If he has not suffered any loss of profits—or if he cannot prove what his profits would have been—he can claim in the alternative the expenditure which has been thrown away, that is, wasted, by reason of the breach. * * *

If the plaintiff claims the wasted expenditure, he is not limited to the expenditure incurred *after* the contract was concluded. He can claim also the expenditure incurred *before* the contract, provided that it was such as would reasonably be in the contemplation of the parties as likely to be wasted if the contract was broken. Applying that principle here, it is plain that, when Mr. Reed entered into this contract, he must have known perfectly well that much expenditure had already been incurred on director's fees and the like. He must have contemplated—or, at any rate, it is reasonably to be imputed to him—that if he broke his contract, all that expenditure would be wasted, whether or not it was incurred before or after the contract. He must pay damages for all the expenditures so wasted and thrown away.

* * *

I think the master was quite right and this appeal should be dismissed.

Problems

1. D, a shipping company, contracted to consign a package to P. D was aware that the package contained motion picture films for exhibition. P

operated a motion picture theater and the films were to be exhibited during Christmas week when attendance is predictably high, but D was unaware that P was the operator of a theater or of the seasonal nature of theater attendance. As a result of D's delay in shipment, P was forced to close its theater during Christmas week. P sues for the profits it would have made during this period. What result?

2. P was the owner of certain shares of D Corp. stock which were virtually unmarketable because they were not registered with the S.E.C. D Corp. promised that the shares would be registered at the same time it registered a block of stock it planned to offer to the public. A public offering was registered and sold to the public. The market price per share soared for a time and has since declined. At the time of the public offering P made numerous suggestions that the stock be registered, but made no firm demand, took no immediate legal action against D and never indicated an intention to sell the shares after registration. In an action for damages, D argues that P's failure to take immediate legal action and failure to inform D of the intention to sell the shares are facts to be taken into account to curtail P's damages award. Is the argument sound?

3. P, a municipality, leased certain premises to D. D agreed to improve the property for an industrial park and P agreed to finance the improvements. To this end P borrowed money from the public by selling municipal bonds. D repudiated and failed to pay the rent. P, as a result, defaulted on the bonds and the market price of the bonds drastically declined. P raised money and called in the bonds at face value plus interest as it had a right to do by virtue of a redemption clause in the bonds. D asserts that P should have mitigated damages by buying the bonds on the open market at the reduced market value as it also had a right to do. Can you formulate an argument to the effect that D's contention is unsound?

4. D contracted with P, a building contractor, to have a house constructed on D's lot. D repudiated after P had just begun to perform. In mitigation, D offers evidence that immediately after the repudiation P entered into another more profitable building contract in the same vicinity. Is this evidence relevant?

5. P provides recorded music to restaurants and other public places. P contracted to provide music to D's place of business for a three year term. After seventeen months, D moved his place of business and repudiated the contract. T, the new tenant in the premises formerly occupied by D, has subscribed to P's services at a higher price than D had contracted to pay. P sues D for damages. D denies that P has suffered any economic injury. What result?

6. P, an author, contracted with D, a publisher, to publish P's manuscript on modern drama within 18 months. D was to pay P a percentage of the retail price of each book sold. Because of a change in its publishing policy D refused to publish the book. P brought suit and the lower court granted $10,000 damages measured by the cost of publication because the value of the lost royalties is speculative. On appeal, what result?

6A. Landlord promised Tenant occupancy of certain retail space for a six-month term, beginning October 1, in exchange for Tenant's promise of $10,000. In September, Tenant ordered and paid for a perishable inventory of $50,000. Landlord totally breached his promise and Tenant was unable to find comparable space for rent. The goods Tenant bought were sold at a distress sale for $9,000. Tenant seeks $41,000 in damages. Will Tenant succeed?

(b) Employment Contracts

(Calamari & Perillo 5th §§ 14.18—14.19)

MISSOURI INTELLIGENCER, OCTOBER 6, 1826

[The following classified ad from this newspaper hangs on the walls of the Kit Carson Museum in Taos, New Mexico.]

Notice is hereby given to all persons that Christopher Carson, a boy of about 16 years old, small for his age, but thick-set; light hair, ran away from the subscriber, living in Franklin, Howard County, Missouri; to whom he had been bound to learn the saddler's trade, on or about the first of September last. He is supposed to have made his way to the upper part of the state. All persons are notified not to harbor, support, or assist said boy under penalty of law. One cent reward will be given to any person who will bring back the said boy.

BALLARD v. EL DORADO TIRE CO.

United States Court of Appeals, Fifth Circuit, 1975.
512 F.2d 901.

COLEMAN, CIRCUIT JUDGE. This diversity action resulted from the allegedly wrongful discharge of plaintiff, Bill L. Ballard, a Florida citizen, by El Dorado Tire Company, a Michigan corporation. The District Court, sitting without a jury, awarded Ballard $46,352.20 in damages.

We affirm the award of damages and remand for further consideration of the other benefits hereinafter discussed.

El Dorado appeals, contending that the District Judge erred in failing to reduce Ballard's damages by the amount he might have earned in other employment during the unexpired term of his contract. Ballard cross appeals, contending that the District Court's calculation of damages erroneously failed to take into account certain fringe benefits due under the employment contract.

The employment contract was executed on May 31, 1969. It called for Ballard, an experienced tire salesman, to work in Orlando, Florida, for a 5 year term as Executive Vice President and General Manager of El Dorado's Florida subsidiary. The contract provided Ballard with generous compensation:

> COMPENSATION: BALLARD shall receive a base salary of $18,000.00 per year. * * * In addition to the base salary, BALLARD shall receive a commission based upon one per cent of the gross sales of the Florida subsidiary corporation. * * * In addition to the base

salary and commission, BALLARD shall receive additional compensation in the form of a credit towards the purchase of stock in the Florida subsidiary company and hereinafter provided.

* * *

In addition Ballard was entitled, upon meeting certain conditions, to 20% of the subsidiary stock.

Other relevant contract provisions dealt with termination and non-competition:

TERMINATION: BALLARD may terminate this employment agreement at any time, upon thirty days written notice to EL DORADO. EL DORADO may, at its option, accept any such resignation without said thirty day notice. EL DORADO may terminate this employment agreement for just cause with either thirty days notice or thirty days base salary in lieu of notice. Upon termination of this agreement by either party as provided herein, BALLARD shall promptly account to EL DORADO and/or the Florida subsidiary corporation for all property of EL DORADO and/or its subsidiary corporation in his hands effective as of the termination date. Upon such termination, BALLARD shall no longer be entitled to any salary or benefits except as may be provided herein or except as may be provided in the aforesaid El Dorado Pension Plan.

NON–COMPETITION: BALLARD agrees that upon his voluntary termination of this agreement or upon the expiration of this agreement by the passage of time and the failure of BALLARD to renew the same, he will refrain from, directly or indirectly, carrying on or engaging in the tire business and from soliciting old customers of EL DORADO and/or its Florida subsidiary within the State of Florida for a period of two years, or for so long as EL DORADO and/or its Florida subsidiary continue to engage in the tire business in the State of Florida, if for less than two years. EL DORADO may enforce this agreement by injunction in a court of competent jurisdiction.

This stipulation *does not* prevail in the event of termination by El Dorado.

/s/ H.W.D

The Ballard–El Dorado relationship was soon jeopardized by negotiations between El Dorado and one of its stockholders, Dodenhoff, who wanted to move to Florida to take over management of the Florida subsidiary. These negotiations culminated in El Dorado's selling all its stock in the Florida subsidiary to Dodenhoff. The contract of sale was executed on July 11, 1971. The sales price included the 31,000 shares Dodenhoff held in El Dorado.

Ballard filed this action to determine his rights under his employment contract on October 19, 1971.

Upon receiving a copy of the complaint, Dodenhoff wrote Ballard telling him that the filing of suit constituted a "breach of contract" and a "voluntary resignation".

The District Court did not agree with Dodenhoff's assessment. It held El Dorado's sale of the subsidiary constituted a breach of contract, and that holding is not appealed.

El Dorado does appeal the Court's refusal to mitigate Ballard's damages by what he might have earned in other employment.

Ballard cross appeals the Court's holding that he was not entitled to compensation for loss of pension benefits and stock in El Dorado.

I.   The El Dorado Appeal—Did the District Court Err in
Failing to Mitigate Ballard's Damages by the Amount
He Might Have Earned in Other Employment?

The District Court found as a fact that Ballard has not sought other employment.[1] Furthermore, the Court took note of the general principle that an employee's damages will be mitigated by what he could have earned in similar employment. * * * The District Court's refusal to allow mitigation was based upon the theory that the burden to prove the existence of similar employment was upon the employer, and that El Dorado had failed to show that similar employment was available.

Our examination of the cases and of other authorities demonstrates that the District Court was correct. The universal rule is that an employee's damages will be mitigated only if the employer proves that similar employment opportunity was available. As explained in Dobbs, Remedies, § 12.25, p. 925:

> The recovery is based on contract price, not on the contract price/market value differential so commonly used in sales cases. The employee need only prove the breach and the contract price when he is wrongfully discharged and this will warrant a judgment in his favor for all future installments due him, reduced to present value. If the employee has obtained a substitute job, or could obtain one by reasonable effort, he is chargeable with the income he obtains or could reasonably obtain in this fashion, but only if the employer sustains the burden of proving these facts.

* * *

Sensing the weight of authority against its position, El Dorado attempts to escape the burden of proving the existence of similar employment in two ways.

First, it points to the Non–Competition Clause in the contract. El Dorado says that by preventing Ballard from engaging in similar employ-

---

1. Ballard's inaction is the result of the advice of a lawyer who told him that seeking similar employment might violate the non-competition clause in the contract, thereby subjecting Ballard to a law suit. The lawyer's advice was based in part on a letter by Dodenhoff telling Ballard that his filing suit constituted a "voluntary resignation". Voluntary resignation is the act that triggered the operation of the non-competition clause.

ment, the clause gave rise to a duty to mitigate by seeking *any* employment. It says, in other words, that the effect of an agreement not to compete in similar work is to change the employee's common law duty to mitigate by seeking *similar* employment to a duty to mitigate by seeking *any* employment. Ballard's damages therefore should be mitigated not by what he could have earned in similar employment but by what he could have earned in any employment.

The ready answer to this contention is that there is no such term in the contract. The contract speaks of a negative duty—the duty not to compete with the former employer by seeking similar employment. It does not include an affirmative promise to mitigate damages by seeking dissimilar employment.[2]

A second and equally persuasive answer to El Dorado's argument is that the non-competition clause did not govern this termination. By its literal terms, the promise not to compete applied only to a *voluntary* termination. Ballard's termination was not voluntary. El Dorado's sale of the subsidiary made it impossible for it to perform its promises to Ballard. Ballard was powerless to prevent the contract termination. His employment termination was involuntary; therefore, the contract promise not to seek similar employment did not come into play.

As its next argument for escaping the burden of proving existence of similar employment, El Dorado cites our decision in Nello L. Teer Company v. Hollywood Golf Estates, Inc., 5 Cir., 1963, 324 F.2d 669, 672, cert. denied, 377 U.S. 909, 84 S.Ct. 1169, 12 L.Ed.2d 178, where we said that an independent contractor, whose contract had been breached, must prove the non-existence of similar employment opportunities in order to escape mitigation. This language is consistent with the holdings of many courts which have reasoned that an independent contractor is in a much more favorable position to know the availability of other contracts than is his employee who is likely to be unfamiliar with the contracting business. See, e.g., the leading case of Green v. Nelson, 120 Utah 155, 232 P.2d 776 (1951).

Decisions like *Teer* and *Green* have always been distinguished from master-servant contracts since "the employer may in fact know as much or more about the job market than the employee". Dobbs, Remedies, § 12.25, p. 925. The independent contractor cases are simply an exception to the general rule that the burden to prove the existence of similar employment opportunity is upon the employer.

* * *

El Dorado could meet its burden of proof only by showing the availability of a managerial type position in the tire industry. Were the contrary true, the rule requiring the employer to prove the availability of

2. Nevertheless, a Florida court has indicated that a non-competition clause has the effect El Dorado attributes to it. See Reed Construction Corporation v. Zimmerman, 133 So.2d 579, 580 (Fla.App.1961). In *Reed,* the employee had actually obtained other work, so the issue of whether damages is mitigated by any type work where the work is not actually obtained was not at issue.

similar employment would be meaningless. The employer could always meet the so-called "burden" simply by introduction of the help-wanted ads of a local newspaper. The law does not allow contract breachers to escape consequences of their wrongful acts in such a perfunctory fashion.

The District Court was correct in refusing to mitigate Ballard's damages by what he might have earned in other employment.

* * *

Problems

7. Shirley MacLaine, contracted with D to play the female lead in "Bloomer Girl," a musical to be filmed in California for a minimum guaranteed compensation of $750,000. D decided it would not produce "Bloomer Girl." In substitution D offered Miss MacLaine the lead in "Big Country," a Western to be filmed in Australia. She declined to play in "Big Country" and sues for $750,000 damages. What result?

8. Jack was a highly skilled production manager in the ladies' ready-to-wear industry. He entered into a three-year contract with defendant to work in this capacity in Dallas, a city in which positions of this type were rare. Soon after the performance of the contract began, Jack was fired without cause. He spent over $1300 in advertising and travel costs in an unsuccessful attempt to find a comparable position. He ultimately took a temporary and less skilled job at a lesser salary for a period of time that was less than the unexpired contract term. Under the principle of mitigation of damages how should his expenses and his temporary job earnings be treated?

9. Employee entered into a contract for 16-years-employment with Employer at $100,000 per year. Since the employment was predicated on Employee's great expertise in managing a process on which Employer owned a patent, there was no similar employment available to Employee elsewhere. At the end of one year Employer wrongfully terminated Employee's employment. Upon finding that Employee could not mitigate damages, the trial court entered judgment for Employee for $1,500,000. Was the court's judgment mathematically sound?

10. P was hired as a radio "talk show" host for one year on station WMCA at a salary of $50,000 per year. In mid year he was discharged without cause. The balance of his salary for the year was tendered. He refused the tender and sued for $500,000 claiming damages for "lost publicity." What result?

11. Defendant, a highly skilled hairdresser entered into a bilateral contract with plaintiff to work for plaintiff for one year at $75 per week. Defendant quit without cause to take a job at $100 per week. Are damages sufficiently shown by the facts stated?

12. D contracted with P whereby D would play the leading role in a motion picture. D knew that P had contracted with T, a distributor, whereby T would pay P $900,000 for the distribution rights plus a share of the distribution receipts after the $900,000 had been recouped. D also knew that P had contracted with X whereby X would produce the picture for $750,000. P's contracts with T and X were both predicated on D's playing the leading

role. D breached the contract by refusing to appear for the filming of the picture. What is D's liability?

(c) Sale of Goods and Realty

———

(Calamari & Perillo 5th §§ 14.20—14.27, 14.30)

CHRONISTER OIL CO. v. UNOCAL REFINING AND MARKETING

United States Court of Appeals, Seventh Circuit, 1994.
34 F.3d 462.

POSNER, CHIEF JUDGE. Chronister Oil Company brought this diversity suit for breach of contract against Union Oil Company (Unocal), to which Chronister had agreed to sell 25,000 barrels of gasoline. Unocal counterclaimed, charging that it was Chronister, not Unocal, that had broken their contract. The case is governed by the Uniform Commercial Code as interpreted by the Illinois courts; and the magistrate judge, to whom the case was assigned for trial by consent of the parties, held after a bench trial that Chronister had broken the contract, and he awarded damages of $26,000 to Unocal, precipitating this appeal.

The contract, made February 9, 1990, provided that Chronister, an oil trader, would deliver the 25,000 barrels to Colonial Pipeline (for shipment to Unocal) on the "front seventh cycle," and fixed a price of 60.4 cents a gallon. The term "front cycle" is pipelinese for the first half of what is normally a ten-day period for shipping a particular grade of product in a petroleum pipeline. The cycles begin on January 1, so the "front seventh cycle" would be approximately the first five days of March—apparently no effort is made to pin down the dates of the cycles and half cycles more precisely. To fulfill the contract, Chronister on March 1, 1990, made a contract with another oil trader, Enron, which in turn made a contract with a supplier, Crown Petroleum, to deliver the 25,000 barrels to Colonial Pipeline's pipeline at Pasadena, Texas for shipment east and north to terminals from which Unocal would deliver the gasoline to its dealers. Enron decided to have the gasoline delivered to Colonial's pipeline on March 5. But when the day arrived and Colonial tested the gasoline preparatory to taking it into its pipeline, it found that the gasoline contained too much water, and refused to take it. Unocal was informed on the morning of March 6 (which apparently was still within the front seventh cycle) and immediately called Chronister, demanding (at least implicitly, as we'll explain) assurances that Chronister would comply with the contract. Chronister got in touch with Enron, which agreed to supply another 25,000 barrels, but for shipment on the back seventh cycle, that is, later in March, or on the eighth cycle, later still. Unocal wasn't interested, and within hours, while Chronister was trying to solve the problem, Unocal took the precaution of diverting 25,000 barrels of gasoline that it already owned and that were in the pipeline in transit to a storage facility to Baton Rouge to its distribution terminals farther up the line—a measure Unocal describes as "provisional cover"—in effect supplying the 25,000 barrel deficit from inventory, but giving Chronister until the following day (March 7) to come up with conforming product.

Yet later the same day (March 6), Chronister, despite Unocal's adamant refusal to accept anything but front seventh cycle gasoline, accepted Enron's offer of substitute performance on the back seventh cycle and again offered this to Unocal. Again Unocal insisted that it would take only front seventh cycle product—either the Crown Petroleum gasoline drained of its water or other product that could be injected into the pipeline in time. With Unocal unwilling to accept the 25,000 barrels on the back seventh cycle that Chronister had perhaps precipitately agreed to take from Enron, Chronister sold this gasoline to another company, Aectra Refining, at 55.3 cents a gallon. Claiming that by refusing to accept the substitute performance Unocal had broken the contract, Chronister filed this suit for damages based on the difference between the contract price and the lower price at which it sold the 25,000 barrels to Aectra. Unocal counterclaimed, contending that it was Chronister that had broken the contract and seeking damages equal to the difference between the contract price and the average cost of its inventory (63.14 cents), from which it had made up the loss of the 25,000 barrels promised by Chronister. The district court agreed with Unocal that Chronister, not Unocal, had broken the contract, and it awarded damages to Unocal on its counterclaim. [The court affirms the finding that Chronister is the party in breach.]

* * *

We move to the issue of damages. The point of an award of damages, whether it is for a breach of contract or for a tort, is, so far as possible, to put the victim where he would have been had the breach or tort not taken place. Nicolet Instrument Corp. v. Lindquist & Vennum, 34 F.3d 453, 457 (7th Cir.1994). Unocal had, back in February, promised to pay Chronister 60.4 cents a gallon. By the first week of March the price of gasoline for delivery to the Colonial Pipeline had fallen. On March 6, Chronister sold 25,000 barrels to Aectra at 55.3 cents a gallon, and it is not argued that Chronister could have gotten a higher price. Uncontradicted evidence revealed that there had been a similar sale at a similar price on March 2. Had Unocal gone out in the market and covered by buying 25,000 barrels on March 6 or 7 it would have paid somewhere in the neighborhood of 55 cents a gallon and thus would have saved 5 cents a gallon as a result of Chronister's breach. It makes no difference that instead of buying the gasoline on the open market it took it from inventory. As a matter of fact, because of an impending change in pressure by Colonial Pipeline that would make Unocal's inventory, stored mainly in a 300,000 barrel storage facility in Baton Rouge, shortly unshippable, Unocal had a strong interest in drawing down its inventory. The breach was a godsend. At argument Unocal's counsel candidly acknowledged that Unocal was made better off as a result of the breach and that this was evident not only by the time of trial, and hence early enough to figure in the calculation of damages, *Rea* v. *Ford Motor Co.*, 560 F.2d 554, 557 (3d Cir.1977), but within fifteen days after Chronister's breach.

Nevertheless, argues Unocal, it was entitled by UCC § 2–712 to cover by obtaining a substitute for the lost 25,000 barrels, even from itself, and to obtain as damages the difference between the cover price, which it deems to be 63.14 cents a gallon, the average cost of the inventory from which it obtained the substitute supply of gasoline, and the contract price of 60.4 cents. This is a misreading of section 2–712. . . . Section 2–712 defines cover as purchasing or making a contract to purchase a substitute good. Unocal did not purchase any gasoline to take the place of the lost 25,000 barrels. It decided not to purchase a substitute good but instead to use a good that it already owned. You can't "purchase," whether in ordinary language or UCC speak (see § 1–201(32)), what you already own. The purpose of the cover provision is not to allow buyers to obtain damages when they have not been hurt, but to provide a market measure of the hurt. Taking a good out of your inventory and selling it is not a purchase in a market. There is no purchase price to use as a ready index of the harm that the buyer incurred by the seller's breach.

Two cases from other jurisdictions have shoehorned this kind of "self-cover" into section 2–712. *Cives Corp.* v. *Callier Steel Pipe & Tube, Inc.*, 482 A.2d 852, 858 (Me.1984); *Dura–Wood Treating Co.* v. *Century Forest Industries, Inc.*, 675 F.2d 745, 753–54 (5th Cir.1982). They had no need to do this violence to the text. Section 2–712 is not the only buyer's remedy that the UCC authorizes. The very next section allows the buyer to obtain damages measured by the difference between market price and contract price. If a reasonable response for the buyer to the breach would be to make the product itself, then the difference between the market price of that product and the contract price would be an appropriate measure of the harm from the breach. * * * That is what *Cives* and *Dura–Wood* hold; they merely cite the wrong section.

Unocal's response in diverting gasoline in transit to storage was reasonable; the only question, upon which its damages if any turn, is what that cost it. What it had paid for the gasoline—even less, the average price that it had paid for all the gasoline that it had not yet sold (the average cost of its inventory, in other words)—was not the cost of diverting the gasoline from storage to sale. At least it was not cost in a sense relative to damages. The object of an award of damages, as we have already noted, is to put the victim in the same place that he would have been in had the breach or other wrong of which he complains not occurred. It is to compensate him for a loss *that he would have avoided* had the violation not occurred. The concept of loss that underlies the computation of legal damages thus resembles the economist's concept of "opportunity cost": the opportunity one gives up by engaging in some activity is the cost of that activity, [citation omitted]. We must ask what

Unocal gave up as a consequence of the breach, and whether it was something of value.

By diverting the gasoline in order to protect itself against Chronister's breach of contract, Unocal gave up the opportunity either to sell the gasoline on the market (in order to lighten its inventory), which we know would have yielded it substantially less than the average cost of its inventory because the market price was much lower than that cost, or to have a larger—an unnecessarily and, it would soon prove, unusably larger—inventory. Neither course of action would have yielded value equal to Unocal's average cost of inventory or equal to the contract price. The first point shows that the average cost of inventory was the wrong figure to use in estimating Unocal's damages, and the second point shows that it had no damages. The 25,000 barrels it diverted to its dealers cost it less—was worth less—than the 25,000 barrels that Chronister failed to deliver to it as promised. Sellers usually break their contracts in a rising market, where they can get more for the product by selling to someone other than the buyer with whom they signed the contract. Here a seller in a declining market broke a contract that he desperately wanted to perform, conferring a windfall gain on the buyer—which the latter would like as it were to double with the help of the courts. The judgment of the district court is affirmed insofar as it determined that Chronister broke its contract with Unocal. But it is reversed with respect to damages and remanded with directions to enter judgment for Unocal for nominal damages (to which for reasons we do not understand every victim of a breach of contract, unlike a tort victim, is entitled *Stromberger* v. *3M Co.*, 990 F.2d 974, 976 (7th Cir.1993)) only.

AFFIRMED IN PART, REVERSED IN PART.

NATIONAL CONTROLS, INC. v. COMMODORE BUSINESS MACHINES, INC.

Court of Appeal, First District, Division 3, California, 1985.
163 Cal.App.3d 688, 209 Cal.Rptr. 636 (1985).

Scott, Associate Justice. Respondent National Controls, Inc. (NCI) brought an action for breach of contract against appellant Commodore Business Machines, Inc. (Commodore). After a court trial, judgment was entered awarding NCI over $280,000 in damages, and Commodore has appealed.

I

NCI manufactures electronic weighing and measuring devices. Among its products is the model 3221 electronic microprocessor technology load cell scale (the 3221), which is designed to interface with a cash register for use at check-out stands. NCI sells the 3221 to cash register manufacturers, also termed original equipment manufacturers, or O.E.M.s. NCI does not maintain an inventory stock of the scales, but builds them to specific order by an O.E.M. The 3221 is a standard unit, which is modified by NCI to meet the specifications of each O.E.M. with respect to cash register compatability, paint, and logo.

In November 1980, Commodore had initial discussions with NCI about the possibility of Commodore becoming an O.E.M. customer. By telephone, Commodore purchased one 3221, which was sent by NCI to Commodore's Texas facility, along with NCI's standard specifications for the 3221 and its standard price schedule. In December 1980, Commodore ordered and paid for four more scales. Again, the orders were made by telephone. NCI did not receive a purchase order from Commodore; instead, Commodore merely gave NCI a Commodore purchase order number over the phone; that number was written on the sales order prepared by NCI and sent to Commodore.

In March 1981, Terry Rogers of Commodore ordered an additional 30 scales. The order was placed by telephone, and once again Commodore did not send NCI a purchase order. Instead, Rogers gave Wiggins of NCI a purchase order number by telephone; that number was entered by Wiggins on NCI's sales order.

On March 31, 1981, in a phone conversation with Wiggins, Rogers placed a firm order for 900 scales: 50 to be delivered in May, 150 in June, 300 in July, and 400 in August. Wiggins and Rogers agreed on quantity, price, and delivery schedule. As in the previous transactions, Rogers gave Wiggins a purchase order number over the telephone, Wiggins then prepared an NCI sales order, entered on it the Commodore purchase order number, and mailed a copy of that sales order to Commodore. NCI also sent a copy of its sales order to its Florida manufacturing facility, which began manufacture of the units.

* * *

Delivery was made to Commodore of the first 200 units, and 300 units were ready to ship in June of 1981. As of that date, the remaining 400 units of the order were nearly complete. However, Commodore accepted only the first 50 scales, and did not or pay for the remaining 850 units. Thereafter, all of the 850 units were resold to National Semiconductor, an existing O.E.M. customer. NCI's vice president and general manager in charge of its Florida manufacturing facility testified that in 1980 and 1981, the plant had the production capacity to more than double its output of 3221's.

Among its findings and conclusions, the trial court concluded that the terms of the parties' contract were those established during their telephone discussions prior to and on March 31, 1981, and in the November 1980 letter from NCI to Commodore enclosing a price schedule, as well as "the terms" of NCI's prior sales orders. * * * The court also found that NCI was a "lost volume seller" who was entitled to recover the loss of profit it would have made on the sale of the 850 units to Commodore, notwithstanding its subsequent resale of those units to another customer.

[Section II of the opinion which discusses the terms of the contract is omitted. Ed.]

III

Commodore also contends that the trial court erred when it relied on section 2–708, subdivision (2), to award NCI damages by way of lost profits. In a related argument, Commodore contends that if lost profits were the proper measure of damages, it was entitled under the plain language of section 2–708 to credit for the proceeds of NCI's resale of the contract goods to National Semiconductor.

Damages caused by a buyer's breach or repudiation of a sales contract are usually measured by the difference between the resale price of the goods and the contract price, as provided by Uniform Commercial Code section 2–706. When it is not appropriate to use this difference to measure the seller's loss (as when the goods have not been resold in a commercially reasonable manner), the seller's measure of damages is the difference between the market and the contract prices as provided in Uniform Commercial Code section 2–708, subdivision (1). Ordinarily, this measure will result in recovery equal to the value of the seller's bargain. However, under certain circumstances this formula is also not an adequate means to ascertain that value, and the seller may recover his loss of expected profits on the contract under subdivision (2) of Uniform Commercial Code section 2–708. (3 Hawkland, Uniform Commercial Code Series (1982–1984) §§ 2–708–2–708:04.)

Section 2–708 provides: "(1) Subject to subdivision (2) and to the provisions of this division with respect to proof of market price (Section 2–723), the measure of damages for nonacceptance or repudiation by the buyer is the difference between the market price at the time and place for tender and the unpaid contract price together with any incidental damages provided in this division (Section 2–710), but less expenses saved in consequence of the buyer's breach.

"(2) If the measure of damages provided in subdivision (1) is inadequate to put the seller in as good a position as performance would have done then the measure of damages is the profit (including reasonable overhead) which the seller would have made from full performance by the buyer, together with any incidental damages provided in this division (Section 2–710), due allowance for costs reasonably incurred and due credit for payments or proceeds of resale."

When buyers have repudiated a fixed price contract to purchase goods, several courts elsewhere have construed subdivision (2) of Uniform Commercial Code section 2–708 or its state counterpart to permit the award of lost profits under the contract to the seller who establishes that he is a "lost volume seller," i.e. one who proves that even though he resold the contract goods, that sale to the third party would have been made regardless of the buyer's breach. (*Neri v. Retail Marine Corporation* (1972) 30 N.Y.2d 393, 334 N.Y.S.2d 165, 168, 285 N.E.2d 311, 314; *Snyder v. Herbert Greenbaum & Assoc., Inc.* (1977) 38 Md.App. 144, 380 A.2d 618, 624–625; *Teradyne, Inc. v. Teledyne Industries, Inc.* (1st Cir.1982) 676 F.2d 865, 866–868; *Nederlandse, etc. v. Grand Pre-Stressed Corp.* (E.D.N.Y.1979) 466 F.Supp. 846, affd. (2nd Cir.) 614 F.2d 1289.) The lost volume seller must establish that had the breaching buyer performed, the seller would have realized profits from two sales. (See Goetz & Scott, *Measuring Sellers' Damages: The Lost–Profits Puzzle* (1979) 31 Stan.L.Rev. 323, 326.)

In *Neri v. Retail Marine Corporation, supra,* 285 N.E.2d 311, seller contracted to sell a new boat, which it ordered and received from its supplier. The buyer then repudiated the contract. Later, seller sold the boat to another buyer, for the same price. The court relied on Uniform Commercial Code section 2–708, subdivision (2), to award the seller its lost profits under the contract, reasoning that the record established that market damages would be inadequate to put the seller in as good a position as performance would have done. The court drew an analogy to an auto dealer with an inexhaustible supply of cars. A breach of an agreement to buy a car at a standard price would cost that dealer a sale even though he was able to resell the car at the same price. In other words, had the breaching buyer performed, seller would have made two sales instead of one. (*Id.,* at pp. 312–315.)

While the seller in *Neri* was a retailer, the lost volume seller rule is also applicable to manufacturers. (*Nederlandse, etc. v. Grand Pre–Stressed Corp., supra,* 466 F.Supp. 846.) In *Nederlandse,* seller, a manufacturer of steel strand, brought an action against buyer for breach of an agreement to purchase approximately 1,180 metric tons of strand. Defendant had accepted only about 221 tons, and repudiated the remaining 958 tons, of which 317 tons had been already produced by seller. Seller resold the 317 tons to various third party purchasers. (*Id.,* at p. 849.)

The court held that seller was entitled to lost profits under Uniform Commercial Code section 2–708, subdivision (2), and that no set-off would be allowed for profits earned through the sales to third parties. The evidence established that seller had sufficient production capacity to supply not only the 1,180 tons required by the contract, but also the 317 tons sold to third parties. The fact that seller was a manufacturer rather than a retailer, and that he produced only to order rather than maintaining an inventory, was of no significance in determining the applicability of Uniform Commercial Code section 2–708. (*Id.,* at pp. 853–854.)

Commodore accurately points out that the lost volume seller rule has been criticized by some commentators as overly simplistic. (Goetz & Scott, *supra,* 31 Stan.L.Rev. 323, 330–354.) Nevertheless, those courts considering the question have held that Uniform Commercial Code section 2–708 does allow lost profits to a "lost volume seller" and that criticism has not resulted in any revision of the section.

Commodore also contends that if NCI was entitled to lost profits under the contract, Commodore should have received credit for the proceeds of the resale.

The literal language of section 2–708, subdivision (2), does provide some support for that contention: "If the measure of damages provided in subdivision (1) is inadequate to put the seller in as good a position as performance would have done then the measure of damages is the profit (including reasonable overhead) which the seller would have made from full performance by the buyer, *together with ... due credit for payments or proceeds of resale."* (Emphasis added.) However, courts elsewhere have uniformly held that the underscored language does not apply to a lost volume seller. (See *Neri v. Retail Marine Corporation, supra,* 285 N.E.2d at p. 314, fn. 2; *Famous Knitwear Corporation v. Drug Fair, Inc.* (4th Cir.1974) 493 F.2d 251, 254, fn. 7; *Snyder v. Herbert Greenbaum & Assoc., Inc., supra,* 380 A.2d at pp. 625–626; *Teradyne, Inc. v. Teledyne Industries, Inc., supra,* 676 F.2d 865, 868.)

As the court in *Snyder v. Herbert Greenbaum & Assoc., Inc., supra,* 380 A.2d 618 explained, "Logically, lost volume status, which entitles the seller to the § 2–708(2) formula rather than the formula found in § 2–708(1), is inconsistent with a credit for the proceeds of resale. The whole concept of lost volume status is that the sale of the goods to the resale purchaser could have been made with other goods had there been no breach. In essence, the original sale and the second sale are independent events, becoming related only after breach, as the original sale goods are applied to the second sale. To require a credit for the proceeds of resale is to deny the essential element that entitles the lost volume seller to § 2–708(2) in the first place—the mutual independence of the contract and the resale.

"Practically, if the 'due credit' clause is applied to the lost volume seller, his measure of damages is no different from his recovery under § 2–708(1). Under § 2–708(1) he recovers the contract/market differential and the profit he makes on resale. If the 'due credit' provision is applied, the seller recovers only the profit he makes on resale plus the difference between the resale price and the contract price, an almost identical measure to § 2–708(1). If the 'due credit' clause is applied to the lost volume seller, the damage measure of 'lost profits' is rendered nugatory, and he is not put in as good a position as if there had been performance." (*Id.,* at p. 625.)

In this case, the evidence was undisputed that in 1980 and 1981, NCI's manufacturing plant was operating at approximately 40 percent capacity. The production of the 900 units did not tax that capacity, and the plant could have more than doubled its output of 3221's and still have stayed within its capacity. That evidence was sufficient to support the court's findings that NCI had the capacity to supply both Commodore and National Semiconductor, and that had there been no breach by Commodore, NCI would have had the benefit of both the original contract and the resale contract. Accordingly, the trial court correctly determined that NCI was a lost volume seller, that the usual "contract price minus market price" rule set forth in subdivision (1) of section 2–708 was inadequate to put NCI in as good a position as performance would have done, and that NCI was therefore entitled to its lost profits on the contract with Commodore, without any set-off for profits on the resale to National Semiconductor.

Judgment is affirmed.

WHITE, P.J., and BARRY-DEAL, J., concur.

LUCAS, J., is of the opinion the petition should be granted.

DONOVAN v. BACHSTADT

Supreme Court of New Jersey, 1982.
91 N.J. 434, 453 A.2d 160.

SCHREIBER, J.

The central legal issue in this case concerns the damages to which a buyer of realty is entitled upon the breach of the executory agreement by the seller. * * *

* * * Though the record is sparse, the following uncontroverted facts appear.

On December 1, 1977, Joan Lowden acquired a deed from Middletown Township to Lots 25 and 26 in Block F as shown on a certain map duly filed in the Monmouth Clerk's Office. The defendant, Bachstadt, advanced the funds for the purchase of land. Ms. Lowden gave Bachstadt a deed to the property that he never recorded. Bachstadt constructed a house on the property and on January 19, 1980 entered into a contract to sell the premises to the Donovans.

The contract was on a standard form prepared by an association of realtors. Bachstadt had no attorney. The record does not disclose if the Donovans were represented at the time the contract was executed. Indeed, Bachstadt never met the Donovans until after the contract had been signed, the realtor having been the only link between the parties.

The contract recited that the purchase price was $58,900. A deposit of $5,890 was paid to and held by the broker. At the closing scheduled for May 1, 1980, the Donovans were to pay an additional $9,010 in cash and the balance was to consist of a purchase money bond or note and mortgage in the principal amount of $44,000, for 30 years, at an interest rate of [10]%. The conveyance was to be made subject to easements and restrictions of record and facts disclosed in an accurate survey, provided that these would not render the title unmarketable. The contract also stated that title "shall be marketable and insurable . . . by any reputable title insurance company. . . ." There was no liquidated damage provision.

A title search obtained by the Donovans from Lawyers Title Insurance Corporation disclosed that title was presently in Anthony and Jane Mettrich, and not in Middletown Township or Joan Lowden. This was brought to Bachstadt's attention. Middletown had foreclosed its tax lien on other property owned by the Mettrichs, but it had inadvertently failed to foreclose on Lots 25 and 26 in Block F, the land sold to Joan Lowden.

The Donovans, fully aware of the title problem, filed a complaint for specific performance * * *. * * * The trial court entered an order * * * decreeing specific performance. No appeal was taken from that judgment.

When defendant could not obtain marketable title, the Donovans commenced this suit for compensatory and punitive damages. [T]he trial court granted plaintiffs' motion for summary judgment. It was indisputable that the defendant had breached the agreement. The only issue was damages. The trial court held that plaintiffs were entitled under N.J.S.A. 2A:29–1 to recovery of their costs for the title search and survey. Plaintiffs had apparently in the interim purchased a home in Middlesex County and obtained a mortgage loan bearing interest at the rate of 13 1/4% per annum. Plaintiffs sought the difference between 10 1/2% and 13 1/4% as compensatory damages, representing their loss of the benefit of the bargain. The trial court denied recovery because the contract was for the sale of the property and the financing "was only incidental to the basic concept."

The Appellate Division reversed. 181 N.J.Super. 367, 437 A.2d 728 (1981). * * * The court concluded [that] the statute intended that the general law of damages for breach of a contract applies and stated that the difference in interest rates could be the basis for a measure of damages depending on whether the plaintiffs "have entered into a comparable transaction for another home ... or are likely to do so in the near future...." Id. at 376, 437 A.2d 728. The Appellate Division cautioned that any award of future damages should represent the true life of the mortgage and be reduced to present value. Further, the plaintiffs should be held to a duty to mitigate. Lastly, if the proofs should demonstrate that plaintiffs have not purchased and are not likely to purchase a home in the near future, their damages would be remote and speculative. The cause was remanded for a plenary hearing.

I

The initial inquiry is whether plaintiffs are entitled to compensatory damages. We had occasion recently to discuss the measure of damages available when a seller breaches an executory contract for the sale of real property. *St. Pius X House of Retreats v. Diocese of Camden*, 88 N.J. 571, 582–87, 443 A.2d 1052 (1982). We noted that New Jersey follows the English rule, which generally limits a buyer's recovery to the return of his deposit unless the seller wilfully refuses to convey or is guilty of fraud or deceit. The traditional formulation of the English rule has been expressed by T. Cyprian Williams, an English barrister, as follows:

> Where the breach of contract is occasioned by the vendor's inability, without his own fault, to show a good title, the purchaser is entitled to recover as damages his deposit, if any, with interest, and his expenses incurred in connection with the agreement, but not more than nominal damages for the loss of his bargain. [*T.C. Williams, The Contract of Sale of Land* 128 (1930)]

* * *

[In New Jersey] the common law governs the measure of damages apart from those guaranteed in the statute. There is nothing in the statute that prevents the Court from adopting the American rule and awarding loss of the benefit of the bargain damages.

We are satisfied that the American rule is preferable. The English principle developed because of the uncertainties of title due to the complexity of the rules governing title to land during the eighteenth and nineteenth centuries. Oakley, "Pecuniary Compensation for Failure to Complete a Contract for the Sale of Land," 39 Cambridge L.J. 58, 69 (1980). At that time the only evidence of title was contained in deeds which were in a phrase attributed to Lord Westbury, "difficult to read, disgusting to touch, and impossible to understand." The reason for the English principle that creates an exception to the law governing damages for breaches of executory contracts for the sale of property is no longer valid, and the exception should be eliminated. *Cessante ratione legis, cessat et ipsa lex* (the reason for a law ceasing, the law itself ceases) * * *. Indeed in England the rule has been modified by placing the burden of proof on the vendor to establish that he has done everything within his power to carry out the contract. *Malhotra v. Choudhury*, [1978] 3 W.L.R. 825; [1979] 1 All E.R. 186 (C.A.).

Whether titles are clear may be ascertained by record searches. * * * Moreover, limitation periods may be applicable. * * * Thus, it is standard practice for title examiners to search the back title for 60 years and until a warranty deed is found in the chain of title. * * * Further the parties may insert appropriate provisions in their agreements protecting them from title defects so that to a very large extent sellers may control the measure of redress.

There is no sound basis why benefit of the bargain damages should not be awarded whether the subject matter of the contract is realty or personalty. Serious losses should not be borne by the vendee of real estate to the benefit of the defaulting vendor. This is particularly so when an instalment purchase contract is involved that extends over a period of years during which the vendee makes substantial payments upon the principal, as well as extensive improvements to the property.

The innocent purchaser should be permitted to recover benefit of the bargain damages irrespective of the good or bad faith of the seller. Contract culpability depends on the breach of the contractual promise. 4 A. Corbin, Contracts §§ 943–44, at 806–08 (1951). Where, as here, the seller agreed that title would be marketable, the seller's liability should depend upon his breach of that promise.

Many commentators have advocated the adoption of the American rule. 11 S. Williston, A Treatise on the Law of Contracts § 1399 at 524 (3d ed. 1968); 5A Corbin on Contracts § 1097 at 523 (1964); D. Dobbs, Handbook on the Law of Remedies § 12.8 at 835–36 (1973); 3 American Law of Property § 11.67 at 168 (1952). English commentators have also sharply criticized the English rule and advocated permitting the buyer to recover damages for loss of profit. * * * Many states now follow the American rule.[5] 5A Corbin, *supra*, § 1098 at 525–35; 11 S. Williston, *supra*, at 524–28.

* * *

We are satisfied that a buyer should be permitted to recover benefit of the bargain damages when the seller breaches an executory contract

---

5. The dissent recommends adoption of the Uniform Land Transactions Act. 13 U.L.A. 638 (1975). No state has enacted this proposed law.

to convey real property. Here the defendant agreed to convey marketable title. He made that bargained-for promise and breached it and is responsible to the plaintiff for the damages occasioned thereby. The next question is how to compute those compensatory damages.

II

* * *

"Compensatory damages are designed 'to put the injured party in as good a position as he would have had if performance had been rendered as promised.' 5 Corbin, Contracts § 992, p. 5 (1951)." * * * What that position is depends upon what the parties reasonably expected. It follows that the defendant is not chargeable for loss that he did not have reason to foresee as a probable result of the breach when the contract was made. *Hadley v. Baxendale*, 9 Exch. 341, 5 Eng. Rul. Case 502, (1854); * * *. Further the loss must be a reasonably certain consequence of the breach although the exact amount of the loss need not be certain. * * *

* * *

The plaintiffs here assert that their damages are equivalent to the difference in interest costs incurred by them in purchasing a different home at another location. This claim assumes that the financial provision of the contract concerning the purchase money mortgage that the defendant agreed to accept was independent and divisible from the purchase of the land and house. The defendant contends that he did not agree to loan these funds in connection with the purchase of some other property, but that this provision was incidental to the sale of the house. Neither position is entirely sound. This financing was an integral part of the transaction. It can be neither ignored nor viewed as an isolated element.

The relationship of the financing to the purchase of a home has changed in recent years. As interest rates rose and the availability of first mortgage funds was sharply reduced, potential homeowners, though desirous of purchasing homes, found financing difficult to obtain. The seller's acceptance of a purchase money mortgage became an important factor in effecting a sale. See Rand, "Home Resale Market: Pattern Shift," N.Y. Times, March 22, 1981, § 11, at 18, col. 3. In evaluating a contract such a financial arrangement could play an important part in determining price. * * *

In some circumstances interest rate differentials are an appropriate measure of damages. Where the buyer has obtained specific performance, but because of the delay has incurred higher mortgage rates, then his loss clearly should include the higher financing cost. *Godwin v. Lindbert*, 101 Mich.App. 754, 300 N.W.2d 514 (1981), is illustrative. The buyers lost their commitment for a mortgage with an interest rate of 8 3/4% when the seller refused to convey. The buyers succeeded in obtaining specific performance but were compelled to borrow funds at 11 1/2%. They were awarded the difference reduced to present value. *See also Reis v. Sparks*, 547 F.2d 236 (4th Cir.1976). Moreover, we are not unmindful of the possibility that a buyer might demonstrate that a lending institution's commitment to advance the funds initially at a certain interest rate was due to the buyer's financial condition. The particular realty might well be a secondary and incidental consideration for the loan. Therefore an interest differential occasioned by the seller's default might be a proper factor in fixing damages where the buyer shortly thereafter purchased another property financed at a higher interest rate.

This is not such a situation. The defendant's motive was to sell a house and not to lend money. In measuring the plaintiffs' loss there should be a determination of the fair market value of the property and house that could be acquired with a purchase money mortgage in the principal amount of $44,000 at an interest rate of 10 1/2% (no appeal was taken from the judgment of reformation) for a 30–year term. The valuation should be at the time the defendant failed to comply with the judgment of specific performance. The plaintiffs would be entitled to the difference between $58,900 and that fair market value. If the fair market value was not more than the contract price, the plaintiffs would not have established any damage ascribable to the loss of the bargain. They are also entitled to their expenditures for the survey, search, and counsel fees for services rendered in preparation of the aborted closing. The plaintiffs have hitherto received the return of the deposit.

The judgment of the Appellate Division is modified and, as so modified, remanded to the trial court for further proceedings consistent with this opinion.

O'HERN, J., dissenting.

I must respectfully dissent from the opinion and judgment of the Court. The issue is whether out-of-pocket costs or benefit-of-the-bargain damages are to be awarded for breach of an executory contract for the sale of real estate when the contract does not close because of a defect in title unknown to the seller at the time of execution of the contract.

Although commentators advocate the adoption of the "American rule" as suggested by the majority, there remains sufficient flexibility in the rule that would except its application to the circumstances of this case. While both Williston and Corbin suggest that the only rule defensible on principle is allowing the purchaser the difference between the contract price and the market value of the land, it is put this way: the rule "is applied in every case where the vendor *breaks* his contract *without legal excuse.*" 11 Williston, Contracts (3 ed. Jaeger 1968), § 1399 at 527 (emphasis supplied). Accord, 5 Corbin, Contracts (1964) § 1098 at 525. Most of the recent American cases cited in both treatises do not sustain a conclusion that such a rule would be applied to a case where the seller was wholly without fault with respect to the existence of a defect in title that prevents closing.

I believe that the rule the Court adopts can unnecessarily penalize the unwary. Although it is true that a skilled commercial conveyancer can draft provisions to protect a seller from the principle of law adopted by the Court, it is also true that many people enter residential real estate transactions without the benefit of counsel. * * * In New Jersey, a contract for sale of real estate of this type is a consumer contract and should be expressed in plain English, without legalisms, that ordinary people can understand. See N.J.S.A. 56:12–1 *et seq.* In my view, that policy is not furthered by a rule of law that leaves the ordinary homeowner to the consolation that better drafting would have dealt with the unforeseen consequences of an unknown title problem.

I would adhere to the rule that an award of damages should be just under the circumstances. In *Zeliff v. Sabatino*, 15 N.J. 70, 104 A.2d 54 (1954), this Court said:

> We rather are of the opinion that this State is not so inexorably wedded to the "out-of-pocket" rule as to the measure of damages that "the benefit-of-the-bargain" rule cannot be applied where justice requires. . . .

> . . . The just method of determining damages necessarily varies with the facts of the particular case. . . . No rule of damages capable of precise application in all cases can be laid down and followed. [*Id.* at 74, 104 A.2d 54].

* * *

If any modifications of existing law were to be made under the circumstances of this case, I would recommend that the Court follow the recommendations of the Commissioners on Uniform State Laws * * * as follows:

Section 2–510 [Buyer's Damages for Seller's Failure to Convey]

(a) Except as provided in subsection (b), the measure of damages for a seller's repudiation or wrongful failure to convey is the difference between the fair market value at the time for conveyance and the contract price and any incidental and consequential damages (Section 2–514), less expenses avoided because of the seller's breach.

(b) Unless the title defect is an encumbrance securing an obligation to pay money which could be discharged by application of all or a portion of the purchase price, if a seller is unable to convey because of a title defect of which the seller had no knowledge at the time of entering into the contract, the buyer is entitled only to restitution of any amounts paid on the contract price and incidental damages (Section 2–514). [Unif. Land Transactions Act § 2–510, 13 U.L.A. 638 (1980)].

If I were to reach the issue of increased financing costs, I would agree with the majority that such are appropriate for consideration. * * *

I would, however, reverse and reinstate the trial court's judgment.

Problems

13. B contracted with S whereby S agreed to sell steel to B for use in a project to build a dredge for the United States. S was aware that B's contract

with the United States contained provisions requiring the payment of liquidated damages in the event of delay. At the time of contracting steel was readily available on the market. S breached by delivering late. At the time of the breach, because of supervening wartime shortages, steel was not generally available on the market. B seeks to hold S liable for damages measured by the amount it was required to pay the United States in damages. What result?

14. B bought a Ford truck from an authorized dealer in Mobile, Alabama. He received a written warranty whereby the Ford Motor Company promised that within the warranty period certain repairs would be made by the dealer. It also provided: "If the owner is traveling * * * any authorized Ford dealer will perform the repairs." Because of a defect in manufacture the truck broke down in Orlando, Florida, within the warranty period. The dealer in Orlando refused to make the necessary repairs and Ford Motor Company officials on the scene wrongfully refused to recognize the warranty. B has had the repairs done elsewhere and was deprived of the use of the truck for four months. He seeks to recover the value of the loss of use of the truck. His evidence showed that if the truck had been operative he could have used the truck in his business or leased the truck with a driver to others for $22.50 per hour. What is B entitled to?

15. B purchased machinery from S which S warranted for 12 months. The warranty was limited to repair or replacement of defective parts or equipment. Liability for consequential damages was excluded. When the machinery broke down, S repudiated its warranty obligations. B sues, claiming consequential damages. What result?

16. The defendant, an automobile dealer in Maryland, had a quota available to it of 10 or 11 Rolls–Royce automobiles for the model year. Mrs. Kaiden learned, through a dealer in New York, that defendant had on order a Rolls–Royce of the style and color that she wanted. In August, through her dealer, she placed an order with the defendant and made a deposit of $5,000 on a price of $29,000. The order contained no delivery date and expressly disclaimed liability for delays in delivery not within the dealer's control. Through no fault of the dealer, it did not come into possession of a conforming model until November 29. Meanwhile, on November 21, Mrs. Kaiden notified the defendant that she had obtained another Rolls–Royce elsewhere. On January 17, the defendant sold the vehicle intended for Mrs. Kaiden to a buyer in Atlanta for $26,495. The dealer gave Mrs. Kaiden no notice of the intended sale. She sued for the return of her deposit. The dealer counterclaimed for the difference between the contract price and the resale price plus incidental damages (commissions on the second sale, interest on the cost of the car for 52 days and shipping expenses for sending the car to Atlanta). The finder of facts was justified in finding that Mrs. Kaiden breached the contract. Resolve the damages questions.

17. S contracted with B whereby S would manufacture a specially designed stud driving machine for $11,750. Production was about one half completed when B repudiated the contract. S ceased manufacture. The half completed machine had a salvage value of about $1,500. (a) What is the proper measure of damages? (b) Do you have sufficient information to calculate damages?

18. B, a law firm, bought a copier from S. Despite 39 maintenance service calls in 9 months, the copier never worked properly. In an action for breach of warranty, B proved the warranty, the breach, the cost of the copier, and that the "machine has absolutely no value to our firm...." On this evidence what damages may B recover?

19. Seller contracted to sell 1,875 hundredweight (cwt) of beans for $16 a cwt, to be delivered at harvest time. Seller repudiated the contract at a time when the price for forward contracts for beans was still $16. Because of a drought, at harvest time the price of beans had risen to $36 a cwt. What measure of damages should be applied to Buyer's claim?

(d) Construction Contracts

(Calamari & Perillo 5th §§ 14.28—14.29)

JACOB & YOUNGS v. KENT
230 N.Y. 239, 129 N.E. 889, 23 A.L.R. 1429.
See p. 480 supra.

EMERY v. CALEDONIA SAND AND GRAVEL CO., INC.
Supreme Court of New Hampshire, 1977.
117 N.H. 441, 374 A.2d 929.

Bois, Justice. The plaintiffs, husband and wife farm operators, entered into a landfill removal contract with the defendant road construction company. Under the terms of the several written agreements, the plaintiffs allowed the defendant to remove earthfill from a certain site on their farmland at a specified unit charge. The agreements imposed upon the company the obligation to restore the "pit" (excavation area) upon completion of its operations. The defendant was obligated, *inter alia,* to leave the area "reasonably level with all back slopes no steeper 6:1"; to replace all topsoil; to spread all disturbed areas "with the original topsoil or strippings, or with some other material capable of supporting vegetation"; to fertilize and seed the pit area; and to clean up all areas disturbed by the operation to the owners' specifications.

The plaintiffs were fully paid for the fill removed but were dissatisfied with defendant's restoration of the land. Suit was brought to recover damages alleging defendant was in breach of its restoration obligations. The Trial Court (Douglas, J.) found for the plaintiffs in the sum of $17,520. Defendant's exceptions to the verdict and various rulings by the court have been reserved and transferred.

The evidence was undisputed that the defendant had failed to render the back slopes "no steeper than 6:1." There was also substantial evidence that much of the original topsoil from the pit area had been "lost" during the removal operation, and that topsoil depth had deteriorated from twelve inches before the operation to four inches or less after.

Finally, there was evidence that the area had been the source of a substantial hay crop prior to the removal, but was later able to support only a meager stand of grass. The trial court found that the Emerys had been damaged in the following amounts:

1. $3,000 for the cost of 2,000 cubic yards of fill needed to bring the back slopes to the specified grade;

2. $10,500 for the cost of 6,000 cubic yards of topsoil required to restore the topsoil to its original depth;

3. $3,000 as the fair and reasonable value of lost hay crops for the years 1972 to 1975; and

4. $1,020 as the fair and reasonable cost of plowing, harrowing, disking, fertilizing, seeding and feathering the disturbed area (as specified by the owners) in order that the fertility of the topsoil would be restored.

Defendant's principal contention on appeal is that the court erred in considering certain parol evidence relative to plaintiffs' understanding that their land would be restored so as to be usable as a hayfield. The written agreements made no mention of use of the land as a hayfield, and defendant contends that the oral statements should have been excluded under the "parol evidence rule." This common law rule provides:

> "When two parties have made a contract and have expressed it in a writing to which they have both assented as the complete and accurate integration of that contract, evidence, whether parol or otherwise, of antecedent understandings and negotiations will not be admitted for the purpose of varying or contradicting the writing."

3 A. Corbin, Contracts § 573, at 357 (1960).

We find no merit to defendant's contention. The written agreements provided that the defendant would replace all topsoil and otherwise prepare the soil to the owners' specifications. If these undertakings had been performed the land would have been usable as a hayfield. Thus the parol evidence in question did not vary or contradict contractual duties as expressed in the writing.

The defendant may not complain that the trier of fact considered the hayfield evidence. In awarding damages, it was incumbent on the court to grant compensation for those injuries the defendant had reason to foresee as a probable result of its breach when the contract was made. " 'If the injury is one that follows the breach in the usual course of events, there is sufficient reason for the defendant to foresee it; otherwise, it must be shown specifically that the defendant had reason to know the facts and to foresee the injury.' " Johnson v. Waisman Bros., 93 N.H. 133, 135, 36 A.2d 634, 636 (1944); Restatement, Contracts § 330 (1932). The court could properly consider the hayfield evidence in determining whether the claimed lost crops were a probable result of the defendant's breach. There was no damage limitation provision in the written agreements, and the evidence cannot be said to present any parol evidence problem.

The defendant also complains that the court erred in using the ordinary contract measure of compensatory damages. Under this measure, an effort is made "to put the injured party in as good a position, so far as money damages can put him, as he would have occupied had the defendant fully performed." Dunn & Sons, Inc. v. Paragon Homes of New Eng. Inc., 110 N.H. 215, 218, 265 A.2d 5, 8 (1970) * * *.

The defendant relies on a tort case, Moulton v. Groveton Papers Co., 114 N.H. 505, 323 A.2d 906 (1974), involving damages to real property occasioned by flooding resulting from the breach of a dam. In *Moulton* we stated:

> "These plaintiffs allege that their properties have unique value to them and that they do not seek to sell, but rather restore them. If it can be found on the evidence that these properties can and will be restored to their prior conditions without costs disproportionate to the actual injury, the cost of such restoration is the measure of damages. If restoration is impracticable, the difference between the value of the properties before and after the injury is the measure of damages."

114 N.H. at 513, 323 A.2d at 911. The defendant here argues that "there is no evidence that the plaintiffs will restore the premises to their alleged prior condition if awarded damages," and thus that compensatory damages are inappropriate.

We note initially that *Moulton* is a tort case and it is thus readily distinguishable: "In a case of tort * * * the general purpose of compensation is to give a sum of money to the person wronged which as nearly as possible, will restore him to the position he would be in if the wrong had not been committed. In the case of a breach of contract, the goal of compensation is not the mere restoration to a former position, as in tort, but the awarding of a sum which is the equivalent of performance of the bargain—the attempt to place the plaintiff in the position he would be in if the contract had been fulfilled." C. McCormick, Law of Damages § 137 at 560–61 (1935).

Further, assuming that the *Moulton* standard were applicable here, the court denied the defendant's proposed finding to the effect that there was "no evidence" that the plaintiffs would restore the land. It is a fair inference from plaintiff's testimony that restoration is contemplated, and we cannot say that the denial of the requested finding was clearly erroneous.

We agree that there are occasions when it would be economically wasteful to place the aggrieved party under the contract in the "same place" he would have occupied had the contract been fully performed, and on such occasions the ordinary measure of contract damages may not be employed. For example, in the context of a construction contract, the usual measure of damages may be withheld if "physical reconstruction and completion in accordance with the contract [would] involve unreasonable economic waste by destruction of usable property or otherwise." J. Calamari and J. Perillo, Contracts § 230, at 363 (1970); see Danforth v. Freeman, 69 N.H. 466, 43 A. 621 (1898). It is said that the "true rationale" underlying this rule of damages is one of unjust enrichment since "[i]n all likelihood if the owner were to recover this [disproportionate] amount in such circumstances he would pocket the recovery." J. Calamari and J. Perillo supra. However, there is no showing of disproportionality in this case. A valuable income-producing asset has been rendered unproductive; the damages awarded constitute a reasonable means of bringing that asset back to life. If the plaintiffs choose to "pocket" their recovery, they will have foregone the restoration of their land; they will not have been unjustly enriched.

The defendant further complains that the damage award is excessive in that the plaintiffs failed to mitigate and avoid damages. Relying on testimony by the plaintiff husband that he witnessed the defendant's deficient restoration of the topsoil, the defendant argues that plaintiff should "have spoken up at that time"; additionally, defendant argues that plaintiffs could have taken steps to do what had to be done for the damaged land. The trial court denied defendant's proposed findings on this issue, holding that the expenditures required by plaintiffs would have been prohibitive.

We find no reason to disturb the rulings of the trial court. The law requires reasonable efforts by a plaintiff to curtail his loss. * * * Recovery will not be permitted of damages which could have been "avoided by reasonable effort without undue risk, expense, or humiliation." Restatement, Contracts, § 336(1) (1932). The evidence in this case is clear that no hay crop would be possible without the restoration of topsoil. Since this would involve a $10,500 expenditure it was not error for the court to conclude that the expenditure was not within the plaintiffs' duty to mitigate. See Chambers v. Belmore Land Co., 33 Cal.App. 78, 164 P. 404 (1917). This case is obviously distinguishable from the situation where the required expenditure is one for seed only. Defendant's reliance on Wavra v. Karr, 142 Minn. 248, 172 N.W. 118 (1919), is thus misplaced.

* * *

Exceptions overruled.

Problems

20. D contracted to build on D's land and to convey to P a suburban house with a garage and driveway. Rather than excavate a rock formation, D built the driveway with a 22½% grade, which is so steep the driveway cannot be used safely and conveniently. A 12% grade is considered the permissible maximum. The evidence showed that the cost of redoing the driveway and lowering the garage would be $20,000. The full purchase price was $68,000. D offered evidence to show that the property's value, despite the existence of the defect, exceeded the purchase price. The trial judge excluded this

evidence and entered judgment on the jury's verdict for $20,000. Should the judgment be affirmed?

21. L, a municipality, owned a waterfront pier which it leased to T for a ten-year term at $200,000 per year. T agreed to keep the pier in good and sufficient repair at T's expense. At the expiration of the leasehold L discovered that T had failed to maintain the pier in good repair and that costs of repair would be about $200,000. Soon thereafter L demolished the pier for replacement by a containership terminal. In an action by L for damages, T argues that L suffered no damages as the pier had been scheduled for demolition and was, in fact, demolished. What result?

22. P contracted with the United States to improve certain runways at a naval air station. After P had completed about 50 percent of the work on schedule, P was denied access to the runways because they were needed for military operations. After unreasonable delays caused by the government, P was allowed to continue work and completed performance of the contract. During the periods of delay, P's equipment was at the job site, but could not be used. What damages may P recover?

23. P, a potato farmer in Idaho, contracted with D whereby D would construct a potato cellar for frost-free protection of stored potatoes. The agreed completion date was September 1st. Construction, however, was not completed until October 28. As a result of the delay a large part of P's crop was destroyed by frost. It is predictable that killing frost will arrive in Idaho prior to October 28. Is D liable for the loss? *Yes*

Foreseeable as a consequence?

Yes, a consequential Damage

(e) Punitive Damages, Penalties, Efficient Breach, Agreed Damages and Limitations of Liability

(Calamari & Perillo 5th §§ 14.3, 14.31—14.36)

PATTON v. MID–CONTINENT SYSTEMS, INC.

United States Court of Appeals, Seventh Circuit, 1988.
841 F.2d 742.

POSNER, CIRCUIT JUDGE.

[The plaintiffs operated truck stops on I–94 in Indiana and Michigan. The defendant entered into a franchise agreement with them, giving them an exclusive territory, wherein no other truck stops would be franchised, to accept defendant's credit cards in payment of fuel and related items. The jury found that defendant had breached its contracts with plaintiffs by franchising other truck stops, starting with a franchise to Truck–O–Mat, within the plaintiffs' exclusive territorial area. The jury awarded compensatory damages to the plaintiffs and in addition awarded them $2,250,000 in punitive damages, reduced by the district judge to $100,000. The case involved a number of issues, including the choice of Indiana law by acquiescence. After determining that the award of compensatory damages was excessive, the court turned to the question of punitive damages.]

Rule

Indiana allows punitive damages to be awarded in suits for breach of contract if, "mingled" with the breach, are "elements of fraud, malice, gross negligence or oppression." *Travelers Indemnity Co. v. Armstrong, supra,* 442 N.E.2d [349] at 359. . . . In trying to give concrete meaning to these terms (especially "oppression"), it is important to bear in mind certain fundamentals of contractual liability. First, liability for breach of contract is, prima facie, strict liability. That is, if the promisor fails to perform as agreed, he has broken his contract even though the failure may have been beyond his power to prevent and therefore in no way blameworthy. The reason is that contracts often contain an insurance component. The promisor promises in effect either to perform or to compensate the promisee for the cost of nonperformance; and one who voluntarily assumes a risk will not be relieved of the consequences if the risk materializes. See *Field Container Corp. v. ICC,* 712 F.2d 250, 257 (7th Cir.1983); *Fidelity & Deposit Co. v. City of Sheboygan Falls,* 713 F.2d 1261, 1269–70 (7th Cir.1983).

Even if the breach is deliberate, it is not necessarily blameworthy. The promisor may simply have discovered that his performance is worth more to someone else. If so, efficiency is promoted by allowing him to break his promise, provided he makes good the promisee's actual losses. If he is forced to pay more than that, an efficient breach may be deterred, and the law doesn't want to bring about such a result. See *J. Yanan & Associates, Inc. v. Integrity Ins. Co.,* 771 F.2d 1025, 1034 (7th Cir.1985). Suppose that by franchising Truck–O–Mat in the plaintiffs' territory, Mid–Continent increased its own profits by $150,000 and inflicted damages of $75,000 on the plaintiffs. That would be an efficient breach. But if Mid–Continent had known that it would have to pay in addition to compensatory damages $100,000 in punitive damages, the breach would not have been worthwhile to it and efficiency would have suffered because the difference between Mid–Continent's profits of $150,000 and the plaintiffs' losses of $75,000 would (certainly after the plaintiffs were compensated) represent a net social gain.

Not all breaches of contract are involuntary or otherwise efficient. Some are opportunistic; the promisor wants the benefit of the bargain without bearing the agreed-upon cost, and exploits the inadequacies of purely compensatory remedies (the major inadequacies being that pre- and post-judgment interest rates are frequently below market levels when the risk of nonpayment is taken into account and that the winning party cannot recover his attorney's fees). This seems the common element in most of the Indiana cases that have allowed punitive damages to be awarded in breach of contract cases; see the discussion of cases in *Travelers Indemnity Co. v. Armstrong, supra,* 442 N.E.2d at 359. Granted, this is not how the legal test is phrased; in particular the category of "gross negligence" seems unrelated to opportunistic breach. We may have captured the core of the Indiana rule but missed the periphery. But whatever the exact dimensions of the rule, the facts of the present case are pretty clearly outside it.

There is no evidence that the action of Mid–Continent in franchising Truck–O–Mat in the plaintiffs' exclusive territory was opportunistic or even deliberate. So far as can be discerned from the record it was an honest mistake resulting from the ambiguous description of the territory in the franchise agreement with the plaintiffs. However, Mid–Continent's failure to correct the violation year after year after the plaintiffs had called its attention to it—even after it acknowledged the violation—converted an innocent breach into a deliberate one; but no clear and convincing evidence enables the breach to be characterized as malicious, fraudulent, oppressive, or even grossly negligent. As we saw in discussing the issue of compensatory damages, the breach did little, perhaps no, damage to either plaintiff, and it is therefore quite possible that it was an efficient breach in the sense that it increased Mid–Continent's profits by more than it caused anyone losses. If so, the refusal to rectify the breach, while deliberate, would not justify an award of punitive damages. See *J. Yanan & Associates, Inc. v. Integrity Ins. Co., supra*, 771 F.2d at 1034. Mid–Continent's unfulfilled promises to rectify the breach could be viewed as a form of deceit designed to prevent the plaintiffs from resorting to legal remedies, but this is just the kind of conjecture that seems excluded by the requirement of proving entitlement to punitive damages by clear and convincing evidence.

* * *

The award of punitive damages must be vacated. The finding of breach of contract is affirmed and the case remanded for a new trial limited to compensatory damages.

DANIEL FRIEDMANN, RESTITUTION OF PROFITS GAINED BY PARTY IN BREACH OF CONTRACT

104 Law Quarterly Review 383 (1988).

The Supreme Court of Israel has recently rendered a decision of major importance on the issue of restitution of profits gained by a party in breach of a contract. The question arose in further hearing $^{20}\!/\!_{82}$ *Adras Ltd.* v. *Harlow & Jones GmbH* (to be published in (1988) 42(1) P.D.) in which the defendant, a German corporation, contracted in 1973 to sell to the plaintiff, an Israeli corporation, 7,000 tons of iron c.i.f. Haifa at a price of 570 German marks per ton. Because of the October (Yom Kippur) war there was delay in delivery. But some 5,025 tons were shipped to the plaintiff between January and April 1974.

On April 8, 1974 the seller (the defendant) notified the purchaser (the plaintiff) that because of high storage costs, it had to sell the remaining quantity of iron. Three days later the purchaser replied demanding the remaining 1,925 tons of iron. The defendant did not comply and it was not disputed that about this quantity of iron was sold by the defendant in Hamburg, to third parties, for 804.70 German marks per ton f.o.b. In 1976 the plaintiff sued for damages claiming in the alternative restitution of the defendant's gains.

* * *

The majority (Levin, Barak and Bach JJ.) held that restitution was available and that the plaintiff was entitled to recover the profits which the defendant had gained by selling to third parties that which was promised to the plaintiff. Levin and Barak JJ. in detailed and thorough opinions discussed the views expressed in Anglo–American and Israeli legal literature on the subject. They preferred the approach supported by Professors J. Dawson (1959) 20 Ohio L.J. 175, G. Jones (1983) 99 L.Q.R. 443, G. Palmer, *The Law of Restitution* (1978) vol 2, pp. 439–441 and myself (1980) 80 Col.L.R. 504, to a more restrictive view. Levin J. was sympathetic to the view that the concept of "property" can be broadened to encompass contractual rights and other legally protected interests. He added, however, that it was not essential to follow this since there is no need to confine restitution to the infringement of strict property rights. The general principle against unjust enrichment is broad enough to enable restitution of gains made at the expense of another, even if no property right in the strict sense is involved. Barak J. adopted a similar approach. He pointed out that in Anglo–American law restitution of profits is granted to the purchaser of land, if the vendor, in breach of the contract, sells it to a third party. Such recovery is predicated on the purchaser's equitable ownership (*Lake* v. *Bayliss* [1974] 1 W.L.R. 1073). But in his view it should suffice for recovery that the purchaser's contractual right has been infringed.

Both Levin and Barak JJ. pointed out that under Israeli law specific performance is the primary remedy to which a contracting party is prima facie entitled. There is no reason to treat a breach lightly. Restitution of gains may thus serve an additional function of deterrence. They also rejected the idea of "efficient breach," under which a breach should be allowed or even encouraged, if the benefit to the party in breach exceeds the loss to the other party (Posner, *Economic Analysis of Law* (2nd ed., 1977), pp. 89–90).

* * *

DANIEL FRIEDMANN, THE EFFICIENT BREACH FALLACY

18 J. Legal Studies 1 (1989).

The only universal consequence of a legally binding promise is that the law makes the promisor pay damages if the promised event does not come to pass. In every case it leaves him free from interference until the time for fulfillment has gone by, and therefore free to break his contract if he chooses.[1]

So wrote Oliver Wendell Holmes in his seminal discussion of contract remedies in The Common Law. That position, while widely discussed, is not acceptable as a normative (nor, as will be shown, as a positive) account of the question of contract remedies. Stated in a

---

1. O.W. Holmes, Jr., The Path of the Law, in Collected Legal Papers 167, 175 (1920); and O.W. Holmes, Jr., The Common Law, 300–301 (1881).

phrase, the weakness of Holmes's approach lies in its conclusion that the remedy provides a perfect substitute for the right, when in truth the purpose of the remedy is to vindicate that right, not replace it. Holmes's analysis mistakenly converts the remedy into a kind of indulgence that the wrongdoer is unilaterally always entitled to purchase. As with any unifying ideal, Holmes's proposition is difficult to confine to the contract cases to which it was originally applied. Why not generalize the proposition so that every person has an "option" to transgress another's rights and to violate the law, so long as he is willing to suffer the consequences? The legal system could thus be viewed only as establishing a set of prices, some high and some low, which then act as the only constraints to induce lawful conduct.

The modern theory of "efficient breach" is a variation and systematic extension of Holmes's outlook on contractual remedy. It assumes that role because of the dominance that it gives to the expectation measure of damages in cases of contract breach: the promisor is allowed to breach at will so long as he leaves the promisee as well off after breach as he would have been had the promise been performed, while any additional gain is retained by the contract breakers.

* * *

I.   ENTITLEMENT AND ECONOMIC EFFICIENCY

Proponents of the efficient breach theory have embraced Holmes's approach and endowed it with economic apparel and terminology. In their view, if the promisor's profits from the breach exceed the loss of the promisee, the breach is to be permitted or even encouraged on the ground that it leads to maximization of resources.[2] Under this theory of efficient breach, the promisor is given the option not to perform his contract as long as he is prepared to pay plaintiff his expectation damages, that is, a sum necessary to make the plaintiff indifferent between the performance of the contract and the damages so paid. The theory of efficient breach is that the defendant will exercise this option only if the gains from breach are greater than the moneys so paid over. The pristine form of the theory implies that the plaintiff is left as well off from the breach as before, while the defendant is made better off. If so, the program of expectations damages, if faithfully implemented, satisfies not only the Kaldor–Hicks standard of hypothetical compensation but the more restrictive Pareto standards of efficiency as well: not only is there a net social gain for the contracting parties, but no one is left worse off after breach than before. Consequently, under either view of efficiency the optimal level of damages is that which compensates the plaintiff only for this loss, and no more.

Originally, this theory was religiously preached and was hardly capable of suffering any qualification. Its modern version, as formulated in the latest (1986) edition of Posner's Economic Analysis of Law, evidences a certain retreat from this extreme position. A distinction is

---

2. Richard A. Posner, Economic Analy-   sis of Law 107 (3d ed. 1986).

drawn between "opportunistic breach" and other breaches of contract. Breaches in the latter category still enjoy respectability and, if considered efficient, are lauded. Opportunistic breaches have lost the patronage of the efficient breach theory and are harshly denounced. The distinction is unsatisfactory[6] and in fact undermines much of the efficient breach theory. Indeed, Posner states that the opportunistic contract breaker should be made to "hand over all his profits from the breach to the promisee." Recovery of these gains is diametrically opposed to the efficient breach theory, the essence of which is that the promisor should be allowed or even encouraged to commit a breach whenever his gains exceed the promisee's loss. The theory clearly assumes that the promisor should be allowed to keep his gain, for otherwise he would lose interest in committing the breach that is supposedly so desirable. It is not explained why opportunistic breaches should be discouraged even if they are efficient. Is it because they are morally reprehensible? Is morality more important than efficiency? Or is it because they undermine the institution of contract in general?

Return profits wrongfully gained

A. Contracts Relating to Existing Property

The essence of the theory is "efficiency." The "right" to break a contract is not predicated on the nature of the contractual right, its relative "weakness," or its status as merely in personam, as opposed to the hardier rights in rem. Rather it is on the ground that the breach is supposed to lead to a better use of resources. The theory, therefore, is, in principle, equally applicable to property rights, where it leads to the adoption of a theory of "efficient theft" or "efficient conversion." To see the point, observe how this account of efficiency plays out in two cases. In the first, A promises to sell a machine to B for $10,000 but then turns around and sells it instead to C for $18,000. In the second, B owns a machine for which he has paid $10,000, which A takes and sells to C for $18,000.

To keep matters simple, assume that B values the machine at exactly $12,000 in both cases. If the willful contract breach is justified in the first case, then the willful conversion is justified in the second. In the first, B gets $2,000 in expectation damages and is released from paying the $10,000 purchase price. In the second, B obtains damages for conversion equal to $12,000 because he has already paid the $10,000 purchase price to his seller. The two cases thus look identical even though they derive from distinct substantive fields.

---

6. Opportunism means taking advantage of the promisee's vulnerability. Posner regards the vulnerability mainly as created by the sequential character of performance under the contract. Hence, if A pays in advance for goods or services to be supplied by B in the future, A is vulnerable until B performs ... However, the sequence in which the performances are to be made is only one relevant factor. Thus, suppose A paid part of the price in advance while B has not yet performed. Although A has already partly performed, B may be more vulnerable if his need to receive the remaining part of A's payment is greater than A's payment is greater than A's need for B's promised performance. In fact, vulnerability is a matter of degree. The greater the need for other party's performance and the more difficult it is to obtain a substitute, the greater the vulnerability.

No doubt in the contract situation, A may negotiate with B a release from his contractual obligation. But this, in Posner's view, would lead to additional transaction costs. It is, therefore, preferable to permit the "efficient breach." But the property example is indistinguishable on this ground, for in the second, A, when he takes the machine from B, avoids the transaction cost of having to purchase it from him. The similarity between the two situations (breach of contract and conversion) becomes more striking if the converter did not wrongfully deprive the owner of his possessions. Thus, suppose that A is a bailee who keeps B's goods. C offers A for the goods an amount that exceeds their value to B. A can negotiate with B for the purchase of the goods and, if he is successful, sell them to C at a profit. The cost of this transaction could be saved, just as in the contract example, if A were allowed to sell the goods to C, while limiting his liability to B's expectation-like damages. Nevertheless, the better rule, which has been universally adopted by Anglo–American law, is that the plaintiff is entitled to recover in restitution the proceeds of the sale from the defendant who converted the plaintiff's property and sold it to a third party. Efficient breach theory does not provide an explanation why the promisee in a contract of sale should not be accorded similar rights.

There are, of course, refinements. Where the promisor is a merchant engaged in selling these types of goods, he may be in a better position to find a buyer willing to pay a higher price for them, so that his transaction costs may be somewhat lower. This however, is not necessarily the case, and in any event it does not justify the breach. Again, the situation can be compared to conversion. The fact that A, for example, is a car dealer who is likely to know that C is an excellent buyer for B's car does not justify him to take B's car from hi driveway in order to sell it to C. Nor if B's car has been left with A for repairs can A sell it to C.

The real issue in both the conversion and the breach situation is who should benefit from C's willingness to pay a high price for the goods owned by B (the conversion example) or promised to him (the breach example). In principle, there should be in both situations only one transaction; in my view it should be between C and B (the owner or the promisee). If A promised to sell a piece of property to B for $10,000 and C is willing to have it for $18,000, he should negotiate its purchase from B. A is simply not entitled to sell to C something he has promised to return or transfer to B, the promisee. Similarly, with a bailment, C must negotiate with B (the owner) and not with the bailee. Hence, the question of additional transaction costs does not arise.

It is, of course, conceivable that a person (in the above example, A) would like to take advantage of a potential transaction between two other parties (B and C) . In some instances, this can legitimately be done. A may know that C is the best buyer for B's property (or for the property promised to B), while B and C are unaware of each other. A may buy the property from B and sell it to C, or he may reach an agreement (with B or C or with both) for the payment of a commission. If this is done, the inevitable result would be that the transfer from B to

C would involve two or more transactions (and, arguably, additional transaction costs). This course of dealing is not objectionable. What is, however, objectionable is an attempt by A to obtain through the commission of a wrong (breach of contract or a tort such as conversion) the benefit of a transaction that should have been concluded between B and C.

Moreover, the efficient breach rule is inefficient on its own terms. Neither it nor the analogous efficient conversion rule has the desired effect of minimizing either the number of transactions or, more decisively, the total amount of transaction costs. In fact these rules may often lead to an increase in total transaction costs. In the above contract example, the breach is likely to require two transactions instead of one. If a performs his contract with B, there will be only one additional transaction, that between B and C. If, however, A is "allowed" to break his contract with B, there will be two transactions: one between A and C over the sale of property promised to of damages. The implied assumption in Posner's analysis is that the payment of damages by A to B entails no transaction costs. This, however, is totally unrealistic. The payment of damages is hardly ever a standard of the type the parties are routinely engaged in. It is likely to follow protracted negotiations, or even litigation, over difficult questions of fact and law. Finally, the breach may lead to an expensive tort action for inducement of breach of contract by the promisee (B) against the third party (C). This claim may breed another transaction between C and A regarding A's liability for losses suffered by C.

Hence, the set of remedies that deter breach (such as specific enforcement, injunction, punitive damages or restitution of gains acquired through breach of contract) are likely to reduce the number of transactions as compared to situations in which expectation damages provide the sole remedy. It is, of course, conceivable that the promisor (A) will commit a breach when these rules are in place, forcing the promisee to claim specific performance or restitution of gains.

* * *

The relaxation of contract remedies also has deleterious effects on the willingness of parties to enter into mutually beneficial contracts in the first place. If the legal system imposes severe limitations on specific performance (irrespective of whether they are based on the right to break the contract theory or its modern "efficient breach" (offshoot), it undermines the parties' faith in getting what they bargained for, and the consequence is inefficiency and a waste of resources.[15] If a party in need of contracting with another cannot rely on the contract to guarantee performance, then he may turn to another more costly and less efficient means (for example, becoming a self-supplier or vertically integrating

---

15. See also Alan Schwartz, The Case for Specific Performance, 89 Yale L.J. 271 (1979), who points out that the availability of specific performance would not generate greater transaction costs than the damages remedy ... and that it would actually produce certain efficiency gains....

with his supplier) to gain greater assurance that he will get what he seeks.

This insistence on the respect of both property and contract rights will cause some hardship where there is bargaining breakdown and the parties cannot agree on the terms under which property should be sold. Thus, suppose that A can profitably use a machine that is owned by B or promised to him. A cannot get the machine elsewhere. B, who has no use for the machine, is willing to sell or rent it, but the parties cannot agree on the price. If A takes B's machine (or B's contractual right to receive it), he could gain use of a machine that would otherwise remain idle. Hence, greater efficiency. But this obviously cannot be allowed. The inefficiency resulting from failure of the bargaining process is inherent in the market system. If failure to reach an agreement created a license to take another's property (including contractual rights), then a complete breakdown of the market economy could follow. Why negotiate with a determined owner to buy something that can be taken, subject only to a court's subsequent appraisal of its value? Hence, in the context of a sale of existing property, the contract situation is (as far as efficiency is concerned) indistinguishable from the property situation.

WASSENAAR v. PANOS

Supreme Court of Wisconsin, 1983.
111 Wis.2d 518, 331 N.W.2d 357, 40 A.L.R.4th 266.

ABRAHAMSON, JUSTICE. * * * The circuit court entered a judgment in favor of an employee, Donald Wassenaar, against his former employer, Theanne Panos, d/b/a The Towne Hotel, enforcing the stipulated damages clause in the employment contract and confirming a $24,640 jury award. The circuit court interpreted the stipulated damage clause in the contract as providing that in the event of wrongful discharge the employee was to be paid a sum equal to his salary for the unexpired term of the contract. The court of appeals reversed, holding the stipulated damages clause unenforceable as a penalty and remanding the cause to the circuit court for a new trial on the issue of damages only.

* * *

The employer terminated Wassenaar's employment as of March 31, 1978, 21 months prior to the contract's expiration date. Wassenaar was unemployed from April 1, 1978, until June 14, 1978, when he obtained employment in a Milwaukee area hotel where he remained employed at least until the time of trial in May, 1981.

* * *

After a trial * * * the jury found that the employer terminated the employment without just cause. The circuit court, over the employee's objection, submitted to the jury the question of what sum of money would compensate the employee for his losses resulting from the breach of the employment agreement. The jury answered $24,640, which is the

~~sum the employee had calculated as his damages on the basis of the stipulated damages clause of the contract, that is, his salary for 21 months, the unexpired term of the contract~~.

On review, the court of appeals characterized the question of whether a stipulated damages clause should be held void as a penalty because it fixes unreasonably large damages as a question of law to be determined independently by the reviewing court. It then scrutinized the stipulated damages clause and decided that the clause was void as a penalty. The court of appeals reached that conclusion reasoning that the amount of damages for breach of an employment contract could easily be measured and proved at trial and that the contractual formula fixing damages at full salary without considering how long the employee would need to find a new job or the probable earnings from substitute employment was unreasonable on its face. In its analysis, the court of appeals did not consider any facts other than the actual contract language and the black-letter law relating to the measure of damages for breach of employment contracts.

We agree with the court of appeals that the validity of a stipulated damages clause is a question of law for the trial judge rather than a mixed question of fact and law for the jury. The validity of a stipulated damages clause is a matter of public policy, and as in other contract cases the question of contractual validity as a matter of public policy is an issue the trial judge initially decides. But we disagree with the court of appeals that the label of "question of law" automatically relieves the trial court from its duty to consider evidence or gives the appellate court free rein in reviewing the trial court's decision.

Even though the trial court's conclusion regarding the validity of the stipulated damages clause is a legal conclusion—a policy judgment—that legal conclusion will frequently be derived from a resolution of disputed facts or inferences. The trial judge, not the jury, determines these facts and inferences. In deciding whether a stipulated damages clause is valid, then, the trial judge should inquire into all relevant circumstances, including such matters as the existence and extent of the anticipated and actual injury to the nonbreaching party.

The trial court's decision that a clause is or is not valid involves determinations of fact and law and will be reviewed as such. * * * [O]rdinarily the appellate court need not defer to the trial court's determination of a question of law. United Leasing & Financial Services, Inc. v. R.F. Optical, 103 Wis.2d 488, 492, 309 N.W.2d 23 (Ct.App.1981). Nevertheless, because the trial court's legal conclusion, that is, whether the clause is reasonable, is so intertwined with the factual findings supporting that conclusion, the appellate court should give weight to the trial court's decision, although the trial court's decision is not controlling. [Citations omitted].

* * *

Because the employer sought to set aside the bargained-for contractual provision stipulating damages, it had the burden of proving facts which would justify the trial court's concluding that the clause should not be enforced. * * *

We turn now to the test that the trial court (and the appellate court) should apply in deciding whether a stipulated damages clause is valid. The overall single test of validity is whether the clause is reasonable under the totality of circumstances. See sec. 356(1), Restatement (Second) of Contracts (1979), and sec. 402.718(1), Stats.1979–80.

The reasonableness test is a compromise the courts have struck between two competing viewpoints toward stipulated damages clauses, one favoring enforcement of stipulated damages clauses and the other disfavoring such clauses.

Enforcement of stipulated damages clauses is urged because the clauses serve several purposes. The clauses allow the parties to control their exposure to risk by setting the payment for breach in advance. They avoid the uncertainty, delay, and expense of using the judicial process to determine actual damages. They allow the parties to fashion a remedy consistent with economic efficiency in a competitive market, and they enable the parties to correct what the parties perceive to be inadequate judicial remedies by agreeing upon a formula which may include damage elements too uncertain or remote to be recovered under rules of damages applied by the courts. In addition to these policies specifically relating to stipulated damages clauses, considerations of judicial economy and freedom of contract favor enforcement of stipulated damages clauses.

A competing set of policies disfavors stipulated damages clauses, and thus courts have not been willing to enforce stipulated damages clauses blindly without carefully scrutinizing them. Public law, not private law, ordinarily defines the remedies of the parties. Stipulated damages are an exception to this rule. Stipulated damages allow private parties to perform the judicial function of providing the remedy in breach of contract cases, namely, compensation of the nonbreaching party, and courts must ensure that the private remedy does not stray too far from the legal principle of allowing compensatory damages. Stipulated damages substantially in excess of injury may justify an inference of unfairness in bargaining or an objectionable in terrorem agreement to deter a party from breaching the contract, to secure performance, and to punish the breaching party if the deterrent is ineffective.

The reasonableness test strikes a balance between the two competing sets of policies by ensuring that the court respects the parties' bargain but prevents abuse. See Macneil, Power of Contract and Agreed Remedies, 47 Cornell L.Q. 495 (1962).

Over time, the cases and commentators have established several factors to help determine whether a particular clause is reasonable:(1) Did the parties intend to provide for damages or for a penalty? (2) Is the injury caused by the breach one that is difficult or incapable of accurate estimation at the time of contract? and (3) Are the stipulated damages a reasonable forecast of the harm caused by the breach?

Recent discussions of the test of reasonableness have generally discarded the first factor, subjective intent of the parties, because subjective intent has little bearing on whether the clause is objectively reasonable. The label the parties apply to the clause, which might indicate their intent, has some evidentiary value, but it is not conclusive. Seeman v. Biemann, 108 Wis. 365, 374, 84 N.W. 490 (1900).

The second factor, sometimes referred to as the "difficulty of ascertainment" test, is generally viewed as helpful in assessing the reasonableness of the clause. The greater the difficulty of estimating or proving damages, the more likely the stipulated damages will appear reasonable. * * *

The third factor concerns whether the stipulated damages provision is a reasonable forecast of compensatory damages. Courts test the reasonableness of the parties' forecast, as they test the "difficulty of ascertainment" by looking at the stipulated damages clause from the perspective of both the time of contracting and the time of the breach (or trial).

The second and third factors are intertwined, and both use a combined prospective-retrospective approach. Although courts have frequently said that the reasonableness of the stipulated damages clause must be judged as of the time of contract formation (the prospective approach) and that the amount or existence of actual loss at the time of breach or trial is irrelevant, except as evidence helpful in determining what was reasonable at the time of contracting (the retrospective approach), the cases demonstrate that the facts available at trial significantly affect the courts' determination of the reasonableness of the stipulated damages clause. * * *

* * *

With the reasonableness test and the policies underlying the test in mind, we now consider the circuit court's conclusion that the stipulated damages clause is reasonable. The employer argues that the stipulated damages clause is void as a penalty because the harm to the employee was capable of estimation at the formation of the contract and was relatively easy to prove at trial. The employer further contends that calculating damages based on the entire wage for the unexpired term of the employment contract does not reasonably forecast the loss caused by the breach because such a calculation gives the employee a windfall recovery. * * *

When the parties to an employment contract estimate the harm which might result from the employer's breach, they do not know when a breach might occur, whether the employee will find a comparable job, and if he or she does, where the job will be or what hardship the employee will suffer. Nevertheless, the standard measure of damages provides, as the court of appeals noted in its opinion, a simple formula which is generally fairly easy to apply. According to black-letter law, when an employee is wrongfully discharged, damages are the salary the employee would have received during the unexpired term of the contract plus the expenses of securing other employment reduced by the income which he or she has earned, will earn, or could with reasonable diligence earn, during the unexpired term. These damages are usually easily ascertainable at the time of trial.

The standard calculation of damages after breach, however, may not reflect the actual harm suffered because of the breach. In addition to the damages reflected in the black-letter formulation, an employee may suffer consequential damages, including permanent injury to professional reputation, loss of career development opportunities, and emotional stress. When calculating damages for wrongful discharge courts strictly apply the rules of foreseeability, mitigation, and certainty and rarely award consequential damages. Damages for injury to the employee's reputation, for example, are generally considered too remote and not in the parties' contemplation. Thus, actual harm suffered and damages that would be awarded in a legal action for breach of contract may not be the same. Nevertheless, in providing for stipulated damages, the parties to the contract could anticipate the types of damages not usually awarded by law. The usual arguments against allowing recovery for consequential damages—that they are not foreseeable and that no dollar value can be set by a court—fail when the parties foresee the possibility of such harm and agree on an estimated amount.

In examining the instant stipulated damages clause and the record, we conclude that the parties' estimate at the time of contract formation of anticipated damages was reasonable when consequential damages are taken into account. Consequential damages may be difficult to ascertain at the time of contracting or breach and are difficult to prove at trial. The contract formula of full salary for the period after breach seems to be a simple and fair way of calculating all damages.

* * *

In this case we find it difficult to uphold the employer's position that the employee suffered no harm, because there is evidence in the record that the employee did suffer harm in being unemployed for approximately two and a half months after his discharge. At the end of this time, the employee obtained employment at another hotel, but there is no evidence that the jobs he held were comparable in terms of salary, opportunity for advancement, etc., to the job he held as manager of the Towne Hotel. There is no evidence that the employee's total compensation from the new job was equal to or exceeded the salary under the breached contract, and the record does not reveal whether the employee suffered consequential damages. All we know is that the employee appears to have suffered some harm. This case is therefore distinguishable from Fields Foundation, Ltd. v. Christensen, 103 Wis.2d 465, 476, 309 N.W.2d 125 (Ct.App.1981), upon which the employer relies, where the court held the stipulated damages clause unenforceable when the record established that the non-breaching party suffered no harm.

Since the record in this case can be read to show that the employee suffered some harm, the question remains whether the stipulated damages are so much greater than the loss suffered by the employee that the stipulated damages constitute a penalty.

The employer has repeatedly asserted that this clause is a penalty because it does not take into account the amount the employee earned during the unexpired term of the contract. The employer argues that allowing the employee to recover the stipulated damages in this case gives the employee a windfall because he receives both the agreed upon salary and the ability to sell his services to another employer during the unexpired term of the contract: the employee will receive 21 months salary from the defendant employer and 18 months salary from the new employer. Ordinarily the circuit court would, in this type of stipulated damages case, use evidence of the employee's actual or potential earnings in assessing the overall reasonableness of the clause, since subsequent earnings would be relevant to the issue of the employee's actual loss resulting from the breach. In this case, as we discuss further below, there is no evidence in the record showing the employee's subsequent earnings, so there is no evidence supporting the employer's position that the employee would get a windfall from enforcement of the stipulated damages clause.

* * *

* * * In short, the employer did not meet his burden of proof on the unreasonableness of the stipulated damages clause. Since we conclude that the record shows that the employee suffered some actual injury and that the record does not show that actual damages are disproportionate to the stipulated damages, we affirm the circuit court's ruling that the stipulated damages provision is reasonable and enforceable.

This court asked the parties to brief what it characterized as a subissue, namely, the employee's duty to mitigate damages. In breach of contract cases not involving liquidated damages clauses, this court has consistently held that a discharged employee has a duty to use ordinary care and reasonable efforts to seek other comparable employment and that in calculating damages the employer should be credited to the extent that the employee obtains work and earns wages or might have done so. [Citations omitted].

* * *

Recalculating liquidated damages to credit the breaching party with the amount the employee earned or could have earned is antithetical to the policies favoring liquidated damages clauses. * * *

[T]he judgment of the circuit court should be affirmed.

KVASSAY v. MURRAY

Court of Appeals of Kansas, 1991.
15 Kan.App.2d 426, 808 P.2d 896.

RICHARD B. WALKER, DISTRICT JUDGE, Assigned: Plaintiff Michael Kvassay, d/b/a Kvassay Exotic Food, appeals the trial court's finding that a liquidated damages clause was unenforceable and from the court's finding that damages for lost profits were not recoverable. Kvassay contends these damages occurred when Great American Foods, Inc., (Great American) breached a contract for the purchase of baklava. * * * [The court affirmed a holding that Great American was the alter ego of the Murrays, the defendants in this case.]

On February 22, 1984, Kvassay, who had been an independent insurance adjuster, contracted to sell 24,000 cases of baklava to Great American at $19.00 per case. Under the contract, the sales were to occur over a one-year period and Great American was to be Kvassay's only customer. The contract included a clause which provided: "If Buyer refuses to accept or repudiates delivery of the goods sold to him, under this Agreement, Seller shall be entitled to damages, at the rate of $5.00 per case, for each case remaining to be delivered under this Contract."

Problems arose early in this contractual relationship with checks issued by Great American being dishonored for insufficient funds. Frequently one of the Murrays issued a personal check for the amount due. After producing approximately 3,000 cases, Kvassay stopped producing the baklava because the Murrays refused to purchase any more of the product. * * *

In April 1985, Kvassay filed suit for damages arising from the collapse of his baklava baking business. * * * The court conducted bench hearings on the validity of the liquidated damages clause . * * * [and] ruled that liquidated damages could not be recovered . * * *

Kvassay first attacks the trial court's ruling that the amount of liquidated damages sought by him was unreasonable and therefore the liquidated damages clause was unenforceable. Kvassay claimed $105,000 in losses under the liquidated damages clause of the contract, representing $5 per case for the approximately 21,000 cases of baklava which he was not able to deliver. The trial court determined that Kvassay's use of expected profits to formulate liquidated damages was improper because the business enterprise lacked duration, permanency, and recognition. The court then compared Kvassay's previous yearly income (about $20,000) with the claim for liquidated damages ($105,000) and found "the disparity becomes so great as to make the clause unenforceable."

Since the contract involved the sale of goods between merchants, the Uniform Commercial Code governs. See K.S.A. 84–2–102. "The Code does not change the pre-Code rule that the question of the propriety of liquidated damages is a question of law for the court." 4 Anderson, Uniform Commercial Code § 2–718:6, p. 572 (3d ed. 1983). Thus, this court's scope of review of the trial court's ruling is unlimited. Hutchinson Nat'l Bank & Tr. Co. v. Brown, 12 Kan.App.2d 673, 674, 753 P.2d 1299, rev. denied 243 Kan. 778 (1988).

Liquidated damages clauses in sales contracts are governed by K.S.A. 84–2–718, which reads in part:

"(1) Damages for breach by either party may be liquidated in the agreement but only at an amount which is reasonable in the light of the anticipated or actual harm caused by the breach, the difficulties of proof of loss, and the inconvenience or nonfeasibility of otherwise obtaining an adequate remedy. A term fixing unreasonably large liquidated damages is void as a penalty."

To date, the appellate courts have not interpreted this section of the UCC in light of facts similar to those presented in this case. In ruling on this issue, the trial court relied on rules governing liquidated damages as expressed in *U.S.D. No. 315* v. *DeWerff*, 6 Kan.App.2d 77, 626 P.2d 1206 (1981). *DeWerff*, however, involved a teacher's breach of an employment contract and was not governed by the UCC. Thus, the rules expressed in that case should be given no effect if they differ from the rules expressed in 84–2–718.

In *DeWerff*, this court held a "stipulation for damages upon a future breach of contract is valid as a liquidated damages clause if the set amount is determined to be reasonable and the amount of damages is difficult to ascertain." 6 Kan.App.2d at 78, 626 P.2d 1206. This is clearly a two-step test: Damages must be reasonable and they must be difficult to ascertain. Under the UCC, however, reasonableness is the only test. K.S.A. 84–2–718. K.S.A. 84–2–718 provides three criteria by which to measure reasonableness of liquidated damages clauses: (1) anticipated or actual harm caused by breach; (2) difficulty of proving loss; and (3) difficulty of obtaining an adequate remedy.

In its ruling, the trial court found the liquidated damages clause was unreasonable in light of Kvassay's income before he entered into the manufacturing contract with Great American. There is no basis in 84–2–718 for contrasting income under a previous unrelated employment arrangement with liquidated damages sought under a manufacturing contract. Indeed, the traditional goal of the law in cases where a buyer breaches a manufacturing contract is to place the seller " 'in the same position he would have occupied if the vendee had performed his contract.' " *Outcault Adv. Co.* v. *Citizens Nat'l Bank*, 118 Kan. 328, 330–31, 234 P. 988 (1925). Thus, liquidated damages under the contract in this case must be measured against the anticipated or actual loss under the baklava contract as required by 84–2–718. The trial court erred in using Kvassay's previous income as a yardstick. Was the trial court correct when it invalidated the liquidated damages clause, notwithstanding the use of an incorrect test? If so, we must uphold the decision even though the trial court relied on a wrong ground or assigned an erroneous reason for its decision. Sutter Bros. Constr. Co. v. City of Leavenworth, 238 Kan. 85, 93, 708 P.2d 190 (1985). To answer this question, we must look closer at the first criteria for reasonableness under 84–2–718, anticipated or actual harm done by the breach.

Kvassay produced evidence of anticipated damages at the bench trial showing that, before the contract was signed between Kvassay and Great American, Kvassay's accountant had calculated the baklava production costs. The resulting figure showed that, if each case sold for $19, Kvassay would earn a net profit of $3.55 per case after paying himself for time and labor. If he did not pay himself, the projected profit was $4.29

per case. Nevertheless, the parties set the liquidated damages figure at $5 per case. In comparing the anticipated damages of $3.55 per case in lost net profit with the liquidated damages of $5 per case, it is evident that Kvassay would collect $1.45 per case or about 41 percent over projected profits if Great American breached the contract. If the $4.29 profit figure is used, a $5 liquidated damages award would allow Kvassay to collect 71 cents per case or about 16 ½ percent over projected profits if Great American breached the contract.

An examination of these pre-contract comparisons alone might well lead to the conclusion that the $5 liquidated damages clause is unreasonable because enforcing it would result in a windfall for Kvassay and serve as a penalty for Great American. A term fixing unreasonably large liquidated damages is void as a penalty under 84–2–718.

A better measure of the validity of the liquidated damages clause in this case would be obtained if the actual lost profits caused by the breach were compared to the $5 per case amount set by the clause. However, no attempt was made by Kvassay during the bench trial to prove actual profits or actual costs of production. Thus, the trial court could not compare the $5 liquidated damages clause in the contract with the actual profits lost by the breach. It was not until the jury trial that Kvassay attempted to prove his actual profits lost as part of his damages. Given the trial court's ruling that lost profits were not recoverable and could not be presented to the jury, it is questionable whether the court would have permitted evidence concerning lost profits at the bench trial.

The trial court utilized an impermissible factor to issue its ruling on the liquidated damages clause and the correct statutory factors were not directly addressed. We reverse the trial court on this issue and remand for further consideration of the reasonableness of the liquidated damages clause in light of the three criteria set out in 84–2–718. . . .

LAKE RIVER CORP. v. CARBORUNDUM CO.

United States Court of Appeals, Seventh Circuit, 1985.
769 F.2d 1284.

Posner, Circuit Judge. This diversity suit between Lake River Corporation and Carborundum Company requires us to consider questions of Illinois commercial law, and in particular to explore the fuzzy line between penalty clauses and liquidated-damages.

Carborundum manufactures "Ferro Carbo," an abrasive powder used in making steel. To serve its midwestern customers better, Carborundum made a contract with Lake River by which the latter agreed to provide distribution services in its warehouse in Illinois. Lake River would receive Ferro Carbo in bulk from Carborundum, "bag" it, and ship the bagged product to Carborundum's customers. [The contract provided that Carborundum guaranteed that Lake River would bag and ship a minimum of 22,500 tons and if the guarantee were not met, Carborundum would pay the going rate for bagging and shipping of the unshipped quantity. Because the demand for the product radically diminished, if the minimum guarantee clause were valid, Carborundum would owe $241,000].

The hardest issue in the case is whether the formula in the minimum-guarantee clause imposes a penalty for breach of contract or is merely an effort to liquidate damages. Deep as the hostility to penalty clauses runs in the common law, see Loyd, *Penalties and Forfeitures*, 29 Harv.L.Rev. 117 (1915), we still might be inclined to question, if we thought ourselves free to do so, whether a modern court should refuse to enforce a penalty clause where the signator is a substantial corporation, well able to avoid improvident commitments. Penalty clauses provide an earnest of performance. The clause here enhanced Carborundum's credibility in promising to ship the minimum amount guaranteed by showing that it was willing to pay the full contract price even if it failed to ship anything. On the other side it can be pointed out that by raising the cost of a breach of contract to the contract breaker, a penalty clause increases the risk to his other creditors; increases (what is the same thing and more, because bankruptcy imposes "deadweight" social costs) the risk of bankruptcy; and could amplify the business cycle by increasing the number of bankruptcies in bad times, which is when contracts are most likely to be broken. But since little effort is made to prevent businessmen from assuming risks, these reasons are no better than makeweights.

A better argument is that a penalty clause may discourage efficient as well as inefficient breaches of contract. Suppose a breach would cost the promisee $12,000 in actual damages but would yield the promisor $20,000 in additional profits. Then there would be a net social gain from breach. After being fully compensated for his loss the promisee would be no worse off than if the contract had been performed, while the promisor would be better off by $8,000. But now suppose the contract contains a penalty clause under which the promisor if he breaks his promise must pay the promisee $25,000. The promisor will be discouraged from breaking the contract, since $25,000, the penalty, is greater than $20,000, the profits of the breach; and a transaction that would have increased value will be forgone.

On this view, since compensatory damages should be sufficient to deter inefficient breaches (that is, breaches that cost the victim more than the gain to the contract breaker), penal damages could have no effect other than to deter some efficient breaches. But this overlooks the earlier point that the willingness to agree to a penalty clause is a way of making the promisor and his promise credible and may therefore be essential to inducing some value-maximizing contracts to be made. It also overlooks the more important point that the parties (always assuming they are fully competent) will, in deciding whether to include a penalty clause in their contract, weigh the gains against the costs—costs that include the possibility of discouraging an efficient breach somewhere down the road—and will include the clause only if the benefits exceed those costs as well as all other costs.

On this view the refusal to enforce penalty clauses is (at best) paternalistic—and it seems odd that courts should display parental solicitude for large corporations. But however this may be, we must be on guard to avoid importing our own ideas of sound public policy into an area where our proper judicial role is more than usually deferential. The responsibility for making innovations in the common law of Illinois rests with the courts of Illinois, and not with the federal courts in Illinois. And like every other state, Illinois, untroubled by academic skepticism of the wisdom of refusing to enforce penalty clauses against sophisticated promisors, see, e.g., Goetz & Scott, *Liquidated Damages, Penalties and the Just Compensation Principle,* 77 Colum.L.Rev. 554 (1977), continues steadfastly to insist on the distinction between penalties and liquidated damages. * * * To be valid under Illinois law a liquidation of damages must be a reasonable estimate at the time of contracting of the likely damages from breach, and the need for estimation at that time must be shown by reference to the likely difficulty of measuring the actual damages from a breach of contract after the breach occurs. If damages would be easy to determine then, or if the estimate greatly exceeds a reasonable upper estimate of what the damages are likely to be, it is a penalty. * * *

Mindful that Illinois courts resolve doubtful cases in favor of classification as a penalty, * * * we conclude that the damage formula in this case is a penalty and not a liquidation of damages, because it is designed always to assure Lake River more than its actual damages. The formula—full contract price minus the amount already invoiced to Carborundum—is invariant to the gravity of the breach. When a contract specifies a single sum in damages for any and all breaches even though it is apparent that all are not of the same gravity, the specification is not a reasonable effort to estimate damages; and when in addition the fixed sum greatly exceeds the actual damages likely to be inflicted by a minor breach, its character as a penalty becomes unmistakable. * * * This case is within the gravitational field of these principles even though the minimum-guarantee clause does not fix a single sum as damages.

* * *

AFLAC, INC. v. WILLIAMS

Supreme Court of Georgia, 1994.
264 Ga. 351, 444 S.E.2d 314.

FLETCHER, JUSTICE. We granted the writ of certiorari to determine whether a client must pay legal fees to an attorney under a long-term retainer contract after terminating the contract. Reversing the Court of Appeals, we hold that an attorney may not recover damages under a penalty clause when a client exercises the legal right to terminate the attorney's retainer contract.

John Amos, chairman and chief executive officer of AFLAC, Incorporated and Peter Williams, an attorney in private practice, entered into a seven-year agreement in 1987 for Williams to provide legal advice to company officers on an "as needed" basis. Williams was not required to devote 100 percent of his time to the company's business. He was to be paid a monthly retainer and was entitled to additional compensation for work on assigned projects that required an "extraordinary" amount of his time. The contract provided for automatic renewal in 1995 for an additional five years unless terminated. If the company ended the contract, even for good cause, it agreed to pay "as damages an amount equal to 50 percent of the sums due under the remaining terms, plus renewal of this agreement."[2]

After Amos died in 1990, AFLAC's new CEO terminated Williams' monthly retainer in 1991. AFLAC filed a declaratory judgment action to determine the validity of the contract. Williams filed a counterclaim, seeking more than $1 million in damages for breach of contract. Declaring the 1987 contract unenforceable, the trial court granted summary judgment to AFLAC in its declaratory judgment action and on Williams' counterclaim. The Court of Appeals reversed in part, holding valid the retainer agreement and Williams' claim for damages under the original term of the contract, but disallowing his claim based on the renewal provision. See Williams v. AFLAC, Inc., 209 Ga.App. 841, 434 S.E.2d 725 (1993).

1.   This court has the duty to regulate the practice of law. Sams v. Olah, 225 Ga. 497, 501, 169 S.E.2d 790 (1969), cert. denied, 397 U.S. 914, 90 S.Ct. 916, 25 L.Ed.2d 94 (1970). In exercising this duty, we have sought to assure the public that the practice of law "will be a professional service and not simply a commercial enterprise. The primary distinction is that a profession is a calling which demands adherence to the public interest as the foremost obligation of the practitioner." * * * As an officer of the court, the lawyer's obligation to the courts and the public is as significant as the obligation to clients. * * *

The relationship between a lawyer and client is a special one of trust that entitles the client to the attorney's fidelity. * * * This "unique" relationship is "founded in principle upon the elements of trust and confidence on the part of the client and of undivided loyalty and devotion on the part of the attorney." Demov, Morris, Levin & Shein v. Glantz, 53 N.Y.2d 553, 556, 428 N.E.2d 387, 389, 444 N.Y.S.2d 55, 57 (1981). To force all attorney-client agreements into the conventional status of commercial contracts ignores the special fiduciary relationship created when an attorney represents a client. * * *

Because of this fiduciary relationship, "a client has the absolute right to discharge the attorney and terminate the relation at any time, even without cause." White v. Aiken, 197 Ga. 29, 32, 28 S.E.2d 263 (1943). A client's discharge of his attorney "is not a breach of the contract of employment but the exercise of his right." Dorsey v. Edge, 75 Ga.App. 388, 392, 43 S.E.2d 425 (1947). This right to terminate is a term

---

2.   The disputed provision of the contract provides specifically: "This agreement will automatically renew on the same terms and conditions beginning December 31, 1995, for an additional 5 years, unless terminated for just cause at least ninety (90) days prior to the expiration of the term, in which [case] the Company will pay you as damages an amount equal to 50 percent of the sums due under the remaining terms, plus renewal of this agreement."

of the contract implied by public policy because of the peculiar relationship between attorney and client. See Martin v. Camp, 219 N.Y. 170, 114 N.E. 46, 48 (1916). A client must be free to end the relationship whenever " 'he ceases to have absolute confidence in either the integrity, or the judgment or the capacity of the attorney.' " Fracasse v. Brent, 6 Cal.3d 784, 494 P.2d 9, 100 Cal.Rptr. 385 (1972) (quoting Gage v. Atwater, 136 Cal. 170, 172, 68 P. 581 (1902)).

Our obligation to regulate the legal profession in the public's interest causes us to favor AFLAC's freedom in ending the attorney-client relationship without financial penalty over Williams' right to enforce the damages provision in his retainer contract. Requiring a client to pay damages for terminating its attorney's employment contract eviscerates the client's absolute right to terminate. A client should not be deterred from exercising his or her legal right because of economic coercion. Since the contract improperly imposes a penalty by requiring AFLAC to pay damages equal to half Williams' retainer, we conclude that the provision is unenforceable.

2. We reach the same conclusion even when evaluating the damages provision under contract law. [The court notes that even if the contract were a commercial transaction, the clause would be a void as a penalty. Worse yet, the court notes in footnote 6 that] "[t]he effect of this provision would be to require a client to pay an attorney terminated for embezzling client funds." Judgment reversed.

WEDNER v. FIDELITY SECURITY SYSTEMS, INC.

Superior Court of Pennsylvania, 1973.
228 Pa.Super. 67, 307 A.2d 429.

Watkins, Judge, in support of affirmance. This is an appeal from the judgment of the Court of Common Pleas of Allegheny County entered after a non-jury trial on a burglar alarm system contract, in the amount of $312.00 in favor of Charles Wedner, doing business as Wedner Furs, the appellant, and against Fidelity Security Systems, Inc., the appellee.

This action involved a contract for a burglar alarm system. There was a burglary involving the loss of $46,180.00 in furs. It was first tried by Judge Silvestri without a jury and a nonsuit resulted. The nonsuit was removed and a new trial granted. It was then tried by Judge McLean without a jury and although he found the contract had been negligently breached, the appellant was only entitled to liquidated damages in the amount of $312.00 by the terms of the contract. Exceptions were filed and the Court En Banc by a majority vote dismissed the exceptions. This appeal followed.

The appellant suffered a loss of $46,180.00 due to the appellee's wrongful failure to perform under a burglary protection service contract, but because of a contract provision he was allowed recovery of only $312.00. The contract provided that the appellee, FEPS, was not to be liable for any loss or damages to the goods of the appellant and then continued: "If there shall, notwithstanding the above provisions, at any time arise any liability on the part of FEPS by virtue of this agreement, whether due to the negligence of FEPS or otherwise, such liability is and shall be limited to a sum equal in amount to the yearly service charge hereunder, which sum shall be paid and received by the Subscriber as liquidated damages." The appellant contends that this is an unreasonable forecast of the probable damages resulting from a breach of the contract.

The court below treated the matter as one of liquidated damages and said:

"In his decision the trial judge pointed out, and the parties agree, that there is a well settled general principle that courts will not give effect to a provision in a contract which is a penalty, but will give effect to a provision in a contract which is deemed a liquidated damages provision. The trial judge further noted that deciding which is which can be difficult. In the absence of any Pennsylvania cases making the determination in the context of a contract for burglary alarm protection, the trial judge determined that the instant provision was one for liquidated damages, rather than a penalty, on the reasoning and analysis of A.G. Schepps v. American District Telegraph Company of Texas, 286 S.W.2d 684 (Texas Court of Appeals) (1956); Better Food Markets v. American Dist. Tel. Co., 40 Cal.2d 179, [253] 353 P.2d 10 (1953); Atkinson v. Pacific Fire Extinguisher Company, 40 Cal.2d 192, 253 P.2d 18 (1953)."

However, although he ably supported his judgment on the theory of liquidated damages, he did not have to decide the matter on the premise alone.

Much reliance is placed upon the Restatement of Contracts § 339, but the appellant disregards Comment [g], which provides:

"An agreement limiting the amount of damages recoverable for breach is not an agreement to pay either liquidated damages or a penalty. Except in the case of certain public service contracts, the contracting parties can by agreement limit their liability in damages to a specified amount, either at the time of making their principal contract, or subsequently thereto. Such a contract, or subsequent thereto, does not purport to make an estimate of the harm caused by a breach; nor is its purpose to operate in terrorem to induce performance."

It can hardly be contended that the words "liability is and shall be limited" to the yearly service charge of $312 are anything but a limitation of liability and not really a liquidated damage clause. Surely, if the loss to the customer was $150, the expressed mutual assent was that recovery should be $150 and not $312.

The fact that the words "liquidated damages" were used in the contract has little bearing on the nature of the provision. It is well settled that in determining whether a particular clause calls for liquidated damages or for a penalty, the name given to the clause by the parties "is but of slight weight, and the controlling elements are the

intention of the parties and the special circumstances of the case."
Laughlin v. Baltalden, Inc., 191 Pa.Super. 611, 617, 159 A.2d 26, 29
(1960). The same principle applies here. Nor can it be argued that the
use of these words automatically creates an ambiguity to be resolved
against the appellee as the drafter of the instrument. The meaning of the
words is clear—the fixed limit of liability was $312. We are, therefore,
not dealing with a liquidated damage problem.

The real question is whether any reason exists why the limitation on
liability should not be given effect. There is no doubt as to its legality as
between ordinary business men. "The *validity* of a contractual provision
which exculpates a person from liability for his own acts of negligence is
well settled if the contract is between persons relating entirely to their
own private affairs." Dilks v. Flohr Chevrolet, 411 Pa. 425, 433, 192 A.2d
682, 687 (1963). * * *

In accord is the Restatement of Contracts §§ 574, 575. It is also the
rule with respect to the sale of goods under the Uniform Commercial
Code, 12A P.S. § 2–719(3), which provides:

"Consequential damages may be limited or excluded unless the
limitation or exclusion is unconscionable. Limitation of consequential damages for injury to the person in the case of consumer goods
is prima facie unconscionable but limitation of damages where the
loss is commercial is not."

The common law exception as to public utilities, Turek v. Pennsylvania R.R. Co., 361 Pa. 512, 64 A.2d 779 (1949), has been expanded to
some extent by Thomas v. First Nat. Bank of Scranton, 376 Pa. 181,
185–186, 101 A.2d 910, 912 (1954), where the court concluded:

"Banks, like common carriers, utility companies, etc., perform an
important public service. The United States Government and the
Commonwealth respectively stipulate how banks under their respective jurisdictions shall be incorporated and organized. All banks are
examined and supervised by government or state officers with
extreme particularity. The United States insures deposits in banks
up to a stipulated amount. If a person desires to deposit money in a
bank, necessarily, he is relegated to a governmental or state regulated banking institution. The situation of a depositor is quite analogous to that of a passenger on a public carrier who is required to
accept such means of transportation and to purchase a ticket in the
nature of a contract. This Court has consistently decided that it is
against public policy to permit a common carrier to limit its liability
for its own negligence: (Citations)."

In this case, however, we have a private arrangement between two
firms without the attendant state regulation that exists with banks and
public utilities. The appellant had a choice as to how to protect his
property, and whether or not he should obtain insurance. Although
protection against burglary is becoming increasingly important, we believe that it has not yet reached the level of necessity comparable to that
of banking and other public services.

Nor do we consider this a case of an unconscionable provision, assuming that unconscionability is applicable by adoption of the prevailing rule with respect to the sale of goods. Even under the foregoing reference to the Uniform Commercial Code the limitation of liability under the facts of the case is prima facie conscionable. Furthermore, there is this significant fact pointed out in the opinion of the trial judge:

> "In our case both plaintiff and defendant are experienced, established business persons. Additionally, plaintiff had for some 20 days prior to the instant contract had a similar type protection service with similar type clause, with a competitor of defendant."

Thus in this respect the case is comparable to K & C, Inc. v. Westinghouse Elec. Corp., 437 Pa. 303, 308, 263 A.2d 390, 393 (1970), where the court concluded that "it is clear that the exclusion was not unconscionable here, where the buyer was hardly the sheep keeping company with wolves that it would have us believe."

I would affirm the judgment of the court below.

CERCONE, JUDGE, in support of reversal. The facts in this case as found by the trial judge who sat as the fact-finder are as follows:

> Plaintiff, who was in the retail fur business, entered into a contract with defendant Security Systems whereby defendant was to provide plaintiff's store with electronic burglar alarm protection. While this contract was in full force and effect, and had been for several years, a burglary occurred, setting off devices at defendant's headquarters. Plaintiff brought suit in trespass against defendant for losses ensuing from the said burglary, plaintiff alleging negligence, willfulness, and wantonness of the defendant in failing to carry out its duties towards plaintiff's establishment. After trial, the trial judge found, as stated in his opinion, "defendant negligently failed to carry out those duties and render those services which its contract required of it upon the receipt of such alarm, with the result that the burglars were able to get away with merchandise of the value of $38,862.00. The loss of merchandise put plaintiff out of business until he could replenish his stock of goods, to the further loss of $7,318." The trial judge entered an award for the plaintiff, but limited that award to the amount of $312 (plus interest from the date of loss). This award was based on the trial judge's conclusion that this was the sum of the "liquidated damages" provided for in the contract. The provision so relied upon by the trial judge reads as follows: "If there shall, notwithstanding the above provisions, at any time arise any liability on the part of FEPS by virtue of this agreement, whether due to the negligence of FEPS or otherwise, such liability is and shall be limited to a sum equal in amount to the yearly service charge hereunder, which sum shall be paid and received by the Subscriber as liquidated damages."

The plaintiff took exceptions to the findings and conclusions of the trial judge, which exceptions were dismissed by the court en banc with one judge dissenting. This appeal by plaintiff followed.

Neither the court below nor any of the parties to this action at any time prior to oral argument before this court regarded the provision in question as other than what the parties expressed it to be, to wit: a "liquidated damages" clause. The affirming opinion, however, views the language differently than did the lower court and the parties and refers to it as a "limitation of liability" clause. It apparently views a "limitation of liability" clause as more binding than a "liquidated damages" clause under the circumstances. I cannot agree. If the parties can escape their contractual provisions for liquidated damages because the amount stated is unreasonably disproportionate (either higher or lower) to the actual damages involved, there is no logical reason why the same test of reasonableness should not apply to a contractual limitation of liability. I would hold therefore, that a contractual *limitation,* as well as a contractual *liquidation* of damages, is not binding where unreasonable and bearing no relation to the loss that would result from defendant's failure to fulfill the terms of its contract. The limitation in this case "to a sum equal in amount to the yearly service charge hereunder" was clearly unreasonable and arbitrary, bearing no relationship whatever to the damages flowing from defendant's breach. In my opinion this provision, whether viewed as one of liquidated damages or as a limitation of damages, should not be enforced.

Section 2–718 of the Uniform Commercial Code of Sales, which by its expressed title "Liquidation *or Limitation of Damages*" necessarily refers to limitation as well as liquidation of damages, provides: "(1) Damages for breach by either party may be liquidated in the agreement but only at an amount which is reasonable in the light of the anticipated or actual harm caused by the breach, the difficulties of proof of loss, and the inconvenience or nonfeasibility of otherwise obtaining an adequate remedy. A term fixing unreasonably large liquidated damages is void as a penalty." The Uniform Commercial Code comment to that subsection 1 is: "A term fixing unreasonably large liquidated damages is expressly made void as a penalty. *An unreasonably small amount would be subject to similar criticism and might be stricken under the section on unconscionable contracts or clauses.*" (emphasis added)

Section 2–719 of the Code is entitled "Contractual Modification or *Limitation of Remedy*" and subsection 1 of that section states that "subject to the provisions * * * of the preceding section on liquidation *and limitation of damages,* (a) the agreement * * * may limit or alter the measure of damages recoverable under this Article * * *" The official comment to that section is: "1. Under this section parties are left free to shape their remedies to their particular requirements and *reasonable* agreements *limiting* or modifying remedies are to be given effect.

"However, it is of the very essence of a sales contract that at least minimum adequate remedies be available. If the parties intend to conclude a contract for sale within this Article they must accept the legal consequence that there be at least a fair quantum of remedy for breach of the obligations or duties outlined in the contract. *Thus any clause purporting to modify or limit the remedial provisions of this Article in an unconscionable manner is subject to deletion* and in that event the remedies made available by this Article are applicable as if the stricken clause had never existed. Similarly, under subsection (2), where an apparently fair and reasonable clause because of circumstances fails in its purpose or operates to deprive either party of the substantial value of the bargain, it must give way to the general remedy provisions of this Article." (emphasis added)

The clause here in question (whether viewed as a liquidated damages clause or a limitation of damages clause) unreasonably limits plaintiff's recovery to a return of the service charge and deprives plaintiff of the bargain of his contract. As construed in the affirming opinion, the clause in effect works a rescission of the contract, completely freeing defendant from proper performance of its terms and requiring only a return of the service charge when defendant has failed to properly perform thereunder. The contract thus becomes, in effect, an illusory one with defendant not being bound to perform and plaintiff not being entitled to performance by defendant. By limiting plaintiff's remedy upon defendant's breach to a return of the service charge, the defendant is permitted to effectuate a cancellation of its duties to perform under the contract, leaving plaintiff without the bargained-for performance and without any reasonable compensation for defendant's failure to perform as contracted.

It is my opinion, therefore, that the clause in question is unreasonable and unconscionable and should not be enforced.

I therefore respectfully, but vigorously, dissent from the affirming opinion in this case.

Problems

24.   P sold to D the timber on his land to be severed by D. Payment was based on the amount of timber cut. It was further agreed that the land would be clear-cut and in the event D left any merchantable trees standing D would pay P $1 per tree. D left 1339 such trees standing. D resists payment of P's claim for $1339 by asserting that since the breach the market value of the remaining trees has markedly increased. (a) What result? (b) Would the result be different if the contract were for the sale of goods?

25.   A contract for the purchase and sale of lumber contained this provision:

"If the Buyer breaches this contract and the enforcement thereof, or any provision thereof, or the collection of any monies due thereunder is turned over to an attorney, the Buyer herein agrees to pay, in addition to all of Seller's expenses, a reasonable counsel fee; and in the event the matter turned over is the collection of monies, such reasonable counsel fee is hereby agreed to be Thirty (30%) per cent. The guarantor shall also be liable for such counsel fee and expenses."

Is the provision valid?

26.   Schlitz Brewing Company entered into merger negotiations with Heilman Brewing Company looking towards the takeover of Schlitz by

Heilman. In order to retain key executives in its employ during the merger talks, it entered into "golden parachute" contracts with them, promising that, in the event of their termination or their resignation because of a substantial reduction in their duties, their salaries would be paid in full until the end of the contract terms. K, a member of Schlitz's legal staff, entered into such a contract. The merger talks were unsuccessful but subsequent negotiations resulted in Schlitz's takeover by Stroh's. K's duties were reduced. He resigned and immediately obtained other employment at his then current salary. He claims $44,000, the balance that would be payable during the remaining twelve months of the contract with Schlitz. In the light of his other employment, is he entitled to recover this sum?

27. The United States contracted with D to repair an embankment. The contract provided that in the event the contract was not completed by December 1, D would pay $100 per day as liquidated damages. Another clause stated that "the contractor shall pay, in addition to the liquidated damages hereinbefore specified, all expenses for inspection and superintendence [during the period of delay]." Is this a valid liquidated damages clause?

28. Southern Bell publishes a telephone directory which includes "yellow pages" in which businesses publish their readiness to do business. P paid Southern Bell $4.70 to publish its name and number under the heading "Gas–Liquified Petroleum–Bottled & Bulk." Instead the name and number were published under "Gas–Industrial & Medical–Cylinder & Bulk." P sells no industrial or medical gases and claims that its business has been damaged in the amount of $100,000. The contract provided that "liability on account of errors in or omissions of such advertising shall in no event exceed the amount of charges for the advertising * * *." Southern Bell tenders $4.70 to P, relying on this clause. P refuses the tender and sues. What result?

SECTION 2. RESTITUTION

(Calamari & Perillo 5th §§ 15.1—15.7)

OLIVER v. CAMPBELL

Supreme Court of California, In Bank. 1954.
43 Cal.2d 298, 273 P.2d 15.

CARTER, J. Plaintiff appeals from a judgment for defendant, administratrix of the estate of Roy Campbell, deceased, in an action for attorney's fees.

Plaintiff's cause of action was stated in a common count alleging that Roy Campbell became indebted to him in the sum of $10,000, the reasonable value of services rendered as attorney for Campbell; that no part had been paid except $450. Campbell died after the services were rendered by plaintiff. Plaintiff filed a claim against his estate for the fees which defendant rejected. Defendant in her answer denied the allegations made and as a "further" defense alleged that plaintiff and Campbell entered into an "express written contract" employing plaintiff as attorney for a stated fee of $750, and all work alleged to have been performed by plaintiff was performed under that contract.

According to the findings of the trial court the claim against the estate was founded on the alleged reasonable value of legal services rendered by plaintiff for Campbell in an action for separate maintenance by defendant, Campbell's wife, against Campbell and in which the latter cross-complained for a divorce. Plaintiff was not counsel when the pleadings in that action were filed. He came into the case on December 16, 1949, before trial of the action. He and Campbell entered into a written contract on that date for plaintiff's representation of Campbell in the action, the contract stating that plaintiff agrees to represent Campbell in the separate maintenance and divorce action which has been set for trial in the superior court for a "total fee" of $750 plus court costs and other incidentals in the sum of $100 making a total of $850. The fees were to be paid after trial. Plaintiff represented Campbell at the trial consuming 29 days and lasting until May, 1950. (Defendant's complaint for separate maintenance was changed to one for divorce.) After the trial ended the court indicated its intention to give Mrs. Campbell a divorce. But while her proposed findings were under consideration by plaintiff and the court, defendant Campbell substituted himself instead of plaintiff and thereby the representation by plaintiff of Campbell was "terminated." The findings in the divorce action were filed in May, 1951. Plaintiff's services were furnished pursuant to the contract. The reasonable value of the services was $5,000. Campbell paid $450 to plaintiff and the $100 costs.

The court concluded that plaintiff should take nothing because neither his claim against the estate nor his action was on the contract but were in quantum meruit and no recovery could be had for the reasonable value of the services because the compensation for those services was covered by the express contract.

According to plaintiff's undisputed testimony Campbell told him after defendant had offered proposed findings in the divorce action that he was dissatisfied with plaintiff as his counsel and would discharge him and asked him if he would sign a substitution of attorneys under which Campbell would represent himself. Plaintiff replied that he recognized Campbell had a right to discharge him but that he was prepared to carry the case to conclusion; that he expected to be paid the reasonable value of his services which would be as much as defendant's counsel in the divorce action received, $9,000, to which Campbell replied he was not going to pay "a cent more." (At that time Campbell had paid $450.) Thereupon the substitution (dated January 25, 1951) was signed and Campbell took plaintiff's file in the divorce case with him.

It seems that the contract of employment contemplated that plaintiff was to continue his services and representation at least until and including final judgment in the divorce action. (See Neblett v. Getty, 20 Cal.App.2d 65 [66 P.2d 473].) It might thus appear that plaintiff was discharged before he had fully completed his services under the contract and the discharge prevented him from completing his performance. (That question is later discussed.)

One alleged rule of law applied by the trial court and that urged by defendant is that where there is a contract of employment for a definite term which fixes the compensation, there cannot be any recovery for the reasonable value of the services even though the employer discharges the employee-repudiates the contract before the end of the term; that the only remedy of the employee is an action on the contract for the fixed compensation or damages for the breach of the contract. The trial court accepted that theory and rendered judgment for defendant because plaintiff did not state a cause of action on the contract nor for damages for its breach; it was for the reasonable value of the services performed before plaintiff's discharge. Accordingly there is no express finding on whether the discharge was wrongful or whether there was a rescission of the contract by plaintiff because of Campbell's breach of it, or whether plaintiff had substantially performed at the time of this discharge.

The rule applied is not in accord with the general contract law, the law applicable to employment contracts or employment of an attorney by a client. (1) The general rule is stated: "... that one who has been injured by a breach of contract has an election to pursue any of three remedies, to wit: 'He may treat the contract as rescinded and may recover upon a quantum meruit so far as he has performed; or he may keep the contract alive, for the benefit of both parties, being at all times ready and able to perform; or, third, he may treat the repudiation as putting an end to the contract for all purposes of performance, and sue for the profits he would have realized if he had not been prevented from performing.'" (Alder v. Drudis, 30 Cal.2d 372, 381 [182 P.2d 195]; see 12 Cal.Jur.2d, Contracts, § 253; Rest. Contracts, § 347.) It is the same in agency or contract for services cases.

* * *

It should further be noted that under the only evidence on the subject, above mentioned, plaintiff in effect promptly notified Campbell of the rescission of the contract when he advised him that he would execute the substitution of attorneys when he was discharged by Campbell but told Campbell he would hold him for the reasonable value of the services. (8) On the issue of the necessity of restoration or offer to restore the part payment for the services which Campbell had made, the rule applies that such restoration is not necessary where plaintiff would be entitled to it in any event. * * * It is clear that plaintiff was entitled to receive the $450 paid to him either under the contract or for the reasonable value of his services.

The question remains, however, of the application of the foregoing rules to the instant case. Plaintiff had performed practically all of the services he was employed to perform when he was discharged. The trial was at an end. The court had indicated its intention to give judgment against Campbell and all that remained was the signing of findings and judgment. The full sum called for in the contract was payable because the trial had ended. (9) Under these circumstances it would appear that in effect, plaintiff had completed the performance of his services and the rule would apply that: "The remedy of restitution in money is not available to one who has fully performed his part of a contract, if the only part of the agreed exchange for such performance that has not been rendered by the defendant is a sum of money constituting a liquidated debt; but full performance does not make restitution unavailable if any part of the consideration due from the defendant in return is something other than a liquidated debt." (Rest. Contracts, § 350; Locke v. Duchesnay, 84 Cal.App. 448 [258 P. 418]; Willett & Burr v. Alpert, 181 Cal. 652 [185 P. 976]; Williston on Contracts (rev.ed.), § 1459; Corbin on Contracts, § 1110; Civ. Code, § 3302.) In such cases he recovers the full contract price and no more. As we have seen, as far as pleading is concerned, however, the action may be stated as a common count other than a declaration on the special contract. Here plaintiff alleged an indebtedness on defendant's part for services performed by plaintiff of a reasonable value of $10,000 of which only $450 had been paid. (10) While it may have been more appropriate for him to have alleged that the price of such services was the contract figure, any deficiency of the pleading is eliminated by defendant's answer setting forth that factor. Plaintiff's action can thus be said to be common count indebitatus assumpsit, and there being no dispute as to the amount called for in the contract, the services having been in effect fully performed, the court should have rendered judgment for the balance due on the contract which is conceded to be $300.

The judgment is therefore reversed and the trial court is directed to render judgment in favor of plaintiff for the sum of $300.

SCHAUER, J. I dissent. I agree with a great deal of the discussion in the majority opinion, and even to a larger extent with the authorities therein cited, relative to the rules of law which should govern this case but I think this court misapplies the very rules it cites.

Specifically, I think this court errs when it says "there being no dispute as to the amount called for in the contract, the services having been in effect fully performed, the court should have rendered judgment for the balance due on the contract which is conceded to be $300." The foregoing statement is neither supported factually by the record nor legally by the authorities cited. [The dissent stated its agreement with the opinion of Justice Vallee in the District Court of Appeal which it quotes.]

"I am of the opinion that the judgment should be reversed with directions to the superior court to render judgment for plaintiff for $5,000. The court found that the reasonable value of the services performed by plaintiff is $5,000. Plaintiff was the only witness who testified concerning his discharge by Dr. Campbell. The opinion of this court fails to state all of the testimony of plaintiff with respect to his discharge. I set it forth in toto in the margin. I think no reasonable conclusion can be drawn from the evidence other than that the discharge amounts to a clear repudiation and abrogation of the contract in its entirety, in which case plaintiff is entitled to recover the reasonable value of the service performed. The contract plaintiff made with Dr. Campbell did not limit his services to the trial of the case. Under the contract he agreed to represent the doctor until final judgment, and he told the doctor that he 'thought the case would be reversed on appeal.' * * * "

Problems

29.   P, an architect, was retained by D to design a 56 unit motel and draw up the final working plans. P's fee was to be 4% of the construction costs. P drew up the preliminary plans. D decided not to build the motel because a survey revealed D's land was insufficient in size to accommodate a 56 unit motel with sufficient parking facilities. This constituted a breach by D as D knew the size of the plot while P did not. P sues for the reasonable value of the architectural services performed. D defends, claiming that P's services were of no value to D. What result?

30.   P conveyed a tract of land to D in consideration of a promise by D to construct a railway adjacent to P's remaining land. The railway would enhance the value of P's land. On D's failure to construct the railroad, P sues in equity to cancel the deed to D. What result?

31.   P bought a horse known as Cur–Non for breeding purposes for $3,500. Cur–Non was warranted by D to be a stallion. In fact it was a gelding. After the purchase, P incurred expenses for medical care of Cur–Non relating to an old fracture. Expenses were also incurred in routine care and feeding of the horse. Upon discovering that Cur–Non was a gelding, P offered to return the horse, demanding return of the purchase price, veterinary fees and maintenance costs. D refused the demand. (a) In an action by P against D, what result? (b) Suppose P could show that if Cur–Non had in fact been a stallion its market value would be $5000. How would this fact affect your answer to (a)?

SECTION 3.   SPECIFIC PERFORMANCE

(a) Substantive Basis for Equitable Relief

(Calamari & Perillo 5th §§ 16.1—16.6)

CENTEX HOMES CORP. v. BOAG

Superior Court of New Jersey, 1974.
128 N.J.Super. 385, 320 A.2d 194.

GELMAN, J. S. C., Temporarily Assigned. Plaintiff Centex Homes Corporation (Centex) is engaged in the development and construction of a luxury high-rise condominium project in the Boroughs of Cliffside Park and Fort Lee. The project when completed will consist of six 31–story buildings containing in excess of 3600 condominium apartment units, together with recreational buildings and facilities, parking garages and other common elements associated with this form of residential development. As sponsor of the project Centex offers the condominium apartment units for sale to the public and has filed an offering plan covering such sales with the appropriate regulatory agencies of the States of New Jersey and New York.

On September 13, 1972 defendants Mr. & Mrs. Eugene Boag executed a contract for the purchase of apartment unit No. 2019 in the building under construction and known as "Winston Towers 200." The contract purchase price was $73,700, and prior to signing the contract defendants had given Centex a deposit in the amount of $525. At or shortly after signing the contract defendants delivered to Centex a check in the amount of $6,870 which, together with the deposit, represented approximately 10% of the total purchase of the apartment unit. Shortly thereafter Boag was notified by his employer that he was to be transferred to the Chicago, Illinois, area. Under date of September 27, 1972 he advised Centex that he "would be unable to complete the purchase" agreement and stopped payment on the $6,870 check. Centex deposited the check for collection approximately two weeks after receiving notice from defendant, but the check was not honored by defendants' bank. On August 8, 1973 Centex instituted this action in Chancery Division for specific performance of the purchase agreement or, in the alternative, for liquidated damages in the amount of $6,870. The matter is presently before this court on the motion of Centex for summary judgment.

Both parties acknowledge, and our research has confirmed, that no court in this State or in the United States has determined in any reported decision whether the equitable remedy of specific performance will lie for the enforcement of a contract for the sale of a condominium apartment. The closest decision on point is Silverman v. Alcoa Plaza Associates, 37 A.D.2d 166, 323 N.Y.S.2d 39 (App.Div.1971), which involved a default by a contract-purchaser of shares of stock and a proprietary lease in a cooperative apartment building. The seller, who was also the sponsor of the project, retained the deposit and sold the stock and the lease to a third party for the same purchase price. The original purchaser thereafter brought suit to recover his deposit, and on appeal the court held that the sale of shares of stock in a cooperative apartment building, even though associated with a proprietary lease, was a sale of personalty and not of an interest in real estate. Hence, the seller was not entitled to retain the contract deposit as liquidated damages.[1]

As distinguished from a cooperative plan of ownership such as involved in *Silverman,* under a condominium housing scheme each condominium apartment unit constitutes a separate parcel of real property which may be dealt with in the same manner as any real estate. Upon closing of title the apartment unit owner receives a recordable

---

1. Under New York law, if the contract was deemed to be for the sale of realty, the seller could retain the deposit in lieu of damages.

deed which confers upon him the same rights and subjects him to the same obligations as in the case of traditional forms of real estate ownership, the only difference being that the condominium owner receives in addition an undivided interest in the common elements associated with the building and assigned to each unit. See the Condominium Act, N.J.S.A. 46:8B–1 et seq.; 15 Am.Jur.2d, Condominiums and Cooperative Apartments, at 977 et seq.; Note, 77 Harv.L.Rev. 777 (1964).

Centex urges that since the subject matter of the contract is the transfer of a fee interest in real estate, the remedy of specific performance is available to enforce the agreement under principles of equity which are well-settled in his state.

The principle underlying the specific performance remedy is equity's jurisdiction to grant relief where the damage remedy at law is inadequate. The text writers generally agree that at the time this branch of equity jurisdiction was evolving in England, the presumed uniqueness of land as well as its importance to the social order of that era led to the conclusion that damages at law could never be adequate to compensate for the breach of a contract to transfer an interest in land. Hence specific performance became a fixed remedy in this class of transactions. See 11 Williston on Contracts (3d ed. 1968) § 1418A; 5A Corbin on Contracts § 1143 (1964). The judicial attitude has remained substantially unchanged * * *

While the inadequacy of the damage remedy suffices to explain the origin of the vendee's right to obtain specific performance in equity, it does not provide a *rationale* for the availability of the remedy at the instance of the vendor of real estate. Except upon a showing of unusual circumstances or a change in the vendor's position, such as where the vendee has entered into possession, the vendor's damages are usually measurable, his remedy at law is adequate and there is no jurisdictional basis for equitable relief. But see Restatement, Contracts § 360, comment c.[2] The early English precedents suggest that the availability of the remedy in a suit by a vendor was an outgrowth of the equitable concept of mutuality, i.e., that equity would not specifically enforce an agreement unless the remedy was available to both parties.

* * *

No other *rationale* has been offered by our decisions subsequent to Hopper [v. Hopper, 16 N.J.Eq. 147 (Ch.1863)], and specific performance

---

2. The Restatement's reasoning, as expressed in § 360, comment c amounts to the inconsistent propositions that (1) because the vendor may not have sustained any damage which is actionable at law, specific performance should be granted, and (2) he would otherwise sustain damage equal to the loss of interest on the proceeds of the sale. Yet loss of interest is readily measurable and can be recovered in an action at law, and to the extent that the vendor has sustained no economic injury, there is no compelling reason for equity to grant to him the otherwise extraordinary remedy of specific performance. At the end of the comment, the author suggests that the vendor is entitled to specific performance because that remedy should be mutual, a concept which is substantially rejected as a decisional basis in §§ 372 and 373 of the Restatement.

has been routinely granted to vendors without further discussion of the underlying jurisdictional issue.

Our present Supreme Court has squarely held, however, that mutuality of remedy is not an appropriate basis for granting or denying specific performance. Fleischer v. James Drug Stores, 1 N.J. 138, 62 A.2d 383 (1948); see also, Restatement, Contracts § 372; 11 Williston, Contracts (3d ed. 1968), § 1433. The test is whether the obligations of the contract are mutual and not whether each is entitled to precisely the same remedy in the event of a breach. * * *

The disappearance of the mutuality of remedy doctrine from our law dictates the conclusion that specific performance relief should no longer be automatically available to a vendor of real estate, but should be confined to those special instances where a vendor will otherwise suffer an economic injury for which his damage remedy at law will not be adequate, or where other equitable considerations require that the relief be granted. Cf. Dover Shopping Center, Inc. v. Cushman's Sons, Inc., 63 N.J.Super. 384, 394, 164 A.2d 785 (App.Div.1960). As Chancellor Vroom noted in King v. Morford, 1 N.J.Eq. 274, 281–282 (Ch.Div.1831), whether a contract should be specifically enforced is always a matter resting in the sound discretion of the court and

> * * * considerable caution should be used in decreeing the specific performance of agreements, and * * * the court is bound to see that it really does the complete justice which it aims at, and which is the ground of its jurisdiction.

Here the subject matter of the real estate transaction—a condominium apartment unit—has no unique quality but is one of hundreds of virtually identical units being offered by a developer for sale to the public. The units are sold by means of sample, in this case model apartments, in much the same manner as items of personal property are sold in the market place. The sales prices for the units are fixed in accordance with schedule filed by Centex as part of its offering plan, and the only variance as between apartments having the same floor plan (of which six plans are available) is the floor level or the building location within the project. In actuality, the condominium apartment units, regardless of their realty label, share the same characteristics as personal property.

From the foregoing one must conclude that the damages sustained by a condominium sponsor resulting from the breach of the sales agreement are readily measurable and the damage remedy at law is wholly adequate. No compelling reasons have been shown by Centex for the granting of specific performance relief and its complaint is therefore dismissed as to the first count.

Centex also seeks money damages pursuant to a liquidated damage clause in its contract with the defendants. It is sufficient to note only that under the language of that clause (which was authored by Centex) liquidated damages are limited to such moneys as were paid by defendant at the time the default occurred. Since the default here consisted of the defendant's stopping payment of his check for the balance of the down-payment, Contex's liquidated damages are limited to the retention of the "moneys paid" prior to that date, or the initial $525 deposit. Accordingly, the second count of the complaint for damage relief will also be dismissed.

LACLEDE GAS CO. v. AMOCO OIL CO.

United States Court of Appeals, Eighth Circuit, 1975.
522 F.2d 33.

ROSS, CIRCUIT JUDGE. The Laclede Gas Company (Laclede), a Missouri corporation, brought this diversity action alleging breach of contract against the Amoco Oil Company (Amoco), a Delaware corporation. It sought relief in the form of a mandatory injunction prohibiting the continuing breach or, in the alternative, damages. The district court held a bench trial on the issues of whether there was a valid, binding contract between the parties and whether, if there was such a contract, Amoco should be enjoined from breaching it. It then ruled that the "contract is invalid due to lack of mutuality" and denied the prayer for injunctive relief. The court made no decision regarding the requested damages. Laclede Gas Co. v. Amoco Oil Co., 385 F.Supp. 1332, 1336 (E.D.Mo. 1974). This appeal followed, and we reverse the district court's judgment.

* * *

* * * As a practical matter, * * * Laclede is bound to buy all the propane it distributes from Amoco in any subdivision to which the supplemental agreement applies and for which the distribution system has been established.

When analyzed in this manner, it can be seen that the contract herein is simply a so-called "requirements contract." Such contracts are routinely enforced by the courts where, as here, the needs of the purchaser are reasonably foreseeable and the time of performance is reasonably limited. We conclude that there is mutuality of consideration within the terms of the agreement and hold that there is a valid, binding contract between the parties as to each of the developments for which supplemental letter agreements have been signed.

II.

Since he found that there was no binding contract, the district judge did not have to deal with the question of whether or not to grant the injunction prayed for by Laclede. He simply denied this relief because there was no contract. Laclede Gas Co. v. Amoco Oil Co., supra, 385 F.Supp. at 1336.

Generally the determination of whether or not to order specific performance of a contract lies within the sound discretion of the trial court. Landau v. St. Louis Public Service Co., 364 Mo. 1134, 273 S.W.2d 255, 259 (1954). However, this discretion is, in fact, quite limited; and it is said that when certain equitable rules have been met and the contract is fair and plain "specific performance goes as a matter of right." Miller v. Coffeen, 365 Mo. 204, 280 S.W.2d 100, 102 (1955), quoting, Berberet v. Myers, 240 Mo. 58, 77, 144 S.W. 824, 830 (1912). (Emphasis omitted.)

With this in mind we have carefully reviewed the very complete record on appeal and conclude that the trial court should grant the injunctive relief prayed. We are satisfied that this case falls within that category in which specific performance should be ordered as a matter of right. See Miller v. Coffeen, supra, 280 S.W.2d at 102.

Amoco contends that four of the requirements for specific performance have not been met. Its claims are: (1) there is no mutuality of remedy in the contract; (2) the remedy of specific performance would be difficult for the court to administer without constant and long-continued supervision; (3) the contract is indefinite and uncertain; and (4) the remedy at law available to Laclede is adequate. The first three contentions have little or no merit and do not detain us for long.

There is simply no requirement in the law that both parties be mutually entitled to the remedy of specific performance in order that one of them be given that remedy by the court. * * *

While a court may refuse to grant specific performance where such a decree would require constant and long-continued court supervision, this is merely a discretionary rule of decision which is frequently ignored when the public interest is involved.

Here the public interest in providing propane to the retail customers is manifest, while any supervision required will be far from onerous.

Section 370 of the Restatement of Contracts (1932) provides:

Specific enforcement will not be decreed unless the terms of the contract are so expressed that the court can determine with reasonable certainty what is the duty of each party and the conditions under which performance is due.

We believe these criteria have been satisfied here. As discussed in part I of this opinion, as to all developments for which a supplemental agreement has been signed, Amoco is to supply all the propane which is reasonably foreseeably required, while Laclede is to purchase the required propane from Amoco and pay the contract price therefor. The parties have disagreed over what is meant by "Wood River Area Posted Price" in the agreement, but the district court can and should determine with reasonable certainty what the parties intended by this term and should mold its decree, if necessary accordingly. Likewise, the fact that the agreement does not have a definite time of duration is not fatal since the evidence established that the last subdivision should be converted to natural gas in 10 to 15 years. This sets a reasonable time limit on performance and the district court can and should mold the final decree to reflect this testimony.

It is axiomatic that specific performance will not be ordered when the party claiming breach of contract has an adequate remedy at law.

* * * This is especially true when the contract involves personal property as distinguished from real estate.

However, in Missouri, as elsewhere, specific performance may be ordered even though personalty is involved in the "proper circumstances." Mo.Rev.Stat. § 400.2–716(1); Restatement of Contracts, supra, § 361. And a remedy at law adequate to defeat the grant of specific performance "must be as certain, prompt, complete, and efficient to attain the ends of justice as a decree of specific performance." * * *

[T]he evidence indicates that at the present time propane is readily available on the open market. However, this analysis ignores the fact that the contract involved in this lawsuit is for a long-term supply of propane to these subdivisions. * * * Additionally, there was uncontradicted expert testimony that Laclede probably could not find another supplier of propane willing to enter into a long-term contract such as the Amoco agreement, given the uncertain future of worldwide energy supplies. And, even if Laclede could obtain supplies of propane for the affected developments through its present contracts or newly negotiated ones, it would still face considerable expense and trouble which cannot be estimated in advance in making arrangements for its distribution to the subdivisions.

Specific performance is the proper remedy in this situation, and it should be granted by the district court.

[Reversed and remanded for entry of] a decree of specific performance * * *.

NORTHERN INDIANA PUBLIC SERVICE CO. v. CARBON COUNTY COAL CO.

United States Court of Appeals, Seventh Circuit, 1986.
799 F.2d 265.

[NIPSCO, an electrical utility, agreed to purchase 1.5 million tons of coal every year for 20 years from Carbon County Coal at $24 a ton, subject to various provisions for escalation, which had raised the price to $44. Time has shown that this is an onerous contract for NIPSCO as the market has shifted from a shortage of energy producing fuels to a glut. Carbon County's cost of production is now greater than the market price. NIPSCO repudiated. The trial judge entered judgment for Carbon County on the jury's verdict for $181 million, but denied Carbon County's alternative request for a decree of specific performance. Affirmed. The court's discussion of a defense of illegality is reported at p. 828 *infra*.]

POSNER, CIRCUIT JUDGE. [T]he request for specific performance has no merit. Like other equitable remedies, specific performance is available only if damages are not an adequate remedy, Farnsworth, [Contracts], § 12.6, and there is no reason to suppose them inadequate here. The loss to Carbon County from the breach of contract is simply the difference between (1) the contract price (as escalated over the life of the contract in accordance with the contract's escalator provisions) times quantity, and (2) the cost of mining the coal over the life of the contract. Carbon County does not even argue that $181 million is not a reasonable estimate of the present value of the difference. Its complaint is that although the money will make the owners of Carbon County whole it will do nothing for the miners who have lost their jobs because the mine is closed and the satellite businesses that have closed for the same reason. Only specific performance will help them.

But since they are not parties to the contract their losses are irrelevant. Indeed, specific performance would be improper as well as unnecessary here, because it would force the continuation of production that has become uneconomical. Cf. Farnsworth, *supra*, at 817–18. No one wants coal from Carbon County's mine. With the collapse of oil prices, which has depressed the price of substitute fuels as well, this coal costs far more to get out of the ground than it is worth in the market. Continuing to produce it, under compulsion of an order for specific performance, would impose costs on society greater than the benefits. NIPSCO's breach, though it gave Carbon County a right to damages, was an efficient breach in the sense that it brought to a halt a production process that was no longer cost-justified. * * * The reason why NIPSCO must pay Carbon County's loss is not that it should have continued buying coal it didn't need but that the contract assigned to NIPSCO the risk of market changes that made continued deliveries uneconomical. The judgment for damages is the method by which that risk is being fixed on NIPSCO in accordance with its undertakings.

With continued production uneconomical, it is unlikely that an order of specific performance, if made, would ever actually be implemented. If, as a finding that the breach was efficient implies, the cost of a substitute supply (whether of coal, or of electricity) to NIPSCO is less than the cost of producing coal from Carbon County's mine, NIPSCO and Carbon County can both be made better off by negotiating a cancellation of the contract and with it a dissolution of the order of specific performance. Suppose, by way of example, that Carbon County's coal costs $20 a ton to produce, that the contract price is $40, and that NIPSCO can buy coal elsewhere for $10. Then Carbon County would be making a profit of only $20 on each ton it sold to NIPSCO ($40–$20), while NIPSCO would be losing $30 on each ton it bought from Carbon County ($40–$10). Hence by offering Carbon County more than contract damages (i.e., more than Carbon County's lost profits), NIPSCO could induce Carbon County to discharge the contract and release NIPSCO to buy cheaper coal. For example, at $25, both parties would be better off than under specific performance, where Carbon County gains only $20 but NIPSCO loses $30. Probably, therefore, Carbon County is seeking specific performance in order to have bargaining leverage with NIPSCO, and we can think of no reason why the law should give it such leverage. We add that if Carbon County obtained and enforced an order for specific performance this would mean that society was spending $20 (in our hypothetical example) to produce coal that could be gotten elsewhere for $10—a waste of scarce resources.

As for possible hardships to workers and merchants in Hanna, Wyoming, where Carbon County's coal mine is located, we point out that none of these people were parties to the contract with NIPSCO or third-party beneficiaries. They have no legal interest in the contract. * * * Of course the consequences to third parties of granting an injunctive remedy, such as specific performance, must be considered, and in some cases may require that the remedy be withheld. * * * The frequent references to "public interest" as a factor in the grant or denial of a preliminary injunction invariably are references to third-party effects. * * * But even though the formal statement of the judicial obligation to consider such effects extends to orders denying as well as granting injunctive relief, * * * the actuality is somewhat different: when the question is whether third parties would be injured by an order denying an injunction, always they are persons having a legally recognized interest in the lawsuit, so that the issue really is the adequacy of relief if the injunction is denied. In *Mississippi Power & Light Co. v. United Gas Pipe Line Co.*, 760 F.2d 618 (5th Cir.1985), for example, a public utility sought a preliminary injunction against alleged overcharges by a supplier. If the injunction was denied and later the utility got damages, its customers would be entitled to refunds; but for a variety of reasons explained in the opinion, refunds would not fully protect the customers' interests. The customers were the real parties in interest on the plaintiff side of the case, and their interests had therefore to be taken into account in deciding whether there would be irreparable harm (and how much) if the preliminary injunction was denied. See *id.* at 623–26. Carbon County does not stand in a representative relation to the workers and businesses of Hanna, Wyoming.

Moreover, the workers and merchants in Hanna assumed the risk that the coal mine would have to close down if it turned out to be uneconomical. The contract with NIPSCO did not guarantee that the mine would operate throughout the life of the contract but only protected the owners of Carbon County against the financial consequences to them of a breach. As Carbon County itself emphasizes in its brief, the contract was a product of the international oil cartel, which by forcing up the price of substitute fuels such as coal made costly coalmining operations economically attractive. The OPEC cartel is not a source of vested rights to produce substitute fuels at inflated prices.

* * *

AMERICAN BRANDS, INC. v. PLAYGIRL, INC.

United States Court of Appeals, Second Circuit, 1974.
498 F.2d 947.

MULLIGAN, CIRCUIT JUDGE. This is an appeal by the plaintiff American Brands, Inc. (American) from an order of the United States District Court, Southern District of New York, Hon. Charles L. Brieant, Jr., entered March 8, 1974, denying American's motion for a preliminary injunction seeking to enjoin the defendant, Playgirl, Inc. (Playgirl), from refusing to publish American's advertisement on the back cover of its magazine and from accepting other advertisements for its back cover. Affirmed.

American, formerly known as the American Tobacco Company, is a New Jersey corporation which is basically a manufacturer and distributor of tobacco products. Playgirl is a California corporation which commenced the publication of Playgirl Magazine in May, 1973. The magazine has a current circulation of about 2,000,000 copies, a rapid increase from its initial publication of about 600,000. Playgirl boasts that its publication is "Unconventional. Unprecedented. Unparalleled.", and that it alone delivers the "young, affluent and malleable female audience for your advertising message."

On February 13, 1974, American commenced an action against Playgirl in the Supreme Court, State of New York, County of New York, seeking a declaratory judgment as well as injunctive relief. The case was removed on February 27, 1974, to the United States District Court for the Southern District of New York, pursuant to 28 U.S.C. §§ 1441 & 1446. On March 4, 1974, American obtained an order to show cause seeking a preliminary injunction. After oral argument before Judge Brieant on March 6, 1974, the injunction was denied. Judge Brieant found that the case presented "fair grounds for litigation. That is close to the question of probability of success." He also held there was no showing of irreparable harm which would justify a mandatory injunction since money damages would be adequate. He determined that the equities tipped in favor of Playgirl and further indicated his willingness to provide the parties a speedy trial.

American claims that on January 26, 1973, Playgirl entered into a contract for the placement of American's advertisements on the back cover of Playgirl Magazine. Playgirl had contracted with the Carl Vann Company to solicit orders for advertisements for the new magazine. Vann negotiated the contract at issue, which reserved eight back covers of Playgirl for the advertising of Tareyton cigarettes, manufactured by American. The contract, apparently a form agreement provided by American, had two clauses specifically typed in. One, appearing on the back of the form, provided:

> YOUR ACCEPTANCE BELOW OF THIS AGREEMENT SHALL ALSO SERVE TO ACKNOWLEDGE OUR UNDERTSANDING [SIC] THAT WE HAVE THE CONTINUING AND IRREVOCABLE RIGHT, AT OUR OPTION, TO BUY THE BACK COVER OF PLAYGIRL EACH AND EVERY TWELVE MONTH PERIOD, FOR EACH ISSUE OF PLAYGIRL WITHIN THAT PERIOD, FOR AS LONG A TIME AS PLAYGIRL SHALL CONTINUE TO BE PUBLISHED.

The contract also contained a clause which provided: "We reserve a cancellation privilege as to the use of this space." That sentence was followed by a typed-in sentence which read: "WE HAVE THE RIGHT TO CANCEL THE SUBSEQUENT ISSUES WITHOUT PENALTY IF

THE PREMIERE ISSUE IS UNSATISFACTORY TO US." Playgirl published American's advertisements on the back cover of each of its first 11 issues commencing in June, 1973, and further agreed to accept American's advertisement for the last issue of the first publication year, May, 1974.

By letter dated September 25, 1973, Vann advised American that it was against the policy of Playgirl to afford an advertiser "a position of protection in perpetuity." Playgirl repeated its position in a letter to American dated December 3, 1973, indicating that it had elected to diversify its back cover advertisers. By letter dated December 20, 1973, Playgirl stated that this policy would be effective with the June, 1974 issue.

The standard which governs the trial court in the determination of whether or not a preliminary injunction should issue is whether or not the moving party has carried the burden of clearly demonstrating a combination of either probable success on the merits and the possibility of irreparable damage, or the existence of serious questions going to the merits and the tipping of the balance of hardships sharply in its favor. * * *

The court below in denying injunctive relief placed its greatest emphasis on the failure of the plaintiff to establish that its injury was not compensable by an award of monetary damages. The court observed that Playgirl is not unique, that there are other magazines and other back pages, and it suggested that American's damages should be limited to the difference, if any, between the rates paid at Playgirl and those payable elsewhere. * * *

On appeal, American insists that back cover advertising space is not fungible, and that Playgirl alone and uniquely provides an advertising audience composed of young, malleable and affluent females. In proof of this proposition, American only provides us with the understandably exuberant puffing of Playgirl's vice president, which touts the periodical as standing alone among magazines for women. To further justify the granting of an injunction, American states in its brief on appeal that Playgirl has suggested no basis upon which American might calculate its loss in monetary terms. Since monetary damages cannot be calculated, American argues, an injunction is required to avoid irreparable injury. See Interphoto Corp. v. Minolta Corp., 417 F.2d 621, 622 (2d Cir.1969). However, the burden of establishing its right to relief here is clearly upon American (Robert W. Stark, Jr., Inc. v. New York Stock Exchange, 466 F.2d 743, 744 (2d Cir.1972) (*per curiam*)), and Playgirl does not have the initial obligation of establishing that monetary damages are an appropriate remedy. While we fail to share the confidence of the court below that American's loss can be ultimately measured by the difference between advertising rates at Playgirl and those at some other comparable periodical, we do not find that American has, on the record before us, established that Playgirl is unique.

It would appear to be basic that American is obligated to mitigate its damages. If American can reasonably place its advertising on the back pages of other periodicals of comparable circulation, it would seem likely that its profits picture would be the same whether the tobacco consumers are malleable young ladies or more jaded aging males. If it had been shown that such advertising space is not readily available because of commitments to other national advertisers, American might well have established a case for equitable intervention, but the record before us is barren of any such proof. Again, American might have been able to demonstrate that Playgirl's readership is distinctly advantageous to it and that it cannot be reached by other media. However, except for Playgirl's own rodomontade, we have no documentation or proof that this is so. There is nothing in the record before us to indicate what segment of the populace is titillated by Playgirl and why in any event it is not susceptible to the lure of tobacco by American's blandishment in other and more pedestrian periodicals. The record does not indicate whether American's advertising was prepared particularly for Playgirl and its alleged audience of affluent malleables. The record contains no samples of American's advertisements and no copy of Playgirl. This reticence is perhaps explainable because of the claim of the plaintiff that Playgirl is not a magazine which everyone may find acceptable. In sum, we conclude that, on the basis of the record before the court, the trial judge did not err in holding that American had failed to establish clearly that its damages cannot be calculated and that consequently it cannot be made whole by monetary relief.

American has further failed to clearly establish that it will probably succeed on the merits. The trial court commented that it came close, but this is not enough absent a heavy tipping of the equities in its favor. Pride v. Community School Bd., supra, 482 F.2d at 264.

* * *

Playgirl, perhaps appropriately, claims that the arrangement was in any event *nudum pactum* since an absolute right to cancel was retained by American. Playgirl relies, *inter alia,* upon Miami Coca–Cola Bottling Co. v. Orange Crush Co., 296 F. 693 (5th Cir.1924), which represents a line of authority received with something less than enthusiasm in this circuit in Sylvan Crest Sand & Gravel Co. v. United States, 150 F.2d 642, 644–645 (1945). Cf. Richard Bruce & Co. v. J. Simpson & Co., 40 Misc.2d 501, 243 N.Y.S.2d 503 (Sup.Ct.1963). See also J. Calamari & J. Perillo, Contracts § 70 (1970); 1A A. Corbin, Contracts § 163 (1963). American contends that its right of cancellation is not absolute but was limited to its dissatisfaction with the premiere issue. Whether the right to cancel survived, and whether other consideration to support the contract was given may again depend upon the custom and practice of the advertising and publishing business. The contract is in the form of a brief letter agreement contained on one page with but a single additional paragraph on the back. It provides few details and the interstices must be supplied by evidence of business practice not present in the evidence before us. In short, we cannot say that the plaintiff has made a clear showing of probable success at this stage of the proceedings. The speedy trial which has been promised below provides the proper forum for determining these issues.

Finally, we note that American has failed to persuade us that, even short of probable success, it is nonetheless entitled to injunctive relief because the equities tip strongly in its favor. Dino DeLaurentiis Cinematografica, S.p.A. v. D–150, Inc., 366 F.2d 373 (2d Cir.1966). American urges that denial of the injunctive relief sought will irreparably injure its commercial good will. However, the case upon which it relies (Dino DeLaurentiis Cinematografica, S.p.A., supra) is distinguishable. There, a new motion picture film process was to be utilized for the exhibition of a particular motion picture, "The Bible." It was alleged that the contract bound the producer to exclusively utilize this process in the exhibition of the film. The loss of the opportunity to launch the heavily advertised new process with the particular motion picture provided in the contract was found by this court to create public confusion, with resultant loss of credibility and good will which were not monetarily compensable. Here, of course, the relationship between American and Playgirl was not monogamous. No trade or public identification of American with Playgirl has been established. Neither is there any claim that the marketing of some new tobacco product has been frustrated by the unavailability of Playgirl's back page. On the other hand, forcing Playgirl to leave the back page blank or accepting American's material rather than that of other advertisers, who have presumably entered into arrangements with Playgirl, would obviously force losses and litigation upon the publisher.

While other issues have been raised, they need not be considered. The judgment of the court below is affirmed.

BEVERLY GLEN MUSIC, INC. v. WARNER COMMUNICATIONS, INC.

Court of Appeal, Second District, Division 4, California, 1986.
178 Cal.App.3d 1142, 224 Cal.Rptr. 260.

KINGSLEY, ACTING P. J.—The plaintiff appeals from an order denying a preliminary injunction against the defendant, Warner Communications, Inc. We affirm.

FACTS

In 1982, plaintiff Beverly Glen Music, Inc., signed to a contract a then-unknown singer, Anita Baker. Ms. Baker recorded an album for Beverly Glen which was moderately successful, grossing over $1 million. In 1984, however, Ms. Baker was offered a considerably better deal by defendant Warner Communications. As she was having some difficulties with Beverly Glen, she accepted Warner's offer and notified plaintiff that she was no longer willing to perform under the contract. Beverly Glen then sued Ms. Baker and sought to have her enjoined from performing for any other recording studio. The injunction was denied, however, as, under Civil Code section 3423, subdivision Fifth, California courts will not enjoin the breach of a personal service contract unless the service is unique in nature and the performer is guaranteed annual compensation of at least $6,000,*** which Ms. Baker was not.

Following this ruling, the plaintiff voluntarily dismissed the action against Ms. Baker. Plaintiff, however, then sued Warner Communications for inducing Ms. Baker to breach her contract and moved the court for an injunction against Warner to prevent it from employing her. This injunction, too, was denied, the trial court reasoning that what one was forbidden by statute to do directly, one could not accomplish through the back door. It is from this ruling that the plaintiff appeals.

DISCUSSION

From what we can tell, this is a case of first impression in California. While there are numerous cases on the general inability of an employer to enjoin his former employee from performing services somewhere else, apparently no one has previously thought of enjoining the new employer from accepting the services of the breaching employee. While we commend the plaintiff for its resourcefulness in this regard, we concur in the trial court's interpretation of the maneuver.

(1) "It is a familiar rule that a contract to render personal services cannot be specifically enforced." (Foxx v. Williams (1966) 244 Cal.App.2d 223, 235 [52 Cal.Rptr. 896].) An unwilling employee cannot be compelled to continue to provide services to his employer either by ordering specific performance of his contract, or by injunction. To do so runs afoul of the Thirteenth Amendment's prohibition against involuntary servitude. (Poultry Producers etc. v. Barlow (1922) 189 Cal.278, 288 [208 P. 93].) However, beginning with the English case of Lumley v. Wagner (1852) 42 Eng. Rep. 687, courts have recognized that, while they cannot directly enforce an affirmative promise (in the Lumley case, Miss Wagner's promise to perform at the plaintiff's opera house), they can enforce the negative promise implied therein (that the defendant would not perform for someone else that evening). Thus, while it is not possible to compel a defendant to perform his duties under a personal service contract, it is possible to prevent him from employing his talents anywhere else. The net effect is to pressure the defendant to return voluntarily to his employer by denying him the means of earning a living. Indeed, this is its only purpose, for, unless the defendant relents and honors the contract, the plaintiff gains nothing from having brought the injunction.

The California Legislature, however, did not adopt this principle when in 1872 it enacted Civil Code section 3423, subdivision Fifth, and Code of Civil Procedure section 526, subdivision 5. These sections both provided that an injunction could not be granted: "To prevent the breach of a contract the performance of which would not be specifically enforced." In 1919, however, these sections were amended, creating an exception for: "a contract in writing for the rendition or furnishing of personal services from one to another where the minimum compensation

*** [Even as this statute was amended in 1993, the provision is of doubtful constitutionality as the court indicates below. Ed.]

for such service is at the rate of not less than six thousand dollars per annum and where the promised service is of a special, unique, unusual, extraordinary or intellectual character . . .".

(2) The plaintiff has already unsuccessfully argued before the trial court that Ms. Baker falls within this exception. It has chosen not to appeal that judgment, and is therefore barred from questioning that determination now. The sole issue before us then is whether plaintiff-although prohibited from enjoining Ms. Baker from performing herself-can seek to enjoin all those who might employ her and prevent them from doing so, thus achieving the same effect.

We rule that plaintiff cannot. Whether plaintiff proceeds against Ms. Baker directly or against those who might employ her, the intent is the same: to deprive Ms. Baker of her livelihood and thereby pressure her to return to plaintiff's employ. Plaintiff contends that this is not an action against Ms. Baker but merely an equitable claim against Warner to deprive it of the wrongful benefits it gained when it "stole" Ms. Baker away. Thus, plaintiff contends, the equities lie not between the plaintiff and Ms. Baker, but between plaintiff and the predatory Warner Communications company. Yet if Warner's behavior has actually been predatory, plaintiff has an adequate remedy by way of damages. An injunction adds nothing to plaintiff's recovery from Warner except to coerce Ms. Baker to honor her contract. Denying someone his livelihood is a harsh remedy. The Legislature has forbidden it but for one exception. To expand this remedy so that it could be used in virtually all breaches of a personal service contract is to ignore over 100 years of common law on this issue. We therefore decline to reverse the order. The order is affirmed.

McClosky, J., and Arguelles, J., concurred.

Problems

32. Seller entered into a contract with Buyer for the sale of a large quantity of lipsticks and containers of nail polish at cut-rate prices. Seller repudiated the contract. Buyer brought an action for specific performance. What will be the outcome?

33. P, a social club, entered into a contract with D whereby D would lend to P $125,000, to be secured by a mortgage. The funds were to be used to build a new clubhouse which was to be mortgaged to D. P then sold its existing clubhouse, purchased land and entered into construction contracts for building the new clubhouse. D refused to honor the agreement and P sues for specific performance. What result?

34. D contracted to sell to P 5,000 shares of stock in a publicly traded but closely held mining company. D, who holds sufficient shares to perform, refuses to deliver. The evidence also shows that D is insolvent. P sues for specific performance. What result?

35. M, an unwed pregnant woman, entered into a contract with F, the putative father of the expected child. F contracted to pay M $10 per week until the child's eighteenth birthday. After eleven years F ceased making payments. M seeks a decree for specific performance. What result? Consider

the material in § 12.9 of Calamari & Perillo 5th in addition to the assigned readings to arrive at your conclusion.

(b) Equitable Defenses

———

(Calamari & Perillo 5th §§ 16.7—16.18)

SCHLEGEL v. MOORHEAD

Supreme Court of Montana, 1976.
170 Mont. 391, 553 P.2d 1009.

JOHN C. HARRISON, JUSTICE. Plaintiff appeals from the judgment of the district court dismissing his complaint for specific performance of an option to purchase a federal oil and gas lease from the defendant.

The pertinent facts are set forth as shown by the district court findings of fact and the record. Defendant Sherman Moorhead has been the owner since 1956 of federal oil and gas lease number 073 151(a), consisting of 120 acres in Glacier County, Montana. He acquired the lease for salvage and has maintained only one producing well on the acreage. Said well has not produced sufficient revenue to pay the annual royalty. At all times pertinent hereto Moorhead employed a pumper who operated the well.

Moorhead worked in the oil fields in Glacier County from 1937 to 1964 and is familiar with oil field operations and terms. He has little experience with the business end of oil operations, and no previous experience with options. Within three years of the time of the option in dispute here, he twice attempted to sell the lease with no success. At no time relevant to this case did he make any effort to learn of oil field developments in the vicinity of his lease by making inquiries of his pumper, his attorney in the area, or the public records at the Oil and Gas Commission office in Shelby, Montana. Moorhead lived in Butte, Montana from 1964 to the time of this lawsuit.

Plaintiff Schlegel is a United States citizen who lived in Calgary, Alberta, Canada from 1952 to 1973. He has been engaged in oil fields as a roughneck, has sold real estate, and has bought and sold oil leases. He decided to leave Canada in 1973 due to his dissatisfaction with Canadian politics, and resolved to engage in the oil business in Montana.

In November 1973, Schlegel visited the Oil and Gas Commission offices in Shelby, Montana and met a geologist. The geologist recommended Township 37 N. Range 5 W as an area to review for possible lease opportunities. This township is where Moorhead's lease is located. From the public records in the Shelby office of the Oil and Gas Commission Schlegel learned that most of the acreage in that area was held by Union Oil. Union Oil declined to farm out any acreage to Schlegel. From his review of the records, Schlegel became aware of the lease held by Moorhead.

Schlegel learned from his examination of the public records at Shelby that Union Oil recently had brought in a well designated as "Kruger 4E13", and that the well was capable of producing oil and gas in commercial quantities. He also learned the figures reported for the early stages of oil and gas flow, that the well was located on acreage adjoining land covered by the Moorhead lease, and that Union Oil had located another drilling site, known as "Kruger 5E13", also on land adjacent to the Moorhead lease.

On a date prior to January 12, 1974, Schlegel made a telephone call to Moorhead and asked him whether he was interested in selling his lease. Moorhead replied that he was, and set a price of $5,000. Three subsequent telephone calls by Schlegel to Moorhead established further information about the lease, and set the purchase price at $5,000 provided that Moorhead give Schlegel a 90–day option to purchase for a $100 consideration. On January 18, 1974, Schlegel called Moorhead and advised him that he had prepared the option and would come to Butte to meet Moorhead on the following day to close the deal. Moorhead agreed.

On January 19, 1974, Schlegel and his wife met with Moorhead at a motel in Butte. Schlegel brought with him a form of option agreement which he had prepared. Moorhead then read over the option. There was no further discussion of the terms of the option, but in the course of conversation Moorhead asked Schlegel why he was interested in the lease and Schlegel replied that he had a general interest in the area and had become dissatisfied with the political situation in Canada. Schlegel did not then or at any time tell Moorhead of the information which Schlegel had obtained relative to the well Kruger 4E13 or the location of Kruger 5E13, both on land adjoining land covered by the Moorhead lease. The option was signed by the parties in the presence of a signing witness. Moorhead accepted from Schlegel a draft for $100 as payment of the option consideration.

Thereafter, on two occasions within the option period, Schlegel accepted and exercised the option to purchase Moorhead's lease and tendered $4,900 to Moorhead as payment therefor. Moorhead refused the tender and refused to carry out the option on both occasions.

Schlegel sued for specific performance of the option to purchase the oil and gas lease. Moorheads answered and counterclaimed for: (1) cancellation or rescission of the option on the ground of fraud; (2) damages of $5,000 for slander of title; and (3) actual damages and exemplary damages for fraud, totalling $56,000.

The district court of the ninth judicial district, sitting without a jury, Honorable B.W. Thomas presiding, concluded as a matter of law that neither plaintiff nor defendant-counterclaimants were entitled to the relief prayed for. Judgment was entered in favor of defendants against plaintiff's complaint; the complaint was dismissed; and judgment was entered in favor of plaintiffs against defendants' counterclaim. Only the plaintiff Schlegel appeals from the judgments of the district court.

We preface our discussion of the issues with a statement of the rule enunciated in Interior Securities Co. v. Campbell, 55 Mont. 459, 470, 178 P. 582, 585:

> "A decree for specific performance is not granted as a matter of abstract right, but in every instance the application for such relief is addressed to the sound, legal discretion of the court. * * * The case comes within the general rule, often adverted to by this court, that in the absence of a clear showing of abuse of discretion the decision of the lower court will be affirmed."

See also: Babcock v. Engel, 58 Mont. 597, 194 P. 137.

The focus of Schlegel's assignments of error is upon the district court's finding of fact No. 25 and conclusion of law No. 3. The former reads:

> "25. Enforcement of the option agreement would be unjust and unreasonable as to Moorhead because of (a) the inadequacy of the consideration, and, (b) the failure of Schlegel to fully and candidly inform Moorhead of the completion of Kruger well 4E13 and the location of Kruger 5E13 when he replied to Moorhead's January 19th inquiry as to why he was interested in the lease."

Conclusions of law No. 3 is similar, omitting the words "fully and candidly".

* * *

As to the first issue, Schlegel contends that the option transaction was at arms length and there was no duty upon him to disclose to Moorhead his knowledge gained from public records which were equally accessible to Moorhead. On the other hand, Moorhead argues that Schlegel is guilty of a multitude of frauds, a position which was rejected by the district court. However, our task is to determine whether the district court abused its discretion in refusing specific performance, and we need not resolve the conflicting arguments of the parties concerning actual and constructive fraud and the like.

It is undisputed that Schlegel was aware of the Kruger wells on January 19, 1974, and of the fact that they had substantial production potential. It is also established that when asked "why" he was interested in Moorhead's lease, Schlegel said he had a "general" interest in the area. The question is not whether Schlegel's answer was fraudulent or not, but whether Moorhead's assent was obtained by the "misrepresentations, concealment, circumvention, or unfair practices" of Schlegel. Section 17–808(3), R.C.M.1947. This distinction is significant because under section 17–808 a court in equity has far more latitude in assessing the conduct of the parties before it than does a court determining the legal elements of fraud. As stated in *Interior Securities,* supra:

> " * * * To secure the desired relief [specific performance] in this instance, appellants were required to come into court with clean

hands and with a cause whose ethical qualities were such as to commend it to the conscience of the chancellor. * * * "

The district court specifically found that Schlegel did not affirmatively misrepresent a lack of development in the area, and this finding is not challenged here. However, it is not necessarily inconsistent for the district court to hold that enforcement against Moorhead would be unjust and unreasonable due to Schlegel's concealment or circumvention in answer to Moorhead's question. In short, we do not find an abuse of discretion on this point.

The second issue concerns the inadequacy of the consideration. * * * [T]here is evidence to sustain the district court's finding of inadequacy of consideration independently of Chamberlain's testimony. Therefore, assuming any error in the admission of said testimony, it is harmless and cannot be the basis of a reversal on appeal. Cf. Benner v. B.F. Goodrich Co., 150 Mont. 97, 430 P.2d 648.

In view of the foregoing, we hold that the district court did not abuse its discretion by refusing to grant to Schlegel specific performance of the option to purchase Moorhead's oil and gas lease.

The judgment of the district court is affirmed.

SCHLEGEL v. MOORHEAD

Supreme Court of Montana, 1978.
177 Mont. 456, 582 P.2d 336.

HASWELL, CHIEF JUSTICE. This is an action for damages for the alleged breach of a written contract for the sale of an oil and gas lease. The same contract was the subject of previous litigation between these same parties. In Schlegel v. Moorhead (1976), 170 Mont. 391, 553 P.2d 1009, this Court unanimously affirmed dismissal of Schlegel's complaint for specific performance. The facts which gave rise both to this appeal and the prior case are articulated in detail in our previous opinion and will not be repeated here.

In affirming the dismissal of the original complaint for specific performance, we agreed with the District Court's finding of fact that enforcement of the option would be unjust and unreasonable because of inadequacy of the proposed consideration and because Schlegel failed to divulge on Moorhead's inquiry, information known to him indicating that the value of the lease was far in excess of the amount he had offered for it. We cited section 17–808, R.C.M.1947, which provides that specific performance cannot be enforced against a party under such circumstances. In the case on appeal, Schlegel seeks to secure through an action for damages that which he was denied in the earlier case for specific performance.

In support of his position that an action for damages can be prosecuted by him, Schlegel cites several authorities to the effect that where a plaintiff brings a suit in equity for the specific performance of a contract and judgment is given for the defendant for a reason applicable only to the equitable remedy the plaintiff is not precluded from maintaining an action at law for money damages. We conclude that Schlegel's reliance on these authorities is misplaced in this appeal because the legal deficiencies of inadequate consideration and lack of consent (present here because Moorhead's assent was obtained by concealment) are equally applicable to bar the enforcement of the contract at law as in equity. Section 13–102, R.C.M.1947. Consequently, we hold that this appeal should be summarily dismissed.

* * *

Affirmed.

MEYER v. BENKO

Court of Appeal, Second District, 1976.
55 Cal.App.3d 937, 127 Cal.Rptr. 846.

[Meyer agreed to buy and Benko agreed to sell a residence for $23,500. The agreement was entitled "Deposit Receipt and Agreement of Sale." The lower court ruled that the agreement did not constitute a contract, and, in the alternative, that specific performance would be denied because of the inadequacy of the consideration.]

STEPHENS, ASSOCIATE JUSTICE.

* * *

Having established that the Deposit Receipt constitutes a valid enforceable contract, we proceed to a determination of the proper remedy in this case.

The trial court found that there was inadequate consideration to justify specific performance. "The proper time for testing the adequacy of consideration is as of the formation of the contract." (Henderson v. Fisher, 236 Cal.App.2d 468, 474, 46 Cal.Rptr. 173, 178.) Various items of testimonial evidence were presented regarding the market value of the residence at the time the Deposit Receipt was executed. The listing real estate sales agent testified that she believed the value of the property to be "down a little" from the earlier listing price of $24,950. On the other hand, defendant Irene Benko testified that she believed that the residence was then worth $30,000 to *her,* although conceding that she was unaware of its market value. Defendant Howard Benko testified that he believed that the residence had a market value of $29,000 or $30,000 at that time. However, he also testified that he signed the Deposit Receipt at the sales price of $23,500 in order to sell the residence more quickly. "In determining whether consideration was fair and adequate, all circumstances surrounding the transfer of the property as they existed at that time, must be considered." (Lundgren v. Lundgren, 245 Cal.App.2d 582, 589, 54 Cal.Rptr. 30, 34.) "A consideration, to be adequate, need not amount to the full value of the property." (Foley v. Cowan, 80 Cal. App.2d 70, 76, 181 P.2d 410, 413.) The test "is not whether the [vendor] received the highest price obtainable for his property, but whether the price he received is fair and reasonable under the circumstances." (Henderson v. Fisher, supra, 236 Cal.App.2d 468, 474, 46 Cal.Rptr. 173, 178.) Defendants' desire to quickly consummate a sale explains the difference between the sale price agreed to and the alleged full value of the property. (Williams v. Rush, 134 Cal.App. 554, 560, 25 P.2d 888.) Therefore, the trial court's finding of inadequate consideration was clearly erroneous and unsupported by the evidence adduced at the trial.

* * *

The judgment is reversed.

DUANE SALES, INC. v. CARMEL

N.Y. Supreme Court, Appellate Division, Third Department, 1977.
57 A.D.2d 1003, 394 N.Y.S.2d 307.

MEMORANDUM DECISION. Appeal (1) from an order of the Supreme Court at Special Term, entered October 27, 1976, which granted plaintiff's motion for summary judgment, and (2) from the judgment entered thereon.

This action to compel specific performance of an option agreement for the purchase and sale of real property was before this court on a prior occasion. In reversing Special Term we concluded that, as a matter of law, plaintiff's complaint stated a cause of action for specific performance of the option agreement; that upon the record then before the court the matter should be considered by Special Term for summary judgment pursuant to CPLR 3211 (subd. [c]), and we remitted the matter to Special Term for further proceedings (53 A.D.2d 988, 385 N.Y.S.2d 870).

On this appeal defendants seek to raise again the same issues that were decided by this court on the previous appeal. The doctrine of the "law of the case" is therefore applicable * * * and the order of Special Term should be affirmed on the basis of our prior determination as to those issues * * *.

The defendants make the additional argument on this appeal that, should the plaintiff be entitled to specific performance of the option agreement, then an accounting should be directed to the respective losses and gains during the period of litigation. Special Term did not pass upon this contention. It is clear that in decreeing specific performance equity requires not only that the contract provisions to be enforced be just and equitable, but that the consequences of specific performance likewise be just and equitable. The relief should not be granted if, under the circumstances of the case, the result of the specific enforcement of the contract would be harsh or oppressive, or result in an unconscionable advantage to the plaintiff (55 N.Y.Jur., Specific Performance, § 34, and cases cited therein).

We conclude, therefore, that an accounting should be had which should take into consideration, among other things, the following: the rents received by defendants during the period from the date of the conveyance of the title to the premises; any profits resulting to the defendants in their operation of the property; any losses sustained by the plaintiff because of the delay in conveyance of title; necessary expenses incurred by the defendants in the operation of the property, such as payments of principal and interest on the mortgage, property taxes, insurance, and minor repairs; the benefits to the plaintiff in retaining the use of the purchase money during the pendency of the litigation. As to the defendants' claim that major improvements to the property in question made during the time of their ownership should also be included in the accounting, the record is vague and unclear as to the nature of, or necessity for, such improvements. Consequently, it should be left for the determination of Special Term whether or not defendants are entitled to be compensated for such major improvements.

Judgment modified, on the law and the facts, so as to direct that an accounting should be made, and matter remitted for further proceedings not inconsistent herewith, and, as so modified, affirmed, without costs.

ALAN SCHWARTZ, THE CASE FOR SPECIFIC PERFORMANCE

89 Yale L.J. 272 (1979).

The purpose of contract remedies is to place a disappointed promisee in as good a position as he would have enjoyed had his promisor performed. Contract law has two methods of achieving this "compensation goal": requiring the breaching party to pay damages, either to enable the promisee to purchase a substitute performance, or to replace the net gains that the promised performance would have generated; or requiring the breaching party to render the promised performance. Although the damages remedy is always available to a disappointed promisee under current law, the remedy of specific performance is available only at the discretion of the court. Moreover, courts seldom enforce contract clauses that explicitly provide for specific performance in the event of breach.

* * *

It is useful to begin by examining the paradigm case for granting specific performance under current law, the case of unique goods. When a promisor breaches and the promisee can make a transaction that substitutes for the performance the promisor failed to render, the promisee will be fully compensated if he receives the additional amount necessary to purchase the substitute plus the costs of making a second transaction. In some cases, however, such as those involving works of art, courts cannot identify which transactions the promisee would regard as substitutes because that information often is in the exclusive possession of the promisee. Moreover, it is difficult for a court to assess the accuracy of a promisee's claim. For example, if the promisor breaches a contract to sell a rare emerald, the promisee may claim that only the Hope Diamond would give him equal satisfaction, and thus may sue for the price difference between the emerald and the diamond. It would be difficult for a court to know whether this claim is true. If the court seeks to award money damages, it has three choices: granting the price differential, which may overcompensate the promisee; granting the dollar value of the promisee's forgone satisfaction as estimated by the court, which may overcompensate or undercompensate; or granting restitution of any sums paid, which under-compensates the promisee. The promisee is fully compensated without risk of overcompensation or undercompensation if the remedy of specific performance is available to him and its use encouraged by the doctrine that damages must be foreseeable and certain.

If specific performance is the appropriate remedy there are three reasons why it should be routinely available. The first reason is that in many cases damages actually are undercompensatory. Although promisees are entitled to incidental damages, such damages are difficult to monetize. They consist primarily of the costs of finding and making a second deal, which generally involve the expenditure of time rather than cash; attaching a dollar value to such opportunity costs is quite difficult. Breach can also cause frustration and anger, especially in a consumer context, but these costs also are not recoverable.

Substitution damages, the court's estimate of the amount the promisee needs to purchase an adequate substitute, also may be inaccurate in many cases less dramatic than the emerald hypothetical discussed above. This is largely because of product differentiation and early obsolescence. As product differentiation becomes more common, the supply of products that will substitute precisely for the promisor's performance is reduced. For example, even during the period when there is an abundant supply of new Datsuns for sale, two-door, two-tone Datsuns with mag wheels, stereo, and air conditioning may be scarce in some local markets. Moreover, early obsolescence gives the promisee a short time in which to make a substitute purchase. If the promisor breaches late in a model year, for example, it may be difficult for the promisee to buy the exact model he wanted. For these reasons, a damage award meant to enable a promisee to purchase "another car" could be undercompensatory.

In addition, problems of prediction often make it difficult to put a promisee in the position where he would have been had his promisor performed. If a breach by a contractor would significantly delay or prevent completion of a construction project and the project differs in important respects from other projects—for example, a department store in a different location than previous stores—courts may be reluctant to award "speculative" lost profits attributable to the breach.

Second, promisees have economic incentives to sue for damages when damages are likely to be fully compensatory. A breaching promisor is reluctant to perform and may be hostile. This makes specific performance an unattractive remedy in cases in which the promisor's performance is complex, because the promisor is more likely to render a defective performance when that performance is coerced, and the defectiveness of complex performances is sometimes difficult to establish in court. Further, when the promisor's performance must be rendered over time, as in construction or requirements contracts, it is costly for the promisee to monitor a reluctant promisor's conduct. If the damage remedy is compensatory, the promisee would prefer it to incurring these monitoring costs. Finally, given the time necessary to resolve lawsuits, promisees would commonly prefer to make substitute transactions promptly and sue later for damages rather than hold their affairs in suspension while awaiting equitable relief. The very fact that a promisee requests specific performance thus implies that damages are an inadequate remedy.****

The third reason why courts should permit promisees to elect routinely the remedy of specific performance is that promisees possess better information than courts as to both the adequacy of damages and the difficulties of coercing performance. Promisees know better than courts whether the damages a court is likely to award would be adequate because promisees are more familiar with the costs that breach imposes on them. In addition, promisees generally know more about their promisors than do courts; thus they are in a better position to predict whether specific performance decrees would induce their promisors to render satisfactory performances.

In sum, restrictions on the availability of specific performance cannot be justified on the basis that damage awards are usually compensatory. On the contrary, the compensation goal implies that specific performance should be routinely available. This is because damage awards actually are under compensatory in more cases than is commonly supposed; the fact of a specific performance request is itself good evidence that damages would be inadequate; and courts should delegate to promisees the decision of which remedy best satisfies the compensation goal. Further, expanding the availability of specific performance would not result in greater exploitation of promisors. Promisees would seldom abuse the power to determine when specific performance should be awarded because of the strong incentives that promisees face to seek damages when these would be even approximately compensatory.

Problems

36. M was the mother of C, an infant who was in the care and custody of an uncle in Holland. D promised M that if M would go to Holland, induce the uncle to surrender custody of the infant, and bring the infant to New York, D would support the infant and direct his moral education and training for the balance of the infant's life. M performed the requested acts and D performed for two years. Thereafter D repudiated. M sues for specific performance on the grounds that damages are uncertain. D argues lack of mutuality as the contract is unilateral: M has not promised that D can direct the infant's moral education. Moreover, M cannot bind the infant after he attains majority. D moves to dismiss the complaint on grounds that it does not state a cause of action for specific performance. What result?

**** Noneconomic motives could sometimes impel a promisee to seek specific performance; the German experience, however, provides some confirmation of this point. Although specific performance is much more widely available in Germany than in the United States, promisees there seek the damage remedy "in a high percentage of cases" [Citations omitted].

37. P, as tenant, operated a gasoline station on a portion of a large lot. His lease gave him an option to purchase the entire parcel. The owner of the land conveyed the entire parcel, subject to the lease, to D, the Board of Education. D, at considerable expense, built a new elementary school on the premises. P then duly exercised the option. P sues for specific performance. D counterclaims for ejectment on grounds that the location of the station was hazardous to schoolchildren. The trial court refused to order specific performance, awarded damages to P, and decreed that P could remain in possession until such time as the damages were paid. On appeal, what result?

38. A railroad owned large tracts of land on which many "squatters" resided. The railroad announced in 1881 that it would sell its land, with preference to be given to those who had made improvements on the land. Cole had improved a certain parcel. One Kelly went to the railroad's land agent, represented himself as the improver of the parcel and in reliance on this representation the railroad entered into a contract to convey the parcel to Kelly. In an action for specific performance, Kelly argued that his misrepresentation was not fraudulent as the railroad suffered no injury. Consult Calamari & Perillo 5th § 9.16, as well as the preceding materials. What result?

39. P, a labor union representing fire fighters in the City of Long Beach, entered into a collective bargaining agreement with the City. The agreement provided that in no event would the City reduce the complement of fire fighters below 34 persons. The purpose of the provision, recited in the contract, was to "assure * * * minimum job protection for the fire fighters." Because of a fiscal crisis, the City dismissed 13 of 34 fire fighters in violation of the contract. In an equitable action by P for reinstatement, what factors will the court take into consideration?

40. Decedent, a 73 year old victim of Parkinson's disease, entered into a written contract with P, a friend and neighbor, on May 3, whereby P would take care of Decedent, providing food and nursing care for the rest of her life. In exchange Decedent agreed to leave her 160 acre farm to P by will. On May 6, P quit her job so as to be able to perform under the contract. On the same day, Decedent suffered a stroke, was taken to the hospital and died in the hospital on June 14th. P sues the estate for specific performance. The estate defends on the ground of gross inadequacy of consideration. What result?

41. D contracted to purchase certain lots from P. P was aware that D intended to build a piano warehouse on the premises after the purchase. Prior to the date set for the conveyance, a new zoning ordinance was enacted restricting the area to residential uses. D repudiated the contract and P sues for specific performance. What result?

42. P was the owner of an easement thirty-three feet in width which ran from his lot to a public street. His use of the easement was infrequent. D built an extension onto her house that encroached eighteen inches onto the easement. When P had the easement surveyed and confronted D with the survey, D agreed that, in exchange for his forbearance, within 8 months she would either have her house moved (which would cost $40,000) or have the encroaching portion removed (at a cost of $8,000 and resulting in a severe

diminution in the utility of the extension). When D failed to perform, P sued for specific performance. What result?

43. The owner of a building leased the exterior wall of a building to plaintiff for a term, with options, of ten years. The premises were strategically located for the placement of a billboard at a major entrance to Manhattan Island, the Queens–Midtown Tunnel. Soon thereafter the building was sold to the defendant who assumed the lease but planned to demolish the building along with neighboring buildings it had purchased in order to construct more modern structures. When the defendant repudiated the lease, plaintiff sued for specific performance. Construct an argument for the defendant.

44. Defendant Killefer had played baseball for the 1913 season with Philadelphia. His contract provided that he would play for Philadelphia the next season. Killefer was induced by plaintiff to disaffirm that contract on grounds of infancy and to sign a contract with the plaintiff to play for Chicago for the next three seasons at an increased salary. Philadelphia then lured him away, after he reached the age of majority, at a still higher salary for the same three seasons. Plaintiff sought to enjoin Killefer from playing with Philadelphia because of the prior binding contract to play for Chicago. What defense is available to Killefer?

45. On November 29, Vendor contracted to sell 667 acres of farmland to the State Fish and Game Commission at a price of $67 per acre. On February 19, the State retained a local attorney to search title and prepare an abstract of title. Sporadically, the State contacted its attorney to attempt to expedite the preparation of the abstract. His frequent promises were not fulfilled. Finally, in exasperation, on January 22 of the following year, the State fired the attorney and an attorney on the staff of the Fish and Game Commission prepared the abstract. On April 30, the Commission tendered the purchase price, which Vendor refused. In the time between contracting and the time of tender, the property had doubled in value. The State sues for specific performance. What defense may the Vendor raise?

(c) Covenants Not to Compete

(Calamari & Perillo 5th §§ 16.19—16.22)

KARPINSKI v. INGRASCI

Court of Appeals of New York, 1971.
28 N.Y.2d 45, 320 N.Y.S.2d 1, 268 N.E.2d 751.

Fuld, Chief Judge. This appeal requires us to determine whether a covenant by a professional man not to compete with his employer is enforceable and, if it is, to what extent.

The plaintiff, Dr. Karpinski, an oral surgeon, had been carrying on his practice alone in Auburn—in Cayuga County—for many years. In 1953, he decided to expand and, since nearly all of an oral surgeon's business stems from referrals, he embarked upon a plan to "cultivate connections" among dentists in the four nearby Counties of Tompkins, Seneca, Cortland and Ontario. The plan was successful, and by 1962 twenty per cent of his practice consisted of treating patients referred to him by dentists located in those counties. In that year, after a number of those dentists had told him that some of their patients found it difficult to travel from their homes to Auburn, the plaintiff decided to open a second office in centrally-located Ithaca. He began looking for an assistant and, in the course of his search, met the defendant, Dr. Ingrasci, who was just completing his training in oral surgery at the Buffalo General Hospital and was desirous of entering private practice. Dr. Ingrasci manifested an interest in becoming associated with Dr. Karpinski and, after a number of discussions, they reached an understanding; the defendant was to live in Ithaca, a locale with which he had no prior familiarity, and there work as an employee of the plaintiff.

A contract, reflecting the agreement, was signed by the defendant in June, 1962. It was for three years and, shortly after its execution, the defendant started working in the office which the plaintiff rented and fully equipped at his own expense. The provision of the contract with which we are concerned is a covenant by the defendant not to compete with the plaintiff. More particularly, it recited that the defendant

> "promises and convenants that while this agreement is in effect and forever thereafter, he will never practice dentistry and/or Oral Surgery in Cayuga, Cortland, Seneca, Tompkins or Ontario counties except: (a) In association with the [plaintiff] or (b) If the [plaintiff] terminates the agreement and employs another oral surgeon".

In addition, the defendant agreed, "in consideration of the * * * terms of employment, and of the experience gained while working with" the plaintiff, to execute a $40,000 promissory note to the plaintiff, to become payable if the defendant left the plaintiff and practiced "dentistry and/or Oral Surgery" in the five enumerated counties.*

When the contract expired, the two men engaged in extended discussions as to the nature of their continued association—as employer and employee or as partners. Unable to reach an accord, the defendant, in February, 1968, left the plaintiff's employ and opened his own office for the practice of oral surgery in Ithaca a week later. The dentists in the area thereupon began referring their patients to the defendant rather than to the plaintiff, and in two months the latter's practice from the Ithaca area dwindled to almost nothing and he closed the office in that city. In point of fact, the record discloses that about 90% of the defendant's present practice comes from referrals from dentists in the counties specified in the restrictive covenant, the very same dentists who had been referring patients to the plaintiff's Ithaca office when the defendant was working there.**

---

* Either party was privileged to terminate the agreement on 60 days' notice within the three-year period and, if the plaintiff were to do so, the contract recited, the defendant was released from the restrictive covenant and the note.

** There are two other oral surgeons, in addition to the plaintiff and the defendant, serving the Ithaca area.

The plaintiff, alleging a breach of the restrictive covenant, seeks not only an injunction to enforce it but also a judgment of $40,000 on the note. The Supreme Court, after a nonjury trial, decided in favor of the plaintiff and granted him both an injunction and damages as requested. On appeal, however, the Appellate Division reversed the resulting judgment and dismissed the complaint; it was that court's view that the covenant was void and unenforceable on the ground that its restriction against the practice of both dentistry *and* oral surgery was impermissibly broad.

There can be no doubt that the defendant violated the terms of the covenant when he opened his own office in Ithaca. But the mere fact of breach does not, in and of itself, resolve the case. Since there are "powerful considerations of public policy which militate against sanctioning the loss of a man's livelihood," the courts will subject a covenant by an employee not to compete with his former employer to an "overriding limitation of 'reasonableness' ". * * *

Each case must, of course, depend, to a great extent, upon its own facts. It may well be that, in some instances, a restriction not to conduct a profession or a business in two counties or even in one, may exceed permissible limits. But, in the case before us, having in mind the character and size of the counties involved, the area restriction imposed is manifestly reasonable. The five small rural counties which it encompasses comprise the very area from which the plaintiff obtained his patients and in which the defendant would be in direct competition with him. Thus, the covenant's coverage coincides precisely with "the territory over which the practice extends", and this is proper and permissible. In brief, the plaintiff made no attempt to extend his influence beyond the area from which he drew his patients, the defendant being perfectly free to practice as he chooses outside the five specified counties.

Nor may the covenant be declared invalid because it is unlimited as to time, forever restricting the defendant from competing with the plaintiff. It is settled that such a covenant will not be stricken merely because it "contains no time limit or is expressly made unlimited as to time." * * * In the present case, the defendant opened an office in Ithaca, in competition with the plaintiff, just one week after his employment had come to an end. Under the circumstances presented, we thoroughly agree with the trial judge that it is clear that nearly all of the defendant's practice was, and would be, directly attributable to his association with his former employer.

This brings us to the most troublesome part of the restriction imposed upon the defendant. By the terms of the contract, he agreed not to practice "dentistry and/or Oral Surgery" in competition with the plaintiff. Since the plaintiff practices only "oral surgery," and it was for the practice of that limited type of "dentistry" that he had employed the defendant, the Appellate Division concluded that the plaintiff went beyond permissible limits when he obtained from the defendant the covenant that he would not engage in any "dentistry" whatsoever. The restriction, *as formulated,* is, as the Appellate Division concluded, too broad; it is not reasonable for a man to be excluded from a profession for which he has been trained when he does not compete with his former employer by practicing it.

The plaintiff seeks to justify the breadth of the covenant by urging that, if it had restricted only the defendant's practice of oral surgery and permitted him to practice "dentistry"—that is, to hold himself out as a dentist generally—the defendant would have been permitted, under the Education Law (§ 6601, subd. 3), to do all the work which an oral surgeon could. We have no sympathy with this argument; the plaintiff was not privileged to prevent the defendant from working in an area of dentistry in which he would not be in competition with him. The plaintiff would have all the protection he needs if the restriction were to be limited to the practice of oral surgery, and this poses the question as to the court's power to "sever" the impermissible from the valid and uphold the covenant to the extent that it is reasonable.

Although we have found no decision in New York directly in point, cases in this court support the existence of such a power. (See, e.g., Purchasing Assoc. v. Weitz, 13 N.Y.2d 267, 272, 246 N.Y.S.2d 600, 603, supra; Carpenter & Hughes v. De Joseph, 10 N.Y.2d 925, 224 N.Y.S.2d 9, 179 N.E.2d 854, affg 13 A.D.2d 611, 213 N.Y.S.2d 860; Interstate Tea Co. v. Alt, 271 N.Y. 76, 80, 2 N.E.2d 51, 53, supra.) Moreover, a number of out-of-state decisions, and they are supported by authoritative texts and commentators, explicitly recognize the court's power of severance and divisibility in order to sustain the covenant insofar as it is reasonable. As Professor Blake put it (73 Harv.L.Rev., at pp. 674–675), "If in balancing the equities the court decides that his [the employee's] activity would fit within the scope of a reasonable prohibition, it is apt to make use of the tool of severance, paring an unreasonable restraint down to appropriate size and enforcing it." In short, to cull from the Washington Supreme Court's opinion in Wood v. May, 73 Wash.2d 307, 314, 438 P.2d 587, 591, "We find it just and equitable to protect appellant [employer] by injunction to the extent necessary to accomplish the basic purpose of the contract insofar as such contract is reasonable." Accordingly, since his practice is solely as an oral surgeon, the plaintiff gains all the injunctive protection to which he is entitled if effect be given only to that part of the covenant which prohibits the defendant from practicing oral surgery.

The question arises, however, whether injunctive relief is precluded by the fact that the defendant's promissory note for $40,000 was to become payable if he breached the agreement not to compete. We believe not. The mere inclusion in a covenant of a liquidated damages provision does not automatically bar the grant of an injunction * * *; Diamond Match Co. v. Roeber, 106 N.Y. 473, 486, 13 N.E. 419, 423. As this court wrote in the *Diamond Match Co.* case (106 N.Y., at p. 486, 13 N.E., at p. 424.), "It is a question of intention, to be deduced from the whole instrument and the circumstances; and if it appear that the performance of the covenant was intended, and not merely the payment of damages in case of a breach, the covenant will be enforced." The covenant under consideration in this case may not reasonably be read to render "the liquidated damages provision * * * the sole remedy." (Rubinstein v. Rubinstein, 23 N.Y.2d 293, 298, 296 N.Y.S.2d 354, 358, 244 N.E.2d 49, 51, supra.) On the other hand, it would be grossly unfair to grant the plaintiff, in addition to an injunction, the full amount of damages ($40,000) which the parties apparently contemplated for a total breach of the covenant, since the injunction will halt any further violation. The proper approach is that taken in *Wirth* (265 N.Y. 214, 192 N.E. 297 * * *.) The court, there faced with a similar situation, granted the injunction sought and, instead of awarding the amount of liquidated damages specified, remitted the matter for determination of the *actual* damages suffered during the period of the breach.

The hardship necessarily imposed on the defendant must be borne by him in view of the plaintiff's rightful interest in protecting the valuable practice of oral surgery which he built up over the course of many years. The defendant is, of course, privileged to practice "dentistry" generally in Ithaca or continue to practice "oral surgery" anywhere in the United States outside of the five small rural counties enumerated. The covenant, part of a contract carefully negotiated with no indication of fraud or overbearing on either side, must be enforced, insofar as it reasonably and validly may, according to its terms. In sum, then, the plaintiff is entitled to an injunction barring the defendant from practicing oral surgery in the five specified counties and to damages actually suffered by him in the period during which the defendant conducted such a practice in Ithaca after leaving the plaintiff's employ.

The order appealed from should be reversed, with costs, and the case remitted to Supreme Court, Cayuga County, for further proceedings in accordance with this opinion.

HOWARD SCHULTZ & ASSOCIATES v. BRONIEC

Supreme Court of Georgia, 1977.
239 Ga. 181, 236 S.E.2d 265.

HILL, JUSTICE. This case involves a covenant not to compete and a covenant against disclosure of confidential information. In Rita Personnel Services v. Kot, 229 Ga. 314, 191 S.E.2d 79 (1972), this court was called upon to adopt or reject the "blue-pencil theory of severability" as to a covenant not to compete. In deciding that issue, the court was called upon to decide whether covenants not to compete should or should not be favored, and it was decided that they should not be favored. Thus the "blue-pencil" case, as *Rita Personnel* is known here, is somewhat of a landmark in this area of Georgia law and as such may even represent a turning point. In this case we are asked to overrule *Rita Personnel* if the restriction on competition is found to be overly broad.

At the outset it is necessary to determine whether the contract under consideration here is to be treated for these covenant purposes as an employment agreement in view of the fact that it expressly declares that it creates only the relationship of independent contractor and not that of master and servant. *Rita Personnel,* supra, involved a franchise agreement which was treated as an employment agreement. We find that the agreement here under review is to be treated similarly. Having made this determination, the parties can be identified by use of the traditional labels of "employer" and "employee."

An employer sought an injunction to enforce a covenant not to compete contained in an employment agreement and to restrain the former employee from divulging confidential and privileged information received by him during his employment. After hearing evidence and argument the trial court dismissed the complaint. The employer appeals.

On November 20, 1972, Frank D. Broniec (employee) entered into an agreement with Edward C. Aubitz by which the employee was to audit the accounts of clients of Aubitz and his principal, Howard Schultz and Associates, Inc., to determine if the clients had overpaid accounts payable because they were unaware of the availability of special discounts or allowances. The agreement contained a restrictive covenant whereby employee "will not, for a period of two years after the termination of this agreement, for any reason thereafter, engage, directly or indirectly, as principal, agent, employer, employee, or in any capacity whatsoever, in any business, activity, auditing practice, or any other related activities, in competition with the principal [Howard Schultz & Associates] or associate's [Aubitz] business within any area or areas from time to time constituting the principal's or associate's area of activity in the conduct of their respective businesses, as of the date of said termination. * * * "

The agreement also contained a paragraph concerned with confidential and privileged information which stated that employee "shall receive information and knowledge with reference to clients, customers, and other sources of income of the principal and the associate, and with reference to auditing techniques, forms, standards, and other practices of the principal and the associate in performing the services in which the principal and the associate are engaged, and that all of said knowledge and information is confidential and privileged, and * * * [employee] agrees to keep said information confidential and not reveal the same to any party. * * * "

* * *

1. By both constitutional and legislative provision, Georgia prohibits contracts or agreements in general restraint of trade. Const. 1976, Art. III, Sec. VIII, Par. VIII, Code Ann. § 2–1409; Code Ann. § 20–504. Georgia courts have consistently held that the prohibition does not impose an absolute bar against every kind of restrictive agreement. A covenant not to compete ancillary to an employment contract is enforceable only where it is strictly limited in time and territorial effect and is otherwise reasonable considering the business interest of the employer sought to be protected and the effect on the employee.

Insofar as territorial restrictions are concerned, some of them relate to the territory in which the employee was employed; others relate to the territory in which the employer does business. The former generally will be enforced. The latter generally are unenforceable absent a showing by the employer of the legitimate business interests sought to be protected. * * * It appears that the justification for this difference in treatment is that a court will accept as prima facie valid a covenant related to the territory where the employee was employed as a legitimate protection of the employer's investment in customer relations and good will. Thus a court will enforce an agreement prohibiting an employee from pirating his former employer's customers served by the employee, during the employment, at the employer's direct or indirect expense. Conversely, a court will not accept as prima facie valid a covenant related to the territory where the employer does business where the only justification is that the employer wants to avoid competition by the employee in that area.

In the case before us the employee was prohibited from engaging in competition within "any area or areas from time to time constituting the principal's or associate's area of activity in the conduct of their respective businesses, as of the date of said termination." This area would be, as to the employer's territory, not to mention the principal's territory, Alabama, Georgia, Florida, North Carolina, South Carolina and Tennessee. The employer has not justified this territorial restriction. It therefore stands as a bald attempt by the employer to prevent competition by the employee and is unenforceable.

2. This covenant not to compete must fall for two more reasons. This court has held on several occasions that a covenant wherein the employee agreed not to accept employment with a competitor "in any capacity" imposes a greater limitation upon the employee than is necessary for the protection of the employer and therefore is unenforceable.

A covenant not to compete is also unreasonable where the nature of the business activities in which the employee is forbidden to engage is not specified with particularity. These indefinite business activities generally are identified by reference to the employer's business; e.g., the employee agrees not to engage in or be employed by any "business similar to employer's business."

The restrictive covenant here prohibits the employee from engaging *"in any capacity* whatsoever, in any business, activity, auditing practice, or in any other related activities, in competition with the principal or associate's business." We find that the covenant is unreasonable because the employee is prohibited from working in any capacity for a competitor. The covenant also fails to specify with any particularity the nature and kind of business which is or will be competitive with the employer; i.e., the covenant fails to specify with particularity the activity which the employee is prohibited from performing.

3. The employer urges us to overrule Rita Personnel Services v. Kot, 229 Ga. 314, 191 S.E.2d 79, supra, and adopt the "blue-pencil theory" of severability. In *Rita Personnel* this court considered the

severance theory and declined to apply it. The court has consistently followed *Rita Personnel.* * * *

The employer argues that the Restatement of Contracts, § 518, approves the blue-pencil theory. However, Draft No. 12 of Restatement of the Law, Second, Contracts, § 326, pp. 95–96 (March 1, 1977) [now § 184], approved by the American Law Institute, rejects the blue-pencil theory as contrary to the weight of recent authority. *Rita Personnel* is cited with approval.·

* * *

According to the contract before us the employee agreed that for a period of two years he would not engage, directly or indirectly, as principal, agent, employer, employee, or in any capacity whatsoever, in any business activity, auditing practice, or any other related activity, in competition with the employer in Alabama, Georgia, Florida, North Carolina, South Carolina and Tennessee, or in competition with employer's principal wherever it may operate. The employer requests us to restrict the territory, to strike the offensive words "in any capacity" and to add words of our choosing to specify the activity forbidden to the employee.

It is these very requests which are the reason for rejecting severability of employee covenants not to compete. Employers covenant for more than is necessary, hope their employees will thereby be deterred from competing, and rely on the courts to rewrite the agreements so as to make them enforceable if their employees do compete. When courts adopt severability of covenants not to compete, employee competition will be deterred even more than it is at present by these overly broad covenants against competition. We choose to reaffirm *Rita Personnel Services v. Kot,* supra.

4. We next must consider whether the trial court erred in not issuing an injunction with reference to the employee's covenant against disclosure of confidential information. In Durham v. Stand–By Labor, Inc., supra, we made it clear that a nondisclosure covenant in an employment agreement could be enforced independently from a claim under a covenant not to compete such as has been discussed above. See also Aladdin v. Krasnoff, supra.

Also, at the outset, it is important to note that here the employer does not have a "trade secret" such as can be protected by law absent a contract provision. "A trade secret, within the rules pertaining to the rights which can be protected by injunction, is a plan, process, tool, mechanism, or compound, known only to its owner and those of his employees to whom it must be confided in order to apply it to the uses intended."

Judgment affirmed.

Problems

46. A law partnership agreement provided that upon termination of the partnership the clients of the partnership were to be allocated to individual members of the firm. It further provided " * * * all partners shall be restricted from doing business with a client designated as that of another partner for a period of 5 years." The Code of Professional Responsibility of the A.B.A. provides: "A lawyer shall not be a party to or participate in a partnership or employment agreement with another lawyer that restricts the right of a lawyer to practice law after the termination of the relationship created by the agreement except as may be provided in a bona fide retirement plan * * *." (This provision is substantially replicated in the later A.B.A. Model Rules.) (a) Upon termination of the partnership is the quoted clause of the partnership agreement enforceable?

(b) Suppose, instead, the parties were physicians. Would the result be the same?

47. P, a large nation-wide firm that specialized in advising businesses on how to minimize their unemployment compensation costs, hired D in 1962. D's employment contract provided that after a voluntary termination of D's employment D would refrain for three years from entering any competing business in 7 named counties, one of which was the place of his employment. D rose to the position of vice-president in charge of operations and was thoroughly conversant with all aspects of the operation, but had little involvement with sales. P's services were sold to major companies listed in industrial directories. After eleven years, D resigned and set up a competing business in the same community. P seeks an injunction: (1) prohibiting D from operating a competing business for three years within the designated area and (2) permanently enjoining D from soliciting P's customers. What analysis and result in (a) New York, (b) in Georgia?

Chapter 11

THIRD PARTY BENEFICIARIES

SECTION 1. INTENDED, INCIDENTAL, CREDITOR AND DONEE BENEFICIARIES

(Calamari & Perillo 5th §§ 17.1—17.9)

LAWRENCE v. FOX

Court of Appeals of New York, 1859.
20 N.Y. 268.

Appeal from the Superior Court of the city of Buffalo. On the trial before Mr. Justice Masten, it appeared by the evidence of a bystander, that one Holly, in November, 1857, at the request of the defendant, loaned and advanced to him $300, stating at the time that he owed that sum to the plaintiff for money borrowed of him, and had agreed to pay it to him the then next day; that the defendant in consideration thereof, at the time of receiving the money, promised to pay it to the plaintiff the then next day. Upon this state of facts the defendant moved for a nonsuit, upon three several grounds, viz.: That there was no proof tending to show that Holly was indebted to the plaintiff; that the agreement by the defendant with Holly to pay the plaintiff was void for want of consideration, and that there was no privity between the plaintiff and defendant. The court overruled the motion, and the counsel for the defendant excepted. The cause was then submitted to the jury, and they found a verdict for the plaintiff for the amount of the loan and interest, $344.66, upon which judgment was entered; from which the defendant appealed to the Superior Court, at general term, where the judgment was affirmed, and the defendant appealed to this court. The cause was submitted on printed arguments.

H. GRAY, J. The first objection raised on the trial amounts to this: That the evidence of the person present, who heard the declarations of Holly giving directions as to the payment of the money he was then advancing to the defendant, was mere hearsay and therefore not competent. Had the plaintiff sued Holly for this sum of money no objection to the competency of this evidence would have been thought of; and if the defendant had performed his promise by paying the sum loaned to him to the plaintiff, and Holly had afterwards sued him for its recovery, and this evidence had been offered by the defendant, it would doubtless have been received without an objection from any source. All the defendant had the right to demand in this case was evidence which, as between Holly and the plaintiff, was competent to establish the relation between them of debtor and creditor. For that purpose the evidence was clearly competent; it covered the whole ground and warranted the verdict of the jury. But it is claimed that notwithstanding this promise was established by competent evidence, it was void for the want of consideration. It is now more than a quarter of a century since it was settled by the Supreme Court of this State—in an able and pains-taking opinion by the late Chief Justice Savage, in which the authorities were fully examined and carefully analysed—that a promise in all material respects like the one under consideration was valid; and the judgment of that court was unanimously affirmed by the Court for the Correction of Errors. (Farley v. Cleaveland,* 4 Cow., 432; *same case in error,* 9 id., 639.) In that case one Moon owed Farley and sold to Cleaveland a quantity of hay, in consideration of which Cleaveland promised to pay Moon's debt to Farley; and the decision in favor of Farley's right to recover was placed upon the ground that the hay received by Cleaveland from Moon was a valid consideration for Cleaveland's promise to pay Farley, and that the subsisting liability of Moon to pay Farley was no objection to the recovery. The fact that the money advanced by Holly to the defendant was a loan to him for a day, and that it thereby became the property of the defendant, seemed to impress the defendant's counsel with the idea that because the defendant's promise was not a trust fund placed by the plaintiff in the defendant's hands, out of which he was to realize money as from the sale of a chattel or the collection of a debt, the promise although made for the benefit of the plaintiff could not enure to his benefit. The hay which Cleaveland delivered to Moon was not to be paid to Farley, but the debt incurred by Cleaveland for the purchase of the hay, like the debt incurred by the defendant for money borrowed, was what was to be paid. That case has been often referred to by the courts of this State, and has never been doubted as sound authority for the principle upheld by it. (Barker v. Bucklin, 2 Denio, 45; Hudson Canal Company v. The Westchester Bank, 4 id., 97.) It puts to rest the objection that the defendant's promise was void for want of consideration. The report of that case shows that the promise was not only made to Moon but to the plaintiff Farley. In this case the promise was made to Holly and not expressly to the plaintiff; and this difference between the two cases presents the question, raised by the defendant's objection as to the want of privity between the plaintiff and defendant. * * *

But it is urged that because the defendant was not in any sense a trustee of the property of Holly for the benefit of the plaintiff, the law will not imply a promise. I agree that many of the cases where a promise was implied were cases of trusts, created for the benefit of the promiser. The case of Felton v. Dickinson (10 Mass., 189, 190), and others that might be cited, are of that class; but concede them all to have been cases

* [Spelled "Cleaveland" throughout this published opinion, but "Cleveland" in the   published reports of Farley v. Cleveland. Ed.]

of trusts, and it proves nothing against the application of the rule to this case. The duty of the trustee to pay the *cestuis que trust,* according to the terms of the trust, implies his promise to the latter to do so. In this case the defendant, upon ample consideration received from Holly, promised Holly to pay his debt to the plaintiff; the consideration received and the promise to Holly made it as plainly his duty to pay the plaintiff as if the money had been remitted to him for that purpose, and as well implied a promise to do so as if he had been made a trustee of property to be converted into cash with which to pay. The fact that a breach of the duty imposed in the one case may be visited, and justly, with more serious consequences than in the other, by no means disproves the payment to be a duty in both. The principle illustrated by the example so frequently quoted (which concisely states the case in hand) "that a promise made to one for the benefit of another, he for whose benefit it is made may bring an action for its breach," has been applied to trust cases, not because it was exclusively applicable to those cases, but because it was a principle of law, and as such applicable to those cases. It was also insisted that Holly could have discharged the defendant from his promise, though it was intended by both parties for the benefit of the plaintiff, and therefore the plaintiff was not entitled to maintain this suit for the recovery of a demand over which he had no control. It is enough that the plaintiff did not release the defendant from his promise, and whether he could or not is a question not now necessarily involved; but if it was, I think it would be found difficult to maintain the right of Holly to discharge a judgment recovered by the plaintiff upon confession or otherwise, for the breach of the defendant's promise; and if he could not, how could he discharge the suit before judgment, or the promise before suit, made as it was for the plaintiff's benefit and in accordance with legal presumption accepted by him (Berly v. Taylor, 5 Hill, 577–584, et seq.), until his dissent was shown. The cases cited, and especially that of Farley v. Cleaveland, establish the validity of a parol promise; it stands then upon the footing of a written one. Suppose the defendant had given his note in which, for value received of Holly, he had promised to pay the plaintiff and the plaintiff had accepted the promise, retaining Holly's liability. Very clearly Holly could not have discharged that promise, be the right to release the defendant as it may. No one can doubt that he owes the sum of money demanded of him, or that in accordance with his promise it was his duty to have paid it to the plaintiff; nor can it be doubted that whatever may be the diversity of opinion elsewhere, the adjudications in this State, from a very early period, approved by experience, have established the defendant's liability; if, therefore, it could be shown that a more strict and technically accurate application of the rules applied, would lead to a different result (which I by no means concede), the effort should not be made in the face of manifest justice.

The judgment should be affirmed.

JOHNSON, CH. J., DENIO, SELDEN, ALLEN and STRONG, JS., concurred. JOHNSON, CH. J., and DENIO, J., were of opinion that the promise was to be regarded as made to the plaintiff through the medium of his agent, whose action he could ratify when it came to his knowledge, though taken without his being privy thereto.

COMSTOCK, J. (Dissenting.) The plaintiff had nothing to do with the promise on which he brought this action. It was not made to him, nor did the consideration proceed from him. If he can maintain the suit, it is because an anomaly has found its way into the law on this subject. In general, there must be privity of contract. The party who sues upon a promise must be the promisee, or he must have some legal interest in the undertaking. In this case, it is plain that Holly, who loaned the money to the defendant, and to whom the promise in question was made, could at any time have claimed that it should be performed to himself personally. He had lent the money to the defendant, and at the same time directed the latter to pay the sum to the plaintiff. This direction he could countermand, and if he had done so, manifestly the defendant's promise to pay according to the direction would have ceased to exist. The plaintiff would receive a benefit by a complete execution of the arrangement, but the arrangement itself was between other parties, and was under their exclusive control. If the defendant had paid the money to Holly, his debt would have been discharged thereby. So Holly might have released the demand or assigned it to another person, or the parties might have annulled the promise now in question, and designated some other creditor of Holly as the party to whom the money should be paid. It has never been claimed, that in a case thus situated, the right of a third person to sue upon the promise rested on any sound principle of law. We are to inquire whether the rule has been so established by positive authority.

* * *

The cases in which some trust was involved are also frequently referred to as authority for the doctrine now in question, but they do not sustain it. If A delivers money or property to B, which the latter accepts upon a trust for the benefit of C, the latter can enforce the trust by an appropriate action for that purpose. (Berly v. Taylor, 5 Hill, 577.) If the trust be of money, I think the beneficiary may assent to it and bring the action for money had and received to his use. If it be of something else than money, the trustee must account for it according to the terms of the trust, and upon principles of equity. There is some authority even for saying that an express promise founded on the possession of a trust fund may be enforced by an action at law in the name of the beneficiary, although it was made to the creator of the trust. Thus, in *Comyn's Digest (Action on the case upon Assumpsit, B. 15)*, it is laid down that if a man promise a pig of lead to A, and his executor give lead to make a pig to B, who assumes to deliver it to A, an assumpsit lies by A against him. The case of The Delaware and Hudson Canal Company v. The Westchester County Bank (4 Denio, 97), involved a trust because the defendants had received from a third party a bill of exchange under an agreement that they would endeavor to collect it, and would pay over the proceeds when collected to the plaintiffs. A fund received under such an agreement does not belong to the person who receives it. He must account for it specifically; and perhaps there is no gross violation of principle in permitting the equitable owner of it to sue upon an express promise to pay it over. Having a specific interest in the thing, the undertaking to account for it may be regarded as in some sense made with him through the author of the trust. But further than this we cannot go without violating plain rules of law. In the case before us there was nothing in the nature of a trust or agency. The defendant borrowed the money of Holly and received it as his own. The plaintiff had no right in the fund, legal or equitable. The promise to repay the money created an obligation in favor of the lender to whom it was made and not in favor of any one else.

* * *

GROVER, J., also dissented.

Judgment affirmed.

VROOMAN v. TURNER

Court of Appeals of New York, 1877.
69 N.Y. 280.

Appeal from judgment of the General Term of the Supreme Court in the second judicial department, affirming a judgment in favor of plaintiff, entered upon the report of a referee. (Reported below, 8 Hun, 78.)

This was an action to foreclose a mortgage.

The mortgage was executed in August, 1873, by defendant Evans, who then owned the mortgaged premises. He conveyed the same to one Mitchell, and through various mesne conveyances the title came to one Sanborn. In none of these conveyances did the grantee assume to pay the mortgage. Sanborn conveyed the same to defendant Harriet B. Turner, by deed which contained a clause stating that the conveyance was subject to the mortgage, "which mortgage the party hereto of the second part hereby covenants and agrees to pay off and discharge, the same forming part of the consideration thereof."

The referee found that said grantee, by so assuming payment of the mortgage, became personally liable therefor, and directed judgment against her for any deficiency. Judgment was entered accordingly.

ALLEN, J. The precise question presented by the appeal in this action has been twice before the courts of this State, and received the same solution in each. It first arose in King v. Whitely, 10 Paige, 465, decided in 1843. There the grantor of an equity of redemption in mortgaged premises, neither legally nor equitably interested in the payment of the bond and mortgage except so far as the same were a charge upon his interest in the lands, conveyed the lands subject to the mortgage, and the conveyance recited that the grantees therein assumed the mortgage, and were to pay off the same as a part of the consideration of such conveyance, and it was held that as the grantor in that conveyance was not personally liable to the holder of the mortgage to pay the same, the grantees were not liable to the holder of such mortgage for the deficiency upon a foreclosure and sale of the mortgaged premises. It was conceded by the chancellor that if the grantor had been personally liable to the holder of the mortgage for the payment of the mortgage debt, the holder of such mortgage would have been entitled in equity to the benefit of the agreement recited in such conveyance, to pay off the mortgage and to a decree over against the grantees for the deficiency. This would have been in accordance with a well established rule in equity, which gives to the creditor the right of subrogation to and the benefit of any security held by a surety for the re-enforcement of the principal debt, and in the case supposed, and by force of the agreement recited in the conveyance, the grantee would have become the principal debtor, and the grantor would be a *quasi* surety for the payment of the mortgage debt. (Halsey v. Reed, 9 Paige, 446; Curtis v. Tyler, id., 432; Burr v. Beers, 24 N.Y., 178.)

* * *

It is true there need be no privity between the promissor and the party claiming the benefit of the undertaking, neither is it necessary that the latter should be privy to the consideration of the promise, but it does not follow that a mere volunteer can avail himself of it. A legal obligation or duty of the promisee to him, will so connect him with the transaction as to be a substitute for any privity with the promissor, or the consideration of the promise, the obligation of the promisee furnishing an evidence of the intent of the latter to benefit him, and creating a privity by substitution with the promissor. A mere stranger cannot intervene, and claim by action the benefit of a contract between other parties. There must be either a new consideration or some prior right or claim against one of the contracting parties, by which he has a legal interest in the performance of the agreement.

It is said in Garnsey v. Rogers (47 N.Y., 233), that it is not every promise made by one person to another from the performance of which a third person would derive a benefit that gives a right of action to such third person, he being privy neither to the contract nor the consideration. In the language of Judge Rapallo, "to entitle him to an action, the contract must have been made for his benefit. He must be the party intended to be benefited." See, also, Turk v. Ridge (41 N.Y., 201), and Merrill v. Green (55 id., 270), in which, under similar agreements third parties sought to maintain an action upon engagements by the performance of which they would be benefited, but to which they were not parties, and failed. The courts are not inclined to extend the doctrine of Lawrence v. Fox to cases not clearly within the principle of that decision. Judges have differed as to the principle upon which Lawrence v. Fox and kindred cases rest, but in every case in which an action has been sustained there has been a debt or duty owing by the promisee to the party claiming to sue upon the promise. Whether the decisions rest upon the doctrine of agency, the promisee being regarded as the agent for the third party, who, by bringing his action adopts his acts, or upon the doctrine of a trust, the promissor being regarded as having received money or other thing for the third party, is not material. In either case there must be a legal right, founded upon some obligation of the promisee, in the third party, to adopt and claim the promise as made for his benefit.

In Lawrence v. Fox a prominent question was made in limine, whether the debt from Halley* to the plaintiff was sufficiently proved by the confession of Halley* made at the time of the loan of the money to the defendant. It was assumed that if there was no debt proved the action would not lie, and the declaration of Halley* the debtor was held sufficient evidence of the debt. Gray, J., said: "All the defendant had the right to demand in this case was evidence which as between Halley* and the plaintiff was competent to establish the relation between them of debtor and creditor." In Burr v. Beers, (24 N.Y., 178), and Thorp v. Keokuk Coal Co., (48 N.Y., 253), the grantor of the defendant was personally liable to pay the mortgage to the plaintiff, and the cases were therefore clearly within the principle of Lawrence v. Fox, Halsey v. Reed, and Curtis v. Tyler, supra. See also per BOSWORTH, J., Doolittle v. Naylor, (2 Box., 225); and Ford v. David (1 Bos., 569). It is claimed that King v. Whitely and the cases following it were overruled by Lawrence v. Fox. But it is very clear that it was not the intention to overrule them, and that the cases are not inconsistent. The doctrine of Lawrence v. Fox, although questioned and criticised, was not first adopted in this state by the decision of that case. It was expressly adjudged as early as 1825, in Farley v. Cleveland, (4 Cow., 432), affirmed in the court for the correction of errors in 1827, *per totam curiam,* and reported in 9 Cow., 639. The chancellor was not ignorant of these decisions when he decided King v. Whitely, nor was Judge Denio and his associates unaware of them when Trotter v. Hughes was decided, and Judge Gray in Lawrence v. Fox says the case of Farley v. Cleveland had never been doubted.

The court below erred in giving judgment against the appellant for the deficiency after the sale of the mortgaged premises, and so much of the judgment as directs her to pay the same must be reversed with costs.

All concur, except EARL, J., dissenting.

Judgment accordingly.

SEAVER v. RANSOM

Court of Appeals of New York, 1918.
224 N.Y. 233, 120 N.E. 639.

POUND, J. Judge Beman and his wife were advanced in years. Mrs. Beman was about to die. She had a small estate consisting of a house and lot in Malone and little else. Judge Beman drew his wife's will according to her instructions. It gave $1,000 to plaintiff, $500 to one sister, plaintiff's mother, and $100 each to another sister and her son, the use of the house to her husband for life, remainder to the American

---

* [Spelled "Holly" in the Lawrence v. Fox printed opinion. Probably should be "Haw- ley." See Waters, The Property in The Promise, 98 Harv.L.Rev. 1109 (1985).]

Society for the Prevention of Cruelty to Animals. She named her husband as residuary legatee and executor. Plaintiff was her niece, thirty-four years old, in ill health, sometimes a member of the Beman household. When the will was read to Mrs. Beman she said that it was not as she wanted it; she wanted to leave the house to plaintiff. She had no other objection to the will, but her strength was waning and although the judge offered to write another will for her, she said she was afraid she would not hold out long enough to enable her to sign it. So the judge said if she would sign the will he would leave plaintiff enough in his will to make up the difference. He avouched the promise by his uplifted hand with all solemnity and his wife then executed the will. When he came to die it was found that his will made no provision for the plaintiff.

This action was brought and plaintiff recovered judgment in the trial court on the theory that Beman had obtained property from his wife and induced her to execute the will in the form prepared by him by his promise to give plaintiff $6,000, the value of the house, and that thereby equity impressed his property with a trust in favor of plaintiff. Where a legatee promises the testator that he will use property given him by the will for a particular purpose, a trust arises. * * * Beman received nothing under his wife's will but the use of the house in Malone for life. Equity compels the application of property thus obtained to the purpose of the testator, but equity cannot so impress a trust except on property obtained by the promise. Beman was bound by his promise, but no property was bound by it; no trust in plaintiff's favor can be spelled out.

An action on the contract for damages or to make the executors trustees for performance stands on different ground. (Farmers' Loan & Trust Co. v. Mortimer, 219 N.Y. 290, 294, 295.) The Appellate Division properly passed to the consideration of the question whether the judgment could stand upon the promise made to the wife, upon a valid consideration, for the sole benefit of plaintiff. The judgment of the trial court was affirmed by a return to the general doctrine laid down in the great case of Lawrence v. Fox (20 N.Y. 268) which has since been limited as herein indicated.

Contracts for the benefit of third persons have been the prolific source of judicial and academic discussion. * * * The general rule, both in law and equity * * *, was that privity between a plaintiff and a defendant is necessary to the maintenance of an action on the contract. The consideration must be furnished by the party to whom the promise was made. The contract cannot be enforced against the third party and, therefore, it cannot be enforced by him. On the other hand, the right of the beneficiary to sue on a contract made expressly for his benefit has been fully recognized in many American jurisdictions, either by judicial decision or by legislation, and is said to be "the prevailing rule in this country." (Hendrick v. Lindsay, 93 U.S. 143; Lehow v. Simonton, 3 Col. 346.) It has been said that "the establishment of this doctrine has been gradual, and is a victory of practical utility over theory, of equity over technical subtlety." (Brantly on Contracts [2d ed.], p. 253.) The reasons for this view are that it is just and practical to permit the person for whose benefit the contract is made to enforce it against one whose duty it is to pay. Other jurisdictions still adhere to the present English rule * * * that a contract cannot be enforced by or against a person who is not a party * * *. In New York the right of the beneficiary to sue on contracts made for his benefit is not clearly or simply defined. It is at present confined, *first,* to cases where there is a pecuniary obligation running from the promisee to the beneficiary; "a legal right founded upon some obligation of the promisee in the third party to adopt and claim the promise as made for his benefit." * * * *Secondly,* to cases where the contract is made for the benefit of the wife * * *, affianced wife * * *, or child * * * of a party to the contract. The close relationship cases go back to the early King's Bench case (1677), long since repudiated in England, of Dutton v. Poole (2 Lev. 210; s. c., 1 Ventris, 318, 332). * * * The natural and moral duty of the husband or parent to provide for the future of wife or child sustains the action on the contract made for their benefit. "This is the farthest the cases in this state have gone," says Cullen, J., in the marriage settlement case of Borland v. Welch (162 N.Y. 104, 110).

The right of the third party is also upheld in, *thirdly,* the public contract cases * * * where the municipality seeks to protect its inhabitants by covenants for their benefit and, *fourthly,* the cases where, at the request of a party to the contract, the promise runs directly to the beneficiary although he does not furnish the consideration. * * * It may be safely said that a general rule sustaining recovery at the suit of the third party would include but few classes of cases not included in these groups, either categorically or in principle.

The desire of the childless aunt to make provision for a beloved and favorite niece differs imperceptibly in law or in equity from the moral duty of the parent to make testamentary provision for a child. The contract was made for the plaintiff's benefit. She alone is substantially damaged by its breach. The representatives of the wife's estate have no interest in enforcing it specifically. It is said in Buchanan v. Tilden that the common law imposes moral and legal obligations upon the husband and the parent not measured by the necessaries of life. It was, however, the love and affection or the moral sense of the husband and the parent that imposed such obligations in the cases cited rather than any common-law duty of husband and parent to wife and child. If plaintiff had been a child of Mrs. Beman, legal obligation would have required no testamentary provision for her, yet the child could have enforced a covenant in her favor identical with the covenant of Judge Beman in this case. (De Cicco v. Schweizer, supra.) The constraining power of conscience is not regulated by the degree of relationship alone. The dependent or faithful niece may have a stronger claim than the affluent or unworthy son. No sensible theory of moral obligation denies arbitrarily to the former what would be conceded to the latter. We might consistently either refuse or allow the claim of both, but I cannot reconcile a decision in favor of the wife in Buchanan v. Tilden based on the moral obligations arising out of near relationship with a decision against the niece here on the ground that the relationship is too remote for equity's ken. * * *

KELLOGG, P.J., writing for the court below well said: "The doctrine of Lawrence v. Fox is progressive, not retrograde. The course of the late decisions is to enlarge, not to limit the effect of that case." The court in that leading case attempted to adopt the general doctrine that any third person, for whose direct benefit a contract was intended, could sue on it. * * *

[O]n principle, a sound conclusion may be reached. If Mrs. Beman had left her husband the house on condition that he pay the plaintiff $6,000 and he had accepted the devise, he would have become personally liable to pay the legacy and plaintiff could have recovered in an action at law against him, whatever the value of the house. * * * That would be because the testatrix had in substance bequeathed the promise to plaintiff and not because close relationship or moral obligation sustained the contract. The distinction between an implied promise to a testator for the benefit of a third party to pay a legacy and an unqualified promise on a valuable consideration to make provision for the third party by will is discernible but not obvious. The tendency of American authority is to sustain the gift in all such cases and to permit the donee-beneficiary to recover on the contract. * * * The equities are with the plaintiff and they may be enforced in this action, whether it be regarded as an action for damages or an action for specific performance to convert the defendants into trustees for plaintiff's benefit under the agreement.

The judgment [for plaintiff] should be affirmed, with costs.

Judgment affirmed. [Three of the seven judges dissented without opinion.]

SEAVER v. RANSOM

N.Y. Supreme Court, Appellate Division, Third Department, 1917.
180 A.D. 734, 168 N.Y.S. 454, 460.

[This is an excerpt from the intermediate appellate court in the prior case.]

The Judge was a legal adviser as well as the husband of the testatrix. He owed a duty to her, and he owed a duty to the plaintiff when he was informed by his wife that she intended to devise the house to the plaintiff. The court will not allow its officer to commit such as fraud upon the plaintiff as would result if relief were denied her here. It is better not to draw close legal distinctions, but to say that on the facts the law will get at an attorney who seeks to avoid such a contract and will compel performance.

H.R. MOCH CO. v. RENSSELAER WATER CO.

Court of Appeals of New York, 1928.
247 N.Y. 160, 159 N.E. 896.

CARDOZO, CH. J. The defendant, a water works company under the laws of this State, made a contract with the city of Rensselaer for the supply of water during a term of years. Water was to be furnished to the city for sewer flushing and street sprinkling; for service to schools and public buildings; and for service at fire hydrants, the latter service at the rate of $42.50 a year for each hydrant. Water was to be furnished to private takers within the city at their homes and factories and other industries at reasonable rates, not exceeding a stated schedule. While this contract was in force, a building caught fire. The flames, spreading to the plaintiff's warehouse near by, destroyed it and its contents. The defendant according to the complaint was promptly notified of the fire, "but omitted and neglected after such notice, to supply or furnish sufficient or adequate quantity of water, with adequate pressure to stay, suppress or extinguish the fire before it reached the warehouse of the plaintiff, although the pressure and supply which the defendant was equipped to supply and furnish, and had agreed by said contract to supply and furnish, was adequate and sufficient to prevent the spread of the fire to and the destruction of the plaintiff's warehouse and its contents." By reason of the failure of the defendant to "fulfill the provisions of the contract between it and the city of Rensselaer," the plaintiff is said to have suffered damage, for which judgment is demanded. A motion, in the nature of a demurrer, to dismiss the complaint, was denied at Special Term. The Appellate Division reversed by a divided court.

Liability in the plaintiff's argument is placed on one or other of three grounds. The complaint, we are told, is to be viewed as stating: (1) A cause of action for breach of contract within Lawrence v. Fox (20 N.Y. 268); (2) a cause of action for a common-law tort, within MacPherson v. Buick Motor Company (217 N.Y. 382); or (3) a cause of action for the breach of a statutory duty. These several grounds of liability will be considered in succession.

(1) We think the action is not maintainable as one for breach of contract.

No legal duty rests upon a city to supply its inhabitants with protection against fire (Springfield Fire Ins. Co. v. Village of Keeseville, 148 N.Y. 46). That being so, a member of the public may not maintain an action under Lawrence v. Fox against one contracting with the city to furnish water at the hydrants, unless an intention appears that the promisor is to be answerable to individual members of the public as well as to the city for any loss ensuing from the failure to fulfill the promise. No such intention is discernible here. On the contrary, the contract is significantly divided into two branches: one a promise to the city for the benefit of the city in its corporate capacity, in which branch is included the service at the hydrants; and the other a promise to the city for the benefit of private takers, in which branch is included the service at their homes and factories. In a broad sense it is true that every city contract, not improvident or wasteful, is for the benefit of the public. More than this, however, must be shown to give a right of action to a member of the public not formally a party. The benefit, as it is sometimes said, must be one that is not merely incidental and secondary (cf. Fosmire v. Nat. Surety Co., 229 N.Y. 44). It must be primary and immediate in such a sense and to such a degree as to bespeak the assumption of a duty to make reparation directly to the individual members of the public if the benefit is lost. The field of obligation would be expanded beyond reasonable limits if less than this were to be demanded as a condition of liability. A promisor undertakes to supply fuel for heating a public building. He is not liable for breach of contract to a visitor who finds the building without fuel, and thus contracts a cold. The list of illustrations can be indefinitely extended. The carrier of the mails under contract with the government is not answerable to the merchant who has lost the benefit of a bargain through negligent delay. The householder is without a remedy against manufacturers of hose and engines, though prompt performance of their contracts would have stayed the ravages of fire. "The law does not spread its protection so far" (Robins Dry Dock & Repair Co. v. Flint, 275 U.S. 303).

So with the case at hand. By the vast preponderance of authority, a contract between a city and a water company to furnish water at the city hydrants has in view a benefit to the public that is incidental rather than immediate, an assumption of duty to the city and not to its inhabitants. Such is the ruling of the Supreme Court of the United States (German Alliance Ins. Co. v. Home Water Supply Co., 226 U.S. 220). Such has been the ruling in this state * * * though the question is still open in this court. * * * Such with few exceptions has been the ruling in other jurisdictions. The diligence of counsel has brought together decisions to that effect from twenty-six States. * * * Only a few States have held otherwise (Page, Contracts, § 2401). An intention to assume an obligation of indefinite extension to every member of the public is seen to be the more improbable when we recall the crushing burden that the obligation would impose. * * * The consequences invited would bear no reasonable proportion to those attached by law to defaults not greatly different. A wrongdoer who by negligence sets fire to a building is liable in damages to the owner where the fire has its origin, but not to other owners who are injured when it spreads. The rule in our State is settled to that effect, whether wisely or unwisely * * *. If the plaintiff is to prevail, one who negligently omits to supply sufficient pressure to extinguish a fire started by another, assumes an obligation to pay the ensuing damage, though the whole city is laid low. A promisor will not be deemed to have had in mind the assumption of a risk so overwhelming for any trivial reward.

The cases that have applied the rule of Lawrence v. Fox to contracts made by a city for the benefit of the public are not at war with this conclusion. Through them all there runs as a unifying principle the presence of an intention to compensate the individual members of the public in the event of a default. For example, in Pond v. New Rochelle Water Co. (183 N.Y. 330) the contract with the city fixed a schedule of rates to be supplied not to public buildings but to private takers at their homes. In Matter of International Railway Co. v. Rann (224 N.Y. 83, 85) the contract was by street railroads to carry passengers for a stated fare. In Smyth v. City of N.Y. (203 N.Y. 106) and Rigney v. N.Y.C. & H.R.R.R. Co. (217 N.Y. 31) covenants were made by contractors upon public works, not merely to indemnify the city, but to assume its liabilities. These and like cases come within the third group stated in the comprehensive opinion in Seaver v. Ransom * * *. The municipality was contracting in behalf of its inhabitants by covenants intended to be enforced by any of them severally as occasion should arise.

(2) We think the action is not maintainable as one for a common law tort.

* * *

(3) We think the action is not maintainable as one for the breach of a statutory duty.

* * *

The judgment should be affirmed with costs.

WESTERN WATERPROOFING CO. v. SPRINGFIELD HOUSING AUTHORITY

United States District Court, C.D. Illinois, 1987.
669 F.Supp. 901.

MILLS, DISTRICT JUDGE: As far as the Court and the parties can discern, this case presents a novel issue under Illinois law.

The ultimate issue: Whether a third party beneficiary contract action may be asserted by an unpaid subcontractor against a public entity where such entity has failed to procure from a general contractor a payment bond as required by the Illinois Bond Act.

The case is before this Court on cross motions for summary judgment. Under Count III of their complaint, Plaintiff Western Waterproofing Company, Inc., prays for judgment in the amount of $129,000. Under Count VI of their complaint, Mid–Continental Restoration Company, Inc., prays for judgment in the amount of $22,456. Defendant Springfield Housing Authority prays for judgment dismissing Counts III and VI of Plaintiffs' complaint.

* * *

The pertinent facts of this suit are undisputed. Plaintiffs were subcontractors for a federally funded construction project of the Defendant, Springfield Housing Authority (SHA). In January 1985, the SHA entered into an agreement with Bildoc, Inc. (Bildoc), for the waterproofing and weatherization of five hi-rise apartment buildings. The general contractor, Bildoc, then entered into contracts with various subcontractors which included Plaintiffs Western Waterproofing Company, Inc. (Western) and Mid–Continental Restoration Company, Inc. (Mid–Continental). Both Plaintiffs contributed labor and materials toward the completion of the project. Both were to receive payment 63 days from completion of the project. Work was completed and final payment, less retainage in the amount of $12,481.16, was made to Bildoc on December 13, 1985.

Western was to be paid $129,000 under its agreement with Bildoc. Mid–Continental was to be paid $22,456 under its agreement with Bildoc. Neither Plaintiff has received any payments for work performed.

Plaintiffs filed their complaint on May 2, 1986. They secured a default judgment against Defendant Bildoc based on Counts I and IV of the complaint in a judgment order entered July 11, 1986. The Plaintiffs have been unable to collect on this judgment. Plaintiffs then resumed proceedings in this case in February 1987 against the SHA. Plaintiffs confessed SHA's motion to strike Counts II and V of the complaint. Thus, Counts III and VI of the complaint, which allege that the Plaintiffs are third party beneficiaries of SHA's contract with Bildoc, remain unlitigated and are the subject of the cross motions for summary judgment.

I.

The basis of the Plaintiffs' claim as a third party beneficiary of the contract between SHA and Bildoc stems from the following provision in the general contract:

Performance and Payment Bond

A performance bond in the amount of total amount of contract for cost of installation of windows will be furnished to the authority as a separate cost item and will be added to the contract price. After the first shipment of windows and payment thereof by SHA, the Contractor shall provide SHA with a Waiver of Lien against all materials on site.

The SHA failed to procure from Bildoc either a performance bond or a payment bond. Both parties agree that had a payment bond been secured the Plaintiffs, as subcontractors, would have collected monies due them under such bond. The parties further agree that subcontractors have no rights under a performance bond. Thus, the initial bone of contention is, what exactly was required under the contract. If only a performance bond was required, as stated in the body of the provision, then Western and Mid–Continental as subcontractors have no claim. If, however, a payment bond was also required as stated in the heading of the provision, then Plaintiffs have stated a colorable claim.

The nature of the bonds involved is as follows. Generally, as a condition of the construction contract between an owner (SHA) and a general contractor (Bildoc), the owner requires the contractor to obtain a surety bond. "There are two kinds of surety bonds, performance bonds and payment bonds. A performance bond simply insures that the contractor will perform the work as contracted.... A payment bond, on the other hand, requires that the contractor pay all subcontractors and materialmen before the owner will make final payment." *Taylor Woodrow Blitman Const. Corp. v. Southfield Gardens Co.,* 534 F.Supp. 340, 344 (D.Mass.1982) (footnotes omitted); *see also* J. Calamari & J. Perillo, The Law of Contracts 621 (2d ed. 1977). Thus, although the two bonds can be combined into a single bond, they serve separate and distinct purposes. J. Calamari & J. Perillo, *supra.*

It is the SHA's contention that although the above quoted "section is entitled Performance and Payment Bond, it requires only a Performance Bond. There is nothing that requires Bildoc to supply a Payment Bond under the contract." The Court disagrees with this interpretation for two reasons. First, under 29 Ill.Rev.Stat. ¶ 15 (1985), An Act in Relation to Bonds of Contractors Entering into Contracts for Public Construction (Bond Act),

> all officials, boards, commissions or agents of this State, or of any political subdivision thereof in making contracts for public work of any kind to be performed for the State, or a political subdivision thereof *shall require* every contractor for such work to furnish, supply and deliver a bond to the State, or to the political subdivision thereof entering into such contract, as the case may be, with good and sufficient sureties. The amount of such bond shall be fixed by such officials, boards, commissions, commissioners or agents, and such bond, among other conditions, shall be conditioned for the completion of the contract, for the payment of material used in such work and for all labor performed in such work, *whether by subcontractor or otherwise.*

Id. (emphasis added).[1] The Act contains mandatory language directing the requirement of a payment bond to protect materialmen and subcontractors. *Fodge v. Board of Educ. of the Village of Oak Park, Dist. 97,* 309 Ill.App. 109, 124, 32 N.E.2d 650 (1941).

Under Illinois law, "statutory provisions applicable to a contract ... are deemed to form a part of that contract and must be construed in connection therewith." *DC Electronics, Inc. v. Employers Modern Life Co.,* 90 Ill.App.3d 342, 348, 45 Ill.Dec. 690, 413 N.E.2d 23 (1st Dist. 1980). * * * Similarly, this same rule should apply to the Bond Act where a contract for public work is involved as it has been held that "paragraphs 15 and 16 (of Chapter 29) are remedial and were intended to protect subcontractors and materialmen for whom no right of mechanic's lien exists against a public work." *Board of Educ., ex rel. Palumbo v. Pacific Nat'l Fire Ins. Co.,* 19 Ill.App.2d 290, 299, 153 N.E.2d

---

1. It has been held that a housing authority is a political subdivision and therefore subject to the provisions of the Bond Act. *Housing Authority of Franklin, Illinois* *ex rel. Smith–Alsop Paint & Varnish Co. v. Holtzman,* 120 Ill.App.2d 226, 241, 256 N.E.2d 873 (5th Dist.1970).

498 (1st Dist.1958). Thus, because the mechanic's lien was inapplicable under this public works contract, and because the Bond Act was established to achieve the same remedial goal as the mechanic's lien in a public works situation, it follows that the Bond Act should be read into the public works contract between SHA and Bildoc, requiring the procurement of a payment bond as required by the Bond Act.

The second reason a payment bond and not simply a performance bond is held to be required under the contract is that ambiguous contractual language is to be construed against the drafter of the language. *Duldulao v. St. Mary of Nazareth Hosp. Center*, 115 Ill.2d 482, 106 Ill.Dec. 8, 505 N.E.2d 314 (1987). The contract was apparently drawn by the SHA and would therefore be construed against it. Under this rule, again, a payment bond would be required under the contract. Additionally, it should be noted that, the contract language notwithstanding, the Executive Director of SHA stated in his deposition that: "It is our policy there should be a performance and payment bond. So—I am not sure how to phrase this. Our directors just didn't follow their responsibilities and duties here in regard to that [getting a performance and payment bond from Bildoc]."

II.

Having established that a payment and performance bond was necessary under the contract, the Court must now decide whether Plaintiffs are third party beneficiaries under the contract and are, therefore, able to assert the bond provision. The Court determines that they are.

There is no question that had a payment bond been procured Plaintiffs would have been third party beneficiaries under it. The question arises here, however, whether Plaintiffs are third party beneficiaries under the contract provision to procure a bond where none has been procured. The answer in Illinois appears to be that they are.

The general rule with respect to third party beneficiary actions in Illinois is well settled. If the contract is entered into for a direct benefit of a third person, not party to the contract, such third person may sue for breach thereof. The test is whether the benefit to the third person is direct or incidental. If direct, he may sue on the contract; if incidental, there is no right of recovery. *Carson Pirie Scott & Co. v. Parrett*, 346 Ill. 252, 257, 178 N.E. 498 (1931).

The [Avco court] (*Avco Delta Corp. Canada Ltd. v. United States*, 484 F.2d 692 (7th Cir.1973), *cert. denied, sub nom. Canadian Parkhill Pipe Stringing, Ltd. v. United States*, 415 U.S. 931, 94 S.Ct. 1444, 39 L.Ed.2d 490 (1974)) * * * determined that the subcontractors were third party beneficiaries under a provision in a construction contract providing for retainage by the owner until the general contractor provided to the owner an affidavit stating that all the general contractor's bills were paid. It is only logical, then, that a subcontractor would also be a third party beneficiary of a contract provision to procure a payment bond since a payment bond is, by definition, for the protection of subcontractors.

See Ill.Rev.Stat. ch. 29, ¶ 15 (1985). In fact, the Seventh Circuit stated in *Avco:*

> A materialman may be a third party beneficiary of a promise by a general contractor to obtain a surety bond for the prompt payment of all laborers and materialmen, and, in the context of a government contract, an unpaid materialman of a subcontractor was allowed to sue the general contractor who had failed to provide such a bond as he had covenanted in the construction contract.

Avco, 484 F.2d at 702 (*citing Strong v. American Fence Constr. Co.,* 245 N.Y. 48, 156 N.E. 92, 94 (1927) (opinion by Cardozo, C.J.)). Thus, this Court holds that Plaintiffs are third party beneficiaries under the SHA–Bildoc contract.

* * *

Ergo, for the reasons given above, the Court ALLOWS Plaintiffs' motion for summary judgment. * * *

LUCAS v. HAMM

Supreme Court of California, In Bank, 1961.
56 Cal.2d 583, 15 Cal.Rptr. 821, 364 P.2d 685, cert. denied
368 U.S. 987, 82 S.Ct. 603, 7 L.Ed.2d 525 (1962).

GIBSON, CHIEF JUSTICE. Plaintiffs, who are some of the beneficiaries under the will of Eugene H. Emmick, deceased, brought this action for damages against defendant L.S. Hamm, an attorney at law who had been engaged by the testator to prepare the will. They have appealed from a judgment of dismissal entered after an order sustaining a general demurrer to the second amended complaint without leave to amend.

The allegations of the first and second causes of action are summarized as follows: Defendant agreed with the testator, for a consideration, to prepare a will and codicils thereto for him by which plaintiffs were to be designated as beneficiaries of a trust provided for by paragraph Eighth of the will and were to receive 15% of the residue as specified in that paragraph. Defendant, in violation of instructions and in breach of his contract, negligently prepared testamentary instruments containing phraseology that was invalid by virtue of section 715.2 and former sections 715.1 and 716 of the Civil Code relating to restraints on alienation and the rule against perpetuities. * * *

After the death of the testator the instruments were admitted to probate. Subsequently defendant, as draftsman of the instruments and as counsel of record for the executors, advised plaintiffs in writing that the residual trust provision was invalid and that plaintiffs would be deprived of the entire amount to which they would have been entitled if the provision had been valid unless they made a settlement with the blood relatives of the testator under which plaintiffs would receive a lesser amount than that provided for them by the testator. As the direct and proximate result of the negligence of defendant and his breach of contract in preparing the testamentary instruments and the written advice referred to above, plaintiffs were compelled to enter into a settlement under which they received a share of the estate amounting to $75,000 less than the sum which they would have received pursuant to testamentary instruments drafted in accordance with the directions of the testator.

* * *

It was held in Buckley v. Gray, 110 Cal. 339, 42 P. 900, 31 L.R.A. 862, that an attorney who made a mistake in drafting a will was not liable for negligence or breach of contract to a person named in the will who was deprived of benefits as a result of the error. The court stated that an attorney is liable to his client alone with respect to actions based on negligence in the conduct of his professional duties, and it was reasoned that there could be no recovery for mere negligence where there was no privity by contract or otherwise between the defendant and the person injured. 110 Cal. at pages 342–343, 42 P. 900. The court further concluded that there could be no recovery on the theory of a contract for the benefit of a third person, because the contract with the attorney was not expressly for the plaintiff's benefit and the testatrix only remotely intended the plaintiff to be benefited as a result of the contract. 110 Cal. at pages 346–347, 42 P. 900. For the reasons hereinafter stated the case is overruled.

* * *

Neither do we agree with the holding in Buckley that beneficiaries damaged by an error in the drafting of a will cannot recover from the draftsman on the theory that they are third-party beneficiaries of the contract between him and the testator. Obviously the main purpose of a contract for the drafting of a will is to accomplish the future transfer of the estate of the testator to the beneficiaries named in the will, and therefore it seems improper to hold, as was done in Buckley, that the testator intended only "remotely" to benefit those persons. It is true that under a contract for the benefit of a third person performance is usually to be rendered directly to the beneficiary, but this is not necessarily the case. (See Rest., Contracts, § 133, com. d; 2 Williston on Contracts (3rd ed. 1959) 829.) For example, where a life insurance policy lapsed because a bank failed to perform its agreement to pay the premiums out of the insured's bank account, it was held that after the insured's death the beneficiaries could recover against the bank as third-party beneficiaries. * * * Persons who had agreed to procure liability insurance for the protection of the promisees but did not do so were also held liable to injured persons who would have been covered by the insurance, the courts stating that all persons who might be injured were third-party beneficiaries of the contracts to procure insurance. * * * Since, in a situation like those presented here and in the Buckley case, the main purpose of the testator in making his agreement with the attorney is to benefit the persons named in his will and this intent can be effectuated, in the event of a breach by the attorney, only by giving the beneficiaries a right of action, we should recognize, as a matter of policy, that they are entitled to recover as third-party beneficiaries. See 2 Williston on Contracts (3rd ed. 1959) pp. 843–844; 4 Corbin on Contracts (1951) pp. 8, 20.

Section 1559 of the Civil Code, which provides for enforcement by a third person of a contract made "expressly" for his benefit, does not preclude this result. The effect of the section is to exclude enforcement by persons who are only incidentally or remotely benefited. * * * As we have seen, a contract for the drafting of a will unmistakably shows the intent of the testator to benefit the persons to be named in the will, and the attorney must necessarily understand this.

Defendant relies on language in Smith v. Anglo–California Trust Co., 205 Cal. 496, 502, 271 P. 898, and Fruitvale Canning Co. v. Cotton, 115 Cal.App.2d 622, 625, 252 P.2d 953, that to permit a third person to bring an action on a contract there must be "an intent clearly manifested by the promisor" to secure some benefit to the third person. This language, which was not necessary to the decision in either of the cases, is unfortunate. Insofar as intent to benefit a third person is important in determining his right to bring an action under a contract, it is sufficient that the promisor must have understood that the promisee had such intent. (Cf. Rest., Contracts, § 133, subds. 1(a) and 1(b); 4 Corbin on Contracts (1951) pp. 16–18; 2 Williston on Contracts (3rd ed. 1959) pp. 836–839.) No specific manifestation by the promisor of an intent to benefit the third person is required. The language relied on by defendant is disapproved to the extent that it is inconsistent with these views.

We conclude that intended beneficiaries of a will who lose their testamentary rights because of failure of the attorney who drew the will to properly fulfill his obligations under his contract with the testator may recover as third-party beneficiaries.

However, an attorney is not liable either to his client or to a beneficiary under a will for errors of the kind alleged in the first and second causes of action.

The general rule with respect to the liability of an attorney for failure to properly perform his duties to his client is that the attorney, by accepting employment to give legal advice or to render other legal services, impliedly agrees to use such skill, prudence, and diligence as lawyers of ordinary skill and capacity commonly possess and exercise in the performance of the tasks which they undertake. * * * The attorney is not liable for every mistake he may make in his practice; he is not, in the absence of an express agreement, an insurer of the soundness of his opinions or of the validity of an instrument that he is engaged to draft; and he is not liable for being in error as to a question of law on which reasonable doubt may be entertained by well-informed lawyers. * * * These principles are equally applicable whether the plaintiff's claim is based on tort or breach of contract.

The complaint, as we have seen, alleges that defendant drafted the will in such a manner that the trust was invalid because it violated the rules relating to perpetuities and restraints on alienation. These closely akin subjects have long perplexed the courts and the bar. Professor

Gray, a leading authority in the field, stated: "There is something in the subject which seems to facilitate error. Perhaps it is because the mode of reasoning is unlike that with which lawyers are most familiar. * * * A long list might be formed of the demonstrable blunders with regard to its questions made by eminent men, blunders which they themselves have been sometimes the first to acknowledge; and there are few lawyers of any practice in drawing wills and settlements who have not at some time either fallen into the net which the Rule spreads for the unwary, or at least shuddered to think how narrowly they have escaped it." Gray, The Rule Against Perpetuities (4th ed. 1942) p. xi; see also Leach, Perpetuities Legislation (1954) 67 Harv.L.Rev. 1349 [describing the rule as a "technicality-ridden legal nightmare" and a "dangerous instrumentality in the hands of most members of the bar"]. Of the California law on perpetuities and restraints it has been said that few, if any, areas of the law have been fraught with more confusion or concealed more traps for the unwary draftsman; that members of the bar, probate courts, and title insurance companies make errors in these matters; that the code provisions adopted in 1872 created a situation worse than if the matter had been left to the common law, and that the legislation adopted in 1951 (under which the will involved here was drawn), despite the best of intentions, added further complexities. (See 38 Cal.Jur.2d 443; Coil, Perpetuities and Restraints; A Needed Reform (1955) 30 State Bar J. 87, 88–90.)

In view of the state of the law relating to perpetuities and restraints on alienation and the nature of the error, if any, assertedly made by defendant in preparing the instrument, it would not be proper to hold that defendant failed to use such skill, prudence, and diligence as lawyers of ordinary skill and capacity commonly exercise. * * *[2]

The judgment is affirmed.

Problems

1. A Corp. was indebted to a number of creditors. A asked C for a loan with which to pay its debts. C promised to make the loan. Are the creditors of A third party beneficiaries of the arrangement between A and C?

2. D contracted with the City of Duluth to do certain work, including blasting, in connection with the construction of a sewer. The contract provided that the D would "be liable for any damages done to the work or other structure or public or private property and injuries sustained by persons" in the operation. P's property, located some 100 yards outside the City's boundaries, was damaged by blasting. May P recover in a contract action against D?

3. The New York State Thruway Authority entered into an agreement with defendant under which defendant was granted the exclusive franchise

---

2. ["After the family have got rid of the Undertaker, then comes the Lawyer, with the Bonze, to read the *Will* of the deceased. This is a new departure (as the English call it) in the family voyage of life. The Barbarian law is so erratic and confused that no one knows what the dead man may have ordered to do with his money." Ah–Chin–Le, Some Observations Upon the Civilization of the Western Barbarians 159 (1876). Ed.]

for automobile servicing along the Thruway. Plaintiff's car became disabled due to a flat tire. Despite many calls for assistance, the defendant did not respond. After three hours, plaintiff, a middle aged accountant who was unaccustomed to physical exertion, attempted to change the tire and died of a heart attack. The contract between the defendant and the Authority expressly provided that defendant "agrees that it will have sufficient road-side automotive services vehicles, equipment and personnel to provide road-side automotive services to disabled vehicles within a maximum of thirty (30) minutes from the time a call is assigned to service vehicle * * *." Is plaintiff an intended beneficiary?

4. PepsiCo entered into agreements with numerous franchisees. Each contract provides the franchisee with an exclusive territory in which to bottle and distribute Pepsi–Cola and forbids the franchisee from distributing Pepsi–Cola into the territory of any other franchisee. Plaintiff has the franchise for described areas in Kansas and Missouri. Defendant has a neighboring franchise. Plaintiff alleges that Defendant has repeatedly made large sales to buyers in Plaintiff's territory in breach of Defendant's contract with PepsiCo. Has Plaintiff stated a cause of action?

5. A Co., a manufacturer of automobiles, entered into an agreement with P Co. by which P Co. was to supply electric power to the plant. P breached its contract by failing to supply power to the plant for one month. Employees of A bring an action against P for lost wages. What result?

6. H (husband) and W (wife) entered into a separation agreement. In that agreement there were provisions for the support of the children. Are the children third party beneficiaries of the agreement?

7. Owner (O) of property had a mortgage loan from B Bank. O was obligated to make monthly payments to the bank. In return, B promised to obtain liability insurance to cover B and O. B failed to do this. Plaintiff was injured as a result of O's negligence in the maintenance of his property. Does plaintiff have a cause of action against B?

8. A Corp. obtained a policy of fidelity insurance from I (Insurance Co.) under which I agreed to indemnify A against any loss which A might sustain through the fraudulent or dishonest acts of any of its own employees. A did become liable to C as a result of the dishonesty of one of its own employees. Does C have a cause of action against I? Does A have a cause of action against I? If so, when?

9. A, a municipality, owes a duty to the public to keep its streets in good repair. B promises A to keep the streets in good repair and fails to do so. As a result, C is injured. Does C have a cause of action against B?

10. In January 1999, a union local entered into a two year contract with Mfg. Co. The contract provided that the union would not call a strike for the two year term of the contract. A strike was called by the union in violation of this promise. Does Customer Co., which had entered into a contract in Dec. 1998 to purchase Mfg. Co.'s entire output for 1999 and 2000 have a cause of action against the union if the strike caused Mfg. Co.'s output to decrease drastically?

11. Landlord contracted with Macy's to construct a large shopping center on Landlord's land and Macy's agreed to lease 60% of the shopping

center. Landlord then contracts with Contractor to construct the center. Contractor defaults. Does Macy's have a cause of action versus Contractor? Versus Landlord?

12.   In a case such as Lucas v. Hamm, does the plaintiff have a cause of action in tort as well as in contract?

SECTION 2.   DEFENSES, VESTING AND RELATIVE RIGHTS OF THE PARTIES

––––––

(Calamari & Perillo 5th §§ 17.10—17.14)

ERICKSON v. GRANDE RONDE LUMBER CO.

Supreme Court of Oregon, 1939.
162 Or. 556, 94 P.2d 139.

ROSSMAN, J.

* * *

The petitioners argue that after the Stoddard Company had agreed to pay the Grande Ronde Company's debts, the plaintiff, as a creditor of the Grande Ronde Company, was not entitled to judgment against both of these companies. They insist that he was entitled to a remedy against only one of them, and that it was incumbent upon him to make an election. The respondents argue: "It may even be that so far as the commencement of the action was concerned that he had a right to pursue his remedy against both, but manifestly when the time came for the case to be decided he was not entitled to judgment against both." They argue that since he took judgment against the Grande Ronde Company he made his election and, therefore, cannot have relief against the Stoddard Company. In support of these contentions, the respondents cite Wood v. Moriarty, 15 R.I. 518, 9 A. 427; Bohanan v. Pope, 42 Me. 93; Verrill v. Weinstein, 135 Me. 126, 190 A. 634; 13 C.J., p. 705 § 815; and 12 Am.Jur., p. 841, § 288.

The first two of the decisions just cited support the respondents' position. The section of Corpus Juris on which they rely is not concerned with the precise problem with which we are now dealing. It states that the English doctrine which denies to the beneficiary the right to maintain an action against the promisor is not the prevailing rule in the United States. The section of American Jurisprudence upon which they rely is concerned with the problem whether the beneficiary must formally accept the promise made in his behalf by the promisor. The essence of the section is stated in the following words which we quote from it: "By suing on the contract, the beneficiary accepts or adopts the same." Neither of these treatises considers the question of whether judgment may be entered against both the promisor and the promisee. In the Verrill case, the defendant in purchasing a parcel of real property from one Katz signed a note and mortgage which finally came into the ownership of the plaintiff. Before maturity of the note the defendant conveyed her equity in the property to two individuals named Hecht who assumed and agreed to pay the mortgage debt. Thereafter the defendant made no payments upon the note, but payments were made by the Hechts. The question before the court was whether the payments made by the Hechts interrupted the running of the limitation period against the liability of the defendant. The plaintiff argued that the promisor is in effect the agent of the original debtor, and that accordingly his payments interrupt the running of the statutory period against the latter. In rejecting this argument, the court said [135 Me. 126, 190 A. 635]: "Such claim misconceives the theory on which the liability of the promisor is based. His obligation is not on the note, not as agent of the mortgagor, but to pay a debt of his own."

We stated that the Bohanan and Wood decisions support the plaintiff's position, but both of them regarded the new promise as the consummation of a novation; and, of course, a novation is the substitution of a new right for an existing obligation. Williston on Contracts, Rev.Ed., § 393, referring to these two decisions, among others, states: "Courts which hold that the original contract is in effect an offer of novation to the creditor naturally hold that if the creditor accepts the promisor as his debtor he releases the original debtor, and on the other hand, if he elects to sue the original debtor he thereby rejects the proffered novation and cannot afterwards sue the new promisor." From § 353 of the same treatise, we quote: " * * * A few states, however, have erroneously resorted to an implied novation theory for enforcement of the creditor beneficiary type of third party contract." Among the decisions which he states "have erroneously resorted to an implied novation theory" he cites the Bohanan and Wood decisions. In § 393, after the language quoted above, Williston continues: "The weight of authority, however, in the jurisdictions which allow a creditor beneficiary a direct right against the promisor supports the conclusion that the creditor has rights against both the promisor and the promisee, not merely a choice of rights; being entitled, of course, to but a single satisfaction. And in some states he is allowed to join both as defendants in the same action. He ought to be compelled to do so."

From Restatement of the Law, Contracts, § 141, we quote: "(1) A creditor beneficiary who has an enforceable claim against the promisee can get judgment against either the promisee or the promisor or against each of them on their respective duties to him. Satisfaction in whole or in part of either of these duties, or of judgments thereon, satisfies to that extent the other duty or judgment."

The principle embraced in the Restatement represents the law of this state. From the carefully prepared annotations to § 141, subd. 1, of the Restatement of the Law of Contracts prepared by Professor Charles G. Howard (12 Oregon Law Review 283), we quote: "Oregon cases are in accord with this section and hold uniformly that there can be but one satisfaction, though both promisor and promisee are liable. . . ." We have read the decisions cited by Professor Howard and are satisfied that he correctly stated their essence.

We conclude that the plaintiff was entitled to maintain this action against the promisor (the Stoddard Company) as well as against his original debtor (the Grande Ronde Company). He was entitled to judgment against both; however, to only one complete satisfaction.

* * *

[Petition denied.]

ALEXANDER H. REVELL & CO. v. C.H. MORGAN GROCERY CO.

Appellate Court of Illinois, 1919.
214 Ill.App. 526.

MR. JUSTICE O'CONNOR delivered the opinion of the court.

Plaintiff brought suit in the Municipal Court of Chicago against the defendant, and in its final statement of claim sought to recover $671.80. There was a finding and judgment in favor of the defendant, to reverse which this appeal is prosecuted.

So far as it is necessary to state them, the facts are these: The defendant, C.H. Morgan Grocery Company, entered into a contract with one William Lidke, whereby he was to perform certain work and furnish and install certain fixtures in one of defendant's stores. Lidke proceeded with the work and purchased the fixtures from plaintiff and installed them in the store. The work was not done by Lidke satisfactorily to the defendant, and on May 22nd they entered into a written agreement which plaintiff makes the basis of its claim in this suit. The contract provided: "As per our recent agreement regarding the completion of all work as per contract with you, I will do as follows: (Item specified.) In return you are to pay the balance of Eleven Hundred ($1,100) Dollars due me in full, as follows: To Alexander H. Revell & Co., the sum of $671.80," etc. Lidke did not do any part of the work which he agreed to do. Afterwards plaintiff brought this suit to recover the $671.80.

Plaintiff's position, as we understand it, is that Lidke's promise to do the work was the consideration for the defendant's promise to Lidke to pay the $671.80 to plaintiff, and that plaintiff may maintain an action on the defendant's promise, although Lidke did not fulfil his part of the contract by doing the work specified. * * *

In the instant case, the promise to the defendant to pay the money to plaintiff was upon condition that Lidke would perform certain work. This condition, it is conceded, was not carried out by Lidke. It would be a strange rule of law that would permit the plaintiff to recover in this case. Plaintiff admits, as of course it must since the contract on which liability is claimed is in writing, that Lidke was to do certain work for the defendant, and in consideration defendant was to pay plaintiff the amount specified, and it is admitted that Lidke did not do any part of the work, and yet in the face of this admission plaintiff maintains that it is entitled to the $671.80. It is obvious that this contention is against all sense of justice and fair dealing—contrary to common sense. Of course Lidke could not recover without performing the work. * * *

MR. JUSTICE TAYLOR dissenting. Lidke having done certain work for and furnished certain materials to the defendant, they got into a controversy, the defendant claiming that some portions of the work were not properly done, Lidke claiming otherwise. There was due the latter at that time, according to his claim, about $1,100. To settle that controversy, amicably between them, they met, and on May 22, 1916, entered into the written contract which is in question in the instant case. By that contract Lidke makes a promise to do certain work and to waive payment for certain extra labor and material and the defendant promises to pay the plaintiff $671.80 and to each of four other parties a certain sum. Nothing was to be paid Lidke, himself. It was a bilateral contract made up of their mutual promises, those promises being, according to the law of contract, sufficient consideration for each other. The contract, as soon as signed, created mutual obligations, one of which was to pay the plaintiff $671.80. That promise, according to the writing, was unconditional; it was not provided that it should be paid at some future time or dependent in any way upon Lidke's future conduct. The consideration of the promise of the defendant to Revell was not the doing of the work by Lidke, but Lidke's promise to do that work. In the eyes of the law, a very different thing. The moment the binding written contract was made and the obligations of the defendant and Lidke fixed and specified, the defendant became bound, unconditionally, to pay Revell, the plaintiff. He had so promised; that was unalterable either by him or Lidke. Though the consideration for it moved from Lidke, being Lidke's promise to do certain things, it, nevertheless, was as binding upon the defendant as though the plaintiff, himself, had furnished certain materials as a consideration for the defendant's promise. Being a binding promise upon the defendant, the plaintiff had a right to sue to have it carried out. If it be admitted, as the opinion of the majority imports, that the contract was binding at the time it was executed and made and gave rise to the obligations it recites, it follows, as the writing mentions no condition, that the plaintiff was entitled at once to the sum promised him. If the promise to pay the plaintiff had been qualified, as, for example, to pay on a certain date, or when Lidke gets so far along in the fulfillment of his obligations, or when Lidke had done all he promised to do, then the plaintiff might not sue until the specified condition was fulfilled. But, the written promise is unqualified and the writing alone contains the contract.

* * *

DETROIT BANK AND TRUST CO. v. CHICAGO FLAME HARDENING CO.

United States District Court, N.D. Indiana, 1982.
541 F.Supp. 1278.

Lee, District Judge.

* * *

Findings of Fact

* * *

In 1956, Chicago Flame Hardening Company (hereinafter referred to as "Chicago Flame"), was founded in East Chicago, Indiana by Marvin R. Scott, a Michigan domiciliary, and Gainor D. Scott and John R. Keeler, Indiana domiciliaries. * * *

Marvin R. Scott, although continuing to reside in Michigan, visited the new firm periodically and acted as its President while utilizing his expertise in the flame hardening industry to establish the East Chicago, Indiana operation as an investment and a means of livelihood for his brother, Gainor D. Scott, and brother-in-law, John R. Keeler.

On July 29, 1964, Marvin R. Scott, Gainor D. Scott and John R. Keeler, the owners of the entire issue of Chicago Flame's capital stock, unanimously agreed by corporate resolution that upon the death of these specifically named shareholders (M.R. Scott, G.D. Scott and J.D. Keeler), the corporation would pay to his wife, if then living, commencing with the date of her husband's death, a graduated monthly stipend over a fifteen (15) year period totaling $150,300 to terminate in the event of her death if prior to the expiration of the payment period.

The signatories to this 1964 resolution did not expressly reserve the right to alter and/or amend.

* * *

Within a reasonable time following the adoption of this resolution Marvin R. Scott's wife, Roxanne, became aware that this document's beneficial terms were potentially available to her in the future. She then "forgot the whole thing." (Transcript of testimony, December 22, 1980, pp. 19–20).

The provisions of the 1964 widow's resolution were initially implemented on July 12, 1967 when Marjorie Scott Keeler signed the requisite statement agreeing to abide by the resolution's consideration requirements, following the July 8, 1967 death of her husband, John R. Keeler.

Marjorie Scott Keeler thereinafter continually received a monthly stipend pursuant to the express terms of this agreement, except for an eighteen (18) month period during 1971 and 1972 when she voluntarily consented to a postponement in recognition of Chicago Flame's deteriorating financial posture.

Marvin R. Scott's wife, Roxanne, was fully and continuously aware that Marjorie Scott Keeler (her sister-in-law) was receiving the benefits provided by the 1964 resolution for surviving spouses of the original signatories.

On February 15, 1971 Marvin R. Scott participated in and approved the adoption of a second corporate resolution along with the other owners of the entire issue of Chicago Flame's capital stock, Gainor D. Scott and Marjorie Scott Keeler. This subsequent agreement was executed to rescind the right of Marvin R. Scott's surviving spouse to receive graduated monthly payments as formerly provided in the 1964 resolution.

Marvin R. Scott's motivation for entering into this second resolution was to sustain the future financial integrity of Chicago Flame.

Following a lengthy period of convalescence, Marvin R. Scott died on October 31, 1971 leaving plaintiff's current ward, Roxanne Scott, as his surviving spouse.

Although there remains conflicting testimony, it is the determination of the Court that, while Mrs. Roxanne Scott may not have actually seen the February 15, 1971 rescission document prior to the instigation of this suit, she became aware of her husband's relinquishment of the widow's benefits during the interim following his death and the filing of this suit.

* * *

APPLICATION OF LAW

Plaintiff initiated this litigation on September 19, 1977 by way of a complaint which seeks to enforce the terms of the 1964 widow's resolution for the benefit of its ward, Mrs. Roxanne Scott. Plaintiff asserts its contentions on the basis of (1) the failure to expressly reserve the right to rescind, (2) a presumption of acceptance for a donee beneficiary, (3) Roxanne Scott's medical condition precluding the earlier assertion of her rights as a means of acceptance, and (4) that this agreement vested a right in its ward which could not be denied by the 1971 rescission. * * *.

The old Restatement rule provided that the promisor and promisee could make no change in the promise made to a donee beneficiary unless such a power is reserved.[9] Restatement of Contracts § 142 at 168 (1932). Nor could a change be made by the promisor and promisee in their promise to a creditor beneficiary if he has changed his position in reliance on that promise. *Id.; see* Page, *The Power of Contracting Parties to Alter a Contract for Rendering Performance to a Third Person,* 12 Wis.L.Rev. 141, 149–50 (1937). Evolutionary changes in the law, however, have transformed the aforementioned position of the original Restatement. The Second Restatement of Contracts as adopted and promulgat-

---

9. This position promulgated by the initial restatement was not followed by the vast majority of states even at the time of its adoption. The express reservation requirement was thereafter abandoned in tentative drafts and the final adopted version of the Restatement (Second); *see* 2 Williston, Contracts §§ 396–97 (3d Ed.1959).

ed, eliminates this distinction between a donee and creditor beneficiary and recognizes that modification on the part of the promisor and promisee is ineffective only if the agreement so provides, unless the third party beneficiary has changed his position in reliance on the promise or has accepted, adopted or acted upon it. Restatement (Second) of Contracts § 142* (1979). * * *

Indiana specifically reaffirmed its adoption of this majority view as later expressed in the Second Restatement. * * *

In the case of contracts entered into for the benefit of a third party,[11] Indiana follows the rule found in most jurisdictions. That is, the parties to a third party beneficiary contract may rescind, vary or abrogate the contract as they see fit, without the approval of the third party, at any time before the contract is accepted, adopted or acted upon by a third party beneficiary. *Fanning,* 333 N.E.2d at 84; *accord Jackman Cigar Co. v. Berger,* 114 Ind.App. 437, 52 N.E.2d 363 (1944). A rescission prior to the required change in position by a third party deprives that third party of any rights under or because of the contract. *Id.; see* 17 Am.Jur.2d Contracts § 317 (1979).

In this case the 1964 agreement was adopted as a corporate resolution by Chicago Flame Hardening, Inc. All of the officers and shareholders of the corporation approving the initial agreement. On February 15, 1971 the officers and shareholders mutually agreed to rescind the July 29, 1964 resolution. Recognizing the majority view followed by Indiana, the rescission of the prior agreement is valid without a specific reservation of the power to rescind so long as the third-party beneficiary, Mrs. Roxanne Scott, had not accepted, adopted or acted upon the original widow's resolution. Therefore, an express reservation of the right to rescind is not required to abrogate the third party beneficiary agreement.

Plaintiff next contends that since Mrs. Roxanne Scott had knowledge of the original 1964 resolution, her acceptance of this beneficial agreement must be presumed. In support of this position plaintiff offers three vintage cases which recognize a presumption of acceptance.

These cases are clearly distinguishable from the present cause. The primary and controlling distinction is that while acceptance was presumed in cases cited by plaintiff, the intended beneficiaries were infants at the time of the transaction. A presumption is necessary in such instances to protect the interests of minor beneficiaries. Mrs. Scott, however, was an adult at the time of the 1964 widow's resolution, completely able to assert her own rights, and as such is not afforded the

---

* The citation was doubtless intended to be § 311. Ed.

11. As neither the general common law nor related statutes from other jurisdictions distinguish between various types of beneficiaries, between release and rescission, between unilateral and bilateral, or between partially executed and wholly executory contracts, this Court will not. *See* 2 Williston, Contracts, §§ 396–398 (3d Ed.1959); *see also Holbrook v. Pitt,* 643 F.2d 1261, 1271 (7th Cir.1981) (While addressing federal common law the three classes of beneficiaries [donee, creditor, and incidental] were disdained in favor of the Second Restatement's two divisions [intended and incidental] which permitted review of intent without further distinction.)

same protection. Moreover, the same authority submitted by plaintiff in support of a presumption of acceptance provides a fortiori a strong argument for the opposite proposition—a lack of such protection for a competent adult through negative implication.

* * *

Plaintiff's next focus theorizes that "but for" Roxanne Scott's declining health, she would have instituted this litigation at an earlier date. Plaintiff attempts thereby to utilize its ward's acknowledged mental and physical difficulties as a vehicle to excuse not only the failure to sue before rescission, but also to demonstrate why prompt commencement of this action to preserve her benefits was prevented. The net effect of this proposition is to attempt to transform this 1977 litigation into a belated substitute for acceptance prior to rescission.

Although the Court recognizes that the filing of a suit by a third party beneficiary may be considered as acceptance by that individual, *Zimmerman v. Zehender,* 164 Ind. 466, 73 N.E. 920 (1905); *Blackard v. Monarch,* 131 Ind.App. 514, 169 N.E.2d 735 (1960), the Court may not consider Mrs. Scott's health as dispositive of the issue before it. Perhaps equity might demand some presumption of acceptance had Mrs. Scott been totally incapacitated prior to rescission; however, plaintiff's own evidence makes it clear that the February 15, 1971 rescission took place before Mrs. Scott's inhibiting physical and mental decline occurred and the appointment of guardians to represent her interests.

* * *

The analysis above establishes that acceptance may not be presumed by this Court and that this contract for the benefit of a third party is enforceable only if the third party beneficiary has accepted, adopted or acted upon it prior to rescission. Because prior decisions fail to provide an adequate definition, the Court must examine the somewhat nebulous term "acceptance" in an effort to identify if some form of assent took place on the part of Mrs. Roxanne Scott if it is to conclude that the 1971 rescission was ineffective and that her derivative rights were preserved. *See e.g., United States v. Winnicki,* 151 F.2d 56, 57 (7th Cir.1945) (words "receive" and "accept" are legal equivalents).

Acceptance may be an overt act, or the adoption of a benefit which is a question of intent and thereby also a factual determination. *See* Corbin, *supra,* §§ 782–793; Jones, *Legal Protection of Third Party Beneficiaries: On Opening Courthouse Doors,* 46 Cinn.L.Rev. 313 (1977). Nevertheless, even in instances such as this where plaintiff has provided no specific evidence of an overt act or of a change in position, it must still be remembered that "the power of promisor and promisee to vary the promisor's duty to an intended beneficiary is terminated when the beneficiary manifests assent to the promise in a manner invited by the promisor or promisee." Restatement (Second) on Contracts, *supra,* § 311 at comment (h). This rule utilizes an analogy to the law of offer and acceptance by recognizing that a third party beneficiary may well rely in ways difficult or impossible to prove. *Id.*

Fortunately for this Court, the narrow question currently before it does not present this circumstance characterized by an impossibility of proof. The converse is true as the Court's determination of the factual question regarding Roxanne Scott's intent to accept the benefits afforded by the 1964 resolution was answered in the negative by her own sworn testimony. While facing cross-examination, Mrs. Scott was specifically asked whether she made any long range plans or depended upon the 1964 widow's resolution. Her answer was, "No, I forgot the whole thing." (Transcript of testimony, December 22, 1980, pp. 19–20). In addition to this testimonial controversion, the Court also failed to discern any other corroborative evidence which might sustain plaintiff's claim of acceptance or change in position in reliance on that resolution. *See generally* Note, *The Requirements of Promissory Estoppel as Applied to Third Party Beneficiaries,* 30 U.Pitt.L.Rev. 174 (1968). Furthermore, the Court's position regarding the failure to establish adoptive intent is not gleaned from this single negatory response, but is supported by a detailed review of the entire record. It is therefore the conclusion of the Court that Roxanne Scott failed to accept, adopt or act upon the 1964 resolution prior to the 1971 rescission. Consequently, the Court must hold that Mrs. Scott's failure to act or rely upon the original agreement extinguished any benefits which might have accrued to her from the 1964 agreement.

* * *

It is hereby ORDERED that Judgment be entered for the defendant, Chicago Flame Hardening Company, Inc., consistent with this Memorandum Decision and the findings and conclusions herein.

DREWEN v. BANK OF MANHATTAN CO.

Supreme Court of New Jersey, 1959.
31 N.J. 110, 155 A.2d 529, 76 A.L.R.2d 221.

PROCTOR, J. This suit was brought in the Superior Court, Chancery Division, by John Drewen, administrator *c.t.a.* of the estate of Doris Ryer Nixon, to enforce a contract executed by the plaintiff's decedent and her husband, Stanhope Wood Nixon, the defendant's decedent. On motion addressed to the complaint, the Chancery Division dismissed the administrator's suit, and the dismissal was affirmed by the Appellate Division. 55 N.J.Super. 331, 150 A.2d 779 (1959). Certification was granted. 30 N.J. 154, 152 A.2d 171 (1959).

The complaint sets forth the following allegations: Doris Ryer Nixon and Stanhope Wood Nixon were married in 1917. They had two children, Lewis and Blanche. On July 27, 1945, the husband and wife executed an agreement settling the rights of each in the other's property in contemplation of a divorce which was granted some months later. As part of that agreement, Stanhope Wood Nixon promised never to reduce the quantity or quality of the children's interest in his estate, as set forth in a will executed on the same day as the agreement. By that will, each child was to receive about 30% of Nixon's estate in fee. If one child were to predecease the testator without leaving issue, the surviving child would take the other's share.

In 1948 Doris Ryer Nixon died testate in California. An executor was appointed there and undertook the administration of her estate. In 1951 Stanhope Wood Nixon executed a new will, which revoked his 1945 will, changed the outright gifts to his children to life estates, with life estates over to surviving issue and, finally, remainders to charities. The will also contained an *in terrorem* clause which would void the bequests made to any one who should "directly or indirectly * * * call in question before any tribunal the provisions of any legacy, devise or provision herein, * * *." The daughter, Blanche, died in 1955 without issue, and the son, Lewis, survived and succeeded to her share under either of the father's wills. Stanhope Wood Nixon died in 1958, and his 1951 will was admitted to probate by the Surrogate of Middlesex County. The defendant is the executor and trustee under that will.

* * *

The Chancery Division dismissed the complaint on the ground that the administrator *c.t.a.* had no standing to prosecute the suit, since no benefit could accrue from it to the estate. The Appellate Division affirmed, holding that "[a]s administrator with the will annexed, he has shown no right, power or duty to maintain this action." 55 N.J.Super. at page 336, 150 A.2d at page 781.

On this appeal plaintiff contends that his decedent, Doris Ryer Nixon, had in her lifetime a sufficient interest as promisee of the contract to enforce it, and that upon her death her right passed to her California executor and in turn to the plaintiff. On the other hand, the defendant contends that the only rights passing to her personal representatives are those whose enforcement would result in the realization of assets for distribution to the creditors and beneficiaries of her estate. It urges that the rights of Lewis Nixon belong to him as third party beneficiary of the 1945 contract, and not as beneficiary of the estate of Doris Ryer Nixon, and that under N.J.S. 2A:15–2, N.J.S.A., he has the right to enforce the contract, and is capable of instituting the necessary suit himself. Furthermore, it argues that if Stanhope Wood Nixon breached the contract, he did so at his death, which was after the death of plaintiff's decedent; no cause of action accrued to plaintiff's decedent during her lifetime and therefore none passed to the plaintiff.

It is beyond question that a person may bind himself by contract to make a particular will. * * * It is equally clear that Lewis Nixon, the third party beneficiary of the 1945 contract, could have maintained a suit for specific performance. * * * Our courts have long recognized the right of a third party beneficiary to enforce a simple contract. * * *

A promisee of a contract for the benefit of a third party donee has a sufficient interest in the enforcement of the promise to entitle him to sue for damages. Restatement, Contracts, § 135(b) (1932); see also O'Neill v. Supreme Council, Am.L. of Honor, 70 N.J.L. 410, 57 A. 463 (Sup.Ct. 1904). He may also invoke the aid of a court of equity, for the general reason that his remedy at law is inadequate, and he should not be denied an effective means of compelling fulfillment of a promise that he bought and paid for. * * * In the case of a suit on a contract to make a will, there is the additional reason that breach of such a contract is deemed to be a fraud against which equity will afford relief. * * *

* * *

For affirmance: JUSTICES BURLING and HALL—2.
[Reversed.]

ROUSE v. UNITED STATES

United States Court of Appeals, District of Columbia Circuit, 1954.
215 F.2d 872, 94 U.S.App.D.C. 386.

* * *

EDGERTON, CIRCUIT JUDGE. Bessie Winston gave Associated Contractors, Inc., her promissory note for $1,008.37, payable in monthly installments of $28.01, for a heating plant in her house. The Federal Housing Administration guaranteed the note and the payee endorsed it for value to the lending bank, the Union Trust Company.

Winston sold the house to Rouse. In the contract of sale Rouse agreed to assume debts secured by deeds of trust and also "to assume payment of $850 for heating plant payable $28 per Mo." Nothing was said about the note.

Winston defaulted on her note. The United States paid the bank, took an assignment of the note, demanded payment from Rouse, and sued him for $850 and interest.

Rouse alleged as defenses (1) that Winston fraudulently misrepresented the condition of the heating plant and (2) that Associated Contractors did not install it satisfactorily. The District Court struck these defenses and granted summary judgment for the plaintiff. The defendant Rouse appeals.

Rouse * * * is not liable to the United States at all unless his contract with Winston makes him so. The contract says the parties to it are not "bound by any terms, conditions, statements, warranties or representations, oral or written" not contained in it. But this means only that the written contract contains the entire agreement. It does not mean that fraud cannot be set up as a defense to a suit on the contract.[1] Rouse's promise to "assume payment of $850 for heating plant" made him liable to Associated Contractors, Inc., only if and so far as it made him liable to Winston; one who promises to make a payment to the promisee's creditor can assert against the creditor any defense that the promisor could assert against the promisee. Accordingly Rouse, if he had

---

1. 3 Williston, Contracts § 811A (Rev. Ed.1936).

been sued by the corporation, would have been entitled to show fraud on the part of Winston. He is equally entitled to do so in this suit by an assignee of the corporation's claim. It follows that the court erred in striking the first defense. We do not consider whether Winston's alleged fraud, if shown, would be a complete or only a partial defense to this suit, since that question has not arisen and may not arise.

We think the court was right in striking the second defense. "If the promisor's agreement is to be interpreted as a promise to discharge whatever liability the promisee is under, the promisor must certainly be allowed to show that the promisee was under no enforceable liability. * * * On the other hand, if the promise means that the promisor agrees to pay a sum of money to A, to whom the promisee says he is indebted, it is immaterial whether the promisee is actually indebted to that amount or at all. * * * Where the promise is to pay a specific debt * * * this interpretation will generally be the true one."[3]

The judgment is reversed and the cause remanded with instructions to reinstate the first defense.

Reversed and remanded.

Problems

13. M, mortgagee, brings an action under the standard mortgage clause of a fire insurance policy which provides that the coverage of the mortgagee "shall not be invalidated by any act or neglect of the mortgagor or owner". Defendant, insurer, seeks to set up as a defense to the action the fact that the owner who had procured the insurance was guilty of a breach of warranty. May the defense be raised? *No.*

Mortgage situation — some defenses are limited.

14. Employer promised Employee to pay certain sums to Employee's minor son if Employee died before the son reached the age of 21. Later, Employer and Employee modified the agreement so that payments were to be made to Employee's wife rather than his son. What are the rights of the parties?

15. Does the promisee in a donee beneficiary case have a claim against the promisor if the beneficiary validly agrees to release his claim? *No.*

16. A gave a bond and a mortgage to B in exchange for a loan of $10,000. A subsequently sold the property to C for an agreed purchase price of $25,000. C paid A $15,000 and agreed to assume the mortgage. A had a defense of fraud against B. Does C have the same defense? *Yes (same case as Rouse)*

3. 2 id. § 399.

Chapter 12

ASSIGNMENT AND DELEGATION

SECTION 1. THE NATURE AND EFFECT OF AN ASSIGNMENT

(Calamari & Perillo 5th §§ 18.1—18.5)

DONOVAN v. MIDDLEBROOK

Appellate Division of the Supreme Court of New York, 1904.
95 App.Div. 365, 88 N.Y.S. 607.

McLaughlin, J. This appeal is from a judgment dismissing the complaint at the close of plaintiff's case. The action was brought to recover one-half of brokers' commissions in the sale of real estate under an alleged assignment. The complaint alleged, in substance, that in March or April, 1903, the defendants employed one Joseph Toch to secure a purchaser for certain real estate in the city of New York, and agreed if successful to pay him a commission of two per cent of the purchase money; that Toch, with the aid and influence of one Horowitz, procured a purchaser to whom the property was sold for $325,000; that Toch thereupon, in consideration of the services of Horowitz, entered into the following agreement with him, which was confirmatory of a previous oral agreement:

> "In consideration of one (1) dollar I hereby agree with Salo A. Horowitz, representing Mr. Ralph C. Gerlach in the purchase of the Ryan property from Mary Ryan and Frederic J. Middlebrook, executor, that said Horowitz is entitled to one-half of the commission earned, amounting to $3,250.00, resulting from said sale.

> "Dated New York, *April 6th*, 1903.

> "JOSEPH TOCH."

That, by this agreement, Toch assigned to Horowitz one-half of the commission earned, of which fact the defendants were informed, and prior to the commencement of the action such claim was duly assigned to the plaintiff and judgment demanded for $3,250. The answer, among other defenses pleaded, denied substantially all of the material allegations of the complaint upon which plaintiff's right to a recovery was predicated.

800

At the trial the agreement above set forth between Toch and Horowitz was introduced in evidence and this constituted plaintiff's entire proof as tending to show that any claim which Toch had against the defendants for the commissions earned had been assigned by him to the plaintiff's assignor. Upon this proof the complaint was dismissed, the trial court holding that such agreement did not constitute an assignment of the commission alleged to have been earned by Toch, or any part of it. This ruling of the trial court is challenged, it being urged that the instrument constituted an assignment of one-half of the commissions. The action is at law. The plaintiff predicates his right to a recovery upon the fact that the defendants were indebted to Toch, and Toch assigned a portion of that indebtedness to his assignor. The only evidence of the assignment is the paper referred to, and a bare inspection of it shows, as it seems to me, that it did not constitute an assignment. There are no words in it which either expressly or inferentially can be said to transfer any interest in the claim which Toch had against the defendants to plaintiff's assignor. The agreement is between Toch and Horowitz. At most it is an agreement on the part of Toch to pay to Horowitz one-half of what the defendants are to pay to him. The fact that the plaintiff called this paper an assignment did not make it so. (Wemple v. Hauenstein, 19 App.Div. 552.) To constitute a valid assignment there must be a perfected transaction between the parties intended to vest in the assignee a present right in the thing assigned. An agreement to pay a certain sum out of, or that one is entitled to receive, from a designated fund, when received, does not operate as a legal or equitable assignment, since the assignor in either case retains control over the subject-matter. "The test is," even of an equitable assignment, "whether the debtor would be justified in paying the debt or the portion contracted about to the person claiming to be assignee." (Fairbanks v. Sargent, 117 N.Y. 320.) "It is the settled doctrine in this State," says the court in Thomas v. N.Y. & G.L.R. Co. (139 N.Y. 163), "that an agreement, either by parol or in writing, to pay a debt out of a designated fund, does not give an equitable lien upon the fund or operate as an equitable assignment thereof." In Williams v. Ingersoll (89 N.Y. 508) Judge EARL said: "Whatever the law may be elsewhere, it must be regarded as the settled law of this State, that an agreement either by parol or in writing to pay a debt out of a designated fund does not give an equitable lien upon the fund or operate as an equitable assignment thereof. It was so decided in Rogers v. Hosack's Executors (18 Wend. 319). That case was followed, and the same rule laid down in Christmas v. Russell (14 Wall. 69) and Trist v. Child (21 id. 441)."

The paper in question, as already indicated, did not constitute an assignment and the trial court was correct in so holding.

The judgment is right and should be affirmed, with costs.

Problems

1. Mr. Cobb owned a wholesale meat business. Although he had accounts receivable which were payable weekly or, in some cases, monthly, he was short of cash. He entered into a written agreement with Mrs. Baxter in which he stated that he had "sold" certain described accounts to Mrs. Baxter at a specified discount. Does the writing amount to an assignment?

2. C had some money which was being held for him by the Continental Escrow Company. When C hired A, an attorney, C told A that, "If I get this money, I will pay you from this fund." Does this amount to an assignment?

3. D owes C $1,000. C writes to D, "Please pay the balance due me to A." Does this amount to an assignment?

4. Morale was the attorney for the Pelletiers who were claimants in a personal injury action. When a settlement seemed imminent, they purchased a new car, partially on credit. The seller prepared a letter, which was signed by the Pelletiers and delivered to Morale, instructing him to assign to the seller $4,132.45 from the proceeds of the accident settlement. When Morale later received the settlement proceeds, his clients instructed him to prepare a check in the amount of $4,132.45, payable to them. They told Morale that they would make arrangements with the seller to settle their obligations for the purchase of the car. Morale complied with their instructions. They failed to pay the seller. The latter brings this action against Morale, claiming to be an assignee. What result?

5. Futterman, a lawyer representing Martinez, drafted the following instrument at the request of Martinez and Leon: "I give to Gina Leon 5% of any recovery that I may get after deducting all disbursements, expenses and attorney's fees from the case of Wilfredo Martinez v. Hertz Corporation." When a settlement was reached with Hertz, Futterman, at Martinez's request, disbursed the entire sum, less his fees and expenses to Martinez. Ms. Leon sues Futterman. What result?

SECTION 2.   DEVIANTS FROM THE NORM

(Calamari & Perillo 5th §§ 18.6—18.9, 18.21—18.23)

SPEELMAN v. PASCAL

Court of Appeals of New York, 1961.
10 N.Y.2d 313, 222 N.Y.S.2d 324, 178 N.E.2d 723.

DESMOND, CH. J. Gabriel Pascal, defendant's intestate who died in 1954, had been for many years a theatrical producer. In 1952, an English corporation named Gabriel Pascal Enterprises, Ltd., of whose 100 shares Gabriel Pascal owned 98, made an agreement with the English Public Trustee who represented the estate of George Bernard Shaw. This agreement granted to Gabriel Pascal Enterprises, Ltd., the exclusive world rights to prepare and produce a musical play to be based on

Shaw's play "Pygmalion" and a motion picture version of the musical play. The agreement recited, as was the fact, that the licensee owned a film scenario written by Pascal and based on "Pygmalion". In fact Pascal had, some time previously, produced a nonmusical movie version of "Pygmalion" under rights obtained by Pascal from George Bernard Shaw during the latter's lifetime. The 1952 agreement required the licensee corporation to pay the Shaw estate an initial advance and thereafter to pay the Shaw estate 3% of the gross receipts of the musical play and musical movie with a provision that the license was to terminate if within certain fixed periods the licensee did not arrange with Lerner and Loewe [sic] or other similarly well-known composers to write the musical play and arrange to produce it. Before Pascal's death in July, 1954, he had made a number of unsuccessful efforts to get the musical written and produced and it was not until after his death that arrangements were made, through a New York bank as temporary administrator of his estate, for the writing and production of the highly successful "My Fair Lady". Meanwhile, on February 22, 1954, at a time when the license from the Shaw estate still had two years to run, Gabriel Pascal, who died four and a half months later, wrote, signed and delivered to plaintiff a document as follows:

> "Dear Miss Kingman
>
> This is to confirm to you our understanding that I give you from my shares of profits of the Pygmalion Musical stage version five per cent (5%) in England, and two per cent (2%) of my shares of profits in the United States. From the film version, five per cent (5%) from my profit shares all over the world.
>
> As soon as the contracts are signed, I will send a copy of this letter to my lawyer, Edwin Davies, in London, and he will confirm to you this arrangement in a legal form.
>
> This participation in my shares of profits is a present to you, in recognition for your loyal work for me as my Executive Secretary.

Very sincerely yours,

Gabriel Pascal."

The question in this lawsuit is: Did the delivery of this paper constitute a valid, complete, present gift to plaintiff by way of assignment of a share in future royalties when and if collected from the exhibition of the musical stage version and film version of "Pygmalion"? A consideration was, of course, unnecessary (Personal Property Law, § 33, subd. 4).[a]

* * *

The only real question is as to whether the 1954 letter above quoted operated to transfer to plaintiff an enforcible right to the described

---

a. [Ed. This section provided: "An assignment shall not be denied the effect of irrevocably transferring the assignor's rights because of the absence of consideration, if such assignment is in writing and signed by the assignor, or by his agent." This section has been carried forward as McKinney's N.Y. Gen'l Oblig.L. § 5–1107.]

percentages of the royalties to accrue to Pascal on the production of a stage or film version of a musical play based on "Pygmalion". We see no reason why this letter does not have that effect. It is true that at the time of the delivery of the letter there was no musical stage or film play in existence but Pascal, who owned and was conducting negotiations to realize on the stage and film rights, could grant to another a share of the moneys to accrue from the use of those rights by others. There are many instances of courts enforcing assignments of rights to sums which were expected thereafter to become due to the assignor. A typical case is Field v. Mayor of New York (6 N.Y. 179). One Bell, who had done much printing and similar work for the City of New York but had no present contract to do any more such work, gave an assignment in the amount of $1,500 of any moneys that might thereafter become due to Bell for such work. Bell did obtain such contracts or orders from the city and money became due to him therefor. This court held that while there was not at the time of the assignment any presently enforcible or even existing chose in action but merely a possibility that there would be such a chose of action, nevertheless there was a possibility of such which the parties expected to ripen into reality and which did afterwards ripen into reality and that, therefore, the assignment created an equitable title which the courts would enforce. * * * The cases cited by appellant (Young v. Young, 80 N.Y. 422; Vincent v. Rix, 248 N.Y. 76; Farmers' Loan & Trust Co. v. Winthrop, 207 App.Div. 356, mod. 238 N.Y. 477) are not to the contrary. In each of those instances the attempted gifts failed because there had not been such a completed and irrevocable delivery of the subject matter of the gift as to put the gift beyond cancellation by the donor. In every such case the question must be as to whether there was a completed delivery of a kind appropriate to the subject property. Ordinarily, if the property consists of existing stock certificates or corporate bonds, as in the Young and Vincent cases (supra), there must be a completed physical transfer of the stock certificates or bonds. * * * In our present case there was nothing left for Pascal to do in order to make an irrevocable transfer to plaintiff of part of Pascal's right to receive royalties from the productions.

* * *

Judgment affirmed.

Assignments as security interests. This chapter concentrates on outright assignments. Some explanation of the use of assignments as security for a loan is in order, because most assignments are of this second type. Suppose a manufacturer (M) assigns its accounts receivables, including those accounts that are not yet in being, to F, a factor. (Many financial institutions that specialize in taking assignments as security for loans are known as factors.) Suppose M soon thereafter declares bankruptcy. Secured creditors of a bankrupt are much better protected than general creditors. A general creditor might be a supplier that furnished M with goods on credit and had no security interest. An example of a secured creditor is a mortgagee. The mortgagee can foreclose on the mortgaged real property and, unless the real property has declined in value, is likely to get repaid in full.

Similarly, the assignee who took an assignment for security can collect from the obligor and may be able to collect the amount of its loan and receive 100 cents on the dollar. If the obligor owes more than the value of the loan, the excess will be given to the general creditors. General creditors are lucky to get a few pennies on the dollar.

An important question is the respective rights of the trustee in bankruptcy and the assignee of accounts that were not yet in being at the time of the assignment. A trustee in bankruptcy is treated as a hypothetical attaching creditor. Prior to the UCC, the trustee in bankruptcy would prevail because the rights of an assignee of future rights (an equitable assignee) were deemed inferior to the rights of a subsequent attaching creditor. Under the UCC, to the extent of its coverage, the assignment of a future right is treated as a legal assignment, and the result would be different from the pre-UCC result. See Text § 18.9. The assignee will prevail.

SECTION 3.   ARE THE RIGHTS ASSIGNABLE AND PERFORMANCES DELEGABLE?

(a) General principles

(Calamari & Perillo 5th §§ 18.10—18.15, 18.28—18.29, 18.31—18.32)

MACKE CO. v. PIZZA OF GAITHERSBURG, INC.

Court of Appeals of Maryland, 1970.
259 Md. 479, 270 A.2d 645.

SINGLEY, JUDGE. The appellees and defendants below, Pizza of Gaithersburg, Inc.; Pizzeria, Inc.; The Pizza Pie Corp., Inc. and Pizza Oven, Inc., four corporations under the common ownership of Sidney Ansell, Thomas S. Sherwood and Eugene Early and the same individuals as partners or proprietors (the Pizza Shops) operated at six locations in Montgomery and Prince George's Counties. The appellees had arranged to have installed in each of their locations cold drink vending machines owned by Virginia Coffee Service, Inc., and on 30 December 1966, this arrangement was formalized at five of the locations, by contracts for terms of one year, automatically renewable for a like term in the absence of 30 days' written notice. A similar contract for the sixth location, operated by Pizza of Gaithersburg, Inc., was entered into on 25 July 1967.

On 30 December 1967, Virginia's assets were purchased by The Macke Company (Macke) and the six contracts were assigned to Macke by Virginia. In January, 1968, the Pizza Shops attempted to terminate the five contracts having the December anniversary date, and in February, the contract which had the July anniversary date.

Macke brought suit in the Circuit Court for Montgomery County against each of the Pizza Shops for damages for breach of contract. From judgments for the defendants, Macke has appealed.

The lower court based the result which it reached on two grounds: first, that the Pizza Shops, when they contracted with Virginia, relied on its skill, judgment and reputation, which made impossible a delegation of Virginia's duties to Macke * * *.

In the absence of a contrary provision—and there was none here— rights and duties under an executory bilateral contract may be assigned and delegated, subject to the exception that duties under a contract to provide personal services may never be delegated, nor rights be assigned under a contract where *delectus personae* was an ingredient of the bargain.[1] 4 Corbin on Contracts § 865 (1951) at 434; 6 Am.Jur.2d, Assignments § 11 (1963) at 196. Crane Ice Cream Co. v. Terminal Freezing & Heating Co., 147 Md. 588, 128 A. 280 (1925) held that the right of an individual to purchase ice under a contract which by its terms reflected a knowledge of the individual's needs and reliance on his credit and responsibility could not be assigned to the corporation which purchased his business. In Eastern Advertising Co. v. McGaw & Co., 89 Md. 72, 42 A. 923 (1899), our predecessors held that an advertising agency could not delegate its duties under a contract which had been entered into by an advertiser who had relied on the agency's skill, judgment and taste.

* * *

We cannot regard the agreements as contracts for personal services. They were either a license or concession granted Virginia by the appellees, or a lease of a portion of the appellees' premises, with Virginia agreeing to pay a percentage of gross sales as a license or concession fee or as rent and were assignable by Virginia unless they imposed on Virginia duties of a personal or unique character which could not be delegated.

The appellees earnestly argue that they had dealt with Macke before and had chosen Virginia because they preferred the way it conducted its business. Specifically, they say that service was more personalized, since the president of Virginia kept the machines in working order, that commissions were paid in cash, and that Virginia permitted them to keep keys to the machines so that minor adjustments could be made when needed. Even if we assume all this to be true, the agreements with Virginia were silent as to the details of the working arrangements and contained only a provision requiring Virginia to "install * * * the above listed equipment and * * * maintain the equipment in good operating

---

1. Like all generalizations, this one is subject to an important exception. Uniform Commercial Code § 9–318 makes ineffective a term in any contract prohibiting the assignment of a contract right: i.e., a right to payment. Compare Restatement, Contracts § 151(c) (1932).

order and stocked with merchandise." We think the Supreme Court of California put the problem of personal service in proper focus a century ago when it upheld the assignment of a contract to grade a San Francisco street:

> "All painters do not paint portraits like Sir Joshua Reynolds, nor landscapes like Claude Lorraine, nor do all writers write dramas like Shakespeare or fiction like Dickens. Rare genius and extraordinary skill are not transferable, and contracts for their employment are therefore personal, and cannot be assigned. But rare genius and extraordinary skill are not indispensable to the workmanlike digging down of a sand hill or the filling up of a depression to a given level, or the construction of brick sewers with manholes and covers, and contracts for such work are not personal, and may be assigned."
> Taylor v. Palmer, 31 Cal. 240 at 247–248 (1866).

See also Devlin v. Mayor, Aldermen and Commonalty of the City of New York, 63 N.Y. 8, at 17 (1875). Moreover, the difference between the service the Pizza Shops happened to be getting from Virginia and what they expected to get from Macke did not mount up to such a material change in the performance of obligations under the agreements as would justify the appellees' refusal to recognize the assignment, Crane Ice Cream Co. v. Terminal Freezing & Heating Co., supra, 147 Md. 588, 128 A. 280.

In support of the proposition that the agreements were for personal services, and not assignable, the Pizza Shops rely on three Supreme Court cases, Burck v. Taylor, 152 U.S. 634, 14 S.Ct. 696, 38 L.Ed. 578 (1894); Delaware County Comm'rs v. Diebold Safe & Lock Co., 133 U.S. 473, 10 S.Ct. 399, 33 L.Ed. 674 (1890); and Arkansas Valley Smelting Co. v. Belden Mining Co., 127 U.S. 379, 8 S.Ct. 1308, 32 L.Ed. 246 (1888), all of which were cited with approval by our predecessors in Tarr v. Veasey, 125 Md. 199, 207, 93 A. 428 (1915). We find none of these cases persuasive. Burck held that the contractor for the state capitol in Texas, who was prohibited by the terms of his contract from assigning it without the state's consent, could not make a valid assignment of his right to receive three-fourths of the proceeds. In *Delaware County*, Diebold Safe and Lock, which was a subcontractor in the construction of a county jail, was barred from recovering from the county commissioners for its work on the theory that there had been a partial assignment of the construction contract by the prime contractor, which had never been assented to by the commissioners. This result must be limited to the facts: i.e., to the subcontractor's right to recover under the assignment, and not to the contractor's right to delegate. See Taylor v. Palmer and Devlin v. Mayor, Aldermen and Commonalty of the City of New York, both supra. *Arkansas Valley*, which held invalid an attempt to assign a contract for the purchase of ore, is clearly distinguishable because of a contract provision which stipulated that payment for the ore was to be made after delivery, based on an assay to be made by the individual purchaser named in the contract. The court concluded that this was a confidence imposed in the individual purchaser's credit and responsibility and that his rights under the contract could not be transferred to another. Tarr v. Veasey involved a situation where duties were delegated to one person and rights assigned to another and our predecessors held the rights not to be assignable, because of the parties' intention that duties and rights were interdependent.

We find more apposite two cases which were not cited by the parties. In The British Waggon Co. & The Parkgate Waggon Co. v. Lea & Co., 5 Q.B.D. 149 (1880), Parkgate Waggon Company, a lessor of railway cars, who had agreed to keep the cars "in good and substantial repair and working order," made an assignment of the contract to British Waggon Company. When British Waggon Company sued for rent, the lessee contended that the assignment had terminated the lease. The court held that the lessee remained bound under the lease, because there was no provision making performance of the lessor's duty to keep in repair a duty personal to it or its employees.

Except for the fact that the result has been roundly criticized, see Corbin, supra, at 448–49, the Pizza Shops might have found some solace in the facts found in Boston Ice Co. v. Potter, 123 Mass. 28 (1877). There, Potter, who had dealt with the Boston Ice Company, and found its service unsatisfactory, transferred his business to Citizens' Ice Company. Later, Citizens' sold out to Boston, unbeknown to Potter, and Potter was served by Boston for a full year. When Boston attempted to collect its ice bill, the Massachusetts court sustained Potter's demurrer on the ground that there was no privity of contract, since Potter had a right to choose with whom he would deal and could not have another supplier thrust upon him. Modern authorities do not support this result, and hold that, absent provision to the contrary, a duty may be delegated, as distinguished from a right which can be assigned, and that the promisee cannot rescind, if the quality of the performance remains materially the same.

Restatement, Contracts § 160(3) (1932) reads, in part:

"Performance or offer of performance by a person delegated has the same legal effect as performance or offer of performance by the person named in the contract, unless,

(a) performance by the person delegated varies or would vary materially from performance by the person named in the contract as the one to perform, and there has been no * * * assent to the delegation * * *."

In cases involving the sale of goods, the Restatement rule respecting delegation of duties has been amplified by Uniform Commercial Code § 2–210(5), Maryland Code (1957, 1964 Repl.Vol.) Art. 95B § 2–210(5), which permits a promisee to demand assurances from the party to whom duties have been delegated. * * *

As we see it, the delegation of duty by Virginia to Macke was entirely permissible under the terms of the agreements. In so holding, we do not put ourselves at odds with Eastern Advertising Co. v. McGaw, supra, 89 Md. 72, 42 A. 923, for in that case, the agreement with the agency contained a provision that "the advertising cards were to be 'subject to the approval of Eastern Advertising Company as to style and contents' ", at 82, 42 A. at 923, which the court found to import that reliance was being placed on the agency's skill, judgment and taste, at 88, 42 A. 923.

* * *

Special Skill ?

Delegation of duty amounts towards

[Reversed and remanded.]

SALLY BEAUTY CO. v. NEXXUS PRODUCTS CO.

United States Court of Appeals, Seventh Circuit, 1986.
801 F.2d 1001.

CUDAHY, CIRCUIT JUDGE. Nexxus Products Company ("Nexxus") entered into a contract with Best Barber & Beauty Supply Company, Inc. ("Best"), under which Best would be the exclusive distributor of Nexxus hair care products to barbers and hair stylists throughout most of Texas. When Best was acquired by and merged into Sally Beauty Company, Inc. ("Sally Beauty"), Nexxus cancelled the agreement. Sally Beauty is a wholly-owned subsidiary of Alberto–Culver Company ("Alberto–Culver"), a major manufacturer of hair care products and a competitor of Nexxus'. Sally Beauty claims that Nexxus breached the contract by cancelling; Nexxus asserts by way of defense that the contract was not assignable or, in the alternative, not assignable to Sally Beauty. The district court granted Nexxus' motion for summary judgment, ruling that the contract was one for personal services and therefore not assignable. We affirm on a different theory—that this contract could not be assigned to the wholly-owned subsidiary of a direct competitor under section 2–210 of the Uniform Commercial Code.

I.

Only the basic facts are undisputed and they are as follows. Prior to its merger with Sally Beauty, Best was a Texas corporation in the business of distributing beauty and hair care products to retail stores, barber shops and beauty salons throughout Texas. Between March and July 1979, Mark Reichek, Best's president, negotiated with Stephen Redding, Nexxus' vice-president, over a possible distribution agreement between Best and Nexxus. Nexxus, founded in 1979, is a California corporation that formulates and markets hair care products. Nexxus does not market its products to retail stores, preferring to sell them to independent distributors for resale to barbers and beauticians. On August 2, 1979, Nexxus executed a distributorship agreement with Best, in the form of a July 24, 1979 letter from Reichek, for Best, to Redding, for Nexxus * * *.

In July 1981 Sally Beauty acquired Best in a stock purchase transaction and Best was merged into Sally Beauty, which succeeded to Best's rights and interests in all of Best's contracts. Sally Beauty, a Delaware corporation with its principal place of business in Texas, is a wholly-owned subsidiary of Alberto–Culver. Sally Beauty, like Best, is a distributor of hair care and beauty products to retail stores and hair styling salons. Alberto–Culver is a major manufacturer of hair care products and, thus, is a direct competitor of Nexxus in the hair care market.

Shortly after the merger, Redding met with Michael Renzulli, president of Sally Beauty, to discuss the Nexxus distribution agreement. After the meeting, Redding wrote Renzulli a letter stating that Nexxus would not allow Sally Beauty, a wholly-owned subsidiary of a direct competitor, to distribute Nexxus products:

> As we discussed in New Orleans, we have great reservations about allowing our NEXXUS Products to be distributed by a company which is, in essence, a direct competitor. We appreciate your argument of autonomy for your business, but the fact remains that you are totally owned by Alberto–Culver.

> Since we see no way of justifying this conflict, we cannot allow our products to be distributed by Sally Beauty Company.

* * *

II.

Sally Beauty's breach of contract claim alleges that by acquiring Best, Sally Beauty succeeded to all of Best's rights and obligations under the distribution agreement. It further alleges that Nexxus breached the agreement by failing to give Sally Beauty 120 days notice prior to terminating the agreement and by terminating it on other than an anniversary date of its formation. Nexxus, in its motion for summary judgment, argued that the distribution agreement it entered into with Best was a contract for personal services, based upon a relationship of personal trust and confidence between Reichek and the Redding family. As such, the contract could not be assigned to Sally without Nexxus' consent.

In opposing this motion Sally Beauty argued that the contract was freely assignable because (1) it was between two corporations, not two individuals and (2) the character of the performance would not be altered by the substitution of Sally Beauty for Best. It also argued that "the Distribution Agreement is nothing more than a simple, non-exclusive contract for the distribution of goods, the successful performance of which is in no way dependent upon any particular personality, individual skill or confidential relationship."

In ruling on this motion, the district court framed the issue before it as "whether the contract at issue here between Best and Nexxus was of a personal nature such that it was not assignable without Nexxus' consent." * * *

* * *

We cannot affirm this summary judgment on the grounds relied on by the district court.* * *

We may affirm this summary judgment, however, on a different ground if it finds support in the record. * * * We agree with Sally that the provisions of the UCC govern this contract and for that reason hold that the assignment of the contract by Best to Sally Beauty was barred by the UCC rules on delegation of performance, UCC § 2–210(1) * * *.

III.

The UCC codifies the law of contracts applicable to "transactions in goods." UCC § 2–102 * * *. Texas applies the "dominant factor" test to determine whether the UCC applies to a given contract or transaction: was the essence of or dominant factor in the formation of the contract the provision of goods or services? * * * No Texas case addresses whether a distribution agreement is a contract for the sale of goods, but the rule in the majority of jurisdictions is that distributorships (both exclusive and non-exclusive) are to be treated as sale of goods contracts under the UCC. * * *

* * *

IV.

The fact that this contract is considered a contract for the sale of goods and not for the provision of a service does not, as Sally Beauty suggests, mean that it is freely assignable in all circumstances. The delegation of performance under a sales contract (whether in conjunction with an assignment of rights, as here, or not) is governed by UCC section 2–210(1) * * *. The UCC recognizes that in many cases an obligor will find it convenient or even necessary to relieve himself of the duty of performance under a contract, see Official Comment 1, UCC § 2–210 ("[T]his section recognizes both delegation of performance and assignability as normal and permissible incidents of a contract for the sale of goods."). The Code therefore sanctions delegation except where the delegated performance would be unsatisfactory to the obligee: "A party may perform his duty through a delegate unless otherwise agreed to or unless the other party has a substantial interest in having his original promisor perform or control the acts required by the contract." UCC § 2–210(1) * * *. Consideration is given to balancing the policies of free alienability of commercial contracts and protecting the obligee from having to accept a bargain he did not contract for.

We are concerned here with the delegation of Best's duty of performance under the distribution agreement, as Nexxus terminated the agreement because it did not wish to accept Sally Beauty's substituted performance. * * *

In the exclusive distribution agreement before us, Nexxus had contracted for Best's "best efforts" in promoting the sale of Nexxus products in Texas. UCC § 2–306(2) * * *. It was this contractual undertaking which Nexxus refused to see performed by Sally.

In ruling on Nexxus' motion for summary judgment, the district court noted: "Unlike Best, Sally Beauty is a subsidiary of one of Nexxus' direct competitors. This is a significant distinction and in the court's view, it raises serious questions regarding Sally Beauty's ability to perform the distribution agreement in the same manner as Best." * * * We agree * * * and hold that Sally Beauty's position as a wholly-owned subsidiary of Alberto–Culver is sufficient to bar the delegation of Best's duties under the agreement.

We do not believe that our holding will work the mischief with our national economy that the appellants predict. We hold merely that the duty of performance under an exclusive distributorship may not be delegated to a competitor in the market place—or the wholly-owned subsidiary of a competitor—without the obligee's consent. We believe that such a rule is consonant with the policies behind section 2–210, which is concerned with preserving the bargain the obligee has struck. Nexxus should not be required to accept the "best efforts" of Sally Beauty when those efforts are subject to the control of Alberto–Culver. It is entirely reasonable that Nexxus should conclude that this performance would be a different thing than what it had bargained for. At oral argument, Sally Beauty argued that the case should go to trial to allow it to demonstrate that it could and would perform the contract as impartially as Best. It stressed that Sally Beauty is a "multi-line" distributor, which means that it distributes many brands and is not just a conduit for Alberto–Culver products. But we do not think that this creates a material question of fact in this case. When performance of personal services is delegated, the trier merely determines that it is a personal services contract. If so, the duty is per se nondelegable. There is no inquiry into whether the delegate is as skilled or worthy of trust and confidence as the original obligor: the delegate was not bargained for and the obligee need not consent to the substitution. And so here: it is undisputed that Sally Beauty is wholly owned by Alberto–Culver, which means that Sally Beauty's "impartial" sales policy is at least acquiesced in by Alberto–Culver—but could change whenever Alberto–Culver's needs changed. Sally Beauty may be totally sincere in its belief that it can operate "impartially" as a distributor, but who can guarantee the outcome when there is a clear choice between the demands of the parent-manufacturer, Alberto–Culver, and the competing needs of Nexxus? The risk of an unfavorable outcome is not one which the law can force Nexxus to take. Nexxus has a substantial interest in not seeing this contract performed by Sally Beauty, which is sufficient to bar the delegation under section 2–210 * * *. Because Nexxus should not be forced to accept performance of the distributorship agreement by Sally, we hold that the contract was not assignable without Nexxus' consent.

The judgment of the district court is AFFIRMED.

Posner, Circuit Judge, dissenting. My brethren have decided, with no better foundation than judicial intuition about what businessmen consider reasonable, that the Uniform Commercial Code gives a supplier an absolute right to cancel an exclusive-dealing contract if the dealer is acquired, directly or indirectly, by a competitor of the supplier. I interpret the Code differently.

Nexxus makes products for the hair and sells them through distributors to hair salons and barbershops. It gave a contract to Best, cancellable on any anniversary of the contract with 120 days' notice, to be its exclusive distributor in Texas. Two years later Best was acquired by and merged into Sally Beauty, a distributor of beauty supplies and wholly owned subsidiary of Alberto–Culver. Alberto–Culver makes "hair care" products, too, though they mostly are cheaper than Nexxus's, and are sold to the public primarily through grocery stores and drugstores. My brethren conclude that because there is at least a loose competitive relationship between Nexxus and Alberto–Culver, Sally Beauty cannot— as a matter of law, cannot, for there has been no trial on the issue— provide its "best efforts" in the distribution of Nexxus products. Since a commitment to provide best efforts is read into every exclusive-dealing contract by section 2–306(2) of the Uniform Commercial Code, the contract has been broken and Nexxus can repudiate it. Alternatively, Nexxus had "a substantial interest in having his original promisor perform or control the acts required by the contract," and therefore the delegation of the promisor's (Best's) duties to Sally Beauty was improper under section 2–210(1).

* * *

My brethren find this a simple case—as simple (it seems) as if a lawyer had undertaken to represent the party opposing his client. But notions of conflict of interest are not the same in law and in business, and judges can go astray by assuming that the legal-services industry is the pattern for the entire economy. The lawyerization of America has not reached that point. Sally Beauty, though a wholly owned subsidiary of Alberto–Culver, distributes "hair care" supplies made by many different companies, which so far as appears compete with Alberto–Culver as vigorously as Nexxus does. Steel companies both make fabricated steel and sell raw steel to competing fabricators. General Motors sells cars manufactured by a competitor, Isuzu. What in law would be considered a fatal conflict of interest is in business a commonplace and legitimate practice. The lawyer is a fiduciary of his client; Best was not a fiduciary of Nexxus.

* * *

How likely is it that the acquisition of Best could hurt Nexxus? Not very. Suppose Alberto–Culver had ordered Sally Beauty to go slow in pushing Nexxus products, in the hope that sales of Alberto–Culver "hair care" products would rise. Even if they did, since the market is competitive Alberto–Culver would not reap monopoly profits. Moreover, what guarantee has Alberto–Culver that consumers would be diverted from Nexxus to it, rather than to products closer in price and quality to Nexxus products? In any event, any trivial gain in profits to Alberto– Culver would be offset by the loss of goodwill to Sally Beauty; and a cost to Sally Beauty is a cost to Alberto–Culver, its parent. Remember that Sally Beauty carries beauty supplies made by other competitors of Alberto–Culver; Best alone [also?] carries "hair care" products manufactured by Revlon, Clairol, Bristol–Myers, and L'Oreal, as well as Alberto–Culver. Will these powerful competitors continue to distribute their products through Sally Beauty if Sally Beauty displays favoritism for Alberto–Culver products? Would not such a display be a commercial disaster for Sally Beauty, and hence for its parent, Alberto–Culver? Is it really credible that Alberto–Culver would sacrifice Sally Beauty in a vain effort to monopolize the "hair care" market, in violation of section 2 of the Sherman Act? Is not the ratio of the profits that Alberto–Culver obtains from Sally Beauty to the profits it obtains from the manufacture of "hair care" products at least a relevant consideration?

Another relevant consideration is that the contract between Nexxus and Best was for a short term. Could Alberto–Culver destroy Nexxus by failing to push its products with maximum vigor in Texas for a year? In the unlikely event that it could and did, it would be liable in damages to Nexxus for breach of the implied best-efforts term of the distribution contract. Finally, it is obvious that Sally Beauty does not have a bottleneck position in the distribution of "hair care" products, such that by refusing to promote Nexxus products vigorously it could stifle the distribution of those products in Texas; for Nexxus has found alternative distribution that it prefers—otherwise it wouldn't have repudiated the contract with Best when Best was acquired by Sally Beauty.

Not all businessmen are consistent and successful profit maximizers, so the probability that Alberto–Culver would instruct Sally Beauty to cease to push Nexxus products vigorously in Texas cannot be reckoned at zero. On this record, however, it is slight. And there is no principle of law that if something happens that trivially reduces the probability that a dealer will use his best efforts, the supplier can cancel the contract. Suppose there had been no merger, but the only child of Best's president had gone to work for Alberto–Culver as a chemist. Could Nexxus have canceled the contract, fearing that Best (perhaps unconsciously) would favor Alberto–Culver products over Nexxus products? That would be an absurd ground for cancellation, and so is Nexxus's actual ground. At most, so far as the record shows, Nexxus may have had grounds for "insecurity" regarding the performance by Sally Beauty of its obligation to use its best efforts to promote Nexxus products, but if so its remedy was not to cancel the contract but to demand assurances of due performance. See UCC § 2–609; Official Comment 5 to § 2–306. No such demand was made. An anticipatory repudiation by conduct requires conduct that makes the repudiating party unable to perform. Farnsworth, Contracts 636 (1982). The merger did not do this. At least there is no evidence it did. The judgment should be reversed and the case remanded for a trial on whether the merger so altered the conditions of performance that Nexxus is entitled to declare the contract broken.

Problems

7. S and B entered into a contract under which S agreed to furnish B with its requirements of ice in his business as an ice cream manufacturer up

to 250 tons per week for five years. B agreed not to purchase elsewhere except if B's needs exceeded the weekly maximum. After one year, B sold its plant to C and, at the same time, assigned its rights and delegated performance of its duties under the contract with S to C. While B did business only in one plant in Maryland, C was a large corporation and was engaged in the ice cream business in several states. Are the rights assignable and performance of the duties delegable? No

8. S and B entered into a contract for the purchase and sale of a piece of real property. B was to pay one half of the purchase price in cash and the other half by giving a bond and mortgage. Before closing, B assigned his rights and delegated performance of his duties to A. When A tendered cash and his own bond, S refused. (a) What result? (b) What result if A had tendered a bond of B?

9. A client retains a lawyer for a certain task. Unknown to the client, the lawyer delegates performance of the duties and assigns the right to payment of the fee to a second lawyer. The second lawyer, without the client's knowledge, performs, and the performance is successful. To whom, if anyone, does the client owe a fee?

10. George had a bad back. He consulted Dr. Doolittle who recommended surgery. George consented in writing to having Dr. Doolittle operate. When George was anesthetized, Dr. Doolittle left the room and Dr. Domuch operated. The surgery was not successful. What recourse does George have?

11. Peterson was the anchorman on channel 9 in Washington, D.C. under a contract that had several years to go when the owners of channel 9 sold it to the plaintiff. Prior to the sale, Peterson had a close personal relationship with his managers and was able to discuss programming options as an equal. When the station was sold, Peterson declared that the contract had been breached by the sale and commenced working for a competitive channel. The new owners of channel 9 sued to enjoin Peterson from working for the competition. What result?

(b) Contractual Prohibitions Against Assignment

(Calamari & Perillo 5th § 18.16)

ALDANA v. COLONIAL PALMS PLAZA, LTD.

District Court of Appeal of Florida, Third District, 1991.
591 So.2d 953.

Per Curiam. The appellant, Robert Aldana, appeals an adverse summary judgment in favor of appellee, Colonial Palms Plaza, Inc. and an order awarding Colonial Palms Plaza, Inc. attorney's fees pursuant to the offer of judgment rule. We reverse.

Colonial Palms Plaza, Inc. [Landlord], entered into a lease agreement with Abby's Cakes On Dixie, Inc. [Tenant] for commercial space in a shopping center. The lease included a provision in which Landlord agreed to pay Tenant a construction allowance of up to $11,250 after Tenant satisfactorily completed certain improvements to the rented premises.

Prior to the completion of the improvements, Tenant assigned its right to receive the first $8,000 of the construction allowance to Robert Aldana [Assignee]. In return, Assignee loaned Tenant $8,000 to finance the construction. Assignee recorded the assignment and sent notice of the assignment by certified mail to Landlord.

When Tenant completed the improvements to the rented premises, Landlord ignored the assignment and paid Tenant the construction allowance. Assignee sued Landlord for the money due pursuant to the assignment. The trial court granted Landlord's motion for summary judgment. The trial court also awarded Landlord attorney's fees pursuant to the offer of judgment rule, Fla.R.Civ.P. 1.442, and costs pursuant to section 57.041, Florida Statutes (1989).

Landlord relies on an anti-assignment clause in the lease agreement to argue that the assignment was void and unenforceable. The clause states in part:

> TENANT agrees not to assign, mortgage, pledge, or encumber this Lease, in whole or in part, or to sublet the whole or any part of the DEMISED PREMISES, or to permit the use of the whole or any part of the DEMISED PREMISES by any licensee or concessionaire, without first obtaining the prior, specific written consent of LANDLORD at LANDLORD'S sole discretion.... Any such assignment, encumbrance or subletting without such consent shall be void and shall at LANDLORD'S option constitute a default.

On this appeal, Assignee has two main arguments. First, he claims that the anti-assignment clause is rendered ineffective by Article 9 of the Uniform Commercial Code. Assignee argues that the construction allowance provision in the lease was an "account" or "general intangible" as defined by section 679.106, Florida Statutes (1989). Assignee argues that consequently, subsection 679.318(4), Florida Statutes (1989), serves to invalidate the anti-assignment clause. That subsection states:

> (4) A term in any contract between an account debtor and an assignor is ineffective if it prohibits assignment of an account or prohibits creation of a security interest in a general intangible for money due or to become due or requires the account debtor's consent to such assignment or security interest. § 679.318(4), Fla. Stat. (1989).

Assignee asserts that subsection 679.318(4) applies to this case and renders the anti-assignment clause ineffective. In the absence of the anti-assignment clause, Assignee argues the assignment is valid and binding upon Landlord.

However, Landlord correctly points out that leases are excluded from the provisions of chapter 679 (with an exception not applicable here) and therefore, subsection 679.318(4) does not apply to this case. Subsection 679.104(10) provides "[t]his chapter does not apply.... to the creation or transfer of an interest in or lien on real estate, including a lease or rents thereunder." (emphasis added). Therefore, Assignee's first argument fails.

Assignee argues alternatively that under ordinary contract principles, the lease provision at issue here does not prevent the assignment of the right to receive contractual payments. We agree.

So far as pertinent here, the lease provides that "TENANT agrees not to assign ... this lease, in whole or in part...." Tenant did not assign the lease, but instead assigned a right to receive the construction allowance.

The law in this area is summarized in Restatement (Second) of Contracts, § 322(1), as follows:

> (1) Unless the circumstances indicate the contrary, a contract term prohibiting assignment of "the contract" bars only the delegation to an assignee of the performance by the assignor of a duty or condition.

As a rule of construction, in other words, a prohibition against assignment of the contract (or in this case, the lease) will prevent assignment of contractual duties, but does not prevent assignment of the right to receive payments due—unless the circumstances indicate the contrary. [Citations omitted.]

Landlord was given notice of the assignment. Delivery of the notice of the assignment to the debtor fixes accountability of the debtor to the assignee. * * * Therefore, Landlord was bound by the assignment. * * * The trial court improperly granted final summary judgment in favor of Landlord and the judgment must be reversed. Consequently, the trial court's award of attorney's fees and costs to Landlord must also be reversed. The cause is remanded for further proceedings consistent herewith.

Reversed and remanded.

Problem

12. M & M, the owner of extensive timberlands, contracted with Hull whereby the latter could log 250 million board feet of redwood at $6 per thousand board feet from M & M's lands. The contract provided that Hull's rights could not be assigned without the approval of M & M and that approval would not be unreasonably withheld. Hull had financial problems and reached agreement with Union whereby Hull assigned his rights and Union assumed Hull's duties, subject to M & M's approval. When M & M's approval was sought, internal memoranda showed that some of M & M's board members and executives recommended against approval because Union's principals were "untrustworthy", and "litigious", were guilty of "sharp practices", and had an "unsavory reputation." Others within M & M's organization saw Hull's difficulties as a convenient opportunity to cancel the contract and to have the redwood tract "to ourselves" so as to reap a greater profit in a rising market. Approval was denied and M & M canceled the contract because Hull was unable to perform. Hull sued M & M. The trial judge found that the non-approval was proper. On appeal, what result?

(c) Option Contracts

(Calamari & Perillo 5th § 18.32)

FRANKLIN v. JORDAN

Supreme Court of Georgia, 1968.
224 Ga. 727, 164 S.E.2d 718.

FRANKUM, JUSTICE. Franklin filed a complaint against Jordan in which he sought to require the defendant to specifically perform an option contract which granted to the plaintiff's assignor, Ackerman, "his heirs, executors, successors and assigns," the exclusive right to purchase a described tract of land located in Cobb County. The option contract contains the following stipulation: "Purchaser's rights under this contract shall be transferable and assignable at or prior to the closing by purchaser, to any individual, corporation, or partnership, but such assignment or transfer shall in no way release or relieve the purchaser from [his] liability, obligations or any of the provisions of this agreement." It appears that subsequent to exercising the option Ackerman assigned the same to the complainant. While the contract in one place refers to Ackerman, the optionee, as the "grantee" and in another place refers to "purchaser's rights," etc., it is apparent from a reading of the entire contract which was signed by Ackerman as "grantee" that the terms "purchaser" and "grantee" both refer to the optionee. It is equally apparent that one of the obligations undertaken by Ackerman as optionee was to give a note signed by him personally promising to pay the balance of the purchase price, due after the initial payment. This was one of the liabilities from which Ackerman was not released by his assignment of the option to Franklin. To the complaint seeking specific performance of the contract Franklin attached as an exhibit a promissory note signed only by him as maker which he tendered to the defendant as a part of his offer to perform the agreement. This note was not signed by Ackerman, either as maker or endorser, and it thus appears that the performance tendered by the plaintiff was not strictly in accordance with the terms of the agreement sued on. Plaintiff was not entitled, therefore, to have specific performance of the agreement. * * *

Judgment affirmed.

Problems

13.   S offers to sell a specific car to B for $10,000. B assigns the offer to C who tenders $10,000 to S. Is A bound to take the money?

14.   S offers to sell a certain car to B if B drives the car in the Indianapolis 500 and wins, and if B pays $52,000 thereafter, and if B gives $100 to keep the offer open until after the race. B gives S $100. May B now assign the rights and delegate the performance of the conditions to C?

(d) *Improper Assignment or Delegation—Effect of Waiver*

(Calamari & Perillo 5th §§ 18.14 and 18.29

SEALE v. BATES

Supreme Court of Colorado, 1961.
145 Colo. 430, 359 P.2d 356.

DOYLE, JUSTICE. Plaintiffs in error will be referred to by name or as they were designated in the trial court where they were plaintiffs in an action against John Bates, individually, the Bates Dance Studio, Inc. and the Dance Studio of Denver, Inc. The Seales sought to recover $2,040 which had been paid to the Bates Dance Studio to defray the cost of 300 hours of dance instruction. The plaintiff Hanscome sought to recover $4,131.34 which he had paid to the Bates Dance Studio for 612 hours of dance instruction. From their complaints it would appear that the contracts which the plaintiffs entered into with the Bates Dance Studio had been assigned to the Dance Studio of Denver, doing business as Dale Dance Studio. It is alleged that the defendants refused to carry out their obligations and duties under the said contracts.

The Seales started taking dance lessons at the Dale Dance Studios in June of 1956. They signed up for a series of lessons costing in excess of $200, but in a short time they became dissatisfied with the arrangement and had the contract cancelled upon the basis that they would be allowed to take the balance of their lessons at the Bates Studio. After completion of this first series they entered into a new contract with the Bates Dance Studio whereby they undertook to take a total of 600 one-half hour lessons. These lessons were interrupted due to illness in the family and upon the Seales' resuming classes they were told that the remainder of the lessons would be given at the Dale Studio. They then went to the Dale Studio to discuss the situation and were there advised by one of the former Bates employees, who was then working for Dale, that the latter had assumed the obligations of the Bates contracts. The Seales were told that the "students and the instructors, the entire organization was transferred to the Dale Studios; that we would have the same instructors, the same instruction, a continuation of what we had had at Bates." They proceeded to take lessons at Dale, but after some 30 one-half hours of instruction they became dissatisfied with the conditions. This dissatisfaction arose from the fact that the room was much smaller and more crowded and the music from another room interfered with the lessons. Each of the Seales did not have his or her own instructor, Mr. Seale being required to take his lessons from a male instructor; there were difficulties in getting appointments and on some occasions when appointments were made an instructor would not be available. Mr. and Mrs. Seale complained to the management of the Dale Studio, but the conditions did not improve. After two or three lessons at Dale, Mr. Seale had demanded that he have a former instructor, Miss Valie, and though he was assured that he could and although he made repeated requests, Miss Valie was never available to him. As a result of this dissatisfaction, Mr. and Mrs. Seale stopped taking lessons in May of 1957. The following August they complained to Mr. John Bates of the Bates Studio and demanded that he refund their money or make proper arrangements for completing their contract. Bates informed them that his school was then closed and that there was no money to reimburse them. Later, in August of 1957, Mr. Bates attended a meeting of 13 or 14 of his former pupils for the purpose of discussing the problems which had arisen as a result of the assignment of the contracts. He then assured the persons in attendance that he would speak to the manager of the Dale Studio and he did so. At the trial, in answer to a question as to why he continued to take lessons at the Dale Studios, Seale explained "I kept hoping that somebody would get the thing arranged to where we could continue as had been promised."

The grievances of the plaintiff Hanscome are similar to those of the Seales. * * *

* * *

The cause was tried to the court and at the close of plaintiffs' testimony, which included cross-examination of Bates, the court dismissed the plaintiffs' claims and entered informal findings and conclusions, giving these reasons:

The complaint against Bates was dismissed on the ground that the Bates Dance Studio, Inc., a corporation, was the contracting party. The basis for dispositions as to the Bates and Dale Studios was the assent of the plaintiffs to the assumption by Dale of the obligations under the contracts; that this acceptance of Dale was apparent from the plaintiffs' conduct. The court further found that neither Dale nor Bates had defaulted; that the contract did not require that a certain instructor be furnished or that instruction be given at appointed times. It was also pointed out that there was no evidence of refusal on the part of the defendants to give the number of lessons guaranteed by the contract. The court rejected plaintiffs' theory that the plaintiffs consented to the assignment on any kind of conditional basis and that essentially dissatisfaction did not arise from the assignment but rather arose in connection with the terms of performance.

* * *

A further stipulation of the form contract signed by both the plaintiffs is relevant. It provides:

"I fully understand that *this agreement cannot be cancelled,* that my failure to take the lessons contracted for shall not relieve me of my obligations hereunder; and that any delay on your part in proceeding against me after any default by me shall not be deemed a waiver of any of your rights. This agreement expresses our entire understanding and agreement, and neither you nor I shall be bound by any statements, representations or understandings not stated and set forth herein."

* * *

The argument of plaintiffs that this was a personal service contract and therefore non-assignable without their consent is valid. This assignment did not result in release of the assignor. 4 Corbin, Contracts, 476 (1951). 1 Restatement, Contracts, § 160(4) (1932). This, however, does not furnish a reason for holding that plaintiffs are now entitled to recover. On the contrary, there *is* evidence to support the trial court's finding and conclusion that the plaintiffs accepted the assignment as such; they did not elect to rescind when it was brought to their attention that the contracts had been assigned to Dale Dance Studio. The undisputed evidence shows that they accepted the assignment and proceeded to take lessons from the Dale Dance Studio. This conduct is inconsistent with plaintiffs' present theory that they at all times objected to the assignment. Had they refused to receive instruction from Dale and had they taken the position that their contract was with Bates and no other, there would be substance to their present contention that this violation justified the rescission.

We turn now to the question of whether the matters of complaint appearing in the evidence were sufficiently substantial to justify rescission. It is to be noted that none of these matters are specifically treated in the contract. In other words, there are no stipulations relative to the size of the ballroom or the number of people participating, or that the instruction will always be given by one of the opposite sex. While we sympathize with Mr. Seale's preference for Miss Valie over Mr. Ritchie, we do not consider this a breach of a promise implicit in the contract. Apparently Mr. Ritchie was assigned to Mr. and Mrs. Seale. It is probable that Mrs. Seale preferred to be taught by Mr. Ritchie. It thus appears to us that the proper remedy for this problem is an express stipulation in the contract requiring a partner of the opposite sex.

We are called upon to determine whether from the nature of this instruction contract we must imply stipulations of the kind which plaintiffs say existed and were violated. Considered in this context, we conclude that the plaintiffs cannot succeed. *First,* the warranties which the plaintiffs would have us read into the contracts do not arise by necessary implication. *Secondly,* these breaches cannot be regarded as sufficiently substantial to justify the remedy of rescission. *Thirdly,* there is a failure of proof with respect to the essential element set forth in the complaint, namely, a refusal on the part of the Dale Dance Studio to furnish lessons. All of the evidence supports the finding that Dale was willing to continue the lessons.

The above factors and considerations must be weighed in the light of the express stipulation in the contract that it is non-cancellable and that the monies cannot be returned. Its presence in the contract is entitled to some weight against the contentions of plaintiffs that implied provisions of the contract have been violated. In the light of such a stipulation, the plaintiffs cannot raise the inconsequential variations in the course of instruction as a ground for rescission. Stipulations of the contract will not be implied unless the surrounding circumstances require it.

* * *

The case of Barngrover v. Maack, 46 Mo.App. 407, further illustrates the workings of the applicable principle. There the proprietor of a school undertook in his prospectus to teach specific branches of study by thus advertising. It was held that he had undertaken to teach in the listed areas and it was also held that there was an inability to speak English and thus be able to communicate with the students. It was concluded that there was sufficient evidence to justify submission of the case to the jury. See also Kentucky Military Institute v. Cohen, 131 Ark. 121, 198 S.W. 874, L.R.A. 1918B, 709. There it was held that mistreatment of a student justified his withdrawal from the school. Restitution plus incidental damages were there held to be recoverable. Here again the case illustrates that breach of an implied stipulation must involve an important or substantial part of the performance. Cf. Timmerman v. Stanley, 123 Ga. 850, 51 S.E. 760, 1 L.R.A., N.S., 379, wherein the school abandoned the contract and ceased the teaching after payment had been made. Cf. also 5 Williston on Contracts 4069, sec. 1457.

It follows that the only substantial breach of the contract apparent from a careful reading of the record here is the assignment to the Dale Dance Studio. Had plaintiffs refused to accept this, there would have been a remedy by rescission or perhaps in breach of contract and they could have recovered at least the unused portion of the consideration. Accordingly the trial court's finding and conclusion that the plaintiffs waived any rights which may have arisen from the assignment must be upheld. Plaintiffs' conduct in accepting the transfer to Dale was in effect a waiver of this breach, and the evidence does not undisputedly show that the consent thereto was in any way conditional.

* * *

The judgment is affirmed.

SECTION 4. OTHER PROBLEMS RELATING TO ASSIGNMENT AND DELEGATION

(Calamari & Perillo 5th §§ 18.24—18.27, 18.30)

WESTERN OIL SALES CORP. v. BLISS & WETHERBEE

Commission of Appeals of Texas, 1927.
299 S.W. 637.

HARVEY, P.J. On March 7, 1923, McCamey, Sheerin & Dumas, a partnership, who will be designated herein as the sellers, held certain tracts of land under oil leases, from which they were producing oil. On that day they made and entered into the following contract of sale with Western Oil Sales Corporation, the plaintiff in error, to wit:

"Agreement made and entered into on this 7th day of March, A.D.1923, by and between J.E. McCamey, J.J. Sheerin, and H.O.

Dumas a partnership, as party of the first part, and the Western Oil Sales Corporation, a corporation, as party of the second part, witnesseth:

"That the party of the first part, in consideration of the premises and agreements hereinafter contained, and by the party of the second part to be done, kept, paid, performed, and carried out, hereby sells and agrees to deliver to said party of the second part, in tanks, at its wells, all of the crude oil produced from said wells located in what is known as the Pioneer oil field at Pioneer, Eastland county, Tex., and on four leases known as the Armstrong lease consisting of 20 acres more or less; the Armstrong lease consisting of 60 acres more or less; the Moore lease consisting of 30 acres more or less; the Moore lease consisting of 10 acres more or less.

"The party of the first part agrees to sell and deliver the oil from the above-described leases to the party of the second part for a period of six months from the date the party of the second part connects up and begins running the oil, subject to the terms and conditions of a certain division order, a copy of which is hereto attached. It is agreed that in case of any conflict of terms between the said division order and this contract, the terms of this contract shall govern.

"In consideration whereof, party of the second part hereby agrees to lay its gathering lines to and connect same with the tanks of the party of the first part and to run oil therefrom, and to pay therefor the posted market price of the Prairie Pipe Line Company for crude oil on the date said oil is run by the party of the second part, plus 25 cents per barrel premium.

"This agreement shall extend to and be binding on the parties hereto, their heirs, executors, administrators, successors, and assigns.

"In witness whereof, the parties hereto have hereunto set their hands and seals on the day and year hereinabove written."

By mutual consent of the contracting parties, no division order was attached to the contract, as mentioned therein, and the contract was put in operation without such division order. The terms of the contract were carried out by the parties for about three months, when the plaintiff in error, who will be designated herein as the Western Corporation, assigned the foregoing instrument to the American Oil Company; the latter company assuming all obligations of the Western Corporation under the instrument, and acquiring all its rights thereunder. Thereupon the Western Corporation notified the sellers of such assignment, demanding that they look to the American Oil Company for their pay for all future deliveries of oil under the contract of sale, and disclaiming and renouncing all liability on the part of said corporation for any future deliveries of oil under the contract. The American Oil Company, claiming to have succeeded to all the obligations of the Western Corporation under the contract of sale, as well as to the rights of the corporation thereunder, made demand of the sellers that the latter continue to make deliveries of oil to said oil company under the sale contract; the said oil company being solvent at the time. This demand was refused by the sellers, except upon condition that the Western Corporation should recognize its liability under the contract, which the said corporation refused to do, but reiterated its renunciation of liability thereunder. This attitude of the Western Corporation was maintained by it on the asserted ground, which is urged here also, that because the contract of sale, by its terms, ran to the assigns of the contracting parties, the assignment that had been made to the American Oil Company had effect to transfer to that company the obligations of the Western Corporation under the contract of sale and to relieve the corporation of those obligations. The sellers treated the contract of sale in question as terminated. On July 13, 1923, they conveyed their leaseholds to the defendants in error, Bliss & Wetherbee, and assigned to them all their rights and claims against the Western Corporation growing out of the contract of sale in question. The defendants in error thereafter brought this suit against the Western Corporation for damages resulting from its alleged breach of said contract of sale in repudiating its liability under the contract, as stated above. The trial court found as a fact that the sellers and their assignees, the defendants in error, exercised due diligence in minimizing their damage resulting from said breach, and rendered judgment for the defendants in error for $4,420.25 damages. The Court of Civil Appeals affirmed that judgment. 292 S.W. 640.

The contract of sale, at the time it was made, was wholly executory, and was constituted of the promise of the sellers, on the one hand, to the effect that they or their assigns would sell and deliver to the Western Corporation, or its assigns, the oil produced from the leaseholds named, as it was produced during the six months' period named in the contract, and, on the other hand, of the promise of that corporation to the effect that it or its assigns would pay for the oil thus delivered, as stipulated in the contract. These obligations of the respective parties were interdependent, and there is no provision in the contract for the release of either promisor by the substitution of the promise of another. The provision declaring that the agreement should extend to and be binding on the assigns of the parties is not to be construed as authorizing such a release.

The mere fact that a contract is invested, by consent of the parties or otherwise, with the quality of assignability, does not signify that either party may, by assigning the contract, release himself from liability under it. When a contract is assignable, a party may assign the benefits of his contract to another, and delegate to his assignee the performance of his obligations under the contract; but he remains liable for the proper performance of those obligations, unless the other party to the contract consents for the assignment to have the effect of releasing him. 5 C.J. § 45, p. 878, and authorities there cited.

The Western Corporation was not released from its contract by the assignment to the American Oil Company. The unexecuted portion of the contract remained constituted, as it was in the beginning, of the mutual promises of the contracting parties. When, therefore, the corporation repudiated all liability for future deliveries of oil, it committed an anticipatory breach, and the sellers thereupon became entitled to terminate the contract. * * *

The contract having been thus terminated, the sellers' obligation to make future deliveries of oil under it was released; and the sellers were under no obligation which required them to substitute the promise of the American Oil Company for that of the Western Corporation which had been repudiated. Nor was it the duty of the sellers, in order to minimize their damage, to waive the breach and continue to deliver oil to the oil company under the contract. Nor is the evidence such as to establish, as a matter of law, that the sellers, or the defendants in error, failed to exercise ordinary prudence and diligence to mitigate the damage flowing from said breach.

We recommend that the judgment of the Court of Civil Appeals affirming the judgment of the trial court be affirmed.

KAGAN v. K–TEL ENTERTAINMENT, INC.

N.Y. Supreme Court, Appellate Division, 1991.
172 A.D.2d 375, 568 N.Y.S.2d 756.

MEMORANDUM DECISION. Order of the Supreme Court, New York County (William Davis, J.), entered December 22, 1989, which denied defendant Metro–Goldwyn–Mayer/United Artists Entertainment Company's motion for summary judgment dismissing the complaint, unanimously reversed, on the law, and the complaint dismissed, without costs. The Clerk is directed to enter judgment in favor of said defendant dismissing the complaint as to it.

Plaintiffs International Program Consultants, Inc. ("IPC") and its principal shareholder, officer and director, Russell J. Kagan, were engaged by defendant K–Tel Entertainment, Inc. ("K–Tel") to place a pilot and locate a distributor for a successful television series entitled "Kids, Incorporated." Plaintiffs placed the series with defendant Metro–Goldwyn–Mayer/United Artists Entertainment Company ("MGM/UA") which entered into a written agreement with K–Tel dated February 8, 1984 pursuant to which MGM/UA agreed to pay certain fixed amounts for each episode.

It does not appear that the agreement between K–Tel and plaintiffs was ever reduced to writing. However, IPC was paid $15,000 for the sale of the pilot by K–Tel, which also paid a $10,000 advance towards sums due on the first eight programs in the series. K–Tel had produced only those eight episodes when it fell into financial difficulty. MGM/UA thereupon notified K–Tel that it intended to remove it as producer of the series pursuant to paragraph 12 of their agreement. At this time, MGM/UA had paid K–Tel all monies due under the written agreement.

In an attempt to cure its default under the contract with MGM/UA, K–Tel assigned its rights and obligations thereunder to Hal Roach

Entertainment, Inc. ("Roach"). MGM/UA was not a party to the assignment agreement but, in a separate agreement signed by K–Tel, Roach and MGM/UA, it agreed to the substitution of Roach as producer in K–Tel's stead. On October 25, 1984, K–Tel filed a voluntary bankruptcy petition under Chapter 11 of the Bankruptcy Code (11 USC). Plaintiffs, in their brief, state that Roach has now also filed a similar petition.

In this action, plaintiffs seek to recover from MGM/UA the amount allegedly agreed to be paid to them by the producer (K–Tel and, later, Roach), that is, 10 percent of the amount paid by MGM/UA for the entire series of some 26 episodes. While plaintiffs purport to state six causes of action, the gravamen of their complaint is that MGM/UA received the benefits associated with being the distributor for the series and should therefore be held liable to plaintiffs for their 10 percent fee on a theory of unjust enrichment.

Plaintiffs' claim is without merit. As reflected in the common law of the various states, to recover under a theory of quasi contract, a plaintiff must demonstrate that services were performed for the defendant resulting in its unjust enrichment (Kapral's Tire Svc. v. Aztek Tread Corp., 124 A.D.2d 1011, 1013, 508 N.Y.S.2d 777). It is not enough that the defendant received a benefit from the activities of the plaintiff (Armstrong v. I.T.T.S. Corp., 10 A.D.2d 711, 198 N.Y.S.2d 641); if services were performed at the behest of someone other than the defendant, the plaintiff must look to that person for recovery (Citrin v. Columbia Broadcasting, 29 A.D.2d 740, 286 N.Y.S.2d 706). Plaintiffs have offered no authority which indicates that California law is any different in this regard (see, Truestone, Inc. v. Simi West Indus. Park II, 163 Cal.App.3d 715, 209 Cal.Rptr. 757; Neptune Gunite Co. v. Monroe Ents, 229 Cal.App.2d 439, 40 Cal.Rptr. 367).

The case of Callano v. Oakwood Park Homes Corp. (91 N.J.Super. 105, 219 A.2d 332) is illustrative. There, the plaintiff planted shrubbery on property owned by the defendant at the request of one Pendergast who was the contract vendee. Pendergast died without paying for the shrubbery, his estate cancelled the contract of sale, and the defendant sold the lot, improved with the plaintiff's shrubbery, to another buyer. It was held that the defendant's enrichment was not unjust because the plaintiff expected payment from Pendergast, not the defendant, and because there was no privity of contract between the plaintiff and the defendant.

The matter under review is not distinguishable. Plaintiffs performed services at the request of K–Tel, locating MGM/UA as distributor for the series. K–Tel went bankrupt without making full payment under its contract with plaintiffs, Roach was substituted as producer, and defendant MGM/UA continued distribution of the series. Plaintiffs expected payment from K–Tel and lacked privity of contract with MGM/UA.

Plaintiffs' obvious remedy was to pursue their claim against K–Tel in the bankruptcy proceeding. Their failure to do so gives them no right to proceed against MGM/UA, just as the plaintiff's failure in Callano (supra) to pursue a claim against Pendergast's estate afforded no right to proceed against the seller of the property.

The assignment by K–Tel to Roach of its production agreement with MGM/UA likewise provides no basis for recovery. The mere acquiescence in the assignment by MGM/UA does not imply any obligation to assume duties owed by either the assignee or the assignor under K–Tel's separate agreement with plaintiffs. Even if, as plaintiffs assert, MGM/UA could be considered a party to the assignment, in the absence of an express assumption of those duties, it incurred no obligation. As the rule has been stated: "The mere assignment of a bilateral executory contract may not be interpreted as a promise by the assignee to the assignor to assume the performance of the assignor's duties, so as to have the effect of creating a new liability on the part of the assignee to the other party to the contract assigned" (Langel v. Betz, 250 N.Y. 159, 161–162, 164 N.E. 890). Moreover, plaintiffs do not explain why MGM/UA, which has paid the producer (K–Tel and, later Roach) pursuant to the production contract, should be required to make a duplicate payment of the amount of plaintiffs' fee, which is the producer's obligation.

Plaintiffs' other contentions have been examined and found to be without merit.

Problems

15. O, the owner of a mare, leased her to L with a guarantee of restitution if she proved barren. Soon thereafter O transferred ownership in the mare to D in partial satisfaction of a debt owed by O to D. When L was notified of the transaction L wrote to D, informing D that the mare was barren, offering to return her, and requesting a refund of the rental payments. D refused and L brought suit against D. What result?

16. X Corp. leased 125 air conditioning units from P. The lease was for a period of five years at a stipulated monthly rental. The lease contained an acceleration clause. There was also a realty mortgage on X's property which required the presence of 125 air conditioning units. The lease was recorded. X failed to make payments in June and July, and P invoked the acceleration clause. In July, X sold the property to the defendant. P notified defendant that it was owed $29,000. Defendant replied that it had not assumed any contractual obligation to P and agreed that P could remove the air conditioners. However, when the mortgagee of the realty learned of this, it informed defendant that the mortgage would be foreclosed if the units were removed and not replaced by similar units. Defendant then refused to allow P to remove the units. Is defendant contractually obligated to P?

17. D Inc. obtained approval for a subdivision on the Oregon coast. It contracted to sell the lots to purchasers who agreed to pay the price in installments prior to receipt of their deeds (what in many jurisdictions are known as contracts for deed). Each of the contracts contained a promise by D to install a water supply system for use of the purchasers. D assigned some of these contracts to X, Y and Z, giving them a deed to the parcels to which the contracts related. The balance of the contracts were assigned to K, who agreed to assume D's obligation to install the water supply system that

would service each of the lots in the subdivision. K failed to provide the water system and has been declared bankrupt. Because of the lack of water the contract purchasers have ceased to pay X, Y, and Z and the lots are practically worthless. X, Y, and Z would like to make a claim against D. Under what theory should they proceed?

SECTION 5. DEFENSES, COUNTERCLAIMS, VESTING AND LATENT EQUITIES

(Calamari & Perillo 5th §§ 18.17—18.20)

ASSOCIATES LOAN CO. v. WALKER

Supreme Court of New Mexico, 1966.
76 N.M. 520 416 P.2d 529.

SPIESS, JUDGE, Court of Appeals. The appellant, Associates Loan Company, brought suit against appellees, Earl Walker and his wife, Billie Walker, upon a written contract executed by them and involving the sale of a mechanical water softener. Appellant will be referred to as Associates, and appellees as Walkers.

Walkers were the owners of and operated a dairy farm in Roosevelt County. One, Daniel R. Partin, was engaged in the business of selling mechanical water softeners under the trade name of Lindsay Soft Water Company of Portales. On or about May 1, 1962, Partin solicited Walkers to purchase a water softener to be used by Walkers to improve the drinking water for their dairy herd. Partin represented to Walkers that through use of the device their milk production would be increased and the water softener could be paid for through such increased production.

Walkers were interested in purchasing the device if it, in fact, would increase their milk production. It was accordingly orally agreed that Partin would install a water softener at the Walker farm upon a trial basis. If, through use of the device, milk production was actually increased then Walkers would buy it. If the condition did not happen and the device did not serve to increase production as represented by Partin, the Walkers would not be obligated to buy the device and Partin would remove it from the farm.

At the time of, or subsequent to the making of the oral agreement, and at Partin's request, Walkers executed an instrument entitled "All Goods Retail Installment Contract", being the contract upon which suit was brought. The contract states that Walkers purchased the water softener for a stated sum to which was added a finance charge. The total amount was to be paid in monthly installments commencing June 6, 1962.

The contract, in addition to containing usual remedies in the event of default, provided that title to the device would remain in the seller until the price was fully paid. Partin orally agreed that the contract would not be assigned or transferred. After Partin had obtained the execution of the instrument by Walkers he caused it to be assigned to Associates. The device was installed on the Walker farm and after trial it was determined by Walkers and Partin that it had not and would not increase milk production.

Walkers made no payments upon the contract which had been assigned to Associates. A number of payments, however, were made to Associates by Partin and by a Stirman Rivers, who acquired the Partin business and assumed payment of the particular contract held by Associates, which was treated by both Partin and Rivers as Partin's obligation. The water softener was ultimately removed by Rivers from the Walker farm.

* * *

The defense, in substance, in that Partin and Walkers agreed that there would be no sale and the contract would not be effective unless after trial the water softener served to increase Walkers' milk production. This agreement was made orally at the time, or prior to the signing of the written contract. Walkers contend that the oral agreement created a condition precedent to the written contract becoming a valid obligation.

It is further asserted that since the condition failed the contract did not come into existence.

The trial court found the issues in favor of Walkers and entered judgment against Associates from which it has appealed.

It is first contended that the transaction falls within the Uniform Commercial Code, and in accordance with its provisions an assignee takes an assigned chose in action subject only to such equities and defenses between the debtor and assignee as are specified in Sec. 50A–9–318(1), N.M.S.A., 1953. It is argued that the equities or defenses so specified do not include the type of defense interposed by Walkers. Therefore, the trial court was in error in permitting Walkers to raise the defense against Associates.

The cited section is as follows:

"(1) Unless an account debtor has made an enforceable agreement not to assert defenses or claims arising out of a sale as provided in section 9–206 (50A–9–206) the rights of an assignee are subject to

(a) all the terms of the contract between the account debtor and assignor and any defense or claim arising therefrom; and

(b) any other defense or claim of the account debtor against the assignor which accrues before the account debtor receives notification of the assignment."

* * *

The fundamental rule of law, unchanged by the quoted section of the Uniform Commercial Code, is that an assignee of a chose in action acquires by virtue of his assignment nothing more than the assignor had and all equities and defense which could have been raised by the debtor against the assignor are available to the debtor against the assignee.

This rule is so well recognized and settled that it needs no authoritative support. In our opinion, under both the statute and the rule of law, if the contract in Partin's hands was subject to a condition precedent under which it was not to become effective until the happening of a contingency, upon assignment the assignee took the contract subject to the same condition. The trial court correctly held that the defense raised by Walkers was available against the assignee, Associates.

Associates also invokes the parol evidence rule contending that under the rule the court should have disregarded the oral agreement between Walkers and Partin in that it contradicted and varied the terms of the written contract. Further, contention is made that Walkers are estopped to deny that the written contract represents a complete, exclusive and final agreement.

While both contentions may have merit, these questions were not urged in the trial court and thus such issues may not be raised for the first time on appeal. [Citations omitted.]

We find no error in the judgment of the district court. It is, accordingly affirmed. It is so ordered.

COOPER v. HOLDER

Supreme Court of Utah. 1968.
21 Utah 2d 40, 440 P.2d 15.

CROCKETT, CHIEF JUSTICE: The defendant City of Moab here challenges a ruling of the District Court that service upon its mayor of notice of an assignment to Joe W. Cooper of money payable by the City to the assignor, defendant Davis C. Holder, constituted notice to the City and was binding upon it.

In January of 1961, Holder borrowed $50,000 from Cooper and in March of that year entered into a contract with Moab to perform certain engineering services in the construction of water and sewer improvements. In April 1961 he borrowed $10,000 more from Cooper. As security for this second loan Holder assigned to Cooper his rights to receive the proceeds of his contract with Moab. A notice of assignment was served upon the Moab City Mayor, Kenneth E. McDougald, who accepted it and signed an acknowledgment which recited that payment would be made in accordance therewith. For some reason of which we are not aware, the City did not honor the assignment, but made the payment directly to Holder.

In October 1963 plaintiff commenced this suit against Holder for about $26,000 unpaid on the January loan, and in another count sued Moab City for $5,000 remaining unpaid upon the $10,000 loan, based on the proposition that the City had wrongfully ignored the assignment in paying money over to Holder. This appeal is taken by the City of Moab from findings and judgment against it on the latter issue.

The contention of the City is that the acknowledgment of notice of the assignment by the mayor should not be considered as creating any obligation on its behalf. It relies on Secs. 10–6–3, 10–6–5, and 10–6–9, U.C.A.1953, which set forth the powers of government of cities of the third class (Moab City) as vested in a mayor and city council of five who must vote on and approve 'all propositions to create any liability against the City'; and Sec. 10–10–61, which requires that every contract to which the City is a party must be signed by the city recorder. Upon the basis of these statutes the City urges that the mayor himself cannot enter into any contract on its behalf and that it was therefore not bound by the assignment.

This limitation upon the mayor's authority to enter into an original contract for the City is not to be questioned. There are undoubtedly sound reasons why the legislature thought that the full city council as the policy-making body should pass upon the problems involved in determining what can be done within the limits of the prerogatives of city government and its available resources to carry on the affairs of the City and provide for the needs of its inhabitants. However, when these problems have been so considered and resolved, and a contract has been entered into for that purpose, the city council's function of policy making has been fulfilled; and there is then no policy decision to be made as to whether the City will pay what it owes for the services received.

The obligation of a debtor to honor an assignment of a right to receive money payable is plainly something quite different in nature from the negotiation for and the entering into a contract for goods, property, or services in the first instance. In this case the problems involved in whether the City should enter into the contract for water and sewer improvements had been resolved when the original contract was entered into with Holder. Our concern is only with the payment by the City of money it owed for his services. Once he had acquired the right to receive the money, it was his prerogative to assign it to whomsoever he chose. When this has been done it is not essential that the debtor agree to that arrangement. Except under unusual circumstances, where the assignment relates to personal services, or something of a unique character where a party would be put to a distinct disadvantage, when the obligor receives proper notice of the assignment, he must honor it. It has been specifically so adjudged where the debtor is a municipal corporation and money due under a contract is assigned.

The question then becomes whether notice to the mayor should be deemed proper notice to the City. A study of the authorities dealing with this question indicates that the requirement of proper notice is satisfied by serving it upon an official whose duty it would be to either act upon it himself or to communicate it to others who had such duty. Instructive on this point and closely related to our case is that of Bank of Spring City v. Rhea County, wherein it was held that notice of an assignment to the plaintiff of the right to receive money payable on construction of a bridge given to one county commissioner was notice to 'the whole body of commissioners' and binding on the county. There should be no question but that this doctrine would apply to the mayor of Moab. He is the chief executive officer of the City, Sec. 10–6–23, U.C.A.1953; is affirmatively charged with the duty of giving the council information concerning the business of the City, Sec. 10–6–24, U.C.A.1953.

From what we have stated herein it will be seen that an assignment directing the City to pay money it owes to an assignee is not the kind of claim required to be submitted to the City in accordance with Sec. 10–7–77, U.C.A.1953. The City's contention in that regard is likewise without merit.

Judgment affirmed. Costs to plaintiff (respondent).

FEDERAL DEPOSIT INSURANCE CORP.
v. REGISTRY HOTEL CORP.

United States District Court, N.D. Texas, 1986.
658 F.Supp. 311.

Fish, District Judge.

This case is before the court on the motion for summary judgment of defendants Registry Hotel Corporation and Registry Dallas Associates ("Registry"). After considering the arguments of counsel and the supporting affidavits, the court concludes that the motion should be denied.

Posture of the Case

On December 10, 1985, the court denied Registry's motion for summary judgment, holding that Tex.Bus. & Com.Code § 9.318(b) (Vernon Supp.1986) governed the transaction at issue and that material issues of fact existed as to whether the assigned contract was terminated "in good faith and in accordance with reasonable commercial standards." After plaintiff, Federal Deposit Insurance Corporation ("FDIC"), apparently satisfied itself through pretrial discovery that Registry had acted in good faith and in accordance with reasonable commercial standards, it requested the opportunity to brief another issue in response to Registry's motion. The court granted the request and now addresses the newly raised issue.

* * *

Factual Background

FDIC, as receiver of Indian Springs State Bank of Kansas City, Kansas ("the Bank"), filed this case to recover loans extended to Frownfelter Construction Company ("FCC"). The following facts are undisputed:

1. The Bank made a series of loans to FCC in the total principal amount of $102,217.92. Repayment was due in May and June 1983.

2. On February 24, 1982, FCC and Registry executed a $170,000 construction contract.

3. In consideration for the loans, Stanley Frownfelter ("Frownfelter"), owner and president of FCC, signed a security agreement giving the Bank a security interest in the Registry contract.

4. On April 16, 1982, Registry accepted the assignment by executing the following acknowledgment:

> This assignment is acknowledged and accepted this 16th day of April, 1982, and assignee will be named as co-payee on any disbursement of above named contract.

J.R. Thoele, vice-president and secretary-treasurer of the Registry Hotel Corporation, signed the acknowledgment and acceptance.

5. Prior to November of 1982, Registry terminated the contract for failure of FCC to obtain the necessary bonds.

6. In November of 1982, Registry contracted with Uni–Lock Pavestone ("Pavestone"), FCC's former subcontractor, to perform the work FCC was to perform.

7. In January of 1983, Pavestone subcontracted with Frownfelter's company Pave–Lock Systems to provide labor for the installation of paving stones.

8. FCC defaulted on the loans, and FDIC sued Registry for the $102,217.92 deficiency.

BASIS OF THE SUIT

* * * The court concludes that the assignment of the Registry–FCC contract was effective.

If an account debtor fails to comply with a valid assignment and improperly pays the assignor, the account debtor may be liable to the assignee for the amount of the improper payment. * * *

FDIC contends that Registry failed to pay the Bank in accordance with the assignment. It therefore seeks to recover from Registry the outstanding amount of Frownfelter's debt.

PRELIMINARY ISSUES

Registry argues that it is not liable to FDIC as a matter of law because, as a result of FCC's breach of a material bonding condition, it terminated FCC's contract and made no payments to FCC from the date of the assignment until the present date. Thus, it concludes, termination relieved it of any obligation it may have had to FDIC.

Tex.Bus. & Com.Code Ann. § 9.318(b) (Vernon Supp.1986) provides for modification or substitution of an assigned contract:

> So far as the right to payment or a part thereof under an assigned contract has not been fully earned by performance, and notwithstanding notification of the assignment, any modification of or substitution for the contract made in good faith and in accordance with reasonable commercial standards is effective against an assignee unless the account debtor has otherwise agreed but the assignee

acquires corresponding rights under the modified or substituted contract.

Pretermitting its "good faith" argument for purposes of the present motion, FDIC contends that it acquired "corresponding rights under the modified or substituted contract," and that Registry waived any defense it might have had to the original contract by entering into the new agreement. The court need not address the latter contention because its conclusion as to the former argument is dispositive.

FDIC contends that "[d]etermining whether the particular contractual gyrations between Registry, Frownfelter, and Pavestone constitute the type of arrangement that qualifies as a substituted or modified contract with concommitant corresponding rights for the assignee is necessarily a factual issue" (Letter Brief of February 11, 1986 at 2). To substantiate its proposition, FDIC relies on the following portion of a law review article written by the assistant reporter and later reporter of Article Nine of the Uniform Commercial Code:

> If the new arrangement is far enough removed, in time or in subject matter, from the original contract, it may be assumed that the "corresponding rights" claim would fail. On the other hand, if the new arrangement follows hard on the heels of the original contract and deals roughly with the same subject matter, then it seems that the assignee should be entitled to his "corresponding rights".…

Gilmore, *The Assignee of Contract Rights and His Precarious Security,* 74 Yale L.J. 217, 258 (1964). FDIC contends that Gilmore enunciates a "reasonableness" standard which necessarily is a factual issue.

The court concludes that, as least for purposes of this case, the issue of corresponding rights is a legal question. Resolution of the instant motion does not require resolving the temporal connection or the subject matter identity of the various contracts but, rather, requires construction of a statute, an issue of law.

FDIC argues that § 9.318(b) is not limited strictly to modifications or substitutions but encompasses a termination or rescission of a contract. For purposes of this motion, the court assumes, without deciding, that the terms "modification" and "substitution" include terminations and rescissions.

ANALYSIS

FDIC argues that it has corresponding rights in the new contract because, in spite of the termination of the FCC contract, Frownfelter performed an active role throughout the construction project. Thus, regardless of the entrance of a third party (Pavestone) into the contractual relationships, FDIC reasons, the same parties performed the same functions. Consequently, according to FDIC, money paid to Frownfelter, either directly by Registry or indirectly through Pavestone, should have been paid to FDIC, so that Registry is liable to FDIC for amounts so paid.

FDIC does not identify in which of the two new contracts it claims corresponding rights. Registry originally contracted with FCC. Upon FCC's failure to secure the requisite bonds, Registry terminated the original agreement and contracted with Pavestone to perform the work FCC was to perform. Pavestone then subcontracted with Pave–Lock, Frownfelter's new company, for labor on the project.

Consequently, no single contract was substituted for the original agreement. Pavestone was not a party to the original contract and there is no showing that it knew of the prior financing arrangement. Further, Registry could not pay FDIC by withholding a portion of the money contractually owed Pavestone without breaching the Pavestone agreement. Nor could Pavestone pay FDIC sums it contractually owed Pave–Lock. Apparently, no contract in any form between Registry and Pavestone, on the one hand, or Pavestone and Pave–Lock on the other, was ever assigned, and neither Registry nor Pave–Lock ever executed an acknowledgment of assignment of the new contracts. Neither contract existed in a prior form so as to qualify as a substitution or modification of an earlier contract.

Thus, since the original parties to the assigned contract were not in privity after the breach, FDIC could not acquire corresponding rights in any new contracts. The new contracts simply did not correspond to the original agreement, and the twin facts that both Registry and Frownfelter were parties to the same general transaction and that Registry was aware of Frownfelter's new role at the time the Registry–Pavestone contract was executed are of no legal effect for purposes of FDIC's claim to corresponding rights.

FDIC contends that Comment 2 to 9–318 supports its claim to corresponding rights. That Comment posits a government agency forced to cut back or modify existing contracts. Section 9–318(2), according to the Comment, permits the prime contractor, the account debtor, to make comparable arrangements with its subcontractors "without undertaking the task of procuring assets from the many banks to whom rights under the contracts may have been assigned."

The court concludes that the Comment does not fortify FDIC's position. The example contemplates execution of new contracts between parties to the original contracts, not the addition of a third party to a transaction and an alteration of contractual privity.

The construction of 9–318(2) advanced herein does not leave an aggrieved assignee without recourse. The assignee is protected by the provision of § 9–318(2) requiring good faith and commercial reasonableness. Thus, modifications or substitutions that are fraudulent or intended to circumvent the assignee's rights are ineffective against the assignee.

CONCLUSION

The court reaffirms its prior order, concluding that the only remaining factual issues, if any, are whether the modification or substitution at issue was undertaken in good faith and in accordance with commercial reasonableness. Accordingly, Registry's motion for summary judgment is DENIED.

SO ORDERED.

FALL RIVER TRUST CO. v. B.G. BROWDY, INC.

Supreme Judicial Court of Massachusetts, 1964.
346 Mass. 614, 195 N.E.2d 63.

WHITTEMORE, JUSTICE. This is the defendant's appeal from an order for judgment for the plaintiff for $7,596.93 in an action on assigned accounts. The defendant declared in set-off to the extent of the plaintiff's claim—in count 1 for the value of goods delivered to the plaintiff's assignor subject to the defendant's order and not returned, and in count 2 for money had and received.

* * *

The agreement as to the facts presented a case stated. Quintin Vespa Co., Inc. v. Construction Serv. Co., 343 Mass. 547, 551–552, 179 N.E.2d 895. It is our duty to order the correct judgment on the auditor's report. Ibid. We may draw inferences. G.L., c. 231, § 126. The facts, however, are inadequate for a conclusion.

The facts shown by the auditor's scanty report are these: Watuppa Finishing Corp. (Watuppa) was engaged in the dyeing and finishing business in Fall River and was adjudicated a bankrupt in July of 1959. The defendant (Browdy) from time to time delivered goods to Watuppa for dyeing and finishing. "Watuppa had an arrangement with the bank under which the bank advanced money from time to time and took assignments of accounts receivable as security and notified Browdy of the assignment in each instance before payment, and payment was made by Browdy to the bank in each instance, excepting the unpaid accounts" in litigation. These are the accounts outstanding at the time of the bankruptcy in the amount of $9,496.16 assigned as security for advances of $7,596.93. The accounts represent work done on goods delivered to Watuppa between February 6, 1959, and June 6, 1959. These accounts were assigned to the bank on various days from June 12 through June 26, 1959.

The auditor found that Watuppa had received from Browdy 89,199 yards of goods valued at $42,393.10, that these goods had not been returned, and that "Watuppa owes Browdy at least $7,596.93 * * *." The financing statements required by G.L. c. 106, § 9–302(1), were duly executed and filed October 8, 1958.

The case is governed by G.L. c. 106, § 9–318(1). Browdy contends that it is to be inferred that the $42,393.10 represents the goods delivered to Watuppa between February 6, 1959, and June 6, 1959. If this were so and the missing goods were processed under the contracts which gave rise to the assigned accounts, it would make no difference when the plaintiff gave Browdy notice of the assignment. The rights of the assignee would be subject to any defense or claim arising from the terms of the bailment contract between the assignor and the account debtor regardless of notice. G.L. c. 106, § 9–318(1)(a). However, the auditor's report does not show whether the missing goods were processed under the contracts which gave rise to the assigned accounts. The facts stated are insufficient satisfactorily to support an inference and we may not speculate.

If the goods now missing were other than those on which the accounts arose, G.L. c. 106, § 9–318(1)(b), would be applicable and whether the bank's rights would be subject to Browdy's claim would hinge on whether Browdy's claim accrued before it received notice of the assignments. The auditor's report does not show when notice of the various assignments was sent or received nor does it show when the claim of the defendant accrued. The facts do not show, as the defendant contends, that its claim accrued at the time the goods were delivered to the assignor. The record fails to show whether the claim arose because the goods were destroyed as a result of the assignor's negligence (compare Rourke v. Cadillac Auto. Co., 268 Mass. 7, 167 N.E. 231), or because the assignor intentionally departed from the terms of the bailment by an act inconsistent with the defendant's ownership (compare Spooner v. Manchester, 133 Mass. 270, 274–275), or because there was a contractual extension of the bailee's common law liability by an unconditional promise to return the goods (compare Amiro v. Crowley, 256 Mass. 53, 57, 152 N.E. 78).

* * *

The order for judgment is reversed and the case is remanded to the Superior Court for a determination of the necessary facts either on a recommittal or a new reference or by the court as it shall determine.

Problems

18. D, a distributor, who sold goods and billed customers in D's own name was in fact the agent of M, a manufacturer. A is the assignee of D. What are the relative rights of A and M?

19. B and O entered into a building contract. B (builder) assigned its rights under the contract to C, a Bank. C immediately gave notice of its assignment to O. At the time of the assignment, O owed B $100,000. However, B defaulted in the work, and became liable to O in the amount of $150,000. What are the rights of the parties?

Chapter 13

THE STATUTE OF FRAUDS

SECTION 1. THE ONE YEAR PROVISION

(Calamari & Perillo 5th §§ 19.1, 19.35, 19.17—19.22, 19.36, 19.25)

C.R. KLEWIN, INC. v. FLAGSHIP PROPERTIES, INC.

Supreme Court of Connecticut, 1991.
220 Conn. 569, 600 A.2d 772.

PETERS, CHIEF JUSTICE. The sole question before us in this certified appeal is whether the provision of the statute of frauds, General Statutes § 52–550(a)(5), requiring a writing for an "agreement that is not to be performed within one year from the making thereof," renders unenforceable an oral contract that fails to specify explicitly the time for performance when performance of that contract within one year of its making is exceedingly unlikely. This case comes to this court upon our grant of an application for certification from the United States Court of Appeals for the Second Circuit pursuant to General Statutes § 51–199a. C.R. Klewin, Inc. v. Flagship Properties, Inc., 936 F.2d 684 (2d Cir.1991).

The Second Circuit has provided us with the following facts. * * * The plaintiff, C.R. Klewin, Inc. (Klewin), is a Connecticut based corporation that provides general construction contracting and construction management services. The defendants, Flagship Properties and DKM Properties (collectively Flagship), are engaged in the business of real estate development; although located outside Connecticut, they do business together in Connecticut under the trade name Conn–Tech.

Flagship became the developer of a major project (ConnTech Project) in Mansfield, near the University of Connecticut's main campus. The master plan for the project included the construction of twenty industrial buildings, a 280 room hotel and convention center, and housing for 592 graduate students and professors. The estimated total cost of the project was $120 million.

In March, 1986, Flagship representatives held a dinner meeting with Klewin representatives. Flagship was considering whether to engage Klewin to serve as construction manager on the ConnTech Project. During the discussions, Klewin advised that its fee would be 4 percent of the cost of construction plus 4 percent for its overhead and profit. This fee structure was, however, subject to change depending on when different phases of the project were to be constructed. The meeting ended with Flagship's representative shaking hands with Klewin's agent and saying, "You've got the job. We've got a deal." No other specific terms or conditions were conclusively established at trial. The parties publicized the fact that an agreement had been reached and held a press conference, which was videotaped. Additionally, they ceremoniously signed, without filling in any of the blanks, an American Institute of Architects Standard Form of Agreement between Owner and Construction Manager.

Construction began May 4, 1987, on the first phase of the ConnTech Project, called Celeron Square. The parties entered into a written agreement regarding the construction of this one part of the project. Construction was fully completed by the middle of October, 1987. By that time, because Flagship had become dissatisfied with Klewin's work, it began negotiating with other contractors for the job as construction manager on the next stage of the ConnTech Project. In March, 1988, Flagship contracted with another contractor to perform the sitework for Celeron Square II, the next phase of the project.

After having been replaced as construction manager, Klewin filed suit in the United States District Court for the District of Connecticut, claiming (1) breach of an oral contract to perform as construction manager on all phases of the project; (2) quantum meruit recovery for services performed in anticipation of future stages of the project; and (3) detrimental reliance on Flagship's promise to pay for preconstruction services. Flagship moved for summary judgment, claiming, inter alia, that enforcement of the alleged oral contract was barred by the statute of frauds. The district court granted summary judgment, reasoning that (1) "the contract was not of an indefinite duration or open-ended" because full performance would take place when all phases of the ConnTech Project were completed, and (2) the contract "as a matter of law" could not possibly have been performed within one year. In drawing this second conclusion, the court focused on the sheer scope of the project and Klewin's own admission that the entire project was intended to be constructed in three to ten years.

Klewin appealed to the United States Court of Appeals for the Second Circuit. The Court of Appeals held that "the issues presented involve substantial legal questions for which there is no clear precedent under the decisions of the Connecticut Supreme Court"; * * * and certified to this court the following questions:[1]

"A. Whether under the Connecticut Statute of Frauds, Conn.Gen. Stat. § 52–550(a)(5), an oral contract that fails to specify explicitly the time for performance is a contract of 'indefinite duration,' as that term has been used in the applicable Connecticut precedent, and therefore outside of the Statute's proscriptions?

---

1. These certified questions do not involve the question, which these facts raise, of whether the alleged oral contract was too vague to be enforceable. See Dunham v. Dunham, 204 Conn. 303, 313, 528 A.2d 1123 (1987).

"B. Whether an oral contract is unenforceable when the method of performance called for by the contract contemplates performance to be completed over a period of time that exceeds one year, yet the contract itself does not explicitly negate the possibility of performance within one year?" * * * We answer "yes" to the first question, and "no" to the second.

I

The Connecticut statute of frauds has its origins in a 1677 English statute entitled "An Act for the prevention of Fraud and Perjuries." See 6 W. Holdsworth, A History of English Law (1927) pp. 379–84. The statute appears to have been enacted in response to developments in the common law arising out of the advent of the writ of assumpsit, which changed the general rule precluding enforcement of oral promises in the King's courts. Thereafter, perjury and the subornation of perjury became a widespread and serious problem. Furthermore, because juries at that time decided cases on their own personal knowledge of the facts, rather than on the evidence introduced at trial, a requirement, in specified transactions, of "some memorandum or note ... in writing, and signed by the party to be charged" placed a limitation on the uncontrolled discretion of the jury. See 2 A. Corbin, Contracts (1950) § 275, pp. 2–3; 6 W. Holdsworth, supra, pp. 387–89; An Act for Prevention of Fraud and Perjuries, 29 Car. 2, c. 3, § 4 (1677), quoted in J. Perillo, "The Statute of Frauds in the Light of the Functions and Dysfunctions of Form," 43 Fordham L.Rev. 39, 39 n. 2 (1974). Although the British Parliament repealed most provisions of the statute, including the one-year provision, in 1954; see The Law Reform (Enforcement of Contracts) Act, 2 & 3 Eliz. 2, c. 34 (1954); the statute nonetheless remains the law virtually everywhere in the United States.[5]

Modern scholarly commentary has found much to criticize about the continued viability of the statute of frauds. The statute has been found wanting because it serves none of its purported functions very well; see J. Perillo, supra; and because it permits or compels economically wasteful behavior; see M. Braunstein, "Remedy, Reason, and the Statute of Frauds: A Critical Economic Analysis," 1989 Utah L.Rev. 383. It is, however, the one-year provision that is at issue in this case that has caused the greatest puzzlement among commentators. As Professor Farnsworth observes, "of all the provisions of the statute, it is the most difficult to rationalize."

"If the one-year provision is based on the tendency of memory to fail and of evidence to go stale with the passage of time, it is ill-contrived because the one-year period does not run from the making of the contract to the proof of the making, but from the making of the contract to the completion of performance. If an oral contract that cannot be performed within a year is broken the day after its making, the provision applies though the terms of the contract are fresh in the minds of the

---

5. "The one-year provision has been omitted in North Carolina and Pennsylvania." 2 E. Farnsworth, Contracts (2d Ed.1990) § 6.4, p. 110 n. 5.

parties. But if an oral contract that can be performed within a year is broken and suit is not brought until nearly six years (the usual statute of limitations for contract actions) after the breach, the provision does not apply, even though the terms of the contract are no longer fresh in the minds of the parties.

"If the one-year provision is an attempt to separate significant contracts of long duration, for which writings should be required, from less significant contracts of short duration, for which writings are unnecessary, it is equally ill-contrived because the one-year period does not run from the commencement of performance to the completion of performance, but from the making of the contract to the completion of performance. If an oral contract to work for one day, 13 months from now, is broken, the provision applies, even though the duration of performance is only one day. But if an oral contract to work for a year beginning today is broken, the provision does not apply, even though the duration of performance is a full year." 2 E. Farnsworth, Contracts (2d Ed.1990) § 6.4, pp. 110–11 (footnotes omitted); see also Goldstick v. ICM Realty, 788 F.2d 456, 464 (7th Cir.1986); D & N Boening, Inc. v. Kirsch Beverages, Inc., 63 N.Y.2d 449, 454, 472 N.E.2d 992, 483 N.Y.S.2d 164 (1984); 1 Restatement (Second), Contracts (1979) § 130, comment a; J. Calamari & J. Perillo, Contracts (3d Ed.1987) § 19–18, p. 807.

Historians have had difficulty accounting for the original inclusion of the one-year provision. Some years after its enactment, one English judge stated that "the design of the statute was, not to trust to the memory of witnesses for a longer time than one year." Smith v. Westall, 1 Ld.Raym. 316, 317, 91 Eng.Rep. 1106, 1107 (1697). That explanation is, however, unpersuasive, since, as Farnsworth notes, the language of the statute is ill suited to this purpose. One eminent historian suggested that because such contracts are continuing contracts, it might be very difficult to give evidence of their formation, inasmuch as the rules of evidence of that time prohibited testimony by the parties to an action or any person who had an interest in the litigation. 6 W. Holdsworth, supra, 392. That argument, however, proves too much, since it would apply equally to all oral contracts regardless of the duration of their performance. The most extensive recent study of the history of English contract law offers plausible explanations for all of the other provisions, but acknowledges that this one is "curious." A. Simpson, A History of the Common Law of Contract (1975) p. 612. More recently, it has been suggested that the provision "may have been intended to prevent oral perjury in actions of assumpsit against customers who had forgotten the details of their purchases." P. Hamburger, "The Conveyancing Purposes of the Statute of Frauds," 27 Am.J.Leg.Hist. 354, 376 n. 85 (1983).

In any case, the one-year provision no longer seems to serve any purpose very well, and today its only remaining effect is arbitrarily to forestall the adjudication of possibly meritorious claims. For this reason, the courts have for many years looked on the provision with disfavor, and have sought constructions that limited its application. See, e.g., Landes Construction Co. v. Royal Bank of Canada, 833 F.2d 1365, 1370

(9th Cir.1987) (noting policy of California courts "of restricting the application of the statute to those situations precisely covered by its language"); Cunningham v. Healthco, Inc., 824 F.2d 1448, 1455 (5th Cir.1987) (one-year provision does not apply if the statute "conceivably" can be performed within one year); Hodge v. Evans Financial Corporation, 823 F.2d 559, 561 (D.C.Cir.1987) (statute of frauds "has long been construed narrowly and literally"); Goldstick v. ICM Realty, supra, at 464 ("Courts tend to take the concept of 'capable of full performance' quite literally ... because they find the one-year limitation irksome.")

II

Our case law in Connecticut, like that in other jurisdictions, has taken a narrow view of the one-year provision of the statute of frauds now codified as § 52–550(a)(5). In Russell v. Slade, 12 Conn. 455, 460 (1838), this court held that "it has been repeatedly adjudged, that unless it appear from the agreement itself, that it is not to be performed within a year, the statute does not apply.... The statute of frauds plainly means an agreement not to be performed within the space of a year, and expressly and specifically so agreed. A contingency is not within it; nor any case that depends upon contingency. It does not extend to cases where the thing only may be performed within the year." (Emphases in original; citation and internal quotation marks omitted.)

* * *

More recently, in Finley v. Aetna Life & Casualty Co., 202 Conn. 190, 197, 520 A.2d 208 (1987), we stated that " '[u]nder the prevailing interpretation, the enforceability of a contract under the one-year provision does not turn on the actual course of subsequent events, nor on the expectations of the parties as to the probabilities. Contracts of uncertain duration are simply excluded; the provision covers only those contracts whose performance cannot possibly be completed within a year.' (Emphasis added.) 1 Restatement (Second), Contracts, supra."

In light of this unbroken line of authority, the legislature's decision repeatedly to reenact the provision in language virtually identical to that of the 1677 statute suggests legislative approval of the restrictive interpretation that this court has given to the one-year provision. "[T]he action of the General Assembly in re-enacting the statute, including the clause in question ... is presumed to have been done in the light of those decisions." Turner v. Scanlon, 146 Conn. 149, 156, 148 A.2d 334 (1959); see also Ralston Purina Co. v. Board of Tax Review, 203 Conn. 425, 439–40, 525 A.2d 91 (1987).

III

Bearing this history in mind, we turn to the questions certified to us by the federal court. Our case law makes no distinction, with respect to exclusion from the statute of frauds, between contracts of uncertain or indefinite duration and contracts that contain no express terms defining the time for performance. The two certified questions therefore raise only one substantive issue. That issue can be framed as follows: in the exclusion from the statute of frauds of all contracts except those "whose performance cannot possibly be completed within a year"; (emphasis omitted) Finley v. Aetna Life & Casualty Co., supra, 202 Conn. at 197, 520 A.2d 208; what meaning should be attributed to the word "possibly"? One construction of "possibly" would encompass only contracts whose completion within a year would be inconsistent with the express terms of the contract. An alternate construction would include as well contracts such as the one involved in this case, in which, while no time period is expressly specified, it is (as the district court found) realistically impossible for performance to be completed within a year. We now hold that the former and not the latter is the correct interpretation. "The critical test ... is whether 'by its terms' the agreement is not to be performed within a year," so that the statute will not apply where "the alleged agreement contain[s] [no] provision which directly or indirectly regulated the time for performance." Freedman v. Chemical Construction Corporation, 43 N.Y.2d 260, 265, 372 N.E.2d 12, 401 N.Y.S.2d 176 (1977). "It is the law of this state, as it is elsewhere, that a contract is not within this clause of the statute unless its terms are so drawn that it cannot by any possibility be performed fully within one year." (Emphasis added.) Burkle v. Superflow Mfg. Co., supra, 137 Conn. [488] at 492, 78 A.2d 698 [1951].

Flagship contends, to the contrary, that the possibility to which this court referred in Burkle must be a reasonable possibility rather than a theoretical possibility. It is true that in Burkle this court rejected the argument that "since all the members of a partnership [that was a party to the contract] may possibly die within a year, the contract is not within the statute." We noted that "[n]o case has come to our attention where the rule that the possibility of death within a year removes a contract from the statute has been extended to apply to the possibility of the death of more than one individual." Id., at 494, 78 A.2d 698. In Burkle, however, we merely refused to extend further yet another of the rules by which the effect of the provision has been limited. Burkle did not purport to change the well-established rule of narrow construction of the underlying one-year provision.

Most other jurisdictions follow a similar rule requiring an express contractual provision specifying that performance will extend for more than one year. Only "[a] few jurisdictions, contrary to the great weight of authority ... hold that the intention of the parties may put their oral agreement within the operation of the Statute." 3 S. Williston, Contracts (3d Ed. W. Jaeger 1960) § 495, pp. 584–85. In "the leading case on this section of the Statute"; id., p. 578; the Supreme Court of the United States undertook an extensive survey of the case law up to that time and concluded that "[i]t ... appears to have been the settled construction of this clause of the statute in England, before the Declaration of Independence, that an oral agreement which, according to the intention of the parties, as shown by the terms of the contract, might be fully performed within a year from the time it was made, was not within the statute, although the time of its performance was uncertain, and might probably extend, and be expected by the parties to extend, and did in fact extend, beyond the year. The several States of the Union, in reenacting this provision of the statute of frauds in its original words, must be taken to have adopted the known and settled construction which it had received by judicial decisions in England." (Emphasis added.) Warner v. Texas & Pacific R. Co., 164 U.S. 418, 422–23, 17 S.Ct. 147, 149–50, 41 L.Ed. 495 (1896). The agreement at issue was one in which a lumbermill agreed to provide grading and ties and the railway agreed to construct rails and a switch and maintain the switch as long as the lumbermill needed it for shipping purposes. Although the land adjoining the lumbermill contained enough lumber to run a mill for thirty years, and the lumbermill used the switch for thirteen years, the court held that the contract was not within the statute. "The parties may well have expected that the contract would continue in force for more than one year; it may have been very improbable that it would not do so; and it did in fact continue in force for a much longer time. But they made no stipulation which in terms, or by reasonable inference, required that result. The question is not what the probable, or expected, or actual performance of the contract was; but whether the contract, according to the reasonable interpretation of its terms, required that it should not be performed within the year." (Emphasis added.) Id., at 434, 17 S.Ct. at 153–54; see also Walker v. Johnson, 96 U.S. 424, 427, 24 L.Ed. 834 (1877); McPherson v. Cox, 96 U.S. 404, 416–17, 24 L.Ed. 746 (1877).

Because the one-year provision "is an anachronism in modern life ... we are not disposed to expand its destructive force." Farmer v. Arabian American Oil Co., 277 F.2d 46, 51 (2d Cir.1960). When a contract contains no express terms about the time for performance, no sound reason of policy commends judicial pursuit of a collateral inquiry into whether, at the time of the making of the contract, it was realistically possible that performance of the contract would be completed within a year. Such a collateral inquiry would not only expand the "destructive force" of the statute by extending it to contracts not plainly within its terms, but would also inevitably waste judicial resources on the resolution of an issue that has nothing to do with the merits of the case or the attainment of a just outcome. See 2 A. Corbin, supra, § 275, p. 14 (the statute "has been in part the cause of an immense amount of litigation as to whether a promise is within the statute or can by any remote possibility be taken out of it. This latter fact is fully evidenced by the space necessary to be devoted to the subject in this volume and by the vast number of cases to be cited").

We therefore hold that an oral contract that does not say, in express terms, that performance is to have a specific duration beyond one year is, as a matter of law, the functional equivalent of a contract of indefinite duration for the purposes of the statute of frauds. Like a contract of indefinite duration, such a contract is enforceable because it is outside the proscriptive force of the statute regardless of how long completion of performance will actually take.

The first certified question is answered "yes." The second certified question is answered "no."

No costs will be taxed in this court to either party.

In this opinion the other Justices concurred.

J. M. PERILLO, THE STATUTE OF FRAUDS IN THE LIGHT OF THE FUNCTIONS AND DYSFUNCTIONS OF FORM

43 Fordham L. Rev. 39, 77 (1974).

No one knows why agreements not performable within a year were selected to be within the Statute. Usually, it is speculated that the selection of this class was motivated by a policy akin to that of the statute of limitations, *i.e.*, if the interval between the making of the promise and its proof in court is overly long, the difficulties of proof make desirable a more cogent type of evidence than testimony. If this is indeed the rationale the statute serves it poorly.[1]

———

ERHLICH v. DIGGS

United States District Court, E.D.N.Y., 2001.
169 F.Supp.2d 124.

DEARIE, DISTRICT JUDGE. Plaintiff David M. Ehrlich, a manager of musical groups, seeks a portion of defendant Robert Diggs's earnings arising from his activities as a member the Gravediggaz, a rap music group, and as a solo artist. Defendant moves to dismiss and, in the alternative, for summary judgment. The critical issues raised concern the enforceability of an oral management contract between plaintiff and the Gravediggaz. The resolution of this question, and the appropriateness of dismissal or of summary judgment, depends on the choice of law to be applied.

BACKGROUND

Plaintiff David Ehrlich is a manager of musical groups and an attorney. He conducts business under the name DME Management, and he formerly worked under the name DuKane Management. Plaintiff is a resident of California and is admitted to practice law in New York. Defendant Robert Diggs is a popular rap artist, professionally known as RZA and Prince Rakim. He is a resident of New York. Although defendant maintains an affiliation with his original musical group, known as the Gravediggaz, he has gone on to an extremely successful

---

1. It seems quite likely, however, that, as in the case of the other subdivisions, the draftsmen had in mind a transaction type: employment and similar relationships such as apprenticeships and fiduciary retainers. The common law rule was that a general hiring was presumed to be for a one-year term. 1 W. Blackstone Commentaries *425. But long-term apprenticeships, clerkships, etc. were commonplace.

career as a solo recording artist, producer and member of another rap group, the Wu Tang Clan.

On July 1, 1993, plaintiff and the Gravediggaz entered into a written contract under which the Gravediggaz retained plaintiff as their exclusive representative in negotiating a record contract with a major record label (the "Shopping/Finders Agreement"). On July 2, 1993, allegedly as a result of plaintiff's efforts, the Gravediggaz entered into a written contract with Gee Street Records (the "Gravediggaz/Gee Street Contract"). This contract contains a provision giving Gee Street an option for the recording services of defendant as a solo artist. See Ehrlich Aff. ¶ 38.

In August 1993, plaintiff was hired as the manager of the Gravediggaz pursuant to an oral agreement (the "Management Agreement"). See Ehrlich Aff. ¶ ¶ 15–23. The Management Agreement was never reduced to writing. Plaintiff claims that he was to receive fifteen percent of the gross earnings of the Gravediggaz and each of its members for "all entertainment-related employment, engagements or agreements commenced or entered into" while he served as manager of the group. In addition, the Management Agreement was terminable by either plaintiff or the group at any time. See Ehrlich Aff. ¶ 23. The enforceability of this oral contract is the primary focus of this dispute. Plaintiff contends that the duties of a manager, including the duty to advise and counsel each member of a group individually, are universally known in the music recording industry and that these understandings were shared by all parties, including defendant, at the time the oral Management Agreement was made. See Ehrlich Aff. ¶ ¶ 18–23. Moreover, according to plaintiff, it is standard industry practice that the manager of a musical group is entitled to commissions on entertainment-related work by each member of the group, whether performed individually or performed as a group member. See Complaint ¶ 13; Ehrlich Aff. ¶ ¶ 31–33.

On December 20, 1996, defendant entered into a written contract with Gee Street as a solo recording artist (the "Gee Street/Diggs Contract"). Defendant argues that this contract is independent of the earlier relationship between plaintiff and defendant. Plaintiff counters that the option given to Gee Street for defendant's individual recording services at ¶ 22 of the Gravediggaz/Gee Street Contract was largely the result of discussions between plaintiff and defendant regarding the possibility of defendant working solo and was negotiated by plaintiff at defendant's specific request. See Ehrlich Aff. ¶ 38. Because defendant ultimately contracted with Gee Street to record as an individual, the 1993 Gravediggaz/Gee Street Contract and the 1996 Gee Street/Diggs Contract are, according to plaintiff, "inextricably linked." See Ehrlich Aff. ¶ 39.

The complaint asserts five claims based on the written and oral contracts between the parties relating to periods in which defendant was a member of the Gravediggaz as well as subsequent periods in which defendant was a solo artist and member of the Wu Tang Clan. In the first claim, plaintiff seeks commissions based on defendant's earnings from individual work, both as a recording artist and as a producer. In the second claim, he seeks a portion of the "ancillary sums" earned by defendant as a result of defendant's work as a member of the Gravediggaz. Plaintiff seeks a percentage of earnings from defendant's production of two Gravediggaz albums and direction of a Gravediggaz music video in the third claim. In the fourth claim, plaintiff seeks an accounting of all sums of money received by defendant and seeks commissions due on such sums as a result of his efforts. Finally, in the fifth claim, plaintiff seeks damages for substantial cost overruns and depressed album sales suffered as a result of defendant's late or canceled appearances for Gravediggaz tours, concerts, events, recording and video sessions.

* * * Defendant * * * contends that the claims must be dismissed because enforcement of the Management Agreement is barred by the statute of frauds.

Notwithstanding defendant's detailed arguments that plaintiff's claims based on the Shopping/Finders Agreement must be dismissed, the gravamen of the complaint is that defendant breached the oral Management Agreement. See Plaintiff's Opposition to Defendant's Motion at 19; Complaint ¶ 10. Accordingly, this Court will not address the defendant's contentions with respect to the Shopping/Finders Agreement. The remaining issues are whether the enforcement of the Management Agreement is barred by the statute of frauds and whether the agreement is too indefinite to be enforced. For the reasons set forth below, this Court finds that enforcement is not barred and the agreement is not void for indefiniteness. Accordingly, defendant's motion is denied.

Discussion

The California and New York Statutes of Frauds

Defendant contends that New York law applies and that New York's Statute of Frauds bars enforcement of the oral Management Agreement. Plaintiff counters that California law should apply and that under the California Statute of Frauds, the Management Agreement is enforceable. To resolve the issue, this Court must apply New York's choice of law rules. * * * *

The relevant New York and California provisions are nearly facially identical. New York's Statute of Frauds provides:

> [e]very agreement, promise or undertaking is void, unless it or some note or memorandum thereof be in writing, and subscribed by the party to be charged therewith, or by his lawful agent, if such agreement, promise or undertaking: 1. By its terms is not to be performed within one year from the making thereof ... N.Y.Gen. Oblig.Law § 5–701(a)(1).

Similarly, California's statute provides:

> [t]he following contracts are invalid, unless they, or some note or memorandum thereof, are in writing and subscribed by the party to be charged or by the party's agent: (1) An agreement that by its

terms is not to be performed within a year from the making thereof. Cal.Civ.Code § 1624(a)(1).

However, as set forth more fully below, the statutes have been interpreted differently. California's statute has been interpreted literally and narrowly. Rosenthal v. Fonda, 862 F.2d 1398, 1401 (9th Cir.1988). Court's [sic] have held that employment contracts that are terminable at the will of either party fall outside the bar. Id. In contrast, the New York Statute of Frauds has been interpreted to bar enforcement of an employment contract requiring commission payments unless after the plaintiff has performed, "the defendant can unilaterally terminate the contract, discharging all promises made to the plaintiff including the promise to make commission payments." Id.

California Law

An oral contract is unenforceable under California law only if it expressly precludes performance within one year or by its terms cannot possibly be performed within one year. [Citations Omitted]. This has been interpreted to exempt contracts that are terminable within one year by either party from the Statute of Frauds. As set forth in Plumlee [v. Poag],

> [a]lthough the majority of jurisdictions have held that a party's option to put an end to a contract within a year does not take it out of the operation of the statute of frauds, on the grounds that to be discharged from liability under a contract is not to 'perform' it, the California rule is to the contrary: A contract ... may be taken out of [the statute of frauds's] operation by the fact that a party (or at least a defendant) may rightfully terminate it within a year.

150 Cal.App.3d at 550, 198 Cal.Rptr. 66 (footnote omitted). Because contracts that may be terminated at will by either party can, by their terms, be "performed" within one year, they are enforceable. [Citations omitted] Jenkins v. Family Health Program, 214 Cal.App.3d 440, 445–46, 262 Cal.Rptr. 798 (Cal.Dist.Ct.App.1989) (if plaintiff employee can terminate at will and defendant employer can terminate for cause, the contract is enforceable); Moreover, employment contracts providing for payment upon termination of the employment relationship or payment of a bonus ascertainable only after one year are not barred. White Lighting [Co. v. Wolfson], 68 Cal.2d at 344, 66 Cal.Rptr. 697, 438 P.2d 345.

Thus, under California law, the oral Management Agreement, as alleged, is not barred by the Statute of Frauds. Rosenthal v. Fonda, 862 F.2d 1398 (9th Cir.1988), supports this conclusion in dicta. In Rosenthal, plaintiff alleged that defendant actress Jane Fonda entered into an oral contract with him for a variety of services in exchange for a percentage of income derived from projects initiated during his tenure. Although the court ultimately applied New York law, it concluded that because the oral contract was terminable at the will of either party, the contract would fall outside California's Statute of Frauds as a contract capable of being performed within one year. Rosenthal, 862 F.2d at 1401.

New York

New York courts have interpreted the Statute of Frauds somewhat differently. The key issue in determining the applicability of New York's Statute of Frauds is whether the defendant can unilaterally terminate the contract, discharging all promises made. * * * North Shore Bottling Co. v. C. Schmidt & Sons, Inc., 22 N.Y.2d 171, 176–77, 239 N.E.2d 189, 292 N.Y.S.2d 86 (N.Y.1968); Rosenthal v. Fonda, 862 F.2d 1398, 1401 (9th Cir.1988). Contracts involving performance which is dependent on the will of a third party, and not solely upon the will of the parties to the contract, fall within the Statute of Frauds. * * * Commission sales arrangements that extend beyond an employee's termination, therefore, are barred. See, e.g, Zupan v. Blumberg, 2 N.Y.2d 547, 141 N.E.2d 819, 161 N.Y.S.2d 428 (N.Y.1957) (agreement for 25% commission on any account brought so long as account was active barred); * * * .

As alleged by plaintiff, defendant does not have a unilateral right to terminate the Management Agreement. Defendant is obligated to turn over fifteen percent of his gross earnings "for all entertainment-related employment, engagements or agreements commenced or entered into while [plaintiff] served as manager of the [Gravediggaz]." See Ehrlich Aff. ¶ 23. The earnings in which plaintiff has an interest may continue indefinitely, as recordings and other musical works sold to third parties will generate earnings far into the future. Thus, defendant has an ongoing obligation to pay plaintiff that he cannot terminate. This open-ended interest is squarely within the Statute of Frauds under New York law. See, e.g., Grossberg v. Double H. Licensing Corp., 86 A.D.2d 565, 446 N.Y.S.2d 296 (1982) (agreement to produce a record in exchange for a royalty on all records sold barred; "defendants' liability endured so long as a single record … was sold anywhere in the world"); Kantor v. Watson, 167 A.D.2d 297, 298, 562 N.Y.S.2d 39 (N.Y.App.Div.1990) (agreement to develop, produce and market screenplay based on defendant's childhood barred; "payments to plaintiff contemplated under the alleged agreement clearly could not be accomplished within one year, as plaintiff was to share any compensation received from exploitation of defendant's screenplay").[4]

[The court determined that California law governed because the "center of gravity" of the transaction was in California and California had the greatest interest in the litigation. The court next held that the contract was sufficiently definite for enforcement.]

---

4. Cron v. Hargro Fabrics, Inc., 91 N.Y.2d 362, 694 N.E.2d 56, 670 N.Y.S.2d 973 (N.Y.1998), enforcing an alleged oral agreement to pay a bonus consisting of a percentage of a company's annual pretax profits, calculable after the close of the year, does not alter treatment of continuing commission arrangements like the one at issue. The ruling represents only a "slight modification of the language in previous case law concerning the necessity of full payment by all parties within a year to satisfy the Statute of Frauds." Id. at 370, 670 N.Y.S.2d 973, 694 N.E.2d 56.

Conclusion

For the reasons set forth above, the Court concludes that California law applies to this contract dispute and that the oral Management Agreement is not barred by the California Statute of Frauds. Further, the Court concludes that the oral contract as alleged is sufficiently definite to be enforced. Accordingly, defendant's motion to dismiss and, in the alternative, for summary judgement is denied. * * * * In addition, the Court denies defendant's motion to dismiss plaintiff's fifth claim seeking damages as a result of defendant's late or canceled appearances.

Problems

1. Plaintiff and defendant entered into an oral contract for services for one year to be rendered by plaintiff. The term of service was to commence as soon as plaintiff could amicably sever his employment with his present employer. Is the contract within the Statute of Frauds?

2. On November 20 plaintiff and defendant entered into an oral agreement whereby plaintiff would be employed as defendant's advertising manager. The employment term was to be one year, commencing the following January 1st. Plaintiff commenced working for defendant, on January 1st as agreed, and on January 2nd plaintiff and defendant had a conversation in which the terms and conditions of employment, including the period of employment, were again discussed and agreed to. On June 15, plaintiff's employment was terminated. Plaintiff sues and defendant raises the defense of the Statute of Frauds. What result?

3. P entered Georgetown Law School as a first year student. D, an old friend of the family, hired P to be a part-time resident manager of an apartment complex controlled by D. P was promised a rent-free apartment plus a salary. The agreement, which was oral, provided that the position was to continue "until P completed his law studies at Georgetown or was obliged to discontinue these studies." Five weeks after the agreement was made, P was dismissed from his job at the apartment complex. When P sued for breach, D raised the defense of the Statute of Frauds. What result?

4. Which, if any, of the following contracts is within the Statute of Frauds?

(a) A agrees to work for B for two years.

(b) A agrees to work for B for A's lifetime, not exceeding two years.

(c) A agrees to work for B for two years if A lives that long.

(d) A agrees to work for B for two years but if A dies the contract shall be terminated.

5. Ohanian, who was employed by Avis on the West Coast, was offered a promotion to a managerial job in the East. He was reluctant to relocate, but finally agreed to take the promotion on the oral promise: "You can have the job until you reach retirement age unless you totally screw up." He was dismissed prior to his reaching retirement age as defined in the Avis pension plan or the Social Security laws. Will the Statute of Frauds bar evidence of this promise?

6. Defendant, a grocer, sold his stock of groceries and his good will to the plaintiff and orally agreed that he would not re-enter the grocery business in the City of Chicopee for five years. Plaintiff sues for breach of this oral promise. Defendant raises the defense of the Statute of Frauds. What result?

SECTION 2.   THE MEMORANDUM

(Calamari & Perillo 5th §§ 19.26—19.33)

CRABTREE v. ELIZABETH ARDEN SALES CORP.

Court of Appeals of New York, 1953.
305 N.Y. 48, 110 N.E.2d 551.

FULD, JUDGE. In September of 1947, Nate Crabtree entered into preliminary negotiations with Elizabeth Arden Sales Corporation, manufacturers and sellers of cosmetics, looking toward his employment as sales manager. Interviewed on September 26th, by Robert P. Johns, executive vice-president and general manager of the corporation, who had apprised him of the possible opening, Crabtree requested a three-year contract at $25,000 a year. Explaining that he would be giving up a secure well-paying job to take a position in an entirely new field of endeavor—which he believed would take him some years to master—he insisted upon an agreement for a definite term. And he repeated his desire for a contract for three years to Miss Elizabeth Arden, the corporation's president. When Miss Arden finally indicated that she was prepared to offer a two-year contract, based on an annual salary of $20,000 for the first six months, $25,000 for the second six months and $30,000 for the second year plus expenses of $5,000 a year for each of those years, Crabtree replied that that offer was "interesting". Miss Arden thereupon had her personal secretary make this memorandum on a telephone order blank that happened to be at hand:

> "EMPLOYMENT AGREEMENT WITH
>
> NATE CRABTREE   Date Sept. 26–1947
> At 681—5th Ave   6: PM
>   * * *
>
> Begin   20000.
> 6 months   25000.
> 6   "   30000.
>   5000.—per year
>   Expense money
>   [2 years to make good]
>   Arrangement with Mr. Crabtree
>   By Miss Arden
>   Present Miss Arden
>   Mr. John
>   Mr. Crabtree

Miss OLeary"

A few days later, Crabtree phoned Mr. Johns and telegraphed Miss Arden; he accepted the "invitation to join the Arden organization", and Miss Arden wired back her "welcome". When he reported for work a "pay-roll change" card was made up and initialed by Mr. Johns, and then forwarded to the payroll department. Reciting that it was prepared on September 30, 1947, and was to be effective as of October 22d, it specified the names of the parties, Crabtree's "Job Classification" and, in addition, contained the notation that "This employee is to be paid as follows:

> "First six months of employment $20,000. per annum
> Next six months of employment   25,000.   "   "
> After one year of employment   30,000.   "   "
>
>   Approved by RPJ [initialed]"

After six months of employment, Crabtree received the scheduled increase from $20,000 to $25,000, but the further specified increase at the end of the year was not paid. Both Mr. Johns and the comptroller of the corporation, Mr. Carstens, told Crabtree that they would attempt to straighten out the matter with Miss Arden, and, with that in mind, the comptroller prepared another "pay-roll change" card, to which his signature is appended, noting that there was to be a "Salary increase" from $25,000 to $30,000 a year, "per contractual arrangements with Miss Arden". The latter, however, refused to approve the increase and, after further fruitless discussion, plaintiff left defendant's employ and commenced this action for breach of contract.

At the ensuing trial, defendant denied the existence of any agreement to employ plaintiff for two years, and further contended that, even if one had been made, the statute of frauds barred its enforcement. The trial court found against defendant on both issues and awarded plaintiff damages of about $14,000, and the Appellate Division, two justices dissenting, affirmed. Since the contract relied upon was not to be performed within a year, the primary question for decision is whether there was a memorandum of its terms, subscribed by defendant, to satisfy the statute of frauds, Personal Property Law, § 31.

Each of the two payroll cards—the one initialed by defendant's general manager, the other signed by its comptroller—unquestionably constitutes a memorandum under the statute. That they were not prepared or signed with the intention of evidencing the contract, or that they came into existence subsequent to its execution, is of no consequence; * * * it is enough to meet the statute's demands, that they were signed with intent to authenticate the information contained therein and that such information does evidence the terms of the contract. Those two writings contain all of the essential terms of the contract—the parties to it, the position that plaintiff was to assume, the salary that he was to receive—except that relating to the duration of plaintiff's employment. Accordingly, we must consider whether that item, the length of the contract, may be supplied by reference to the earlier unsigned office memorandum, and, if so, whether its notation, "2 years to make good", sufficiently designates a period of employment.

The statute of frauds does not require the "memorandum * * * to be in one document. It may be pieced together out of separate writings, connected with one another either expressly or by the internal evidence of subject-matter and occasion." Marks v. Cowdin, supra, 226 N.Y. 138, 145, 123 N.E. 139, 141, see, also, 2 Williston, op. cit., p. 1671; Restatement, Contracts, § 208, subd. [a]. Where each of the separate writings has been subscribed by the party to be charged, little if any difficulty is encountered. See, e.g., Marks v. Cowdin, supra, 226 N.Y. 138, 144–145, 123 N.E. 139, 141. Where, however, some writings have been signed, and others have not—as in the case before us—there is basic disagreement as to what constitutes a sufficient connection permitting the unsigned papers to be considered as part of the statutory memorandum. The courts of some jurisdictions insist that there be a reference, of varying degrees of specificity, in the signed writing to that unsigned, and, if there is no such reference, they refuse to permit consideration of the latter in determining whether the memorandum satisfies the statute. * * *That conclusion is based upon a construction of the statute which requires that the connection between the writings and defendant's acknowledgment of the one not subscribed, appear from examination of the papers alone, without the aid of parol evidence. The other position—which has gained increasing support over the years—is that a sufficient connection between the papers is established simply by a reference in them to the same subject matter or transaction. * * * The statute is not pressed "to the extreme of a literal and rigid logic", Marks v. Cowdin, supra, 226 N.Y. 138, 144, 123 N.E. 139, 141, and oral testimony is admitted to show the connection between the documents and to establish the acquiescence, of the party to be charged, to the contents of the one unsigned.

The view last expressed impresses us as the more sound, and, indeed—although several of our cases appear to have gone the other way * * *—this court has on a number of occasions approved the rule, and we now definitively adopt it, permitting the signed and unsigned writings to be read together, provided that they clearly refer to the same subject matter or transaction.

The language of the statute—"Every agreement * * * is void, unless * * * some note or memorandum thereof be in writing, and subscribed by the party to be charged", Personal Property Law, § 31—does not impose the requirement that the signed acknowledgment of the contract must appear from the writings alone, unaided by oral testimony. The danger of fraud and perjury, generally attendant upon the admission of parol evidence, is at a minimum in a case such as this. None of the terms of the contract are supplied by parol. All of them must be set out in the various writings presented to the court, and at least one writing, the one establishing a contractual relationship between the parties, must bear the signature of the party to be charged, while the unsigned document must on its face refer to the same transaction as that set forth in the one that was signed. Parol evidence—to portray the circumstances surrounding the making of the memorandum—serves only to connect the separate documents and to show that there was assent, by the party to be charged, to the contents of the one unsigned. If that testimony does not convincingly connect the papers, or does not show assent to the unsigned paper, it is within the province of the judge to conclude, as a matter of law, that the statute has not been satisfied. True, the possibility still remains that, by fraud or perjury, an agreement never in fact made may occasionally be enforced under the subject matter or transaction test. It is better to run that risk, though, than to deny enforcement to all agreements, merely because the signed document made no specific mention of the unsigned writing. As the United States Supreme Court declared, in sanctioning the admission of parol evidence to establish the connection between the signed and unsigned writings. "There may be cases in which it would be a violation of reason and common sense to ignore a reference which derives its significance from such [parol] proof. If there is ground for any doubt in the matter, the general rule should be enforced. But where there is no ground for doubt, its enforcement would aid, instead of discouraging, fraud." Beckwith v. Talbot, 95 U.S. 289, 292, 24 L.Ed. 496.

Turning to the writings in the case before us—the unsigned office memo, the payroll change form initialed by the general manager Johns, and the paper signed by the comptroller Carstens—it is apparent, and most patently, that all three refer on their face to the same transaction. The parties, the position to be filled by plaintiff, the salary to be paid him, are all identically set forth; it is hardly possible that such detailed information could refer to another or a different agreement. Even more, the card signed by Carstens notes that it was prepared for the purpose of a "Salary increase per contractual arrangements with Miss Arden". That certainly constitutes a reference of sorts to a more comprehensive "arrangement," and parol is permissible to furnish the explanation.

The corroborative evidence of defendant's assent to the contents of the unsigned office memorandum is also convincing. Prepared by defendant's agent, Miss Arden's personal secretary, there is little likelihood that that paper was fraudulently manufactured or that defendant had not assented to its contents. Furthermore, the evidence as to the conduct of the parties at the time it was prepared persuasively demonstrates defendant's assent to its terms. Under such circumstances, the courts below were fully justified in finding that the three papers constituted the "memorandum" of their agreement within the meaning of the statute.

Nor can there be any doubt that the memorandum contains all of the essential terms of the contract. Only one term, the length of the employment, is in dispute. The September 26th office memorandum contains the notation, "2 years to make good". What purpose, other than to denote the length of the contract term, such a notation could have, is hard to imagine. Without it, the employment would be at will, see Martin v. New York Life Ins. Co., 148 N.Y. 117, 121, 42 N.E. 416, 417, and its inclusion may not be treated as meaningless or purposeless.

Quite obviously, as the courts below decided, the phrase signifies that the parties agreed to a term, a certain and definite term, of two years, after which, if plaintiff did not "make good", he would be subject to discharge. And examination of other parts of the memorandum supports that construction. Throughout the writings, a scale of wages, increasing plaintiff's salary periodically, is set out; that type of arrangement is hardly consistent with the hypothesis that the employment was meant to be at will. The most that may be argued from defendant's standpoint is that "2 years to make good", is a cryptic and ambiguous statement. But, in such a case, parol evidence is admissible to explain its meaning. Having in mind the relations of the parties, the course of the negotiations and plaintiff's insistence upon security of employment, the purpose of the phrase—or so the trier of the facts was warranted in finding—was to grant plaintiff the tenure he desired.

The judgment should be affirmed, with costs.

Problems

7. Plaintiff and the defendant railroad reached an oral contract whereby for a five year term plaintiff would have the exclusive concession for advertising on defendant's rights of way, stations and cars. A written memorandum of the agreement was drawn up by defendant's staff, approved by its president and signed by the vice-president in charge. One hour after he signed it, the vice-president was called by the president who told him that he had changed his mind. The vice-president struck off his signature and placed the memorandum in the company's files. Defendant refuses to honor the agreement and plaintiff sues. What result?

8. Defendant wrote to plaintiff offering a franchise for a two year term on given terms. Plaintiff accepted orally. In an action by plaintiff for breach, the defendant pleads the Statute of Frauds. What result?

9. The president of defendant XYZ company dictated a memorandum of an oral contract within the Statute of Frauds to his secretary in plaintiff's presence. The memorandum on plain white paper started out as follows: "XYZ undertakes to perform the following services: * * *" After dictating the memorandum he left the premises, stating he had to rush to catch a plane and directing his secretary to give plaintiff a copy of the memorandum once it was typed. The secretary followed this direction. In a suit for breach of the contract, defendant pleads the Statute of Frauds, arguing that the memorandum is unsigned. What result?

10. A and B entered into a contract within the one year provision of the Statute of Frauds. A writing was signed by both parties. Neither party noticed that the typist had mistakenly typed $40,000, where $90,000 was intended. How does this error affect the rights of the parties?

11. Assume the same facts as in case 10. However, assume that $40,000 was typed instead of $90,000 to confuse any unauthorized third persons who might read the document. What are the rights of the parties?

SECTION 3. EFFECT OF PART OR FULL PERFORM-ANCE, RESCISSION AND MODIFICA-TION AND THE ONE YEAR PROVI-SION

(Calamari & Perillo 5th §§ 19.23—19.24, 19.37—19.48)

McINTOSH v. MURPHY

Supreme Court of Hawai'i, 1970.
52 Haw. 29, 469 P.2d 177.

LEVINSON, JUSTICE. This case involves an oral employment contract which allegedly violates the provision of the Statute of Frauds requiring "any agreement that is not to be performed within one year from the making thereof" to be in writing in order to be enforceable. HRS § 656–1(5). In this action the plaintiff-employee Dick McIntosh seeks to recover damages from his employer, George Murphy and Murphy Motors, Ltd., for the breach of an alleged one-year oral employment contract.

While the facts are in sharp conflict, it appears that defendant George Murphy was in southern California during March, 1964 interviewing prospective management personnel for his Chevrolet–Oldsmobile dealerships in Hawai'i. He interviewed the plaintiff twice during that time. The position of sales manager for one of the dealerships was fully discussed but no contract was entered into. In April, 1964 the plaintiff received a call from the general manager of Murphy Motors informing him of possible employment within thirty days if he was still available. The plaintiff indicated his continued interest and informed the manager that he would be available. Later in April, the plaintiff sent Murphy a telegram to the effect that he would arrive in Honolulu on Sunday, April 26, 1964. Murphy then telephoned McIntosh on Saturday, April 25, 1964 to notify him that the job of assistant sales manager was open and work would begin on the following Monday, April 27, 1964. At that time McIntosh expressed surprise at the change in job title from sales manager to assistant sales manager but reconfirmed the fact that he was arriving in Honolulu the next day, Sunday. McIntosh arrived on Sunday, April 26, 1964 and began work on the following day, Monday, April 27, 1964.

As a consequence of his decision to work for Murphy, McIntosh moved some of his belongings from the mainland to Hawai'i, sold other possessions, leased an apartment in Honolulu and obviously forwent any other employment opportunities. In short, the plaintiff did all those things which were incidental to changing one's residence permanently from Los Angeles to Honolulu, a distance of approximately 2200 miles. McIntosh continued working for Murphy until July 16, 1964, approximately two and one-half months, at which time he was discharged on the grounds that he was unable to close deals with prospective customers and could not train the salesmen.

At the conclusion of the trial, the defense moved for a directed verdict arguing that the oral employment agreement was in violation of the Statute of Frauds, there being no written memorandum or note thereof. The trial court ruled that as a matter of law the contract did not come within the Statute, reasoning that Murphy bargained for acceptance by the actual commencement of performance by McIntosh, so that McIntosh was not bound by a contract until he came to work on Monday, April 27, 1964. Therefore, assuming that the contract was for a year's employment, it was performable within a year exactly to the day and no writing was required for it to be enforceable. Alternatively, the court ruled that if the agreement was made final by the telephone call between the parties on Saturday, April 25, 1964, then that part of the weekend which remained would not be counted in calculating the year, thus taking the contract out of the Statute of Frauds. With commendable candor the trial judge gave as the motivating force for the decision his desire to avoid a mechanical and unjust application of the Statute.[1]

The case went to the jury on the following questions: (1) whether the contract was for a year's duration or was performable on a trial basis, thus making it terminable at the will of either party; (2) whether the plaintiff was discharged for just cause; and (3) if he was not discharged for just cause, what damages were due the plaintiff. The jury returned a verdict for the plaintiff in the sum of $12,103.40. The defendants appeal to this court on four principal grounds, three of which we find to be without merit. The remaining ground of appeal is whether the plaintiff can maintain an action on the alleged oral employment contract in light of the prohibition of the Statute of Frauds making unenforceable an oral contract that is not to be performed within one year.

I. TIME OF ACCEPTANCE OF THE EMPLOYMENT AGREEMENT

The defendants contend that the trial court erred in refusing to give an instruction to the jury that if the employment agreement was made more than one day before the plaintiff began performance, there could be no recovery by the plaintiff. The reason given was that a contract not to be performed within one year from its making is unenforceable if not in writing.

The defendants are correct in their argument that the time of acceptance of an offer is a question of fact for the jury to decide. But the trial court alternatively decided that even if the offer was accepted on the Saturday prior to the commencement of performance, the intervening Sunday and part of Saturday would not be counted in computing the

---

1. THE COURT: You make the law look ridiculous, because one day is Sunday and the man does not work on Sunday; the other day is Saturday; he is up in Fresno. He can't work down there. And he is down here Sunday night and shows up for work on Monday. To me that is a contract within a year. I don't want to make the law look ridiculous, Mr. Clause, because it is one day later, one day too much, and that one day is a Sunday, and a non-working day.

year for the purposes of the Statute of Frauds. The judge stated that Sunday was a non-working day and only a fraction of Saturday was left which he would not count. In any event, there is no need to discuss the relative merits of either ruling since we base our decision in this case on the doctrine of equitable estoppel which was properly briefed and argued by both parties before this court, although not presented to the trial court.

II. ENFORCEMENT BY VIRTUE OF ACTION IN RELIANCE ON THE ORAL CONTRACT

In determining whether a rule of law can be fashioned and applied to a situation where an oral contract admittedly violates a strict interpretation of the Statute of Frauds, it is necessary to review the Statute itself together with its historical and modern functions. * * *

The first English Statute was enacted almost 300 years ago to prevent "many fraudulent practices, which are commonly endeavored to be upheld by perjury and subornation of perjury". 29 Car. 2, c. 3 (1677). Certainly, there were compelling reasons in those days for such a law. At the time of enactment in England, the jury system was quite unreliable, rules of evidence were few, and the complaining party was disqualified as a witness so he could neither testify on direct-examination nor, more importantly, be cross-examined. Summers, The Doctrine of Estoppel and the Statute of Frauds, 79 U.Pa.L.Rev. 440, 441 (1931). The aforementioned structural and evidentiary limitations on our system of justice no longer exist.

Retention of the Statute today has nevertheless been justified on at least three grounds: (1) the Statute still serves an evidentiary function thereby lessening the danger of perjured testimony (the original rationale); (2) the requirement of a writing has a cautionary effect which causes reflection by the parties on the importance of the agreement; and (3) the writing is an easy way to distinguish enforceable contracts from those which are not, thus channelling certain transactions into written form.

In spite of whatever utility the Statute of Frauds may still have, its applicability has been drastically limited by judicial construction over the years in order to mitigate the harshness of a mechanical application.[3] Furthermore, learned writers continue to disparage the Statute regarding it as "a statute for promoting fraud" and a "legal anachronism."

Another method of judicial circumvention of the Statute of Frauds has grown out of the exercise of the equity powers of the courts. Such

---

3. Thus a promise to pay the debt of another has been construed to encompass only promises made to a creditor which do not benefit the promisor (Restatement of Contracts § 184 (1932); 3 Williston, Contracts § 452 (Jaeger ed. 1960)); a promise in consideration of marriage has been interpreted to exclude mutual promises to marry (Restatement, supra § 192; 3 Williston, supra § 485); a promise not to be performed within one year means a promise not per-formable within one year (Restatement, supra § 198; 3 Williston, supra, § 495); a promise not to be performed within one year may be removed from the Statute of Frauds if one party has fully performed (Restatement, supra § 198; 3 Williston, supra § 504); and the Statute will not be applied where all promises involved are fully performed (Restatement, supra § 219; 3 Williston, supra § 528).

judicially imposed limitations or exceptions involved the traditional dispensing power of the equity courts to mitigate the "harsh" rule of law. When courts have enforced an oral contract in spite of the Statute, they have utilized the legal labels of "part performance" or "equitable estoppel" in granting relief. Both doctrines are said to be based on the concept of estoppel, which operates to avoid unconscionable injury. 3 Williston, Contracts § 553A at 791 (Jaeger ed. 1960), Summers, supra at 443–49; Monarco v. Lo Greco, 35 Cal.2d 621, 220 P.2d 737 (1950) (Traynor, J.).

Part performance has long been recognized in Hawai'i as an equitable doctrine justifying the enforcement of an oral agreement for the conveyance of an interest in land where there has been substantial reliance by the party seeking to enforce the contract. * * * Other courts have enforced oral contracts (including employment contracts) which failed to satisfy the section of the Statute making unenforceable an agreement not to be performed within a year of its making. This has occurred where the conduct of the parties gave rise to an estoppel to assert the Statute. * * *

It is appropriate for modern courts to cast aside the raiments of conceptualism which cloak the true policies underlying the reasoning behind the many decisions enforcing contracts that violate the Statute of Frauds. There is certainly no need to resort to legal rubrics or meticulous legal formulas when better explanations are available. The policy behind enforcing an oral agreement which violated the Statute of Frauds, as a policy of avoiding unconscionable injury, was well set out by the California Supreme Court. In Monarco v. Lo Greco, 35 Cal.2d 621, 623, 220 P.2d 737, 739 (1950), a case which involved an action to enforce an oral contract for the conveyance of land on the grounds of 20 years performance by the promisee, the court said:

> The doctrine of estoppel to assert the statute of frauds has been consistently applied by the courts of this state to prevent fraud that would result from refusal to enforce oral contracts in certain circumstances. Such fraud may inhere in the unconscionable injury that would result from denying enforcement of the contract after one party has been induced by the other seriously to change his position in reliance on the contract * * *.

In seeking to frame a workable test which is flexible enough to cover diverse factual situations and also provide some reviewable standards, we find very persuasive section 217A [now § 139] of the Second Restatement of Contracts. That section specifically covers those situations where there has been reliance on an oral contract which falls within the Statute of Frauds. Section [139] states:

> (1) A promise which the promisor should reasonably expect to induce action or forbearance on the part of the promisee or a third person and which does induce the action or forbearance is enforceable notwithstanding the Statute of Frauds if injustice can be

avoided only by enforcement of the promise. The remedy granted for breach is to be limited as justice requires.

(2) In determining whether injustice can be avoided only by enforcement of the promise, the following circumstances are significant: (a) the availability and adequacy of other remedies, particularly cancellation and restitution; (b) the definite and substantial character of the action or forbearance in relation to the remedy sought; (c) the extent to which the action or forbearance corroborates evidence of the making and terms of the promise, or the making and terms are otherwise established by clear and convincing evidence; (d) the reasonableness of the action or forbearance; (e) the extent to which the action or forbearance was foreseeable by the promisor.

We think that the approach taken in the Restatement is the proper method of giving the trial court the necessary latitude to relieve a party of the hardships of the Statute of Frauds. Other courts have used similar approaches in dealing with oral employment contracts upon which an employee had seriously relied. See Alaska Airlines, Inc. v. Stephenson, 217 F.2d 295 (9th Cir.1954); Seymour v. Oelrichs, 156 Cal. 782, 106 P. 88 (1909). This is to be preferred over having the trial court bend over backwards to take the contract out of the Statute of Frauds. In the present case the trial court admitted just this inclination and forthrightly followed it.

There is no dispute that the action of the plaintiff in moving 2200 miles from Los Angeles to Hawai'i was foreseeable by the defendant. In fact, it was required to perform his duties. Injustice can only be avoided by the enforcement of the contract and the granting of money damages. No other remedy is adequate. The plaintiff found himself residing in Hawai'i without a job.

It is also clear that a contract of some kind did exist. The plaintiff performed the contract for two and one-half months receiving $3,484.60 for his services. The exact length of the contract, whether terminable at will as urged by the defendant or for a year from the time when the plaintiff started working, was up to the jury to decide.

In sum, the trial court might have found that enforcement of the contract was warranted by virtue of the plaintiff's reliance on the defendant's promise. Naturally, each case turns on its own facts. Certainly there is considerable discretion for a court to implement the true policy behind the Statute of Frauds, which is to prevent fraud or any other type of unconscionable injury. We therefore affirm the judgment of the trial court on the ground that the plaintiff's reliance was such that injustice could only be avoided by enforcement of the contract.

Affirmed.

ABE, JUSTICE (dissenting).

* * *

* * * I cannot agree, as intimated by this court, that we should circumvent the Statute of Frauds by the exercise of the equity powers of courts. As to statutory law, the sole function of the judiciary is to interpret the statute and the judiciary should not usurp legislative power and enter into the legislative field. Thus, if the Statute of Frauds is too harsh as intimated by this court, and it brings about undue hardship, it is for the legislature to amend or repeal the statute and not for this court to legislate.

Problems

12. C loaned D $4,000 two years ago, payable last month at a specified interest rate. The oral loan agreement had no prepayment provision. D has repudiated the agreement and C has sued. D has interposed the defense of the Statute of Frauds. Can C recover?

13. For over ten years P, an independent insurance agent, represented D, a life insurer, pursuant to an oral contract. P alleges that the contract provided that after ten years of a continuous contractual relation all commissions on renewals of policies procured by P would be paid to P and P's spouse for their joint lives. P's relationship with D came to an end when P refused to sign a proposed agreement whereby P was asked to agree to represent D exclusively. When D refused to pay the renewal commissions as promised, P sued. D pleaded the defense of the Statute of Frauds and moved to dismiss. What result?

14. A and B entered into an oral contract whereby A agreed to render periodic services to B for a two-year term for the sum of $5,000 payable at the end of the term.

     a) At the end of the two-year period, A brought suit for the reasonable value of the services. What result?

     b) Suppose, instead, that after six months A refused to perform unless the compensation was raised to $7,500. B refused. A discontinued services and brought suit for the reasonable value of the services rendered prior to this disagreement. What result?

     c) Suppose, instead, that after six months A offered to sign a memorandum, asked B to sign a memorandum, and B refused. A discontinued services and sued for the reasonable value of A's services. What result?

15. Plaintiff entered into a written contract for two years' employment as a physician with the defendant clinic. After six weeks the parties orally agreed that the agreement would be rescinded immediately. Plaintiff soon thereafter, and before any change of position by defendant, changed his mind, tendered his services which were refused, and brought suit to enforce the written contract. What result?

16. Assume the same facts as case 15 except that the oral conversation resulted in an agreement that the employment term would expire in two months. What result?

17. Assume the same facts as case 15 except that the oral conversation resulted in an agreement that the employment term would be extended an additional 6 months. What result?

18. Five years ago Cain promised the plaintiff that he would leave his entire estate consisting of securities and realty to plaintiff if plaintiff would take care of him for the rest of Cain's life. Plaintiff duly performed until Cain's death last year. Cain left no will. The court-appointed administrator refuses to honor Cain's agreement, basing his refusal on the Statute of Frauds. Plaintiff sues. What result?

SECTION 4. STATUTE OF FRAUDS AND SALES OF GOODS

(Calamari & Perillo 5th §§ 19.16, 19.34)

AZEVEDO v. MINISTER

Supreme Court of Nevada, 1970.
86 Nev. 576, 471 P.2d 661.

MOWBRAY, JUSTICE. This case centers about the enforceability of an oral agreement to purchase 1500 tons of hay. The principal issue presented for our determination is whether the periodic accountings prepared by the seller and sent to the buyer covering the sale of the hay constituted confirming memoranda within the provisions of NRS 104.2201(2) of the Uniform Commercial Code and, if so, whether the seller sent them within a reasonable time as required by that statute so that the oral agreement is not barred by the statute of frauds. The district judge ruled that the mandates of NRS 104.2201(2) had been satisfied, and he upheld the validity of the agreement. We agree, and we affirm the judgment of the lower court.

1. THE FACTS

Appellant J.L. Azevedo is a rancher who buys and sells hay. * * * Respondent Bolton F. Minister operates the Minister Ranch near Yerington, Nevada, where he raises and sells large quantities of hay.

In early November 1967, Azevedo approached Minister for the purpose of buying hay. Terms were discussed. Several days later an agreement was reached by telephone. Both parties acknowledge that Azevedo agreed to purchase hay from Minister at a price of $26.50 per ton for the first and second cuttings and $28 per ton for the third cutting and that the parties opened an escrow account in a Yerington Bank in Minister's favor, where Azevedo agreed to deposit sufficient funds to cover the cost of the hay as he hauled it from the Minister Ranch. The parties are in dispute as to the total quantity of hay Azevedo agreed to purchase. Minister claims Azevedo contracted to purchase 1,500 tons. Azevedo maintains that they never had an agreement as to quantity. Soon after this telephone conversation, Azevedo deposited $20,000 in the designated escrow account and began hauling hay from the Minister Ranch. As Azevedo hauled the hay, Minister furnished him with periodic accountings, commencing December 4, which specified the dates the hay was hauled, names of the truckers, bale count, and weight. This arrangement was satisfactory to the parties, and it continued until the latter part of March 1968, when Minister loaded only two of four trucks sent by Azevedo for hay, because the funds on deposit in the escrow account were insufficient to cover all four loads. Azevedo then refused to buy any more hay, and Minister commenced this action in district court.

2. THE STATUTE OF FRAUDS

The determination of the legal issues presented for our consideration will turn on our interpretation of NRS 104.2201(2) of the Uniform Commercial Code. Since the enactment of the Uniform Commercial Code, sweeping changes have been effectuated in the law of commercial transactions. * * *

* * *

As with all codifications, it was impossible for the Uniform Commercial Code to encompass every conceivable factual situation. Realizing this limitation, its drafters couched much of the language of the text and comments in broad generalities, leaving many problems to be answered by future litigation.

The development of the action of *assumpsit* in the fourteenth century gave rise to the enforceability of the oral promise. Although parties to an action could not be witnesses, the alleged promise could be enforced on the strength of oral testimony of others not concerned with the litigation. Because of this practice, a party could readily suborn perjured testimony, resulting in marked injustice to innocent parties who were held legally obligated to promises they had never made. The statute of frauds was enacted to preclude this practice. The passage of the statute did not eliminate the problem, but rather, has precipitated a controversy as to the relative merits of the statute. Those favoring the statute of frauds insist that it prevents fraud by prohibiting the introduction of perjured testimony. They also suggest that it deters hasty action, in that the formality of a writing will prevent a person from obligating himself without a full appreciation of the nature of his acts. Moreover, it is said, since business customs almost entirely conform to the mandates of the statute, an abolition of the statute would seriously disrupt such affairs.

On the other hand, in England the statute of frauds has been repealed. The English base their position upon the reasoning that the assertion of the technical defense of the statute aids a person in breaking a contract and effects immeasurable harm upon those who have meritorious claims.

It is further maintained by the advocates of the English position that the rationale for the necessity of the statute has been vitiated, because parties engaged in litigation today may testify as witnesses and readily defend against perjured testimony.[9]

The Uniform Commercial Code, however, has attempted to strike a balance between the two positions by seeking to limit the defense of the statute to only those cases where there is a definite possibility of fraud.

It is in the light of this historical background that we turn to consider whether the oral agreement of the parties in this case is barred by the statute of frauds.

There is no question that the Azevedo–Minister agreement was oral and that its enforceability is governed by NRS 104.2201(2), supra. The sale of hay is included within the definition of the sale of "goods" as defined by NRS 104.2105(1) and NRS 104.2107(2), which when read together provide that the sale of "growing crops," when they are to be "severed by the buyer or by the seller," constitutes the sale of goods within the definition of that expression in the Uniform Commercial Code. The parties agree that they are "merchants" within the meaning of that term as defined in the Code.

It is also true that the statute of frauds is no defense to that portion of the contract that has been performed under the provisions of NRS 104.2201(3)(c), supra, which makes enforceable an oral contract "[w]ith respect to goods * * * which have been received and accepted."

The legal issues are, therefore, (1) whether Minister's accountings constituted confirming memoranda within the standards of NRS 104.2201(2) and, if so, (2) whether Minister sent them within a reasonable time as required by the statute.

3. THE CONFIRMING MEMORANDA

(a) The Accounting of January 21, 1968

In addition to the data set forth in the periodic accountings covering the dates on which hay was hauled, the names of the truckers, and the bale counts and weights, Minister added the following statement in his January 21 accounting to Azevedo:

"From your original deposit of $20,000.00 there is now a balance of $1819.76. *At this time there remains [sic] approximately 16,600 bales of hay yet to be hauled on your purchase,* about 9200 of which are first crop, 7400 of which are second crop.

"We would appreciate hearing when you plan to haul the *balance of the hay.* Also please make a deposit to cover the hay, sufficient in amount to pay for the hay you will be currently hauling. At this time you have only about *$2.25 deposit per ton on the remaining balance*

---

9. L. Vold, Sales § 14, at 88 (2d ed. 1959). Advocates of The Sales Act have advanced the argument that the technical safeguard of a writing is more important in the United States than in England because in this country a litigant has a basic right to demand trial by jury. In England such a right is within the discretion of the court; thus, in most instances the court and not the jury will make the ultimate determination as to the existence of the contract. 68 Harv.L.Rev. 383, 384 (1954).

of the hay, and we cannot permit a lower deposit per ton and still consider the hay as being sold." (Emphasis added.)

Azevedo did not challenge or reply to Minister's accountancy of January 21. Rather, he deposited an additional $3,000 in the escrow account and continued hauling hay.

(b) The Accounting of February 22, 1968

In the regular accounting of February 22, Minister added the following:

> "Balance of deposit on approximately 14000 bales remaining to be hauled—$1635.26."

Azevedo did not challenge or reply to the February 22 accounting.

It is these two accountings that the district judge found constituted confirming memoranda within the meaning of NRS 104.2201(2). There is little authority articulating the meaning of a confirming memorandum as used in the Code. The official Comment, Uniform Laws Annotated, Uniform Commercial Code § 2–201 (1968), states at 90, 91:

> "Only three definite and invariable requirements as to the [confirming] memorandum are made by this subsection. First, it must evidence a contract for the sale of goods; second, it must be 'signed', a word which includes any authentication which identifies the party to be charged; and third, it must specify a quantity."

The parties concede that the memoranda were "signed" within the meaning of the statute, but appellant Azevedo urges that neither memorandum confirms the existence of an oral contract.

While § 2–201(2) of the Code is entirely new in the commercial law field, its only effect is to eliminate the defense of the statute of frauds. The party alleging the contract still has the burden of proving that an oral contract was entered into *before* the written confirmation. The purpose of the subsection of the Code is to rectify an abuse that had developed in the law of commerce. The custom arose among business people of confirming oral contracts by sending a letter of confirmation. This letter was binding as a memorandum on the sender, but not on the recipient, because he had not signed it.[12] The abuse was that the recipient, not being bound, could perform or not, according to his whim and the market, whereas the seller had to perform.[13] Obviously, under these circumstances, sending any confirming memorandum was a dangerous practice. Subsection (2) of Section 2–201 of the Code cures the abuse by holding a recipient bound unless he communicates his objection within 10 days.

Appellant urges that the January and February accountings do not meet the standards of the subsection because neither memorandum

---

12. As indicated in the instant case, Minister, who signed the memorandum, could be held to deliver to Azevedo the balance of the hay on the terms indicated.

13. The record reflects the price of hay was lower in March than in the previous November, when the parties had agreed on a tonnage price.

makes reference to any oral agreement between the parties. A fair reading of the memoranda shows otherwise. The January memorandum states that, "At this time there remains [sic] approximately 16,600 bales of hay yet to be hauled on your purchase", and, further, that, "We [Minister] would appreciate hearing when you plan to haul the balance of the hay." Although neither the January nor the February memorandum refers to the previous November agreement by telephone, the language clearly demonstrates that the referred-to agreement between the parties was not an *in futuro* arrangement, but a pre-existing agreement between Azevedo and Minister. As the court said in Harry Rubin & Sons, Inc. v. Consolidated Pipe Co., 396 Pa. 506, 153 A.2d 472, 476 (1959), in ruling on a case involving subsection (2) of section 2–201:

> "Under the statute of frauds as revised in the Code[,] 'All that is required is that the writing afford a basis for believing that the offered oral evidence rests on a real transaction.' " (Footnote omitted.)

The district judge found that it did so in the instant case, and the record supports his finding.

4. The "Reasonable Time" Factor

Subsection 2 of NRS 104.2201 provides that the confirming memorandum must be sent within a reasonable time after the oral contract is made. Appellant argues that the delay of 10 weeks (November 9 to January 21) as a matter of law is an unreasonable time. We do not agree. What is reasonable must be decided by the trier of the facts under all the circumstances of the case under consideration. Subsection 2 of NRS 104.1204 provides:

> "What is a reasonable time for taking any action depends on the nature, purpose and circumstances of such action."

In this case, the parties commenced performance of their oral agreement almost immediately after it was made in early November. Azevedo deposited $20,000 in the designated escrow account and began hauling hay. Minister commenced sending his periodic accounting reports to Azevedo on December 14. It is true that the accounting containing the confirming memorandum was not sent until January 21. It was at that time that Azevedo's deposit of $20,000 was nearing depletion. Minister so advised Azevedo in the January memorandum. Azevedo responded by making an additional deposit. He did not object to the memorandum, and he continued to haul the hay until the latter part of March. Under "the nature, purpose and circumstances" of the case, we agree with the district judge that the delay was not unreasonable.

The judgment is affirmed.

COHN v. FISHER

Superior Court of New Jersey, Law Div., 1972.
118 N.J.Super. 286, 287 A.2d 222.

ROSENBERG, J.C.C. (temporarily assigned). Plaintiff Albert L. Cohn (hereinafter Cohn) moves for summary judgment against defendant Donal L. Fisher (hereinafter Fisher). The controversy concerns an alleged breach of contract for the sale of Cohn's boat by Fisher.

On Sunday, May 19, 1968, Fisher inquired of Cohn's advertisement in the New York Times for the sale of his 30–foot auxiliary sloop. Upon learning the location of the sailboat, Fisher proceeded to the boatyard and inspected the sloop. Fisher then phoned Cohn and submitted an offer of $4,650, which Cohn accepted. Both agreed to meet the next day at Cohn's office in Paterson. At the meeting on Monday, May 20, Fisher gave Cohn a check for $2,325 and affixed on same: "Deposit on aux. sloop, D'Arc Wind, full amount $4,650." Both parties agreed to meet on Saturday, May 25, when Fisher would pay the remaining half of the purchase price and Cohn would presumably transfer title.

A few days later Fisher informed Cohn that he would not close the deal on the weekend because a survey of the boat could not be conducted that soon. Cohn notified Fisher that he would hold him to his agreement to pay the full purchase price by Saturday. At this point relations between the parties broke down. Fisher stopped payment on the check he had given as a deposit and failed to close the deal on Saturday.

Cohn then re-advertised the boat and sold it for the highest offer of $3,000. In his suit for breach of contract Cohn is seeking damages of $1,679.50 representing the difference between the contract price with Fisher and the final sales price together with the costs incurred in reselling the boat.

* * *

As to the element of formality of memorialization, N.J.S.A. 12A:2–201 requires that a contract for the sale of goods for the price of $500 or more, to be enforceable, must comply with the statute of frauds.

* * *

[I]n the present case, there are three alternatives by which the contract could be held enforceable:

    (1) under N.J.S.A. 12A:2–201(1) the check may constitute a sufficient written memorandum;

    (2) under N.J.S.A. 12A:2–201(3)(b) defendant's testimony in depositions and his answers to demands for admission may constitute an admission of the contract or

    (3) under N.J.S.A. 12A:2–201(3)(c) payment and acceptance of the check may constitute partial performance.

The above issues, arising under the Uniform Commercial Code adopted by this State on January 1, 1963, are novel to the courts of New Jersey. For such reason this court will determine the enforceability of the contract under each of the alternatives. Ample authority for resolving the issues is found in the notes provided by the framers of the Code and in the decisions of our sister states.

With regard to the question of whether the check satisfies the statute of frauds as a written memorandum, N.J.S.A. 12A:2-201(1) requires (1) a writing indicating a contract for sale, (2) signed by the party to be charged, and (3) the quantity term must be expressly stated. The back of the check in question bore the legend "deposit on aux. sloop, D'Arc Wind, full amount $4,650." Thus the check seems to *prima facie* satisfy the requirements in that: it is a writing which indicates a contract for sale by stating the subject matter of the sale (aux. sloop, D'Arc Wind), the price ($4,650), part of the purchase terms—50% down (deposit of $2,325), and by inferentially identifying the seller (Albert Cohn, payee) and the purchaser (Donal Fisher, drawer); it is signed by the party against whom enforcement is sought (Donal Fisher); and it expressly states the quantity term (the D'Arc Wind). Thus the check, although not a sales contract, would comply with the requirements of the statute of frauds under N.J.S.A. 12A:2-201(1).

Such a result, however, would be in conflict with the case law of New Jersey. As noted in the New Jersey Study Comment to § 12A:2-201, par. 3, under both the Uniform Sales Act and the Uniform Commercial Code a sales contract not in writing is not unenforceable if there is a memorandum of the agreement in writing signed by the party to be charged or his authorized agent. Although the Uniform Sales Act was silent as to the required terms for a satisfactory memorandum, the courts of New Jersey had restrictively interpreted "memorandum" to mean a writing containing the *full terms of the contract*. See Bauer v. Victory Catering Co., 101 N.J.L. 364, 370, 128 A. 262 (E. & A. 1925). N.J.S.A. 12A:2-201(1), in stating, with the exception of the quantity term, that "A writing is not insufficient because it omits or incorrectly states a term agreed upon * * *," clearly changes the law in New Jersey as to the requirements of the memorandum exception to the statute of frauds. As evidenced by the Uniform Commercial Code Comment to § 12A:2-201, par. 1, such a change was clearly intended:

> The required writing need not contain all the material terms of the contract and such material terms as are stated need not be precisely stated. All that is required is that the writing afford a basis for believing that the offered oral evidence rests on a real transaction. * * * The price, time and place of payment or delivery, the general quality of the goods, or any particular warranties may all be omitted.

* * *

Only three definite and invariable requirements as to the memorandum are made by this subsection. First, it must evidence a contract for the sale of goods; second, it must be 'signed,' a word which includes any authentication which identifies the party to be charged; and third, it must specify a quantity.

In holding that the check in the present litigation sufficiently satisfies the requirements of N.J.S.A. 12A:2–201(1) to constitute a memorandum of the agreement, this court is not without judicial authority. In Herzog v. Tidaback, 67 N.J.Super. 14, 169 A.2d 726 (Ch.Div.1961), the court took a half step in such a direction. There the court held that where a purchaser of real estate gave the seller's agent a check which bore the notation that it was a deposit on specific premises in accordance with a listing agreement, and where the seller's agent accepted, endorsed and cashed said check, the notation together with the endorsement of seller's authorized agent would be sufficient to satisfy the requirements of the statute of frauds. Thus, in order for a check to satisfy the memorandum exception, *Herzog* required that an outside agreement be incorporated by reference. But this distinction is due to the fact that the sale in *Herzog* involved real estate rather than goods, as in the present case. This distinction between a contract for the sale of land which requires that a check refer to a written agreement, and a contract for the sale of goods which does not require incorporation by reference on a check, has been clearly drawn. See 20 A.L.R. 363; 153 A.L.R. 1112. The decisions under the Uniform Commercial Code involving a contract for the sale of goods are to the effect that a check alone is sufficient to constitute a writing in compliance with the statute of frauds. * * *

Accordingly, this court concludes that by the adoption of the Uniform Commercial Code in New Jersey, the case law concerning the sufficiency of memorandum has been changed. It therefore appears to the satisfaction of this court that the check in the case at bar satisfies the requirements of N.J.S.A. 12A:2–201(1) and thereby renders the contract enforceable under the statute of frauds.

Had the check not satisfied the requirements of N.J.S.A. 12A:2–201(1), the check, together with defendant's admission of a contract in his depositions and demands for admission, may satisfy N.J.S.A. 12A:2–201(3)(b). This subsection states, in effect, that where the requirements of 12A:2–201(1) have not been satisfied, an otherwise valid contract will be held enforceable if the party charged admits that a contract was made. Such a contract would be enforceable only with respect to the quantity of goods admitted.

The New Jersey Study Comment to § 12A:2–201, par. 7, points out that "The cases from other states are in disagreement on the question of giving effect to admissions in court for purposes of satisfying the statute of frauds." The theory behind the dissension under § 2–201(3)(b) seems to be that " * * * the defendant should be privileged not to make the admission if it has the legal effect of depriving him of the defense of the Statute of Frauds." Hawkland, Sales and Bulk Sales, 31 (1958).

This court is of the opinion that if a party admits an oral contract, he should be held bound to his bargain. The statute of frauds was not designed to protect a party who made an oral contract, but rather to aid a party who did not make a contract, though one is claimed to have been made orally with him. This court would therefore hold that the check, together with defendant's admission of an oral contract, would constitute an enforceable contract under N.J.S.A. 12A:2–201(3)(b).

Finally, under N.J.S.A. 12A:2–201(3)(c) the check may constitute partial performance of the contract in that payment for goods was made and accepted, and, as such, the contract would be held enforceable under the statute of frauds. N.J.S.A. 12A:2–201(3)(c) provides that although the requirements of N.J.S.A. 12A:2–201(1) have not been met, an otherwise valid contract will be held enforceable with respect to goods (1) for which payment has been made and accepted, or (2) which have been received and accepted.

As noted in the New Jersey Study Comment to § 2–201, par. 8, this subsection partially changes New Jersey case law which held that either part payment or the actual receipt and acceptance of part of the goods satisfies the statute of frauds for the entire contract. See Field and Field v. Runk, 22 N.J.L. 525 (Sup.Ct.1850); Casey v. Leslie, 59 N.J.L. 6, 35 A. 6 (Sup.Ct.1896). Under the Code oral contracts would be held enforceable only to the extent that goods have been paid for or received. Thus, part payment or receipt and acceptance of part of the goods would satisfy the statute of frauds, not for the entire contract, but only for the *quantity* of goods which have been received and accepted or for which payment has been made and accepted.

In the present case, since the quantity term has been clearly indicated by the check itself, namely "aux. sloop, D'Arc Wind," the check, by representing that payment had been made and accepted, would constitute partial performance and the contract would be held enforceable under N.J.S.A. 12A:2–201(3)(c). That such a decision results in upholding the entire contract is due solely to the fact that the entire contract concerned only the sale of one boat.

* * *

In sum, the case at bar has fully complied with the statute of frauds in that under each of the alternative subsections—N.J.S.A. 12A:2–201(1), (3)(b), and (3)(c)—the enforceability of the contract is upheld.

POTTER v. HATTER FARMS, INC.

Court of Appeals of Oregon, 1982.
56 Or.App. 254, 641 P.2d 628.

Gillette, Presiding Judge. In this oral contract action, defendant appeals from a jury verdict in favor of plaintiffs (Potters). Defendant argues that: there was no substantial evidence that a contract existed between it and Potters; even if an oral agreement was reached, it was unenforceable because it violated the Uniform Commercial Code (UCC) Statute of Frauds; and plaintiffs were not entitled to raise promissory estoppel as a bar to their Statute of Frauds defense. We affirm.

Plaintiffs operate a turkey hatchery in Oregon. The hatchery processes turkey eggs through incubation to hatching, at which time new turkey "poults" are sold to growers. Defendant is a turkey grower in Oklahoma; it raises turkeys and sells them to food processing companies.

The arrangement between the parties began with a telephone call. Plaintiff Charles Potter testified that Gil Kent, production manager of Hatter Farms, first contacted him by phone in November or December, 1978, and stated an interest in purchasing some poults from the Potters' company. The men then met in January, 1979, at the Tulsa, Oklahoma, airport. At that time, according to Potter, he and Kent entered into an oral contract. Potter testified that he agreed to sell and Kent agreed that Hatter Farms would buy 192,000 poults for eighty cents per poult, plus charges for egg dipping, inspections and toe clipping.

The men also discussed transportation of the poults during the January meeting, but the exact means of transportation was left undecided. They agreed at that time that, because poults are neither fed nor watered in transit, transportation from Oregon to Oklahoma should take no longer than 40 hours. Potter testified, however, that the 40–hour figure was merely a goal set by the parties and that the agreement was not contingent upon finding transportation to attain that goal. In essence, Potter testified that he and Kent reached an oral contract for sale of the poults with the exact method of transportation left to be decided later. The parties agreed, according to Potter, to find transportation that was as quick and inexpensive as possible. Potter stated that, aside from the open transportation term, there was no disagreement whatsoever as to the terms of the contract.

Subsequent to their January discussion, both parties investigated transportation possibilities. One was to fly the poults to Chicago and truck them from there to Oklahoma. Robert Hatter, the president of defendant corporation, claimed at trial that such a method of transportation was not practical. He admitted, however, that it was possible to transport the poults in that manner. Potter testified that the cost of trucking the poults from Chicago to Oklahoma was too high, but that it was "not totally out of reason," because the alleged agreement occurred during the off-season when demand for turkey poults was high and supply was low. William Lewis, who had 30 years experience buying and selling turkey poults, testified that the estimated cost of the poults, including transportation, was "not too exorbitant" for poults during the off-season.

Potter met with defendant's representatives again in June, 1979. He had been contacted by two customers in California who expressed interest in buying the poults involved in this case, and the purpose of the June meeting was to determine if Hatter Farms still needed the poults. He explained:

"My purpose in selling turkeys is to protect our customer to the utmost, and in order to do that I make very solid commitments, and the people in California understood when the poults were going and that I had been back there and they had been confirmed and sold in January, and I told them I would go back and see if there was any problem with them taking them, or if they needed them, and I got no indication that they didn't need them."

Gil Kent testified that he told Potter that it was unwise for Potter to hold the poults for defendant, because neither party had arranged a suitable means of transportation. Potter testified, however, that he was certain at the end of the meeting that defendant still intended to buy the poults from him and that there were no contractual terms left to be worked out. Potter subsequently turned down an offer from the California buyer to buy the poults.

In August, 1979, Gil Kent informed Potter that defendant would be unable to use the poults. This action followed.

Defendant first claims that no contract for the sale of poults existed. It argues that transportation was so essential an element of any such contract that failure to agree on it indicates a lack of intent to contract. Alternatively, it argues that, even if a contract existed, it was conditioned upon the occurrence of and agreement upon transportation, which never occurred.

We cannot overturn the jury's decision on the basis of insufficient evidence unless there was no evidence to support the verdict. *Allison v. Shepherd*, 285 Or. 447, 454, 591 P.2d 735 (1979). There was evidence here, based on Potter's testimony, that he and defendant's representatives entered into an oral contract. The fact that the transportation term was left open is not fatal to the agreement, because Potter testified that the agreement was not conditioned upon finding ideal transportation. The cost of the poults shipped by the available transportation was, according to the evidence, high but not unreasonable. ORS 72.2040(3) states:

> "(3) Even though one or more terms are left open a contract for sale does not fail for indefiniteness if the parties have intended to make a contract and there is a reasonably certain basis for giving an appropriate remedy."

We hold that there is sufficient evidence that the requirements of this statute were fulfilled.

Defendant next argues that the trial court erred by not granting defendant's motions for summary judgment, for directed verdict and for judgment n.o.v., because the alleged oral contract was unenforceable in that it violated the UCC Statute of Frauds. ORS 72.2010. Plaintiffs respond that the defendant was barred on the basis of promissory estoppel from raising the Statute of Frauds as a defense.

Traditionally, a promissory estoppel claim has been used to supply the element of consideration where to refuse to enforce an otherwise valid promise would work an injustice on a party who relied to his detriment on the promise. Calamari & Perillo, *The Law of Contracts*, §§ 99–105 (1970). In *Stevens v. Good Samaritan Hosp.*, 264 Or. 200, 504 P.2d 749 (1972), however, the Oregon Supreme Court held that promissory estoppel could be used to defeat the application of Oregon's general Statute of Frauds. * * *

The issue in the present case is whether promissory estoppel should be allowed as an exception to the *UCC* Statute of Frauds. ORS 72.2010. * * *

Estoppel is introduced into the Code through [U.C.C. § 1–103] which states:

> "*Unless displaced by the particular provisions of the Uniform Commercial Code*, the principles of law and equity, including the law merchant and the law relative to capacity to contract, principal and agent, *estoppel*, fraud, misrepresentation, duress, coercion, mistake, bankruptcy, or other validating or invalidating cause shall supplement its provisions." (Emphasis supplied.)

Our examination of those two provisions leads us to the conclusion that promissory estoppel should be allowed to defeat reliance upon the UCC Statute of Frauds. The central issue is whether promissory estoppel is specifically displaced by [U.C.C. 2–201]. Because it is not mentioned in the statute, the only arguable means of displacement is the legislature's silence. We do not believe that silence constitutes displacement of estoppel from the Statute of Frauds. In light of [U.C.C. § 1–103], we hold that if the legislature did not want estoppel to apply to application of the Statute of Frauds, it would have stated that intent expressly.

Our conclusion is also influenced by [U.C.C. § 1–203], which states:

> "Every contract or duty within the Uniform Commercial Code imposes an obligation of good faith in its performance or enforcement."

Allowing promissory estoppel as an exception to the Statute of Frauds is consistent with the obligation of good faith. Exclusion of promissory estoppel, on the other hand, would allow a party to enter into an oral contract, induce the other party to rely to its detriment and yet completely escape liability under the contract. We do not believe the legislature intended such a result. *See* J. White and R. Summers, *Uniform Commercial Code,* § 2–6 at 69–70 (2d ed. 1980).

Defendant argues that allowing promissory estoppel to defeat the Statute of Frauds would render the statute meaningless. It is true that any exception to such a writing requirement increases the possibility of fraud through perjury. Despite that fact, the Supreme Court has created exceptions to the general Statute of Frauds for both promissory estoppel and for part performance, and the Code's Statute of Frauds contains some express exceptions. * * * Neither the Oregon court nor the legislature apparently believed that creating exceptions to the statute render it a nullity. As the court made clear in *Stevens v. Good Samaritan Hosp., supra,* a promissory estoppel exception essentially enhances the Statute of Frauds by preventing its use as an instrument of fraud. Neither do we believe that a promissory estoppel exception eliminates the incentive for merchants to memorialize their agreements in writing. Those who would comply with the statute to avoid unenforcibility of their agreements would likewise comply to avoid the uncertainty and difficulty of having to prove the elements of promissory estoppel at trial.

To avoid a Statute of Frauds defense through promissory estoppel, it is necessary to prove 1) actual reliance on a promise, 2) a definite and substantial change of position occasioned by the promise and 3) foreseeability to the promisor, as a reasonable person, that the promise would induce conduct of the kind that occurred. *Schafer et al. v. Fraser et ux.*, 206 Or. 446, 472, 290 P.2d 190 (1956). The difficulty of meeting that burden of proof should both encourage merchants to put agreements into writing and decrease the likelihood of a proponent of a contract being able to prove its existence through perjury.

It has been suggested that allowing a reliance exception to the statute would make it possible for one party unilaterally to create an enforceable contract simply by relying substantially on discussions that did not, in fact, result in any actual agreement. It is highly unlikely, however, that any merchant would rely to his significant detriment on a nonexistent agreement in hope that he could convince a trier of fact that an agreement was actually reached and that the elements of promissory estoppel were satisfied.

Defendant also argues that the promissory estoppel exception would hamper the consistency and predictability which the Code was designed to bring to commercial transactions. As the Code provisions cited above concerning the application of good faith and estoppel suggest, the legislature did not intend to provide predictability and consistency at the expense of equitable principles. The Code's Statute of Frauds provides a means of assuring certainty in dealings between merchants. The promissory estoppel exception assures that, when merchants do not avail themselves of the protections provided by the Statute of Frauds, the requirement of good faith is not abrogated. We are convinced that such a balance between predictability and good faith is consistent with the legislature's intent.

Finally, we must decide whether there was substantial evidence to satisfy the requirements of promissory estoppel. As we pointed out above, Potter's testimony provides substantial evidence that a promise was made. Potter's testimony that he turned down offers to sell the poults to buyers in California in reliance on defendant's promise satisfies the actual reliance and substantial change of position requirements. His testimony that he reached an agreement with Gil Kent in January, 1979, that in June of that year he told defendant of the offers he had from other buyers and that Hatter Farms did not indicate to him that it was no longer interested in the poults satisfies the reasonable foreseeability requirement.

There was substantial evidence of the existence of an oral contract between plaintiff and defendant. Although the contract would otherwise be unenforceable for violating the Statute of Frauds, there was substantial evidence here of promissory estoppel barring defendants' assertion of that defense.

Affirmed.

Problems

19. X, a salesman for S, visited B, a physician, at his office and attempted to sell him a sailboat. B asked for a week or two to think it over. X falsely reported to S that an oral agreement was reached and S sent B a written confirmation of the alleged sale. B, in annoyance, ripped up and threw the paper into the wastebasket. A month later, S tendered delivery of the boat, B refused to accept it and S sues. What result?

20. S & B entered into an oral contract for the purchase and sale of specified quantities of oats to be delivered over a 16 month period. S sent B a written confirmation of the oral contract bearing number 6077. After several months B wrote S, stating: "We have no further need for oats, consequently we will accept no further deliveries under contract number 6077." S brought suit and B pleads the U.C.C. and the one year provisions of the Statute of Frauds. What result?

21. Plaintiff, a construction contractor, was preparing to bid on a government reclamation contract. It requested and received a bid from defendant by telephone whereby defendant would furnish the pumps needed on the project for $1,000,000. Because this was the low bid received by plaintiff, it was used by plaintiff in calculating its successful $15,000,000 bid. Before the government accepted plaintiff's bid, defendant revoked its offer. Plaintiff purchased pumps from another supplier and sues defendant for damages. The litigation takes place in California where all the operative facts occurred. Defendant pleads the Statute of Frauds. What result? Consider the Drennan case (Ch. 4 supra).

SECTION 5.   THE SURETYSHIP STATUTE OF FRAUDS

(Calamari & Perillo 5th §§ 19.2—19.12)

LAWRENCE v. ANDERSON

Supreme Court of Vermont, 1936.
108 Vt. 176, 184 A. 689.

POWERS, CHIEF JUSTICE. Answering an emergency call from an unknown source, the plaintiff, a licensed physician, administered to John Anderson, who had suffered severe injuries in an automobile accident somewhere on the "Williston Road" outside of the city of Burlington. This was on October 1, 1933. When the plaintiff arrived at the scene of the accident, he found there the defendant, a daughter of the injured man; and when he had introduced himself to her, she directed him, as he testified, to "do everything you can under the sun to see this man is taken care of." Thereupon, the plaintiff called an ambulance, in which Anderson was taken to a hospital where the plaintiff treated him until the next morning, when he was discharged by the defendant after she had conferred with her father about it. The patient died from the effects of the injuries a few days later. The plaintiff made his charges for his services to Mr. Anderson, and sent bills to his estate. He engaged a Burlington lawyer to proceed against the estate, for the collection of his charges, and some effort in that direction was made, but nothing came of it. About a year after the accident, the plaintiff began sending bills to Anderson's widow, but nothing came from that. Finally, about a year and half after the accident, this suit was brought. It was returnable to the Chittenden municipal court, and there tried to a jury. At the close of the plaintiff's evidence, on motion therefor, a verdict was ordered for the defendant. The plaintiff excepted.

It is apparent that the facts above stated, standing alone, did not make a case for the jury; and if nothing more had been shown, the judgment would have to be affirmed. For it fully appears that the defendant's relations with her father were such that she was not liable for the plaintiff's services unless she became so by reason of what she said or did. The rule is fully established that one who merely calls a physician to render services to another is not liable therefor in the absence of an express agreement, unless he is legally bound to furnish such service, as it is a fair inference from the evidence that it was the intention of both parties that he should pay for it. The services here sued for were not, so far as the above recited facts show, beneficial, in a legal sense, to the defendant, and she would not be liable therefor. Smith v. Watson, 14 Vt. 332, 337.

But in addition to what has been recited, one Charles Brown, who was at the scene of the accident when the plaintiff arrived there, testified that in his presence the defendant said to the plaintiff, "I want my father taken care of, and give him the best care you can give him, and what the charges are * * * I will pay for it."

Ordinarily, this statement might make an entirely different case for the plaintiff. It shows that the defendant not only requested the services, but also that she made a direct promise to pay the plaintiff. Such a promise is not collateral or secondary, but primary and original. It comes within the law as laid down in Pocket v. Almon, 90 Vt. 10, 96 A. 421, and Enos v. Owens Slate Co., 104 Vt. 329, 160 A. 185. To such a contract the statute of frauds (P.L. 1675) does not apply, for the simple reason that it is not a promise to pay the debt of another, but is a promise to pay the debt of the promisor—one that he makes his own by force of his engagement.

But before we can apply this rule to the case in hand, we must consider the effect of the plaintiff's conduct.

When the defendant made the promise that Brown testified to, the plaintiff was at liberty to accept it and to rely upon it. But he was not obliged to do so. He could, if he chose, treat Anderson on his own credit. But he could not hold both Anderson and the defendant. If he gave the credit to Anderson, he could not hold the defendant, though she had tendered an engagement direct, in form. The plaintiff could not turn the defendant's sole obligation into a joint obligation without her concurrence. If he gave any credit to Anderson, he elected to accept the defendant's engagement as collateral to that of Anderson. Of course it is only where the promise sued on is primary and direct that this question we are now discussing arises. 27 C.J. p. 42. But in such cases, the extension of any credit to the third party involved requires a written promise on the part of the promisor. Blodgett v. Town of Lowell, 33 Vt. 174, 175, 176.

As we have seen, it appears here that the plaintiff made his original charges against Anderson. Such a fact is not always conclusive evidence of the person who is to be regarded as the original debtor. It is subject to explanation, to be sure, Greene v. Burton and Sowles, 59 Vt. 423, 425, 10 A. 575, but to rebut the inference arising from the fact that the charges were so made, the proof must be of a strong character. Hardman v. Bradley, 85 Ill. 162. As we said in Enos v. Owens Slate Co., 104 Vt. 329, 333, 160 A. 185, the quality of a defendant's promise may usually be found by ascertaining whether the third person continues to be liable after the defendant's oral promise is made. In that case, it did not appear that the original charges for the services rendered by the plaintiff were made against the third person; and the plaintiff explained why he attempted to collect his pay from such person. Here no explanation is made or attempted. No reason is given why these charges were made against Anderson. So it must be taken that it was because the plaintiff considered him responsible therefor. Lomax v. McKinney, 61 Ind. 374; Langdon v. Richardson, 58 Iowa 610, 12 N.W. 622. Having given credit to Anderson, the plaintiff cannot collect from the defendant. There being no error in the ruling on the motion for a verdict, there is no occasion to consider the other exceptions argued.

Judgment affirmed.

YARBRO v. NEIL B. McGINNIS EQUIPMENT CO.

Supreme Court of Arizona, In Banc, 1966.
101 Ariz. 378, 420 P.2d 163.

BERNSTEIN, VICE CHIEF JUSTICE.

This case is before us on an appeal from a judgment of the Superior Court of Maricopa County. The appellee, McGinnis Equipment Co., brought suit to recover payments due it pursuant to a conditional sales contract for the sale of one used Allis–Chalmers Model HD–5G tractor. The contract was negotiated in August of 1957 and called for twenty-three monthly installments of $574.00 each. The buyer, Russell, failed to make the first monthly payment, and on his suggestion a McGinnis company representative met with the appellant, Yarbro, to ask if he would help with the payments. As a result of this meeting Yarbro agreed to, and did, pay the September installment.

In the months that followed there was a continued failure on the part of Russell to make any of the monthly installment payments. During the late months of 1957 and the early months of 1958, there were numerous discussions between McGinnis Co., Russell and Yarbro relative to these monthly payments and at various times during this period, the defendant orally agreed to make some of the payments for Russell. Late in December of 1957, Yarbro gave the McGinnis Co. a check to cover one of the delinquent payments but the check was returned due to insufficient funds. In March of 1958, Yarbro agreed to bring the account of Russell current and allocated $2,378.00 of a check for this purpose. This check, however, was also returned by the bank for lack of sufficient funds.

In May, 1958 when McGinnis Co. indicated that the tractor soon would have to be repossessed, Yarbro again assured the company that it would be paid as soon as two pending real estate escrows were closed. This promised payment was not made. A similar promise was made by Yarbro in July on the strength of proceeds that were to be forthcoming from an oat crop in New Mexico but again no payment was made. An ultimatum was issued by the McGinnis Co. at the end of July, 1958 and finally steps to repossess were taken in August of 1958.

Persons at the Yarbro ranch prevented the repossession, leading to further negotiations which also provided unfruitful. The tractor was finally repossessed in January of 1959. Subsequently, the McGinnis Co. brought an action to recover the payments due under the conditional sales contract, naming Russell and Yarbro as defendants. A default judgment was entered against Russell and the only question before this court now concerns the liability of the defendant, Yarbro. The trial court found Yarbro liable for the entire balance under the conditional sales contract ($8,751.95).

The errors assigned by the defendant on this appeal are threefold. First, he contends that his promises to pay the debts of Russell, being oral, are unenforceable by reason of the Statute of Frauds. § 44–101, subsec. 2. Second, he contends that there was insufficient consideration to support the promise assuming it was otherwise enforceable. Third, he contends that if the Statute of Frauds were held to be inapplicable to this case, the judgment rendered by the trial court was excessive. The third assignment of error is based on defendant's arguments that he only promised to pay four, rather than all, of the unpaid monthly installments. We will consider these contentions separately.

Although the promises made by Yarbro clearly were of the type covered in the [suretyship Statute of Frauds], the plaintiff contends that the leading object or primary purpose exception recognized by this court in the case of Steward v. Sirrine, 34 Ariz. 49, 267 P. 598, is applicable. Simply stated, this rule provides that where the leading object of a person promising to pay the debt of another is actually to protect his own interest, such promise if supported by sufficient consideration, is valid, even though it be oral. This rule has been adopted by a great number of states although the rationale has often been stated in varying terms. This exception to the Statute of Frauds no matter how stated, is based upon the underlying fact that the Statute does not apply to promises related to debts created at the instance, and for the benefit, of the promisor, (i.e. "original" promises) but only to those by which the debt of one party is sought to be charged upon and collected from another (i.e. "collateral" promises). Although a third party is the primary debtor, situations may arise where the promisor has a personal, immediate and pecuniary interest in the transaction, and is therefore himself a party to be benefitted by the performance of the promisee. In such cases the reason which underlies and which prompted the above statutory provision fails, and the courts will give effect to the promise. * * *

Recognizing the leading object rule as a well reasoned exception, the question remains whether the facts presently before this court make the exception applicable. There are no easy, mathematical guidelines to such a determination. To ascertain the character of the promise in question and the intention of the parties as to the nature of the liability created, regard must be had to the form of expression, the situation of the parties, and to all the circumstances of each particular case. * * * The assumption behind the exception is that it is possible for a court to infer from the circumstances of any given case whether the "leading object" of the promisor was to become a surety for another or whether it was to secure a pecuniary advantage to himself and so, in effect, to answer for his own debt. The leading object may be inferred from that which he expected to get as the exchange for his promise. Thus, it is neither "consideration" alone (for there must be consideration to make any promise enforceable, including one of guaranty) nor "benefit" alone (for in most every guaranty situation at least some benefit will flow to the promisor-guarantor) that makes an oral promise to pay the debt of another enforceable. Rather, there must be consideration and benefit *and* that benefit must be the primary object of making the promise as distinguished from a benefit which is merely incidental, indirect, or remote. It is when the leading and main object of the promisor is *not* to become surety or guarantor of another, even though that may be the effect, but is to serve some purpose or interest of his own, that the oral promise becomes enforceable. * * *

The facts in the present case show that before the McGinnis Co. ever began its dealings with Russell, Yarbro had sought to purchase the tractor in question for himself, but that no sale had resulted because the financing institution with which the McGinnis Equipment Co. financed such deals would not accept Yarbro's credit. It was at this point that Yarbro said that he thought he could get Russell to buy the tractor. Further evidence of Yarbro's interest in the tractor comes from the fact that after its purchase he had borrowed it on a series of occasions. When repairs were needed shortly after Yarbro had made the first installment payment, the McGinnis Co. repairman found the machine on Yarbro's land. He admits that a number of times he used the tractor for jobs around his ranch, and witnesses stated at the trial that Yarbro had asked on several occasions that the McGinnis Co. not repossess the tractor because he needed it. These requests were usually in conjunction with a promise to pay what was owing on the tractor.

We have often stated that this court will not disturb the findings and judgment of the trial court when supported by substantial evidence and that all the evidence and inferences therefrom must be viewed in a manner strongest in favor of the appellees. * * * We find that there was substantial evidence to support the trial court's conclusion that the main and leading object of Yarbro in making his promises to McGinnis Co. was not to become Russell's guarantor but rather was to serve interests of his own.

Yarbro further contends that if the oral character of the promise does not prevent its enforcement, then a failure of consideration does. We, of course, recognize that a promise must be supported by consideration or some substitute in order to be legally enforceable, but find this requirement to be fulfilled in the present instance. In Cavanagh v. Kelly, 80 Ariz. 361, 297 P.2d 1102, we held that a benefit to a promisor or a loss or detriment to the promisee is good consideration to legally support a promise. In the present case, the McGinnis Co. had a legal right to repossess the subject of its conditional sales contract, but the evidence shows that it forbore from doing so because Yarbro promised that he would pay the delinquent installment payments. This forbearance was not only a legal detriment to the McGinnis Co., but as previously noted, was a substantial benefit to Yarbro. Forbearance by a creditor to seize his debtor's property or enforce a lien against it, has often been held to be sufficient consideration to support an oral promise of guaranty when such forbearance enables the promisor to obtain an advantage or benefit. * * *

Thus, when the main purpose of the promisor is not to answer for the debt of another, but to obtain a substantial benefit to himself, which he actually secures as the consideration for his promise, then not only is the promise valid though oral, it is supported by good and sufficient consideration.

The defendant also contends that assuming his promise was not within the contemplation of the Statute of Frauds, the eventual judgment rendered against him was excessive. With this contention, we agree.

The trial court granted judgment in the amount of $8,751.95 which represents the entire unpaid balance of the contract purchase price reduced by the $5,000 received by the plaintiff at an auction sale of the repossessed machine. To hold Yarbro liable for the complete contract price, the evidence must indicate that his promises to pay went not only to delinquent payments but also to the remainder of the payments under the contract. The evidence, however, does not show this.

It is clear from the testimony of the creditor's agents that each time they visited Yarbro and Russell, only past due payments were requested. It is also clear from their testimony that there were no promises by Yarbro to assume future installment payments. The only evidence regarding a promise to pay in the future appears in Yarbro's own testimony on direct examination, and is as follows:

"Q. What was said by you concerning the * * * Russell obligation?

"A. I told them that * * * if they would give me time I would pay for this tractor and take it over."

The creditors failed to make any such arrangements, and under such circumstances the above statement cannot be considered to rise to the dignity necessary to obligate the defendant to pay future installment payments. When one assumes a portion of the debt of another it does not necessarily follow that he has assumed his entire debt.

The record indicates that the last time that Yarbro was contacted prior to repossession was shortly after the July, 1958 installment came due. At this time, claiming anticipated crop proceeds for assurance, he promised to make all past due payments on the equipment. No later promises were made. Accordingly, we find Yarbro liable for the monthly installments from October, 1957 through July, 1958 only. The trial court judgment is reduced correspondingly.

Judgment affirmed as modified.

Problems

22. D says to C, "Deliver these goods to TP and I will see that you are paid." C delivers the goods to TP but manifests an intent not to treat TP as his debtor, relying solely on the credit of D. Is D's promise enforceable?

23. TP orders goods from C. D orally promises C to act as surety for TP. C insists that they undertake a joint obligation, the parties agree, and C delivers the goods. Is D's promise enforceable?

24. TP owes C $1,000. D says to C, release TP and I will pay. C releases TP. Is D's promise enforceable?

25. TP owes C $1,000. TP and D enter into an oral contract by the terms of which D, for a consideration, agrees to assume the obligation. Is D's promise enforceable?

26. TP owes C $1,000. For a consideration, D orally promises to become a surety. Is D's promise enforceable?

27. TP owes C $1,000. C is about to levy an attachment on TP's factory. D, who is an unsecured creditor of TP, orally promises that if C forbears D will pay TP's debt if TP does not. Is D's promise enforceable?

28. TP is indebted to C and as a result C has a lien upon TP's property. D orally promises to pay the debt if TP does not, provided that C discharges the lien of the mortgage. C discharges the lien of the mortgage. Is D's promise enforceable?

29. A, for a consideration, orally promises B that, in the event B's car is damaged in a collision, A will reimburse B for the loss. C and B have a collision for which C is responsible. Is A's promise enforceable?

30. A, for a consideration, orally promises B that in the event that C, B's employee, steals money from B, A will reimburse B. Is A's promise enforceable?

SECTION 6.   STATUTE OF FRAUDS AND MARRIAGE

(Calamari & Perillo 5th § 19.13)

DIENST v. DIENST

Supreme Court of Michigan, 1913.
175 Mich. 724, 141 N.W. 591.

McAlvay, J. Complainant filed her bill of complaint against defendant, praying for divorce on the ground of extreme cruelty. Defendant appeared and filed an answer to said bill of complaint, coupled with a cross-bill, wherein he set up a verbal antenuptial contract, by which it is claimed that she agreed to make provision for him after the marriage by executing a will of all her property in his favor in case he survived her. The relief prayed for in said cross-bill is that complainant produce and file such will, which is claimed to have been made soon after the marriage, and that it be declared binding as a settlement of the property rights of the parties; that in case the will has been destroyed by her she be required to make and execute a duplicate thereof; that in case she refuses so to do within the period of five days after decree, the decree stand in the place and stead of said will and be final; that the rights and interest of defendant in said property be declared fixed, binding, and vested; that complainant be enjoined from disposing of any of her property except in accordance with the agreement claimed, and for general relief. He does not pray for a decree of divorce. Issue was joined by a replication to the answer.

A general demurrer was interposed by complainant to the cross-bill of defendant on the ground of want of equity for several reasons, the chief of which was that the claimed antenuptial contract was within the statute of frauds. This provision of the statute reads: "Every agreement, promise or undertaking, made upon consideration of marriage, except the mutual promises to marry, shall be void unless such agreement, contract or promise, or some note or memorandum thereof, be in writing signed by the party to be charged therewith." Section 9515, subd. 3, C.L.1897.

* * *

A very brief statement of the circumstances which brought about the marriage between these parties will be made. It appears that in November, 1908, a correspondence between them was begun, the initial letter having been written by complainant. Both were subscribers to the publication of a marriage brokerage called "The Correspondent," in which complainant discovered an attractive description of defendant. Complainant was of the age of 62 years and defendant 66 years. Both had been previously married, and each had been widowed by death. She was possessed of an estate, real and personal, in her own right, of between sixty and seventy thousand dollars. Defendant was penniless. A lurid correspondence, thus begun between the parties, of which we are furnished only that of complainant, appears as exhibits to his cross-bill (he modestly withholding his contributions to the same), and within a few months culminated in their engagement, which was speedily followed by a marriage, growing out of which this litigation, to sever the marital relations between them, naturally followed.

Counsel for defendant apparently appreciates and admits that if the agreement sought to be enforced was made and entered into upon consideration of marriage, not having been reduced to writing, it is void under the statute of frauds. However, he contends that the agreement relied upon by him was "not made upon consideration of marriage"; that the agreement was that if defendant would give up his home and employment and abandon prospective political preferment, come to Kalamazoo, marry, and reside with complainant and not return to Kansas, she would not only support him, but would make a will, as already stated. It appears, however, that the only agreement which defendant charges in his cross-bill was entered into by complainant, and which he avers he relied upon, is the agreement set forth in the excerpt from his cross-bill above quoted, to the effect that she *"then and there, as a further consideration for the consummation of such engagement of marriage promised and agreed* that she would, immediately after their said marriage, make such provision that the said defendant would come into possession and ownership of all of her said property upon her death." That this was the inducement appears from his averment as follows: "And that thereupon immediately thereafter, relying upon such representations, promises, and agreements on the part of the said plaintiff, and in consideration thereof, he gave up and abandoned his employment, position, and prospects, * * * which he then and there had, and immediately proposed marriage to the said complainant," which proposal complainant immediately accepted. It is clear to us that this claimed agreement and undertaking between these parties was made upon consideration of marriage, and was within the prohibition of the statute of frauds. It was therefore void and not enforceable.

The other questions discussed in the briefs of the parties do not require consideration.

The order and decree of the circuit court in sustaining the demurrer of complainant is affirmed, and the cross-bill is dismissed, with costs of both courts to complainant. The cause will be remanded, and will proceed in due course.

Problems

31. A and B, an engaged couple, orally agree that after their marriage they will live in A's house. In exchange B agrees to pay $70,000 to A. Is the agreement within the Statute of Frauds?

32. A and B were engaged to be married. C, who is A's mother, orally promised A and B a new Jaguar automobile as a wedding gift. She subsequently repudiated. Is her promise enforceable?

SECTION 7. STATUTE OF FRAUDS AND REAL PROPERTY

(Calamari & Perillo 5th §§ 19.14—19.15)

SHAUGHNESSY v. EIDSMO

Supreme Court of Minnesota, 1946.
222 Minn. 141, 23 N.W.2d 362, 166 A.L.R. 435.

MATSON, JUSTICE. In an action for specific performance, defendant Bernt Eidsmo appeals from an order denying his motion for a new trial.

Plaintiffs, husband and wife, on April 5, 1943, by oral agreement, leased from the defendant Bernt Eidsmo a dwelling house and lot * * * for a term of one year from May 1, 1943, at a rental of $47.50 per month, and, in consideration for the making of said lease and as a part thereof, defendant agreed to give, and gave, plaintiffs an option to purchase said property at the expiration of the lease term at a price between $4,750 and $5,000 on a contract for deed, subject to the proviso that plaintiffs should be allowed as a credit on the purchase price the total rent paid for the lease term with the balance of the purchase price to be paid in monthly installments of $32.50, inclusive of unpaid taxes and five percent interest per annum on the unpaid balance. Defendant also agreed to sell plaintiffs a stove for $119.50, payable in installments of $4 per month without interest. Plaintiffs entered into possession May 1, 1943, and continued in possession throughout the one-year lease term ending April 30, 1944, and paid during said term a total rental of $570 and a total of $48 on the purchase price of the stove. At and before the expiration of said lease term, plaintiffs notified defendant that they wished to exercise their option of purchase according to the terms thereof, and on several occasions they demanded of defendant that he deliver a contract for deed as agreed. On each of these occasions, defendant told plaintiffs that he did not have time to have a contract drawn, but that his word was good and they should not worry. Plaintiffs fully performed their part of the option agreement and have at all times been ready, willing, and able to execute a contract for deed. Since the expiration of the lease term, plaintiffs have continued in possession, and from May 1, 1944, to May 1, 1945, have paid an additional $570 on the purchase of said property and a further sum on the purchase of the stove. When the option and lease agreement were made, the premises were subject to a $4,200 mortgage of which no mention was made to the plaintiffs and in regard to which no agreement was made that plaintiffs should assume said mortgage or take the property subject to the same.

* * *

The trial court decreed that plaintiffs have a vendees' interest in the property and that they were entitled to a contract for deed from defendant specifying a purchase price of $5,000, subject to a credit on said price for the gross sum of all rents and purchase money paid, with a proviso that the balance of the price should be paid in monthly installments of $32.50 each, inclusive of taxes and interest at five percent per annum.

* * *

The instant * * * plaintiffs exercised their option by notifying defendant of their election to buy the premises a new contract, an oral contract for the purchase and sale of land, came into being. It was clearly within the statute of frauds (§ 513.04 [§ 8459]), unless taken therefrom by part performance, § 513.06 (§ 8461). According to Restatement, Contracts, § 197, the applicable rule is as follows:

> "Where, acting under an oral contract for the transfer of an interest in land, the purchaser with the assent of the vendor

* * *

> "(b) takes possession thereof or retains a possession thereof existing at the time of the bargain, and also pays a portion or all of the purchase price,

> the purchaser or the vendor may specifically enforce the contract."

In other words, the acts of taking possession and of making part payment, when they are performed under or in reliance upon the oral contract as to be unequivocally referable to the vendor-vendee relationship and not referable to any other relation between the parties, are sufficient to remove the contract from the statute of frauds. The doctrine of part performance, exemplified by the above rule, was followed by this court in Wentworth v. Wentworth, 2 Minn. 277, 2 Gil. 238, 72 Am.Dec. 97; Gill v. Newell, 13 Minn. 462, 13 Gil. 430; and Bresnahan v. Bresnahan, 71 Minn. 1, 73 N.W. 515. In Brown v. Hoag, 35 Minn. 373, 375, 29 N.W. 135, 137, however, the court expressly rejected the unequivocal reference theory upon which the earlier cases were based and adopted the fraud theory under which the plaintiff must show that his acts or part performance in reliance upon the contract so altered his position that he would incur an unjust and irreparable injury in the event the defendant were permitted to rely on the statute of frauds. This latter decision, though apparently overlooked in Bresnahan v. Bresnahan, supra, has been followed in subsequent cases. We now adopt the Restatement principle to the effect that the taking of possession, coupled with the making of part payment, in reliance upon and with unequivocal reference to the vendor-vendee relationship, *without proof of irreparable injury through fraud,* is sufficient to avoid the statute. Brown v. Hoag, supra, and subsequent decisions based thereon, in so far as they require proof of irreparable injury or great hardship in addition to part performance, are expressly overruled. In other jurisdictions, as well as our own, in losing sight of historical antecedents considerable confusion has resulted in determining the basis for the removal of cases from purview of the statute of frauds. See 13 Minn.L.Rev. 744; Annotation, 101 A.L.R. 923, 943.

"The origin of the doctrine of the part performance as applied to permit the specific performance of an oral contract for the sale of real estate may be traced to a rule of equity which, antedating the English statute of frauds, required as a prerequisite of the enforcement of parol contracts concerning land that the plaintiff show that the contract had been partly performed, *or* that he had so altered his position in reliance on the agreement that a refusal to enforce it would amount to a fraud upon him." (Italics supplied.) 49 Am.Jur., Statute of Frauds, § 420.

Dean Pound, The Progress of the Law, in 33 Harv.L.Rev. 929, 937, with clarity explains the basis for the confusion that has arisen in so many American jurisdictions:

"* * * It is important to insist that the taking of cases out of the statute is a historical anomaly, only to be understood by reference to seventeenth-century and eighteenth-century legal institutions and modes of thought in equity and that, like all historical anomalies of the sort, it defies logically satisfactory analytical treatment.

"What is the actual situation? We say that for the purposes of courts of equity, cases are taken out of the purview of the statute in either of two ways: by fraud *or* by part performance. Recently there has been a tendency to run the two together, largely under the influence of Pomeroy's doctrine of 'equitable fraud.' But they had an independent origin and have developed along independent lines. Hence they call first for independent consideration." (Italics supplied.) and Id., at pp. 939, 940: "Before a decade had passed after its [statute of frauds] enactment, the Court of Chancery began to take cases out of the operation of the statute where purchaser had been put in possession under the contract. Sugden [Vendor and Purchaser (14 ed.) 152, note p] long ago called attention to some old cases which indicate that this was the result of ideas as to livery of seisin. *Putting the purchaser in possession was taken to be the substance of a common-law conveyance.* The rule thus derived became established in England and in a majority of American jurisdictions. But its original basis was soon overlooked and attempts to rationalize the subject led writers and courts to turn to the idea of 'fraud' in order to make a reasoned doctrine of 'part performance' on the basis of the old cases where the chancellor had dispensed with the statute. Different developments of this idea gave rise to many varieties of doctrine. Thus we get to-day cases taken out by possession alone; cases taken out by possession coupled with something else, arbitrarily prescribed by judicial decision or by statute; cases taken out by possession when joined to circumstances of great hardship upon purchaser; cases of part performance other than by taking possession, where there are acts solely referable to a contract as to the very land or showing a change in the character of the preexisting possession, and cases where it is not possible to take possession but relief is given on a theory of fraud or of irreparable injury to purchaser, without more." (Italics supplied.)

* * *

Samuel Williston, under whose direction Restatement, Contracts, § 197, was drafted, in Commentaries on Contracts, Restatement No. 4, pp. 14, 15, dated February 23, 1928, states: " * * * Courts of equity early adopted the doctrine that such acts as the taking of possession, making of improvements, and the like by the purchaser with consent of the vendor make the contract enforceable though there is no written memorandum. This doctrine has been rested upon two main reasons: (1) that the rule of the Statute of Frauds is an evidential rule and that any acts clearly and solely referable to the existence of the contract satisfy in equity the purpose of the Statute; (2) that equity should relieve against the operation of the Statute in cases where it would be unconscionable for the vendor to rely upon it in defense."

These two main reasons given by Williston correspond to Dean Pound's analysis that "cases are taken out of the purview of the statute in either of two ways: by fraud *or* by part performance." (Italics supplied.) Obviously, the evidential purpose of the statute is fully satisfied by adequate part performance without proof of irreparable injury. * * *

Whether the acts of part performance are unequivocally referable to the vendor-vendee relationship under the oral contract is (in this case) a question of fact for the trier of fact. * * *

In the instant case, the two essential elements of possession and part payment are present. Defendant contends, however, that possession is not unequivocally referable to the vendor-vendee relationship, but is equally referable to the relation of landlord and tenant. The entire record, however, is pregnant with indications of a dominant intent of the parties from the inception of their transaction that a purchase-and-sale relation should be established upon the expiration of the lease term. The purchase of the stove also indicated an understanding that plaintiffs were to occupy the premises permanently. After plaintiffs exercised their option and an oral contract of purchase and sale then came into being, defendant's conduct and statements were consistent only with a mutual understanding that plaintiffs' possession of the premises was no longer that of a tenant but that of a vendee with unequivocal reference to the oral contract. When plaintiffs, on several occasions, requested the preparation of a contract for deed, defendant, instead of rejecting the vendor-vendee relationship, affirmed it by stating "that he did not have time to have a contract drawn; that his word was good; that plaintiff Mark Shaughnessy was not to worry about getting his contract." In fact, defendant finally presented to plaintiffs a written memorandum to be used as a basis for drawing a contract for deed. The conduct of the parties indicated no misunderstanding as to the nature of their transaction and the relation that each bore to the other. There was a dispute as to the amount of the purchase price and the terms of payment, but as to these matters the findings of the court are sustained by the evidence. Similar considerations support the findings that the payments made by plaintiffs were solely referable to the oral contract of purchase and sale.

The order denying a new trial is affirmed.

Problems

33. S orally retained X, a licensed real estate broker, to procure a buyer who would pay $10,000 cash for Blackacre. S promised X a commission of 6%. X produced B who purchased Blackacre for $10,000. In an action by X against S for the commission, S pleads the Statute of Frauds. What result?

34. D orally contracted with P to build a one family residential structure for P's use. As part of the deal, D orally warranted that the house would be free of defects for one year after completion of construction. The house was completed and P took possession of it. Within a year certain defects became apparent. When D refused to repair them, P sued and D raised the defense of the Statute of Frauds. Is the defense sound?

35. S, the owner of Blackacre, orally authorized A to sell Blackacre for $10,000 and to sign any necessary papers. A, as agent, agreed to sell Blackacre to B for $10,000 in a writing signed by A but not by S. Raise and resolve the Statute of Frauds problems in this case.

36. S made a written offer to sell Blackacre to B. B accepted orally. B breached the contract. When sued by S, B sets up the defense of the Statute of Frauds. What result?

37. S made an oral offer to sell Blackacre to B for $10,000. B accepted and paid the $10,000 to S. S now refuses to convey. In an action by B, S raises the defense of the Statute of Frauds. What result?

38. S orally agreed to transfer Blackacre to B. B agreed to pay the purchase price in one year. Pursuant to further terms of the agreement, S conveyed the property to B. At the end of the year B has not paid. Is the Statute of Frauds a defense to S's action for the price?

Chapter 14

DISCHARGE OF CONTRACTS

SECTION 1. MUTUAL RESCISSION

(Calamari & Perillo 5th §§ 21.1—21.2)

COPELAND PROCESS CORP. v. NALEWS, INC.

Supreme Court of New Hampshire, 1973.
113 N.H. 612, 312 A.2d 576.

DUNCAN, JUSTICE. In 1966 the plaintiff was under contract with the Franconia Paper Corporation to furnish a chemical recovery system at the Franconia plant in Lincoln. It was also under contract with the town of Lincoln to install pollution control equipment at the same plant to solve a water pollution problem. The town project, financed by federal funds and proceeds of bonds issued by the town, had a completion date in November 1968. This action of assumpsit was brought to recover damages alleged to have been suffered by the plaintiff as the result of alleged breach by the defendant of a subcontract entered into in May 1966, by which the defendant undertook to furnish labor, materials and services in connection with construction and installation of the town sulphite disposal system pursuant to the plaintiff's contract with the town.

Thereafter the parties to the action stipulated as follows: "To submit for the decision of the Court for a hearing on the merits the question of fact and law as to what effect, if any, a document signed by the parties dated October 2, 1968, a copy of which is attached hereto, had on the rights and duties of the parties relating to the plaintiff's purchase order #6605 901–3 dated May 1, 1968, together with all correspondence incorporated thereto by reference and as subsequently modified by change orders CO 1, 2, 3 and 4."

The agreement referred to as the document of October 2, 1968 was on stationery of the plaintiff company addressed to the defendant company, attention of Mr. Phil Swett, President. It read as follows: "Gentlemen: You and we hereby agree, for and on behalf of our separate companies, that as of 4:30 P.M. of this date of October 2, 1968, the contract agreement entered into by our companies for the Lincoln N.H. project and covered by our purchase order 6605–901–3 of May 1, 1968,

889

together with change orders CO #1, CO #2, CO #3 & CO #4 are hereby cancelled without prejudice by mutual agreement.

"We also agree that as quickly as possible, an accounting of all costs on the contract will be assembled and settlement made between Copeland Process Corp & Nalews Inc.

"Nalews will promptly submit a statement of cost under the contract to date together with an inventory of pipes, valves, fittings purchased and on site at the job. Copeland Process Corp will purchase those materials, already on the site, which have not previously been included in cost statements.

"Agreed & Accepted for Copeland Process Corp. GG Copeland President Accepted & Agreed Upon for Nalew's Inc. Philip E. Swett President."

The issue presented by the stipulation was tried to the Court (Keller, C.J.), and resulted in findings and rulings favorable to the defendant. The plaintiff excepted to the findings and rulings and to certain rulings made in the course of the trial, and its exceptions were reserved and transferred by the presiding justice.

At the trial the plaintiff excepted to receipt of evidence of circumstances surrounding execution of the agreement of October 2, 1968. The plaintiff maintains that the agreement is unambiguous, and that parol evidence was inadmissible to vary its meaning. It contends that by agreeing that the contract of May 1, 1966 should be "cancelled without prejudice", the parties intended that their rights and obligations under the contract should be unaffected by the termination of the defendant's services on October 2, 1968.

In addition to ruling upon requests for findings and rulings submitted by the parties, the trial court found and ruled as follows:

"It is found that in cancelling the contract of May 1st, the parties intended to cancel all rights and obligations of both parties, past, present and future, arising out of the contract, including rights and obligations relative to any breaches of the contract; also, that in cancelling it 'without prejudice' they intended that the cancellation itself should not give rise to any liability; and it is further found that they intended that there would be a settlement between the parties relative to work done and materials furnished by the defendant prior to cancellation, and that this would be on a cost basis. In such a settlement, the defendant is entitled to be credited with the cost of work done and materials furnished, and the plaintiff is entitled to a credit for payments made, and for the cost of rectifying any defective work and/or materials."

In finding and ruling that the parties intended to cancel all rights and obligations arising out of any breaches of the subcontract, the trial court in response to a request by the defendant also found and ruled as follows: "Nalews is an experienced contracting firm and would not voluntarily default on its contract resulting in the work being performed at cost-plus, with excess cost being assessed against it."

The problems presented by an agreement to cancel or rescind a contract after part performance have been outlined by Professor Corbin in his treatise on contracts. In 5A A. Corbin, Contracts § 1229 at 508 (1964), under the heading of " 'Discharge', 'Termination' and 'Cancellation' ", this comment is made: "[I]t is a common supposition that when a 'contract' is said to be * * * cancelled, all of these legal relations cease to exist, the rights and duties of both parties, alike being ended." However, under the heading "Discharge by rescission", § 1236 points out at pages 535–538 the questions which arise where rescission is agreed upon after part performance or a breach: "Is any compensation to be made for a part performance rendered? Does the agreement discharge all right to compensatory damages for a breach that has already been committed? * * * Does the rescission operate only in futuro, making the contract inoperative as to matters yet unperformed, but leaving it still operative as to performances fully or defectively rendered under it?" We think the conclusion therein stated is applicable to the circumstances of this case: "The answers to such questions as these can be made only after interpretation of the terms of the agreement of rescission [or cancellation], and in the light of the circumstances that surrounded its making." 5A A. Corbin, supra § 1236, at 538.

On its face and without the aid of extrinsic evidence, the agreement of the parties that the subcontract should be "cancelled" might seem without ambiguity to mean that their rights and duties under the contract should be terminated. However, other provisions of the cancellation agreement indicated that the intention was otherwise with respect to specific past performance. The use of the words "without prejudice" served to heighten the ambiguity. To a legal mind this expression might suggest that rights arising out of the subcontract were to remain unaffected by termination of performance. But it could well mean something different to the laymen who drafted and executed the agreement without benefit of legal advice. In this situation, the evidence of the circumstances surrounding integration of the agreement was properly received. * * *

In the interpretation of a contract the findings of the trial court based upon evidence of the surrounding circumstances are findings of fact which are binding in this court if supported by the evidence. * * * Thus in Pettee v. Chapter, 86 N.H. 419, 425, 170 A. 1, 4 (1934), after adverting to the statement by *Doe*, C.J., in Brown v. Bartlett, 58 N.H. 511 (1879), that "the question of intention is ordinarily determined as a question of fact, by the natural weight of competent evidence, * * * " this court said: "Undoubtedly the question of intention is for the court. It is equally true that all evidence tending to show material circumstances is admissible in the attempt to establish their existence. But the ascertainment of their existence is clearly and appropriately a function of the court, to which the determination of issues of fact is generally committed." Pettee v. Chapter, supra at 428, 170 A. at 5.

The cancellation agreement was entered into in some haste, on the verge of a meeting with representatives of the town and the paper company and their engineers for the purpose of determining what should be done to assure completion of the project by the date fixed by the various contracts between the interested parties. Copeland Process and Nalews both were under the gun, and Copeland pointed out to Swett that the companies which they represented were both in danger of being discharged, with ensuing damage to their professional standing. The subcontract provided in terms that Copeland could terminate the contract on ten days' notice, for violation of its terms by Nalews, and that Copeland Process could complete the work at Nalews' expense. Copeland assured Swett that he did not wish to injure Nalews' standing by following such a course. He therefore proposed that the parties terminate their relationship by agreement, so that he might satisfy the forthcoming meeting that completion of the project would be expedited. In the brief course of negotiations Swett offered little comment concerning proposed terms, except to express concern over payment for work already performed and materials on hand. Thus the agreement also concerned itself with these considerations.

The question of who would be responsible for the completion of the contract was not discussed in terms of liability for the cost, nor did the cancellation agreement advert to this. Copeland's expression of a purpose not to harm Nalews coupled with his phraseology of cancellation "without prejudice", could reasonably be found to have given Swett to understand that Nalews would be under no responsibility or liability for the cost of completion; and Copeland could reasonably be found to have had reason to know both that Swett so understood, and that Swett acted in reliance upon that understanding. In such case, it is fundamental contract law that Copeland Process would be bound by Swett's understanding. * * *

Since the findings and rulings of the trial court are supported by both the law and the evidence, its decree for the defendant on the issue submitted by stipulation of the parties is sustained. * * *

Remanded.

U.C.C. § 1–107. Waiver or Renunciation of Claim or Right After Breach

Any claim or right arising out of an alleged breach can be discharged in whole or in part without consideration by a written waiver or renunciation signed and delivered by the aggrieved party.

U.C.C. § 1–306 (2001 revision). WAIVER OR RENUNCIATION OF CLAIM OR RIGHT AFTER BREACH.

A claim or right arising out of an alleged breach may be discharged in whole or in part without consideration by agreement of the aggrieved party in an authenticated record.

U.C.C. § 2–720. Effect of "Cancellation" or "Rescission" on Claims for Antecedent Breach (Unchanged in revision).

Unless the contrary intention clearly appears, expressions of "cancellation" or "rescission" of the contract or the like shall not be construed as a renunciation or discharge of any claim in damages for an antecedent breach.

U.C.C. § 3–604 (2002 revision). Discharge by Cancellation or Renunciation.

(a) A person entitled to enforce an instrument, with or without consideration, may discharge the obligation of a party to pay the instrument (i) by an intentional voluntary act, such as surrender of the instrument to the party, destruction, mutilation, or cancellation of the instrument, cancellation or striking out of the party's signature, or the addition of words to the instrument indicating discharge, or (ii) by agreeing not to sue or otherwise renouncing rights against the party by a signed record.

(b) Cancellation or striking out of an indorsement pursuant to subsection (a) does not affect the status and rights of a party derived from the indorsement.

(c) In this section, "signed," with respect to a record that is not a writing, includes the attachment to or logical association with the record of an electronic symbol, sound, or process with the present intent to adopt or accept the record.

Problems

1. A and B enter into a binding contract by the terms of which A agrees to work for B for a period of one year and B agrees to pay $500 to A each week. The parties mutually agree to rescind their duties under the contract before performance begins. Is their rescission effective?

2. In problem 1, if A works for a week and then the parties mutually rescind, should A be paid for the week's work?

3. In problem 1, would an agreement to mutually rescind be effective if A has completely performed?

4. A promises B that a structure will be completed before Jan. 1, and it is agreed that time is of the essence. B permits A to complete the structure despite A's late performance. Is A entitled to recover? Does B have a claim?

5. A agreed to furnish specifications for a unique machine and B agreed to furnish machine design drawings. Both parties failed to cooperate and to act in good faith in trying to create such a machine. What are the rights of the parties?

SECTION 2. RELEASE, EXECUTORY ACCORD, AND SUBSTITUTED AGREEMENT

(Calamari & Perillo 5th §§ 21.3—21.7, 21.10—21.11)

GREENFIELD v. PHILLES RECORDS, INC.

Court of Appeals of New York, 2002.
98 N.Y.2d 562, 780 N.E.2d 166, 750 N.Y.S.2d 565.

GRAFFEO, J. In this contract dispute between a singing group and their record producer, we must determine whether the artists' transfer of full ownership rights to the master recordings of musical performances carried with it the unconditional right of the producer to redistribute those performances in any technological format. In the absence of an explicit contractual reservation of rights by the artists, we conclude that it did.

In the early 1960s, Veronica Bennett (now known as Ronnie Greenfield), her sister Estelle Bennett and their cousin Nedra Talley, formed a singing group known as "The Ronettes." They met defendant Phil Spector, a music producer and composer, in 1963 and signed a five-year "personal services" music recording contract (the Ronettes agreement) with Spector's production company, defendant Philles Records, Inc. The plaintiffs agreed to perform exclusively for Philles Records and in exchange, Philles Records acquired an ownership right to the recordings of the Ronettes' musical performances. The agreement also set forth a royalty schedule to compensate plaintiffs for their services. After signing with Philles Records, plaintiffs received a single collective cash advance of approximately $15,000.

The Ronettes recorded several dozen songs for Philles Records, including "Be My Baby," which sold over a million copies and topped the music charts. Despite their popularity, the group disbanded in 1967 and Philles Records eventually went out of business. Other than their initial advance, plaintiffs received no royalty payments from Philles Records.

Beyond their professional relationship, however, was the story of the personal relationship between Spector and plaintiff Ronnie Greenfield. They married in 1968 but separated after a few years. Greenfield initiated a divorce proceeding against Spector in California and a settlement was reached in 1974. As part of that agreement, Spector and Greenfield executed mutual general releases that purported to resolve all past and future claims and obligations that existed between them, as well as between Greenfield and Spector's companies.

Defendants subsequently began to capitalize on a resurgence of public interest in 1960s music by making use of new recording technologies and licensing master recordings of the Ronettes' vocal performances for use in movie and television productions, a process known in entertainment industry parlance as "synchronization." The most notable example was defendants' licensing of "Be My Baby" in 1987 for use in the motion picture "Dirty Dancing." Defendants also licensed master recordings to third parties for production and distribution in the United States (referred to as domestic redistribution), and sold compilation albums containing performances by the Ronettes. While defendants earned considerable compensation from such licensing and sales, no royalties were paid to any of the plaintiffs.

As a result, plaintiffs commenced this breach of contract action in 1987, alleging that the 1963 agreement did not provide Philles Records with the right to license the master recordings for synchronization and domestic redistribution, and demanded royalties from the sales of compilation albums. Although defendants initially denied the existence of a contract, in 1992 they stipulated that an unexecuted copy of the contract would determine the parties' rights. Defendants thereafter argued that the agreement granted them absolute ownership rights to the master recordings and permitted the use of the recordings in any format, subject only to royalty rights. Following extensive pretrial proceedings (160 A.D.2d 458, 553 N.Y.S.2d 771, 243 A.D.2d 353, 674 N.Y.S.2d 1, 248 A.D.2d 212, 670 N.Y.S.2d 73), Supreme Court ruled in plaintiffs' favor and awarded approximately $3 million in damages and interest.

The Appellate Division affirmed, concluding that defendants' actions were not authorized by the agreement with plaintiffs because the contract did not specifically transfer the right to issue synchronization and third-party domestic distribution licenses. Permitting plaintiffs to assert a claim for unjust enrichment, the Court found that plaintiffs were entitled to the music recording industry's standard 50% royalty rate for income derived from synchronization and third-party licensing. We granted leave to appeal.

* * *

[The contract provided: "Without limitation of the foregoing, [Philles] shall have the right to make phonograph records, tape recordings or other reproductions of the performances embodied in such recordings by any method now or hereafter known, * * * ." Under the "plain meaning" rule, the court held that defendant's had the absolute right, without royalties, to reproduce the recordings in media that were not in existence at the time of the contract. Ed.]

We realize that our conclusion here effectively prevents plaintiffs from sharing in the profits that defendants have received from synchronization licensing. However sympathetic plaintiffs' plight, we cannot resolve the case on that ground under the guise of contract construction. Our guiding principle must be to neutrally apply the rules of contract interpretation because only in this way can we ensure stability in the law and provide guidance to parties weighing the risks and advantages of entering a binding agreement.

Defendants acknowledge that the royalty schedule for domestic sales encompasses the sale of records, compact discs and other audio reproductions by entities holding domestic third-party distribution licenses from Philles Records. In light of that concession, we remit this case to Supreme Court to recalculate plaintiffs' damages for royalties due on all such sales. Damages should be determined pursuant to the applicable schedule incorporated in the agreement rather than based on industry standards.

Defendants further claim that Greenfield is barred from sharing in those royalties because she executed a general release in connection with her divorce from Spector. We look to California law to analyze the scope of Greenfield's release because that is the state where the release was executed and the divorce was finalized. In contrast to the "four corners" rule that New York has long applied * * *, California courts preliminarily consider all credible evidence of the parties' intent in addition to the language of the contract—"[t]he test of admissibility of extrinsic evidence to explain the meaning of a written instrument is not whether it appears to the court to be plain and unambiguous on its face, but whether the offered evidence is relevant to prove a meaning to which the language of the instrument is reasonably susceptible" (*Pacific Gas & Elec. Co. v. G.W. Thomas Drayage & Rigging Co.*, 69 Cal.2d 33, 37, 442 P.2d 641, 644 [1968]).

During proceedings in New York, Supreme Court determined that the extrinsic evidence supported Greenfield's allegation that her right to compensation under the 1963 recording contract was not an intended subject of the release. That finding of fact, affirmed by the Appellate Division, is supported by the record. We find no reason to reverse the Appellate Division's interpretation of California law (*see e.g. Rudman v. Cowles Communications*, 30 N.Y.2d 1, 10, 330 N.Y.S.2d 33, 280 N.E.2d 867 [1972]). Plaintiff Greenfield is therefore entitled to her share of any damages assessed against defendants.

We have reviewed the parties' remaining contentions; they are either academic or meritless. Accordingly, the order of the Appellate Division should be modified, without costs, and the case remitted to Supreme Court for further proceedings in accordance with this opinion and, as so modified, affirmed.

GOLDBARD v. EMPIRE STATE MUTUAL LIFE INS. CO.

Supreme Court of New York, Appellate Division, 1958.
5 A.D.2d 230, 171 N.Y.S.2d 194.

BREITEL, J. Plaintiff appeals from a determination of the Appellate Term modifying a judgment rendered in his favor against defendant after trial without a jury in the Municipal Court. The Appellate Term modification, one Justice dissenting, reduced plaintiff's recovery from $2,800 to $800. That court granted leave for plaintiff to appeal to this court.

Plaintiff is the insured under an accident and health insurance policy providing monthly indemnity; defendant is the insurer. * * *

The issue which divided the Appellate Term is whether plaintiff insured settled and compromised his claims against defendant insurer prior to suit, with finality, and, as a consequence, is limited in recovery to the settlement figure of $800. The trial court found that insured was not so limited, but a majority of the Appellate Term disagreed.

It is concluded that the settlement negotiations between insured and insurer did not constitute either a substituted agreement or an enforcible executory accord; and, that therefore, insured is not prevented from pursuing his original claim. * * *

Insured is a barber by trade. Before his illness he ran his own one-man shop. In December, 1951 insurer issued its annually renewable policy to insured, who maintained his payments of premiums as required by the policy. In 1955 insured filed claims based upon a fungus hand infection from which he was suffering and which he asserted totally disabled him from engaging in his occupation. If true, he was entitled to monthly indemnity at fixed amounts under the policy. There then ensued a sequence of events in which some payments, vouchered as final, were offered by insurer, which insured refused to accept, believing they were less than that to which he was entitled. Insurer had misgivings concerning the nature of insured's illness and the extent of its disabling character. The parties remained in genuine dispute. In the early fall of 1955 insured made complaint to the State Insurance Department, and this triggered the occurrence upon which the main issue on this appeal is based.

While the disputants were before the department representative, insurer offered to settle the claims for $800, conditioned on a surrender of the policy, with consequent termination of its renewability. Insured, concededly, refused. He was willing to accept the $800, but not to surrender the renewable policy. However, later that day insured telephoned the department representative and asked him to advise insurer that he would accept the $800, without requiring that the policy be renewed. The department representative relayed the call. Insurer thereupon wrote insured a letter asking him to call at the office with his policy for surrender and advising, in effect, that he would then be paid the $800 upon signing a release. Insured ignored the letter, and in due time started this action.

Insurer contends that on the facts related there was a "settlement and compromise" which limits insured's right of recovery. Insured, on the other hand, contends that there was no more involved than a new offer by insurer, not accepted by insured, or, at best, an executory accord which is unenforcible for lack of a writing as required by section 33–a of the Personal Property Law.*

There is no magic to the words "settlement" or "compromise" in deciding whether a disputed claim has been discharged with such finality that no action may be brought upon it, but only upon the later agreement. As a matter of fact, the words are used interchangeably to describe either a subsequent agreement which discharges an earlier agreement, that is, a substituted or superseding agreement (Morehouse v. Second Nat. Bank, 98 N.Y. 503), or an executory accord which does not (Larscy v. Hogan & Sons, 239 N.Y. 298). Consequently, one does not advance the

* [Now § 15–501 of McKinney's N.Y.Gen'l Obl.L. See Calamari & Perillo 5th § 21.4 n.11. Ed.]

solution of any problem in this area by attaching either label, or presuming to conclude the discussion by making an initial determination that a negotiation has or has not achieved a "settlement" or a "compromise". (6 Corbin on Contracts, § 1268.)

The question always is whether the subsequent agreement, whatever it may be, and in whatever form it may be, is as a matter of intention, expressed or implied, a superseder of, or substitution for, the old agreement or dispute; or whether it is merely an agreement to accept performance, *in futuro,* as future satisfaction of the old agreement or dispute. The literature on the subject is voluminous. * * * There is, then, no simple rule to be applied, as a matter of law, to determine in all given situations whether the subsequent agreement extinguishes the old.

Nevertheless, there are principles which occasionally assist in the determination of the question of intention where settlement negotiations have consummated in an agreement. The Restatement has described these as giving rise to presumptions. (See Restatement, Contracts, § 419, Comment a.) The New York Law Revision Commission takes the same view (1937 Report, p. 213). This court recently followed a similar analysis (Blair & Co. v. Otto V., 5 A.D.2d 276).

There has arisen, however, a certain class of cases which have given color to the view that some settlements are, as a matter of law, superseding or substituted agreements discharging the old obligations, without involving the determination of intention. Nothing said, or held, in those cases, however, warrants such a conclusion. In each there were circumstances pointed to, at least impliedly, as grounding the findings of intention to supersede the old agreement with the new. [Citations omitted.] The persistent principle to be applied is that of determination of the intention of the parties, as objectively manifested [Citations omitted.]

Sometimes, of course, the matter of intention may be determined from documents exclusively, in which event the conclusion may be drawn, as a matter of law, by the court (e.g., Moers v. Moers, [229 N.Y. 294, 301]). At other times, the determination of intention will depend upon conversation, surrounding circumstances, or extrinsic proof, in addition to documentation, if any exist, in which event the issue is one of fact, for the trier of the facts, be it court or jury (e.g., Katz v. Bernstein, 236 App.Div. 456; 6 Corbin on Contracts, § 1293, pp. 148–149).

The complex of facts—conversations, circumstances and documents, if there be any—presents the basis for making inferences. Both experience and logic suggest that some recurring factors are more indicative of intention than others. These have given rise to what have been earlier described as presumptions. So it is that the courts hasten to find an intention to have a substituted or superseding agreement discharging the old where the settlement has resulted in formalized papers with unequivocal language (as in Blair & Co. v. Otto V., supra), or in formalized or deliberate proceedings in court during the pendency of an action (see Langlois v. Langlois, supra, and the cases cited therein). These, of course, are not the only relevant recurring factors, or the only bases for presumptions; nor would it be true to suggest that the search for evidentiary inferences has not been influenced by various policy considerations. * * *

When, however, it is concluded that the settlement negotiations have resulted in no more than in an agreement to accept a future performance, albeit by a promise presently made, in future satisfaction of the old obligations—in this State especially—another principle of law intervenes. In New York, an executory accord not fully performed was, prior to the enactment of section 33–a of the Personal Property Law, unenforcible. It was not even available as a defense. This was the rule at common law. (1937 Report of N.Y.Law Rev.Comm., pp. 211–217; Restatement, Contracts, § 417, N.Y. Annotations.) Since the enactment of section 33–a an executory accord may be enforced provided it is in writing and signed by the party to be held. If it remain unperformed, the promisee may elect to sue on the accord or the original obligation.

On this analysis, one does not reach the requirements for a writing provided in section 33–a, unless one has first found that the subsequent agreement is not one that supersedes or substitutes for the old one, and, therefore, extinguishes it. Such a subsequent agreement need not be in writing, unless, of course, a writing is required by some independent statute, such as a Statute of Frauds. But, if it is determined that the intention of the parties, expressed by their conduct or words, is that the subsequent agreement was designed to do no more than result in agreement that a future performance, albeit of a promise presently made, would be accepted as future satisfaction of the old obligations, then section 33–a comes into play and the subsequent agreement is unenforcible unless it is in writing and signed.

Applying these principles to the facts in this case, the question is whether there was a substituted agreement, an executory accord, or no contract at all.

In the first place, we have a series of distinctly informal conversations with bargaining give and take. At no time are the bargainers, and the intermediary, agreeing on one occasion and in one place as to what the settlement should be. Instead, there was a triangular operation, the purportedly final terms of which were never expressed in the presence of all. Secondly, at no point do the conversations and communications converge on the precise terms, time or place for consummation. These were the facts that impelled the trial court to find no contract at all.

Thirdly, and crucially, there is nothing in the record, which would support an inference that insured ever intended, let alone agreed, to accept only a promise of $800 to be paid in the future (as distinguished from an actual payment here and now) as a present discharge and satisfaction of the insurer's obligations.

Taking the three enumerated elements outlined above, they do not suggest the finality, the deliberateness, or the occasional formalization with which one associates substituted agreements and the specific intention to discharge pre-existing obligations. They do not attain the considered resolution of the entire dispute between the parties that moved the court in Moers v. Moers (supra) or in Langlois v. Langlois (supra) to find a superseding agreement. Indeed, they fall far short of the circumstances which the court held insufficient to infer a superseding agreement in cases like Atterbury v. Walsh Paper Corp. (261 App.Div. 529, affd. 286 N.Y. 578, supra).

Generally, it is assumed that one does not surrender an existing obligation for a promise to perform in the future (Moers v. Moers, supra, p. 300; see 6 Williston on Contracts [rev. ed.], § 1847, where it was said: "it is not a probable inference that a creditor intends merely an exchange of his present cause of action for another. It is generally more reasonable to suppose that he bound himself to surrender his old rights only when the new contract of accord was performed"; 6 Corbin on Contracts, §§ 1268, 1271, 1293). The Restatement would seem to have taken a somewhat more advanced position (Restatement, Contracts, § 419***), but it is explicitly stated to be merely a guide for interpretation in case of doubt. So treated it is akin to a canon of construction, rather than a presumption that a court is bound to follow in the absence of proof to the contrary. Considering the inchoate and staccato negotiations that ensued in this case, culminating in a relayed telephone call, there is no warrant for inferring the making of a superseding agreement which thereby discharged insured's claims and his renewable policy.

Assuming then, although the trial court found to the contrary, that there was a contract, the factors present in this case, whether subsumed under some rule of interpretation or examined on an *ad hoc* basis, suggest that if any settlement was reached it was not a superseding or substituted agreement but at best only an executory accord. (Actually there is still another possibility applicable to this case, but it is not one urged here: the conversations which took place may have never achieved the finality of concluding a settlement. All negotiations in which parties verbally, and especially, if orally, concur on a settlement are not necessarily intended, instanter, to be binding. Just as often, in quite informal settings, the parties do no more than agree to agree, and consummation awaits some degree of implementation. This, of course, is also merely a matter of intention.) * * *

And, of course, on the principles earlier discussed, if all that resulted from the telephone conversations and the letter written by insurer was an executory accord, it was not cognizable under New York law for lack of a writing as required by section 33–a of the Personal Property Law.

Accordingly, the determination of the Appellate Term modifying the judgment rendered in favor of plaintiff against defendant in the Municipal Court by reducing the recovery from $2,800 to $800 should be

---

*** "Where a contract is made for the satisfaction of a pre-existing contractual duty, or duty to make compensation, the interpretation is assumed in case of doubt, if the pre-existing duty is an undisputed duty either to make compensation or to pay a liquidated sum of money, that only performance of the subsequent contract shall discharge the pre-existing duty; but if the pre-existing duty is of another kind, that the subsequent contract shall immediately discharge the pre-existing duty, and be substituted for it." For applications of this rule in New York, see Restatement, N.Y. Annotations, to this section. (See, also, 6 Corbin on Contracts, § 1271.)

modified, on the law and on the facts, to reinstate the judgment of the Municipal Court, except as modified, in accordance with the concession of plaintiff, by reduction to the sum of $2,600, together with costs and disbursements of this appeal to plaintiff-appellant.

Problems

6. P commenced an action against defendant, an auto dealer, for restitution of financing charges that exceeded the maximum allowed by state law, plus a penalty. P's total claim was about $6,000. After settlement discussions, P signed a release of this claim that recited a consideration of "$5 and other consideration." P subsequently pursued the claim. The dealer pleaded an affirmative defense based on the release. P testifies that the "other consideration" was supposed to be title to a described used Thunderbird automobile which was never delivered. P's testimony was credited by the trial court. What effect does the failure to deliver the Thunderbird have upon the release?

7. A is indebted to B and they enter into an agreement by the terms of which B presently discharges A's debt in exchange for a promise made by A. A materially breaches the promise. May B still successfully sue A on the original claim?

8. C has a claim against D in the amount of $1,000. C and D agree that C will take a horse worth $500 in exchange. D tenders the horse and C refuses to take it. What are the rights of the parties. Would the result be different if the horse were worth $2,000?

9. A is a mortgagee and B is a mortgagor. A agrees to take $5,000 less than the face amount of the mortgage loan if B will tender the amount prior to July 1. B makes the tender which A refuses to accept. What are the rights of the parties?

SECTION 3. NOVATION, ACCOUNT STATED, TENDER, AND UNION OF RIGHT AND DUTY

(Calamari & Perillo 5th §§ 21.8, 21.9, 21.12—21.15)

FIRST AMERICAN COMMERCE CO. v. WASHINGTON MUTUAL SAVINGS BANK

Supreme Court of Utah, 1987.
743 P.2d 1193.

DURHAM, JUSTICE: In this interlocutory appeal, First American Commerce (Borrower) seeks relief from a summary judgment entered against it dismissing all but its claim for fraud against First Security Realty Services (Lender).

* * *

The facts as asserted by Borrower are that Borrower received a loan from Lender, securing repayment with a deed of trust and an assignment of rents on a commercial building owned by Borrower. Under the loan documents, Lender's written approval was required on new leases and a percentage of the loan was withheld in a "hold-back" fund pending the completion of certain tenant improvements. On the day the loan documents were signed, Lender assigned the loan to Washington Mutual Savings Bank (Assignee). The assignment was made with the knowledge and consent of Borrower. Borrower desired to lease space in the building and contacted both Lender and Assignee, neither of which would give written consent. Borrower lost the opportunity to lease the space. Upon completion of the tenant improvements, Borrower made a written request that Lender release the held-back funds. Lender refused to release the funds on the theory that its duty to do so had been delegated to Assignee. Borrower sued Lender and Assignee.

Lender obtained summary judgment on the theory that when it assigned the loan documents to Assignee, it ceased to have any responsibility to Borrower, including the duty to release the held-back funds. Borrower argues that although Lender assigned its right to receive payments, it remained obligated to perform its duties under the loan agreement. In the absence of a novation agreement between Lender and Borrower whereby Assignee's performance would be substituted for that of Lender, Lender remained responsible for its duties under the loan. We believe that Borrower is correct.

A review of basic contract law vocabulary is helpful to a resolution of the issue. An assignment is the transfer of rights; a delegation is the transfer of duties. J. Calamari & J. Perillo, *Contracts* § 18–24 (2d ed. 1977). The term "assignment" is often used imprecisely by courts. We agree with the Second Circuit Court of Appeals that "lawyers seem prone to use the word 'assignment' inartfully, frequently intending to encompass within the term the distinct [concept] of delegation...." *Contemporary Mission, Inc. v. Famous Music Corp.*, 557 F.2d 918, 924 (2d Cir.1977) (quoting J. Calamari & J. Perillo, *Contracts* § 254 (1970)). *Cf. Pemberton v. Arkansas State Highway Commission*, 268 Ark. 929, 597 S.W.2d 605 (Ark.Ct.App.1980) (demonstrating an imprecise use of the terminology). Regardless of the terminology they use, courts agree that a party who delegates his duties under a contract to a third person is not relieved of his responsibilities, but rather remains ultimately responsible to the party with whom he contracted for guaranteeing the successful execution of the contractual duties. * * *

Lender contends that ordinary contract law principles do not apply to bank loans and that the language of the loan documents contemplated a novation rather than an assignment. Lender's argument is that while the usual rules of contract law should apply when a party delegates a duty to provide goods or services, a bank that delegates duties under a loan agreement should have no further liability. * * * An examination of the policy underlying the general rule demonstrates the weakness of Lender's position. The usual rule requiring that a delegating party remain liable is designed to protect the expectations of the party receiving the performance. The delegating party should not be able to foist upon the other party to the contract a performer whose skills, goods, reliability, or solvency might differ from those of the delegator. *See Foster v. Cross,* 650 P.2d 406, 410–11 (Alaska 1982). That reasoning applies equally to duties under loan documents. Borrower is entitled to look to Lender's reasonableness and policies respecting the approval of leases and to Lender's solvency to guarantee the release of the remainder of the loan funds.

Lender insists that whether a novation occurred is a matter of law, not of fact. Lender asserts that the language of the loan documents clearly describes a novation. We disagree with Lender on both assertions. Whether an agreement is a novation is a matter of intent. The essential element of a novation is the discharge of one of the parties to a contract and the acceptance of a new performer by the other party as a substitute for the first original party. *See Kennedy v. Griffith,* 98 Utah 183, 187, 95 P.2d 752 (1939). A novation must be intended by the parties to the original contract.

> [T]he burden of proof as to a novation by the transaction in question rests upon the party who asserts it; … an intention to effect a novation will not be presumed; … in the absence of evidence indicating a contrary intention, it will be presumed, prima facie, that the new obligation was accepted merely as additional or collateral security, or conditionally, subject to the payment thereof; and that the intention to effect a novation must be clearly shown.

D.A. Taylor Co. v. Paulson, 552 P.2d 1274, 1275 (Utah 1976) (footnote omitted).

Borrower filed an affidavit from one of its general partners stating that Borrower at all times intended to look to Lender for the held-back funds and intended to acknowledge only the assignment of money due in repayment of the loan when it acknowledged the assignment. While it is possible that a document could by its unambiguous terms provide for a novation, the documents in this case do not. Lender argues that the duties under the contract belong to the "Beneficiary," who is defined as "the holder of the note, whether or not named herein," and that by calling Assignee the holder of the note, the contract relieved Lender of its obligations. That interpretation ignores another clause in the loan documents which defines the beneficiary by name as Lender and a provision stating that the agreements bind the parties to the documents *and* their heirs and assigns, not the parties *or* their assigns, as a novation would. Further, if the parties had intended to draft a novation agreement, we think that Lender's counsel would have called the arrangement a novation or at least provided clear language consistent with the intent to substitute Assignee for Lender.

We reverse the grant of summary judgment and remand the matter to the trial court in order to determine the intent of the parties and the other factual issues.

OLD WEST ENTERPRISES, INC.
v. RENO ESCROW CO.

Supreme Court of Nevada, 1970.
86 Nev. 727, 476 P.2d 1.

MOWBRAY, JUSTICE. This is an appeal from an order of the district court granting summary judgment to respondent-plaintiff, Reno Escrow Company, who had commenced an action against appellant-defendant, Old West Enterprises, Inc., to recover $6,836.89 on an alleged account stated for legal services received by Old West over a 5–year period.[1]

Reno Escrow filed its complaint in district court on November 17, 1969, and its motion for summary judgment on December 10, 1969, accompanied by the attorney's supporting affidavit, which set forth in detail the legal services performed, fees charged, and statements rendered, to which, affiant claimed, Old West did not object.

Old West answered the complaint on December 15, 1969, and on December 22, 1969, responded to the motion for summary judgment by filing three counteraffidavits that challenged the propriety of the charges on the grounds that the $6,836.89 figure was excessive and that, further, the affiants had, during the period of the billings, questioned the attorney "regarding the propriety, justifiability and excessiveness of the legal charges."

On December 30, 1969, the district judge entered an order granting summary judgment in favor of Reno Escrow. Hence this appeal.

1.   THE SUMMARY JUDGMENT

This court has ruled that the trial court may grant summary judgment only when the proofs received show that there is no genuine issue as to any material fact. * * *

* * *

2.   THE ACCOUNT STATED

An account stated may be broadly defined as an agreement based upon prior transactions between the parties with respect to the items composing the account and the balance due, if any, in favor of one of the parties. To effect an account stated, the outcome of the negotiations must be the recognition of a sum due from one of the parties to the other with a promise, express or implied, to pay that balance. The amount or balance so agreed upon constitutes a new and independent cause of action. The genesis of an account stated is the *agreement* of the parties, express or implied.

Reno Escrow argues that implication of acceptance of the account rendered in this case may be drawn from its retention without objection

---

1. The attorney who had performed the services had assigned his claim to Reno   Escrow Company for collection.

by Old West.[2] To give an account rendered the force of an account stated because of silence on the part of the one receiving the account, the circumstances must be such as to support an inference of agreement as to the correctness of the account. Such an inference may be rebutted. As the court said in Karnofsky v. 4548 Main St., Inc., Sup., 192 N.Y.S.2d 577 at 582 (1959):

> "Where the terms of an oral contract between bitterly disputing parties are in issue, a trial is the only remedy. * * *

> "* * * Although a sum due for attorney's services may properly be the subject of an account stated, the omission to object to an account rendered raises only a rebuttable inference that the debtor consents to such account, giving rise to a triable issue; * * * In such a case, the value of the professional services rendered and the amount thereof unpaid are to be assessed before a jury * * *"

The reason back of the rule is well expressed in Cooper v. Conklin, 197 App.Div. 205, 189 N.Y.S. 552, 553 (1921):

> "The rule is a just one, and imposes no unreasonable burden upon the attorney. The underlying reason for the rule is that the relations between attorney and client are so confidential, and the client relies so fully upon his attorney for the protection of his legal rights, and is by the nature of their relations so subject to the advice of the attorney, that in all such contracts the attorney cannot rely upon the face of the agreement itself, but is compelled by the law to show, in addition thereto, that the contract is fair and reasonable, and that the client was fully informed of all the facts which enabled him to judge its fairness and reasonableness."

Since the proofs received present a material factual issue that must be resolved by the trier of the facts, the order granting summary judgment must be reversed.

It is so ordered, and the case is remanded to the district court for a trial on the merits.

Problems

10. D owes C $1,000. T agreed with D to assume this debt for a consideration. Is there a novation? Would the result be different if C *promised* to release D from liability in exchange for T's promise?

11. A is indebted to B. C executed a promissory note in favor of B to pay A's indebtedness. B accepted the note. Does A continue to remain liable to B?

12. In an action for recovery of the unpaid balance for merchandise sold and delivered, S was able to show that B received and retained the goods without objection. He also did not object to the invoices and demands for payment submitted by S. May S proceed upon a theory of account stated?

2. Although the counteraffidavits tendered by Old West assert that the state-   ments were challenged.

13. D, a contractor, bought lumber on credit. Monthly statements sent by C, the lumber supplier, stated that all statements not paid within 10 days would be charged interest at a specified rate. D was considerably in arrears. When litigation ensued, C claimed interest, as well as principal. Is C entitled to interest?

14. A is a mortgagor. B is the mortgagee. At the maturity of the obligation, A makes a valid tender of payment which B refuses. What effect does this have on the rights of the parties?

15. A is a mortgagor. B is a first mortgagee and C is a second mortgagee. A conveys the fee to B. Is the first mortgage merged into the fee?

Chapter 15

BARGAINS THAT ARE ILLEGAL OR AGAINST PUBLIC POLICY

SECTION 1. SOME VARIETIES OF PUBLIC POLICIES

(Calamari & Perillo 5th § 22.1)

HEWITT v. HEWITT

Supreme Court of Illinois, 1979.
77 Ill.2d 49, 31 Ill.Dec. 827, 394 N.E.2d 1204.

UNDERWOOD, JUSTICE: The issue in this case is whether plaintiff Victoria Hewitt, whose complaint alleges she lived with defendant Robert Hewitt from 1960 to 1975 in an unmarried, family-like relationship to which three children have been born, may recover from him "an equal share of the profits and properties accumulated by the parties" during that period.

Plaintiff initially filed a complaint for divorce, but at a hearing on defendant's motion to dismiss, admitted that no marriage ceremony had taken place and that the parties have never obtained a marriage license. In dismissing that complaint the trial court found that neither a ceremonial nor a common law marriage existed,* that since defendant admitted the paternity of the minor children, plaintiff need not bring a separate action under the Paternity Act (Ill.Rev.Stat.1975, ch. 1063/4, par. 51 *et seq.*) to have the question of child support determined; and directed plaintiff to make her complaint more definite as to the nature of the property of which she was seeking division.

Plaintiff thereafter filed an amended complaint alleging the following bases for her claim: (1) that because defendant promised he would "share his life, his future, his earnings and his property" with her and all of defendant's property resulted from the parties' joint endeavors, plaintiff is entitled in equity to a one-half share; (2) that the conduct of the parties evinced an implied contract entitling plaintiff to one-half the

---

* [In the past, a "common law marriage" could be created by mutual agreement without state or church intervention. This form of marriage has been abolished in most jurisdictions. Clark states that the institution survives in 13 U.S. jurisdictions. Clark on Domestic Relations § 2.4 (2d ed., 1988). Ed.]

property accumulated during their "family relationship"; (3) that because defendant fraudulently assured plaintiff she was his wife in order to secure her services, although he knew they were not legally married, defendant's property should be impressed with a trust for plaintiff's benefit; (4) that because plaintiff has relied to her detriment on defendant's promises and devoted her entire life to him, defendant has been unjustly enriched.

The factual background alleged or testified to is that in June 1960, when she and defendant were students at Grinnell College in Iowa, plaintiff became pregnant; that defendant thereafter told her that they were husband and wife and would live as such, no formal ceremony being necessary, and that he would "share his life, his future, his earnings and his property" with her; that the parties immediately announced to their respective parents that they were married and thereafter held themselves out as husband and wife; that in reliance on defendant's promises she devoted her efforts to his professional education and his establishment in the practice of pedodontia, obtaining financial assistance from her parents for this purpose; that she assisted defendant in his career with her own special skills and although she was given payroll checks for these services she placed them in a common fund; that defendant, who was without funds at the time of the marriage, as a result of her efforts now earns over $80,000 a year and has accumulated large amounts of property, owned either jointly with her or separately; that she has given him every assistance a wife and mother could give, including social activities designed to enhance his social and professional reputation.

The amended complaint was also dismissed, the trial court finding that Illinois law and public policy require such claims to be based on a valid marriage. The appellate court reversed, stating that because the parties had outwardly lived a conventional married life, plaintiff's conduct had not "so affronted public policy that she should be denied any and all relief" (62 Ill.App.3d 861, 869, 20 Ill.Dec. 476, 482, 380 N.E.2d 454, 460), and that plaintiff's complaint stated a cause of action on an express oral contract. We granted leave to appeal. Defendant apparently does not contest his obligation to support the children, and that question is not before us.

The appellate court, in reversing, gave considerable weight to the fact that the parties had held themselves out as husband and wife for over 15 years. The court noted that they lived "a most conventional, respectable and ordinary family life" (62 Ill.App.3d 861, 863, 20 Ill.Dec. 476, 478, 380 N.E.2d 454, 457) that did not openly flout accepted standards, the "single flaw" being the lack of a valid marriage. Indeed the appellate court went so far as to say that the parties had "lived within the legitimate boundaries of a marriage and family relationship of a most conventional sort" (62 Ill.App.3d 861, 864, 20 Ill.Dec. 476, 479, 380 N.E.2d 454, 457), an assertion which that court cannot have intended to be taken literally. Noting that the Illinois Marriage and Dissolution of Marriage Act (Ill.Rev.Stat.1977, ch. 40, par. 101 *et seq.*) does not prohibit nonmarital cohabitation and that the Criminal Code of 1961 (Ill.Rev.Stat.1977, ch. 38, par. 11–8(a)) makes fornication an offense only if the behavior is open and notorious, the appellate court concluded that plaintiff should not be denied relief on public policy grounds.

In finding that plaintiff's complaint stated a cause of action on an express oral contract, the appellate court adopted the reasoning of the California Supreme Court in the widely publicized case of *Marvin v. Marvin* (1976), 18 Cal.3d 660, 134 Cal.Rptr. 815, 557 P.2d 106, quoting extensively therefrom. In *Marvin*, Michelle Triola and defendant Lee Marvin lived together for 7 years pursuant to an alleged oral agreement that while "the parties lived together they would combine their efforts and earnings and would share equally any and all property accumulated as a result of their efforts whether individual or combined." (18 Cal.3d 660, 666, 134 Cal.Rptr. 815, 819, 557 P.2d 106, 110.) In her complaint she alleged that, in reliance on this agreement, she gave up her career as a singer to devote herself full time to defendant as "companion, home-maker, housekeeper and cook." (18 Cal.3d 660, 666, 134 Cal.Rptr. 815, 819, 557 P.2d 106, 110.) In resolving her claim for one-half the property accumulated in defendant's name during that period the California court held that "The courts should enforce express contracts between nonmar-ital partners except to the extent that the contract is explicitly founded on the consideration of meretricious sexual services" and that "In the absence of an express contract, the courts should inquire into the conduct of the parties to determine whether that conduct demonstrates an implied contract, agreement of partnership or joint venture, or some other tacit understanding between the parties. The courts may also employ the doctrine of quantum meruit, or equitable remedies such as constructive or resulting trusts, when warranted by the facts of the case." (18 Cal.3d 660, 665, 134 Cal.Rptr. 815, 819, 557 P.2d 106, 110.) The court reached its conclusions because:

> "In summary, we believe that the prevalence of nonmarital relationships in modern society and the social acceptance of them, marks this as a time when our courts should by no means apply the doctrine of the unlawfulness of the so-called meretricious relation-ship to the instant case. * * *

> The mores of the society have indeed changed so radically in regard to cohabitation that we cannot impose a standard based on alleged moral considerations that have apparently been so widely abandoned by so many." 18 Cal.3d 660, 683–84, 134 Cal.Rptr. 815, 831, 557 P.2d 106, 122.

It is apparent that the *Marvin* court adopted a pure contract theory, under which, if the intent of the parties and the terms of their agree-ment are proved, the pseudo-conventional family relationship which impressed the appellate court here is irrelevant; recovery may be had unless the implicit sexual relationship is made the explicit consideration for the agreement. In contrast, the appellate court here, as we under-stand its opinion, would apply contract principles only in a setting where the relationship of the parties outwardly resembled that of a traditional family. It seems apparent that the plaintiff in *Marvin* would not have been entitled to recover in our appellate court because of the absence of that outwardly appearing conventional family relationship.

The issue of whether property rights accrue to unmarried cohabitants can not, however, be regarded realistically as merely a problem in the law of express contracts. Plaintiff argues that because her action is founded on an express contract, her recovery would in no way imply that unmarried cohabitants acquire property rights merely by cohabitation and subsequent separation. However, the *Marvin* court expressly recognized and the appellate court here seems to agree that if common law principles of express contract govern express agreements between unmarried cohabitants, common law principles of implied contract, equitable relief and constructive trust must govern the parties' relations in the absence of such an agreement. (18 Cal.3d 660, 678, 134 Cal.Rptr. 815, 827, 557 P.2d 106, 118; 62 Ill.App.3d 861, 867–68, 20 Ill.Dec. 476, 380 N.E.2d 454.) In all probability the latter case will be much the more common, since it is unlikely that most couples who live together will enter into express agreements regulating their property rights. (Bruch, *Property Rights of De Facto Spouses, Including Thoughts on the Value of Homemakers' Services,* 10 Fam.L.Q. 101, 102 (1976).) The increasing incidence of nonmarital cohabitation referred to in *Marvin* and the variety of legal remedies therein sanctioned seem certain to result in substantial amounts of litigation, in which, whatever the allegations regarding an oral contract, the proof will necessarily involve details of the parties' living arrangements.

Apart, however, from the appellate court's reliance upon *Marvin* to reach what appears to us to be a significantly different result, we believe there is a more fundamental problem. We are aware, of course, of the increasing judicial attention given the individual claims of unmarried cohabitants to jointly accumulated property, and the fact that the majority of courts considering the question have recognized an equitable or contractual basis for implementing the reasonable expectations of the parties unless sexual services were the explicit consideration. (See cases collected in Annot., 31 A.L.R.2d 1255 (1953) and A.L.R.2d Later Case Service supplementing vols. 25 to 31.) The issue of unmarried cohabitants' mutual property rights, however, as we earlier noted, cannot appropriately be characterized solely in terms of contract law, nor is it limited to considerations of equity or fairness as between the parties to such relationships. There are major public policy questions involved in determining whether, under what circumstances, and to what extent it is desirable to accord some type of legal status to claims arising from such relationships. Of substantially greater importance than the rights of the immediate parties is the impact of such recognition upon our society and the institution of marriage. Will the fact that legal rights closely resembling those arising from conventional marriages can be acquired by those who deliberately choose to enter into what have heretofore been commonly referred to as "illicit" or "meretricious" relationships encourage formation of such relationships and weaken marriage as the foundation of our family-based society? In the event of death shall the survivor have the status of a surviving spouse for purposes of inheritance, wrongful death actions, workmen's compensation, etc.? And still more important-ly: what of the children born of such relationships? What are their support and inheritance rights and by what standards are custody questions resolved? What of the sociological and psychological effects upon them of that type of environment? Does not the recognition of legally enforceable property and custody rights emanating from nonmar-ital cohabitation in practical effect equate with the legalization of com-mon law marriage—at least in the circumstances of this case? And, in summary, have the increasing numbers of unmarried cohabitants and changing mores of our society * * * reached the point at which the general welfare of the citizens of this State is best served by a return to something resembling the judicially created common law marriage our legislature outlawed in 1905?

Illinois' public policy regarding agreements such as the one alleged here was implemented long ago in *Wallace v. Rappleye* (1882), 103 Ill. 229, 249, where this court said: "An agreement in consideration of future illicit cohabitation between the plaintiffs is void." This is the traditional rule, in force until recent years in all jurisdictions. (See, *e.g., Gauthier v. Laing* (1950), 96 N.H. 80, 70 A.2d 207; *Grant v. Butt* (1941), 198 S.C. 298, 17 S.E.2d 689.) Section 589 of the Restatement of Con-tracts (1932) states, "A bargain in whole or in part for or in consider-ation of illicit sexual intercourse or of a promise thereof is illegal." See also 6A Corbin, Contracts sec. 1476 (1962), and cases cited therein.

It is true, of course, that cohabitation by the parties may not prevent them from forming valid contracts about independent matters, for which it is said the sexual relations do not form part of the consideration. (Restatement of Contracts secs. 589, 597 (1932); 6A Cor-bin, Contracts sec. 1476 (1962).) Those courts which allow recovery generally have relied on this principle to reduce the scope of the rule of illegality. Thus, California courts long prior to *Marvin* held that an express agreement to pool earnings is supported by independent consid-eration and is not invalidated by cohabitation of the parties, the agree-ments being regarded as simultaneous but separate. (See, *e.g., Trutalli v. Meraviglia* (1932), 215 Cal. 698, 12 P.2d 430; see also Annot., 31 A.L.R.2d 1255 (1953), and cases cited therein.) More recently, several courts have reasoned that the rendition of housekeeping and homemak-ing services such as plaintiff alleges here could be regarded as the consideration for a separate contract between the parties, severable from the illegal contract founded on sexual relations. (*Kozlowski v. Kozlowski* (1979), 80 N.J. 378, 403 A.2d 902; *Marvin v. Marvin* (1976), 18 Cal.3d 660, 670 n. 5, 134 Cal.Rptr. 815, 822 n. 5, 557 P.2d 106, 113 n. 5; *Tyranski v. Piggins* (1973), 44 Mich.App. 570, 205 N.W.2d 595, 597; contra, *Rehak v. Mathis* (1977), 239 Ga. 541, 238 S.E.2d 81.)

* * *

The real thrust of plaintiff's argument here is that we should abandon the rule of illegality because of certain changes in societal norms and attitudes. It is urged that social mores have changed radically in recent years, rendering this principle of law archaic. It is said that because there are so many unmarried cohabitants today the courts must confer a legal status on such relationships. This, of course, is the rationale underlying some of the decisions and commentaries. (*See, e.g., Marvin v. Marvin* (1976), 18 Cal.3d 660, 683, 134 Cal.Rptr. 815, 831, 557 P.2d 106, 122; *Beal v. Beal* (1978), 282 Or. 115, 577 P.2d 507; Kay & Amyx, *Marvin v. Marvin: Preserving the Options,* 65 Cal.L.Rev. 937 (1977).) If this is to be the result, however, it would seem more candid to acknowledge the return of varying forms of common law marriage than to continue displaying the naivete we believe involved in the assertion that there are involved in these relationships contracts separate and independent from the sexual activity, and the assumption that those contracts would have been entered into or would continue without that activity.

Even if we were to assume some modification of the rule of illegality is appropriate, we return to the fundamental question earlier alluded to: If resolution of this issue rests ultimately on grounds of public policy, by what body should that policy be determined? *Marvin,* viewing the issue as governed solely by contract law, found judicial policy-making appropriate. Its decision was facilitated by California precedent and that State's no-fault divorce law. In our view, however, the situation alleged here was not the kind of arm's length bargain envisioned by traditional contract principles, but an intimate arrangement of a fundamentally different kind. The issue, realistically, is whether it is appropriate for this court to grant a legal status to a private arrangement substituting for the institution of marriage sanctioned by the State. The question whether change is needed in the law governing the rights of parties in this delicate area of marriage-like relationships involves evaluations of sociological data and alternatives we believe best suited to the superior investigative and fact-finding facilities of the legislative branch in the exercise of its traditional authority to declare public policy in the domestic relations field. * * * That belief is reinforced by the fact that judicial recognition of mutual property rights between unmarried cohabitants would, in our opinion, clearly violate the policy of our recently enacted Illinois Marriage and Dissolution of Marriage Act. Although the Act does not specifically address the subject of nonmarital cohabitation, we think the legislative policy quite evident from the statutory scheme.

* * *

We cannot confidently say that judicial recognition of property rights between unmarried cohabitants will not make that alternative to marriage more attractive by allowing the parties to engage in such relationships with greater security. As one commentator has noted, it may make this alternative especially attractive to persons who seek a property arrangement that the law does not permit to marital partners.

(Comment, 90 Harv.L.Rev. 1708, 1713 (1977).) This court, for example, has held void agreements releasing husbands from their obligation to support their wives. * * * In thus potentially enhancing the attractiveness of a private arrangement over marriage, we believe that the appellate court decision in this case contravenes the Act's policy of strengthening and preserving the integrity of marriage.

The Act also provides: "Common law marriages contracted in this State after June 30, 1905 are invalid." (Ill.Rev.Stat.1977, ch. 40, par. 214.) The doctrine of common law marriage was a judicially sanctioned alternative to formal marriage designed to apply to cases like the one before us. In *Port v. Port* (1873), 70 Ill. 484, this court reasoned that because the statute governing marriage did not "prohibit or declare void a marriage not solemnized in accordance with its provisions, a marriage without observing the statutory regulations, if made according to the common law, will still be a valid marriage." (70 Ill. 484, 486.) This court held that if the parties declared their present intent to take each other as husband and wife and thereafter did so a valid common law marriage existed. (*Cartwright v. McGown* (1887), 121 Ill. 388, 398, 12 N.E. 737.) Such marriages were legislatively abolished in 1905, presumably because of the problems earlier noted, and the above-quoted language expressly reaffirms that policy.

* * *

In our judgment the fault in the appellate court holding in this case is that its practical effect is the reinstatement of common law marriage, as we earlier indicated, for there is no doubt that the alleged facts would, if proved, establish such a marriage under our pre–1905 law. (*Cartwright v. McGown* (1887), 121 Ill. 388, 12 N.E. 737.) The concern of both the *Marvin* court and the appellate court on this score is manifest from the circumstance that both courts found it necessary to emphasize marital values ("the structure of society itself largely depends upon the institution of marriage") (*Marvin v. Marvin* (1976), 18 Cal.3d 660, 684, 134 Cal.Rptr. 815, 831, 557 P.2d 106, 122) and to deny any intent to "derogate from" (18 Cal.3d 660, 684, 134 Cal.Rptr. 815, 831, 557 P.2d 106, 122) or "denigrate" (*Hewitt v. Hewitt* (1978), 62 Ill.App.3d 861, 868, 20 Ill.Dec. 476, 380 N.E.2d 454) that institution. Commentators have expressed greater concern: "[T]he effect of these cases is to reinstitute common-law marriage in California after it has been abolished by the legislature." (Clark, *The New Marriage*, Williamette L.J. 441, 449 (1976).) "*[Hewitt]* is, if not a direct resurrection of common-law marriage contract principles, at least a large step in that direction." Reiland, *Hewitt v. Hewitt: Middle America, Marvin and Common–Law Marriage*, 60 Chi.B.Rec. 84, 88–90 (1978).

We do not intend to suggest that plaintiff's claims are totally devoid of merit. Rather, we believe that our statement in *Mogged v. Mogged* (1973), 55 Ill.2d 221, 225, 302 N.E.2d 293, 295, made in deciding whether to abolish a judicially created defense to divorce, is appropriate here:

"Whether or not the defense of recrimination should be abolished or modified in Illinois is a question involving complex public-policy considerations as to which compelling arguments may be made on both sides. For the reasons stated hereafter, we believe that these questions are appropriately within the province of the legislature, and that, if there is to be a change in the law of this State on this matter, it is for the legislature and not the courts to bring about that change."

We accordingly hold that plaintiff's claims are unenforceable for the reason that they contravene the public policy, implicit in the statutory scheme of the Illinois Marriage and Dissolution of Marriage Act, disfavoring the grant of mutually enforceable property rights to knowingly unmarried cohabitants. The judgment of the appellate court is reversed and the judgment of the circuit court of Champaign County is affirmed.

Appellate court reversed; circuit court affirmed.

TROUTMAN v. SOUTHERN RAILWAY CO.

United States Court of Appeals, Fifth Circuit, 1971.
441 F.2d 586, cert. den. 404 U.S. 871, 92 S.Ct. 81, 30 L.Ed.2d 115.

WISDOM, CIRCUIT JUDGE. Robert B. Troutman, Jr., a member of the State Bar of Georgia, brought this diversity action against the Southern Railway Company seeking to recover the sum of $200,000 as the reasonable value of legal services rendered to Southern in two separate matters—the Central of Georgia case and the grain rate case—during the years 1962 and 1963. On Southern's motion for summary judgment, the district court ruled that Troutman's claim with respect to the Central of Georgia matter was barred by the Georgia four-year statute of limitations. Troutman v. Southern Ry. Co., N.D.Ga.1968, 296 F.Supp. 963. Troutman took no appeal from that ruling, and the Central of Georgia matter has dropped out of the case. A jury awarded Troutman the sum of $175,000 as the reasonable value of his services in the grain rate case. We affirm.

I

In 1963 the Interstate Commerce Commission issued an order directing Southern to increase certain rates on grain shipments from the Midwest to the Southeast by approximately 16 percent. The order created a difficult situation for Southern: if allowed to stand, the order, according to Southern, would result in its losing a $13,000,000 investment in "Big John" railroad cars plus a "tremendous" loss of revenue in the future. Sim S. Wilbanks, a vice president and assistant to the president of Southern, turned for help to Troutman, who had only recently come to Southern's aid in the Central of Georgia case. Troutman, an Atlanta attorney, had no experience in I.C.C. matters, but he was known to Wilbanks as a personal friend and political ally of President John F. Kennedy. Wilbanks told Troutman that Southern was filing suit in a federal district court in Ohio to enjoin the order of the

I.C.C. He asked Troutman to persuade the President and the Department of Justice, then headed by the President's brother, Robert F. Kennedy, to "ditch" the I.C.C. and enter the case on the side of Southern. What Wilbanks actually told Troutman, what he engaged Troutman to do, and what Troutman eventually did are of course the crucial issues in this case, and we shall deal with them later in this opinion. Troutman's efforts were successful: the Department of Justice filed an answer in the Ohio lawsuit opposing the I.C.C. and supporting Southern's position. As a result of the Ohio litigation (in which Troutman played no further part), the I.C.C. order was struck down. In return for Troutman's services (in connection with the Central of Georgia case as well as the grain rate case), Southern agreed to look into the joint development of air rights that Troutman owned on property in downtown Atlanta adjacent to property owned by Southern. Efforts to work out the joint development of the air rights continued for several years. When it became apparent, however, that Southern would not join in the development of the air rights, Troutman demanded compensation for his services in the grain rate case in "the usual manner"—i.e., by the payment of money. When Southern refused to pay, Troutman filed suit.

Southern defended the action on three grounds: (1) that Troutman's claim was barred by the Georgia four-year statute of limitations; (2) that Troutman's activities on behalf of Southern were not legal services and were gratuitously rendered; and (3) that because of the nature of the services rendered, it would be contrary to public policy to enforce a claim for compensation. On these grounds Southern moved for the entry of summary judgment in its favor. The district court denied the Motion, Troutman v. Southern Ry. Co., N.D.Ga.1968, 296 F.Supp. 963, and a jury returned a verdict for Troutman in the amount of $175,000. The court denied Southern's motion for judgment notwithstanding the verdict or for a new trial, and Southern appealed.

II

Southern's first contention is that the district court erred in refusing to grant Southern's motion for judgment notwithstanding the verdict because the evidence conclusively establishes that the contract upon which Troutman sued was "to exert his personal and political influence upon the President of the United States." Southern argues that such a contract is in violation of public policy and unenforceable; therefore, the court erred as a matter of law in failing to render judgment for Southern. We cannot agree.

It is of course true that a contract to influence a public official in the exercise of his duties is illegal and unenforceable when that contract contemplates the use of personal or political influence rather than an appeal to the judgment of the official on the merits of the case. * * * Nevertheless, all citizens possess the right to petition the government for redress of their grievances. United States Constitution, Amendment I. To that end, one may employ an agent or attorney to use his influence to gain access to a public official. Moreover, once having obtained an audience, the attorney may fairly present to the official the merits of his client's case and urge the official's support for that position. * * * As the district court well stated in its opinion overruling Southern's motion for summary judgment, it is "only the elements of 'personal influence' and 'sinister means' [that] will void the contract and deny it enforcement." Troutman v. Southern Ry. Co., N.D.Ga.1968, 296 F.Supp. 963, 972. * * * Moreover, the illegal or sinister nature of a contract for professional services will not be presumed; the burden of proving the illegality of the contract is clearly upon the party asserting it. * * *

It necessarily follows then that the decision whether to enforce a claim for compensation for these kinds of legal services will depend largely upon the facts of each case. * * * Whether the parties in fact entered into a contract calling for the improper exercise of personal influence upon a public official is therefore a question for the jury, guided of course by proper instructions. * * * In this case the jury concluded that Troutman had agreed with Southern to use his influence merely to gain access to the President and present to him the merits of Southern's case; therefore, the contract was valid and enforceable. On appeal from the order of the district court denying Southern's motion for judgment notwithstanding the verdict, it is our task to examine the record to see whether substantial evidence supports the jury's conclusion. * * *

Troutman himself testified that Wilbanks asked him to go to the President and persuade him "to listen to the case and to see if [the I.C.C.'s order] was not truly against the national interest of this country." He testified that Wilbanks did not ask him to use personal or political influence to get the President to do something for that reason alone. Because he was convinced of the merit of Southern's position, Troutman went to Washington and talked with the President, the President's Special Deputy Counsel Myer Feldman, Assistant Attorney General William H. Orrick, Jr., and officials in the Department of Agriculture.

Feldman testified by deposition that upon being advised of the grain rate problem the President asked him to look into it and "to report back to him on the merits of the case." He said that Troutman supplied him with material helpful to an understanding of the issues and that their conversations dealt with what was in the best interest of the nation, the South, and the farm community. After carefully studying the matter, Feldman reported to the President that he thought that the I.C.C.'s order would adversely affect the economy of the South and therefore was not in the national interest. Finally, Feldman testified that Troutman did not make any request of the President that Feldman considered in any way improper; he did not consider it improper to bring the grain rate case to the attention of the President.

Orrick testified, also by deposition, that he and his staff studied the legal questions and that the decision of the Department of Justice to file an answer in the Ohio court contrary to the position of the I.C.C. was based entirely on the merits of the case, unaffected by any outside influence. He also stated that it was not unusual for an attorney to call upon him for the purpose of presenting to him, as an Assistant Attorney General, the contentions, both legal and economic, of the attorney's client; and such activities come within the general scope of the performance of legal services for the client.

From this evidence we conclude that a jury could reasonably find that Troutman was employed to use his influence, such as it was, merely to obtain an audience with the President and there to present to him the merits of Southern's position. Such an employment contract is not in violation of public policy and is therefore enforceable. It follows then that the district court did not err in refusing to grant Southern's motion for judgment notwithstanding the verdict.

* * *

Therefore, the judgment of the district court is affirmed.

IN RE JAMES H. HIMMEL, ATTORNEY

Supreme Court of Illinois, 1988.
125 Ill.2d 531, 533 N.E.2d 790, 127 Ill.Dec. 708.

* * *

JUSTICE STAMOS delivered the opinion of the court: This is a disciplinary proceeding against respondent, James H. Himmel. On January 22, 1986, the Administrator of the Attorney Registration and Disciplinary Commission (the Commission) filed a complaint with the Hearing Board, alleging that respondent violated Rule 1–103(a) of the Code of Professional Responsibility (the Code) (107 Ill.2d R. 1–103(a)) by failing to disclose to the [Attorney Registration and Disciplinary] Commission information concerning attorney misconduct. On October 15, 1986, the Hearing Board found that respondent had violated the rule and recommended that respondent be reprimanded. The Administrator filed exceptions with the Review Board. The Review Board issued its report on July 9, 1987, finding that respondent had not violated a disciplinary rule and recommending dismissal of the complaint. We granted the Administrator's petition for leave to file exceptions to the Review Board's report and recommendation. 107 Ill.2d R. 753(e)(6).

We will briefly review the facts, which essentially involve three individuals: respondent, James H. Himmel, licensed to practice law in Illinois on November 6, 1975; his client, Tammy Forsberg, formerly known as Tammy McEathron; and her former attorney, John R. Casey.

The complaint alleges that respondent had knowledge of John Casey's conversion of Forsberg's funds and respondent failed to inform the Commission of this misconduct. The facts are as follows.

In October 1978, Tammy Forsberg was injured in a motorcycle accident. In June 1980, she retained John R. Casey to represent her in any personal injury or property damage claim resulting from the accident. Sometime in 1981, Casey negotiated a settlement of $35,000 on Forsberg's behalf. Pursuant to an agreement between Forsberg and

Casey, one-third of any monies received would be paid to Casey as his attorney fee.

In March 1981, Casey received the $35,000 settlement check, endorsed it, and deposited the check into his client trust fund account. Subsequently, Casey converted the funds.

Between 1981 and 1983, Forsberg unsuccessfully attempted to collect her $23,233.34 share of the settlement proceeds. In March 1983, Forsberg retained respondent to collect her money and agreed to pay him one-third of any funds recovered above $23,233.34.

Respondent investigated the matter and discovered that Casey had misappropriated the settlement funds. In April 1983, respondent drafted an agreement in which Casey would pay Forsberg $75,000 in settlement of any claim she might have against him for the misappropriated funds. By the terms of the agreement, Forsberg agreed not to initiate any criminal, civil, or attorney disciplinary action against Casey. This agreement was executed on April 11, 1983. Respondent stood to gain $17,000 or more if Casey honored the agreement. In February 1985, respondent filed suit against Casey for breaching the agreement, and a $100,000 judgment was entered against Casey. If Casey had satisfied the judgment, respondent's share would have been approximately $25,588.

The complaint stated that at no time did respondent inform the Commission of Casey's misconduct. According to the Administrator, respondent's first contact with the Commission was in response to the Commission's inquiry regarding the lawsuit against Casey.

In April 1985, the Administrator filed a petition to have Casey suspended from practicing law because of his conversion of client funds and his conduct involving moral turpitude in matters unrelated to Forsberg's claim. Casey was subsequently disbarred on consent on November 5, 1985.

* * *

Before retaining respondent, Forsberg collected $5,000 from Casey. After being retained, respondent made inquiries regarding Casey's conversion, contacting the insurance company that issued the settlement check, its attorney, Forsberg, her mother, her fiancé and Casey. Forsberg told respondent that she simply wanted her money back and specifically instructed respondent to take no other action. Because of respondent's efforts, Forsberg collected another $10,400 from Casey. Respondent received no fee in this case.

The Hearing Board found that respondent received unprivileged information that Casey converted Forsberg's funds, and that respondent failed to relate the information to the Commission in violation of Rule 1–103(a) of the Code. The Hearing Board noted, however, that respondent had been practicing law for 11 years, had no prior record of any complaints, obtained as good a result as could be expected in the case, and requested no fee for recovering the $23,233.34. Accordingly, the Hearing Board recommended a private reprimand.

* * *

The Administrator now raises three issues for review: (1) whether the Review Board erred in concluding that respondent's client had informed the Commission of misconduct by her former attorney; (2) whether the Review Board erred in concluding that respondent had not violated Rule 1–103(a); and (3) whether the proven misconduct warrants at least a censure.

As to the first issue, the Administrator contends that the Review Board erred in finding that Forsberg informed the Commission of Casey's misconduct prior to retaining respondent. In support of this contention, the Administrator cites to testimony in the record showing that while Forsberg contacted the Commission and received a complaint form, she did not fill out the form, return it, advise the Commission of the facts, or name whom she wished to complain about. The Administrator further contends that even if Forsberg had reported Casey's misconduct to the Commission, such an action would not have relieved respondent of his duty to report under Rule 1–103(a). Additionally, the Administrator argues that no evidence exists to prove that respondent failed to report because he assumed that Forsberg had already reported the matter.

* * *

We begin our analysis by examining whether a client's complaint of attorney misconduct to the Commission can be a defense to an attorney's failure to report the same misconduct. Respondent offers no authority for such a defense and our research has disclosed none. Common sense would dictate that if a lawyer has a duty under the Code, the actions of a client would not relieve the attorney of his own duty. * * *

As to the second issue, the Administrator argues that the Review Board erred in concluding that respondent did not violate Rule 1–103(a). The Administrator urges acceptance of the Hearing Board's finding that respondent had unprivileged knowledge of Casey's conversion of client funds, and that respondent failed to disclose that information to the Commission. The Administrator states that respondent's knowledge of Casey's conversion of client funds was knowledge of illegal conduct involving moral turpitude under In re Stillo (1977), 68 Ill.2d 49, 54, 11 Ill.Dec. 289, 368 N.E.2d 897. Further, the Administrator argues that the information respondent received was not privileged under the definition of privileged information articulated by this court in People v. Adam (1972), 51 Ill.2d 46, 48, 280 N.E.2d 205, cert. denied (1972), 409 U.S. 948, 93 S.Ct. 289, 34 L.Ed.2d 218. Therefore, the Administrator concludes, respondent violated his ethical duty to report misconduct under Rule 1–103(a). According to the Administrator, failure to disclose the information deprived the Commission of evidence of serious misconduct, evidence that would have assisted in the Commission's investigation of Casey.

Respondent contends that the information was privileged information received from his client, Forsberg, and therefore he was under no obligation to disclose the matter to the Commission. Respondent argues that his failure to report Casey's misconduct was motivated by his respect for his client's wishes, not by his desire for financial gain. To support this assertion, respondent notes that his fee agreement with Forsberg was contingent upon her first receiving all the money Casey originally owed her. Further, respondent states that he has received no fee for his representation of Forsberg.

Our analysis of this issue begins with a reading of the applicable disciplinary rules. Rule 1–103(a) of the Code states:

"(a) A lawyer possessing unprivileged knowledge of a violation of Rule 1–102(a)(3) or (4) shall report such knowledge to a tribunal or other authority empowered to investigate or act upon such violation." 107 Ill.2d R. 1–103(a).

Rule 1–102 of the Code states:

"(a) A lawyer shall not

(1) violate a disciplinary rule;

(2) circumvent a disciplinary rule through actions of another;

(3) engage in illegal conduct involving moral turpitude;

(4) engage in conduct involving dishonesty, fraud, deceit, or misrepresentation; or

(5) engage in conduct that is prejudicial to the administration of justice." 107 Ill.2d R. 1–102.

These rules essentially track the language of the American Bar Association Model Code of Professional Responsibility, upon which the Illinois Code was modeled. (See 107 Ill.2d Rules art. VIII, Committee Commentary, at 604.) * * *

The record does not suggest that this information was communicated by Forsberg to the respondent in confidence. We have held that information voluntarily disclosed by a client to an attorney, in the presence of third parties who are not agents of the client or attorney, is not privileged information. (People v. Williams (1983), 97 Ill.2d 252, 295, 73 Ill.Dec. 360, 454 N.E.2d 220, cert. denied (1984), 466 U.S. 981, 104 S.Ct. 2364, 80 L.Ed.2d 836.) In this case, Forsberg discussed the matter with respondent at various times while her mother and her fiancé were present. Consequently, unless the mother and fiancé were agents of respondent's client, the information communicated was not privileged. Moreover, we have also stated that matters intended by a client for disclosure by the client's attorney to third parties, who are not agents of either the client or the attorney, are not privileged. (People v. Werhollick (1970), 45 Ill.2d 459, 462, 259 N.E.2d 265.) The record shows that respondent, with Forsberg's consent, discussed Casey's conversion of her funds with the insurance company involved, the insurance company's lawyer, and with Casey himself. Thus, under Werhollick and probably Williams, the information was not privileged.

Though respondent repeatedly asserts that his failure to report was motivated not by financial gain but by the request of his client, we do not deem such an argument relevant in this case. This court has stated that discipline may be appropriate even if no dishonest motive for the misconduct exists. [Citations omitted.] In addition, we have held that client approval of an attorney's action does not immunize an attorney from disciplinary action. [Citations omitted.] We have already dealt with, and dismissed, respondent's assertion that his conduct is acceptable because he was acting pursuant to his client's directions.

* * *

The third issue concerns the appropriate quantum of discipline to be imposed in this case. The Administrator contends that respondent's misconduct warrants at least a censure, although the Hearing Board recommended a private reprimand and the Review Board recommended dismissal of the matter entirely. In support of the request for a greater quantum of discipline, the Administrator cites to the purposes of attorney discipline, which include maintaining the integrity of the legal profession and safeguarding the administration of justice. The Administrator argues that these purposes will not be served unless respondent is publicly disciplined so that the profession will be on notice that a violation of Rule 1–103(a) will not be tolerated. The Administrator argues that a more severe sanction is necessary because respondent deprived the Commission of evidence of another attorney's conversion and thereby interfered with the Commission's investigative function under Supreme Court Rule 752 (107 Ill.2d R. 752). Citing to the Rule 774 petition (107 Ill.2d R. 774) filed against Casey, the Administrator notes that Casey converted many clients' funds after respondent's duty to report Casey arose. The Administrator also argues that both respondent and his client behaved in contravention of the Criminal Code's prohibition against compounding a crime by agreeing with Casey not to report him, in exchange for settlement funds.

* * *

In evaluating the proper quantum of discipline to impose, we note that it is this court's responsibility to determine appropriate sanctions in attorney disciplinary cases. [Citations omitted.] We have stated that while recommendations of the Boards are to be considered, this court ultimately bears responsibility for deciding an appropriate sanction. [Citations omitted.] We reiterate our statement that " '[w]hen determining the nature and extent of discipline to be imposed, the respondent's actions must be viewed in relationship "to the underlying purposes of our disciplinary process, which purposes are to maintain the integrity of the legal profession, to protect the administration of justice from reproach, and to safeguard the public." [Citations omitted.]

Bearing these principles in mind, we agree with the Administrator that public discipline is necessary in this case to carry out the purposes of attorney discipline. While we have considered the Boards' recommendations in this matter, we cannot agree with the Review Board that respondent's conduct served to rectify a wrong and did not injure the bar, the public, or the administration of justice. Though we agree with the Hearing Board's assessment that respondent violated Rule 1–103 of the Code, we do not agree that the facts warrant only a private reprimand. As previously stated, the evidence proved that respondent possessed unprivileged knowledge of Casey's conversion of client funds, yet respondent did not report Casey's misconduct.

This failure to report resulted in interference with the Commission's investigation of Casey, and thus with the administration of justice. Perhaps some members of the public would have been spared from Casey's misconduct had respondent reported the information as soon as he knew of Casey's conversions of client funds. We are particularly disturbed by the fact that respondent chose to draft a settlement agreement with Casey rather than report his misconduct. As the Administrator has stated, by this conduct, both respondent and his client ran afoul of the Criminal Code's prohibition against compounding a crime, which states in section 32–l:

> "(a) A person compounds a crime when he receives or offers to another any consideration for a promise not to prosecute or aid in the prosecution of an offender.
>
> (b) Sentence. Compounding a crime is a petty offense." (Ill.Rev. Stat.1987, ch. 38, par. 32–1.)

Both respondent and his client stood to gain financially by agreeing not to prosecute or report Casey for conversion. According to the settlement agreement, respondent would have received $17,000 or more as his fee. If Casey had satisfied the judgment entered against him for failure to honor the settlement agreement, respondent would have collected approximately $25,588.

We have held that fairness dictates consideration of mitigating factors in disciplinary cases. [Citations omitted.] Therefore, we do consider the fact that Forsberg recovered $10,400 through respondent's services, that respondent has practiced law for 11 years with no record of complaints, and that he requested no fee for minimum collection of Forsberg's funds. However, these considerations do not outweigh the serious nature of respondent's failure to report Casey, the resulting interference with the Commission's investigation of Casey, and respondent's ill-advised choice to settle with Casey rather than report his misconduct.

Accordingly, it is ordered that respondent be suspended from the practice of law for one year. Respondent suspended.

Problems

1.   P, a woman, and D, a man, lived together while unmarried. During their relationship they had acquired a truck, a car, and two motorcycles. P paid substantially all of the purchase prices of the vehicles, but they were registered in D's name to save on insurance premiums. At the breakup of their relationship P seeks to obtain title and possession of the vehicles. Frame an argument for P before an Illinois court in the light of *Hewitt v. Hewitt.*

2.   Defendant operated a "dating service" which was a front for the providing of prostitutes. Idaho law made it a crime to knowingly receive "without consideration" the earnings of a woman engaged in prostitution. The customers paid fifty dollars for each act of prostitution. Of this sum, the defendant received twenty-five dollars plus one-half of any tips received. The defendant appeals from a conviction, arguing that his services—advertising, maintaining files, providing a telephone and a place of business—constituted consideration. What result?

3.   The City of Eastport in partial exchange for a Federal grant contracted to maintain an airport for twenty years or for its useful life whichever was longer. While the airport was still in operation the city contracted to sell the airport to Pittston so that Pittston could close down the airport and build an oil refinery on the site. Resident taxpayers bring an action to enjoin the sale. On what theory related to this chapter might the injunction be granted?

There is nothing in the text or case readings to assist you in the proper resolution of problems 4 and 5. Assume there is no case on point. It is up to you to determine public policy.

4.   "Plaintiff was a Democrat, publishing a Democratic newspaper of independent proclivities. The defendant was a Republican, seeking a nomination to Congress from a Republican convention." The parties agreed that for a fee the plaintiff's "services as editor would be at the command of the defendant for the campaign" and that he "was to do all he could to influence the choice of delegates and secure the defendant's nomination...." Assuming the agreement was made and the services performed, should Plaintiff be able to recover judgment for his fee?

5.   Plaintiff's wife was a compulsive gambler. She was indebted to the defendant, a legal card club, because some checks she had cashed bounced for insufficient funds. Plaintiff agreed to pay her debt provided the defendant would deny his wife access to the club in the future. Defendant agreed and plaintiff paid. The defendant nevertheless permitted plaintiff's wife to patronize the club where she lost about $30,000. Much of this money was made available to her by the defendant's cashing of her checks. Plaintiff sues for breach. Defendant argues that denial of access to the wife would violate a statute that provides "[a]ll persons ... are free and equal, and no matter what their sex, race, color, religion, ancestry, or national origin are entitled to the full and equal accommodations, advantages, facilities, privileges, or services in all business establishments...." Is the agreement illegal and therefore void?

SECTION 2. EFFECT OF ILLEGALITY

(Calamari & Perillo 5th §§ 22.2—22.9)

NORTHERN INDIANA PUBLIC SERVICE CO. v. CARBON COUNTY COAL CO.

United States Court of Appeals, Seventh Circuit, 1986.
799 F.2d 265.

[NIPSCO, an electrical utility, agreed to purchase 1.5 million tons of coal every year for 20 years from Carbon County Coal at $24 per ton subject to various provisions for escalation. Time has shown that this was an onerous agreement for NIPSCO. It now seeks a declaratory judgment to the effect that it need not honor the agreement for various reasons, including that the agreement violated § 2(c) of the Federal Mineral Land Leasing Act of 1920. Carbon County Coal counterclaimed for breach of contract. The district court entered a judgment for damages on behalf of the seller.]

POSNER, CIRCUIT JUDGE. * * *

Section 2(c) of the Mineral Lands Leasing Act of 1920 provides in pertinent part that "no company or corporation operating a common-carrier railroad shall be given or hold a permit or lease under the provisions of this chapter [relating to federal lands] for any coal deposits except for its own use for railroad purposes. . . ." Oddly in this litigious age, no reported decision has interpreted section 2(c) in the 66 years since its enactment. NIPSCO contends that if the statute is not to be made a dead letter, it must be read to forbid a railroad's affiliate to hold a mineral lease or permit on federal lands. Roughly 15 percent of Carbon County's projected output for the contract with NIPSCO was to come from federal lands that Carbon County had a permit to mine, and Carbon County is a partnership of two firms (each with a half interest in the partnership), Dravo Coal Company and Rocky Mountain Energy Company, the latter a wholly owned subsidiary of the Union Pacific Corporation, whose principal subsidiary is the Union Pacific Railroad Company.

* * *

Since this is not a case where the contract itself is illegal—as it would be if it were a contract in restraint of trade and therefore a violation of section 1 of the Sherman Act, or a contract to commit a bank robbery and therefore a criminal conspiracy—it is not governed by *Kaiser Steel Corp. v. Mullins,* 455 U.S. 72, 77–83, 102 S.Ct. 851, 856–59, 70 L.Ed.2d 833 (1982). Kaiser agreed to make extra contributions to a union welfare fund if Kaiser failed to adhere to an allegedly illegal boycott; the Court sustained the defense of illegality to a suit to enforce the agreement. The extra contributions were in effect a penalty for abandoning the boycott; the underlying agreement that the penalty was designed to enforce was thus an agreement to participate in the boycott. See also *Somerset Importers, Ltd. v. Continental Vintners,* 790 F.2d 775 (9th Cir.1986). In contrast, the contract in this case is not "intrinsically illegal," *Trustees of the Operative Plasterers' and Cement Masons' Local Union Officers & Employees Pension Fund v. Journeyman Plasterers' Protective & Benevolent Soc'y, Local Union No. 5,* 794 F.2d 1217, 1220 (7th Cir.1986); and the defense of illegality does not come into play just because a party to a lawful contract (here a contract to supply coal to an electric utility) commits unlawful acts to carry out his part of the bargain. * * *

Second, supposing that the contract does violate section 2(c) of the Mineral Lands Leasing Act, this does not necessarily make it unenforceable. This issue, too, is one of federal rather than state law, though we have no reason to think Indiana law would require a different resolution of it; federal and state law on the contract defense of illegality—the latter well described in Farnsworth, Contracts §§ 5.5, 5.6 (1982)—seem quite similar. When the statute is federal, federal law determines not only whether the statute was violated but also, if so, and assuming the statute itself is silent on the matter, the effect of the violation on the enforceability of the contract. * * *

But when we ask what is the federal rule on illegality as a contract defense, we find, alas, that the course of decision has not run completely true. Compare, for example, the hard line taken in government-contract cases such as *United States v. Mississippi Valley Generating Co.,* 364 U.S. 520, 563–66, 81 S.Ct. 294, 316–17, 5 L.Ed.2d 268 (1961), where the defense seems almost automatic (see also *Comdisco, Inc. v. United States,* 756 F.2d 569, 576 (7th Cir.1985); but cf. *United States v. Medico Industries, Inc.,* 784 F.2d 840, 845 (7th Cir.1986)), with the very soft line taken in antitrust cases such as *Kelly v. Kosuga, supra,* and *Delta Marina, Inc. v. Plaquemine Oil Sales, Inc.,* 644 F.2d 455, 458–59 (5th Cir.1981); but cf. *Kaiser Steel Corp. v. Mullins, supra,* 455 U.S. at 79–82, 102 S.Ct. at 857–59. The best generalization possible is that the defense of illegality, being in character if not origins an equitable and remedial doctrine, is not automatic but requires (as NIPSCO's counsel acknowledged at argument) a comparison of the pros and cons of enforcement. * * *

There are, after all, statutory remedies (e.g., cancellation of the lease or permit, see 30 U.S.C. § 188(b)) for violations of section 2(c); the question is whether there should be an additional, a judge-made, remedy. To decide whether there should be, we must consider the reciprocal dangers of overdeterrence and underdeterrence. Applied too strictly, the doctrine that makes the unenforceability of a contract an additional remedy for the violation of a statute can produce a disproportionately severe sanction; and the overdeterrence of illegality is as great a danger to freedom and prosperity as underdeterrence. The benefits of enforcing the tainted contract—benefits that lie in creating stability in contract relations and preserving reasonable expectations—must be compared with the costs in forgoing the additional deterrence of behavior forbidden by statute that is brought about by refusing to let the violator enforce the contract.

The balance in this case favors enforcement. This makes it irrelevant whether the district judge improperly instructed the jury that in order to uphold the defense of illegality, it must find both that Carbon County was an alter ego of the railroad and that NIPSCO had been injured by the violation of section 2(c), or even whether the contract itself could be viewed as illegal under any interpretation of the statute. * * * In any event the violation of section 2(c) (if any) was trivial given the attenuated linkage between the Union Pacific Railroad and Carbon County, and so far as appears completely harmless. No competitor of Union Pacific in the railroad business, and no competitor of Rocky Mountain Energy Company in the coal business who might be dependent on Union Pacific to transport his coal—no competitor of any member of the Union Pacific "family," however broadly defined—has complained that Carbon County is violating section 2(c). Nor has the Department of the Interior or the Department of Justice. Nor has any customer of any of the entities involved (however peripherally) in this lawsuit. * * * Only NIPSCO complains.

Section 2(c) is an anachronism—a regulatory statute on which the sun set long ago. It could serve as Exhibit A to Dean Calabresi's proposal that courts be empowered to invalidate obsolete statutes without having to declare them unconstitutional. See Calabresi, A Common Law for the Age of Statutes (1982). We do not believe that we have the power to declare a constitutional statute invalid merely because we, or for that matter everybody, think the statute has become obsolete. But the question in this case is not whether section 2(c) is enforceable but whether an alleged violation of the statute makes a contract unenforceable, and the obsolescence of the statute may be relevant to that determination.

NIPSCO does not argue that Carbon County's alleged violation of the statute hurt NIPSCO or that invalidating this contract under section 2(c) would help anyone, anywhere, at any time. The only consequence, other than to the parties to this suit, would be to throw a cloud of uncertainty over hundreds, perhaps thousands, of contracts for the supply of coal by firms affiliated with railroads, and to inject uncertainty into the contracting process generally. Persons negotiating contracts would have to worry about whether their contract might someday be found to have violated some old, little-known, and newly reinterpreted statute. Lawyers would benefit from the need to do more legal research before signing a contract, but no one else would. We conclude that the Mineral Lands Leasing Act is not a defense to the enforcement of this contract.

* * *

BATEMAN EICHLER, HILL RICHARDS, INC. v. BERNER

Supreme Court of the United States, 1985.
472 U.S. 299, 105 S.Ct. 2622, 86 L.Ed.2d 215.

JUSTICE BRENNAN delivered the opinion of the Court.

The question presented by this case is whether the common-law *in pari delicto* defense bars a private damages action under the federal securities laws against corporate insiders and broker-dealers who fraudulently induce investors to purchase securities by misrepresenting that they are conveying material nonpublic information about the issuer.

I

The respondent investors filed this action in the United States District Court for the Northern District of California, alleging that they incurred substantial trading losses as a result of a conspiracy between Charles Lazzaro, a registered securities broker employed by the petitioner Bateman Eichler, Hill Richards, Inc. (Bateman Eichler), and Leslie Neadeau, President of T.O.N.M. Oil & Gas Exploration Corporation (TONM), to induce them to purchase large quantities of TONM over-the-counter stock by divulging false and materially incomplete information about the company on the pretext that it was accurate inside information. Specifically, Lazzaro is alleged to have told the respondents that he personally knew TONM insiders and had learned, *inter alia*, that (a) "[v]ast amounts of gold had been discovered in Surinam, and TONM had options on thousands of acres in gold-producing regions of Surinam"; (b) the discovery was "not publically known, but would subsequently be announced"; (c) TONM was currently engaged in negotiations with other companies to form a joint venture for mining the Surinamese gold; and (d) when this information was made public, "TONM stock, which was then selling from $1.50 to $3.00/share, would increase in value from $10 to $15/share within a short period of time, and ... might increase to $100/share" within a year. Complaint ¶¶ 16–17, App. 10–12. Some of the respondents aver that they contacted Neadeau and inquired whether Lazzaro's tips were accurate; Neadeau stated that the information was "not public knowledge" and "would neither confirm nor deny those claims," but allegedly advised that "Lazzaro was a very trustworthy and a good man." *Id.* ¶ 19, App. 12.

The respondents admitted in their complaint that they purchased TONM stock, much of it through Lazzaro, "on the premise that Lazzaro was privy to certain information not otherwise available to the general public." *Id.* ¶ 15, App. 10. Their shares initially increased dramatically in price, but ultimately declined to substantially below the purchase price when the joint mining venture fell through. *Id.* ¶¶ 22–26, App. 13–14.

Lazzaro and Neadeau are alleged to have made the representations set forth above knowing that the representations "were untrue and/or contained only half-truths, material omissions of fact and falsehoods," intending that the respondents would rely thereon, and for the purpose of "influenc[ing] and manipulat[ing] the price of TONM stock" so as "to profit themselves through the taking of commissions and secret profits." *Id.* ¶¶ 23, 30, 38, App. 13, 15–16. The respondents contended that this scheme violated, *inter alia,* § 10(b) of the Securities Exchange Act of 1934, 48 Stat. 891, 15 U.S.C. § 78j(b), and Securities and Exchange Commission (SEC) Rule 10b–5 promulgated thereunder, 17 CFR § 240.10b–5 (1984). They sought capital losses and lost profits, punitive damages, and costs and attorney's fees. App. 26.

The District Court dismissed the complaint for failure to state a claim. The court reasoned that "trading on insider information is itself a violation of rule 10b–5" and that the allegations in the complaint demonstrated that the respondents themselves had "violated the particular statutory provision under which recovery is sought." App. to Pet. for Cert. C–2. Thus, the court concluded, the respondents were *in pari delicto* with Lazzaro and Neadeau and absolutely barred from recovery. *Ibid.*

The Court of Appeals for the Ninth Circuit reversed. *Berner v. Lazzaro,* 730 F.2d 1319 (1984). Although it assumed that the respondents had violated the federal securities laws, *id.,* at 1324, the court nevertheless concluded that "securities professionals and corporate officers who have allegedly engaged in fraud should not be permitted to invoke the *in pari delicto* doctrine to shield themselves from the consequences of their fraudulent misrepresentation," *id.,* at 1320. The Court of Appeals noted that this Court had sharply restricted the availability of the *in pari delicto* defense in antitrust actions, see *Perma Life Mufflers, Inc. v. International Parts Corp.,* 392 U.S. 134, 88 S.Ct. 1981, 20 L.Ed.2d 982 (1968), and concluded that, essentially for three reasons, there was no basis "for creating a different rule for private actions initiated under the federal securities laws," 730 F.2d, at 1322. First, the court reasoned that, in cases such as this, defrauded tippees are not in fact "equally responsible" for the violations they allege. *Ibid.* Second, the court believed that allowing the defense in these circumstances would be "totally incompatible with the overall aims of the securities law" because the threat of a private damages action is necessary to deter "insider-tipster[s]" from defrauding the public. *Id.,* at 1323. Finally, the court noted the availability of means other than an outright preclusion of suit to deter tippees from trading on inside information. *Id.,* at 1324, n. 3.

The lower courts have divided over the proper scope of the *in pari delicto* defense in securities litigation. We granted certiorari. 469 U.S. 1105, 105 S.Ct. 776, 83 L.Ed.2d 772 (1985). We affirm.

II

The common-law defense at issue in this case derives from the Latin, *in pari delicto potior est conditio defendentis:* "In a case of equal or mutual fault . . . the position of the [defending] party . . . is the better one." The defense is grounded on two premises: first, that courts should not lend their good offices to mediating disputes among wrongdoers;[12] and second, that denying judicial relief to an admitted wrongdoer is an effective means of deterring illegality.[13] In its classic formulation, the *in pari delicto* defense was narrowly limited to situations where the plaintiff truly bore at least substantially equal responsibility for his injury, because "in cases where both parties are in delicto, concurring in an illegal act, it does not always follow that they stand in pari delicto; for there may be, and often are, very different degrees in their guilt." 1 J. Story, Equity Jurisprudence 304–305 (13th ed. 1886) (Story). Thus there might be an "inequality of condition" between the parties, *id.*, at 305, or "a confidential relationship between th[em]" that determined their "relative standing" before a court, 3 J. Pomeroy, Equity Jurisprudence § 942a, p. 741 (5th ed. 1941) (Pomeroy). In addition, the public policy considerations that undergirded the *in pari delicto* defense were frequently construed as precluding the defense even where the plaintiff bore substantial fault for his injury: "[T]here may be on the part of the court itself a necessity of supporting the public interests or public policy in many cases, however reprehensible the acts of the parties may be." 1 Story 305. Notwithstanding these traditional limitations, many courts have given the *in pari delicto* defense a broad application to bar actions where plaintiffs simply have been involved generally in "the same sort of wrongdoing" as defendants. *Perma Life Mufflers, Inc. v. International Parts Corp.*, 392 U.S., at 138, 88 S.Ct., at 1984.

In *Perma Life,* we emphasized "the inappropriateness of invoking broad common-law barriers to relief where a private suit serves important public purposes." *Ibid.* 138, 88 S.Ct., at 1984. That case involved a treble-damages action against a Midas Muffler franchisor by several of its dealers, who alleged that the franchise agreement created a conspiracy to restrain trade in violation of the Sherman and Clayton Acts. The lower courts barred the action on the grounds that the dealers, as parties to the agreement, were *in pari delicto* with the franchisor. In reversing that determination, the opinion for this Court emphasized that there was no indication that Congress had intended to incorporate the defense

12. See, *e.g., Higgins v. McCrea,* 116 U.S. 671, 685, 6 S.Ct. 557, 564, 29 L.Ed. 764 (1886); *Austin's Adm'x v. Winston's Ex'x,* 11 Va. 33, 47 (1806) ("He who comes here for relief must draw his justice from pure fountains"). See also *Holman v. Johnson,* 1 Cowp. 341, 343, 98 Eng.Rep. 1120, 1121 (K.B.1775):

"The objection, that a contract is immoral or illegal as between plaintiff and defendant, sounds at all times very ill in the mouth of the defendant. It is not for his sake, however, that the objection is ever allowed.... The principle of public policy is this; ex dolo malo non oritur actio [out of fraud no action arises].... It is upon that ground the Court goes; not for the sake of the defendant, but because they will not lend their aid to such a plaintiff."

13. See, *e.g., McMullen v. Hoffman,* 174 U.S. 639, 669–670, 19 S.Ct. 839, 850–851, 43 L.Ed. 1117 (1899):

"To refuse to grant either party to an illegal contract judicial aid for the enforcement of his alleged rights under it tends strongly towards reducing the number of such transactions to a minimum. The more plainly parties understand that when they enter into contracts of this nature they place themselves outside the protection of the law, so far as that protection consists in aiding them to enforce such contracts, the less inclined will they be to enter into them. In that way the public secures the benefit of a rigid adherence to the law."

into the antitrust laws, which "are best served by insuring that the private action will be an ever-present threat to deter anyone contemplating [illegal] business behavior." *Id.,* at 139, 88 S.Ct., at 1984. Accordingly, the opinion concluded that "the doctrine of *in pari delicto,* with its complex scope, contents, and effects, is not to be recognized as a defense to an antitrust action." *Id.,* at 140, 88 S.Ct., at 1985. The opinion reserved the question whether a plaintiff who engaged in "truly complete involvement and participation in a monopolistic scheme"—one who "aggressively support[ed] and further[ed] the monopolistic scheme as a necessary part and parcel of it"—could be barred from pursuing a damages action, finding that the muffler dealers had relatively little bargaining power and that they had been coerced by the franchisor into agreeing to many of the contract's provisions. *Ibid.*

In separate opinions, five Justices agreed that the concept of "equal fault" should be narrowly defined in litigation arising under federal regulatory statutes. "[B]ecause of the strong public interest in eliminating restraints on competition, . . . many of the refinements of moral worth demanded of plaintiffs by . . . many of the variations of *in pari delicto* should not be applicable in the antitrust field." *Id.,* at 151, 88 S.Ct., at 1991 (Marshall, J., concurring in result). The five Justices concluded, however, that where a plaintiff truly bore at least substantially equal responsibility for the violation, a defense based on such fault—whether or not denominated *in pari delicto*—should be recognized in antitrust litigation.

Bateman Eichler argues that *Perma Life*—with its emphasis on the importance of analyzing the effects that fault-based defenses would have on the enforcement of congressional goals—is of only marginal relevance to a private damages action under the federal securities laws. Specifically, Bateman Eichler observes that Congress *expressly* provided for private antitrust actions—thereby manifesting a "desire to go beyond the common law in the antitrust statute in order to provide substantial encouragement to private enforcement and to help deter anticompetitive conduct"—whereas private rights of action under § 10(b) of the Securities Exchange Act of 1934 are merely *implied* from that provision—thereby, apparently, supporting a broader application of the *in pari delicto* defense. Brief for Petitioner 32. Bateman Eichler buttresses this argument by observing that, unlike the Sherman and Clayton Acts, the securities laws contain savings provisions directing that "[t]he rights and remedies provided by [those laws] shall be in addition to any and all other rights and remedies that may exist at law or in equity"—again, apparently, supporting a broader scope for false-based defenses than recognized in *Perma Life.*

We disagree. Nothing in *Perma Life* suggested that public policy implications should govern only where Congress expressly provides for private remedies; the classic formulation of the *in pari delicto* doctrine itself required a careful consideration of such implications before allowing the defense. See *supra,* at 2627. Moreover, we repeatedly have emphasized that implied private actions provide "a most effective weapon in the enforcement" of the securities laws and are "a necessary supplement to Commission action." *J.I. Case Co. v. Borak,* 377 U.S. 426, 432, 84 S.Ct. 1555, 1560, 12 L.Ed.2d 423 (1964); see also *Blue Chip Stamps v. Manor Drug Stores,* 421 U.S. 723, 730, 95 S.Ct. 1917, 1922, 44 L.Ed.2d 539 (1975). In addition, we have eschewed rigid common-law barriers in construing the securities laws. See, *e.g., Herman & MacLean v. Huddleston,* 459 U.S. 375, 388–389, 103 S.Ct. 683, 690–691, 74 L.Ed.2d 548 (1983) (common-law doctrines are sometimes of "questionable pertinence" in applying the securities laws, which were intended "to rectify perceived deficiencies in the available common-law protections by establishing higher standards of conduct in the securities industry"); *A.C. Frost & Co. v. Coeur d'Alene Mines Corp.,* 312 U.S. 38, 43, 61 S.Ct. 414, 417, 85 L.Ed. 500 (1941) (rejecting the unclean hands defense on the facts of the case because it would "seriously hinder rather than aid the real purpose" of the securities laws). We therefore conclude that the views expressed in *Perma Life* apply with full force to implied causes of action under the federal securities laws. Accordingly, a private action for damages in these circumstances may be barred on the grounds of the plaintiff's own culpability only where (1) as a direct result of his own actions, the plaintiff bears at least substantially equal responsibility for the violations he seeks to redress, and (2) preclusion of suit would not significantly interfere with the effective enforcement of the securities laws and protection of the investing public.

* * *

B

We also believe that denying the *in pari delicto* defense in such circumstances will best promote the primary objective of the federal securities laws—protection of the investing public and the national economy through the promotion of "a high standard of business ethics ... in every facet of the securities industry." *SEC v. Capital Gains Research Bureau, Inc.,* 375 U.S. 180, 186–187, 84 S.Ct. 275, 280, 11 L.Ed.2d 237 (1963). Although a number of lower courts have reasoned that a broad rule of *caveat tippee* would better serve this goal, we believe the contrary position adopted by other courts represents the better view.

To begin with, barring private actions in cases such as this would inexorably result in a number of alleged fraudulent practices going undetected by the authorities and unremedied. The SEC has advised us that it "does not have the resources to police the industry sufficiently to ensure that false tipping does not occur or is consistently discovered," and that "[w]ithout the tippees' assistance, the Commission could not effectively prosecute false tipping—a difficult practice to detect." Brief for SEC as *Amicus Curiae* 25. See also H.R.Rep. No. 98–355, p. 6 (1983) ("In recent years, the securities markets have grown dramatically in size and complexity, while Commission enforcement resources have declined"). Thus it is particularly important to permit "litigation among guilty parties [that will serve] to expose their unlawful conduct and render them more easily subject to appropriate civil, administrative, and criminal penalties." *Kuehnert v. Texstar Corp.,* 412 F.2d 700, 706, n. 3 (CA5 1969) (Godbold, J., dissenting). The *in pari delicto* defense, by denying any incentive to a defrauded tippee to bring suit against his defrauding tipper, would significantly undermine this important goal.

Moreover, we believe that deterrence of insider trading most frequently will be maximized by bringing enforcement pressures to bear on the sources of such information—corporate insiders and broker-dealers.

> "The true insider or the broker-dealer is at the fountainhead of the confidential information.... If the prophylactic purpose of the law is to restrict the use of all material inside information until it is made available to the investing public, then the most effective means of carrying out this policy is to nip in the bud the source of the information, the tipper, by discouraging him from 'making the initial disclosure which is the first step in the chain of dissemination.' This can most readily be achieved by making unavailable to him the defense of in pari delicto when sued by his tippee upon charges based upon alleged misinformation." *Nathanson v. Weis, Voisin, Cannon, Inc.,* 325 F.Supp. 50, 57–58 (SDNY 1971).

In addition, corporate insiders and broker-dealers will in many circumstances be more responsive to the deterrent pressure of potential sanctions; they are more likely than ordinary investors to be advised by counsel and thereby to be informed fully of the "allowable limits on their conduct." *Kuehnert v. Texstar Corp.,* 412 F.2d, at 706 (Godbold, J., dissenting). Although situations might well arise in which the relative culpabilities of the tippee and his insider source merit a different mix of deterrent incentives, we therefore conclude that in tipper-tippee situations such as the one before us the factors discussed above preclude recognition of the *in pari delicto* defense.[30]

Lower courts reaching a contrary conclusion have typically asserted that, absent a vigorous allowance of the *in pari delicto* defense, tippees would have, "in effect, an enforceable warranty that secret information is true," *id.,* at 705, and thus no incentive *not* to trade on that information. These courts have reasoned, in other words, that tippees in such circumstances would be in "the enviable position of 'heads-I-win tails-you-lose,'" *Wolfson v. Baker,* 623 F.2d 1074, 1082 (CA5 1980), cert. denied, 450 U.S. 966, 101 S.Ct. 1483, 67 L.Ed.2d 615 (1981)—if the tip is correct, the tippee will reap illicit profits, while if the tip fails to yield the expected return, he can sue to recover damages.

---

30. Some courts have suggested that "even in a case where the fault of plaintiff and defendant were relatively equal, simultaneous and mutual, the court might still reject the [*in pari delicto*] defense if it appeared that the defendant's unlawful activities were of a sort likely to have a substantial impact on the investing public, and the primary legal responsibility for and ability to control that impact is with defendant." *Woolf v. S.D. Cohn & Co.,* 515 F.2d, at 604; see also *Mallis v. Bankers Trust Co.,* 615 F.2d, at 76, n. 6. Because there is no basis at this stage of the litigation for concluding that the respondents bore substantially equal responsibility for the violations they seek to redress, we need not address the circumstances in which preclusion of suit might otherwise significantly interfere with the effective enforcement of the securities laws and protection of the investing public.

We believe the "enforceable warranty" theory is overstated and overlooks significant factors that serve to deter tippee trading irrespective of whether the *in pari delicto* defense is allowed. First, tippees who bring suit in an attempt to cash in on their "enforceable warranties" expose themselves to the threat of substantial civil and criminal penalties for their own potentially illegal conduct. Second, plaintiffs in litigation under § 10(b) and Rule 10b–5 may only recover against defendants who have acted with scienter. See *Ernst & Ernst v. Hochfelder,* 425 U.S. 185, 96 S.Ct. 1375, 47 L.Ed.2d 668 (1976). Thus "if the tip merely fails to 'pan out' or if the information itself proves accurate but the stock fails to move in the anticipated direction, the investor stands to lose all of his investment. Only in the situation where the investor has been deliberately defrauded will he be able to maintain a private suit in an attempt to recoup his money." 730 F.2d, at 1324, n. 3.

We therefore conclude that the public interest will most frequently be advanced if defrauded tippees are permitted to bring suit and to expose illegal practices by corporate insiders and broker-dealers to full public view for appropriate sanctions. As the Ninth Circuit emphasized in this case, there is no warrant to giving corporate insiders and broker-dealers "a license to defraud the investing public with little fear of prosecution." *Id.,* at 1323.

Affirmed.

CHIEF JUSTICE BURGER concurs in the judgment.

JUSTICE MARSHALL took no part in the decision of this case.

SINGLETON v. FOREMAN

United States Court of Appeals, Fifth Circuit, 1970.
435 F.2d 962.

GOLDBERG, CIRCUIT JUDGE. Once again—it seems to be habitual—we are confronted with a case demonstrating the dangers of rendering a judgment of dismissal on the basis of bare-bone pleadings. Finding that the plaintiff did plead facts sufficient to state a claim upon which relief can be granted, we reverse.

We must here review an unseemly and deplorable belligerency between an attorney, Percy Foreman, and his client, Mrs. Geneva Singleton. The difficulties began in February 1969 when Mrs. Singleton who was apparently experiencing marital difficulties traveled from her home in Tampa, Florida, to Memphis, Tennessee, to consult with the defendant, a Texas attorney. Following consultation Mrs. Singleton retained Mr. Foreman to represent her in a divorce action in the State of Florida. The parties entered into the following contract pertaining to Mr. Foreman's employment:

"This is to make a record of our agreement concerning my employment as your principal attorney to represent you in a divorce action to be filed in the Circuit Court of Hillsborough Co., Florida, within the near future. I am not licensed to practice law in Florida, but I have never been refused permission to try an isolated case there, and I anticipate engaging a licensed lawyer who maintains offices in Tampa and with whom I have previously worked.

"My normal retainer for accepting a case outside Texas, where there is child custody and/or a considerable estate to establish, is $25,000.00. This is not applied to the per diem but is a retainer paid soley [sic] for my agreement to represent the client. My actual fee in your case is to be one-third of the value of any recovery that may be obtained for you, plus a reasonable fee of any alimony and or support payments the Court may grant or allow, such reasonable fee of such installment payments is to be fixed by the Court.

"The one-third of the base recovery in property or money is to be my property absolutely, whether obtained by me or anyone else. That is, should you elect to dispense with my services and engage another lawyer, I am still entitled to receive the one-third of any recovery and a reasonable amount of any payments made after the divorce.

"I agree to pay any local lawyer that I may engage out of the above fee arrangement. But it is anticipated that he and I will apply for an advance for attorneys fees and trial expenses. Any such fees so advanced by order of the Court will apply to our total or over all fee.

"I have made no statement, representation or warranty concerning the outcome of this case. We both know that it is a hard fight. But I have promised to appear at the final trial of this case in person and to try to be present at the first hearing. I will prepare all pleadings and have the final decision on all important matters, subject, of course, to consultation with you when such is possible.

"To secure the payment of my $25,000.00 retainer, you have given me this date the following jewelry and personal property, to-wit: [jewelry listed]

"You will note the total value of the above are less than my stated retainer fee. But, since you have evidenced a willingness to do whatever you could in the way of placing your jewels with me, I agree to hold all the above until the final disposition of your case, including any appeals, and that you shall have all the above personal property returned to you upon payment to me out of your portion of the recovery, in addition to by [sic] one-third fee aforesaid, the total value of each or any of the above items you may care to redeem.

"The above jewels are not a part of the fee provided in the court's advance order or the one-third attorney fee but are to be considered soley [sic] as my separate retainer in the case. It is not contemplated that any local attorney will have any claim on them whatsoever.

"As evidence that the above is our agreement, you will sign the original and two copies of this agreement.

Yours very truly,

/S/ PERCY FOREMAN

"The above is our agreement and I have signed each page of the original and two copies of same. I fully understand it.

/S/ GENEVA A. SINGLETON"

By February 28, 1969, 21 days after their initial meeting and approximately 10 days after the plaintiff's divorce petition was filed in Florida, discord and dissent between the parties had reached such a crescendo that Mrs. Singleton dismissed Mr. Foreman as her attorney. Subsequently Mrs. Singleton brought this suit in a Florida court against Mr. Foreman, alleging the following:

* * *

7. That the defendant then entered upon a course of abuse and oppression directed toward plaintiff which caused the plaintiff extreme mental pain and suffering; that the defendant cursed the plaintiff, and in some instances the plaintiff's mother in the presence of the plaintiff, with language so vile, scurrilous, and indecent that plaintiff is embarrassed to repeat them in this pleading and to spread said language upon the public records.

* * *

10. That while attempting to discuss the terms of settlement that plaintiff desired, the defendant exploded into a torrent of abuse, cursing and vile language directed at plaintiff. In the course of said obscenities, the defendant told the plaintiff that she was a 'stupid _____'; that plaintiff did not 'have any more to say in this case than a chair in the Court room'; and that if plaintiff attempted to obtain the services of another lawyer that, 'I'll ruin you and that _____ husband of yours.'

11. That the alleged agreement, Exhibit A, was and is offensive to and violative of public policy and is void ab initio.

* * *

WHEREFORE, plaintiff demands a judgment from the defendant for the value of the jewels which defendant has converted to his own use, plus compensatory and punitive damages in the total sum alleged."

* * *

The central issue in this case, therefore, is whether the trial court was in error in dismissing the action on the pleadings. * * *

* * *

It is immediately apparent to us that at the very least Mrs. Singleton's complaint states a cognizable claim for a return of the retainer paid to Mr. Foreman. The contract provided for a retainer and a contingent fee out of the proceeds from the divorce settlement. Contracts for a contingent fee in divorce cases are void and unenforceable under Florida law. Salter v. St. Jean, Fla.App. 1964, 170 So.2d 94; Sobieski v. Maresco, Fla.Ct.App.1962, 143 So.2d 62. Although Florida follows the general rule that courts will not aid either party to an illegal contract but will leave them where they place themselves, Florida also recognizes an exception to this rule when "law or public policy requires action by the courts, or where the parties are not in pari delicto." Stewart v. Sterns and Culver Lumber Co., 1908, 56 Fla. 570, 48 So. 19, 25. Since on the pleadings Mrs. Singleton can in no manner be considered in pari delicto with Mr. Foreman, we think the courts of Florida would go to her aid to the extent of returning the consideration which she tendered in performance of her part of the invalid contract. Restatement of Contracts § 604 (1932).

Foreman, however, contends that even if the contract is invalid as to the contingent fee, the retainer should be allowed to stand since the contract is divisible. We do not agree. Florida law provides that "a contract should be treated as entire when, by a consideration of its terms, nature, and purpose, each and all of its parts appear to be interdependent and common to one another and to the consideration." Local No. 234 of United Association of Journeymen and Apprentices of Plumbing and Pipefitting Industry of United States and Canada v. Henley and Beckwith, Inc., Fla.1953, 66 So.2d 818, 821. Similarly, "a contract is indivisible where the entire fulfillment of the contract is contemplated by the parties as the basis of the arrangement." Id. at 821. Judged by this standard, we think the contract here was clearly non-divisible. The retainer and contingent fee were related to the sole object of employment, the divorce. The parties did not contemplate a piece work relationship. We think it obvious that Mr. Foreman did not agree and would not have agreed to handle the divorce for the retainer alone. With the illegal portion of the contract excised, the greater portion of the consideration was eliminated. It is impossible to think that a portion of the contract with this much significance could be entirely "eliminated from the contract and still leave a valid working arrangement fairly reflecting the original mutual understanding between the parties." Local No. 234 v. Henley and Beckwith, Inc., supra, at 822. The contract is thus not subject to divisible quantification. The retainer and the contingent fee both related to the whole obligation. We conclude, therefore, that the invalid contingent fee made the entire contract void and unenforceable.

* * *

In the instant case we can form no other conclusion but that the alleged acts of Mr. Foreman constitute an absolute refusal to perform substantial duties under the contract, rendering his entire performance unsuccessful. If we assume that he did and said that which Mrs. Singleton alleges, his conduct was so pockmarked with hostility and arrogance that Mrs. Singleton was justified in rescinding the entire contract and demanding the return of her consideration. We therefore hold that Mrs. Singleton's complaint states a valid cause of action for the return of the jewels or their value since she paid this much on the contract which Mr. Foreman did not successfully perform.

* * *

Reversed and remanded.

COCHRAN v. DELLFAVA

City Court, City of Rochester, Monroe County, Small Claims Branch, 1987.
136 Misc.2d 38, 517 N.Y.S.2d 854.

JOHN R. SCHWARTZ, JUDGE. The issue here is whether the plaintiff can recover from the defendant the Two Thousand Two Hundred Dollars ($2,200.00) she gave to him to play in the so-called "airplane game".

The game consists of a total of fifteen players or investors. Each player must initially pay Two Thousand Two Hundred Dollars ($2,200.00) to enter the airplane game. There is an out-going pilot, two co-pilots, four flight attendants, and eight passengers. The pilot, co-pilots and flight attendants are already on the plane and they attempt to sell tickets to eight new passengers. As each of these eight passengers boards the airplane, he [she] pays $2,200.00 for his [her] ticket to the flight attendant, who in turn passes the money onto the co-pilot, who in turn gives it to the out-going pilot. When the eight passenger tickets are sold, the out-going pilot collects a total of Seventeen Thousand Two Hundred Dollars ($17,200.00) for his or her original $2,200.00 investment. After all eight passenger tickets are sold, the out-going pilot leaves the game and the plane is split off into two new airplanes. Each co-pilot becomes an out-going pilot of his or her own plane; the four flight attendants split off and each becomes a co-pilot of one of the new planes. The passengers split off and become flight attendants of the new planes. The members of the new airplane then try to solicit eight new passengers and the game goes on as explained.

Clearly this is a "chain distribution scheme" as defined in General Business Law 359–fff(2): "... a chain distribution scheme is a sales device whereby a person, upon condition that he make an investment, is granted a license or right to solicit or recruit for profit or economic gain one or more additional persons who are also granted such license or right upon condition of making an investment and may further perpetuate the chain of persons who are granted such license or right upon such condition ..."

It is illegal and prohibited for any person to promote, offer or grant participation in a chain distribution scheme, General Business Law 359–fff(1), and anyone who does shall be guilty of an unclassified misdemeanor. General Business Law 359–g(2).

FACTS

On January 13, 1987, the plaintiff went to a meeting called by the defendant whereby she was persuaded by the defendant to join the so-called "airplane game". She alleged that he was the pilot but the facts revealed he was only the co-pilot, and therefore, he had not started to make a profit yet. The plaintiff stated that she knew it was illegal to play in the game but she was assured by the defendant that "if they got caught, he would take all responsibility". After the meeting, she gave

Two Thousand Two Hundred Dollars ($2,200.00) to her friend, another participant, who gave it to the defendant, who gave it to the pilot. At the next meeting, the plaintiff found out that she had become a flight attendant on a plane she did not wish to be on and asked the defendant for her money back. He told her that he did not have her money because he gave it to the pilot. He suggested that she call the pilot. The pilot refused to give the plaintiff her money back. The plane crashed and the plaintiff never recovered her initial investment or made a profit. She brings this action against the defendant for the return of her money.

LAW

The issue here is, does the plaintiff have a cause of action to recover her money in a civil court?

It is illegal and criminal "to promote, offer or grant participation in" the so-called "airplane game". (See General Business Law 359–fff(1) and 359–g(2)). "It is settled law in this State (and probably of every other state) that a party to an illegal contract cannot ask a court of law to help him [her] carry out his [her] illegal object, nor can such a person plead or prove in any court a case in which he [she], as a basis for his [her] claim, must show forth his [her] illegal purpose. * * * For no court should be required to serve as a paymaster of the wages of crime, or referee between thieves. Therefore, the law 'will not extend its aid to either of the parties' or 'listen to their complaints against each other, but will leave them where their own acts have left them' ". (*Stone v. Freeman*, 298 N.Y. 268, 271, 82 N.E.2d 571, quoting *Schermerhorn v. Talman*, 14 N.Y. 93, 141).

However, there are exceptions to this general principal of law. Courts have allowed recovery by a plaintiff to an illegal contract provided the plaintiff's conduct was *malum prohibitum* and not *malum in se.* Here, the plaintiff's conduct was only *malum prohibitum* (conduct prohibited by statute) as opposed to *malum in se* (conduct prohibited by the nature of the act). To fall under the exception to the general principal of law, not only must the plaintiff establish that the agreement was only *malum prohibitum,* but she must also establish that she entered the agreement under duress or undue influence and that the defendant's conduct was more culpable. Courts have permitted recovery to a widow who became involved in an illegal marriage brokerage contract (*Duvall v. Wellman*, 127 N.Y. 156) and to a Russian Jewish family who illegally loaned money to another Russian Jewish family so that family could emigrate from a communist country (*Birger v. Tuner*, 104 Misc.2d 63, 427 N.Y.S.2d 904). A court has also mandated the return of a plaintiff's money based on an illegal agreement for the proprietary operation by plaintiff of defendant's restaurant, including plaintiff's use of defendant's liquor license, which was against public policy. (*Smith v. Pope*, 72 A.D.2d 913, 422 N.Y.S.2d 192; see also 21 N.Y.Jur Contracts § 183).

In each of the cases, the courts held that the parties were not *in pari delicto.* The plaintiff either acted under duress, undue influence, or out of good will.

Therefore, plaintiff's standing to bring this lawsuit stands or falls on whether she violated General Business Law Section 359–fff(1). Did she, by contributing her Two Thousand Two Hundred Dollars ($2,200.00) to the airplane game in the first instance, "promote" the game as declared illegal in the statute?

This Court finds, as a matter of law, that by entering the so-called "airplane game" as a passenger, one is in fact "promoting" the game in violation of the General Business Law (e.g. encouraging the pilot to make an illegal profit; encouraging others to enter the game by example; and eventually hoping to make an illegal profit). Therefore, plaintiff's cause of action must fail as a matter of law. It matters not whether the defendant was the more culpable party, whether the defendant was a pilot, as plaintiff testified, and did actually recover a profit or whether he took money because he never made out-going pilot as defendant testified.

The plaintiff by entering the game had larceny in her heart. If the plane did not crash she would have made a substantial illegal profit. If this Court permitted her to recover, in effect this Court would become a referee amongst thieves. The law will not extend its aid to the parties to such an agreement. (See *Stone v. Freeman*, 298 N.Y. 268, 82 N.E.2d 571). Therefore, the complaint is dismissed.

Problems

6. Plaintiff, mother, is suing her son for specific performance of a contract to convey. She wished to buy a house. She was informed that it would be difficult for her to obtain mortgage financing and was advised that a male family member would more likely be able to obtain such financing. Her son (the defendant) agreed to apply for mortgage financing, take title in his name and then convey to her. He successfully applied for a GI mortgage (a government guaranteed loan at reduced interest available only to veterans). Plaintiff paid the down payment and closing costs. Defendant now refuses to convey and points out that his agreement with his mother is expressly illegal under the Servicemen's Readjustment Act. She points out that she was unaware of the kind of financing he had applied for. What result?

7. Seller sues purchaser on a $147,196 note given in connection with credit sales of electronic components which purchaser smuggled into Mexico. Seller, knowing of the purchaser's purpose, removed the components from their original labeled packages and packed them in unlabeled packages and delivered them in loads of 1200 to 1400 lbs., the capacity of the smugglers' airplane. Will seller recover?

8. Plaintiff rendered housekeeping services for decedent. She also surrendered her daughter to decedent for adoption. In exchange for the services and the adoption of the daughter, decedent promised plaintiff that she would be the beneficiary of decedent's entire estate. It is illegal to surrender a child for adoption for a consideration. May plaintiff recover for the value of her concededly lawful services?

9. A and B entered into two agreements at the same time and place. The first gave B an option to purchase certain real property in exchange for

a promissory note which was given to A in the amount of $10,000. The purchase price was $260,000. The second agreement was a pasturing agreement which was entered into by both parties in violation of Bureau of Land Management regulations and was performed in a way to cover up the illegality. B never exercised his option and A sues upon the promissory note. What result?

10. A sold milk to B in excess of 3,000 pounds in one month. The agreed price was $11,000. Both were milk dealers. In an action for the price B set up as an affirmative defense the fact that A was not licensed as required by State law. The relevant statute provided in part that it shall be unlawful for an unlicensed milk dealer to sell milk to another dealer. It also provided: "The commissioner may by official order exempt from the license requirements provided by this article, milk dealers who purchase or handle milk in total quantity not exceeding three thousand pounds in any month, and/or milk dealers selling milk in any quantity in markets of one thousand population or less." The primary requirement for obtaining a license was proof of financial soundness. Violation of the statute is a misdemeanor which is punishable by imprisonment or fine. What result?

11. Plaintiff was duly licensed as a contractor at the time of contracting with defendant to grade and fill certain land. The license expired while plaintiff was performing the contract. It was not renewed until after performance was complete. Failure to renew earlier was due to oversight and not to any substantive reasons having to do with plaintiff's suitability to be licensed. Plaintiff has fully performed and seeks to obtain the balance of $432,000 out of a total price of $740,000. A statute provides that no contractor may recover "without alleging and proving that he was a duly licensed contractor at all times during the performance of such act or contract." Frame an argument for plaintiff.

12. Plaintiff, a firm of licensed lawyers, had no partners or associates who were licensed in California. Several members of the firm went to California to represent a client in arbitration proceeding and settlement discussions. They billed the client for over $1 million. The client refused to pay. The plaintiff sued and the client raised the defense of illegality. Will the defense succeed?

13. At all relevant times the sale of Irish Sweepstakes lottery tickets was illegal in Michigan. Plaintiff and defendant were nonetheless jointly engaged in the business of selling these illegal tickets in Michigan. As compensation, they received two free tickets for every twenty they sold. They agreed that they would split the proceeds of any winning ticket that either of them possessed. A ticket entered in defendant's name won $500,000. Upon his refusal to share the winnings with plaintiff, the latter brought this action to claim 50% of the winnings. Defendant raises the defense of illegality. Will the defense be successful?

14. Plaintiff contracted with defendant whereby plaintiff became defendant's exclusive distributor for defendant's sprinkler system in Thailand. Plaintiff alleges that in breach of the agreement defendant refused to supply a sprinkler system to fulfill a contract plaintiff had entered into with the Thai army and had instead made a sale to the Thai army through another distributor. In reply, defendant alleges that plaintiff had obtained the Thai

army contract by bribing Thai officials thereby rendering void the exclusive distributorship. Assuming the allegations of both parties are true, what should be the result?

15. Pamela's husband brought divorce proceedings. She retained plaintiff as her attorney in the proceedings. Legal fees were not discussed until a property settlement seemed to be at hand at which point plaintiff prepared and Pamela signed an agreement to pay a fee of 15% of any settlement that might be made. Assuming the contingent fee arrangement is void, is plaintiff entitled to anything?

16. D, the president of X Creamery, visited K and offered him a "Grade A" contract for the sale of K's milk to X, if K would pay him a rebate or "kickback" of 4½ cents a gallon during the lifetime of the contract. K accepted the offer because no other "Grade A" contracts were available and "he had no other choice" because his economic survival was dependent upon his ability to obtain a "Grade A" milk contract in a locality where such contracts were extremely scarce. K brings an action to recover the rebates paid. What result?

17. I (investigator) entered into a contract with A (attorney) under which it was agreed that if I would investigate cases assigned to him by A, A would pay I an amount equal to ⅓ of net attorney's fees received by A in the cases investigated. A has refused to pay I for his investigations. What result?

18. S turned over $10,000 to his agent, A, which A was to use in bribing purchasing agents to facilitate the sale of S's goods. A has used $5,000 for this purpose. S demanded that the remaining $5,000 be returned and A refused. S sues A. What result? Would the result be different if S had demanded the return of the money before any part of the $10,000 was used?

19. A statute forbade the construction of a class of buildings in Boston with a roof having a pitch of more than 20 degrees. Defendant's architect designed a hotel within this class having a roof pitch of 30 degrees. Plaintiff contractor agreed to erect the building in accordance with the architect's plan and in conformity with all applicable statutes. When the time came to construct the roof, plaintiff learned that construction would violate the statute and attempted to negotiate for the revision of the plans. Defendant adamantly insisted that the plans be followed. Plaintiff refused, abandoned the job, and sues for the reasonable value of the work done. What result?

20. In December 1966 the Maryland Court of Appeals reaffirmed its traditional rule that contracts made on Sunday are illegal and unenforceable. In the opinion so holding it invited the legislature to change the Sunday law. On Sunday, March 19, 1967, the parties entered into a signed agreement for the sale of real property, postdating it to March 20. The purchaser made a down payment of $3,500. On April 14, 1967 the governor signed into law a bill enacted by the legislature permitting Sunday contracts. On June 20, 1967, the purchasers brought a bill in equity for rescission of the contract of sale and restitution of its down payment. What arguments are likely to be made by the parties?

Appendix A

UNIFORM COMMERCIAL CODE

1991 OFFICIAL TEXT
ARTICLE 1
GENERAL PROVISIONS

PART 1

SHORT TITLE, CONSTRUCTION, APPLICATION
AND SUBJECT MATTER OF THE ACT

§ 1–101. Short Title

This Act shall be known and may be cited as Uniform Commercial Code.

§ 1–102. Purposes; Rules of Construction; Variation by Agreement

(1) This Act shall be liberally construed and applied to promote its underlying purposes and policies.

(2) Underlying purposes and policies of this Act are

(a) to simplify, clarify and modernize the law governing commercial transactions;

(b) to permit the continued expansion of commercial practices through custom, usage and agreement of the parties;

(c) to make uniform the law among the various jurisdictions.

(3) The effect of provisions of this Act may be varied by agreement, except as otherwise provided in this Act and except that the obligations of good faith, diligence, reasonableness and care prescribed by this Act may not be disclaimed by agreement but the parties may by agreement determine the standards by which the performance of such obligations is to be measured if such standards are not manifestly unreasonable.

(4) The presence in certain provisions of this Act of the words "unless otherwise agreed" or words of similar import does not imply that the effect of other provisions may not be varied by agreement under subsection (3).

(5) In this Act unless the context otherwise requires

(a) words in the singular number include the plural, and in the plural include the singular;

(b) words of the masculine gender include the feminine and the neuter, and when the sense so indicates words of the neuter gender may refer to any gender.

§ 1–103. Supplementary General Principles of Law Applicable

Unless displaced by the particular provisions of this Act, the principles of law and equity, including the law merchant and the law relative to capacity to contract, principal and agent, estoppel, fraud, misrepresentation, duress, coercion, mistake, bankruptcy, or other validating or invalidating cause shall supplement its provisions.

§ 1–104. Construction Against Implicit Repeal

This Act being a general act intended as a unified coverage of its subject matter, no part of it shall be deemed to be impliedly repealed by subsequent legislation if such construction can reasonably be avoided.

§ 1–105. Territorial Application of the Act; Parties' Power to Choose Applicable Law

(1) Except as provided hereafter in this section, when a transaction bears a reasonable relation to this state and also to another state or nation the parties may agree that the law either of this state or of such other state or nation shall govern their rights and duties. Failing such agreement this Act applies to transactions bearing an appropriate relation to this state.

(2) Where one of the following provisions of this Act specifies the applicable law, that provision governs and a contrary agreement is effective only to the extent permitted by the law (including the conflict of laws rules) so specified:

Rights of creditors against sold goods. Section 2–402.

Applicability of the Article on Leases. Sections 2A–105 and 2A–106.

Applicability of the Article on Bank Deposits and Collections. Section 4–102.

Bulk transfers subject to the Article on Bulk Transfers. Section 6–102.

Applicability of the Article on Investment Securities. Section 8–106.

Perfection provisions of the Article on Secured Transactions. Section 9–103.

As amended in 1972 and 1987.

§ 1–106. Remedies to Be Liberally Administered

(1) The remedies provided by this Act shall be liberally administered to the end that the aggrieved party may be put in as good a position as if the other party had fully performed but neither consequential or special

nor penal damages may be had except as specifically provided in this Act or by other rule of law.

(2) Any right or obligation declared by this Act is enforceable by action unless the provision declaring it specifies a different and limited effect.

§ 1–107. Waiver or Renunciation of Claim or Right After Breach

Any claim or right arising out of an alleged breach can be discharged in whole or in part without consideration by a written waiver or renunciation signed and delivered by the aggrieved party.

§ 1–108. Severability

If any provision or clause of this Act or application thereof to any person or circumstances is held invalid, such invalidity shall not affect other provisions or applications of the Act which can be given effect without the invalid provision or application, and to this end the provisions of this Act are declared to be severable.

§ 1–109. Section Captions

Section captions are parts of this Act.

PART 2

GENERAL DEFINITIONS AND PRINCIPLES OF INTERPRETATION

§ 1–201. General Definitions

Subject to additional definitions contained in the subsequent Articles of this Act which are applicable to specific Articles or Parts thereof, and unless the context otherwise requires, in this Act:

(1) "Action" in the sense of a judicial proceeding includes recoupment, counterclaim, set-off, suit in equity and any other proceedings in which rights are determined.

(2) "Aggrieved party" means a party entitled to resort to a remedy.

(3) "Agreement" means the bargain of the parties in fact as found in their language or by implication from other circumstances including course of dealing or usage of trade or course of performance as provided in this Act (Sections 1–205 and 2–208). Whether an agreement has legal consequences is determined by the provisions of this Act, if applicable; otherwise by the law of contracts (Section 1–103). (Compare "Contract".)

(4) "Bank" means any person engaged in the business of banking.

(5) "Bearer" means the person in possession of an instrument, document of title, or certificated security payable to bearer or indorsed in blank.

(6) "Bill of lading" means a document evidencing the receipt of goods for shipment issued by a person engaged in the business of

transporting or forwarding goods, and includes an airbill. "Airbill" means a document serving for air transportation as a bill of lading does for marine or rail transportation, and includes an air consignment note or air waybill.

(7) "Branch" includes a separately incorporated foreign branch of a bank.

(8) "Burden of establishing" a fact means the burden of persuading the triers of fact that the existence of the fact is more probable than its non-existence.

(9) "Buyer in ordinary course of business" means a person who in good faith and without knowledge that the sale to him is in violation of the ownership rights or security interest of a third party in the goods buys in ordinary course from a person in the business of selling goods of that kind but does not include a pawnbroker. All persons who sell minerals or the like (including oil and gas) at wellhead or minehead shall be deemed to be persons in the business of selling goods of that kind. "Buying" may be for cash or by exchange of other property or on secured or unsecured credit and includes receiving goods or documents of title under a pre-existing contract for sale but does not include a transfer in bulk or as security for or in total or partial satisfaction of a money debt.

(10) "Conspicuous": A term or clause is conspicuous when it is so written that a reasonable person against whom it is to operate ought to have noticed it. A printed heading in capitals (as: NON-NEGOTIABLE BILL OF LADING) is conspicuous. Language in the body of a form is "conspicuous" if it is in larger or other contrasting type or color. But in a telegram any stated term is "conspicuous". Whether a term or clause is "conspicuous" or not is for decision by the court.

(11) "Contract" means the total legal obligation which results from the parties' agreement as affected by this Act and any other applicable rules of law. (Compare "Agreement".)

(12) "Creditor" includes a general creditor, a secured creditor, a lien creditor and any representative of creditors, including an assignee for the benefit of creditors, a trustee in bankruptcy, a receiver in equity and an executor or administrator of an insolvent debtor's or assignor's estate.

(13) "Defendant" includes a person in the position of defendant in a cross-action or counterclaim.

(14) "Delivery" with respect to instruments, documents of title, chattel paper, or certificated securities means voluntary transfer of possession.

(15) "Document of title" includes bill of lading, dock warrant, dock receipt, warehouse receipt or order for the delivery of goods, and also any other document which in the regular course of business or financing is treated as adequately evidencing that the person in possession of it is entitled to receive, hold and dispose of the document and the goods it covers. To be a document of title a document must purport to be issued

by or addressed to a bailee and purport to cover goods in the bailee's possession which are either identified or are fungible portions of an identified mass.

(16) "Fault" means wrongful act, omission or breach.

(17) "Fungible" with respect to goods or securities means goods or securities of which any unit is, by nature or usage of trade, the equivalent of any other like unit. Goods which are not fungible shall be deemed fungible for the purposes of this Act to the extent that under a particular agreement or document unlike units are treated as equivalents.

(18) "Genuine" means free of forgery or counterfeiting.

(19) "Good faith" means honesty in fact in the conduct or transaction concerned.

(20) "Holder" means a person who is in possession of a document of title or an instrument or a certificated investment security drawn, issued, or indorsed to him or his order or to bearer or in blank.

(21) To "honor" is to pay or to accept and pay, or where a credit so engages to purchase or discount a draft complying with the terms of the credit.

(22) "Insolvency proceedings" includes any assignment for the benefit of creditors or other proceedings intended to liquidate or rehabilitate the estate of the person involved.

(23) A person is "insolvent" who either has ceased to pay his debts in the ordinary course of business or cannot pay his debts as they become due or is insolvent within the meaning of the federal bankruptcy law.

(24) "Money" means a medium of exchange authorized or adopted by a domestic or foreign government as a part of its currency.

(25) A person has "notice" of a fact when

    (a) he has actual knowledge of it; or

    (b) he has received a notice or notification of it; or

    (c) from all the facts and circumstances known to him at the time in question he has reason to know that it exists.

A person "knows" or has "knowledge" of a fact when he has actual knowledge of it. "Discover" or "learn" or a word or phrase of similar import refers to knowledge rather than to reason to know. The time and circumstances under which a notice or notification may cease to be effective are not determined by this Act.

(26) A person "notifies" or "gives" a notice or notification to another by taking such steps as may be reasonably required to inform the other in ordinary course whether or not such other actually comes to know of it. A person "receives" a notice or notification when

    (a) it comes to his attention; or

    (b) it is duly delivered at the place of business through which the contract was made or at any other place held out by him as the place for receipt of such communications.

(27) Notice, knowledge or a notice or notification received by an organization is effective for a particular transaction from the time when it is brought to the attention of the individual conducting that transaction, and in any event from the time when it would have been brought to his attention if the organization had exercised due diligence. An organization exercises due diligence if it maintains reasonable routines for communicating significant information to the person conducting the transaction and there is reasonable compliance with the routines. Due diligence does not require an individual acting for the organization to communicate information unless such communication is part of his regular duties or unless he has reason to know of the transaction and that the transaction would be materially affected by the information.

(28) "Organization" includes a corporation, government or governmental subdivision or agency, business trust, estate, trust, partnership or association, two or more persons having a joint or common interest, or any other legal or commercial entity.

(29) "Party", as distinct from "third party", means a person who has engaged in a transaction or made an agreement within this Act.

(30) "Person" includes an individual or an organization (See Section 1–102).

(31) "Presumption" or "presumed" means that the trier of fact must find the existence of the fact presumed unless and until evidence is introduced which would support a finding of its non-existence.

(32) "Purchase" includes taking by sale, discount, negotiation, mortgage, pledge, lien, issue or re-issue, gift or any other voluntary transaction creating an interest in property.

(33) "Purchaser" means a person who takes by purchase.

(34) "Remedy" means any remedial right to which an aggrieved party is entitled with or without resort to a tribunal.

(35) "Representative" includes an agent, an officer of a corporation or association, and a trustee, executor or administrator of an estate, or any other person empowered to act for another.

(36) "Rights" includes remedies.

(37) "Security interest" means an interest in personal property or fixtures which secures payment or performance of an obligation. The retention or reservation of title by a seller of goods notwithstanding shipment or delivery to the buyer (Section 2–401) is limited in effect to a reservation of a "security interest". The term also includes any interest of a buyer of accounts or chattel paper which is subject to Article 9. The special property interest of a buyer of goods on identification of those goods to a contract for sale under Section 2–401 is not a "security interest", but a buyer may also acquire a "security interest" by complying with Article 9. Unless a consignment is intended as security, reservation of title thereunder is not a "security interest", but a consignment in any event is subject to the provisions on consignment sales (Section 2–326).

Whether a transaction creates a lease or security interest is determined by the facts of each case; however, a transaction creates a security interest if the consideration the lessee is to pay the lessor for the right to possession and use of the goods is an obligation for the term of the lease not subject to termination by the lessee, and

(a) the original term of the lease is equal to or greater than the remaining economic life of the goods,

(b) the lessee is bound to renew the lease for the remaining economic life of the goods or is bound to become the owner of the goods,

(c) the lessee has an option to renew the lease for the remaining economic life of the goods for no additional consideration or nominal additional consideration upon compliance with the lease agreement, or

(d) the lessee has an option to become the owner of the goods for no additional consideration or nominal additional consideration upon compliance with the lease agreement.

A transaction does not create a security interest merely because it provides that

(a) the present value of the consideration the lessee is obligated to pay the lessor for the right to possession and use of the goods is substantially equal to or is greater than the fair market value of the goods at the time the lease is entered into,

(b) the lessee assumes risk of loss of the goods, or agrees to pay taxes, insurance, filing, recording, or registration fees, or service or maintenance costs with respect to the goods,

(c) the lessee has an option to renew the lease or to become the owner of the goods,

(d) the lessee has an option to renew the lease for a fixed rent that is equal to or greater than the reasonably predictable fair market rent for the use of the goods for the term of the renewal at the time the option is to be performed, or

(e) the lessee has an option to become the owner of the goods for a fixed price that is equal to or greater than the reasonably predictable fair market value of the goods at the time the option is to be performed.

For purposes of this subsection (37):

(x) Additional consideration is not nominal if (I) when the option to renew the lease is granted to the lessee the rent is stated to be the fair market rent for the use of the goods for the term of the renewal determined at the time the option is to be performed, or (ii) when the option to become the owner of the goods is granted to the lessee the price is stated to be the fair market value of the goods determined at the time the option is to be performed. Additional consideration is nominal if it is less than the lessee's reasonably predictable cost of performing under the lease agreement if the option is not exercised;

(y) "Reasonably predictable" and "remaining economic life of the goods" are to be determined with reference to the facts and circumstances at the time the transaction is entered into; and

(z) "Present value" means the amount as of a date certain of one or more sums payable in the future, discounted to the date certain. The discount is determined by the interest rate specified by the parties if the rate is not manifestly unreasonable at the time the transaction is entered into; otherwise, the discount is determined by a commercially reasonable rate that takes into account the facts and circumstances of each case at the time the transaction was entered into.

(38) "Send" in connection with any writing or notice means to deposit in the mail or deliver for transmission by any other usual means of communication with postage or cost of transmission provided for and properly addressed and in the case of an instrument to an address specified thereon or otherwise agreed, or if there be none to any address reasonable under the circumstances. The receipt of any writing or notice within the time at which it would have arrived if properly sent has the effect of a proper sending.

(39) "Signed" includes any symbol executed or adopted by a party with present intention to authenticate a writing.

(40) "Surety" includes guarantor.

(41) "Telegram" includes a message transmitted by radio, teletype, cable, any mechanical method of transmission, or the like.

(42) "Term" means that portion of an agreement which relates to a particular matter.

(43) "Unauthorized" signature or indorsement means one made without actual, implied or apparent authority and includes a forgery.

(44) "Value". Except as otherwise provided with respect to negotiable instruments and bank collections (Sections 3–303, 4–208 and 4–209) a person gives "value" for rights if he acquires them

(a) in return for a binding commitment to extend credit or for the extension of immediately available credit whether or not drawn upon and whether or not a charge-back is provided for in the event of difficulties in collection; or

(b) as security for or in total or partial satisfaction of a pre-existing claim; or

(c) by accepting delivery pursuant to a pre-existing contract for purchase; or

(d) generally, in return for any consideration sufficient to support a simple contract.

(45) "Warehouse receipt" means a receipt issued by a person engaged in the business of storing goods for hire.

(46) "Written" or "writing" includes printing, typewriting or any other intentional reduction to tangible form.

As amended in 1962, 1972, 1977 and 1987.

§ 1–202. Prima Facie Evidence by Third Party Documents

A document in due form purporting to be a bill of lading, policy or certificate of insurance, official weigher's or inspector's certificate, consular invoice, or any other document authorized or required by the contract to be issued by a third party shall be prima facie evidence of its own authenticity and genuineness and of the facts stated in the document by the third party.

§ 1–203. Obligation of Good Faith

Every contract or duty within this Act imposes an obligation of good faith in its performance or enforcement.

§ 1–204. Time; Reasonable Time; "Seasonably"

(1) Whenever this Act requires any action to be taken within a reasonable time, any time which is not manifestly unreasonable may be fixed by agreement.

(2) What is a reasonable time for taking any action depends on the nature, purpose and circumstances of such action.

(3) An action is taken "seasonably" when it is taken at or within the time agreed or if no time is agreed at or within a reasonable time.

§ 1–205. Course of Dealing and Usage of Trade

(1) A course of dealing is a sequence of previous conduct between the parties to a particular transaction which is fairly to be regarded as establishing a common basis of understanding for interpreting their expressions and other conduct.

(2) A usage of trade is any practice or method of dealing having such regularity of observance in a place, vocation or trade as to justify an expectation that it will be observed with respect to the transaction in question. The existence and scope of such a usage are to be proved as facts. If it is established that such a usage is embodied in a written trade code or similar writing the interpretation of the writing is for the court.

(3) A course of dealing between parties and any usage of trade in the vocation or trade in which they are engaged or of which they are or should be aware give particular meaning to and supplement or qualify terms of an agreement.

(4) The express terms of an agreement and an applicable course of dealing or usage of trade shall be construed wherever reasonable as consistent with each other; but when such construction is unreasonable express terms control both course of dealing and usage of trade and course of dealing controls usage of trade.

(5) An applicable usage of trade in the place where any part of performance is to occur shall be used in interpreting the agreement as to that part of the performance.

(6) Evidence of a relevant usage of trade offered by one party is not admissible unless and until he has given the other party such notice as the court finds sufficient to prevent unfair surprise to the latter.

§ 1–206. Statute of Frauds for Kinds of Personal Property Not Otherwise Covered

(1) Except in the cases described in subsection (2) of this section a contract for the sale of personal property is not enforceable by way of action or defense beyond five thousand dollars in amount or value of remedy unless there is some writing which indicates that a contract for sale has been made between the parties at a defined or stated price, reasonably identifies the subject matter, and is signed by the party against whom enforcement is sought or by his authorized agent.

(2) Subsection (1) of this section does not apply to contracts for the sale of goods (Section 2–201) nor of securities (Section 8–319) nor to security agreements (Section 9–203).

§ 1–207. Performance or Acceptance Under Reservation of Rights

(1) A party who with explicit reservation of rights performs or promises performance or assents to performance in a manner demanded or offered by the other party does not thereby prejudice the rights reserved. Such words as "without prejudice", "under protest" or the like are sufficient.

(2) Subsection (1) does not apply to an accord and satisfaction. Added 1990.

§ 1–208. Option to Accelerate at Will

A term providing that one party or his successor in interest may accelerate payment or performance or require collateral or additional collateral "at will" or "when he deems himself insecure" or in words of similar import shall be construed to mean that he shall have power to do so only if he in good faith believes that the prospect of payment or performance is impaired. The burden of establishing lack of good faith is on the party against whom the power has been exercised.

§ 1–209. Subordinated Obligations

An obligation may be issued as subordinated to payment of another obligation of the person obligated, or a creditor may subordinate his right to payment of an obligation by agreement with either the person obligated or another creditor of the person obligated. Such a subordination does not create a security interest as against either the common debtor or a subordinated creditor. This section shall be construed as declaring the law as it existed prior to the enactment of this section and not as modifying it. Added 1966.

Note: *This new section is proposed as an optional provision to make it clear that a subordination agreement does not create a security interest unless so intended.*

ARTICLE 2
SALES

PART 1
SHORT TITLE, GENERAL CONSTRUCTION AND SUBJECT MATTER

§ 2-101. Short Title

This Article shall be known and may be cited as Uniform Commercial Code—Sales.

§ 2-102. Scope; Certain Security and Other Transactions Excluded From This Article

Unless the context otherwise requires, this Article applies to transactions in goods; it does not apply to any transaction which although in the form of an unconditional contract to sell or present sale is intended to operate only as a security transaction nor does this Article impair or repeal any statute regulating sales to consumers, farmers or other specified classes of buyers.

§ 2-103. Definitions and Index of Definitions

(1) In this Article unless the context otherwise requires

    (a) "Buyer" means a person who buys or contracts to buy goods.

    (b) "Good faith" in the case of a merchant means honesty in fact and the observance of reasonable commercial standards of fair dealing in the trade.

    (c) "Receipt" of goods means taking physical possession of them.

    (d) "Seller" means a person who sells or contracts to sell goods.

(2) Other definitions applying to this Article or to specified Parts thereof, and the sections in which they appear are:

"Acceptance". Section 2-606.

"Banker's credit". Section 2-325.

"Between merchants". Section 2-104.

"Cancellation". Section 2-106(4).

"Commercial unit". Section 2-105.

"Confirmed credit". Section 2-325.

"Conforming to contract". Section 2–106.

"Contract for sale". Section 2–106.

"Cover". Section 2–712.

"Entrusting". Section 2–403.

"Financing agency". Section 2–104.

"Future goods". Section 2–105.

"Goods". Section 2–105.

"Identification". Section 2–501.

"Installment contract". Section 2–612.

"Letter of Credit". Section 2–325.

"Lot". Section 2–105.

"Merchant". Section 2–104.

"Overseas". Section 2–323.

"Person in position of seller". Section 2–707.

"Present sale". Section 2–106.

"Sale". Section 2–106.

"Sale on approval". Section 2–326.

"Sale or return". Section 2–326.

"Termination". Section 2–106.

(3) The following definitions in other Articles apply to this Article:

"Check". Section 3–104.

"Consignee". Section 7–102.

"Consignor". Section 7–102.

"Consumer goods". Section 9–109.

"Dishonor". Section 3–507.

"Draft". Section 3–104.

(4) In addition Article 1 contains general definitions and principles of construction and interpretation applicable throughout this Article.

§ 2–104. Definitions: "Merchant"; "Between Merchants"; "Financing Agency"

(1) "Merchant" means a person who deals in goods of the kind or otherwise by his occupation holds himself out as having knowledge or skill peculiar to the practices or goods involved in the transaction or to whom such knowledge or skill may be attributed by his employment of an agent or broker or other intermediary who by his occupation holds himself out as having such knowledge or skill.

(2) "Financing agency" means a bank, finance company or other person who in the ordinary course of business makes advances against goods or documents of title or who by arrangement with either the seller

or the buyer intervenes in ordinary course to make or collect payment due or claimed under the contract for sale, as by purchasing or paying the seller's draft or making advances against it or by merely taking it for collection whether or not documents of title accompany the draft. "Financing agency" includes also a bank or other person who similarly intervenes between persons who are in the position of seller and buyer in respect to the goods (Section 2–707).

(3) "Between merchants" means in any transaction with respect to which both parties are chargeable with the knowledge or skill of merchants.

§ 2–105. Definitions: Transferability; "Goods"; "Future" Goods; "Lot"; "Commercial Unit"

(1) "Goods" means all things (including specially manufactured goods) which are movable at the time of identification to the contract for sale other than the money in which the price is to be paid, investment securities (Article 8) and things in action. "Goods" also includes the unborn young of animals and growing crops and other identified things attached to realty as described in the section on goods to be severed from realty (Section 2–107).

(2) Goods must be both existing and identified before any interest in them can pass. Goods which are not both existing and identified are "future" goods. A purported present sale of future goods or of any interest therein operates as a contract to sell.

(3) There may be a sale of a part interest in existing identified goods.

(4) An undivided share in an identified bulk of fungible goods is sufficiently identified to be sold although the quantity of the bulk is not determined. Any agreed proportion of such a bulk or any quantity thereof agreed upon by number, weight or other measure may to the extent of the seller's interest in the bulk be sold to the buyer who then becomes an owner in common.

(5) "Lot" means a parcel or a single article which is the subject matter of a separate sale or delivery, whether or not it is sufficient to perform the contract.

(6) "Commercial unit" means such a unit of goods as by commercial usage is a single whole for purposes of sale and division of which materially impairs its character or value on the market or in use. A commercial unit may be a single article (as a machine) or a set of articles (as a suite of furniture or an assortment of sizes) or a quantity (as a bale, gross, or carload) or any other unit treated in use or in the relevant market as a single whole.

§ 2–106. Definitions: "Contract"; "Agreement"; "Contract for Sale"; "Sale"; "Present Sale"; "Conforming" to Contract; "Termination"; "Cancellation"

(1) In this Article unless the context otherwise requires "contract" and "agreement" are limited to those relating to the present or future

sale of goods. "Contract for sale" includes both a present sale of goods and a contract to sell goods at a future time. A "sale" consists in the passing of title from the seller to the buyer for a price (Section 2–401). A "present sale" means a sale which is accomplished by the making of the contract.

(2) Goods or conduct including any part of a performance are "conforming" or conform to the contract when they are in accordance with the obligations under the contract.

(3) "Termination" occurs when either party pursuant to a power created by agreement or law puts an end to the contract otherwise then for its breach. On "termination" all obligations which are still executory on both sides are discharged but any right based on prior breach or performance survives.

(4) "Cancellation" occurs when either party puts an end to the contract for breach by the other and its effect is the same as that of "termination" except that the cancelling party also retains any remedy for breach of the whole contract or any unperformed balance.

§ 2–107. Goods to Be Severed From Realty: Recording

(1) A contract for the sale of minerals or the like (including oil and gas) or a structure or its materials to be removed from realty is a contract for the sale of goods within this Article if they are to be severed by the seller but until severance a purported present sale thereof which is not effective as a transfer of an interest in land is effective only as a contract to sell.

(2) A contract for the sale apart from the land of growing crops or other things attached to realty and capable of severance without material harm thereto but not described in subsection (1) or of timber to be cut is a contract for the sale of goods within this Article whether the subject matter is to be severed by the buyer or by the seller even though it forms part of the realty at the time of contracting, and the parties can by identification effect a present sale before severance.

(3) The provisions of this section are subject to any third party rights provided by the law relating to realty records, and the contract for sale may be executed and recorded as a document transferring an interest in land and shall then constitute notice to third parties of the buyer's rights under the contract for sale.

As amended in 1972.

PART 2

FORM, FORMATION AND READJUSTMENT OF CONTRACT

§ 2–201. Formal Requirements; Statute of Frauds

(1) Except as otherwise provided in this section a contract for the sale of goods for the price of $500 or more is not enforceable by way of

action or defense unless there is some writing sufficient to indicate that a contract for sale has been made between the parties and signed by the party against whom enforcement is sought or by his authorized agent or broker. A writing is not insufficient because it omits or incorrectly states a term agreed upon but the contract is not enforceable under this paragraph beyond the quantity of goods shown in such writing.

(2) Between merchants if within a reasonable time a writing in confirmation of the contract and sufficient against the sender is received and the party receiving it has reason to know its contents, it satisfies the requirements of subsection (1) against such party unless written notice of objection to its contents is given within 10 days after it is received.

(3) A contract which does not satisfy the requirements of subsection (1) but which is valid in other respects is enforceable

(a) if the goods are to be specially manufactured for the buyer and are not suitable for sale to others in the ordinary course of the seller's business and the seller, before notice of repudiation is received and under circumstances which reasonably indicate that the goods are for the buyer, has made either a substantial beginning of their manufacture or commitments for their procurement; or

(b) if the party against whom enforcement is sought admits in his pleading, testimony or otherwise in court that a contract for sale was made, but the contract is not enforceable under this provision beyond the quantity of goods admitted; or

(c) with respect to goods for which payment has been made and accepted or which have been received and accepted (Sec. 2–606).

§ 2–202. Final Written Expression: Parol or Extrinsic Evidence

Terms with respect to which the confirmatory memoranda of the parties agree or which are otherwise set forth in a writing intended by the parties as a final expression of their agreement with respect to such terms as are included therein may not be contradicted by evidence of any prior agreement or of a contemporaneous oral agreement but may be explained or supplemented

(a) by course of dealing or usage of trade (Section 1–205) or by course of performance (Section 2–208); and

(b) by evidence of consistent additional terms unless the court finds the writing to have been intended also as a complete and exclusive statement of the terms of the agreement.

§ 2–203. Seals Inoperative

The affixing of a seal to a writing evidencing a contract for sale or an offer to buy or sell goods does not constitute the writing a sealed instrument and the law with respect to sealed instruments does not apply to such a contract or offer.

§ 2–204. Formation in General

(1) A contract for sale of goods may be made in any manner sufficient to show agreement, including conduct by both parties which recognizes the existence of such a contract.

(2) An agreement sufficient to constitute a contract for sale may be found even though the moment of its making is undetermined.

(3) Even though one or more terms are left open a contract for sale does not fail for indefiniteness if the parties have intended to make a contract and there is a reasonably certain basis for giving an appropriate remedy.

§ 2–205. Firm Offers

An offer by a merchant to buy or sell goods in a signed writing which by its terms gives assurance that it will be held open is not revocable, for lack of consideration, during the time stated or if no time is stated for a reasonable time, but in no event may such period of irrevocability exceed three months; but any such term of assurance on a form supplied by the offeree must be separately signed by the offeror.

§ 2–206. Offer and Acceptance in Formation of Contract

(1) Unless otherwise unambiguously indicated by the language or circumstances

    (a) an offer to make a contract shall be construed as inviting acceptance in any manner and by any medium reasonable in the circumstances;

    (b) an order or other offer to buy goods for prompt or current shipment shall be construed as inviting acceptance either by a prompt promise to ship or by the prompt or current shipment of conforming or non-conforming goods, but such a shipment of non-conforming goods does not constitute an acceptance if the seller seasonably notifies the buyer that the shipment is offered only as an accommodation to the buyer.

(2) Where the beginning of a requested performance is a reasonable mode of acceptance an offeror who is not notified of acceptance within a reasonable time may treat the offer as having lapsed before acceptance.

§ 2–207. Additional Terms in Acceptance or Confirmation

(1) A definite and seasonable expression of acceptance or a written confirmation which is sent within a reasonable time operates as an acceptance even though it states terms additional to or different from those offered or agreed upon, unless acceptance is expressly made conditional on assent to the additional or different terms.

(2) The additional terms are to be construed as proposals for addition to the contract. Between merchants such terms become part of the contract unless:

(a) the offer expressly limits acceptance to the terms of the offer;

(b) they materially alter it; or

(c) notification of objection to them has already been given or is given within a reasonable time after notice of them is received.

(3) Conduct by both parties which recognizes the existence of a contract is sufficient to establish a contract for sale although the writings of the parties do not otherwise establish a contract. In such case the terms of the particular contract consist of those terms on which the writings of the parties agree, together with any supplementary terms incorporated under any other provisions of this Act.

§ 2–208. Course of Performance or Practical Construction

(1) Where the contract for sale involves repeated occasions for performance by either party with knowledge of the nature of the performance and opportunity for objection to it by the other, any course of performance accepted or acquiesced in without objection shall be relevant to determine the meaning of the agreement.

(2) The express terms of the agreement and any such course of performance, as well as any course of dealing and usage of trade, shall be construed whenever reasonable as consistent with each other; but when such construction is unreasonable, express terms shall control course of performance and course of performance shall control both course of dealing and usage of trade (Section 1–205).

(3) Subject to the provisions of the next section on modification and waiver, such course of performance shall be relevant to show a waiver or modification of any term inconsistent with such course of performance.

§ 2–209. Modification, Rescission and Waiver

(1) An agreement modifying a contract within this Article needs no consideration to be binding.

(2) A signed agreement which excludes modification or rescission except by a signed writing cannot be otherwise modified or rescinded, but except as between merchants such a requirement on a form supplied by the merchant must be separately signed by the other party.

(3) The requirements of the statute of frauds section of this Article (Section 2–201) must be satisfied if the contract as modified is within its provisions.

(4) Although an attempt at modification or rescission does not satisfy the requirements of subsection (2) or (3) it can operate as a waiver.

(5) A party who has made a waiver affecting an executory portion of the contract may retract the waiver by reasonable notification received by the other party that strict performance will be required of any term waived, unless the retraction would be unjust in view of a material change of position in reliance on the waiver.

§ 2–210. Delegation of Performance; Assignment of Rights

(1) A party may perform his duty through a delegate unless otherwise agreed or unless the other party has a substantial interest in having his original promisor perform or control the acts required by the contract. No delegation of performance relieves the party delegating of any duty to perform or any liability for breach.

(2) Unless otherwise agreed all rights of either seller or buyer can be assigned except where the assignment would materially change the duty of the other party, or increase materially the burden or risk imposed on him by his contract, or impair materially his chance of obtaining return performance. A right to damages for breach of the whole contract or a right arising out of the assignor's due performance of his entire obligation can be assigned despite agreement otherwise.

(3) Unless the circumstances indicate the contrary a prohibition of assignment of "the contract" is to be construed as barring only the delegation to the assignee of the assignor's performance.

(4) An assignment of "the contract" or of "all my rights under the contract" or an assignment in similar general terms is an assignment of rights and unless the language or the circumstances (as in an assignment for security) indicate the contrary, it is a delegation of performance of the duties of the assignor and its acceptance by the assignee constitutes a promise by him to perform those duties. This promise is enforceable by either the assignor or the other party to the original contract.

(5) The other party may treat any assignment which delegates performance as creating reasonable grounds for insecurity and may without prejudice to his rights against the assignor demand assurances from the assignee (Section 2–609).

PART 3

GENERAL OBLIGATION AND CONSTRUCTION OF CONTRACT

§ 2–301. General Obligations of Parties

The obligation of the seller is to transfer and deliver and that of the buyer is to accept and pay in accordance with the contract.

§ 2–302. Unconscionable Contract or Clause

(1) If the court as a matter of law finds the contract or any clause of the contract to have been unconscionable at the time it was made the court may refuse to enforce the contract, or it may enforce the remainder of the contract without the unconscionable clause, or it may so limit the application of any unconscionable clause as to avoid any unconscionable result.

(2) When it is claimed or appears to the court that the contract or any clause thereof may be unconscionable the parties shall be afforded a reasonable opportunity to present evidence as to its commercial setting, purpose and effect to aid the court in making the determination.

§ 2–303. Allocation or Division of Risks

Where this Article allocates a risk or a burden as between the parties "unless otherwise agreed", the agreement may not only shift the allocation but may also divide the risk or burden.

§ 2–304. Price Payable in Money, Goods, Realty, or Otherwise

(1) The price can be made payable in money or otherwise. If it is payable in whole or in part in goods each party is a seller of the goods which he is to transfer.

(2) Even though all or part of the price is payable in an interest in realty the transfer of the goods and the seller's obligations with reference to them are subject to this Article, but not the transfer of the interest in realty or the transferor's obligations in connection therewith.

§ 2–305. Open Price Term

(1) The parties if they so intend can conclude a contract for sale even though the price is not settled. In such a case the price is a reasonable price at the time for delivery if

    (a) nothing is said as to price; or

    (b) the price is left to be agreed by the parties and they fail to agree; or

    (c) the price is to be fixed in terms of some agreed market or other standard as set or recorded by a third person or agency and it is not so set or recorded.

(2) A price to be fixed by the seller or by the buyer means a price for him to fix in good faith.

(3) When a price left to be fixed otherwise than by agreement of the parties fails to be fixed through fault of one party the other may at his option treat the contract as cancelled or himself fix a reasonable price.

(4) Where, however, the parties intend not to be bound unless the price be fixed or agreed and it is not fixed or agreed there is no contract. In such a case the buyer must return any goods already received or if unable so to do must pay their reasonable value at the time of delivery and the seller must return any portion of the price paid on account.

§ 2–306. Output, Requirements and Exclusive Dealings

(1) A term which measures the quantity by the output of the seller or the requirements of the buyer means such actual output or requirements as may occur in good faith, except that no quantity unreasonably disproportionate to any stated estimate or in the absence of a stated estimate to any normal or otherwise comparable prior output or requirements may be tendered or demanded.

(2) A lawful agreement by either the seller or the buyer for exclusive dealing in the kind of goods concerned imposes unless otherwise agreed an obligation by the seller to use best efforts to supply the goods and by the buyer to use best efforts to promote their sale.

§ 2–307. Delivery in Single Lot or Several Lots

Unless otherwise agreed all goods called for by a contract for sale must be tendered in a single delivery and payment is due only on such tender but where the circumstances give either party the right to make or demand delivery in lots the price if it can be apportioned may be demanded for each lot.

§ 2–308. Absence of Specified Place for Delivery

Unless otherwise agreed

(a) the place for delivery of goods is the seller's place of business or if he has none his residence; but

(b) in a contract for sale of identified goods which to the knowledge of the parties at the time of contracting are in some other place, that place is the place for their delivery; and

(c) documents of title may be delivered through customary banking channels.

§ 2–309. Absence of Specific Time Provisions; Notice of Termination

(1) The time for shipment or delivery or any other action under a contract if not provided in this Article or agreed upon shall be a reasonable time.

(2) Where the contract provides for successive performances but is indefinite in duration it is valid for a reasonable time but unless otherwise agreed may be terminated at any time by either party.

(3) Termination of a contract by one party except on the happening of an agreed event requires that reasonable notification be received by the other party and an agreement dispensing with notification is invalid if its operation would be unconscionable.

§ 2–310. Open Time for Payment or Running of Credit; Authority to Ship Under Reservation

Unless otherwise agreed

(a) payment is due at the time and place at which the buyer is to receive the goods even though the place of shipment is the place of delivery; and

(b) if the seller is authorized to send the goods he may ship them under reservation, and may tender the documents of title, but the buyer may inspect the goods after their arrival before payment is due unless such inspection is inconsistent with the terms of the contract (Section 2–513); and

(c) if delivery is authorized and made by way of documents of title otherwise than by subsection (b) then payment is due at the time and place at which the buyer is to receive the documents regardless of where the goods are to be received; and

(d) where the seller is required or authorized to ship the goods on credit the credit period runs from the time of shipment but post-dating the invoice or delaying its dispatch will correspondingly delay the starting of the credit period.

§ 2–311. Options and Cooperation Respecting Performance

(1) An agreement for sale which is otherwise sufficiently definite (subsection (3) of Section 2–204) to be a contract is not made invalid by the fact that it leaves particulars of performance to be specified by one of the parties. Any such specification must be made in good faith and within limits set by commercial reasonableness.

(2) Unless otherwise agreed specifications relating to assortment of the goods are at the buyer's option and except as otherwise provided in subsections (1)(c) and (3) of Section 2–319 specifications or arrangements relating to shipment are at the seller's option.

(3) Where such specification would materially affect the other party's performance but is not seasonably made or where one party's cooperation is necessary to the agreed performance of the other but is not seasonably forthcoming, the other party in addition to all other remedies

(a) is excused for any resulting delay in his own performance; and

(b) may also either proceed to perform in any reasonable manner or after the time for a material part of his own performance treat the failure to specify or to cooperate as a breach by failure to deliver or accept the goods.

§ 2–312. Warranty of Title and Against Infringement; Buyer's Obligation Against Infringement

(1) Subject to subsection (2) there is in a contract for sale a warranty by the seller that

(a) the title conveyed shall be good, and its transfer rightful; and

(b) the goods shall be delivered free from any security interest or other lien or encumbrance of which the buyer at the time of contracting has no knowledge.

(2) A warranty under subsection (1) will be excluded or modified only by specific language or by circumstances which give the buyer reason to know that the person selling does not claim title in himself or that he is purporting to sell only such right or title as he or a third person may have.

(3) Unless otherwise agreed a seller who is a merchant regularly dealing in goods of the kind warrants that the goods shall be delivered free of the rightful claim of any third person by way of infringement or the like but a buyer who furnishes specifications to the seller must hold

the seller harmless against any such claim which arises out of compliance with the specifications.

§ 2–313. Express Warranties by Affirmation, Promise, Description, Sample

(1) Express warranties by the seller are created as follows:

(a) Any affirmation of fact or promise made by the seller to the buyer which relates to the goods and becomes part of the basis of the bargain creates an express warranty that the goods shall conform to the affirmation or promise.

(b) Any description of the goods which is made part of the basis of the bargain creates an express warranty that the goods shall conform to the description.

(c) Any sample or model which is made part of the basis of the bargain creates an express warranty that the whole of the goods shall conform to the sample or model.

(2) It is not necessary to the creation of an express warranty that the seller use formal words such as "warrant" or "guarantee" or that he have a specific intention to make a warranty, but an affirmation merely of the value of the goods or a statement purporting to be merely the seller's opinion or commendation of the goods does not create a warranty.

§ 2–314. Implied Warranty; Merchantability; Usage of Trade

(1) Unless excluded or modified (Section 2–316), a warranty that the goods shall be merchantable is implied in a contract for their sale if the seller is a merchant with respect to goods of that kind. Under this section the serving for value of food or drink to be consumed either on the premises or elsewhere is a sale.

(2) Goods to be merchantable must be at least such as

(a) pass without objection in the trade under the contract description; and

(b) in the case of fungible goods, are of fair average quality within the description; and

(c) are fit for the ordinary purposes for which such goods are used; and

(d) run, within the variations permitted by the agreement, of even kind, quality and quantity within each unit and among all units involved; and

(e) are adequately contained, packaged, and labeled as the agreement may require; and

(f) conform to the promises or affirmations of fact made on the container or label if any.

(3) Unless excluded or modified (Section 2–316) other implied warranties may arise from course of dealing or usage of trade.

§ 2–315. Implied Warranty; Fitness for Particular Purpose

Where the seller at the time of contracting has reason to know any particular purpose for which the goods are required and that the buyer is relying on the seller's skill or judgment to select or furnish suitable goods, there is unless excluded or modified under the next section an implied warranty that the goods shall be fit for such purpose.

§ 2–316. Exclusion or Modification of Warranties

(1) Words or conduct relevant to the creation of an express warranty and words or conduct tending to negate or limit warranty shall be construed wherever reasonable as consistent with each other; but subject to the provisions of this Article on parol or extrinsic evidence (Section 2–202) negation or limitation is inoperative to the extent that such construction is unreasonable.

(2) Subject to subsection (3), to exclude or modify the implied warranty of merchantability or any part of it the language must mention merchantability and in case of a writing must be conspicuous, and to exclude or modify any implied warranty of fitness the exclusion must be by a writing and conspicuous. Language to exclude all implied warranties of fitness is sufficient if it states, for example, that "There are no warranties which extend beyond the description on the face hereof."

(3) Notwithstanding subsection (2)

    (a) unless the circumstances indicate otherwise, all implied warranties are excluded by expressions like "as is", "with all faults" or other language which in common understanding calls the buyer's attention to the exclusion of warranties and makes plain that there is no implied warranty; and

    (b) when the buyer before entering into the contract has examined the goods or the sample or model as fully as he desired or has refused to examine the goods there is no implied warranty with regard to defects which an examination ought in the circumstances to have revealed to him; and

    (c) an implied warranty can also be excluded or modified by course of dealing or course of performance or usage of trade.

(4) Remedies for breach of warranty can be limited in accordance with the provisions of this Article on liquidation or limitation of damages and on contractual modification of remedy (Sections 2–718 and 2–719).

§ 2–317. Cumulation and Conflict of Warranties Express or Implied

Warranties whether express or implied shall be construed as consistent with each other and as cumulative, but if such construction is unreasonable the intention of the parties shall determine which warranty is dominant. In ascertaining that intention the following rules apply:

    (a) Exact or technical specifications displace an inconsistent sample or model or general language of description.

(b) A sample from an existing bulk displaces inconsistent general language of description.

(c) Express warranties displace inconsistent implied warranties other than an implied warranty of fitness for a particular purpose.

§ 2–318. Third Party Beneficiaries of Warranties Express or Implied

Note: *If this Act is introduced in the Congress of the United States this section should be omitted. (States to select one alternative.)*

Alternative A

A seller's warranty whether express or implied extends to any natural person who is in the family or household of his buyer or who is a guest in his home if it is reasonable to expect that such person may use, consume or be affected by the goods and who is injured in person by breach of the warranty. A seller may not exclude or limit the operation of this section.

Alternative B

A seller's warranty whether express or implied extends to any natural person who may reasonably be expected to use, consume or be affected by the goods and who is injured in person by breach of the warranty. A seller may not exclude or limit the operation of this section.

Alternative C

A seller's warranty whether express or implied extends to any person who may reasonably be expected to use, consume or be affected by the goods and who is injured by breach of the warranty. A seller may not exclude or limit the operation of this section with respect to injury to the person of an individual to whom the warranty extends.

As amended in 1966.

§ 2–319. F.O.B. and F.A.S. Terms

(1) Unless otherwise agreed the term F.O.B. (which means "free on board") at a named place, even though used only in connection with the stated price, is a delivery term under which

(a) when the term is F.O.B. the place of shipment, the seller must at that place ship the goods in the manner provided in this Article (Section 2–504) and bear the expense and risk of putting them into the possession of the carrier; or

(b) when the term is F.O.B. the place of destination, the seller must at his own expense and risk transport the goods to that place and there tender delivery of them in the manner provided in this Article (Section 2–503);

(c) when under either (a) or (b) the term is also F.O.B. vessel, car or other vehicle, the seller must in addition at his own expense and risk load the goods on board. If the term is F.O.B. vessel the buyer must name the vessel and in an appropriate case the seller must comply with the provisions of this Article on the form of bill of lading (Section 2–323).

(2) Unless otherwise agreed the term F.A.S. vessel (which means "free alongside") at a named port, even though used only in connection with the stated price, is a delivery term under which the seller must

(a) at his own expense and risk deliver the goods alongside the vessel in the manner usual in that port or on a dock designated and provided by the buyer; and

(b) obtain and tender a receipt for the goods in exchange for which the carrier is under a duty to issue a bill of lading.

(3) Unless otherwise agreed in any case falling within subsection (1)(a) or (c) or subsection (2) the buyer must seasonably give any needed instructions for making delivery, including when the term is F.A.S. or F.O.B. the loading berth of the vessel and in an appropriate case its name and sailing date. The seller may treat the failure of needed instructions as a failure of cooperation under this Article (Section 2–311). He may also at his option move the goods in any reasonable manner preparatory to delivery or shipment.

(4) Under the term F.O.B. vessel or F.A.S. unless otherwise agreed the buyer must make payment against tender of the required documents and the seller may not tender nor the buyer demand delivery of the goods in substitution for the documents.

§ 2–320. C.I.F. and C. & F. Terms

(1) The term C.I.F. means that the price includes in a lump sum the cost of the goods and the insurance and freight to the named destination. The term C. & F. or C.F. means that the price so includes cost and freight to the named destination.

(2) Unless otherwise agreed and even though used only in connection with the stated price and destination, the term C.I.F. destination or its equivalent requires the seller at his own expense and risk to

(a) put the goods into the possession of a carrier at the port for shipment and obtain a negotiable bill or bills of lading covering the entire transportation to the named destination; and

(b) load the goods and obtain a receipt from the carrier (which may be contained in the bill of lading) showing that the freight has been paid or provided for; and

(c) obtain a policy or certificate of insurance, including any war risk insurance, of a kind and on terms then current at the port of shipment in the usual amount, in the currency of the contract, shown to cover the same goods covered by the bill of lading and providing for payment of loss to the order of the buyer or for the account of whom it may concern; but the seller may add to the price the amount of the premium for any such war risk insurance; and

(d) prepare an invoice of the goods and procure any other documents required to effect shipment or to comply with the contract; and

(e) forward and tender with commercial promptness all the documents in due form and with any indorsement necessary to perfect the buyer's rights.

(3) Unless otherwise agreed the term C. & F. or its equivalent has the same effect and imposes upon the seller the same obligations and risks as a C.I.F. term except the obligation as to insurance.

(4) Under the term C.I.F. or C. & F. unless otherwise agreed the buyer must make payment against tender of the required documents and the seller may not tender nor the buyer demand delivery of the goods in substitution for the documents.

§ 2–321. C.I.F. or C. & F.: "Net Landed Weights"; "Payment on Arrival"; Warranty of Condition on Arrival

Under a contract containing a term C.I.F. or C. & F.

(1) Where the price is based on or is to be adjusted according to "net landed weights", "delivered weights", "out turn" quantity or quality or the like, unless otherwise agreed the seller must reasonably estimate the price. The payment due on tender of the documents called for by the contract is the amount so estimated, but after final adjustment of the price a settlement must be made with commercial promptness.

(2) An agreement described in subsection (1) or any warranty of quality or condition of the goods on arrival places upon the seller the risk of ordinary deterioration, shrinkage and the like in transportation but has no effect on the place or time of identification to the contract for sale or delivery or on the passing of the risk of loss.

(3) Unless otherwise agreed where the contract provides for payment on or after arrival of the goods the seller must before payment allow such preliminary inspection as is feasible; but if the goods are lost delivery of the documents and payment are due when the goods should have arrived.

§ 2–322. Delivery "Ex-ship"

(1) Unless otherwise agreed a term for delivery of goods "ex-ship" (which means from the carrying vessel) or in equivalent language is not restricted to a particular ship and requires delivery from a ship which has reached a place at the named port of destination where goods of the kind are usually discharged.

(2) Under such a term unless otherwise agreed

(a) the seller must discharge all liens arising out of the carriage and furnish the buyer with a direction which puts the carrier under a duty to deliver the goods; and

(b) the risk of loss does not pass to the buyer until the goods leave the ship's tackle or are otherwise properly unloaded.

§ 2–323. Form of Bill of Lading Required in Overseas Shipment; "Overseas"

(1) Where the contract contemplates overseas shipment and contains a term C.I.F. or C. & F. or F.O.B. vessel, the seller unless otherwise agreed must obtain a negotiable bill of lading stating that the goods have been loaded on board or, in the case of a term C.I.F. or C. & F., received for shipment.

(2) Where in a case within subsection (1) a bill of lading has been issued in a set of parts, unless otherwise agreed if the documents are not to be sent from abroad the buyer may demand tender of the full set; otherwise only one part of the bill of lading need be tendered. Even if the agreement expressly requires a full set

(a) due tender of a single part is acceptable within the provisions of this Article on cure of improper delivery (subsection (1) of Section 2–508); and

(b) even though the full set is demanded, if the documents are sent from abroad the person tendering an incomplete set may nevertheless require payment upon furnishing an indemnity which the buyer in good faith deems adequate.

(3) A shipment by water or by air or a contract contemplating such shipment is "overseas" insofar as by usage of trade or agreement it is subject to the commercial, financing or shipping practices characteristic of international deep water commerce.

§ 2–324. "No Arrival, No Sale" Term

Under a term "no arrival, no sale" or terms of like meaning, unless otherwise agreed,

(a) the seller must properly ship conforming goods and if they arrive by any means he must tender them on arrival but he assumes no obligation that the goods will arrive unless he has caused the non-arrival; and

(b) where without fault of the seller the goods are in part lost or have so deteriorated as no longer to conform to the contract or arrive after the contract time, the buyer may proceed as if there had been casualty to identified goods (Section 2–613).

§ 2–325. "Letter of Credit" Term; "Confirmed Credit"

(1) Failure of the buyer seasonably to furnish an agreed letter of credit is a breach of the contract for sale.

(2) The delivery to seller of a proper letter of credit suspends the buyer's obligation to pay. If the letter of credit is dishonored, the seller may on seasonable notification to the buyer require payment directly from him.

(3) Unless otherwise agreed the term "letter of credit" or "banker's credit" in a contract for sale means an irrevocable credit issued by a financing agency of good repute and, where the shipment is overseas, of good international repute. The term "confirmed credit" means that the credit must also carry the direct obligation of such an agency which does business in the seller's financial market.

§ 2–326. Sale on Approval and Sale or Return; Consignment Sales and Rights of Creditors

(1) Unless otherwise agreed, if delivered goods may be returned by the buyer even though they conform to the contract, the transaction is

(a) a "sale on approval" if the goods are delivered primarily for use, and

(b) a "sale or return" if the goods are delivered primarily for resale.

(2) Except as provided in subsection (3), goods held on approval are not subject to the claims of the buyer's creditors until acceptance; goods held on sale or return are subject to such claims while in the buyer's possession.

(3) Where goods are delivered to a person for sale and such person maintains a place of business at which he deals in goods of the kind involved, under a name other than the name of the person making delivery, then with respect to claims of creditors of the person conducting the business the goods are deemed to be on sale or return. The provisions of this subsection are applicable even though an agreement purports to reserve title to the person making delivery until payment or resale or uses such words as "on consignment" or "on memorandum". However, this subsection is not applicable if the person making delivery

(a) complies with an applicable law providing for a consignor's interest or the like to be evidenced by a sign, or

(b) establishes that the person conducting the business is generally known by his creditors to be substantially engaged in selling the goods of others, or

(c) complies with the filing provisions of the Article on Secured Transactions (Article 9).

(4) Any "or return" term of a contract for sale is to be treated as a separate contract for sale within the statute of frauds section of this Article (Section 2–201) and as contradicting the sale aspect of the contract within the provisions of this Article on parol or extrinsic evidence (Section 2–202).

§ 2–327. Special Incidents of Sale on Approval and Sale or Return

(1) Under a sale on approval unless otherwise agreed

(a) although the goods are identified to the contract the risk of loss and the title do not pass to the buyer until acceptance; and

(b) use of the goods consistent with the purpose of trial is not acceptance but failure seasonably to notify the seller of election to return the goods is acceptance, and if the goods conform to the contract acceptance of any part is acceptance of the whole; and

(c) after due notification of election to return, the return is at the seller's risk and expense but a merchant buyer must follow any reasonable instructions.

(2) Under a sale or return unless otherwise agreed

(a) the option to return extends to the whole or any commercial unit of the goods while in substantially their original condition, but must be exercised seasonably; and

(b) the return is at the buyer's risk and expense.

§ 2–328. Sale by Auction

(1) In a sale by auction if goods are put up in lots each lot is the subject of a separate sale.

(2) A sale by auction is complete when the auctioneer so announces by the fall of the hammer or in other customary manner. Where a bid is made while the hammer is falling in acceptance of a prior bid the auctioneer may in his discretion reopen the bidding or declare the goods sold under the bid on which the hammer was falling.

(3) Such a sale is with reserve unless the goods are in explicit terms put up without reserve. In an auction with reserve the auctioneer may withdraw the goods at any time until he announces completion of the sale. In an auction without reserve, after the auctioneer calls for bids on an article or lot, that article or lot cannot be withdrawn unless no bid is made within a reasonable time. In either case a bidder may retract his bid until the auctioneer's announcement of completion of the sale, but a bidder's retraction does not revive any previous bid.

(4) If the auctioneer knowingly receives a bid on the seller's behalf or the seller makes or procures such a bid, and notice has not been given that liberty for such bidding is reserved, the buyer may at his option avoid the sale or take the goods at the price of the last good faith bid prior to the completion of the sale. This subsection shall not apply to any bid at a forced sale.

PART 4

TITLE, CREDITORS AND GOOD FAITH PURCHASERS

§ 2–401. Passing of Title; Reservation for Security; Limited Application of This Section

Each provision of this Article with regard to the rights, obligations and remedies of the seller, the buyer, purchasers or other third parties applies irrespective of title to the goods except where the provision refers to such title. Insofar as situations are not covered by the other provisions of this Article and matters concerning title become material the following rules apply:

(1) Title to goods cannot pass under a contract for sale prior to their identification to the contract (Section 2–501), and unless otherwise explicitly agreed the buyer acquires by their identification a special property as limited by this Act. Any retention or reservation by the seller of the title (property) in goods shipped or delivered to the buyer is limited in effect to a reservation of a security interest. Subject to these provisions and to the provisions of the Article on Secured Transactions (Article 9), title to goods passes from the seller to the buyer in any manner and on any conditions explicitly agreed on by the parties.

(2) Unless otherwise explicitly agreed title passes to the buyer at the time and place at which the seller completes his performance with reference to the physical delivery of the goods, despite any reservation of a security interest and even though a document of title is to be delivered at a different time or place; and in particular and despite any reservation of a security interest by the bill of lading

(a) if the contract requires or authorizes the seller to send the goods to the buyer but does not require him to deliver them at destination, title passes to the buyer at the time and place of shipment; but

(b) if the contract requires delivery at destination, title passes on tender there.

(3) Unless otherwise explicitly agreed where delivery is to be made without moving the goods,

(a) if the seller is to deliver a document of title, title passes at the time when and the place where he delivers such documents; or

(b) if the goods are at the time of contracting already identified and no documents are to be delivered, title passes at the time and place of contracting.

(4) A rejection or other refusal by the buyer to receive or retain the goods, whether or not justified, or a justified revocation of acceptance revests title to the goods in the seller. Such revesting occurs by operation of law and is not a "sale".

§ 2–402. Rights of Seller's Creditors Against Sold Goods

(1) Except as provided in subsections (2) and (3), rights of unsecured creditors of the seller with respect to goods which have been identified to a contract for sale are subject to the buyer's rights to recover the goods under this Article (Sections 2–502 and 2–716).

(2) A creditor of the seller may treat a sale or an identification of goods to a contract for sale as void if as against him a retention of possession by the seller is fraudulent under any rule of law of the state where the goods are situated, except that retention of possession in good faith and current course of trade by a merchant-seller for a commercially reasonable time after a sale or identification is not fraudulent.

(3) Nothing in this Article shall be deemed to impair the rights of creditors of the seller

(a) under the provisions of the Article on Secured Transactions (Article 9); or

(b) where identification to the contract or delivery is made not in current course of trade but in satisfaction of or as security for a pre-existing claim for money, security or the like and is made under circumstances which under any rule of law of the state where the goods are situated would apart from this Article constitute the transaction a fraudulent transfer or voidable preference.

§ 2–403. Power to Transfer; Good Faith Purchase of Goods; "Entrusting"

(1) A purchaser of goods acquires all title which his transferor had or had power to transfer except that a purchaser of a limited interest acquires rights only to the extent of the interest purchased. A person with voidable title has power to transfer a good title to a good faith purchaser for value. When goods have been delivered under a transaction of purchase the purchaser has such power even though

(a) the transferor was deceived as to the identity of the purchaser, or

(b) the delivery was in exchange for a check which is later dishonored, or

(c) it was agreed that the transaction was to be a "cash sale", or

(d) the delivery was procured through fraud punishable as larcenous under the criminal law.

(2) Any entrusting of possession of goods to a merchant who deals in goods of that kind gives him power to transfer all rights of the entruster to a buyer in ordinary course of business.

(3) "Entrusting" includes any delivery and any acquiescence in retention of possession regardless of any condition expressed between the parties to the delivery or acquiescence and regardless of whether the procurement of the entrusting or the possessor's disposition of the goods have been such as to be larcenous under the criminal law.

(4) The rights of other purchasers of goods and of lien creditors are governed by the Articles on Secured Transactions (Article 9), Bulk Transfers (Article 6) and Documents of Title (Article 7).

PART 5

PERFORMANCE

§ 2–501. Insurable Interest in Goods; Manner of Identification of Goods

(1) The buyer obtains a special property and an insurable interest in goods by identification of existing goods as goods to which the contract

refers even though the goods so identified are non-conforming and he has an option to return or reject them. Such identification can be made at any time and in any manner explicitly agreed to by the parties. In the absence of explicit agreement identification occurs

(a) when the contract is made if it is for the sale of goods already existing and identified;

(b) if the contract is for the sale of future goods other than those described in paragraph (c), when goods are shipped, marked or otherwise designated by the seller as goods to which the contract refers;

(c) when the crops are planted or otherwise become growing crops or the young are conceived if the contract is for the sale of unborn young to be born within twelve months after contracting or for the sale of crops to be harvested within twelve months or the next normal harvest season after contracting whichever is longer.

(2) The seller retains an insurable interest in goods so long as title to or any security interest in the goods remains in him and where the identification is by the seller alone he may until default or insolvency or notification to the buyer that the identification is final substitute other goods for those identified.

(3) Nothing in this section impairs any insurable interest recognized under any other statute or rule of law.

§ 2–502.   Buyer's Right to Goods on Seller's Insolvency

(1) Subject to subsection (2) and even though the goods have not been shipped a buyer who has paid a part or all of the price of goods in which he has a special property under the provisions of the immediately preceding section may on making and keeping good a tender of any unpaid portion of their price recover them from the seller if the seller becomes insolvent within ten days after receipt of the first installment on their price.

(2) If the identification creating his special property has been made by the buyer he acquires the right to recover the goods only if they conform to the contract for sale.

§ 2–503.   Manner of Seller's Tender of Delivery

(1) Tender of delivery requires that the seller put and hold conforming goods at the buyer's disposition and give the buyer any notification reasonably necessary to enable him to take delivery. The manner, time and place for tender are determined by the agreement and this Article, and in particular

(a) tender must be at a reasonable hour, and if it is of goods they must be kept available for the period reasonably necessary to enable the buyer to take possession; but

(b) unless otherwise agreed the buyer must furnish facilities reasonably suited to the receipt of the goods.

(2) Where the case is within the next section respecting shipment tender requires that the seller comply with its provisions.

(3) Where the seller is required to deliver at a particular destination tender requires that he comply with subsection (1) and also in any appropriate case tender documents as described in subsections (4) and (5) of this section.

(4) Where goods are in the possession of a bailee and are to be delivered without being moved

    (a) tender requires that the seller either tender a negotiable document of title covering such goods or procure acknowledgment by the bailee of the buyer's right to possession of the goods; but

    (b) tender to the buyer of a non-negotiable document of title or of a written direction to the bailee to deliver is sufficient tender unless the buyer seasonably objects, and receipt by the bailee of notification of the buyer's rights fixes those rights as against the bailee and all third persons; but risk of loss of the goods and of any failure by the bailee to honor the non-negotiable document of title or to obey the direction remains on the seller until the buyer has had a reasonable time to present the document or direction, and a refusal by the bailee to honor the document or to obey the direction defeats the tender.

(5) Where the contract requires the seller to deliver documents

    (a) he must tender all such documents in correct form, except as provided in this Article with respect to bills of lading in a set (subsection (2) of Section 2–323); and

    (b) tender through customary banking channels is sufficient and dishonor of a draft accompanying the documents constitutes non-acceptance or rejection.

§ 2–504.   Shipment by Seller

Where the seller is required or authorized to send the goods to the buyer and the contract does not require him to deliver them at a particular destination, then unless otherwise agreed he must

    (a) put the goods in the possession of such a carrier and make such a contract for their transportation as may be reasonable having regard to the nature of the goods and other circumstances of the case; and

    (b) obtain and promptly deliver or tender in due form any document necessary to enable the buyer to obtain possession of the goods or otherwise required by the agreement or by usage of trade; and

    (c) promptly notify the buyer of the shipment.

Failure to notify the buyer under paragraph (c) or to make a proper contract under paragraph (a) is a ground for rejection only if material delay or loss ensues.

§ 2–505.   Seller's Shipment Under Reservation

(1) Where the seller has identified goods to the contract by or before shipment:

(a) his procurement of a negotiable bill of lading to his own order or otherwise reserves in him a security interest in the goods. His procurement of the bill to the order of a financing agency or of the buyer indicates in addition only the seller's expectation of transferring that interest to the person named.

(b) a non-negotiable bill of lading to himself or his nominee reserves possession of the goods as security but except in a case of conditional delivery (subsection (2) of Section 2–507) a non-negotiable bill of lading naming the buyer as consignee reserves no security interest even though the seller retains possession of the bill of lading.

(2) When shipment by the seller with reservation of a security interest is in violation of the contract for sale it constitutes an improper contract for transportation within the preceding section but impairs neither the rights given to the buyer by shipment and identification of the goods to the contract nor the seller's powers as a holder of a negotiable document.

§ 2–506.   Rights of Financing Agency

(1) A financing agency by paying or purchasing for value a draft which relates to a shipment of goods acquires to the extent of the payment or purchase and in addition to its own rights under the draft and any document of title securing it any rights of the shipper in the goods including the right to stop delivery and the shipper's right to have the draft honored by the buyer.

(2) The right to reimbursement of a financing agency which has in good faith honored or purchased the draft under commitment to or authority from the buyer is not impaired by subsequent discovery of defects with reference to any relevant document which was apparently regular on its face.

§ 2–507.   Effect of Seller's Tender; Delivery on Condition

(1) Tender of delivery is a condition to the buyer's duty to accept the goods and, unless otherwise agreed, to his duty to pay for them. Tender entitles the seller to acceptance of the goods and to payment according to the contract.

(2) Where payment is due and demanded on the delivery to the buyer of goods or documents of title, his right as against the seller to retain or dispose of them is conditional upon his making the payment due.

§ 2–508.   Cure by Seller of Improper Tender or Delivery; Replacement

(1) Where any tender or delivery by the seller is rejected because non-conforming and the time for performance has not yet expired, the

seller may seasonably notify the buyer of his intention to cure and may then within the contract time make a conforming delivery.

(2) Where the buyer rejects a non-conforming tender which the seller had reasonable grounds to believe would be acceptable with or without money allowance the seller may if he seasonably notifies the buyer have a further reasonable time to substitute a conforming tender.

§ 2–509. Risk of Loss in the Absence of Breach

(1) Where the contract requires or authorizes the seller to ship the goods by carrier

    (a) if it does not require him to deliver them at a particular destination, the risk of loss passes to the buyer when the goods are duly delivered to the carrier even though the shipment is under reservation (Section 2–505); but

    (b) if it does require him to deliver them at a particular destination and the goods are there duly tendered while in the possession of the carrier, the risk of loss passes to the buyer when the goods are there duly so tendered as to enable the buyer to take delivery.

(2) Where the goods are held by a bailee to be delivered without being moved, the risk of loss passes to the buyer

    (a) on his receipt of a negotiable document of title covering the goods; or

    (b) on acknowledgment by the bailee of the buyer's right to possession of the goods; or

    (c) after his receipt of a non-negotiable document of title or other written direction to deliver, as provided in subsection (4)(b) of Section 2–503.

(3) In any case not within subsection (1) or (2), the risk of loss passes to the buyer on his receipt of the goods if the seller is a merchant; otherwise the risk passes to the buyer on tender of delivery.

(4) The provisions of this section are subject to contrary agreement of the parties and to the provisions of this Article on sale on approval (Section 2–327) and on effect of breach on risk of loss (Section 2–510).

§ 2–510. Effect of Breach on Risk of Loss

(1) Where a tender or delivery of goods so fails to conform to the contract as to give a right of rejection the risk of their loss remains on the seller until cure or acceptance.

(2) Where the buyer rightfully revokes acceptance he may to the extent of any deficiency in his effective insurance coverage treat the risk of loss as having rested on the seller from the beginning.

(3) Where the buyer as to conforming goods already identified to the contract for sale repudiates or is otherwise in breach before risk of their loss has passed to him, the seller may to the extent of any deficiency in his effective insurance coverage treat the risk of loss as resting on the buyer for a commercially reasonable time.

§ 2–511. Tender of Payment by Buyer; Payment by Check

(1) Unless otherwise agreed tender of payment is a condition to the seller's duty to tender and complete any delivery.

(2) Tender of payment is sufficient when made by any means or in any manner current in the ordinary course of business unless the seller demands payment in legal tender and gives any extension of time reasonably necessary to procure it.

(3) Subject to the provisions of this Act on the effect of an instrument on an obligation (Section 3–802), payment by check is conditional and is defeated as between the parties by dishonor of the check on due presentment.

§ 2–512. Payment by Buyer Before Inspection

(1) Where the contract requires payment before inspection non-conformity of the goods does not excuse the buyer from so making payment unless

(a) the non-conformity appears without inspection; or

(b) despite tender of the required documents the circumstances would justify injunction against honor under the provisions of this Act (Section 5–114).

(2) Payment pursuant to subsection (1) does not constitute an acceptance of goods or impair the buyer's right to inspect or any of his remedies.

§ 2–513. Buyer's Right to Inspection of Goods

(1) Unless otherwise agreed and subject to subsection (3), where goods are tendered or delivered or identified to the contract for sale, the buyer has a right before payment or acceptance to inspect them at any reasonable place and time and in any reasonable manner. When the seller is required or authorized to send the goods to the buyer, the inspection may be after their arrival.

(2) Expenses of inspection must be borne by the buyer but may be recovered from the seller if the goods do not conform and are rejected.

(3) Unless otherwise agreed and subject to the provisions of this Article on C.I.F. contracts (subsection (3) of Section 2–321), the buyer is not entitled to inspect the goods before payment of the price when the contract provides

(a) for delivery "C.O.D." or on other like terms; or

(b) for payment against documents of title, except where such payment is due only after the goods are to become available for inspection.

(4) A place or method of inspection fixed by the parties is presumed to be exclusive but unless otherwise expressly agreed it does not postpone identification or shift the place for delivery or for passing the risk of loss. If compliance becomes impossible, inspection shall be as provided

in this section unless the place or method fixed was clearly intended as an indispensable condition failure of which avoids the contract.

§ 2–514. When Documents Deliverable on Acceptance; When on Payment

Unless otherwise agreed documents against which a draft is drawn are to be delivered to the drawee on acceptance of the draft if it is payable more than three days after presentment; otherwise, only on payment.

§ 2–515. Preserving Evidence of Goods in Dispute

In furtherance of the adjustment of any claim or dispute

(a) either party on reasonable notification to the other and for the purpose of ascertaining the facts and preserving evidence has the right to inspect, test and sample the goods including such of them as may be in the possession or control of the other; and

(b) the parties may agree to a third party inspection or survey to determine the conformity or condition of the goods and may agree that the findings shall be binding upon them in any subsequent litigation or adjustment.

PART 6

BREACH, REPUDIATION AND EXCUSE

§ 2–601. Buyer's Rights on Improper Delivery

Subject to the provisions of this Article on breach in installment contracts (Section 2–612) and unless otherwise agreed under the sections on contractual limitations of remedy (Sections 2–718 and 2–719), if the goods or the tender of delivery fail in any respect to conform to the contract, the buyer may

(a) reject the whole; or

(b) accept the whole; or

(c) accept any commercial unit or units and reject the rest.

§ 2–602. Manner and Effect of Rightful Rejection

(1) Rejection of goods must be within a reasonable time after their delivery or tender. It is ineffective unless the buyer seasonably notifies the seller.

(2) Subject to the provisions of the two following sections on rejected goods (Sections 2–603 and 2–604),

(a) after rejection any exercise of ownership by the buyer with respect to any commercial unit is wrongful as against the seller; and

(b) if the buyer has before rejection taken physical possession of goods in which he does not have a security interest under the provisions of this Article (subsection (3) of Section 2–711), he is under a duty after rejection to hold them with reasonable care at the seller's disposition for a time sufficient to permit the seller to remove them; but

(c) the buyer has no further obligations with regard to goods rightfully rejected.

(3) The seller's rights with respect to goods wrongfully rejected are governed by the provisions of this Article on Seller's remedies in general (Section 2–703).

§ 2–603. Merchant Buyer's Duties as to Rightfully Rejected Goods

(1) Subject to any security interest in the buyer (subsection (3) of Section 2–711), when the seller has no agent or place of business at the market of rejection a merchant buyer is under a duty after rejection of goods in his possession or control to follow any reasonable instructions received from the seller with respect to the goods and in the absence of such instructions to make reasonable efforts to sell them for the seller's account if they are perishable or threaten to decline in value speedily. Instructions are not reasonable if on demand indemnity for expenses is not forthcoming.

(2) When the buyer sells goods under subsection (1), he is entitled to reimbursement from the seller or out of the proceeds for reasonable expenses of caring for and selling them, and if the expenses include no selling commission then to such commission as is usual in the trade or if there is none to a reasonable sum not exceeding ten per cent on the gross proceeds.

(3) In complying with this section the buyer is held only to good faith and good faith conduct hereunder is neither acceptance nor conversion nor the basis of an action for damages.

§ 2–604. Buyer's Options as to Salvage of Rightfully Rejected Goods

Subject to the provisions of the immediately preceding section on perishables if the seller gives no instructions within a reasonable time after notification of rejection the buyer may store the rejected goods for the seller's account or reship them to him or resell them for the seller's account with reimbursement as provided in the preceding section. Such action is not acceptance or conversion.

§ 2–605. Waiver of Buyer's Objections by Failure to Particularize

(1) The buyer's failure to state in connection with rejection a particular defect which is ascertainable by reasonable inspection precludes him from relying on the unstated defect to justify rejection or to establish breach

(a) where the seller could have cured it if stated seasonably; or

(b) between merchants when the seller has after rejection made a request in writing for a full and final written statement of all defects on which the buyer proposes to rely.

(2) Payment against documents made without reservation of rights precludes recovery of the payment for defects apparent on the face of the documents.

§ 2–606. What Constitutes Acceptance of Goods

(1) Acceptance of goods occurs when the buyer

(a) after a reasonable opportunity to inspect the goods signifies to the seller that the goods are conforming or that he will take or retain them in spite of their non-conformity; or

(b) fails to make an effective rejection (subsection (1) of Section 2–602), but such acceptance does not occur until the buyer has had a reasonable opportunity to inspect them; or

(c) does any act inconsistent with the seller's ownership; but if such act is wrongful as against the seller it is an acceptance only if ratified by him.

(2) Acceptance of a part of any commercial unit is acceptance of that entire unit.

§ 2–607. Effect of Acceptance; Notice of Breach; Burden of Establishing Breach After Acceptance; Notice of Claim or Litigation to Person Answerable Over

(1) The buyer must pay at the contract rate for any goods accepted.

(2) Acceptance of goods by the buyer precludes rejection of the goods accepted and if made with knowledge of a non-conformity cannot be revoked because of it unless the acceptance was on the reasonable assumption that the non-conformity would be seasonably cured but acceptance does not of itself impair any other remedy provided by this Article for non-conformity.

(3) Where a tender has been accepted

(a) the buyer must within a reasonable time after he discovers or should have discovered any breach notify the seller of breach or be barred from any remedy; and

(b) if the claim is one for infringement or the like (subsection (3) of Section 2–312) and the buyer is sued as a result of such a breach he must so notify the seller within a reasonable time after he receives notice of the litigation or be barred from any remedy over for liability established by the litigation.

(4) The burden is on the buyer to establish any breach with respect to the goods accepted.

(5) Where the buyer is sued for breach of a warranty or other obligation for which his seller is answerable over

(a) he may give his seller written notice of the litigation. If the notice states that the seller may come in and defend and that if the seller does not do so he will be bound in any action against him by his buyer by any determination of fact common to the two litigations, then unless the seller after seasonable receipt of the notice does come in and defend he is so bound.

(b) if the claim is one for infringement or the like (subsection (3) of Section 2–312) the original seller may demand in writing that his buyer turn over to him control of the litigation including settlement or else be barred from any remedy over and if he also agrees to bear all expense and to satisfy any adverse judgment, then unless the buyer after seasonable receipt of the demand does turn over control the buyer is so barred.

(6) The provisions of subsections (3), (4) and (5) apply to any obligation of a buyer to hold the seller harmless against infringement or the like (subsection (3) of Section 2–312).

§ 2–608. Revocation of Acceptance in Whole or in Part

(1) The buyer may revoke his acceptance of a lot or commercial unit whose non-conformity substantially impairs its value to him if he has accepted it

(a) on the reasonable assumption that its non-conformity would be cured and it has not been seasonably cured; or

(b) without discovery of such non-conformity if his acceptance was reasonably induced either by the difficulty of discovery before acceptance or by the seller's assurances.

(2) Revocation of acceptance must occur within a reasonable time after the buyer discovers or should have discovered the ground for it and before any substantial change in condition of the goods which is not caused by their own defects. It is not effective until the buyer notifies the seller of it.

(3) A buyer who so revokes has the same rights and duties with regard to the goods involved as if he had rejected them.

§ 2–609. Right to Adequate Assurance of Performance

(1) A contract for sale imposes an obligation on each party that the other's expectation of receiving due performance will not be impaired. When reasonable grounds for insecurity arise with respect to the performance of either party the other may in writing demand adequate assurance of due performance and until he receives such assurance may if commercially reasonable suspend any performance for which he has not already received the agreed return.

(2) Between merchants the reasonableness of grounds for insecurity and the adequacy of any assurance offered shall be determined according to commercial standards.

(3) Acceptance of any improper delivery or payment does not prejudice the aggrieved party's right to demand adequate assurance of future performance.

(4) After receipt of a justified demand failure to provide within a reasonable time not exceeding thirty days such assurance of due performance as is adequate under the circumstances of the particular case is a repudiation of the contract.

§ 2–610. Anticipatory Repudiation

When either party repudiates the contract with respect to a performance not yet due the loss of which will substantially impair the value of the contract to the other, the aggrieved party may

    (a) for a commercially reasonable time await performance by the repudiating party; or

    (b) resort to any remedy for breach (Section 2–703 or Section 2–711), even though he has notified the repudiating party that he would await the latter's performance and has urged retraction; and

    (c) in either case suspend his own performance or proceed in accordance with the provisions of this Article on the seller's right to identify goods to the contract notwithstanding breach or to salvage unfinished goods (Section 2–704).

§ 2–611. Retraction of Anticipatory Repudiation

(1) Until the repudiating party's next performance is due he can retract his repudiation unless the aggrieved party has since the repudiation cancelled or materially changed his position or otherwise indicated that he considers the repudiation final.

(2) Retraction may be by any method which clearly indicates to the aggrieved party that the repudiating party intends to perform, but must include any assurance justifiably demanded under the provisions of this Article (Section 2–609).

(3) Retraction reinstates the repudiating party's rights under the contract with due excuse and allowance to the aggrieved party for any delay occasioned by the repudiation.

§ 2–612. "Installment Contract"; Breach

(1) An "installment contract" is one which requires or authorizes the delivery of goods in separate lots to be separately accepted, even though the contract contains a clause "each delivery is a separate contract" or its equivalent.

(2) The buyer may reject any installment which is non-conforming if the non-conformity substantially impairs the value of that installment and cannot be cured or if the non-conformity is a defect in the required documents; but if the non-conformity does not fall within subsection (3) and the seller gives adequate assurance of its cure the buyer must accept that installment.

(3) Whenever non-conformity or default with respect to one or more installments substantially impairs the value of the whole contract there is a breach of the whole. But the aggrieved party reinstates the contract if he accepts a non-conforming installment without seasonably notifying of cancellation or if he brings an action with respect only to past installments or demands performance as to future installments.

§ 2–613. Casualty to Identified Goods

Where the contract requires for its performance goods identified when the contract is made, and the goods suffer casualty without fault of either party before the risk of loss passes to the buyer, or in a proper case under a "no arrival, no sale" term (Section 2–324) then

(a) if the loss is total the contract is avoided; and

(b) if the loss is partial or the goods have so deteriorated as no longer to conform to the contract the buyer may nevertheless demand inspection and at his option either treat the contract as avoided or accept the goods with due allowance from the contract price for the deterioration or the deficiency in quantity but without further right against the seller.

§ 2–614. Substituted Performance

(1) Where without fault of either party the agreed berthing, loading, or unloading facilities fail or an agreed type of carrier becomes unavailable or the agreed manner of delivery otherwise becomes commercially impracticable but a commercially reasonable substitute is available, such substitute performance must be tendered and accepted.

(2) If the agreed means or manner of payment fails because of domestic or foreign governmental regulation, the seller may withhold or stop delivery unless the buyer provides a means or manner of payment which is commercially a substantial equivalent. If delivery has already been taken, payment by the means or in the manner provided by the regulation discharges the buyer's obligation unless the regulation is discriminatory, oppressive or predatory.

§ 2–615. Excuse by Failure of Presupposed Conditions

Except so far as a seller may have assumed a greater obligation and subject to the preceding section on substituted performance:

(a) Delay in delivery or non-delivery in whole or in part by a seller who complies with paragraphs (b) and (c) is not a breach of his duty under a contract for sale if performance as agreed has been made impracticable by the occurrence of a contingency the non-occurrence of which was a basic assumption on which the contract was made or by compliance in good faith with any applicable foreign or domestic governmental regulation or order whether or not it later proves to be invalid.

(b) Where the causes mentioned in paragraph (a) affect only a part of the seller's capacity to perform, he must allocate production and deliveries among his customers but may at his option include regular customers not then under contract as well as his own requirements for further manufacture. He may so allocate in any manner which is fair and reasonable.

(c) The seller must notify the buyer seasonally that there will be delay or non-delivery and, when allocation is required under paragraph (b), of the estimated quota thus made available for the buyer.

§ 2–616. Procedure on Notice Claiming Excuse

(1) Where the buyer receives notification of a material or indefinite delay or an allocation justified under the preceding section he may by written notification to the seller as to any delivery concerned, and where the prospective deficiency substantially impairs the value of the whole contract under the provisions of this Article relating to breach of installment contracts (Section 2–612), then also as to the whole,

(a) terminate and thereby discharge any unexecuted portion of the contract; or

(b) modify the contract by agreeing to take his available quota in substitution.

(2) If after receipt of such notification from the seller the buyer fails so to modify the contract within a reasonable time not exceeding thirty days the contract lapses with respect to any deliveries affected.

(3) The provisions of this section may not be negated by agreement except in so far as the seller has assumed a greater obligation under the preceding section.

PART 7

REMEDIES

§ 2–701. Remedies for Breach of Collateral Contracts Not Impaired

Remedies for breach of any obligation or promise collateral or ancillary to a contract for sale are not impaired by the provisions of this Article.

§ 2–702. Seller's Remedies on Discovery of Buyer's Insolvency

(1) Where the seller discovers the buyer to be insolvent he may refuse delivery except for cash including payment for all goods theretofore delivered under the contract, and stop delivery under this Article (Section 2–705).

(2) Where the seller discovers that the buyer has received goods on credit while insolvent he may reclaim the goods upon demand made within ten days after the receipt, but if misrepresentation of solvency has been made to the particular seller in writing within three months before delivery the ten day limitation does not apply. Except as provided

in this subsection the seller may not base a right to reclaim goods on the buyer's fraudulent or innocent misrepresentation of solvency or of intent to pay.

(3) The seller's right to reclaim under subsection (2) is subject to the rights of a buyer in ordinary course or other good faith purchaser under this Article (Section 2–403). Successful reclamation of goods excludes all other remedies with respect to them. As amended in 1966.

§ 2–703. Seller's Remedies in General

Where the buyer wrongfully rejects or revokes acceptance of goods or fails to make a payment due on or before delivery or repudiates with respect to a part or the whole, then with respect to any goods directly affected and, if the breach is of the whole contract (Section 2–612), then also with respect to the whole undelivered balance, the aggrieved seller may

(a) withhold delivery of such goods;

(b) stop delivery by any bailee as hereinafter provided (Section 2–705);

(c) proceed under the next section respecting goods still unidentified to the contract;

(d) resell and recover damages as hereafter provided (Section 2–706);

(e) recover damages for non-acceptance (Section 2–708) or in a proper case the price (Section 2–709);

(f) cancel.

§ 2–704. Seller's Right to Identify Goods to the Contract Notwithstanding Breach or to Salvage Unfinished Goods

(1) An aggrieved seller under the preceding section may

(a) identify to the contract conforming goods not already identified if at the time he learned of the breach they are in his possession or control;

(b) treat as the subject of resale goods which have demonstrably been intended for the particular contract even though those goods are unfinished.

(2) Where the goods are unfinished an aggrieved seller may in the exercise of reasonable commercial judgment for the purposes of avoiding loss and of effective realization either complete the manufacture and wholly identify the goods to the contract or cease manufacture and resell for scrap or salvage value or proceed in any other reasonable manner.

§ 2–705. Seller's Stoppage of Delivery in Transit or Otherwise

(1) The seller may stop delivery of goods in the possession of a carrier or other bailee when he discovers the buyer to be insolvent

(Section 2–702) and may stop delivery of carload, truckload, planeload or larger shipments of express or freight when the buyer repudiates or fails to make a payment due before delivery or if for any other reason the seller has a right to withhold or reclaim the goods.

(2) As against such buyer the seller may stop delivery until

(a) receipt of the goods by the buyer; or

(b) acknowledgment to the buyer by any bailee of the goods except a carrier that the bailee holds the goods for the buyer; or

(c) such acknowledgment to the buyer by a carrier by reshipment or as warehouseman; or

(d) negotiation to the buyer of any negotiable document of title covering the goods.

(3)(a) To stop delivery the seller must so notify as to enable the bailee by reasonable diligence to prevent delivery of the goods.

(b) After such notification the bailee must hold and deliver the goods according to the directions of the seller but the seller is liable to the bailee for any ensuing charges or damages.

(c) If a negotiable document of title has been issued for goods the bailee is not obliged to obey a notification to stop until surrender of the document.

(d) A carrier who has issued a non-negotiable bill of lading is not obliged to obey a notification to stop received from a person other than the consignor.

§ 2–706. Seller's Resale Including Contract for Resale

(1) Under the conditions stated in Section 2–703 on seller's remedies, the seller may resell the goods concerned or the undelivered balance thereof. Where the resale is made in good faith and in a commercially reasonable manner the seller may recover the difference between the resale price and the contract price together with any incidental damages allowed under the provisions of this Article (Section 2–710), but less expenses saved in consequence of the buyer's breach.

(2) Except as otherwise provided in subsection (3) or unless otherwise agreed resale may be at public or private sale including sale by way of one or more contracts to sell or of identification to an existing contract of the seller. Sale may be as a unit or in parcels and at any time and place and on any terms but every aspect of the sale including the method, manner, time, place and terms must be commercially reasonable. The resale must be reasonably identified as referring to the broken contract, but it is not necessary that the goods be in existence or that any or all of them have been identified to the contract before the breach.

(3) Where the resale is at private sale the seller must give the buyer reasonable notification of his intention to resell.

(4) Where the resale is at public sale

(a) only identified goods can be sold except where there is a recognized market for a public sale of futures in goods of the kind; and

(b) it must be made at a usual place or market for public sale if one is reasonably available and except in the case of goods which are perishable or threaten to decline in value speedily the seller must give the buyer reasonable notice of the time and place of the resale; and

(c) if the goods are not to be within the view of those attending the sale the notification of sale must state the place where the goods are located and provide for their reasonable inspection by prospective bidders; and

(d) the seller may buy.

(5) A purchaser who buys in good faith at a resale takes the goods free of any rights of the original buyer even though the seller fails to comply with one or more of the requirements of this section.

(6) The seller is not accountable to the buyer for any profit made on any resale. A person in the position of a seller (Section 2–707) or a buyer who has rightfully rejected or justifiably revoked acceptance must account for any excess over the amount of his security interest, as hereinafter defined (subsection (3) of Section 2–711).

§ 2–707. "Person in the Position of a Seller"

(1) A "person in the position of a seller" includes as against a principal an agent who has paid or become responsible for the price of goods on behalf of his principal or anyone who otherwise holds a security interest or other right in goods similar to that of a seller.

(2) A person in the position of a seller may as provided in this Article withhold or stop delivery (Section 2–705) and resell (Section 2–706) and recover incidental damages (Section 2–710).

§ 2–708. Seller's Damages for Non-acceptance or Repudiation

(1) Subject to subsection (2) and to the provisions of this Article with respect to proof of market price (Section 2–723), the measure of damages for non-acceptance or repudiation by the buyer is the difference between the market price at the time and place for tender and the unpaid contract price together with any incidental damages provided in this Article (Section 2–710), but less expenses saved in consequence of the buyer's breach.

(2) If the measure of damages provided in subsection (1) is inadequate to put the seller in as good a position as performance would have done then the measure of damages is the profit (including reasonable overhead) which the seller would have made from full performance by the buyer, together with any incidental damages provided in this Article (Section 2–710), due allowance for costs reasonably incurred and due credit for payments or proceeds of resale.

§ 2–709. Action for the Price

(1) When the buyer fails to pay the price as it becomes due the seller may recover, together with any incidental damages under the next section, the price

(a) of goods accepted or of conforming goods lost or damaged within a commercially reasonable time after risk of their loss has passed to the buyer; and

(b) of goods identified to the contract if the seller is unable after reasonable effort to resell them at a reasonable price or the circumstances reasonably indicate that such effort will be unavailing.

(2) Where the seller sues for the price he must hold for the buyer any goods which have been identified to the contract and are still in his control except that if resale becomes possible he may resell them at any time prior to the collection of the judgment. The net proceeds of any such resale must be credited to the buyer and payment of the judgment entitles him to any goods not resold.

(3) After the buyer has wrongfully rejected or revoked acceptance of the goods or has failed to make a payment due or has repudiated (Section 2–610), a seller who is held not entitled to the price under this section shall nevertheless be awarded damages for non-acceptance under the preceding section.

§ 2–710. Seller's Incidental Damages

Incidental damages to an aggrieved seller include any commercially reasonable charges, expenses or commissions incurred in stopping delivery, in the transportation, care and custody of goods after the buyer's breach, in connection with return or resale of the goods or otherwise resulting from the breach.

§ 2–711. Buyer's Remedies in General; Buyer's Security Interest in Rejected Goods

(1) Where the seller fails to make delivery or repudiates or the buyer rightfully rejects or justifiably revokes acceptance then with respect to any goods involved, and with respect to the whole if the breach goes to the whole contract (Section 2–612), the buyer may cancel and whether or not he has done so may in addition to recovering so much of the price as has been paid

(a) "cover" and have damages under the next section as to all the goods affected whether or not they have been identified to the contract; or

(b) recover damages for non-delivery as provided in this Article (Section 2–713).

(2) Where the seller fails to deliver or repudiates the buyer may also

(a) if the goods have been identified recover them as provided in this Article (Section 2–502); or

(b) in a proper case obtain specific performance or replevy the goods as provided in this Article (Section 2–716).

(3) On rightful rejection or justifiable revocation of acceptance a buyer has a security interest in goods in his possession or control for any payments made on their price and any expenses reasonably incurred in their inspection, receipt, transportation, care and custody and may hold such goods and resell them in like manner as an aggrieved seller (Section 2–706).

§ 2–712. "Cover"; Buyer's Procurement of Substitute Goods

(1) After a breach within the preceding section the buyer may "cover" by making in good faith and without unreasonable delay any reasonable purchase of or contract to purchase goods in substitution for those due from the seller.

(2) The buyer may recover from the seller as damages the difference between the cost of cover and the contract price together with any incidental or consequential damages as hereinafter defined (Section 2–715), but less expenses saved in consequence of the seller's breach.

(3) Failure of the buyer to effect cover within this section does not bar him from any other remedy.

§ 2–713. Buyer's Damages for Non-delivery or Repudiation

(1) Subject to the provisions of this Article with respect to proof of market price (Section 2–723), the measure of damages for non-delivery or repudiation by the seller is the difference between the market price at the time when the buyer learned of the breach and the contract price together with any incidental and consequential damages provided in this Article (Section 2–715), but less expenses saved in consequence of the seller's breach.

(2) Market price is to be determined as of the place for tender or, in cases of rejection after arrival or revocation of acceptance, as of the place of arrival.

§ 2–714. Buyer's Damages for Breach in Regard to Accepted Goods

(1) Where the buyer has accepted goods and given notification (subsection (3) of Section 2–607) he may recover as damages for any non-conformity of tender the loss resulting in the ordinary course of events from the seller's breach as determined in any manner which is reasonable.

(2) The measure of damages for breach of warranty is the difference at the time and place of acceptance between the value of the goods accepted and the value they would have had if they had been as warranted, unless special circumstances show proximate damages of a different amount.

(3) In a proper case any incidental and consequential damages under the next section may also be recovered.

§ 2–715. Buyer's Incidental and Consequential Damages

(1) Incidental damages resulting from the seller's breach include expenses reasonably incurred in inspection, receipt, transportation and care and custody of goods rightfully rejected, any commercially reasonable charges, expenses or commissions in connection with effecting cover and any other reasonable expense incident to the delay or other breach.

(2) Consequential damages resulting from the seller's breach include

(a) any loss resulting from general or particular requirements and needs of which the seller at the time of contracting had reason to know and which could not reasonably be prevented by cover or otherwise; and

(b) injury to person or property proximately resulting from any breach of warranty.

§ 2–716. Buyer's Right to Specific Performance or Replevin

(1) Specific performance may be decreed where the goods are unique or in other proper circumstances.

(2) The decree for specific performance may include such terms and conditions as to payment of the price, damages, or other relief as the court may deem just.

(3) The buyer has a right of replevin for goods identified to the contract if after reasonable effort he is unable to effect cover for such goods or the circumstances reasonably indicate that such effort will be unavailing or if the goods have been shipped under reservation and satisfaction of the security interest in them has been made or tendered.

§ 2–717. Deduction of Damages From the Price

The buyer on notifying the seller of his intention to do so may deduct all or any part of the damages resulting from any breach of the contract from any part of the price still due under the same contract.

§ 2–718. Liquidation or Limitation of Damages; Deposits

(1) Damages for breach by either party may be liquidated in the agreement but only at an amount which is reasonable in the light of the anticipated or actual harm caused by the breach, the difficulties of proof of loss, and the inconvenience or nonfeasibility of otherwise obtaining an adequate remedy. A term fixing unreasonably large liquidated damages is void as a penalty.

(2) Where the seller justifiably withholds delivery of goods because of the buyer's breach, the buyer is entitled to restitution of any amount by which the sum of his payments exceeds

(a) the amount to which the seller is entitled by virtue of terms liquidating the seller's damages in accordance with subsection (1), or

(b) in the absence of such terms, twenty per cent of the value of the total performance for which the buyer is obligated under the contract or $500, whichever is smaller.

(3) The buyer's right to restitution under subsection (2) is subject to offset to the extent that the seller establishes

(a) a right to recover damages under the provisions of this Article other than subsection (1), and

(b) the amount or value of any benefits received by the buyer directly or indirectly by reason of the contract.

(4) Where a seller has received payment in goods their reasonable value or the proceeds of their resale shall be treated as payments for the purposes of subsection (2); but if the seller has notice of the buyer's breach before reselling goods received in part performance, his resale is subject to the conditions laid down in this Article on resale by an aggrieved seller (Section 2–706).

§ 2–719.   Contractual Modification or Limitation of Remedy

(1) Subject to the provisions of subsections (2) and (3) of this section and of the preceding section on liquidation and limitation of damages,

(a) the agreement may provide for remedies in addition to or in substitution for those provided in this Article and may limit or alter the measure of damages recoverable under this Article, as by limiting the buyer's remedies to return of the goods and repayment of the price or to repair and replacement of non-conforming goods or parts; and

(b) resort to a remedy as provided is optional unless the remedy is expressly agreed to be exclusive, in which case it is the sole remedy.

(2) Where circumstances cause an exclusive or limited remedy to fail of its essential purpose, remedy may be had as provided in this Act.

(3) Consequential damages may be limited or excluded unless the limitation or exclusion is unconscionable. Limitation of consequential damages for injury to the person in the case of consumer goods is prima facie unconscionable but limitation of damages where the loss is commercial is not.

§ 2–720.   Effect of "Cancellation" or "Rescission" on Claims for Antecedent Breach

Unless the contrary intention clearly appears, expressions of "cancellation" or "rescission" of the contract or the like shall not be construed as a renunciation or discharge of any claim in damages for an antecedent breach.

§ 2–721.   Remedies for Fraud

Remedies for material misrepresentation or fraud include all remedies available under this Article for non-fraudulent breach. Neither rescission or a claim for rescission of the contract for sale nor rejection or return of the goods shall bar or be deemed inconsistent with a claim for damages or other remedy.

§ 2–722. Who Can Sue Third Parties for Injury to Goods

Where a third party so deals with goods which have been identified to a contract for sale as to cause actionable injury to a party to that contract

(a) a right of action against the third party is in either party to the contract for sale who has title to or a security interest or a special property or an insurable interest in the goods; and if the goods have been destroyed or converted a right of action is also in the party who either bore the risk of loss under the contract for sale or has since the injury assumed that risk as against the other;

(b) if at the time of the injury the party plaintiff did not bear the risk of loss as against the other party to the contract for sale and there is no arrangement between them for disposition of the recovery, his suit or settlement is, subject to his own interest, as a fiduciary for the other party to the contract;

(c) either party may with the consent of the other sue for the benefit of whom it may concern.

§ 2–723. Proof of Market Price: Time and Place

(1) If an action based on anticipatory repudiation comes to trial before the time for performance with respect to some or all of the goods, any damages based on market price (Section 2–708 or Section 2–713) shall be determined according to the price of such goods prevailing at the time when the aggrieved party learned of the repudiation.

(2) If evidence of a price prevailing at the times or places described in this Article is not readily available the price prevailing within any reasonable time before or after the time described or at any other place which in commercial judgment or under usage of trade would serve as a reasonable substitute for the one described may be used, making any proper allowance for the cost of transporting the goods to or from such other place.

(3) Evidence of a relevant price prevailing at a time or place other than the one described in this Article offered by one party is not admissible unless and until he has given the other party such notice as the court finds sufficient to prevent unfair surprise.

§ 2–724. Admissibility of Market Quotations

Whenever the prevailing price or value of any goods regularly bought and sold in any established commodity market is in issue, reports in official publications or trade journals or in newspapers or periodicals of general circulation published as the reports of such market shall be admissible in evidence. The circumstances of the preparation of such a report may be shown to affect its weight but not its admissibility.

§ 2–725. Statute of Limitations in Contracts for Sale

(1) An action for breach of any contract for sale must be commenced within four years after the cause of action has accrued. By the original agreement the parties may reduce the period of limitation to not less than one year but may not extend it.

(2) A cause of action accrues when the breach occurs, regardless of the aggrieved party's lack of knowledge of the breach. A breach of warranty occurs when tender of delivery is made, except that where a warranty explicitly extends to future performance of the goods and discovery of the breach must await the time of such performance the cause of action accrues when the breach is or should have been discovered.

(3) Where an action commenced within the time limited by subsection (1) is so terminated as to leave available a remedy by another action for the same breach such other action may be commenced after the expiration of the time limited and within six months after the termination of the first action unless the termination resulted from voluntary discontinuance or from dismissal for failure or neglect to prosecute.

(4) This section does not alter the law on tolling of the statute of limitations nor does it apply to causes of action which have accrued before this Act becomes effective.

Appendix B

UNIFORM COMMERCIAL CODE [REVISED] ARTICLE 1

GENERAL PROVISIONS

[Revised Article 1 was approved in 2001.]

PART 1
GENERAL PROVISIONS

§ 1–101. Short Titles

(a) This [Act] may be cited as the Uniform Commercial Code.

(b) This article may be cited as Uniform Commercial Code–General Provisions.

Official Comments

Source: Former Section 1–101.

Changes from former law: Subsection (b) is new. It is added in order to make the structure of Article 1 parallel with that of the other articles of the Uniform Commercial Code.

1. Each other article of the Uniform Commercial Code (except Articles 10 and 11) may also be cited by its own short title. See Sections 2–101, 2A–101, 3–101, 4–101, 4A–101, 5–101, 6–101, 7–101, 8–101, and 9–101.

§ 1–102. Scope of Article

This article applies to a transaction to the extent that it is governed by another article of [the Uniform Commercial Code].

§ 1–103. Construction of [Uniform Commercial Code] to Promote Its Purposes and Policies; Applicability of Supplemental Principles of Law

(a) [The Uniform Commercial Code] must be liberally construed and applied to promote its underlying purposes and policies, which are:

(1) to simplify, clarify, and modernize the law governing commercial transactions;

(2) to permit the continued expansion of commercial practices through custom, usage, and agreement of the parties; and

(3) to make uniform the law among the various jurisdictions.

(b) Unless displaced by the particular provisions of [the Uniform Commercial Code], the principles of law and equity, including the law merchant and the law relative to capacity to contract, principal and agent, estoppel, fraud, misrepresentation, duress, coercion, mistake, bankruptcy, and other validating or invalidating cause supplement its provisions.

§ 1–104. Construction Against Implied Repeal

[The Uniform Commercial Code] being a general act intended as a unified coverage of its subject matter, no part of it shall be deemed to be impliedly repealed by subsequent legislation if such construction can reasonably be avoided.

§ 1–105. Severability

If any provision or clause of [the Uniform Commercial Code] or its application to any person or circumstance is held invalid, the invalidity does not affect other provisions or applications of [the Uniform Commercial Code] which can be given effect without the invalid provision or application, and to this end the provisions of [the Uniform Commercial Code] are severable.

§ 1–106. Use of Singular and Plural; Gender

In [the Uniform Commercial Code], unless the statutory context otherwise requires:

(1) words in the singular number include the plural, and those in the plural include the singular; and

(2) words of any gender also refer to any other gender.

§ 1–107. Section Captions

Section captions are part of [the Uniform Commercial Code].

§ 1–108. Relation to Electronic Signatures in Global and National Commerce Act

This article modifies, limits, and supersedes the Federal Electronic Signatures in Global and National Commerce Act, 15 U.S.C. § 7001 *et seq..*, Except That Nothing In This Article Modifies, Limits, Or supersedes section 7001(c) of that act or authorizes electronic delivery of any of the notices described in section 7003(b) of that Act.

PART 2

GENERAL DEFINITIONS AND PRINCIPLES OF INTERPRETATION

§ 1–201. General Definitions

(a) Unless the context otherwise requires, words or phrases defined in this section, or in the additional definitions contained in other articles of [the Uniform Commercial Code] that apply to particular articles or parts thereof, have the meanings stated.

(b) Subject to definitions contained in other articles of [the Uniform Commercial Code] that apply to particular articles or parts thereof:

(1) "Action", in the sense of a judicial proceeding, includes recoupment, counterclaim, set-off, suit in equity, and any other proceeding in which rights are determined.

(2) "Aggrieved party" means a party entitled to pursue a remedy.

(3) "Agreement", as distinguished from "contract", means the bargain of the parties in fact, as found in their language or inferred from other circumstances, including course of performance, course of dealing, or usage of trade as provided in Section 1–303.

(4) "Bank" means a person engaged in the business of banking and includes a savings bank, savings and loan association, credit union, and trust company.

(5) "Bearer" means a person in possession of a negotiable instrument, document of title, or certificated security that is payable to bearer or indorsed in blank.

(6) "Bill of lading" means a document evidencing the receipt of goods for shipment issued by a person engaged in the business of transporting or forwarding goods.

(7) "Branch" includes a separately incorporated foreign branch of a bank.

(8) "Burden of establishing" a fact means the burden of persuading the trier of fact that the existence of the fact is more probable than its nonexistence.

(9) "Buyer in ordinary course of business" means a person that buys goods in good faith, without knowledge that the sale violates the rights of another person in the goods, and in the ordinary course from a person, other than a pawnbroker, in the business of selling goods of that kind. A person buys goods in the ordinary course if the sale to the person comports with the usual or customary practices in the kind of business in which the seller is engaged or with the seller's own usual or customary practices. A person that sells oil, gas, or other minerals at the wellhead or minehead is a person in the business of selling goods of that kind. A buyer in ordinary course of business may buy for cash, by exchange of other property, or on secured or unsecured

credit, and may acquire goods or documents of title under a preexisting contract for sale. Only a buyer that takes possession of the goods or has a right to recover the goods from the seller under Article 2 may be a buyer in ordinary course of business. "Buyer in ordinary course of business" does not include a person that acquires goods in a transfer in bulk or as security for or in total or partial satisfaction of a money debt.

(10) "Conspicuous", with reference to a term, means so written, displayed, or presented that a reasonable person against which it is to operate ought to have noticed it. Whether a term is "conspicuous" or not is a decision for the court. Conspicuous terms include the following:

   (A) a heading in capitals equal to or greater in size than the surrounding text, or in contrasting type, font, or color to the surrounding text of the same or lesser size; and

   (B) language in the body of a record or display in larger type than the surrounding text, or in contrasting type, font, or color to the surrounding text of the same size, or set off from surrounding text of the same size by symbols or other marks that call attention to the language.

(11) "Consumer" means an individual who enters into a transaction primarily for personal, family, or household purposes

(12) "Contract", as distinguished from "agreement", means the total legal obligation that results from the parties' agreement as determined by [the Uniform Commercial Code] as supplemented by any other applicable laws.

(13) "Creditor" includes a general creditor, a secured creditor, a lien creditor, and any representative of creditors, including an assignee for the benefit of creditors, a trustee in bankruptcy, a receiver in equity, and an executor or administrator of an insolvent debtor's or assignor's estate.

(14) "Defendant" includes a person in the position of defendant in a counterclaim, cross-claim, or third-party claim.

(15) "Delivery", with respect to an instrument, document of title, or chattel paper, means voluntary transfer of possession.

(16) "Document of title" includes bill of lading, dock warrant, dock receipt, warehouse receipt or order for the delivery of goods, and also any other document which in the regular course of business or financing is treated as adequately evidencing that the person in possession of it is entitled to receive, hold, and dispose of the document and the goods it covers. To be a document of title, a document must purport to be issued by or addressed to a bailee and purport to cover goods in the bailee's possession which are either identified or are fungible portions of an identified mass.

(17) "Fault" means a default, breach, or wrongful act or omission.

(18) "Fungible goods" means:

(A) goods of which any unit, by nature or usage of trade, is the equivalent of any other like unit; or

(B) goods that by agreement are treated as equivalent.

(19) "Genuine" means free of forgery or counterfeiting.

(20) "Good faith," except as otherwise provided in Article 5, means honesty in fact and the observance of reasonable commercial standards of fair dealing.

(21) "Holder" means:

(A) the person in possession of a negotiable instrument that is payable either to bearer or to an identified person that is the person in possession; or

(B) the person in possession of a document of title if the goods are deliverable either to bearer or to the order of the person in possession.

(22) "Insolvency proceeding" includes an assignment for the benefit of creditors or other proceeding intended to liquidate or rehabilitate the estate of the person involved.

(23) "Insolvent" means:

(A) having generally ceased to pay debts in the ordinary course of business other than as a result of bona fide dispute;

(B) being unable to pay debts as they become due; or

(C) being insolvent within the meaning of federal bankruptcy law.

(24) "Money" means a medium of exchange currently authorized or adopted by a domestic or foreign government. The term includes a monetary unit of account established by an intergovernmental organization or by agreement between two or more countries.

(25) "Organization" means a person other than an individual.

(26) "Party", as distinguished from "third party", means a person that has engaged in a transaction or made an agreement subject to [the Uniform Commercial Code].

(27) "Person" means an individual, corporation, business trust, estate, trust, partnership, limited liability company, association, joint venture, government, governmental subdivision, agency, or instrumentality, public corporation, or any other legal or commercial entity.

(28) "Present value" means the amount as of a date certain of one or more sums payable in the future, discounted to the date certain by use of either an interest rate specified by the parties if that rate is not manifestly unreasonable at the time the

transaction is entered into or, if an interest rate is not so specified, a commercially reasonable rate that takes into account the facts and circumstances at the time the transaction is entered into.

(29) "Purchase" means taking by sale, lease, discount, negotiation, mortgage, pledge, lien, security interest, issue or reissue, gift, or any other voluntary transaction creating an interest in property.

(30) "Purchaser" means a person that takes by purchase.

(31) "Record" means information that is inscribed on a tangible medium or that is stored in an electronic or other medium and is retrievable in perceivable form.

(32) "Remedy" means any remedial right to which an aggrieved party is entitled with or without resort to a tribunal.

(33) "Representative" means a person empowered to act for another, including an agent, an officer of a corporation or association, and a trustee, executor, or administrator of an estate.

(34) "Right" includes remedy.

(35) "Security interest" means an interest in personal property or fixtures which secures payment or performance of an obligation. "Security interest" includes any interest of a consignor and a buyer of accounts, chattel paper, a payment intangible, or a promissory note in a transaction that is subject to Article 9. "Security interest" does not include the special property interest of a buyer of goods on identification of those goods to a contract for sale under Section 2–401, but a buyer may also acquire a "security interest" by complying with Article 9. Except as otherwise provided in Section 2–505, the right of a seller or lessor of goods under Article 2 or 2A to retain or acquire possession of the goods is not a "security interest", but a seller or lessor may also acquire a "security interest" by complying with Article 9. The retention or reservation of title by a seller of goods notwithstanding shipment or delivery to the buyer under Section 2–401 is limited in effect to a reservation of a "security interest." Whether a transaction in the form of a lease creates a "security interest" is determined pursuant to Section 1–203.

(36) "Send" in connection with a writing, record, or notice means:

   (A) to deposit in the mail or deliver for transmission by any other usual means of communication with postage or cost of transmission provided for and properly addressed and, in the case of an instrument, to an address specified thereon or otherwise agreed, or if there be none to any address reasonable under the circumstances; or

    (B) in any other way to cause to be received any record or notice within the time it would have arrived if properly sent.

(37) "Signed" includes using any symbol executed or adopted with present intention to adopt or accept a writing.

(38) "State" means a State of the United States, the District of Columbia, Puerto Rico, the United States Virgin Islands, or any territory or insular possession subject to the jurisdiction of the United States.

(39) "Surety" includes a guarantor or other secondary obligor.

(40) "Term" means a portion of an agreement that relates to a particular matter.

(41) "Unauthorized signature" means a signature made without actual, implied, or apparent authority. The term includes a forgery.

(42) "Warehouse receipt" means a receipt issued by a person engaged in the business of storing goods for hire.

(43) "Writing" includes printing, typewriting, or any other intentional reduction to tangible form. "Written" has a corresponding meaning.

§ 1–202. Notice; Knowledge

(a) Subject to subsection (f), a person has "notice" of a fact if the person:

(1) has actual knowledge of it;

(2) has received a notice or notification of it; or

(3) from all the facts and circumstances known to the person at the time in question, has reason to know that it exists.

(b) "Knowledge" means actual knowledge. "Knows" has a corresponding meaning.

(c) "Discover", "learn", or words of similar import refer to knowledge rather than to reason to know.

(d) A person "notifies" or "gives" a notice or notification to another person by taking such steps as may be reasonably required to inform the other person in ordinary course, whether or not the other person actually comes to know of it.

(e) Subject to subsection (f), a person "receives" a notice or notification when:

(1) it comes to that person's attention; or

(2) it is duly delivered in a form reasonable under the circumstances at the place of business through which the contract was made or at another location held out by that person as the place for receipt of such communications.

(f) Notice, knowledge, or a notice or notification received by an organization is effective for a particular transaction from the time it is brought to the attention of the individual conducting that transaction and, in any event, from the time it would have been brought to the individual's attention if the organization had exercised due diligence. An organization exercises due diligence if it maintains reasonable routines for communicating significant information to the person conducting the transaction and there is reasonable compliance with the routines. Due diligence does not require an individual acting for the organization to communicate information unless the communication is part of the individual's regular duties or the individual has reason to know of the transaction and that the transaction would be materially affected by the information.

§ 1–203.   Lease Distinguished From Security Interest

(a) Whether a transaction in the form of a lease creates a lease or security interest is determined by the facts of each case.

(b) A transaction in the form of a lease creates a security interest if the consideration that the lessee is to pay the lessor for the right to possession and use of the goods is an obligation for the term of the lease and is not subject to termination by the lessee, and:

(1) the original term of the lease is equal to or greater than the remaining economic life of the goods;

(2) the lessee is bound to renew the lease for the remaining economic life of the goods or is bound to become the owner of the goods;

(3) the lessee has an option to renew the lease for the remaining economic life of the goods for no additional consideration or for nominal additional consideration upon compliance with the lease agreement; or

(4) the lessee has an option to become the owner of the goods for no additional consideration or for nominal additional consideration upon compliance with the lease agreement.

(c) A transaction in the form of a lease does not create a security interest merely because:

(1) the present value of the consideration the lessee is obligated to pay the lessor for the right to possession and use of the goods is substantially equal to or is greater than the fair market value of the goods at the time the lease is entered into;

(2) the lessee assumes risk of loss of the goods;

(3) the lessee agrees to pay, with respect to the goods, taxes, insurance, filing, recording, or registration fees, or service or maintenance costs;

(4) the lessee has an option to renew the lease or to become the owner of the goods;

(5) the lessee has an option to renew the lease for a fixed rent that is equal to or greater than the reasonably predictable fair market rent for the use of the goods for the term of the renewal at the time the option is to be performed; or

(6) the lessee has an option to become the owner of the goods for a fixed price that is equal to or greater than the reasonably predictable fair market value of the goods at the time the option is to be performed.

(d) Additional consideration is nominal if it is less than the lessee's reasonably predictable cost of performing under the lease agreement if the option is not exercised. Additional consideration is not nominal if:

(1) when the option to renew the lease is granted to the lessee, the rent is stated to be the fair market rent for the use of the goods for the term of the renewal determined at the time the option is to be performed; or

(2) when the option to become the owner of the goods is granted to the lessee, the price is stated to be the fair market value of the goods determined at the time the option is to be performed.

(e) The "remaining economic life of the goods" and "reasonably predictable" fair market rent, fair market value, or cost of performing under the lease agreement must be determined with reference to the facts and circumstances at the time the transaction is entered into.

§ 1–204. Value

Except as otherwise provided in Articles 3, 4, [and] 5, [and 6], a person gives value for rights if the person acquires them:

(1) in return for a binding commitment to extend credit or for the extension of immediately available credit, whether or not drawn upon and whether or not a charge-back is provided for in the event of difficulties in collection;

(2) as security for, or in total or partial satisfaction of, a preexisting claim;

(3) by accepting delivery under a preexisting contract for purchase; or

(4) in return for any consideration sufficient to support a simple contract.

§ 1–205. Reasonable Time; Seasonableness

(a) Whether a time for taking an action required by [the Uniform Commercial Code] is reasonable depends on the nature, purpose, and circumstances of the action.

(b) An action is taken seasonably if it is taken at or within the time agreed or, if no time is agreed, at or within a reasonable time.

§ 1–206. Presumptions

Whenever [the Uniform Commercial Code] creates a "presumption" with respect to a fact, or provides that a fact is "presumed," the trier of fact must find the existence of the fact unless and until evidence is introduced that supports a finding of its nonexistence.

Legislative Note: Former Section 1–206, a Statute of Frauds for sales of "kinds of personal property not otherwise covered," has been deleted. The other articles of the Uniform Commercial Code make individual determinations as to requirements for memorializing transactions within their scope, so that the primary effect of former Section 1–206 was to impose a writing requirement on sales transactions not otherwise governed by the UCC. Deletion of former Section 1–206 does not constitute a recommendation to legislatures as to whether such sales transactions should be covered by a Statute of Frauds; rather, it reflects a determination that there is no need for uniform commercial law to resolve that issue.

PART 3

TERRITORIAL APPLICABILITY AND GENERAL RULES

§ 1–301. Territorial Applicability; Parties' Power to Choose Applicable Law

(a) In this section:

(1) "Domestic transaction" means a transaction other than an international transaction.

(2) "International transaction" means a transaction that bears a reasonable relation to a country other than the United States.

(b) This section applies to a transaction to the extent that it is governed by another article of the [Uniform Commercial Code].

(c) Except as otherwise provided in this section:

(1) an agreement by parties to a domestic transaction that any or all of their rights and obligations are to be determined by the law of this State or of another State is effective, whether or not the transaction bears a relation to the State designated; and

(2) an agreement by parties to an international transaction that any or all of their rights and obligations are to be determined by the law of this State or of another State or country is effective, whether or not the transaction bears a relation to the State or country designated.

(d) In the absence of an agreement effective under subsection (c), and except as provided in subsections (e) and (g), the rights and obligations of the parties are determined by the law that would be selected by application of this State's conflict of laws principles.

(e) If one of the parties to a transaction is a consumer, the following rules apply:

(1) An agreement referred to in subsection (c) is not effective unless the transaction bears a reasonable relation to the State or country designated.

(2) Application of the law of the State or country determined pursuant to subsection (c) or (d) may not deprive the consumer of the protection of any rule of law governing a matter within the scope of this section, which both is protective of consumers and may not be varied by agreement:

(A) of the State or country in which the consumer principally resides, unless subparagraph (B) applies; or

(B) if the transaction is a sale of goods, of the State or country in which the consumer both makes the contract and takes delivery of those goods, if such State or country is not the State or country in which the consumer principally resides.

(f) An agreement otherwise effective under subsection (c) is not effective to the extent that application of the law of the State or country designated would be contrary to a fundamental policy of the State or country whose law would govern in the absence of agreement under subsection (d).

(g) To the extent that [the Uniform Commercial Code] governs a transaction, if one of the following provisions of [the Uniform Commercial Code] specifies the applicable law, that provision governs and a contrary agreement is effective only to the extent permitted by the law so specified:

(1) Section 2–402;

(2) Sections 2A–105 and 2A–106;

(3) Section 4–102;

(4) Section 4A–507;

(5) Section 5–116;

[(6) Section 6–103;]

(7) Section 8–110;

(8) Sections 9–301 through 9–307.

§ 1–302. Variation by Agreement

(a) Except as otherwise provided in subsection (b) or elsewhere in [the Uniform Commercial Code], the effect of provisions of [the Uniform Commercial Code] may be varied by agreement.

(b) The obligations of good faith, diligence, reasonableness, and care prescribed by [the Uniform Commercial Code] may not be disclaimed by agreement. The parties, by agreement, may determine the standards by which the performance of those obligations is to be measured if those standards are not manifestly unreasonable. Whenever [the Uniform Commercial Code] requires an action to be taken within a reasonable time, a time that is not manifestly unreasonable may be fixed by agreement.

(c) The presence in certain provisions of [the Uniform Commercial Code] of the phrase "unless otherwise agreed", or words of similar import, does not imply that the effect of other provisions may not be varied by agreement under this section.

§ 1–303. Course of Performance, Course of Dealing, and Usage of Trade

(a) A "course of performance" is a sequence of conduct between the parties to a particular transaction that exists if:

(1) the agreement of the parties with respect to the transaction involves repeated occasions for performance by a party; and

(2) the other party, with knowledge of the nature of the performance and opportunity for objection to it, accepts the performance or acquiesces in it without objection.

(b) A "course of dealing" is a sequence of conduct concerning previous transactions between the parties to a particular transaction that is fairly to be regarded as establishing a common basis of understanding for interpreting their expressions and other conduct.

(c) A "usage of trade" is any practice or method of dealing having such regularity of observance in a place, vocation, or trade as to justify an expectation that it will be observed with respect to the transaction in question. The existence and scope of such a usage must be proved as facts. If it is established that such a usage is embodied in a trade code or similar record, the interpretation of the record is a question of law.

(d) A course of performance or course of dealing between the parties or usage of trade in the vocation or trade in which they are engaged or of which they are or should be aware is relevant in ascertaining the meaning of the parties' agreement, may give particular meaning to specific terms of the agreement, and may supplement or qualify the terms of the agreement. A usage of trade applicable in the place in which part of the performance under the agreement is to occur may be so utilized as to that part of the performance.

(e) Except as otherwise provided in subsection (f), the express terms of an agreement and any applicable course of performance, course of dealing, or usage of trade must be construed whenever reasonable as consistent with each other. If such a construction is unreasonable:

(1) express terms prevail over course of performance, course of dealing, and usage of trade;

(2) course of performance prevails over course of dealing and usage of trade; and

(3) course of dealing prevails over usage of trade.

(f) Subject to Section 2–209, a course of performance is relevant to show a waiver or modification of any term inconsistent with the course of performance.

(g) Evidence of a relevant usage of trade offered by one party is not admissible unless that party has given the other party notice that the court finds sufficient to prevent unfair surprise to the other party.

§ 1–304. Obligation of Good Faith

Every contract or duty within [the Uniform Commercial Code] imposes an obligation of good faith in its performance and enforcement.

§ 1–305. Remedies to Be Liberally Administered

(a) The remedies provided by [the Uniform Commercial Code] must be liberally administered to the end that the aggrieved party may be put in as good a position as if the other party had fully performed but neither consequential or special damages nor penal damages may be had except as specifically provided in [the Uniform Commercial Code] or by other rule of law.

(b) Any right or obligation declared by [the Uniform Commercial Code] is enforceable by action unless the provision declaring it specifies a different and limited effect.

§ 1–306. Waiver or Renunciation of Claim or Right After Breach

A claim or right arising out of an alleged breach may be discharged in whole or in part without consideration by agreement of the aggrieved party in an authenticated record.

§ 1–307. Prima Facie Evidence by Third–Party Documents

A document in due form purporting to be a bill of lading, policy or certificate of insurance, official weigher's or inspector's certificate, consular invoice, or any other document authorized or required by the contract to be issued by a third party is prima facie evidence of its own authenticity and genuineness and of the facts stated in the document by the third party.

§ 1–308. Performance or Acceptance Under Reservation of Rights

(a) A party that with explicit reservation of rights performs or promises performance or assents to performance in a manner demanded or offered by the other party does not thereby prejudice the rights reserved. Such words as "without prejudice," "under protest," or the like are sufficient.

(b) Subsection (a) does not apply to an accord and satisfaction.

§ 1–309. Option to Accelerate at Will

A term providing that one party or that party's successor in interest may accelerate payment or performance or require collateral or additional collateral "at will" or when the party "deems itself insecure," or words of similar import, means that the party has power to do so only if that party in good faith believes that the prospect of payment or performance is impaired. The burden of establishing lack of good faith is on the party against which the power has been exercised.

§ 1–310. Subordinated Obligations

An obligation may be issued as subordinated to performance of another obligation of the person obligated, or a creditor may subordinate its right to performance of an obligation by agreement with either the person obligated or another creditor of the person obligated. Subordination does not create a security interest as against either the common debtor or a subordinated creditor.

AMENDMENTS TO
UNIFORM COMMERCIAL CODE
ARTICLE 2—SALES

April 2003

Table of Contents

PART 6. BREACH, REPUDIATION AND EXCUSE

PART 7. REMEDIES

PART 8. TRANSITION PROVISIONS

PART 1

SHORT TITLE, GENERAL CONSTRUCTION AND SUBJECT MATTER

§ 2–103. Definitions and Index of Definitions.

(1) In this article unless the context otherwise requires

(a) "Buyer" means a person ~~who~~ that buys or contracts to buy goods.

(b) "Conspicuous", with reference to a term, means so written, displayed, or presented that a reasonable person against which it is to operate ought to have noticed it. A term in an electronic record intended to evoke a response by an electronic agent is conspicuous if it is presented in a form that would enable a reasonably configured electronic agent to take it into account or react to it without review of the record by an individual. Whether a term is "conspicuous" or not is a decision for the court. Conspicuous terms include the following:

(i) for a person:

(A) a heading in capitals equal to or greater in size than the surrounding text, or in contrasting type, font, or color to the surrounding text of the same or lesser size;

(B) language in the body of a record or display in larger type than the surrounding text, or in contrasting type, font, or color to the surrounding text of the same size, or set off from surrounding text of the same size by symbols or other marks that call attention to the language; and

(ii) for a person or an electronic agent, a term that is so placed in a record or display that the person or electronic agent cannot proceed without taking action with respect to the particular term.

(c) "Consumer" means an individual who buys or contracts to buy goods that, at the time of contracting, are intended by the individual to be used primarily for personal, family, or household purposes.

(d) "Consumer contract" means a contract between a merchant seller and a consumer.

(e) "Delivery" means the voluntary transfer of physical possession or control of goods.

(f) "Electronic" means relating to technology having electrical, digital, magnetic, wireless, optical, electromagnetic, or similar capabilities.

(g) "Electronic agent" means a computer program or an electronic or other automated means used independently to initiate an action or respond to electronic records or performances in whole or in part, without review or action by an individual.

(h) "Electronic record" means a record created, generated, sent, communicated, received, or stored by electronic means.

(i) "Foreign exchange transaction" means a transaction in which one party agrees to deliver a quantity of a specified money or unit of account in consideration of the other party's agreement to deliver another quantity of a different money or unit of account either currently or at a future date, and in which delivery is to be through funds transfer, book entry accounting, or other form of payment order, or other agreed means to transfer a credit balance. The term includes a transaction of this type involving two or more moneys and spot, forward, option, or other products derived from underlying moneys and any combination of these transactions. The term does not include a transaction involving two or more moneys in which one or both of the parties is obligated to make physical delivery, at the time of contracting or in the future, of banknotes, coins, or other form of legal tender or specie.

(b) (j) "Good faith" in the case of a merchant means honesty in fact and the observance of reasonable commercial standards of fair dealing in the trade.

(k) "Goods" means all things that are movable at the time of identification to a contract for sale. The term includes future goods, specially manufactured goods, the unborn young of animals, growing crops, and other identified things attached to realty as described in Section 2–107. The term does not include information, the money in which the price is to be paid, investment securities under Article 8, the subject matter of foreign exchange transactions, or choses in action.

(c) (l) "Receipt of goods" means taking physical possession of them.

(m) "Record" means information that is inscribed on a tangible medium or that is stored in an electronic or other medium and is retrievable in perceivable form.

(n) "Remedial promise" means a promise by the seller to repair or replace the goods or to refund all or part of the price of goods upon the happening of a specified event. (d) (o) "Seller" means a person who that sells or contracts to sell goods.

(p) "Sign" means, with present intent to authenticate or adopt a record:

(i) to execute or adopt a tangible symbol; or

(ii) to attach to or logically associate with the record an electronic sound, symbol, or process. . . .

§ 2–104. Definitions: "Merchant"; "Between Merchants"; "Financing Agency".

(1) "Merchant" means a person ~~who~~ that deals in goods of the kind or otherwise ~~by his occupation holds himself out~~ holds itself out by occupation as having knowledge or skill peculiar to the practices or goods involved in the transaction or to ~~whom~~ which ~~such~~ the knowledge or skill may be attributed by ~~his~~ the person's employment of an agent or broker or other intermediary ~~who by his occupation holds himself out~~ that holds itself out by occupation as having ~~such~~ the knowledge or skill.

(2) "Financing agency" means a bank, finance company or other person ~~who~~ that in the ordinary course of business makes advances against goods or documents of title or ~~who~~ that by arrangement with either the seller or the buyer intervenes in ordinary course to make or collect payment due or claimed under the contract for sale, as by purchasing or paying the seller's draft or making advances against it or by merely taking it for collection whether or not documents of title accompany the draft. "Financing agency" includes also a bank or other person ~~who~~ that similarly intervenes between persons ~~who~~ that are in the position of seller and buyer in respect to the goods (Section 2–707).

(3) "Between merchants" means in any transaction with respect to which both parties are chargeable with the knowledge or skill of merchants.

§ 2–105. Definitions: Transferability; ~~"Goods";~~ "Future" Goods; "Lot"; "Commercial Unit".

~~(1) "Goods" means all things (including specially manufactured goods) which are movable at the time of identification to the contract for sale other than the money in which the price is to be paid, investment securities (Article 8) and things in action. "Goods" also includes the unborn young of animals and growing crops and other identified things attached to realty as described in the section on goods to be severed from realty (Section 2–107).~~

~~(2)~~ (1) Goods must be both existing and identified before any interest in them can pass. Goods which are not both existing and identified are "future" goods. A purported present sale of future goods or of any interest therein operates as a contract to sell.

~~(3)~~ (2) There may be a sale of a part interest in existing identified goods.

~~(4)~~ (3) An undivided share in an identified bulk of fungible goods is sufficiently identified to be sold although the quantity of the bulk is not determined. Any agreed proportion of such a bulk or any quantity thereof agreed upon by number, weight or other measure may to the extent of the seller's interest in the bulk be sold to the buyer ~~who~~ that then becomes an owner in common.

~~(5)~~ (4) "Lot" means a parcel or a single article which is the subject matter of a separate sale or delivery, whether or not it is sufficient to perform the contract.

~~(6)~~ (5) "Commercial unit" means such a unit of goods as by commercial usage is a single whole for purposes of sale and division of which materially impairs its character or value on the market or in use. A commercial unit may be a single article (as a machine) or a set of articles (as a suite of furniture or an assortment of sizes) or a quantity (as a bale, gross, or carload) or any other unit treated in use or in the relevant market as a single whole.

§ 2–108. Transactions Subject to Other Law.

(1) A transaction subject to this article is also subject to any applicable:

(a) [list any certificate of title statutes of this State covering automobiles, trailers, mobile homes, boats, farm tractors, or the like], except with respect to the rights of a buyer in ordinary course of business under Section 2–403(2) which arise before a certificate of title covering the goods is effective in the name of any other buyer;

(b) rule of law that establishes a different rule for consumers; or

(c) statute of this state applicable to the transaction is subject, such as a statute dealing with:

(i) the sale or lease of agricultural products;

(ii) the transfer of human blood, blood products, human tissues, or parts;

(iii) the consignment or transfer by artists of works of art or fine prints;

(iv) distribution agreements, franchises, and other relationships through which goods are sold;

(v) the misbranding or adulteration of food products or drugs; and

(vi) dealers in particular products, such as automobiles, motorized wheelchairs, agricultural equipment, and hearing aids.

(2) Except for the rights of a buyer in ordinary course of business under subsection (1)(a), in the event of a conflict between this article and a law referred to in subsection (1), that law governs.

(3) For purposes of this article, failure to comply with a law referred to in subsection (1) has only the effect specified in that law.

(4) This article modifies, limits, and supersedes the federal Electronic Signatures in Global and National Commerce Act, 15 U.S.C. Section 7001 et seq., except that nothing in this article modifies, limits, or

supersedes Section 7001(c) of that Act or authorizes electronic delivery of any of the notices described in Section 7003(b) of that Act.

PART 2

FORM, FORMATION, TERMS AND READJUSTMENT OF CONTRACT; ELECTRONIC CONTRACTING

§ 2–201. Formal Requirements; Statute of Frauds.

(1) ~~Except as otherwise provided in this section a~~ A contract for the sale of goods for the price of ~~$500~~ $5,000 or more is not enforceable by way of action or defense unless there is some ~~writing~~ record sufficient to indicate that a contract for sale has been made between the parties and signed by the party against ~~whom~~ which enforcement is sought or by ~~his~~ the party's authorized agent or broker. A ~~writing~~ record is not insufficient because it omits or incorrectly states a term agreed upon but the contract is not enforceable under this subsection beyond the quantity of goods shown in ~~such~~ the ~~writing~~ record.

(2) Between merchants if within a reasonable time a ~~writing~~ record in confirmation of the contract and sufficient against the sender is received and the party receiving it has reason to know its contents, it satisfies the requirements of subsection (1) against ~~such party~~ the recipient unless ~~written~~ notice of objection to its contents is given in a record within 10 days after it is received.

(3) A contract which does not satisfy the requirements of subsection (1) but which is valid in other respects is enforceable

(a) if the goods are to be specially manufactured for the buyer and are not suitable for sale to others in the ordinary course of the seller's business and the seller, before notice of repudiation is received and under circumstances which reasonably indicate that the goods are for the buyer, has made either a substantial beginning of their manufacture or commitments for their procurement; or

(b) if the party against ~~whom~~ which enforcement is sought admits in ~~his~~ the party's pleading, or in the party's testimony or otherwise ~~in court~~ under oath that a contract for sale was made, but the contract is not enforceable under this ~~provision~~ paragraph beyond the quantity of goods admitted; or

(c) with respect to goods for which payment has been made and accepted or which have been received and accepted (Sec. 2–606).

(4) A contract that is enforceable under this section is not unenforceable merely because it is not capable of being performed within one year or any other period after its making.

§ 2–202. Final ~~Written~~ Expression in a Record: Parol or Extrinsic Evidence.

(1) Terms with respect to which the confirmatory ~~memoranda~~ records of the parties agree or which are otherwise set forth in a ~~writing~~

record intended by the parties as a final expression of their agreement with respect to such terms as are included therein may not be contradicted by evidence of any prior agreement or of a contemporaneous oral agreement but may be ~~explained or~~ supplemented by evidence of:

(a) ~~by course of dealing or usage of trade (Section 1B205) or by course of performance (Section 2–208)~~ course of performance, course of dealing or usage of trade (Section 1–303); and

(b) ~~by evidence of~~ consistent additional terms unless the court finds the ~~writing~~ record to have been intended also as a complete and exclusive statement of the terms of the agreement.

(2) Terms in a record may be explained by evidence of course of performance, course of dealing, or usage of trade without a preliminary determination by the court that the language used is ambiguous.

§ 2–203. Seals Inoperative.

The affixing of a seal to a ~~writing~~ record evidencing a contract for sale or an offer to buy or sell goods does not constitute the ~~writing~~ record a sealed instrument and the law with respect to sealed instruments does not apply to such a contract or offer.

§ 2–204. Formation In General.

(1) A contract for sale of goods may be made in any manner sufficient to show agreement, including offer and acceptance, conduct by both parties which recognizes the existence of such a contract, the interaction of electronic agents, and the interaction of an electronic agent and an individual.

(2) An agreement sufficient to constitute a contract for sale may be found even though the moment of its making is undetermined.

(3) Even though one or more terms are left open a contract for sale does not fail for indefiniteness if the parties have intended to make a contract and there is a reasonably certain basis for giving an appropriate remedy.

(4) Except as otherwise provided in Sections 2–211 through 2–213, the following rules apply:

(a) A contract may be formed by the interaction of electronic agents of the parties, even if no individual was aware of or reviewed the electronic agents' actions or the resulting terms and agreements.

(b) A contract may be formed by the interaction of an electronic agent and an individual acting on the individual's own behalf or for another person. A contract is formed if the individual takes actions that the individual is free to refuse to take and makes a statement that the individual has reason to know will:

(i) cause the electronic agent to complete the transaction or performance; or

(ii) indicate acceptance of an offer, regardless of other expressions or actions by the individual to which the electronic agent cannot react.

§ 2–205. Firm Offers.

An offer by a merchant to buy or sell goods in a signed record which by its terms gives assurance that it will be held open is not revocable, for · lack of consideration, during the time stated or if no time is stated for a reasonable time, but in no event may such period of irrevocability exceed three months, but any such term of assurance ~~on a form~~ in a form supplied by the offeree must be separately signed by the offeror.

§ 2–206. Offer and Acceptance in Formation of Contract.

(1) Unless otherwise unambiguously indicated by the language or circumstances

(a) an offer to make a contract shall be construed as inviting acceptance in any manner and by any medium reasonable in the circumstances;

(b) an order or other offer to buy goods for prompt or current shipment shall be construed as inviting acceptance either by a prompt promise to ship or by the prompt or current shipment of conforming or nonconforming goods, but ~~such a~~ the shipment of nonconforming goods is not an acceptance if the seller seasonably notifies the buyer that the shipment is offered only as an accommodation to the buyer.

(2) Where the beginning of a requested performance is a reasonable mode of acceptance an offeror ~~who~~ that is not notified of acceptance within a reasonable time may treat the offer as having lapsed before acceptance.

(3) A definite and seasonable expression of acceptance in a record operates as an acceptance even if it contains terms additional to or different from the offer.

§ 2–207. ~~Additional Terms In Acceptance Or~~ Terms Of Contract; Effect Of Confirmation.

(1) ~~A definite and seasonable expression of acceptance or a written confirmation which is sent within a reasonable time operates as an acceptance even though it states terms additional to or different from those offered or agreed upon, unless acceptance is expressly made conditional on assent to the additional or different terms.~~

(2) ~~The additional terms are to be construed as proposals for addition to the contract. Between merchants such terms become part of the contract unless:~~

(a) ~~the offer expressly limits acceptance to the terms of the offer;~~

(b) ~~they materially alter it; or~~

~~(c) notification of objection to them has already been given or is given within a reasonable time after notice of them is received.~~

~~(3) Conduct by both parties which recognizes the existence of a contract is sufficient to establish a contract for sale although the writings of the parties do not otherwise establish a contract. In such case the terms of the particular contract consist of those terms on which the writings of the parties agree, together with any supplementary terms incorporated under any other provisions of this Act.~~

Subject to Section 2–202, if (i) conduct by both parties recognizes the existence of a contract although their records do not otherwise establish a contract, (ii) a contract is formed by an offer and acceptance, or (iii) a contract formed in any manner is confirmed by a record that contains terms additional to or different from those in the contract being confirmed, the terms of the contract, are:

(a) terms that appear in the records of both parties;

(b) terms, whether in a record or not, to which both parties agree; and

(c) terms supplied or incorporated under any provision of this Act.

§ 2–208. ~~Course of Performance on Practical Construction~~ <u>Reserved</u>.

~~(1) Where the contract for sale involves repeated occasions for performance by either party with knowledge of the nature of the performance and opportunity for objection to it by the other, any course of performance accepted or acquiesced in without objection shall be relevant to determine the meaning of the agreement.~~

~~(2) The express terms of the agreement and any such course of performance, as well as any course of dealing and usage of trade, shall be construed whenever reasonable as consistent with each other; but when such construction is unreasonable, express terms shall control course of performance and course of performance shall control both course of dealing and usage of trade (Section 1B205).~~

~~(3) Subject to the provisions of the next section on modification and waiver, such course of performance shall be relevant to show a waiver or modification of any term inconsistent with such course of performance.~~

§ 2–209. Modification; Rescission and Waiver.

(1) An agreement modifying a contract within this Article needs no consideration to be binding.

(2) ~~A signed agreement~~ An agreement in a signed record which excludes modification or rescission except by a signed ~~writing~~ record cannot be otherwise modified or rescinded, but except as between merchants such a requirement ~~on a form~~ in a form supplied by the merchant must be separately signed by the other party.

(3) The requirements of the statute of frauds section of this Article (Section 2–201) must be satisfied if the contract as modified is within its provisions.

(4) Although an attempt at modification or rescission does not satisfy the requirements of subsection (2) or (3) it can operate as a waiver.

(5) A party ~~who~~ that has made a waiver affecting an executory portion of the contract may retract the waiver by reasonable notification received by the other party that strict performance will be required of any term waived, unless the retraction would be unjust in view of a material change of position in reliance on the waiver.

§ 2–210.   Delegation of Performance; Assignment of Rights.

~~(1) A party may perform his duty through a delegate unless otherwise agreed or unless the other party has a substantial interest in having his original promisor perform or control the acts required by the contract. No delegation of performance relieves the party delegating of any duty to perform or any liability for breach.~~

~~(2) Unless otherwise agreed all rights of either seller or buyer can be assigned except where the assignment would materially change the duty of the other party, or increase materially the burden or risk imposed on him by his contract, or impair materially his chance of obtaining return performance. A right to damages for breach of the whole contract or a right arising out of the assignor's due performance of his entire obligation can be assigned despite agreement otherwise.~~

~~(3) Unless the circumstances indicate the contrary a prohibition of assignment of "the contract" is to be construed as barring only the delegation to the assignee of the assignor's performance.~~

~~(4) An assignment of "the contract" or of "all my rights under the contract" or an assignment in similar general terms is an assignment of rights and unless the language or the circumstances (as in an assignment for security) indicate the contrary, it is a delegation of performance of the duties of the assignor and its acceptance by the assignee constitutes a promise by him to perform those duties. This promise is enforceable by either the assignor or the other party to the original contract.~~

~~(5) The other party may treat any assignment which delegates performance as creating reasonable grounds for insecurity and may without prejudice to his rights against the assignor demand assurances from the assignee (Section 2–609).~~

(1) If the seller or buyer assigns rights under a contract, the following rules apply:

(a) Subject to paragraph (b) and except as otherwise provided in Section 9–406 or as otherwise agreed, all rights of the seller or the buyer may be assigned unless the assignment would materially change the duty of the other party, increase materially the burden or risk imposed on that party by the contract, or impair materially that party's chance of obtaining return performance. A right to damages for breach of the whole contract or a right arising out of the assignor's due performance of its entire obligation may be assigned despite an agreement otherwise.

(b) The creation, attachment, perfection, or enforcement of a security interest in the seller's interest under a contract is not an assignment that materially changes the duty of or materially increases the burden or risk imposed on the buyer or materially impairs the buyer's chance of obtaining return performance under paragraph (a) unless, and only to the extent that, enforcement of the security interest results in a delegation of a material performance of the seller. Even in that event, the creation, attachment, perfection, and enforcement of the security interest remain effective. However, the seller is liable to the buyer for damages caused by the delegation to the extent that the damages could not reasonably be prevented by the buyer, and a court may grant other appropriate relief, including cancellation of the contract or an injunction against enforcement of the security interest or consummation of the enforcement.

(2) If the seller or buyer delegates performance of its duties under a contract, the following rules apply:

(a) A party may perform its duties through a delegate unless otherwise agreed or unless the other party has a substantial interest in having the original promisor perform or control the acts required by the contract. Delegation of performance does not relieve the delegating party of any duty to perform or liability for breach.

(b) Acceptance of a delegation of duties by the assignee constitutes a promise to perform those duties. The promise is enforceable by either the assignor or the other party to the original contract.

(c) The other party may treat any delegation of duties as creating reasonable grounds for insecurity and may without prejudice to its rights against the assignor demand assurances from the assignee under Section 2–609.

(d) A contractual term prohibiting the delegation of duties otherwise delegable under paragraph (a) is enforceable, and an attempted delegation is not effective.

(3) An assignment of "the contract" or of "all my rights under the contract" or an assignment in similar general terms is an assignment of rights and unless the language or the circumstances, as in an assignment for security, indicate the contrary, it is also a delegation of performance of the duties of the assignor.

(4) Unless the circumstances indicate the contrary a prohibition of assignment of "the contract" is to be construed as barring only the delegation to the assignee of the assignor's performance.

§ 2–211. Legal Recognition of Electronic Contracts, Records and Signatures.

(1) A record or signature may not be denied legal effect or enforceability solely because it is in electronic form.

(2) A contract may not be denied legal effect or enforceability solely because an electronic record was used in its formation.

(3) This article does not require a record or signature to be created, generated, sent, communicated, received, stored, or otherwise processed by electronic means or in electronic form.

(4) A contract formed by the interaction of an individual and an electronic agent under Section 2–204(4)(b) does not include terms provided by the individual if the individual had reason to know that the agent could not react to the terms as provided.

§ 2–212. Attribution.

An electronic record or electronic signature is attributed to a person if the record was created by or the signature was the act of the person or the person's electronic agent or the person is otherwise legally bound by the act.

§ 2–213. Electronic Communication.

(1) If the receipt of an electronic communication has a legal effect, it has that effect even if no individual is aware of its receipt.

(2) Receipt of an electronic acknowledgment of an electronic communication establishes that the communication was received but, in itself, does not establish that the content sent corresponds to the content received.

PART 3

GENERAL OBLIGATION AND CONSTRUCTION OF CONTRACT

§ 2–302. Unconscionable Contract or ~~Clause~~ Term.

(1) If the court as a matter of law finds the contract or any ~~clause~~ term of the contract to have been unconscionable at the time it was made the court may refuse to enforce the contract, or it may enforce the remainder of the contract without the unconscionable ~~clause~~ term, or it may so limit the application of any unconscionable ~~clause~~ term as to avoid any unconscionable result.

(2) When it is claimed or appears to the court that the contract or any ~~clause~~ term thereof may be unconscionable the parties shall be afforded a reasonable opportunity to present evidence as to its commercial setting, purpose and effect to aid the court in making the determination.

§ 2–304. Price Payable in Money, Goods, Realty, or Otherwise.

(1) The price can be made payable in money or otherwise. If it is payable in whole or in part in goods each party is a seller of the goods which ~~he~~ that party is to transfer.

(2) Even though all or part of the price is payable in an interest in realty the transfer of the goods and the seller's obligations with reference to them are subject to this Article, but not the transfer of the interest in realty or the transferor's obligations in connection therewith.

§ 2–305. Open Price Term.

(1) The parties if they so intend can conclude a contract for sale even though the price is not settled. In such a case the price is a reasonable price at the time for delivery if

(a) nothing is said as to price; or

(b) the price is left to be agreed by the parties and they fail to agree; or

(c) the price is to be fixed in terms of some agreed market or other standard as set or recorded by a third person or agency and it is not so set or recorded.

(2) A price to be fixed by the seller or by the buyer means a price ~~for him to fix~~ to be fixed in good faith.

(3) When a price left to be fixed otherwise than by agreement of the parties fails to be fixed through fault of one party the other may at ~~his~~ the party's option treat the contract as canceled or ~~himself~~ the party may fix a reasonable price.

(4) Where, however, the parties intend not to be bound unless the price be fixed or agreed and it is not fixed or agreed there is no contract. In such a case the buyer must return any goods already received or if unable so to do must pay their reasonable value at the time of delivery and the seller must return any portion of the price paid on account.

§ 2–308. Absence of Specified Place for Delivery.

Unless otherwise agreed

(a) the place for delivery of goods is the seller's place of business or if ~~he~~ it has none ~~his~~ the seller's residence; but

(b) in a contract for sale of identified goods which to the knowledge of the parties at the time of contracting are in some other place, that place is the place for their delivery; and

(c) documents of title may be delivered through customary banking channels.

§ 2–309. Absence of Specific Time Provisions; Notice of Termination.

(1) The time for shipment or delivery or any other action under a contract if not provided in this Article or agreed upon shall be a reasonable time.

(2) Where the contract provides for successive performances but is indefinite in duration it is valid for a reasonable time but unless otherwise agreed may be terminated at any time by either party.

(3) Termination of a contract by one party except on the happening of an agreed event requires that reasonable notification be received by the other party and an agreement dispensing with notification is invalid if its operation would be unconscionable. <u>A term specifying standards for the nature and timing of notice is enforceable if the standards are not manifestly unreasonable.</u>

§ 2–310. Open Time for Payment or Running of Credit Authority to Ship Under Reservation.

Unless otherwise agreed

(a) payment is due at the time and place at which the buyer is to receive the goods even though the place of shipment is the place of delivery; and

(b) if the seller is <u>required or</u> authorized to send the goods ~~he~~ <u>the seller</u> may ship them under reservation, and may tender the documents of title, but the buyer may inspect the goods after their arrival before payment is due unless such inspection is inconsistent with the terms of the contract (Section 2–513); and

(c) if <u>tender of</u> delivery is ~~authorized and~~ <u>agreed to</u> be made by way of documents of title otherwise than by subsection (b) then payment is due at the time and place at which the buyer is to receive the documents regardless of where the goods are to be received; and

(d) where the seller is required or authorized to ship the goods on credit the credit period runs from the time of shipment but postdating the invoice or delaying its dispatch will correspondingly delay the starting of the credit period.

§ 2–311. Options and Cooperation Respecting Performance.

(1) An agreement for sale which is otherwise sufficiently definite (subsection (3) of Section 2–204) to be a contract is not made invalid by the fact that it leaves particulars of performance to be specified by one of the parties. Any such specification must be made in good faith and within limits set by commercial reasonableness.

(2) Unless otherwise agreed specifications relating to assortment of the goods are at the buyer's option and ~~except as otherwise provided in subsections (1)(c) and (3) of Section 2–319~~ specifications or arrangements relating to shipment are at the seller's option.

(3) Where such specification would materially affect the other party's performance but is not seasonably made or where one party's cooperation is necessary to the agreed performance of the other but is not seasonably forthcoming, the other party in addition to all other remedies

(a) is excused for any resulting delay in ~~his own~~ <u>that party's</u> performance; and

(b) may also either proceed to perform in any reasonable manner or after the time for a material part of ~~his~~ that party's ~~own~~ performance treat the failure to specify or to cooperate as a breach by failure to deliver or accept the goods.

§ 2–312. Warranty of Title and Against Infringement; Buyer's Obligation Against Infringement.

(1) Subject to subsection (3) there is in a contract for sale a warranty by the seller that

(a) the title conveyed shall be ~~good,~~ good and its transfer rightful and shall not, unreasonably expose the buyer to litigation because of any colorable claim to or interest in the goods; and

(b) the goods shall be delivered free from any security interest or other lien or encumbrance of which the buyer at the time of contracting has no knowledge.

~~(2) A warranty under subsection (1) will be excluded or modified only by specific language or by circumstances which give the buyer reason to know that the person selling does not claim title in himself or that it is purporting to sell only such right or title as it or a third person may have.~~

~~(3) Unless otherwise agreed a seller who is a merchant regularly dealing in goods of the kind warrants that the goods shall be delivered free of the rightful claim of any third person by way of infringement or the like but a buyer who furnishes specifications to the seller must hold the seller harmless against any such claim which arises out of compliance with the specifications.~~

(2) Unless otherwise agreed a seller that is a merchant regularly dealing in goods of the kind warrants that the goods shall be delivered free of the rightful claim of any third person by way of infringement or the like but a buyer that furnishes specifications to the seller must hold the seller harmless against any such claim that arises out of compliance with the specifications.

(3) A warranty under this section may be disclaimed or modified only by specific language or by circumstances that give the buyer reason to know that the seller does not claim title, that the seller is purporting to sell only the right or title as the seller or a third person may have, or that the seller is selling subject to any claims of infringement or the like.

§ 2–313. Express Warranties by Affirmation, Promise, Description, Sample; Remedial Promise.

(1) In this section, "immediate buyer" means a buyer that enters into a contract with the seller.

~~(1)~~ (2) Express warranties by the seller to the immediate buyer are created as follows:

(a) Any affirmation of fact or promise made by the seller ~~to the buyer~~ which relates to the goods and becomes part of the basis of the bargain creates an express warranty that the goods shall conform to the affirmation or promise.

(b) Any description of the goods which is made part of the basis of the bargain creates an express warranty that the goods shall conform to the description.

(c) Any sample or model which is made part of the basis of the bargain creates an express warranty that the whole of the goods shall conform to the sample or model.

~~(2)~~ (3) It is not necessary to the creation of an express warranty that the seller use formal words such as "warrant" or "guarantee" or that ~~he~~ the seller have a specific intention to make a warranty, but an affirmation merely of the value of the goods or a statement purporting to be merely the seller's opinion or commendation of the goods does not create a warranty.

(4) Any remedial promise made by the seller to the immediate buyer creates an obligation that the promise will be performed upon the happening of the specified event.

§ 2–313A. Obligation to Remote Purchaser Created by Record Packaged With or Accompanying Goods.

(1) In this section:

(a) "Immediate buyer" means a buyer that enters into a contract with the seller.

(b) "Remote purchaser" means a person that buys or leases goods from an immediate buyer or other person in the normal chain of distribution.

(2) This section applies only to new goods and goods sold or leased as new goods in a transaction of purchase in the normal chain of distribution.

(3) If in a record packaged with or accompanying the goods the seller makes an affirmation of fact or promise that relates to the goods, provides a description that relates to the goods, or makes a remedial promise, and the seller reasonably expects the record to be, and the record is, furnished to the remote purchaser, the seller has an obligation to the remote purchaser that:

(a) the goods will conform to the affirmation of fact, promise or description unless a reasonable person in the position of the remote purchaser would not believe that the affirmation of fact, promise or description created an obligation; and

(b) the seller will perform the remedial promise.

(4) It is not necessary to the creation of an obligation under this section that the seller use formal words such as "warrant" or "guarantee" or that the seller have a specific intention to undertake an obligation, but an affirmation merely of the value of the goods or a

statement purporting to be merely the seller's opinion or commendation of the goods does not create an obligation.

(5) The following rules apply to the remedies for breach of an obligation created under this section:

    (a) The seller may modify or limit the remedies available to the remote purchaser if the modification or limitation is furnished to the remote purchaser no later than the time of purchase or if the modification or limitation is contained in the record that contains the affirmation of fact, promise or description.

    (b) Subject to a modification or limitation of remedy, a seller in breach is liable for incidental or consequential damages under Section 2–715, but not for lost profits.

    (c) The remote purchaser may recover as damages for breach of a seller's obligation arising under subsection (2) the loss resulting in the ordinary course of events as determined in any reasonable manner.

(6) An obligation that is not a remedial promise is breached if the goods did not conform to the affirmation of fact, promise or description creating the obligation when the goods left the seller's control.

§ 2–313B. Obligation to Remote Purchaser Created by Communication to the Public.

(1) In this section:

    (a) "Immediate buyer" means a buyer that enters into a contract with the seller.

    (b) "Remote purchaser" means a person that buys or leases goods from an immediate buyer or other person in the normal chain of distribution.

(2) This section applies only to new goods and goods sold or leased as new goods in a transaction of purchase in the normal chain of distribution.

(3) If in an advertisement or a similar communication to the public a seller makes an affirmation of fact or promise that relates to the goods, provides a description that relates to the goods, or makes a remedial promise, and the remote purchaser enters into a transaction of purchase with knowledge of and with the expectation that the goods will conform to the affirmation of fact, promise, or description, or that the seller will perform the remedial promise, the seller has an obligation to the remote purchaser that:

    (a) the goods will conform to the affirmation of fact, promise or description unless a reasonable person in the position of the remote purchaser would not believe that the affirmation of fact, promise or description created an obligation; and

    (b) the seller will perform the remedial promise.

(4) It is not necessary to the creation of an obligation under this section that the seller use formal words such as "warrant" or "guarantee" or that the seller have a specific intention to undertake an obligation, but an affirmation merely of the value of the goods or a statement purporting to be merely the seller's opinion or commendation of the goods does not create an obligation.

(5) The following rules apply to the remedies for breach of an obligation created under this section:

(a) The seller may modify or limit the remedies available to the remote purchaser if the modification or limitation is furnished to the remote purchaser no later than the time of purchase. The modification or limitation may be furnished as part of the communication that contains the affirmation of fact, promise or description.

(b) Subject to a modification or limitation of remedy, a seller in breach is liable for incidental or consequential damages under Section 2–715, but not for lost profits.

(c) The remote purchaser may recover as damages for breach of a seller's obligation arising under subsection (2) the loss resulting in the ordinary course of events as determined in any reasonable manner.

(6) An obligation that is not a remedial promise is breached if the goods did not conform to the affirmation of fact, promise or description creating the obligation when the goods left the seller's control.

§ 2–314. Implied Warranty: Merchantability; Usage of Trade.

(1) Unless excluded or modified (Section 2–316), a warranty that the goods shall be merchantable is implied in a contract for their sale if the seller is a merchant with respect to goods of that kind. Under this section the serving for value of food or drink to be consumed either on the premises or elsewhere is a sale.

(2) Goods to be merchantable must be at least such as

(a) pass without objection in the trade under the contract description; and

(b) in the case of fungible goods, are of fair average quality within the description; and

(c) are fit for the ordinary purposes for which ~~such~~ goods <u>of that description</u> are used; and

(d) run, within the variations permitted by the agreement, of even kind, quality and quantity within each unit and among all units involved; and

(e) are adequately contained, packaged, and labeled as the agreement may require; and

(f) conform to the promise or affirmations of fact made on the container or label if any.

(3) Unless excluded or modified (Section 2–316) other implied warranties may arise from course of dealing or usage of trade.

§ 2–316. Exclusion or Modification of Warranties.

(1) Words or conduct relevant to the creation of an express warranty and words or conduct tending to negate or limit warranty shall be construed wherever reasonable as consistent with each other; but subject to the provisions of this Article on parol or extrinsic evidence (Section 2–202) negation or limitation is inoperative to the extent that such construction is unreasonable.

(2) Subject to subsection (3), to exclude or modify the implied warranty of merchantability or any part of it in a consumer contract the language must be in a record, be conspicuous, and state "The seller undertakes no responsibility for the quality of the goods except as otherwise provided in this contract," and in any other contract the language must mention merchantability and in case of a ~~writing~~ record must be conspicuous~~, and to~~. Subject to subsection (3), to exclude or modify the implied warranty of fitness, the exclusion must be ~~by a writing~~ in a record and be conspicuous. Language to exclude all implied warranties of fitness in a consumer contract must state "The seller assumes no responsibility that the goods will be fit for any particular purpose for which you may be buying these goods, except as otherwise provided in the contract," and in any other contract the language is sufficient if it states, for example, that "There are no warranties that extend beyond the description on the face hereof." Language that satisfies the requirements of this subsection for the exclusion and modification of a warranty in a consumer contract also satisfies the requirements for any other contract.

(3) Notwithstanding subsection (2):

(a) unless the circumstances indicate otherwise, all implied warranties are excluded by expressions like "as is," "with all faults" or other language which in common understanding calls the buyer's attention to the exclusion of warranties ~~and~~, makes plain that there is no implied warranty, and, in a consumer contract evidenced by a record, is set forth conspicuously in the record; and

(b) when the buyer before entering into the contract has examined the goods or the sample or model as fully as ~~he~~ desired or has refused to examine the goods after a demand by the seller there is no implied warranty with regard to defects which an examination ought in the circumstances to have revealed to ~~him~~ the buyer; and

(c) an implied warranty can also be excluded or modified by course of dealing or course of performance or usage of trade.

(4) Remedies for breach of warranty can be limited in accordance with the provisions of this article on liquidation or limitation of damages and on contractual modification of remedy (Sections 2–718 and 2–719).

§ 2–318. Third Party Beneficiaries of Warranties Express or Implied.

(1) In this section:

(a) "Immediate buyer" means a buyer that enters into a contract with the seller.

(b) "Remote purchaser" means a person that buys or leases goods from an immediate buyer or other person in the normal chain of distribution.

Alternative A to subsection (2)

(2) A seller's warranty whether express or implied extends to any natural person who is in the family or household of his buyer or who is a guest in his home if it is reasonable to expect that such person may use, consume or be affected by the goods and who is injured in person by breach of the warranty. A seller's warranty to an immediate buyer, whether express or implied, a seller's remedial promise to an immediate buyer, or a seller's obligation to a remote purchaser under Section 2–313A or 2–313B extends to any natural person who is in the family or household of the immediate buyer or the remote purchaser or who is a guest in the home of either if it is reasonable to expect that the person may use, consume or be affected by the goods and who is injured in person by breach of the warranty, remedial promise or obligation. A seller may not exclude or limit the operation of this section.

Alternative B to subsection (2)

(2) A seller's warranty whether express or implied extends to any natural person who may reasonably be expected to use, consume or be affected by the goods and who is injured in person by breach of the warranty. A seller's warranty to an immediate buyer, whether express or implied, a seller's remedial promise to an immediate buyer, or a seller's obligation to a remote purchaser under Section 2–313A or 2–313B extends to any natural person who may reasonably be expected to use, consume or be affected by the goods and who is injured in person by breach of the warranty, remedial promise or obligation. A seller may not exclude or limit the operation of this section.

Alternative C to subsection (2)

(2) A seller's warranty whether express or implied extends to any person who may reasonably be expected to use, consume or be affected by the goods and who is injured by breach of the warranty. A seller's warranty to an immediate buyer, whether express or implied, a seller's remedial promise to an immediate buyer, or a seller's obligation to a remote purchaser under Section 2–313A or 2–313B extends to any person that may reasonably be expected to use, consume or be affected by the goods and that is injured by breach of the warranty, remedial promise or obligation. A seller may not exclude or limit the operation of this section with respect to injury to the person of an individual to whom the warranty, remedial promise or obligation extends.

§ 2–319. ~~F.O.B. and F.A.S. Terms~~ Reserved.

~~(1) Unless otherwise agreed the term F.O.B. (which means "free on board") at a named place, even though used only in connection with the stated price, is a delivery term under which~~

~~(a) when the term is F.O.B. the place of shipment, the seller must at that place ship the goods in the manner provided in this Article (Section 2–504) and bear the expense and risk of putting them into the possession of the carrier; or~~

~~(b) when the term is F.O.B. the place of destination, the seller must at his own expense and risk transport the goods to that place and there tender delivery of them in the manner provided in this Article (Section 2–503);~~

~~(c) when under either (a) or (b) the term is also F.O.B. vessel, car or other vehicle, the seller must in addition at his own expense and risk load the goods on board. If the term is F.O.B. vessel the buyer must name the vessel and in an appropriate case the seller must comply with the provisions of this Article on the form of bill of lading (Section 2–323).~~

~~(2) Unless otherwise agreed the term F.A.S. vessel (which means "free alongside") at a named port, even though used only in connection with the stated price, is a delivery term under which the seller must~~

~~(a) at his own expense and risk deliver the goods alongside the vessel in the manner usual in that port or on a dock designated and provided by the buyer; and~~

~~(b) obtain and tender a receipt for the goods in exchange for which the carrier is under a duty to issue a bill of lading.~~

~~(3) Unless otherwise agreed in any case falling within subsection (1)(a) or (c) or subsection (2) the buyer must seasonably give any needed instructions for making delivery, including when the term is F.A.S. or F.O.B. the loading berth of the vessel and in an appropriate case its name and sailing date. The seller may treat the failure of needed instructions as a failure of cooperation under this Article (Section 2–311). He may also at his option move the goods in any reasonable manner preparatory to delivery or shipment.~~

~~(4) Under the term F.O.B. vessel or F.A.S. unless otherwise agreed the buyer must make payment against tender of the required documents and the seller may not tender nor the buyer demand delivery of the goods in substitution for the documents.~~

§ 2–320. ~~C.I.F. And C. & F. Terms~~ Reserved.

~~(1) The term C.I.F. means that the price includes in a lump sum the cost of the goods and the insurance and freight to the named destination. The term C. & F. or C.F. means that the price so includes cost and freight to the named destination.~~

(2) Unless otherwise agreed and even though used only in connection with the stated price and destination, the term C.I.F. destination or its equivalent requires the seller at his own expense and risk to

(a) put the goods into the possession of a carrier at the port for shipment and obtain a negotiable bill or bills of lading covering the entire transportation to the named destination; and

(b) load the goods and obtain a receipt from the carrier (which may be contained in the bill of lading) showing that the freight has been paid or provided for; and

(c) obtain a policy or certificate of insurance, including any war risk insurance, of a kind and on terms then current at the port of shipment in the usual amount, in the currency of the contract, shown to cover the same goods covered by the bill of lading and providing for payment of loss to the order of the buyer or for the account of whom it may concern; but the seller may add to the price the amount of the premium for any such war risk insurance; and

(d) prepare an invoice of the goods and procure any other documents required to effect shipment or to comply with the contract; and

(e) forward and tender with commercial promptness all the documents in due form and with any indorsement necessary to perfect the buyer's rights.

(3) Unless otherwise agreed the term C. & F. or its equivalent has the same effect and imposes upon the seller the same obligations and risks as a C.I.F. term except the obligation as to insurance.

(4) Under the term C.I.F. or C. & F. unless otherwise agreed the buyer must make payment against tender of the required documents and the seller may not tender nor the buyer demand delivery of the goods in substitution for the documents.

§ 2–321.   C.I.F. Or C. & F.: "Net Landed Weights"; "Payment On Arrival"; Warranty Of Condition On Arrival Reserved.

Under a contract containing a term C.I.F. or C. & F.

(1) Where the price is based on or is to be adjusted according to "net landed weights", "delivered weights", "out turn" quantity or quality or the like, unless otherwise agreed the seller must reasonably estimate the price. The payment due on tender of the documents called for by the contract is the amount so estimated, but after final adjustment of the price a settlement must be made with commercial promptness.

(2) An agreement described in subsection (1) or any warranty of quality or condition of the goods on arrival places upon the seller the risk of ordinary deterioration, shrinkage and the like in transportation but has no effect on the place or time of identification to the contract for sale or delivery or on the passing of the risk of loss.

(3) Unless otherwise agreed where the contract provides for payment on or after arrival of the goods the seller must before payment allow such preliminary inspection as is feasible; but if the goods are lost delivery of the documents and payment are due when the goods should have arrived.

§ 2–322. ~~Delivery "Ex–Ship"~~ Reserved.

(1) Unless otherwise agreed a term for delivery of goods "ex-ship" (which means from the carrying vessel) or in equivalent language is not restricted to a particular ship and requires delivery from a ship which has reached a place at the named port of destination where goods of the kind are usually discharged.

(2) Under such a term unless otherwise agreed

(a) the seller must discharge all liens arising out of the carriage and furnish the buyer with a direction which puts the carrier under a duty to deliver the goods; and

(b) the risk of loss does not pass to the buyer until the goods leave the ship's tackle or are otherwise properly unloaded.

§ 2–323. ~~Form Of Bill Of Lading Required In Overseas Shipment; "overseas"~~ Reserved.

(1) Where the contract contemplates overseas shipment and contains a term C.I.F. or C. & F. or F.O.B. vessel, the seller unless otherwise agreed must obtain a negotiable bill of lading stating that the goods have been loaded in board or, in the case of a term C.I.F. or C. & F., received for shipment.

(2) Where in a case within subsection (1) a bill of lading has been issued in a set of parts, unless otherwise agreed if the documents are not to be sent from abroad the buyer may demand tender of the full set; otherwise only one part of the bill of lading need be tendered. Even if the agreement expressly requires a full set

(a) due tender of a single part is acceptable within the provisions of this Article on cure of improper delivery (subsection (1) of Section 2–508); and

(b) even though the full set is demanded, if the documents are sent from abroad the person tendering an incomplete set may nevertheless require payment upon furnishing an indemnity which the buyer in good faith deems adequate.

(3) A shipment by water or by air or a contract contemplating such shipment is "overseas" insofar as by usage of trade or agreement it is subject to the commercial, financing or shipping practices characteristic of international deep water commerce.

§ 2–324. ~~"No Arrival, No Sale"~~ Term Reserved.

Under a term "no arrival, no sale" or terms of like meaning, unless otherwise agreed,

(a) the seller must properly ship conforming goods and if they arrive by any means he must tender them on arrival but he assumes no obligation that the goods will arrive unless he has caused the non-arrival; and

(b) where without fault of the seller the goods are in part lost or have so deteriorated as no longer to conform to the contract or arrive after the contract time, the buyer may proceed as if there had been casualty to identified goods (Section 2–613).

§ 2–325. "Letter Of Credit" Term; "Confirmed Credit" Failure To Pay By Agreed Letter Of Credit.

(1) Failure of the buyer seasonably to furnish an agreed letter of credit is a breach of the contract for sale.

(2) The delivery to seller of a proper letter of credit suspends the buyer's obligation to pay. If the letter of credit is dishonored, the seller may on seasonable notification to the buyer require payment directly from him.

(3) Unless otherwise agreed the term "letter of credit" or "banker's credit" in a contract for sale means an irrevocable credit issued by a financing agency of good repute and, where the shipment is overseas, of good international repute. The term "confirmed credit" means that the credit must also carry the direct obligation of such an agency which does business in the seller's financial market.

If the parties agree that the primary method of payment will be by letter of credit, the following rules apply:

(a) The buyer's obligation to pay is suspended by seasonable delivery to the seller of a letter of credit issued or confirmed by a financing agency of good repute in which the issuer and any confirmer undertake to pay against presentation of documents that evidence delivery of the goods.

(b) Failure of a party seasonably to furnish a letter of credit as agreed is a breach of the contract for sale.

(c) If the letter of credit is dishonored or repudiated, the seller, on seasonable notification, may require payment directly from the buyer.

§ 2–326. Sale On Approval And Sale Or Return; Consignment Sales And Rights Of Creditors.

(1) Unless otherwise agreed, if delivered goods may be returned by the buyer even though they conform to the contract, the transaction is

(a) a "sale on approval" if the goods are delivered primarily for use, and

(b) a "sale or return" if the goods are delivered primarily for resale.

(2) Except as provided in subsection (3), goods Goods held on approval are not subject to the claims of the buyer's creditors until acceptance; goods held on sale or return are subject to such claims while in the buyer's possession.

(3) Where goods are delivered to a person for sale and such person maintains a place of business at which he deals in goods of the kind involved, under a name other than the name of the person making delivery, then with respect to claims of creditors of the person conducting the business the goods are deemed to be on sale or return. The provisions of this subsection are applicable even though an agreement purports to reserve title to the person making delivery until payment or resale or uses such words as "on consignment" or "on memorandum". However, this subsection is not applicable if the person making delivery

(a) complies with an applicable law providing for a consignor's interest or the like to be evidenced by a sign, or

(b) establishes that the person conducting the business is generally known by his creditors to be substantially engaged in selling the goods of others, or

(c) complies with the filing provisions of the Article on Secured Transactions (Article 9).

(4) (3) Any "or return" term of a contract for sale is to be treated as a separate contract for sale within the statute of frauds section of this Article (Section 2–201) and as contradicting the sale aspect of the contract within the provisions of this Article on parol or extrinsic evidence (Section 2–202).

§ 2–328. Sale By Auction.

(1) In a sale by auction if goods are put up in lots each lot is the subject of a separate sale.

(2) A sale by auction is complete when the auctioneer so announces by the fall of the hammer or in other customary manner. Where a bid is made while the hammer is falling in acceptance of during the process of completing the sale but before a prior bid is accepted the auctioneer may in his has discretion to reopen the bidding or to declare the goods sold under the prior bid on which the hammer was falling.

(3) Such a sale is with reserve unless the goods are in explicit terms put up without reserve. In an auction with reserve the auctioneer may withdraw the goods at any time until he announces completion of the sale. In an auction without reserve, after the auctioneer calls for bids on an article or lot, that article or lot cannot be withdrawn unless no bid is made within a reasonable time. In either case a bidder may retract his bid until the auctioneer's announcement of completion of the sale, but a bidder's retraction does not revive any previous bid. A sale by auction is subject to the seller's right to withdraw the goods unless at the time the goods are put up or during the course of the auction it is announced in express terms that the right to withdraw the goods is not reserved. In an auction in which the right to withdraw the goods is reserved, the auctioneer may withdraw the goods at any time until completion of the sale is announced by the auctioneer. In an auction in which the right to withdraw the goods is not reserved, after the auctioneer calls for bids on an article or lot, the article or lot cannot be withdrawn unless no bid is

made within a reasonable time. In either case a bidder may retract a bid until the auctioneer's announcement of completion of the sale, but a bidder's retraction does not revive any previous bid.

(4) If the auctioneer knowingly receives a bid on the seller's behalf or the seller makes or procures such a bid, and notice has not been given that liberty for such bidding is reserved, the buyer may at ~~his~~ the buyer's option avoid the sale or take the goods at the price of the last good faith bid prior to the completion of the sale. This subsection shall not apply to any bid at ~~a forced sale~~ an auction required by law.

PART 4

TITLE, CREDITORS AND GOOD FAITH PURCHASERS

§ 2–401. Passing of Title; Reservation for Security; Limited Application of This Section.

Each provision of this Article with regard to the rights, obligations and remedies of the seller, the buyer, purchasers or other third parties applies irrespective of title to the goods except where the provision refers to such title. Insofar as situations are not covered by the other provisions of this Article and matters concerning title become material the following rules apply:

(1) Title to goods cannot pass under a contract for sale prior to their identification to the contract (Section 2–501), and unless otherwise explicitly agreed the buyer acquires by their identification a special property as limited by this Act. Any retention or reservation by the seller of the title (property) in goods shipped or delivered to the buyer is limited in effect to a reservation of a security interest. Subject to these provisions and to the provisions of the Article on Secured Transactions (Article 9), title to goods passes from the seller to the buyer in any manner and on any conditions explicitly agreed on by the parties.

(2) Unless otherwise explicitly agreed title passes to the buyer at the time and place at which the seller completes ~~his~~ performance with reference to the ~~physical~~ delivery of the goods, despite any reservation of a security interest and even though a document of title is to be delivered at a different time or place; and in particular and despite any reservation of a security interest by the bill of lading

    (a) if the contract requires or authorizes the seller to send the goods to the buyer but does not require ~~him~~ the seller to deliver them at destination, title passes to the buyer at the time and place of shipment; but

    (b) if the contract requires delivery at destination, title passes on tender there.

(3) Unless otherwise explicitly agreed where delivery is to be made without moving the goods,

(a) if the seller is to deliver a document of title, title passes at the time when and the place where ~~he~~ the seller delivers such documents; or

(b) if the goods are at the time of contracting already identified and no documents are to be delivered, title passes at the time and place of contracting.

(4) A rejection or other refusal by the buyer to receive or retain the goods, whether or not justified, or a justified revocation of acceptance revests title to the goods in the seller. Such revesting occurs by operation of law and is not a "sale".

§ 2–402. Rights of Seller's Creditors Against Sold Goods.

(1) Except as provided in subsections (2) and (3), rights of unsecured creditors of the seller with respect to goods which have been identified to a contract for sale are subject to the buyer's rights to recover the goods under this Article (Sections 2–502 and 2–716).

(2) A creditor of the seller may treat a sale or an identification of goods to a contract for sale as void if as against ~~him~~ the creditor a retention of possession by the seller is fraudulent under any rule of law of the state where the goods are situated, except that retention of possession in good faith and current course of trade by a merchant-seller for a commercially reasonable time after a sale or identification is not fraudulent.

(3) ~~Nothing~~ Except as otherwise provided in Section 2–403(2), nothing in this Article shall be deemed to impair the rights of creditors of the seller

(a) under the provisions of the Article on Secured Transactions (Article 9); or

(b) where identification to the contract or delivery is made not in current course of trade but in satisfaction of or as security for a pre-existing claim for money, security or the like and is made under circumstances which under any rule of law of the state where the goods are situated would apart from this Article constitute the transaction a fraudulent transfer or voidable preference.

§ 2–403. Power To Transfer; Good Faith Purchase of Goods; "Entrusting".

(1) A purchaser of goods acquires all title which ~~his~~ the purchaser's transferor had or had power to transfer except that a purchaser of a limited interest acquires rights only to the extent of the interest purchased. A person with voidable title has power to transfer a good title to a good faith purchaser for value. When goods have been delivered under a transaction of purchase the purchaser has such power even though

(a) the transferor was deceived as to the identity of the purchaser, or

(b) the delivery was in exchange for a check which is later dishonored, or

(c) it was agreed that the transaction was to be a "cash sale", or

(d) the delivery was procured through criminal fraud ~~punishable as larcenous under the criminal law~~.

(2) Any entrusting ~~of possession~~ of goods to a merchant ~~who~~ that deals in goods of that kind gives ~~him~~ the merchant power to transfer ~~all rights of the entruster~~ all of the entruster's rights to the goods and to transfer the goods free of any interest of the entruster to a buyer in ordinary course of business.

(3) "Entrusting" includes any delivery and any acquiescence in retention of possession regardless of any condition expressed between the parties to the delivery or acquiescence and regardless of whether the procurement of the entrusting or the possessor's disposition of the goods have been such as to be ~~larcenous~~ punishable under the criminal law.

[Legislative Note: If a state adopts the repealer of Article 6—Bulk Transfers (Alternative A), subsection (4) should read as follows:]

(4) The rights of other purchasers of goods and of lien creditors are governed by the Articles on Secured Transactions (Article 9) and Documents of Title (Article 7).

[Legislative Note: If a state adopts revised Article 6—Bulk Sales (Alternative B), subsection (4) should read as follows:]

(4) The rights of other purchasers of goods and of lien creditors are governed by the Articles on Secured Transactions (Article 9), Bulk Sales (Article 6) and Documents of Title (Article 7).

PART 5

PERFORMANCE

§ 2–501. Insurable Interest in Goods; Manner of Identification of Goods.

(1) The buyer obtains a special property and an insurable interest in goods by identification of existing goods as goods to which the contract refers even though the goods so identified are non-conforming and ~~he~~ the buyer has an option to return or reject them. Such identification can be made at any time and in any manner explicitly agreed to by the parties. In the absence of explicit agreement identification occurs

(a) when the contract is made if it is for the sale of goods already existing and identified;

(b) if the contract is for the sale of future goods other than those described in paragraph (c), when goods are shipped, marked or otherwise designated by the seller as goods to which the contract refers;

(c) when the crops are planted or otherwise become growing crops or the young are conceived if the contract is for the sale of unborn young to be born within twelve months after contracting or for the sale of crops to be harvested within twelve months or the next normal harvest season after contracting whichever is longer.

(2) The seller retains an insurable interest in goods so long as title to or any security interest in the goods remains in ~~him~~ the seller and where the identification is by the seller alone ~~he~~ the seller may until default or insolvency or notification to the buyer that the identification is final substitute other goods for those identified.

(3) Nothing in this section impairs any insurable interest recognized under any other statute or rule of law.

§ 2–502. Buyer's Right to Goods on Seller's Insolvency.

(1) Subject to ~~subsection (2)~~ subsections (2) and (3) and even though the goods have not been shipped a buyer ~~who~~ that has paid a part or all of the price of goods in which ~~he~~ the buyer has a special property under the provisions of the immediately preceding section may on making and keeping good a tender of any unpaid portion of their price recover them from the seller ~~if the seller becomes insolvent within ten days after receipt of the first installment on their price.~~ if:

(a) in the case of goods bought by a consumer, the seller repudiates or fails to deliver as required by the contract; or

(b) in all cases, the seller becomes insolvent within ten days after receipt of the first installment on their price.

(2) The buyer's right to recover the goods under subsection (1) vests upon acquisition of a special property, even if the seller had not then repudiated or failed to deliver.

~~(2)~~ (3) If the identification creating ~~his~~ the special property has been made by the buyer ~~he,~~ the buyer acquires the right to recover the goods only if they conform to the contract for sale.

§ 2–503. Manner of Seller's Tender of Delivery.

(1) Tender of delivery requires that the seller put and hold conforming goods at the buyer's disposition and give the buyer any notification reasonably necessary to enable ~~him~~ the buyer to take delivery. The manner, time and place for tender are determined by the agreement and this Article, and in particular

(a) tender must be at a reasonable hour, and if it is of goods they must be kept available for the period reasonably necessary to enable the buyer to take possession; but

(b) unless otherwise agreed the buyer must furnish facilities reasonably suited to the receipt of the goods.

(2) Where the case is within the next section respecting shipment tender requires that the seller comply with its provisions.

(3) Where the seller is required to deliver at a particular destination tender requires that ~~he~~ the seller comply with subsection (1) and also in any appropriate case tender documents as described in subsections (4) and (5) of this section.

(4) Where goods are in the possession of a bailee and are to be delivered without being moved

(a) tender requires that the seller either tender a negotiable document of title covering such goods or procure acknowledgment by the bailee to the buyer of the buyer's right to possession of the goods; but

(b) tender to the buyer of a non-negotiable document of title or of a ~~written direction to~~ a record directing the bailee to deliver is sufficient tender unless the buyer seasonably objects, and except as otherwise provided in Article 9 receipt by the bailee of notification of the buyer's rights fixes those rights as against the bailee and all third persons; but risk of loss of the goods and of any failure by the bailee to honor the non-negotiable document of title or to obey the direction remains on the seller until the buyer has had a reasonable time to present the document or direction, and a refusal by the bailee to honor the document or to obey the direction defeats the tender.

(5) Where the contract requires the seller to deliver documents

(a) ~~he~~ the seller must tender all such documents in correct form~~, except as provided in this Article with respect to bills of lading in a set (subsection (2) of Section 2–323)~~; and

(b) tender through customary banking channels is sufficient and dishonor of a draft accompanying the documents constitutes non-acceptance or rejection.

§ 2–504. Shipment By Seller.

Where the seller is required or authorized to send the goods to the buyer and the contract does not require ~~him~~ the seller to deliver them at a particular destination, then unless otherwise agreed ~~he~~ the seller must

(a) put ~~the~~ conforming goods in the possession of ~~such~~ a carrier and make ~~such~~ a proper contract for their transportation, ~~as may be reasonable~~ having regard to the nature of the goods and other circumstances of the case; and

(b) obtain and promptly deliver or tender in due form any document necessary to enable the buyer to obtain possession of the goods or otherwise required by the agreement or by usage of trade; and

(c) promptly notify the buyer of the shipment.

Failure to notify the buyer under paragraph (c) or to make a proper contract under paragraph (a) is a ground for rejection only if material delay or loss ensues.

§ 2–505. Seller's Shipment Under Reservation.

(1) Where the seller has identified goods to the contract by or before shipment:

(a) ~~his~~ the seller's procurement of a negotiable bill of lading to ~~his~~ the seller's own order or otherwise reserves in ~~him~~ the seller a security interest in the goods. ~~His~~ The seller's procurement of the bill to the order of a financing agency or of the buyer indicates in addition only the seller's expectation of transferring that interest to the person named.

(b) a non-negotiable bill of lading to ~~himself~~ the seller or ~~his~~ the seller's nominee reserves possession of the goods as security but except in a case ~~of conditional delivery~~ when a seller has a right to reclaim the goods under ~~(subsection (2) of Section 2–507)~~ a non-negotiable bill of lading naming the buyer as consignee reserves no security interest even though the seller retains possession of the bill of lading.

(2) When shipment by the seller with reservation of a security interest is in violation of the contract for sale, it constitutes an improper contract for transportation within the preceding section but impairs neither the rights given to the buyer by shipment and identification of the goods to the contract nor the seller's powers as a holder of a negotiable document.

§ 2–506. Rights of Financing Agency.

(1) ~~A~~ Except as otherwise provided in Article 5, a financing agency by paying or purchasing for value a draft which relates to a shipment of goods acquires to the extent of the payment or purchase and in addition to its own rights under the draft and any document of title securing it any rights of the shipper in the goods including the right to stop delivery and the shipper's right to have the draft honored by the buyer.

(2) The right to reimbursement of a financing agency which has in good faith honored or purchased the draft under commitment to or authority from the buyer is not impaired by subsequent discovery of defects with reference to any relevant document which was apparently regular on its face.

§ 2–507. Effect of Seller's Tender; Delivery on Condition.

(1) Tender of delivery is a condition to the buyer's duty to accept the goods and, unless otherwise agreed, to ~~his~~ the buyer's duty to pay for them. Tender entitles the seller to acceptance of the goods and to payment according to the contract.

(2) Where payment is due and demanded on the delivery to the buyer of goods or documents of title, ~~his right as against the seller to retain or dispose of them is conditional upon his making the payment due~~ the seller may reclaim the goods delivered upon a demand made

within a reasonable time after the seller discovers or should have discovered that payment was not made.

(3) The seller's right to reclaim under subsection (2) is subject to the rights of a buyer in ordinary course or other good-faith purchaser for value under this Article (Section 2–403).

§ 2–508. Cure By Seller of Improper Tender or Delivery; Replacement.

~~(1) Where any tender or delivery by the seller is rejected because non-conforming and the time for performance has not yet expired, the seller may seasonably notify the buyer of his intention to cure and may then within the contract time make a conforming delivery.~~

~~(2) Where the buyer rejects a non-conforming tender which the seller had reasonable grounds to believe would be acceptable with or without money allowance the seller may if he seasonably notifies the buyer have a further reasonable time to substitute a conforming tender.~~

(1) Where the buyer rejects goods or a tender of delivery under Section 2–601 or 2–612 or, except in a consumer contract, justifiably revokes acceptance under Section 2–608(1)(b) and the agreed time for performance has not expired, a seller that has performed in good faith, upon seasonable notice to the buyer and at the seller's own expense, may cure the breach of contract by making a conforming tender of delivery within the agreed time. The seller shall compensate the buyer for all of the buyer's reasonable expenses caused by the seller's breach of contract and subsequent cure.

(2) Where the buyer rejects goods or a tender of delivery under Section 2–601 or 2–612 or, except in a consumer contract, justifiably revokes acceptance under Section 2–608(1)(b) and the agreed time for performance has expired, a seller that has performed in good faith, upon seasonable notice to the buyer and at the seller's own expense, may cure the breach of contract, if the cure is appropriate and timely under the circumstances, by making a tender of conforming goods. The seller shall compensate the buyer for all of the buyer's reasonable expenses caused by the seller's breach of contract and subsequent cure.

§ 2–509. Risk of Loss in the Absence of Breach.

(1) Where the contract requires or authorizes the seller to ship the goods by carrier

(a) if it does not require ~~him~~ the seller to deliver them at a particular destination, the risk of loss passes to the buyer when the goods are ~~duly~~ delivered to the carrier even though the shipment is under reservation (Section 2–505); but

(b) if it does require ~~him~~ the seller to deliver them at a particular destination and the goods are there ~~duly~~ tendered while in the possession of the carrier, the risk of loss passes to the buyer when the goods are there ~~duly~~ so tendered as to enable the buyer to take delivery.

(2) Where the goods are held by a bailee to be delivered without being moved, the risk of loss passes to the buyer

(a) on ~~his~~ the buyer's receipt of a negotiable document of title covering the goods; or

(b) on acknowledgment by the bailee to the buyer of the buyer's right to possession of the goods; or

(c) after ~~his~~ the buyer's receipt of a non-negotiable document of title or other ~~written~~ direction to deliver in a record, as provided in subsection (4)(b) of Section 2–503.

(3) In any case not within subsection (1) or (2), the risk of loss passes to the buyer on ~~his~~ the buyer's receipt of the goods ~~if the seller is a merchant; otherwise the risk passes to the buyer on tender of delivery~~.

(4) The provisions of this section are subject to contrary agreement of the parties and to the provisions of this Article on sale on approval (Section 2–327) and on effect of breach on risk of loss (Section 2–510).

§ 2–510. Effect of Breach on Risk of Loss.

(1) Where a tender or delivery of goods so fails to conform to the contract as to give a right of rejection the risk of their loss remains on the seller until cure or acceptance.

(2) Where the buyer rightfully revokes acceptance ~~he~~ the buyer may to the extent of any deficiency in ~~his~~ the buyer's effective insurance coverage treat the risk of loss as having rested on the seller from the beginning.

(3) Where the buyer as to conforming goods already identified to the contract for sale repudiates or is otherwise in breach before risk of their loss has passed to ~~him~~ the buyer, the seller may to the extent of any deficiency in ~~his~~ the seller's effective insurance coverage treat the risk of loss as resting on the buyer for a commercially reasonable time.

§ 2–512. Payment By Buyer Before Inspection.

(1) Where the contract requires payment before inspection non-conformity of the goods does not excuse the buyer from so making payment unless

(a) the non-conformity appears without inspection; or

(b) despite tender of the required documents the circumstances would justify injunction against honor under this Act (Section 5B109(b)).

(2) Payment pursuant to subsection (1) does not constitute an acceptance of goods or impair the buyer's right to inspect or any of ~~his~~ the buyer's remedies.

§ 2–513. Buyer's Right to Inspection of Goods.

(1) Unless otherwise agreed and subject to subsection (3), where goods are tendered or delivered or identified to the contract for sale, the

buyer has a right before payment or acceptance to inspect them at any reasonable place and time and in any reasonable manner. When the seller is required or authorized to send the goods to the buyer, the inspection may be after their arrival.

(2) Expenses of inspection must be borne by the buyer but may be recovered from the seller if the goods do not conform and are rejected.

(3) Unless otherwise agreed ~~and subject to the provisions of this Article on C.I.F. contracts (subsection (3) of Section 2–321)~~, the buyer is not entitled to inspect the goods before payment of the price when the contract provides

(a) for delivery ~~"C.O.D." or on other like terms~~ <u>on terms that under applicable course of performance, course of dealing, or usage of trade are interpreted to preclude inspection before payment</u>; or

(b) for payment against documents of title, except where such payment is due only after the goods are to become available for inspection.

(4) A place ~~or method~~ <u>, method or standard</u> of inspection fixed by the parties is presumed to be exclusive but unless otherwise expressly agreed it does not postpone identification or shift the place for delivery or for passing the risk of loss. If compliance becomes impossible, inspection shall be as provided in this section unless the place ~~or method~~ <u>, method or standard</u> fixed was clearly intended as an indispensable condition failure of which avoids the contract.

§ 2–514. When Documents Deliverable on Acceptance; When on Payment.

Unless otherwise agreed <u>and except as otherwise provided in Article 5,</u> documents against which a draft is drawn are to be delivered to the drawee on acceptance of the draft if it is payable more than three days after presentment; otherwise, only on payment.

PART 6

BREACH, REPUDIATION AND EXCUSE

§ 2–601. Buyer's Rights on Improper Delivery.

Subject to the provisions of this Article on breach in installment contracts (Section 2–612) <u>and on shipment by seller (Section 2–504),</u> and unless otherwise agreed under the sections on contractual limitations of remedy (Sections 2–718 and 2–719), if the goods or the tender of delivery fail in any respect to conform to the contract, the buyer may

(a) reject the whole; or

(b) accept the whole; or

(c) accept any commercial unit or units and reject the rest.

§ 2–602. Manner and Effect of ~~Rightful~~ Rejection.

(1) Rejection of goods must be within a reasonable time after their delivery or tender. It is ineffective unless the buyer seasonably notifies the seller.

(2) Subject to Sections 2–603, 2–604 and Section 2–608(4),

(a) after rejection any exercise of ownership by the buyer with respect to any commercial unit is wrongful as against the seller; and

(b) if the buyer has before rejection taken physical possession of goods in which ~~he~~ the buyer does not have a security interest under the provisions of this Article (subsection (3) of Section 2–711), ~~he~~ the buyer is under a duty after rejection to hold them with reasonable care at the seller's disposition for a time sufficient to permit the seller to remove them; but

(c) the buyer has no further obligations with regard to goods rightfully rejected.

(3) The seller's rights with respect to goods wrongfully rejected are governed by the provisions of this Article on seller's remedies in general (Section 2–703).

§ 2–603. Merchant Buyer's Duties as to ~~Rightfully~~ Rejected Goods.

(1) Subject to any security interest in the buyer (subsection (3) of Section 2–711), when the seller has no agent or place of business at the market of rejection a merchant buyer is under a duty after rejection of goods in ~~his~~ the buyer's possession or control to follow any reasonable instructions received from the seller with respect to the goods and in the absence of such instructions to make reasonable efforts to sell them for the seller's account if they are perishable or threaten to decline in value speedily. ~~Instructions~~ In the case of a rightful rejection instructions are not reasonable if on demand indemnity for expenses is not forthcoming.

(2) When the buyer sells goods under subsection (1) following a rightful rejection, ~~he~~ the buyer is entitled to reimbursement from the seller or out of the proceeds for reasonable expenses of caring for and selling them, and if the expenses include no selling commission then to such commission as is usual in the trade or if there is none to a reasonable sum not exceeding ten per cent on the gross proceeds.

(3) In complying with this section the buyer is held only to good faith and good faith conduct hereunder is neither acceptance nor conversion nor the basis of an action for damages.

§ 2–604. Buyer's Options as to Salvage of ~~Rightfully~~ Rejected Goods.

Subject to the provisions of the immediately preceding ~~section on perishables if the seller gives no instructions within a reasonable time after notification of rejection~~ section, the buyer may store the rejected goods for the seller's account or reship them to ~~him~~ the seller or resell them for the seller's account with reimbursement as provided in the preceding section. Such action is not acceptance or conversion.

§ 2–605.   Waiver of Buyer's Objections by Failure to Particularize.

(1) The buyer's failure to state in connection with rejection a particular defect <u>or in connection with revocation of acceptance a defect that justifies revocation</u> ~~which is ascertainable by reasonable inspection~~ precludes ~~him~~ <u>the buyer</u> from relying on the unstated defect to justify rejection or ~~to establish breach~~ <u>revocation of acceptance if the defect is ascertainable by reasonable inspection</u>

> (a) where the seller <u>had a right to cure the defect and</u> could have cured it if stated seasonably; or

> (b) between merchants when the seller has after rejection made a request in ~~writing~~ <u>a record</u> ~~and~~ <u>for</u> a full and final ~~written~~ statement <u>in record form</u> of all defects on which the buyer proposes to rely.

(2) ~~Payment~~ <u>A buyer's</u> against documents <u>tendered to the buyer</u> made without reservation of rights precludes recovery of the payment for defects apparent on the face of the documents.

§ 2–606.   What Constitutes Acceptance of Goods.

(1) Acceptance of goods occurs when the buyer

> (a) after a reasonable opportunity to inspect the goods signifies to the seller that the goods are conforming or that ~~he~~ <u>the buyer</u> will take or retain them in spite of their non-conformity; or

> (b) fails to make an effective rejection (subsection (1) of Section 2–602), but such acceptance does not occur until the buyer has had a reasonable opportunity to inspect them; or

> (c) <u>except as otherwise provided in Section 2–608(4),</u> does any act inconsistent with the seller's ownership~~; but~~ if ~~such~~ <u>the</u> act is ~~wrongful as against the seller it is an acceptance only if ratified by him~~ <u>ratified by the seller.</u>

(2) Acceptance of a part of any commercial unit is acceptance of that entire unit.

§ 2–607.   Effect of Acceptance; Notice of Breach; Burden of Establishing Breach After Acceptance; Notice of Claim or Litigation to Person Answerable Over.

(1) The buyer must pay at the contract rate for any goods accepted.

(2) Acceptance of goods by the buyer precludes rejection of the goods accepted and if made with knowledge of a non-conformity cannot be revoked because of it unless the acceptance was on the reasonable assumption that the non-conformity would be seasonably cured but

acceptance does not of itself impair any other remedy provided by this Article for non-conformity.

(3) Where a tender has been accepted

(a) the buyer must within a reasonable time after ~~he~~ the buyer discovers or should have discovered any breach notify the seller ~~of breach or be barred from any remedy.~~ However, failure to give timely notice bars the buyer from a remedy only to the extent that the seller is prejudiced by the failure and

(b) if the claim is one for infringement or the like (subsection (3) of Section 2–312) and the buyer is sued as a result of such a breach ~~he~~ the buyer must so notify the seller within a reasonable time after ~~he~~ the buyer receives notice of the litigation or be barred from any remedy over for liability established by the litigation.

(4) The burden is on the buyer to establish any breach with respect to the goods accepted.

(5) Where the buyer is sued for indemnity, breach of a warranty or other obligation for which ~~his seller~~ another party is answerable over

(a) ~~he~~ the buyer may give ~~his seller~~ the other party ~~written~~ notice of the litigation in a record. If the notice states that the ~~seller~~ other party may come in and defend and that if the ~~seller~~ other party does not do so ~~he~~ the other party will be bound in any action against ~~him~~ the other party by ~~his~~ the buyer by any determination of fact common to the two litigations, then unless the ~~seller~~ other party after seasonable receipt of the notice does come in and defend ~~he~~ the other party is so bound.

(b) if the claim is one for infringement or the like (subsection (3) of Section 2–312) the original seller may demand in ~~writing~~ a record that ~~his~~ its buyer turn over to ~~him~~ it control of the litigation including settlement or else be barred from any remedy over and if ~~he~~ it also agrees to bear all expense and to satisfy any adverse judgment, then unless the buyer after seasonable receipt of the demand does turn over control the buyer is so barred.

(6) The provisions of subsections (3), (4) and (5) apply to any obligation of a buyer to hold the seller harmless against infringement or the like (subsection (3) of Section 2–312).

§ 2–608.   Revocation of Acceptance in Whole or in Part.

(1) The buyer may revoke ~~his~~ acceptance of a lot or commercial unit whose non-conformity substantially impairs its value to ~~him~~ the buyer if ~~he~~ the buyer has accepted it

(a) on the reasonable assumption that its non-conformity would be cured and it has not been seasonably cured; or

(b) without discovery of such non-conformity if ~~his~~ the buyer's acceptance was reasonably induced either by the difficulty of discovery before acceptance or by the seller's assurances.

(2) Revocation of acceptance must occur within a reasonable time after the buyer discovers or should have discovered the ground for it and before any substantial change in condition of the goods which is not caused by their own defects. ~~It~~ The revocation is not effective until the buyer notifies the seller of it.

(3) A buyer ~~who~~ that so revokes has the same rights and duties with regard to the goods involved as if ~~he~~ the buyer had rejected them.

(4) If a buyer uses the goods after a rightful rejection or justifiable revocation of acceptance, the following rules apply:

(a) Any use by the buyer which is unreasonable under the circumstances is wrongful as against the seller and is an acceptance only if ratified by the seller.

(b) Any use of the goods which is reasonable under the circumstances is not wrongful as against the seller and is not an acceptance, but in an appropriate case the buyer is obligated to the seller for the value of the use to the buyer.

§ 2–609. Right to Adequate Assurance of Performance.

(1) A contract for sale imposes an obligation on each party that the other's expectation of receiving due performance will not be impaired. When reasonable grounds for insecurity arise with respect to the performance of either party the other may ~~in writing~~ demand in a record adequate assurance of due performance and until ~~he~~ the party receives the assurance may if commercially reasonable suspend any performance for which ~~he~~ it has not already received the agreed return.

(2) Between merchants the reasonableness of grounds for insecurity and the adequacy of any assurance offered shall be determined according to commercial standards.

(3) Acceptance of any improper delivery or payment does not prejudice the aggrieved party's right to demand adequate assurance of future performance.

(4) After receipt of a justified demand failure to provide within a reasonable time not exceeding thirty days such assurance of due performance as is adequate under the circumstances of the particular case is a repudiation of the contract.

§ 2–610. Anticipatory Repudiation.

(1) When either party repudiates the contract with respect to a performance not yet due the loss of which will substantially impair the value of the contract to the other, the aggrieved party may

(a) for a commercially reasonable time await performance by the repudiating party; or

(b) resort to any remedy for breach (Section 2–703 or Section 2–711), even though ~~he~~ the aggrieved party has notified the repudiating party that ~~he~~ it would await the latter's performance and has urged retraction; and

(c) in either case suspend ~~his own~~ performance or proceed in accordance with the provisions of this Article on the seller's right to identify goods to the contract notwithstanding breach or to salvage unfinished goods (Section 2–704).

(2) Repudiation includes language that a reasonable person would interpret to mean that the other party will not or cannot make a performance still due under the contract or voluntary, affirmative conduct that would appear to a reasonable person to make a future performance by the other party impossible.

§ 2–611. Retraction of Anticipatory Repudiation.

(1) Until the repudiating party's next performance is due ~~he~~ that party can retract ~~his~~ the repudiation unless the aggrieved party has since the repudiation canceled or materially changed ~~his~~ position or otherwise indicated that ~~he considers~~ the repudiation is final.

(2) Retraction may be by any method which clearly indicates to the aggrieved party that the repudiating party intends to perform, but must include any assurance justifiably demanded under the provisions of this Article (Section 2–609).

(3) Retraction reinstates the repudiating party's rights under the contract with due excuse and allowance to the aggrieved party for any delay occasioned by the repudiation.

§ 2–612. "Installment Contract"; Breach.

(1) An "installment contract" is one which requires or authorizes the delivery of goods in separate lots to be separately accepted, even though the contract contains a clause "each delivery is a separate contract" or its equivalent.

(2) The buyer may reject any installment which is non-conforming if the non-conformity substantially impairs the value of that installment ~~and cannot be cured~~ to the buyer or if the non-conformity is a defect in the required documents; but if the non-conformity does not fall within subsection (3) and the seller gives adequate assurance of its cure the buyer must accept that installment.

(3) Whenever non-conformity or default with respect to one or more installments substantially impairs the value of the whole contract there is a breach of the whole. But the aggrieved party reinstates the contract if ~~he~~ the party accepts a non-conforming installment without seasonably notifying of cancellation or if ~~he~~ the party brings an action with respect only to past installments or demands performance as to future installments.

§ 2–613. Casualty to Identified Goods.

Where the contract requires for its performance goods identified when the contract is made, and the goods suffer casualty without fault of either party before the risk of loss passes to the buyer, ~~or in a proper case under a "no arrival, no sale" term (Section 2–324)~~ then

    (a) if the loss is total the contract is ~~avoided~~ terminated; and

    (b) if the loss is partial or the goods have so deteriorated as no longer to conform to the contract the buyer may nevertheless demand inspection and at ~~his~~ its option either treat the contract as ~~avoided~~ terminated or accept the goods with due allowance from the contract price for the deterioration or the deficiency in quantity but without further right against the seller.

§ 2–615. Excuse by Failure of Presupposed Conditions.

Except so far as a seller may have assumed a greater obligation and subject to the preceding section on substituted performance:

    (a) Delay in ~~delivery or non-delivery~~ performance or non-performance in whole or in part by a seller ~~who~~ that complies with paragraphs (b) and (c) is not a breach of ~~his~~ the seller's duty under a contract for sale if performance as agreed has been made impracticable by the occurrence of a contingency the non-occurrence of which was a basic assumption on which the contract was made or by compliance in good faith with any applicable foreign or domestic governmental regulation or order whether or not it later proves to be invalid.

    (b) Where the causes mentioned in paragraph (a) affect only a part of the seller's capacity to perform, ~~he~~ the seller must allocate production and deliveries among ~~his~~ its customers but may at ~~his~~ its option include regular customers not then under contract as well as ~~his~~ its own requirements for further manufacture. ~~He~~ The seller may so allocate in any manner which is fair and reasonable.

    (c) The seller must notify the buyer seasonably that there will be delay or non-delivery and, when allocation is required under paragraph (b), of the estimated quota thus made available for the buyer.

§ 2–616. Procedure on Notice Claiming Excuse.

(1) Where the buyer receives notification of a material or indefinite delay or an allocation justified under the preceding section ~~he~~ it may by ~~written~~ notification in a record to the seller as to any delivery concerned, and where the prospective deficiency substantially impairs the value of the whole contract under the provisions of this Article relating to breach of installment contracts (Section 2–612), then also as to the whole,

    (a) terminate and thereby discharge any unexecuted portion of the contract; or

    (b) modify the contract by agreeing to take ~~his~~ its available quota in substitution.

(2) If after receipt of ~~such~~ notification from the seller the buyer fails ~~so~~ to modify the contract within a reasonable time not exceeding thirty

days the contract ~~lapses~~ is terminated with respect to any ~~deliveries~~ performance affected.

(3) The provisions of this section may not be negated by agreement except in so far as the seller has assumed a greater obligation under the preceding section.

PART 7

REMEDIES

§ 2–702. Seller's Remedies on Discovery of Buyer's Insolvency.

(1) Where the seller discovers the buyer to be insolvent ~~he~~ the seller may refuse delivery except for cash including payment for all goods theretofore delivered under the contract, and stop delivery under this Article (Section 2–705).

(2) Where the seller discovers that the buyer has received goods on credit while insolvent ~~he~~ the seller may reclaim the goods upon demand made within ~~ten days~~ a reasonable time after the buyer's receipt of the goods, ~~but if misrepresentation of solvency has been made to the particular seller in writing within three months before delivery the ten day limitation does not apply~~. Except as provided in this subsection the seller may not base a right to reclaim goods on the buyer's fraudulent or innocent misrepresentation of solvency or of intent to pay.

(3) The seller's right to reclaim under subsection (2) is subject to the rights of a buyer in ordinary course or other good-faith purchaser for value under this Article (Section 2–403). Successful reclamation of goods excludes all other remedies with respect to them.

§ 2–703. Seller's Remedies in General.

~~Where the buyer wrongfully rejects or revokes acceptance of goods or fails to make a payment due on or before delivery or repudiates with respect to a part or the whole, then with respect to any goods directly affected and, if the breach is of the whole contract (Section 2–612), then also with respect to the whole undelivered balance, the aggrieved seller may~~

~~(a) withhold delivery of such goods;~~

~~(b) stop delivery by any bailee as hereafter provided (Section 2–705);~~

~~(c) proceed under the next section respecting goods still unidentified to the contract;~~

~~(d) resell and recover damages as hereafter provided (Section 2–706);~~

~~(e) recover damages for non-acceptance (Section 2–708) or in a proper case the price (Section 2–709);~~

~~(f) cancel.~~

(1) A breach of contract by the buyer includes the buyer's wrongful rejection or wrongful attempt to revoke acceptance of goods, wrongful failure to perform a contractual obligation, failure to make a payment when due, and repudiation.

(2) If the buyer is in breach of contract the seller, to the extent provided for by this Act or other law, may:

(a) withhold delivery of the goods;

(b) stop delivery of the goods under Section 2–705;

(c) proceed under Section 2–704 with respect to goods unidentified to the contract or unfinished;

(d) reclaim the goods under Section 2–507(2) or 2–702(2);

(e) require payment directly from the buyer under Section 2–325(c);

(f) cancel;

(g) resell and recover damages under Section 2–706;

(h) recover damages for nonacceptance or repudiation under Section 2–708(1);

(i) recover lost profits under Section 2–708(2);

(j) recover the price under Section 2–709;

(k) obtain specific performance under Section 2–716;

(*l*) recover liquidated damages under Section 2–718;

(m) in other cases, recover damages in any manner that is reasonable under the circumstances.

(3) If a buyer becomes insolvent, the seller may:

(a) withhold delivery under Section 2–702(1);

(b) stop delivery of the goods under Section 2–705;

(c) reclaim the goods under Section 2–702(2).

§ 2–704. Seller's Right to Identify Goods to the Contract Notwithstanding Breach or to Salvage Unfinished Goods.

(1) An aggrieved seller under the preceding section may

(a) identify to the contract conforming goods not already identified if at the time ~~he~~ the seller learned of the breach ~~they~~ the goods are in ~~his~~ the seller's possession or control;

(b) treat as the subject of resale goods which have demonstrably been intended for the particular contract even though those goods are unfinished.

(2) Where the goods are unfinished an aggrieved seller may in the exercise of reasonable commercial judgment for the purposes of avoiding loss and of effective realization either complete the manufacture and

wholly identify the goods to the contract or cease manufacture and resell for scrap or salvage value or proceed in any other reasonable manner.

§ 2–705. Seller's Stoppage of Delivery in Transit or Otherwise.

(1) The seller may stop delivery of goods in the possession of a carrier or other bailee when ~~he~~ the seller discovers the buyer to be insolvent (Section 2–702) ~~and may stop delivery of carload, truckload, planeload or larger shipments of express or freight~~ or when the buyer repudiates or fails to make a payment due before delivery or if for any other reason the seller has a right to withhold or reclaim the goods.

(2) As against such buyer the seller may stop delivery until

(a) receipt of the goods by the buyer; or

(b) acknowledgment to the buyer by any bailee of the goods, except a carrier, that the bailee holds the goods for the buyer; or

(c) such acknowledgment to the buyer by a carrier by reshipment or as warehouse; or

(d) negotiation to the buyer of any negotiable document of title covering the goods.

(3)(a) To stop delivery the seller must so notify as to enable the bailee by reasonable diligence to prevent delivery of the goods.

(b) After such notification the bailee must hold and deliver the goods according to the directions of the seller but the seller is liable to the bailee for any ensuing charges or damages.

(c) If a negotiable document of title has been issued for goods, the bailee is not obliged to obey a notification to stop until surrender of the document.

(d) A carrier ~~who~~ that has issued a non-negotiable bill of lading is not obliged to obey a notification to stop received from a person other than the consignor.

§ 2–706. Seller's Resale Including Contract for Resale.

(1) ~~Under the conditions stated in Section 2–703 on seller's remedies~~ In an appropriate case involving breach by the buyer, the seller may resell the goods concerned or the undelivered balance thereof. Where the resale is made in good faith and in a commercially reasonable manner the seller may recover the difference between the contract price and the resale price ~~and the contract price~~ together with any incidental or consequential damages allowed under the provisions of this Article (Section 2–710), but less expenses saved in consequence of the buyer's breach.

(2) Except as otherwise provided in subsection (3) or unless otherwise agreed resale may be at public or private sale including sale by way of one or more contracts to sell or of identification to an existing contract of the seller. Sale may be as a unit or in parcels and at any time and

place and on any terms but every aspect of the sale including the method, manner, time, place and terms must be commercially reasonable. The resale must be reasonably identified as referring to the broken contract, but it is not necessary that the goods be in existence or that any or all of them have been identified to the contract before the breach.

(3) Where the resale is at private sale the seller must give the buyer reasonable notification of ~~his~~ an intention to resell.

(4) Where the resale is at public sale

(a) only identified goods can be sold except where there is a recognized market for a public sale of futures in goods of the kind; and

(b) it must be made at a usual place or market for public sale if one is reasonably available and except in the case of goods which are perishable or threaten to decline in value speedily the seller must give the buyer reasonable notice of the time and place of the resale; and

(c) if the goods are not to be within the view of those attending the sale the notification of sale must state the place where the goods are located and provide for their reasonable inspection by prospective bidders; and

(d) the seller may buy.

(5) A purchaser ~~who~~ that buys in good faith at a resale takes the goods free of any rights of the original buyer even though the seller fails to comply with one or more of the requirements of this section.

(6) The seller is not accountable to the buyer for any profit made on any resale. A person in the position of a seller (Section 2–707) or a buyer ~~who~~ that has rightfully rejected or justifiably revoked acceptance must account for any excess over the amount of ~~his~~ the buyer's security interest, as hereinafter defined (subsection (3) of Section 2–711).

(7) Failure of a seller to resell under this section does not bar the seller from any other remedy.

§ 2–707. "Person in the Position of a Seller".

(1) A "person in the position of a seller" includes as against a principal an agent ~~who~~ that has paid or become responsible for the price of goods on behalf of ~~his~~ the principal or anyone ~~who~~ that otherwise holds a security interest or other right in goods similar to that of a seller.

(2) A person in the position of a seller ~~may as provided in this Article withhold or stop delivery (Section 2–705) and resell (Section 2–706) and recover incidental damages (Section 2–710)~~ has the same remedies as a seller under this Article.

§ 2–708. Seller's Damages for Non–Acceptance or Repudiation.

(1) Subject to subsection (2) and to the provisions of this Article with respect to proof of market price (Section 2–723):

(a) the measure of damages for non-acceptance ~~or repudiation~~ by the buyer is the difference between the <u>contract price and the</u> market price at the time and place for tender ~~and the unpaid contract price~~ together with any incidental <u>or consequential</u> damages provided in this Article (Section 2–710), but less expenses saved in consequence of the buyer's ~~breach.~~ <u>breach; and</u>

(b) <u>the measure of damages for repudiation by the buyer is the difference between the contract price and the market price at the place for tender at the expiration of a commercially reasonable time after the seller learned of the repudiation, but no later than the time stated in paragraph (a), together with any incidental or consequential damages provided in this Article (Section 2–710), less expenses saved in consequence of the buyer's breach.</u>

(2) If the measure of damages provided in subsection (1) <u>or in Section 2–706</u> is inadequate to put the seller in as good a position as performance would have done then the measure of damages is the profit (including reasonable overhead) which the seller would have made from full performance by the buyer, together with any incidental <u>or consequential</u> damages provided in this Article (Section 2–710)~~, due allowance for costs reasonably incurred and due credit for payments or proceeds of resale~~.

§ 2–709. Action for the Price.

(1) When the buyer fails to pay the price as it becomes due the seller may recover, together with any incidental <u>or consequential</u> damages under the next section, the price

(a) of goods accepted or of conforming goods lost or damaged within a commercially reasonable time after risk of their loss has passed to the buyer; and

(b) of goods identified to the contract if the seller is unable after reasonable effort to resell them at a reasonable price or the circumstances reasonably indicate that such effort will be unavailing.

(2) Where the seller sues for the price ~~he~~ <u>the seller</u> must hold for the buyer any goods which have been identified to the contract and are still in ~~his~~ <u>the seller's</u> control except that if resale becomes possible ~~he~~ <u>the seller</u> may resell them at any time prior to the collection of the judgment. The net proceeds of any such resale must be credited to the buyer and payment of the judgment entitles ~~him~~ <u>the buyer</u> to any goods not resold.

(3) After the buyer has wrongfully rejected or revoked acceptance of the goods or has failed to make a payment due or has repudiated (Section 2–610), a seller ~~who~~ <u>that</u> is held not entitled to the price under this section shall nevertheless be awarded damages for non-acceptance under the preceding section.

§ 2–710.   Seller's Incidental <u>and Consequential</u> Damages.

<u>(1)</u> Incidental damages to an aggrieved seller include any commercially reasonable charges, expenses or commissions incurred in stopping delivery, in the transportation, care and custody of goods after the buyer's breach, in connection with return or resale of the goods or otherwise resulting from the breach.

(2) <u>Consequential damages resulting from the buyer's breach include any loss resulting from general or particular requirements and needs of which the buyer at the time of contracting had reason to know and which could not reasonably be prevented by resale or otherwise.</u>

<u>(3) In a consumer contract, a seller may not recover consequential damages from a consumer.</u>

§ 2–711.   Buyer's Remedies in General; Buyer's Security Interest in Rejected Goods.

~~(1) Where the seller fails to make delivery or repudiates or the buyer rightfully rejects or justifiably revokes acceptance then with respect to any goods involved, and with respect to the whole if the breach goes to the whole contract (Section 2–612), the buyer may cancel and whether or not he has done so may in addition to recovering so much of the price as has been paid~~

~~(a) "cover" and have damages under the next section as to all the goods affected whether or not they have been identified to the contract; or~~

~~(b) recover damages for non-delivery as provided in this Article (Section 2–713).~~

~~(2) Where the seller fails to deliver or repudiates the buyer may also~~

~~(a) if the goods have been identified recover them as provided in this Article (Section 2–502); or~~

~~(b) in a proper case obtain specific performance or replevy the goods as provided in this Article (Section 2–716).~~

<u>(1) A breach of contract by the seller includes the seller's wrongful failure to deliver or to perform a contractual obligation, making of a nonconforming tender of delivery or performance, and repudiation.</u>

<u>(2) If a seller is in breach of contract under subsection (1) the buyer, to the extent provided for by this Act or other law, may:</u>

<u>(a) in the case of rightful cancellation, rightful rejection or justifiable revocation of acceptance recover so much of the price as has been paid;</u>

<u>(b) deduct damages from any part of the price still due under Section 2–717;</u>

<u>(c) cancel;</u>

<u>(d) cover and have damages under Section 2–712 as to all goods affected whether or not they have been identified to the contract;</u>

(e) recover damages for non-delivery or repudiation under Section 2–713;

(f) recover damages for breach with regard to accepted goods or breach with regard to a remedial promise under Section 2–714;

(g) recover identified goods under Section 2–502;

(h) obtain specific performance or obtain the goods by replevin or similar remedy under Section 2–716;

(i) recover liquidated damages under Section 2–718;

(j) in other cases, recover damages in any manner that is reasonable under the circumstances.

(3) On rightful rejection or justifiable revocation of acceptance a buyer has a security interest in goods in ~~his~~ the buyer's possession or control for any payments made on their price and any expenses reasonably incurred in their inspection, receipt, transportation, care and custody and may hold such goods and resell them in like manner as an aggrieved seller (Section 2–706).

§ 2–712. "Cover"; Buyer's Procurement of Substitute Goods.

(1) ~~After a breach within the preceding section~~ If the seller wrongfully fails to deliver or repudiates or the buyer rightfully rejects or justifiably revokes acceptance, the buyer may "cover" by making in good faith and without unreasonable delay any reasonable purchase of or contract to purchase goods in substitution for those due from the seller.

(2) The buyer may recover from the seller as damages the difference between the cost of cover and the contract price together with any incidental or consequential damages as hereinafter defined (Section 2–715), but less expenses saved in consequence of the seller's breach.

(3) Failure of the buyer to effect cover within this section does not bar ~~him~~ the buyer from any other remedy.

§ 2–713. Buyer's Damages for Non–Delivery or Repudiation.

(1) Subject to the provisions of this Article with respect to proof of market price (Section 2–723), if the seller wrongfully fails to deliver or repudiates or the buyer rightfully rejects or justifiably revokes acceptance:

(a) the measure of damages ~~for non-delivery or repudiation~~ in the case of wrongful failure to deliver by the seller or rightful rejection or justifiable revocation of acceptance by the buyer is the difference between the market price at the time ~~when the buyer learned of the breach~~ for tender under the contract and the contract price together with any incidental ~~and~~ or consequential damages provided in this Article (Section 2–715), but less expenses saved in consequence of the seller's ~~breach.~~ breach; and

(b) the measure of damages for repudiation by the seller is the difference between the market price at the expiration of a commercially reasonable time after the buyer learned of the repudiation, but no later than the time stated in paragraph (a), and the contract price together with any incidental or consequential damages provided in this Article (Section 2–715), less expenses saved in consequence of the seller's breach.

(2) Market price is to be determined as of the place for tender or, in cases of rejection after arrival or revocation of acceptance, as of the place of arrival.

§ 2–714. Buyer's Damages for Breach in Regard to Accepted Goods.

(1) Where the buyer has accepted goods and given notification (subsection (3) of Section 2–607) ~~he~~ the buyer may recover as damages for any non-conformity of tender the loss resulting in the ordinary course of events from the seller's breach as determined in any manner which is reasonable.

(2) The measure of damages for breach of warranty is the difference at the time and place of acceptance between the value of the goods accepted and the value they would have had if they had been as warranted, unless special circumstances show proximate damages of a different amount.

(3) In a proper case any incidental and consequential damages under the next section may also be recovered.

§ 2–716. ~~Buyer's Right to~~ Specific Performance ~~or~~; Buyer's Right Replevin.

(1) Specific performance may be decreed where the goods are unique or in other proper circumstances. In a contract other than a consumer contract, specific performance may be decreed if the parties have agreed to that remedy. However, even if the parties agree to specific performance, specific performance may not be decreed if the breaching party's sole remaining contractual obligation is the payment of money.

(2) The decree for specific performance may include such terms and conditions as to payment of the price, damages, or other relief as the court may deem just.

(3) The buyer has a right of replevin or similar remedy for goods identified to the contract if after reasonable effort ~~he~~ the buyer is unable to effect cover for such goods or the circumstances reasonably indicate that such effort will be unavailing or if the goods have been shipped under reservation and satisfaction of the security interest in them has been made or tendered.

(4) The buyer's right under subsection (3) vests upon acquisition of a special property, even if the seller had not then repudiated or failed to deliver.

§ 2–717. Deduction of Damages From the Price.

The buyer on notifying the seller of ~~his~~ <u>an</u> intention to do so may deduct all or any part of the damages resulting from any breach of the contract from any part of the price still due under the same contract.

§ 2–718. Liquidation or Limitation of Damages; Deposits.

(1) Damages for breach by either party may be liquidated in the agreement but only at an amount which is reasonable in the light of the anticipated or actual harm caused by the breach <u>and, in a consumer contract,</u> the difficulties of proof of ~~loss,~~ <u>loss</u> and the inconvenience or nonfeasibility of otherwise obtaining an adequate remedy. ~~A term fixing unreasonably large liquidated damages is void as a penalty.~~ <u>Section 2–719 determines the enforceability of a term that limits but does not liquidate damages.</u>

(2) Where the seller justifiably withholds delivery of goods <u>or stops performance</u> because of the buyer's breach <u>or insolvency</u>, the buyer is entitled to restitution of any amount by which the sum of ~~his~~ <u>the buyer's</u> payments exceeds ~~(a)~~ the amount to which the seller is entitled by virtue of terms liquidating the seller's damages in accordance with subsection (1)~~, or (b) in the absence of such terms, twenty per cent of the value of the total performance for which the buyer is obligated under the contract or $500, whichever is smaller~~.

(3) The buyer's right to restitution under subsection (2) is subject to offset to the extent that the seller establishes

    (a) a right to recover damages under the provisions of this Article other than subsection (1), and

    (b) the amount or value of any benefits received by the buyer directly or indirectly by reason of the contract.

(4) Where a seller has received payment in goods their reasonable value or the proceeds of their resale shall be treated as payments for the purposes of subsection (2); but if the seller has notice of the buyer's breach before reselling goods received in part performance, ~~his~~ <u>the</u> resale is subject to the conditions laid down in this Article on resale by an aggrieved seller (Section 2–706).

§ 2–722. Who Can Sue Third Parties for Injury to Goods.

Where a third party so deals with goods which have been identified to a contract for sale as to cause actionable injury to a party to that contract

    (a) a right of action against the third party is in either party to the contract for sale ~~who~~ <u>that</u> has title to or a security interest or a special property or an insurable interest in the goods; and if the goods have been destroyed or converted a right of action is also in the party ~~who~~ <u>that</u> either bore the risk of loss under the contract for sale or has since the injury assumed that risk as against the other;

(b) if at the time of the injury the party plaintiff did not bear the risk of loss as against the other party to the contract for sale and there is no arrangement between them for disposition of the recovery, ~~his~~ the party plaintiff's suit or settlement is, subject to ~~his~~ its own interest, as a fiduciary for the other party to the contract;

(c) either party may with the consent of the other sue for the benefit of ~~whom~~ which it may concern.

§ 2–723. Proof of Market: Time and Place.

~~(1) If an action based on anticipatory repudiation comes to trial before the time for performance with respect to some or all of the goods, any damages based on market price (Section 2–708 or Section 2–713) shall be determined according to the price of such goods prevailing at the time when the aggrieved party learned of the repudiation.~~

~~(2)~~ (1) If evidence of a price prevailing at the times or places described in this Article is not readily available the price prevailing within any reasonable time before or after the time described or at any other place which in commercial judgment or under usage of trade would serve as a reasonable substitute for the one described may be used, making any proper allowance for the cost of transporting the goods to or from such other place.

~~(3)~~ (2) Evidence of a relevant price prevailing at a time or place other than the one described in this Article offered by one party is not admissible unless and until he has given the other party such notice as the court finds sufficient to prevent unfair surprise.

§ 2–724. Admissibility of Market Quotations.

Whenever the prevailing price or value of any goods regularly bought and sold in any established commodity market is in issue, reports in official publications or trade journals or in newspapers ~~or periodicals~~ , periodicals or other means of communication in ~~of~~ general circulation published as the reports of such market shall be admissible in evidence. The circumstances of the preparation of such a report may be shown to affect its weight but not its admissibility.

§ 2–725. Statute of Limitations in Contracts for Sale.

~~(1) An action for breach of any contract for sale must be commenced within four years after the cause of action has accrued. By the original agreement the parties may reduce the period of limitation to not less than one year but may not extend it.~~

~~(2) A cause of action accrues when the breach occurs, regardless of the aggrieved party's lack of knowledge of the breach. A breach of warranty occurs when tender of delivery is made, except that where a warranty explicitly extends to future performance of the goods and discovery of the breach must await the time of such performance the cause of action accrues when the breach is or should have been discovered.~~

(1) Except as otherwise provided in this section, an action for breach of any contract for sale must be commenced within the later of four years after the right of action has accrued under subsection (2) or (3) or one year after the breach was or should have been discovered, but no longer than five years after the right of action accrued. By the original agreement the parties may reduce the period of limitation to not less than one year but may not extend it. However, in a consumer contract, the period of limitation may not be reduced.

(2) Except as otherwise provided in subsection (3), the following rules apply:

(a) Except as otherwise provided in this subsection, a right of action for breach of a contract accrues when the breach occurs, even if the aggrieved party did not have knowledge of the breach.

(b) For breach of a contract by repudiation, a right of action accrues at the earlier of when the aggrieved party elects to treat the repudiation as a breach or when a commercially reasonable time for awaiting performance has expired.

(c) For breach of a remedial promise, a right of action accrues when the remedial promise is not performed when performance is due.

(d) In an action by a buyer against a person that is answerable over to the buyer for a claim asserted against the buyer, the buyer's right of action against the person answerable over accrues at the time the claim was originally asserted against the buyer.

(3) If a breach of a warranty arising under Section 2–312, 2–313(2), 2–314, or 2–315, or a breach of an obligation other than a remedial promise arising under Section 2–313A or 2–313B, is claimed the following rules apply:

(a) Except as otherwise provided in paragraph (c), a right of action for breach of a warranty arising under Section 2–313(2), 2–314 or 2–315 accrues when the seller has tendered delivery to the immediate buyer, as defined in Section 2–313, and has completed performance of any agreed installation or assembly of the goods.

(b) Except as otherwise provided in paragraph (c), a right of action for breach of an obligation other than a remedial promise arising under Section 2–313A or 2–313B accrues when the remote purchaser, as defined in sections 2–313A and 2–313B, receives the goods.

(c) Where a warranty arising under Section 2–313(2) or an obligation other than a remedial promise arising under Section 2–313A or 2–313B explicitly extends to future performance of the goods and discovery of the breach must await the time for performance the right of action accrues when the immediate buyer as defined in Section 2–313 or the remote purchaser as defined in Sections 2–313A and 2–313B discovers or should have discovered the breach.

(d) A right of action for breach of warranty arising under Section 2–312 accrues when the aggrieved party discovers or should have discovered the breach. However, an action for breach of the warranty of non-infringement may not be commenced more than six years after tender of delivery of the goods to the aggrieved party.

(3) (4) Where an action commenced within the time limited by subsection (1) is so terminated as to leave available a remedy by another action for the same breach such other action may be commenced after the expiration of the time limited and within six months after the termination of the first action unless the termination resulted from voluntary discontinuance or from dismissal for failure or neglect to prosecute.

(4) (5) This section does not alter the law on tolling of the statute of limitations nor does it apply to causes of action which have accrued before this Act becomes effective.

PART 8

TRANSITION PROVISIONS

§ 2–801. Effective Date.

This [Act] takes effect on _____, 20__.

§ 2–802. Amendment of Existing Article 2.

This [Act] amends [insert citation to existing Article 2].

§ 2–803. Applicability

This [Act] applies to a transaction within its scope that is entered into on or after the effective date of this [Act]. This [Act] does not apply to a transaction that is entered into before the effective date of this [Act] even if the transaction would be subject to this [Act] if it had been entered into after the effective date of this [Act]. This [Act] does not apply to a right of action that accrued before the effective date of this [Act]. Section 2–313B of this [Act] does not apply to an advertisement or similar communication made before the effective date of this [Act].

§ 2–804. Savings Clause.

A transaction entered into before the effective date of this [Act], and the rights, obligations, and interests flowing from that transaction, are governed by any statute or other law amended or repealed by this [Act] as if amendment or repeal had not occurred and may be terminated, completed, consummated, or enforced under that statute or other law.

APPENDIX C

MODEL ANSWERS TO SELECT EXAMINATION PROBLEMS

The Plumber and His Suppliers (Chapter 4, p. 353)

1. A catalog is not an offer to sell. It is an invitation to potential buyers to place offers.

2. B's letter is an inquiry. It is a request for an offer since it asks for a promise from S.

3. S's reply is an offer to a requirements contract.

4. (a) B's reply as a common law proposition is a counter-offer that results in a rejection when received. (b) One could argue that the brand name provision and the rush provision are implied. However, the provision with respect to special situations is not.

5. Under the UCC, which governs as we are dealing with the sale of goods, the first question about B's reply is:

(a) Was there a definite and seasonable expression of acceptance? On the one hand, the language is definite: "I agree with what you insist on." However, there is authority for the proposition that if a reasonable commercial person would conclude a deal has *not* closed (or there is a disparity in the dickered terms), the expression of acceptance, taken as a whole cannot be a definite expression of acceptance. Thus, we are uncertain about how a court would rule on the point.

(b) Assuming the court finds a definite expression of acceptance, it must then determine whether it was expressly made conditional on assent to the additional or different terms. There is no language of express condition present here.

(c) Assuming a contract is formed by the writings, what happens to B's terms? Are B's terms additional or different? B's reply embraces the central term of requirements and raises points not dealt with in the offer, so B's terms are probably additional.

(d) Assuming B's terms are additional, since the parties are both merchants, the terms become part of the contract automatically unless they are material alterations, or notification of objection is given. [There is no language in the offer expressly limiting acceptance to the terms of the offer.] There has been no prior or subsequent objection by S (but the reasonable time for notice would only begin when notice of the additional terms is *received*). Are the terms material alterations? This is generally a question of fact. While the provisions with respect to brand names and rush orders are probably immaterial, we have no idea of the scale of B's requirements in relation to Jones' inventory.

(e) If S's terms are deemed to be "different" there are three views, the most popular of which is the "knock out rule." However, applying that rule to these facts would eliminate both parties' quantity terms and result in a void contract. This result would more properly be achieved by concluding that S's communication was not a definite expression of acceptance at all. (See part 5(a) above.)

6. Assuming an acceptance, the above analysis is based on the assumption that the mailbox rule applies to the case. The UCC has no general rule on the mailbox question, so the common law governs (UCC 1–103).

7. If a contract was made and the "special situation" was not part of the contract, B's purchase from Jones was a breach of B's contract with S. If it was material, S could cancel the contract and demand the 10% increase; if immaterial, S's demand was a breach of the contract. [See Chapter 8.]

B and C

8. C gave B a price quote. It was not an offer because there was no quantity term. Even if it was, say, an implicit offer to a requirements contract, B never expressed assent. Could it be an offer to a series of contracts (I will sell you whatever you may order from time to time)? If so, B's first order would be an acceptance (creating a bilateral contract for that quantity alone) but C's revocation would be effective as to the future.

9. Assuming no offer by C, is C liable on promissory estoppel grounds? C made a promise on which B relied. Did C have reason to foresee B's reliance? Probably some reliance was foreseeable, but was the extent of B's reliance (3 contracts) foreseeable?

B and Jones

10. The original sale by Jones to B appears to be valid. There is (a) a possible unconscionability (or duress) argument but distress sales at greatly reduced prices are commonplace. B did not apply the coercion, the State did. A detailed examination of all the circumstances is required. [See Chapter 7.] (b) Did Jones lack capacity ("I wasn't thinking straight")? Again a detailed factual exploration would be needed. [See Chapter 6.]

11. The letter from jail was an offer which invited acceptance by performance. (a) Under the orthodox view of the matter, a promise made in reply is ineffective. (b) Since what is involved is arguably the renegotiation of a sales contract, the UCC arguably applies and it allows acceptance to be in any reasonable manner unless the offer is unequivocal on the manner of acceptance. B's promise in response is reasonable. Even if the UCC does not apply on the theory that the sales contract is fully executed, the modern common law view agrees with the UCC.

12. Was there consideration for B's promise to pay $10,000 to Jones? (a) Jones has given up his right to "pester." This can be taken to mean he is surrendering the claim stated by him in his letter. Under the first Restatement view, this is consideration only if the claim is both objectively doubtful and asserted in good faith; under the Restatement (Second) either one is sufficient. (b) At any rate, since we are dealing with a contract for the sale of goods, is consideration necessary? UCC 2–209 dispenses with the need for consideration for modifications. But inasmuch as the sales contract is fully executed, can we characterize B's promise (assuming Jones' assent is assumed) as a modification? If not, B's promise is not binding.

FLOOD AND THE WELL (CHAPTER 5, p. 363)

1. The option is clearly irrevocable. The promise to pay the monthly rental of $1,000 for 10 years is consideration for both the lease and the option. One consideration will support many promises. Consequently, it is not material whether the recited $1 was nominal or even sham.

2. Was the promise with respect to water too vague and indefinite and even illusory? No. It is an output arrangement. It requires Lessor to exercise good faith in the management of the water supply.

3. Was there consideration for Lessor's promise to pay one-half the cost of the well? (Obviously, Lessor's promise is consideration because Lessor had no duty to supply additional water.) Lessee's promise is consideration because (a) Lessee's paying half the cost of drilling a well on Lessor's land is not a preexisting duty. Moreover (b), we do not know the nature of the dispute. If Lessee had a good faith (and/or reasonable) belief that Lessor was not fulfilling Lessor's obligation under the lease, or that Lessor had fraudulently misrepresented the water supply, surrender of that claim is consideration. (Essentially the each-pay-half agreement is a settlement of a good faith dispute.) Furthermore, (c), there was a signed writing. In some states, e.g., N.Y. and Michigan, no consideration is needed if a lease is modified in writing. In addition (d), if this arrangement could be characterized as a sale of water to Lessee, under the UCC no consideration is needed for a modification.

4. (a) Under the orthodox view, there is no consideration for Lessor's & Lessee's promise to pay Flood more than the contract price. (b) However, under the view of the second Restatement, because the promise is made to compensate for unanticipated circumstances, a modification without consideration is permitted. (c) We are not told whether the modification is in writing. If it is, in some jurisdictions a modification is binding without consideration when it is made in a signed writing.

5. [This thought was not on the grading chart, but a number of students mentioned it]. There are no facts to indicate that either the modification of the lease or of the well-drilling contract was made under duress. There is nothing to indicate that the promisors had no reasonable alternative or that their free wills were overcome.

6. Assuming the modification was valid, is Flood's claim for the balance discharged by an accord and satisfaction? There is: (a) mutual

assent to discharge the claim, and (b) consideration if Lessor and Lessee asserted a good faith (and/or reasonable) claim that they were not bound by the modification agreement. (c) Moreover, in a number of states a claim can be discharged by a signed writing without consideration. There is such a writing here signed by Flood.

7. (a) Is Lessor's testimony as to the modification of the option barred by the parol evidence rule? It is subsequent to the lease, consequently it is not barred by the lease. (b) It is contemporaneous with the modification agreement and is therefore conceivably barred for that reason. Without further information about the modification agreement; e.g., was it in writing, was the writing complete, etc., it is not possible to rule on the question.

8. The Statute of Frauds bars proof of oral agreements with respect to leases of land for over a year. Assuming that the modification agreement was not made in the last year of the ten year lease, the statute applies. If the evidence of the oral agreement is not barred by the parol evidence rule, the oral agreement may be introduced into evidence to show that the written modification of the lease did not satisfy the Statute of Frauds and therefore the modification was unenforceable and the original lease is still binding on the parties. [This paragraph is here for completeness, but we realize that the Statute of Frauds has not yet been covered in this casebook].

Index

References are to Pages

1067

†